The Blackwell Companion to Modern Irish Culture

Edited by

W. J. McCormack

assisted by

Patrick Gillan

BLACKWELL
Publishers

First published 1999
First published in paperback 2001

Blackwell Publishers Ltd
108 Cowley Road
Oxford OX4 1JF
UK

Blackwell Publishers Inc.
350 Main Street
Malden, Massachusetts 02148
USA

British Library Cataloguing in Publication Data

A CIP catalogue record for this book is available from the British Library.

Library of Congress Cataloging-in-Publication Data

The Blackwell companion to Modern Irish culture / edited by W. J. McCormack.
    p.   cm.
    Includes bibliographical references (p.   ) and index.
    ISBN 0–631–16525–8 (hbk. acid-free paper). 0–631–22817–9 (pbk. acid-free paper)

    1. Ireland—Civilization—Handbooks, manuals, etc.   I. McCormack, W. J.

DA925.B47 1998   98–5572
941.5—dc21   CIP

Typeset in 10 on 12 pt Ehrhardt by Kolam Information Services Pvt. Ltd, Pondicherry
http://www.kolamindia.com
Printed in Great Britain by T. J. International, Padstow, Cornwall
This book is printed on acid-free paper

Contents

Illustrations

The illustrations appear between pages 26 and 27.

1. Cathedral of St Patrick, Armagh

2. Cathedral of St Colman, Cobh, County Cork, drawing from north elevation

3. Leinster House complex, Dublin

4. Government Buildings, Merrion Street, Dublin

5. Parliament House, College Green, Dublin (now the Bank of Ireland), interior of House of Lords

6. Maynooth College, County Kildare

7. Our Lady's Hospital, Cork, formerly Eglington Asylum

8. Parliament Buildings Stormont

9. Sandford parish church, Dublin

10. St Finbarre's Cathedral, Cork

11. University College, Galway, the Quadrangle

12. Berkley Library, Trinity College, Dublin

Acknowledgements

The editor and publishers wish to thank the following copyright holders for permission to reproduce the illustrations:

Plates 1, 2, 4, 7, 8, 9 and 10 are reproduced by permission of The Irish Architectural Archive.
Plate 3 is reproduced by permission of the Irish Tourist Board.
Plate 5 is reproduced courtesy of the Bank of Ireland.
Plate 6 is reproduced by permission of The Irish Architectural Archive/Army Air Corps.
Plate 11 is reproduced courtesy of the National University of Ireland, Galway.
Plate 12 is reproduced courtesy of Trinity College, Dublin.

Introduction

The Irish – Samuel Johnson is reported to have said – are a very fair-minded people; 'they never speak well of one another'. This too-frequently misused observation deserves a little close analysis by anyone about to dip into *The Blackwell Companion to Modern Irish Culture*. First, Johnson's emphasis on language, especially on spoken language, deserves attention in itself. Whatever else may follow from this characteristic engagement in linguistic communion, few will challenge the implication that Irish people have been acutely responsive to language over the centuries, have contributed extensively to literature and song in several languages, and have eloquently tolerated the transformation of an Irish place-name (Blarney, in County Cork) into a doubtful term for rhetorical success. Language in its many manifestations will be extensively treated in the pages which follow.

But there is more to be said about Johnson's remark, just as there is more to Irish culture than poetry, drama and fiction. Quoted to suggest a national trait of backbiting or mutual recrimination, the doctor's words might be better understood as suggesting a radical division. This division would not mark off the Irish from the rest of humanity so much as it would emphasize a more

complex differentiation: between the Irish considered as a whole – as a group, even as a nation – on the one hand, and individual Irish men and women on the other. Fair-minded in one frame of reference, they become something unexpected when, as individuals, they are distinguished in or from the group. This less than serenely balanced antithesis transports us rapidly from the late-Augustan occasion of Johnson's declaration to the unstable and perhaps unreliable categories of the present day – of the postmodern age.

The same consideration concentrates the general editor's mind wonderfully on what is covered by the *Companion* and what is not. As so often happens in discussing Irish questions, we must have recourse to history. Blackwell Publishers was so impressed by public response to Derick Thomson's *Companion to Scotland* (1983) that it decided to 'do' the other Celtic countries. Wales proved to be trouble-free. In Ireland, however, it became clear that the very long and richly documented tradition of Gaelic culture could not be effectively treated together with the massive contribution of twentieth-century Irish writers – Yeats, Joyce, Synge, Beckett, etc. – to Anglophone Modernism. There was, quite simply, too much for one companion to bear. Accordingly, the decision was made on

1

expert advice in Dublin to commission two Irish companions – one attending to Gaelic culture from the Old Irish Period (or earlier) down to the residual Gaelic present, the other treating a culture predominantly mediated through the English language from – say – the mid-sixteenth century onwards. The present writer was appointed to edit the second of these two Irish companions, but soon found himself – so to speak – companionless. No *Companion to Gaelic Ireland* could be commissioned to the publisher's satisfaction.

The point must be made in this plain fashion in order to dispel the suspicion – otherwise plausible – that the present book has been based on some apartheid-like exclusion of Gaelic culture. As it became clear that some among the Celticists did not 'speak well of each other' to the point where their co-operation on a companion was feasible, I began to commission bridging entries for the present book which would signal to readers that Anglophone Irish culture was only part of a wider picture, though a part of increasing dimensions as Gaelic declined as a vernacular throughout the last two centuries. These entries include certain vitally important and distinctive features of early modern Ireland – for example, the survival of bardic poetry into the Elizabethan period – and also include accounts of some contemporary and near-contemporary writers in modern Gaelic (e.g. Máirtín Ó Cadhain). They now resemble crossing-posts on a border which has not been opened, and the interested reader must gain admission to Gaelic Ireland by some means other than the companion originally proposed for this *Companion*.

In fairness, it should be noted that a major difficulty facing the hypothetical contributors to the lost volume would have been that of balancing a highly specialized discipline (Celtic philology and its attendant subdivisions) against the needs of the general reader. Perhaps no reader who would eagerly turn to an entry on 'cattle as legal fee' – the illustration is purely my invention – could be described as general, but then the problem of defining readership for works of companionable reference is no easy one. What the hypothetic instance about cattle neatly illustrates is that no account of Irish culture, neither in its Gaelic nor its Anglophone vector, can be restricted to linguistic matters. There is a great deal in this *Companion* on cultural matters (such as abortion, the Baptist church, conacre, the Depositions of 1641, electrification, and so on through the alphabet) which were rarely considered as such until recently.

Traditionally, of course, the literary achievement of Yeats, Joyce and company has so dominated discussion of the arts in Ireland that the co-existence of lively work in music, painting, sculpture, etc., has often gone unnoticed. In drawing up the initial word list for the present *Companion* – a list some five times the length of the present one – I found that recent work in art history and musicology greatly altered one's perspective on the pre-eminence of literature. Accordingly, this book will serve the needs of readers whose interests lie well beyond the familiar boundary marks of Irish culture, while it will also provide fresh critical insights into the well-known heroes – and even a few heroines – of the traditional discourse.

At the same time, it is worth noting as a historical phenomenon that Irish literature in English has entered a phase of some complex uncertainty. Popularity can be measured in terms of poetry readings, book prizes and postgraduate dissertations, but the intellectual and spiritual rigour previously found in (say) the work of Maria Edgeworth and Samuel Beckett is now also discovered in the painters James Barry and Mainie Jellett. Nor is this simply a matter of revisionism, in which the past is acknowledged as having produced vital work in modes additional to the literary. There is a more distinctly contemporary, even urgent, sense in which the music of Frederick May or the sculpture of Edward Delaney extends the range of reference, allusion and implicated feeling beyond the secured territory of a tradition defined largely in literary terms.

This is to say something, inevitably, about Irish nationality, about Ireland's very recent trauma, and about its developing relationships with continental Europe and with what was once known as the Third World. During the period when literature dominated discussion of Irish culture, the idea of fictional setting dominated discussion of fiction. (Thus, for years, Samuel Beckett scarcely featured in the bookshops of Dublin.) A reliance on geographical setting in determining what constituted 'an Irish novel', a predicating of Irish political thought on the identification of the nation with the territory of the whole island – these were two related aspects of a cultural nationalism which had little time for those arts in which crude representationalism showed up as just that – crude. The account of music which is discretely provided in the *Companion to Modern Irish Culture* is for the most part concerned with an artistic practice conceived in European terms, and even when folk-motifs are employed the example of the Hungarians, Béla Bartok and Zoltán Kodaly, is as significant as any internal national tradition. The case of twentieth-century painting is even more instructive. For here one sees how an ideological breach occurred in the 1920s, with a new breadth of idiom and technique introduced notably by women painters who looked to Paris, to Cubism, and to successor movements rather than back to the practice of Sean Keating and the early Jack Yeats. To be sure, Jack Yeats also transformed his art in the years leading up to World War II, but the example is set earlier by Jellett and others.

Naturally, readers come to a work like the present one with certain predispositions and needs. Many will be looking for precise bits of information – when was Daniel O'Connell born? how many times did Arkle win the Cheltenham Gold Cup? It is to be hoped that these inquirers are not disappointed in what they find. But the *Companion* is not an encyclopedia. Inevitably there are omissions. More fundamentally, the book was designed to be companionable, to entertain as well as to inform, to entertain or even provoke as well as to inform. The entries contain opinion as well as information, and the opinion is by no means always dressed up to look like unchallengeable judgement. Readers will probably find contradictory verdicts returned in some entries which relate to a shared topic. Readers are expected to find this stimulating of further research and thought on their own part. Some entries are unexpectedly long – one of the longest deals with the position of women – while others are deliberately kept brief because there is little point in duplicating matter which can also be found in – say – the *Dictionary of National Biography*. The index is strongly recommended as an integral part of the book itself.

An effort was made to keep the number of biographical entries under control. The first reason for this was a desire to avoid the mechanical inscription of crude data where the reader might prefer a more concentrated account of specific achievements. For example, many dictionaries of biography faithfully record whether X was the second or third son while the person's real achievement remains isolated from that of others working in the same field. In the *Companion to Modern Irish Culture*, however, a number of important Irish men and women are treated under collective headings – booksellers, classicists and classical studies, Nobel Prize winners, women artists, and so forth. In addition, certain eminent names will be found through entries devoted to a larger circle – the Arne family, Guinness family, Hone family, Sheridan family, Yeats family. Here the belief was that a new perspective could be gained on, for example, William Butler Yeats by treating in the same article the careers of his father, his brother, and his sisters. At the same time, Lily and Lolly Yeats gain a degree of attention which reference works of the more doggedly 'Great Men of Letters' variety never afforded them. Perhaps the policy of collective entries should have been taken further, but one has to recognize the actual state of practice in the field; that is, a general editor cannot compel contributors to adopt approaches with which they are uncomfortable.

The mention of contributors prompts consideration of non-contributors. But first it should be recognized that those who have written for the *Companion* constitute a very large proportion of the experts available in Ireland and a good number of other highly qualified people living and working elsewhere. One had a sense of testing, even straining, the available resources of the Irish higher education system, where lecturers and professors teach for much longer hours than is the case in Britain or the United States. Sometimes a contracted contributor found it impossible to fulfil all the commissions he or she had undertaken. Most of these individuals not only kept the editor informed of their difficulty but often helped to recruit their own replacements. There were moments, of course, when undertakings were silently abandoned, the editor's and the publisher's letters left unanswered. Among these cases one might list – but will not list – the names of several eminences. The point depends not on personal recrimination but, once again, on a phenomenon of some historical significance. The thinking classes in Ireland are hard pressed, relatively, and underpaid, relatively; there are easier ways of stretching an academic salary or a ministerial pension than writing for a *Companion*.

The collection of diligent and authoritative contributors remains a matter of pride. Two former taoisigh (prime ministers), former leaders of the British Labour Party and of the Fine Gael party mix happily with leading professors, distinguished poets and composers, retired polymaths, one of England's finest post-war dramatists, energetic up-and-coming critics, dwellers in Lebanon, Romania and the Netherlands, a senior Irish army officer and an ordained minister of the Mennonite church. But in particular, the contribution of younger writers, scholars by profession for the most part but some of them *amateurs* in the best sense, should be noted.

The book is organized along dictionary lines. That is to the say the entries appear alphabetically under headwords. Naturally, the choice of headword sometimes involves decisions which relegate a term to a secondary place (for example, 'labour and trade union movement', rather than 'trade unions', 'Travellers', not 'itinerants'). Consequently, the index has been designed as an integral part of the work and should be consulted freely. Despite its resemblance to dictionaries, the book is *not* a dictionary: entries differ in tone and length and in the degree to which they can be definitive. The book *is* a companion: it can be taken up for a brief consultation or cradled for an hour's contemplation. I hope it contains a few laughs, some disturbing thoughts, much sound information, and a generous verbal image of a culture in transition, an Irish kaleidoscope.

By the way, the man to whom Johnson made his fair-minded comment was the bishop of Killaloe. They became good friends. Two lifelong companions.

A

Abbey Theatre The opening of the Abbey Theatre on 27 December 1904 followed from the Irish Literary Theatre (1899–1901) created by W.B. Yeats and Lady Gregory, with Edward Martyn and George Moore, to produce a 'school of Celtic and Irish dramatic literature'. When Yeats joined forces with the self-trained Fay brothers – William the stage manager and comedian, and Frank the verse-speaker – their company (augmented importantly by Synge and the talented Allgood sisters) had the potential to create an entirely new kind of Irish theatre, one which aimed, as a later Abbey playwright, Thomas Kilroy, put it, to 'weld the fracture between the Anglo-Irish and Gaelic Ireland'. The Irish National Theatre Society became in 1904 the National Theatre Society (NTS) Ltd, familiarly known from its inception as the Abbey Theatre. The ruling perspective in the early years was Anglo-Irish but the dramatic repertoire contained many cultural strands, including plays written in Irish by Douglas Hyde, founding president of the Gaelic League.

The company's need for a building and subsidy was met, ironically, by an English-woman, Annie F. Horniman, who admired Yeats and his repertory ideal (though not its nationalist aspect). The theatre, built in 1904 from a conversion of the Mechanics' Hall in Lower Abbey Street and a disused morgue, was small, with a shallow stage which dictated simple sets. But though poorly equipped, the early Abbey was aesthetically innovative. Robert Gregory and Charles Ricketts designed for it, Gordon Craig's screens were first used on its stage, and Ninette de Valois set up a ballet school for theatre use. In 1905 a permanent salaried company was established and controlling powers were given to the directors (some actors seceded, thinking the changes contrary to nationalist principles).

The Abbey's claim to be a national theatre was aggressively tested by Catholics and nationalists in their audiences. The peasant drama was the field where cultural interests clashed most spectacularly. Lady Gregory popularized the genre with one-act comedies like *Spreading the News*, which shared the Abbey's opening bill with Yeats's heroic verse play, *On Baile's Strand*. These were acceptable even to ardent nationalists, committed to faith in an idealized peasantry, but the plays of J.M. Synge, best proof of the Abbey's early distinction, were not. For those who rioted nightly for a week at performances of *The Playboy of the Western World* in 1907 the idea of a murderer being taken for a hero in Mayo was slander (on the 'Pure,

Honest and Noble characteristics of the Irish people', as the Liverpool Irish put it). Police protection was required for the actors in Dublin and on their first (lucrative) American tour in 1911. But as Synge wrote to Molly Allgood (Maire O'Neill), rows were preferable to apathy: 'We're an event in the history of the Irish stage.'

Their distinctive repertoire, natural acting style and commitment to the ensemble won the Abbey a high reputation in their tours abroad (beginning as early as 1903 with the first of many to London). At home they had to defend themselves equally against censorship from the Gaelic League and Dublin Castle, as in 1909 when they defiantly performed Shaw's *The Showing up of Blanco Posnet*. Tensions within the company led to the departure of the Fays in 1908 and in 1910 of Miss Horniman, dissatisfied with management policy: she withdrew her subsidy but transferred the theatre to the NTS on generous terms.

Realism rooted itself early in the Abbey repertoire, despite Yeats's wish for a more poetic theatre. A view of Ireland in all its regional variety was built up on the little stage by writers who came to realize, as Lennox Robinson did on first seeing the Abbey players in Cork, that 'play-material could be found outside one's own door'. From Padraic Colum (*Broken Soil*, 1903) and William Boyle (*The Building Fund*, 1905) at the start, the line of realism was carried into the forties and beyond by writers such as Denis Johnston (*The Moon in the Yellow River*, 1931), Paul Vincent Carroll (*Shadow and Substance*, 1937) and George Shiels (*The Rugged Path*, 1940). Lennox Robinson combined writing for the theatre (*The Clancy Name*, 1909) with managing and directing for it (1910–14, 1919–35). As a founder of the Dublin Drama League, he opened the Abbey stage to productions of foreign plays; an attempt, like the inclusion of Molière in the early repertoire, to maintain an international perspective in a theatre at some risk from parochialism. During this time actors of outstanding talent emerged, celebrated for their skill in combining the comic and the poignant. Among them, Barry Fitzgerald, F.J. McCormick, Siobbhain McKenna and Cyril Cusack became known world-wide (often through Hollywood).

Sean O'Casey, in 1923, brought the Abbey its greatest fame since Synge. Much-needed audiences crowded in, electrified by *Juno and the Paycock* (1925) and *The Plough and the Stars* (1926), with their profoundly lifelike portrayal of the Dublin tenements during the Easter Rising (1916) and the Civil War. The closeness in time of the plays to the events they portrayed and O'Casey's sardonic view of nationalist idealism made disturbances inevitable. But as Yeats said, in one of his combative speeches from the stage when rioting broke out over *The Plough and the Stars*, passionate responses were a kind of tribute: 'Dublin has once more rocked the cradle of a reputation.' The sadly mistaken rejection of *The Silver Tassie* brought O'Casey's association with the Abbey to a premature end, but his Dublin plays remained their classic texts.

A government subsidy in 1925 gave the Abbey some financial security at the cost of increasing control over artistic policy by government nominees among the directors. Yeats continued to write for their stage (*Purgatory*, 1938), but on his death in 1939 the Abbey's Anglo-Irish phase ended and a narrower idea of a national theatre emerged in the long regime of Ernest Blythe (board of directors 1935–41, managing director 1941–67). As minister of finance he had negotiated the subsidy but did not want a 'cosmopolitan arts theatre'. His policy required Abbey actors to be bilingual, provoking the criticism that dramatic quality was being sacrificed on the altar of the Irish language revival. A decline in standards in the forties and fifties was exacerbated by the fire which destroyed the theatre in 1951, necessitating a move to the run-down Queen's Theatre. Its size had adverse effects on the Abbey's repertory system and on an acting style which had already coarsened. There was a tendency for actors to play 'Abbey characters' and for playwrights (with some valued exceptions, such as Hugh Leonard in *A Leap in the Dark*, 1957) to write the safe 'Abbey play'.

A Renaissance dawned for the Abbey with the completion of their handsome new 828-seat theatre (and the small-scale Peacock Theatre) in Lower Abbey Street in 1966. Its spacious stage and sophisticated equipment gave a series of artistic directors the opportunity (taken with varying degrees of confidence) to initiate bolder programmes. Neglected plays from an older Irish tradition were revived (Boucicault's *The Shaughraun* was the success of 1968) and foreign plays and directors reintroduced. In the seventies and eighties the Abbey again participated in a major dramatic revival. Most of Tom Murphy's plays (*The Gigli Concert*, 1983) were seen there for the first time, as were plays by Thomas Kilroy (*Talbot's Box*, 1977), Tom MacIntyre (*The Great Hunger*, 1983) and others who were evolving new dramatic forms to express an Ireland in transition. The Abbey's association with Brian Friel, begun in the seventies, gave them the first Dublin productions of his Field Day plays and the première of *Dancing at Lughnasa* (1990), which won awards in London and New York. Frank McGuinness, leading playwright of a younger generation, joined the board of directors in 1991; a hopeful augury for an enterprising future policy.

Famed especially as a writers' theatre, the Abbey has not always maintained production standards equal to that fame (choice of repertoire and casting have been under the pressures commonly experienced by theatres with a board conscious of its national role, and a core of permanent, salaried actors). Directorial styles have fluctuated within an artistic policy that sometimes seemed to lack driving purpose. After a rapid sequence of short-lived directorships following an expansive period under Joe Dowling (1978–85), the appointment of Garry Hynes as the first woman artistic director in 1990 opened a new phase of experiment. A Synge-like storm of criticism greeted her production of John McGahern's *The Power of Darkness* (1991), a play which made no attempt to mitigate the shock of its savage action (adapted from Tolstoy) being set in rural Ireland. *The Plough and the Stars* in 1991 raised protests about Hynes's radical, Brechtian handling of a 'sacred text'. Supporters argued that a strong breath of fresh air was revitalizing the Abbey tradition. The productions of *Hedda Gabler* in 1991 and *The Iceman Cometh* in 1992 stressed a European and American context for a theatre which no longer needed to insist in narrow ways on its Irishness. Hynes left the Abbey in 1993, to be succeeded by Patrick Mason who, in turn, was succeeded by Ben Barnes in 2000. The annual W.B. Yeats International Festivals launched at the Peacock in 1989 celebrated not only the achievement of Yeats but that of an Abbey Theatre newly poised to become a unique European cultural institution.

KATHERINE WORTH

abortion In Ireland the law on abortion is governed both by the criminal law, under sections 58 and 59 of the Offences Against the Person Act, 1861, and by the Constitution, under Article 40.3. The Act of 1861 provides that any woman who is pregnant and who administers to herself 'with Intent to procure her own Miscarriage ... any Poison or other noxious Thing, or shall unlawfully use any Instrument or other Means whatsoever', shall be guilty of a criminal offence. In addition, it is a criminal offence for any other person to do any of the above mentioned activities with the intent of procuring a miscarriage, whether the woman is pregnant or not. The criminal law does not provide for any exceptions or extenuating circumstances. There are very few reported decisions of prosecutions under this statute and there are no reported Irish cases on its exact scope.

As Irish women had access to legal abortion services in Britain from 1967, abortion was not an issue in Irish politics until the early 1980s. Then several organizations succeeded in obtaining the support of the Taoiseach, Garret Fitzgerald, for holding a referendum on amending the constitution of Ireland to provide for constitutional guarantees concerning the right to life of a foetus. Despite the Society for the Protection of the Unborn Child (SPUC) having the support of the hierarchy of the Catholic church, the referendum was vigorously fought by both sides and is generally considered to have been an extremely divisive social debate, as Catholics walked out of their churches and politicians spoke out against their party's position. In terms of Irish politics, it created some strange alliances, with fundamentalist Protestant churches in Northern Ireland coming out in support of the amendment whilst many Northern Catholics supported the position of the Church of Ireland and the Presbyterian, Quaker and Jewish churches in the Republic, which questioned the wisdom of using a constitutional prohibition to deal with such a complex moral and social problem. The Methodist church was totally opposed to any constitutional amendment on abortion. On 7 September 1983, 35 per cent of the electorate voted in favour of the eighth amendment to the Irish Constitution. The majority of 'yes' votes over 'no' votes was 425,096, out of a total electorate of 2,358,651.

The constitution was, therefore, amended as follows: 'The State acknowledges the right to life of the unborn and, with due regard to the equal right to life of the mother, guarantees in its laws to respect, and, as far as practicable, by its laws to defend and vindicate that right.' To date the Irish legislature has not enacted any statute or adopted any regulations to implement this amendment. As a result, there are no guidelines for the medical profession as to how to balance the equal right to life of the mother and of the foetus or in what circumstances the right of the foetus to life should be superior to the mother's right to life. It is as if, in the United States, no civil rights legislation was enacted after the 14th Amendment was passed.

There have been, however, several cases brought by the SPUC seeking injunctions to stop abortion counselling and the giving of information which would facilitate women's obtaining abortions in Britain. The legal basis for these actions was the very terms of Article 40.3.

The first case to come before the courts was *The Attorney General (SPUC)* v. *Open Door Counselling Limited and Dublin Wellwoman Centre Limited*. Both defendants carried on pregnancy counselling services, including abortion counselling and giving of names and addresses of clinics in Britain which performed those services. The Supreme Court ordered that both companies and their employees be perpetually restrained from assisting pregnant women within Ireland 'to travel abroad to obtain abortions by referral to a clinic, by the making for them of travel arrangements, or by informing them of the identity and location of and the method of communication with a specified clinic or clinics or otherwise'. This decision was challenged before the European Court of Human Rights.

The second case, *SPUC* v. *S. Grogan and others*, resulted from SPUC seeking to restrain university students from including in their publications the identity and location of abortion clinics outside Ireland. Before those proceedings were finally determined by the High Court, several questions were referred to the European Court of Justice for a preliminary ruling as to the effect of European Union law on the restriction of information concerning services which are lawfully performed in other EU member states. On 11 June 1991 the Advocate General advised that:

The Treaty provisions with regard to the freedom to provide services do not prevent a Member State where the protection of unborn life is recognized in the Constitution and in its legislation as a fundamental principle from imposing a general prohibition, applying to everyone regardless of their nationality or place of establishment, on the provision of assistance to pregnant women, regardless of their nationality, with a view to the termination of their pregnancy, more specifically through the distribution of information as to the identity and location of and method of communication with clinics located in another Member State where abortions are carried out, even though the services of medical termination of pregnancy and the information relating thereto are provided in accordance with the law in force in that second Member State.

A Supreme Court decision of 1992 overturned a High Court decision banning an under-age rape victim from travelling abroad to obtain an abortion. As a result, a referendum held later that year resulted in the constitution being amended to take into account the right to travel and freedom of access to information on abortion.

So far, therefore, the practical effects of Article 40.3 of the constitution are that whilst a woman may receive non-directive counselling as to whether or not she should decide to terminate her pregnancy she cannot be given any information as to where she can obtain that termination. Books which contain information about abortion have been removed from bookshops, and British magazines which have included articles on abortion have arrived in Ireland with those pages missing or with blank passages. The full implications of Article 40.3 are still unknown and will remain so until the legislature brings in either a statute or regulations, or until further cases are brought before the courts whereby the judiciary will interpret the amendment.

CATHERINE FORDE

absenteeism Although the landed classes, in the decades following the Battle of the Boyne (1690), were intensely English-oriented in culture-political and constitutional outlook, there was a growing awareness that their Irish economic interests did not coincide with those of England. Restrictions on trade and manufacture, imposed on Ireland by the English government, meant that, increasingly, Ireland came to be seen as a single, discrete economic system *vis-à-vis* England. One of the drains on this system was the fact that many landlords resided in England. They took their Irish income out of the country without reinvesting, spending, or adequately managing their Irish estates. Frequently 'middlemen' were appointed to take care of their absent landlords' Irish affairs; this practice imposed a second unproductive layer of wealth extraction, which increased rents for the actual tenants, and came to epitomize the awareness that Ireland, though a sister kingdom in name, was really in a colonial position. Thus the absenteeism of Anglo-Irish landowners became a symbol of the inherent corruptness of the landlord system. Many activists in the Patriot movement tried to combat absenteeism. Throughout the eighteenth century, absentees were publicly denounced in published lists containing estimates 'of the yearly value of their estates and incomes spent abroad' – the earliest example compiled in 1729. Repeatedly the suggestion was made (by Swift, among others) to tax absentee incomes at a rate of four or even five shillings per pound. Maria Edgeworth's novel *The Absentee* (1812) still echoes this Patriot disgust with absenteeism, which continued to persist, however, until the abolition of the landlord system.

JOEP LEERSSEN

abstraction A key feature of early Irish art just as it was of the Gothic art of northern Europe. Its religious justification within the Judaeo-Christian tradition may be found in Exodus 20:4, and it is an important element in Islamic art for similar reasons. Its philosophical justification goes back to Plato, who spoke (*Philebus*) of the beauty of 'straight lines and curves and the surfaces or solid forms produced out of these by lathes and rulers and squares...These things are not beautiful relatively, like other things, but always and naturally and absolutely.' In a modern context, Clement Greenberg justified the abstractionist tendency by defining the prime features of painting as being two-dimensionality and self-interrogation.

The tendency towards abstraction, based on the assumption that forms and colours in themselves embody aesthetic values, is a key element of Irish Modernism, particularly in its earlier phases, and has remained an important feature of the visual arts in Ireland up to the present. The most important Irish abstractionist is usually taken to be Mainie Jellett, who together with Evie Hone was a pioneer in Ireland of Cubism. Cubism sacrificed the representation of things as they appear in favour of an attempt to describe the whole structure of an object and its spatial situation. (It can thus be seen from one standpoint as an extreme form of realism and its relationship with abstraction is complicated and problematic.) Hone's work always retained an 'intuitive' element which came to displace the Cubist influence. Her work later moved away from a focus on painting to the use of stained glass.

From an Irish 'Ascendancy' background, Jellett studied under Walter Sickert, and in Paris under Lhote and the 'synthetic Cubist' Gleizes (who published *Du Cubisme* with Metzinger in 1912 and whose theoretical perspective was influenced by both Catholicism and philosophical idealism). Jellett's later work contains a strong devotional element, characterized by a search for the 'inner principle'. Others influenced by Cubism included Mary Swanzy, May Guinness, Ralph Cusack and Norah McGuinness.

Laurence Campbell's sculpture is perhaps influenced by elements of Jellett's work, though his work became more academic as it developed. Paul Henry's painting, particularly that of his earlier stage, evidences a sense of abstraction deriving ultimately from Whistler. Of the White Stag Group artists of the 1940s, Bobby Dawson, influenced by Paul Klee, was perhaps the most abstract in orientation, but the group also included Patrick Scott, with his semi-abstract animal imagery, and Paul Egestorff, who studied under Jellett. Doreen Vanston's work of the early 1940s shows evidence of the influence of Picasso. The Cubist influence of Lhote continued to make itself felt in the late 1940s in the work of Elizabeth Rivers. William Scott has had a

recurring concern with abstraction from the 1940s onwards, and the work of Camille Souter has been marked by the style at times. Other artists who should be mentioned in this context include Colin Middleton, Nano Reid and Patrick Collins. With the Irish Exhibition of Living Art, abstraction emerged as a dominant force and became, in Aidan Dunne's words, 'a virtual orthodoxy in the heyday of the early 1970s', though under sustained attack by Neo-Expressionism in the 1980s. Criticisms of abstraction included its tendency towards institutionalization, its comfortable relationship with business patronage, and its association with the much-criticized (particularly in Dublin) style of architectural Modernism.

Michael Farrell moved from figuration to 'hard-edge' abstraction, and, finding abstraction to be an overly 'aesthetic' style, returned to figuration as a better means of making the kinds of statement that interested him. Tony O'Malley attempts to evoke the essential character of rural landscape, while Barrie Cooke also goes to nature for abstract shapes to explore questions of growth and structure. Cecily Brennan's painting explores issues linking landscape and the sublime, while Gwen O'Dowd's work is gaining increasing recognition for the sensitivity combined with force of her response to natural forms.

Sculptors who work or have worked in the abstract tradition include Gerda Froemel, Deborah Brown, Edward Delaney (who is also well-known for figurative bronze works), Brian King, Michael Bulfin, John Aiken, Noel Hoare, John Burke, Eilis O'Connell and Michael Warren (whose highly finished smaller work shows the influence of his training in Italy). Alexandra Wejchert's work is reminiscent of aspects of constructivism and kinetic art, while some of Dorothy Cross's work falls into the category of abstraction.

The later painting of Patrick Scott shows a recurring interest in the sphere, and in the 1960s he began his 'gold' paintings, balancing gold, canvas and tempera. Cecil King has produced works in a Minimal 'hard-edge' style which eliminates all but the essential elements of a picture: 'This is a cool, classical art in which precise visual problems have been considered with a calm intelligence' (Frances Ruane). Theo McNab's paintings are characterized by a sense of architectural precision, while Felim Egan has been inspired by Kandinsky, specifically his notion of musical analogies in painting. Charles Tyrrell's early colour field paintings gave way to a sense of landscape and the organic through the 1980s, while Roy Johnston, beginning with the examination of natural forms, developed to a geometrical concern, and later still to an exploration of some aspects of Expressionism. Samuel Walsh's painting, though abstract, is influenced by the seasonal and agricultural changes of the countryside where he lives, the theme of the rural and of landscape being one that, for purely geographical reasons, is difficult for Irish artists to escape. Mary Fitzgerald's work embodies an element of Orientalism deriving from her time spent in Japan. Other names that should be mentioned in the context of abstraction are Anne Madden, Erik van der Grijn, Michael Coleman, Richard Gorman and Ciaran Lennon.

The relationship in Ireland between abstraction, Expressionism and Romanticism is often ill defined, though modern Irish art, including much that passes for abstraction, is marked by a recurring element of 'naturist' Romanticism, deriving originally from Yeats, that marks it off from mainstream Continental developments. Whether Romanticism, and as a consequence the Irish art that is marked by it, is due for a new revival with the current interest in ecology is too soon to tell.

Reading

Arnold, Bruce, *Mainie Jellett and the Modern Movement in Ireland* (New Haven CT: Yale University Press, 1991).
Douglas Hyde Galley, *The Allied Irish Bank Collection: Twentieth Century Irish Art*, intro. Frances Ruane (Dublin: DHG, 1986).

Dunne, Aidan, 'Saving the phenomena: formalist painting in the 1980s', in Douglas Hyde Gallery, *A New Tradition: Irish Art of the Eighties* (Dublin: DHG, 1990).
Irish Museum of Modern Art, *Mainie Jellett: 1897–1944* (Dublin: IMOMA, 1991).
Kennedy, S.B., *Irish Art and Modernism, 1880–1950* (Belfast: Institute of Irish Studies/Queens University, 1991).
Knowles, Roderic, *Contemporary Irish Art* (Dublin: Wolfhound, 1982).

PAUL O'BRIEN

abuse and power The word 'abuse' has now become associated with the physical or sexual mistreatment of children. Sexual abuse, or the involvement in sexual activity by an older person of a child too young to give informed consent, became an issue after the establishment of the Sexual Assault Unit in the Rotunda Hospital, Dublin, in 1985. Though established for adult rape victims, children, not adults, became the largest group of victims brought forward. Because of the numbers involved – about 50 confirmed cases of abuse a month in Dublin – two specialist units were subsequently established in the Children's Hospitals at Temple Street and Crumlin.

In 1994, child sexual abuse became a political issue when the sexual abuse perpetrated over years by the paedophile priest Brendan Smyth led to the fall of Albert Reynolds's Fianna Fáil–Labour coalition government. On 11 November, Harry Whelehan, the attorney general, was appointed president of the High Court at the insistence of Reynolds, even after Labour walked out of the cabinet meeting in protest. The new attorney general, Eoghan Fitzsimons, was then asked to re-examine the Smyth case to explain a seven-month delay after the UK authorities requested his extradition to Belfast. On 14 November, Fitzsimons told Fianna Fáil ministers the delay was unacceptable as an earlier case provided precedent. The taoiseach deliberately omitted this Duggan case in his explanation of the delay to the Dail on 15 November, and when Dick Spring, the

Labour leader, learned of this omission the next day, he pulled his party out of government. On 17 November, both Reynolds and Whelehan resigned. On 19 November, Bertie Ahern was appointed Fianna Fáil leader and began negotiations with Labour to form a new government. It was then revealed that Fianna Fáil ministers not only knew of the Duggan case, but also knew of its significance. When the extent of a deliberate cover-up was revealed, Labour turned to Fine Gael and the Democratic Left to form a 'rainbow coalition'.

The Smyth case brought home to the powerful institutions of church and state that they could no longer expect to rule without being accountable to the public. Because of the Whelehan appointment, the method of making judicial appointments was changed to prevent party leanings being the main consideration. Above all, the Smyth case proved that live television coverage of Dáil debates is an important democratic advance. It allowed the public to judge for themselves the characters and performances of their elected representatives. Television proved that honest speeches can be more important than great orations.

FRED LOWE

Academy of Letters Founded by George Bernard Shaw and W.B. Yeats in 1932 to combat literary censorship by 'giving authority to the utterance' of Irish writers. Membership is by invitation only, although membership offers have been rejected, notably by James Joyce and Sean O'Casey. From the 1940s until the early 1980s the Irish Academy of Letters carried out functions similar to those now performed by the Arts Council, offering awards to new writers and honouring established writers. Today it has only a nominal existence, meeting rarely and providing its members with a prized, if arcane, form of peer recognition. Although the Academy is constituted to admit 35 members, there are now only 19: John Banville, Eavan Boland, Brian Friel, Seamus Heaney,

Jennifer Johnston, Benedict Kiely, Thomas Kilroy, Mary Lavin, Hugh Leonard, Michael McLaverty, Bryan McMahon, John Montague, Thomas Murphy, Edna O'Brien, James Plunkett, Francis Stuart, William Trevor, Mervin Wall, and Terence de Vere White.

CHRIS MORASH

Adams, Gerry (1948–) President of Sinn Féin since 1983. Born Belfast. He joined the republican movement in 1964 and sided with the Provisionals in the IRA split of 1969–70. He was one of six leading Provisionals who in 1972 met William Whitelaw, Secretary of State for Northern Ireland. While in Long Kesh Adams wrote for *Republican News* under the pen-name 'Brownie'; his articles led to the 'Armalite and the ballot-box' strategy. Following the hunger strikes of 1981, support for the Provisionals grew and, in 1983, Adams was elected MP for West Belfast, a seat he lost in 1992. Adams engaged in talks with the Social Democratic and Labour Party (SDLP) in 1988, which ended when the IRA refused to abandon violence. The Hume/Adams talks of 1993 were more successful, however, and prepared the ground for the IRA cease-fire of 1994. But as Adams told a Belfast rally in August 1995: 'They [the IRA] haven't gone away, you know.' His words were borne out by the London Docklands bomb in February 1996 which ended the IRA cease-fire. Sinn Féin increased its vote in the subsequent Forum elections, standing on an abstentionist platform, but continuing IRA violence excluded the party from the inter-party talks. Adams regained his Westminster seat in May 1997. The IRA declared a second 'unequivocal' cease-fire in July 1997 which, in September, enabled Adams to lead Sinn Féin into the Stormont talks and stand for election as a Sinn Féin candidate to the New Northern Ireland Assembly in June 1998. His 1996 autobiography, *Before the Dawn*, was a bestseller in Ireland. The resumption of violence undermined sales in the US, but the achievement of a peace settlement in Northern

Ireland has since enhanced his international reputation.

PATRICK GILLAN

Addison, Joseph (1672–1719) Essayist, poet, dramatist and statesman. Born 1 May at Milston in Wiltshire, the son of the dean of Lichfield. He was educated at Charterhouse, as a contemporary of Richard Steele, and at Queen's College and Magdalen, Oxford. During 1708, he and Steele dominated the Whig literary circle which then included Swift. It was the very English Addison, however, not his politically aspiring Irish friends, who first rose to Irish prominence. On 6 December 1708, he was appointed chief secretary to the lord lieutenant of Ireland, Lord Wharton. This post, already wrongly referred to as that of the secretary of state, was filled by Addison with such diligence and integrity that he won friends everywhere. Elected MP for Cavan in 1709, he was able to overcome his shyness at speaking in the smaller Irish House of Commons. He was made keeper of the records in Bermingham's Tower, a sinecure post with a nominal salary, but one which Addison took seriously, for he began to rehouse and rearrange the public records.

Steele launched the *Tatler* while Addison was in Ireland, and soon involved Addison, who proved to be an essayist without equal.

When the Whig Ministry fell in 1710, Addison lost his post as secretary to the lord lieutenant. In 1714, he was reappointed, this time to the Earl of Sunderland, until 1715, when he moved to the Board of Trade. He rose to be secretary of state in 1717, but retired that year through illness. He died on 17 June 1719.

FRED LOWE

Agar, Charles (1736–1809) Ecclesiastic and politician. He was born in Dublin on 22 December, the third son of Henry Agar of Gowran Castle, Country Kilkenny, and he died in London in July 1809. Successively archbishop of Cashel (1779–1801) and of Dublin (1801–9), he was the last of the 'political bishops' of the eighteenth century. His influence was at its height in the 1790s. He is credited with being the first to raise the king's coronation oath as a constitutional obstacle to Catholic emancipation.

Reading

Cokayne, George E., *The Complete Peerage*, 12 vols (London: St Catherine's Press, 1910–59).
Malcomson, A.P.W., *John Foster* (Oxford: Oxford University Press, 1978).

JAMES KELLY

agents and middlemen Represented two faces of the Irish landholding evil known as absenteeism. The land agent was a common feature of the Irish countryside during the long neglectful period between the Boyne (1690) and independence (1922). He was the landowner's personal and professional representative on his Irish estates, acting as steward, manager and sometimes financial adviser also. The extent of his influence depended partly on the closeness of his relationship with his employer but mainly on his efficiency in making the estate pay for itself. In the case of long-term absentee owners the agent often occupied the manor house and his lifestyle was a satisfying if slightly paler reflection of that of his opulent master. The middleman leased land from an estate owner and then became a 'professional' landlord, subletting land to tenants and usually subsisting on the income derived therefrom. Often the subtenants would relet the land or portions of it and so themselves become a further layer of middlemen. Both institutions were frowned on by contemporary economists and later historians. The land, it was felt, was being managed by persons who had no direct interest in it other than commercial, and who moreover disrupted and undermined the deference relationship and formed a barrier between the landlord and his tenants.

GERARD O'BRIEN

agriculture The dominant form of economic activity in Ireland at the turn of the century. At independence it accounted for just over half of total employment, about three-quarters of merchandise exports and about one-third of gross domestic product. By the early 1990s its economic importance had shrunk to the point where less than 15 per cent of the population classified themselves as farmers, and agricultural production accounted for around 10 per cent of national output. Ireland's social and cultural evolution in this century reflects this transition from a largely agrarian to a mainly urban society, albeit one in which the imprint of its agricultural past is rarely far below the surface.

Irish agriculture has a predominantly pastoral orientation for both climatic and economic reasons. Cattle and dairy products produced mainly from grass form the backbone of agricultural production. The cattle economy has been based on a complex division of labour between different geographical regions. Traditionally, calves born in the south were purchased for rearing on small western farms and then sold on to the larger grazing farms of the midlands and east for fattening and subsequent export or slaughter. Animals were traded many times. While fair days provided much life and colour in rural towns in the past, by the mid-1960s they had been largely superseded by the more efficient, if more clinical, service provided by the livestock marts.

Irish agriculture has had few golden moments during the twentieth century. The great agricultural depression at the end of the nineteenth century came to an end when for a brief few years during World War I farmers earned high prices from a British market starved of food. But depression quickly returned in the 1920s and was exacerbated by the effects of the economic war with Britain in the 1930s, whose costs were borne largely by the farming class. World War II, provided no respite, although in the 1950s there was a brief glimmer of hope that prosperity could be achieved by exporting beef

and butter to the expanding UK market. The British, however, alarmed by the consequences of having to rely on food imports during the war, embarked on a policy of increased self-sufficiency through state support for their own production. Combined with the extensive protection of Continental European agriculture, this meant markets for increased Irish production could only be found with the aid of increasing, and increasingly expensive, Exchequer subsidies.

Accession to the European Economic Community (as it was then called) in 1973 dramatically altered the fortunes of Irish agriculture (and of the Irish economy) by extending to farmers the high farm prices paid at the expense of European consumers and taxpayers under the Common Agricultural Policy. These subsidies are now so important to farm incomes that farmers have developed one of the most powerful and effective political lobby groups to defend and extend them.

The Land Acts of the nineteenth and early twentieth centuries saw the abolition of the historical form of Irish landlordism and vested the land of the country in tenants who worked it. But while peasant proprietorship gave the farmer ownership of the land, it could not guarantee him a living. Even at the turn of the century many farms were too small to yield an adequate income. Furthermore, there were many landless families who agitated for land redistribution. Despite the efforts of the Land Commission in redistributing some 2.8 million acres to about 140,000 allottees until it ceased operations in the mid-1980s, the subsistence groups in rural society – landless men, the sons and daughters of small farmers – were gradually squeezed out.

The social mechanisms which governed this process revolved around the patriarchal role of the farmer, which was greatly strengthened by peasant proprietorship. The farm had to be handed on intact to a single son and non-inheriting children had to make their own way in the world. In well-to-do families there were opportunities in the professions or in the state or local bureaucracy, but for many children of smallholders or landless families emigration to the cities of Britain and North America was the only outlet.

This small farm economy remained viable until the late 1950s. The collapse, when it came, was sharp and sudden. Output per acre on larger farms, which in the 1920s had been only one-third the level on smaller farms, grew level in the 1950s and rapidly surpassed small farm levels in the 1970s. Important small farm enterprises, such as pigs and poultry, migrated to industrial units.

Demographic statistics complete the story. Up to the 1950s marriage rates in the west were higher than in the east. After the 1950s the typical figure on small farms became the elderly, bachelor farmer without an heir. Farm surveys showed that these farmers were least likely to be engaged in modern farm practices. Production stagnated and in many cases contracted. The high prices of the EC boom in the 1970s came too late to help these farmers. The demographic collapse was too deep-rooted to allow them to respond, although higher incomes did permit more to be spent on material comforts and the rural housing stock was radically improved.

In other countries the co-operative movement provided the means for small farms to unite to overcome some of the disadvantages of lack of scale. In Ireland the co-operative message was preached by Sir Horace Plunkett (1854–1932) and the Irish Agricultural Organization Society (today the Irish Co-operative Organization Society), which he founded in 1894. The movement's main success was in dairy processing, where eventually 100 per cent of the industry came under farmer control, and in the establishment of livestock marts to replace the traditional fairs. Yet it may be doubted if the co-operative spirit ever really took root in the Irish countryside.

On the more commercial farms the opportunities provided by EC membership were eagerly grasped as farmers sought to undo the consequences of decades of underinvestment in the space of a few years. Land prices hit record levels. In one year (1979) average farm incomes exceeded average non-farm incomes for possibly the first time ever. Rural industrialization has provided some off-farm employment opportunities, particularly for women, and in recent years much has been made of the income potential of forestry and agri-tourism. Ireland's rural areas face a much more diversified future in which agriculture will be just one of the shaping forces.

Reading

Breen, Richard, 'Agriculture: policy and politics', in Richard Breen, Damian Hannan, David Rottman and Christopher Whelan (eds), *Understanding Contemporary Ireland* (Dublin: Gill and Macmillan, 1990).

Crotty, Raymond, *Irish Agricultural Production: Its Volume and Structure* (Cork: Cork University Press, 1966).

Drudy, P.J., ed. *Ireland: Land, Politics and People* (Cambridge: Cambridge University Press, 1982).

Matthews, Alan, 'Agriculture and rural development', in John O'Hagan (ed.), *The Economy of Ireland: Policy and Performance*, (Dublin: Irish Management Institute, 1991).

ALAN MATTHEWS

Ahern, Bartholomew (Bertie) (1951–) Leader of Fianna Fáil since November 1994; briefly tánaiste during the hiatus after the collapse of the Fianna Fáil/Labour government (1992–4). Born Dublin. Ahern's parents were both staunch Fianna Fáil supporters and, at the age of 13, he was constituency 'director of lamp-post boys' in the 1965 general election. Later, while employed by the Mater Hospital, he became a member of the Federated Workers' Union of Ireland. Ahern was elected to the Dáil in the Fianna Fáil landslide of 1977 and was appointed assistant government whip in 1980; after he topped the poll in elections in 1981 and 1982, he became chief whip. A Haughey loyalist, he held various front bench positions during 1982–7; he also served as lord mayor of Dublin (1986–7). He was appointed minister for labour on Fianna Fáil's return to power in 1987. He facilitated the merger of the FWUI and the ITGWU to create SIPTU in 1990. However, many trade unionists felt that the Industrial Relations Act (1990) tilted the balance in favour of employers. He served as minister for finance (1991–4) and, in 1993, introduced a controversial amnesty for income-tax evaders.

When Haughey stood down as taoiseach in 1992, Ahern was widely seen as indecisive when he failed to stand in the leadership contest. He remained at Finance under taoiseach Albert Reynolds and retained the portfolio in the Fianna Fáil/Labour government that was formed in December 1992. His defence of the púnt during the 1992–3 currency crisis was criticized by business interests and he was eventually forced to reverse his policy.

Following the collapse of the government in 1994, Ahern was elected leader of Fianna Fáil. A song commissioned to celebrate his victory, *The Man They Call Ahern*, proved so embarrassing that it was quickly jettisoned. He was a lacklustre leader of the opposition and found it difficult to motivate his parliamentary colleagues. He did, however, obtain expert advice on policy development and commissioned an independent consultant's report on the future of the party. Fianna Fáil's electoral strategy was drawn up and the party's image revamped in good time for the 1997 general election. Although the party's share of the vote increased only marginally compared to 1992, astute vote management resulted in a gain of ten seats. Thus Ahern was elected taoiseach in June 1997 and became leader of a Fianna Fáil/Progressive Democrats minority government supported by three independent deputies. Ahern scored a considerable political victory in 1998, when he gained a mandate from the Irish people to drop Ireland's constitutional claim over Northern Ireland, in an effort to aid the peace process there. Ten years earlier,

he described politics as 'rough, tough, hard'. According to his mentor, Charles Haughey, Ahern was ideally suited to this milieu: 'He's the best, the most skilful, the most devious and the most cunning.'

PATRICK GILLAN

AIDS It held a mirror to Irish society, revealing hidden parts that challenged traditional views and icons. AIDS and HIV infection were confined to risk groups at the beginning: male homosexuals and then intravenous drug abusers. Initial fears of society's reacting with homophobia were put aside as more was learnt about the disease and society saw the benefit of the advice and positive contribution of the gay organizations and self-help groups. Drug abusers unfortunately did not have the advantage of such an organized caring infrastructure, and HIV infection and AIDS put another burden upon their shattered lives.

Whilst treatment can now offer substantial benefit, there is no cure for AIDS. 'Knowledge is the only vaccine', and there is a duty incumbent upon education and health-care workers to provide the ways and means to allow the behaviour modification that protects against infection.

Behavioural modification of such a strong primordial instinct as sex requires explicit information and messages on topics from which Irish society had previously been sheltered. This posed a challenge to the traditional tenets of church and state. That innocuous piece of rubber, the condom, became the centre of many people's attention and emotion. The adoption of a Scandanavian model of health education against sexually transmitted diseases with a primary emphasis upon partner selection and fidelity, and with condom usage as a secondary protection for those not so fortunate in choice of partner, provided a solution that was received as being not only practical and sensible but one that could be supported by all bodies. The more explicit messages of safe-sex practices were left to the voluntary sector.

The statutory bodies had difficulty in coping with the problems raised by covert groups and behaviour in society. The voluntary groups received no direct support, despite the high value put upon their efforts by all concerned. Some indirect funding was furnished through the AIDS Fund and Irish cultural life has been enhanced by a number of events and performances for AIDS charities.

The 1990s saw the beginning of some action by the statutory bodies with the provision of walk-in needle-exchange clinics in Dublin, which also distributed condoms. AIDS forced the issue of sex education with the commencement of a pilot programme in schools and the promise of full programmes in the future.

Surveys of public knowledge of and information on AIDS in the 1980s showed that Ireland coped surprisingly well in the face of a rather limp performance by the statutory bodies. This has been largely due to the persistence of a few individuals and media personalities who kept the topic alive in the public eye in a rational and non-sensational manner, and whom the public felt they could relate to and trust.

The silent and sad face of AIDS in Irish society is the loss of many talented and gifted contributors to all aspects of Irish culture as well as to their family and friends.

DAVID FREEDMAN

Aiken, John (1950–) Sculptor. Born Belfast. Aiken works in certain types of materials that can roughly be associated with landscape, but in an unusual way. Influenced very much by Robert Smithson's land art and process art, his sculpture and installations use sand, wood/timber, metal/steel and marble/stone, and rely a lot on geometric pattern and organization of space. His formal fusing of steel and marble displays and contrasts the relative softness of the stone and the rigidity of the cast metal, foregrounding the formal properties of each of these materials in an elegant fashion.

Reading

Lampert, Catherine 1988: 'The poetry of strange bedfellows'.

MARTIN MCCABE AND MICHAEL WILSON

aisling Means 'dream' or 'vision' in Gaelic and refers to a stylized form of eighteenth-century Gaelic political verse. The genre was established in Munster by Aogán Ó Rathaille (*c*.1670–*c*.1726) and typically features a dream encounter between the poet and a beautiful fairy woman who symbolizes Ireland. She tells him of her current distress and desired deliverance; he responds with hope or despair, depending upon the actual prospects of the return of a Stuart king – seen as a potential saviour by Irish Catholics – to the English throne. Late eighteenth-century aisling poems lack political realism, since hopes of a Jacobite restoration ended with the defeat of Prince Charles Stuart at the battle of Culloden in 1746.

Reading

Murphy, Gerard, 'Notes on aisling poetry', *Éigse*, 1 (1939), pp. 40–50.
Ó Buachalla, Breandán, 'Irish Jacobite poetry', *Irish Review*, 12 (Spring/Summer 1992), pp. 40–9.

LIAM HARTE

alcoholism Ireland has a higher rate of alcoholism than other European countries. It is the second most common cause of admissions to psychiatric hospitals, comprising 26 per cent of all cases. Cirrhosis rates are low, however, for the typical drinking pattern involves binges rather than tippling. Ireland also has a high proportion of teetotallers (25 per cent).

Historically, the rural Irish indulged in drinking at special occasions like markets, festivals, Christenings and weddings. Wakes were an important part of this circumstantial drinking. Ale was part of Celtic tradition, but by the eighteenth century it was too expensive, and the common people drank whiskey.

Poteen (illegal spint) was distilled in the north and west.

In the 1790s, the government, concerned at heavy whiskey drinking, abolished tax on beer, but its consumption was restricted to towns like Dublin and Cork until the 1850s. In the 1920s, when Kevin O'Higgins legislated to curb the abuses of the liquor trade, he met with such opposition that he remarked that the publicans of Ireland were far harder to deal with than the Republicans.

Many famous persons have suffered from alcoholism. Anthony Cronin's *Dead as Doornails* describes the excesses of Brendan Behan, Patrick Kavanagh and Flann O'Brien, whose writing, however, also reflects the humour found in the traditional Dublin public house.

FRED LOWE

Alcorn, Michael (1962–) Born Belfast, 22 January. He studied at the University of Ulster with David Morris, and at Durham University with John Casken. He was composer in residence at Queen's University, Belfast, before being appointed lecturer in music in 1989. Influenced by electronic and computer music techniques, his works have been performed and broadcast in Ireland, Great Britain and Denmark. They include *Hanging Stones* for tape and slide projection, *In dulci jubilo* for chorus and organ (both 1985), *Time Domains* for piano (1986), *Jubilate* for piano and computer, *Incantation* for orchestra (both 1987), and the piano quartet *Making a Song and Dance* (1989).

PETER DOWNEY

Allingham, William (1824–89) Ballyshannon-born poet who worked as a Donegal customs official before taking up a literary life in England, publishing his *Poems* (1850) and becoming editor of *Fraser's Magazine* (1874–9). Anti-imperialist and sympathetic to the Irish peasantry, his enthusiasm for Irish folk literature was channelled into a collection of his own ballads in 1864. In the same year his long narrative poem *Lawrence Bloomfield in Ireland* advocated a policy of liberal paternalism in the escalating landlord–tenant conflict. His diary (published 1907, reprinted 1967) provides an entertaining and useful chronicle of Victorian London's literary milieu in accounts of his relationships with Tennyson, Carlyle, Rossetti and Browning.

EVE PATTEN

American Conference for Irish Studies Two University College, Dublin, historians a generation apart, Eoin MacNeill and R. Dudley Edwards, can claim credit for inspiring the formation of the American Conference (originally Committee) for Irish Studies. Some thirty years later the conference hosts academic symposia, encourages study in Ireland and publishes an ever-expanding guide to Irish Studies courses in US colleges.

JOHN B. BRESLIN

Andrews, Christopher Stephen ('Todd') (1901–85) Revolutionary and public servant. Born in Summerhill, Dublin, 6 October; died in Dundrum, County Dublin, 11 October. A member of the Dublin Brigade, Irish Volunteers, from 1916, he was imprisoned in Mountjoy in April 1920. Interned in the Curragh in 1921, he escaped by tunnelling out. He took the anti-Treaty side in the Civil War, and was interned by the Free State Government until 1924. He then returned to University College, Dublin, and graduated BComm.

Andrews was employed by the Irish Tourist Association between 1926 and 1930, and as accounts inspector in the ESB between 1930 and 1933. In 1933, he was put in charge of the Turf Development Board, which became Bord na Mona in 1946. The board expanded rapidly under his direction. In 1958, he became chairman of Coras Iompair Éireann (the Transport Organization of Ireland) and oversaw a major reorganization programme. In June 1966, he was appointed chairman of the RTE Authority, resigning in 1970 when his son David was appointed chief whip of Fianna Fáil.

The New University of Ireland, Trinity College, Dublin, and Queen's University, Belfast, conferred honorary doctorates on him. He wrote an autobiography in two volumes.

Reading

Andrews, Christopher, *Dublin Made Me*, (Dublin and Cork: Mercier Press, 1979).
——*Man of no Property* (Dublin and Cork: Mercier Press, 1982).

ALAN DUKES

annals Some medieval monasteries kept annual records of notable events, and compiled obituaries of prominent individuals, ecclesiastical and lay. The resultant annals are the most comprehensive native record of the history of Gaelic Ireland down to the end of the sixteenth century. Medieval Irish annals were local rather than national in scope, reflecting the limited world view of the compilers, who by the sixteenth century were usually lay men. Major surviving compilations in Gaelic are the *Annals of Ulster*, the *Annals of Connacht* and the *Annals of Loch Cé*. Some annals were also produced in the Pale, notably those of John Clyn and Thady Dowling. One major seventeenth-century research undertaking of the Irish Franciscans at Louvain produced the last great Irish manuscript history of Ireland in the form of annals: the *Annals of the Kingdom of Ireland* by the Four Masters. It was first published in a classic edition with English translation by John O'Donovan in the mid-nineteenth century.

Reading

Mac Niocaill, Gearóid, *The Medieval Irish Annals* (Dundalk: Dublin Historical Association, 1975).

BERNADETTE CUNNINGHAM

Anthologia Hibernica A monthly periodical published in Dublin during 1793 and 1794 'to diffuse knowledge and rational amusement throughout the kingdom' without becoming 'the organ of any sect or party'. In February 1793, for instance, it offered subscribers 'Curious Accounts of Our Round Towers' (illustrated with an engraving), comic pieces, 'Remarks on the Book of Revelations' couched in surprisingly ecumenical language, a study of Aeschylus' *Agamemnon*, and a 'Scale of Genius for 1792' (Richard Brinsley Sheridan scored highest; Edmund Burke, penalized for lack of 'humour', ranked second). Each edition also carried 'Domestic', British and 'Foreign' news, accounts of scientific discoveries, theatre listings, notices of new publications, complex mathematical questions, poetry (often in Latin or French), and a lively readers' correspondence. Conducted with support from members of Trinity College and the Royal Irish Academy, the *Anthologia* provided reading material for an erudite intelligentsia whose interests extended beyond local political and sectarian power struggles.

CHRIS MORASH

antiquarianism Generally, the pre-scientific investigation of the past, mainly as pursued in the seventeenth and eighteenth centuries; in the course of the nineteenth century, antiquarianism was split asunder by the emergence of academic disciplines such as philology, archaeology and the new post-Walter Scott historiography. Some Irish antiquaries were great scholars of European stature, such as Archbishop James Ussher and Sir James Ware; others were enthusiastic amateurs who sacrificed critical analysis for colourful speculation, such as Charles Vallancey. All of them worked at a time when no evidence had yet come to light which allowed scholars to see world history in other than biblical terms: antiquarianism traces humanity from the Garden of Eden, and the human languages and races from the sons of Noah. The main preoccupations of antiquarianism were non-classical antiquity, comparative linguistics, and the recuperation of non-classical older literature from medieval oral sources.

Antiquarianism in Ireland was a local variation on British antiquarianism generally; thus, Charlotte Brooke's *Reliques of Ancient Irish Poetry* (1789) was a counterpart to Bishop Percy's *Reliques of Ancient English Poetry* (1765), and the archaeological investigation of Ireland's Gaelic past matched growing interest in pre-Conquest, Anglo-Saxon England. What made the Irish situation special, however, was that the pre-Conquest antiquity of Ireland was not quite a closed book or a bygone period: it was still remembered by a living (though rapidly fading) tradition of native Gaelic scholarship. That tradition was largely active in religious exile in the Irish colleges on the Continent, but to some extent within Ireland as well. Thus, it was usual for antiquarians to rely for information on native assistance. Ware employed, in the 1650s, the bardic scholar Dubhaltach Mac Fir Bhisigh; the Welsh antiquarian Edward Lhuyd was helped, in his Irish investigations *c.*1700, by Roderic O'Flaherty; Walter Harris in the 1740s drew on Hugh Mac Curtin; Vallancey relied, in the 1770s, on Charles O'Conor of Belanagar; Charlotte Brooke and Joseph Cooper Walker were assisted in the 1780s by Theophilus O'Flanagan. That model persisted into the nineteenth century, when Gaelic scholars like Edward O'Reilly and Eugene O'Curry provided native expertise to the Ulster king-of-arms Sir William Betham and to the Royal Irish Academy.

Another specific feature of Irish antiquarianism was the fact that its researches had direct political importance. English supremacy in Ireland had from the beginning been based on the axiom that England was entitled to rule Ireland owing to its superior civility and culture, as opposed to the benighted barbarianism of the natives. It was this perception which the Gaelic, bardic intelligentsia was trying to controvert by pointing out its rich cultural legacy and the ancient achievements of the Gaels in arts and letters. Such insights squared oddly with the contemporary culture-political relations (of perceived Gaelic squalor and rusticity) that Anglo-Irish antiquarians worked in. Various hypotheses were advanced to account for the contradiction. One school (the more conservative, anglocentric one) dismissed the stories of ancient Gaelic greatness and civility as mere boastful invention and held that Ireland had until the advent of English-imported civility been buried in barbarbism; they tended to see the Gaels as a branch of Scytho-Celtic tribes, and their dour scepticism could vindicate itself by pointing out the patent absurdities of some of the other, more credulous and speculative antiquaries. These latter accepted that there had been an ancient, refined Gaelic culture (traced back, in accordance with native mythography, to Phoenician or Carthaginian roots), but that it had been destroyed in internecine wars; or that it had been destroyed by the spoliations of the Danes; and there were some who said that the barbarous policy of English hegemonism was to blame. This last interpretation was closest to the one advanced by the native scholars themselves, and had the most subversive and politically dangerous implications.

Thus the speculations of Irish antiquarianism were not only of a scholarly nature, but had political overtones as well. The most positive, appreciative interest in Gaelic antiquity was taken by those closest to the Patriot movement end of the political spectrum. Similarly, the decline of such appreciative antiquarianism after 1800 was partly dictated by an anti-patriotic backlash after the 1798 rebellion, as well as by the advent of new, more scientific methods of investigating the past.

The most important long-term effect of Irish antiquarianism was probably that the Anglo-Irish intelligentsia (which until 1700 had been fervently aware of its English roots and its non-Irishness) slowly came to see itself as the cultural heir of Gaelic antiquity, and began to affiliate itself at the affective level to Ireland's Gaelic past. In short, Anglo-Irish historical self-awareness 'went native'. This development made it possible for Ireland's urban, English-speaking population to adopt a Gaelic iconography for its cultural nationalism.

Reading

de Valera, Ann, 'Antiquarian and historical investigations in Ireland in the eighteenth century', MA thesis, University College Dublin, 1978.

Leerssen Joep, 'On the edge of Europe: Ireland in search of Oriental roots, 1650–1850', *Comparative Criticism*, 8 (1987), pp. 91–112.

O'Halloran Clare, Golden Ages and barbarous nations: antiquarian debate on the Celtic past in Ireland and Scotland in the eighteenth century', PhD thesis, Cambridge, 1991.

Vance Norman, 'Celts, Carthaginians and constitutions: Anglo-Irish literary relations, 1780–1820', *Irish Historical Studies*, 22, no. 87 (March 1981) pp. 216–38.

JOEP LEERSSEN

Aosdána Established by An Comhairle Ealaíon, the Irish Arts Council, with the support and encouragement of the Irish government in 1982.

Its purpose is to honour those artists whose work has made an outstanding contribution to the arts in Ireland and to encourage and assist them to devote their energies fully to their art. Membership is limited to 150 artists of distinction and vacant places are filled by a democratic if rather complicated process of election.

Members are eligible to receive an annuity, known as a Cnuas, to enable them to concentrate their time and energies on the full-time pursuit of their art. There is no doubt that eligibility for this has released many from the sorts of exigency which were once endemic in the artist's situation.

Aosdána meets in general assembly at least once a year to discuss issues of concern to it as a body or generally relevant to the status of the artist and the arts in society. It recognizes especially significant achievement in an art form by electing members as Saoi. To date those elected include Samuel Beckett, Sean O'Faolain, Patrick Collins and Francis Stuart.

Aosdána came into existence partly as a result of the realization that while provision for the performance and dissemination of works of art had improved, not enough was being done to honour individual artists for their achievement or to enable them to go on producing works of art. One of the most remarkable things about its inception was the welcome accorded to it by the general public.

C.J. HAUGHEY

Apprentice Boys of Derry On 7 December 1688, 13 apprentices shut the Ferryquay gate minutes before Lord Antrim's Catholic forces would have gained entry. This inauguration of the siege became the focal point of Protestant/loyalist enthusiasm in Derry and beyond. Apprentice boys' clubs developed, the earliest in 1714, but especially in the mid-nineteenth century. A general committee was established in 1859. A memorial hall, with elaborately furnished council chambers, opened in 1877 overlooking the city wall, the Walker Pillar and the Bogside. In 1988 the Apprentice Boys claimed 12,000 members in 200 branch clubs. Annual siege commemorations have been organized every 12 August. The Boys' insistence on marching on 5 October 1968 and on 12 August 1969 helped precipitate the disturbances in Derry, the latter leading to the introduction of British troops on 14 August.

Reading

Apprentice Boys of Derry Association, *Official Brochure of the Tercentenary Celebrations* (1988).

Lacy, Brian, *Siege City* (Belfast: Blackstaff, 1990), pp. 113–27.

W. HARVEY COX

Aran Islands (Oileáin Árann) Three islands famous for Celtic grandeur, medieval sanctity, persistence of folk-ways and flourishing Gaelic. Administratively part of County Galway, geologically and ecologically they belong to the Burren, being the broken remains of a limestone escarpment extending west-north-west across the mouth of Galway Bay.

The smallest island, Inis Oírr (from 'Inis Oirthir', island of the east, anglicized as Inisheer), has close social ties with Doolin on the Clare coast. Inis Méain (middle island, anglicized as Inishmaan), the least visited, was selected by J.M. Synge for his sojourns in 1898–1902, as its life was perhaps the most primitive left in Europe. The largest, Árainn or Inis Mór (big island, Inismore), has the islands' capital, Cill Rónáin (Kilronan), home to a small but modern fishing fleet, and greets perhaps a hundred thousand tourists each year. Many of these are drawn by the spectacular triple-ramparted cashel, Dún Aonghasa, on the brink of a 300-foot cliff over the Atlantic, and traditionally ascribed to Aonghas, a leader of the mythical Fir Bolg.

There are also five substantial inland cashels, a fine promontory fort, and several early oratories and medieval chapels in the islands. Cill Éinne in Arainn was the site of a monastery said to have been founded by St Enda in about AD 480 and to have numbered such celebrities as Columcille Ciaráin of Clonmacnois and Jarlath of Tuam among its alumni. But perhaps the islands' most amazing monument is the nineteenth-century field system, defined by about a thousand miles of drystone walling, which is largely intact, modern farming being impracticable in this terrain.

The islands belonged to the O'Briens of Munster, who built a towerhouse in Inis Oírr, until they were ousted by the O'Flahertys of Connemara in the 1570s. Because of the islands' strategic importance in the context of her Spanish wars, Queen Elizabeth bestowed them on an Englishman in 1582 on condition he kept a force there. A fort was built at Cill Éinne, which saw some action after the surrender of Galway to Cromwell's general in 1651: when it was finally secured by the Cromwellians, it was rebuilt and enlarged with stone from the long-deserted monasteries close by. The absentee landlords of Aran from 1744 onwards were the Digbys of Landenstown, County Kildare, by whom it was rackrented and neglected until the 1880s, when the Congested Districts Board began to develop the fishing industry. In 1922 the estate was bought out and divided among the tenants.

The population was at its peak (3,521) just before the Great Famine, which it seems was less severe there than in neighbouring mainland areas. Nevertheless, emigration had started as early as 1822, and the current population is about 1,350. The island community responded to its rediscovery by the Irish cultural revival of the late nineteenth century by producing its own writers, including Máirtín Ó Direáin (1910–88) and Liam O'Flaherty (1897–1984). Breandán Ó hEithir (1930–90), the latter's nephew, was also born in Árainn.

Reading

Ó hEithir, B. and Ó hEithir, R. (eds), *An Aran Reader* (Dublin: 1991).

Oileáin Árann: The Aran Islands, a Map and Guide (Roundstone, 1992).

Powell, Antoine, *Oileáin Árann: stair na n-oileán anuas go dtí* (Dublin: n.d., *c*.1983).

Robinson, T., *Stones of Aran* (Dublin: 1986, repr. Penguin, 1990).

Synge, J.M., *The Aran Islands* (London: 1907; repr. Penguin, 1992).

TIM ROBINSON

architecture

Ecclesiastical Architecture from 1829

The immediate post-Emancipation Irish church was typically a rectangular box with a low-pitched roof, usually Perpendicular Gothic in the provinces and classical in Dublin. Only the largest examples had internal columns, usually wooden as at Naas, Tuam Cathedral and Ennis Pro-cathedral. Among the more elaborate Gothic designs was the T-shaped St Malachy's, Belfast (Thomas Jackson, 1840–4). Neo-classical churches included St Mary's, Pope's Quay, Cork (Kearns Deane, 1832–9), Longford Cathedral (J.B. Keane, 1840–56) and, in Dublin, St Paul's, Arran Quay (1837),

St Audeon's, High Street (1841), and Rathmines (1854), all by Patrick Byrne. Byrne also worked in the Gothic idiom and became aware of the archaeologically correct Gothic revival being wrought in Britain by the young architect and writer Augustus Welby Pugin. Pugin assisted Byrne with the chapel at Loreto Convent, Rathfarnham, County Dublin (1839). Through connections in County Wexford Pugin obtained further commissions, including Enniscorthy Cathedral (1842). His Irish masterpiece was undoubtedly Killarney Cathedral (also 1842), of which only the walls had been built at the time of his death in 1852.

Pugin's influence was to dominate Irish ecclesiastical architecture for the rest of the century, though his successors were to introduce French elements into the Early English and Decorated Gothic styles that he had advocated. From the 1850s the most significant architect was Pugin's sometime Irish associate J.J. McCarthy, known as the 'Irish Pugin', who cultivated the hierarchy and obtained commissions for four cathedrals – Derry (1851), the completion of Armagh (1853), Monaghan (1861) and Thurles (1865) – as well as numerous churches throughout the country. The majority were Gothic, though Thurles is Pisan Ronanesque. From 1860 the practice set up by Pugin's son Edward and George Coppinger Ashlin competed with McCarthy for major jobs, of which Cobh Cathedral (1867–1919) was the most important. Although the partnership broke up in 1868, Ashlin was to become the foremost church architect after McCarthy's death in 1882, designing substantial buildings like the O'Connell Memorial Church, Cahirciveen (1886), and, with his partner Thomas A. Coleman, completing Killarney Cathedral in 1908–12.

After Pugin, the only English church architect with a significant Irish practice was George Goldie, who obtained commissions as far apart as Waterford, Cork, Limerick and Sligo, where he designed the cathedral (1869–75). Another Englishman, P.C. Hardwick, architect to Lord Dunraven,

designed Limerick Cathedral (1856–61), spire by M.A. Hennessy (1878). Among the more significant late Victorian church architects were William Hague (Letterkenny Cathedral, 1891–1901) and William H. Byrne (Loughrea Cathedral, 1897–1901). The critic Robert Elliott's remark, in 1907, that Loughrea was an example of worn-out Puginism, coupled with his comment that Gothic was a British style, effectively marked the end of the Gothic revival and sent architects and clergy off in a hunt for a national style. Elliott's friend William A. Scott had just designed a church at Spiddal in the Hiberno-Romanesque style, but this and Scott's later basilica at Lough Derg (1921) were too individual to be copied, the mainstream of Romanesque revival churches being distinguished from their Gothic predecessors more by detail than by form. Tired and shopworn as it soon became itself, the Romanesque revival was accompanied by a major encouragement of native artists and craftsmen, with stained glass artists like Michael Healy and Harry Clarke supplanting the ubiquitous Mayer of Munich.

During the inter-war years some architects managed to design interesting buildings within the stylistic constraints of the Romanesque theme, among them Padraic Gregory (St Malachy's, Coleraine, 1937) and the firm of Robinson and Keefe, whose Dublin churches included the Italianate Foxrock (1934) and the Byzantine Deco Whitehall (1938). The only really modern church of the period, Turner's Cross, Cork (Barry Byrne of Chicago, 1927–31), proved to be too controversial for the experiment to be repeated. The master of combining details from different classical and European sources was undoubtedly Ralph Byrne (son of William H.), whose major works were Mullingar Cathedral (1932–6), SS Peter and Paul, Athlone (1935–7), and Cavan Cathedral (1937–41).

The growth of Irish cities after World War II saw the construction of many new suburban churches, the Dublin examples being mostly Romanesque and red-brick, giving way in the early 1960s to the modern basilica, typified by low-pitched roofs and angular or angled windows. After the introduction, from 1963, of the liturgical reforms of Vatican II, new plan forms, often based on a circle or square, replaced the basilica layout. Among the more interesting are the churches of Liam McCormick, the most striking being the award winning Burt, County Donegal (1967). The liturgical reforms also led to the remodelling of existing churches and regrettably many fine vernacular and High Victorian interiors and fittings were lost in the scramble for modernity.

The Church of Our Lady of Refuge, Rathmines, Dublin dates from 1854. The last of Patrick Byrne's great Dublin classical churches, it is said to have been built with the contributions of servants in this expanding suburb. Unusually for Dublin, its plan is a Greek cross, with a dome, originally slated, rising above the crossing. As with Byrne's earlier St Audoen's (1841), the walls are built of calp limestone. The facade, though, is faced with granite ashlar, and the Portland stone tetrastyle corinthian porticos were completed in the 1880s by William M. Byrne. Following a serious fire in 1920, the church was rebuilt by his son Ralph Byrne, with a copper dome of Roman proportions. Internally, the original pilasters and frieze were integrated into an elaborate scheme of stucco decoration.

The original design for the *Cathedral of St Patrick, Armagh*, was an exercise in Perpendicular Gothic with two towers at the west end and a great tower over the crossing. This was the work of the Newry architect Thomas Duff, under whose supervision building began in 1840, only to be suspended during the famine years. Work did not recommence until 1854, Duff having died in the interval. The new architect J.J. McCarthy preferred Decorated Gothic, so that the building, above the level of the aisles, was completed in that style (but without the central tower) in 1873. A remarkable and costly scheme of interior decoration was undertaken in 1900–4

by Cardinal Logue. Of this, the intricately carved marble pulpit and rood screen were removed in 1982.

Work on Augustus Welby Pugin's great *St Mary's Cathedral, Killarney, County Kerry*, began in 1842. The design, in Early English Gothic, was relatively severe, depending on contrasting stonework, form and massing for effect, rather than an elaboration of carved detail. Work was suspended between 1848 and 1853, when the shell was open to the elements. Pugin having died in 1852, it was left to his associate J.J. McCarthy and son Edward Welby Pugin to resume construction and roof the cathedral, enabling it to be opened for worship in 1855. A major building programme in 1908–12 saw the erection of the 285-foot spire under the supervision of Ashlin and Coleman. By the 1970s, it was felt that the interior was a 'museum of Victoriana' inappropriate to the modern liturgy, so that all the plaster was stripped out, together with the floors, altar, pulpit and reredos.

The Church of SS Augustine and John, John's Lane, Dublin was the first and best of Pugin and Ashlin's Dublin churches, commissioned apparently in 1860, but not begun until 1862 and not finished (by William Hague) until 1895. Major design credit must go to Edward Welby Pugin, who sent his pupil George Coppinger Ashlin over to open a Dublin office on the strength of the job. The *Dublin Builder* wrote that 'this church promises to be one of the finest in the kingdom'. The design exploited a dramatic site on falling ground, the composition, in polychromatic sandstone with limestone dressings, rising to a 160-foot stone spire (not completed until 1884).

Pugin and Ashlin were one of three firms asked to submit designs in 1867 for a new *Cathedral of St Colman at Cobh, County Cork* (then Queenstown). Following a row between the other competitors and the building committee, partly over the £25,000 cost limit, the commission went to Pugin and Ashlin. Owing to a difficult site and a client intent on elaborating the design after work had begun, construction was extremely protracted. The final

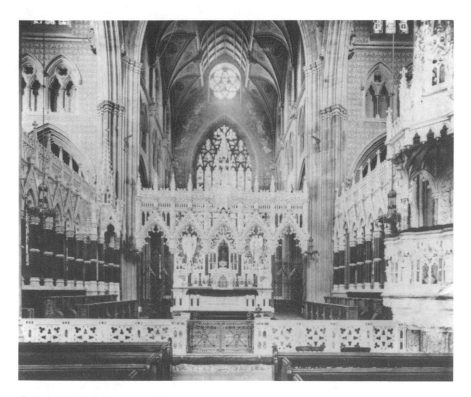

Cathedral of St. Patrick, Armagh.

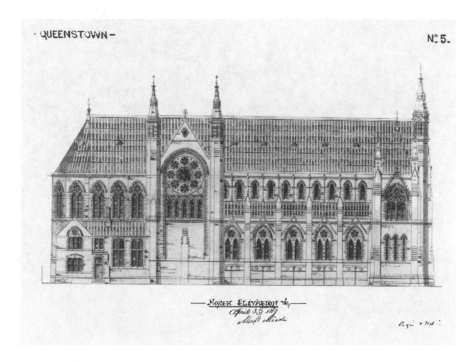

Cathedral of St. Colman, Cobh, Co. Cork, drawing of the North Elevation

Leinster House complex, Dublin

Government Buildings, Merrion Street, Dublin

Parliament House, College Green, Dublin (now the bank of Ireland), interior of the House of Lords

Maynooth College, Co. Kildare

Our Lady's Hospital, Cork, formerly Eglinton Asylum

Parliament House, College Green, Dublin (now the bank of Ireland), interior of the House of Lords

Maynooth College, Co. Kildare

Our Lady's Hospital, Cork, formerly Eglinton Asylum

Parliament Buildings, Stormont

Sandford parish church, Dublin

St. Finbarre's Cathedral, Cork

University College, Galway, the Quadrangle

University College, Galway, the Quadrangle

cost, in 1919, was £235,000, making it probably the most expensive single building constructed in Ireland to that date. The walls are faced externally with Dalkey granite with Mallow limestone dressings. The 300-foot spire, one of the landmarks of Cork harbour, was erected in 1911–13.

Spiddal Church, County Galway, a compact Hiberno-Romanesque building, was built in 1904–7 from the designs of William A. Scott of Dublin. The claim of the commissioning parish priest Fr. Mark Conroy that it was 'the first effort at a revival of the native architecture developed by the Gael before the coming of the Gall' ignores the scholarly examples, including some churches with round towers, erected by the Church of Ireland as early as the 1860s. Spiddal, which almost got a round tower, owed much to Scott's Arts and Crafts training in London and was more a building of its time than a revived form.

The Church of St Patrick, Newport, County Mayo, built by Sisks in 1917–18, was R.M. Butler's attempt at adopting the Hiberno-Romanesque style for a relatively large building. Its construction, on the hilltop site of its predecessor, was made possible by the £10,000 legacy of a parishioner. It is faced with local red sandstone, with Dumfries sandstone for the entrance and carved work, complemented by a roof of green Tilbertwaithe slates. The interior, which tapers towards the east end (with Harry Clark window), has classical columns and a fibrous-plaster vault not stylistically related to the elevations. The west end square tower, surmounted by a flagstaff, gives it the appearance of an English parish church.

In 1937, the newly appointed Bishop of Kilmore, Dr Lyons, commissioned Ralph Byrne of Wm H. Byrne and Son to design a new *Cathedral of SS Patrick and Felim, Cavan*, after seventeen years of fundraising. It was begun by Sisks in September 1938 and completed in 1941. Like Byrne's earlier cathedral at Mullingar and church at Athlone, the style is classical. Gothic was

considered too expensive, but Dr Lyons wanted a spire and got one, based on Francis Johnston's (Protestant) church of St George's, Dublin. The nave is of the Roman basilica type, with a richly plastered ceiling, dome over the crossing and coffered vaults over the transepts.

Other Public Architecture
Leinster House, which today as part of the *Leinster House Complex* houses the Irish Parliament, was built from 1745 for James, Earl of Kildare, to the designs of the German-born architect Richard Castle. Its plan and generous site gave it the appearance of a country house. In 1815 it was sold to the Royal Dublin Society (RDS), which added new drawing schools to the north in 1827 (architect H.A. Baker). The Natural History Museum, on the south side of Leinster Lawn, built by the government in 1856–7 (architect F.V. Clarendon), was subsequently mirrored by the elevation of the National Gallery, privately promoted in 1853, but completed with Treasury funding in 1864 (architect Captain Francis Fowke CE, in succession to Charles Lanyon). The complex, the Dublin equivalent of South Kensington, was completed with the erection of the National Library and National Museum in 1885–90 (architects T.N. Deane and Son). Leinster House became the temporary home of Dáil Éireann in 1922, and was subsequently purchased by the state, the RDS erecting new premises at Ballsbridge.

The Government Buildings, Merrion Street, Dublin, a quadrangular Edwardian baroque building faced with Portland stone and granite, was built in 1904–22 to house the College of Science (opened by King George V in 1911) and, facing Merrion Street, the offices of the Department of Agriculture and Technical Instruction, and the Department of Local Government. The design was entrusted to Sir Aston Webb of London, with Thomas Manly Deane as local executant architect. Although traditional in appearance, it had such novel features as concrete floors and roofs, electric power and elevators. In 1990–1 the College of Science (latterly the School of Engineering of University College, Dublin) was converted to house the offices of the Department of the Taoiseach.

The Parliament House, College Green, Dublin, now the Bank of Ireland, was built in 1728–39 on the site of its predecessor Chichester House, where the Irish Lords and Commons had sat since 1661. The design of the new building was entrusted not to the then surveyor-general Thomas Burgh, but to the young Edward Lovett Pearce, a protégé of the speaker William Conolly. Pearce had probably been a pupil of his cousin Vanbrugh and had studied Palladian architecture at first hand in the Veneto. The octagonal Commons chamber, at the centre of the plan, has been destroyed, but the House of Lords survives. James Gandon made additions to the House of Lords (1784–*c*.9) and was one of the architects involved in the Foster Place extension to the Commons (1786–93). The conversion to a bank was carried out by Francis Johnston in 1804–8.

The design of the *Belfast Custom House* was entrusted by the Board of Public Works to the local firm Lanyon and Lynn. The building, erected in 1854–7, is in the form of an Italian palazzo, a style previously used by Lanyon for country houses. The leading architect in Ulster, Lanyon was the son-in-law of the board's architect Jacob Owen. Built to an E-shaped plan on an island site, the elevations are faced with Glasgow freestone. As well as the customs, the building originally housed several other government departments as well as a post office. The carved figures in the pediment and spandrils of the east front were designed by S.F. Lynn, sculptor brother of the architect, and executed by Thomas Fitzpatrick.

In 1845 two Irish education acts were passed. Under the first, *Maynooth College*, the national seminary, was to get £30,000 for extensions and repairs. Under the second, £100,000 was provided 'to endow [three] new [Queen's] colleges for the advancement of learning in Ireland'. Maynooth and the *Queen's Colleges* were placed under the charge of the Board of Public Works, each college being entrusted to a private architect: Maynooth (A.W.N. Pugin), Belfast (Charles Lanyon), Cork – now University College, Cork (Sir Thomas Deane) and Galway – now University College, Galway (John B. Keane). All the designs were Gothic, Cork and Maynooth being the most interesting. The Cork contract ran smoothly, but the Belfast and Maynooth designs were over budget and had to be cut back, while both the builder and the architect for Galway got into financial difficulties, the Board of Works taking over the supervision after Keane's imprisonment in the Dublin Marshalsea.

Our Lady's Hospital (formerly Eglinton Asylum), Cork, was built to house 500 patients. It was the largest of seven district lunatic asylums commissioned by the Board of Public Works in the late 1840s to supplement the nine establishments erected by Johnston and Murray in 1820–35. Like the earlier buildings, the new institutions were 'corridor asylums', but with the emphasis on wards rather than cells. There was a change in style from classical to Gothic. Designed by local architect William Atkins, the Cork asylum was one of the longest buildings in Ireland (almost 1,000 feet), originally split into three blocks, punctuated with towers and gables. Atkins made good use of polychromy, contrasting Glanmire sandstone with limestone dressings. The elevated site, overlooking the River Lee at Shanakiel, appears to have been chosen by the local governors for dramatic effect rather than practicality, great difficulty being encountered in providing exercise yards on the steep slope.

Parliament Buildings, Stormont, County Down, was the last great neo-classical building erected in Ireland (1927–32). It was built on a dramatic hillside site approached by a three-quarter-mile-long avenue. The 27-bay facade has a hexastyle Ionic portice and a richly carved attic storey over the breakfront. Like the Dublin Government Buildings, it is faced with Portland stone on a granite base.

The original proposal, in 1922, was for three blocks – a parliament house and two administrative buildings as at Pretoria and New Delhi. After the parliament house was begun, the architect Arnold Thornley of Liverpool was asked to incorporate all the offices within it. The main interiors are the travertine-clad central hall and the Commons and Senate Chambers, fitted up by the firm that did the transatlantic liners.

Reading

de Courcy, Catherine, *The Foundation of the National Gallery of Ireland* (Dublin: National Gallery of Ireland, 1985).

Duffy, Rev. Francis 'The Cathedral of SS Patrick and Felim, Cavan', *Breifne* VIII, no. 3 (1992–3).

Elliott, Robert, *Art in Ireland* (Dublin: Sealy, Bryers and Walker, 1906).

Gaffney, V. Rev. Patrick (ed.), *The Book of Kilmore Cathedral* (Cavan: 1947).

The Georgian Society Records of Eighteenth-Century Domestic Architecture and Decoration in Dublin, IV, (Dublin: 1912; repr. Shannon: Irish University Press, 1969).

Henry, Hanora M., *Our Lady's Psychiatric Hospital, Cork* (Cork: Haven Books, 1989).

Hurley, Richard, 'Irish church architecture 1839–1989', in John Graby (ed.), *150 Years of Architecture in Ireland* (Dublin: RIAI/Eblana Editions, 1989).

Larmour, Paul, *Belfast, An Illustrated Architectural Guide* (Belfast: Friar's Bush Press, 1987).

McParland, Edward, 'The Bank and the visual arts', in *Bicentenary Essays: Bank of Ireland 1783–1983* (Dublin: Gill and Macmillan, 1983).

——'Edward Lovett Pearce and the Parliament House in Dublin', *Burlington Magazine* CXXXI, no. 1031 (February 1989).

Moody, Theodore William and Beckett, James Camlin, *Queen's Belfast 1845–1949: The History of a University*, 2 vols (London: Faber, 1959).

'New Church, Newport, Co. Mayo', *Irish Builder and Engineer* (26 May 1917).

'New Church Spiddal', *Irish Builder and Engineer* (24 August 1907).

Newman, Jeremiah, *Maynooth and Victorian Ireland* (Galway: Kenny, 1983).

O Caoimh, Tomas, *Killarney Cathedral* (Dublin: Eason and Son, 1990).

O'Dwyer, Frederick, 'The architecture of the Board of Public Works 1831–1922', in Ciaran O'Connor and John O'Regan (eds) *Public Works* (Dublin: Architectural Association of Ireland, 1987).

——'A Victorian partnership – the architecture of Pugin & Ashlin', in John Graby (ed.), *150 Years of Architecture in Ireland* (Dublin: RIAI/Eblana Editions, 1989).

Ó Fiaich, Tomás, *St Patrick's Cathedral, Armagh* (Dublin: Eason and Son, 1987).

Raftery, Patrick, 'The last of the traditionalists: Patrick Byrne 1783–1864', *Irish Georgian Society Bulletin* vii, nos. 2, 3, 4 (Apr.–Dec. 1964).

Rothery, Sean, *Ireland and the New Architecture* (Dublin: Lilliput Press, 1991).

Shechy, Jeanne, *J.J. McCarthy and the Gothic Revival in Ireland* (Belfast: Ulster Architectural Heritage Society, 1977).

Stanton, Phoebe, *Pugin* (London: Thames and Hudson, 1971).

Thompson, Patrick (ed.), *St Colman's Cathedral, Cobh* (Cobh: c.1983).

Turpin, John, 'The Dublin Society's School of Architectural Drawing', *Irish Georgian Society Bulletin* xxviii (1985).

Walker, Brian and Dixon, Hugh, *In Belfast Town, 1864–1880* (Belfast: Friar's Bush Press, 1984).

Williams, Jeremy, 'William Atkins 1812–1887, a forgotten Cork Pre-Raphealite', in Agnes Bernelle (ed.), *Decantations* (Dublin: Lilliput Press, 1992).

FREDERICK O'DWYER

archives There are three official archival repositories for records relating to the government of Ireland: the National Archives, Dublin, the Public Record Office of Northern Ireland in Belfast and the Public Record Office in London. The Public Record Office of Ireland was established in 1867 in the Four Courts building in Dublin. In the succeeding 40 years local and central government records were transferred there and a guide to the contents was published in 1919. But in 1922, at the beginning of the Irish Civil War, the four courts building was attacked and the Public Record Office destroyed by fire. All that survived was a small collection of original records and transcripts and calendars of the burnt manuscripts. Fortunately the records of the Chief Secretary's office which were kept in a tower in Dublin Castle (the State Paper Office) escaped the fire, as did some government records which had not yet been transferred to the Four Courts building. Among these were land surveys from the seventeenth century in the Quit Rent Office and records concerned with law and order in the eighteenth century. These records were subsequently deposited in the Record Office: but generally, government departments in the new state were reluctant to allow public access to their archives and were under no legal or official pressure to do so.

In 1991, however, as a consequence of the National Archives Act (1988), the management of Irish government archives was transformed. Under the act the Public Record Office was renamed the National Archives and its premises moved from the Four Courts to Bishop Street, Dublin. The records in the State Paper Office were relocated in the new premises. The legislation also facilitated the depositing of official records in the National Archives. From January 1991, government records can be made available for public inspection after 30 years. It is left to the discretion of individual government departments to withhold confidential or sensitive material; but in the first year of its operation, historians were agreeably surprised at the wealth of records made available for public consultation. Apart from official documentation, the National Archives has a large collection of business records from offices and companies all over Ireland, and a smaller collection of private papers. The National Archives receives court and probate records 20 years after their creation and also has responsibility for pre-disestablishment parish registers of the Church of Ireland.

The Public Record Office of Northern Ireland (PRONI) in Belfast was established under legislation passed in 1923. It is the depository for the records of Northern Ireland government departments and also holds records relating to the six countries which pre-date the founding of the state and were transferred to Belfast from government offices in Dublin. A 30-year rule applies to government records in Northern Ireland, as in the rest of the United Kingdom; in recent years, because of the troubles, access to what are considered sensitive files has been restricted. Apart from central government records, local authorities in Northern Ireland deposit records in PRONI, as do some church authorities. PRONI also has an excellent collection of private papers. Among the most important are the estate papers of the Downshire and Gosford families and those of the marquis and marchioness of Dufferin and Ava. PRONI is also the repository for the papers of prominent Ulster unionist and nationalist politicians, including Lord Edward Carson and Viscount Craigavon. In addition, there is a large collection of papers from solicitor's offices and archives of many organizations and societies based in Northern Ireland. These include the records of the Irish Unionist Association and the Irish Unionist Council as well as many Orange lodges. PRONI has also collected archives and documents relating to industrial and commercial development in the province. Among the most substantial collections in this category is the archive of the shipbuilders Harland and Wolfe.

The Public Record Office (PRO) in London holds a very large collection of documentary material relating to Ireland. One of the most continuous series is that of the Irish state papers from the earliest years of Henry VIII's reign to 1782. These papers contain a great variety of documents relating to Ireland including the correspondence of successive Irish administrations, financial accounts, military surveys and reports from government commissions. They have been calendared for the sixteenth and seventeenth centuries. Since the destruction of the Irish Public Record Office, the state papers in the PRO have been the main source for the history of early modern Ireland. The records of the Home Office, which had overall responsibility for the affairs of Ireland until 1922 and for Northern Ireland 1922–72, have a great deal of material concerning most of the main political events in Ireland from the late eighteenth to the early twentieth century. The Home Office also had responsibility for Irish public services and institutions such as hospitals and the Royal Irish Constabulary. After 1922, the Colonial Office dealt with the Irish Free State, and its records contain documentation on the Irish Free State as well as Northern Ireland in the 1920s. The records of the British Cabinet after 1916 are also available in the PRO and include many references to Ireland.

Local government archives are deposited in a variety of institutions including town and county halls and local libraries. In recent years many local authorities have begun to provide facilities for researchers. The largest collection of municipal records is in Dublin and can be consulted in the manuscripts room in the City Hall. Records of local institutions such as hospitals and schools are usually still preserved *in situ* and may be consulted by private arrangement.

The records of the Roman Catholic church are organized on a diocesan basis, with the largest archive to be found in the Dublin Diocesan Library. The Church of Ireland has its own library and archive (in the Representative Church Body Library in Dublin), as do the Quakers. The Presbyterian and Methodist churches have archieves and libraries in Belfast. The Jewish Museum, Dublin, can provide information on records relating to the community in Ireland. Copies of parish records can be found in PRONI, the National Archive and the National Library of Ireland; or can be seen, with the permission of the relevant ecclesiastical authorities, in local parish churches. Other ecclesiastical institutions such as convents, friaries and schools have archives usually dating back to the nineteenth century, and these can often be consulted on inquiry. Public libraries, founded by ecclesiastical figures in the eighteenth century, such as Marsh's Library, Dublin, Armagh Public Library and the Guinness

Peat Library, Cashel, all have archival collections which are mainly concerned with Church of Ireland affairs.

The largest public library in Ireland, the National Library of Ireland, has a large miscellaneous collection of manuscript material, mainly in the form of private or family papers. Among the most important are the estate papers of the Leinster (Fitzgerald), Ormonde (Butler) and Devonshire (Boyle) families. Papers relating to prominent political figures such as Daniel O'Connell, Patrick Pearse, Roger Casement and John Redmond can also be found in the National Library. Irish writers represented in the library's collections include Maria Edgeworth, Patrick Sheehan, W.B. Yeats and Patrick Kavanagh. The library has also accumulated a significant number of manuscripts in Irish. In addition it has a collection of Irish maps, topographical prints, portraits and original drawings as well as an impressive collection of early photographs of Irish towns in the Lawrence Collection. Attached to the National Library is the Genealogical Office, which has a small archive of genealogical material relating to Irish families.

All Irish universities have archive collections. The manuscripts room in Trinity College, Dublin, has manuscripts relating to many individuals associated with the college including James Ussher, William King and Jonathan Swift. The papers of the Land League leader Michael Davitt and the playwright John Millington Synge are also in Trinity. The library has as well an important collection of early Irish manuscripts including the Book of Kells, the Book of Armagh and the Book of Durrow.

The Archives Department in University College, Dublin, has over the last 25 years accumulated a large collection of papers relating to government ministers of the Irish Free State, including Richard Mulcahy and Desmond Fitzgerald; and for more recent times, the papers of Desmond's son, Garret. The papers of Eamon de Valera were left to the Franciscan Library in Killiney.

The Chester Beatty Library in Dublin was the private library of Sir Alfred Chester Beatty and was bequeathed on his death to the Irish people in 1968. It has an internationally respected collection of eastern manuscripts including clay tablets as well as Arabic, Indian, Burmese, Siamese, Tibetan and Mongolian manuscripts.

Other, smaller and more specialized collections of archives in Ireland include literary manuscripts in Irish in the Royal Irish Academy, trade union records in the Irish Labour History Museum, legal records in the library of King's Inns, Dublin, and architectural drawings and photographs in the Irish Architectural Archive, also in Dublin.

Apart from the PRO in London, the most important collections of manuscript material relating to Ireland in Britain are in the British Library and the Bodleian Library, Oxford. The Irish material in these institutions has never been adequately catalogued but includes a wide variety of material relating to Irish officials, politicians and literary figures.

Reading

Edwards, R.W. Dudley and O'Dowd, Mary, *Sources for Early Modern Irish History*, (Cambridge: Cambridge University Press, 1985).

Elmes, Rosalind M., *Catalogue of Irish Topographical Prints and Original Drawings*, new edn. rev. and enlarged by Michael Hewson (Dublin: Malton Press for National Library of Ireland Society, 1975).

Hayes Richard, J., *Manuscript Sources for the History of Irish Civilisation*, 11 vols (Boston MA: G.K. Hall, 1965; 3-vol. supplement, Boston MA: 1979).

Helferty, Seamus and Refausse, Raymond (eds), *Directory of Irish Archives* (Dublin: Irish Academic Press, 1988).

Irish Archives, 2, no. 1 (Summer 1992): special issue on maritime history sources.

Prochaska, Alice, *Irish History from 1700: A Guide to Sources in the Public Record Office* (London: British Records Association, 1986).

Reports of the Deputy Keeper of the Records of the Public Record Office of Northern Ireland 1925–72 (Belfast: HMSO).

Reports of the Public Records and Keeper of the State Papers in Ireland, 55–59 (Dublin, 1928–61).

MARY O'DOWD

Arms Trial On 5 May 1970 Jack Lynch dismissed his finance minister, Charles Haughey, from his cabinet. Later the same year Haughey and others went on trial accused of illegally attempting to import arms. All were acquitted. The trial, the sensation of the decade, was notable *inter alia* for a conflict of evidence between Haughey and James Gibbons, who had served with him in cabinet as defence minister. Afterwards the Dáil committee of public accounts investigated the disposal of £100,000 voted for relief of distress in Northern Ireland and concluded that a large proportion of the money had been appropriated to other purposes. In May 1980 *Magill* magazine stated that almost one-third of the money had gone to the two wings of the IRA. The circumstances of Haughey's dismissal in 1970 alarmed many opposition, especially Labour, politicians, some of whom claimed that the purpose of the attempted importation was to mount a *coup d'état*. There is no doubt that an attempt at importation was made, but that the arms were meant for the use of 'Republican' elements in the North. After his acquittal Haughey, believing correctly that he had no political future outside Fianna Fáil, set about reconstructing his position and was ultimately rewarded by his election as Fianna Fáil leader, and as taoiseach, in December 1979. But the 'arms crisis' shadowed the whole of his later career.

JAMES DOWNEY

Arne family

Thomas Augustine (1710–78)
English composer and violinist; the leading figure in English theatrical music in the mid-eighteenth century, and teacher of

numerous singers. He paid extended visits to Dublin between 1742 and 1756, conducting theatrical works and oratorios. His *Alfred* and *Comus* became perennial favourites there. His sister Susanna Maria was the singing actress Mrs Cibber, who took part in the first performance of *Messiah*.

Cecilia (née Young) (1711–89)

Soprano. A sister of Mrs J.F. Lampe and pupil of Geminiani, she came to Dublin with her husband Thomas, remaining there after the marriage broke up, where she followed her career as a singer and looked after her niece, Polly Young the singer. They both returned to London in 1762.

Michael (c.1740–86)

Composer and organist. He came to Dublin with his third wife, the singer Anne Venables, in 1775, remaining for about five years. He performed his father's organ concertos and operas, and conducted his own opera *Cymon*. The lure of alchemy led him into debt and confinement in the Marshalsea prison.

BRIAN BOYDELL

art 1913–23 Throughout the years from 1913 until 1923, a momentous period in Irish history, the development of art was determined more than anything else by the growing ascendancy of the international modern movement. This, however, was linked to and influenced by the nationalism of contemporary politics and the desire among many to establish a distinct Irish school of art, what at the time was often referred to as a 'national' art.

In the visual arts, the period is not self-contained; rather, those forces which we find present in 1913 have their beginnings a decade or more earlier, during the *fin de siècle*, and they were to reach their natural conclusion later in the century. Yet, nevertheless, the period did see the formalization of those paths which both the Modernist and the nationalist painters would pursue in the future.

By 1913 Modernism, that is, that which is generally understood as representing the main stream of development in art from the time of Manet and the Impressionists in France, was already well established in Ireland. As early as 1884 the Dublin Sketching Club had exhibited paintings by James McNeill Whistler, the leading avant-garde painter in England. In 1899 George Russell, better know as 'AE', a painter, poet and writer, had arranged in Dublin an exhibition of '*Modern Paintings*' which included, amongst others, works by the better-known French Impressionists. Russell's hope was that the exhibition might stimulate the development of modern painting in Ireland and, more importantly, encourage artists to draw upon Irish themes, as the literary men had done, and so create a distinct Irish school of art. In 1901 Sarah Purser arranged the celebrated exhibition of paintings by John Butler Yeats and Nathaniel Hone, held in St Stephen's Green, Dublin, and this event saw the introduction of Hugh (later Sir Hugh) Lane to Irish art. Lane, as is well known, hoped to establish a recognizably Irish art, and in 1908 his activities culminated in the opening of the Dublin Municipal Gallery of Modern Art, which he considered a prerequisite to this. Other important exhibitions which promoted Modernism in Ireland were '*Works by Post-Impressionist Painters*' and '*Modern French Pictures*', held at the United Arts Club, Dublin, in 1911 and 1912 respectively. These years, 1901–11, also coincided with the residence in Dublin of George Moore, who had known Manet in Paris, and who was then at the height of his powers as a novelist and critic. It was through Moore that William Orpen, one of the most distinguished painters of the time, became involved with the Irish cultural revival.

Of these events, the appearance of Hugh Lane was the most consequential and with him the two strands of development, namely Modernism and the search for an Irish school of art, are united. To begin with the Municipal Gallery had opened in temporary premises, but the Dublin Corporation had undertaken to erect a suitable building to

31

house the collection. Lane in turn agreed to donate to the Gallery a group of 39 important French Impressionist pictures if the corporation kept to its word. By 1912, however, no final decision having been made on the matter, Lane began to feel that the corporation was procrastinating and he removed his 39 Impressionist works to the National Gallery, London. In 1913 he made a will bequeathing these pictures to London, but in 1915, before sailing to America, wrote a codicil to this will leaving the pictures to Dublin provided that a suitable building was found for them within five years of his death. However, the codicil was unwitnessed and was therefore invalid when Lane drowned in the *Lusitania* later in 1915. Subsequent events regarding the pictures – of which the best known are, perhaps, Degas's *Sur la Plage*, Manet's *Éva Gonzalès*, Monet's *Vétheuil: Sunshine and Snow*, Pissarro's *Printemps, vue de Louveciennes* and Renoir's *Les Parapluies* – stem from this point. In brief, despite well-substantiated protestations from Lane's executor, his aunt, Lady Gregory, and others that the pictures should be returned to Dublin, they remained in London, and in 1924 the British government appointed a committee of inquiry to determine whether Lane, when he signed the codicil, thought it to have legal force. This committee published its findings in 1926 and decided in favour of the Dublin argument, but resolved that had Lane known of recent developments at the Tate Gallery he would have destroyed the codicil. While the legal aspect of this whole affair has never been in doubt, the moral aspect is not yet permanently resolved. The Hugh Lane Municipal Gallery of Modern Art, as the institution is now called, is the most tangible memorial we have to Lane and his efforts to stimulate the development of Irish painting, yet the gallery has never been at the forefront of developments in Irish art.

The years before 1920 in Ireland saw a growing awareness of national identity. The literary revivalists had contributed to this awareness and in the visual arts William Orpen raised the issue in a number of compositions such as *Sowing New Seed* (1913), a picture symbolizing Irish rejuvination, *The Western Wedding* (1914) and *The Holy Well* (1916). But Orpen, who had a flourishing portrait practice in London, was to an extent ambivalent towards events in Ireland, although as a part-time teacher at the Dublin Metropolitan School of Art he exerted an enormous influence on a younger generation of painters. Orpen, however, never returned to Ireland after the end of World War I, so that his essays in the cause of a distinct Irish art must be treated with some circumspection.

Sean Keating studied under Orpen at the Metropolitan School and later worked in London as his studio assistant. In 1916 he returned to Ireland to find his inspiration in the west, in particular in the Aran Islands, which he had first visited in about 1913 or 1914. Henceforth, the area dominated much of his subject matter and he forged from it a strongly nationalist art. From 1916, in compositions such as *The Men of the West*, until the Civil War – with *Men of the South* (1922), *On the Run: War of Independence* (*c*.1924) – and later, Keating chronicled Ireland's emergence to nationhood; while in *An Aran Fisherman and his Wife* of the 1920s, *Half Flood* and *The Race of the Gael*, both of the 1930s, he set down an idyllic vision of rural Irish life and character which perfectly matched the mood of the period.

Ireland's struggle for independence greatly affected Jack B. Yeats, the most important Irish painter to have emerged this century. In a number of paintings done in the years immediately before and after the gaining of independence Yeats recorded the revolutionary events of the time. *Bachelors Walk, In Memory* (1915), a seminal image of the period, *On Drumcliffe Strand* (1918), *The Island Funeral* (1923), *A Westerly Wind* (1921), a picture rich in metaphor, and *Communicating with Prisoners* (1924), for example, show him at his best and illustrate his sense of universal human experience which characterizes so much of his work. Yeats, who was something of a loner, was an observer of events, working from what he called 'a pool of memories', and throughout his career he recorded the changing circumstances of Irish life.

In August 1920, amid the uncertainties of the time, Jack B. Yeats, Paul and Grace Henry, Mary Swanzy, E.M.O'R. Dickey, Letitia Hamilton and a few others founded the Society of Dublin Painters, their aim being to circumvent the hostility of the art establishment towards avant-garde painting. With the Dublin Painters we see the beginning of the steady ascendancy of Modernism in Irish painting. The society took rooms at 7 St Stephen's Green, Dublin, and there held regular single and group exhibitions of members' work. From its inception until the 1940s the Dublin Painters' Society represented all that was progressive in Irish painting. Its members espoused no common aesthetic, but rather were united in their individuality and common interest in avant-garde painting.

Paul Henry, a prominent member of the society in its early days, had spent much of the decade before 1920 living and working on Achill Island, where he recorded the harsh life of the people in images set down with a Post-Impressionist rigour. In 1919, however, Henry and his wife, Grace, settled in Dublin and the following year conceived the idea of founding the Dublin Painters' Society. These and the immediately subsequent years saw Henry at the height of his powers with compositions such as the various versions of his *Potato Diggers* (1910–12), which show his debt to the French painter J.F. Millet, or *Dawn, Killary Harbour* (1922–3) which, with its closely modulated forms and atmospheric tones, betrays the influence of Whistler, whom Henry knew and admired as a student in Paris.

Another founder-member of the Dublin Painters' Society was Mary Swanzy. Like many of her contemporaries, she had studied art in Paris and in the early years of the century had developed a style which, in terms of her use of bright colours briskly applied, was greatly influenced by French Fauvism. She had first shown such paintings in Ireland at her exhibition in the Mills' Hall, Dublin, in 1919 and thus when she joined the Dublin Painters her work was already known. In the mid-1920s she developed a style which, in terms of the simplification of forms and sense of dynamic energy, is part Cubist and part Futurist in derivation, but she did not long persist in this.

In 1923, at the Dublin Painters' autumn exhibition, Mainie Jellett showed two abstract paintings which were a development from her experiments with Cubism. These works, both simply titled *Decoration*, were the most advanced paintings by an Irish artist to have been exhibited in Ireland by that time. The pictures caused a considerable stir in the press, George Russell (AE), for example, betraying the critical mood of the period, describing them as examples of 'artistic malaria'! In the following years, however, Jellett and her friend Evie Hone continued to show similar works at the Dublin Painters' gallery, although they met with little acclaim. Mainie Jellett is the most important Irish Cubist painter and she is one of the few Irish artists of her generation to espouse a distinct theory of art, which, in terms of her search for 'inner rhythms' and 'inner principles' derived from nature, she saw as being a spiritual matter.

Those artists whom we have mentioned, without exception, looked to France for their inspiration, but Cecil Salkeld, another member of the Dublin Painters' Society, had studied in Germany and it is due to him that an influence from the *Neue Sachlichkeit* movement, which greatly influenced European art in the inter-war years, can be found in Ireland. Salkeld first exhibited at the Dublin Painters in about 1923 or 1924, showing in all probability works such as *Composition* (1922), a watercolour with extremely angular and stylized forms, *Cinema* (c.1922), a woodcut, and *The Tennis Party*, an oil of 1923. All of these pictures illustrate the German influence on his work at that time. Like

Mainie Jellett, Salkeld held a distinct philosophy of art, which he set down in the journal *To-Morrow* in 1924. There he defined art as 'the crystallisation of idea into form' which the spectator, through thought, transmutes into idea again. This theory, which he held to throughout his life, is essentially Expressionist and again shows the influence of his time in Germany.

In sculpture, the period from 1913 until 1923 saw little innovation. Oliver Sheppard's *Death of Cúchulain*, of 1911–12, which characterizes his work at the time, is in the Belle Époque tradition of late nineteenth-century sculpture, although his '*In Mystery the Soul Abides*' (*c*.1920–8) is less heroic. The work of Sheppard's foremost pupil, Albert Power, is more naturalistic, as can be seen from his *1916 Memorial* in Limerick and his *Madonna and Divine Child* (1921–2). Other, more minor sculptors working in the period include Roasmond Praeger, Frank Wiles, Morris Harding and Joseph Higgins. They are more sentimental in approach than Sheppard and Power, as Praeger's *The Philosopher* (*c*.1920), Wiles's *Dawn of Womanhood* (1918) and Higgins's *Boy with a Boat* (*c*.1910), for example, show, although Higgins's head of *Michael Collins*, carved in wood in 1922, is a boldly Expressionist piece of work.

As we have said, the period under discussion in Irish art is not self-contained, yet in it one sees the gradual polarization of those paths along which future developments were to proceed. Perhaps this polarization was in itself the major achievement of the time, for with it artists both articulated the critical issue facing them – the need for some kind of genuine expression of the national consciousness – and mapped out ways of achieving it.

s.b. KENNEDY

art, contemporary In summarizing the developments in Irish art practice over the last three decades, it is necessary to make some prefacing remarks. These pertain to periodization, patronage and critical structures.

In terms of periodization, the following loose chronology is proposed; 1960–72, 1972–83, 1983–present. Beginning with the establishment of the Independent Artists Group in 1960, we may identify a period characterized by the conflict between the three organizational nodes of the Royal Hibernian Academy (RHA), the Irish Exhibition of Living Art (IELA, founded 1943) and the Independents. This period ends with the reconfiguration of the IELA Committee in 1972, the crisis in art education practice at the National College of Art and Design (NCAD) and the restructuring of the Arts Council of Ireland in 1973.

In the period 1972–83, art practice in Ireland is marked by the conflict between what may be termed an 'internationalist Modernism' and a 'Romantic Modernism', which can be very loosely identified with the IELA and the Independents respectively. This period comes to an end in the controversial exhibition of 1983, '*Making Sense: Ten Artists 1968–83*', and the furore around the selection of the Irish contributors to the international exhibition ROSC 1984. The current period of art production may be identified with the generation of artists in the newly restructured art colleges who have been educated within the framework of the debates around Modernism and postmodernism, identity and difference, and the poststructuralist critique of 'the sign'. The suggestion implicit in this crude chronology is that the development of contemporary art practice in Ireland since 1960 is to some degree autonomous from the extraordinary political, economic and social upheavals of this period. This must, of course, be corrected. Indeed the development of a complex field of contemporary art practices in Ireland in recent decades might itself be seen as a manifestation of the dramatic transformations of Irish political, economic and social life. The proposed chronology might equally be justified in terms of the transformations of political and economic processes.

In terms of patronage, an understanding of the role of state and corporate sponsorship is crucial. The Arts Councils, Allied Irish Banks

(AIB), Guinness Peat Aviation (GPA) and other large financial institutions have played a determining role in the construction of a canonical body of late twentieth-century Irish art. There is a significant overlap between the Arts Council initiatives and, say, those of the AIB Collection, as evidenced in the key role played by Dr Frances Ruane of the NCAD in contributing to Arts Council Exhibitions and ventures both curatorially and critically and in acting as advisor to the AIB on its collection. Correspondingly, the direct involvement of private collectors such as Patrick Murphy with the organization of state cultural initiatives such as the ROSC series of exhibitions from 1967 to 1988 should be remarked as indicative of the concentrated patterns of patronage and exhibition in place.

Finally and in summary, a pattern of criticism can be discerned whereby a handful of practitioners in the 1960s and 1970s championed the cause of certain individual artists in relation to one or more of the valorized terms 'Irishness', 'Modernity', 'individuality', 'expressivity', 'sensitivity' and 'landscape'. Dorothy Walker's writings on the work of Louis Le Brocquy are an appropriate example of this tendency. With the establishment in 1981 of *Circa* by the Artists' Collective of Northern Ireland, the initiation of a critical discourse around contemporary art practices began in earnest. This project, a journal devoted to contemporary visual culture in Ireland, was complemented by the occasional foray into issues of visual culture by a journal such as *Crane Bag*. The importance of *Circa* since 1981 has been its commitment to rigorous public and critical debate around contemporary visual culture. Rather than simply reinscribe the pre-valorized set of terms identified above, *Circa* sought to interrogate these and provide a much-needed critical forum for the discussion of contemporary visual art production.

The dominant mode of art practice in Ireland in the early 1960s was characterized by the academicism of the RHA, which preoccupied itself with landscape, portraiture and to a lesser extent still life. Such a hegemony was maintained by two established RHA figures, Sean Keating and his pupil Maurice McGonigal, and their role in the then National College of Art. They operated within a paradigm of traditional painting techniques harnessed to a conservative nationalist politic which saw painting and sculpture as very much in the service of the nationalist project. Explicit in this project was a resistance to change and a deep suspicion and hostility towards Modernism with its cosmopolitanism and formalist approach to material.

By the late 1960s, there was pressure to change the rigidified aesthetic of the RHA which dominated the National College of Art. An attempt on the part of some staff to produce students with a 'comprehensive vision [and] a flexible critical sensibility' met with resolute resistance. The ensuing conflict led to disputes between the college authorities and the students who were seeking transformations to curricula in line with the limited Modernism of the newly developed foundation studies course. Eventually, after a long and hard dispute, some compromises were achieved. A new managerial system of education was introduced, based on the British model. This brought with it a conception of artistic production which 'laid great emphasis on the evolution of an individual, marketable style on the part of each student'.

Abstract Modernists such as Patrick Scott and Cecil King developed a hard-edged formalism which by 1970 began to acquire a limited hegemony in its promotion as a national style. This was supported at state level by the Arts Council of Ireland led by Donal O'Sullivan SJ. This apparent shift in patronage was greeted with vociferous criticisms on the part of the Independent Artists. Chief amongst the members of this group were Michael Kane and James Mc Kenna, who subscribed neither to the modern abstractionist ILEA nor to the anti-Modernism of the RHA. They advocated a range of informal figurative and semi-abstract styles which they believed constituted a more organic and democratic aesthetic. The Independents further identified this informal aesthetic as particular to Irish experience and culture.

Their position was in some way vindicated by the community of painters living and working in Ireland from the late forties and early fifties. These painters displayed a preoccupation with nature, rural life and the landscape. Patrick Collins, Nano Reid, Tony O'Malley, Camille Souter, and later Sean McSweeney and Barrie Cooke all applied a semi-abstract, lyrical approach to their subject matter, producing a 'poetic genre' of painterly work which represents a school of Irish landscape that spans three decades. This work was produced in a High Romantic mode which treats the landscape as an enduring repository of native value and identity. The personal response to this centrally important motif was posited as an alternative to an imported modernity and celebrated as a moment of transcendence. This work was claimed as quite 'independent of mainstream international movements...not so much a rejection of the international avant-garde, but a tacit recognition that these styles may not be wholly appropriate in an Irish context'. Landscape was promoted as the quintessential subject matter in Irish art, where artists articulate their 'Irishness' and express their 'Celtic imagination'. Beyond landscape as the privileged signifier for this Celtic sensibility, the portraiture of Louis le Brocquy has also been presented by this discourse as essentializing and reifying this Celtic imagination.

The Committee for the Living Art was radically transformed in 1972 by the displacement of the older 1943 membership by a younger generation. Under the chairmanship of sculptor Brian King, IELA changed its complexion and policies. IELA had always been open to international Modernist influences and was represented in Ireland at this time as a conduit for conceptualism and minimalism as these were circulating and diversifying in the international art world. Some of its members included Robert Ballagh,

Charles Harper and Michael O'Sullivan, who were painters and sculptors. Regular participants in IELA exhibitions included Michael Farrell and John Burke. Abstract formalism dominated these shows, although as an organized group the artists managed to maintain a degree of heterogeneity and a plurality of approaches, materials and concerns, such as responses to events in Northern Ireland. However, any antagonisms which may have been subsumed throughout the 1970s between those who pursued an international Modernist aesthetic, on the one hand, and those who pursued a more Romantic Modernism which manifested itself in expressionism and painterliness, on the other, certainly re-emerged in the controversy surrounding the selection of Irish artists for ROSC 1984.

ROSC's importance for contemporary art in Ireland cannot be overstated, in that it became the first showcase of late twentieth-century modern art in Ireland and contributed to an assessment of Irish art in an international context. Its originator, Michael Scott, was well known for his interest in the development of an Irish Modernism with its 'criteria of transcendental excellence and visual poetry'. However, ROSC 1984's committee, which included two European collectors, failed to come to a decision on the 10 places set aside for Irish artists. The strong implication was that Irish art was not on a par with the international work to be shown. Another selection jury was set up to deal with this problem and it too failed, coming up with 22 names instead of 10. When forced to choose, Michael Kane protested and resigned his position. His promotion of Romantic Modernism and neo-Expressionism did not find favour with the ROSC committee. Finally Ronald Tallon, an architect and colleague of Scott, was appointed to complete the list, which ended up reproducing the abstract Modernism that Kane had railed against in his protest. The ROSC episode is instructive in that it brought to the fore the tensions that had crossed the art scene in Ireland over the previous 20 years.

The role of the Arts Council is also crucial to any understanding of contemporary Irish art. In the early eighties, it addressed itself to the visual arts with increased vigour. This development reinforced earlier initiatives such as the radical restructuring in 1973, increased funding and resources, new proactive policies, and the extending of the council's remit to encompass most areas of cultural welfare. In its short history, it has proven a major force in the developing and profiling of the arts and cultural agendas. The Arts Council promoted business sponsorship of the arts, finding its most powerful expression in major financial institutions such as the major banks (Bank of Ireland and AIB) establishing collections of contemporary art.

Arguably the most controversial and remarkable development in the international art world of the early 1980s was the foregrounding and prioritization of a range of expressive, painterly, figurative styles. Particularly central in this renovation of 'Expressionism' was the presentation of this work along national categories, as evidenced in the debates around the 1981 exhibition 'A New Spirit in Painting'. In the art capitals, this neo-Expressionism was based on a reinvigorated art market. It thus seemed that entering into the new decade the Independents and the practices endorsed by this grouping were well positioned to claim the mantle of 'Irish art', particularly within the international arena. Paddy Graham was propelled centre-stage due to the rise of neo-Expressionism, and was joined by a generation of younger artists who were returning to painting as a reaction against the conceptualism and minimalism of the late 1970s. Some of these artists were represented in a show in 1983 which was an attempted response to 'A New Spirit in Painting'. 'Making Sense: Ten Artists 1968–83' was funded by the Arts Council of Ireland. However, as a show it drew criticism for its failure to include any women and for the male artists' obsessive preoccupation with their own identities, thus reaffirming the resolutely masculine myth-making that

neo-Expressionism had established in Europe and North America. The artists Michael Mulcahy and Brian Bourke, for instance, represented the convergence of metaphysical concerns with references to indigenous cultures and symbols using Expressionist gestures which excavated myth and mythologies.

There were of course others, some of whose work roughly fits into the idiom of neo-Expressionism but who had been passed over (Eithne Jordan, Cecily Brennan and Gwen O'Dowd), and others again who sought to move beyond the pure formalism of some of the Modernist work that had preceded them. Sculptors like Eilis O'Connell and Alistair Wilson combined an abstract use of colour and material with formal elaboration. This period is also marked by a dispersal of previous groupings away from the encampments of the previous decades into new configurations. For instance, the Independents' group suffered a major decline and subsequent death in the mid-1980s. IELA was also discontinued at this time, although the annual open 'Exhibition of Visual Arts' (EVA) held in Limerick has in many ways replaced it.

After 1983, Irish art saw the emergence of young artists who had assimilated the debates around the prominent discourse of national/cultural identity and art production in Ireland. This discourse of cultural nationalism in the visual arts may be seen to have culminated in the 'Sense of Ireland' series of exhibitions in London in 1980. A new generation of practitioners were now beginning to articulate themselves outside the ambit of this essentially conservative discursive frame. These would have been seen as continuing the tradition of IELA and its outward-looking attitude to international influences and concerns. Artists such as Alanna O'Kelly, Dorothy Cross, Willie Doherty and Kathy Prendergast engaged with art discourses which privilege conceptual and theoretical concerns, and their work might be termed 'issue-based'. This period also witnessed a more vigorous and concerted effort on the part of these artists to address the social, historical, political and cultural dimensions of the conflict in the North.

Critics have remarked upon an apparent commonality of approach among artists towards issues arising out of the current political crisis. They suggest there is an oblique, often understated mode of address employed which allows critical response to the prevailing rhetorics and media representations. Brian McAvera argues that the northern artists use 'strategies of subtext [whose] angle of approach is layered and subterranean'. This understated and tentative mode of articulation was remarked upon particularly by the US art critic Lucy Lippard in 1984, when she came to Ireland in search of political and activist art. This contention was also made by critics and historians in '*A Sense of Ireland*', where it was suggested that such an approach may well in fact betray an underlying 'Celtic imagination' or some putative notion of 'Irishness'. Later in 1988, McAvera went even further and termed this a 'genetic' predisposition to oblique modes of address within Irish culture. It may be remarked that the work of Willie Doherty has contained within its thematic concerns and rhetorical strategies an implicit critique of power and domination played out not on human bodies, although this is certainly implied, but on the borderlands – cityscapes and militarized zones – through surveillance. Doherty's photo-texts continue the landscape tradition so privileged within the canon of art production in Ireland, and yet they undermine the neutrality and 'innocence' of any representation of the land. Likewise Victor Sloan's images, through their violation and disruption of the pristine surface of photographic meaning, produce critiques of the triumphalism of the Loyalist community. Some Northern painters also combine comment on the historical roots of the conflict with the tradition of landscape. Dermot Seymour employs ironic images of the militarization of the landscape, while Micky Donnelly makes use of symbol and

political allegory in elaborating the conjunction of landscape and the contestation of power. Rita Duffy's tragi-comic paintings seek to represent women in their quotidian existence and share with John Kindness's work a wit and incisiveness that deconstructs traditional and dominant images of Ireland and Irish culture. The late eighties were marked by the rejection of the earlier, unreflexive debates around 'Irishness', while an investigation of the politics of place and the local has emerged. Important in this development beyond the narrow preoccupation with the particularity of the 'Irish' is the assertion by key artists of the politics of gender as the premise and agenda for their work.

Coming to the fore with this work are women artists who have been politicized and galvanized by critiques of Modernism's seeming intractable gender bias, and the debates around gender and representation which emanated from feminist art practices and theories and cultural criticism in North America and Britain during the 1970s. This process of politicization must be seen as concomitant with the socio-political cultural upheavals and controversies of the 1980s in the Republic. These have arguably impinged very differently on women's lives and on men's: the abortion and divorce referenda, the feminization of poverty and the rapid growth in unemployment. A number of women artists were producing critiques of the traditional role and image of women in Ireland that they found oppressive. Much of the art of this period concerned itself with the representation of the nation as female. Produced across diverse media, this work has engaged a broad series of thematics and concerns related to the (female) body, identity, history and the land. There is too a concerted effort to articulate a gender specificity in this art with a particular feminist revision of landscape. These developments may be identified in the work of Kathy Prendergast and Alanna O'Kelly. Dorothy Cross's sculptures and installations are preoccupied with the issues of sexual identity, gendered power relations and the gendering of objects and processes. The problematics of the 'gaze' and the 'fetish' may be said to operate as pivotal elements in many of her installations.

It would be difficult not to remark upon the significance of James Coleman's contribution to the development of avant-garde art practices in the Irish context. Since the late sixties Coleman has acted as an invaluable agent for international influences and developments around time-based art, performance and video art in particular. He is not, however, the only art practitioner working in these media. Nigel Rolfe from England and Alastair McLennan from Scotland arrived in the 1970s, and have through their own practices and their teaching acted as considerable forces in the initiation of an indigenous performance praxis. Symptomatic of the general postmodern pluralization of practices are the difficulties presented by any attempt to summarize the period from 1983 to the present. The older blocks of affiliations have dissipated. Thus, the cosmopolitan pop art of Elizabeth Magill and the theory-based multimedia group Blue Funk co-exist with the Expressionism of David Crone, Michael Cullen and Anita Groener. Abstraction and formalism, so dominant in Irish painting and sculpture in the 1970s, continued into the 1980s and 1990s. The paintings of Mary Fitzgerald, Richard Gorman and Felim Egan, and the sculpture of John Aiken, all indicate that the impact of abstract formalism has been formidable in contemporary art practice in Ireland.

Contemporary art in Ireland bears the traces and marks of a series of struggles and institutional shifts that have occurred in the last 30 years. This has amply demonstrated the need to examine the institutional frames of art education and production when seeking to identify the continuities and discontinuities, movements and traditions, that make up the contemporary art environment. Contemporary art production and consumption in Ireland is a complex of sites where particular contestations around representation are being

acted out. In the past the agenda has been to establish a canon of specifically Irish art and the legitimacy of a given practice as appropriate to Ireland, and hence the correctness of a particular conception of Ireland. Recent work has attempted to change this agenda and establish a plurality of concerns and alternative models of artistic value. However, this very pluralism is in itself a contestable and contested frame. On the one hand it can be mobilized as a testament to the advanced cultural life of Ireland in the interests of cultural diplomacy or international business. On the other hand the seeming pluralism may erase the unresolved conflicts central to contemporary social experience.

Reading

Dunne, Aidan, 'Back to the future: a context for Irish art of the 1980s', in *A New Tradition: Irish Art of the Eighties* (Dublin: Douglas Hyde Gallery, 1990).

Fowler, Joan, 'Locating the context – art and politics in the eighties' in *A New Tradition: Irish Art of the Eighties* (Dublin: Douglas Hyde Gallery, 1990).

——'Speaking of gender...Expressionism, feminism and sexuality', in *A New Tradition: Irish Art of the Eighties* (Dublin: Douglas Hyde Gallery, 1990).

Hutchinson, John, 'The nature of landscape', in *A New Tradition: Irish Art of the Eighties* (Dublin: Douglas Hyde Gallery, 1990).

McAvera, Brian, Catalogue essays for '*Directions Out*' (Dublin: Douglas Hyde Gallery, 1988).

Ruane, Frances, 'An aspect of Irish painting', in *Six Artists from Ireland*, catalogue essay for the Arts Council and Department of Foreign Affairs, Dublin, 1983.

MARTIN MCCABE AND MICHAEL WILSON

art education A significant development in Irish art since the 1970s is that the majority of younger artists to have emerged since then hold academic qualifications in their subject. The 'self-taught' artist and the artist who trained through evening classes are now in a minority. Today there is a marked distinction between the amateur artist and the concerns and practices which constitute the professional artist, even while very few Irish artists earn a living through their art alone. In secondary education, art is a recognized subject and is taught in the vast majority of schools, though its prestige is slight compared to the traditional academic subjects and, particularly in the Republic of Ireland, 'art' is predominantly understood in terms of naturalism. This view has been contested within tertiary education since the 1970s largely as a result of the introduction of Modernist and, latterly, postmodernist concepts, which coincide with a general expansion of art courses in the sector during the period.

The philosophy and structure of art courses in tertiary education is similar to the model established in England in the 1960s, which, in turn, is based on the Bauhaus school in Weimar Germany. The course structure is built around an induction to various materials in which the nature of the end product is open-ended. The course develops through increasing specialization in an area of study. For the most part this has been governed by Modernist beliefs; for example, the integrity of the material and work processes and an emphasis on individual interpretation and understanding.

Prior to this the old system of art education was centred in schools in Dublin, Belfast, Cork and Limerick. These institutions survive but they have been transformed into the National College of Art and Design, the University of Ulster at Belfast, the Crawford Municipal School of Art and the Limerick College of Art, Commerce and Technology, respectively. The oldest of these, dating from 1746, is the National College of Art and Design in Dublin, which, until it was restructured in the early 1970s, epitomized the eighteenth-century academy by its exclusive emphasis on the learning of techniques, particularly drawing. The nineteenth-century schools at Cork and Limerick had similar emphases.

The school in Belfast was established as a school of design in 1849 and was one of several created by the British government to encourage better standards of design. While the Belfast school had closer links with industry than its counterparts in the rest of Ireland, it too developed art classes, which became central to its existence. Since the 1960s, the school has undergone dramatic structural changes, and is now part of a university. In the Republic, the art schools experienced a dormant period after the Irish Free State was established in 1922. It was not until after (though not as a direct result of) student protests at the National College of Art between 1969 and 1971 over the perceived irrelevance of their courses that the present system was created.

A major development in tertiary education in the Republic since the 1970s is the emergence of the Regional Technical Colleges. The purpose of the RTCs is to provide higher technical education, and to provide higher-level courses in regions of the country where these were not previously available. Art and design courses were part of the new development, and art courses became available in RTCs at Waterford, Galway, Sligo and Letterkenny. Meanwhile diploma-level art courses were also offered at Dun Laoghaire School of Art, and later at the College of Marketing and Design in Dublin. As a necessary part of this expansion, new teaching posts were created, which brought an influx of teacher-artists, many of whom were from the United Kingdom and who introduced the philosophy and attitudes of the new English system. The art departments within the RTCs, as well as those within the older colleges, became sites of conflict between Modernists and traditionalists. By the 1980s, the Modernists had gained the upper hand within tertiary art education, but in the 1990s this dominance is under threat as art colleges and art departments are under increasing pressure to conform to product-based models of higher education with more quantifiable learning outcomes.

Other tensions have emerged. The Republic of Ireland has a highly centralized education system, and the modern, non-university tertiary sector was planned in such a way that 'centres of excellence' were to be identified; many courses are maintained with low-level qualifications in the expectation that students will move elsewhere to achieve higher ones. This may be understandable from a planning point of view in a country with scarce resources, but it creates hierarchies rather than offering genuine differences and therefore choices between courses, and is a source of political rivalry between regions. In art education, only Dublin, Cork and Limerick offer degrees while other colleges offer diplomas and certificates. A comparable situation exists at Belfast, where for decades the college has struggled against a self-image of being small and provincial compared to colleges in mainland Britain. As in the Republic of Ireland, many of the best students move to the larger centres.

Since 1970 art education has witnessed extensive growth. It has also become part of a national system of higher education in both Northern Ireland and the Republic of Ireland. There are many benefits from this development; for example, art is linked to other tertiary subjects, which brings status and opens the possibility of postgraduate study. In this regard, the MA course in fine art at Belfast is well regarded in Ireland and abroad. While greater emphasis on higher qualifications for artists within a national system has helped to establish better standards of professional practice and has helped to reinstate theoretical premises in fine art practices, it also encourages greater conformity than was the case three decades ago. The enhanced institutionalization of art education brings with it a growing inability to directly address changing conditions in art and society.

JOAN FOWLER

Arts and Crafts Movement The visual counterpart to the Yeatsian literary revival and driven by political and romantic nationalist ideologies, it began *c*.1886, when Irish home industries, especially lace, were acclaimed in Edinburgh; by 1925, when the Arts and Crafts Society of Ireland (founded 1894) held its seventh exhibition, the Irish Free State was established and the original momentum had been lost.

Although rooted in the utopian socialism of Ruskin and Morris, the Irish movement was led not by architect/craftsmen but by philanthropic patrons concerned to educate and employ unskilled, mostly rural labour faced with severe poverty. By 1910 the desired skilfully executed, apposite interpretations of a mythical past expressed in a contemporary idiom were being exhibited. While the Dublin School of Art became the centre of activity, with lectures, demonstrations and exhibitions in its immediate vicinity, particularly at the National Museum, there were notable workshops and short-lived industries throughout the country.

Reading

Bowe, Nicola Gordon, 'Aspects of nationalism in the Irish Arts and Crafts Movement 1886–1925: suggested parallels and context', *GPA Irish Arts Review Yearbook* (1991).

NICOLA GORDON BOWE

ascendancy The word (deriving from astrology) first appears with precision in Richard Woodward's *Present State of the Church of Ireland* (1787, *recte* 1786) where it connotes the predominant status of one religious denomination in a state; Protestant ascendancy, with regard to Ireland, is only one of several instances therein. The fuller term is deployed with some conceptual rigour in the February 1792 Irish parliamentary debates on Catholic relief. Edmund Burke's scathing analysis of it – linking it to jobbery and municipal corruption – occurs in his May 1792 'Letter to Richard Burke'. Thereafter, Protestant ascendancy has a mixed press and the term does not occur with any great frequency in the Union debates (1799–1800.) The shift from the term's signifying a political or social condition to its naming a

41

quasi-aristocratic elite is not completed until well into the nineteenth century. Its latter-day connotations (of an early eighteenth-century hegemony based on landed estate) continue to appeal to nationalists and revisionists alike, despite the evidence summarized above. W.B. Yeats (cf. 'Commentary on "A Parnellite at Parnell's Funeral"', 1934) can take some credit for this.

W.J. MCCORMACK

Ashford, William (1746–1824) Painter. Born Birmingham; died Dublin, 17 April. In 1764 he came to Dublin to work in the Ordnance Office and from 1767 exhibited elegant amateur flower-pieces and still lifes with the Society of Artists, perhaps teaching himself. He first showed landscapes in 1772. His fresh topographical views of Dublin and of country houses (engraved by Milton and others), painted with a realism and vitality that differed from the more romantic Irish style, soon became popular. He was honoured by his contemporaries in being chosen first president of the Royal Hibernian Academy in 1823.

Reading

Crookshank, A., and the Knight of Glin, *The Painters of Ireland, c. 1660–1920* (London: Barrie and Jenkins, 1978).
Strickland, W.G., *A Dictionary of Irish Artists* (Shannon: Irish University Press, 1968).
Wynne, M., 'William Ashford and the Royal Charter School Clontarf, County Dublin', *Irish Georgian Society* X, no. 4 (Oct.–Dec. 1967).

HILARY PYLE

association football Football in various forms was played in most parts of medieval Europe, but all the evidence suggests that stick-and-ball games were dominant in Ireland. Football was most probably introduced by the soldiery, and became popular in the garrison towns and their hinterlands in the seventeenth century. O'Maolfabhail argues that the game played at that time was more like modern Rugby, but that two variants of hurling were more widespread.

The rules of modern field sports were codified in the second half of the nineteenth century, and the organized structure of football in Ireland took a form which has changed little in the interim. The Gaelic Athletic Association (GAA) codified a version now called Gaelic football, initially strongest in the towns but eventually through the countryside. The same association inherited hurling, which appears to have been stronger in the early days of the GAA. But the codification in England of the rules of association football resulted in the attraction of adherents in Ireland, especially in Dublin, where the Shelbourne and Bohemians clubs were formed around the time of the GAA's foundation.

The national organization split in the 1920s, the only field sports body to do so. Professional club football in the Republic was at its peak of popularity in the 1930s, when crowds of several thousand people used to gather outside newspaper offices in Dublin on Sunday afternoons to learn the fate of their teams playing in Cork or Limerick. Club matches between the top Dublin teams attracted crowds of 30,000 and upwards on a regular basis.

As a participation sport, soccer was largely confined to the urban areas until recent times, but there has been a rapid expansion in rural areas. In 1991, a survey by the Football Association of Ireland found that there were over 3,000 clubs registered, with 110,000 players (excluding schools). This included active junior leagues in every county in the Republic. The professional club game has, however, declined dramatically, with the better players opting to ply their trade in Britain and the leading English and Scottish clubs enjoying active support, including regular travelling spectators, from Ireland. The Republic's clubs have lost out to television.

The international team has, after decades of near misses, enjoyed great success since the mid-eighties. The team, consisting entirely of players from British clubs, reached the quarter-finals of the 1990 World Cup in

Italy, and each of their games there attracted record television audiences in Ireland. The game in which they were eliminated, in Rome, attracted over 20,000 spectators who had travelled from Ireland.

Eamonn de Valera remarked that Rugby and hurling were the games most suited to the Irish temperament, but the public appear to have, as in other matters, voted with their feet.

Reading

O Maolfabhail, *2,000 Years of Hurling in Ireland* (Dundalk: Dundalgan Press, 1973).

COLM MCCARTHY

astronomy The remarkable blossoming of astronomical activity which took place in Ireland during the nineteenth century was influenced by the founding of observatories at Dunsink near Dublin in 1783 and at Armagh in 1790. These institutions were later complemented by private observatories at Markree, Parsonstown and Daramona and by the work of many talented individuals who made useful contributions both within Ireland and abroad. The scientific activity provided a stimulus for the successful telescope-making firm of Thomas and Howard Grubb.

Dunsink Observatory was established by Trinity College as a result of a bequest of a former provost of the college, Francis Andrews. The first professor of astronomy, Henry Ussher, was responsible for choosing the site and for designing the building, which was completed in 1785. The main objective of astronomy at that time was the accurate measurement of the positions of stars, and special attention was paid to the circulation of air around the telescopes in order to achieve observations of the highest possible quality.

The first student at Dunsink was a 14-year-old lad, Francis Beaufort, from Navan, County Meath, who had a passion for the sea. During 1788 he spent five months with Ussher studying astronomy and meteorology before embarking on a naval career. He

was a courageous captain and devoted himself to making meticulous surveys of uncharted coasts, perhaps motivated by being shipwrecked at the age of 15. He was appointed hydrographer of the Admiralty in 1829, a post he held for 26 years. He is probably best remembered for his table for estimating the force of wind at sea – the Beaufort Scale. It was Beaufort who got approval for Charles Darwin to sail with Fitzroy on board the *Beagle*.

The most renowned resident of Dunsink was William Rowan Hamilton. Born in Dublin in 1805 and educated by his uncle, he had a prodigious command of languages. While still an undergraduate, he was appointed professor of astronomy and he lived at Dunsink until his death in 1865. He made fundamental contributions to the mathematical theory of optics and mechanics and is regarded as Ireland's greatest mathematician. He is probably best known for his idea of quaternions, which came to him in a flash of inspiration on 16 October 1843 when he was walking with his wife to a meeting of the Royal Irish Academy, of which he was president. He recorded the famous quaternion equations in his diary and scratched them with his penknife on the stonework of Brougham Bridge, which crosses the Royal Canal. Each year it is the custom for mathematics students to retrace his steps along the canal, perhaps in the hope that they may have an idea that will make them as famous as Hamilton.

Hamilton was followed in the chair of astronomy by F.F. Brunnow, R.S. Ball, A.A. Rambaut and C.J. Joly, all of whom pursued observational work, which had been somewhat neglected under Hamilton's tenure. Robert Ball went to Dunsink in 1874, where most of his observational work was done with the 12-inch refracting telescope, erected in 1868. He is best remembered as an accomplished public lecturer and for his many popular books on astronomy. In 1892 he was appointed Lowndean professor of astronomy and geometry at Cambridge.

The story of Armagh Observatory is dominated by two men named Robinson: its founder, Archbishop Richard Robinson, and its long-serving director, T.R. Robinson. Thomas Romney Robinson was born in Dublin in 1793 and spent his childhood in Belfast. A child prodigy with a reputation as a poet, he was appointed director at Armagh in 1823. His manual and observational skills enabled him to make many technical improvements in telescope design and he became one of the most respected practical astronomers of his time. He played a key role in encouraging Thomas Grubb to establish his telescope-making firm in Dublin. His varied interests included meteorology, to which he contributed by his invention of the cup anemometer for measuring windspeed. Beset by financial problems and failing eyesight, Romney Robinson died in 1882 after being in office for 59 years, a record unlikely to be surpassed.

The next director was J.L.E. Dreyer, who was born in Copenhagen in 1852. Dreyer's work on nebulae at Birr led him to revise John Herschel's catalogue of galaxies and to produce in 1888 a *New General Catalogue of Nebulae and Clusters of Stars*, which is still widely consulted; this is the origin of the prefix 'NGC' used for such objects.

The earliest private observatory of significance was built at Markree Castle near Sligo, the home of the Cooper family. Edward J. Cooper was born in Dublin in 1798 and he spared no expense in equipping his observatory. In 1831 he bought a 13.3-inch lens (then the largest in the world) which had been made by Cauchoix in Paris and mounted it on a temporary wooden stand. Acting on advice from Romney Robinson, Cooper ordered a permanent mounting from Thomas Grubb of Dublin and this was put in place in 1834. Cooper employed several assistants, the longest serving being Andrew Graham, who discovered the minor planet Metis in 1848.

The best-known private observatory in Ireland was at Birr where William Parsons, the third earl of Rosse, completed a 36-inch reflector in 1839. It was surpassed in 1845 by his great 72-inch telescope, the 'Leviathan of Parsonstown'. Among the assistant astronomers attracted to Birr were G.J. Stoney, W.H. Rambaut, R.S. Ball, C.E. Burton, R. Copeland, J.L.E. Dreyer and O. Boeddiker, all of whom made significant contributions.

Daramona Observatory was set up by William E. Wilson on the family estate at Streete, County Westmeath. In 1870, at the age of 19, Wilson took part in an expedition to Iran to observe a total eclipse of the sun, and the following year he bought a 12-inch reflector from Grubb. Ten years later it was replaced by a 24-inch Grubb reflector, which was used for stellar photography and for pioneering experiments to measure starlight electrically. Wilson measured the temperature of the sun's surface and obtained a value which compares favourably with modern estimates.

The existence of these institutions inspired many private individuals to attempt astronomical work; the most eminent include:

1 Wentworth Erck (1827–90) of Bray, County Wicklow, had an observatory equipped with a fine 7.5-inch refractor. In 1877 he was the first in the British Isles to observe the two moons of Mars, which had been discovered a few weeks previously in Washington with a much larger telescope.

2 Isaac Ward (1832–1916) of Belfast had a 4.3-inch refractor and was renowned for his keen vision. In August 1885 he discovered a new star in the Andromeda nebula. When the distance of the nebula was estimated 30 years later it was realized that Ward had actually observed a supernova – the first to be seen in an external galaxy.

3 William H.S. Monck (1839–1915) was born near Borris-in-Ossory, not far from Parsonstown. A lawyer by profession, he bought Erck's telescope and in August 1892 made the first electrical measurements of starlight from his Dublin home

at 16 Earlsfort Terrace. He was among the first to realize the existence of giant and dwarf stars and has been described as 'a brilliant amateur astronomer'.

4 Agnes M. Clerke (1842–1907), born in Skibbereen, County Cork, is best known for her *Popular History of Astronomy during the Nineteenth Century*, which was acclaimed on its publication in 1885. As a result of the high quality of her work, she became an internationally recognized authority on astrophysics.

5 John E. Gore (1845–1910) grew up near Cooper's observatory at Markree. After a short career as a civil engineer in India he returned to Ireland at the age of 34. He was a skilled observer of variable stars and published eight books and over 80 papers, as well as a translation of Flammarion's best-selling *Popular Astronomy*.

6 Charles E. Burton (1846–82) was born in Cheshire of Irish parents. He was employed at Birr, Dunsink and Greenwich. He learnt the art of grinding speculum at Birr and made his own high-quality silver-on-glass mirrors. An expert planetary observer, he made many original observations of the planet Mars. He suffered from persistent ill health and died suddenly at the age of 35.

7 Margaret L. Huggins, née Murray (1848–1915), was born in Monkstown, County Dublin. She married William Huggins, who was 24 years her senior and who had his own observatory in London, where he carried out fundamental work in stellar spectroscopy. The marriage has been described as 'one of the most successful husband-and-wife partnerships in the whole of astronomy'.

The nineteenth century was a golden age for astronomy in Ireland. In spite of a poor climate, the observational work was pursued with considerable success and much of the theoretical work was of lasting benefit to science.

IAN ELLIOTT

Atkinson, Sarah (1823–93) Writer. Born 13 July, in Athlone. At 25 she married a young Dublin physician, George Atkinson, following the death of her only child. She ploughed her energies into writing and charitable works. With her friend Ellen Woodlock, she established a school in Dublin, St Joseph's Industrial Institute, and organized a girls' school inside the South Dublin Workhouse. Their aim was to train girls to earn an honest livelihood.

Sarah Atkinson's writings include biographies of Mary Aikenhead (the foundress of the Irish Sisters of Charity), John Hogan, and studies of various Irish saints.

She died 8 July.

Reading

Irish Monthly, XXI–XXIII.

RACHEL FURMSTON

autobiography Modern Irish autobiographical writing dates, roughly speaking, from 1800, and its history may be divided into three main periods. These loosely correspond to the major phases in the articulation of modern Ireland's political and cultural consciousness. Distinct though these periods are, their autobiographies share certain thematic, formal and ideological interests. Among the most persistent of these are a preoccupation with the fashioning of social and cultural identity, an ethnographic approach to place and people, and an oppositional point of view. The relative prominence given each of these interests distinguishes a particular period's autobiographies. From within the familiar spectrum of reminiscences, diaries, letters and other conventional autobiographical outlets, each period produces a particular autobiographical pretext which typifies, for the time being, the form's possibilities and establishes its specific cultural relevance and aesthetic presuppositions.

The prototype for the narratives of opposition and recuperation which are representative of the first period of modern Irish autobiography is *The Life of Wolfe Tone* (1826). Foremost among other noteworthy works in the same vein is John Mitchel's *Jail Journal* (1854), and from that date to the end of the nineteenth century there is a steady flow of similar titles, culminating in the autobiographies of William O'Brien. This period's themes are legitimacy, empowerment, agency and integrity. These are articulated as correctives to the clandestinity, subversion, deracination and judicial reprisal in terms of which a ruling oligarchy allegedly characterizes the matter of Ireland. The tone of these narratives is extrovert, and their focus is on action, organization and the discovery that public events possess a permeable structure. The narrators speak as embodiments of a collective aspiration rather than as instances of individuation. The point of view is retrospective and compensatory, not reconstitutive and analytical. Print bears permanent witness to the values which action was unable to install, with the result that the personal dimension of autobiography is subsidiary to the form's putative power as a manual of possibility and a rhetoric of commitment.

The personal element, critically considered, typifies the second period of modern Irish autobiography. Dating from George Moore's *Confessions of a Young Man* (1888), this period features not only autobiographies by, most notably, W.B. Yeats, in addition to Moore's *Hail and Farewell* trilogy, but also reformulations of the autobiographical impulse in works as diverse as James Joyce's *A Portrait of the Artist as a Young Man* and the travel works of J.M. Synge. In a period when the political aspirations of earlier radical autobiographers appeared to be realized in action, autobiography as a form virtually overlooked the fact, Ernie O'Malley's *On Another Man's Wound* (1936) being the most outstanding exception. Dissident thought, shaped by the oppositional personality, keynotes the moral landscape of Irish autobiography during the period of the separatist climacteric.

This shift in emphasis replaces self-aggrandisement with self-awareness, a change accompanied by innovative formal developments. Among these may be noted the imaginative deployment of commonplace autobiographical forms such as diaries, the compression of temporal and spatial conditions for dramatic effect, and a tendency towards a pictorial aesthetic. In terms of content, these works deal intimately with family matters, with a particular emphasis on childhood. Structures of inner life, dwelling on sexual identity and theoretical thought, are also to the fore. Mind is considered of more consequence than world. Criticism is implicitly claimed to be a higher form of politics, thereby becoming synonymous with a rhetoric of self-actualization. The enactment of this synonymity, and the ethos of modernization to which it subscribes, constitute the presence of these autobiographies' most important innovation, the persona. The intellectual sophistication implict in this ethos appears under stress in Sean O'Casey's sequence *Mirror in My House* (1939–54), and is absent from the personae of the autobiographical romances of Liam O'Flaherty and Francis Stuart, works which have been virtually overshadowed by modern Irish autobiography's third period.

Inaugurated by such works as *Twenty Years A-Growing* (1933), *The Islandman* (1937) and *An Old Woman's Reflections* (1939), this period rejects the persona and opposition in favour of community and recuperation. The works in question not only encode a nativist moment in modern Irish letters but establish expectations which subsequent autobiographies have found difficult to outgrow. These nativist works convey recollection as self-possession, and provide a repertoire of themes concerning affiliation, language, place, and the rituals which inhere in them. The reactionary appeal of these themes is unwittingly identified in Patrick Kavanagh's *The Green Fool* (1938), while the response to them of even writers with the nationalist credentials of Frank O'Connor and Sean O'Faolain is ambivalent, as may be noted by comparing their autobiographical works with Robert Harbinson's tetralogy depicting Northern Irish realities, or with Brendan Behan's *Borstal Boy* (1958). Despite its problematic populism, the nativist narrative of communal and cultural integrity still informs much contemporary Irish autobiography, where it appears as self-deceiving nostalgia. Notable exceptions are Noel Browne's *Against the Tide* (1986), Denis Donoghue's *Warrenpoint* (1991) and Hubert Butler's republished essays. The huge international success of Seamus Deane's autobiographical novel *Reading in the Dark* and the much-acclaimed *Angela's Ashes* by Frank McCourt both attest to a powerful new trend in Irish autobiographical writing which is now exploring the darker and more disturbing aspects of growing up in Ireland. Without the insights of feminism, the testimony of emigrants, and other sources likely to develop the form, the third period of Irish autobiography is typified by a glut of works whose uncertainty and evasiveness perhaps reveal a larger cultural anomie but which seem to counteract modern Irish autobiography's literary and historical significance.

GEORGE O'BRIEN

aviation The first aircraft to fly successfully in Ireland was built and piloted by Harry Ferguson – better known for his tractors – in County Down in December 1909, six years after that of the Wright brothers. In the following decade serious flying was largely confined to the operations of the British Royal Flying Corps, which set up bases in several parts of the country; but following independence in 1921 the growing importance of both military and civil aviation was recognized with the establishment of an Army Air Corps in June 1922 and of a national airline, Aer Lingus, in April 1936. The latter's first revenue flight, from Dublin to Bristol, took place on 27 May utilizing the company's first aircraft, a DH84 Dragon named *Iolar* (*Eagle*).

Whilst Aer Lingus was to confine itself until 1958 to European operations, Ireland's geographical position caused it at an early stage to become the focus for those attempting, in both a public and a private capacity, to fly the Atlantic. The pioneer crossings of Alcock and Brown (west–east, 1919) and *The Bremen* (east–west, 1928) either began or terminated in Ireland, and in the 1930s international interest in the opening of commercial flying-boat services resulted in the establishment of a base at Foynes on the Shannon estuary and the first proving flights by Pan-American and Imperial Airways of Britain in July 1937. At the same time work had started on the site of a landplane base – Rineanna – on the opposite Clare shore; and with the supremacy of the landplane established following World War II this airport, thereafter known as Shannon, became a mandatory refuelling stop for transatlantic services until the advent of the big jets. In the meantime Foynes had created Irish Coffee to warm flying-boat passengers ferried ashore in inclement conditions, and Rineanna had inaugurated the world's first duty-free shop.

Though Cork airport was opened in 1961, domestic routes were not seriously developed until the 1980s with the establishment of a private airline, Ryanair, which began serving provincial centres, linking them directly with British destinations. Aer Lingus responded, but some of these routings have proved at best marginally viable.

Reading

Byrne, Liam, *History of Aviation in Ireland* (Dublin: Blackwater, 1980).
Corlett, John, *Aviation in Ulster* (Belfast: Blackstaff, 1981).
Share, Bernard, *The Flight of the Iolar: The Aer Lingus Experience 1936–1986* (Dublin: Gill and Macmillan, 1986).

BERNARD SHARE

B

Bale, John (1495–1563) Dramatist and churchman. Born at Cove, Suffolk, 21 November; died at Canterbury, November. Educated at a Carmelite priory from 1507, and at Cambridge University from 1514, he obtained his BD in 1529. In about 1534 he converted to Protestantism, and became a violent anti-Catholic polemicist ('bilious Bale'), in prose writings and verse plays, five of which survive. Imprisoned in 1540, he fled to the continent, where he wrote a history of English literature (the *Summarium*). Returning to England, he was appointed bishop of Ossory in 1551. His attempts to convert his Catholic flock by performances of his plays in Kilkenny led to civil unrest, and, with Catholic Mary on the throne, he again fled. He reached Switzerland after being captured by pirates. In England again after Mary's death, he was made Prebendary of Canterbury in 1560. He married his 'faithful Dorothy' in 1537.

Reading

Happé, P. (ed.), *The Complete Plays of John Bale*, 5 vols (*King Johan, Johan Baptystes Preachynge, God's Promises, Three Laws, The Temptation of Our Lord*) (Cambridge: D.S. Brewer, 1985–).

DAVID SMITH

Balfe, Michael William (1808–70) Composer and Singer. Born Dublin, 15 May; died Rowney Abbey, Hertfordshire, 20 October. From a musical and theatrical family, he became famous throughout Europe. He sang leading baritone roles in France (where he was much admired by Cherubini and Rossini) and Italy before settling in London in 1833. He had already composed Italian operas, but in London he quickly achieved extraordinary acclaim with two English operas, *The Siege of Rochelle* (1835) and *The Maid of Artois* (1836). Even greater success came with *The Bohemian Girl* (1843), which ran for over 100 nights and was performed all over Europe and the Americas. The appeal of these works depends not on vocal display or spectacle or characterization, but on their simple ballads, over which he took great pains, and which he would use several times in the course of an opera. He also wrote similar operas in French, while his Italian works are after the manner of Rossini. He also had great success with some non-dramatic ballads, notably 'By Killarney's Lakes', 'Come into the garden, Maud' and 'Excelsior'. In his retirement he lived on his estate at Rowney Abbey in Hertfordshire, where he worked on his last and unfinished opera, *The Knight of the Leopard* (based on Scott).

Reading

Temperley, Nicholas (ed.), *Music in Britain: The Romantic Age 1800–1914* (London: Athlone Press, 1981).

White, Eric Walter, *A History of English Opera* (London: Faber, 1983).

DAVID GREER

Ballagh, Robert (1943–) Painter. Studied architecture before beginning to paint in 1966. Ballagh has exhibited throughout Europe; he represented Ireland at the Paris Biennale in 1969, and held a retrospective in Sweden in 1982. He is a member of Aosdána, an honorary president of the International Association of Art, a fellow of the World Academy of Art and Science, and an active supporter of republican causes. Ballagh has also worked in graphic and set design. His painting is strictly representational and reveals the commitment to social equality which Ballagh sees as pivotal to his work.

Reading

Ballagh, Robert, *Robert Ballagh on Stage* (Dublin: Project Arts Centre, 1990).

Carty, Ciaran, *Robert Ballagh* (Dublin: Magill, 1986).

Knowles, Roderic, *Contemporary Irish Art* (Dublin: Wolfhound Press, 1982).

DERVAL TUBRIDY

ballet From 1927 to 1934, at the suggestion of W.B. Yeats, Ninette de Valois ran a ballet school at the Abbey Theatre, Dublin, for which she choreographed 24 ballets, several subsequently staged in London. Pupils included Jill Gregory, later soloist with Sadler's Wells Ballet and ballet mistress with the Royal Ballet, as well as well-known dance teachers Cepta Cullen in Dublin and Arthur Hamilton in Belfast. De Valois also choreographed a version of Yeats's *The Only Jealousy of Emer*, called *Fighting the Waves* (1929), with herself as a dancing, non-speaking Fand. This was followed by six more of his *Plays for Dancers* between 1931 and 1934, notably *At the Hawk's Well*, with herself as the Guardian of the Well.

During this period, John Regan was dancing with the major companies of Europe. Regan (1905–88) was born in Mulrany, County Mayo, and trained with Cecchetti, Legat and Espinosa. He danced with Diaghilev's Ballets Russes, de Basil's Ballet Russe de Monte Carlo, Woizikowski's Ballet Russe de Paris, Balanchine's Ballet Russe de 1932, Nijinska's Warsaw Opera Ballet, the Georgian State Dancers and the Markova–Dolin Company, before founding the Ballet Trois Arts in 1937. Later he founded his own ENSA dance company to entertain the troops during World War II. He was a soloist in the film *The Red Shoes*, produced the BBC series *Ballet for Beginners*, and also worked for television in Paris. After several years as director of the Spanish Conservatorio de Musica in Pamplona, he returned to Ireland in 1977 to found the Limerick School of Classical Ballet and Theatre Omnibus.

In the mid-fifties, Legat School-trained Patricia Ryan directed the National Ballet School in Dublin, with Nadine Nicolaeva-Legat as patron. Performing at the Olympia and Abbey Theatres in the early sixties with guest artists from both the Royal Ballet and the Soviet Union, the company premièred three ballets with choreography by Ryan to A.J. Potter scores: *Careless Love* (1961) with libretto by Donagh MacDonach, *Gamble No Gamble* (1962) to a Patrick Kavanagh poem, and *Caillin Bhocht* (1963). Pupils included Deirdre O'Donoghue, who, after going on to the Royal Ballet School, became a soloist with Western Theatre Ballet and the Stuttgart Ballet. When injury ended her dancing career, she became ballet mistress with companies including the Nederlands Dans Theater and Deutsche Oper, Berlin, and is currently director of the Royal Academy of Dance Teachers' Training Course at the Dublin College of Dance.

Meanwhile Jean Denise Moriarty, who trained in the Rambert School, was developing ballet in Cork. In 1947, she founded the amateur Cork Ballet Company, later directing the short-lived semi-professional Irish Theatre Ballet, which toured small Irish towns. In 1972 she was awarded state funding to establish the fully professional Irish Ballet Company, with Ninette de Valois as patron. Its principal dancer was Ballinasloe-born Anna Donovan, later ballet mistress and *repetiteur* to the Dallas Ballet, Texas, and guest teacher to the College of Dance, Dublin. Another of its principal dancers, Joanna Banks, who previously danced with the Royal Ballet, Ballet Rambert, Canadian National Ballet, and the Bavarian State Opera Ballet, Munich, became a principal teacher at the Dublin College of Dance, also serving on the executive of the Dance Council of Ireland.

In 1983 the Irish Ballet Company became Irish National Ballet and, though based in Cork, performed regularly at the Abbey Theatre, Dublin, and toured to London, New York and Europe, as well as throughout Ireland. It presented small-scale works from the international repertoire as well as performing new ballets, including Moriarty's, which used Irish themes and dancing, such as her *Playboy of the Western World*. Based on J.M. Synge's play, the music was by the Chieftains, who performed live at all performances. The company was forced to disband when Arts Council funding was withdrawn in 1989.

In 1979 Louis O'Sullivan founded Dublin City Ballet, with Anton Dolin as patron. It presented classical and jazz ballet until its grant was withdrawn in 1985. In 1989 O'Sullivan founded a short-lived dance-in-education company called Dublin Metropolitan Ballet, engaging as director Gavin Dorrian, who danced with Scottish Ballet, La Scala, Ballet Theatre Russillo and London City Ballet. He became principal male teacher at the Dublin College of Dance as well as serving on the executive of the Dance Council of Ireland.

Except when it was cut off by war, Dublin was a popular venue with touring companies, which went on to the Grand Opera House, Belfast, and these attracted capacity audiences.

They included Stars from the Bolshoi and Kirov Ballets (Gaiety, 1965, 1968), Sadler's Wells Theatre Ballet (Gaiety, 1948, 1949, and Olympia, 1955), the Royal Ballet (Theatre Royal, 1957, Olympia, 1958, and Gaiety, 1962), Anton Dolin's London Festival Ballet (Gaiety, 1952, 1953, 1954, 1958, and Olympia, 1956, 1962), John Regan's Ballet Trois Arts (Gaiety, 1940), Mona Ingoldsby's International Ballet (Gaiety, 1952, 1953), Ballet Rambert (Gaiety, 1963, 1964), Walter Gore's London Ballet (Olympia, 1961, 1962), Peter Darrell's Western Theatre Ballet (Gaiety, 1958), Ballets Joos (Olympia, 1953), American Ballet Theatre (Olympia, 1958), Royal Danish Ballet (Gaiety, 1956), Janine Charrat's Les Ballets de France (Olympia, 1954, 1955, 1956), Maurice Bejart's Ballet Theatre de Paris (Olympia, 1957) and Ballet Miskovitch (Olympia), with many folk groups such as Ballet Folclorico Grancolombiano (Gaiety, 1964) and Ballets Basques et Choeurs Etorki (Olympia, 1954). There were also frequent visits from six different Spanish dance companies and Indian, Pakistani, African, Brazilian and Japanese groups. When the political situation made companies reluctant to visit Belfast, however, Dublin dates became uneconomic and visits were mostly confined to events under the umbrella of the Dublin Theatre Festival. Happily, both Belfast and Dublin once more regularly host touring companies.

A new international dance festival for Ireland is planned which will showcase local companies such as Coiscéim, Ballet Ireland, and Irish Modern Dance Theatre as well as international artistes and companies.

CAROLYN SWIFT

Banville, John (1945–) James Joyce always considered himself a European writer despite the relentlessly Irish settings of his fiction. Until recently John Banville was best known outside Ireland for his award-winning historical novels about the tangled beginnings of European science, *Doctor Copernicus* (1976) and *Kepler* (1981). Together with *The Newton Letter* (1982) and *Mefisto* (1986), set in

Ireland, these form a tetralogy of sorts on the interplay of intuition and hard slogging in the making of scientific genius and on the way neither of these assures harmony in the life of the knower.

In his two later novels, *The Book of Evidence* (1989) and *Ghosts* (1992), which form a pair of their own, Banville pursues a second path in the solitary ego's search for some correspondence between the promised harmony of science or of art and the fractured world of compulsion, conspiracy and guilt that ensnares his characters. Obsessed with a painting sold out of his family, the first-person narrator of *Evidence* murders the young woman who witnesses his theft and goes into hiding, but the novel, written as an artful 'confession', cares more about the painting and its allure than the homicide. When the same character (nameless this time) shows up again in *Ghosts*, it is on an island presided over by a professor, who may also be a counterfeiter, of art. Is art's promise of a golden world equally a fake, or worse, a fatal delusion? Banville's own high art only underlines the question and he has continued to challenge the reader with *Athena* (1995), *The Untouchable* (1996) and *Eclipse* (2000).

JOHN B. BRESLIN

Baptist church In many Irish garrison towns, Cromwellian soldiers and chaplains introduced Baptist congregations, including extant ones in Cork, Dublin and Waterford. The Baptist church today, however, is a Northern Ireland-based product of the evangelical revival. Of existing congregations, 97 per cent date from 1795 onward, and 95 per cent of Irish Baptists live in the North.

Almost all Baptist congregations belong to the Baptist Union of Ireland, which in 1992 included 105 congregations and 8,613 members. However, adding children and non-members who attend regularly, the total Baptist community probably numbers around 20,000.

In Ireland, Baptists are a conservative denomination, whose typically evangelical emphasis on a conversion experience is reinforced by their practice of adult baptism. While Baptists work with other evangelicals, they are the largest church choosing to remain outside the Irish Council of Churches, due to what they see as the compromising liberalism of the ecumenical movement.

JOSEPH LIECHTY

Barber, Mary (*c*.1685–1757) Poet. She was probably born in Dublin and she probably died there. Her maiden name cannot be traced. Her husband, Jonathan, was a woollen draper in Capel street, Dublin, and she had several children before coming to prominence *c*.1724 through a poem she wrote about the plight of an officer's widow and her blind child, 'The Widow Gordon's Petition'. The poem gained her an introduction to Swift, who was henceforth to prove an influential and generous friend to her. Largely through Swift sufficient subscribers were found to enable her collection of verse to be published in 1734. During the 1730s she spent much of her time in Bath, hoping for some amelioration of the gout. Her declining years were spent in Glasnevin. Her verse is for the most part trite and pedestrian, but the occasional poem is worth reading for the light it sheds on living conditions in Dublin in her time.

Reading

Barber, Mary, *Poems on Several Occasions* (London: 1734).

PATRICK FAGAN

Bardic poetry in the early modern period Bardic poetry in the narrowest sense consists of syllabic verse in classical, or early modern, Irish (*c*.1200–1650 AD), the bulk of it composed by trained professionals from the Uí Dhálaigh (O'Dalys), Uí Uiginn (O'Higgins) and other Gaelic families of hereditary praise-poets. In its traditional form this verse was designed for public recitation at banquets, to a musical accompaniment. It was characterized by ornate, very complex metres and an abundance of inherited motifs, celebrating the reign of a just king or a victorious battle, or lamenting the passing of an allegedly popular chieftain – themes that were also used figuratively of God and Christ in bardic religious verse, composed by the same professional practitioners. However, the higher survival rate of late manuscripts has meant that about half the extant corpus of 1,800–2,000 poems dates to the late sixteenth or early seventeenth century. In this period anthologies of famous medieval odes were compiled for the entertainment of aristocratic connoisseurs, both Gaelic and Anglo-Irish, and such literate amateurs tried their hand at composing verse themselves, using the bardic language and metres but imitating English court poetry of the period in subject matter, writing love poems, letter poems, lines in praise or dispraise of womankind, riddles, acrostics and sometimes short humorous or obscene pieces.

The Nugent manuscript, National Library of Ireland MS G 992, is an anthology which testifies to the close association between the barons of Delvin and a neighbouring poetic school run by the Ó Cobhthaigh (O'Coffey) family in the later sixteenth century. The baron's younger son, William Nugent, was listed in 1577 by the Dublin writer Richard Stanihurst as author of a number of English sonnets, but his only surviving compositions are a group of Irish poems in faultless bardic metre, written while William was a student at Oxford. In these he expresses alienation from his English surroundings and nostalgic longing for the mixed Gaelic and Anglo-Irish society in which he was reared, especially for the bardic poets and musicians. A friend of the Nugents, Giolla Brighde Ó hEoghusa, typified another variation from bardic tradition when he resigned his post as court poet in Fermanagh to become a Franciscan friar in Louvain, where as Brother Bonaventura he published religious tracts in prose and deliberately simple verse,

designed to promote the Counter-Reformation.

The works of two other major bards in this period foreshadow future developments. Tadhg Dall Ó hUiginn (d. *c*.1591) experimented with the use of stressed ballad metre (*amhrán*) in formal praise poetry, and composed two of the earliest known aisling or 'vision' poems, in which the poet describes a ravishingly beautiful woman who visits his dreams, and questions her identity. In later generations this vision was to symbolize Ireland and such poems acquired a political import. Eochaidh Ó hEoghusa (d. 1613) forsook on occasion his complex court poetry for love verses in the amateur style, but also set a trend in stately lamentation for the passing of the old Gaelic ways, the triumph of English culture and the neglect of the bards. Both the patriotic and the Counter-Reformation themes were to be taken up by the new generation of middle-class *amhrán* poets from Munster, such as Geoffrey Keating and Pádraigín Haicéad, who maintained friendly contacts with some of the last professional bards. The 1641 uprising and rule by the Catholic Confederation of Kilkenny led to a brief revival in local autonomy, and hence to some renewal of patronage for the hereditary bards, whose trade was the celebration of sovereignty. In fact certain noble families, including the viscounts Dillon and the O'Neills of Clandeboye, continued to reward compositions in the bardic style up to the battle of Aughrim (1691) and beyond, but the masters of this dying art could no longer support themselves on the profits of poetry alone.

Reading

Bergin, O., *Irish Bardic Poetry*, eds D. Greene and F. Kelly (Dublin: Dublin Institute for Advanced Studies, 1970).

Carney, J., *The Irish Bardic Poet* (Dublin: Dolmen Press, 1985).

Knott, E. (ed.), *The Bardic Poems of Tadhg Dall Ó nUiginn*, 2 vols (London: 1922, 1926).

Murphy, G. (ed.), 'Poems of exite by William Nuinseann mac Banúin Dealbhna', *Éigse* 6 (1948), pp. 8–15.

O Riordan, M., *The Gaetic Mind and the Collapse of the Gaelic World* (Cork: Cork University Press, 1990).

Simms, K., 'Bards and barons: the Anglo-Irish aristocracy and the native culture', in *Medieval Frontier Societies*, eds R. Bartlett and A. MacKay (Oxford: Clarendon Press, 1989).

KATHERINE SIMMS

Baron Rev. Bartholomew/Bonaventura (*c.*1610–96) Franciscan and writer. Born in Clonmel, County Tipperary, and the nephew of Luke Wadding, founder of St Isidore's College in Rome. He was an eminent writer, publishing ten volumes of Latin prose and verse. Furthermore he was a theologian of some repute, enjoying the friendship of popes Urban IV and Alexander VII. His early published writings include a diary of the siege of Duncannon and *Panegyrici Sacroprophani*, published in 1643 whilst he was a professor at St Isidore's. In 1653 he published a four-volume treatise on the work of Boethius, *Boetius Absolutus; sive de Consolatione Theologiae*. In 1656, whilst in Hungary, he published a collection of his poems concerning various Irish saints and his family. He spent much of his life studying the works of Duns Scotus, publishing many tracts and a three-volume treatise on the subject. In 1676 he was appointed to the office of historiographer by Cosmo de Medici, grand duke of Tuscany, for whom he published *Trias Tusca* and a treatise on the de Medici family *Orbes Medicei*. His last published work was a history of the Order for Redemption of Captives. On many occasions he declined the offer of a bishopric in Ireland. He died at St Isidore's College in Rome.

Reading

Millett, Benignus, 'Irish literature in Latin 1550–1700', in *New History of Ireland*, vol. 3 (Oxford: Clarendon Press, 1976).

Wall, Thomas, 'A distinguished Irish humanist: Bonaventure Baron, O.F.M., of Clonmel (1610–96)', *Irish Ecclesiastical Record*, 5th series, Lxvii (1946), pp. 92–102, 317–27.

BRIAN DONOVAN

Barret, George (1728 or 1732–84) Painter. Born in the Dublin Liberties, died London 29 May. He studied under Robert West in the Dublin Society's School. His early Italianate rococo style was soon exchanged for a more romantic manner taken from nature, influenced by Edmund Burke's philosophy of 'the Sublime and the Beautiful'. He moved to London *c.*1763, where his premium-winning landscape at the Free Society in 1764 was compared with Claude. His most notable views, rivalling Wilson's, were painted in Wales, and at Norbury Park. He was a founder member of the Royal Academy in 1768, and master painter to Chelsea Hospital in 1782.

Reading

Bodkin, T., *Four Irish Landscape Painters* (Dublin: Maunsell Press, 1920).

Crookshank, A., and the Knight of Glin, *The Painters of Ireland, c. 1660–1920* (London: Barrie and Jenkins, 1978).

Strickland, W.G., *A Dictionary of Irish Artists* (Shannon: Irish University Press, 1968).

HILARY PYLE

Barrington, Sir Jonah (1760–1834) Politician, lawyer and memoir writer. Jonah was the fourth of sixteen children born to John Barrington, a middle-sized landowner in Queen's County in 1760. He died in Paris on 8 April. An unabashed careerist, Barrington entered the law after graduation from Trinity College, and purchased a parliamentary seat in the borough of Tuam in 1790 in the knowledge that this was the most effective way to secure the attention of Dublin Castle, which was the key to professional advancement. He ostentatiously supported the Castle in the early 1790s, and it led directly to a sinecure position worth £1,000 in 1793. He declined to repurchase his seat in 1797, but he re-entered parliament in 1798 and voted against the Act of Union, though it cost him his sinceure. Having failed to be elected to the imperial parliament in 1802, Barrington accepted the government's offer of a judgeship in the Admiralty Court and a knighthood. While in office, he misappropriated court funds to finance his extravagant lifestyle. He was not discovered and removed from the bench until 1830, by which time he had an established reputation as the raciest memorialist of his generation.

Reading

Barrington, Sir Jonah, *Personal Sketches of My Own Times*, 3 vols (London: 1827–32).

JAMES KELLY

Barry, Gerald (1952–) Composer. Born County Clare. Gained BMus and MA degrees at University College, Dublin, and then studied composition in the Netherlands (with Peter Schat), Germany (with Stockhausen and Kagel), and Austria (with Friedrich Cerha). In Germany, where he lived for five years, many works were commissioned, performed and broadcast. In 1980 the City of Bremen Theatre commissioned music for Reinhild Hoffman's ballet *Unkraugarten*, which subsequently toured Europe, and in the same year his ensemble piece was chosen by Kagel to represent the younger generation at the Festival St Denis in Paris, where it was performed by Ensemble Musique Vivant, conducted by Vinko Globokar. From 1982 to 1986 Barry lectured in music at University College, Cork, until devoting himself to composition full-time on his election to Aosdána, Ireland's government-sponsored body honouring creative artists. Major works to date include the orchestral pieces *Of Queen's Gardens* (1986) and *Chevaux de Frise* (1987–8), the latter commissioned by the BBC and premièred at the 1988 Henry Wood Promenade Concerts by the Ulster Orchestra, conducted by Robert Houlihan. Chamber music includes *Handel's Favourite*

Song (1981), *Sur les Pointes* (1981) and *Sweet Punishment* (1987). In 1990 his full-length opera, *The Intelligence Park* (1982–7), was premièred in London at the Almeida Festival and performed in Dublin. In 1992 *Flamboys for Orchestra* was commissioned by Trinity College Dublin and premièred as part of the quatercentenary celebrations of the College. Barry has been described as 'an individual voice, sure of intention and accomplished of execution. He has selected an artistic stance unusual among his contemporaries; there is more of Kagel than of Stockhausen in his work, and a marked preference for the fringes of "music theatre"'.

EVE O'KELLY

Barry, James (1741–1806) Painter and critic. Born Water Lane (now Seminary Road), Cork, 11 October. His father, John Barry, was a publican and small-time ship owner; his mother, Juliana Reardon, belonged to a Catholic family dispossessed after the Williamite wars. In Cork, Barry studied painting under the landscape artist John Butts, and in 1763 transferred to West's Academy in Dublin, where he was awarded a premium for his picture *The Baptism of the King of Cashel by St Patrick* at the Exhibition of the Dublin Society for the Encouragement of Arts, Manufactures and Commerce. This is believed to be the first painting of an Irish historical theme, and it brought the young painter to the attention of Edmund Burke. In 1764, at Burke's expense, Barry moved to London and subsequently to the Continent, where he studied for five years (1765–71) in Paris and Rome, also financed by Burke. He first exhibited a painting, *Adam and Eve*, at the Royal Academy on his return to London in 1771. In 1775 he was elected to the Royal Academy, and in 1782 he was elected professor of painting.

Barry's early paintings were thoroughly imbued with neo-classical ideals, and it was the civic humanism and universal vision of antiquity which attracted him to Republicanism. In 1776 his print *The Phoenix, or the*

Resurrection of Freedom depicted the flight of liberty from Britain to revolutionary America, a theme addressed more obliquely in his painting *Ulysses and a Companion*, in which Burke appears to caution Barry on his excessive political ardour. In 1777, Barry dedicated a print of his 1770 painting *Philoctetes* to Sir George Savile, who, at Burke's behest, led the campaign for the Catholic Relief Act in 1778. Prints of both *Philoctetes* and *The Phoenix* circulated among political radicals in the Patriot movement in Ireland.

In 1777 Barry commenced work on a monumental series of history paintings, 'The Progress of Human Culture', to decorate the Great Room of the (Royal) Society of Arts in the Adelphi. This project, undertaken without remuneration save his materials and 'my two-penny loaf, my cheese, and my pot of porter', occupied Barry in one way or another for the rest of his life, and led to his rapid descent into poverty, lamented by his friend William Blake. These paintings traced the rise of culture from the time of Orpheus to its ultimate flowering in the republican principles of liberty and progress as represented in the final massive painting, *Elysium and Tartarus or the State of Final Retribution*. In this sprawling canvas 125 great figures (artists, statesmen, etc.) are celebrated for their contributions to humanity, but Barry's own particular political agenda is clear from the inclusion of a substantial number of Catholics, and Irish figures such as William Molyneux and Ossian, thus reinforcing Irish claims for repeal of the penal laws and for political independence.

In his extensive critical writings, Barry defended the beleaguered genre of history painting because of its devotion to the 'public sphere', to citizenship and liberty. His first publication, *An Inquiry into the Real and Imaginary Obstructions to the Acquisition of the Arts in England* (1775), took issue with Continental theories that national character (and hence potential for progress) was determined by climate rather than social and political conditions. Throughout his subsequent writings and artistic practice, he attempted to reconcile the universal and future-oriented ideals of the Enlightenment with what were later seen as opposing Romantic sentiments – an emphasis on locality, and the native history of ancient Britain or Gaelic Ireland. In 1799, his accusations of corruption in the artistic establishment in *A Letter to the Dillettanti Society* led to his expulsion from the Royal Academy. In 1799–1801 he worked on a new version of *The Baptism of the King of Cashel by St Patrick*, and in his final paintings and drawings, he alternated between an increasingly feminist-inspired classicism (*The Birth of Pandora*, 1804–5; *Agrippina Mourning over the Ashes of Germanicus*, 1790s; and *Jupiter and Juno on Mount Ida*, 1785–1805) and a sense of political desperation evident in his bleak Irish drawings, most notably his depiction of the false promise of the Act of Union in 1800, *Passive Obedience* (1802–5). Barry died in destitution and is buried in St Paul's Cathedral.

LUKE GIBBONS

Barton, Rose (1856–1929) Watercolourist. Born Dublin. Her father was a lawyer from Rochestown, County Tipperary. After a private education, in 1874 she went to Brussels to train with Henri Gervex, a *plein air* painter. She frequently exhibited her broad-wash watercolours at the Royal watercolour Society, only becoming a full member of that institution in 1911 (the first woman to be so elected). She produced a large number of scenes of Dublin and London, both topographical and of social interest; her Anglo-Irish background often dictating the subject – a levée at Dublin Castle or the interior of a great house on St Stephen's Green.

Reading

Nugent, Charles and Rowe, Rebecca, *Rose Barton RWS (1856–1929)* (Cork: Crawford Municipal Art Gallery; London: Fine Art Society, and elsewhere, 1987).

FINTAN CULLEN

Bax, Arnold (1883–1953) Composer. A prolific English musician who was much drawn to the people and land of Ireland. This sympathy was enkindled through the poetry of Yeats, which inspired much of Bax's early creative work. In 1902 Bax paid the first of his many visits to Ireland, where he first came to attention as an aspiring literary figure publishing under the pseudonym Dermot O'Byrne. His affinity with burgeoning nationalist sentiment was given musical expression in the tone poems *Into the Twilight* (1908), *In the Faery Hills* (1909) and *Roscatha* (1910), works that anticipate his surpassing achievement from this period of enthralment with Ireland, *The Garden of Fand* (1913). The impressive *Moy Mell*, described as a tone poem for two pianos, followed three years later. He was conscious of the beauty of Irish folk music but did not resort to direct quotation. Later works, including seven symphonies, are less indebted to the Celtic spirit, although Bax did set poems by his friend, the poet Padraic Colum, and completed a setting of *St Patrick's Breastplate* (1923) for chorus and orchestra. Ties with Ireland remained close and Bax frequently acted as extern examiner for the National University, from which he received an honorary DMus in 1947. It was while engaged on these duties that Bax died in Cork, and he remains buried there.

Reading

Foreman, L., *Bax: A Composer and His Times* (Scolar Press, 1988). Dent, Scott-Sutherland, C., *Arnold Bax* (London: 1973).

JOSEPH RYAN

Beaufort Family Of Huguenot ancestry, the Irish branch of the Beaufort family was founded by Daniel Cornelius Beaufort (1700–88), who came to Ireland in 1746 as chaplain to the Lord Lieutenant, Earl Hartington. His son Daniel Augustus (1739–1821), who was born in London in 1739 and died in Cork in 1821, and who also took holy orders, was a man of many talents. He was one of the 'foundation membership' of the Royal Irish Academy, an active member of the Dublin Society, a talented architect with many buildings to his credit in County Meath, and inveterate travel-journal writer, and a topographer who produced the wonderful 6-inch map of 'Ireland, Civil and Ecclesiastical' in 1792. Of his two sons and three daughters, Francis (1774–1857) had a distinguished naval career; Frances (1769–1865), who married R.L. Edgeworth, helped edit Maria Edgeworth's letters for publication; Henrietta (1778–1865) wrote children's books; and Louisa (1781–1763) wrote on architecture and entomology.

Reading

Ellison, C.C., 'Remembering Dr Beaufort', *Quarterly Bulletin of the Irish Georgian Society*, 18 (1975).
——The Hopeful Traveller: The Life and Times of Daniel Augustus Beaufort (Kilkenny: Boethius Press, 1987).

JAMES KELLY

Beckett, Brian (1950–) Composer and pianist. Born Dublin, nephew of Walter Beckett. He studied composition with Dr A. J. Potter and with James Wilson, and his compositions are mainly in the areas of chamber music and solo piano music. He has taught piano at the Royal Irish Academy of Music since 1974 and is actively involved in music education.

BARRA BOYDELL

Beckett family Described by Vivian Mercier as coming from 'the same rather philistine Irish Protestant background' as himself, Samuel Beckett was the grandson of a prosperous Dublin builder-contractor and the son of an equally successful quantity surveyor, William Frank Beckett (1871–1933). It is believed that the family was of Huguenot descent. His maternal grandfather was Samuel Roe of Roe Hall, Leixlip, County Kildare, owner of a grain mill though described as a 'gentleman' on Beckett's parents' marriage certificate, and his mother Mary Jones Roe (1871–1950) had been a nurse at the Adelaide Hospital in Dublin, where she met and nursed her future husband, before their marriage on 31 August 1901. Photographs of Beckett's parents – his father, at Leopardstown Race course, in a bowler hat that seems slightly too small for him, his mother, always fashionably hatted whether hearing her son's prayers, driving a donkey cart, or seated with her Pomeranian on a hillside (and somewhat incongruosly wearing an apron) – tellingly convey the difference in their temperaments: the father, jovial and amiable, his rotund figure belying his height; the tall, slender mother, handsome, austere and forbidding. Beckett, who was preceded by an elder brother, Frank Edward (1902–54), was born at the family home, Coodrinagh, Foxrock, on 13 April (or May) 1906. His birth was not registered until 14 June, and Beckett always claimed Good Friday, 13 April, as his birthday, though his birth certificate, perhaps due to an oversight on his father's part, dates the event a month later. Significantly, Beckett's mother was known in the family as 'May'.

Samuel Beckett (1906–89)

Born Dublin; died Paris, December, having lived in that city virtually continuously since 1945. His life and writing career are punctuated by the Irish struggle for independence, the rise of fascism that he witnessed in his travels in Germany in the 1930s, and World War II, which he experienced both as a Resistance worker and in hiding in Vichy France. His subsequent life in France also saw its wars of decolonization, in Vietnam and in Algeria, and the major intellectual movements there which during the same period radically transformed western conceptions of humanity and of culture. He was intimate with James Joyce and with the younger avant-garde poets of his generation – Coffey, Devlin and McGreevy. He was a close friend of the painter Jack B. Yeats and wrote criticism on many of the principal figures of the post-war avant-garde. At

the same time, he collaborated with Octavio Paz on translations of Mexican poets. He is, in other words, a writer whose life and work to an exceptional extent intersect with the complex intellectual and political currents of his time. If Yeats and Joyce may be said to be the writers who most fully map the terrain of pre-independence Ireland as it intersects with international Modernism, Beckett is the writer whose work most intricately addresses the difficult relations of a post-colonial and postmodern world.

Beckett's *oeuvre* may indeed be seen as working out the consequences of what he saw in France at the end of the war while working as a hospital orderly: 'the conception of humanity in ruins'. But his perception of the disorder of post-war Europe was prepared for by his previous work, which had already commenced a relentless dismantling of the literary and aesthetic forms intrinsic both to dominant European cultures and to those nationalisms, like that of Ireland, which emerged in opposition to them. His writing, from his earliest critical texts, is deeply antagonistic to the 'literature of notations' against which he posed the example of *Finnegans Wake* in 'Dante . . . Bruno. Vico . . . Joyce', or to the 'eyes of building contractors' which he sees as underlying the European tradition in painting. In every case, what he poses against the domination of mimesis in either art is the process of an art which explores the predicament of its own incapacity. Devoted from the start to the pursuit of 'the core of the eddy' and yet driven by the knowledge that 'asserting unity denies unity', Beckett's work is a deconstruction *avant la lettre*, working from within certain aesthetic and philosophical presuppositions in order to show how their own logic issues in contradiction or aporia. He is, as he wrote of Jack B. Yeats, seeking 'to reduce the dark where there might have been, mathematically at least, a door'.

His *oeuvre* in consequence is a continual paring down, both within individual works and from work to work, a *via negativa* whose end might be, as his character Molloy remarks of anthropology, the 'definition of man, as though he were no better than God, in terms of what he is not'. At the 'core of the eddy' is the problem of the self and identity, those conditions of both knowledge and social being that the novel, even up to Proust, had always taken as a given. For Beckett, however, the very process of socialization narrated in the great nineteenth-century novels is intrinsically contradictory. The problem he faces is to find the literary means not simply to state but to enact the interminable, logically aporetic pursuit of the 'I am' on which philosophy since Descartes had predicated our certainty of self and of truth.

Beckett's early poem *Whoroscope* (1930) is testimony at once to his fascination with Descartes, whose semi-autobiographical musings it enacts, and to the kind of difficulty presented by his early writings. The fiction and poetry of the 1930s is itself often a kind of literature of notations, its obscurities for the most part resolvable by reference to encyclopedia or dictionary. With a handful of exceptions like 'Malacoda' in *Echo's Bones* (1935), the early poems lack the intensity of ambivalence which the later work so forcefully carries. Likewise, the stories of *More Pricks than Kicks* (1934) are often seen to betray the influence of Joyce pushed, as in his contemporary Flann O'Brien, to mannerist extremes. The novel *Murphy* (1938), however, begins to trace the failure of its eponymous protagonist to attain to quiescence of self in the logic of that quest itself, entertaining throughout not only the tension between the desire for quiescence and its interruption by successive contingent events, but also the contradiction between intense self-consciousness and the project of self-abnegation which is its end. This is famously dramatized in Murphy's interminable chess game with the psychotic Mr Endon, who refuses all engagement and in whose eyes Murphy finally becomes, to his horror and delight, a non-entity.

Beckett's last novel to be written in English, *Watt* (1945), composed mostly in hiding in Vichy France, pushes the derangement of language and its referential functions to their limits in the form of linguistic and logical games. These dramatize the gradual disintegration in the enigmatic Mr Knott's house of Watt's naive desire for a fit between representation and reality. Remarkable both for the virtuosity of its linguistic and logical play and for its simulation of schizophrenic thought processes, *Watt* continues none the less to present the crisis of language and representation as if it inhered between increasingly complex and ornate language systems, verging often on idiosyncratic language games, and the evacuated domain of 'things in themselves'. It situates, that is, the problem of knowledge between subject and object, self and world, even as it radically destabilizes the 'building contractor's' perspective.

Beckett's celebrated decision to write and publish in French coincides with a crucial move beyond the stylistic impasse presented by *Watt*. Several reasons have been suggested for this decision beyond the simple desire to write in the language of what had become his adopted country. Beckett's own terse account was that in French it was easier to write without style, a remark that has variously been taken to mean that only in French was it possible for him to escape the overwhelming influence of Joyce or that as a foreign language it permitted a further move into linguistic dispossession or impoverishment. It is certainly the case that already in the early French texts, such as *Premier Amour/ First Love* or *L'expulsé/ The Expelled* (1945–6), a drastic simplification of language and technique has taken place in comparison to *Murphy* or *Watt*. There is also an increasingly intent focus on certain thematic motifs which will recur throughout Beckett's later work: exile or expulsion, the desire for self-identity figured as death or suspension of animation, the gradual decay of the body. These themes are most fully explored in the trilogy of novels, *Molloy* (1951), *Malone Dies* (1951) and *The Unnamable* (1953), that stands as Beckett's principal prose work.

It has often been said that the trilogy brought Beckett to an impasse from which the fragmentary *Texts for Nothing* (1958) scrabbled to pass. The reasons for this sense are not hard to decipher, as the series of novels gradually reduces the means of expression, the projects of the protagonists and the scope of representation towards degree zero. At the same time, Beckett gradually exhausts the capacities of the forms or genres of prose fiction: the *Bildungsroman* or novel of self-formation, the detective novel, the quest or homing narration, the autobiography or confessional, and implicitly the dialectical master narratives of idealist philosophy for which the alienation of self-consciousness is only a stage in a return of the spirit to self-identity. The relentlessness of Beckett's excoriation of fictions of identity, not to mention the insistently caustic humour of his protagonists, over and over confronts systematic interpretations of the trilogy with Beckett's own ironic dictum concerning *Finnegans Wake*: 'The danger is in the neatness of identifications' ('Dante... Bruno. Vico... Joyce'). Such interpretations have been manifold – Jungian, Freudian, Christian, existentialist – but each takes the reader only so far before the deliberate referential instability of the novels twists away from neat allegorization. Even the assumption that the quartet of protagonists, Molloy and Moran, Malone and the Unnamable, are one devolving persona founders in their reappearances throughout as fictional figurations of the self sought.

Perhaps the most consistent readings of the work are those which see it as an allegory of the Cartesian split between mind and body. Beckett's interest in Descartes is well documented and the novels certainly dramatize a dysfunction of both the mind and the body. Yet it is significant that for all his ageing protagonists, always on the threshold of a perpetually deferred death, language and the body are simultaneously disintegrating. The dilemma is not that of a mind unable to be in the body or in the world but that of a subject whose vehicles of being in the world (to cite the phenomenologists) operate through an irredeemably alienating grammar. The body, in the nice phrase of the Unnamable, is always a tympanum, an interface between self and other. Its disintegration or malfunctioning is only the accentuation of the predicament of non-identity. By the same token, the subject is always an effect of a language not its own – 'I'm in words, made of words, others' words', as Molloy puts it – and submitted to the logic of self-predication. It is as if Beckett's rejoinder to Descartes is to remind us that what 'I am' means is the impossible 'I am that I am', an identity logically unattainable. Writing becomes a process of deferral in every domain: Malone's death-bed inventories as much as his fictional inventions reduce the panorama of European self-hood and its 'properties' to the minimum of elements, as if to highlight the contradictions of the desire for identity and substance that underlies not only our aesthetic but also our legal and political formations.

The caustic humour of the trilogy lies in the novels' propensity for verbal and logical slapstick, a theatrical device which always attracted Beckett. It is at once a 'low' form, a counterpart to the carnivalesque scatology of so much of his work, and a form which demands a maximum of elegant control and timing as a means to perform dysfunction. Beckett's earliest and still best-known plays exhibit an extraordinary combination of slapstick routine with the most exacting of classical forms. *Waiting for Godot* (1952), famously described as a play in which nothing happens, twice, and *Endgame* (1956), both conform with a rigour rare in English-language drama to the classical unities of time, place and action. At the same time, both are disconcertingly evacuated of content. Nothing happens, except that Vladimir and Estragon wait for a Godot who never arrives, and Hamm and Clov kill time rather than one another. The time of the plays is filled with the exchange of banalities, philosophical fragments, literary allusions, the high and the low reduced equally to the formality of clichés in a radical parody of the western tradition their empty forms evoke. As with the trilogy, no interpretation, whether of the teasing religious suggestiveness of *Godot* or of the world catastrophe apparently in process in *Endgame*, can withstand the corrosive power of these plays. 'Neatness of identification' succumbs again to the slapstick which the plays' couples counterpoint with their verbal patter.

Beckett's subsequent dramatic works continue to exhibit extraordinary formal exactitude in whatever medium he explores. From radio plays, like *All that Fall* (1957: the first work composed in English after 1945), *Cascando* (1963) or *Embers* (1959), to television plays like *Eh Joe* (1966), to his single film, *Film* (1965), all his dramatic works explore with absolute economy the specific potential of their media. The concentration of sound permitted by radio permits the orchestration of *Cascando*, a play for words and music; variations of camera angle, depth of field and reverse shots provide the means in *Film* to present the agony of self-perception fled by its protagonist, played by Buster Keaton as if in silent homage to the slapstick tradition; in *Eh Joe*, the intimacy of television is exploited in the increasingly tight series of close-ups that dramatize Joe's inability to escape the interior voice. Beckett's own demanding participation in many of these productions emphasized the precision required by their intense formal structures. And with that precision goes an unrelenting paring away of the medium to its minimal elements: the single spotlight which successively interrogates the banal characters of *Play* (1963), each immobilized in an urn and only speaking under the spot's duress, weaves the pattern of their manipulative relationships; the total darkness of *Not I* (1972), relieved only by the isolated, illuminated mouth of an old woman, babbling furiously in order not to utter the word 'I', and her scarcely visible auditor; the scarcely moving, identical figures of *Ohio Impromptu* (1982), reading and listening. In the precise economy of these works, literal reduction has the effect of making the medium itself a protagonist in the dramas of alienation and self-perception: the medium becomes an allegory for the constantly, inevitably frustrated attempts of Beckett's characters to flee from self-perception into self-identity.

Beckett's late prose similarly dramatizes its medium, not in mere play with self-referentiality, but in the desire to explore the constitutive tension of narrative that subsists between the necessary temporality of language and the desire to come to rest, a tension captured in titles like *Still* (1974), *Stirrings Still* (1989) and *For to End Yet Again* (1975). Many of the texts of the 1960s, such as *Imagination Dead Imagine* (1966), *Ping* (1967) and *Lessness* (1969), render a single image constantly displaced from immediacy of apprehension by the linked temporal and predicative functions of language. It could be said that the longer, quasi-narrative texts like *Worstward Ho* (1983), *Ill Seen, Ill Said* (1982) or *Company* (1980), dramatize a similar predicament in the genre of biography or autobiography around the idea of self-portraiture. The comparative richness of these texts, after the extreme dessication of works like *Lessness*, does not come at the expense of Beckett's coninuing interrogation of the conditions of subjectivity. *Company*, for instance, is a deeply ironic autobiography, possibly written in response to Deirdre Bair's desperately fixing biography, and plays dislocated stills from a life against the splitting of a narrative persona into voice and hearer, heard and overheard, while never offering the assurance of conclusion or fixed identity.

Indeed, Beckett's whole *oeuvre* might be encapsulated in the single word 'still', which recurs insistently throughout the later work. The term at once for fixity and for a continuing process, it expresses both the desire of the subject and the displacement that very desire entails. 'At the same time it is over and it goes on, and is there any tense for that?', asks Molloy. The immanent logic of Beckett's work refuses recuperation either into the pathos of the 'human condition' or by way of explanatory interpretation. The conditions by which the the western subject emerges and is sustained as the foundation of truth, law and order are too thoroughly dismantled in these texts for such fictions to survive. Lodged in the vision of 'humanity in ruins', Beckett's work is an irreducible critique at the level of the individual subject of the terrible but contradictory logic of domination.

Reading

Adorno, T.W., 'Trying to understand *Endgame*', *New German Critique*, 26 (Summer 1982), pp. 119–50.

Bair, Deirdre, *Samuel Beckett: A Biography* (London: Jonathan Cape, 1978).

Bernal, Olga, *Langage et fiction dans le roman de Samuel Beckett* (Paris: Gallimard, 1969).

Friedman, Melvin J. (ed.), *Samuel Beckett Now* (Chicago: University of Chicago Press, 1970).

Harvey, Lawrence E., *Samuel Beckett. Poet and Critic*. (Princeton NJ: Princeton University Press, 1970).

Hill, Leslie, *Beckett's Fiction. In Different Words* (Cambridge: Cambridge University Press, 1990).

Kenner, Hugh, *Samuel Beckett: A Critical Study* (Berkeley: University of California Press, 1961).

Lloyd, David, 'Writing in the shit: Beckett, nationalism and the colonial subject', in *Anomalous States: Irish Writing and the Post-Colonial Moment* (Dublin: Lilliput Press, 1992).

Locatelli, Carla, *Unwording the World: Samuel Beckett's Prose Works after the Nobel Prize* (Philadelphia: University of Pennsylvania Press, 1990).

O'Brien, Eoin, *The Beckett County: Samuel Beckett's Ireland* (Dublin: Black Cut Press, 1986).

MARY LYDON AND DAVID LLOYD

Beckett, John (1927–) Born Dublin, cousin of Walter Beckett. Harpsichordist and conductor. He studied in London and has divided his career between Dublin and London. He conducted the pioneering early music ensemble Musica Reservata from 1961 to 1971, taught harpsichord, viol consort and baroque chamber music, and conducted an annual series of Bach contatas in Dublin between 1973 and 1983. He subsequently returned to London to work as a music producer with Radio 3.

BARRA BOYDELL

Beckett, Walter (1914–96) Composer. Born Dublin. Influenced by Delius, Vaughan Williams, Fauré and Janacek, Beckett's music is romantic in concept, with traditional Irish music also being influential. His output includes symphonic, chamber, vocal and organ music. He held a MusD from Trinity College, Dublin, and was a member of Aosdána. He wrote the volume on Liszt for the Master Musicians series (Dent), and for many years taught at the Royal Irish Academy of Music.

BARRA BOYDELL

Bedell, William (1571–1642) Bishop. For someone who only desired a quiet parochial ministry, Bedell had a remarkably varied career. Born at Black Notley in Essex in 1571, educated at Emmanuel College, Cambridge (MA 1592, Fellow 1593, BD 1599), in 1602 he was appointed to the church of St Mary's, Bury St Edmunds. From 1607 to 1610 he was chaplain to the British Ambassador to Venice, Sir Henry Wotton, becoming closely involved in the dispute between city and papacy. In 1627 he was again plucked out of pastoral obscurity, this time to become provost of Trinity College. As provost (1627–9), he reformed the college, seeking to ensure that its clerical graduates were able to preach in Irish. Appointed bishop of Kilmore and Ardagh in 1629 (though he resigned Ardagh in 1633), he tried to put into practice his commitment to an indigenous reformation, encouraging Irish-speaking clergy, and sponsoring the translation of the Old Testament into Irish. Though his success was limited, two contemporary biographies have ensured that his ministry was preserved as an ideal of that rare figure in the seventeenth century – a tolerant and culturally sensitive Church of Ireland prelate.

Reading

Clarke, Aidan, 'Bishop William Bedell (1571–1642) and the Irish reformation', in C.F. Brady (ed.), *Worsted in the Game: Losers in Irish History* (Dublin: 1989).

Ford, Alan, *The Protestant Reformation in Ireland, 1590–1641* (Frankfurt: 1987).

Rupp, E.G., 'William Bedell, 1571–1642', in *Just Men* (London: 1977).

Shuckburgh, E.S. (ed.), *Two Biographies of William Bedell Bishop of Kilmore with a Selection of his Letters and an Unfinished Treatise* (Cambridge: 1902).

ALAN FORD

Behan family Literary members include not only Brendan (1923–64) but his brothers Brian (1925–) and Dominic (1928–89). Their father Stephen, a housepainter, was a socialist and IRA man, in jail when Brendan was born (in Dublin). Republicanism, jail and literature are key elements of the Behans' early and later lives.

Their mother, born Kathleen Kearney (a sister of Peader Kearney, stage manager of the Abbey, and author of 'The Soldier's Song', adopted as the Irish national anthem) had two boys, Rory and Sean Furlong, by an earlier marriage, whom Brendan liked because they did not write. A Kearney aunt was married into the Bourkes, a Dublin theatrical family. Cathal Goulding, Marxist chief of staff of the Official IRA in the 1960s, was another family connection. Song and theatre came early to all the boys.

Brendan, widely well read, left school aged 14. Joining the IRA, he went to England in 1939 to play a part in the terrorist bombing campaign in which the Coventry killings (August) were an ugly incident. He was arrested for possession of explosives in Liverpool and sent to Walton Jail and later to Hollesley Bay Borstal. Released (1941) and deported back to Ireland, he was jailed (1942) for attempting to murder a policeman, and sent to Mountjoy Jail (where he experienced the prisoners' reactions to the execution of fratricide Bernard Kirwan), and later to Arbour Hill and the Curragh. Freed in 1946, he combined housepainting with occasional journalism, before becoming notorious as a playwright, raconteur and drunk a decade later.

His first play was *The Quare Fellow* inspired by the Kirwan execution. After a successful low-key production in Dublin (9 November 1954), it was remounted by Joan Littlewood in her unique style at the Theatre Royal, Stratford East (24 May 1956). It was followed by *The Hostage* (also inspired by an actual event), originally produced in Dublin in Gaelic as *An Giall* (16 June 1958; at Stratford 14 October 1958), and by *Borstal Boy* (1958), an account of his years as a revolutionary delinquent. Later books were largely easy going and amusing rambles, though his Gaelic poems have won praise. Afflicted with alcoholism, diabetes and jaundice, he died in Dublin on 20 March.

Brian Behan was active for many years as a notorious radical trade unionist in London, and is now an anarchist, the author of a memoir *With Breast Expanded* (1964), a play, a novel, an autobiography of his mother (a woman as unusual as her children), and a saga novel based on her life, *Kathleen* (1988).

Dominic Behan became first known as an anti-IRA dramatist (*Posterity Be Damned*, 1960), much to Brendan's chagrin. His account of the family appears in *Teems of Times and Happy Returns* (1961) and *My Brother Brendan* (1965). After a great deal of journalism and some years as a singer (famous for his ballad 'The Patriot Game'), he wrote a novel followed by a biography of Spike Milligan (1988). Though lacking the charming fecklessness of Brendan, the harder lives and thwarted ambitions of Brian and Dominic made tougher books, not negligible among the literary outpourings of a remarkable family.

Reading

Jeffs, Rae, *Brendan Behan: Man and Showman* (London: Hutchinson, 1966).

O'Connor, Ulick, *Brendan Behan* (London: Hamilton, 1970).

PETER COSTELLO

Behan, John (1938–) Sculptor. Born in Dublin, Behan worked in the metal industry from 1953 to 1960 and studied art at evening classes at the National College of Art and Design. He then attended Ealing College of Art, London, full-time 1960–2 and also studied in Oslo. In 1970 he jointly set up the Dublin Art Foundry. Behan is a figurative sculptor who works primarily in bronze. He has consistently drawn inspiration from Irish mythology, especially the Tain, and the bull is one of his best-known motifs. A well-known sculpture on public display is *Birds* in the Irish Life Centre on Abbey Street; birds in flight are another recurring theme in Behan's work. Behan now lives and works in Galway.

FELICITY WOOLF

Belfast Belfast is a city of paradoxes: Irish, yet not entirely Irish: a capital city, yet not quite a capital city; at once civilized and barbarous.

It received its first charter in 1613; overtook Carrickfergus as the principal seaport of the north in the mid-seventeenth century; and grew steadily throughout the eighteenth century. By 1800, it was a sober, mainly Protestant, mercantile town, just beginning to take on its industrial character. Whilst not untouched by the enlightenment of the French Revolution and the American War of Independence, it was not really another 'Athens of the North', although its citizens would have liked to think so.

Alone in Ireland, Belfast in the ensuing century benefited from, and suffered, the full gale-force of the industrial revolution. Its population increased from 20,000 in 1800 to 350,000 in 1900; in 1888 it became a city. For the first third of the nineteenth century it remained predominantly Presbyterian, but by degrees the Great Famine, the upsurge in trade caused by the American Civil War, and growing prosperity brought to the city an influx of labour, much of it from rural Roman Catholic districts. Between 1830 and 1960, the citizens were roughly one-third Catholic and nationalist, two-thirds Protestant and Unionist, a deep gulf dividing the parties. Having reached a peak of 450,000 in 1951, the population began to fall, and has continued to do so ever since: in 1993 it was probably under 280,000. The result is disconcerting; Protestants have mostly moved out, for safety, to the periphery; Catholics have largely moved in, for safety, nearer the city centre. The factions are now almost evenly balanced. Soon Belfast may become the predominantly Catholic capital of a predominantly Protestant province in a predominantly Catholic island.

Although there had been serious earlier disturbances, Gladstone's Home Rule Bill of 1886 led to sectarian troubles of a kind, and on a scale, which have continued at intervals ever since, with intervening periods of delusive peace. The divisions are very deep and, at times, very savage. Belfast has an image as a city divided comparable with that of Beirut, Dubrovnik, Jerusalem or Jaffna. In the early 1970s, fear led to drastic population movements, polarization, the almost total segregation of the Protestant and Catholic communities, the establishment of physical so-called 'peace lines' to keep apart the factions along the sectarian interfaces, and a so-called 'ring of steel' to protect the city centre from car-bombers. The fear is fully justified. Despite the peace process of the late 1990s there are still parts of the city where no Protestant feels it safe to walk alone at night; other parts where no Catholic feels it safe to do so; and frontiers where neither can feel safe. The passionate partisanship of each side has its roots in the working classes; the dichotomy is not amenable to democratic resolution, a fact reflected in both the composition and the conduct of the elected city council. The overwhelming motivation of the hard men on each side is to assert the predominance of their faction over the other.

Other paradoxes there are aplenty. Belfast has high unemployment, low average earnings; yet some of its shops are the most profitable in the British Isles. The expression 'ghetto' is loosely used; yet Belfast has some of the best modern public housing in Europe, most of it occupied by the minority. Pious Christian church-going is the norm; yet barbarous murder regularly took place there in the name of religion during the 30 years of the Troubles, 1968–98. Beautiful seacoast, mountains, lakes and countryside are easily accessible, at least to those with jobs, however grim the urban image.

The fabric of the city is predominantly Victorian and Edwardian. Bombers and developers between them have greatly prejudiced the integrity of its very individual character over the past 30 years; but there remain many handsome churches, warehouses, banks and public buildings, often with exuberant stone-carving or woodwork. In flavour, Belfast more nearly resembles Glasgow than either Dublin or Liverpool, the other seaport cities of the Irish Sea quadrilateral.

Belfast has never been noted for eminence in the arts, but it has produced some good (if sometimes slightly homespun) artists, novelists, playwrights and musicians: only in poetry has the local culture in recent years excelled. It has a concert hall and an opera house; the first public museum in Ireland (now an arts centre), and the newer Ulster Museum; theatres; three daily newspapers; and the 200-year-old Linenhall Library, consistently a haven of civilization. There are also, at a less highbrow level, strong local traditions of gable-painting, Lambeg drumming, bandsmanship, folk song and hymn-singing; not to mention play-acting, story-telling, and 'craic' or 'crack' (according to the preferred tradition).

Many of its citizens have chosen to shake the dust of Belfast off their feet: Louis MacNeice, Brian Moore and Maurice Craig, whose wounding jingle still hangs in the air over the city:z

> Red brick in the suburbs, white horse on the wall,
> Eyetalian marbles in the City Hall,
> O stranger from England, why stand so aghast?
> May the Lord in His mercy be kind to Belfast.

Others, of both cultural traditions, feel a deep sense of belonging – blood, bone, gristle, proud flesh and all: John Hewitt and Michael Longley; Martin Lynch and Ciaran Carson.

Belfast is a city which deeply engages its citizens whether in old bigotries and old atavisms, or old loyalties and old loves. It is hard to believe that it could ever be quite like any other place. At the time of writing, suggestions of change are in the wind. Even the oldest inhabitant may wonder, wistfully perhaps: can the tiger change its stripes?

Reading

Bardon, Jonathan, *Belfast: An Illustrated History* (Belfast: Blackstaff, 1982).

Beckett, J.C. and Glasscock, R.E. (eds), *Belfast: Origin and Growth of an Industrial City* (London: BBC, 1967).

Jones, Emrys, *A Social Geography of Belfast* (London: Oxford University Press, 1960).

Larmour, Paul, *Belfast: An Illustrated Architectural Guide* (Belfast: FBP, 1987).

Maguire, W.A., *Belfast* (Keele University Press, 1993).

C.E.B. BRETT

The *Bell* Monthly magazine founded in Dublin in 1940 by Sean O Faolain, and edited by him until 1946. Described as 'A Survey of Irish Life', it encompassed more than straightforward literary material, and carried articles of social and personal observation as well as poems and short stories – pieces such as 'A Day in the Life of a Dublin Mechanic', 'Two Years in a Sanatorium', 'I Did Penal Servitude' and 'A Month on the Bog'. Among its contributors were Patrick Kavanagh, Frank O'Connor, Elizabeth Bowen, Padraic Fallon and Anthony Cronin. Actively reformist, the *Bell* offered a continuing critique of Ireland at a time when the country and its society had become isolated by post-independence politics, wartime neutrality and the ideology of censorship. It had an average sale of about 3,000. In April 1946

Peadar O'Donnell took over the editorship; from 1948 the magazine became irregular in its publication, and the final issue appeared in 1954.

PETER DENMAN

Bell, John Stewart (1928–90) Physicist. No book on the modern view of the nature of reality is complete without a discussion of Bell's Theorem. Regarded by many as one of the most fundamental insights in the history of science, this piece of mathematics offers a sharply defined test of some of the weirder aspects of quantum mechanics. So far it has passed the test and we are thereby forced to contemplate a world in which things far apart are linked by instantaneous connections. Popularizers of eastern mysticism have latched on to this enthusiastically. Physicists have pondered it ruefully, as it contradicts a longstanding prejudice against non-local effects.

Bell was born in one of the humbler districts of Belfast, and went to Queen's University. At the time of his death, which came as a great shock to his many admirers, he was a staff member of CERN.

DENIS L. WEAIRE

Bell, Sam Hanna (1909–90) Novelist and broadcaster. Born in Glasgow of Ulster parents and raised in County Down, Bell worked at a wide variety of jobs before joining the BBC in Belfast in 1945 as a radio producer. His first novel, *December Bride* (1951), is a classic of Ulster fiction, remarkable for its authentic recreation of the physical and mental landscapes of a Presbyterian farming community in rural County Down. It is the story of a strange *ménage à trois* between Sarah Gomartin and the brothers Frank and Hamilton Echlin, and has as its theme the clash between passionate individualism and pious conformity. Bell published three other novels, *The Hollow Ball* (1961), *A Man Flourishing* (1973) and *Across the Narrow Sea* (1987), as well as works on Ulster folklore and drama.

Reading

Carson, Douglas, 'Sam Hanna Bell 1901–1990', *Honest Ulsterman*, 89 (Summer 1990), pp. 43–52.

LIAM HARTE

Benedict, Sir Julius (1804–85) English composer and conductor of German birth. Born Stuttgart, 27 November; died London, 5 June. After studying with Weber (whose biography he wrote), he held conducting posts in Vienna and Naples before settling in London in 1835, becoming a leading figure in English musical life. As musical director at Drury Lane (1838–48) he was responsible for *The Bohemian Girl*, *Maritana* and other operas by Balfe and Wallace. The most successful of his own operas was *The Lily of Killarney*, produced at Covent Garden in 1862. This three-act opera, to a libretto by John Oxenford and Dion Boucicault based on the latter's *The Colleen Bawn* (1859), has been described as the first convincing English opera on an Irish theme. It was also produced in New York, and in Germany as *Die Rose von Erin*. Benedict's musical style was based on Rossini, but he gradually adopted a more English idiom, and in *The Lily of Killarney* even achieved a touch of Irishness. He also composed choral and orchestral music, songs and piano pieces. He was knighted in 1871.

Reading

Temperley, Nicholas (ed.), *Music in Britain: The Romantic Age 1800–1914* (London: Athlone Press, 1981).
White, Eric Walter, *A History of English Opera* (London: Faber, 1983).

DAVID GREER

Bennett, Louie (1870–1956) Socialist. Born Temple Hill, Dublin; died Killiney, 25 November. She was educated in Dublin, London and Bonn. Her early interests were in music and imaginative literature; she published two novels in her thirties, and believed that novelists had helped the cause of

65

women's emancipation. In 1911 she helped to form the Irishwomen's Suffrage Federation, and from 1916 became active in the trade union and labour movement. Influenced by James Connolly's ideas, she believed that the struggles for social and for national justice were closely linked. In the 1920s she represented Ireland on the International Executive of the Women's League for Peace and Freedom, and in 1932 became the first woman president of the Irish Trades Union Congress, a post she held again in 1947–8. She remained politically active until her death.

Reading

Fox, R.M., *Louie Bennett: Her Life and Times* (Dublin: Talbot Press, 1958).
Murphy, C., *The Women's Suffrage Movement and Irish Society in the Early Twentieth Century* (Brighton: Harvester-Wheatsheaf, 1987).

DAVID SMITH

Beresford family The founder of the Beresford political dynasty was Sir Tristam Beresford, who came to Ireland as a manager for the London Company in the early seventeenth century. By the end of the century, the family had seats at Coleraine, Country Derry, and Curraghmore, County Waterford; and following the death of Sir Tristam (third baronet) in 1701, his son, Marcus Beresford, piloted them to the forefront of Irish Protestant society. Having represented the constituency of Coleraine for five years (1715–20), he was raised to the peerage as Baron Beresford and Viscount Tyrone in consequence of his marriage in 1721 to Katherine Power, the daughter of the third earl of Tyrone. Twenty-five years later he became an earl. His heir, George de la Poer Beresford (1735–1816), first marquess of Waterford from 1789, was a leading member of the House of Lords in the second half of the eighteenth century, and one of the most enthusiastic proponents of a legislative union with Britain. However, it was his brother John (1738–1805) who was the real political force in the family. John was first elected to the House of Commons in 1761, and from the outset his administrative abilities and his support for British government in Ireland destined him for high office. In 1770, he was made one of the commissioners of the revenue, and ten years later he became chief commissioner of the revenue. Between this date and his death 25 years later, Beresford was one of Ireland's most influential politicians. He played a prominent part in the House of Commons in the Dublin Castle interest, helped maintain the Anglo-Irish connection, and exercised enormous influence on the growth of Dublin in his capacity as wide streets commissioner.

The influence of the Beresfords remained strong in the early nineteenth century. Marcus, John's son, was an MP and a leading figure in the Orange Order; Lord John George Beresford, the marquess of Waterford's youngest son, became archbishop of Armagh in 1822 and a key figure in the rebuilding of the Church of Ireland; while other members of the family, notably Sir John Poo Beresford (1766–1844) and William Carr Beresford (1768–1854), served with distinction in the British army.

Reading

Cokayne, George E., *The Complete Peerage*, 12 vols (London: St Catherine's Press, 1910–59). Beresford, William (ed.) *Correspondence of John Beresford*, 2 vols (London, 1854).

JAMES KELLY

Berkeley, George (1685–1753) Philosopher and churchman. George Berkeley, Ireland's most important philosopher, was born in County Kilkenny on 12 March. He died on 14 January, and is buried in the Chapel of Christ Church, Oxford. Berkeley entered Kilkenny College at the age of 11, and went to Trinity College, Dublin, in 1700, where he graduated BA in 1704 and MA in 1707, the year in which he was elected to a fellowship. He was appointed librarian in 1709, junior dean in 1710, and lectured in Greek, Hebrew and Divinity. In 1713 he left Ireland for about 20 years, retaining his fellowship at Trinity College to 1724, when he became (an absentee) dean of Derry. In 1734 he returned to Ireland as lord bishop of Cloyne, where he remained until he retired to Oxford in 1752.

Berkeley contributed to many fields: to natural science and theology, mathematics and psychology, philosophy and metaphysics, and even medicine and the theory of economics. In the history of philosophy he is known as one of the British empiricists (with John Locke and David Hume).

He wrote his most important books while still at Trinity College in Dublin. The first of these was *An Essay Towards A New Theory of Vision* (1709), later commented on in *The Theory of Vision Vindicated and Explained* (1733). It was regarded as *the* book in psychology, or 'the science of man', from the 1730s to the end of the nineteenth century. He studied what he styled 'the proper objects of sight', that is to say, our sensations of light and colour, and asked 'How do we perceive the distance, magnitude, or situation of objects by sight?' Examining what we are actually aware of in different situations (an object brought near the eye looks fuzzy or blurred, for instance), he tried to identify the means by which we form our conception of the environment (just as fuzziness is taken as one sign of near distance). He also emphasized the heterogeneity between sensations of different senses, sight and touch in particular, and asked 'How do we come to think of these *different* sensations as being perceptions of *one* thing?' His answer was that visual appearances 'suggest' to the imagination what other sensations we are likely to experience. In this way they act as 'signs', 'whereby we are instructed how to regulate our actions'.

As a metaphysician, he shocked the world in 1710 (and ever since) by his challenging denial of the existence of matter in *A Treatise Concerning the Principles of Human Knowledge*. He opens with a strict empiricist 'survey of the objects of human knowledge'. The most basic of these objects are sensations of light and colour, of smells, tastes, sounds, and tactual sensations of hard and soft, heat and cold, motion and resistance. These sensations may form more complex units, which Berkeley calls 'collections of ideas' or 'sensible things'. When I speak or think about an apple, for instance, then I am thinking about 'a certain colour, taste, smell, figure and consistence having been observed to go together'. Berkeley's famous thesis, *esse est percipi* (to be is to be perceived), applies to these 'sensible things' or 'collections of ideas'. If we would object that the 'real' apple cannot be identified by those qualities which we are actually aware of by sense, then Berkeley's answer is 'For my part I might as easily divide a thing from itself.' If I subtract from my conception of an apple the colour and shape that I perceive by sight, as well as its smell and taste, and my tactual sensations of a certain figure and consistence, then there is nothing left in my thought about which I can affirm or deny anything at all. The allegedly 'real apple' is then an empirically empty conception, according to Berkeley, and propositions about it are meaningless. The concepts of matter which Berkeley examines are rejected as either meaningless or contradictory.

Most of his contemporaries regarded his immaterialism as too absurd to be taken seriously. One of his friends wrote to him: 'A physician of my acquaintance undertook to describe your person, and argued you must be mad, and that you ought to take remedies.'

Berkeley produced a brilliant defence of his seemingly impossible view in *Three Dialogues Between Hylas and Philonous* (1713). Apart from its philosophical qualities, these dialogues are still regarded as a masterpiece in Anglo-Irish literature.

In January 1713, Berkeley went to London in order to publish his *Dialogues*. He became a friend of John Arbuthnot and Alexander Pope, was presented to the court by his countryman Jonathan Swift, became acquainted with Richard Steele and Joseph Addison, and contributed to Steele's *Guardian* 'many excellent Arguments in Honour of Religion and Virtue'. In October 1713 he left London for his first Continental tour as the chaplain of the British ambassador to the king of Sicily. When he returned in August 1714, the political situation was unstable, following the death of Queen Anne. Berkeley had earlier argued – in *Passive Obedience* (1712) – that morality must be founded on religion. As 'Whoever resisteth the power, resisteth the ordinance of God' (Romans 12: 2), then rebellion – even the Glorious Revolution – was immoral, according to Berkeley. This was taken as a pro-Jacobite stand. But, again defending passive obedience, he now criticized the Jacobite rebellion in his *Advice to the Tories* (1715), to which the Oath of Allegiance was appended. He argued that George I was now the lawful king, to whom the Tories should be loyal for both legal and moral reasons.

In the autumn of 1716 Berkeley went abroad again as the tutor of George Ashe, son of the Bishop of Clogher. His second Continental tour lasted until the late autumn of 1720. During his travels, mostly in Italy, he wrote a Latin tract, *De Motu* (published in 1721), in which he develops a theory of relativity, attacking Isaac Newton's concepts of absolute space, absolute time and absolute motion. According to Sir Karl Popper, Berkeley proved himself 'a precursor to Mach and Einstein' in this book.

When he returned to London in 1720, he reacted against the South Sea Bubble in *An Essay towards Preventing the Ruin of Great Britain* (1721). In this pamphlet he proposed remedies for economical and moral recovery. The means to the latter was religion. But he seems to have given up the hope for the Old World a few years later, when he published *A Proposal for the Better Supplying of Churches in our Foreign Planatations and for Converting the Savage Americans to Christianity* (1725). His plan was to build a college on Bermuda, a place equidistant from all plantations. It has been argued that his project was perhaps greater than the subtitle indicates: that he intended to establish 'Christ's Kingdom on earth' – with Berkeley himself as the spiritual leader. He received a royal charter, and was promised a grant from the House of Commons. Before he sailed for America in 1729, he married Anne, eldest daughter of John Forster, former speaker of the Irish House of Commons and chief justice.

But the grant from the House of Commons was never paid, and the Bermuda project failed. He did not even reach Bermuda, but landed in Newport, Rhode Island, where he lived between 1729 and 1731. Through the collections of books, which he gave to Harvard and Yale, and his acquaintance with (the American) Samuel Johnson (the first president of King's College, now Columbia University), he had a remaining influence on education in America. Berkeley University, California, is named after him.

When he returned from the New World to London, he published *Alciphron or the Minute Philosopher* (1732). It is, as the subtitle informs us, 'an apology for the Christian Religion, against those who are called Freethinkers'. One commentator has described this book as a work by 'the last strongminded theologean'. He also published *The Analyst* (1734), sometimes regarded as 'the most spectacular event of the century in the history of British mathematics'.

In 1734 Berkeley was consecrated lord bishop of Cloyne, returned to Ireland, and became deeply engaged in social and economical problems. Ireland suffered a long period of depression as a result of prohibitive legislation by the English Parliament against Irish exportation, such as the woollen goods export prohibition Acts of 1698–9. In his *Essay towards preventing the Ruin of Great Britain*, Berkeley took a conventional approach to economical issues. But, in order to solve the urgent problems of the Irish economy, he was breaking new ground in *The Querist*, published in three parts (1735–7). He objected to measuring 'the wealth of a nation by its gold and silver'. Such a concept of 'universal wealth' was no more than an abstract idea. Real wealth consists in the proper feeding, clothing and housing of the population. In a poor country, such as Ireland, exportation of goods necessary for establishing real wealth must be strictly controlled, according to Berkeley. The basic national policy should be to establish well-being through full employment.

Berkeley's major contribution to monetary doctrine is his attack on the traditional way of identifying money with gold and silver. The 'right conception of money', he says, is 'that of a ticket, entitling to power' over goods and services. As 'the true idea of money' is 'that of a ticket or counter' paper money would do the job without backing of precious metals. In *A Letter on the Project of a National Bank* (1737), he argued (in vain) that a National Bank, owned by the public, should be established in order to solve some urgent monetary problems, and to adjust the Irish currency value.

His last book, the *Siris* (1744), contains a series of metaphysical reflections on a great variety of issues. Its medical observations made tar water famous almost as a panacea.

In *A Word to the Wise* (1749), Berkeley asked for tolerance between Protestants and Roman Catholics in Ireland. 'We are indeed (to our shame be it spoken) more inclined to hate for those articles wherein we differ', he said, 'than to love one another for those wherein we agree.'

Reading

Belfrage, Bertil, 'The contructivism of Berkeley's *New Theory of Vision*', Phillip D. Cummins and Guenter Zoeller, eds, *Minds, Ideas, and Objects: Essays on the Theory of Representation in Modern Philosophy*, vol. 2 NAKS Studies in Philosophy (Atascadero CA: Ridgeview, 1982).

Berkeley, George, *The Works of George Berkeley*, 9 vols, eds A.A. Luce and T.E Jessop (London: Thomas Nelson, 1948–57; repr. 1964, 1967; Kraus repr. 1979).

——*Philosophical Commentaries*, ed. G.H. Thomas, notes A.A. Luce (Alliance OH: Thomas Edition, 1976; repr. New York: Garland, 1989).

——*George Berkeley's Manuscript Introduction*, editio diplomatica transcr. and ed. with intro. and commentary by Bertil Belfrage (Oxford: Doxa, 1987).

Berman, David, *George Berkeley: Idealism and the Man* (Oxford: Clarendon Press, 1993).

Bracken, H.M., *The Early Reception of Berkeley's Immaterialism: 1710–1733* (The Hague: Martinus Nijhoff, 1959; rev. edn 1965).

Brykman, Geneviève, *Berkeley et le voile des mots* (Paris: Librairie Philosophique J. Vrin, 1993).

Grayling, A.C., *Berkeley: The Central Arguments* (London: Ducksworth, 1986).

Luce, A.A., *The Life of George Berkeley* (Edinburgh, Nelson, 1949; repr. 1969, 1992, with new intro. by David Berman).

Pitcher, George, *Berkeley* (London: Routledge and Kegan Paul, 1977).

Tipton, I.C., *Berkeley: The Philosophy of Immaterialism*, (London: Methuen, 1974; Garland repr. 1988).

Winkler, Kenneth P., *Berkeley: An Interpretation* (Oxford: Clarendon Press, 1989).

BERTIL BELFRAGE

Bernal, (John) Desmond (1901–71) Scientist and political activist. Born Nenagh, County Tipperary, 10 May; died London, 17 September. At Emmanuel College, Cambridge (1919–23), he joined the Communist Party, never to leave it. A pioneer in crystallography and founder of molecular biology, he also wrote extensively on the history and social functions of science. He made notable contributions to the British war effort, but his politics led subsequently to the withholding of funds for his scientific research. He was awarded both the United States Medal of Freedom and the Lenin Peace Prize, and helped to found UNESCO.

Reading

Goldsmith, M., *Sage: A Life of J.D. Bernal* (London: Hutchinson, 1980).

Hodgkin, D., 'Memoir of J.D. Bernal', *Biographical Memoirs of Fellows of the Royal Society xxvi* (1980).

DAVID SMITH

Bewerunge, Heinrich (1862–1923) German music scholar and teacher. Born Letmathe, Westphalia, 7 December; died Maynooth, 2 December. He received his early music education in a classical *Gymnasium* in Düsseldorf. He thereafter entered the university of Würzburg (Bavaria) as a student of theology. In the summer of 1885, he was ordained a priest in the college of Eichstadt. During his studentship there, he also enrolled at the Royal School of Church Music at Würzburg, and after ordination he undertook a course of study at the Royal School of Church Music established at Regensburg in 1874 by F.X. Haberl. On his return to the Rhineland, Bewerunge was appointed secretary to the vicar-general of Cologne Diocese, and chanter in Cologne cathedral.

On 26 June 1888, a chair of church chant and organ was established at St Patrick's College, Maynooth, and the Trustees of the college invited Bewerunge to take up this position, which he accepted in the autumn of that year. He occupied this chair for a period of some 35 years in total, although the outbreak of World War I in 1914 ultimately enforced his absence from Ireland for a period of four years (1916–1920), which he spent in Cologne. From 1914 to 1916 he also occupied the chair of music at University College, Dublin. On his return to Maynooth in 1920, Bewerunge resumed his professorial duties there, although his health had visibly declined during the war years.

During his tenure at Maynooth, many of Bewerunge's activities were practical rather than academic. His responsibilites centred upon the reformation and training of the college choir and the systematic instruction of all seminarians in the elements of chant. He also established a smaller, more specialized *schola cantorum* for the peformance of the more complex parts of the chant repertory and sixteenth-century polyphonic mass and motet settings. He arranged several of Palestrina's works and those of his contemporaries for male-voice choir, and he introduced to Maynooth the works of so-called 'Cecilian' composers, pre-eminently Haller, who wrote in the 'Palestrina' style, as it was then understood. Bewerunge's extensive knowledge of organ building led him to commission the magnificent Stalhuth instrument, which was installed in the equally imposing and recently constructed college chapel in 1890.

Apart from his writings on church music, music education, and the history of the chant and its various editions, Bewerunge's non-professorial activities were directly related to the propagation of the Cecilian movement in Ireland. This movement, established initially at Regensburg, sought to restore to pre-eminence the music of the Italian Renaissance and the chant in church services throughout Europe. Bewerunge edited *Lyra Ecclesiastica*, the journal of the Irish Society of St Cecilia (1891–3), and he participated in several Cecilian festivals in Maynooth, Dublin and Continental Europe. As a member of the Feis Ceoil Committee and the Incorporated Society of Musicians, Bewerunge was a frequent and lively correspondent in newspapers and journals on many aspects of music in Ireland. He also introduced to Ireland German organists who filled positions in cathedrals and larger churches throughout the country, even as he strongly advocated the training of Irish musicians for the same purpose.

His most important scholarly writings on music are contained in the *Irish Theological Quarterly*, the *Irish Ecclesiastical Record*, *Kirchenmusikalisches Jahrbuch*, *Musica Sacra*, the *New Ireland Review* and *Lyra Ecclesiastica*. Bewerunge also published English translations of treatises by Hugo Riemann. His extensive review of the Vatican Edition of the Plain Chant was published in Düsseldorf as *Die Vatikanische Choralausgabe: eine kritische Studie* in two parts (1906–7).

Bewerunge ranks as a vital figure in the history of church music in Ireland.

Reading

Lawrence, Frank and White, Harry, 'Heinrich Bewerunge (1862–1923). Zur Geschichte des Caecilianismus auf Irland', *Kirchenmusikalishces Jahrbuch*, 74 (1990).

HARRY WHITE

Big Wind, Night of the (Oíche na Gaoithe Móire) An appalling storm on the night of 6–7 January 1839. The deaths and damage done passed into folk memory, the topic of many Gaelic poems. In 1909, on the introduction of the state old age pension, knowledge of the night was used as an age test. A modern scientific study concluded, however, that 'the storm was not quite such an unusual event as folk memory would have us believe', being equalled or surpassed by other storms.

The 'Big Wind' alluded to in *Ulysses*, on 26–7 February 1903, also caused nationwide damage, trees in the Phoenix Park being uprooted.

PETER COSTELLO

bilingual writing since 1960 It is an irony of Irish literary history since 1960 that its two most acclaimed bilingual writers should have combined English not with Gaelic but with French (Samuel Beckett) and Spanish (Ian Gibson). Beckett published a succession of novels, novellas and short stories in both languages and in translation, while Gibson's work varies from *Un Irlandés En España* (1981) – interviews with Spanish writers and politicians – to *The English Vice* (1976) – a history of flagellation – as well as his biography, *Federico García Lorca* (1989), originally published in Spanish as two volumes.

In spite of Thomas Kinsella's claim that 'most of Ireland's comtemporary writers in English ... know modern Irish reasonably well,' works in Gaelic by established writers in English are few indeed. John B. Keane's novel *Dan Pheadaí Aindí* (1977) is an exception, but hardly a significant one. However, many writers of Gaelic have also written in English, often using English for work outside their specialized creative fields. Raymond Murray published poetry collections in 1964 and 1970 (*Athphreabadh na hóige, Arán ar an Tábla*), but his numerous pamphlets on issues of justice arising from events in Northern Ireland since 1969 and his *The SAS in Ireland* (1990) were in English, causing the critic Maolmhaodhóg Ó Ruairc to interpret his poetic silence in the face of political events as evidence of the essentially hobbyist nature of much poetry in Gaelic.

Even the irredentist genius Máirtín Ó Cadhain resorted to English for his polemical tracts *Mr Hill and Mr Tara* and *Irish Above Politics* (both 1964), as did the novelist Diarmaid Ó Suílleabháin for *Ireland: Free State or Nation?*, written for Sinn Féin in 1977. Other instances are Micheál Ó hAodha (drama in Gaelic/theatrical history in English); Edward Mac Lysaght (journals/history); Breandán Ó hEithir (novels/sport, politics) and Máirtín Ó Corrbuí (novels/local history).

Linguistic tensions have characterized the attempt by a number of poets to write in both languages. Eoghan Ó Tuairisc/Eugene Watters published his poem *The Weekend of Dermot and Grace* and his collection of poetry in Gaelic, *Lux Aeterna*, in 1964, but by 1975 was indicating his despair at 'the degeneration of written English ... from now on I am an Irish writer writing in Irish ... Irish is a vital force in a devitalised society ... my fate is to spend the rest of my creative life as Eoghan Ó Tuairisc'. Similarly and in the same year, Michael Hartnett's collection *A Farewell to English* marked a resolution to write in Gaelic, finding 'English a necessary sin / the perfect language to sell pigs in'. However, the resolution was not maintained and following two dual-language volumes, he returned to English 10 years later with *Inchicore Haiku*.

Two writers heavily influenced by Ó Tuairisc, Rita Kelly and Conleth Ellis, followed his lead by publishing poetry in both languages. Micheál O'Siadhail followed three collections in Gaelic with three in English and the latter seems destined to remain his creative medium, marking, in the opinion of Máire Mhac an tSaoi, a mistaken direction in his work. Pearse Hutchinson and Eithne Strong have also published collections in both languages, as has Criostóir Ó Floinn, who has also written numerous plays and short stories in both languages. Seán Mac Mathúna and Dónall Mac Amhlaigh substantially rewrote their books *Ding agus Scéalta Eile* (1983) and *Schnitzer O Sé* (1974) when they appeared in English as *The Atheist and Other Stories* (1987) and *Schnitzer O'Shea* (1985). *Bláth agus Taibhse*, the 1964 poetry collection from Micheál Mac Liammóir, was his final work in Gaelic, but was followed by memoirs and other works in English.

The Arts Council has been encouraging the translation of works in Gaelic since 1984 and, to quote Kinsella again, there has been an 'enlarging sympathy' between writers in the two traditions.

PROINSIAS Ó DRISCEOIL

Binchy, Maeve (1940–) Writer. Born Dublin and educated at the Holy Child convent, Killiney, and University College, Dublin. After teaching history in girls' schools, she began writing a regular column in the *Irish Times* in 1968. In 1978 she published *Central Line*, a collection of short stories, and this was followed by further collections, including *Victoria Line* (1980) *Dublin Four* (1982) and *Silver Wedding* (1988). Also in 1982, her first novel *Light a Penny Candle* was an instant popular success, which she followed with a string of other novels, including *Firefly Summer* (1987), *Circle of Friends* (1990, which was well-received critically in a 1995 film version), *Copper Beech* (1992), *The Glass Lake* (1994), *Evening Class* (1996) and *Scarlet Feather* (2000). Her brand of light romantic fiction, distinguished by wry humour and sharp observation, enjoys a wide appeal, and her books have frequently been bestsellers in both Ireland and Britain. She is married to the writer and broadcaster Gordon Snell.

TONY STEWART

Blackburne, Helen (1842–1903) Suffragist. Born 25 May, Valentia Island, County Kerry; died 11 January. She moved to London with her family in 1859 and became involved in the Women's Suffrage Movement. Between 1874 and 1985 she was secretary of the National Society for Women's Suffrage, and she edited the *English Women's Review* 1881–90. In 1895 she gave up most of her public works in order to look after her father, who died two years later.

Helen Blackburne published *Women's Suffrage: A Record of the Movement in the British Isles* in 1902. She also wrote several other books which examined the position of women in industry.

RACHEL FURMSTON

Blackshaw, Basil (1932–) Painter. Born Glengormley, County Antrim. He studied at Belfast College of Art and in 1951 visited Paris on a CEMA scholarship. He exhibited regularly in Belfast and Dublin, was included in 'The Delighted Eye' in London (1980), and was given a retrospective exhibition at the Arts Council Gallery in Belfast. Blackshaw's paintings reflect his love of animals – he has trained horses and dogs, as a hobby – but he is also a noted portraitist and landscape painter in a free, loosely brushed style. More recently, he was included in the 1988 Rosc exhibition in Dublin. Many regard him as the most gifted Northern artist of his generation.

BRIAN FALLON

Blasket islands A cluster of precipitous, rocky islands and islets which lie facing Dún Chaoin in the barony of Corca Dhuibhne, just north of the entrance to Dingle Bay, County Kerry. The largest of the group, An Blascaod Mór – the Great Blasket Island – had a totally Gaelic-speaking fishing community but its numbers were gradually reduced from 200 during World War I to 20 when the island was finally evacuated in 1953.

The material culture of the island was poor and conditions were harsh. The surf blown from the sea frequently covered the village and the island was often shrouded in mist. The islanders had, however, a very rich oral culture. They practised the traditional arts of story-telling, poetry and song. The whole tradition was shared equally by all. Their language was rich, representing as it did a wide experience of hard work on sea and land. Out of this remote island culture came a little 'library' of books written by the islanders themselves, in Gaelic, about their island life. There is nothing like this 'library' to be found in any other culture.

The principal volumes in the island 'library' are those by Tomás Ó Criomhthain (1855–1937) and Muiris Ó Súilleabháin (1904–50), as well as two autobiographical volumes by Peig Sayers (1873–1958), whom could neither read nor write in Gaelic, but whose poet son Micheál Ó Gaoithín (1909–74) was her amanuensis. This first shelf of books was followed by a second containing those of Ó Gaoithín, Ó Criomhthain's son Seán (1898–1975). Seán Sheáin Ó Cearnaigh (1912–), Lís Ní Shúilleabháin (1911–71), Máire Ní Ghuithín (1900–88), Muiris Ó Catháin (1870–1961) and Pádraig Ua Maoileoin (1913–).

The explanation for this extraordinary output from a remote island community is fourfold: the nature of the island's oral culture; the introduction of literacy in the Gaelic language into the Great Blasket in the latter part of the nineteenth century; the arrival of scholar visitors to learn Gaelic and study the oral culture, and their contact in particular with Ó Criomhthain; and the friendship between Ó Criomhthain and Brian Ó Ceallaigh (1889–1936), who persuaded Ó Criomhthain to write his two volumes when he was over 60.

Ó Criomhthain, a fisherman, learnt to write and read in Gaelic when he was over 40. Carl Marstrander (1883–1965), a Norwegian linguistics scholar, came to the island in 1907 and worked with Ó Criomhthain. When teaching Old Irish in Dublin, Marstrander persuaded a student of his, Robin Flower (1881–1946) of the British Musuem, to go to the Great Blasket to learn Gaelic. Flower came in 1910, worked with Ó Criomhthain and continued to visit the island for many years. He wrote a seminal book on the island culture, and in turn influenced two other English scholars, George Thomson (1903–87) and Kenneth Jackson (1909–91), to come to the island. Thomson, later to be professor of Greek at Birmingham, persuaded Ó Súilleabháin to write *Fiche Blian ag Fás* while a gárda in Connemara. Jackson published a collection of Peig Sayers' stories, and later became professor of Celtic at Edinburgh.

Reading

Flower, Robin, *The Western Island* (Oxford: Clarendon Press, 1944).

Mac Conghail, Muiris, *The Blaskets: A Kerry Library* (Dublin: Country House, 1987).

Ó Criomhthain, Tomás, *Allagar na hLnise* (Dublin: 1928, 1977; tr. as *Island Cross-Talk*, Oxford University Press, 1986).

——*An tOileánack* (Dublin: 1929, 1973; tr. as *The Islandman*, London: 1934).

Ó Súilleabháin, Muiris, *Fiche Blain ag Fás* (Dublin: 1933; tr. as *Twenty Years A-Growing*, London: 1933).

Sayers, Peig, *Peig* (Dublin: 1936; English tr., Dublin: 1974).

——*Scéalta ón mBlascaod*, ed. K. Jackson (Dublin: Béaloideas, 1938).

——*Machtramh Seanmhná* (Dublin: 1939; tr. as *An Old Woman's Reflections*, Oxford: Oxford University Press, 1962).

Thomson, George, *Island Home: The Blasket Heritage* (Dingle: Brandon, 1988).

MUIRIS MACCONGHAIL

Boate, Arnold (1600–53) and **Gerard** (1603–50) Hebrew scholar; topographer. Born Gorcum, Holland. They were medical graduates of Leyden University. Arnold took up biblical studies and corresponded with Archbishop Ussher of Armagh, who persuaded him to settle in Dublin and establish a medical practice. He was physician to the army in Leinster during the Confederate Wars, but moved in 1644 to Paris, where he published several medical and Biblical works.

Gerard came to London as physician to Charles I, but he is today remembered for his *Natural History of Ireland*, a survey of the island's resources for the use of English merchants who speculated in Irish land under the Adventurers Act of 1642. The information was supplied by **Arnold**. **Gerard** eventually reached Ireland as Cromwell's physician in 1649, but died soon afterwards. The *Natural History* was published by Hartlib in 1652.

Reading

Barnard, T.C., *Cromwellian Ireland* (Oxford: Oxford University Press, 1975).

Canny, Nicholas, *Kingdom and Colony: Ireland in the Atlantic World* (Baltimore and London: Johns Hopkins University Press, 1982).

TONY STEWART

Bodley, Seóirse (1933–) Composer, academic, conductor. Born Dublin, 4 April. Bodley received his early musical education at the Royal Irish Academy of Music and University College, Dublin (UCD), where he graduated with a BMus in 1955. A postgraduate travelling studentship took him to the Stuttgart Musikhochschule, where he studied composition in the class of J.N. David. On returning to Dublin Bodley joined the staff of the music department of UCD in 1959 and was awarded a DMus in 1960. He later became associate professor and acting head of the music department in his *alma mater*.

Since the 1970s his compositions (hitherto mainstream contemporary European in style) have experimented in wedding the melodic and rhythmic nuances of Irish folk music (which has also been one of Bodley's scholarly interests) to the sophisticated language of late twentieth-century art music. His works include *Music for Strings* (1952), five symphonies (1958–9, 1980, 1981, 1990, 1991), two chamber symphonies (1964, 1982), *Configurations* (1967), *Never To Have Lived Is Best* (song cycle for soprano and orchestra, 1965),

Meditations on Lines from Patrick Kavanagh (for contralto and orchestra, 1972), *A Small White Cloud Drifts over Ireland* (1976), *A Chill Wind* (choral suite, 1978), and *Beanshee* for electronically modulated voices.

GERARD GILLEN

Boland, Eavan (1944–) Poet and critic. Born Dublin. Educated at Trinity College, Boland emerged in the sixties as one of the most talented in a technically gifted generation of Irish poets. Her chief thematic concern has been the relation between ethical responsibility and artistic expression. Her poems canvass tensions between home and exile, myth and history, art and ornament, subject and object. Influenced heavily by both W.B. Yeats and Adrienne Rich, Boland has pushed the political poem into a new context in Ireland by insisting that women's voices are central, not marginal, to the interests of Irish poetry. Stylistically, there has been a darkening of tone in Boland's work during the nineties, *Outside History* (1990) and *In a Time of Violence* (1994), which examines history's exclusions, and the violences of time and aging. A selection of her reviews and essays was published in *Selected Prose* (1994). She now holds a professorship at Stanford University, California.

Reading

Irish University Review (Spring/Summer 1993): *Special Issue: Eavan Boland.*

JODY ALLEN-RANDOLPH

Bolger, Dermot (1959–) Poet, playwright and novelist. Born Dublin. His work is engaged largely with modern urban life, unreconciled with the past or future. He was known first as a poet (with collections such as *The Habit of Flesh* (1979)) and then as a dramatist; his novels finally received wide notice. He founded the Raven Arts Centre, publishing his own and others' work. He is fascinated by the life of Dublin, which is small enough to be a community but large enough for vital contrasts. His plays are collected in *A Dublin Quartet* (1991); his novels are *Night Shift* (1985), *The Journey Home* (1990), *The Woman's Daughter* (first edn 1987; enlarged edn 1991) *Emily's Shoes* (1992), *A Second Life* (1994), *Father's Music* (1997) and *Temptation* (2000).

PETER COSTELLO

Booksellers, printers and 'publishers' in the eighteenth century Throughout the century Dublin remained without rival as the chief centre of book production, and Dublin practices are described here. Even in Dublin the book trade did not become as demarcated and specialized as the London trade did and, unlike the Stationers' Company, the Dublin Guild took no part in regulating the trade.

The bookseller's most important job was obviously the selling and publishing of books and pamphlets. As a salesman he served the customer in his shop, and might supply the 'country trade', selling wholesale to pedlars and chapmen. He imported books, chiefly from Britain but also from the Continent, and when trade was freed in 1782 he exported large quantities to North America. He might specialize in legal, medical or foreign books; he might also be an auctioneer or run a circulating library. Economic survival often depended on the sale of stationery, patent medicines and lottery tickets, and most booksellers stocked old books as well as new.

The term 'publisher' in its modern sense is not normally applied to the eighteenth-century bookseller, because in London it was reserved for front men employed to sell and distribute the books by the undertaking bookseller who held the copyright. There is no evidence that the practice operated in this way in Dublin. Here the bookseller according to his imprints sold his own publications, as did others who bought from him or, more usually, exchanged their own publications.

In publishing he might finance the whole operation himself, or join with others in publishing a particular title; this form of tem-porary partnership grew till, in 1777, 46 names appeared in the imprint of Robertson's *History of America*. It was used mainly in publishing reprints and how it was organized is not clear. Perhaps one or two put up the production costs and ensured an adequate return by persuading others to take multiple copies at discount. In practice perhaps two-thirds or three-quarters of a bookseller's list might consist of reprinted London editions, the remainder of original editions of native writers' work, chiefly on subjects restricted to Irish matters – politics, history, local causes, verse by unknown poets. None of this would find much sale in London, where the ambitious Irish writer would prefer to publish for its highly organized methods of advertising and distribution; and more importantly, where the British Copyright Act enabled him to sell his work.

Publication by subscription was a method of financing the edition and of testing the market. The undertaker issued proposals and named the booksellers, often provincial, who would take in subscriptions. Unless he could find a bookseller to take the initial risk, publication by subscription was the only way open to an Irish writer with neither wealth nor reputation. As well as original work, extensive reprints were sometimes published by subscription, the public response guaranteeing the heavy outlay against loss.

The bookseller, once preliminary matters were settled and having announced his intention to publish to deter rival editions, either sent his copy to the printer, supplying him with paper for the edition, or set about printing it himself. Unlike in London, in Dublin there was no clear separation of the two jobs; many booksellers were also printers and the printers who did not also sell and publish books were very few.

To the printer, jobbing work was as necessary as book work in keeping his presses busy and productive, and here appointment as printer to an institution or society such as the House of Commons or the Dublin Society offered the best prospect of a regular and assured income. Government work made the King's Printers comparatively wealthy men. In the early days several bookseller-printers compiled and ran a twice-weekly newspaper, which gave the press regular work and the printer a little daily bread for the limited time of the paper's survival; later a few presses concentrated on printing the more frequent papers.

Throughout the century the book trade in Ireland suffered restraint by the censorship of seditious libel in the courts of law and Parliament, but remained uncontrolled by statute law till the first Stamp Act of 1774. From then on legal restraint increased and in 1798 licences for individual presses were enforced. The trade's autonomy ended with the Act of Union and the Copyright Act of 1801.

Reading

Pollard, M. *Dublin's Trade in Books 1550–1800* (Oxford: Clarendon Press, 1989).

M. POLLARD

Boole, George (1815–64) Mathematician. Born Lincoln, 2 November; died Blackrock, near Cork, 8 December. Largely self-taught in mathematics, he published mathematical papers while schoolteaching in Lincoln, until his appointment as professor of mathematics at Queen's College, Cork, in 1849. His major work is *The Mathematical Analysis of Logic* (1847), from which the term 'Boolean algebra' derives. He had many cultural and literary interests, and is a seminal figure in modern mathematics.

Reading

Kneale, W., 'Boole and the revival of logic', *Mind* 57 (1948).
Taylor, G., 'George Boole, F.R.S., 1815–1864', *Notes and Records of the Royal Society of London* 12 (1956).

DAVID SMITH

Boucicault, Dion (1820–90) Playwright and actor-manager. Boucicault himself gave only guarded accounts of his own early years. His mother, Anne, was married to Samuel Boursiquot (thus spelt), an unsuccessful wine merchant of Dublin, but evidently Dion's true father was the Boursiquots' lodger, Dionysius Lardner, encylopedist, engineer and womanizer, of Trinity College, Dublin. In 1828 Anne and her children followed her lover to London; in 1836, when Anne's relationship with Lardner ended, they returned to Dublin. In 1837 Dion was sent back to England, ostensibly as apprentice to Lardner. But by 1838 he was making his own way, establishing himself as an actor and, with *London Assurance* in 1841, as a playwright. By 1846, after a visit to France, Boucicault had settled on that spelling of the family name. Thereafter followed an extraordinary world-wide career, as actor, playwright and showman, with wives, lovers, scandals, and fortunes won and lost.

Boucicault did much to establish now generally accepted theatre practices, like protected copyright, royalties and the role of the director. He wrote over 140 plays, most now forgotten. The plays of his 'Irish Tryptych' have had a longer-lasting influence: three comedy melodramas, with rural Irish settings (far removed from Boucicault's own experience) and aggressively Gaelic titles, *The Colleen Bawn* (1860), *Arrah na Pogue* (1864) and *The Shaughraun* (1874). The Irish-American theatre managers first suggested the drawing power of Boucicault's name linked to plays with Irish subject matter, and they suggested the approach of, for example, *The Shaugraun* to its subject matter: their audiences wanted to laugh, not think. In America, Britain and Australia, Irish migrants flocked to see Boucicault's plays, in a sacramental celebration of Irishness. In Ireland, helped by this international success, the three plays laid the foundation of an Irish dramatic tradition. Shaw, Synge and O'Casey all stole from Boucicault, and his influence can be seen in Augusta Gregory, Behan and Beckett. O'Casey first experienced the theatre when he was asked to step into the part of Father Dolan in *The*

Shaugraun. Boucicault's achievement with characters like Conn the Shaugraun is that he not so much subverts as commandeers the stock character of the stage Irishman: thus, for good or ill, the structures of comic melodrama were built into the nascent Irish national theatre.

Reading

Fawkes, Richard, *Dion Boucicault: A Biography* (London: Quartet, 1979).
Thomson, Peter (ed.), *Plays by Dion Boucicault* (Cambridge: Cambridge University Press, 1984).

PATRICK O'SULLIVAN

Bourke, Brian (1936–) Painter and sculptor. Born Dublin. Bourke studied at the National College of Art and Design, Dublin, and at St Martin's School of Art and Goldsmith's College in London. His work is figurative and is mainly concerned with landscape and portraiture. His landscapes are executed in dramatic, Fauve-like colours, and in 1988 provided a setting for a series of paintings exploring the myth of the mad bird-king, Sweeney, some of which were included in the international exhibition ROSC. Although often untitled, his portraits are usually of family, friends and himself. The style of his figures suggests the influence of African sculptures.

Reading

White, James, *The Art of Brian Bourke* (Newbridge, Co. Kildare: Goldsmith Press, 1982).
Sharpe, Henry J., *Making Sense – Ten Irish Artists 1963–83* (Dublin: 1983).
Walker, Sarah, 'Heaney, Sweeney and Brian Bourke's drawings', *Irish Arts Review*, 4, no. 4 (1987), pp. 68–71.

FELICITY WOOLF

Bowen, Elizabeth (1899–1973) Novelist and short story writer. Bowen moved from Ireland to southern England aged 7, but returned for frequent visits, especially after 1930 when she inherited the family mansion,

Bowen's Court, in County Cork. She also commuted between the two countries in her fictions, though only ten of her nearly eighty short stories and two of her ten novels – *The Last September* (1929) and *A World of Love* (1955) – have an Irish setting.

Bowen's Court (1942), a history of the Bowens from the Cromwellian settlements to 1914, is more celebratory of the Ascendancy class than *The Last September*, which is set in the last months of the War of Independence and represents this colonial caste as socially isolated and ineffectual. The novel concludes with the burning of the Big House, but it is anticipatory as well as valedictory, since its heroine, Lois, is a young woman heading out into the modern world.

Bowen lived in London throughout World War II and captured the fraught, edgy, surreal atmosphere of this period, especially in the short story collection *The Demon Lover* (1945) and the novel *The Heat of the Day* (1949). This novel is a subtle study of love in a climate of secrecy and treason.

Permanence and stability are always at risk in Bowen's world. Her fictions are peopled with threatening older women, deracinated adults seeking a secure relationship, and orphaned or only children in search of fosterage or emotional support. Her narratives focus on the psychological and the psychic, on sensibility and ambience, yet her romances are laced with irony. She is an elegant, mannered stylist, who maintains a cool distance from her protagonists and analyses their plight with a wry, precise detachment.

ANTOINETTE QUINN

Bowles, Michael (1909–98) Conductor, composer, administrator, and teacher. Born Sligo. Bowles worked as a clerk in the Department of Education before joining the Army School of Music in 1932 as an officer cadet under Colonel Fritz Brase. As part of his training, Bowles studied with Professor John Larchet and Robert O'Dwyer at University College, Dublin where he took his primary degree in 1936, in which year he was also commissioned, eventually attaining the rank of captain. He was seconded to the broadcasting service in 1940, where he was to remain with dual responsibility as director of music and principal conductor. During this productive period he augmented the station orchestra, with which he instituted a successful series of public concerts; he also founded the Concert Orchestra and Cór Radio Éireann. Bowles resigned his positions under unhappy circumstances in 1948 and conducted and taught in New Zealand and the United States before eventually returning to Ireland in 1970. He published a number of articles and *The Art of Conducting* (1959). His compositions include some two dozen original songs which demonstrate a sensitive response to chosen texts.

JOSEPH RYAN

boycott Organized ostracism of an individual, group or country for retaliatory or punitive reasons. The term derives from the treatment of Charles Cunningham Boycott (1832–97), Lord Erne's land agent at Lough Mack, County Mayo. In autumn 1880, Erne refused to lower rents despite a bad harvest year; tenant eviction notices were served. Parnell, speaking at Ennis on 19 September 1880, had urged the shunning of settlers of evictee homesteads. A fortnight later tenants convinced local merchants and even Boycott's servants to abandon the Boycott family to complete isolation. The word first appeared in an October 1880 *Inter-Ocean* article on Boycott's dilemma by American journalist James Redpath. The film *Captain Boycott* (1947) starred Stewart Granger and Alastair Sims.

AMY L. FRIEDMAN

Boydell, Brian (1917–2000) Composer, academic and conductor. Born Dublin, 17 March. Educated at Cambridge, where he obtained a first in the natural science tripos in 1938, Boydell studied music at the Royal College of Music (composition with Patrick Hadley and Herbert Howells) and Heidel-

berg, before taking the extern MusB degree from Trinity College, Dublin, in 1942 and the MusD in 1959. He became professor of music at the university in 1962 and retired in 1982 to devote himself to composition and research.

As a composer Boydell embraced a great variety of forms in a style that is basically tonal and showing some indebtedness to Hindemith. His principal orchestral works include *In Memoriam Mahatma Gandhi* (1948), *Violin Concerto* (1953), *Megalithic Ritual Dances* (1956), *Shielmartin Suite* (1958) and *Symphonic Inscapes* (1968). His chamber music includes three string quartets, and his various choral compositions show the influence of the composer's life-long scholarly and practical interest in Renaissance vocal polyphony. His principal research interest was musical life in eighteenth-century Dublin, which has resulted in his *A Dublin Musical Calendar 1700–1760* (1988). He also contributed chapters on music and society to the *Oxford New History of Ireland*.

GERARD GILLEN

Boyle family The founder of the Boyle political family, successive generations of which were a force in Irish politics and society in the seventeenth and eighteenth centuries, was Richard Boyle, Earl of Cork (1566–1643). He fathered a large and talented family of which Robert Boyle, the scientist, Roger, Earl of Orrery, and Richard, Earl of Burlington, were the most prominent. The Cork Boyles were eclipsed in the late seventeenth and early eighteenth centuries by the Brodrick family of Midleton, but following the death of Lord Midleton in 1728 Henry Boyle (1682–1764), the grandson of Lord Orrery, took command of the Brodrick interest. He used his formidable political talent to build up a network of parliamentary support that left the duke of Dorset with little option but to ask him to undertake to secure a working majority in the House of Commons. He was also entrusted with the management of the estates and parliamentary boroughs of his kinsman, the earl of Burlington. As the 'Undertaker' and holder of several of the key political offices in the land, Boyle effectively managed the Irish House of Commons for a generation. The beginning of the end was signalled when John Ponsonby and Primate Stone challenged Boyle's political ascendancy in the 1750s. Boyle overcame this threat to his position, but his political influence was never the same thereafter. He resigned the speakership of the House of Commons and accepted a peerage as Earl Shannon in 1756, eight years before his death.

His son and heir, Richard Boyle, second Earl of Shannon (1728–1807), did not possess the political talent which had enabled his father to dominate the Irish House of Commons for so long. He remained a force in domestic politics, however, even after the Undertaker system was undermined by Lord Townshend, because of the parliamentary interest he commanded. Throughout most of the 1770s and 1780s, he supported Dublin Castle, as a result of which he secured a British peerage in 1786. He broke with the administration during the regency crisis (1789), but he was back in the Castle fold by the mid-1790s, and he strongly supported the Act of Union, though it resulted in the abolition of his parliamentary base.

Reading

Canny, Nicholas, *The Upstart Earl: A Study of the Social and Mental World of Richard Boyle, First Earl of Cork* (Cambridge: Cambridge University Press, 1982).

Hewitt, Esther (ed.), *Lord Shannon's Letters to His Son* (Belfast: Public Record Office of Northern Ireland, 1982).

JAMES KELLY

Boyle, Ina (1892–1967) Composer. Boyle lived and worked in Enniskerry, County Wicklow. She studied in both Dublin and London, most notably with Ralph Vaughan Williams, whose evocative modal approach was to exercise a perceptible influence on her creative style. Her compositions embrace a wide variety of forms, with the majority of

her work emanating from the first half of her life. The many compositions for solo voice and for choir demonstrate an eclectic literary taste, while her last completed work was the short opera *Maudlin of Paplewick* (1966), to her own libretto after Ben Jonson's 'The Sad Shepherd'. Her sole symphony, entitled *Glencree* (1927), and the pastoral *Colin Clout* (1921) provoked a warm response when given in Dublin and London. Her final piece for this medium, *Wild Geese* (1942), which she described as a 'sketch for small orchestra', is representative in its rhythmic flexibility and adherence to the tonal system. Her scores and MSS are housed in Trinity College Library.

JOSEPH RYAN

Brabazon, Hercules Brabazon (1821–1906) Watercolourist. An amateur artist, born Hercules Brabazon Sharpe, in Paris on 21 November, he took his maternal name when he inherited the Brabazon properties in 1847. His mother was Anne Mary, daughter of Sir Anthony Brabazon of New Park, County Mayo; his father was Hercules Sharpe, author and antiquarian. Brabazon never lived on his Irish estates but spent his time travelling throughout Europe, the Middle East and North Africa, producing a vast body of watercolours. He was much praised by John Ruskin as a true follower of Turner, especially in his minimalist technique. Brabazon did not make his professional debut until 1892, when he was in his seventies.

Brabazon produced watercolours noticeable for their omissions rather than their inclusions. His work has been referred to as Impressionist, but this is a mistaken use of the term. Like many Irish and British artists of his generation (e.g. John Butler Yeats) he favoured tonal values rather than lines, while also painting subjects from modern life.

Reading

Faberman, Hilarie, *Hercules Brabazon Brabazon* (New York: Godwin-Ternbach Museum, Queen's College, 1985).

Hind, C. Lewis, *Hercules Brabazon Brabazon 1821–1906: His Art and Life* (London: G. Allen, 1912).

FINTAN CULLEN

Brady, Charles (1926–97) Born New York. Brady moved to Ireland in the mid-1960s after travelling around Europe. The flatness characteristic of Abstract Expressionism (e.g. De Kooning, Rothko and Pollack) dominates his painting. His small-scale paintings of everyday domestic items (vegetables, envelopes, wallets and pencils) are isolated and flat, in lyrical colours. In the 1980s, Brady began to work with sculpture representing those same commonplace domestic objects. His work is very much respected for its gentle epiphanic qualities and its sensitivity to colour and form. He was a member of Aosdána.

MARTIN MCCABE AND MICHAEL WILSON

Brady Hugh (*c.*1527–84) Bishop of Meath (1563–84). Born Dunboyne, County Meath. He was probably a graduate of Oxford, and was a noted reforming cleric and strong advocate of the founding of a university at St Patrick's in Dublin. He was a member of the Irish Privy Council and considered the religious reformation of the Irish as a necessary precondition for the complete conquest of the country. His views became increasingly isolated from the majority of the administration, who advocated military conquest and enforced conversion. Even though he was considered a gifted ecclesiastic, the Reformation made little progress in Meath diocese.

Reading

Bradshaw, Brendan, 'Sword, word and strategy in the Reformation in Ireland', *Historical Journal*, xxi (1978), pp. 475–502.
Ronan, Myles V., *The Reformation in Ireland under Elizabeth* (London: Longmans, Green, 1930).
Walshe, Helen Coburn, 'Enforcing the Elizabethan settlement: the vicissitudes of Hugh Brady, bishop of Meath, 1563–84', *Irish Historical Studies*, xxvi (1989), pp. 352–76.

BRIAN DONOVAN

Brady, Liam (1956–) Football player. After almost a decade at English club Arsenal, Brady was signed by Italian club Juventus, becoming their top goal-scorer. He went on to play for Sampdoria, Inter Milan and Ascoli. A former schoolboy international, Brady was capped 71 times at senior level for the Republic of Ireland, 12 as captain, and ended his playing career in 1990. A brief career in management, first with Celtic and then Brighton, followed. In 1996 Brady returned to Arsenal where he became head of youth development.

Reading

Brady, Liam, *So Far So Good: A Decade in Football* (London: S. Paul, 1980).
Walsh, David (ed.), *The Liam Brady Story* (Dublin: 1990).

TREVOR BUTTERWORTH

Bramhall, John (1594–1663) Archbishop of Armagh (1661–3). Born in Cheshire. A graduate of Cambridge, he came to Ireland in 1633 as Lord Deputy Wentworth's chaplain, and was consecrated bishop of Derry in 1634. Bramhall was an energetic anti-papal theologian, writing five treatises against the Roman Catholic church. He was centrally involved in the 1634 Irish Convocation and was rigidly opposed to the translation of the Bible into Irish. His activities in Ulster were primarily aimed against the Presbyterians, who in 1641 had him impeached in the Irish Parliament. He remained a stringent royalist throughout his life, publishing many tracts in defence of the Anglican faith and the royalist cause. He also published three works against the views of Hobbes in Paris in the 1640s. With the restoration he was consecrated archbishop of Armagh.

Reading

Phillips, W.A. (ed.), *History of the Church of Ireland*, 3 vols (Oxford: Oxford University Press, 1933–4).
Vesey, John, *Life of Archbishop Bramhall Prefixed to his Works* (Dublin: 1676, repr. Oxford: 1842–5).

BRIAN DONOVAN

Brehon law in the early modern period

'Brehon law' took its name from the brehons or *breitheamhain*, judges trained in Irish customary law. Their profession was normally hereditary, the most frequently occurring surnames being MacAodhagáin (MacEgan) and MacFhlannchadha (MacClancy). In the sixteenth century they were widely employed as the 'lord's judge' by Gaelic or Anglo-Irish magnates who exercised jurisdiction in Ireland outside the royal system of sheriffs and county courts. They were also used to arbitrate civil disputes between private individuals.

The fact that such brehons are described as conducting their cases in the open air, sitting under a thorn tree, is a reminder of the ancient pagan origins of their order, but the law they administered in the later sixteenth century had many strands. Succession to inherited family lands and to a Gaelic chieftainship, the prosecution of cattle-rustling and the institutions of marriage and fosterage were still influenced by the old customary law or *féineachas*. Indeed the succession customs, which were known to the English as 'gavelkind' and 'tanistry', received some recognition in the Dublin government's Court of Chancery, established *c*.1570. On the other hand, the disposition of newly acquired lands or movable property, dowries and settlements, wills and testaments, bonds and mortgages, were negotiated largely according to English common law principles, with some influence from Roman civil law and the canon law of the Catholic church. Consequently one finds much borrowed vocabulary in the texts of such brehon deeds and documents as survive from the late fifteenth to the early seventeenth century. In addition, trespasses, disputes and debts involving parties from independent neighbouring jurisdictions were arbitrated under the hybrid 'law of the march' (or 'frontier'), which combined principles of Irish custom with common law. Finally, the proclamations issued by the judge's own lord on matters such as taxation or policing had the force of law for inhabitants of the local territory. Tenants of the ninth earl of Kildare, for instance, were said to be ruled by a combination of brehon law, common law and the earl's own proclamations.

This pot-pourri of laws did not result simply from Gaelic political decline and the culture clash occurring in the late sixteenth century. Already *c*.700 AD the Old Irish law tract *Críth Gablach* spoke of four kinds of law in Irish society. The decrees of king and church, and treaty regulations between local kingdoms, operated side by side with inherited custom or *fénechus*. In the period between *c*.650 and 850 AD customary laws, which had their origin in pagan times or even Indo-European prehistory, achieved written form in the monastic schools of early Christian Ireland, having been censored, selected and combined with much scriptural teaching and church legislation. Thereafter these written compilations were regarded as authoritative texts, to be studied by means of glosses and commentaries as law schools and universities elsewhere in Europe studied civil and canon law.

When the church reform of the twelfth century swept Irish studies out of the monasteries, the Old Irish law tracts were transcribed and commented on in secular schools held in the residences of heads of eminent legal families up to the end of the sixteenth century. Brehons thus trained in the ancient *féineachas* might subsequently acquire a smattering of civil and canon law, and when conducting cases they could also be advised by men versed in English common law. However, with the extension of royal jurisdiction by means of sheriffs and country courts to all parts of Ireland by the early seventeenth century and the extinction of sovereign local lordships, the brehons and their eclectic system of laws also became obsolete.

Reading

MacNiocaill, G., 'The interaction of laws', in J. Lydon (ed.), *The English in Medieval Ireland* (Dublin: Royal Irish Academy, 1984).

Nicholls, K.W., *Land, Law and Society in Sixteenth-Century Ireland* (Cork: Irish Academic Press in Association with the Irish Legal History Society, 1976).

—— 'Irishwomen and property in the sixteenth century', in M. MacCurtain and M. O'Dowd (eds), *Women in Early Modern Ireland* (Edinburgh: 1991).

Simms, K., 'The brehons of later medieval Ireland', in D. Hogan and W.N. Osborough (eds), *Brehons, Serjeants and Attorneys* (Dublin: National University of Ireland, 1990).

KATHERINE SIMMS

Brennan, Cecily (1955–) Painter. Born Athenry, County Galway. Brennan studied at the National College of Art and Design, Dublin (1974–8). Her paintings are personal responses to, rather than representations of, specific landscapes or places, such as Wicklow (1982), the rhododendron garden at Howth (1985) and Iceland (1991). She works on a large scale, making expressionistic paintings with vigorously applied bright colours. Her work uses landscape as a metaphor to explore personal themes such as sexuality and the unconscious; this is clearly manifest in the recent series made after a visit to Iceland, a volatile landscape, in a constant state of powerful change.

Reading

Gibbons, Luke, 'Displacing landscape' and Curtis, Penelope, 'Natural selection', in *Cecily Brennan* (Dublin: Douglas Hyde Gallery: 1991).

FELICITY WOOLF

brewing Irish brewing is dominated by one name, Guinness, on which the world-wide reputation of Irish beer largely rests.

The Guinness brewery in Dublin was founded in 1759 when Arthur Guinness took over a small, disused brewery at St James's Gate, leasing it for 9,000 years at an annual rent of £45 per year. Guinness started by brewing ales, but soon moved to a new product, made with roasted barley. This was first known as porter and eventually as stout. By 1833 Guinness's was the largest brewery in Ireland, and by 1914 the largest in the world.

The Guinness name has been spread not just because of the innate qualities of the brew, but also on the back of an always innovative advertising strategy, dating back at least to 1929 when the famous slogan 'Guinness is Good for You' was first coined. Today, the Dublin brewery exports to 27 markets world-wide. In the domestic beer market (the equivalent of 850,000,000 pints per year), stout, not just Guinness but also the rival brands of Murphy and Beamish, accounts for just over 50 per cent, with lager occupying a 38-per-cent market share and ale 11.7 per cent.

ENDA O'DOHERTY

Brigades, Irish These surfaced on several occasions in Irish history, in different contexts and with different meanings. The 'Brigade' made its first appearance as a proposed adjunct to the royalist force of the earl of Newcastle, who planned to import it for use in the north of England during the 1640s, had it ever been formed. But Irish Brigades are best remembered as organized groups of Irish gentlemen (or nearly so) who fought in the service of foreign armies in eighteenth-century wars against England. As autocracy yielded to republicanism in Europe, an Irish legion fought under Napoleon in the campaign against Prussia. Later still, different Irish Brigades fought for the Union in the American Civil War and for the pope in Italy in 1860. In Irish domestic politics the term 'Irish Brigade' was associated with those liberal MPs who joined forces to conduct a campaign both within and without Parliament in opposition to the Ecclesiastical Titles Bill of 1851.

GERARD O'BRIEN

broadcasting On the evening of New Year's Day 1926, in a heavily draped room over a Dublin employment exchange, Seamus Hughes announced three times 'This is 2RN' before introducing Douglas Hyde, who formally opened the modest service. There had been earlier broadcasts – one, in Morse code in the course of the 1916 rising, having some claim to being the first news transmission in the world – but the radio service proper had its origins in a White Paper laid before the Dáil in 1923. A subsequent committee recommended that 'broadcasting should be a State service purely – the installation and the working of it to be solely in the hands of the Postal Ministry'. The model was the BBC, but Irish conditions produced a very different organization. Civil Service control and Department of Finance parsimony made the job of the first director, Seamus Clandillon, a continuing frustration, whilst programme content was governed both by financial restrictions and by restricted transmission areas (national coverage was not achieved until 1932, with the opening of the Athlone transmitter), and was subject to political pressures. The Gaelic League, for example, objected strongly to jazz and other alien influences. (The word 'jazz', as Myles na gCopaleen was to point out, contained three letters not found in the Irish language.)

When T.J. Kiernan became director in 1935, licences were held by no more than 2.2 per cent of the population – half that of Northern Ireland, where the BBC had begun regional broadcasting from Belfast on 15 September 1924. The onset of war (otherwise 'the Emergency') in 1939 saw the service in decline; but the effect of de Valera's measured reply on radio to an attack by Churchill in 1947 brought to the attention of the then taoiseach the importance of the medium as a means of addressing a world audience, and the staff and resources of Radio Éireann, as it had become, were substantially expanded and a national radio symphony orchestra established. Under the Broadcasting Authority Act of 1960 the service was removed from departmental control and placed under an independent authority appointed by the minister.

This Act also provided for a television service to be operated by the state, even though a commission had recommended it be run by private enterprise under the control of a public authority. The service opened on the night of 31 December 1961 from a makeshift Studio 3 in a partially completed building. The first chairman of the new Radio Telefis Éireann Authority was Eamonn Andrews, an Irishman who had made his reputation in Britain, and from the outset both the staffing and content of the new service stimulated vigorous debate. The 1960 Act had required the broadcasting services to encourage the restoration of the Irish language, preserve the national culture, and present matters of controversy in an objective matter. Perceived shortcomings in respect of the first two requirements were quickly overshadowed by serious controversy over the station's presentation of social and political questions, the long-running *Late Late Show* offering a platform to many seeking social change. Political dissent culminated in the dismissal of the entire authority by the government on 24 September 1972 following the transmission of a report on an interview with Seán Mac Stiofán, then head of the Provisional IRA. This was held to be in breach of the controversial Section 31 of the 1960 Act, subsequently redrafted in 1976, which banned interviews, or reported interviews, with members of organizations deemed to be subversive. Section 31 was dropped in 1994 in the context of the Northern Ireland peace process.

Other development have included the opening of the Irish-language radio service, Radió na Gaeltachta, in 1972 and a second TV channel, RTÉ 2 (now Network 2), in 1978. Telefis na Gaeilge (now TG4) followed in 1996 and the commercial channel TV3 went on air in 1998. RTÉ has met the challenge of commercial broadcasting which began in 1989, and its main radio rival Today FM (formerly Radio Ireland) has struggled to establish a viable market share. RTÉ's arts and music channel, Lyric FM, began broadcasting in 1999.

Reading

Cathcart, Rex, 'Broadcasting – the early decades' in *Communications and Community in Ireland* (Cork: Mercier, 1984).

——*The Most Contrary Region: The BBC in Northern Ireland 1924–1984* (Belfast: Blackstaff, 1984).

Fisher, Desmond, *Broadcasting in Ireland* (London: Routledge, 1978).

Mac Conghail, Muiris, 'The creation of RTE and the impact of television', in *Communications and Community in Ireland* (Cork: Mercier, 1984).

BERNARD SHARE

Brocas family

1 Henry Brocas Sr (1766–1837) Born and died Dublin.
2 James Henry Brocas (1790–1846) Born Dublin, died Cork.
3 Samuel Frederick Brocas (1792–1897) Born and died Dublin.
4 William Brocas (1794–1868) Born and died Dublin.
5 Henry Brocas Jr (*c*.1798–1873) Born and died Dublin.

The Brocas family of painters is made up of a father and four sons, their periods of activity stretching from the 1780s to the 1860s. A family of mainly landscape painters, they worked on a small scale, mainly in watercolour and in engraving. Views of Dublin, other Irish towns, animals and antiquities predominate, together with engraved portraiture. Henry Brocas Sr was a prolific engraver and an occasional landscape painter. His achievements in landscape were recognized in 1801 when he was appointed master of the Landscape and Ornament School of the Royal Dublin Society. As an engraver Brocas Sr is memorable for his portraits and caricatures of Dublin figures of the late eighteenth century. Many of these were published in the *Hibernian Magazine*. James Henry Brocas is remembered largely as an animal painter. Although the occasional painter of animal scenes, Samuel Frederick is best remembered for his views of Dublin. He worked closely with his brother Henry Jr in producing a set of twelve views of Dublin (1818–28). Samuel Frederick did the drawings, his brother the engravings. William Brocas was alone among his family in becoming a Royal Hibernian Academician. He specialized in portraits and figure subjects, in particular scenes from Irish rural life.

Reading

Butler, Patricia, *Three Hundred Years of Irish Watercolours and Drawings* (London: Weidenfeld and Nicolson, 1990).

Strickland, Walter, *A Dictionary of Irish Artists* (Shannon: Irish University Press, 1968).

FINTAN CULLEN

Brontë, Patrick (1777–1861), Clergyman and father of novelists. Born, most probably on St Patrick's Day, in Imdel, Co Down, the first of the ten children of Hugh and Alice Brunty (sometimes given as Prunty or Pronty: in the accents of Down all such names would sound alike). Alice had become estranged from her Catholic family through her love match with Protestant and reportedly free-thinking Hugh. Young Patrick worked as a weaver, but by the age of 16 had acquired enough education (reading his books while he worked at the loom) to run a small parish school. A local Protestant clergyman helped Patrick to enter St John's College, Cambridge, in 1802 as a mature student. At Cambridge Patrick experimented with the spelling of the family name: a college register gives 'Branty'. By 1804 Patrick had settled on 'Brontë', in imitation perhaps of one of the titles of his hero, Horatio Nelson. After graduating in 1806 he was ordained within the Church of England and served as curate in a number of places in England. In 1820 he secured the post of perpetual curate at Haworth, Yorkshire, where he stayed until his death, outliving all his talented children.

The memory and the meaning of Ireland are explored in Patrick Brontë's own writing. Many find hints of 'Irishness' in the novels of his daughters, but it is difficult to pinpoint any specific Irish traits (melancholy introspection, anguish) that might not simply be products of Yorkshire weather. The tensions around Catholicism in Charlotte Brontë's novels seem simply an aspect of the Protestantism of her time. However, the Brontë sisters were certainly aware of their Irish heritage, in the form of family stories: grandfather Hugh Brunty was a famous story-teller, and so was Patrick, in his way. Hugh's adoptive father, 'Welsh' Brunty, the cuckoo-like foundling who disrupted the Brunty family, might be the origin of Heathcliff in Emily Brontë's *Wuthering Heights*. And Jane in Charlotte Brontë's *Jane Eyre*, declaring her love for Rochester, echoes a line from a poem written in Ireland by grandfather Hugh to grandmother Alice.

Reading

Cannon, John, *The Road to Haworth: The Story of the Brontës' Irish Ancestry* (London: Weidenfeld and Nicolson, 1980).
Chitham, Edward, *The Brontës' Irish Background* (London: Macmillan, 1986).

PATRICK O'SULLIVAN

Brounker, William (*c*.1620–84) 2nd viscount Brounker of Castle Lyons. Educated in Oxford, he was made doctor of medicine in 1647. He was an eminent mathematician, making important discoveries, the chief of which were published in *Continued Fractions*, *Quadrature of a Portion of the Equilateral Hyperbola* and *Experiments of the Recoiling of Forces*. He also published a translation of Descartes's *Musical Compendium* in 1653, with his own annotations and criticisms. He was founder and first president of the Royal Society (1662–77), chancellor to Queen Catherine, and commissioner for executing the office of lord high admiral.

BRIAN DONOVAN

Brown, George (d. 1556) Archbishop of Dublin (1535–54). As first Reformation arch-

bishop of Dublin he presided over the dissolution of the monasteries and the enactment of the English Reformation in Ireland. He journeyed over much of the country, publishing the new injunctions and enforcing the 'form of the beads' – bidding prayers which affirmed the royal supremacy. He spent much of his career dealing with both the opposition within the church to the Reformation (particularly archbishop Dowdall of Armagh) and the charges of corruption and incompetence levelled at him by members of the Irish Council and the energetic Edwardian reformer John Bale, bishop of Ossory. In 1554 his see was revoked with the reintroduction of Roman Catholicism under Queen Mary.

Reading

Bradshaw, Brendan, 'George Browne, first Reformation archbishop of Dublin, 1536–1554', *Journal of Ecclesiastical History*, xxi (1970).
Ronan, M.V., 'Cardinal Pole's absolution of George Browne, Henry VIII's Archbishop of Dublin', *Irish Ecclesiastical Record*, 5th series, LXXII (1949), pp. 193–205.

BRIAN DONOVAN

Browne, Noel Christopher (1915–97) Doctor and politician. Born Waterford, 20 December. Though brought up in poverty he received, owing to strokes of good fortune, a first-class education at Beaumont College, Windsor, and Trinity College, Dublin. Elected as a Clann na Poblachta deputy in 1948, he became minister for health in the coalition government under John A. Costello on his first day in the Dáil. He quarrelled with his party leader, Sean MacBride, and the Catholic hierarchy over his mother-and-child scheme, and joined Fianna Fáil, but left when denied a Dáil nomination in 1957. In 1958 he founded, with Jack McQuillan, the National Progressive Democrats. Both joined the Labour Party in 1963, but Browne split with Labour over coalition with Fine Gael and other issues. He was later associated with the left-wing Socialist Labour party.

Though difficult to work with and mercurial on policy matters, he had great public appeal because of his manifest courage and compassion and his successful work as health minister in combating tuberculosis, a disease from which he himself had suffered. He demonstrated his popularity by being re-elected several times under different banners. His autobiography, *Against the Tide* (1986), was a bestseller.

JAMES DOWNEY

Buckley, John (1951–) Composer and teacher. Born Templeglantine, County Limerick, 19 December. Having trained as a primary schoolteacher in Dublin, Buckley studied composition with James Wilson at the Royal Irish Academy of Music and later with Alun Hoddinott in Wales. In 1979 he gained an MA in composition from University College, Cork, and was awarded the Macaulay Fellowship by the Irish Arts Council in 1978 and the Council's Composer Bursary in 1982. In the same year he retired from his school teaching position to devote himself fulltime to composition, and in 1984 he was elected to membership of Aosdána, the government-sponsored body honouring creative artists.

Buckley's output includes many commissions for solo instruments, chamber ensembles, choirs, bands and large-scale orchestras. His music has received many international performances in recent years and was chosen to represent Ireland on four occasions at the International Rostrum of Composers and at the Prix Italia in 1990. He has also been active as a composer of film music. His principal compositions include *Quintet for Wind* (1976), *Missa Brevis* (1979), *Concerto for Chamber Orchestra* (1981), *Sonata for Unaccompanied Violin* (1983), *At the Round Earth's Imagin'd Corners* for organ (1985), *Millennium Fanfare* for brass or military band (1987), *Symphony No. 1* (1988), *A Thin Halo of Blue* for orchestra, choir and narrator (1990), and *The Words upon the Window Pane*, a chamber opera (1991).

GERARD GILLEN

Bunting, Edward (1773–1893) Collector of Irish folk music and organist. Born Armagh, February; died Dublin, 21 December. Son of an English father and an Irish mother, Bunting received his early musical training from the organist of Armagh Cathedral and obtained his first organist's position at the age of 11 when he was appointed sub-organist at St Anne's Church, Belfast. He later became organist of St George's, High Street, and acquired a considerable reputation as a pianist and teacher in the city. On his marriage in 1819 he moved to Dublin, where he became organist of St Stephen's Church.

In July 1792 Bunting was appointed by the organizers of the Belfast Harp Festival to annotate the various melodies played by the great harpers assembled for the occasion. This stimulated him to make the study and preservation of Irish folk music the main work of his life, and the fruits of his labours can be seen in his *A General Collection of Irish Music*, which appeared in three volumes, the first containing 66 tunes (1796), the second having 75 melodies (1809), and the third consisting of some 150 tunes together with a 100-page essay on the history of music in Ireland (1840). He was a founding member of the Belfast Harp Society (1808–13) and of the Irish Harp Society (1819–39).

Reading

O'Sullivan, Donal (ed.), *The Bunting Collection of Irish Folk Music and Songs*, 6 vols (Dublin: Cork University Press, 1927–39).

GERARD GILLEN

Burke, Edmund (1729–97) Statesman. Born in Dublin to a father recently converted from Catholicism to the established church and to a mother who remained a Catholic, Edmund Burke was educated at the Quaker School at Ballitore, County Kildare, and at Trinity College, Dublin. After an apprenticeship in journalism, he attached himself to the Whig interest in English politics. Though he never ceased to write, his career from 1765 onwards was made in British parliamentary circles. He held office only briefly, as paymaster of the forces in 1782–3. His publications include *A Vindication of Natural Society* (1756), *On the Sublime and Beautiful* (1756), *Thoughts on the Present Discontents* (1770), and – climatically – *Reflections on the French Revolution* (1790). In addition to these, his speeches on American affairs and his publicly issued letters on Irish affairs contribute to a massive, if informally organized body of thoughtful, stylish prose.

Burke is now so familiar a figure that a conventional account of his life serves little purpose in a *Companion* of the present kind. Borrowing a phrase from Friedrich Nietzsche, it may be more fruitful to consider 'The Uses and Abuses' to which he had been put in recent decades, with special reference to Irish cultural debates. In the nineteenth century, Burke came to be regarded as the founder of British Conservatism, in both its pragmatic and imperial guises. This did not prevent Matthew Arnold from mobilizing him in the context of the Home Rule agitation of the late Victorian decades; see, in particular, his edition of writings and speeches, *Edmund Burke on Irish Affairs* (1881). Half a century later, W.B. Yeats recruited Burke (with Oliver Goldsmith, Henry Grattan and Jonathan Swift) to the cause of a Protestant Ascendancy more of Yeats's making than Swift's or Burke's. The canonical – and canon-creating – texts here are mainly to be found in the collection *The Tower* (1928), though it is arguable that the frenzied mood of Burke's last utterances served as a model for Yeats's autocratic politics throughout the 1930s. In both cases, Burke is taken as a writer whose words are helpfully malleable in any anti-revolutionary cause, though Arnold's instincts were imperial/liberal and Yeats's nationalistic/authoritarian in undertaking the task.

Even at this point, one might ask what in Burke's writings facilitated such diversity of exploitation. But Arnold and Yeats had no monopoly on the author of the *Reflections*.

As early as 1918, A.V. Dicey had spotted an opportunity to apply Burke to contemporary affairs; see his article 'Burke on Bolshevism' in *The Nineteenth Century and After*. After World War II, American commentators sought to establish Burke as a systematic philosopher of natural law, in the heated context of the Cold War. This involved a concentrated neglect of *A Vindication of Natural Society* and, less methodically, of the occasional, tactical and – yes – opportunistic basis of some of Burke's pronouncements. A *Burke Newsletter* was founded, with highly politicized contributions from Russell Kirk, Peter Stanlis and others. This was, in Stanlis's words, 'a counterrevolution on traditional grounds' in the study of the great parliamentarian. A late contribution to this genre may be discerned in Paul Hollander's *Political Pilgrims* (1981) as cited in Steven Blakemore's *Burke and the Fall of Language* (1988); subtitling his work *Travels of Western Intellectuals to the Soviet Union, China, and Cuba*, Hollander has – in including Castro's island – left no stone unthrown.

Cold War Burke was made up of suitably public texts, in which the *Reflections* naturally played a major part, with the substitution of the Soviet Union for Jacobin France already recommended by Dicey at the time of the Bolsheviks. To counter such blatant exploitation, a number of American, British and Irish scholars came together to edit a full edition of Burke's letters, including especially his private letters. Appearing in ten volumes between 1958 and 1968, the *Correspondence* has had the effect of revealing a Burke who is far less consistent than the inspirer of the *Newsletter*, who is occasionally at odds with himself and his friends, who is embroiled in an immense dossier of local complaint and historical precedent, of private speculation, personal grief and philological analysis. Apart from contributing to the release of Burke from the crusade against Moscow, the editors of the *Correspondence* may also have facilitated a shift of attention away from Burke on American Affairs (in the 1770s, etc.) and towards Burke on Irish Affairs (in the 1790s). This has had its own ironic repercussions in latter-day Irish cultural disputations.

Before coming to these, some details of less obviously partisan commentary on Burke may be helpful. Carl B. Cone's two-volume biography, *Burke and the Nature of Politics* (1957, 1964), was the first to employ the wealth of papers preserved in the Fitzwilliam collection (Sheffield Public Library) and elsewhere. James Boulton's *The Language of Politics in the Age of Wilkes and Burke* (1963) still holds its own in the ever-expanding library of works on the linguistic revolution of the late eighteenth century. Gerald W. Chapman's *Edmund Burke, the Practical Imagination* (1967) is a useful, short but lucid introduction. The edition of the *Reflections* appearing with an introduction by Conor Cruise O'Brien (1968) generated a great deal of interest, especially in directing attention towards Burke's allegedly Janus-like position *vis-à-vis* the conflict of religious denominations in Ireland. But, appearing on the eve of the Northern Ireland 'Troubles', this intervention has proved to be as troublesome as many which it condemns.

In the past quarter of a century, Burke has preoccupied two Irish thinkers whose resemblance to each other each would vigorously deny. In his T.S. Eliot memorial lectures (*The Suspecting Glance*) O'Brien, already mentioned, debated the American Cold War claim that Burke had healed the schism between politics and morality. More recently, he has published a life, *The Great Melody: A Thematic Biography and Commented Anthology of Edmund Burke* (1992), while Seamus Deane has deployed Burke in his *Short History of Irish Literature* and edited a selection of the writings in the first volume of the controversial *Field Day Anthology of Irish Writing* (1991). For each, Burke's attitude towards Irish Catholics in the 1790s is the dominant issue. Both of these mutually repelling Burkeans have retreated from the left-wing positions of their earlier years – Deane to become

a near-uncritical supporter of Ulster Republicanism, and O'Brien to become a member of the Ulster Forum of 1996 in the Unionist interest. Together, they have reassembled, with all the integrity of their ancient quarrel, the Janus-dilemma of Burke himself in the decade when the Dublin authorities refused concessions to Irish Catholics while relying on their loyalty in the struggle against France.

Without suggesting that we can return to the scene of these crimes to examine the evidence afresh, we can surely admit that some closer attention to what Burke actually wrote may demonstrate how the operations of language remain crucial to an understanding of Burke's protean availability. In the theoretical terms of the late twentieth century, Tom Furniss's *Edmund Burke's Aesthetic Ideology* is certainly helpful. But the Cruiser–Deane paradox lies beyond Furniss's remit. Essentially, Deane wishes to recruit Burke's sympathy for disadvantaged Irish Catholics while ignoring Burke's scornful contempt of Irish Jacobin republicanism. To balance this, Cruise O'Brien emphasizes Burke's attention to the 'little platoon' from which he came, while passing over in silence Burke's scornful contempt for the 'junto of jobbers' trade as defenders of Protestant Ascendancy.

Rather than go over once again the complicated, and to some extent inscrutable, utterances of Burke on the last-used phrase, readers might turn to the spendid edition of William Godwin's *Enquiry Concerning Political Justice* (first pub 1793) and his novel *Caleb Williams* (1794) as they are now presented in the multivolume editions edited by Mark Philp. From an examination of the successive editions of the *Enquiry* which Godwin published in the 1790s, we can now trace how positively the founder of modern anarchism responded to Burke; while, in a discussion of Godwin's famous novel, the present writer has drawn out a critique of Ascendancy ideology which clarifies Burke's own contemporaneous response to the phrase in a manner which assists neither Deane nor Cruise O'Brien (McCormack, *From Burke to Beckett*, 1994).

Whether one approaches the historical phenomenon of Burke's writing by the means approved by a James Boulton or a Tom Furniss, linguistic issues remain central. The German romantic Novalis summarized this when he wrote, 'There have been many antirevolutionary books written in favour of the Revolution. Burke has written a revolutionary book against the Revolution.' But one could hardly expect J. Edgar Hoover and the zealots of the *Burke Newsletter* to grasp so unnatural a conception.

W.J. MCCORMACK

Burke's Peerage First published in 1826 by John Burke, an Irish gentleman-genealogist. Although the compiler was Irish, it covered the peerage – and baronetage – of England, Scotland, Great Britain and the UK as well as Ireland, and for the first time arranged the entries in simple, alphabetical order, instead of by chronological order of creation within each rank in the peerage. Under Burke's son, Sir John Bernard Burke, Ulster king-at-arms, it ran through a new edition every year from 1847 to 1892, and it was continued with decreasing frequency down to recent times. The Burkes were fairly complaisant in accepting and even augmenting imaginative pedigrees submitted by their constituents. However, Burke's *Peerage* is of infinitely greater service to the historian than *Debrett's*, which still continues but is essentially a guide to living members of titled families, and also scores over *The Complete Peerage* and *Complete Baronetage* in that it records all cadet branches of the family concerned, not just successive bearers of the title.

Reading

Cokayne, George E., *The Complete Peerage*, 12 vols (London: St Catherine's Press, 1910–59).

A.P.W. MALCOMSON

The Burren The north-west corner of County Clare, principally a plateau at about 1,000 feet divided by a few broad valleys.

Solution of its carboniferous limestone by rainwater has given rise to what is called a karst landscape, which has been further moulded by glaciation. Its principal features are large, closed depressions or poljes (e.g. the two-mile-long Carran valley), extensive caves with subterranean rivers, turloughs (lakes that appear and disappear as the level of ground water fluctuates), and wide areas of bare pavement dissected by deep fissures.

Some 70 neolithic tombs, the magnificent late Bronze Age gold collar found at Gleninsheen and now in the National Museum, 400–500 ring-forts (including dozens of substantial cashels), and numerous towerhouses and ecclesiastical sites attest to the former productivity of his landscape, which probably owes its present ascetic look (and its name, from *boireann*, stony place or hill) to erosion initiated by earlier overuse. Paradoxically its flora is famous: Arctic and Alpine species such as the spring gentian and mountain avens grow in shallow patches of soil on the exposed and heavily grazed pavement surface, close to such Mediterranean plants as the maidenhair fern in the moist shelter of deep rock clefts.

The best-known monuments are the portal tomb at Poulnabrone, recently dated to 3800 BC; the (?Iron Age) cashel of Baile Cinn Mhargaidh, with its abattis of set stones; the inland cliff-top cashel of Cathair Chomain, which seems to have been an important wool-producing centre in the ninth century AD; and the ruins of the Cistercian abbey at Corcomroe, setting of W.B. Yeats's *The Dreaming of the Bones*. The Burren's principal villages are the holiday resort of Ballyvaughan, Kilfencra with its cathedral ruins and twelfth-century high crosses, and Doolin, renowned for its pub culture of folk music. Just beyond its southern margin is the nineteenth-century spa town of Lisdoonvarna.

Reading

O'Connell, J.W. and Korff, A. (eds), *The Book of the Burren* (Kinvara: 1991).

Robinson, Tim, *The Burren: A Map of the Uplands of North-West Clare* (Cill Rónáin: 1977).

TIM ROBINSON

Butler family (of Ormond) In November 1950 an Agreement for Sale was signed between the sixth marquis of Ormonde on the one part and the minister of education and Dr Richard Hayes, director of the National Library, on the other part. By this, in consideration of £20,000, manuscripts, books and documents, together known as the Ormonde Collection of Manuscripts and Deeds, were purchased. They are in the National Collection at the National Library. It is probably true to say that this is the greatest contribution the Ormonde Butlers have made to modern Ireland. It is the largest extant collection of family and state deeds and records from the end of the twelfth century to modern times, and had been housed in the Muniment Room of Kilkenny Castle – the chief seat of the Ormonde Butlers from 1391 until 1936. This collection contributed much to the historian's knowledge of the workings of the feudal system in Ireland, and of the relationship of the crown with the Anglo-Irish barons, with the Old Irish families, and with the church and monastic system.

In 1967, the sixth marquis presented Kilkenny Castle to the local committee. The castle at Carrick-on-Suir, County Tipperary (built *c*.1568 by the tenth earl of Ormaonde) and Cahir Castle, Cahir, County Tipperary, considered to be the largest and best preserved fifteenth–sixteenth century castle in Ireland (also a Butler seat) are owned by the Commissioners of Public Works, who conserve and maintain them. These are just a few examples of the legacies left by the once great Ormond Butler family.

MÁIRE MacCONGHAIL

Butler, Hubert (1900–91) Essayist, translator, and Protestant Republican. Born near Bennetsbridge in County Kilkenny. He was educated at Charterhouse and St John's College, Oxford. A job with the Irish Country Libraries was followed by spells teaching English in Alexandria, Riga and Leningrad. The School of Slavonic Studies, London, funded him for three years (1934–7) in Yugoslavia. By 1938 he was in Vienna assisting in the rescue of Austrian Jews. In 1941 he inherited the family home in Kilkenny, where he and his wife settled. In 1952 he clashed with the papal nuncio over forced conversions in wartime Croatia. He organized the Kilkenny Debates (1954–62) and was a co-founder of the Butler Society, whose *Journal* he edited. The artists' centre at Annaghmakerrig owes much to his foresight. A gifted linguist, his books include translations from the Russian of Leonid Leonov's *The Thief* (1931) and Anton Chekhov's *The Cherry Orchard* (1934). He was review editor of the *Bell* under Peadar O'Donnell, contributed to many other journals, and broadcast for RTE and the BBC. His *Ten Thousand Saints: Studies in Irish and European Origins* was published in 1972, followed by *Escape from the Anthill* (1985), *The Children of Drancy* (1988) and *Grandmother and Wolfe Tone* (1990). In 1986 he won the American-Irish Foundation Award for literature.

PATRICK GILLAN

Butler, Mildred Anne, (1858–1941) Watercolourist. Born and died in her home, Kilmurry, near Thomastown, County Kilkenny. The daughter of Captain Henry Butler, an amateur artist and grandson of the eleventh viscount Mountgarret, she trained at Westminster School of Art and with the animal painter William Frank Calderon and the watercolourist Paul Jacob Naftel. Butler was elected a full member of the Royal Watercolour Society in 1937, though she had work in the Tate Gallery from 1896. Her subject matter was largely composed of garden walks, farm fowl and flowers, all conveyed in a rich, confident colouring, sublimely isolated from the troubled Ireland outside the walls of her Kilkenny demesne.

Reading

Crookshank, Anne and the Knight of Glin, *Mildred Anne Butler 1858–1941* (Kilkenny Castle: Kilkenny Art Gallery Society: Dublin: Bank of Ireland; London: Christies, 1981).

FINTAN CULLEN

Butler, Sarah (d.?1735) Writer. Butler was the author of the posthumously published, *Irish Tales*, with a preface by Charles Gildon. Possibly the widow of James Butler, killed at the Battle of Aughrim, she petitioned the crown for the continuation of a pension awarded by William III.

Irish Tales is one of the earliest examples of anglophone Irish fiction and is significant for its use of Gaelic antiquarianism. The narrative is set in the era of Brian Boru and the preface acknowledges Keating and Walsh as well as citing Bede, Camden and Spenser.

Reading

Butler, Sarah, *Irish Tales or Instructive Histories for the Happy Conduct of Life* (London: E. Curll, 1716, repr. as *Milesian Tales*, 1719, 1727).

Leersen, J., *Mere Irish and Fíor-Ghael* (Amsterdam: John Benjamins, 1986).

SIOBHÁN KILFEATHER

Butt, Isaac (1813–79) Politician and writer. Born 6 September near Stranorlar, County Donegal. Butt was educated at the Royal School, Raphoe, and Trinity College, Dublin. Before graduating he had published translations of Ovid and Virgil, but he had also begun a life-long engagement with Irish political controversy. He was a leader writer for the virulent Irish Tory press from 1833 and, as an active member of the Irish Metropolitan Conservative Society (1836), strove to keep Irish Protestants of all classes united against O'Connell. Already O'Connell's chief opponent in the repeal debates in the reformed Dublin Corporation in 1843, the young Butt combined an idealistic belief in the cause of the Irish Protestant nation with a practical understanding of the devices of modern politics. The latter he had learnt from his tutor and mentor, the Rev. Charles Boyton.

Always implicit in Butt's politics was a belief that loyalty to the legislative union was conditional upon Westminster's treatment of Ireland, but he also believed that it was traitorous to inflame Irish national passions at the expense of imperial interests. Historians have sought to identify a specific moment when Butt converted to Irish nationalism, but this ignores the extent to which there was an underlying consistency to his Irish politics. From the beginning of his public life he had a patriotic feeling for Ireland, suspected the motives of all English politicians in respect of Ireland, and yet retained high hopes of Ireland's imperial partnership with England.

In January 1833 Butt was one of the co-founders of the *Dublin University Magazine*, a literary and political journal which was to remain the leading organ of intellectual Irish Toryism into the 1850s. Butt's political articles for the *DUM* were savage assaults on O'Connell and Whiggery, but his occasional literary manifestoes revealed that he sought to promote an Irish national literature. As the *DUM*'s editor (1834–8), Butt was the hidden patron of an Irish literary revival and responsible for fostering the literary talents of Samuel Ferguson, William Carleton, James Clarence Mangan, Charles Lever and Sheridan Le Fanu.

Butt's own fiction was too melancholic and dry to attract popularity or literary acclaim, but 'Chapters of College Romance' (*DUM*, 1834–6) revealed some talent for caricature and an ability to deliver unsubtle political messages in fictional guise. Butt's later use of fiction is more intriguing. In 1840, while still professedly an unreconstructed Tory, he delivered in his novel *Irish Life in the Castle, the Courts and the Country* a swingeing analysis of Ireland's stultifying sectarianism. However, in 1848, when he was thought of as an associate of the romantic nationalists, he offered in *The Gap of Barnesmore* (one of many attempts to write an Irish *Waverley*) a pessimistic view of a divided Ireland, which needed to look to practical, progressive, Protestant Ulster to pull itself out of the romanticized past in which it wallowed.

Between 1837 and 1841 Butt was professor of political economy at Trinity College, Dublin. He was an original economic thinker who delivered powerful challenges to *laissez faire* orthodoxy. His *Protection to Home Industry* (1846), which argued that in Ireland protective duties acted as 'a national poor law', was thought by John Mitchel to be the most important economic tract published in Ireland since the age of Swift and Berkeley. The Famine exposed the lack of understanding of Ireland inherent in all the English parties, but even in 1837 Butt had criticized the Irish Poor Law as a piece of 'forced legislation', passed to salve English consciences rather than address Ireland's needs. By 1847, in *A Voice for Ireland: Famine in the Land*, there was reference to England's 'moral crime' to Ireland and by 1849 an unequivocal statement of her 'separate nationality': '[L]et acts of parliament declare what they will, Antrim and Cork are parts of the same nation, Mayo and Kent are not . . . [A]fter half a century's experience of the Union, we still feel that Ireland is a separate country' (*The Rate in Aid*).

For all his literary endeavours and economic lessons, however, it was as the legal tribune of nationalist Ireland that Butt first came to prominence as a patriot. Called to the Irish Bar in 1838 (QC, 1844), Butt had used his skill as an advocate to defend, brilliantly but hopelessly, the unreformed Dublin Corporation at the bar of the House of Lords in 1840: but in 1848 he defended William Smith O'Brien and other Young Irelanders in the courts with a passion which revealed that he had more than a professional interest in their cases. He attended the meetings of various quasi-nationalist Irish societies in the aftermath of the Famine, but the lure of Westminster prevented him playing any decisive role in them.

Butt was Liberal-Conservative MP for Youghal (1852–65) and Home Rule MP for Limerick (1871–9). His first 12 years in London were clouded by the spectre of debt and rumours of shady speculation and by the fact of a mistress and illegitimate children. It took the activities of the Fenians to lead Butt to a renewed reflection on the Irish question, most inventively in an updating of Berkeley's Irish tract *The Querist* (1735–7), which he published as *The Irish Querist* in 1867. Butt's decision to associate himself with Berkeley and the Ascendancy tradition of Irish nationalism is revealing, but he wrote other pamphlets which suggested that he accepted a more radical reading of Irish history and politics than had previously been the case. Although he was soon to be outpaced in the field, with *Land Tenure in Ireland: A Plea for the Celtic Race* (1866) and *The Irish People and the Irish Land* (1867), Butt became the chief spokesman of those who believed that offering the Irish tenant some fixity of tenure was unlikely to prove dangerously subversive of the true rights of property.

Having defended many Fenians in the courts from 1865, notably Thomas Clarke Luby and Charles Kickham of the *Irish People*, Butt became president of the Amnesty Association in June 1869. In September 1869 he oversaw the inauguration of the Irish Tenant League and, in September 1870, formalizing his rejection of the union, he presided at the first meeting of the Home Government Association. The philosophy of the new 'Home Rule' movement was outlined in Butt's *Home Government for Ireland: Irish Federalism, its Meaning, its Objects and its Hopes* (1870). He combined strict guidance as to the constitutional path which would be followed to secure a Dublin Parliament with imaginative ideas about the benefits to Great Britain and Ireland of a complete system of imperial devolution.

Butt was for a time the undisputed leader of the Home Rulers, but, in spite of the electoral success of 1874, when the party won 59 seats, his unfaltering constitutionalism and nascent imperialism began to frustrate powerful elements in the party. From 1875, Butt's leadership was increasingly ignored or repudiated by the 'obstructionists', led by Joseph Biggar and Charles Stewart Parnell, and in August 1877, Parnell was elected to succceed him as president of the Home Rule Confederation. Butt continued to be the titular head of the Home Rulers in Parliament, but his health was failing and almost every nationalist was preparing for a future without him. He died in Dundrum, County Dublin, on 5 May and was buried at Stranorlar, the officiating clergyman refusing to utter a word about his life and work.

Isaac Butt has secured a footnote in the history of Ireland as 'the father of Home Rule', but, while Home Rule politics took up all his time and energy in the 1870s, that endeavour does not represent the sum of his work for Ireland. From the age of 20, Butt reflected on the past and present state of Ireland in newspaper articles, academic lectures, legal defences, political and economic tracts, and fiction. He also encouraged others to do the same. He was, therefore, as much a father of Irish cultural nationalism as he was of modern nationalist politics.

Reading

Spence, Joseph, 'Isaac Butt, nationality and Irish Toryism, 1833–52', *Bullan*, 2, no. 1 (Summer 1995).

Thornley, David, *Isaac Butt and Home Rule* (London: Mac Gibbon and Kee, 1964).

White, Terence de Vere, *The Road of Excess* (Dublin: 1946).

JOSEPH SPENCE

Byers, David (1947–) Composer. Born Belfast, 26 January. Byers studied composition at Queen's University, Belfast, with Raymond Warren: at the Royal Academy of Music, London, with James Iliff, and at the Liège Conservatoire with Henri Pousseur. He is senior producer (music) with BBC Northern Ireland. His works, mainly for vocal and chamber ensembles, have been influenced by mediaeval polyphony and Irish traditional music. They include *Night Song* (1972) for choir, *Magnificat* for organ and *A Planxty for the Dancer* for orchestra (both 1983), *Moon is Our Breathing* for chamber ensemble (1985) and for orchestra and narrator (1989), *The Wren's Blether* for four instruments and two actors (1989), and *The Journey of the Magi* for string quartet (1990). He is also active as an editor of music.

PETER DOWNEY

Byrne, Gay (1934–) Broadcaster. Born Dublin, 5 August. Byrne was educated by the Christian Brothers, Synge Street. He married the harpist and broadcaster Kathleen Watkins, and has two daughters. After working in insurance, cinema management, car hire and advertising, he began his career at RTÉ in 1958 (with brief spells at BBC and Granada). Byrne is famous as producer/host of the influential *Late, Late Show* (from 1962 to 1999), which aired many topics once taboo. Credited as a major influence in widening public opinion in Ireland, but later outdistanced by the increasing frankness of other media, he remains the country's most popular broadcaster, one keenly aware of ordinary people's feelings and tastes. In 2000 he became the first host of the Irish version of *Who Wants to be a Millionaire*.

Reading

Byrne, Gay with D. Purcell, *The Time of My Life* (Dublin: 1989).

PETER COSTELLO

C

Campbell, George (1918–79) Painter. Though born in Arklow, he grew up mainly in Belfast and is generally reckoned a Northern artist. With Middleton, O'Neill and Dillon, he formed one of the most talented generation of painters to emerge from Ulster. Largely self-taught, he developed a brilliant, high-toned style with a kind of Cubist armature; his love of Spain is reflected frequently in his subject matter, and he also painted a great deal in and around Roundstone, in Connemara. Campbell, who was a witty, gregarious man and an excellent flamenco guitarist, will always be identified with the early years of the Living Art Exhibition and with the Victor Waddington Gallery in Dublin, which virtually brought Irish Modernism to the public. He is represented in most public collections, North and South.

BRIAN FALLON

Campion, Edmund (1540–81) English Jesuit. Prior to his flight to Europe, Campion went to Ireland, where he wrote his *Two Bokes of the Histories of Ireland* in 1571. He took part in the unsuccessful founding of a university in Dublin. Whilst in Ireland he stayed with the recorder of Dublin, James Stanihurst.

Campion's history of Ireland was based on notes taken in the Stanihurst library, and aided by Lord Deputy Sidney, the brother-in-law of Campion's patron, the earl of Leicester. The work covers many aspects of Irish history and society, emphasizing the importance of education in reforming the Gaelic-Irish. His work was the basis for Stanihurst's various descriptions and histories of Ireland.

Campion left Ireland in 1571, and went to the Continent to commit himself to the work of the Counter-Reformation. He was executed for treason on his return to England in 1581.

Reading

Hogan, Edmund, 'The blessed Edmund Campion's History of Ireland, and its critics', *Irish Ecclesiastical Record*, 3rd series, xii (1891), pp. 629–641, 725–35.
Lennon, Colm, *Richard Stanihurst, the Dubliner, 1547–1618* (Dublin: Irish Academic Press, 1981).
Simpson, Richard, *Edmund Campion: A Bibliography* (London: 1867).

BRIAN DONOVAN

Canada, the nineteenth-century Irish in Emigration to British North America before Confederation was dominated by the Irish, who, by the end of the century, constituted the largest non-French ethnic group in

Canada. Between 1825 and 1845, approximately 475,000 landed there, over half from a Protestant rural background. During the Famine period, a further 340,000 made the journey. Thousands died en route or in the quarantine stations of Grosse Ile (Québec) or Partridge Island (New Brunswick). Although many of the immigrants successfully adapted to rural life in Canada, many others eked out miserable lives as low-paid labourers in canal, lumber or railway camps. Life for them was bedevilled by the same religious bigotry and sectarianism that existed in Ireland, though institutions such as the Orange Order or Catholic benevolent societies did provide a politically cohesive environment of conviviality and fraternalism. The Fenian movement, however, found little support in the country and its futile attempts to invade Upper and Lower Canada served merely to confirm the need for Confederation. The Irish had considerable impact on the political, academic and commercial life of Canada throughout the century, and names such as Eaton, O'Keever, McMaster and D'Arcy McGee are a reminder of Canada's debt to its Irish immigrants.

Reading

Davin, N.F., *The Irishman in Canada* (Toronto: 1877; repr., Shannon: Irish University Press, 1969).

Elliott, Bruce S., *Irish Migrants in the Canadas: A New Approach* (Kingston and Montreal: McGill-Queen's University Press; Belfast: Institute of Irish Studies, 1988).

O'Driscoll, Robert and Reynolds, Lorna, *The Untold Story: The Irish in Canada*, 2 vols (Toronto: Celtic Arts of Canada, 1988).

JAMES JACKSON

Cantillon, Richard (1680/1690–1734) Entrepreneur and economist. Born Ballyronan, Ballyheigus, County Kerry, some time between 1680 and 1690; died London, 14 May. Cantillon successfully applied for French citizenship in 1708 and made a career in trade and banking in France.

He had close associations with James Brydges, paymaster general to British forces during the War of the Spanish Succession, and with John Law, who was appointed controller general of the finances in Paris in 1720, and who was particularly connected with the Mississippi System (1719–29) and the South Sea Bubble. Each of these associations was highly lucrative for Cantillon, who showed a remarkable ability to handle banking and foreign exchange transactions. He was, indeed, one of the few fathers of modern economics who showed flair as a financier. His combination of analytical and financial expertise allowed him to test many of his theories in practice.

Cantillon's *Essai sur la nature du commerce en général* (*Essay on the General Nature of the Economic System*) was not published until 1755, 21 years after his death. The circumstances of its publication are not much less mysterious than those of his death. The purpose of the *Essai* was to create a model of how the economic system worked, which could then be used as the basis for judging the appropriateness of different options in macro-economic policies.

Perhaps because of his experience as a banker and dealer in foreign exchange, Cantillon sought to identify the dynamic agents at work in the economic system. Where Adam Smith attributed the design of the system to an 'invisible hand', Cantillon identified the entrepreneur. He showed how economic society evolved from a centralized command economy to a market economy and, concurrently, from a barter economy to a monetary economy. The themes of his analysis were: the theory of market behaviour and the significance of the entrepreneur in the market; the circular flow of income; the theory of money providing the linkage between the real economy and the monetary economy; and a critique of financial innovations.

ALAN DUKES

Carleton, William 1794–1869 Writer. William Carleton, widely regarded as a father of the Irish short story, records in his work a way of life which he himself abandoned – rural, just emerging from Gaelic into English, Catholic, at best semi-educated. He escaped from the poverty of County Tyrone to Dublin, where he was prompted to write of his background for a Protestant, potentially evangelizing audience.

Most of Carleton's best work is found in the tales, enormously popular in their own time, collected in *Traits and Stories of the Irish Peasantry* (1830s). Often these pieces satirize Catholicism as consisting of a collection of superstitions, now identifiable as pagan survivals. The ease with which Carleton abandoned the religion of his childhood seems explained by the fact that he evidently perceives no genuine spirituality in any religion, although Protestantism for him often represents decent living. His later work, less anti-Catholic, includes several novels and an illuminating, if unfinished, autobiography.

Carleton is among those who created the comic stereotype of the ignorant, hard-drinking, pugnacious and voluble Paddy, yet the grim reality of poverty, oppression and despair which repeatedly emerges in his work provides him with nationalist credentials, as does his pioneering use of the vernacular for literary purposes.

If his prolific work often appears facile, an ill-considered mix of genres and prose styles, he is nevertheless valued highly as a recorder of the rituals and quotidian details of the pre-Famine way of life; in a later generation he might have found a truer vocation as an anthropologist.

RUTH SHERRY

Carolan, Turlough (1670–1738) Composer. Born near Nobber, County Meath; died Ballyfarnon, County Roscommon. Although Carolan may more properly be regarded as part of the native tradition in Irish music and culture, he belongs also to the anglophone tradition, in that he absorbed certain elements and forms of European (especially Italian) music which influenced the shape and structure of his own work in part. As an Irish

harper, Carolan was one of a group of musicians whose livelihood depended on the sporadic patronage of Catholic families of Norman or Irish descent. Grainne Yeats remarks that he was 'the last of the harpers to compose, and the only one about whom much is known'. Although not accounted an outstanding performer, Carolan's gifts as a composer and versifier were highly esteemed. Scholars have imputed to his style the influence of Vivaldi, Corelli and Geminiani, the last of whom was resident periodically in Dublin during Carolan's lifetime. From the vantage point of anglophone culture, Carolan's importance lies pre-eminently in his posthumous reputation as the embodiment of the native tradition.

Charles Burney's characterization of the Irish bard as 'little better than that of piper to the *White Boys* and other savage and lawless ruffians' gives some indication of how this tradition was received by the foremost English music historian of the later eighteenth century. Carolan's achievement, which was understood by Irish commentators (chief among them Joseph Walker, author of the *Historical Memoirs of the Irish Bards*, 1786) as the epitome of a vanished high culture of ethnic origin, has important implications for the reception of music in Ireland throughout the nineteenth century.

Reading

Yeats, Grainne, 'Carolan, Turlough', in *The New Grove Dictionary of Music and Musicians*, ed. Stanley Sadie (London: Macmillan, 1980), vol. 3.

HARRY WHITE

Carroll, Paul Vincent (1899–1968) Playwright. Born Blackrock, near Dundalk, 10 July, to Michael and Kitty Sandys Carroll; died Bromley, Kent, 20 October. Educated to be a national schoolteacher, Carroll emigrated to Glasgow in 1920, where he began to write. In 1932 he won an Abbey Theatre prize for *Things That Are Caesar's*, two years after his first play was staged. Thereafter, Carroll's subject was almost obsessively the battle to preserve freedom of thought and choice in a society dominated by the Catholic church. *Shadow and Substance* (1937), which was successfully staged on Broadway in 1937 and won the New York Drama Critics Circle award, remains Carroll's best play because here his subject finds outstanding representation in the well-drawn characters of Canon Skerritt and schoolteacher O'Flingsley: between them the naive servant girl Bridget, frail symbol of the soul of Ireland, is destroyed. Carroll wrote many plays, after this, tragedies, satires and fantasies, but it is as the author of *Shadow and Substance* he is remembered.

Reading

Doyle, Paul A., *Paul Vincent Carroll* (Lewisburg: Bucknell University Press, 1971).

Hogan, Robert, *After the Irish Renaissance* (Minneapolis: University of Minnesota Press, 1957; London: Macmillan, 1968).

Journal of Irish Literature 1, no. 1 (1972), special issue on Carroll, ed. Robert Hogan.

CHRISTOPHER MURRAY

Carson, Ciaran (1948–) Poet and traditional musician. Born Belfast. Carson was educated at Queen's University, Belfast, his first language being Gaelic. He then worked for the Arts Council of Northern Ireland. Carson's *The New Estate* appeared in 1976 and was followed ten years later by *The Pocket Guide to Irish Traditional Music*. It was under the influence of the narrative procedures of story-teller John Campbell of Mullaghbawn and the unfolding rhymical patterns of American poet C.K. Williams that Carson's *The Irish for No* (1987) and *Belfast Confetti* (1989) struck a new note of powerful vernacular speech coupled with literary sophistication. More recent publications include *The Star Factory* (1997) and *Fishing for Amber* (2000). His work has won Carson several important honours.

Carson, Edward Henry, (1854–1935) Lawyer and politician. Born in Dublin of Scottish ancestry, Carson was educated at Portarlington and Trinity College, Dublin, where he built a reputation as a hard worker though with little academic bent. Called to the Irish bar in 1877, Carson became a most successful barrister, his achievements eventually securing him the solicitor generalships for Ireland (1892) and later for England (1900). As a member of the English bar he conducted the famous cross-examination which ended with the imprisonment of Oscar Wilde. Elected leader of the Irish Unionist Party in 1910, Carson became regarded by many as the personification of opposition to Home Rule. He was prominent in the setting up of the Ulster Volunteer Force and in the general militarization of the Ulster psyche. After the shelving of the Home Rule Act for the duration of World War I, Carson held cabinet office as attorney general and later as first lord of the admiralty. An Irish rather than an Ulster Unionist, he looked on partition with dismay, and his appointment as lord of appeal in 1921 really signified his abandonment of active politics. He died in England in October 1935 and was returned to Belfast for burial.

GERARD O'BRIEN

Carver, Robert (fl. 1750–91) Landscape painter. Born Dublin. The son of the landscape painter Richard Carver (d. 1754), he studied under his father and at the Dublin Society School. He died in Covent Garden, London, in November 1791. After some years as a scene painter in Dublin theatres (both Smock Alley and Crow Street), he was invited by Garrick to London. In 1769 he was made principal scene painter at Drury Lane, where he met with great success. Unfortunately we have no visual record of these designs. At the same time he was exhibiting rather dull, sub-Claudian landscapes at the Free Society's exhibitions in London, becoming president of the society in 1777.

Reading

Strickland, Walter, *A Dictionary of Irish Artists* (Shannon: Irish University Press, 1968).

Crookshank, Anne and the Knight of Glin, *The Painters of Ireland c. 1660–1920* (London: Barrie and Jenkins, 1978).

FINTAN CULLEN

Casement, Sir Roger (1864–1916) Diplomat and revolutionary. Born Sandycove, County Dublin, 1 September; hanged for high treason in Pentonville prison, 3 August. Casement was educated at Ballymena Academy and in 1892 joined the British colonial service in Africa. In 1904 he made a notable report on the inhuman treatment of native workers in the Belgian Congo. Promoted to consul general at Rio de Janeiro, he investigated conditions in the Peruvian rubber plantations, and his report exposing the cruelties practised on the natives by the white traders created an international sensation on its publication in 1912. He was knighted in 1911 for his public service and retired in 1912.

Always of strong nationalist sympathies, he joined the Irish Volunteers in 1913. When World War I broke out, he went to Berlin hoping to obtain German help to win Irish independence. He tried without success to enlist Irish prisoners of war in a brigade for service in an Irish rising, but persuaded the Germans to ship a cargo of arms to Kerry for the rebellion of Easter Week, 1916. The ship was captured by British warships and Casement was arrested when he landed from a submarine. He was tried, convicted of high treason and sentenced to be hanged. Many influential people in England petitioned for a reprieve and in the USA there was strong feeling against the sentence. Copies of diaries alleged to be his, recording homosexual practises, were circulated, it is said, by the British government and had the inevitable effect on public opinion. René MacColl, biographer of Casement, considers that these 'Black Diaries' are authentic; the use alleged to have been made of them is another matter.

HENRY BOYLAN

Catholics and Catholicism Ireland was the only large territory in Western Europe in which, by the close of the religious wars that followed the Reformation, the religion of the majority of the population remained different from that of the state. In the eighteenth and nineteenth centuries, as Ireland came culturally and economically closer to the other regions of the British Isles, religion increasingly stood out as the single most important issue preventing its full integration into a unitary British state. This background has had a lasting influence on the character of Irish Catholicism and on its role in Irish culture.

In Ireland, as elsewhere, the history of Catholicism must begin, not with the medieval Christianity whose glories later generations of Protestant and Catholic were alike to claim for their own, but with the transformation of the whole character of popular religion that took place in the sixteenth and seventeenth centuries. From an early stage it was clear that the Protestant Reformation, starved of resources and too closely linked to the tensions of the Tudor reconquest, was making little head way with the indigenous population, whether Old English or native Irish. But it was only from the 1590s that indifference or hostility towards externally imposed religious innovation began to be transformed into a Counter-Reformation Catholicism of the kind whose outlines had been laid down a few decades earlier at the Council of Trent. The backbone of the new system, as in the rest of Counter-Reformation Europe, was the reaffirmation of a fixed territorial framework of diocese and parish. Within this, a trained and disciplined clergy enforced uniform standards of religious instruction and practice. Popular religious observance was purged of its more blatantly magical elements. Collective rituals expressive of communal solidarity gave way to individual acts of personal devotion. The seminaries and colleges established at Salamanca (1592), Douai (1594), Louvain (1607) and other centres in Continental Europe were crucial to the success of these endeavours. They provided the trained and disciplined clergy essential to the new ecclesiastical order, and at the same time became a base from which exiled Catholic intellectuals began to promulgate a new political ideology, in which Irish political conflicts were reinterpreted as part of the international struggle against heresy.

The creation of a new Catholic identity in late sixteenth- and early seventeenth-century Ireland involved not just the reshaping of religious culture, but the blurring of long-standing political and cultural divisions between Old English descendants of pre-Reformation colonists and Irish 'natives'. The necessity of uniting these traditionally antagonistic groups was a major concern of Counter-Reformation propagandists. Geoffrey Keating's history of Ireland (c.1634), for example, is Gaelic-language text that seeks to create a national history embracing both Old English and Gaelic Irish. By this time the traditional self-image of the Old English as the crown's most loyal servants in Ireland was being eroded by the presence of growing numbers of New English officials and settlers and by the increasing willingness of English government to equate recusancy with disloyalty. These pressures led the Old English, in the crisis precipitated by the rising of October 1641, to join in uneasy alliance with the Gaelic Irish in the Catholic Confederation. But ethnic divisions only gradually lost their relevance. The extension of Tridentine Catholicism was itself in part an assertion of cultural hegemony, with the new discipline being received more readily in the towns and among the Old English than it was in Gaelic Ireland, where the religious orders fought a determined rearguard action against the restraints of parochial and episcopal control. These tensions form part of the background to the downfall of Oliver Plunkett, the Old English archbishop of the ethnically polarized

diocese of Armagh, who was executed on trumped-up charges of treason in 1681.

Defeat in the civil wars of 1641–53 and 1689–91 had far-reaching and irreversible consequences. The campaign of religious repression initiated by the Cromwellian government of the 1650s, the only sustained attempt ever made to stamp out Catholic religious practice in Ireland, was relatively short-lived, and the ecclesiastical structures built up over the preceding half-century were fairly quickly reconstituted in the quieter circumstances that obtained after 1660. But the restored monarchical regime of Charles II was unwilling to tamper drastically with the Cromwellian land settlement. In 1641 Catholics had owned 59 per cent of the profitable land in Ireland; in 1685 they owned 22 per cent. Catholics also remained excluded, in fact if not in law, from most positions of power and influence. In the aftermath of the brief period of Catholic ascendancy under James II, the Irish Parliament introduced a formidable-looking body of penal laws, forbidding Catholics to vote, to sit in Parliament, to hold office in central or local government, to enter the armed services, or to practice law. But these were for the most part a restatement of disabilities that had already existed for decades. The main new feature was the acts of 1704 and 1708 making it illegal for Catholics to acquire land by purchase, marriage or inheritance, and providing for the progressive subdivision of existing estates among all the sons of each deceased proprietor. By the second half of the century the majority of the remaining Catholic landed families had conformed to the established church. Legislation dating from the 1690s also made it illegal for Catholic bishops or regular clergy to reside in the kingdom and for Catholics to run schools. But this was never wholeheartedly enforced, and by the 1720s could be largely ignored.

Irish Catholicism of the eighteenth century, despite its unusual position as an unestablished and technically illegal church serving the great majority of the population, was in many ways a typical institution of the *ancien régime.* Bureaucratic, legalistic, decentralized, disproportionately manned by members of the surviving gentry and aristocracy, its structures preserved the broad outlines of Tridentine discipline, but could not always cope effectively with minor lapses of discipline – excessive financial rapacity, neglect of pastoral or administrative duties, failures in sobriety or chastity. At the top of Catholic society came the surviving propertied class: a handful of landowners, a substantial non-proprietorial landed interest of leaseholders, middlemen and strong farmers, and a significant Catholic mercantile interest. This stratum of Catholic society retained close links with Catholic Europe, through trade, the placing of family members in foreign armies and ecclesiastical benefices, and, in the first half of the century, a mainly passive Jacobitism. Its members exhibited a conventional piety, tending – possibly under the influence of contemporary English Catholic spirituality – towards the morbid and scrupulous. Among the lower classes, particularly in the countryside, religion took a different form. There was a strong attachment to the Christian rites of passage, but Catholic doctrine and ritual were interlaced with other elements: belief in fairies, witchcraft and magical healing, the celebration of ancient festivals like Midsummer's Day or St John's Eve (23 June), and ceremonies at holy wells in which devotion to a Christian saint was combined with protective ritual and carnivalesque celebration. Nor did popular religious practice always conform to the minimum requirements of canon law. Statistics from the mid-1830s suggest that church attendance on a normal Sunday in rural Ireland may have been as low as 40 per cent of the adult population.

Two developments during the nineteenth century transformed the character of Irish Catholicism. The first was the reshaping of popular religious practice. From around the 1780s there began a concerted movement within the Irish church to tighten internal discipline and raise the standard of pastoral services. Already in the first half of the

nineteenth century these reforms had some impact on popular religious practice. But it was the Famine of 1845–51 that provided the opportunity for what Professor Emmet Larkin has called the 'devotional revolution'. Starvation, disease and emigration scythed through the ranks of the rural poor, leaving behind a smaller but more affluent Catholic population, better able to finance a substantial ecclesiastical establishment and at the same time more receptive to the social and religious discipline it promulgated. The period 1850–75, years of general prosperity, saw a massive building programme, as churches, cathedrals, convents, schools, hospitals and orphanages provided visible testimony to an increasingly assertive and self-confident Catholicism. The character of public worship was transformed by the introduction of new services and by a novel emphasis on external magnificence and display. Popular participation in religious services was encouraged and regimented by the proliferation of lay sodalities and confraternities. By the end of the nineteenth century, at a time when organized religion in most parts of Europe was in sharp decline, regular church attendance had become the norm among Irish Catholics, men as well as women.

This explosion of popular religious fervour was closely linked to the changes taking place during the same period in the character of Irish popular culture: the transition, in just two generations, from a predominantly Gaelic-speaking, oral and subsistence-oriented world to an English-speaking, literate and commercialized society. One reason why Catholicism assumed such a central role in popular life was because it offered a symbol of identity and apparent continuity at a time of bewildering cultural dislocation. For their part the clergy of the new Catholic church contributed markedly to the wider process of cultural change. In France and elsewhere the Catholic church of this period sought to regain popular support by taking a more sympathetic view of popular religious traditions. The Catholicism of late Victorian Ireland was by contrast a combination of urban middle-class morality and Roman orthodoxy, with remarkably few roots in indigenous culture. A few traditional festivals, like the annual pilgrimages to Croagh Patrick in County Mayo and Lough Derg in County Donegal, were continued, in a modified form, under clerical patronage and supervision. For the most part, however, such observances were condemned as occasions of superstition, disorder or immorality, and were vigorously suppressed.

The other major development of the nineteenth century was the increasingly close association of Catholicism and nationalism. Up to this point it had been mainly Protestants who had articulated a demand for greater political autonomy. Although some Catholics had joined with Protestant radicals in the United Irish movement of the 1790s, others, including the Catholic bishops and clergy, had instead put their trust in a public stance of conspicuous loyalty to the British government. The Act of Union, however, permanently altered the terms of political debate. Within a short time, Protestants came to look on the union as their only protection against Catholic majority rule. Instead self-government was now overwhelmingly a Catholic demand. Meanwhile, starting with the campaign for Catholic emancipation in 1823–9, the Catholic clergy became directly involved in political agitation. By the second half of the nineteenth century, an informal alliance had taken shape, whereby nationalist politicians received the active support of the bishops and clergy, and in return supported distinctively Catholic interests in such matters as education. This alliance, reaching its highest point in the period between the rise of Parnell and World War I, gave constitutional nationalism additional legitimacy and crucial organizational support, while at the same time further strengthening religious loyalties. In most parts of Europe political divisions, and in particular class conflict, were a major cause of popular alienation from the churches. In Ireland, where religious and political identities reinforced one another, both Catholics and Protestants remained faithful to organized religion on a scale otherwise seen only in the somewhat similar case of Catholic Poland.

Despite these close links between Catholicism and nationalism, independent Ireland after 1922 did not formally become a Catholic state. But in practice the political influence of the church was considerable. Legislation on divorce, contraception and censorship gave legal force to Catholic moral teaching. The bishops and clergy were given substantial control of both primary and secondary education, with separate provision being made for the small Protestant minority. Episodes like the campaign against the appointment of a Protestant, Miss Letitia Dunbar-Harrison, as county librarian for Mayo (1931), and the resignation 20 years later of Noel Browne, minister for health, after a scheme for free health care for mothers and children was declared to be in contravention of Catholic social teaching, confirmed the image of a political establishment unwilling to risk ecclesiastical censure or opposition. Meanwhile levels of popular religious devotion remained by European standards extraordinarily high. Surveys in the early 1970s suggested that nine out of ten adult Catholics attended church at least once a week, with a substantial minority attending far more often. In Northern Ireland a strictly orthodox religious devotion, more conservative even than that of the Irish Republic, remained part of the closed and inward-looking world of the Catholic minority.

It is only since the late 1970s that the face of popular Catholicism has begun to change significantly. The huge crowds mobilized by the visit of Pope John Paul II in 1979 testified to the continued strength of traditional religious allegiances. But since the 1980s there has been evidence of growing indifference, in particular among the urban young. On the newer housing estates to the north and west of Dublin there exists, for the first time in modern Ireland, a substantial population among whom regular religious practice is the exception rather than the rule. Meanwhile there have been significant developments within Catholicism: the continued growth of fringe movements of exceptional religious commitment such as the charismatics, and the emergence of conservative pressure groups, consciously opposed to liberalizing and secularizing influences both within the church and in society as a whole. As a result Irish Catholicism, for so long unique in Western Europe for its uniform devotion, ended the twentieth century in much the same condition as most other denominations, polarized between a largely indifferent majority of nominal adherents and a committed activist minority.

SEAN CONNOLLY

Catholic emancipation The long agitation for civil rights for Roman Catholics culminated in the passing of 'an Act for the relief of His Majesty's Roman Catholic subjects' (1829). This repealed the declarations against transubstantiation, the saints and the Mass hitherto required of elected representatives before taking their seats in Parliament. Instead of the Oaths of Allegiance, Supremacy and Abjuration there was substituted a simple Oath of Allegiance to the crown, which declared that the pope had no right to depose heretical monarchs; accepted the land settlement; and undertook not to exercise any privilege to disturb or weaken the Protestant religion or government in the United Kingdom. Under this Act, Roman Catholics were entitled to hold all civil and military offices except those of regent, chancellor and lord lieutenant. Catholics continued to be debarred from certain specified ecclesiastical offices limited to members of the established church, and from using titles associated with it. Other restrictions applied to the use of the robes of office and the exercise of Roman Catholic rites or ceremonies except in Roman Catholic places of worship.

Since this Act carried none of the 'wings', such as the royal 'veto' on the appointment of bishops, or the payment of clergy, which had been attached to earlier bills, it left the clergy free of state control. The manner in which the Act had been passed and the limitations incorporated in it earned little gratitude. Emancipation had not been graciously conceded: instead the effectiveness of massive organization and agitation had been demonstrated.

Reading

Curtis, E. and McDowell, R.B., *Irish Historical Documents 1172–1922* (London: Methuen, 1977: first pub. 1943).

Machin, G.I.T., *The Catholic Question in English Politics 1820–1830* (Oxford: Clarendon Press, 1964).

O'Farrell, Fergus, *Catholic Emancipation: Daniel O'Connell and the Birth of Irish Democracy 1820–30* (Dublin: Gill and Macmillan, 1985).

Reynolds, James A., *The Catholic Emancipation Crisis in Ireland, 1823–1829* (New Haven CT: Yale University Press, 1954).

DONAL MCCARTNEY

cattle trade Ireland's climate and topography have predisposed its agricultural economy to be based on livestock production rather than arable farming. In early Irish society, however, cattle were more than an economic unit, they were also a measure of status and wealth. The early Irish law tracts, for example, define honour (*enech*) in terms of units of cattle, in line with other legal obligations.

From the early seventeenth century the pattern of the cattle trade began to change. Cross-breeding with English stock improved the strain and live animals began to be exported for fattening in England, largely in response to improving English cattle prices. Between 1607 and 1639 the number of Irish cattle landed at Chester rose from 16 to 15,814. Such an expansion of the Irish cattle trade alarmed the English breeders of the West Country, and during the depressed years of the early 1660s they campaigned for a prohibition of imports of live cattle from Ireland. Against the wish of government, a

Cattle Act was passed in 1663 imposing a temporary ban, and in 1667 a further Act closed the English market completely to Irish cattle apart from a brief period in 1679/80. Even before the Acts the Irish cattle trade was moving away from live exports to barrelled beef and butter, a process speeded up by the passage of the Acts. The market for these products lay in the expanding colonial trade of the Americas and the provisioning trade. After the passage of the 1667 Act the government had licensed beef trade with enemy countries, a practice stopped in 1776, and Ireland was a prime supplier of naval supplies to all sides in the warfare of the early eighteenth century.

In the 1750s the Cattle Acts were relaxed and in 1776 finally repealed. The trade in beef with the American colonies continued into the early nineteenth century, and supplies for armies and navies during the Napoleonic wars also kept that market buoyant. However, the cattle trade was becoming increasingly oriented towards England, where industrialization and urbanization created a market for Irish meat. The introduction of steamships on the Irish sea in the 1820s made the shipping of live cattle easier, and by the time of the Famine the cattle trade had moved back to the export of live animals. After the Famine there was considerable consolidation of land-holdings with the emergence, especially in the west, of large cattle farms concentrating on producing live cattle for the English market. Attempts were made to improve other branches of the trade, notably with Horace Plunkett and the co-operative movement in the dairying sector, but live cattle continued to dominate the trade.

In 1996 the Irish cattle trade was severely affected by the European Union ban on Exports of British beef, in the wake of the outbreak of bovine spongiform encephalopathy (BSE) in Britain. The ban also provoked a slump in beef sales in the home market, with a considerable effect on the livelihoods of Irish farmers. The ban on Irish beef was lifted by the EU in 1998.

Reading

Crotty, Raymond, *Irish Agricultural Production: Its Volume and Structure* (Cork: Cork University Press, 1966).

Lucas, A.T., *Cattle in Ancient Ireland* (Kilkenny: Boethius, 1989).

O'Donovan, John, *The Economic History of Livestock in Ireland* (Cork: Cork University Press, 1940).

Woodward, Donald, 'The Anglo-Irish livestock trade in the seventeenth century', *Irish Historical Studies* xviii, no. 72 (1973).

RAYMOND GILLESPIE

Caulfield, James (1728–99) Nationalist. Born Dublin 18 August; died 4 August. He made the grand tour of Europe in 1746–54 and was created first earl of Charlemont in 1763 for his services against the French in defending Belfast. He built Charlemont House in Rutland (now Parnell) Square, and in his demesne at Marino he built the Casino, one of the most beautiful buildings of its kind anywhere. He was a leader of the liberal and polite society of his day, and devoted himself to literature, architecture and the affairs of the Royal Irish Academy, of which he was the virtual founder in 1785. In middle age his Whig nationalism involved him in the Volunteer movement. He became their commander-in-chief in 1780 and was prominent in the Dungannon Convention of 1782, which gave the final impetus to legislative freedom for the Irish Parliament. The movement aimed to achieve parliamentary reform, the removal of restrictions on Irish commerce, and Catholic emancipation. Reforms proposed at a Volunteer convention in 1783 were defeated in the Commons, and the Volunteers' political influence began to wane from then on.

HENRY BOYLAN

Cavendish diary Sir Henry Cavendish (1732–1804) sat at Westminster and in the Irish Parliament for over 30 years. He is remembered primarily for his accurate recording of parliamentary proceedings and speeches in the Irish House of Commons between June 1776 and August 1785, and also February to April 1789. Using the Gurney system of shorthand, Cavendish, who was present at most Commons debates during this period, recorded the proceedings as they occurred in a series of pocket-sized diaries. These eventually ran to 45 volumes, together with a further 37 volumes of longhand transcription. All were purchased from his descendants by the Library of Congress. The importance of the diaries lies in the fact that Cavendish worked in an age when such detailed parliamentary recording was forbidden by both Irish and British legislatures. Consequently his earlier diaries are the only extant source for Irish parliamentary debates until 1781, and in some respects his account of proceedings thereafter is markedly superior to published debates. The bulk of the Cavendish diaries remain in manuscript, but several volumes have been transcribed by modern scholars for academic purposes.

GERARD O'BRIEN

Celticism Defined by L.P. Curtis Jr in *Anglo-Saxons and Celts* as 'an ethnocentric nationalism with a strong measure of race consciousness which many Irishmen used to arm themselves against Anglo-Saxonist claims of cultural and racial superiority'. The word 'celt' denotes a prehistoric implement with a variety of uses: hoe, chisel or weapon of war. 'Celt' in its racial sense has likewise fulfilled both pejorative and ameliorative purposes. According to Curtis, 'Celticism' developed in reaction to 'Anglo-Saxonism', a system of texts about and images of the Celt which repressed by representation. While Anglo-Saxonism dominated by calumniation, Celticism, as in Douglas Hyde's 1892 lecture 'The Necessity of De-Anglicising Ireland', responded with the celebration of native language and culture. In its analysis of Anglo-Saxonism, *Anglo-Saxons and Celts* anticipates Edward Said's *Orientalism* (1978), which examines how the Orient and its peoples were stereotyped.

One irony of Celticism (besides the way in which its frequent concern with racial purity mimicked Anglo-Saxon exclusivism) was that its advocates often provided ammunition for the Celt's detractors. Ernest Renan, who represented himself as a vindicator of the Celts, none the less argued in 'The Poetry of the Celtic Races' (1859) that because of its 'infinite' imagination the race had 'worn itself out in resistance to its time, and in the defence of desperate causes...in taking dreams for realities, and in pursuing its splendid visions'. Matthew Arnold, adapting Renan, argued in *On the Study of Celtic Literature* (1866) that, because the sentimental Celts chafed 'against the despotism of fact', they were politically incompetent, although the race's 'feminine' sensibility could be a useful weapon (or celt) against Anglo-Saxon philistinism. When W.B. Yeats, in 'The Celtic Element in Literature' (1897), celebrated the Celtic movement as 'a new intoxication for the imagination of the world', he was thus unknowingly endorsing Arnold's estimate of the Celts' ineligibility for self-government. The same could be argued of the treatment of imagination in G.B. Shaw's *John Bull's Other Island* (1904), J.M. Synge's *The Playboy of the Western World* (1907), Sean O'Casey's *Juno and the Paycock* (1924) and even Brian Friel's *Translations* (1980).

Valuable work on connections between Celticism, literature and the Irish national character debate has appeared since Curtis, but because Irish literature, especially in the nineteenth century, was imbricated with travel journals, memoirs, journalism, religious tracts, histories, antiquarianism, and anthologies of myth and superstition, it is clear that a wealth of material remains to be analysed.

RICHARD HASLAM

censorship Books and periodicals are prohibited in Ireland under the Censorship of Publication Acts, 1929, 1946 and 1967. The censorship they authorize is moral instead of political, and unlike Great Britain, Ireland has never had official censorship of theatre. Under the 1929 Act books are banned indefinitely either because they are 'indecent or obscene' or because they advocate 'the unnatural prevention of conception or the procurement of abortion or miscarriage'. Periodicals are banned for varying lengths of time on these two counts and a third, that they devote undue space to crime.

With one exception, the grounds for banning have remained unchanged since 1929, and Ireland is unusual in prohibiting publications for indecency. The Health (Family Planning) Act, 1979, meant that books and periodicals could no longer be banned for advocating contraception. In 1946 an Appeal Board was introduced to which writers, editors, publishers or five members of the Oireachtas could appeal bannings; in fact, few appeals were lodged. In 1967 the period for which books could be prohibited as 'indecent or obscene' was reduced to 12 years; as a result, thousands of books were unbanned.

In Great Britain, as in most democratic countries, banning of publications occurs in the courts. In Ireland it is done by prior restraint, by a Censorship Board of five appointed by the minister for justice. The board is required to examine all books and periodicals submitted by customs officials or any member of the public; however, it is not required to give detailed explanations of why publications are banned. No qualifications are required of board members. Publishers and writers have never been represented on the board, which was dominated for years by the Roman Catholic church and the academic community.

Nationalism, in particular anti-Englishness, and pressure to mould Ireland into a preserve of Catholic morality lay behind the 1929 Act. The first book banned was Aldous Huxley's *Point Counterpoint*. It was followed by Claude McKay's *Home to Harlem*, Radclyffe Hall's *The Well of Loneliness*, which was also banned in Great Britain, and nine books by Marie Stopes and Margaret Sanger.

From 1930 to 1968 a severe literary censorship was imposed. It was supported both directly and indirectly by the Roman Catholic church and made possible by the enthusiasm of a militant public and the vague wording of the Acts, which fail to define obscenity and define indecent as 'suggestive of, or inciting to, sexual immorality or unnatural vice or likely in any other similar way to corrupt or deprave'. Under pressure to read large numbers of books, many of which were submitted with the so-called offensive passages underlined by members of lay Catholic organizations such as the Catholic Truth Society, the board frequently banned books on the basis of these passages even though it was required to consider 'the literary, artistic, scientific or historic merit of a book'. Between 1930 and 1968 major works of Continental literature and the bulk of modern British, American and Irish modern fiction were banned as 'indecent or obscene', including books by Thomas Mann, Marcel Proust, Jean-Paul Sartre, William Faulkner, Ernest Hemingway, Sinclair Lewis, John Updike, Graham Greene, Robert Graves and Lawrence Durrell.

Irish authors in particular were affected and most writers of fiction from this period had at least one book banned. Banned works included: *The House of Gold* by Liam O'Flaherty, *The Adventures of the Black Girl in Her Search for God* by George Bernard Shaw, *Watt* by Samuel Beckett, *Midsummer Night Madness* by Sean O'Faolain, *Dutch Interior* by Frank O'Connor, *Borstal Boy* by Brendan Behan, *Windfalls* by Sean O'Casey, *The Country Girls* by Edna O'Brien, *The Lonely Passion of Judith Hearne* by Brian Moore, and *The Land of Spices* by Kate O'Brien.

This censorship resulted in cultural isolation for both Irish writers and the Irish people, an isolation which was heightened by the unofficial censorship which followed in its wake. Writers of banned books became regarded as legitimate targets of harassment, the most notorious example being that of John McGahern, who lost his job as a National School teacher after *The Dark* was banned in 1965. Instead of protesting or appealing against censorship many writers left Ireland in anger, a notable exception being Sean O'Faolain, who became one of censorship's few vocal opponents. Bookshops and libraries often refused to stock unbanned books by writers whose other books had been prohibited. As a result, virtually an entire generation of Irish writing is still missing from the shelves of many city and county libraries.

An equally impressive array of classics has been banned for advocating abortion or contraception, including *Marriage and Morals* by Bertrand Russell, *Lady into Woman* by Vera Brittain and *The Second Sex* by Simone de Beauvoir. In its enthusiasm the Censorship Board has banned several books which support the Roman Catholic church's position on contraception, including *The Laws of Life* by Halliday Sutherland, which received the *permissu superiorum* of the archbishop of Westminster. A similar comedy of errors occurred in 1987 when the board banned a Thames and Hudson art book, *The Erotic Art of India*, which had been out of print for two years.

Most of the publications now prohibited are erotic or pornographic, but serious works of fiction and non-fiction, sex education books and medically valuable sex guides are still being banned. For example, books by Angela Carter, Monique Wittig and Georges Bataille are now prohibited. In 1987 *The Joy of Sex* by Alex Comfort was banned, apparently on feminist grounds, but that ban has been successfully appealed. The Irish social taboo on homosexuality is still being reflected in the decisions of the Censorship Board, which banned the children's book *Jenny Lives with Eric and Martin* in 1990.

Reading

Adams, Michael, *Censorship: The Irish Experience* (Dublin: Scepter, 1968).

Brown, Terence, *Ireland: A Social and Cultural History, 1922–1985* (London: Fontana, 1987).

Carlson, Julia, *Banned in Ireland* (London: Routledge, 1990).

Register of Prohibited Publications (Dublin: Stationery Office, 1931–85).

Woodman, Kieran, *Media Control in Ireland, 1923–1983* (Galway: Officina Typographica, 1985).

JULIA CARLSON

Centlivre, Susanah (1667–1723) Playwright. Born County Tyrone. At 15, Centlivre ran away to England to seek her fortune. Befriended by Arthur Hammond, she worked in disguise as his valet at Cambridge University, before leaving for London with letters of introduction.

Widowed twice in quick succession, she began writing for the stage, securing the production of her first play, *The Perjured Husband*, by agreeing to play the heroine. The play was attended by Queen Anne's chef, Joseph Centlivre, whom she married.

She wrote 18 plays, including the comedies *The Wonder a Woman Keeps a Secret* (1714) and *A Bold Strike for a Wife* (1718).

RACHEL FURMSTON

Chambers, John (1754–1837) Printer and United Irishman. Son of John, a wine merchant, and Elinor Carter, John Chambers was born in Dublin and died in New York, 8 February. He was apprenticed in 1767 to Oliver Nelson, printer to the City, and in 1780 married Christian Fitzsimon, a Catholic.

In his professional life he was primarily a printer working for others, but he also published in his own name, chiefly in the field of politics. He showed initiative and energy in both printing and editing. An early coup was the reprinting, with William Drennan's pleased permission, of *Letters of Orellana* (1785), and he extensively enlarged the section on Ireland in his reprint of Guthrie's *Modern Geography* (1789), begging authoritative contributions from Charles O'Conor and Drennan amongst others. In his illustrated edition of *Don Quixote* (1796) he made every effort to produce a well-designed and finely printed book.

Chambers was a foundation, and very active, member of the Dublin Society of United Irishmen. He was master of his guild (1793–4), and so supervised the first admission to freedom of Catholics. In the revived United Irishmen in 1797 the spy McNally said he headed 'a committee of fifteen – all men of letters or opulence'. In 1798 as one of the Executive Directory he was banished by Act of Parliament, but then imprisoned for four years in Scotland. After some time in France he settled in 1805 in New York where, with his elder son, he opened a stationery business.

Reading

Pollard, M., 'John Chambers', *Irish Book*, 3 (1964).

M. POLLARD

Chappell, William (1582–1649) Scholar and bishop. Born 10 December at Lexington, Nottinghamshire, Chappell went to Christ's College, Cambridge, where he became a long-serving fellow in 1607. After an early career as a respected teacher, with, if anything, a Puritan reputation, he became in the 1630s closely associated with Archbishop Laud and Lord Deputy Wentworth and their efforts to reform the Irish church and root out Puritanism and non-conformity, serving as provost of Trinity 1634–40 and bishop of Cork and Ross from 1638. Threatened with impeachment by the Parliament in 1641, Chappell was allowed to retire to England after the Rebellion.

Reading

Biographia Britannica, 2nd edn (London: 1784), vol. iii.

Peck, F., *Desiderata curiosa*, 2 vols (London: 1732–5), vol. ii.

ALAN FORD

charter schools Elementary schools for the children of the poor (charity schools), teaching them to read and write, and with a marked emphasis on religious instruction, were a common phenomenon in eighteenth-century Europe. The Church of Ireland saw a particular need for such schools to make the Irish poor loyal, industrious and Protestant.

In 1733 the Incorporated Society in Dublin for Promoting English Protestant Schools in Ireland was established by royal charter (hence 'charter schools'). The role of the society was to encourage clergy and landlords throughout the country to build and endow boarding schools for the poor, and to stipulate regulations in such matters as clothing, curriculum and diet. The children, mainly though not exclusively Catholic, were to be instructed in the Bible and the tenets of the established church, the boys trained in husbandry on the school lands, and the girls prepared for domestic work. Many schools employed the boys in flax-growing and the girls in spinning, and all schools were expected to be to some extent self-supporting. The masters (mistresses in the case of girls' schools) were paid salaries and per capita allowances towards maintaining the children. Each school was under the control of a local committee of gentry and clergy, one of whom was a catechist-visitor.

In the 1760s, to further the society's primary aim, a series of nurseries was set up, taking very young children. A policy of 'transplanting' children to schools remote from the influence of their parents and the Catholic clergy was operated.

The schools suffered grievously from the cupidity and ignorance of masters and mistresses and from neglect by the local committees. John Howard, the prison reformer, made a devastating report on the condition of the schools in 1788, as did a committee of the Irish House of Commons in 1791. Both were largely ignored by government, and the society's genuine efforts to reform were largely frustrated by local indifference, collusion between masters and the Dublin office, and a totally inadequate system of inspection and communications.

KENNETH MILNE

Chenevix, Richard (1774–1830) Chemist. Of Huguenot ancestry, Chenevix was probably born in Dublin, and died in Paris on 5 April 1830. He was educated at Trinity

College, Dublin. The first of his 28 papers to the Royal Society was submitted in 1801; he was elected Fellow that year and awarded their Copley medal in 1803 for his papers on chemistry. His claim to have discovered a new metal, palladium, is now disputed. He moved to France in 1804 and published nine chemical memoirs there. His plays, *Mantuan Revels* and *Henry the Seventh*, were published in London in 1812.

Reading

Chenevix, Richard, *Remarks on Chemical Nomenclature* (London: for J. Bell by Wilks and Taylor, 1802).

HENRY BOYLAN

Cheyne, John (1777–1836) Physician and medical writer. Cheyne was born in Leith, near Edinburgh, into a family with a long medical tradition. In 1795, he qualified at Edinburgh and became surgeon to a horse artillery regiment. He served at the battle of Vinegar Hill in Wexford in 1798. He studied pathology under Sir Charles Bell, specializing in acute and epidemic illnesses, and diseases of children, publishing two essays on this topic in 1801–2. In 1808 he wrote the first detailed description of hydrocephalus. In 1809, Cheyne returned to Dublin, and two years later was appointed physician to the Meath Hospital and, in 1813, professor of the practice of physic at the College of Surgeons, lecturing on military surgery. In 1815, he launched Dublin's first medical journal, *Dublin Hospital Reports*, and moved to the House of Industry Hospital, later the Richmond. He wrote a history of the fever epidemic of 1817, when the hospital treated over 700 patients. In 1818, he described the breathing pattern later known as Cheyne–Stokes Respiration. In 1825, he contracted a nervous fever, and never regained his health. He retired in 1835 to Sherington, Bucks, where he continued to write and treat the poor, until his death.

Reading

Cheyne, John, 'Autobiographical Sketch', *Dublin Journal of Medical Science*, ix (1836).

FRED LOWE

Chief Secretaryship 1690–1800 The Dublin Castle-based executive, which oversaw the administration of the kingdom of Ireland on behalf of the British crown, was dependent on a small troop of secretaries and clerks for the conduct of day-to-day business in the eighteenth century. The most important of these was the 'secretary to the lord lieutenant', or 'chief secretary', as he was better known. As the title implies, the chief secretary's primary function was to serve the lord lieutenant. For this reason, it was the norm throughout most of the eighteenth century for the lord lieutenant to choose his own chief secretary, and for the chief secretary to leave office on the resignation of the lord lieutenant.

Though the role, duties and influence of the chief secretary changed substantially in response to changing political circumstances in the period 1690–1800, much depended on the talent and application of the chief secretary himself. It was quite possible for a modestly talented or unambitious chief secretary to make little impression, particularly in the early eighteenth century when the opportunities for chief secretaries to excel were few. Indeed, quite a number of the incumbents of that office during that period seemed content to leave the business of policy making and political administration to others. They performed the administrative duties given to them by the lord lieutenant; and they maintained a basic level of communication with the secretary of state for the southern department in London, whom they were responsible for keeping informed on events in Ireland; but other than that they left little mark. They had little option but to leave the running of the House of Commons to managers and Undertakers, and the running of the Castle bureaucracy to the under-secretary. This era finally came to an end with the appointment of

Lord Townshend as lord lieutenent in 1767. Townshend reclaimed the initiative in managing the House of Commons for the House of Commons, and one consequence of this was the emergence of the chief secretaryship as one of the most important offices in the land. For this reason, it is both convenient and appropriate to identify two phases in the history of the chief secretaryship in the eighteenth century.

None of the chief secretaries that served in Ireland during the reigns of William and Mary and of Anne (1688–1714) made a significant impact. They were not all poor administrators – Sir Cyril Wyche (1676–82, 1692) was both talented and able – rather they had no defined role in the power struggle between the House of Commons and the lord lieutenant that was one of the main features of Irish parliamentary politics in the 1690s. Following Lord Sydney's failure to make the House of Commons toe the line in 1692, his successor, Lord Capel, concluded that it was preferable to work with rather than against Irish MPs, and when Parliament was reconvened in 1695, he ensured proceedings ran more smoothly by persuading a number of prominent MPs to work with him in securing a parliamentary majority by acceding to a number of their legislative demands and requests for preferment. Capel's successful recourse to management to secure a parliamentary majority offered lords lieutenant and Irish MPs many advantages, and it quickly became the norm following Lord Rochester's pattern-setting decision to reside in Ireland only when Parliament was meeting. As a result, successive chief secretaries received little opportunity to develop a detailed political knowledge of men and measures in Ireland, which was essential if the office was to develop into a position of influence. The chief secretary's main political function in the early eighteenth century was to act as the lord lieutenant's eyes and ears in the House of Commons rather than to lead the Castle phalanx. In truth, it is hard to imagine how such inexperienced chief

secretaries as Sir John Stanley (1713) or Martin Bladen (1715–16) would have managed if they had been given the opportunity, when the intervention of the experienced Whig George Doddington (1707–8) proved disruptive. Joseph Addison (1708–10, 1714–15) was shrewder. He simply left the business of parliamentary management to others. Indeed, only Edward Southwell and Charles Delafaye, who had some knowledge of Ireland, bucked this trend, but their contribution to parliamentary proceedings remained significantly less than that of parliamentary managers.

The essentially subordinate role defined for the Irish chief secretary in the early eighteenth century remained unchanged in subsequent decades. As the authority of individual parliamentary managers grew during the reign of George I (1714–27), the position of successive chief secretaries – Edward Webster (1717–20), Horatio Walpole (1720–1), Edward Hopkins (1721–4) and Thomas Clutterbuck (1722–30) – remained unchanged. The longer a chief secretary stayed in office, the more he learned and the more influential he could become, but though Walter Cary (1730–7), Viscount Duncannon (1741–5) and Edward Weston (1746–50) had longer than usual incumbencies, they were strictly confined in what they could accomplish by the facts that they spent most of the time out of Ireland and the Undertaker system was at its peak during these decades.

The attempt by the duke of Dorset (lord lieutenant 1750–5) to undermine the power of the Undertakers gave the chief secretaryship a higher profile in the early 1750s, but once Dorset and his chief secretary, Sir George Sackville, were removed, the office quickly reverted to its primarily administrative character of earlier decades. It is true that the more active part taken by the duke of Bedford (1757–61), Lord Halifax (1761–3) and the duke of Northumberland (1763–5) did enable their ambitious chief secretaries, Richard Rigby (1757–61) and William Gerard Hamilton (1761–64), to adopt a higher political profile. But for all that, the status of the office remained low, as the modest calibre and general inactivity of the five incumbents between 1764 and 1769 amply attest. However, they were the last such holders of the office.

The decision of George, Lord Townshend, to take on the Undertakers by choosing to reside in Ireland for the duration of his viceroyalty, and to oversee the transfer of the responsibility for managing the Irish House of Commons to Dublin Castle, had a radical impact on the chief secretaryship. Instead of his former peripheral role, the chief secretary was now thrust into the very centre of affairs and given the responsibility, formerly exercised by the Undertakers, of ensuring a majority for government bills in the House of Commons. The first new-style chief secretary was Sir George Macartney (1769–72). He reluctantly embraced the 'ministerial' responsibilities he was asked to shoulder, but once Townshend had broken the resistance of the Undertakers, the political duties Macartney disliked became the main responsibility of incumbents of that office. The implication of these changes was that future chief secretaries had to be capable parliamentarians as well as effective administrators, with the capacity to undertake the onerous burden of work this entailed. Indeed, those that were most successful were politicians first and administrators second. Macartney's successor, Sir John Blaquiere (1772–6), is one such example. He proved an adept parliamentarian, as did William Eden (1781–2) and Lord Castlereagh (1798–1800), though both took up office at difficult moments. By contrast, individuals like Sir Richard Heron (1777–81), Thomas Orde (1784–7) and Robert Hobart (1789–93), who lacked the self-confidence and diplomatic skills of Eden and Castelreagh, found the going much tougher. Heron was so ineffective, he simply foundered. Orde, by contrast, was effective, but he lacked the deftness of touch which would have enabled him to manage the House of Commons to greater effect.

The marked increase in the status of the Irish chief secretaryship in the 1770s and 1780s did not go unnoticed in Whitehall. By the mid-1780s, William Pitt deemed the office sufficiently important to recommend successors for Thomas Orde, while word had got round political circles just how onerous the position was. The fact that the last chief secretary before the Union (Lord Castlereagh) went on to become one of Britain's most influential foreign secretaries in the nineteenth century illustrates the vast improvement in the status and importance of the office since its incumbent became responsible for the management of the Irish House of Commons.

Reading

Bartlett, Thomas, *Macartney in Ireland 1768–72* (Belfast: Public Record Office of Northern Ireland, 1978).

Hayton, David, 'Ireland and the English ministers 1707–16', DPhil thesis, University of Oxford, 1975.

Johnston, E.M., *Great Britain and Ireland 1760–1800* (Edinburgh: Oliver and Boyd for the University Court of the University of St Andrews, 1963).

Kelly, J., 'The search for a commercial arrangement: Anglo-Irish politics in the 1780s', PhD thesis, University College, Dublin, 1985.

JAMES KELLY

Childers, Robert Erskine (1870–1922) Writer and Irish Republican. Born London, 25 June. Childers was the second son of Robert Caesar Childers, Oriental scholar, and Anna Mary, daughter of Thomas Johnson Barton, of Annamoe, County Wicklow. Educated at Haileybury and Cambridge, he was clerk in the House of Commons (1895–1910) and served in the Second Boer War (1899–1902). A skilled yachtsman, he wrote a classic spy novel in 1903, *The Riddle of the Sands*, about a German invasion of Britain. He converted to Irish Home Rule in 1910, influenced by his American wife, Molly, and wrote *The Framework of Home Rule* in 1911, which demanded for Ireland the status of the self-governing dominions. In 1914, he used his yacht, the *Asgard*, to smuggle German arms to the Irish Volunteers in Howth. The next month, solicited by the Admiralty, he joined the Royal Navy, flew in the Royal Navy Air Service, and emerged in 1918 with the rank of major, and the DSC. He returned to Ireland a vehement republican, believing that 'Capitalistic Imperialism...stands or falls by the subjugation or liberation of Ireland.' In 1921, he accompanied de Valera's party to London to meet Lloyd George, and formidably opposed the treaty, because it left Ireland 'under the shadow of Britain'. In the Civil War, he fought against the Free State, was captured, and was executed at the Beggar's Bush Barracks on 24 November 1922. He remains an enigmatic figure, accused by Griffith of being a double agent, and by Churchill of being 'a murderous renegade'. His son, Erskine, became president of Ireland.

FRED LOWE

children's literature The moral and didactic tone popular in late eighteenth-and nineteenth-century writing was, in Ireland, echoed by Maria Edgeworth (1767–1849) in collections of stories such as *Early Lessons* (1802), and by other contemporary authors. A long tradition of mythology and folklore inspired some writers to set their work in a fantasy landscape, like that in *Granny's Wonderful Chair and the Stories it Told* (1857) by Frances Browne (1816–79), *Stories for Children* (1898) by Oscar Wilde (1856–1900) and the *King of Ireland's Son* (1916) by Padraic Colum (1881–1972). Collections of folktales were made by W.B. Yeats (1856–1939), *Irish Fairy Tales* (1892); Ella Young (1865–1951), *Celtic Wonder Tales* (1910); Eileen O'Faolain (1902–88), *Irish Sagas and Folk-Tales* (1954); Michael Scott (1959–), *Irish Hero Tales* (1989).

Patricia Lynch (1898–1972), author of over 50 books, is best remembered for *The Turf-Cutter's Donkey* (1934). English-born Meta Mayne Reid (1905–) set many of her novels in Ulster, and the west of Ireland is the setting for Eilis Dillon's and Walter Macken's children's novels.

The late twentieth century has seen a considerable growth in interest in children's literature, including the founding of the Children's Literature Association of Ireland in 1987 and its publication *Children's Books in Ireland*, and the Irish Children's Books Trust in 1989. Two awards have been established, and this is all matched by an upsurge in writing and publishing. Martin Waddell/Catherine Sefton (1941–) has published almost 90 titles. Other writers making a mark include Margrit Cruickshank, Tom McCaughren, Cormac MacRaois, Michael Mullen, John Quinn and Marita Conlon-McKenna, who in 1991 won an International Reading Association Award for *Under the Hawthorn Tree*.

VALERIE COGHLAN

Cholera epidemics Cholera first appeared in Europe in 1830 and, within three years, spread across the Continent, causing widespread social disruption. Its source, usually water contaminated by infected excreta, was then unknown to medical science.

The first Irish cases were confirmed in Belfast in mid-March 1832, followed within days by cases in Dublin. The epidemic spread rapidly to the rest of the country, reaching its peak in the summer and autumn of 1832 but persisting until 1834. Local outbreaks caused considerable panic. Recorded deaths during 1832 and 1833 amounted to 25,378, almost certainly considerably short of the true figure.

Cholera struck again in late 1848 and early 1849 during the Famine, when there were 19,325 recorded deaths, again an unreliable figure. The last serious Irish outbreak occurred in July 1866, causing 2,501 deaths, mainly in Dublin. By then the scientific facts about the nature of cholera and its control were being established.

Reading

McCoy, Simon, 'Notes on malignant cholera as it appeared in Dublin', *Dublin Journal of Medical and Chemical Science*, 2 and 3 (1833).

Cameron, Charles, 'Asiatic cholera and its invasions of Europe', *Dublin Journal of Medical Science*, 76 (1883).

MacArthur, William P. 'Medical history of the famine', in R. Dudley Edwards and T. Desmond Williams (eds), *The Great Famine* (Dublin: Browne and Nolan, 1956).

Longmate, Norman, *King Cholera: The Biography of a Disease* (London: Hamilton, 1966).

JOSEPH ROBINS

The Christian Examiner and Church of Ireland Magazine Began publication in July 1825, 'conducted by members of the Established Church'. The founders were Rev. Caesaer Otway, evangelist and writer on the Irish scene, and Rev. Joseph Henderson Singer, later regius professor of divinity at Trinity College, Dublin, and bishop of Meath. The *Examiner* was the voice of the evangelical movement, aspiring 'to provide a defence and moderator for the Church of Ireland'. It saw itself as 'an antidote to the ribaldry' of the radical press, while simultaneously engaging in controversy with Rome. Theological issues predominated, but much space was given to the discussion of education and other matters of national concern, and to book reviews. It ceased publication in 1869.

KENNETH MILNE

Church of Ireland 1660–1760 The Church of Ireland, Protestant and episcopalian, was restored in 1660 because Irish Protestant landowners preferred its rigidities to the sectarian mêlée which was engulfing the country. The Irish church was quickly brought into closer conformity to the worship and doctrine of its English counterpart, first by staffing decrepit Englishmen into its bishoprics, and then with an Act of Uniformity in 1666. In the wake of Catholic resurgence in the 1680s and Presbyterian dynamism in the 1690s, and in recognition of its role as a vital agent of anglicization, its privileges were enlarged. In 1704 a Test Act allowed communicant members of the Church of Ireland, in theory at least, to monopolize office holding. Between 1697 and 1709 a series of penal laws hobbled the Catholic majority. Clergymen throughout the eighteenth century energetically and ingeniously defended the church's legal favours as the brittle barricade that alone contained popery, dissent, irreligion, libertinism and lawlessness. Parsons, indeed, proved some of the most eloquent and intemperate apologists of the Irish Protestant 'Ascendancy'.

A church which aspired to be comprehensive and national was inevitably enmeshed in politics and public affairs. Its four archbishops and 18 bishops sat in the House of Lords, where they often constituted a large part of the active membership. Their appointment and conduct mattered in the worlds of high politics and clientage that spanned the Irish Sea. Yet, at best, this church embraced 10 per cent of Ireland's inhabitants, and, ramshackle and penurious behind the grand structures, more nearly resembled a sect. This gap between aspiration and actuality, particularly striking to dignitaries newly arrived from England, bred a defensiveness which too often turned into aggression against critics and competitors. Churchmen inherited, or were taught, theological and racial attitudes which ranged from rigid predestinarian Calvinism through varied local hybrids to a lax Arminianism, and which then inspired the legal harassment or brisk evangelization of the Catholic Irish. A majority of the incumbents – estimated to number anything from 400 to 800 – serviced castle, garrison and mansion, and preached to the converted rather than to convert. A minority interested itself in instructing in the Gaelic language (a Gaelic translation of the Old Testament was first published in 1685 and one of the Book of Common Prayer in 1712), but this arduous activity hardly answered the expectations of mass conversions. Gaelic enthusiasts within the church instead contented themselves with recording and collecting antiquities and curiosities. Strenuous parsons also opened and ran English schools, and prodded the laity to better themselves and the poor Irish through moral and material improvements.

The clergy enjoyed stipends ranging from £30 to £2,200 p.a., and so encompassed the half-witted Trinity graduate who dwelt in the spire of his church at Taghmon in Meath and was handed an annual dole of £20 by his bishop, and the sleek bishops of Derry, one of whom justified his enjoyment of 'the elegant and splendid superfluities of life' by listing the work that was thereby created. The clergy, if not quaffing the restorative waters of Bath or bumpers of claret in Dublin, leavened the Irish provinces. As magistrates, they administered the law; as landowners and active farmers, pioneered new crops and techniques; and as social and intellectual gurus, introduced and popularized unfamiliar tastes and commodities. It was they who wrote and read many of the books printed in Ireland. The bishops, because of their political power, were often imported from England; the other ranks of the clergy, however, were largely staffed by men born and educated in Ireland. Shared origins, training and interests meant that the clergy began to assume some of the attributes of a profession. Also, since many were themselves sons of the clergy, the Church of Ireland clerisy resembled the hereditary clerical lineages of the medieval Gaelic church. Like those predecessors, the parsons generally depended on and deferred to their lay patrons and neighbours, who proved, at best, luke-warm supporters. Schemes to mend the fabric and fortunes of the church, and to augment the glebes and tithes on which incumbents lived, foundered on the material self-interest of the nominally Anglican laity. The Church of Ireland, modelled so slavishly on its sister church in England, when judged by the inappropriate English standards of a national church, invited a harsh verdict. But, concealed under the formal and grandiose armature, there lurked a flexible and vibrant sect.

T.C. BARNARD

Citizen Army, Irish Formed by the labour leader James Larkin in 1913 as a workers' militia, following the bitter and violent Dublin labour dispute of that year. Initially presented as a defence force to protect striking workers from assault, under the leadership of the socialist James Connolly it evolved into a more consciously revolutionary body. In competition for recruits with the much larger Irish Volunteers, the Citizen Army never had more than a few hundred members. However, Connolly was a resolute leader with some grasp of military affairs. His mind was fixed on revolution, and it was only with difficulty that the Military Council of the Irish Republican Brotherhood persuaded him to join them in rising at Easter 1916, rather than acting precipately and independently.

Unlike the Irish Volunteers, the Citizen Army was not reconstituted after the 1916 rebellion.

EUNAN O'HALPIN

civil rights movement The Northern Ireland Civil Rights Association (NICRA) was born in January 1967. It presented itself as a broad coalition of groups ranging from Republicans to Communists, straightforward libertarians and even some liberal unionists, concerned only with promoting civil rights on the American model, specifically on housing allocation, equal voting, an end to job discrimination and the repeal of the Special Powers Act. Gerry Adams later argued that republicans were the largest element, eschewing prominence for tactical reasons. Only four of the 12 original committee could be said to be concerned with civil rights *per se*. For the majority, 'civil rights' was a way of attacking unionism and 'Stormont', putting them morally on the defensive and achieving maximum political mobilization of all anti-unionist elements. The (disputed) decision in mid-1968 to go for street demonstrations was decisive, ensuring an almost inevitable loyalist impulse to counter-demonstrate, and drawing in the state with its policing role.

In the demonstration-packed autumn of 1968 the NICRA often took little official part beyond lending its name as 'sponsor'.

By then civil rights had become a broad, popular, pan-Catholic movement, though one taking on added bite by its claim to be non-sectarian. The Trotskyist-influenced student group People's Democracy took a lead role. Their Belfast–Derry march of New Year 1969, and the loyalist and RUC responses, greatly advanced sectarian polarization. Thenceforth the movement lost unity and coherence, events acquiring a momentum of their own and the initiative passing more unambiguously into the hands of radicals and Republicans. Paradoxically many of the claims of civil rights were conceded (in principle) in 1968–9; but by now the 'factory of grievances' was working overtime on fresh raw material.

Reading

Purdie, Bob, *Politics in the Streets* (Belfast: Blackstaff, 1990).

Bishop, Patrick and Mallie Eamonn, *The Provisional IRA* (London: Heinemann 1989).

W. HARVEY COX

Clarke, Austin (1896–1974) Poet, novelist, verse dramatist and radio broadcaster. Born Dublin. Clarke published 18 poetry volumes, from *The Vengeance of Fionn* (1917) to the posthumous *Collected Poems* (1974). The novels are *The Bright Temptation* (1932), *The Singing Men at Cashel* (1936) and *The Sun Dances at Easter* (1952). *Collected Plays* appeared in 1963. His autobiographical volumes are *Twice round the Black Church* (1962) and *A Penny in the Clouds* (1968).

As a middle-class Catholic the gifted Clarke studied Gaelic and English literature at University College, Dublin. His early adulthood was tumultuous; after rapidly earning his BA and MA, a year in a mental hospital after a nervous breakdown in 1919, a 10-day unconsummated marriage in 1920, and the loss of his University College lectureship in English (due to a registry office instead of church marriage), Clarke fled to England. His exile lasted 15 years while he worked as a journalist and book reviewer, within a second, contented marriage to Nora Walker. He returned to Dublin in 1937.

With the poet, Robert Farren, Clarke founded the Dublin Verse-Speaking Society in 1938, later the Lyric Theatre Company from 1944, to revive and perform poetic verse dramas. Clarke's verse plays were often based on medieval Irish stories. Influenced by Yeats, his early poetry explores Irish legends, literature and history, retelling the stories of early sages. *Pilgrimage* (1929) focuses on the peopling of Irish history, using the patterns and rhythms of Gaelic prosody. Subsequent work reflects a deepening fascination with medieval Ireland, rather than the Yeatsian 'Celtic Twilight'. *Night and Morning* (1938) finds the poet wrestling with his spiritual conscience in the torment of apostasy. The later poetry collections are mature and entertaining: *Ancient Lights* (1955); *Later Poems* (1961), containing a good deal of political satire; *Flight to Africa* (1963); *Mnemosyne Lay in Dust* (1966), a long poem based on Clarke's experiences as a mental patient. The novels, humorous prose romances, juxtapose Christian and natural moralities, satirizing their historical Irish settings and present social and political counterparts.

AMY L. FRIEDMAN

Clarke, Harry (1889–1931) Stained-glass artist and book illustrator. Born Dublin, 17 March, to Brigid (née MacGonigal) and Joshua, from a Leeds printing family. He was educated at nearby Belvedere College and trained in his father's stained-glass and church-decorating business before winning a scholarship to the Metropolitan School of Art in 1910. He died on 6 January at Coire, Switzerland, of tuberculosis.

Clarke was trained in the medievally inspired English Arts and Crafts tradition, and the Symbolist nature of his art found its fullest expression in stained glass. Iconographically rich, the jewel-like colours, sinuous lines, virtuoso technique and dramatic idiosyncrasies of his windows and cabinet panels are an extension of his better-known book illustrations.

Reading

Bowe, Nicola Gordon, 'The miniature stained glass panels of Harry Clarke', *Apollo*, CXV (February 1982).
——*Harry Clarke – His Graphic Art* (Mountrath: Dolmen Press, 1983).
——*The Life and Work of Harry Clarke* (Dublin: Irish Academic Press, 1989).

NICOLA GORDON BOWE

classicists and classical studies Ireland, situated beyond the fringe of the Greco-Roman world, has enjoyed little material prosperity and little stability. Yet, although it has not produced massive works of classical scholarship, its achievements in this area and its relatively great penetration by classical culture are worthy of note. While it seems unlikely that Agricola led an expedition against Ireland in the first century AD, the island nevertheless had definite contact with the north-west Roman world through the movements between Ireland and Roman Britain of Celtic tribes common to both countries, and through warlike forays, travel and trade. The evidence is to be found in Roman remains in Ireland – burials, coins, pieces of silver, sherds, and perhaps some common military-type ground works.

The earliest Latin writings to emerge from Ireland are the *Confession* and *Letter to the Soldiers of Coroticus* of St Patrick in the fifth century, which reflect, naturally, his upbringing in, probably, Britain. The earliest Irish-born writer in Latin was Columbanus, whose *Letters* in the early seventh century displayed acquaintance with Virgil, Horace and, possibly, Ovid, Juvenal and other Latin writers: this has been challenged recently, but still more recently confirmed. By the middle of the ninth century a galaxy of Irish writers, living in north-western Europe, exhibited a knowledge of Latin and Greek which for the time and place was quite remarkable. They manifested some competence not only in grammar and science, but also in Greek language and literature, especially as gleaned from the Greek Fathers of the church. It is sometimes contended that this unusual learning was amassed by them, not in Ireland, but on the Continent – but the phenomenon that when such knowledge was present in that area it was to be found in almost no circles but Irish ones can scarcely be reconciled with such a contention.

At any rate, Dicuil wrote an important work *de mensura orbis terrae* in the year 825, Sedulius Scottus at Liége and Martin and Johannes Erigena Scottus (to be carefully distinguished from John Duns Scotus – a Franciscan of the thirteenth century) at Laon, and other Irishmen towards the middle of the ninth century evinced a knowledge of Greek that was then quite exceptional. Eriugena especially revealed in his lengthy *Periphyseon* (*de divisione naturae*) an intimate knowledge and sympathy with Neoplatonic doctrine, especially in the form bequeathed through Greek Fathers by Proclus (410–85). While this *summa* of the study of all that is and all that is not attempts a profound synthesis of late Hellenic philosophy and Christian thought, it has suffered severely from condemnation by the Latin Christian church.

We have to wait until the foundation of a university (Trinity College) in Dublin in 1592 before we again encounter Irishmen displaying a professional, or something like professional, interest in the classics. J. Ussher not only inflicted on Erigena the pleonastic name of Scotus (*sic*) 'Irish' until the eleventh century) Erigena (*sic*, 'born-in-Ireland'), but also bequeathed to Trinity College two Erigenian manuscripts of some interest. H. Dodwell and Jonathan Swift showed a familier use of classics in the seventeenth century, and J.H. Newman made a stout defence of the classics in inaugurating the Catholic university, of which he was rector, towards the middle of the nineteenth century. But the real *floraison* of professional classicists came a century ago, when the historians J. Mahaffy, J.B. Bury and S. Dill gained international reputation. Bury, under the influence of the scientists of the University of Cambridge (where he migrated in 1902), proclaimed that history was a science – no more – and that the Roman empire declined because of a falling off in intellectual rather than moral qualities. He slightly modified his position on history as a science subsequently. Another impressive historian of the time was W. Ridgeway, of whom R.S. Conway (himself a fine scholar) wrote that 'posterity would surely rank him with Darwin and Mommsen' – this in spite of some audacious, not to say fallacious, views. Apart from these historians there were R.Y. Tyrrell, L. Purser (both associated with an important edition of Cicero's *Correspondence*), A. Palmer (praised – and censored – by A.E. Houseman as a textual critic) and J.G. Smyly, who worked in papyrology. Meanwhile the gifted G.M. Hopkins engaged himself with Greek metres.

In the twentieth century H. Browne carried on a campaign in favour of the enlivening of the classics, particularly in the provision of courses in 'classical civilization'. W.H. Parke and D.E.W. Wormell did an important study on the Delphic Oracle, a subject treated earlier by T. Dempsey. W.B. Stanford wrote perceptively on Greek poetic themes, and L. Bieler earned distinction in medieval studies. In 1968 a Committee for Greek and Latin Studies was founded in the Royal Irish Academy to support research at the academic level, notably in organizing the project of a dictionary of medieval Latin from Celtic sources.

The number of classical scholars born in Ireland who worked abroad is not negligible: one might confine oneself to mentioning only R.C. Jebb, E.R. Dodds and D'Arcy W. Thompson. And as we began this survey by including non-professional people like Ussher and Swift, so we may end by referring to two extraordinary works, the mighty *Aeneidea* of the medical doctor J. Henry, published in 1873–6, and the marvellous translation of Plotinus by Stephen MacKenna, who was born in Liverpool, but counted himself Irish.

Just as Erigena's work, while preserving general allegiance to Augustine, is in fact characterized by its deep preoccupation with solutions proposed by the Greek Fathers, so the Irish, said to be 'as Roman as they are Christian', have tended to be attracted by the Greek mentality. Indeed some have claimed an origin for Irishmen among the Greeks. Irish mythology seized upon and embellished Greek mythological themes at an earlier stage than happened elsewhere and with remarkable intensity. Irish orators fixed avidly upon the concept of liberty, as proclaimed imperishably by Demosthenes, with total conviction and dedication. And Platonic philosophy, particularly in its Neo-Platonic version, has had, and still apparently has, an almost uncanny appeal for the Irish. The unlikely, but for all that genuine, phenomenon of many 'peasants' not only being able to speak fluently a mangled, but still comprehensible, Latin, but also seeking their analogies in Greek history, literature and mythology, amazed travellers from abroad, who thus witnessed how real and intimate some classical themes became to a dispossessed population, through the 'hedge-schools' from the seventeenth to the early nineteenth century. Doubtless the Irish did some leg-pulling here (as they did with Giraldus Cambrensis); and doubtless they indulged in showing-off. But something remains, some humour and irony and exaggeration expressed frequently in terms that were classical. Whether they frequented 'hedge-school' or university, the Irish discovered in the Greeks and Romans, in some small way, some building of their souls.

Reading

Stanford, W.B., *Ireland and the Classical Tradition* (Dublin: Irish Academic Press, 1976).

JOHN J. O'MEARA

Clayton, Robert (1695–1758) Theologian. Born Dublin. Clayton was educated at Westminister School and Trinity College, Dublin, and inherited a good estate on the death of his father in 1728. He was appointed to the bishopric of Killala and Achonry in 1729, and was translated to Cork and Ross in 1735 and to Clogher in 1745. He wrote extensively on theological subjects. His *Essay on Spirit... with some remarks on the Athanasian and Nicene Creeds* (1751), led to a long controversy and lost him the archbishopric of Tuam. More controversy was caused by his *Vindication of the Histories of the Old and New Testaments*, which advocated many doctrines contrary to the Thirty-Nine Articles. The government felt compelled to order a prosecution and he was summoned to a meeting of prelates, but he was seized of a nervous fever and died on 26 February 1758.

Reading

Clayton, Robert, *A Vindication of the Histories of the Old and New Testaments* (Dublin: printed by George Faulkner, 1752–7).
A Journey from Grand Cairo to Mount Sinai and Back Again (London: Bowyer, 1753).

HENRY BOYLAN

Clerke, Agnes Mary (1842–1907) Musician and astronomer. Born Skibbereen; died London. The younger sister of the novelist Ellen Mary Clerke (*The Flying Dutchman*, 1881, and *The Flames of Fire*, 1902), Clerke was a fine musician and one of the few women to achieve fame as an astronomer. She began at the age of 15 to write her *Popular History of Astronomy during the 19th Century* (1885), which became a standard work. She lived in Italy before moving to London in 1877, where she continued to live with her sister until Ellen died in 1906. She also published *System of Stars* (1890) and *Problems in Astrophysics* (1903).

RACHEL FURMSTON

Cobbe, Frances Power (1822–1904) Philosopher, essayist and feminist philanthropist. Born Newbridge, County Kildare, 5 April; died Wales, 4 December. Power received an education which she found deplorably obsessed with 'accomplishments', and later compaigned for women's education. She travelled in Europe and the Middle East. Cobbe wrote extensively on the 'woman question', arguing that celibacy and female friendship offered women a better life than marriage, and campaigned to reform the property laws, for women to have access to university education, and, from the early 1870s on, for female suffrage. Her essays on women's rights include 'Criminals, Idiots, Women and Minors: Is the Classification Sound?' (1868) and 'Wife-Torture in England' (1878). Profoundly religious, Cobbe also wrote extensively on philosophy, religion and morals, and her work includes *Essay on the Theory of Intuitive Morals* (1855), *Darwinism in Morals* (1872) and *The Scientific Spirit of the Age* (1886), *The Duties of Women* (1881) combined her ethical and feminist concerns. Cobbe was also a prominent anti-vivisectionist and philanthropic educationalist.

GERALDINE MEANEY

Coffey, Brian (1905–95) Poet. Born Dun Laoghaire, County Dublin. Coffey was educated at University College, Dublin, in mathematics, physics and chemistry. During the 1930s he researched in Paris in physical chemistry and, under Jacques Maritain, philosophy. He met Samuel Beckett in London (1934) and contributed poetry and reviews to T.S. Eliot's journal, the *Criterion*. He continued to study philosophy (Aquinas). In 1938 he married Bridget Rosalind Baynes and met James Joyce.

Third Person was Coffey's first single volume published, an earlier volume of *Poems* (1930) being shared with his life-long friend Denis Devlin. During World War II, Coffey lived and worked in England before, on completion of his doctoral thesis in 1947, moving to Missouri, where he was appointed assistant professor of philosophy. He returned to England in 1954 after resigning from St Louis University. He published various poems in literary journals in Ireland, such as *University Review* and *Poetry Ireland*, and edited in 1963 for *University Review* the *Collected Poems* of Denis Devlin, subsequently published by Dolmen Press as a book. He also edited Devlin's *The Heavenly Foreigner* for Dolmen Press in 1967.

In 1972 Coffey retired from teaching and moved to Southampton. Coffey is mostly associated with the poets of the 1930s, such as Denis Devlin and Thomas MacGreevy, and forms what Beckett described as 'the nucleus of a living poetic' in the Ireland of that time. His poetry, often published with small presses and in art editions, has been collected in *Poems and Versions, 1929–1990* (1991). This challenging and experimental work is unique in Irish poetic practice. For that reason alone, Coffey's poetry poses difficulties to those readers and critics less accustomed to the Modernist approaches to writing.

Reading

Dawe, Gerald, 'An absence of influence: three Modernist poets', in Terence Brown and Nicholas Grene (eds), *Tradition and Influence in Anglo-Irish Poetry* (London: Macmillan, 1989).

Mays, J.C.C., 'Introductory Essay', *Irish University Review*, 5, no. 1 (Spring 1975).

Smith, Stan, 'On other grounds: the poetry of Brian Coffey', Donglas Dunn (ed.), in *Two Decades of Irish Writing* (Manchester: Caracanet, 1975).

GERALD DAWE

Cogan, Philip (1748–1833) Pianist, organist, composer. Born Cork (?); died Dublin. A chorister at St Finbar's Cathedral Cork as a child, Cogan later moved to Dublin, where he was organist of St Patrick's Cathedral from 1780 to 1810. Although he was reputedly a Doctor of Music, there is no evidence to support this claim. Cogan enjoyed a distinguished reputation as a pianist and composer. As a teacher his pupils included Michael Kelly and Thomas Moore. He helped found the Irish Musical Fund Society and performed regularly in Dublin. His compositions include two piano concertos

and many solo sonatas and arrangements. Although he is known to have composed for the stage, only some isolated songs survive.

BARRA BOYDELL

Cole, Sir William (d. 1653) Ulster planter and first provost of Enniskillen. As an Undertaker in the plantation Cole received a grant of 1,000 acres in Dromskeagh, County Fermanagh, in 1611. He was a noted Puritan member of the Irish Parliament, and was commissioned as a colonel of 500 foot at the outbreak of the 1641 rebellion. In fact he was one of the first to notify the government of the Ulster rising. In 1644 Sir Frederick Hamilton accused Cole of withholding information regarding the 1641 rising from the government. Though Cole was acquitted of the charges, the various documents produced during the case were published in 1645.

Reading

Fitzpatrick, Brendan, *Seventeenth-Century Ireland: The War of Religions* (Dublin: Gill and Macmillan, 1988).

BRIAN DONOVAN

Coleman, James (1941–) Artist. Born Ballaghadereen, County Roscommon. Coleman studied art in Paris, London, Dublin and Milan and currently lives and works in the latter two cities. He had his first individual exhibition at the Molesworth Gallery, Dublin, in 1965 and has since gone on to exhibit in Ireland, England, Europe and the United States. Coleman's work is notable for his use of a variety of media forms as a way of interpeting text and image. He has attracted particular attention with his use of slide projection, as in *Connemara Landscape* (1980). He has also exploited tape-slide, film, video and performance, using actors in order to recreate tableaux such as *So Different... and Yet* (1981) and *Living and Presumed Dead* (1983–5), where the viewer/audience is invited to take part in the interpretative act.

HELEN MCCURDY

Coleman, Michael (1891–1945) Fiddle player. Born County Sligo. Coleman emigrated to America in 1914. In the 1920s the burgeoning American recording industry went to the thriving Irish dance scene in the American cities, to make recordings for the 'ethnic' music market. Coleman, with other south Sligo fiddle players, like Paddy Killoran and James Morrison, made recordings of Irish dance music, and great numbers of these records were sent back to Ireland by Irish emigrants.

The records show Coleman to be a confident and innovative artist, though perhaps ill served by his piano accompanists. Exactly how innovative he was is now hard to say. Coleman can be understood sociologically. In another musical tradition, the New Orleans trumpeter Louis Armstrong went to Chicago, where he was credited with originality and ability to improvize, when he was in fact playing material common in his home town. In the same way Coleman and his peers seem to have drawn on the common storehouse of the local fiddlers, at home in Sligo.

But the records brought the 'Sligo fiddle style', jaunty, flamboyant, highly ornamented, to all parts of Ireland: other local styles and traditions were abandoned. It has been suggested that the records brought with them the prestige of America and of 'modernity'. One player has told how, anticipating the techniques of the ethno-musicologist, he would slow down the rotating disc with his finger, so that he could catch all the detail of Coleman's ornamentation. These records, 'cultural remittances', thus had an extraordinary effect on Irish music within Ireland. They shaped the course of Irish music for the next 50 years, and they contributed to the homogenization of Irish music, but they also indicated the ways that Irish music would find a home within the diaspora, and within the urban world, and survive.

Reading

McCullough, Lawrence, 'Michael Coleman, traditional fiddler', *Eire-Ireland*, 10, no. 1 (1975).

O'Connor, Nuala, *Bringing It All Back Home: The Influence of Irish Music* (London: BBC Books, 1991).
Smith, Graeme, 'My love is in America: emigration and Irish music', in Patrick O'Sullivan (ed.), *The Creative Migrant*, vol. 3 of *The Irish World Wide: History, Heritage, Identity* (London: Leicester University Press, 1994).

PATRICK O'SULLIVAN

Colleges on the Continent For medieval Gaelic literati, the cultivation of learning had been a full-time, professional, all-engrossing calling, under the patronage of powerful local lords. As the campaigns under Henry VIII and Elizabeth broke this clannish social order, many of the intelligentsia turned to holy orders and sought shelter in the church. Most of them gravitated to the Franciscan Order, as opposed to those urban-based Irish recusants of Old English stock, who tended to favour the Jesuit order. (The Dominican Order received an influx of members from both Irish communities.)

Monastic colleges for exiled Irish recusants sprung up all over Europe – the Old English tending to favour France, the Gaelic ones predominantly in Spain. Between 1580 and 1630, 'Irish colleges' were established in Paris, Salamanca, Lisbon, Douai, Seville, Rouen, Bordeaux, Louvain, Rome, Madrid and Prague. Later in the seventeenth century, the establishment of Irish colleges tapered off.

The direct political importance of the exiled clergy within Irish politics was strongest during the Confederation of Kilkenny; but throughout the eighteenth century, while the Penal Laws prohibited Catholic clerical activity and organization within Ireland, many Continental colleges retained an important function. The most important were Paris, Salamanca, Louvain and Rome.

The Irish colleges (that is, the Franciscan ones) were important in the Counter-Reformation and in the revival of Scotistic theology (Duns Scotus being considered a fellow Irishman, through an erroneous confusion with Scotus Erigena). Most importantly, however, the Irish Franciscans were instrumental in committing native bardic lore to paper – be it as part of recusant propaganda, as part of hagiographical enterprises, or out of vestigial bardic chauvinism. The famous *Annals of the Four Masters* are only the best-known instance of this enterprise. (Geoffrey Keating, too, had been ordained on the Continent.) The exile of Irish learning into the monastic colleges on the Continent meant that Gaelic learning could disseminate beyond, and thus ultimately outlast, its traditional clannish environment.

Reading

Bellesheim, Alphons, *Geschichte der katholischen Kirche in Irland von der Einführung des Christenthums bis auf die Gegenwart*, 3 vols (Mainz: 1890–1).

Henchy, Monica, 'The Irish colleges in Spain', *Eire-Ireland*, 24 (1989), pp. 11–27.

Leersen, Joep, *Mere Irish and Fior-Ghael* (Amsterdam, and Philadelphia: John Benjamins, 1986).

O Cléirigh, Tomás, *Aodh Mac Aingil agus an Scoil nua-Ghaedhilge i Lobháin* (Dublin: Oifig an tSoláthair, 1936).

JOEP LEERSSEN

Collins, Michael (1890–1922) Soldier and statesman. Born West Cork, near the small town of Clonakilty. Collins's family farmed there at Sam's Cross, and were linked closely by dense ties of kinship with the farming and shopkeeping society of the area. He had five sisters and two brothers and was the youngest of the family. Inevitably, he was reared almost as much by his sisters as by his parents. His mother was 35 when he was born, and, in a not uncommon pattern of the society and of the time, his father was 75, having been born in 1815, the year of Waterloo.

Old Michael was an impressive figure intellectually, mainly self-taught, as was common, and with much knowledge of local history and genealogy as well as nationalist historiography, and also some grasp of the classical languages and French. Michael's parents were bilingual in Gaelic and English. As was also common in Munster at the time, the parents did not pass the Irish language on to the children, but used it among themselves to ensure that the children did not know what they were saying. Many revolutionaries of the period reported themselves as being the first generation to be denied the Gaelic side of their heritage because of a fixed belief that English was the language of the modern world whereas Irish was the language of backwardness and defeat. Collins, like many others, came to regret this and strove to recapture the lost world of the Irish language in young adulthood. He often remarked that he wished to retire early from politics and learn the language properly in the Gaeltacht.

However, through the English language, Michael imbibed a vision of Irish history that was very much part of the folk culture of the area. The collective memory of the Collins family certainly stretched back to the end of the previous century and contained vivid accounts of the 1798 insurrection, O'Connell, the tithe war, the Famine, the Fenian movement and the Land War. Michael rapidly accepted rather uncritically a conventional view of Irish history as being a struggle between two castes or even civilizations, one English, Protestant and powerful, the other Catholic, Irish and dispossessed. The great age-gap between Michael and his father was not as unusual in Irish rural propertied society as it might have been elsewhere; half-century gaps between parents and children were quite common. This 'long-generation' syndrome assisted in the general extraordinary *immobilisme* of Irish political culture; collective memories were long.

The intense nationalism of the Collins family was given further depth by a local schoolteacher called Lyons whose powerful influence on his personal ideological development Collins later acknowledged. In this, he was again typical; many IRA and Sinn Féin leaders owed their political formation to national schoolmasters of that kind.

Collins, then, inherited a newly articulated version of an old political culture, but, like many others, he seems to have put together an extremist or aggressively activist version of the culture while outside Ireland. It was in London, where he went at age 15 as a boy clerk in the Post Office Savings Bank, that he discovered the Gaelic League and became an enthusiastic promoter of Gaelic games. He loudly supported the 'ban' which forbade Gaelic and hurling players to play soccer, and to the end of his life he held that England's true conquest of Ireland was by peaceful means, economic encroachment and cultural invasion being far more effective than any military conquest or formal political overlordship. It may have been this conviction that made him willing to accept the Treaty in 1921; possibly, had he lived, he would have been as enthusiastic a constructor of cultural and economic iron curtains as his great rival, Éamon de Valera.

He was not, however, untouched by political ideas outside the little world of the Irish-Irelanders. He read the *Leader*, *Sinn Féin*, *United Irishman* and *An Claidheamh Soluis*, like everyone else in Gaelic League circles, but he also read H.G. Wells, George Bernard Shaw (whom he greatly admired), Joseph Conrad, George Meredith and other, mainly 'progressive', mainline writers of the period. Interestingly, he liked Thomas Hardy, who was documenting a dying rural society not altogether unlike that from which Michael had come, and which he seems to have dreamed of preserving and revivifying, like so many other young Leaguers.

Collins soon joined the Irish Republican Brotherhood (IRB) in London, a logical step for someone like him, already quite the young nationalist firebrand. His administrative ability and energy soon got recognition and he became a conspicuous figure in the secret society in England, his growing expertise in financial matters helping his underground political career. His overground career also went well, and he soon moved from the Post Office to a stockbrocking firm. The preparations for 1916, however, caused Seán Mac Diarmada to summon him back to Dublin at the beginning of the year. He played a very

subordinate part during the Rising, and deeply disagreed with the way in which the revolutionaries ran the battle.

Internment gave Michael his chance, and he quickly showed his talent for building large networks of friends and allies, networks which often were known in their entirety only to him. His intelligence system, or rather *systems*, built up during and after internment, were based not only on the IRB, but on networks involving sailors on the Irish Sea, Irish America, the 'West Cork Mafia' which was so conspicuous in the independence movement, the Dáil government, the IRA, sets of relatives, girlfriends and policemen along with others lost to the historical record.

His ability to penetrate the bumbling British governmental structure in Ireland is proverbial, and was very great; at one stage he expressed bewilderment that his apparently spectacularly incompetent British opponents in Dublin had ever managed to put together an empire. He became adept at the surgical strike, having British secret agents and key officials assassinated before they could penetrate his organization. He also had a vengeful side, and had several police officers killed for overenthusiastic performance of their duties or for beating up his comrades. However, he also had a merciful side to his character, once saving a young man from possible exile for making a girl pregnant. His very organizational brilliance made him many enemies. According to de Valera and other observers, Cathal Brugha envied Collins, and was able to lead a faction in the Dáil leadership against him, its most prominent members being Austin Stack and J.J. O'Kelly. This appears to have had the ironic effect of making Collins strike up an apparently unlikely alliance with Arthur Griffith, and seems also to have made him see the limitations to a purist nationalist stance.

De Valera and Collins did not get on very well, being completely different kinds of people. Collins was impatient with de Valera's endless logic-chopping and pedantry, and de Valera seems to have seen Collins as a possibly unprincipled plotter who was using the IRB to take over the movement. De Valera, curiously, refused to go to London to negotiate with Lloyd George, and insisted that Collins go instead. Interestingly, Collins had already been spotted by the British as the Irish leader most likely to do business with them, as he appeared to lack the quasi-religious rigidity of many of his colleagues. Adventurer figures like Alfred Cope and F.E. Smith took to him immediately. Also, Collins knew England well, and had a certain respect for the British elite and even for the empire's future possibilities as a commonwealth of nations. Most of all, perhaps, he had a genius for practical argument and was free of a certain Irish Catholic obsession with the names of things as distinct from the things themselves.

Under the Treaty, Collins busied himself with forming a regular Irish army to replace the territorial, guerrilla IRA in December 1921. It was this that seems to have triggered de Valera's rejection, not only of the Treaty, but of the entire representative democratic political order which was emerging under the leadership of Griffith, Collins, Mulcahy, Cosgrave and O'Higgins. The establishment of a professional Irish army meant the dethronement of the IRA, and the local guerrilla chieftains' control of much of the Second Dáil would disappear if a genuinely competitive election were held; nomenclature apart, the power structure of the revolutionary Republic was going to be transformed decisively to the advantage of the Treatyites. De Valera termed the entire process a mutiny, and proceeded to ratify a mutiny against the new state and army himself.

Collins spent the next seven months desperately trying to keep together a movement which was turning into several movements and a state apparatus: the new Free State, with its army, civil service and police cobbled together from British and Republican elements. On the other side were the Sinn Féin party, the anti-Treaty IRA, and de Valera, almost a party in himself because of his charismatic status. Collins was also trying to

negotiate with the Unionists while supplying the six-county IRA with weapons to defend the Catholics against Orange pogroms and assuring the British that he was being faithful to a Treaty which he did not really like. Eventually the obduracy of the IRA and the conviction of Griffith and the rest of the Cabinet that what they saw as a mutiny should be put down made Collins agree to the attack on the Four Courts. He became commander-in-chief of the new army, and travelled to Cork to negotiate with the leaders of the Republican forces, hoping to stop the Civil War. He was killed by a chance shot from ambush at Béal na Bláth, County Cork, on 22 August 1922.

Michael Collins was not quite 32 when he was killed, which is one of the reasons why he has become a legendary figure. His political career was starting rather than ending, and part of Collins's fascination for posterity was his everyday character; he was very much a child of his generation and did not have political or social views which made him intellectually distinctive, unlike, for example, Arthur Griffith, Patrick Pearse or James Connolly. He was not even physically distinctive, being conventionally handsome, middle-sized and well-built, a fact that served as a disguise during the Troubles. He was 'one of the boys' and attractive to women. His associates, incidentally, were convinced that his love affair with Kitty Kiernan would not have lasted, another speculation which can never be substantiated. The male peer group was important to him, he was fond of horseplay and convivial drinking, he was resourceful, intelligent and, on occasion, utterly ruthless. These qualities were combined with a sentimental streak.

He grew out of much of his earlier ideological fanaticism, and was contemptuous of those of his colleagues who combined practical incapacity with political purism. He was capable of killing, but came to be a firm believer in electoral democracy and the subordination of the military wing of the movement to civilian political leaders. In this he differed from comrades like Rory O'Connor and Liam Lynch. Had he survived, the pro-Treaty group might have put down deeper popular roots in Irish political culture than it in fact did. As it was, de Valera inherited his opponent's political estate.

TOM GARVIN

Collins, Patrick (1911–94) Painter. Collins became a full-time painter in the 1940s. He received the Guggenheim National Section Award for Ireland in 1958. He first exhibited with the Royal Hibernian Academy in 1962 and periodically thereafter. He worked mainly in Dublin apart from a period in France in the 1970s, which helped to temper a leaning towards Romanticism in his work. His paintings are mostly landscape in character with a tendency towards abstraction, and a two-dimensional emphasis which rejects spatial illusionism. They are steeped in a poetic identification with nature and with the Irish past. His lyrical, allusive ('Celtic') painting may be seen as an attempted visual counterpart of the work of, for example, W.B. Yeats – though political events of recent decades have tended to problematize the Romantic, 'naturist' tradition in Irish culture. He exhibited with the Tom Caldwell Galleries. A major retrospective of his work was organized by the Arts Council in Dublin, Cork and Belfast in 1982. He was a member of Aosdána and widely regarded as one of Ireland's leading artists.

Reading

Ruane, Frances, *Patrick Collins* (Dublin: An Chomhairle Ealaíon/Arts Council, 1982).

PAUL O'BRIEN

colonial nationalism The pre-Union ideology which advanced Irish, as opposed to English, constitutional and economic interests while maintaining the prerogatives of the country's Protestant gentry and nobility. Inspired by Molyneux, Swift and Berkeley, the movement gained momentum in the years

1760–90 with figureheads such as Flood and Grattan.

The term 'colonial nationalism' (rather than the more widespread 'patriotism') is used mainly by the Trinity College school of historiography – thus by Simms, who coined the term in 1976, and in the *New History of Ireland*; its phraseology helps to legitimize the Anglo-Irish 'Ascendancy' tradition (treated with suspicion by traditional Gaelocentric historians) as part of the national Irish past. None of the 'colonial nationalists' would have called himself either a colonial or a nationalist. However, the term is more precise than the traditional appellation of 'patriotism', which is of doubtful historiographical value since it also has been, and still is, used in the loose sense of 'love of one's fatherland'. Moreover, 'colonial nationalism' brings out the structural parallels with, for instance, the similar movement which in 1776 led to the declaration of independence of the American colonies. However, unlike the American nationalists, the Irish members of the Patriot movement on the whole advocated regional heteronomy within, rather than autonomous independence from, the British crown; and in this respect, the term is problematic. It anachronistically fixes on a devolutionist movement the appellation of the separatist ideology which subsequently supplanted it.

Reading

Simms, J.G., *Colonial Nationalism 1698–1776* (Cork: Mercier Press for the Cultural Relations Committee of Ireland, 1976).

JOEP LEERSSEN

colonization, theories of Theories of colonization, now frequently derided as cant, were cherished by educated people throughout Europe during the early modern centuries. All such theories proceeded from the assumption that colonial endeavours enjoyed divine approval because the apostles had been directed by Christ to preach his message to all nations. A secular justification for colonial enterprise was also readily available because it could be shown that the ancient Romans had succeeded in extending their civilization beyond its Mediterranean confines through a process of colonization. The corollary to this argument was that people who had not been so disciplined still endured in a condition which was neither Christian nor civil. Those peoples who were first encountered by Europeans during their navigational exploits of the fifteenth and sixteenth centuries obviously existed in such a condition, and it was accepted without dispute that Europeans had a moral responsibility to incorporate them within a Christian and civil order. Some of those who pondered the problem of how this imperative might be fulfilled developed a keen understanding of civil and religious norms, and this brought them to appreciate that there were many within Europe itself who did not conform to these norms. Peoples both within and on the eastern periphery of Europe who had not been subjected to Roman or Norman dominance had long been considered to fall short of these norms, but it was increasingly accepted that the great illiterate mass of the population in even the most civilized parts of Europe were both spiritually and culturally deficient.

Such considerations aroused Europeans to engage upon a renewed effort of reform, which would result in the consolidation of these newly defined Christian values within Europe itself, and in the creation of European-style commonwealths in those areas overseas that had recently come under European influence. Not all theorists were agreed upon how these objectives could be achieved, and opinion was sharply divided about the relative importance of force and persuasion in shaping this ideal world. All were agreed, however, that colonization would be one of the instruments employed, and there was general agreement about what that concept involved. The first necessary steps towards the erection of any colony were the forceful establishment of the authority of the colonizing power over the people to be reformed, and

the acquisition by the colonizers of substantial tracts of land in the area where they wished to settle. Most commentators fostered the optimistic notion that the indigenous population would welcome them, and that only obstinate political and religious leaders and fighting men would deny the social, material and spiritual superiority of the colonizing power. Similarly it was argued that the natives would part easily with their land either because they had more than they could usefully occupy or because they placed great store on what the colonizers offered in exchange for it. In the event of either of these expectations being disappointed, however, it was argued by theorists from all European societies that engaged in colonial exploits that they were fully justified in taking possession of their country by right of conquest.

Once control and possession were established the way would then be open for the erection of a model society by the colonizing power. Many theorists believed that this should be organized on military lines after the manner of the Romans, and all reserved a special position for Christian clergy within the colony. Thereafter, however, the settlers would be miners, artisans and agricultural workers, together with their families, who would exploit the natural resources of the colony. The immediate benefit from this endeavour would be the enrichment of the colonists and the enhancement of the economic position of the mother country that sponsored them. The ultimate objective was, however, the creation of a flourishing society which would absorb many of the native population within its confines and bring the remainder to become subservient to it in both cultural and economic terms.

This ideal was never achieved by anybody and much writing on colonization was devoted to explaining failures and shortfalls. Although frequently disappointed, the sponsors of colonization never despaired, and every reverse seemed to spur the theorists to more strident exhortation. National rivalries within Europe also added a new urgency to their cause, which became acute when the Continent was divided along religious lines following the partial success of the Protestant Reformation. At that point, the Spaniards and Portuguese had got a clear head start in the field of colonization over their northern European rivals. Spanish successes in central America and Peru were thought by many to explain their military and naval prowess, and it wrankled with many Dutch, French and English Protestants that Jesuits and friars should be so 'diligent to destroy souls' at a time when Protestant clergy did not have the opportunity to 'seek the tender lambs'. Some consoled themselves that the ill reputation gained by the Spaniards for this harsh treatment of the Indians would ensure their ultimate failure. For example, one English author, writing in 1609, took satisfaction in the fact that when Spain sent an expeditionary force to Ireland in 1601, ostensibly 'to free their nation from their bondage and tyrannous subjection and to restore Catholicism', it received scant support from the Irish population, who recognized the overtures made by its leader, Don Juan del Aguila, as but 'a plausible pretence, the least end of his thought'.

This reference to Ireland in a pamphlet essentially concerned with settlement in Virginia was unusual only to the extent that it was described as 'a noble civil kingdom where all (except a few renegades) were settled in the truth of religion, and lived by wholesome laws'. References to Ireland in pamphlet literature on colonization, and most especially those emanating from English or Protestant sources, were usually to the effect that Ireland was a wild barbaric land which was itself in need of colonization, and many English colonists and travellers in the New World used Irish practices and customs as a point of cultural reference when describing traits of American Indian life they had witnessed in various places stretching from Newfoundland to the Amazon basin. The Irish, by which was meant the Gaelic Irish, were thus categorized with Turks and Tartars, whose way of life was

also assumed to be typically primitive or barbaric. Such denigration of the Gaelic population of Ireland had its source in the compositions of Giraldus Cambrensis, who had described the incursions of the Anglo-Norman king Henry II into Ireland, and whose writings on the Irish assumed the status of a classic in European ethnographic literature of medieval times. The impressions, descriptions and arguments of Giraldus had been especially fostered during medieval times by the descendants of the medieval Anglo-Norman settlers, who by early modern times had become known as the Old English population in Ireland. The leaders of this community had historically identified themselves as the upholders of English and true Christian standards in Ireland, and had persistently called upon the government in England to further their efforts to complete the conquest of Ireland that had been partially implemented by the Anglo-Normans of the twelfth and thirteenth centuries. Some of these Old English proposals of the sixteenth century specifically favoured colonization as an instrument for reforming the areas still under the control of the Gaelic Irish, and several prominent members of the Old English population wished to become involved in each of the major plantations that were promoted by the English government in Ireland between 1550 and the 1630s.

These plantations or colonies (the words were interchangeable in the English language) in Ireland were first justified on the grounds that had been suggested by the Old English, and were sanctioned by the government in England only when it despaired of the cost of reforming Ireland by more moderate means and feared that the country would come under the influence of Continental foes. Soon, however, it became evident that the Old English were not suited to such colonial endeavours, because they remained firmly attached to Catholicism when the English state and society were becoming stridently Protestant. Many English-born officials in the Dublin government and most English proprietors insisted both that the Old English should be excluded from colonial settlements and that the areas under Old English control should themselves be subjected to plantation. These propositions were detailed in comprehensive works by such authors as Edmund Spenser, Sir John Davies, Sir John Temple, Arnold Boate and Sir William Petty, and echoed in scores of minor texts by obscure authors. They were justified initially on the grounds that all Catholic landowners were a potential threat to a Protestant state, but this pragmatic argument was supplemented by complex theorizing on how, over the passage of time, the Old English had degenerated from their erstwhile civility to the point where they were more desperately in need of reform than the Gaelic Irish.

These texts are of especial interest to our general understanding of theories of colonization because of the emphasis which was placed on degeneracy. This concept had been familiar to the ancestors of the Old English, who, during the later medieval centuries, had taken repeated measures to prevent some of their own borderers from lapsing to Gaelic ways as a consequence of intermarriage or fostering with the Gaelic Irish. Englishmen who led colonial expeditions into foreign parts were also familiar with the phenomenon of some of their followers deserting to the indigenous population and 'going native', and all who had anything to do with colonization recognized that the liberty associated with moving overseas could easily become licence. It was with a view to avoiding such slippage that advocates of colonization attached importance to the need for military discipline in a colonial situation. The English writings on Ireland broke new ground, however, when they contended that such degeneration would inevitably occur unless all traces of barbarism were stamped out by force, and a completely new order was erected in place of the old: this, they contended, had happened to the Old English, and this too would inevitably occur to themselves unless they were given full support and authority to

achieve a complete conquest of Ireland, which would open the way for a comprehensive programme of colonization. These texts were original also in their insistence that a people such as the Old English, who had become barbaric through a process of degeneration, made more formidable opponents than those who had always been uncivil.

The Old English contested these arguments of their Protestant opponents, but in doing so they never became principled opponents of colonization, or at least not until they were completely swept from power by the Cromwellian confiscation of the 1650s. On the contrary, they petitioned for their inclusion within all schemes of plantation that were implemented in Ireland before the 1640s, while, at the same time, Old English merchants from such towns as Dublin and Galway became involved in colonial ventures in the British West Indies. The Gaelic Irish would thus appear to have been the exclusive Irish victims of colonization in both theory and practice, but their response was also ambivalent. There were some who called for a united Catholic stand against what they identified as a Protestant onslaught. Most of these were priests trained in Continental seminaries, who could view events in Ireland from a Continental perspective. Those who remained in Ireland, whether landowners or members of the Gaelic learned classes, did what they could to escape the general cataclysm, and many accepted property within the colonial schemes that were being proceeded with in Ireland. Some also of Gaelic background looked further afield for colonial ventures, and the most amazing experience that can be documented is that of Bernard O'Brien, who became especially familiar with the American Indian tribes in the Amazon basin and successively negotiated with the English and Dutch governments, as well as with the Spanish and Portuguese monarchies, for the necessary support to establish an Irish colony in that torrid area. In each case he pointed to the advantages that would accrue to the government in question as well as to the

American Indians, but we can take it that he, like other theorists of colonization, hoped that the ultimate beneficiary would have been himself. The career of O'Brien is of interest, however, because it demonstrates the unique position of the Irish, who in both the theory and practice of colonization were simultaneously the colonizers and the colonized.

NICHOLAS CANNY

Colum, Padraic (1881–1972) and **Mary** (1884–1957) Writers. Padraic Colum was born in Longford on 8 December 1881 and died in Enfield, Connecticut, 11 January 1972. He started work as a railway clerk in Dublin. He wrote some of the Abbey Theatre's earliest plays and his first book of poems, *Wild Earth*, appeared in 1907. In 1912 he married Mary Maguire, who was born in Collooney, County Sligo, 13 June 1884 and died in New York 22 October 1957. In 1914 they moved to the USA, where they both became teachers of comparative literature at Columbia University, New York. Padraic wrote folk tales for the *New York Tribune*, and in 1923 the Hawaiian legislature commissioned him to make a survey of their native myths and folklore and edit them as stories for Hawaiian school children. His output was prodigious; in addition to plays, poetry and articles, he wrote 61 books. He was the last link with the early days of the Irish literary revival and his great age did not impair his mental vigour. Mary Colum became a well-known literary critic and with Padraic published *Our Friend James Joyce* in 1958.

Reading

Colum, Mary, *Life and the Dream* (London: Macmillan, 1947).
——*Legends of Hawaii*, (New Haven CT: Yale University Press, 1937).
——*Collected Poems* (New York: Devin Adair, 1953).
Colum, Padraic, *Thomas Muskerry* (Dublin: Maunsel, 1910).

HENRY BOYLAN

Commentarius Rinuccinianus The most comprehensive and detailed account of Ireland in the 1640s from the perspective of the clergy was the compilation now known as the *Commentarius Rinuccinianus*, although it was probably originally entitled *A Commentary on the Intrusion of the English Heresy into Ireland and its Progress and on the Catholic War which Began in the Year 1641 and was Waged for Some Years Following*. It was written in Florence between 1661 and 1666. The work falls into three parts. An introduction summarizes Irish history from 1170 to 1642, with particular reference to sixteenth-century religious conflicts. The main body of the work is a narrative account of events in Ireland from 1642 to 1654. A concluding section brings the narrative to 1666. The work has the merit of detailing the later history of the Irish faction, which the other main contemporary narratives by Richard Bellings, secretary to the Confederation, and the anonymous *Aphromisical Discoverer* do not chart in detail.

The *Commentarius* was written to vindicate the actions of Giovanni Battista Rinuccini, the papal nuncio in Ireland (1645–), Rinuccini had not been prepared to accept either the 1646 or the 1648 peace negotiated with the Duke of Ormond by the Old-English-dominated Confederation of Kilkenny. In both cases he excommunicated those prepared to accept the peace, including some clergy, and the Confederates appealed to Rome against Rinuccini. The issue of the excommunications was an important one for the Irish in Europe during the 1650s and 1660s.

The *Commentarius* was begun by the Longford-born Capuchin Richard O'Ferrall, who had supported Rinuccini in Ireland, in response to the pro-Ormond tract *Vindiciarum Catholicorum Iberniae*, published in Paris by Fr. John Callaghan in 1650. The second compiler was another Irish Capuchin, Robert O'Connell, who collaborated with O'Ferrall and completed the work after O'Ferrall's death in 1663. Unlike O'Ferrall, who had spent most of the 1640s in Galway,

O'Connell had not been in Ireland during the 1640s. Both scholars had access to transcripts of Rinuccini's working papers and correspondence contained in the *Nuncii Regestum* together with Rinuccini's private papers. Their original manuscript was not published but survived in the library of the Rinuccini family in Florence. It was later transferred to Milan, where it was destroyed in the bombing in 1943. This version was edited for the Irish Manuscripts Commission before its destruction.

Reading

Corish, P.J., 'Rinuccini's censure of 27 May 1648', *Irish Theological Quarterly* xviii (1951).
—— 'Two contemporary historians of the Confederation of Kilkenny', *Irish Historical Studies* viii (1953).
—— 'John Callaghan and the controversies among the Irish in Paris, 1648–54', *Irish Theological Quarterly* xxi (1954).
Kavanagh, Stanislaus (ed.), *Commentarius Rinuccinianus*, 6 vols (Dublin: Irish Manuscripts Commission, 1932–49).
Ninth Report of the Royal Commission on Historical Manuscripts (1883).

RAYMOND GILLESPIE

Commercial Propositions (1784–5). Devised by Prime Minister William Pitt in order to strengthen the Anglo-Irish connection following the concession of 'legislative independence' to the Irish Parliament in 1782. In essence a scheme to effect a commercial union between Britain and Ireland, the propositions excited intense opposition in Britain from political as well as commercial interests. Following amendments to meet these objections, Irish Patriots objected strenuously to the provision for legislative uniformity in commercial law as an unwarranted intrusion on the legislative authority of the Irish Parliament. Following a narrow victory on the issue in the Irish House of Commons on 13 August 1785, the propositions were withdrawn by Dublin Castle to prevent their being rejected.

Reading

Kelly, James, 'The search for a commercial arrangement: Anglo-Irish politics in the 1780s', PhD thesis, University College, Dublin, 1985.

JAMES KELLY

Composition of Connacht (1585–6) Often regarded as a curious aberration from the general Elizabethan policy of conquest and colonization, or as a temporary expedient in a disturbed province, the Composition of Connacht was in fact a conscious product of the fundamental Tudor aims in Ireland and, in its exceptionalism, a clear demonstration of the failure of those aims elsewhere.

A general term denoting a bargain, commutation or settlement, 'composition' was applied in sixteenth-century Ireland to a series of policies, of varying degrees of sophistication, proposed by the English government to reform the English army's abuse of the royal prerogative to take up supplies, and later to abolish 'coyne and livery' and other forms of extortion exacted by the Gaelic Irish and Anglo-Irish lords throughout the country.

The word appears first to have been used in this specific sense in the early 1560s, when it was reported that a number of English soldiers who had been billeted upon the farmers of the Pale by the Dublin government entered into private arrangements with their hosts under which they agreed to withdraw from the countrymen's houses to local inns in exchange for a fixed monthly payment. But the idea of developing 'composition' as a general scheme for the reform of all bastard feudal and extortionate practices in the island as a whole was first proposed in the early 1570s by Edmund Tremayne, sometime secretary to the Elizabethan viceroy, Sir Henry Sidney.

In a series of memoranda at this time, Tremayne argued that previous attempts to introduce the procedures and institutions of English law in provincial areas had failed because they had been imposed on an existing set of social and political relations (enforced by coyne and livery) which were strongly resistant to change. The only way to extend law was to dismantle this system, and the only way to dismantle the system short of outright war (an option dismissed by Tremayne as impracticable on grounds of uncertainty) was to gain control of it from within. By despatching a large army not to fight but to extort its own maintenance from the countryside, the crown would steadily persuade the provincial and their local juniors to agree to a compromise: a deal by which the army's exactions would be commuted to a much-reduced, fixed, annual sum on condition that the lords themselves entered into similar compositions with their own vassals.

Tremayne's proposals for the introduction of composition on a national basis formed the basis of the programmes for government submitted by Sir Henry Sidney and Sir John Perrot during their respective periods in office (1575–8, 1584–8). But in each case the concessions which the governors were required to make on attaining appointment, concerning costs, army size and timetabling, seriously undermined their ability to make the scheme work with equal effect throughout the provinces of Ireland. Both men encountered sharp resistance in Leinster, where the constitutional sensibilities of the English of the Pale proved impossible to overcome. Sidney's recall before he could finalize composition in Munster helped precipitate rebellion in the province (1579–83); Perrot's disgrace on the point of completing similar arrangements in Ulster was the principal cause of the major war that erupted in the north and spread throughout the country in the years between 1584 and 1603. But in Connacht composition under both men made progress.

Sidney's governor in the province, Sir Nicholas Malby, succeeded in the face of much opposition in establishing the first composition in Galway and Thomond in the late 1570s, which after Sidney's recall he enforced more or less as a personal rent until his death in 1584. But in the following year Lord Deputy Perrot introduced a more extensive and comprehensive scheme. Commissioners visited every shire, dividing each territory into 'quarters' (units of 120 acres) and drawing up detailed tripartite agreements between the crown, the great lords, and the freeholders and tenants of the area concerning the annual commuted taxes which were to be paid to the lords and the government.

In these introductory stages rapid progress was made and the agreements were put in force with little resistance. But there were from the outset serious inconsistencies and imperfections in the scheme, whose implications became critical once the initiating viceroy, Perrot, was dismissed from office, and the composition was allowed to develop independently of central government interference under the supervision of the provincial governor, Sir Richard Bingham. In the southern half of the province, the great earls of Clanrickard and Thomond were given special advantages both in relation to their own freeholders and tenants and in their exemption from composition payments to the crown. In the northern sector no great regional authorities were recognized but the agreements reached with some lesser lords were often generous, in cases artificially so, given the tenuous nature of their claims over the other residents in their territories. The tensions between lords and freeholders, between great lords and lesser lords, and between all groups and the crown which resulted from such discrepancies and inaccuracies in the initial agreements might have been resolved by arbitration and renegotiation. But in the wake of the loss of centralized control they became the source of much internal feuding and dissent, fanned and exploited by Bingham and his subordinates in their attempt to extract more advantageous terms for themselves under the composition.

Bingham's efforts to redesign the composition by force at first provoked rebellion in the north and later led others, dissatisfied with their lot elsewhere in the province, to give succour to or openly join with the rebels. In defeat many who had initially entered the composition had their lands confiscated and granted away to new settlers. But even more seriously, the disruption caused by Bingham's actions and the rebellion which followed from it derailed the promise made to several landholders at the beginning of the scheme to have their titles to property confirmed by royal patent.

The recognition of security of tenure for all involved had been inherent in the policy of composition from the beginning. But in the early seventeenth century, as English adventures were scouring Ireland in search of defective land titles on which to make claims, the failure to honour the undertaking implicit in the composition agreements acquired fateful significance. In 1615 King James authorized the confirmation of all titles under the composition by patent. But due to covert resistance by opponents of the plan in the Dublin administration (many of whom had much to lose by the securing of titles), the patents then drawn up were never formally enrolled in Chancery. Title under the composition remained, therefore, questionable, and in the late 1620s Dublin officials brazenly began drawing up proposals for the confiscation and plantation of composition lands. In 1636 the Connacht landholders' worst fears were realized when Lord Deputy Wentworth moved to find title for the crown in large parts hitherto considered bound by the composition. Local resistance was brusquely repressed, and the efforts of the earl of Clanrickard to defend his Galway interests by appeals at court proved futile. The obstacle then presented proved sufficient to delay a new plantation in Connacht until Wentworth's fall and the outbreak of the English Civil War. But by then the idea of composition was dead, and in the decades that followed the province was to be regarded not as an edifying example of peaceful social reconstruction, but as the dumping ground for the rest of Ireland's victims of war, dispossession and transplantation.

Reading

Brady, Ciaran, *The Chief Governors: The Rise and Fall of Reform Government in Tudor Ireland,* *1536–1588* (Cambridge: Cambridge University Press, 1994).

Cunningham, Bernadette, 'The composition of Connacht in the lordships of Clanrickard and Thomond', *Irish Historical Studies*, xxix (1984).

——'Natives and newcomers in Mayo, 1560–1603', in Gerard Moran and Raymond Gillespie (eds), *'A Various Country': Essays in Mayo history* (Westport CT: 1987).

Kearney, Hugh, *Strafford in Ireland: A Study in Absolutism, 1633–1641* (Manchester, Cambridge University Press, 1958).

O'Dowd, Mary, *Power, Politics and Land: Sligo 1568–1688* (Belfast: Institute of Irish Studies, University of Belfast, 1991).

CIARAN BRADY

conacre The name given a small plot of land hired for the purpose of raising a single crop of potatoes or oats. 'conacre' or 'cornacre' was a form of tenure, whereby the tenant-farmer offered the cornacre plot (from a rood to two acres) to the cottier-labourer for a period of 11 months. In the pre-Famine period, many types of landless people participated in the conacre system as a means of getting acess to land, such as artisans, linen weavers, bound cottiers and wage labourers.

Much of the academic debate over whether the Irish economy was commercialized or not at this period now tends to revolve around the conceptualization of these 'conacre' classes.

Reading

Beames, M. R., 'Cottiers and conacre in pre-famine Ireland', *Journal of Peasant Studies*, 2, no. 3 (April 1975).

Mokyr, Joel, *Why Ireland Starved: A Quantative and Analytical History of the Irish Economy, 1800–1850* (London: George Allen, and Unwin, 1983).

O'Neill, Kevin, *Family and Farm in Pre-Famine Ireland: The Parish of Killashandra* (London: University of Wisconsin Press, 1984).

EAMONN SLATER

Congested Districts Board Set up by Balfour's Land Purchase Act, 1891, to provide assistance in the congested districts. Those districts were those where the inhabitants were never very far from starvation: for administrative purposes, they were originally defined as areas where the PLV was less than £1.10s.0d. per inhabitant.

The board's activities fell into four main categories: promotion of native crafts; the purchase of land to facilitate amalgamation of smallholdings in order to make them viable; the resettlement of tenants on to those holdings; instruction in modern farming methods to encourage the development of products other than the potato.

When the board was set up, it had jurisdiction over 3.6 million acres in parts of counties Donegal, Leitrim, Sligo, Mayo, Roscommon, Galway, Kerry and Cork, with a population of 500,000 people. Its initial funding consisted of the annual interest of the Irish Church Surplus Fund, which amounted to £41,250 per annum. Its jurisdiction, areas of activity and income grew over time. By the time the Board was dissolved in 1923, it had spent £9 million on purchasing land under a succession of Land Acts. It had spent £2.25 million on improving land, on dwellings, on farm buildings, drainage, fences and roads. It had taken over 1,000 estates and created or improved 60,000 holdings. The board was involved also in the promotion of fisheries, constructing piers, harbours and slips.

Although Balfour's objective was represented by some as an attempt to 'kill Home Rule with kindness', the board was held in high regard, its work being described by Michael Davitt as 'enlightened State socialism'. Its functions, together with those of the Land Commission, were abolished in 1923 by the Irish Land Commission.

Reading

Curtis, L.P., Jr, *Coercion and Conciliation in Ireland 1880–1892: A Story in Conservative Unionism* (Princeton NJ: Princeton University Press, 1963).
Shannon, Catherine B., *Arthur J. Balfour and Ireland 1874–1922* (Washington DC: Catholic University of America Press, 1988).

ALAN DUKES

Congregationalism Although Congregationalists (or Independents) came to Ireland with Cromwell, the oldest existing congregations date from the nineteenth-century evangelical revival, in which Congregationalists figured prominently. In 1992 the Congregational Union numbered 27 congregations, all but one in Ulster; 2,081 members were the heart of a broader Congregationalist community of about 6,000.

JOSEPH LIECHTY

Congreve, William (1670–1729) Playwright. Born Yorkshire; died London. Generally regarded as an Irish playwright because his formative years were spent at Kilkenny College and Trinity College, Dublin, and because critics see him as prefiguring Sheridan and Wilde. It is arguable that his view of English society from 1689 is that of the amused outsider. Southerne, the Dublin-born playwright, introduced him to Davenant, lessee of the Theatre Royal, Drury Lane, who produced his first comedy of manners, *The Old Bachelor* (1693). *The Double Dealer* (1694) takes the original step of building the intrigue round a plausible villain. *Love for Love* (1695) shows complete assurance in the genre, and *The Way of the World* (1700) is without doubt the most brilliant comedy of the post-Restoration era, though it was not highly acclaimed when first brought out at the Theatre in Lincoln's Inn Fields – the complexity of its sexual politics may have been too much for that audience. Congreve's sharp delineation of character allied to the most exquisitely barbed yet graceful phrasing – dialogue described by Voltaire as possessing 'extreme finesse' – places him among the half-dozen supreme writers of comedy in the English language. His once highly regarded tragedy *The Mourning Bride* (1697) has not survived in the theatre.

CHRISTOPHER FITZSIMON

Connemara Galway's Atlantic province, of rainbow-haunted mountains, lakes and bogs. The name derives from the Conmaicne Mara (descendants of Conmac, son of the legendary Fergus and Queen Maeve; *mara*, of the sea), whose former territory became the barony of Ballynahinch in Elizabethan times. Nowadays Connemara is taken to include areas to the east of that, and sometimes even all the land west of Lake Corrib. The mountains of the Twelve Bens or Beanna Beoia to the west, and the Maamturks or Sléibhte Mhám Tuirc on its eastern marches, formed in the Caledonian phase of mountain building, have been deeply carved by glaciation. Their glittering, bare, quartzite peaks rise to around 2,000 feet. To north and south of them and between the two ranges are valleys formed in schists, marbles including the famous green Connemara marble, and gneisses. The southern coastal area is a low-lying terrain of boggy hollows and knobbly hillocks on the Galway granite, deeply penetrated by ramifying inlets.

The O'Flahertys, driven out of their lands east of the Corrib by the Normans, were lords of Connemara until dispossessed by the Cromwellians in the 1650s, when much of their territory was granted to Catholic landowners transplanted there from further east. Among these, the Martins of Galway enlarged their holdings into the biggest directly owned estate in either Ireland or Britain, which Humanity Dick (1754–1834, duellist and founder of the RSPCA) ruled over in feudal style from Ballynahinch, while the D'Arcys, also of Galway, founded the region's little market town of Clifden in the 1800s. Both families were bankrupted by the Great Famine, which was a time of mass starvation and emigration throughout the region.

Towards the end of the nineteenth century, this despised and neglected Congested District, and especially its southern, Gaelic-speaking parts, came to be prized as a type of the true Ireland. Pádraig Ó Conaire learned his Gaelic as a child in Ros Muc, and Patrick Pearse dreamed of a Gaelic Ireland and foresaw Easter 1916 by his cottage fireside there. Ros Muc also bore the Gaelic-language writers Pádraig Óg Ó Conaire (1893–1971),

Colm Ó Gaora (1887–1954) and Caitlín Maude (1941–82), while Cois Fharraige, Connemara's south-eastern extension, gave the language its great Modernist Máirtín Ó Cadhain (1907–70). In the 1960s great riches were recorded from traditional story-tellers and singers and the art of sean-nós singing still flourishes throughout the Gaeltacht.

Reading

Gwynn, Stephen, *A Holiday in Connemara* (London: 1909).

Mac Giollarnath, Seán, *Connemara* (Cork: 1954).

O'Flaherty, Roderic, *West or H-liar Connaught*, written 1684, ed. James Hardiman (Dublin: 1846).

Robinson, Tim, *Connemara. Part I: Introduction and Gazetteer*, Part II, a one-inch map (Roundstone, 1990).

Synge, J. M., *In Connemara*, in *Collected Works. Vol. II: Prose*, ed. Alan Price (Oxford: 1966).

TIM ROBINSON

Connolly, James (1868–1916) Marxist socialist, founder of the Irish Labour Party, labour organizer, signatory of the Declaration of Independence of the Irish Republic in 1916. Connolly was born in Edinburgh of working-class Irish parents on 5 June 1868; he was executed by British firing squad in Kilmainham Jail on 12 May 1916, after being court-martialled for his part in the 1916 Rising. After basic schooling and a period in the British army Connolly, who had married an Irish girl, Lillie Reynolds, in 1890, returned to Edinburgh, where he became involved in socialist politics. Rapidly establishing a reputation as an able propagandist, he thenceforth devoted his life to socialist and trade union organization in Scotland, in Dublin (1896–1903), in America (1903–10) working for Daniel DeLeon's Socialist Labour Party and the Industrial Workers of the World (IWW), and, finally, back in Ireland (1910–16), where he worked as union organizer in Belfast and Dublin for Larkin's Irish Transport and General Workers' Union. In 1912 he established the Irish

Labour Party. After the outbreak of the 1914 war he became increasingly involved in opposition to British rule in Ireland, eventually joining with Pearse and the Irish Republican Brotherhood (IRB) in the Easter Rising. After Pearse's surrender, Connolly and the other leaders were court-martialled and executed. Having been wounded during the fighting, he was carried to his execution on a stretcher.

Connolly, a life-long Marxist, produced a significant body of socialist writing. While not a major innovator in fundamental theory, he provided a thoughtful, lucid examination of socialism, against the backdrop of the importance of trade union organization and the dilemmas facing a socialist in a country that was an industrially underdeveloped colony, whose culture was rooted in conservative Catholicism, and where politics were dominated by 'the national question'. The most significant strands in Connolly's thought are his syndicalism, his attempt to resolve the dilemma of preaching socialism to a largely Catholic audience, and his understanding of the relationship between socialism and nationalism.

His syndicalism, deriving from DeLeon and the ideology of the IWW, insisted that workers should be organized in 'One Big Union', the rationale being that a single union, with subdivisions paralleling the functional segmentation of industry, would render strike action maximally effective, provide workers with the weapon of 'the General Strike', as a back-up to parliamentary politics, and, importantly, would prefigure the apolitical structure of the collective control of the economy required by a socialist democracy.

Connolly's approach to the issue of socialism and religion started from the Second International's policy, declaring religion and personal morality 'private' matters, socialism being concerned with economic, class and political issues. Connolly, however, attempted a theoretical resolution of the problem; in a refreshingly undogmatic qualification of historical materialism, he claimed that

theory could only explain the 'general outlines' of society and culture. Then, distinguishing between the conservative manipulation of religion by institutionalized churches and certain core values extractable from religion, he claimed that such core values could provide a normative base for socialism. Emphasizing how Christianity (in particular, Irish Catholicism) had been used as a tool of popular oppression, he argued that the humanist values implicit in Christianity provided a solid basis for socialism, rendering the conservative manipulation of religion guilty of hypocritical inconsistency. Implicit in his argument is the significant thesis that what is produced by an exploitative society, even if it has in fact been used to further that exploitation, is not necessarily tainted by its origin.

Some aspects of Connolly's nationalism are unproblematic. Condemning colonial oppression as a form of economic exploitation, he was committed to its overthrow, while emphasizing that political independence alone, without socialism, would, for the oppressed, mean only a change of oppressors. But what could have led Connolly to participate with non-socialist nationalists in an armed rebellion which, even if successful, would have produced only political independence with little prospect of an advance towards socialism? Interpretations range from those that see his nationalism as a logical development of his socialism to those that see Connolly as having been seduced by the 'mystical' nationalism of the IRB into abandoning his socialist principles, in the desperate circumstances of the failure of the Dublin workers' struggle, the capitulation of the British government to Unionism, the impotence of international socialism in the face of European militarism, and the Redmondite endorsement of Irish involvement in the British war effort.

Connolly's commitment to socialism, and his implacable opposition to oppression of all forms are unquestionable, but perhaps the ultimate sacrifice of his life in the cause of Irish nationalism will always remain an enigma.

Reading

Dudley Edwards, Owen and Ransom, Bernard (eds), *James Connolly, Selected Political Writings* (London: Jonathan Cape, 1973).

Greaves, Desmond, *The Life and Times of James Connolly* (London: Lawrence and Wishart, 1961).

Levenson, Samuel, *James Connolly* (London: Martin Brian and O'Keefe, 1973).

Morgan, Austen, *James Connolly: A Political Biography* (Manchester: Manchester University Press, 1988).

Newsinger, John, 'Connolly and his biographers', *Irish Political Studies*, 5 (1990).

Ransom, Bernard, *Connolly's Marxism* (London: Pluto Press, 1980).

JAMES L. HYLAND

Connolly, Peter (1927–87) Priest and academic. Connolly was ordained a priest in 1951 and subsequently studied for some years at Oxford. He was professor of English at St Patrick's College, Maynooth, from 1954 until 1985, when he retired on health grounds. His teaching had considerable influence on successive classes of clerical students. Although he published little, his courageous articles and lectures, particularly in the areas of film criticism and the morality of censorship, brought a tenuous but much-needed flicker of liberalism to Irish Catholic thought in the late fifties and early sixties.

Reading

Connolly, Peter, *No Bland Facility: Selected Writings on Literature, Religion and Censorship*, ed. James H. Murphy (Colin Smythe: Gerrards Cross, 1991).

PETER DENMAN

constitutional nationalism to 1918 It seems quite probable that the term 'constitutional nationalism' was less a historical description than a device fastened on by historians who sought a means of categorizing patriots who were sophisticated politicians rather than simple gunmen. Ireland by 1800 had had a long constitutional tradition which had nothing to do with separatism or Republicanism and which was connected only obliquely with colonial nationalism. The Irish, the Old English, and eventually the Patriots of the Grattanite period had pursued their aims through debate rather than by arms for centuries in a parliamentary tradition that stretched back to 1264.

For the most part the various respective parliaments represented only part of the island's mixed community. Medieval assemblies were filled with Anglo-Normans and their Old English descendants. The Reformation and the English political disputes of the early seventeenth century saw the intrusion of Protestant planter representation into the hitherto ecclusively Catholic and largely Old English assemblies. It was the English Civil War that forced the Old English and the Irish into each others' arms in the Confederation of Kilkenny, a wartime legislature which represented Catholic Ireland's stand for Charles I and against Protestantism and planters. Military defeat of the Catholics by Cromwell in 1650 meant that when an Irish parliamentary body sat again in 1661 the ephemeral and ill-defined nationalism which had united the Confederates had to give place to a predominantly Protestant interest.

The continuing correspondence between religious belief and political loyalty surfaced again in 1689 when Catholics filled an Irish parliament presided over by James II and apparently plotted the dispossession of their Protestant enemies. Yet again nationalism was subordinated to religious fervour. The strong constitutional machinery which was installed after the Williamite victory of 1690–1 was of course Protestant and determinedly so, and the Irish Parliament's claim to be a representative assembly was based rather shakily on the legal non-existence of Catholics and their exclusion from all political processes. The basis of the eighteenth-century Irish constitutionality was an illusion and its parliamentary processes were founded on venality rather than idealism. The development of colonial nationalism amongst the Protestants was therefore slow and reliant on the extent to which they could free their assembly from the legislative constraints of Westminster and themselves from their historic dependence on the British political connection.

It was not until the 1780s that an appreciable though imperfect degree of legislative independence was secured for the Irish parliament. Even allowing for the facts that any incipient nationalism would necessarily be exclusively Protestant and that the culture of the Irish Protestants was ineffably English, the 20 years of uncertainty and strife which remained to the Irish Parliament left it no time to develop a nationalist character. Opposition politics in the Irish Parliament after 1782 were not so much anti-establishment or pro-patriotic as a continuation on slightly adjusted terms of the old party politics. The most promising proto-nationalist issue amongst the opposition, that of 'responsible government', was counteracted by cunning administration tactics, confounded by the opposition's inability to confront the matter of its own inherent venality, and overtaken by the extra-parliamentary Catholic nationalist threat, which forced even the most liberal MPs to take refuge once again in Protestantism and the siege mentality.

Catholics, united by a new middle-class solidarity and by the common enemy of the Penal Laws, had bonded together with an organizing skill that was, for its time, highly impressive. By late 1792 the endemic Irish social barriers of localism and parochialism had been overcome (however temporarily) and the large community of Irish Catholics had been sufficiently politicized to procure the election of delegates to a Parliament-style Catholic Convention held in Dublin. The delegates, however, were so relatively pro-establishment in their sentiments and the Convention's proceedings so very constitutional that the event was effectively robbed of any significant nationalist overtone, and it succeeded only in the negative sense of giving the already-suspicious government an unpleasant jolt.

Constitutionalism, whether of the Catholic or Protestant variety, was already under threat from the French Revolution. The Revolution was spilling over into Ireland through the United Irishmen. This movement had by the mid-1790s jettisoned its early moderate reform aims and was seeking to harness the thus-far untapped political energy of the lower classes. The more respectable middle-class Catholics withdrew from the movement and the bodies controlled by it when the United Irishmen's nationalist aim of separating the two kingdoms by force became clear. The lower classes for their part may or may not have been tuned in politically to nationalist values by the time violence broke out in 1798. What is clear is that in several areas of the country the rebellion quickly became a sectarian blood-bath.

The 1790s saw both the proscription of Catholic political organizations and the abolition of the Irish Parliament; these years also marked the death of all home-grown Irish constitutionalism for a generation. When it resurfaced it was under the direction of Daniel O'Connell. O'Connell revolutionized nationalism in theory and in practice; it was he who was the originator of modern Irish constitutional nationalism. His political objective, the Repeal of the Act of Union, looked backward to Grattan's Parliament rather than forwards towards national self-determination; but then O'Connell was essentially an eighteenth-century man who had merely lived on into a nineteenth-century world. During the 1830s and 1840s, for the first time since the initial hostile reaction to the Union, Repeal became a popular movement, and Repeal or Home Rule – varying degrees of legislative independence within the British imperial framework – was to remain the goal of constitutional nationalists until the final disappearance of the movement in 1918. It was O'Connell also who established that the Union was the source of Irish grievances; this became a traditional belief which outlived not only O'Connell but even the Union itself. His glorification of the venal and relatively powerless College Green assembly of his youth was a legacy that passed into Irish nationalist folklore.

The scale and havoc of the 1798 rebellion had revealed to O'Connell the potential power at the disposal of anyone who could exert even a modest degree of influence over the lower classes. O'Connell sought to harness those lower classes by careful reinterpretation of their grievances and redirection of their Anglophobic tendencies. Religious animosity and material grievance already had their meeting place on such issues as the Tithe Controversy. O'Connell was to consolidate that connection and give it expression for the first time through a means other than agrarian terrorism.

A peculiarly Irish difficulty was that too many people believed that the achievement of Repeal would signify the establishment of a Catholic-dominated state. Before the Catholic Emancipation campaign of the 1820s, the Irish Protestant establishment had been assailed by Catholics more as a self-contained enemy than as a symbol of British government policy in Ireland. O'Connell tried, not altogether successfully, to reverse this emphasis. His attempt had the long-term effect of consolidating and making permanent the government's tendency to identify disaffection with Catholicism.

Most of O'Connell's methods as well as his nationalist objective were adopted by later successful constitutional nationalists, notably by Charles Stewart Parnell. The value of his educational techniques – the 'know your wrongs' approach – was recognized and closely adhered to by later nationalists of all leanings; it was the life-blood of the Young Ireland movement of the 1840s, and it was the weapon with which Parnellites and their opponents fought throughout the 1890s. The master-tool of constitutional nationalism – agitation within the bounds of legality but with the implicit threat of mass revolt – was used by Parnell with as much success in the 1880s as it was by O'Connell in the early 1840s. O'Connell was closely connected with both Catholic and nationalist objectives; through him and with him began the interchangeability of the terms 'Catholic' and 'nationalist' which later was to be such a feature of both revolutionary and constitutional nationalism. An important factor in the development of this interchangeability was O'Connell's successful wooing of the support of the Catholic clergy for a nationalist objective; this was a link which was revived in the 1880s.

A constitutional nationalist tradition which linked O'Connell and Parnell and, perhaps to a lesser degree, John Redmond, was that of the leadership cult. The natural weakness of such a system was the overdependence of the group upon the individual leader and its failure to inspire confidence in itself as an organization. This weakness manifested itself not only in O'Connell's Repeal movement but also in the parliamentary party of Parnell.

One of O'Connell's most important contributions not only to nationalist methodology but to politics was his establishing of the modern parliamentary party. This weapon was developed to a fine point and used with devastating effect by Parnell and Redmond. The 1914 Home Rule Act remains the most poignant tribute to O'Connell's constitutional achievement.

GERARD O'BRIEN

Contemporary Music Centre Founded in 1986 by the Irish Arts Council to promote contemporary Irish music, it also encourages and assists performances of music by living composers and provides information on all aspects of new Irish music. The centre's library houses a comprehensive collection of scores by over 60 contemporary Irish composers and includes a wide range of orchestral, choral, instrumental and vocal music. The centre is a member of the International Association of Music Information Centres and cooperates with similar institutes in 22 countries. Scores and catalogues of works are available for consultation and in some cases copies of musical works are also available for sale. The centre's founding director, Bernard Harris, was succeeded in 1990 by Eve O'Kelly. The Contemporary Music Centre publishes an information bulletin entitled *New Music News* which details publications by the centre itself, information on competitions, awards and courses, news of contemporary Irish composers and a 'New Music Calendar'.

HARRY WHITE

contraception In 1911, the average family size in Ireland was 7–9 children. By 1946, it was 4–6 children, twice as large as that in the low-fertility countries of Europe. Such high marital fertility was not considered a problem in Ireland, for several reasons. Both church and state prohibited contraception; persistent emigration and high levels of permanent celibacy ensured that the population remained low; and patriarchal state policies restricted married women's opportunities for paid employment.

The Catholic church in Ireland from the 1920s onward feared the erosion of traditional values as a result of exposure to external cultural influences. The state in legislation willingly safeguarded traditional values in relation to sexual morality. In 1929 a Censorship of Publications Act made the publishing, selling or distribution of literature advocating birth control an offence. The Criminal Law Amendment Act 1935, Section 17, prohibited the sale and importation of contraceptives.

In 1969 the Fertility Guidance Clinic opened in Dublin. It was followed a year later by the setting up of a family planning rights group. Due to a legal loophole, clinics could dispense contraceptives freely, while requesting donations from clients. The contraceptive pill was also being prescribed by some general practitioners as a cycle-regulator for health reasons. In 1971, the women's liberation movement demanded legal contraception in its 'Chains or Change' manifesto. While the Catholic Church remained resolutely opposed to contraceptives, public opinion began to favour change.

A Supreme Court ruling in 1973 (*McGee* v. *Attorney General*) declared that the right to marital privacy included the right to use contraceptives. Section 17 of the 1935 Act was therefore deemed unconstitutional. It was not until 1979, however, that the Health (Family Planning) Act was enacted. Described as 'an Irish solution to a an Irish problem', it legalized the sale of contraceptives, including condoms, on prescription, to married couples for medical reasons or bona fide family planning purposes. This situation continued until 1985, when the legislation was amended to permit the sale of condoms, without prescription, to those aged 18 and over. Availability remained uneven, with many rural chemists refusing to stock them. In 1992 legislation reduced the age of purchase to 17, and additional outlets, such as pubs and supermarkets, were licensed to sell condoms if they wished. This change in the legislation was due mainly to increased fears about the spread of AIDS.

Reading

Courtney D., 'Demographic structure and change', in *Ireland: A Sociological Profile*, P. Clancy, S. Drudy, K. Lynch and L. O'Dowd (eds), (Dublin: Gill and Macmillan, 1986).

Mahon, E., 'Women's rights and Catholicism', *New Left Review*, 166 (Nov. Dec. 1987).

Whyte, J. H., *Church and State in Modern Ireland 1923–1979*, 2nd edn (Dublin: Gill and Macmillan, 1980).

EVELYN MAHON

Cooke, Barrie (1931–) Artist. Born in the UK, Cooke came to Ireland in 1954. Prior to this he read art history at Harvard in conjunction with practical art classes during vacations at Skowhegan. Though trained as a realist, he was drawn towards the radicalizing force of abstract Expressionism in 1950s America – and his work reflects a peculiar hybridization of both styles. Initially based in West Clare, his large-scale paintings take as their themes the flow of water and the flux of nature. Concurrently, Cooke has also created a series of perspex boxes containing arrangements of real or artificial bone fragments. According to Frances Ruane, these reveal 'a search for abstract shapes that embody essential principles of natural structure and growth'. As one of Ireland's premier contemporary artists, Cooke has represented Ireland in the 1963 Paris Biennale, exhibited at the international exhibition ROSC in 1980 and 1984, and has held a major retrospective at the Douglas Hyde Gallery in 1986.

TREVOR BUTTERWORTH

Cooke, Edward (1755–1820) Administrator. Born and educated in England, Cooke pursued a career in Irish government. He held various offices from 1778, rising steadily to become under-secretary to the military department in 1789. As one of those dismissed by Earl Fitzwilliam in 1795, his rapid reinstatement raised his standing and influence with senior politicians. He became a close friend of Castlereagh and was one of the principal instruments whereby the Union was procured. A politician also, he sat for Old Leighlin borough from 1790. Cooke followed Pitt and resigned after the Union when further concessions to Catholics were refused. After a further period in government service he retired in 1817.

GERARD O'BRIEN

Cooke, Henry (1788–1868) Presbyterian leader. Born Henry Macook, on 11 May in Grillagh, near Maghera, Henry Cooke became Ulster's greatest Presbyterian leader. His evangelical fervour altered not only the course of Ulster Presbyterianism, but also the political mood of the whole Protestant population.

After failing to graduate at Glasgow College through illness, he obtained his licence to preach and was ordained in 1808. By 1818, he had also studied chemistry, geology, anatomy and medicine at Glasgow, at Trinity College, Dublin, and at the College of Surgeons. A tall man with a powerful voice, he first proved his oratorical powers against the English Unitarian John Smethurst, whom he confronted wherever he spoke on his mission to Antrim. In 1825, he gave evidence before the Royal Commission on Education in Ireland, where he described the Belfast Academical Institution as 'a seminary of Arianism' and warned against undue concessions to Catholic emancipation. He intensified his campaign against the Arians and their leader Henry Montgomery, and by 1829, they were forced to withdraw from the Presbyterian church because Cooke had a motion passed that all ministers would have to subscribe to the doctrine of the Trinity. A church was built for him in May Street, Belfast, where he preached from 1829 to 1867. When the scheme for Irish national education began in 1831, Cooke saw a threat to Protestantism, and organized through the synod a parallel educational scheme, which the government recognized in 1840. At a mass meeting in Hillsborough in 1834 he published the banns of a marriage between the established and Presbyterian churches. 'A minister may and must', he declared, 'interfere with politics whenever politics interfere with religion . . . Never, in the history of Ireland, was Protestantism in greater danger than at this hour.' As Belfast expanded industrially, Catholics in search of work moved into the Presbyterian town, while Protestant immigrants brought in Orangeism. While never an Orangeman, Cooke's increasingly anti-Catholic stance (he treasured a ring engraved with the words 'Nulla pax cum Roma') gave voice to Orange forebodings.

Cooke achieved a famous victory when Daniel O'Connell came to address a meeting in Belfast on the repeal of the Union. Cooke challenged him to a public debate, but O'Connell avoided 'bully Cooke', and slipped quietly into Belfast, speaking not at the Pavilion but from the balcony of the Royal Hotel. Riots ensued, and O'Connell withdrew the next day. Cooke claimed a victory in his pamphlet, 'The Repealer Repulsed'. When Queen's College opened in 1849, he was made professor of sacred rhetoric. Previously, for eliminating heterodoxy from Presbyterianism, he had been given honorary doctorates by Jefferson University and Trinity College, Dublin.

Cooke had his critics, notably John Knox, Jr, who warned Ulster not to oppose civil and religious liberty, but Cooke's view that Protestant Christianity should be 'the law of the empire' prevailed. On his death-bed, he urged Protestant electors to beware 'the insidious advances of popish error and despotism'. Cooke may not have been the first to identify religion with politics, but he undoubtedly laid the foundations for a Protestant party in the politics of Ulster. He died on 13 December 1868, and a statue to him, erected on the site of one to the earl of Belfast known as 'The Black Man', stands fittingly with its back to the Royal Belfast Academical Institution.

Reading

Holmes, Finlay, *Henry Cooke* (Belfast: Christian Journals Ltd, 1981).
Porter, J.L., *The Life and Times of Henry Cooke, D.D., LL.D.* (Belfast: William Mullen, 1875).

FRED LOWE

Cooke, Thomas Simpson (1782–1848) Composer and singer. Born Dublin: died London. Cooke was part of a well-known Dublin musical family and received his earliest musical education from his father. From 1800 he led the orchestra at the annual concerts in Dublin of the Irish Musical Fund, and gained a reputation as an especially versatile instrumentalist in Dublin and Cork. He also achieved success as a singer and made his debut at the English Opera House (the Lyceum) in London in July, 1813. Thereafter he joined Drury Lane theatre as principal tenor for a period of 20 years. He was also appointed director of music at the same house in 1821 and performed at Covent Garden and at the chapel of the Bavarian Embassy in London.

His career as a composer began at Crow Street theatre in Dublin, where he wrote overtures for various productions imported from abroad. Although he also subsequently composed a number of original operas, he is perhaps best known for his adaptations of operatic works by Auber, Boieldieu, Halévy,

Hérold, Rossini and Weber, all of which were given in London. Apart from his operatic enterprises, Cooke was famous as a writer of glees, which were esteemed as the finest of their kind by many of his contemporaries.

Reading

Hogan, Ita M., *Anglo-Irish Music 1780–1830* (Cork: 1966).

HARRY WHITE

co-operative movement The modern co-operative movement originated with the Rochdale Pioneers in England in 1844. The first co-operative society in Ireland was the Ralahine Agricultural and Manufacturing Co-operative Association founded by John Scott Vandaleur in County Clare in November 1831, largely inspired by the writings of Robert Owen (1771–1858). It failed because the law governing property and land tenure provided no means of protecting the members of the association against claims on Vandaleur's property when he lost his estate through gambling.

The philosophy of co-operation was promoted by Sir Horace Plunkett (1854–1932), Rev. T.A. Finlay SJ (1848–1940) and George W. (AE) Russell (1867–1935).

Plunkett's objective was to anticipate the effects of the industrial revolution in Ireland and to provide a new form of economic organization to put people in control of their own destinies. He started a co-operative shop on his family estate in Dunsany, County Meath, followed in 1895 by another in Doneraile, County Cork. The Doneraile Agricultural Bank, modelled on the German *Raiffeisen* system, was set up in 1894.

Plunkett took the view that, if the co-operative movement was to make any head way in Ireland, it had to apply to farming. In the 1880s, the processing and marketing of Irish farm produce were haphazardly organized and biased to suit middlemen and dealers.

The first co-operative creamery was founded in Drumcollogher, County Limerick, in 1889. By 1894, when Plunkett founded the Irish Agricultural Organization Society (IAOS), there were 33 co-operative creameries and 13 co-operative agricultural societies. By 1915, the figures were 344 and 219 respectively. Co-operative creameries played a major role in improving standards of dairy husbandry and milk quality, and in making milk production on small farms a viable enterprise.

From the earliest days, it proved difficult to raise sufficient share capital from co-operative members. Managers were frequently reluctant to press members to subscribe capital, for fear of driving them back to reliance on private merchants and dealers. Banks were reluctant to provide funds without adequate guarantees. The result was that co-operative society committees tended to be dominated by small numbers of almost permanent members whose only qualification was that they were able to provide guarantees acceptable to the banks.

Notwithstanding these problems, the movement achieved significant success in the dairy products area, with creamery co-operatives becoming some of the largest firms in Ireland. This was further reinforced by a series of amalgamations, notably in the period from the mid-sixties to the mid-eighties. The meat sector proved more problematic: meat processing co-operatives did not meet with the same success as the creameries. Co-operative livestock marts, however, have been extremely successful.

In recent years, many of the larger creamery co-operatives, which had engaged in a significant diversification of their operations, converted themselves into private limited companies, perhaps indicating that the co-operative form of organization is no longer as relevant to the needs of the modern market place as it was.

Reading

Bolger, Patrick, *The Irish Co-operative Movement: Its History and Development* (Dublin: Institute of Public Administration).

Smith, Louis P.F., *The Evolution of Agricultural Co-operation* (Oxford: Blackwell, 1961).

ALAN DUKES

copyright and 'piracy' in the eighteenth century Copyright as a legal concept did not exist in Ireland in the eighteenth century. In Britain it was first recognized in 1709 when the Copyright Act gave authors property rights in their works. The Act did not extend to Ireland, therefore printers there could legitimately reprint books first published in London. This advantage was to some extent offset by the attraction for the Irish author of payment for his copy and publication in London; in Dublin he had no bargaining rights.

The London trade was deprived of the most profitable part of the very profitable Irish market once the Irish started to reprint every work they thought would sell, and by using smaller formats and inferior paper they could sell at cheaper rates than London. London naturally resented this and fought the harder to prevent the importation into Britain of the undercutting Dublin reprint, so gaining the British Importation Act in 1739. This forbade the importation of works first printed in Britain and reprinted abroad. The Irish bookseller looking for sales in England, Scotland and America now had to hope his books could be smuggled past the customs officers; all imports from Ireland, including permitted original Irish works, ran the risk of seizure.

London editions were not always printed without permission, and enough examples exist of payment to the British copyright holder for Dublin reprint rights to suggest that this was not unusual. There are also instances of British authors correcting errors of the London edition in the Irish reprint.

Of considerable interest is the Dublin trade's method of regulating rights to copy among themselves. No explicit code exists, but it seems that the process of publication started with the 'posting up' of the book's title by the bookseller as a claim to his copy and advertising his intent to publish. Whoever was first in the possession of a manuscript, or, for a reprint, of sheets of the London edition, had the right of publication. This appears to have worked in most cases, though there was quite frequent trouble over rival editions.

It has been argued that Dublin booksellers committed 'moral piracy', but there was then no notion of international agreement on copyright; London booksellers cannot often have negotiated rights for the French texts they reprinted. Righteous indignation, so ably expressed by Samuel Richardson, can be reserved for Dublin bribery of London journeymen to send over sheets of copy straight from the press.

Although in Ireland the merits of a Copyright Act were occasionally debated, the trade was too firmly dependent on reprints to allow it to recognize property rights in the written word; in 1785, such an Act, suggested in the British commercial propositions, was firmly rejected by Parliament. Ireland became subject to copyright law only when the United Kingdom Act was passed in 1801.

M. POLLARD

Corcoran, Frank (1944–) Composer and lecturer. Born Tipperary. Corcoran studied in Dublin, Maynooth, Rome and Berlin (with Boris Blacher). Since 1983, he has been professor of composition and theory of music in the Hochschüle für Musik, Hamburg. His compositions include two symphonies: *Symphonies of Symphonies of Wind* (Symphony No. 1) and *Symphony No. 2* (both from 1981); an opera, *Gilgamesh* (1990); two string quartets; two wind quintets; much choral, vocal and chamber music; two chamber symphonies; and some electronic music. His works have been widely performed and broadcast in Ireland and abroad. In 1983 he was elected a member of Aosdána, Ireland's government-sponsored body honouring creative artists.

EVE O'KELLY

Cork Ireland's third and the Republic's second city, developed on marshland and islands in the River Lee. Founded by St Finbar early in the seventh century, the settlement continued under the Vikings and Anglo-Normans. The latter dominated its trade and government until the 1640s, when warfare and English reconquest delivered it into the hands of Protestant newcomers. It thrived thanks to the fertility of its hinterland and its easy access by water.

The main point of entry for imports into Munster, by the late seventeenth century it also dominated the export of butter, beef and other provisions popular in Britain, Europe and the North American colonies. The prosperity of its lucrative trade was reflected in population growth (perhaps 6,000 in 1660; 27,000 in 1719; 71,500 by 1821; and about 136,000 today), and in grander public buildings. The South Gate Bridge, Christ Church, St Anne's Shandon and the nearby Skiddy's almshouses all date from the early eighteenth century. Further building in the early nineteenth century utilized the talents of local architects, notably the Pains and Deanes. Survivals from this period include Pain's gaol, with a sombre Doric portico (now part of the university), St Mary Shandon and St Patrick, McCurtain Street.

Meanwhile wealthy merchants and professional people removed to villas along the estuary and around the harbour, giving a distinctive grace which can still be discerned in Montenotte, Tivoli Glanmire and the separate port of Cobh, originally 'the Cove of Cork'.

Political and socio-economic changes in the early nineteenth century dethroned Protestants from their ascendancy. Continuing prosperity left its mark in the striking buildings of the University College (1845–8), Atkins's Lunatic Asylum (soon to be acquired by the university), the Church of Ireland Cathedral rebuilt by William Burges, and the Honan chapel, remarkable for its Celtic revival interior, glass and furnishings. Scarred by the War of Independence, shortly before which the lord mayor, Terence MacSwiney, died on hunger strike, and during which much of the centre was burnt, the city's resilience allowed a swift recovery.

Resolute in its independence from the cultural and economic thrall of Dublin, proud of its sporting prowess, Cork has produced the writers Daniel Corkery, Sean O Faoloin and Frank O'Connor, supports art galleries and an opera house, and achieves a gastronomic excellence unequalled elsewhere in Ireland. Its port continues to link it directly with Europe and the world.

T.C. BARNARD

Corri, Haydn (1785–1860) Pianist, composer and organist of Italian extraction. Born Edinburgh; died Dublin. The son of composer Domenico Corri, he came to Dublin in 1821 to take up a post as a singer in Hawkins Street Theatre. He settled in Dublin thereafter as a teacher of piano and occasionally conducted concerts at the Rotunda. In 1826 he was appointed organist and choirmaster of the pro-cathedral in Dublin, where he remained until 1848. He published a singing tutor in 1827.

HARRY WHITE

Corry, Isaac (1755?–1813) Politician. Corry was the son of a Newry merchant and succeeded his father as MP for that town (1776–1800, 1802–6). His mercantile background, slender means, facile debating style and raffish private life led him to be regarded throughout his career as something of an adventurer. A leading figure in the opposition until 1788, he went over to the government side in that year and held a succession of increasingly important offices culminating in the chancellorship of the Irish Exchequer (1799–1804). He succeeded the blundering but widely popular Sir John Parnell, who had been dismissed from the chancellorship for his opposition to the Union, and in 1800 incurred further notoriety by provoking a duel with Grattan. After the Union, he quarrelled with his ministerial colleagues over his requests for the patronage required to maintain his shaky seat for Newry, and his budgets were inevitably unpopular (and ineffective) because of the combined effects of war and the fiscal provisions of the Act of Union. In 1804 he was replaced, on the formation of Pitt's second ministry, by an old enemy, John Foster (who had previously been chancellor, 1784–5). He thus fell victim to the post-Union process of reconciliation with former opponents of that measure. He was defeated at Newry in 1806, and died in reduced circumstances in 1813.

Reading

Malcomson, A.P.W., *Isaac Corry, 1755–1813: 'An Adventurer in the Field of Politics'* (Belfast: 1974).
Thorne, R.G., *The History of Parliament: The House of Commons, 1790–1820*, 5 vols (London: Secker and Warburg for the History of Parliament Trust, 1986), vol. iii.

A.P.W. MALCOMSON

Council of State Established under the constitution 'to aid and advise' the president. Its advice is required before the president exercises certain functions (referring bills to the Supreme Court, referring a bill to popular referendum after parliamentary petition, addressing messages to the Parliament or people, abridging time for consideration of emergency legislation). The president is not required to follow the council's advice. The council consists of seven *ex officio* members (taoiseach, tánaiste, chief justice, president of the High Court, chairman of dáil, chairman of Seanad, attorney general), all previous holders of the offices of president, chief justice and taoiseach, and up to seven persons appointed by the president.

BRIAN FARRELL

Counter-Reformation A movement within the Catholic church in the early modern period to counteract unorthodoxy and to canalize all impulses for the reform and renewal of religious life. In Ireland the Counter-Reformation, as well as imposing new norms for religious practice and spirituality, fostered a Catholic ideology which became central to the nationalist historiographical tradition.

This was because, after a false start in the 1540s, the reaction to the state-sponsored Reformation became closely identified with political disaffection from and outright opposition to the regime. As a consequence of these developments in the Tudor period, when the agents of the Counter-Reformation began to set up an effective organization in the early seventeenth century they found themselves ministering to the bulk of the island's population, whether of Gaelic or English origin. Uniquely, Ireland was the country in Western Europe in which the religion of the state was not that of the majority of the inhabitants, and accordingly the character of the Irish Counter-Reformation was exceptional.

In 1542 two members of the newly founded Society of Jesus visited the north of Ireland. Their general, Ignatius Loyola, had asked for a report on the royally imposed Reformation, thitherto merely encompassing a break with papal jurisdiction. This initiative, as well as Roman efforts to insert papally approved bishops into Irish dioceses, ran counter to the prevailing impetus of conciliatory English policy within the island, which had resulted in widespead lay and clerical acceptance of Henry VIII's sovereignty in church as well as state. Whatever weak impulses towards reform of the Irish church had existed before the changes of the 1530s were to be subsumed in the policy of royal ecclesiastical management (apart from the notable force of Observantism among the friars, which did feed into the Counter-Reformation). The two Jesuits, Fathers Salmeron and Broet, withdrew from Ireland after a short sojourn, convinced that Ireland was lost to papal control.

The first, failed Counter-Reformation promoted from the Continent was followed by several decades of unco-ordination between Catholic bishops, priests and lay people, as the agents of state Protestantism began evangelizing, albeit tentatively, under Queen Elizabeth after 1560. While credal certitude fostered by the Marian reaction to the advanced Reformation of King Edward VI's ministers may have carried through into the succeeding reign in the form of continuity of ministry, worship and pious practices, neither the decrees of the Council of Trent nor the work of the new orders of the European Counter-Reformation had much impact on Ireland initially. Political issues overshadowed theological ones, though the influence of the confessional divisions in the northern European wars of the time on political dissenters in Ireland was evidenced in the uprisings in Munster, Leinster and later Ulster. A key to the ultimate receptivity of the country to the renewed Counter-Reformation effort was the gradual alienation of the Old English from the state administration. Although complaisant in the face of ecclesiastical innovation in the earlier century and benefiting materially from the distribution of church properties, this community of urban merchants and rural gentry had been confirmed by Marian Catholicism and maintained continuity of pre-Reformation devotional practice at local level without much interference from the authorities. Their religious sensibilities were heightened by the tougher state response to politico-religious opposition, which encompassed the executions of Catholic bishops, clergy and lay people among the dissidents. Although overwhelmingly loyal to the government during the crisis of the rebellion of Hugh O'Neill, earl of Tyrone, the Old English gave every indication that by the last years of the century they had withdrawn from the institution of the state church.

The crucial meshing of the political disaffection of the recusants with the Tridentine reforms took place through the medium of education abroad. During the decades down to the 1590s, the promoters of Reformation and Counter-Reformation alike had pressed schemes for the founding of schools and colleges at all levels for the fostering of their respective creeds, but with little success. As the evangelical thrust of the Protestant Reformation was given an impetus by the establishment of Trinity College in 1592, it was the Continental colleges which galvanized

Counter-Reformation Catholicism in Ireland. Founded principally in Spain, the Spanish Netherlands, France and Italy, these institutions enshrined in their curricula the rules for seminaries as appointed at Trent. In their new environments, the alumni were part of a wider Irish emigré community which comprised soldiers, merchants, diplomats and their families, among whom an Irish Catholic identity emerged in advance of a similar development at home. As priest-graduates, they formed the spearhead of the Counter-Reformation mission in Ireland, the Jesuit residency dating from 1596 and other religious and diocesan clergy returning in numbers in the years from the turn of the century. Although theological disputation with Protestant divines was a new feature of Irish intellectual life, the missionary priests concentrated on reviving worship and sacramental life, and on instructing their hearers in the truths of Catholicism. In doing so, they confirmed the surviving religious life of their congregations, giving Tridentine sophistication to simple faith. When the Jacobean regime decided on a course of prosecution of recusancy, using extraordinary legal instruments, the revelatory force of lay resistance principally in the towns, and specifically the demonstration of Catholic sympathy in Dublin on the execution of the aged bishop of Down and Connor, Cornelius O'Devaney, in 1611, inspirited the work of the Counter-Reformation agents.

Diocesan and parochial organization was fundamental to the success of the Counter-Reformation in setting up a reformed Catholic church in opposition to the state one in the early decades of the seventeenth century. On the basis laid by individual missioners, the vicars general and later resident bishops such as David Rothe of Ossory put in place the machinery whereby the ideals of the Council of Trent were to be realized. Diocesan synods provided for the regulation of parishes, with the parish church being the focus for the celebration of Sunday Mass, the cultivation of sacramental life and the provision of catechetical instruction. Regular visitation of their parishes and religious institutions was made bounden upon the bishops by Trent, and the ranks of the lower clergy contained a significant and growing number of fully trained seminarians. Their methods emphasized the inculcation of Catholic precepts through the catechism of the Council of Trent, an Irish version of which was published in Louvain in 1611. While some of the old devotions were anathema to the seminary-trained clergy, others such as traditional pilgrimages were incorporated within the range of approved pious activities with papal consent. In the towns, the old fraternities and chantries were replaced by clerically supervised sodalities. At the interface of religion and society were many potential sources of conflict, as the Counter-Reformation priests tried to impose patterns of Christian observance on social customs. For example, the ascendancy of parish over kin group was now asserted in the services associated with the 'rites of passage' of the church – baptism, marriage and funerals. Whereas the Old English magnates were happy with the promotion of these socio-religious reforms, which were broadly in line with principles propounded by their progenitors a century previously, for the Gaelic Irish community in particular the acceptance of innovative religious practices brought a painful and unwonted disjunction of the sacred and the secular.

The differing perceptions of the two communities of the nature and implications of the Counter-Reformation foreshadowed major difficulties in the way of a unified approach on the part of church authorities to the implantation of reinvigorated Catholicism. While the challenge from a competing Anglican church, backed up by rigorous but very sporadic state action, was relatively muted in these early seventeenth-century decades, more serious were the internal obstacles to forging a united Catholic body. Conflicting views on the question of relations with the state arose in the pacified island after the treaty of Mellifont (1603). Whereas the Old English clergy were ready by and large to advocate co-operation with the Stuart regime in the quest for toleration if not recognition of Catholic practice, the Gaelic stance was uncompromising in seeking nothing less than the complete re-establishment of the Catholic church in Ireland. These divergent attitudes were seen most clearly in the relations of the Confederate Catholics in the 1640s, and prevented the emergence of a united Catholic front then and later. Internal frictions were the legacy of religious rivalries stretching back into the later medieval period. The new role for Tridentine bishops involving close supervision of clerical and lay institutions in the dioceses was questioned by the increasingly resurgent pre-Reformation orders, especially the Franciscans, Dominicans and Cistericians. These had reconstituted older houses and founded new ones, and were claiming many former rights such as parochial appointments (especially in the case of the Cistercians) and the missionary faculties granted to the friars when they were almost on their own in maintaining a Catholic presence in the later years of the previous century. When clashes occurred over control of burial places and funeral offerings, for example, appeals would be made to Rome. When the newly established Roman Congregation of Propaganda (set up to supervise the Catholic mission in non-Catholic established countries) issued a charter for the Catholic church mission in Ireland in the mid-1630s, disputes, if not eradicated, were controlled, and the work of furthering religious practice based on the Tridentine decrees proceeded apace. Thus the Catholic parish system, manned by a growing supply of priests, many seminary-trained, was well enough rooted to be able to recover, with difficulty, from the turmoil of the mid-seventeenth century. The efforts of Counter-Reformation clergy to catechize, administer the sacraments in the new manner and extirpate superstition continued in successive generations.

Unlike its counterparts elsewhere, the Irish Counter-Reformation did not have to engage with a strong, well-organized Reformed church, but it needed its demonologies as well as its martyrologies. Although the number of those put to death in Ireland for religion was small by comparison with other countries, the concept of persecution was important as a galvanizing force in the writings of Counter-Reformation apologists in the seventeenth century. For the Old English and Gaelic Irish Catholics alike, the growth of self-identity was facilitated by the cultural efflorescence of the Counter-Reformation. For the former, the failure to achieve toleration for their religious practice was all the more galling because of their professed loyalty to the government. The intellectual energies of the scholarly elite were channelled into devotional, apologetic and historical writings, enshrining a self-confident sense of identity with Catholic Europe and asserting the continuity of the Catholic church in Ireland down to their own time. Much of this literary output was in Latin and was aimed at a European readership as well as an Irish one. The Franciscans of Louvain played a major role in formulating a Catholic ideology, underpinned by Counter-Reformation devotion and an awareness of antipathetic forces in Ireland. In this context may be understood their work of gathering Gaelic sources for the presentation of the story of Ireland's past, including the lives of its saints, both national and local. The history of Ireland came to be rendered by the scholars of the Counter-Reformation as the emergence of a Catholic nation, owing complete allegiance to the Roman church. In this way the Counter-Reformation contributed to the course of subsequent Irish historiography.

Reading

Bossy, John, 'The counter reformation and the people of catholic Ireland, 1596–1641', *Historical Studies*, viii (1971).

Canny, Nicholas, 'The formation of the Irish mind: religion, politics and Gaelic Irish literature, 1580–1750', *Past and Present* 95 (1982).

Corish, Patrick J., *The Catholic Community in the Seventeenth and Eighteenth Centuries* (Dublin: Helicon, 1981).

Clarke, Aidan, 'Colonial identity in early seventeenth-century Ireland', in T.W. Moody (ed.), *Nationality and the Pursuit of National Independence: Historical Studies XI* (Belfast: Appletree Press, 1978).

Cregan, Donal, 'The social and cultural background of a Counter-Reformation episcopate, 1618–60', in Art Cosgrove and Donal McCartney (eds), *Studies in Irish History Presented to R. Dudley Edwards* (Naas: Leinster Leader, 1979).

Cunningham, Bernadette, 'The culture and ideology of Irish Franciscan historians at Louvain, 1607–50', in Ciaran Brady (ed.), *Ideology and the Historians* (Dublin: Lilliput Press, 1991).

Hammerstein, Helga, 'Aspects of the continental education of Irish students in the reign of Elizabeth I', *Historical Studies*, viii (1971).

Henry, Grainne, 'The emerging identity of an Irish military group in the Spanish Netherlands, 1586–1610', in R.V. Comerford, M. Cullen, J.R. Hill and C. Lennon (eds), *Religion, Conflict and Coexistence* (Dublin: Gill and Macmillan, 1989).

Jones, Frederick, 'The Counter-Reformation', in Patrick J. Corish (ed.), *A History of Irish Catholicism*, vol. iii (Dublin: Gill and Macmillan, 1967).

Lennon, Colm, 'The Counter Reformation', in Ciaran Brady and Raymond Gillespie (eds), *Natives and Newcomers* (Dublin: Irish Academic Press, 1986).

Millett, Benignus, 'Survival and reorganisation, 1650–95', in Patrick J. Corish (ed.), *A History of Irish Catholicism*, vol. iii (Dublin: Gill and Macmillan, 1968).

O'Riordan, Michelle, *The Gaelic Mind and the Collapse of the Gaelic World* (Cork: Cork University Press, 1991).

COLM LENNON

county At the death of King John in 1216 most of Ireland was covered by large Anglo-Norman lordships and by the remnants of Gaelic kingdoms. Yet already there were royal sheriffs of Dublin, Waterford–Cork and Munster. During the thirteenth century crown administration grew at the expense of Gaelic kings and provincial barons: when local government was reorganized in 1297, there were eleven counties (Louth, Meath, Roscommon, Connacht, Dublin, Kildare, Waterford, Cork, Tipperary, Limerick and Kerry) and five great liberties (Kilkenny, Carlow, Wexford, Trim and Ulster). Central control was far from uniform in the shired areas; even in the south and east, where it was strongest, every county had its zones of upland, woodland or bog, where English administration gave way to a marcher world of cattle raiding and feud. In the late Middle Ages the march areas enlarged, and royal influence slackened. By 1500 only the sheriffs of the Pale were regularly responsive to Dublin, though vestiges of the county structure survived in south Leinster and Munster.

The second phase of county creation belongs to the sixteenth century, in the era of direct rule initiated by the crown in 1534. In 1542 the old county of Meath was divided, and Westmeath created with Athlone as shire town. In 1557 the Gaelic territories represented in the first plantation were designated the counties of King's County (Offaly) and Queen's County (Leix) to provide a new administrative framework. Thereafter the county structure was extended across all Ireland. This was provided for by the 1569 act 'for the turning of countries that be not yet shire ground into shire ground' so that 'her Majesty's laws may have free course... throughout this whole realm of Ireland', and was brought about over the next twenty or so years. In Munster and Connacht the counties were placed under presidencies and councils (abolished, 1672). These proposals for local government under central control, replacing the quasi-autonomy of local lords, contributed to tension and rebellion, and counties with sheriffs and justices of the peace only became effective in Ulster after the Nine Years' War. The county system was functioning from the early seventeenth century and from then also the assize judges went on circuit into all the counties. The 1613 Parliament was the first to draw members from all Irish counties. In 1898 local government was overhauled when democratically elected county councils were created.

Reading

Ellis, S.G., *Reform and Revival: English Government in Ireland 1470–1534* (Woodbridge: Boydell, 1986).
Otway-Ruthven, A.J., 'Anglo-Irish shire government in the thirteenth century', *Irish Historical Studies*, 5 (1946–7).
——*A History of Medieval Ireland* (London: Benn, 2nd edn, 1980).

R.J. FRAME AND R.J. HUNTER

Cousser, Jean Sigismond (Kusser, Johann Sigismund) (1660–1727) Composer. Born (baptized) Pressburg (now Bratislava), 13 February: died Dublin, November. Cousser arrived in Dublin in July 1707, where he composed an annual Royal Birthday Ode for Queen Anne and George I. On 30 October 1727, his birthday ode for George II, a *serenata theatrale* (*sic*), was staged in Dublin Castle. In 1717 he was appointed 'Master of the Musick attending his Majesty's State in Ireland'. Prior to his arrival in Dublin, Cousser had held various appointments as *Kapellmeister* in Germany. He studied with Lully in Paris *c.*1674–82, and was esteemed by Mattheson as an outstanding director of opera.

Reading

Boydell, Brian, *A Dublin Musical Calendar 1700–1760* (Dublin: Irish Academic Press, 1988).
Samuel, Harold, 'John Sigismund Cousser in London and Dublin', *Music and Letters*, 61, no. 2, (1980), pp. 158–71.

HARRY WHITE

Cox, Sir Richard (1650–1733) Lord chancellor of Ireland. He was born at Bandon, County Cork, and spent his early life practising at the bar in Cork. He was a fervent Protestant, and at the accession of James II moved to Bristol, where he wrote *Hibernia Anglicana: or the history of Ireland from the Conquest thereof by the English to the present time*, in 1689. He followed this with a number of publications urging the coronation of the Prince of Orange and the need to subdue Ireland. His support for William was rewarded with a string of offices when he returned to Ireland with the Williamite army, culminating in his brief sojourn on the Irish Privy Council in 1692. Readmitted to the Irish Privy Council in 1701, he was made lord chancellor in 1703. Though he continued to publish tracts on Ireland, his chief work was *Hibernia Anglicana*. This constituted a compilation of previous chronicles and histories of Ireland, with a number of new documents, but is throughout marred by Cox's rabid anti-Catholicism, and his declared intention to show that the Irish would still be barbarous if not for English civility.

Reading

Caulfield, R. (ed.), *Autobiography of Sir Richard Cox, Lord Chancellor of Ireland . . . .* (London: 1860).
Moody, T.W. 'Introduction: early modern Ireland', in *New History of Ireland*, vol. 3 (Dublin: Gill and Macmillan, 1976).
O'Flanagan, J.R., *The Lives of the Lord Chancellors . . . of Ireland*, 2 vols (1870).

BRIAN DONOVAN

Craig, James (1871–1940) Politician. One of the principal founders of the state of Northern Ireland, Craig came of a wealthy Presbyterian family. Born near Belfast, he was educated at a local preparatory school and at Merchiston Castle School, Edinburgh. Following a commercial apprenticeship in Belfast and London, he returned to found his own stockbroking firm and to help establish the Belfast Stock Exchange. He served in the Boer War (1899–1902) and was prominent in the Ulster Unionist movement, becoming Unionist MP for East County Down in 1906. His active wartime service on the Western Front was followed in 1918 by a knighthood and a period as a parliamentary secretary. He succeeded Edward Carson as leader of the Ulster Unionist Party and, following the Government of Ireland Act, 1920, became the first prime minister of Northern Ireland. Craig (Viscount Craigavon from 1927) played a considerable part in keeping the new state as stable and prosperous as the circumstances allowed. Its early survival owed much to his determination and abilities. He underpinned and promoted the state's essentially Protestant identity, not least through the abolition in 1929 of proportional representation. Craig continued in office until his unexpected death in November 1940.

GERARD O'BRIEN

Craig-Martin, Michael (1941–) Born Dublin. Craig-Martin is unusual in that although trained in New York (Yale, 1961–6), he has built his practice in Britain. As an 'international Irish artist', his success and reputation have been gained outside of the country. His practice is very much dominated by the concerns of the mid to late sixties art scene of New York: the minimalism and conceptualism of LeWitt, Judd, André and Morris. His use of mirrors, glasses and buckets of water demonstrates an interest in the interaction between illusion and art. For instance, his *Oak Tree* consists of a glass of water on a glass shelf in a gallery space with the text of an interview discussing it as a work of art. He wanted to create 'a kind of factual illusion using the literalness of the materials as a means of doing it'. In 1994 he held a chair at Goldsmith's College, London.

Reading

Seymour, Anne, 'Commentary', in *Michael Craig-Martin: Selected Works 1966–1975* (Leigh: Turnpike Gallery, 1976).

MARTIN MCCABE AND MICHAEL WILSON

Crawford, William Sharman (1781–1861) Politician. Born County Down, 3 September; died at his home at Crawfordsburn, 18 October. Crawford was elected MP for Dundalk in 1835 but lost his seat in 1837.

In 1841 he was elected for Rochdale but in 1852 he failed to gain a seat in Down. He recognized the Ulster tenant-right custom on his extensive estates and campaigned to have it legalized throughout Ireland. In place of repeal of the Union be advocated a federal parliamentary scheme.

HENRY BOYLAN

Croker, John Wilson (1780–1857) Politician, essayist and critic. Croker became an MP for Downpatrick in 1807 after studying law and being called to the Irish bar in 1802. Rapidly becoming friends with the Duke of Wellington, he was soon a staunch Tory campaigner and was rewarded with the secretaryship of the Admiralty in 1809, a post he held for 22 years. His opposition to the Reform Bill of 1832 led him to resign from Parliament, but he remained a Tory supporter and is acknowledged as the originator of the term 'Conservative'.

In the early 1800s Croker published several satirical sketches. His strong traditionalist views on the arts were later exemplified in his work as a critic for the *Quarterly Review* from 1831 to 1854, where his savage attacks on writers like Keats, Macaulay and Tennyson caused considerable debate and earned him the enmity of Disraeli (among others), who subsequently parodied him in his novel *Coningsby*.

HELEN MCCURDY

Crommellin, Samuel-Louis (1652–1727) Industrialist. Born Armandcourt, Picardy, May; died Lisburn, County Antrim, 14 July. The Crommellin family business of flax-growing was ruined by the revocation of the Edict of Nantes in 1685. In 1699 King William III invited Crommellin to direct the linen manufactures in Lisburn started by exiled Huguenot linen workers. He imported a thousand looms from Flanders and Holland and engaged Dutchmen to superintend bleaching and teach flax-growing. The industry flourished, and Dublin and London were supplied with linens and cambrics of a quality previously obtainable only from abroad.

HENRY BOYLAN

Cromwell, Oliver (1599–1658) Politician and soldier. Cromwell landed near Dublin on 15 August 1649 and embarked again at Youghal on 29 May 1650. Nine months sufficed to convert his name into a by-word for brutality, and the worst personification of that English racial and religious animus against the Irish which stretched over several centuries. Cromwell's impact, then, was both immediate and durable; his importance tangible and symbolic. He arrived as commander of an English army of reconquest, and, thanks to his well-publicized capture of Drogheda and Wexford, was credited with success. But official panegyrists played down the decisive victory at Rathmines on 2 August 1649, which had preceded his arrival, as well as the humiliating losses suffered at Clonmel late in April 1650. His military renown, earned by decisiveness, also owed much to a massive superiority in the number of his troops, and was inflated by English flatterers. There remained much for his subordinates to complete after he had sailed away, and guerilla warfare grumbled on throughout the 1650s.

'Cromwellian' described the settlement to which, after 1650, defeat exposed the Confederate Catholics. Many 'Cromwellian' policies, particularly the forfeiture of the confederates' lands, merely continued what had begun in the sixteenth century or implemented what the English parliaments decreed in 1642, 1652 and 1653. Until December 1653, when he was invested as protector, Cromwell's influence over Irish policy was uncertain and at best intermittent. During his tour of duty in Ireland he admired what the Irish Protestants had achieved and what the Catholics had destroyed; he started summary procedures to provide English law and Protestant preaching. But neither in England nor in Ireland did Cromwell invent new institutions or complex strategies, so it is unlikely that he initiated any important departures in Irish policy, such as the removal of the Irish into Connacht.

What is clear, however, is that Cromwell shared contemporary English prejudices against Ireland and the Irish: the material and moral backwardness; the corrosive effects of the Gaelic social system and Catholic religion; and the innate duplicity, manifest in the uprising and alleged massacres of October 1641. He approved and administered new doses of anglicization. Also, with manic zest, he acted as his countrymen's avenging agent at Drogheda and Wexford. Exhilarated by a sequence of often startling victories throughout the 1640s, he was persuaded of his own and his army's providential mission to advance the cause of godliness and cut down the enemies of the godly.

Even so, once the retributive thirst had been slaked, Cromwellian policy – usually devised and implemented by others – aimed more to conciliate and improve than to punish or destroy. Sometimes the rhetorical generosity, as in the amiable gestures with which he caressed the poorer Irish in 1650, was difficult to translate into actions; equally, the full fury of indiscriminate slaughter and expropriation was impossible to sustain. Cromwell, conventionally, favoured the puny Protestant interest in Ireland, and, without the expected influx of substantial new settlers from England, helped its already well-established members to more lands and power.

Cromwell's (and his son's) rule did not outlast the decade. Nevertheless, in Ireland the material results of the measures imposed in, and associated with, his name endured: Catholics lost land, office and political rights. Simultaneously the Protestant interest had been enlarged, strengthened and splintered. Irish Protestants had responded variously to the Cromwellian usurpation and Stuart restoration in 1660. The religious denominations which had thrived or arrived in the 1650s persisted: Presbyterians most conspicuously, but also small groups of Congregationalists, Baptists and Quakers, thereafter complicated the Irish Protestant community.

After 1660, neither Protestants nor Catholics wrote much of Cromwell. As a villain in Catholic demonologies he was dwarfed by false friends, notably Ormonde and Clarendon, or even Charles II and James II; as a hero, William III embarrassed Protestants less than Cromwell. A grudging admiration for Cromwell's military prowess was usually effaced by the belief, surely accurate, that the 1690s, not the 1650s, had decided definitively Protestant ascendancy and Catholic debasement. Only when the structure and content of Irish politics altered in the late eighteenth and early nineteenth centuries did Cromwell again interest Irish controversialists. Protestant ultras liked his strident anti-Catholicism; irenicists rediscovered but misunderstood his libertarian cant.

Surprisingly little of a continuous folk memory or authentic popular legend of Cromwell, whether black or golden, can be traced before the nineteenth century. Moreover, Protestant celebration and iconography had elevated other eras and conquerors. Only after the 1860s did Unionists and nationalists ransack his published speeches and despatches home for helpful material. The more Unionists annexed Cromwell, the more nationalists vilified him. Much of the popular excoriation of Cromwell dates from this period rather than earlier. Subsequent efforts to return him to his historical context and rehabilitate him stumble against the gratuitous (and militarily unjustified) blood-letting over which he had gleefully presided, and against the intractable problem of who initiated the more imaginative and generous measures which enriched and stabilized Ireland in the later 1650s. The historical Cromwell seems doomed to stand as the type who embodies English non-comprehension of, and insensitivity towards, Ireland.

T.C. BARNARD

Cronin, Anthony (1928–) Poet, critic and publicist. Born Enniscorthy, 28 December, Cronin was educated at Blackrock College and University College, Dublin. He was a barrister of the Kings' Inns. He worked during the early 1950s on the *Bell* under socialist Republican Peadar O'Donnell, and on

John Ryan's *Envoy*. Later he became literary editor of *Time and Tide* in London, founding there in the 1960s (with painter Patrick Swift) *X: A literary journal*. On returning to Ireland Cronin worked largely as a political and social commentator in the *Irish Times* (and sometime racing correspondent of the *Sunday Tribune*). Cultural adviser to C.J. Haughey during his administrations up to 1992, he promoted the Aosdána scheme to give disinction and financial support to Irish artists, and the creation of a museum of modern art in the Royal Hospital Kilmainham. An acute and trenchant critic of Irish life, whose opinions have often aroused anger and resentment, his claims as important writer are supported by his long poem *R.M.S. Titanic* (new edn 1981), by a small number of short poems, to be found in *New and Selected Poems* (1982), and by his novel *The Life of Reilly* (1964). He is also the author of *Dead as Doornails* (1976), a memoir of 1950s literary life in Dublin; a biography of Flann O'Brien, *No Laughing Matter* (1989); and a biography of Samuel Beckett (*The Last Modernist* 1996).

PETER COSTELLO

Cross, Dorothy (1956–) Sculptor. Born in Cork, where she trained initially at the Crawford School of Art (1973–4) and then at Leicester Polytechnic (1974–7) and San Francisco Art Institute (1978–82). Cross's work investigates the ambiguities, conflicts and points of balance in male and female sexuality. It is informed by Jungian and Lacanian psychoanalytic theory. Cross's sculptures consist of various found objects, often old and rusting, combined with photographs and finely made wooden abstract forms. Her installation *Power House* (1991) used imagery and objects from the disused pump house at the Dublin Pigeon House power station.

Reading

Feldman, Melissa E., 'Power plays', in *Dorothy Cross: Power House* (Philadelphia: Institute of Contemporary Art, 1991).

Fowler, Joan, 'Voyages of transformation', in *Dorothy Cross: Ebb* (Dublin: Douglas Hyde Gallery, 1988).

FELICITY WOOLF

CS gas Ortho-chlorobenzal-malononitrile. More than 1,000 canisters of this gas were fired by the Royal Ulster Constabulary in 36 hours during disturbances in Derry in August 1969. A severe irritant, it has induced death in laboratory animals; its effects on humans include damage to the lungs, liver and kidneys. Its use by the RUC and British army in Northern Ireland caused alienation among the Catholic community, but its re-placement by rubber and plastic bullets as methods of crowd control proved even more dangerous.

Reading

McClean, Raymond, *The Road to Bloody Sunday* (Dublin: Ward River Press, 1983).

JAMES DOWNEY

Cuala Press After its split from the Dun Emer Industries in 1908, the Cuala Press continued its role in the Irish literary revival, hand-printing simple yet dignified limited editions of its major authors. It was run prin-cipally by Elizabeth Corbet 'Lolly' Yeats, but other members of the family were closely involved, especially W.B. Yeats, who acted as literary editor and financier as well as writing the majority of the texts. Synge, Lady Gregory, Gogarty and Frank O'Connor were some of the other authors published before Lolly's death in 1940.

The running of the press was continued by Georgie Yeats, widow of the poet, but book production was discontinued in 1946 even though its list had been adventurous and included MacNeice, Donagh MacDonagh, Kavanagh and Bowen. The output now con-sisted of hand-coloured prints and greeting cards. Anne and Michael Yeats decided to revive book publishing in 1969, the year after their mother, Georgie's, death. Thomas Kinsella was among the authors printed, thus continuing the press's tradition of publishing Irish poetry. The final book was issued in 1979, and in 1986 the press finally ceased. Its archive and printing equipment were presented to Trinity College Library, Dublin.

Reading

Kinane, Vincent, 'Some aspects of the Cuala Press', *Private Library*, 2, no. 3 (Autumn 1989).
Miller, Liam, *The Dun Emer Press, Later the Cuala Press* (Dublin: Dolmen, 1973).

VINCENT KINANE

Cubism The first great innovative move-ment in twentieth-century art. Essentially a representational art form, it became the parent of all abstract art. Its formative years lasted from about 1907 until 1914, although its con-sequences were long felt thereafter. The ear-liest Cubist or semi-Cubist picture which can, with certainty, be documented as having been exhibited in Ireland is Picasso's portrait of his friend *Clovis Sagot* (1909, Kunsthalle, Hamburg). This picture was shown during January and February 1911 in the exhibition '*Works by Post-Impressionist Painters*', arranged by Ellen Duncan at the United Arts Club, Dublin. A year later, in March 1912, Ellen Duncan arranged a similar exhibition, '*Modern French Pictures*', at the same venue and included a number of Cubist pictures by Picasso and Juan Gris, although these cannot now be identified. Both of these exhibitions were widely reviewed in the Dublin press, although such avant-garde works found few enthusiasts. However, they did introduce Cubism to a public which, in terms of modern painting, had hitherto seen only Impressionist, Post-Impressionist and Fauvist works.

The next we hear of Cubism in Ireland is in the work of Mainie Jellett (1897–1944) and Evie Hone (1894–1955). In 1917, on leaving the Metropolitan School of Art in Dublin, Jellett worked under Walter Sickert at the Westminster School in London, and there met Evie Hone. In about 1920 Hone and

Jellett met Bernard Meninsky, who succeeded Sickert at the Westminster School, and at his suggestion Hone went to Paris in the autumn of 1920 to work with the Cubist painter André Lhote. Early in 1921 she was joined there by Jellett, but the following December, seeking a more abstract and more spiritual art than that taught by Lhote, they became pupils of Albert Gleizes. Thus began an association with Gleizes which, with Jellett in particular, continued intermittently for most of the rest of her life.

With André Lhote Jellett developed a straightforward form of Cubism, based on the study of natural forms, close in style to early 'Analytical' Cubism. Lhote encouraged his pupils to use colour creatively and not merely descriptively, to emphasize organic structures and rhythmical forms and to think of a picture as an organic whole. Applying these principles Jellett produced a number of works, including her *Seated Female Nude* (1921–2, Ulster Museum). This composition, in the stylized angular forms of the figure, the chair in which she is seated and the drapery in the background, all of which combine to produce a considerable flattening of the picture-plane, well illustrates her grasp of the basics of Cubist theory. Also, as with early Cubism, these works remain representational in concept. At this time Jellett also applied Cubist principles to studies from landscape, the Old Masters and religious subjects. But despite her development with Lhote, Jellett, along with Evie Hone, sought a purer, more abstract form of painting: thus they persuaded Albert Gleizes to take them as pupils.

When Jellett and Hone met Gleizes, he was already recognized as a major theorist on Cubism, his book *Du Cubisme* (1912), written with Jean Metzinger, being the most important study of the movement. *Du Cubisme* is marked throughout by a strong rhetoric and emphasis on principles of colour and surface organization. Moreover, in 1917 Gleizes had undergone a religious conversion and subsequently endeavoured to interpret the 'laws' of art in terms of spiritual experience.

With Gleizes, Jellett and Hone began to work towards a distinct abstract art and, no doubt, the influence of Gleizes's religious views led them to seek the universal, what Jellett called 'the inner principle and not the outer appearance'. With Gleizes, she wrote later, 'our aim was to delve deeply into inner rhythms and constructions of natural forms to create on their pattern, to make a work of art a natural creation complete in itself'. With this in mind, both Jellett and Hone created compositions of forms superimposed one on another with an organic sense of rhythm, and usually displaced a few degrees to the left or right – what they termed 'translation' and 'rotation' of the forms. Jellett's *Decoration* (1923, National Gallery of Ireland), is a supreme example of this technique. It and a similar work, the first completely abstract pictures by an Irish artist, were exhibited at the Dublin Painters' Society in 1923. This was the first time that an Irish public had seen such innovative works, but they bemused the critics, as George Russell's condemnation of them in the *Irish Statesman* as 'artistic malaria' illustrates. However, Jellett and Hone persevered in their work, and in subsequent years exhibited at the Dublin Painters' gallery similar and more elaborate compositions in which the arrangement of imagery became ever more profuse and intricate. At this time their works, due to their experiments with Cubism and abstraction, were often almost indistinguishable. Evie Hone, however, was never as fully committed to Cubism as was Jellett and increasingly lost interest in its theoretical principles. During the later 1920s her work grew more intuitive and in the 1930s she practically abandoned Cubism.

From the mid-1920s Jellett's compositions are characterized by the use of muted colours and an emphasis on line, and often, as in her *Homage to Fra Angelico* (1927), they have a religious significance. The latter work also illustrates how she could combine representational images with Cubist forms, and is a precursor of much of her later work. In general, however, compositions such as *Abstract* (*c*.1932–5, Ulster Museum), or the splendidly colourful and spiritually self-contained *Virgin and Child* of about 1936 characterize her work of the time. By the late 1930s her work became more overtly devotional, although she retained a Cubist approach to composition. Pictures such as *The Ninth Hour* (1939), *I Have Trodden the Winepress Alone* (1943) and *Madonna of Eire* (1943, National Gallery of Ireland), are her most important from this period and, on the eve of war, illustrate her concern for the times. In terms of her work and the theories which underpinned it, Mainie Jellett was Ireland's only true Cubist painter and her untimely death in 1944 was a great loss to Irish painting.

Several other Irish painters of course were influenced by Cubism to some extent at least. Around 1922–5 May Guinness (1863–1955), who had also studied with André Lhote, adopted a Cubist manner, as her *Still Life* (Hugh Lane Municipal Gallery, Dublin) shows, but this did not last long with her. Besides, like many of her contemporaries she had no interest in Cubist theory and her technique, which was to apply Cubist stylization to scenes from everyday life in order to make bold patterns, has only a superficial relationship to Cubism proper. Mary Swanzy (1882–1978), who generally worked in a more Fauvist manner, produced Cubist pictures in about 1925, at which time she was living and working in Samoa. But Swanzy's, too, was a decorative kind of Cubism and lacked theoretical rigour. However, in the late 1920s she evolved a more dynamic style, with an emphasis on movement and energy, which recalls Italian Futurism. *White Tower (San Gimignano)* (*c*.1925–7) is a good example of this phase of her work, but she did not exhibit such pictures in Ireland until 1932, by which time she had turned to a more allegorical kind of painting.

Apart from those whom we have discussed, other Irish painters had a more fleeting association with Cubism. In the 1920s, encouraged by Mainie Jellett, Norah McGuinness

(1903–80) went briefly to André Lhote, but he had little influence on her. In the early 1950s, however, in a few pictures such as *Garden Green* (1952, Hugh Lane Municipal Gallery), she made an excursion into Cubism. Father Jack Hanlon (1913–68) was also with Lhote. In the 1930s he developed a semi-Cubist manner which laid emphasis on colour and light, but which was intuitive in approach. The English painter Elizabeth Rivers (1903–64), too, had been with Lhote before coming to Ireland in 1935. She emphasized angular shapes and flat forms which, as in *The Ark* (1948), were often juxtaposed with bright colours.

Irish sculpture was little influenced by Cubism. In the mid-1930s Laurence Campbell (1911–68), in Dublin, and George MacCann (1909–67) and Elizabeth Clements, in Belfast, made works which were in part inspired by Cubist ideas. Campbell's *Mother and Child* (*c*.1933) has a formal severity and rhythm similar to that found in Mainie Jellett's compositions of the same period, while MacCann and Clements produced works reminiscent of the French sculptor Jacques Lipchitz. In the 1940s, Jocelyn Chewett (1906–79), who exhibited with the White Stag Group, was also influenced by Lipchitz.

By the 1940s and early 1950s Cubism was an influence only in superficial terms. Of the White Stag artists, Basil Rákóczi (1908–79), Phyllis Hayward (1903–85), Doreen Vanston (1903–88) and Ralph Cusack (1912–65) all demonstrated a Cubist sense of form devolved from Picasso, of which Hayward's *Still Life with Guitar*, Vanston's *A Dying Animal* (*c*.1943, Ulster Museum), and Cusack's *Christmas in My Studio* (1943) are good examples. Of those associated with the Irish Exhibition of Living Art (IELA) exhibitions, Gerard Dillon (1916–71), Nevill Johnson (1911–) and Thurloe Conolly (1918–) betray traces of Cubism. The overlapping forms in Dillon's *Angels with Split Voices*, of the early 1940s, are clearly Picassoesque, while Johnson's *The Clown* (*c*.1950) and Conolly's *The Juggler* (1953), for example, though

Cubist-derived, suggest moves towards a more abstract art. Around 1950 Louis le Brocquy (b. 1916), too, adopted a semi-Cubist structural discipline expressed in angular shapes and forms derived from Cézanne and Picasso, as *A Family*, of 1951, demonstrates.

In the mid-1950s Kenneth Mahood (1930–) retained a Cubist sense of form, as did Colin Middleton (1910–83) even till the early 1970s. Traces of Cubism, notably in the use of disjointed forms, can also be seen more recently in the work of T.P. Flangan (1929–), R.J. Croft (1935–), Brian Ferran (1940–) and David Crone (1937–).

S.B. KENNEDY

Cullen, Paul (1803–78) Churchman. Born near Ballitore, County Kildare, 29 April; died Dublin, 24 October. The Cullens were a prosperous family of strong farmers and cattle dealers. Paul attended the Quaker school at Ballitore (1814–17) and Carlow College (1817–20). In 1820 he became a student at the College of Propaganda, Rome. Following ordination to the priesthood he was appointed professor of Greek and Oriental languages at the College of Propaganda in 1830 and became rector of the Irish College, Rome, in 1832. In this position he was admirably placed to act as Roman agent for the bishops of Ireland and of other parts of the English-speaking world. His capacity and flair secured for him a pivotal role in the ecclesiastical politics of Ireland, which he retained until his death. In 1850 Cullen became archbishop of Armagh and returned to Ireland with the additional title of apostolic delegate. He summoned and presided over the Synod of Thurles (1850), which set the tone of his Irish mission. He was translated to the see of Dublin in 1852, becoming in 1866 the first Irish-born cardinal. He was a leading advocate of the definition of papal infallibility at the First Vatican Council.

Cullen has come to personify the political, organizational and devotional triumphs of the post-Famine Catholic church. Assertive ultramontanism was the hallmark of his career. While this left him at odds with older ecclesiastics of a more irenic disposition such as Archbishop Murray of Dublin (1768–1852), he found an ally in John MacHale (1791–1881). When the acceptability of the national school system became an issue in the 1830s, Cullen instinctively joined MacHale in opposing the compromise in church–state relations which it represented, but he subsequently accepted the conciliatory line advocated by most of the bishops and adopted by Rome in 1841. Later Cullen and MacHale successfully advocated Catholic rejection of the Queen's Colleges. They subsequently disagreed about many matters, not least the affairs of the Catholic University. Cullen's sentiments were deeply nationalist but – especially after 1848 – he dreaded the agitations, peaceful or otherwise, inseparable from a nationalist movement.

Reading

Bowen, Desmond, *Paul Cardinal Cullen and the Shaping of Modern Irish Catholicism* (Dublin: Gill and Macmillan, 1983).

Corish, Patrick J., 'Cardinal Cullen and Archbishop MacHale', *Irish Ecclesiastical Records* xci (1959).

Larkin, Emmet, 'The devotional revolution in Ireland, 1850–75', *American Historical Review* lxxvii (1972).

MacSuibhne, Peadar (ed.), *Paul Cullen and his Contemporaries, with their Letters from 1820 to 1902*, 5 vols (Naas: Leinster Leader, 1961–77).

R.V. COMERFORD

Culwick, James C. (1845–1907) English organist and composer. Culwick was a chorister and assistant organist at Lichfield Cathedral before moving to Ireland in 1866. He subsequently held a succession of appointments as organist, first in Birr, County Offaly, then in Bray, County Wicklow, and finally in Dublin. In 1881 he relinquished his post in St Anne's, Dawson Street, to assume the prestigious position of organist and choirmaster at the Chapel Royal in Dublin Castle. He was involved with a number of amateur musical bodies, founded and conducted the Orpheus Choral Society, and was awarded an honorary doctorate from the University of Dublin in 1893. The vocal ascendancy in his original works reflect his preferences and involvement. His output includes church services, anthems, finely crafted secular songs, and notably the dramatic cantata *The Legend of Stauffenberg* (1890).

JOSEPH RYAN

Cumann na mBan Women's organization founded in Dublin in November 1913, at the same time as the Irish Volunteers, of which it became the women's division the following year. Led by Countess Markievicz and Kathleen Clarke, by 1916 it had 43 branches. It supported the 1916 Rising, and worked with the Republican movement throughout the War of Independence. A great majority of its members, together with the women Dáil deputies, opposed the Treaty of 1921. Led by Maude Gonne, they supported the IRA during the following decades and were associated with some of the radical movements of the period.

JAMES KEMMY

Curran, John Philpot (1750–1817) Lawyer and politician. Born in Newmarket, County Cork, Curran is remembered as much for his courtroom performances as for his popular political stance. He was a prominent figure in the Monks of the Screw, one of the earliest ex-parliamentary Patriot clubs and one which endured until 1795. Taking a seat in the Irish Commons in the Longfield 'interest', he was soon in difficulty with his patron for his espousal of popular causes and his obvious connection with the Patriot opposition. He compensated Longfield at considerable personal expense and purchased for himself a seat for Rathcormack. Appointed a king's counsel shortly before entering Parliament, Curran supported a popular but highly unprofitable Patriot career by means of a growing legal practice. An opponent of government patronage systems and a strong supporter of parliamentary reform and Catholic relief, he was known also for his choleric temper and his willingness to engage if necessary in duels. He was legal counsel for Wolfe Tone and Hamilton Rowan and a stout opponent of the Union. Curran was regarded as one of the most colourful characters of his time and has been the subject of several biographies. He died near London in October 1817.

GERARD O'BRIEN

D

Dana (May 1904–April 1905) Radical literary monthly edited by John Eglinton (pseudonym of W.K. Magee, 1868–1961) and Frederick Ryan (1876–1913). It aimed to nourish 'independent thought' in a nationalist context and carried essays by the editors and others criticizing the Catholic hierarchy and the Gaelic League, as well as some responses. Eglinton later attributed its failure to the 'spiritual authorities of Ireland'. There were prose contributions by Stephen Gwynn, George Moore, Horace Plunkett and George Russell; and poems by Jane Barlow, Padraic Colum, James Joyce and Oliver St John Gogarty. *Dana* is best known for rejecting the first draft of Joyce's 'Portrait of the Artist' in essay form, but he was also the only contributor to be paid.

BRUCE STEWART

Danby, Francis (1793–1861) Painter. Born Common, Killinick, near Wexford, 16 November. Danby's father was a small landed proprietor who was both a Protestant and a loyalist. Danby studied at the Dublin Society Drawing Schools, where he befriended George Petrie and James Arthur O Connor. He died in Exmouth in 1861. Primarily a landscape painter, Danby occasionally produced historical and biblical themes.

After training in Dublin he emigrated in 1813 at the age of 20 to Bristol and later London, and is not thought to have ever returned to Ireland. His relationship with Ireland was thus limited; he later claimed that he became an English artist in 1813.

Danby's Irish subject matter dates from his very early years and is in the topographical tradition of the late eighteenth-century country house portraits of William Ashford and Thomas Roberts. There are a few Irish drawings in the National Gallery of Ireland, Dublin, the Ulster Museum, Belfast, and the British Museum, London. Of his mature work, his only known reference to his home country is a now untraced painting exhibited at the Royal Academy in 1837, *Rich and Rare were the Gems she Wore*, a scene from Moore's *Irish Melodies*. It is reported as having been a critical failure.

While working in Bristol, 1813 to 1824, Danby specialized in small, almost Virgilian, genre scenes of children playing and lovers reading to each other in the woods above the city. These subjects are surprisingly similar to the themes of William Mulready, another Irish-born emigrant then working in London.

Danby's career was marked by a variety of dramatic troubles: a great professional disappointment in 1829 when he lost to John

Constable by one vote to be elected a Royal Academician; marital scandal in the same year, leading to his fleeing to Switzerland and later France; and most of all continuous financial problems, leading to his being ostracized by the Royal Academy (RA) for some six years. His great successes were in the area of sublime biblical landscapes, such as *The Opening of the Sixth Seal* (RA, 1828, Dublin, National Gallery of Ireland), which sold for 500 guineas to William Beckford, while Colnaghi bought the print copyright for £300. It was the most popular painting of the year and had to be moved to a separate gallery because of the crowds it attracted. Based on Revelations 6:12, the subject includes a moral justification for the contemporary anti-slavery campaign.

Reading

Adams, Eric, *Francis Danby: Varieties of Poetic Landscape* (New Haven CT and London: 1973).
Art Journal (1855).
Crookshank, Anne and the Knight of Glin, *The Painters of Ireland c.1660–1920* (London: Barrie and Jenkins, 1978).
Greenacre, Francis, *Francis Danby 1793–1861* (London: Tate Gallery, 1988).
Hutchinson, John, *James Arthur O Connor* (Dublin: National Gallery of Ireland, 1985).
Strickland, Walter, *A Dictionary of Irish Artists* (Shannon: Irish University Press, 1968).

FINTAN CULLEN

Darcy, Patrick (1598–1668) Influential Catholic lawyer. Darcy, who came from Galway, represented the Galway landholders in their attempt to circumvent the proposed plantation of Connaught during the 1630s. He was an energetic member of the Irish House of Commons in 1641, and in 1642 was made a member of the Supreme Council of the Catholic Confederacy at Kilkenny, and played a central role throughout the rebellion. His chief work was in refuting the English Parliament's claim that it could legislate for Ireland. Before the rebellion he submitted his 'Argument' to this effect to the judges on behalf of the Commons in June 1641. This document

was published by the Confederacy in 1643, as were other tracts by him on the same topic. His assertion that the Irish Parliament had legislative independence from England represented the political objectives of the Old English in Ireland, and their justification for supporting the confederacy.

Reading

Clarke, Aidan, *The Old English in Ireland 1625–42* (London: 1966).
Coonan, Thomas L., *The Irish Catholic Confederacy and the Puritan Revolution* (New York: Clonmore and Reynolds/Columbia University Press, 1954).
Meehan, C.P., *The Confederation of Kilkenny*, 2nd edn (Dublin: 1882).
O'Malley, L., 'Patrick Darcy, Galway lawyer and politician 1598–1668', in D. O'Cearbhaill (ed.), *Galway: Town and Gown 1484–1984* (Dublin: 1984).

BRIAN DONOVAN

Dargan, William (1799–1867) Engineer. Born Carlow, 28 February: died 2 Fitzwilliam Square, Dublin, 7 February. Dargan trained in England under Telford and then returned to Ireland to start his own contracting business. He was very successful, and by 1853 he had constructed over 600 miles (965 km) of railway, as well as the Ulster canal. The National Gallery was built to commemorate his services in organizing and financing the Dublin Exhibition of 1853. Later ventures outside contracting were unsuccessful. He was unable to attend to business following an accident and suffered acute financial difficulties.

HENRY BOYLAN

Davis, Thomas Osborne (1814–45) Poet and nationalist. Born Mallow, County Cork, 14 October: died of fever in his mother's house, 67 Baggot Street, Dublin, 16 September. The son of a British army surgeon, Davis was educated at Trinity College, Dublin, and was called to the bar in 1838. In a famous speech to the College Historical Society in

1840 he pleaded for Irish historical studies. He became the leader of the younger men who were impatient of O'Connell's constitutional methods. With Gavan Duffy and John Blake Dillon he founded the *Nation* in 1842. His spirited contributions in prose and verse captured the national imagination and inspired his contemporaries with his vision of an Ireland free to pursue its own destiny. His ballads 'A Nation Once Again' and 'The West's Awake' gained an enduring popularity. His influence on movements for political freedom persisted long after his death. Arthur Griffith described him as 'the prophet I followed throughout my life, the man whose words and teachings I tried to translate into practice in politics'.

Reading

Davis, Thomas Osborne, *Essays and Poems* (Dundalk: W. Tempest, 1914).

HENRY BOYLAN

Davitt, Michael (1846–1906) Politician. Born Straide, County Mayo; died Dublin, 31 May. Davitt was the son of a small farmer. The family was evicted in 1850 and emigrated to Lancashire. Aged 11, Michael lost his right arm while working in a cotton mill. He joined the Fenians and the Irish Republican Brotherhood and in 1870 was sentenced to 15 years' penal servitude. He was released from Dartmoor after seven years under harsh conditions and went to America, where with John Devoy he worked out a new national policy aimed at self-government and land reform. He was back in Ireland in 1874 and founded the Land League with Parnell, a Protestant landlord, as president. It combined in one great agrarian movement all nationalists from moderates to revolutionaries, and received strong backing and financial help from America. In the ensuing land war a new word was added to the English language when an evicting landlord's agent, Captain Boycott, was ostracized.

The Land Act of 1881 gave the tenants the 'Three Fs' – fair rent, fixity of tenure and free sale – but the League fought on for tenant ownership. Gladstone arrested the leaders and suppressed the League, but eventually the government yielded, and in 1885 began the process of ending landlordism.

Both Davitt and Parnell saw the winning of the land war as a step to ultimate independence, but the fall of Parnell and the split in the Irish Party set that cause back for generations. Ironically, 'the land for the people' meant to Davitt the nationalization of the land, whereas to the tenants it could mean only one thing: ownership by themselves. Davitt was an MP from 1882 to 1899 and then devoted himself to travel and journalism.

Reading

Davitt, Michael, *Leaves from a Prison Diary* (London: Chapman and Hall, 1885).
—— *The Boer Fight for Freedom* (New York: Funk and Wagnalls, 1902).
—— *The Fall of Feudalism in Ireland* (London, New York: Harper, 1904).

HENRY BOYLAN

Davys, Mary (b. 1670) Born in Ireland. Davys married a clergyman and took up residence in Cambridge, where she lived until her death. Following the demise of her husband, she maintained herself by keeping a coffee house.

She wrote two comedies, *The Northern Heiress* and *The Self Rival*, which were published in 1725 along with some novels, poems and letters, in two volumes entitled *The Works of Mrs Davys*.

Mary Davys was a correspondent of Jonathan Swift, and appears to have enjoyed something of a literary reputation in her day.

Reading

Dublin University Magazine, XLI (Jan. 1855).

RACHEL FURMSTON

Dawe, Gerald Chartres (1952–) Poet and critic. After studying at the University of Ulster and University College Galway, Dawe worked as a librarian and then taught for several years at University College, Galway, before moving to Dublin, where he currently lives and teaches at Trinity College. He published his first collection of poetry, *Sheltering Places*, in 1978, and was awarded the Macaulay Fellowship in Literature for *The Lundys Letter* (1985), which was followed by *Sunday School* (1991), *Heart of Hearts* (1995) and *The Morning Train* (1999). Critical works include *Against Piety* (1995), *The Rest is History* (1998) and *Stray Dogs and Dark Horses* (2000). In 1986 he founded *Krino: The Review*.

HELEN MCCURDY

Deane, Raymond (1953–) Composer. Born Achill Island. Deane read music at University College, Dublin, and later studied composition in Switzerland and Germany with Gerald Bennett, Karlheinz Stockhausen and Isang Yun. In addition to his work as a composer he has been active as a performer, teacher, translator, theatre critic and, most recently, writer. His novel *Death of a Medium* was published in Dublin in 1991. Major compositions to date include *Thresholds* (1987) for orchestra; *Krespel's Concerto* (1989) for solo violin and orchestra; *November Songs* (1990) for voice and chamber ensemble; *The Poet and his Double* (1991), a chamber opera; and *Catenae* (1991) for 11 instruments. Deane has been awarded the Varming Composition Prize (1979), the Macaulay Fellowship (1981) and the Martin Toonder Award (1985). He is a member of Aosdána, Ireland's government-sponsored body honouring creative artists, and now divides his time between Dublin and Paris.

EVE O'KELLY

Deane, Seamus (1940–) Poet, critic and editor. Seamus Deane was professor of modern English and American literature at University College, Dublin, from 1968 to 1977. The Derry-born writer is founder member of Field Day and general editor, with Andrew Carpenter, of *The Field Day Anthology of Irish Writing 550–1991* (1991). Generally regarded as the leading intellectual force behind Field Day, Deane has published three collections of poetry, *Gradual Wars* (1972), *Rumours* (1977) and *History Lessons* (1983). His critical work includes *Celtic Revivals* (1985) and *A Short History of Irish Literature* (1986), followed by *The French Enlightenment and Revolution in England, 1789–1832* (1988), a work which brings together the twin peaks of Deane's preoccupations – enlightenment and revolution. In the 1980s Deane was largely credited with setting the ideological and critical terms of reference within which modern Irish writing has been read. His highly acclaimed autobiographical novel *Reading in the Dark* is a powerful study of life in Derry in the 1940s and 1950s. He followed this with *Strange Country* (1997). In 1993 Deane became Keough Professor of Irish Studies at Notre Dame University, Indiana.

Reading

Deane, Seamus, *Selected Poems* (Dublin: Gallery, 1988).
—— *The Field Day Anthology of Irish Writing 550–1991* (London: Faber, 1991).
—— *Reading in The Dark* (London: Granta, 1992).

GERALD DAWE

de Bromhead, Jerome (1945–) Composer and radio producer. Born Waterford, 2 December. Educated at Glenstal Abbey School and Trinity College, Dublin, de Bromhead studied composition privately at various periods with A.J. Potter, James Wilson, Séoirse Bodley and Franco Donatoni. He has won several prizes for composition in Ireland and was elected a member of Aosdána, the government-sponsored body honouring creative artists. He has received a number of commissions from leading Irish soloists and ensembles, which have resulted in several concert and broadcast performances

159

both in Ireland and abroad. His work has represented Ireland at the International Rostrum of Composers, and his harpsichord piece, *Flux* (1981), was selected by the international jury for performance in the ISCM Musiktage in Germany in 1987. Since 1969 he has been a producer in the music department of RTE. His principal works include *Abstract Variations* for orchestra (1976), *Symphony No. 1* (1985) and *Guitar Concerto* (1991).

GERARD GILLEN

Deevy, Teresa (1903–63) Born and died Waterford. Deevy suffered from almost total deafness from birth. She overcame this disability and became a popular Abbey Theatre dramatist. *Temporal Powers* (1932), *The King of Spain's Daughter* and *Katie Roche* (both 1935) and *The Wild Goose* (1936) were all initially performed at the Abbey, although they were later revived and became popular with amateur companies throughout Ireland. She wrote almost exclusively for radio after 1936, and *Within a Marble City* was widely praised when it was first broadcast. In 1954, she was elected a member of the Irish Academy of Letters.

RACHEL FURMSTON

deism Rejection of revealed religion. Deism played a central role in Irish thought, beginning with John Toland's *Christianity not Mysterious* (1696). His challenge – that mysteries were meaningless, since they did not stand for clear ideas – was taken up in Peter Browne's *Letter* (1697) and Edward Synge's *Appendix* (1698). In defending Christian mysteries they argued that Toland was like a blind person denying that there were colours and sight. The sensible position, as William King urged in his 1709 *Sermon*, was to find the most serviceable theological representations. A more philosophically important response to Toland's challenge came from Berkeley's *Alciphron* (1732), according to which mysteries have emotive meaning. Hence the Holy Trinity is meaningful, even

if it does not stand for ideas, since it can evoke desirable emotions, attitudes and actions.

Another Irish writer who distinguished himself against the deists was Charles Leslie; his often-reprinted *Short Method with the Deists* (1699) brought about the counter-conversion of at least one major deist, Charles Gildon. A later and more sustained critique was Philip Skelton's *Ophiomaches, or Deism Revealed* (1749). The major critical history, *A View of the Principal Deistical Writers* (3 vols, 1754–7), also came from an Irish writer, John Leland. Some of Swift's most forceful satirical essays were written against the deists, particularly his 1711 'Argument against Abolishing the Christian Religion' and *Mr C —— ns's Discourse of Free-thinking . . . put into Plain English* (1713). Another ironic attack, this time aimed against the deism of Lord Bolingbroke, was Burke's 1756 *Vindication of Natural Society*.

Deism did have its Irish sympathizers, amongst, for example, the Molesworth Circle and even (as in the case of Robert Clayton) the higher clergy. Yet, unlike Britain and France, it was the anti-deists who were most original and articulate in Ireland. Probably the last interesting deist was George Ensor of Ardriss, whose *Janus on Sion* (1816) is an often devastating satire on the Bible.

Reading

Berman, David, 'The Irish Counter-Enlightenment', in Richard Kearney (ed.), *The Irish Mind* (Dublin: Wolfhound Press, 1985).

DAVID BERMAN

Delaney, Edward (1930–) Sculptor. Born Claremorris, County Mayo. Delaney studied at the National College of Art and Design, Dublin (1951–4), the Academie der Bildenden Kunst, Munich (1954–9), and the Academie Belle Arte Rosa, Rome (1959–61). He now lives and works in Connemara. Delaney represented Ireland in many international exhibitions during the 1960s. Primarily a sculptor, he is best known for his government commissions on view in Dublin city, such as the statue and fountain to Thomas Davis (1966) in College Green, and the monument to Wolfe Tone on St Stephen's Green (1966), both executed in bronze. More recently, Delaney has explored less figurative subject matter, using stainless steel.

Reading

Delaney, Eamon, 'Kindred: Tone Deft', *Sunday Tribune*, 23 October 1988.

FELICITY WOOLF

depositions of 1641 The name commonly given to a collection of papers, presented by the bishop of Clogher to the library of Trinity College, Dublin, in 1741 to mark the centenary of the rebellion of 1641, which constitutes the chief evidence for the controversial claim that the rebellion was accompanied by a massacre of the Protestant settlers. The collection is composed of five distinct elements:

1   A set of depositions by Protestant refugees taken in Dublin over a period of six years by a group of clergymen, appointed as Commissioners for Despoiled Protestants in December 1641. Their initial terms of reference required them to collect information about robberies and spoils committed against the settlers. Their formal function was to assess and register losses and to issue certificates to the deponents. Informally, the commission acted as an information-gathering agency, and in January 1642, its brief was extended to include the discovery of murders and massacres. Some of the depositions it collected, particularly in the northern counties, testify to atrocities, by no means always at first hand: the large majority deal with the loss of property. In March 1642, under the name of the head of the commission, Henry Jones, it published an influential pamphlet, *Divers remarkable Passages of Church and State in Ireland*, in which the rebellion was characterized as a popish plot and a selection of the depositions was printed as evidence. Extensive use of the more sensational of the materials was made by Sir John Temple in his *History of the Rebellion* (1646).

2   An incomplete set of transcripts of these original depositions, made by the clerk of the Commission, Thomas Waring, with a view to publication.

3   A collection of similar depositions, dealing almost exclusively with the loss of property, taken in Munster between March 1642 and the early autumn of 1643 under the authority of a special commission issued to Archdeacon Philip Bysse.

4   A collection of affidavits, containing information about rebel affairs and activities, made before an officer of state by a variety of individuals, Catholic and Protestant, rebels and refugees, throughout the entire period of the rebellion.

5   Material collected in the course of investigations into specific episodes by a group of commissioners appointed in 1652 to constitute a High Court of Justice 'to hear and determine all murders and massacres of any protestant English or other person' and authorized to collect preparatory evidence by the examination of witnesses on oath.

It seems certain that the five separate groups of papers were brought together as a working collection to service judicial proceedings in 1652, when indexes to Waring's transcripts were prepared, listing references to crimes and their authors. The papers were subsequently used as a reference collection during both the process of transplantation and the assessment of claims for reinstatement after the restoration, when they were commonly known as the 'books of discrimination' (an allusion to the elaborate taxonomy of 'respective demerits' in the 1652 act of settlement). In 1741, the college authorities arranged to have the papers bound in

161

31 uniform volumes, on the principle of grouping the various items according to the county to which they referred: two volumes of related material were added later in the same year. The internal arrangement of the deposition books was entirely haphazard: little effort was made to preserve the integrity or order of the different bodies of material, and the collection, which amounts to more than 19,000 pages, has proved dauntingly difficult to use.

By 1741, the collection was already famous through the publication of lurid selections to illustrate the character of the massacre. From the inference that what had been printed was representative, there had arisen among Protestants the belief that the deposition books were a martyrology in which every page told similar tales of horror. Catholics characterized the material as a crude propaganda exercise designed to prepare the way for the expropriation of Catholic landholders. The availability of the evidence did not affect these entrenched viewpoints: it was used eclectically and uncritically and the assessment of its value was distorted by a protracted and ill-informed controversy about the significance of systematic deletions in both the transcripts and the Munster materials. In reality, the evidence does not support the allegation that the outbreak of rebellion was accompanied by a general massacre: it does show that atrocities were committed and Protestant settlers killed in considerable numbers in the north of Ireland and some other places throughout the first year of the rebellion.

A. CLARKE

Dermody, Thomas (1775–1802) Poet. Born Ennis, County Clare; died Sydenham, Kent, July. The son of a schoolmaster, Dermody was writing verse of some merit from as early as 10 years old. He ran away to Dublin and there managed to make the acquaintance of several influential people who were impressed by his poetic talent. One such was Rev. Henry Boyd of Killeigh, Offaly, with whom Dermody stayed for two years; he celebrated the life of Killeigh in some humorous poems. Another well-wisher, Rev. Gilbert Austin, published a collection of Dermody's verse in 1789. Already a slave to drink and debauchery, Dermody later enlisted in the army, a career which took him to England. He died there in a hovel in miserable circumstances. His output of verse was considerable for such a short life-span, and some of it deserves to be remembered.

Reading

Demody, Thomas, *The Harp of Erin* (London, 1807).

Raymond, James Grant, *The Life of Thomas Dermody* (London: 1806).

PATRICK FAGAN

De Rossa, Proinsias (1940) President of the Labour Party Born Dublin. Interned as a member of Fianna Éireann during the IRA Border Campaign, De Rossa was elected Workers' Party TD for Dublin North West in 1982. Elected president of the Workers' Party (WP) in 1988, he won a European Parliament seat for the Dublin constituency in 1989 and served until 1992, when he resigned to concentrate on national politics. In 1990 he introduced a Private Member's Bill to amend Articles Two and Three of the Irish constitution. In 1992, against a background of allegations of IRA–WP links, he proposed that the party should be reconstituted as an open democratic party, rejecting both 'democratic centralism' and 'revolutionary tactics'. At a special conference he failed to secure the required majority. Together with five of the WP's seven TDs he resigned to form Democratic Left (DL), of which he was elected president. The party lost two seats in the 1992 general election but by-election victories in 1994 restored DL's Dáil strength to six and, in November 1994, it entered government as part of the Rainbow Coalition; De Rossa was appointed minister for social welfare. He returned to the opposition benches following the 1997 general election. In July 1997 he won a libel action against Independent Newspapers. In 1998 DL merged with the Labour Party, and in 1999 De Rossa was again elected to the European Parliament.

PATRICK GILLAN

Derry The name of the town derives from the oak-wood of Calgach (Doire Calgach) where St Columcille (Columba) founded his monastery in 546. It survived Viking raids and eventually became one of the island's most important ecclesiastical centres, see of the diocese of Tir Eoghan (Tyrone) from 1246. In 1600 it fell to the seaborne assault of Sir Henry Docwra, whose soldiers demolished the monastery and churches. Although Sir Cahir O'Doherty destroyed the English garrison in 1608, the city was granted to the Irish Society of London (hence its official name, Londonderry) in 1613 by James I and planted with Protestant settlers. It was held by Parliamentarians against Royalist besiegers in 1648–9, but achieved its special significance in the great siege of 1689, when the Protestant garrison withstood the surrounding Catholic army of James II. Since then, the walled city has been an emblem of Protestant resistance. The name of the governor Lundy, who wished to make terms with James II in 1689, has become the generic Protestant Ulster word for 'traitor'.

Catholic settlers from Donegal immigrated to the city from the seventeenth century, threatening its Protestant character. The influx increased during the Great Famine of 1845–9 and was further accelerated by the city's development as an industrial centre in the late nineteenth century, with shirt-making as its basic industry and low-paid Catholic women as the workforce. The Catholic population settled in the boglands below the city walls and on the hill of Creggan. By the early twentieth century, Catholics formed two-thirds of the total population. After Partition in 1922, Unionist administrations ensured Protestant supremacy by a gross system of gerrymander and discrimination in housing and employment.

The thirty-year period of the 'Troubles' in Northern Ireland began in Derry on 5 October 1968 when a civil rights march was brutally dispersed by the police. On 12 August 1969, the annual Orange parade, commemorating the siege of 1689, was attacked by the youth of the Catholic 'Bogside'. The police counter-attacked; there ensued three days of street fighting, which had violent repercussions in Belfast. The episode ended with the deployment by the British government of troops on the streets. Violence intensified thereafter. The city was badly damaged in the IRA bombing campaigns; and even more so by subsequent 'urban renewal'. On 30 January 1972, a civil rights march was attacked by the British Parachute regiment. Fourteen unarmed civilians were killed. This precipitated a political crisis; Stormont was abolished and direct rule by Britain imposed. 'Bloody Sunday' ended the civil rights campaign and accelerated the IRA's war against the British.

The city is now officially 'Derry'; the county is still 'Londonderry'. Although it was one of the chief sites of the province's guerilla war, it escaped the deep sectarian hatreds of Belfast and business investment in the area has been revitalized. Derry also sees itself as a cultural centre that might provide an exemplary liberation from the effects of a violent history – as in the events of the IMPACT 92 festival, an acronym for International Meeting Place for the Appreciation of Cultural Traditions and the continuing growth of Magee College.

SEAMUS DEANE

Despard, Charlotte (née French) (1844–1939) Suffragette and nationalist. Born in England, of Anglo-Irish descent, in 1870 she married Maximillian Despard and soon afterwards she became a Catholic. Up until the 1920s she was a prominent suffragette. Charlotte Despard had a keen interest in Ireland, visiting the country during the War of Independence. For a while she lived with Maud Gomme and became a Sinn Féiner. Her involvement in nationalist politics led to an estrangement between her and her brother, the Irish viceroy, Sir John French. She supported the anti-Treaty side during the Civil War.

As the years passed, Despard became increasingly left-wing in her politics. She even visited the Soviet Union in 1930.

She died in Belfast.

Reading

Linklater, Andro, *An Unhusbanded Life: Charlotte Despard* (London: Hutchinson).

RACHEL FURMSTON

de Valera, Éamon (1882–1975) Statesman, prime minister and president. Born New York, 14 October, to Catherine Coll and Vivion de Valera, Éamon de Valera was reared by his grandmother in Bruree, County Limerick, following his father's death. Educated by the Christian Brothers in Charleville, he won a scholarship to Blackrock College and graduated with an arts degree from the Royal University, following which he taught mathematics at St Patrick's College, Maynooth. He joined the Gaelic League in 1908 and in the same year met Sinéad Ní Fhlannagáin, whom he married two years later.

In 1913 de Valera joined the Irish Volunteers, and he took part in the Howth gunrunning of 1914. He was the last commandant to surrender after the 1916 Easter Rising. He was sentenced to death, but the sentence was commuted to life imprisonment, and on his release from prison in 1917 he was elected MP for East Clare. In the same year he was elected president of Sinn Féin and leader of the Irish Volunteers. During the anti-conscription campaign he was arrested and imprisoned without trial in Lincoln Jail. De Valera was elected in the Sinn Féin landslide of 1918. With the help of Michael Collins he escaped from prison and in April 1919 was elected *Príomh Aire* of the Irish Republic.

In June 1919 de Valera embarked on a tour of the United States to secure diplomatic recognition of the Irish Republic and to raise funds. Diplomatic recognition was not forthcoming, and while he raised over five million dollars in funds his visit left a legacy of division among Irish-American organizations. On his return to Ireland de Valera criticized the IRA's guerrilla tactics, and his rift with Collins dates from this time. He had a private meeting with Lloyd George in 1921 prior to the Treaty negotiations, which he insisted Collins, and not he, should attend. He opposed the Treaty and used his position as president of the Dáil to dominate the Treaty debates. As an alternative he proposed Document No. 2, a version of his external association proposals that the British had already rejected. De Valera's opposition to the Treaty centred on the Oath of Allegiance; partition was not an issue.

In January 1922 the Dáil voted by 64 votes to 57 to accept the Treaty. De Valera campaigned against the Treaty, declaring that the majority had no right to do wrong. In the 1922 general election pro-Treaty candidates won a three-to-one majority. Continued opposition led to civil war, which began in June 1922 and continued until May 1923 with the defeat of the anti-Treatyites; Michael Collins was among the casualties. De Valera spent most of the Civil War in prison. In 1926 de Valera sought unsuccessfully to change Sinn Féin's abstentionist policy, following which he and his followers formed Fianna Fáil. In 1927 de Valera returned to the United States to raise funds for both the new party and a new national newspaper. The same year Fianna Fáil entered the Dáil on the basis that the Treaty was an 'empty formula', and quickly grew into a well-organized, highly disciplined political party enjoying the tacit support of the IRA.

During the years 1927–9 de Valera engaged in extensive fund-raising in the US, and in 1931 he used American bonds to fund and launch the *Irish Press*. In 1932 he formed his first government, and his abolition of the Oath of Allegiance and removal of the governor general led to economic war with Britain.

This had repercussions in Ireland, among them the formation of the Blueshirts, who came into conflict with both Fianna Fáil and the IRA. De Valera's government neutralized the Blueshirts and in 1936 declared the IRA an illegal organization. Having addressed the League of Nations Assembly in 1934, de Valera introduced a new constitution in 1937 which recognized the 'special position' of the Roman Catholic church and included a territorial claim to Northern Ireland. The ending of the economic war in 1938 enabled de Valera to secure the return of the ports that had been retained by Britain under the Treaty; this facilitated Irish neutrality in World War II. During the war strict censorship was imposed and IRA members were interned and, in some instances, executed under the terms of emergency legislation. De Valera's interpretation of neutrality antagonized the Allies, never more so than when he paid a visit of condolence to the German embassy in Dublin on the death of Hitler.

De Valera lost office in 1948 and the coalition government declared the Irish state a republic. This led the British government to guarantee that Northern Ireland would remain part of the UK so long as a majority of its population so desired. The Mother and Child crisis precipitated the 1951 election, which Fianna Fáil won. Under pressure from the Roman Catholic hierarchy, de Valera amended the Health Bill so that it was 'in harmony with God's law'. Following a further spell in opposition (1954–7), Fianna Fáil was returned to power in 1957. De Valera again introduced internment to deal with the IRA's Border Campaign, and the campaign fizzled out. Ireland's dire economic situation prompted the First Programme for Economic Development in 1958, thus marking the end of economic nationalism. A year later de Valera resigned as taoiseach amid controversy concerning his personal interest in *Irish Press* shares.

He was elected president in June 1959 but his proposal to abolish PR (in order to establish Fianna Fáil as the permanent government) was defeated in a referendum. Among those he welcomed to Ireland were John F. Kennedy, Charles de Gaulle, Haile Selassie and Princess Grace of Monaco. He also addressed a joint session of the US congress. He lived to see both the arms crisis of 1970 and the emergence of the Provisional IRA. He died on 29 August 1975. W.B. Yeats described de Valera as 'a living argument rather than a living man' and John McGahern referred to him as 'a lay cardinal'. He was the dominant, if not the best-loved, political figure of twentieth-century Ireland.

PATRICK GILLAN

de Vere family Anglo-Irish of Norman extraction, related to the earls of Oxford and residing at Curragh Chase, Adare, County Limerick, on land granted in 1657 to Vere Hunt, a Cromwellian officer. During the nineteenth century, family members were known principally for their literary pursuits. Sir Aubrey de Vere (1788–1846) wrote plays and verse which won praise from Wordsworth, a family friend. Aubrey Thomas (1814–1902), his third son, whose circle of friends included eminent writers and churchmen, won acclaim for his prose writings (travelogues, literary and political criticism) and poetry, both lyric and dramatic. Another son, Stephen Edward (1812–1904), fourth and last baronet, MP for Limerick and, like Aubrey, a convert to Catholicism, published verse and translations from Latin. His 1847 visit to Quebec publicized the horror of the coffin ships and helped reform the Passenger Act. Curragh Chase remained the family seat until fire destroyed the house in 1941.

Reading

Reilly, M.P., *Aubrey de Vere, Victorian Observer* (Lincoln NE: University of Nebraska Press, 1953).

de Vere, Joan, *In Ruin Reconciled. A Memoir of Anglo-Ireland, 1913–1959* (Dublin: Lilliput Press, 1990).

JAMES JACKSON

Devlin, Anne (1951–) Dramatist, prose- and screen-writer. Born West Belfast, 13 September. Devlin's father was Paddy Devlin, SDLP MP for Falls Road 1969–71. A Coleraine graduate, she emigrated to Birmingham, where in 1989 she co-wrote a community play about exile. Her major cathartic plays about the hunger strike have yet to be rebroadcast, or staged in Belfast. Influenced by O'Casey, overtly feminist, she has pioneered the exploration of the relationship between political, sexual and religious anxiety, possession and dispossession.

Reading

Devlin, Anne, *Ourselves Alone, The Long March, A Woman Calling, The Waypaver* (London: Faber, 1986).
Watt, Stephen, *O'Casey, Joyce and the Irish Popular Theatre* (Syracuse University Press, 1991).

MEDBH MCGUCKIAN

Devlin, Denis (1908–59) Poet and Diplomat. Born in Greenock, Scotland, Devlin grew up in a comfortable Dublin home whose visitors included Michael Collins and Éamon de Valera. He read languages at University College, Dublin, and studied at the University of Munich and the Sorbonne, developing an enthusiasm for the French symbolist poets. Natural urbanity and personal reserve served his diplomatic career, which included postings in Rome, New York, Washington, London and, again, Rome as ambassador. The major poems emerging in the 1940s, including *Lough Derg*, concern loss of God and loss of love, addressing disillusionment and bitterness, even despair, in dense, elaborately wrought verse which demands and repays the patient reader. *The Heavenly Foreigner* is one of the most important long Irish poems of this century and has correctly been compared to Eliot's *Four Quartets*. *The Colours of Love*, one of the most compelling poems in modern Irish literature, struggles to mitigate loss and betrayal, achieving a final, minimal spiritual subsistence in poetry of great power. To find direct antecedents for Devlin one has to look beyond Eliot, Auden, Yeats, Pound and Stephens, perhaps to Hopkins. The 'difficulty' of Devlin's verse has long concealed its power and importance from general acknowledgement; Samuel Beckett's response to a collected edition of the poems in 1989 was 'Amends at last.'

Reading

Devlin, Denis, *Poems*, with Brian Coffey (A. Thom, 1930).
—— *Intercessions* (Europa Press, 1937).
—— *Lough Derg and Other Poems* (1946).
—— *Selected Poems*, eds Allen Tate and Robert Penn Warren (1963).
—— *The Complete Poems*, ed. Brian Coffey (1963).
—— *Collected Poems of Denis Devlin*, ed. J.C.C. Mays (Dedalus, 1989).

RICHARD RYAN

Devoy, John (1842–1928) Fenian. Born Kill, County Kildare, 3 September; died Atlantic City, New Jersey, 29 September 1928, unmarried and virtually penniless. The son of a smallholder, Devoy joined the Fenians in 1861, and this brought him five years' imprisonment. He was released in 1871 on condition that he lived outside the United Kingdom. He went to New York where he worked as a journalist and became the dominant figure in Clan na Gael, the foremost Irish-American organization, which supported every movement for Irish independence and tried to drive a wedge between America and England.

Reading

Devoy, John, *The Irish Land League* (New York: Patterson and Neilson, 1882).
—— *Recollections of an Irish Rebel* (New York: Young, 1929).
—— *Devoy's Post Bag* (Dublin: Fallon, 1948).

HENRY BOYLAN

Dillon, Gerard (1916–71) Painter. Born, and buried, Belfast. Dillon was apprenticed to a painting and decorating firm before studying art at the Belfast Technical School. He exhibited in Belfast and Dublin, and joined the White Stags and the Dublin Painters' Group, before moving to London in 1946. He represented Britain at the Pittsburgh International Exhibition and Ireland at the Guggenheim International, and travelled in Europe and the USA. In 1968 he returned to Dublin, where he continued to work until his death. He worked primarily in oils, merging the figurative and the abstract through a conjunction of simple but fundamental themes.

Reading

Arnold, Bruce, *A Concise History of Irish Art* (London: Thames and Hudson, 1977).

Pyle, Hilary, *Irish Art 1900–1950* (Cork: Crawford Municipal Art Gallery, 1976).

White, James, *Gerard Dillon* (London: Mercury Gallery).

DERVAL TUBRIDY

Dillon family The best-known members of the family are as follows:

1   John Blake Dillon (1816–66), nationalist. Born Ballaghadereen, County Roscommon; died of cholera, Killarney, 15 September. John Blake Dillon was educated at Trinity College, Dublin, where he formed a close friendship with Thomas Davis, and was called to the Irish bar in 1841. He joined Davis and Gavan Duffy in founding the *Nation* in 1842. He took part in the unsuccessful rising of 1848 and afterwards escaped to France and thence to America, where he practised law until 1855, when an amnesty allowed him to return to Ireland. He was elected MP for Tipperary in 1865, and supported Repeal but opposed Fenianism.

2   John Dillon (1851–1927), nationalist and son of John Blake Dillon. Born Blackrock, County Dublin, 4 September; died London, 4 August. John Dillon was educated at Catholic University Medical

School, but turned to politics and supported Parnell in the Land League. He was elected MP for Tipperary in 1880 and for East Mayo in 1885. He opposed Parnell after the split in the Irish Party in 1891. He showed moral courage in opposing conscription and defending the leaders of the Easter Rising. He led the party in the general election of 1918, when it was virtually wiped out.

3   Myles Dillon (1900–72), Celtic scholar and son of John Dillon. Born Dublin; died there, 18 June. Myles Dillon was educated at Mount St Benedict's, Gorey, University College, Dublin, and the University of Bonn. In a long and distinguished academic career he held posts in the Sorbonne, Trinity College, Dublin, University College, Dublin, the University of Wisconsin and Chicago University, specializing in Celtic studies and Sanskrit. He was director of the school of Celtic Studies in the Dublin Institute of Advanced Studies (1960–8) and president of the Royal Irish Academy (1966).

4   James Dillon (1902–86), politician and fourth son of John Dillon. Born Dublin, 26 September; died there, 10 February. James Dillon was educated at Mount St Benedict's, Gorey, University College, Galway, and the King's Inns. He became manager of the family's general merchant business in Ballaghadereen and was a TD (1932–69). He opposed Irish neutrality in World War II, served two terms as minister for agriculture, and was leader of the Fine Gael party (1959–65). He was regarded in Dáil Éireann as an outstanding parliamentarian and a colourful orator.

HENRY BOYLAN

Dineley, Thomas (d. 1695) Antiquarian. Born Southampton. Dineley travelled through many parts of Europe keeping journals and sketchbooks. He travelled to the Low Countries in 1674, and then to France.

In 1680, he arrived in Ireland, probably in a military capacity, and kept a detailed journal of his observations on Irish society and the economy, notes on Irish history, and graphic illustrations of Irish buildings, cities and other sights. These sketches are among the earliest records of Irish architecture, and include many buildings which have not survived. Similarly, the social and economic details provided by his observations have been much used by historians. Dineley completed further journals, travelling to Wales and to the Midlands of England.

Reading

Cullen, L.M., 'Economic trends, 1660–91', *New History of Ireland*, 3 (1969), pp. 387–407.

MacLysaght, Edward, *Irish Life in the Seventeenth Century* (Dublin: Irish University Press, 1969).

Shirley, E.P. (ed.), 'Extracts from the journal of Thomas Dineley', *Journal of the Royal Society of Antiquaries of Ireland*, iv–v (1856–8), vii–ix (1862–7), xliii (1913).

BRIAN DONOVAN

disestablishment: the Church of Ireland before and after The statute that united Great Britain and Ireland into one United Kingdom from 1 January 1801 also joined the established (Anglican) churches of England and Ireland 'for ever'. In fact, after 70 years they were separated (with effect from 1 January 1871), when the Church of Ireland was disendowed and disestablished.

In keeping with normal European practice in the sixteenth and seventeenth centuries, the people of the kingdom of Ireland were required from the time of the Reformation to adhere to the church of their sovereigns, the Protestant kings and queens of England and Ireland. The Reformation in Ireland had never, however, been a popular movement, being, for one thing, closely associated in the public mind with the English conquest of the country, which was barely achieved by the end of the seventeenth century. Therefore, in the early years of the Reformation, the

established Church of Ireland only took root in those parts of the country (the east and some towns in other parts) where the royal writ ran. Gradually, through conquest, confiscation and settlement of Ireland by English and Scottish planters, the greater part of the country passed into the hands of a Protestant (mainly Anglican) landlord class. A series of late seventeenth- and early eighteenth-century penal laws concentrated political power in the hands of what came to be known as the Protestant Ascendancy, and it was their church alone, the established Church of Ireland, that monopolized social and political status in the country.

The Church of Ireland was not totally preoccupied with exercising its privileged role, and in the early nineteenth century was considerably influenced by the evangelical movement and to a much lesser extent the Oxford Movement of Keble, Pusey and others. It was, indeed, Keble's perception of undue state interference with the spiritualities of the Irish church in the 1830s that led to his historic Assize sermon at Oxford in 1833, which is considered to be the founding of the Oxford Movement. The established status of the Church of Ireland not only exacerbated Catholic resentment at its privileged position and right to tithes, but at the same time placed its property and its liturgy in the power of government and Parliament. An income from tithes was by no means the only benefit that accrued to the established church. Its laws were the laws of the land and its courts could enforce those laws. Some of its bishops sat in the House of Lords. (Before the Union, all had sat in the Irish Lords.) In return, the state had its prerogatives, such as the appointment by the crown of all bishops and deans, and the right to convene convocation, the representative body of the clergy.

The levying of tithes by the clergy of the established church was a source of deep grievance to those Irish Catholics and Presbyterians (Dissenters), often tenant farmers in very reduced circumstances, who had to pay them, and the 1830s saw a fiercely fought resistance to these payments, literally a 'tithe war' in the Irish countryside. Government eased the situation by transferring the payment of tithes to the landlords. A more radical intervention in the life of the church, the occasion of Keble's denunciation, came with the Church Temporalities Act, 1833, when two archbishoprics and eight bishoprics were abolished, and major financial restructuring took place. These 'reforms' owed much to the findings of a series of government enquiries into ecclesiastical revenues. Similarly, the subsequent major transformation of the church's life by disestablishment owed something to the census returns of 1861, which showed the Church of Ireland population to be only 11.9 per cent of the total, and even more to the disclosures of a royal commission that reported in 1867. But the prime impetus to campaign for disestablishment came from William Ewart Gladstone.

Gladstone was a committed Anglican, but he espoused the cause of disestablishment believing that nationalist Ireland and liberal England would rally to this particular policy for reconciling Ireland to the British connection. In April 1868 he tabled in the House of Commons three resolutions that embodied disestablishment proposals. All three were carried. After a general election in which disestablishment of the Irish church was a major issue Gladstone was returned to power, and an 'Irish Church Bill' for the disendowment and disestablishment of the Church of Ireland, largely drafted by the prime minister, was introduced on 1 March 1869. Parliamentary opposition to the bill was determined, especially in the Lords. The queen was strongly against it, and so, with few exceptions, were the dignitaries of the Church of Ireland itself. However, royal assent was given on 26 July 1869.

Disendowment was instantaneous, for on that very day the entire property of the Church of Ireland was placed in the hands of commissioners of church temporalities. Disestablishment took almost a year and a half longer. Gladstone had, in fact, so ordered matters that the Church had adequate time to prepare for its new circumstances. The Irish Church Act made provision for the setting up by royal charter of a Representative Church Body (RCB), comprising bishops, clergy and laity, in which all Church of Ireland churches and schools were vested. Glebes (rectories) could be bought back from the commissioners of temporalities on exceptionally good terms. The RCB was also given half a million pounds, the estimated value of private endowments made to the church since 1660. The personal interests of the clergy were protected by an ingenious scheme that provided funding for the now self-supporting church. The clergy could, if they so wished, receive annuities for life. Alternatively, they could commute this annuity for a lump sum to be paid to the RCB and receive a stipend from it. Most clergy opted for the latter scheme, and the church was thus provided with seven and a half million pounds in capital.

A general convention of representatives of the clergy and laity opened in Dublin on 15 February 1870, and after considerable debate it agreed a constitution that provided for the setting up of a general synod as the supreme governing body of the Church of Ireland, comprising, in parliamentary fashion, two houses: the House of Bishops and the House of Representatives (clerical and lay). The members of the House of Representatives were (and are) elected by diocesan synods on which all clergy of the diocese sit, together with lay representatives of the parishes, who are elected (like the general synod) triennially. Besides the setting up of the RCB and the synodical system of government, the newly disestablised church experienced a third major innovation, that of prayer-book revision, a natural undertaking for a newly independent church. In fact, the Book of Common Prayer as authorized in 1878 saw little radical innovation, despite heated debates, for those counsels that sought to preserve the integrity of Anglican faith and order prevailed.

The century and a quarter since the passing of the Irish Church Act has seen many changes in Ireland, not least the partitioning of the country. The essential structures put in place at disestablishment have stood the test of time, and proved sufficiently flexible to allow for developments in worship and administration that enable the Church of Ireland to address the needs of the times.

KENNETH MILNE

distilling Though gin is manufactured and consumed in Ireland, and imported spirits such as brandy, rum and Scotch whisky enjoy a certain following, distilling for most Irish people means the distilling of the native whiskey (note the distinctive spelling) which is today manufactured in two centres, Bushmills, County Antrim, and Midleton, County Cork, and marketed chiefly under the brand names Old Bushmills, Power's, Jameson, Tullamore Dew and Paddy.

The difference in taste between Irish and Scotch is based on a difference in production methods. The malt for Scotch is dried over an open peat fire, which imparts a characteristic smoky flavour to the whisky. Irish whiskey, on the other hand, is dried in a closed oven and distilled three times in old-fashioned copper pot stills. Most other whiskies are distilled only twice. The whiskey is then left to mature in oak casks for a period of from five to eight years, or in the case of some premium brands even twelve.

The distillery at Bushmills is the oldest licensed whisk(e)y distillery in the world, the first licence having been issued in 1608. The fame of Irish whiskey (from the gaelic *uisce beatha* or water of life) predates that of the Scottish drink by centuries. In the mid-eighteenth century, Dr Samuel Johnson remarked in his dictionary definition of *'uisce beatha'*: 'It is a compounded, distilled spirit, being drawn on aromaticks, and the Irish sort is particularly distinguished for its pleasant and mild flavour. In Scotland it is somewhat hotter, and by corruption in Scottish they call it Whisky.'

During the course of the nineteenth century, Irish whiskey developed a huge export trade, both in the United States and throughout the British empire. Its decline on the world market, relative to Scotch, came as a result of two major catastrophes in the twentieth century.

The Prohibition laws which were in force in the USA between 1919 and 1933 closed down the legal liquor industry there overnight. Just as quickly, a parallel underground 'bootlegging' industry grew up. In a situation where supply was a lot more important than quality, bootleggers often gave their doubtful brews Irish-sounding names in an attempt to cash in on the pre-Prohibition reputation of Irish whiskey. The period of Prohibition coincided with a remarkably turbulent time in Irish history. The War of Independence was followed by a civil war. In the 1930s a trade war with Britain followed, with tariffs being put up in each country against the other's products. In a period of about 15 years, Irish whiskey had lost both the American and British empire markets. Distillers ran down their operations, while many smaller operations closed. When Prohibition was repealed, Ireland was in no position to exploit the reopened market. Scotch was only too glad to fill the gap.

Since the 1960s, a major recovery has taken place. In 1988, the Irish Distillers group was taken over by French company, Pernod Ricard. Sixty per cent of Irish whiskey sales are now exported.

ENDA O'DOHERTY

divorce When the Act of Union was passed in 1801, the law as to divorce was the same in both islands. In Ireland as in England, a divorce *a vinculo matrimonii* (from the bonds of matrimony), the form which enabled the parties to remarry validly, could be obtained only by a private Act of Parliament. With the abolition of the Irish Parliament, an Irish husband or wife seeking such a divorce had to promote a bill in the imperial Parliament at Westminster. Bills could be enacted only on proof of adultery or of cruelty.

There was another form of divorce available in both countries, known as the divorce *a mensa et thoro* (from bed and board). This freed both parties from the legal obligation to cohabit, but did not entitle them to remarry. It was granted by the ecclesiastical courts, in which jurisdiction as to matrimonial cases was then exclusively vested, and the grounds were, again, proof of adultery or cruelty. Since the parties who availed themselves of it were frequently already separated, its principal utility was in enabling question of alimony and child custody to be resolved when the parties could not agree.

Irish law was also similar to English in the importance it attached to the curiously named remedy of 'criminal conversation', usually shortened to 'crim. con.'. This was in effect an action for damages maintainable by a husband against a man whom he could prove to have committed adultery with his wife. It had the important result that, if the jury found the adultery proved, it laid the foundation for the enactment of a private divorce Act. The result was that collusive actions flourished. In both countries, these remedies were in practice available only to the better off, but in Ireland the official hostility of the Catholic church to divorce *a vinculo matrimonii* meant that that remedy was confined in practice to Protestants.

The collusive actions for crim. con. led to growing pressure for the reform of the divorce laws. This resulted in the enactment of the Matrimonial Causes Act 1857, which ended the jurisdiction of the ecclesiastical courts in England and gave the civil courts power to grant divorces *a vinculo matrimonii*. These momentous changes did not apply to Ireland: English governments were concerned to avoid antagonizing the Catholic hierarchy, which had become a formidable leader of majority public opinion and a potential supporter of Irish separatism. The Irish Matrimonial Causes Act, passed in 1871, followed the English model in transferring jurisdiction in matrimonial matters to the civil courts, but contained no provision for divorce *a vinculo matrimonii*.

As a result, Irish couples whose relationships had broken down and who had no religious objection to divorce continued to avail themselves of the parliamentary bill, if they could afford to do so. When the Irish Free State was established in 1921, it appeared that the Parliament established by its wholly secular constitution had inherited the power of the Westminster Parliament to enact divorce legislation. However, there were no standing orders providing for such bills and the Executive Council declined to facilitate them. Their attitude provoked a celebrated outburst in the Senate of the new state from W.B. Yeats. He saw the policy as a narrowly sectarian attack on the civil liberties of Irish Protestants and spoke witheringly of the government's indifference, as he saw it, to the traditions of the stock whence he came: 'we are no petty people'.

The present constitution, enacted in 1937, was strongly influenced by Catholic teaching, and Article 41 expressly prohibited the enactment of divorce legislation. Those whose marriages broke down remained together, separated informally, entered into separation agreements or, less commonly, obtained a divorce *a mensa et thoro*. But changing social patterns from the 1960s onwards led to campaigns for the amendment of the constitution to permit divorce. The most significant factor was the increasing number of people who entered into second relationships and started new families. Much new legislation reached the statute book, designed to protect spouses and children from domestic violence and to facilitate more equitable financial and property arrangements in the event of a marriage breaking down. However, a referendum in 1986 resulted in the defeat by a substantial majority of an amendment which would have enabled the Oireachtas to enact divorce legislation containing specified safeguards for divorced spouses and their children. A referendum on divorce, held in 1995 resulted in a majority of 50.28 per cent in favour of divorce being allowed for those couples who had lived apart for four years.

RONAN KEANE

Doherty, Willie (1959–) Photographer. Born Derry. Doherty studied at Ulster Polytechnic, Belfast (1977–81). He makes black-and-white and colour photographs with texts. His technique was conceived initially as documenting performances and installations, and as a strategy to deconstruct the way the media present the political situation in Derry. The combination of texts and images suggest the political ambiguity, irony and tragedy implicit in the Northern Irish situation. From 1988–90 Doherty's photo works were images of other cities, such as Belfast, Dublin, Cardiff and Glasgow. These works continue to comment on inherent power relations and urban deprivation.

Reading

Coppock, Christopher, 'Interview with Willie Doherty', *CIRCA Art Magazine*, 40 (1988), pp. 68–71.
Doherty, Willie, 'A conversation with Declan McGonagle' (Dublin: Oliver Dowling Gallery, 1988).
Fisher, Jean, 'Seeing beyond the Pale: the photographic works of Willie Doherty', *Willie Doherty: Unknown Depths* (Cardiff: Ffotogallery, 1990).

FELICITY WOOLF

Dolin, Anton (1904–83) Dancer, choreographer and dance director. Of Dublin parents, Dolin was born Patrick Healey Kay at Slinfold, Sussex, 27 July 1904, dying in Paris, 25 November 1983. He trained with Astafieva and Legat. Listed as Patrikieff in Diaghilev's 1921 Stoll production of *The Sleeping Princess*, he became Dolin on joining Ballets Russes as soloist in 1923. He founded the Nemchinova–Dolin Company in 1927 and helped establish the Carmago Society in 1930, creating Satan in de Valois's *Job*. He led the Vic–Wells Ballet from 1931 to 1935, before founding and directing the Markova–Dolin Company, which, in 1950, became London Festival Ballet, after a break from 1940 to 1946 while Dolin was ballet-master, choreographer and *premier danseur* with American Ballet Theatre. He played Cecchetti in the 1980 film *Nijinsky*, and was guest director of Rome Opera Ballet, artistic director of Les Grands Ballets Canadiens, and co-chairman of Indiana University Ballet Department. He choreographed *Variations for Four* (1957) and staged the classics and his own version of *Pas de Quatre* (1941) for many companies, including Irish National Ballet, receiving the Queen Elizabeth Coronation Award (1954), the Peruvian Order of the Sun (1959) and a knighthood (1981). Publications include *Divertissement* (1931), *Ballet-Go-Round* (1938), *Pas de Deux* (1949), *Markova* (1953), *Autobiography* (1960), *The Sleeping Ballerina* (1966) and *Last Words* (1985).

Reading

Gilpin, John, *A Dance With Life* (London: William Kimber, 1982).
Markova, Dame Alicia, *Markova Remembers* (London: Hamish Hamilton, 1986).
Wheatcroft, Andrew, *Dolin, Friends and Memories* (London: Routledge and Kegan Paul, 1982).

CAROLYN SWIFT

Dolmen Press Founded in 1951, at a low point in Irish publishing, by Liam and Josephine Miller to print and issue works by Irish poets. Liam Miller (1924–87), a native of Mountrath, County Laois, had no formal training in printing, but his qualification as an architect provided a disciplined approach to design. The first books were all hand-printed, with the authors often helping to set them, and illustrated by young artists.

In 1956 Miller concentrated full-time on the press and by the early 1960s had established his core list of poets – Austin Clarke, Thomas Kinsella and John Montague. Miller expanded his policy in the 1960s to publish broadly in the field of Irish literature and culture. This period culminated in what many consider to be Dolmen's finest achievement, *The Táin* (1969), an Irish epic translated by Kinsella with illustrations by Louis Le Brocquy.

Miller won many Irish Book Design Awards and in 1981 was awarded a medal at the International Book Design Exhibition, Leipzig, for *Holinshed's Irish chronicle 1577* (1979). The success of Dolmen gave others the courage to found their own publishing houses in Ireland.

Dolmen's printing plant was closed in the late 1970s; Miller regretted the loss of direct control over the printing. At the same time he broadened the output of the press and did more typographic design on commission. One of the last books he produced was a monumental edition of James Joyce's *Dubliners* (1986). Miller was the anima of the press and it did not survive his death in 1987.

Reading

Hayes, Jarlath, 'Liam Miller 1924–1987: an appreciation', *Books Ireland* (July–Aug. 1987).

Miller, Liam, *Dolmen XXV* (Dublin: Dolmen, 1979).

VINCENT KINANE

Donnellan, Anne (*c*.1700–*c*.1761) Founder of the Donnellan lectures at Trinity College, Dublin. Daughter of Chief Baron Nehemiah Donnellan and his second wife Martha Ussher, from 1729 she resided in London. A visit to Ireland with Mary Delany in 1731–3 led to a brief correspondence with Swift. Among her other correspondents were Elizabeth Montagu, the Bluestocking; the poet Edward Young: and the novelist Samuel Richardson; while her musical skills led to friendship with Handel.

Reading

Climenson, E.J., *Elizabeth Montagu, the Queen of the Blue-stockings*, 2 vols (London: 1906).

Donnellan, Anne, *Autobiography and Correspondence of Mary . . . Delany . . . ed. Lady Llanover*, 6 vols (London: 1861–2).

Williams, H. (ed.), *The Correspondence of Jonathan Swift*, vol. iv (Oxford: Oxford University Press 1965).

PATRICK KELLY

Dowden, Edward (1843–1913) Scholar. Born Cork, 3 May; died Dublin, 4 April. Dowden was educated at Queen's College, Cork, and Trinity College, Dublin, graduating in 1863. In 1867 he was appointed to the new chair of English literature, which he held until his death. Of his seven books on literary topics the best known are *Shakspere. His Mind and Art* (1875) and the *Life of Shelley* (1886). He also produced many editions of single Shakespearian plays. He published a volume of verse in 1876, but 'was turned aside to the duty of bread-winning'. His critical approach was to try to find the 'law of a writer's mind' and show how this was expressed in the work. He knew and admired Browning and Whitman, and in politics was a cosmopolitan liberal, opposed to the national movement. He married Mary Clarke in 1866; they had two daughters and one son. Widowed in 1892, he married Elizabeth Dickenson in 1895; they had no children.

DAVID SMITH

Down Survey The survey of Irish lands undertaken in 1654 after the 1640s wars and Cromwell's reduction of Ireland. It was commissioned with a view to distributing to Cromwell's army, in lieu of pay, the lands of all the Irish proprietors who had participated in the 1641 rebellion and who had not been 'of constant good affection' to the parliamentary cause in the subsequent wars. The survey, which remained the most ambitious and largest in scale until the Ordnance Survey of the 1830s, is of interest for two interrelated reasons. One is to do with the development of empirical method, the other with themes recurrent in the history of Anglo-Irish relations, in particular the English tendency, intensified during the Cromwellian era, to perceive Ireland as a *tabula rasa* for English reforming experiment. After some infighting between competing factions of the Dublin administration, the survey was entrusted primarily to William Petty, who made it a modern exercise in practical scientific method. Petty devised for the survey – called 'Down' from his emphasis on doing the empirical work on site – an advanced method, based on a division of labour, which significantly prefigures Adam Smith's thought. His own MS history of the project (first printed by his nineteenth-century successor Larcom) gives an acute account, expressed with Petty's characteristic pragmatism, of the inescapable dependence of the 1650s incomers, however significantly empowered with legal and military force, on the indigenous population: Petty wryly acknowledges that the boundaries of lands could not be determined without Irish 'meresmen'. He perceives as threateningly fluid and verging on indeterminacy the Irish arrangements about land boundaries and measurement, which were in fact based on a predominantly pastoral agriculture and a seasonally nomadic social system. These bring out in Petty an English empiricist exasperation at Irish difference. In practice, the Down Survey did not of itself enable the organized execution of the sweeping shifts in the ownership of Irish land which it was intended to do; those shifts did come about over the fifty years or so up to 1700, but the soldiers were not for long, or the primary, beneficiaries. The traditional lands of the Irish proprietors ultimately passed overwhelmingly into the hands of the powerful group of 'New English' planters already well established before 1641.

Reading

Barnard, T.C., *Cromwellian Ireland* (Oxford: Oxford University Press, 1975).

Coughlan, Patricia, ' "Cheap and common animals": the English anatomy of Ireland in the seventeenth century', in T. Healy, and J. Sawday (eds), *Literature and the English Civil War* (Cambridge: Cambridge University Press, 1990).

Goblet, Y.M. *La transformation de la geographie politique de l'Irlande au 17e siecle dans les cartes et essais anthropogeographiques de Sir William Petty* (Paris: Berger-Levrault, 1930).

Petty, William, *History of the Down Survey*, ed. T.A. Larcom (Dublin: Irish Archaeological Society, 1851; repr. New York: Kelley, 1967).

Webster, Charles, *The Great Instauration: Science, Medicine and Reform 1626–1660* (London: Duckworth, 1975).

PATRICIA COUGHLAN

Downing Street declaration (15 December 1993) Jointly proclaimed by the then taoiseach Albert Reynolds and British prime minister John Major. The declaration was designed to foster agreement and reconciliation, leading to a new political framework founded on consent for arrangements within Northern Ireland, the whole island, and between Ireland and Britain. The British government committed itself to uphold the democratic wish of a greater number of the people of Northern Ireland on the issue of support for the union or a sovereign united Ireland. It pledged to 'encourage, facilitate and enable the achievement of such agreement over a period through a process of dialogue and co-operation based on full respect for the rights and identities of both traditions in Ireland'. The British government further agreed that the right of self-determination was 'for the people of the island of Ireland alone, by agreement between the two parts respectively . . . on the basis of consent, freely and concurrently given, North and South'. The Irish government stated that unity was dependent on 'the freely given consent of a majority of the people of Northern Ireland' and that the democratic right of self-determination by the people of Ireland as a whole must be achieved 'subject to the agreement and consent of a majority of the people of Northern Ireland'. In the event of an overall settlement, the Irish government would, 'as part of a balanced constitutional accommodation, put forward and support proposals for change in the Irish constitution which would fully reflect the principle of consent in Northern Ireland'. Both governments reiterated that peace must involve the permanent end of paramiltary violence. Political talks were open to 'democratically mandated parties which establish a commitment to exclusively peaceful methods and which have shown that they abide by the democratic process'. The Democratic Unionist Party and Sinn Féin were the only political parties to oppose the Declaration.

PATRICK GILLAN

Doyle, James Warren (1786–1834) Churchman. Born near New Ross; died at his house, Braganza, Carlow, 16 June. Doyle was educated at the Augustinian seminary, New Ross, and the University of Coimbra, Portugal. During the Peninsular War he joined Sir Arthur Wellesley's army as a volunteer interpreter. On return to Ireland he was ordained an Augustinian in 1809. After some years' teaching, he was appointed bishop of Kildare and Leighlin in 1819. He identified himself actively with the social struggle of the oppressed Catholics, openly supported O'Connell, and became a formidable opponent of the administration. His trenchant pamphlets, published under the initials 'JKL' (James of Kildare and Leighlin), impressed opponents and allies alike, and he was called to London in 1828, 1830 and 1833 to give evidence on Irish affairs before parliamentary committees.

Reading

Doyle, James Wassen, *A Vindication of the Religious and Civil Principles of the Irish Catholics* (Dublin: printed by R. Coyne, 1824).
—— *Letters on the State of Ireland* (Dublin: printed by R. Coyne, 1824, 1825).

HENRY BOYLAN

Doyle, Roddy (1958–) Novelist and author of film scripts and two plays. Born Dublin. Roddy Doyle grew up in the northside suburb of Kilbarack, where he taught English and geography in a secondary school for 14 years following his education in University College, Dublin. In 1993, after the publication of his fourth novel (*Paddy Clarke HaHaHa*), Doyle left teaching to devote himself to writing. At the end of the same year *Paddy Clarke* won the prestigious Booker Prize and has since been translated into 19 languages. His previous novel, *The Van*, was shortlisted for the Booker in 1991 and, following the successful film versions of the first two parts of his 'Barrytown Trilogy' (*The Commitments*, 1987, and *The Snapper*; 1990), was filmed by Steven Frears in 1996. After the enthusiastic reception of his largely humorous trilogy, the bleaker four-part television series *Family* (broadcast by BBC and RTE in 1994) gave rise to mixed reactions. *The Woman Who Walked into Doors* (1996), is based on the mother character in *Family*, which, like all his previous works, is set in the working-class milieu of Dublin's north side. Doyle's historical novel, *A Star Called Henry* (1999), is the first of a planned trilogy.

ASTRID GERBER

Doyle, Roger (1949–) Composer. Born Dublin. One of Ireland's leading composers of electronic music, Doyle's early works in particular were strongly influenced by pop, rock and jazz. Major compositions for tape include *Thalia* (1976), *Fin-Estra* (1977), *Rapid Eye Movements* (1980), *Light Years* (1983–8) and *Charlotte Corday and the Lament of Louis XVI* (1989). He has written theatre and film music, including the soundtrack for Bob Quinn's silent film *Budawanny* (1986).

In 1991 he began work, with his experimental group IContact, on *Delusional Architecture: The Tower of Babel* a two-hour music-theatre piece integrating live and electronic music, dance and architecture. Doyle is a member of Aosdána.

EVE O'KELLY

drama What constitutes Irish drama before modern times is a difficult question, so much of it having happened outside Ireland. Can the individual work of expatriate playwrights be taken to represent a national drama? Some modern Irish criticism thinks so and has claimed the plays of Goldsmith and the rest for the Irish drama – or Irish theatre, a still more difficult concept, especially in relation to the London-based Irish playwrights who wrote exclusively for the English stage and are an important part of its history. The fostering of Irish talent abroad has, however, helped to nourish a home-based drama. From that viewpoint the expatriates' plays are considered here. Questions of definition arise also with the modern drama of Northern Ireland, which is at once British and Irish. Again, ease of cultural interchange allows Ulster playwrights to be seen in either aspect.

Drama before 1700

Ireland appears to have had no early indigenous drama and none written in Gaelic before modern times. Folk studies have suggested that Gaelic rites such as wake games were a form of folk theatre, but the history of that theatre is yet to be written. Ireland shared in the medieval drama of Europe, as is shown by records of Corpus Christi performances and an occasional standard text like the Dublin 'Quem Queritis'. No immediate development of drama followed, as happened elsewhere in Europe. Only with the building of the first theatre in Dublin in 1637, followed by the Smock Alley Theatre in 1662, did Irish writers turn their attention to the genre of drama. At the same time the exodus to London began.

Eighteenth-Century Anglo-Irish Playwrights

What constitutes Irishness in this period is another vexed question. Proposed criteria have included simple tests such as 'born in Ireland' (ruling out Congreve) or 'educated in Ireland' (ruling out Sheridan). Each case is special in the complex Anglo-Irish situation. Plays written for the Dublin stage, often by Englishmen such as Charles Shadwell, were oriented to English modes even when their context was Irish, as in William Phillips's *St Stephen's Green: or The Generous Lovers*

(1700). John O'Keeffe (1747–1833) set his first play in London though writing it for Dublin. Yet despite the cultural dominance of London, a drama emerged with distinctively Irish features.

In adopting English conventions, the Irish playwrights often exploited 'stage Irish' and the 'stage Irishman' for comic effect, both at home, as in Thomas Sheridan's *Captain O'Blunder*, and abroad (ironically, it was English reviewers who deplored the caricatured Sir Lucius O'Trigger in *The Rivals* as a slight to 'the Irish nation'). But the expatriates also changed the perspectives of English comedy. George Farquhar (1678–1807) shifted the scene from the metropolis: to Shrewsbury in *The Recruiting Officer* (1706), Lichfield in *The Beaux Stratagem* (1707), giving his provincial characters a sturdy independence in tune with the plays' radical social ideas. A shabby country house (trailing associations from Goldsmith's youth in Ireland) is centre stage in *She Stoops to Conquer* (1773) and Sheridan made Bath, a place crucial to his private life, the setting for *The Rivals* (1775). These two greatest writers for the English theatre in the period made the hard, witty 'manners' convention more personal and natural. The move throughout the century to a comedy of feeling was led by Irishmen, from Sir Richard Steele, in moralizing comedies, to Hugh Kelly, arch-exponent of 'sentimental comedy': his *False Delicacy* (1768) typically combined sympathy for fine feeling with irony at its excesses. Goldsmith's genius for the natural sometimes upset his audiences. The 'low' scene with the bailiffs in *The Good-Natur'd Man* (1768) had to be cut but he got his own back with Tony Lumpkin, the spirit of 'lowness' and creative anarchy; a creation probably from the depths of his subconscious.

It was also an oblique comment on the insider/outsider position of the Irish playwrights (true of those at the top as well as minor writers like Arthur Murphy). Their comedy abounds in displaced characters and witty play with the idea of acting, as in Joseph Surface's deployment of his split personality in *The School for Scandal* (1777). Irish playwrights' bravura handling of a stock comic theme, the assumed persona, owed much to their real-life experience of dual identity – spectacularly shown in Charles Macklin's recreation of himself as London actor and playwright, having started life as Cathal MacLochlain, a Gaelic-speaking Catholic peasant from Donegal.

Nineteenth Century: Boucicault, Wilde and Shaw

The move towards an Irish-oriented drama, begun by John O'Keeffe (*The Wicklow Mountains*, 1795) was accelerated by the master of melodrama, Dion Boucicault (1820–90), when he brought Ireland to the transatlantic stage in *The Colleen Bawn: or The Brides of Garryowen* (premièred in New York in 1860). Boucicault's use of the 'stage Irishman', seen by some as pandering to English taste, was cleverly geared to subversive as well as mirthful purposes. Conn in *The Shaughraun* (1874) and his fellow scamps defend 'true' Irishness against pressures from the British military, anglicization (especially of Irish speech modes) and rapacious landlords. Boucicault's easy mix of 'sensation scenes', comedy, song and poignant love relationships, often across the Irish/English divide, contained trenchant criticism of the system it reflected (softened by melodramatic 'happy endings') and provided an influential model for later drama. A line of descent can be traced from his persuasive rogues through those of Synge, O'Casey and Shaw (the trial scene of *The Devil's Disciple* was modelled on Boucicault's in *Arrah na Pogue*, 1864). Echoes with a more tragic ring are heard in Brian Friel's *Translations*.

At the other end of the Dublin–London axis, Wilde and Shaw continued in the established expatriate mode, using comic conventions to overturn convention. Wilde joked that they constituted a Celtic school, with a mission to clear the air ('England is the land of intellectual fog'). He attacked the 'slavery of custom' through witty reversals of standard plots and a dynamic tension between the 'rulers of society' and his sceptical dandies and outcasts. Finally, in *The Importance of being Earnest* (1895), the farce which gave the theme of divided personality an existentialist dimension, he exploded through laughter the patriarchal morality of the Victorian ruling class.

Shaw made himself the Irish gadfly to sting the English into enlightenment. That he wrote for the Dublin theatre only rarely (as in *The Showing-Up of Blanco Posnet*, 1909) was not due entirely to his immersion in the English scene: *John Bull's Other Island* (1904) was rejected by the Abbey as beyond their scope. One of Shaw's most personal plays, it viewed the state of Ireland through a complex multiple perspective, ranging from the absurd romanticism of the English businessman to the debilitating cynicism of his Irish partner. Alongside the (thoroughly guyed) 'stage Irishman' uncomfortably real Irish characters appear; the grasping, narrow Catholic farmer, the unfrocked priest, with his mystical concept of a holy Ireland inaccessible to the 'developers'. Shaw declared himself an Irish playwright throughout his career but would be counted among the potent influences on Irish drama for this play alone.

Modern Irish Drama

The indisputably national drama which began with the Irish Literary Theatre in 1899 was inspired by a great poet and despite phases of more prosaic realism was continually renewed by the poetic imagination of its writers. W.B. Yeats (1865–1939) did what no previous Irish playwright had attempted, put the 'matter of Ireland' on stage, giving it tragic dignity and projecting it into the modern European repertoire through powerful stage images like the bare tree and ruined house of *Purgatory* (1938). Ranging from legend and folk lore to the Easter Rising of 1916 (*The Dreaming of the Bones*, 1919), he probed the inwardness of the Irish experience, inventing an entirely new type of theatre for the dance play *At the Hawk's Well* in 1916. He set the ghosts of Ireland's past – Cuchulain, Swift – in a framing action which questions their meaning for modern Ireland. Yeats could put his finger on the national nerve, as in *Cathleen ni Houlihan* (1899). But he wrote from a larger dimension, European as well as Anglo-Irish, and much of his influence, like that of Wilde and Shaw, was delayed until realism had run its course. He left a cornucopia where future Irish playwrights would find archetypes resonant for their own times, as, famously, did Beckett.

J.M. Synge (1871–1909) and to some extent Lady Gregory (1852–1932) also brought a European imagination to Irish material. The remote places of Wicklow and the West of Ireland, background to Boucicault's simpler romanticism, were drawn by Synge into a modern dimension; poetic, strange, Rabelaisian. In his world of 'violent laughter', lonely beings like the blind couple in *The Well of the Saints* (1905) shape a second world for themselves through that capacity for dreaming which Shaw identified in his Irish play as a national characteristic. Synge set in terms of high symbolic comedy topics that were to engross Irish drama for decades. Nora, trapped in arid marriage in *The Shadow of the Glen* (1903), Christy in *The Playboy of the Western World* (1907) struggling to free himself from his father's shadow, were iconic figures, invested with exhilarating verbal energy. The Irish turns of speech in their style contributed to the shock early audiences suffered over a drama at once so like and so unlike the national idea of rural Ireland.

Synge's plays resonated abroad, and have continued to do so; Lady Gregory's less so. But her version of life in the West of Ireland was more congenial than his to Dublin audiences. She established the peasant drama at the centre of the new Irish theatre. Writing out of a quintessentially Anglo-Irish situation, she unlocked the Gaelic world for the stage with a key made from affectionate knowledge. Her translations into 'Kiltartan' English, including those of Gaelic plays by Douglas Hyde (*Casadh an tSúgháin*, 1901), contribu-

ted importantly to the rooting of drama in Irish culture. Most successful in one-act comedies of peasant life like *The Workhouse Ward* (1908), she could touch deep national chords, as in the poignant *The Rising of the Moon* (1907) and *The Gaol Gate* (1906).

A bevy of playwrights, mostly with Catholic backgrounds, took the Irish drama in the naturalistic direction which every theatre in post-Ibsen Europe seemingly had to experience. The peasant drama, sometimes extended into an urban or middle-class scene (Edward Martyn's *The Heather Field*, 1899), was what a largely rural society called for. Prominent among playwrights from south and north who met the need in early years were Padraic Colum, William Boyle, T. C. Murray, George Fitzmaurice, Lennox Robinson (*The Big House*, 1926), Teresa Deevy, George Shiels and Paul Vincent Carroll. Seamus Byrne and M.J. Molloy (*The King of Friday's Men*, 1948) were among those who added significantly to the repertoire of realism from the forties onward. The Gaelic dramatic movement came to the fore for a time at the Abbey, but has mostly been associated with amateur theatre in the west of Ireland and regional writers such as Siohan O' Suilleabhain.

In 1923 realism was taken into a high, new dimension by Sean O'Casey (1880–1964), who did for the Dublin slums what Synge had done for rural Ireland, but with a colloquial ease and ear for Dublin argot which came from being part of the society he wrote of. He put drama at the centre of Irish cultural life by re-creating on his stage historic events through which his audiences had just passed: the Easter Rising, the Civil War. *Juno and the Paycock* (1924) stamped on the Irish dramatic imagination the disreputable Joxer and the subtly intertwined humour and pain of a tenement world under the shadow of violence. The sardonic view of war fantasies in *The Plough and the Stars* (1926) alienated the nationalists, and when the theatrically innovative *The Silver Tassie* (1929) was rejected by Yeats, O'Casey became one of those who wrote on Irish matters from outside

Ireland. But his plays, with their invigorating application of popular theatre forms to serious issues, continued to feed Irish drama, as very obviously in the epic *The Non-Stop Connolly Show* (1976) of John Arden and Margaretta D'Arcy.

The peasant drama renewed itself intermittently by probing into the dark recesses of Ireland's regional cultures, as in the plays of John Keane, set in rural Kerry (and launched first by local amateurs). In a season of revivals at the Abbey in the eighties, the curious mix of domestic realism, Boucicault-like musicality and gothic horror in plays like *Sive* (1959), a harrowing study of forced marriage, impressed by its 'fearful visceral force'. As late as 1992, John McGahern's adaptation to an Irish setting of Tolstoy's *The Power of Darkness* sent shock waves through Abbey audiences with its unsparing presentation of rural savagery.

Sporadic thrusts towards formal experiment (often under influences from abroad) were made at theatres such as the outward-looking Gate, where Denis Johnston's expressionistic *The Old Lady Says 'No!'* was performed in 1929. Brendan Behan's free-wheeling, improvisatory plays, with their part-knockabout treatment of grim topics, were in the tradition of Boucicault and O'Casey, though *The Hostage* owed much to the workshop techniques of Joan Littlewood, who produced it in London in 1958. In this, and in his moving, colloquial treatment of a prison hanging in *The Quare Fellow* (1954), Behan introduced modern alienation devices which induced the audience to evaluate the dramatic 'happenings' for themselves.

Influence from two mighty Irishmen abroad, Joyce and Beckett, struck Irish drama from the sixties onward. Ironically, given Joyce's commitment to Ibsenism (subtly displayed in his one play, *Exiles*, 1918) it was an adaptation of *Ulysses*, Hugh Leonard's *Stephen D.* (Dublin Festival, 1962), which triggered off a phase of radical experiment. Its technique of dislocated time schemes and unsettling juxtapositions of dream and reality

was apt for the dramatization of an Ireland in a state of bewildering transition between old pieties and a modern commercial culture. Leonard's *Da* trilogy (1973 on) showed the value of the technique in more muted form.

Samuel Beckett (1906–89) wrote for a world stage, always at a distance from Ireland but conveying an intensely felt experience of Irishness in subtly veiled, oblique form. He showed a way to universalize deep private memories, removing them from a narrow, parochial context without losing immediacy. His spectacularly displaced characters, fixed in some unaccountable void which they contrive to fill with humorous, self-searching and haunting words, had a special relevance for Irish drama, with its long-standing uncertainty about its 'natural' identity and language. Beckett created a cornucopia for the next generation of Irish playwrights as surely as Yeats had done for the first.

In Belfast, whose Lyric Theatre was devoted to Yeats, there appeared Yeats's successor in the task of dramatizing the 'matter of Ireland'. Brian Friel created for the stage an Irish landscape, with the mythic Donegal town of Ballybeg as centre, within which he has unrolled a great stretch of Ireland's cultural history. From the complex viewpoint of one brought up a Catholic in Northern Ireland and exposed to the violence renewed there from the late sixties onward, he has extended the limits of realism, using narrators, stage-managing commentators – and in *Philadelphia Here I Come* (1964) a materialized 'private' self – to explore the alternatives open to his self-divided characters. The emphasis is often tragic, as in *The Freedom of the City* (1973), but Friel presents history as a malleable narrative, continually open to reinterpretation, a concept brilliantly illustrated in *Faith Healer* (1979) through four separate narratives which meet only in the audience's mind. Like Yeats, Friel had to create a new stage for a new need. His first play for Field Day, *Translations* (1980), captured attention far beyond Ireland with its portrayal of a Gaelic culture (embodied in a piquantly classical hedge school) disintegrating under pressure from 'English' and the modern world when local place-names are forcibly anglicized by the British. Friel's ability to strike a universal note with his major theme – the deep emotional ambivalence in Irish attitudes to the past – was shown by the huge critical and popular international success of *Dancing at Lughnasa* (1990).

Another major playwright of the new wave, Tom Murphy, has turned the standard conventions of naturalism in a more inward direction, bringing out the many layers of mythic meaning in the stories his characters tell themselves. The obsessive fantasy in *The Gigli Concert* (1983) sets off a chain of subtle revelations, involving Irish/English relationships as well as the inner psychology of the two curiously interlocked characters who represent them. In *Balegangaire* (1985) the story told to her granddaughters by an old, bedridden woman (struggling to surmount a disabling memory block) becomes, obliquely, a story of Ireland, seen from a double perspective, very close and with an effect of infinite distance (Murphy has spoken of the 'objectivity' he gained from spending some years away from Ireland, in London).

Thomas Kilroy, in *The Death and Resurrection of Mr Roche* (1968), and several playwrights of a younger generation, north and south, have focused on the urban working class and a cultural identity under threat – from the security forces' response to sectarian violence in Graham Reid's *Remembrance* (1984); from a Rachmanesque drug culture on a Dublin housing estate in Dermot Bolger's *The Lament for Arthur Cleary* (1989). The 'mapping' of Irish regional life has been continued by Billy Roche in plays known collectively as 'The Wexford Trilogy' (1992: *A Handful of Stars*, *Poor Beast in the Rain*, *Belfry*). Flexible dramatic forms, modulating between naturalism and the surreal, have become a feature of *fin de siècle* Irish drama. Tom McIntyre's *The Great Hunger* (1983) mixes words with arresting visual imagery; Stewart Parker's *Spokesong*

(1975) introduces dream bicycles from a 'safe' past, and a precariously balancing Trick Cyclist to express his Belfast protagonist's sense of lostness. In Bolger's *In High Germany* (1990) a 'new' Irishman conveys his dependence on Irish football teams abroad for a sense of cultural identity through a monologue constructed like an echo chamber. A new wave of younger playwrights includes Marina Carr – whose 1996 play *Portia Coughlan* was seen at both the Abbey and London's Royal Court – and Sebastian Barry – whose *Our Lady of Sligo* was premièred in 1998 at the Royal National Theatre, London.

Irish drama's confidence in its identity has been shown by a spate of Irish-oriented adaptions of foreign classics: three separate versions of *Antigone* in 1984 by writers north and south of the border; Thomas Kilroy's skilful rewriting of *The Seagull* in terms of the Anglo-Irish Big House. 'The expatriates' plays have been reclaimed. Tom Murphy gave *She Stoops to Conquer* an Irish setting (1972); Friel rewrote Macklin's *The True-Born Irishman* (as *The London Vertigo*, 1990); in 1992 Declan Hughes introduced into *Love and a Bottle* a Farquhar persona to speak for that classic figure, the Irish writer abroad.

The drama of the leading Ulster playwright, Frank McGuinness, takes audacious strides into territory few would risk, notably in his visionary portrayal of Northern Irish soldiers in World War I, *Observe the Sons of Ulster Marching Towards the Somme* (1984), and his *Someone Who'll Watch Over Me* (1992), a profoundly sensitive study of three Lebanon hostages, in which old Irish/English antagonisms dissolve. The climax, in one way grim, is touched with hope for closer understanding. McGuinness seems to be continuing the movement, discernible in the great new wave of Irish drama, towards a large perspective and readiness for change in many aspects of cultural life.

KATHARINE WORTH

Drummond, Thomas (1797–1840) Administrator. Born Edinburgh, 10 October; died

Dublin, 15 April. Drummond was educated at Edinburgh University and entered the Royal Engineers after study at Woolwich Academy. He served as under-secretary in Ireland from 1835 until his death. Liberal and fair-minded, he worked to eliminate sectarianism and ensure impartial enforcement of the law. The Orange Order disintegrated and faction fights were curbed. He told the landlords that property had its duties as well as its rights, and agrarian disturbances were reduced. His unremitting labours led to his early death.

HENRY BOYLAN

Dublin, City of The origins of the name Dubhlinn are unknown and tend to enter the realm of legend. Along the old town wall at Wood Quay there would appear to have been an area that flooded at high tide and this possibly was An Linn Dubh, the black pool where the Liffey and Poddle met. The name possibly predates the coming of the Vikings and some sources suggest that the name may have referred to a monastic settlement south of the black pool. Ath Cliath, the old Irish name for the city, to which the word 'Baile' or town was added towards the end of the fourteenth century, refers to hurdles anchored to the bed of the Liffey by heavy stones. Its actual location is not known but it may have been further upstream from Dubhlinn, near Church Street, where the river was shallow and crossing made easy for people and animals to wade across the river bed.

In 1537, Henry VIII ordered the dissolution of the Irish monasteries, and Archbishop George Browne and Sir Anthony St Leger oversaw the division and disposal of the lands of the Dublin monasteries over a period of years. A year later, in 1538, Archbishop Browne made a large bonfire of the city's sacred relics at Christchurch Place.

An important charter of 1547 allowed for the appointment of a sheriff and legally released the city from the county sheriff. Protestantism was declared the official religion of Ireland in 1548, but many of the changes taking place in England were totally rejected by those living within the Pale. Nevertheless, in 1551 the Book of Common Prayer, being the first book printed in Ireland, rolled from the press of Humphrey Powell in Dublin. Ireland was again declared officially Protestant in 1560.

In 1592 Trinity College was founded on the site of the supposed Augustinian monastery of All Hallowes. A charter was provided by Elizabeth I and within two years the college was receiving students. Today, it stands on a 42-acre site. A postal service was established in 1562, with Alderman Nicholas Fitzsimon as the first postmaster in Dublin. This service was extended in 1638 with the opening of a general post office in Castle Street. In 1560 the first public clocks appeared at Dublin Castle, the Tholsel and St Patrick's Cathedral.

The city continued to expand in the seventeenth century, and in 1610 John Speed published the first map of the city of Dublin. The corporation ordered in 1616 that every fifth house should have a lantern and candlelight set forth from six o'clock to nine o'clock every dark night from Hallow-tide until after Christmas. Charles I was executed in 1649, and in the same year Oliver Cromwell arrived at Ringsend with 12,000 troops and stabled his horses in St Patrick's Cathedral. He spent 10 months creating havoc in Ireland. He also introduced cabbages for the first time to Ireland in order to supply green vegetables for his soldiers. For this purpose he rented a garden from Philip Fernley, who owned two houses in St Bride Street and a garden in St Kevin Street. It is now a public park off Kevin Street Lower.

After the restoration of the monarchy, when Charles II returned from exile, the city continued to develop. During the time of Viceroy Lord Essex in 1676 a wealthy merchant, Sir Humphrey Jervis, later to become lord mayor, agreed to build a bridge, and a street named after the viceroy's family (Capel) and a street system were laid out on part of the confiscated lands of St Mary's Abbey. The next year the duke of Ormond, who had replaced Jervis in 1677, suggested that the warehouses and residences which backed on to the river should have a stone quay along the river. The entire system of quays on both sides of the Liffey owes its origin to the prototype built on Ormond Quay.

The office of mayor was established in 1229, but the first lord mayor was Sir Daniel Bellingham, who was elected in 1665. The lord mayor is the first citizen of the city and is elected each year by the city council from among its members. In 1662 both the Phoenix Park and St Stephen's Green were laid out, the former by the duke of Ormond when 2,000 acres surrounding the viceregal residence were acquired to form a royal deer park, and the latter by the corporation, which by 1664 had marked out an area of about 27 acres to be preserved as an open space for the use of citizens.

From 1630 onwards there are records of Huguenots settling in Ireland, but the two greatest influxes were in 1662 and after the Revocation of the Edict of Nantes on 22 October 1685. The Huguenots became part of the existing weaving fraternity in a large industrial area in the Liberties of Thomas Court and Donore, and their expertise contributed to the establishment of a silk and poplin industry.

The Weavers Guild was founded as early as 1446 and their guild hall in the Lower Coombe, built in 1682, was replaced in 1745 by the Huguenot David Digges La Touche, who advanced the £200 needed. In 1689 James II arrived in Dublin and Mass was celebrated in Christ Church cathedral, while in 1690 William of Orange attended thanksgiving service in St Patrick's Cathedral for the defeat of James. The following year, William presented the great chain made of 22-carat gold that was worn until 1988 by the lord mayor. This replaced a chain presented by Charles II in 1660, lost in 1688.

Marsh's Library, designed by Sir William Robinson, who had been architect for the Royal Hospital Kilmainham, was built in 1701 for Archbishop Marsh. This was the first public library in Ireland. The Royal Hospital at Kilmainham was opened in 1684 for the reception and entertainment of ancient, maimed and infirm officers and soldiers.

The eighteenth century was a time of peace and prosperity, and the city as we know it today with its wide streets was constructed. Many of the city's hospitals were opened at this time: the Coombe lying-in hospital in 1770, Bartholomew Mosses Maternity Hospital in 1745, the new Rotunda in 1757, Mercers in 1734 and the Meath in 1753. As well as caring for the sick, there was the problem of the vagabond or sturdy beggar, and in 1704 a 'workhouse' was built, which by 1729 had been transformed into a foundling hospital. By 1772 the workhouse had been divided into two separate institutions, a house of industry (in Channel Row) and the foundling hospital, which had been rebuilt.

By 1707 George Dawson had formed a wide roadway which was considered at the time to be the finest in Dublin. In 1715 the corporation agreed to purchase Mr Dawson's house for £3,500 for the use of the lord mayor, and it has been used for this purpose ever since.

North of the river Liffey in 1714 Luke Gardiner bought the Drogheda Estate, part of the lands of St Mary's Abbey, from Viscount Moore, and in the 1750s Sackville Street, Henry Street, Moore Street and North Earl Street were all being developed. Fashionable living areas like Henrietta Street were commenced again by Luke Gardiner as early as 1721.

Following the passing of an Act of Parliament in 1757 the city experienced the most enlightened period of planning in its history. The Wide Street Commissioners were to transform narrow streets and laneways into the impressive streets that we know today. The commissioners' first task was to make a wide and convenient way from Essex Bridge to the Castle of Dublin. This was named Parliament Street and opened in 1762. They then proceeded to widen Dame Street in 1769. Royal approval was given for a grant of £15,000 towards a new bridge across the Liffey in 1782, and it was decided to extend Sackville Street to the river and to continue it in the opposite direction to Dorset Street and along East Rutland Square and North Frederick Street. Westmoreland Street and D'Olier Street were under way by the beginning of the nineteenth century. The commissioners had achieved their aims by 1800. Merrion Square was laid out in 1752 by John Ensor for the Fitzwilliam Estate.

Fitzwilliam Square was commenced in 1791 but was not completed until the nineteenth-century. On the north side in 1792 the building of houses commenced in Mountjoy Square, while Rutland Street (now Parnell Square) was started as early as 1751. The Grand Canal company opened its canal to cargo-boat traffic in 1779, and the Royal Canal Company was formed in 1789. Both these waterways were set up to link the port of Dublin with its hinterland. Towards the end of the century impressive public buildings were being erected: James Gandon's Customs House was completed in 1791 at a cost of £400,000, while Thomas Cooley's Royal Exchange opened for business in 1779, Parliament having given £13,500 for the site and £40,000 being raised by lotteries conducted by the merchants. Gandon's Four Courts building was completed in 1801. The King's Inns were commenced in 1795 and were designed by James Gandon and his pupil, Henry Aaron Baker.

The disastrous Act of Union in 1801 removed the Dublin Parliament to Westminster, and in spite of the fact that the city continued to expand, many of the Anglo-Irish left their town houses and removed to England. After the Famine of the 1840s country people moved into the empty Georgian houses, which had turned into slums, and it is estimated that one-third of the population living between the canals was housed in slum conditions. The first railway to be built in Ireland was opened for passenger traffic in

1834 and ran between Dublin and Kingstown. As a result of this many Dubliners were introduced to the seaside for the first time. Dun Leary was renamed Kingstown when George IV visited the city in 1821. It became Dun Laoghaire in 1921.

The earliest public transport in the city was operated with horse omnibuses, which ran from about 1836. On 1 February 1872 the first horse tram plied from College Green to Terenure, and on 1 October another line was opened to Sandymount. The Catholic Emancipation Act of 1829 resulted in the building of a large number of Roman Catholic churches. The main part of the guild system was abolished in 1841 by the Municipal Corporations (Ireland) Act, and council members were elected by the rate payers of the city. The Dublin Fire Brigade was established in 1862. Prior to this, insurance companies had their own fire engines.

The Iveagh Trust, founded in 1904, did much to alleviate the hardship of the poor, with the building of red-brick flats around the Nicholas Street area. That same year the Abbey Theatre was opened.

O'Connell Street was badly damaged in 1916 and again in 1922 together with other streets, the Four Courts, the Customs House and the Public Record Office. In the 1960s new building in the form of office blocks began to take shape, and hundreds of houses were demolished to make way for buildings that changed the streetscape and skyline of the city. Today there is a slow move back to the inner city, with attractive red-brick houses being erected and more control over planning laws.

DOUGLAS BENNETT

The *Dublin University Magazine* Founded January 1833 by six Tory dons and undergraduates at Trinity College, Dublin. It emerged from an informal university society called the Porch, whose members wanted to defend the cause of 'the property and intelligence of Protestant Ireland' and to overcome the stigma of Ireland never having supported a good political and literary magazine. Its founders included its first editor, Charles Stuart Stanford, Isaac Butt (editor 1834–8) and Samuel O'Sullivan. The founders put up £10 each to launch the magazine but it proved so successful that, after six months, it was bought by the publisher James McGlashan.

With its abrasive challenge to the liberal reforming spirit of the age, the *DUM* soon attracted the attention of leading Tories in Ireland and England, but it was often read in spite of its politics. Before the end of the 1830s, it had introduced James Clarence Mangan, Sheridan Le Fanu and Charles Lever to the Irish reading public and had brought to national prominence the work of William Carleton and Samuel Ferguson. In its first issue it declared its intention to found an Irish 'school of writing' and advocated a repeal of the literary union, believing that a native press could encourage national feeling as a native Parliament had done before 1800. That the *DUM* was not parochially Irish, however, was revealed in its publishing of specimens from other national literatures. The magazine made a real contribution to popularizing the German Romantics in Britain, most notably through Mangan's 'Anthologia Germanica' (1835–46).

The *DUM* did not have an official association with Dublin University, but its title implied that it was proud of the intellectual heritage bestowed upon Protestant Ireland by Trinity's illustrious graduates, from Ussher, through Swift and Berkeley, to Burke and Grattan. In a 'Gallery of Illustrious Irishmen' (1836–47), which comprised 30 biographies, the *DUM* claimed all the eighteenth-century leaders of public opinion in Ireland as precursors of its own peculiar Irish Toryism. The *DUM* was ambivalent about the Union, highlighting the invariable divergence of 'English theory and Irish Fact'. The magazine's leading political writers in the 1830s and 1840s, notably Samuel and Mortimer O'Sullivan, attacked both the moral evil of popery, for perverting Irish patriotism, and

English misgovernment of Ireland. They also trumpeted the duties of the resident landlord, attacking the Whiggish view that absenteeism was not harmful, and took pride in the un-English but non-Roman roots of Irish Christianity. The *DUM*'s national philosophy was most clearly expressed in Samuel Ferguson's 'Dialogue between the Head and Heart of an Irish Protestant' (November 1833), which captured something of the pride and anxiety of the Anglo-Irish Protestant who wanted to celebrate his dual nationality, but who feared that he was seen as an English colonist by the Catholic Irish and as a mere Irishman by the English.

During Charles Lever's editorship (April 1842–mid-1845), sales of the magazine increased from around 2,500 (itself a respectable figure) to 4,000. There were some who believed that the magazine would become too cosmopolitan under Lever, but he professed himself proud to have achieved the editorship of 'our national magazine'. The writers of the *Nation* accepted this labelling of the *DUM* and, in November 1842, in an early battle between Old and Young Ireland, Thomas Davis defended the journal from the barbed criticisms of O'Connell.

Through the later 1840s the *DUM* still reflected something of the vibrancy of Irish politics but by 1850 it was more evidently a literary than a political journal. McGlashan sold the magazine in 1855 and it was not seen as a genuinely Irish production again. Sheridan Le Fanu bought it in 1861 and edited it until 1869, but he made no attempt to reroot it in the culture of the Irish Protestant nation. He used it as an outlet for his own novels and for those of friends. Its last proprietor took 'Dublin' from the title in 1878 and the unrooted *University Magazine* ceased publication in 1880.

JOSEPH SPENCE

Dublin University Press The printing house in Trinity College, Dublin, was built in 1734–6 using a gift of £1,000 from Bishop John Stearne, and an edition of Plato's dialogues in Greek (1738) was the first book printed. A modest range of volumes was issued by a succession of printers in the eighteenth century, largely classics and texts for the students.

Matters improved somewhat in the early nineteenth-century, and with the appointment of Michael Henry Gill as university printer in 1842 the press at last took on the role of a true university press. Highpoints were Archbishop James Ussher's *Works* (17 vols, 1847–64) and *Annala rioghachta Eireann* (7 vols, 1851). Gill's tenure lasted until 1874, during which time he established the press's reputation for scholarship and high technical skill.

Gill was succeeded by the partnership of Ponsonby, who supplied the capital, and Murphy, who managed the press. In 1878 the Dublin University Press series of scholarly works was initiated. The partnership went through several changes over the years, becoming Ponsonby and Weldrick in 1879 and Ponsonby and Gibbs in 1902.

The twentieth-century saw a gradual shift away from bookwork to scholarly jobbing at the press, especially the high-security production of exam papers. Although the firm had always printed for the trade in general, Trinity College continued to be a major customer. The Allman family took over the press in 1944 and occupied the printing house until early 1976, when the firm moved to the Dublin suburb of Sandymount. There the business continues, the oldest printing firm in Ireland.

Reading

Kinane, Vincent, *A History of the Dublin University Press 1734–1976* (Dublin: Gill and Macmillan, 1994).

VINCENT KINANE

Duff, Arthur Knox (1899–1956) Composer, arranger and music producer. Born Dublin. Knox studied at the Royal Irish Academy of Music and Trinity College, Dublin, where he obtained primary degrees in arts and music and successfully sued for MusD in 1942. He was organist and choirmaster at Christ Church, Bray, before being commissioned as the first native bandmaster in the Army School of Music (1923). Knox resigned from the army in 1931 and was appointed as the first music producer in Radio Eireann in 1937 and eventually as assistant director of music there. A gentle and languid personality, he composed but little music. That which he did is sensitively crafted, the principal works being written for Terry O'Connor and her Dublin String Orchestra. He displayed no inclination to explore larger forms; his works are small and lyrical and frequently employ a modal harmonic resource, all of which point his debt to fellow miniaturists of the early twentieth-century English school. His works include *Meath Pastoral* (1940), *Irish Suite for Strings* (1940), *Music for Strings* (1955) and the two late suites *Echoes of Georgian Dublin* (1955 and 1956).

JOSEPH RYAN

Duffy, Sir Charles Gavan (1816–1903) Politician. Born Monaghan, 12 April; died Nice, 9 February. Virtually self-educated, Duffy became a journalist in Dublin and was called to the bar in 1845. He was a founder and editor of the *Nation* and was elected MP for New Ross in 1852. Despairing of political reform, he emigrated to Australia in 1855. Entering politics, he rose to be prime minister of Victoria in 1871 and was knighted in 1873. He retired to the south of France in 1880 and devoted himself to literary work.

Reading

Duffy, Sir Charles Gavan, *Young Ireland* (London, Paris and New York: Cassell, Petter, Galpin, 1880).

—— *Life of Thomas Davis* (London: Kegan Paul, Trench and Co., 1892).

—— *My Life in Two Hemispheres* (London: Unwin, 1898).

HENRY BOYLAN

Dun Emer Industries 'A wish to find work for Irish hands in the making of beautiful things' was the motivation of Evelyn Gleeson (1885–1944) when she founded the Dun Emer Industries, a women's craft co-operative, in 1902. Tapestry and carpet weaving, embroidery, hand-printing, bookbinding, enamelling and painting classes were all carried on.

The printing was conducted by Elizabeth Corbet Yeats and the first book, *In the seven Woods* by her brother W.B. Yeats, was published in 1903. The press broke away from Dun Emer in 1908 and was renamed the Cuala Press. The other crafts continued in production until the 1960s.

Reading

Miller, Liam, *The Dun Emer Press, Later the Cuala Press* (Dublin: Dolmen, 1973).

VINCENT KINANE

Dungannon Convention (1782) By the midwinter of 1781–2, the Patriots' campaign to secure the repeal of the legislative restrictions binding the Irish Parliament (Poynings' Law (1494) and the Declaratory Act (1719)) was waning. However, the Volunteers of Ulster were determined not to allow the opportunity to pass. Following a call by a number of Armagh corps, it was decided to convene a provincial delegate meeting to deliberate on a series of resolutions calling for legislative independence. The resolutions were approved with acclaim by the representatives of 250 Volunteer corps, and it was the impetus their intervention gave the campaign for legislative independence that won 'the constitution of 1782'.

Reading

O'Connell, M.R., *Irish Politics and Social Conflict in the Age of the American Revolution* (Philadelphia: University of Philadelphia Press, 1965).

Smyth, P.D.H., 'Grattan and 1782: a survey', *Retrospect*, n.s. 3 (1981).

JAMES KELLY

Durcan, Paul (1944–) Poet. Born Dublin. Educated at University College, Cork, where he studied history and archaeology, Durcan is one of the most innovative and distinctive of contemporary Irish poets. His outrageous titles, chatty tones and hyperbolic style belie his penetrating humanism, which exposes the underlying hypocrisies and inadequacies of modern Irish life. A continual experimenter with the techniques of verbal, visual and musical media, his collections, *Crazy about Women* (1991) and *Give Me Your Hand* (1994), consist of poems inspired by paintings in the national galleries of Ireland and Britain. *Greetings to Our Friends in Brazil* was published in 1999.

LIAM HARTE

E

Earls, Flight of the On 4 September 1607 a group of Ulster nobility, including the earls of Tyrone and Tyrconnell and the lord of Fermanagh, Cuconnaught Maguire, left Lough Swilly for Continental Europe. The boat had been hired by Maguire, who had gone to the Low Countries in the summer of 1607, at Rouen with money provided by the archduke Albert of the Spanish Netherlands. The initial aim seemed to be only to bring Tyrconnell and his followers to the Spanish Netherlands, but Tyrone joined at the last moment.

The motivation behind this action, which O'Neill regretted later while in exile in Rome, is unclear. One explanation stresses the imminent discovery of O'Neill's conspiratorial links with Spain after the peace of Mellifont in 1603, but these links consisted only of accepting a Spanish pension. One plot was disclosed by Christopher St Lawrence and the baron Delvin in early 1607, but there was no firm evidence to link Tyrone to it, although the Dublin government clearly suspected that he was involved. Another explanation relies on Tyrone's inability to accept the sorts of restriction on his power that the Dublin government, and especially the solicitor general Sir John Davies, wanted to impose. Dublin was concerned to limit the freedom of action of a potentially 'overmighty subject'. Davies used litigation against Tyrone by one of his followers, Donal O'Cahan, as a test case for the crown to lay hold of the freehold land of the earldom and hence cripple O'Neill economically. Politically, rumours of a presidency of Ulster on the lines of those already existing for Connacht and Munster would have destroyed Tyrone's power within his own lordship. Whatever the motivation, the flight of the earls shaped the history of Ulster, for it was that which formed the basis of the escheatment of the earls' lands and the ensuing plantation of Ulster.

Reading

Canny, Nicholas, 'The flight of the earls, 1607', *Irish Historical Studies* xvii (1971).

Mooney, Canice, 'A noble shipload', *Irish Sword* ii (1955–7).

Ó Cianáin, Tadhg, *The Flight of the Earls*, ed. Paul Walsh (Dublin: 1916).

Walsh, Micheline Kerney, *'Destruction by Peace': Hugh O'Neill after Kinsale* (Armagh: 1986).

RAYMOND GILLESPIE

Easter Rising (1916) The origins of the 1916 rising lay partly in the extraordinary outburst of cultural nationalism that followed in the wake of Parnell's death in 1891. The founding in 1893 of the Gaelic League, a movement to revive the Gaelic language, and the flowering of a literary revival led by the poet W.B. Yeats instilled in the younger generation a strong sense of distinctive cultural identity. Among the seven signatories to the 1916 Proclamation were three Gaelic-speaking poets, Patrick Pearse, Joseph Plunkett and Thomas MacDonagh.

The failure of the British government to implement the Third Home Rule Bill after its passing in 1912 disillusioned many younger nationalists, whose thoughts began to turn towards the possibility of wresting independence by means of physical force. In 1912 Ulster Unionists had set up an armed Ulster Volunteer Force to resist Home Rule. It prompted the founding in Dublin in November 1913 of an Irish Volunteer Force to defend the nationalist claim to Home Rule.

At the outbreak of war in August 1914 the Volunteer movement split. The majority (about 200,000) followed the advice of the parliamentary party leader John Redmond and joined the war to fight for 'the freedom of small nations'. The remainder, about 10,000, followed Eoin MacNeill, the movement's founder, in his insistence that the Volunteers should remain a national defence force.

The plot for a rising, taking advantage of Britain's distraction in the war, now began to take shape within the reduced Volunteer force. It was orchestrated by the veteran Fenian Thomas Clarke, who gathered round him a group of younger conspirators in the secret and oath-bound Irish Republican Brotherhood (IRB). Meanwhile James Connolly, who had helped set up a citizen army to defend the Dublin working class during an all-out strike in 1913, had come to the conclusion that socialism could follow only from political independence on a national basis. He joined forces with the IRB group in the weeks before the rising.

Hopes of foreign aid lay with Germany. Sir Roger Casement had been sent there to raise men and arms. A German boat laden with arms (the *Aud*) arrived off the coast of Kerry on 20 April, but through a mix-up in communications the Volunteers failed to rendezvous with it. Casement was captured and the boat scuttled.

A further blow was delivered to the potential scale of the rebellion when at the last moment Eoin MacNeill, who was against a rebellion that did not stand a chance of success, countermanded mobilization orders issued to the Volunteers for Easter Sunday. Despite this major setback, the planners decided to go ahead with the rising on Easter Monday.

The rising began with Patrick Pearse's reading of the Proclamation of a Republic outside the GPO on Easter Monday morning, 24 April 1916. The rebels held out for a week at strategic buildings around Dublin. Recognizing the hopelessness of the situation and increasingly concerned at the level of civilian casualties, they surrendered on Friday 29 April.

Between 3 and 12 May 1916, 14 of the leaders of the rising were executed in Kilmainham Gaol. Their deaths were the catalyst for a fundamental change in the political mood of Ireland, leading directly to the War of Independence of 1919–21.

PAT COOKE

economic expansion, programmes for There have been 12 programmes for economic expansion: Programme for Economic Expansion (1958); Second Programme for Economic Expansion (1963); Third Programme: Economic and Social Development (1969); National Development (1977–80); Development for Full Employment (1978); Programme for National Development (1978–81); The Way Forward (1982); Proposals for Plan, (1984–7, April 1984); Building on Reality (Autumn 1984); Programme for National Recovery (October 1987); Ireland, National Development Plan (1989–93, March 1989); Programme for Economic and Social Progress (January 1991).

The Programme for Economic Expansion (1958) was based on *Economic Development*, a study prepared by T.K. Whitaker, then secretary of the Department of Finance. That study aimed to set out a five-year framework for economic policy, describe the economy, analyse its strengths and weaknesses, describe the influence on development of external forces and recommend policy options. It placed heavy emphasis on agriculture as the motor of growth. It recommended a number of policy changes to stimulate domestic savings in order to finance development. It also recommended a greater emphasis on 'productive' investment than had previously characterized public investment policies, and a lesser investment in 'social' areas. It forecast 11 per cent overall economic growth for the period from 1959 to 1963. In the event, overall economic growth for the period was 23 per cent, large inflows of private foreign capital eased the domestic financing constraint, the projections of public capital spending were exceeded, agricultural growth played a smaller part than expected, and industrial growth far exceeded expectations. In certain respects, the government's programme departed from the rigour of the proposals set out in Whitaker's study. His systematic analytical framework, however, clearly led to more enlightened economic policy making.

The second and third programmes were based on much more elaborate sectoral analyses than the first.

The second programme (1963) aimed at a 50 per cent increase in GNP at market prices over the period 1960 to 1970, an average annual rate of 4.14 per cent. Within these targets, agriculture, forestry and fishing were expected to grow at 2.7 per cent per annum, while industry was expected to grow at an annual rate of 7.0 per cent and 'other domestic' (including stock appreciation adjustment) at 3.6 per cent. Thus, it marked a major shift from agriculture in the emphasis of expectations. It retained the expectation that most of the resources for increased investment would come from the increased current saving represented by forgoing part of the possible increase in consumption.

The third programme (1969) projected an annual growth rate for the economy over the programme period 1969 to 1972 of 4 per cent, 2 per cent for agriculture, forestry and fishing, 6.5 per cent for industry and 3.3 per cent for the services sector. It forecast a net increase of 16,000 in the numbers at work and an increase in the total population. It still expected external resources to play only a minor part in financing overall investment.

The external environment differed markedly from the expectations set out in the second and third programmes and the growth projections were not realized.

That experience and the activities of OPEC discouraged further planning exercises until 1977. Plans published from 1977 to 1982 proved to be based on excessively optimistic expectations of growth, and of the response of employment to sectoral growth. After 1977, planning was perceived more as a political than as a scientific exercise. Because of that, and perhaps because of the frequency with which new documents were published between 1977 and 1982, together with the apparent failure to integrate annual budgetary policy into the published frameworks, the process suffered a severe loss of public credibility, further confirmed by the failure to reach the employment targets in the 1987 programme and the government's abandonment of the pay commitments in the 1991 document.

ALAN DUKES

ecumenism Began in the 1920s in Ireland but for some forty years did not include the Roman Catholic church, the largest Christian body in the island: in the Republic, Catholics account for 93 per cent of the population (1981 census) and, while in a minority in Northern Ireland, there too they are the largest church, the non-Roman majority being divided between Presbyterians, Church of Ireland (Anglican), Methodists and several smaller groupings. Most Irish Protestants live in the North but all the churches are constituted on an All-Ireland basis.

189

Until quite recently, while personal relations between Protestants and Catholics were generally peaceful, courteous and often cordial, institutionally there was co-existence without co-operation. And though Anglicans and 'Dissenters' often made common cause, formal dialogue between them began only in 1931. But some years earlier the foundations were laid for an Irish Council of Churches, which now has associate status with the Conference of Churches of Britain and Ireland (in which the Church of Ireland and the Methodists enjoy full membership).

Catholic involvement in ecumenical activity hardly began to happen until the Second Vatican Council gave the green light to what had previously been regarded with suspicion and often downright condemnation. The Conciliar Decree on Ecumenism (1964) signalled a new departure, which was generally welcomed in Ireland, especially in the Republic. Catholic attendance at Protestant funerals and weddings, hitherto strictly forbidden, was taken up with enthusiasm, and the religious dimension of civic events became an occasion of inter-church ministry.

Such ministry has found a more urgent task in social work, especially in Northern Ireland, where communal strife, acute since 1969 but rooted in old and deep resentments, often bears religious labels. Church leaders have publicly deplored all sectarian bigotry and violence and have urged reconciliation and co-operation for peace, though, at parish level, a sense of what might be called church tribalism (serving 'our people') is still to be noted, particularly in the wake of each succeeding outrage on the part of the 'others'. But the work of the individual ministers of all churches, frequently undertaken at great personal risk, has been an authentic ministry of healing. And inter-church organizations like the Corymeela Community and the Columbanus Community of Reconciliation in Belfast have provided an effective common witness for peace and understanding in the very eye of the storm.

The guiding spirit of the Columbanus Community is a Jesuit priest from the south, Fr. Michael Hurley, who was the founder and first director of the Irish School of Ecumenics, founded in Dublin in 1970. This unique institution is an independent academic foundation, Christian in inspiration, interdenominational in structure and personnel, of recognized international status, which by the 1990s had a roll of some 70 students drawn from all over the world, and proceeding to degrees and diplomas in ecumenical theology and peace studies awarded by Dublin University (Trinity College) and the University of Ulster. Through teaching, research and certain extra-mural activities, it seeks to promote Christian unity and inter-faith understanding on the global level, as well as peace with justice in Ireland. Its resources are at the disposal of the churches, and of other approved bodies that share its objectives.

Other ecumenical developments worthy of note are the ongoing official Irish Inter-Church meetings (known as the Ballymascanlon conversations) and several unofficial but influential events attracting lay and clerical participants of all traditions. The best known of these is the midsummer conference held annually in Glenstal Benedictine Abbey, County Limerick, since the 1960s.

Considerable progress has been made on both the institutional and the popular level, but it would be too much to say that a Christian consensus has yet been reached, especially on certain moral issues. And in the North, the very idea of ecumenism is seen as a betrayal by fundamentalists and many 'evangelicals', and also by a substantial Presbyterian constituency.

SEÁN MAC RÉAMOINN

education The Irish education system is a centralized one under the supervision of the government Department of Education, with structures for financing schools and regulating curricular and assessment procedures. Yet it also is a system which allows for local freedom for schools, which, though financed by the state, are generally private institutions, and the church authorities have played, and still play, an important historical role in the management of schools. There are no regional structures at primary level, and at secondary level the vocational sector only is controlled by local authorities. The other second-level types of schools, secondary, comprehensive and community, relate directly to the central government department. This system reflects the ideals of the 1937 constitution, which states:

[Article 42.1]

The state acknowledges that the primary and natural educator of the child is the family and guarantees to respect the inalienable right and duty of parents to provide, according to their means, for the religious, moral, intellectual, physical and social education of their children.

State intervention in Irish education dates from Tudor times, but the nineteenth century saw the development of a centralized state bureaucracy. In 1831 the National School system was established to provide primary education for the poor. Under the terms of the 'Stanley Letter' (so called after its author, Lord Edward Stanley, the Irish chief secretary), a Board of Commissioners of National Education was empowered to distribute funds for the building of schools, employing of inspectors, training of teachers and providing grants for school requisites. Applications for aid to the board had to be made by local school patrons and, as the aim of the board was to encourage religious harmony and the 'mixed education' of Catholic and Protestant children, it looked with 'peculiar favour' on 'mixed' applications. Religious instruction was taught separately from moral and secular instruction and strict rules to avoid religious proselytism were laid down. Despite opposition from and distrust among the churches, the National School system developed steadily through the century, albeit, after the 1830s, with each religious denomination applying for its own schools.

By 1900 there were 8,684 National Schools in existence, and the illiteracy rate in Ireland dropped from 51 per cent in 1841 to 14 per cent in 1901. The Powis Commission (1870) on primary education in Ireland recognized that though *de jure* the National School system was non-denominational, *de facto* it had become a denominational one. No changes in the structure of primary education took place with the setting up of the Irish Free State in 1922, and it continues to function in a similar way under the rules for National Schools laid down by the Department of Education. In the 1960s rationalization took place following the publication of the OECD report *Investment in Education* (1965) and the introduction of free school transport (1967). Up to 1,000 one- and two-teacher schools were closed, and the numbers attending primary education rose from 500,000 in 1964/5 to 569,000 by 1980. In the 1970s there was a movement to establish in a number of multi-denominational national schools, and these now number 10. The core curriculum at primary level is prescribed by the Department of Education – a centralized policy adopted from 1831. In the last century the National School Lesson Books, a graded set of five readers published by the National Board which sold widely in the British empire, formed the basis of the core content, which was reading, writing, arithmetic, grammar, geography, and needlework for girls. After 1872, a system of 'payment by results' was introduced, whereby the pupils were examined annually and the teachers duly rewarded. In 1900 a Revised Programme of Primary Instruction was introduced, which was based on heuristic principles and Froebelian ideas and encouraged the teaching of practical subjects such as elementary science, manual training and drill in the core curriculum. In 1922 the *National Programme of Primary Instruction* introduced the compulsory study of the Gaelic language, history and culture and brought a returned emphasis to the '3Rs'. In 1971 a 'new' primary curriculum brought a child-centred approach to the primary schools, and the report of the *Primary Curriculum Review Body* (1990) has, with some amendments, endorsed this approach.

Secondary Education

At secondary level the state did not intervene directly until the Intermediate Education Act (1878), whereby public funds were made available to secondary schools through a system of payment by results based on the pupils' performance in public examinations. The Intermediate Education Board was empowered to organize a scheme of 'Intermediate Examinations' for schools at three levels, junior, middle and senior Grades, and to offer exhibitions and prizes. The scheme proved popular with secondary schools, most of which were managed by religious orders or other voluntary bodies, and as the examinations were open to both boys and girls, the impetus to the development of higher education was considerable. Success in these public examinations increased the demand for university education for both men and women. However, it imposed on the schools a rigid examination-oriented curriculum, which was aptly named by Patrick Pearse *The Murder Machine* (1913).

In 1924 the Department of Education changed to a capitation system of payment to secondary schools and the state examinations were reduced to two: Intermediate (14+) and Leaving (16+) Certificate. The public examinations continued to have a profound influence on the school curriculum. The Gaelic language became an essential subject for a school to be 'recognized' and an obligatory one for the award of the Intermediate Certificate (1928) and the Leaving Certificate (1934).

The numbers attending second-level schooling remained small until the 1960s, when the 'free post-primary education' scheme in 1967 was introduced by the minister for education, Donogh O'Malley. Increased attendance numbers (from 148,000 in 1966–7 to 239,000 in 1974) led to the creation of two new additional types of second-level school, namely comprehensive and community schools, which were funded by the state and offered a broad curriculum both academic and practical. These schools were run by a management board consisting of representatives of the church authorities, local authorities and the state. Free school transport and greater accessibility to post-primary education led to high participation rates in secondary schooling, so that in 1990 nearly 60,000 pupils sat the Leaving Certificate Examination, as compared with 18,975 in 1970. Gaelic ceased to be an obligatory subject for award of the examination certificates in 1973 and the range of subjects for examination broadened. The high participation rates have led to keen competition ('the points race') for third-level places, which are allocated on a basis of performance in the Leaving Certificate Examinations.

In 1984 the government established a Curriculum and Examination Board, which was later dissolved and reconstituted as the National Council for Curriculum and Assessment. It is responsible for the development of curricular policy at both primary and secondary level. In 1989 a new Junior Certificate Syllabus was introduced to replace the old, more formal Intermediate Certificate, and the introduction of a six-year secondary cycle for all schools (1990) has allowed for a 'transition year' as a break from the academic examination curriculum and gives greater flexibility to individual schools.

Technical and Vocational Education

Technical education in Ireland was neglected during the nineteenth century, and despite the fact that the Samuelson Commission on Technical Education (1884) emphasized the importance of extended provision in Ireland, it was not until the establishment of the Department of Agriculture and Technical Instruction (DATI) in 1899 that direct state involvement occurred. Sir Horace Plunkett was the first vice-president of the DATI, and it was due largely to his influence and that of the report of the Recess Committee (1897), which he chaired, that the department was set up. It was seen as part of the movement to make Ireland more self-sufficient and prosperous. The role of the DATI was not to establish technical schools but rather to assist the newly formed local county councils (1898) to do so by providing grants, advice, inspection and examinations. The DATI co-operated closely with the Intermediate Board and developed a joint syllabus in science and drawing for secondary schools, as well as providing grants for equipping school laboratories. The DATI took over responsibility for the grants of the science and art department of South Kensington, and schools in Ireland continued to enter for these examinations until the DATI established its own technical schools examinations in 1913. By 1902, 27 out of 32 counties had established technical school schemes along within the county urban boroughs, and courses in science, commerce, drawing, crafts, building construction, domestic economy and needlework were provided. However, progress was hampered by lack of finance, buildings and trained teachers.

The Ingram Commission on Technical Education (1926–7) recommended that the responsibilities of the local authorities be extended and a system of day continuation education be introduced. The Vocational Education Act (1930) led to the provision of a network of vocational schools under each local authority, which provided both general education and practical courses in preparation for employment in trades. A Group Certificate Examination was introduced as a terminal examination in 1944. The technical schools offered a wide range of evening courses, though higher technical education was confined to the county boroughs.

The expansion of second-level schooling in the 1960s and 1970s greatly increased the numbers attending vocational schools, which from 1966 began to offer the full second-level cycle up to age 18. In addition the Vocational Education Committees participated in the management boards of the community schools and established their own alternative 'community colleges'. In 1969 nine regional technical colleges were opened, which offered advanced third-level type courses, and as the demand for technical education expanded the numbers attending these had reached 5,965 by 1980–1. The setting up of the National Council for Educational Awards (NCEA) in 1972 allowed the non-university colleges to offer degrees as well as diplomas.

Thus the Irish education system is seen essentially as a partnership between the state and voluntary bodies, each respecting and recognizing the other's responsibilities and duties. Historically structured into three sectors, primary, secondary and technical, these still operate independently but with increasing demand for co-ordination and rationalization. In 1984 a government Green Paper, *Partners in Education*, was issued, which proposed the setting up of local education councils to supervise and co-ordinate the work of the three sectors, but no further action was taken. The existence of a common core curriculum at both primary and secondary level undoubtedly contributes towards the creation of a common culture within the community and the make-up of a homogeneous society. Whereas in the 1970s and 1980s the emphasis in education was on 'quantity' and equality of educational opportunity, the emphasis in the 1990s has been more on 'quality' and on the creation of a broad and realistic curriculum which offers a balance between the academic and practical purposes of education. Government proposals have moved towards a more vocational and European-oriented curriculum and more democratic school management structure.

Reading

Coolahan, John, *Irish Education – History and Structure* (Dublin: Institute of Public Administration, 1980).

O'Buachalla, Seamus, *Education Policy in Twentieth Century Ireland* (Dublin: Wolfhound, 1988).

Akenson, D.H., *The Irish Education Experiment: The National System and Education in the Nineteenth Century* (London: Routledge and Kegan Paul, 1970).

——*A Mirror to Kathleen's face: Education in Independent Ireland, 1992–60* (Montreal and London: McGill, Queen's University Press, 1975).

McElligott, T.J., *Secondary Education in Ireland 1870–1921* (Dublin: Institute of Public Administration, 1981).

Randles, Eileen, *Post-Primary Education in Ireland 1957–70*, (Dublin: Veritas, 1975).

Hyland, Aine and Milne, K. (eds), *Irish Educational Documents. Vol I: to 1922* (Dublin: Church of Ireland College of Education, 1987).

Parkes, Susan M., *Guide to Sources in the History of Education – No 5. Irish Education in the British Parliamentary Papers in the Nineteenth Century and after, 1801–1920* (History of Education Society with Cork University Press, 1978).

SUSAN PARKES

Edwards, Hilton (1903–82) Actor who transformed the Irish theatre. Born East Finchley, 2 February. Edwards began his career in 1922 in the Old Vic. He was largely responsible for the highly professional productions which characterized the Gate. He died on 18 November 1982.

PETER COSTELLO

Egan, Felim (1952–) Painter and sculptor. Born Strabane, County Tyrone. Egan studied at Ulster Polytechnic, Belfast (1971–2), Portsmouth Polytechnic (1972–5) and the Slade School of Fine Art, London (1975–7). His paintings are abstract; they consist primarily of lines and abstract shapes on backgrounds of subdued colours. These marks, related to ancient Celtic patterns and spirals, are set on an underlying grid structure, which intermittently breaks them up, creating rhythmical effects similar to those of music. Egan has used neon lights to create three-dimensional lines in his work (1981), and made a series of bronze, linear sculptures (1988). In another series, abstract marks were superimposed on outline drawings of classical figures (ROSC international exhibition, 1984).

Reading

Donnelly, Micky, 'Felim Egan interview', *CIRCA Art Magazine* (Nov./Dec. 1981), pp. 4–7.

Overy, Paul, *Hibernian Inscape*, (Dublin: Douglas Hyde Gallery, 1980).

Smith, Alistair, 'The contemporary hieroglyph', in *Felim Egan* (Dublin: Kerlin Gallery, 1990).

FELICITY WOOLF

electrification, rural The Rural Electrification Scheme was decided by the government on 26 August 1943 and covered by Section 41 of the Electricity (Supply) (Amendment) Act, 1945. In 1946, there were 240,000 consumers of electricity in Ireland, most of them urban; 400,000 rural dwellings were without electricity. The first consumer of the scheme was 'switched on' at Oldtown, County Dublin, on 15 January 1947. At the completion of the scheme in 1976, some 402,000 new consumers had been connected, against the original target of 280,000. The scheme brought light, heat, power, piped running water and water heating to rural households. It vastly improved the material living conditions of rural households, and enabled farmers to equip themselves to reduce the drudgery of much farm work and to raise the quality of their produce to meet the demands of processing industries and consumers.

The use of electricity for domestic purposes expanded rapidly. That of electric power on farms did so less rapidly, and the uptake for pumping water supplies was the slowest to take off.

The Rural Electrification Office was a quasi-autonomous unit, working on a highly decentralized basis. Its staff promoted electrification by direct contact with potential consumers and relied heavily on the support of parish rural electrification committees. Rural organizations such as Muintir na Tíre, Macra na Feirme, the Irish Countrywomen's Association, the National Farmers' Association (later IFA) and the agricultural co-operative societies were closely involved, both directly and through the parish committees.

The programme gave rise to an industrial spin-off in the manufacture in Ireland of transformers, pumps, fractional- and low-horsepower motors, rigid and flexible plastic piping, milking machines and the creosoting of poles.

Up to 1976, the total cost had amounted to £80 million, of which some £28 million represented state subsidy.

Reading

Shiel, Michael, *The Quiet Revolution* (Dublin: O'Brien Press, 1984).

ALAN DUKES

'Emergency' World War II was officially and popularly referred to in Ireland as 'the Emergency' – a term coined by Éamon de Valera to confer *post-factum* constitutionality on an already determined neutrality. If this neutrality was to be theoretically scrupulous in its even-handedness (de Valera was widely criticized for presenting his condolences to the German minister on the death of Hitler), in practice, as the war went on, it increasingly favoured the Allies – their interned airmen, for example, being afforded facilities for evasion witheld from their German opposite numbers.

If Ireland's neutrality was criticized far more than, say, that of Sweden or Switzerland (Ireland was still a member of the British Commonwealth), it enjoyed wide popular support, and many flocked to join the colours to repel – or attempt to repel – invasion threatened at different times by both belligerents. The impact on the civilian population was far-reaching, since for the first time since the gaining of independence the country was obliged to rely almost entirely on its own resources, both cultural and material, and to define itself in terms of the outside world. Whilst some saw this as marginalization, others welcomed it as the first real assumption of the responsibilities of nationhood.

Reading

Fisk, Robert, *In Time of War* (London: Deutsch, 1983).
Share, Bernard, *The Emergency: Neutral Ireland 1939–45* (Dublin: Gill and Macmillan, 1978).

BERNARD SHARE

emigration The Great Irish Famine of the 1840s, a disaster so overwhelming, so obscene, so apocalyptic as to overwhelm the historical imagination, drowns out the smaller voices in the Irish emigration theme in its dreadful cacophany. The potato blight, the death of over one million people, the subsequent surge of emigration, are well known; the searing images of that haunted decade have etched themselves on the Irish psyche – the Famine graves, the *feár gorta*, the workhouse, the coffin ship, Grosse Isle. But in one sense, and without in any way seeking to diminish the horror at the heart of this Irish darkness, Irish emigration and the Irish background were a more complex story than just a lemming-like flight from a doomed land. To understand these complexities, one needs too to grasp the varieties of Irish life, to appreciate that it was not a country swathed in universal poverty and to know that it had profound regional, chronological and structural variation, which underpinned a remarkably varied set of emigration processes.

Irish emigration is unique in its scale, duration and geographical spread. It is also the earliest and, therefore, most consequential episode in the great period of mass transatlantic migration. At least a quarter of a million Irish had entered America prior to 1776; another 100,000 entered between 1776 and 1815, and approximately one million in the three decades before the Great Famine began in 1845. The Irish compose 10 per cent (six million) of the total of 60 million Europeans who migrated in this period – over 10 times what one might expect on the basis of existing population. The eighteenth-century migrations had two principal components: a large flow of Ulster Presbyterians to Pennsylvania and the middle colonies, where they became known as the 'Scotch-Irish', and the smaller flow of south-east Irish Catholics to Newfoundland, eventually overspilling into Atlantic Canada.

A third phase of Irish migration began in the pre-Famine period, and especially post-1815, when the Irish economy began to exhibit marked signs of strain. Uninhibited population growth in the eighteenth century had seen a massive demographic surge (population soared from *c*.1 million in 1600 to 8.5 million by 1840). Now, emigration was increasingly seen as a safety valve in the fraught socio-economic circumstances, and Irish emigration developed an intensity remarkable in contemporary European terms. Located as it was between the two most aggressively expanding labour markets of the nineteenth-century world (both developing an urban-industrial complex with insatiable population demands, both English-speaking, both accessible), it was inevitable that a massive emigration surge would occur. A million Irish crossed the Atantic between 1815 and 1845, establishing a strong Irish footing, especially in the eastern seaboard cities, long before the Famine emigrants arrived. Another half million emigrated to Britain in the same period, making in all the migration of one-fifth of the total population of the country.

The most striking feature of pre-Famine emigration is the extent to which the west of Ireland remained insulated from it. Explanations like poverty, isolation and linguistic preference have been used to explain this, but the single most important determinant was the successful survival of a communal farming system and lifestyle, based on rundale villages, and the accompanying cultural self-sufficiency. There were very few pre-Famine emigrants from Clare, Kerry and Mayo. There was one other unusual feature of this migration; it had a continuously rising proportion of single females. This in turn accounted for another highly unusual feature of Irish emigration – the exceptionally low rate of return migration. The 'returned Yank' was an exotic, not an everyday, creature in nineteenth-century life.

The devastating impact of the Famine was to change this picture irrevocably. Over one million people died and two million emigrated mostly to the United States, between 1845 and 1855. In the peak year of 1851, a quarter of a million emigrated. There were five new features of this Famine and post-Famine emigration. First, its centre of gravity shifted rapidly and irreversibly to the west from its older northern and south-eastern cores. Cork, Kerry, Clare, Galway, Mayo and Donegal became, and remain to the present day, the chief migration centres. Second, there was a drop in the social centre of gravity to encompass the very poor for the first time, including the cottier and the western rundale farmer. Third, the confessional composition shifted markedly from Protestant to Catholic dominance. Fourth, emigration moved away from Canada and overwhelmingly went to the United States, where it sought more urban and less rural settings, and where chain migration was attenuated. Fifth, there was a loosening of the specific port-region nature of emigrant recruitment.

All these changes led cumulatively to one other change: emigration was institutionalized as part of the life cycle, a delayed form of family planning, an Irish solution to an Irish problem. In March 1868, David Moriarty, the Catholic bishop of Kerry, caught the prevailing consensus when writing to Lord Dufferin:

> In point of fact, there is no use in talking for or against emigration. The face of the people is set to the west and they go in obedience to a reasoning or blind instinct of their own. The national schools have superseded the crowbar. Educated youth who leave have had the maps of the world before their eyes for years are not likely to sit down for life on a potato patch.

By the twentieth century, emigration had eaten its way into the heart of the Irish experience. The American traveller Harold Speakman recorded the following scene in his 1931 book, *Here's Ireland*, while visiting a schoolroom:

> Little boys of assorted sizes, resting themselves first on one leg and then on the other, stood against the walls. They seemed to be waiting for something. As I shared my raisin bread with them, there came to my mind the bizarre notion

that they were waiting to grow up and go to America.

A culture of emigration had become endemic; half of all Irish people born in Ireland since 1820 have emigrated. While there are currently five million people in Ireland, there are at least 70 million in the Irish diaspora. Only recently did the Irish state recognize its responsibilities in this aspect, notably in the concern shown by President Mary Robinson to reach out to the Irish overseas.

KEVIN WHELAN

encumbered estates The two Encumbered Estates Acts of 1848 and 1849 can be seen as an attempt to break down the feudal impediments to the sale of the landed estates. Up to this time, the legal transfer of landed property was slow, cumbersome and extremely expensive. This was because of the old feudal law of entail, which secured the freehold from being sold for payments of landlords' debt. In these circumstances, the Irish landlord was able to borrow money on the security of his land by 'confessing to judgment'.

In Irish law the landlord could register his judgment debts in several courts or in the Registry Office of Deeds. As a consequence of this, the landlord could have numerous encumbrances, as either judgments or mortgages, on the same land. Therefore these encumbrances on the landed estates could be beyond the redeemable value of the title deeds. Searching for the title to the land and discovering the history of every encumbrance which had been created on it was extremely time-consuming and expensive. For example, Lord Audley's estate in County Cork incurred legal costs of £16,000, which was reckoned to be beyond the sale value of the estate, in 1838. Between 1848 and 1857 over 3,000 estates were sold under the terms of these Encumbered Estates Acts.

Reading

Anon., 'Incumbered Estates Court', *Dublin University Magazine*, 36 (1850).

Lane, P., 'The Encumbered Estates Court Ireland, 1848–1849', *Economic and Social Review*, 3 (1972).

Osborne, R. 'The transfer of land in relation to the rights of judgment creditors', *Dublin Statistical Society Transactions*, 1 (1850).

EAMONN SLATER

England, the Irish in The Irish have long been the largest minority community in England. Their presence, treated variously as a challenge and a resource by the host society, has had significant impact on the development of their larger neighbour. Second only to the United States as a destination choice for Irish migrants in the nineteenth-century, England has remained the predominant location for Irish settlement since the end of World War I.

However, despite their ubiquity the study of the Irish in England remains in its infancy. The stereotypes of the Irish population as made up of shovel-wielding navvies, nurses and plausible rogues still persist. Only in the last decade has a body of knowledge on the Irish experience in England begun to develop. Research has been hampered by the absence of systematic data on the Irish as a multigenerational ethnic group. It is impossible to say how many people of Irish birth or descent there are living in England today, and estimates range from under one million to over six million people.

Since Victorian times they have been concentrated in the urban, industrial centres of the country. Nearly one-third of the known contemporary population reside in the Greater London area. In this setting their experience is marked by deep contrasts. It reflects successful assimilation and relative prosperity on one hand and some of the worst aspects of the migrant experience on the other; poverty, unemployment, discrimination, high rates of mental hospitalization, alcoholism and premature mortality.

In particular, the resumption of violence in Northern Ireland has had significant impact on Irish migrants. The passing of the Prevention of Terrorism Act in 1974 transformed them into a 'suspect community'. Under its auspices the injustices done to members of the Irish community rank among the worst in English legal history.

Irish migrants have made major contributions to the fabric of English life. Their economic role in the construction of the infrastructure is no less significant than their cultural impact. In providing poets, playwrights and pop singers, nurses, doctors and educators, Irish migrants have benefited the quality of life in England out of all proportion to their numbers. Sadly, it is a contribution which has all too often gone unacknowledged.

Reading

Akenson, Donald Harman, *The Irish Diaspora: A Primer* (Toronto: P.D. Meany, 1993).

Buckland, Patrick and Belchem, John, *The Irish in British Labour History* (Liverpool: Institute of Irish Studies, 1993).

Curtis, Liz, *Nothing But the Same Old Story: The Roots of Anti-Irish Racism* (London: Greater London Council, 1984).

Greenslade, Liam, 'White skin, white masks: psychological distress among the Irish in Britain', in P. O'Sullivan (ed.), *The Irish in the New Communities* (Leicester: Leicester University Press, 1992).

—— *The Irish in Britain in the 1990s: A Preliminary Analysis* (Liverpool: Institute of Irish Studies, 1993).

Hillyard, P., *Suspect Community* (London: Pluto Press, 1993).

Jackson, John, *The Irish in Britain* (London: Routledge and Kegan Paul, 1963).

Lennon, Mary, Macadam, Mary and O'Brien, Joanne, *Across the Water: Irish Women's Lives in Britain* (London: Virago, 1988).

LIAM GREENSLADE

English As We Speak It In Ireland This book, first published in 1910, was the first major study of the Hiberno-English dialect, which both supplied and analysed data assembled by its author, Patrick Weston Joyce (1827–1914). By modern standards, his approach seems amateurish and prolix, but he covered all the essential points. The book has 13 chapters, of which the most important are those on 'Idioms Derived from the Irish Language' and 'Grammar and Pronunciation'. Joyce was a polymath, with a massive range of books to his credit, a late graduate of Trinity College, Dublin (1861), later principal of the Board of Education Training College, Marlborough Street. He died in Rathmines, 7 January 1914.

Reading

Joyce, P.W., *English As We Speak It In Ireland*, intr. Terence Dolan (Dublin: Wolfhound Press, 1991).

T.P. DOLAN

Enlightenment The history of the Enlightenment is a story of intellectual clubs or groups, organized to demonstrate the sovereign rule of reason in political and social matters, hostile to conventional religion and eager to establish the philosopher in place of the priest or the despot. The majority of its most important locales were places in which there was a confrontation between an emergent modern world and a powerfully entrenched backwardness. Naples, Moscow, Koenigsberg, Glasgow, Edinburgh, Genoa, Milan and, above all, Paris were places in which decaying political and social forms came under the surveillance of an increasingly vocal and confident 'cabal' of advanced intellectuals. It was the Paris of the 1750s that crystallized the Enlightenment through its key publication, the *Encyclopédie*. By then, the Irish Enlightenment, was over.

But Dublin had at least the distinction of having created one of the earliest of the Enlightenment 'sects', in the period between 1694, when Robert Molesworth's *An Account of Denmark as it was in the Year 1692* was published, and 1725, the year of Francis Hutcheson's *An Inquiry into the Original of our Ideas of Beauty and Virtue*. In that 30-year period, these writers, along with John Toland (1670–1722), William Molyneux

(1656–98), William King (1650–1729) and George Berkeley (1685–1753) produced works that inaugurated one phase of the European Enlightenment.

Robert (later Viscount) Molesworth (1656–1725) was a republican or commonwealthman in the seventeenth-century mould. He declared that 'all Europe was in a manner a free country till very lately', thereby signalling his preoccupation with what he saw as the rise of despotism and the need to combat it. In his book on Denmark, he described the loss of that country's freedom as a lesson for contemporary Europe; like Italy, it was a free republic that had been swallowed up by emperors, kings, popes, dukes and other tyrants. Freedom could only be defended by education, philosophy and vigilance against encroaching privilege. This was a basic Enlightenment programme that had a direct application to Ireland, where a native polity was in danger of being absorbed within an illiberal and more powerful kingdom.

The most famous and outright defence of Ireland's ancient liberties was made by William Molyneux (1656–98) in his treatise *The Case of Ireland's Being Bound by Acts of Parliament in England. Stated* (1698). His argument was based on a Lockian version of natural rights and legal precedent. But it was condemned by the English Parliament as seditious. Nevertheless, it remained a classic statement of the Protestant Irish claim for independence and was, like Molesworth's book, an important document in the campaign against despotism. This was also true of John Toland's *Christianity Not Mysterious* (1696), which created an uproar in both Ireland and England. Toland queried how it was that Christianity, once simple and comprehensible, had become mysterious. His answer was that it had been made so by those whose interest it was to mystify people in order to exercise dominion over them. Toland's attack on religious superstition and political obscurantism, his defence of rational religion, and his faith in the progress of reason made his book one of the foundational tracts

of deism. The Protestant Irish Parliament was outraged because the book undermined any political system, such as its own, that was founded on religious discrimination. Hence, a series of attacks, led by Anglican clergy, including Peter Browne (1664/5–1735), William King and Edward Synge (1659–1741), was launched against Toland.

Nevertheless, the libertarian tradition, fostered by the Dublin Philosophical Society, and its inner cadre of thinkers, known as the Molesworth circle, survived and reached a culmination with the publication of Francis Hutcheson's *Inquiry* (1725; rev. edn 1738). Hutcheson, as deeply influenced by Shaftesbury as Toland and Molyneux had been by Locke, argued for the existence of a radical benevolence in human nature which was stifled by corrupt political systems. The result was factionalism, despotism and sectarianism. His work clearly and damagingly applied to the established system in Ireland. Hutcheson's book, like Molyneux's, became popular in the Thirteen Colonies; both authors furnished the colonists with arguments against British despotism in the War of American Independence.

Lockian sensationalism was the basis for most Enlightenment forms of reason. Molyneux had first suggested a modification of this, suggesting that there might be a case for admitting the existence of innate ideas. William King and others developed this notion in a theological direction, in order to defend the existence of a God who was above reason but not beyond representation. Ireland's greatest philosopher, George Berkeley, developed this position in a radical manner by formulating a philosophy of immaterialism – that is, by arguing that objects only exist in so far as they are perceived by the mind. His *A New Theory of Vision* (1709) and his *Treatise Concerning the Principles of Human Knowledge* (1710) subvert the radical implications of Lockian epistemology and Shaftesburian benevolence, allowing for an essentially Christian vision of human knowledge and its relation to human feeling. Berkeley is the most important figure of the early Counter-Enlightenment. Like his great contemporary and fellow cleric Jonathan Swift (1667–1745), though with an infinitely greater amenity of style and approach, he defended tradition while still stoutly resisting corruption and oppression.

But it was Edmund Burke (1729–97) who finally formulated the Counter-Enlightenment arguments against reason and revolution in his attacks on the French Revolution, most especially in the *Reflections on the Revolution in France* (1790). In his later life Burke also attacked the Protestant junta that had ruled Ireland since 1688, to the exclusion of the Irish Catholics. Such injustice, he claimed, made Ireland vulnerable to the infection of Enlightenment thought. Oddly, in defending the English Revolution of 1688 and attacking its French counterpart of 1689, he rehearses many of the arguments of Hutcheson and Molesworth, although directing them to a different end. The anomalous position of Protestant Ireland in the Enlightenment is defined when we see how the attitudes that began by sponsoring Enlightenment views against despotism were reproduced in the 1790s to argue that the Enlightenment itself was the producer of despotic rule.

SEAMUS DEANE

enthusiasm The term came into general use in the seventeenth century, especially after 1660, to denigrate all those who made a false or deluded claim of direct divine inspiration, or who indulged in ill-controlled religious emotion. It was particularly used by the established church as a derogatory label for beliefs and sects that threatened schism, whether they were Anglican hereticists, Puritans, millenarians, deists or Catholics. In *A Tale of a Tub* (1707), Jonathan Swift defends his established church against enthusiasms, which he equates with superstition, fanaticism and madness, caused by melancholy vapours.

The reaction against enthusiasm was particularly fierce in Ireland, where Catholicism and dissenting Protestantism posed a double threat. The Irish Anglicans feared that free thought and rational religions like deism would undermine the Protestant ascendancy and allow the Irish Catholics to supplant them. Again, Swift's *An Argument Against the Abolishing of Christianity* is a fine example of a tract illustrating these fears. For these reasons, John Toland's *Christianity not Mysterious* (1696) was burnt by the common hangman and he had to flee to England. In 1702, Thomas Emlyn, a Dublin cleric, was imprisoned for the dissenting views in his *Humble Inquiry into the Scripture Account of Jesus Christ*.

FRED LOWE

Erasmus Smith schools Founded in the seventeenth century by Erasmus Smith (1611–91), a wealthy Cromwellian adventurer who acquired lands in Ireland during the Cromwellian plantations. Under a charter of 1669, the governors of the schools founded by Smith established four grammar schools 'to teach the Greek, Latin and Hebrew tongues' and fit pupils for the university. The first three schools were at Tipperary, Galway and Drogheda, and a fourth later was at Ennis (1773). In the eighteenth century, as the wealth of the endowment grew, five Erasmus Smith chairs were founded at Trinity College, Dublin (professor of Hebrew, 1724; professor of natural and experimental philosophy, 1724; professor of oratory, 1762; professor of mathematics, 1762; and professor of modern history, 1762), as well as a widespread network of 'English' elementary schools (144 in all). A further grammar school in Dublin, the High School, was founded in 1870.

The schools were for Protestant children and the Anglican catechism was taught. However, in the 1880s controversy arose as to whether the endowment was originally intended to include the education of Catholic children as well. The Educational Endowments Commissioners in 1894 were unable to agree; so after a protracted legal battle the trust funds were divided between the governors and the state by the Erasmus Smith Act (1937). The High School, Dublin, is the only school now run by the governors of Erasmus Smith.

SUSAN PARKES

Esposito, Michele (1855–1929) Pianist, composer, teacher and administrator. Esposito was the single most influential musical figure working in Ireland at the turn of the century. As a teacher, he exercised a major influence on a generation of Irish musicians including Hamilton Harty and John Larchet.

Born in Castellammare, south of Naples, Esposito studied at the *conservatoire* there with Cesi (1845–1907) and Serrao (1830–1907), and later in Paris (1878). He accepted a temporary post in the Royal Irish Academy of Music in 1882 and remained there for the rest of his working life. He established there a surpassing piano school, and his influence was such that he was in reality the uncrowned director of the academy. He initiated the scheme of local centre examinations and his industry also led him to the creation of the Dublin Orchestral Society, which from 1899 to 1916 offered Dublin audiences their sole regular opportunity of becoming acquainted with the orchestral repertoire. Under Esposito's direction, the orchestra regularly performed at the Royal Dublin Society, where, in 1886, he had been the prime mover in the decision of the society to embark on its annual series of chamber recitals.

Esposito's many compositions for piano reflect his celebrated pianistic facility, although they are not Italianate in style, demonstrating, rather, his admiration for Brahms and the Germanic school. Indeed, his writings as a whole are consistent with the European aesthetic in which he was grounded, and, with the exception of occasional works such as the secular cantata *Deirdre* (1897) and the Irish Symphony (1902) written for the Feis Ceoil, do not foster a distinctive style.

JOSEPH RYAN

Europe Ireland was an indirect casualty of President Charles de Gaulle's policy of keeping Britain out of the European Economic Community (EEC) in the 1960s. The taoiseach, Seán Lemass, applied for membership unsuccessfully in 1961. His successor, Jack Lynch, failed again in 1967. There is little that either man could have done. But Ireland had not been particularly helped in its application by its central foreign policy stance; neutral since 1939, the Irish government had refused in 1949 to join the North Atlantic Treaty Organization (NATO). Neutrality remained an impediment to membership but no Irish government was ever wedded to the idea of permanent neutrality. Seán Lemass told the *New York Times* in June 1962: 'We recognise that a military commitment will be an inevitable consequence of our joining the Common Market and ultimately we would be prepared to yield even the technical label of our neutrality.' Lemass added that Ireland was prepared to go into an integrated Europe without any reservations as to how far that would take the country in the field of foreign policy and defence. Despite the many twists and turns in Ireland's European policy, the Lemass doctrine has guided successive Irish governments as applicants for, and later as members of, the EEC (after 1973), the European Community (EC, after 1987) and the European Union (EU, after 1992).

During the debate on entry in spring 1972, the minister for external affairs, Dr Patrick Hillery, argued that there was no question whatsoever of Ireland entering into any military or defence commitments as a result of membership: 'We are not, I repeat not, joining NATO, nor are we going to enter into any kind of link with that organisation.' The two largest parties in the country, Fianna Fáil and Fine Gael, supported entry together with the enthusiastic and powerful farming lobby. The Labour Party and the trade union movement officially opposed; in reality, they were divided in their stance. The two wings of Sinn Féin (Official and Provisional) opposed and they were joined by a number of *ad hoc* anti-EEC groups. The referendum was held on 10 May 1972 and the result was an overwhelming rejection of isolationism. The majority was five to one in favour of going into the EEC. In a 71 per cent turnout, 1,041,880 voted in favour and 211,888 were against. That represented an 83 per cent 'yes' vote.

A Jack Lynch-led Fianna Fáil government took the country into the EEC in January 1973. But a year later, a coalition of Fine Gael and Labour took power and remained in office until 1977. Fianna Fáil came back to office under Jack Lynch. He was replaced by Charles Haughey as taoiseach in 1979. The country witnessed three general elections in the early 1980s, with Fianna Fáil first losing power to a Fine Gael/Labour coalition (June 1981–March 1982). Charles Haughey regained power for a short period in 1982 and was replaced in December 1982, again by a Garret FitzGerald-led coalition of Fine Gael and Labour (1982–7). Haughey was returned as taoiseach in 1987 and held that position until he was forced to resign in February 1992. In 1989, he entered into coalition with the Progressive Democrats. His successor, Albert Reynolds, failed to maintain its unity, and following a general election in December 1992, Fianna Fáil and Labour formed a coalition.

Ireland has remained an enthusiastic member of the European Union since 1973. It has meant: (1) new markets for the country's agricultural and industrial products; (2) significant cash transfers from Brussels for improvement to the national economic and agricultural infrastructure, with enhanced international status as a member of a European trading bloc; (3) greater freedom from dependence upon Britain; (4) an extension of the country's influence in the area of foreign policy through participation in the process of European Political Co-operation (EPC). Between 1973 and 1986, Ireland's contribution to the European budget was £1,337.1m; the country's receipts from Brussels were £7,081.7m, making net receipts of £5,744.6m.

Most of this money was paid under FEOGRA, the European Agricultural Guidance and Guarantee Fund. While the country again enjoyed substantial net transfers between 1987 and 1994, Ireland was expected to receive £7.2 billion in structural and cohesion funds between 1994 and 1999 exclusive of payments under EU funds such as the Common Agricultural Policy and the Social and Regional funds. Despite such significant cash transfers, Ireland had over 300,000 unemployed by 1994 and a rising number of people seeking work abroad.

However, the mid-1990s witnessed spectacular change. Between 1994 and 1999 approximately 250,000 new jobs were created. *Newsweek* in December 1996 could report that 'Ireland is booming. We are talking about German style inflation, Asian style growth. Translation: an emerald tiger is at large.' The EU's contribution to this change was significant.

Irish governments and the Irish Civil Service have established a strong reputation in Europe for competence and for professionalism. Irish administrative skills were displayed to good advantage when Ireland took over the presidency of the EEC for the first time in 1975. Despite the apprehensions of the French in particular, Dublin performed the most onerous tasks of the presidency with decisiveness and high competence. That was also done on subsequent occasions when Ireland held the presidency; the country received particular praise for the manner in which the Charles Haughey-led government conducted the EC presidency during the difficult post-Cold War months of early 1990.

The Irish Department of Foreign Affairs was called upon to play a central role in the co-ordination of Irish membership of the community. A healthy tension continued to exist between the taoiseach's office and Iveagh House, the headquarters of the Department of Foreign Affairs, throughout this period. There were occasions, particularly during the Haughey governments in the early 1980s, when Iveagh House suffered a series of reverses. But the department was restored to pre-eminence by the time of the final Haughey government; relations between the taoiseach and the Department of Foreign Affairs were excellent during the 1990 presidency of the EC.

The question of neutrality remained one of the most troubled and contentious issues throughout Ireland's period of membership. The country was the odd man out, being the only non-member of NATO among the Twelve. Neither was Ireland a member of the Western European Union. However, Dublin did seek 'observer status' in 1993. As the community deepened the process of integration in the 1980s, Ireland faced increasing difficulties over neutrality. On the one hand, Dublin had always perceived itself as being very pro-Community and had stoutly and successfully resisted any effort to establish a 'two-speed Europe'. But with the framing of the Single European Act (SEA) in 1986, Ireland had to face up to the consequences of the Lemass doctrine. Title 111 codified the process of EPC, but there was a tension in the wording which revealed the difference between the majority of the member states, which wished to move swiftly towards the establishment of a European defence community, and neutral Ireland. The Irish government was reluctantly obliged to hold a referendum following a successful court case by Dr Raymond Crotty, which questioned the constitutionality of the SEA. The people went to the polls on 28 May 1987. All the major political parties supported ratification with the exception of the Workers' Party. There was a 43.89 per cent turn out, or 1,080,400 out of an electorate of 2,461,790; 69.92 per cent voted in favour and 30.08 per cent against. The low turnout was a disappointment to the political parties, but the result was decisive even if the 'yes' vote was down on the 1972 referendum result.

Irish foreign policy and the future of neutrality were again the focus of concern during the Maastricht referendum campaign, which took place at the end of 1992. Abortion was also an issue in the referendum. The Treaty on European Union was put before the Irish people on 18 June; the total poll was 1,457,219, or a 57.3 per cent turnout. The 'yes' vote was 1,001,076 (69.1 per cent) and the 'no' vote was 448,655 (30.9 per cent). The Irish electorate has been asked to vote four times on Europe, most recently in 1998 on the Amsterdam Treaty. On each occasion there has been a decisive decision in support of the deepening process of integration. By 1995 membership of the community had risen to 15, including Sweden, Austria and Finland. Ireland held the presidency during the latter half of 1996 when the inter-governmental review conference reported on the question of the Common Foreign and Security Policy and supported a major international crackdown on drugs dealing and crime. In order to prepare for the full implementation of the Lemass Doctrine, the tánaiste and minister for foreign affairs, Dick Spring, agreed to publish for the first time a white paper on all aspects of Irish foreign policy in 1995. The process provided for submissions from members of the public and from interest groups.

The outcome may be an end to neutrality. Ireland joined the Partnership for Peace in 1999 and later decided to participate in the European Rapid Reaction Force. The choice facing the Irish public is a two-speed Europe or an end to neutrality. Dublin has fought against the development of the former. The Lemass doctrine is being tested. The outcome is not really in doubt.

DERMOT KEOGH

evangelicalism The founding of the Bethesda Chapel in Dublin (1784) can be regarded as a milestone in the emergence of a distinctive evangelical wing of the Church of Ireland, the turbulent John Walker (who seceded) being followed there by the notable William Benjamin Mathias. Episcopal attitudes towards the evangelicals, cautious, even hostile, at first, softened as their devotion to the Book of Common Prayer, the Sacraments and the threefold order of ministry came to be recognized. Similarly, bishops took different stances with regard to the Ulster Revival that affected all Protestant churches in 1859, some applauding its revitalizing of church life, others suspicious of manifestations that seemed to border on hysteria. The evangelicals placed great emphasis on personal holiness, and Peter Roe, leader of a group of Ossory clergy, was noteworthy as much for the quality of his pastoral ministry as for his advocacy of the evangelical ideals. In time, bishops were themselves being drawn from the ranks of the evangelicals, for example John Gregg of Cork.

Evangelical clergy and laity formed themselves into societies the better to achieve their objectives – the Hibernian Bible Society (1806), launched in the Bethesda Chapel; the Sunday School Society (1809); and the Hibernian Church Missionary Society (1814). Other groups, such as the Religious Tract and Book Society, concerned themselves with evangelism through the printed word, and there were philanthropic bodies, like the Association for the Relief of Distressed Protestants (1836). It was evangelicals who comprised the leadership of bodies specifically devoted to the conversion of Catholics, like Alexander Dallas of the Irish Church Missions and Edward Nangle of the Achill Mission, which worked particularly on the islands and coasts of the west.

KENNETH MILNE

eviction Haunted by the ubiquity of displacement and family disintegration, the Irish popular mentality nurtured as a counterpoise a fierce sense of place, home and family. Any forces which threatened this trinity destabilized the equanimity of the popular imagination. During the landlord era, eviction (the legal or forcible dispossession of a tenant) accordingly acquired a potent penumbra of meaning, hyperbolic to the actual scale or ferocity of the events themselves. It was also, therefore, potentially a highly charged political weapon, wielded with consummate rhetoric and force during the Land League

period as a stick with which to beat landlords. In the aftermath of the Irish tenancy's precocious achievement of dismantling their landlord superstructure, the concept of eviction occupied an ever-more privileged position in the moral narrative of the demise of landlordism.

KEVIN WHELAN

exhibitions pre-1970 Public art exhibitions in Ireland began in 1765. Following on the success of the Society of Artists' Exhibitions in London, a group of Dublin-based artists formed themselves into a like-named society and exhibited some 88 works by 27 artists. Over the next nine years an annual exhibition was held until a schism broke the society, leading to the formation of an alternative group, the Academy of Artists. Both groups exhibited intermittently until 1780, most of the shows being held in the purpose-built exhibition room in William Street. Internal differences and rivalry between the two exhibition societies led in 1780 to a 20-year hiatus in the mounting of public displays of art in Dublin.

The resumption of exhibitions in 1800 by the Society of Artists of Ireland at the print shop, Allens, 32 Dame Street, Dublin, was met with great interest in the city's press. Held during the Anglo-French wars when few could travel, the eight exhibitions of new paintings organized by this group were a welcome contribution to the cultural life of the city. Prominent painters such as Hugh Douglas Hamilton, Vincent Waldre and William Ashford exhibited portraits, history paintings and landscapes, while lengthy reports were carried in such publications as the *Dublin Evening Post* and the *Hibernian Journal*. The level of art criticism was congratulatory and naive. When exhibited in 1800, Hamilton's *Cupid and Psyche in the Nuptial Bower* (1793, Dublin, National Gallery of Ireland) was seen by the *Hibernian Magazine* as 'perhaps the most perfect picture ever produced in this country', while an anonymous writer who privately printed a *Critical Review* claimed that 'the contour of [Cupid's] head breathes the true spirit of the antique... It presents to us that indescribable elegance, that celestial beauty with which the Greek and Roman poets have clothed the deity of the the tenderest passions.' Both reactions excel in hyperbole where they fail in sophistication. Hamilton's up-to-date international neo-classicism is not understood but the critics' enthusiasm for the actuality of exhibitions is infectious:

> We want not talent – we want not genius... we want the grand incentive – Encouragement! – let, then, the men of rank and spirit ably step forward and put the Arts upon a permanent foundation: that accomplished there cannot be a doubt, but that the Irish would soon equal the Flemish or Italian schools.

These exhortations by the *Dublin Evening Post* in 1800 and the calls for the establishment of an 'Irish School' of painting were perhaps laudable, but confused, given the training and economic realities of late eighteenth-century Irish artists. The press display no understanding of what an Irish school could or should be: that is, evidencing local, regional originality and distinction as in the case of the Flemish and Italian schools. Instead these excited demands imply the view that an Irish school will emerge when local painters successfully ape the centre. The result was stylistic and cultural subordination.

Division and rivalry are the hallmarks of art exhibitions in Dublin prior to the establishment of the Royal Hibernian Academy (RHA) in 1823. A plethora of groups held shows, amalgamated, broke up and formed new societies. The range of works on display varied from standard portraits of peers and politicians as well as inoffensive landscapes to amateur drawings and designs. The desire to form an Irish academy that would end the uncertainty of the past led some 30 artists to petition the government for a charter of incorporation. A royal charter was signed in August 1823, by which was founded the Royal Hibernian Academy of Painters, Sculptors, Architects and Engravers. The elderly landscape painter William Ashford was elected the first president, but was quickly succeeded by the architect Francis Johnston. Immediately Johnston built Academy House in Abbey Street, which until it was destroyed in 1916 housed the annual academy exhibition. Ireland now had a training, exhibition and professional institution for the fine arts, which was to hold a dominant place in Irish visual culture for almost a century.

Mediocrity was unfortunately to be a constant feature at the annual RHA exhibitions. The attractions of London to young artists of talent and the dearth of patronage in Ireland hindered the academy. The organization of the annual exhibitions was not helped by the small number of submissions and the seemingly ongoing internal fighting, schisms and the inadequate government grant. As a means of encouraging interest in art the mid-century saw the establishment of the Art Union phenomenon, whereby works displayed at the RHA were distributed by lot as prizes among subscribers, with every member being entitled to an engraving. Works by, among others, Frederick William Burton, Daniel Maclise, J.M.W. Turner and David Wilkie were presented to subscribers.

Loan exhibitions had begun to appear in Ireland with the formation of the Royal Irish Institution in 1814. Old master paintings, seventeenth-century Italian in particular, were exhibited at the Gallery of the Dublin (later Royal) Society's House in Hawkins Street, and this continued until 1832. In 1821, after having exhibited *The Raft of the Medusa* to great success in London, Theodore Gericault took the painting to Dublin for six weeks, where it was on show in the Rotunda buildings. This exhibition was not as financially successful, for a diorama of the same disaster was being shown nearby to the accompaniment of band music. It was not until 1854 that an attempt was made in Dublin to establish a more permanent display of old master paintings. The Irish Industrial Exhibition held there in 1853 acted as the necessary impetus to create a national collection of paintings, leading to the bequest of money by the industrialist William Dargan, whose statue stands to this day in front of the National Gallery of Ireland. In 1854 an Act of Parliament was obtained to establish a gallery, which eventually opened in 1864.

The first recorded exhibition outside of Dublin was the First Munster Exhibition, held in Cork in 1815. Encouraged by the success of the Dublin-based Royal Irish Institution, Cork established its own Society for Promoting the Fine Arts, which held occasional exhibitions until 1833. Contemporary and old master paintings were displayed, with the 1815 exhibition showing some 25 works by the local artist Nathaniel Grogan. In 1819 the Cork society displayed the newly arrived collection of casts from the antique presented by Pope Pius VII to George III and given by George IV to Cork. Limerick and Belfast held occasional exhibitions during the 1820s, 1830s and 1840s. Belfast did not enjoy a long-lived organized exhibiting institution until 1891, with the establishment of the Belfast Ramblers' Sketching Club, later to become the Royal Ulster Academy of Arts.

Founded in 1874, the Dublin Sketching Club was on the whole an amateur organization, which perhaps unwittingly holds a notable place in the history of art exhibitions in Ireland. In 1884 they invited James McNeill Whistler to exhibit with them. He showed among other paintings the famous *Arrangement in Grey and Black: Portrait of the Painter's Mother* (1871, Paris, Musée du Louvre) and the *Arrangement in Grey and Black, No. 2: Portrait of Thomas Carlyle* (1872–3, Glasgow Art Gallery). The exhibition heralded the arrival of Modernism in Ireland. Subsequent exhibitions presented to the Dublin public something very different from the tiresome array of sentimental anecdote to be seen annually at the RHA. The Loan Collection of Pictures by Nathaniel Hone and John Butler Yeats, held at 6 St Stephens Green, Dublin, in 1901 and organized by Sarah Purser, was an example of native artists exhibiting an awareness of newer trends in visual representation. Yeats's portraits were much praised; the *Irish Times* claimed that:

> Mr Yeats is diametrically opposed to those artists who seem to care less for the spirit of man than the body – less for the body than the clothes . . . Mr Yeats has no affinities with this school. He suggests much rather, though at a distance, Mr Watts. There is the same preoccupation with character, the same indifference to the special advantages of his medium – the same difficult and laboured execution, so unlike the dash and showiness of Mr Sargent's followers.

The success of this two-man exhibition encouraged Hugh Lane to see a future for modern Irish painting. By 1908 he had opened, in temporary premises in Harcourt Street, a gallery of modern art. Earlier in 1904 he had organized in London an exhibition of Irish painters, while in Dublin in the same year he showed works from the J. Staats Forbes collection in Abbey Street. Works by Corot and the Barbizon School as well as by Degas (*Two Ballet Dancers, c.*1880, Dublin, National Gallery of Ireland) and Monet (*Waterloo Bridge*, 1900, Dublin, Hugh Lane Municipal Gallery of Modern Art) were put on show along with paintings by such Irish artists as John B. Yeats, Walter Osborne and Roderic O Conor. The RHA was being completely eclipsed by these developments. The continued exhibition of modern painting was of course hindered by the sudden death of Lane and the ensuing legal battles over his will, but alternatives to the academy had been put into place.

Lane's Modern Gallery was a museum and not a temporary exhibition space for new paintings. The dearth of venues for viewing painting led to the formation in 1920 of the Society of Dublin Painters. Founded by Paul Henry, it attracted the support of Jack B. Yeats, Mary Swanzy and others. Active until the 1950s, it held two exhibitions a year at 7 St Stephen's Green. In an attempt to introduce an avant-garde voice into the static world of Irish painting, Henry, who dominated the early years of the society, painted small yet heroicized images of Irish peasants against a western sky. His inspiration may have been Millet, but the visual result is never as harsh nor as unsettling. Equally, his unending series of simplified, almost abstracted views of the west owe a debt to Modernism but diluted of any Expressionist tendencies. Jack Yeats exhibited in the early years of the society frequently, showing work that responded to the political turmoil of the early 1920s, such as *The Funeral of Harry Boland* (1922, Sligo County Library and Museum). In October 1923 Mainie Jellett exhibited her first Cubist-inspired works, the result of her studies with Albert Gleizes in Paris. These abstractions caused savage criticism in the Dublin press, George Russell (AE) going so far as to see her work as part of an 'artistic malaria' that is 'sub-human'.

Although consciously avant-garde, the Society of Dublin Painters should not be seen as the only exhibition venue worthy of discussion during the 1920s. Sean Keating, a later president of the RHA, exhibited annually there but also with the dealer Victor Waddington, who set up a gallery in South Anne Street in 1925. Keatings's paintings of the period represent his deep involvement in the creation of a new Ireland, as Romantic and impossible as that dream was. He perhaps lacked the detachment of the comfortable bourgeois artists who could remove themselves to Paris, but that does not lessen the interest that can be found in his work. His heroic image of gunmen, such as *Men of the West* (1917, RHA, Dublin, Hugh Lane Municipal Gallery of Modern Art), need not be, as it is so often today, dismissed as propaganda, but can be studied in the context of an attempt to deal with the realities of life in Ireland at a particular time.

Jack Yeats was another frequent exhibitor at Waddington's galleries, which moved to Nassau Street in 1938. Waddington took good care of his artists, holding one-painter exhibitions, producing catalogues and monographs as well as promoting his artists abroad. He himself moved to London in 1957 and

many of his artists moved to Leo Smith at the Dawson Gallery, which had been set up in 1944. Maurice MacGonigal, Norah McGuinness, Louis le Brocquy and Mary Swanzy stabled with Smith, who ran his very successful exhibitions until his death in the late 1970s. Many of those who exhibited with Smith were also founders of the Irish Exhibition of Living Art (IELA), which held its first exhibition in 1943. This group was initially reacting against the unacceptable restrictions placed on potential exhibitors at the annual RHA. After failing to have paintings accepted by the selection committee, le Brocquy with the backing of Mainie Jellett and others organized an alternative and far more democratically based exhibition, ironically at the National College of Art in Kildare Street, the same venue as the annual RHA.

The IELA, under the long presidency of Norah McGuinness (1944–72), offered a not necessarily radical alternative to the RHA, but allowed for a strong Modernist voice and one that was fundamentally non-academic. The ILEA nurtured most of Ireland's leading artists of the 1950 and 1960s: Patrick Scott, Oisín Kelly, Brian Bourke, Deborah Brown and Colin Middelton. Controversy was not rare, as when Dublin audiences reacted against le Brocquy's 'grey' paintings of the mid-1950s, which were exhibited both at the ILEA and at Waddington's, objecting to their nudity and social commentary. Yet by the late 1960s the ILEA was becoming somewhat out of date. In 1973 the committee voted itself out of office.

In 1967 the first ROSC exhibition was held in the Royal Dublin Society (RDS). This event marks the internationalization of the Irish art world. Organized by the architect Michael Scott with the advice of the American critic-curator James Johnson Sweeney, the idea was to hold a major exhibition every four years which would expose an Irish audience to the latest trends in world art. The abstract painter Cecil King hung the show, as he did the second ROSC in 1971 (also in the RDS). The significance of ROSC as an inspiration to Irish artists and as an instigator of debate amongst the general public has been immense. An important adjunct to these shows has been a series of historical or retrospective exhibitions dealing with Irish art of a variety of periods.

Reading

Breeze, George *Society of Artists in Ireland. Index of Exhibits, 1765–80* (Dublin: National Gallery of Ireland, 1985).

Crookshank, Anne, and the Knight of Glin, *Painters of Ireland c.1660–1920* (London: Barrie and Jenkins, 1978).

Cullen, Fintan, *The Walpole Society* 50 (1984).

——— *The Drawings of John Butler Yeats* (Albany NY: Albany Institute of History and Art, 1987).

Gilmore Holt, Elizabeth (ed.), *The Triumph of Art for the Public 1785–1848: The Emerging Role of Exhibitions and Critics* (Princeton NJ: Princeton University Press, 1983).

Kennedy, S.B., *Irish Art and Modernism 1880–1950* (Belfast: Institute of Irish Studies at the Queen's University of Belfast, 1991).

——— 'Royal Hibernian Academy', *Martello Arts Review* (1991).

——— *The Irish Imagination 1959–1971* (Dublin: ROSC, 1971).

——— *Irish Art 1943–1973* (Cork: ROSC, 1980).

Stewart, Ann M., *Royal Hibernian Academy of Arts: Index of Exhibitors and their Works, 1826–1979* (Dublin: Manton Publishing, 1985–6).

——— *Irish Art Loan Exhibitions, 1765–1927* (Dublin: Manton 1990–).

Strickland, Walter, *A Dictionary of Irish Artists* (Shannon: Irish University Press, 1968).

FINTAN CULLEN

Expressionism Art in which feeling and emotion dominate over thought and supplant a concern for representational accuracy; in which the subject itself – often grotesque or macabre – evokes strong and disturbing feelings; and in which colour is stressed over line. Expressionism as it developed in the late nineteenth and early twentieth centuries involved distortion, a strong use of colour and an emphasis, as in Romanticism, on the personal vision of the artist, an emphasis intensified by the symbolist and decadent cult of the artist as individualist rebel. Leading European Expressionists included Van Gogh, Munch, Ensor, Kirchner and Beckmann. Expressionism is usually seen as a phenomenon of Protestant northern Europe, and reached a particular intensity in Germany. It was an important element in literature, music and the cinema (e.g. *Metropolis, The Cabinet of Dr Caligari*) as well as in painting. Philosophically its influences included Kierkegaard, Nietzsche and Bergson, and among its artistic forebears might be counted Gruenewald, Bosch, Goya and Breugel. With the anti-Modernist policies of the Nazis – though Goebbels had a sneaking regard for some elements of Expressionism – the movement was severely curtailed. After the war, however, the term received renewed currency with Abstract Expressionism in the US, in which, with the influence of depth psychology and specifically the work of Jung, art was regarded as a means of self-realization – most prominently in the work of Jackson Pollock. More recently, a version of the phenomenon in the form of Neo-Expressionism has surfaced again in Germany and elsewhere as a reaction against abstraction and conceptualism, in the work of Baselitz, Immendorf and Kiefer among others.

In an Irish context Roderic O'Conor, who spent most of his life on the Continent, anticipated his later vivid Expressionism in such early works as *Seascape, Yellow Sky* (1892). His paintings of the early years of the century partake of some of the tendencies of Fauvism, an early manifestation of the style. Cecil Salkeld, one of the few Irish artists of his time with a developed theory of art, held a position influenced by his training in Germany, which might be summed up in his phrase 'the minimum of form with the maximum associations'. (Salkeld's painting was also influenced by the German *Neue Sachlichkeit* movement, which was, in fact, in some ways a reaction against Expressionism.) Edward Gribbon, whose work on occasion reflects the influence of Van Gogh, spent most of his short artistic career working in France – his landscapes have a Mediterranean flavour. Kenneth Hall of the White Stag Group manifested an Expressionist influence, particularly in such paintings as *Après la Guerre* (1941), stimulated by his wartime experience as a pacifist exile in Ireland, as did his colleague Basil Rákóczi. The tendency also prevailed in the painting of another member of the group, Stephen Gilbert. He has cited parallels between his own work and that of the European 'Cobra' painters, and his painting on occasion also shows the influence of surrealism. In S.B. Kennedy's view, apart from some pictures by Jack B. Yeats and Kenneth Hall, Stephen Gilbert's were the only paintings of a boldly Expressionist nature to be made in Ireland before those by Colin Middleton in the late 1940s.

Jack B. Yeats is generally regarded as the most important Irish painter of the twentieth century. His early work was marked by an emphasis on line, which gave way to a more painterly technique, developing into the individualistic Expressionism of his maturity, characterized by paintings such as *A Full Tram* (1923). Influences on Yeats included Sickert, Van Gogh, Rouault, Ensor and Chagall, and he embodies a more Romantic tendency than most of his Continental counterparts, as well as – somewhat anachronistically in European terms – a strong sense of genre and narrative. Kenneth McConkey argues that later visionary works, such as *There is No Night* (1949) and *Shouting* (1950), locate Yeats in the centre of the northern Romantic tradition. Whether he is to be regarded as an important mainstream Expressionist or a gifted throwback to Romanticism is a matter of controversy.

Colin Middleton, an eclectic painter of high technical ability, passed through periods of surrealism, Cubism, Yeats-influenced Romanticism and a relative asceticism. Among his influences have been Vermeer, Mondrian, Miro, Dali, Tanguy and Picasso. His work, predominantly surrealist, manifests

an interest in Jungian thought, in particular the concept of the female principle, and has been affected by the Expressionist tradition of northern Europe. One of his most important works in this style is *Jacob Wrestling with the Angel* (1948). The themes of war and destruction which characterize some of his works embody an element of social consciousness which has been largely absent in Irish Modernist painters; though critics have pointed to a recurrent failure to push his aesthetic explorations to their limits.

The later works of Grace Henry, whose work for a long time tended to be overshadowed by that of her husband Paul, may be seen as having an Expressionist tendency. Nano Reid developed a style in the 1940s reminiscent of the Bruecke group of German painters, and some of her later work is close to that of the Abstract Expressionists. Some of George Campbell's paintings of the early 1950s evidence an Expressionist influence. Dan O'Neill, a self-taught painter, developed a form of Romantic Expressionism indebted to Rouault, and Gerard Dillon worked in an Expressionist manner, manifest in paintings like *Yellow Bungalow* (1954), which shows the influence of Chagall. Other painters whose work at times manifested the tendency were Anne Yeats, Margaret Clarke and Doreen Vanston. Mary Swanzy developed from a sense of lyricism in her pre-war work to the style found in such paintings as *Street Scene II*, of which McConkey writes that 'the viewer is faced with the black despair of the dispossessed'. He notes a theatrical air about the picture which makes it resemble a set piece from some German film like Fritz Lang's *Metropolis*.

Norah McGuinness's work of the early 1960s, which focuses upon Dublin docks and bay, is reminiscent of the earlier phases of Abstract Expressionism. Brian Bourke, who combines a love of the countryside with a jaundiced view of the alleged benefits of technology, has had a deep concern with the figure of Don Quixote: 'presumably', in the words of James White, 'as a reflection of troubled existence and as an illustration of the endeavours of the idealist to surmount the almost impossible obstacles of our time'. Gerard Dillon's work at times evidences an Expressionist tendency, for example in *Pierrot with a Lane*, while Jack Donovan's paintings, with their elements of distortion, embody a sense of shock in some ways reminiscent of Grosz and Dix. Michael Kane's work has been compared by the critic Anthony Cronin to that of the early German Expressionist Schmidt-Rottluff.

With the recent development of Neo-Expressionism on the international scene, Irish artists such as Michael Mulcahy, with his nature mysticism, Patrick Graham, whose art involves a strong sense of spiritual mission, and Brian Maguire, with his concern for social and political issues and alienation, achieved particular prominence. This was in the context of a 1983 exhibition, 'Making Sense', which also included work by Charles Cullen, Brian Bourke and Michael Cullen. This was the culmination of a development going back to 1960, with the formation of the Independent Artists' group committed to 'human' as distinct from stylistic issues, and was part of a reaction against a dominant abstraction that was seen as institutionalized and elitist. The 1984 'October Exhibition' in Dublin, with its Neo-Expressionist tendencies, which included 16 male and only three female painters, was characterized by an overwhelming use of masculine imagery, which from a feminist perspective might be seen as anachronistic.

In terms of the exploration of male sexuality, however, the paintings of Martin Wedge examine the negative elements of sexuality with a feeling for the ugly and the distorted that gives his work something of the grotesque vitality of early German Expressionism. The term 'Expressionist' may also be attached to the art of some Irish women painters of recent times, including Eithne Jordan, Rita Duffy; and Alice Maher; Maher's work uses violent imagery in an attempt to explode conventional images of women.

Outside of the realm of painting, the sculpture of John Behan and of F.E. McWilliam, who has made some striking images responding to the violence in Northern Ireland, may be described by the term 'Expressionist', which could also be applied to the sculpture of Cathy Carman and to some of the three-dimensional work of Graham Gingles. The 'human sculpture' of Vernon Carter might be similarly described.

Although Expressionism is a major theme of recent Irish painting in particular, it seldom achieves the combination of forceful feeling and technical ability that marked its earlier Continental counterpart. This may be due in part to Irish creative tendencies and predispositions, which perhaps express themselves in a more layered, ambiguous and complex way than their Continental, and specifically German, counterparts. It may also be due to the relative weakness in Ireland of industrial capitalism and the forms of dehumanization which it can engender (manifested in their extreme form in fascism) and which German Expressionism was, perhaps, in large measure a reaction against. Despite a traditional hostility among Irish artists to the exploration of social issues, the most recent work of an Expressionist tendency tends to be dominated by the examination of sexual themes. Given the importance of this issue over a wide intellectual spectrum, together with the forms of repression that continue to characterize the Irish scene, this is an exploration which might be expected to continue.

Reading

Arnold, Bruce, *Irish Art: A Concise History* (London: Thames and Hudson, 1977).

Denvir, Bernard, 'Fauvism and Expressionism', in David Britt (ed.), *Modern Art: Impressionism to Post-Modernism* (London: Thames and Hudson, 1974).

Dunne, Aidan, 'Back to the future: a context for Irish art of the 1980s', and Fowler, Joan, 'Speaking of gender: Expressionism, feminism and sexuality', in Douglas Hyde Gallery, *A New*

Tradition: Irish Art of the Eighties (Dublin: Douglas Hyde Gallery, 1990).

Kennedy, S.B., *Irish Art and Modernism: 1880–1950* (Belfast: Institute of Irish Studies/Queens University, 1991).

McConkey, Kenneth, *A Free Spirit: Irish Art 1860–1960* (London: Antique Collectors Club/ Pyms Gallery, 1990).

PAUL O'BRIEN

F

Fagan, Robert (1761–1816) Painter and dealer. Born in London of Irish parents, his father being a baker in Long Acre. After training at the Royal Academy Schools, Fagan travelled to Italy, where he remained for the rest of his life. He committed suicide in Rome in 1816. Fagan specialized in portraits of grand tourists and fashionable emigrés, invariably placing them within sight of ancient monuments. His style can at times be severely classical, no doubt inspired by his own passion for buying and selling classical artifacts to English collectors. His most famous coup as a dealer was to smuggle the Altieri Claudes to William Beckford (now at Anglesey Abbey, National Trust). His relationship with Ireland seems to have been slight.

Reading

Crookshank, Anne and the Knight of Glin, *Irish Portraits 1660–1860*, exhibition catalogue (London: 1969).
—— *The Painters of Ireland, c. 1660–1920* (London: Barrie and Jenkins, 1978).
Trevelyan, Raleigh, *Apollo*, XCVI (October 1972).

FINTAN CULLEN

Fallon, Padraic (1905–74) Poet and playwright whose work was undervalued in his lifetime. After joining Customs and Excise in Dublin, Fallon spent most of his life based in Wexford. Here in the rural isolation of a 20-acre farm he wrote poetry and radio plays inspired by Irish saga and legend. His plays *Diarmuid and Grainne* (1950) and *The Vision of Mac Conglinne* (1953) are particularly successful reworkings of old Irish literary themes. In addition to 17 radio plays, Fallon wrote two better-known stage plays, *The Seventh Step* (1954) and *Sweet Love Till Morn* (1971). Although many of his poems were published in Irish, English and American periodicals, Fallon's first collected edition did not appear until after his death (*Poems*, 1974).

HELEN MCCURDY

Famine, Great (1846–50) Stands out in European history for both its lateness and its context. In England nothing comparable had occurred since Tudor times, and in France not since the early eighteenth century. An added irony is that Ireland in the 1840s formed part of the most industrialized, if not the richest, nation in the world, the United Kingdom. The Act of Union of 1800, which created the United Kingdom of Great Britain and Ireland, had led to legislative and monetary integration, but the Great Famine was a reminder of how unequally the benefits of the new technology were being divided. Though the aggregate income of Ireland had risen between the Union and the Famine, there can be little doubt but that the lot of the poor – the bottom third or so of the population – had worsened.

The population of Ireland had grown faster than that of any other Western European country for several decades after 1750. By the eve of the Famine, it had reached nearly one-third that of the United Kingdom. Irish income per head was only two-fifths that of Great Britain, however, and contemporary travellers often claimed that Irish poverty was unequalled in Western Europe. That is not to say that nearly everybody in Ireland was poor; such claims refer to the underemployed and landless bottom third or so of the population. Most of that bottom third derived a living from agriculture, bartering labour with farmers for the use of an acre of potato ground. The travellers' claims are quite valid in the sense that before the Famine the Irish poor lacked basics such as decent clothes and housing. Irish poverty was not unmitigated, however. Recent research shows that, in part-compensation, the poor were tolerably well supplied with cheap food and fuel. The monotonous dict, dominated by potatoes and skim milk, and supplemented on occasion by items such as fish, oatmeal and cabbage, constituted a humble 'health food'. Regional contrasts in well-being within Ireland should not be ignored; in the east housing was better and literacy levels higher, and the north-east was experiencing an industrial revolution like that transforming parts of England and the Scottish central belt. Poverty was greatest in counties in the west and south-west. The Famine would claim most of its victims there.

Pre-Famine Adjustment

The Great Famine is usually put down to one simple fact – overpopulation. The overwhelming dependence of a sizeable minority of the people on a cheap food from which there could be no trading down in the event of a crop failure provides strong evidence in support of the case. However, it must be stressed too that failures of the kind encountered after 1845 were quite unprecedented in the history of the potato. This raises the question of how much prescience should be expected of the Irish poor before the Famine. Note too that in a typical year only about one-half of the pre-1845 potato crop was consumed by humans; the potato was the staple food of hens and pigs, and was also used to feed cattle and horses. The animals got the worst potatoes, but their share nevertheless acted as a kind of buffer stock when the crop was poor. Thus modest failures killed pigs rather than people. In retrospect, the Great Famine convinced some observers that the less serious famines afflicting Ireland in the eighteenth and early nineteenth centuries should have been taken more seriously as warning shots. It is always easy to be wise after the event. Ireland suffered severely from famine in 1800–1 and 1817–19. However, excess mortality from these crises was miniscule compared to that of the Great Famine, and those crises prompted policies that minimized excess mortality in future crises. Thus the threat of famine in 1822 was efficiently averted through a combination of private charity and government measures. Excess mortality in 1831, another bad year, was small compared to that in either 1800–1 or 1817–19.

Preventive action was prompted in part by middle-class fears of contagion from typhus. That few excess deaths occurred in the first year of potato failure is an indication of the resilience of the system and the capacity of the authorities and private charity to cope. There is evidence too of demographic adjustment in Ireland before 1845. Population growth was slowing, and had even come to a halt in a few pockets by the early 1840s. Admittedly it remained fastest in the poorest areas, though even there it was decelerating. A rising emigration rate was mainly responsible for the adjustment, though there is evidence also for a decline in nuptiality. Evidence for a rise in mortality, however plausible, is lacking: what straws in the wind there are suggest a reduction in the pre-famine half-century. While the wartime requirements and the Corn Laws increased the demand for agricultural labour in Ireland after the 1790s, other factors reduced it. The mysterious disappearance of the herring shut off one source of food, and the decline of rural industry in parts of the west and north-west was marked. The poor in those areas responded by increasing reliance on food production and seasonal migration. Adjustment did not imply economic convergence between Ireland and Britain, and the gap between richest and poorest counties may well also have been increasing in the pre-famine era.

The Potato

The dominance of the potato in Ireland on the eve of the Famine was unequalled anywhere else. For the landless and semi-landless poor, consumption per adult male reached 12 lb daily throughout most of the year. Consumption declined with income, but Irishmen and Irishwomen of all classes liked their potatoes. Introduced first in the south-west of Ireland, probably in the early seventeenth century, the potato had made its first successful inroads there. Diffusion was a gradual process; it was still proceeding in parts of the east and north in the late eighteenth century. The early history of the potato in Ireland remains a mystery. Over time, the number of varieties sown increased and by the late eighteenth century potatoes were available nearly all year. The most notorious variety is the Lumper, introduced from Scotland around 1810. A frequently noted attribute of watery and bland-tasting Lumper was its ability to produce a generous crop in poor soil. For this reason it was widely adopted by the poor. Because it failed disastrously during the Famine, it earned a doubly poor reputation. It is ironic, then, that part of the reason for its original diffusion was its resistance to pests.

The Blight

The potato blight (*Phytophthera infestans*) was first noted in Ireland early in September 1845. The disease caused the potato crop to rot in the ground and omit an unpleasant stench. This first onslaught of the blight turned out to be most serious in the east of Ireland, and certain pockets in the extreme west seem to have escaped virtually scot-free in the first year. A special crop return by the constabulary implies an overall shortfall of somewhat less than one-half in 1845/6. The rise in potato prices was greatest in certain eastern counties. The blight baffled contemporary scientific expertise. One expert correctly diagnosed the mould on diseased tubers as a 'vampire' fungus, but most influential botanists declared it a kind of dry rot. However, since no cure for such fungi would be forthcoming until the 1880s, accurate diagnosis did not count for much.

In the following year (1846) the blight's conquest was almost complete, and the real beginnings of the Famine date from that autumn. By late 1846 famine conditions were widespread. Nature played a cruel trick on people's expectations in 1847. Because of the scarcity of seed and the negative signals given by the failures of 1845 and 1846, the acreage planted in 1847 was small. Yields per acre turned out to be generous, however. That encouraged people to revert to planting a bigger acreage in 1848, but that year's crop also failed disastrously. In effect, therefore, the Famine was the product of four years of poor potato harvests. Thus food shortages rather than entitlement shifts were the main cause of famine. Moreover, while Ireland continued to export grain during the crisis, the trade in grain was two-way, and the overall balance was markedly negative in the late 1840s.

Chronology

Deaths began to mount in late 1846, and graphic accounts of the crisis soon reached London papers such as the *Illustrated London*

News and *The Times*. By spring 1847 the price of potatoes had reached four times their pre-blight norm. Grain prices rose too, though less dramatically. Deaths became commonplace. As is generally the case with famines, literal starvation claimed relatively few lives, dysentery and typhoid fever being the main killers. The incidence of dietary deficiency diseases such as scurvy, previously uncommon in Ireland, also rose.

Tragic and horrific scenes ensued all over the island; mass graves, corpses gnawed by rats, hunger marches, roadside deaths, the dying left unassisted for fear of contagion. Crimes against property rocketed, and were severely dealt with. Some landed proprietors acquitted themselves well, committing time and money to relief. Others evicted without compunction. It must be said that the difficulties facing landlords, on whom the main burden of relief charges fell, were real. Nevertheless, the eviction statistics in the wake of the Famine make for shocking reading: the official count is well over 200,000 people between 1849 and 1854, and that excludes those who voluntarily surrendered possession in exchange for a relief entitlement or subsidized emigration.

Like pre-famine poverty, the famine had an important regional dimension. Mapping the proportion of the population on food rations at the height of the crisis by poor law union produces a striking pattern. East of a line linking Wexford and Sligo, the proportion on relief rarely exceeded one-third. To the west of that line, recourse to the soup kitchen was much greater, exceeding four-fifths in much of Mayo and Galway. It was hoped that the high prices would encourage Irish merchants to purchase and mill foreign grain. That happened eventually; by summer 1847, prices had fallen back considerably.

Relief

The first attack of *Phytophthera infestans* occurred while Sir Robert Peel was prime minister. Peel had personal experience of dealing with famine in Ireland, and took forceful measures to prevent excess mortality in 1845/6. These included public works and the repeal of the Corn Laws, which entailed the virtual freeing of the trade in grain. The repeal caused Peel's Tories to split and forced his resignation, and he was succeeded by Lord John Russell. The challenge facing Russell's Whigs was far more serious. Substantial loss of life in 1846–7 was probably unavoidable under either Tories or Whigs. Nevertheless, there are instances of counter productive measures, and the Treasury was undoubtedly mean-minded. By and large, the Whigs were obsessive about letting public funds allow Irish landlords to shirk their responsibilities to the poor, and about crowding out private charity. They also worried about the moral hazard implications of relief, that is, the danger that in relieving the Irish they would only be paving the way for an even more serious crisis in the future.

Peel relied on providing employment through public works. The Whigs stuck with this policy for a time, and numbers on the works increased greatly in late 1846 and early 1847. However, it was soon realized that task work was not geared to helping those most in need; employers and relief officials feared that public works were competing with 'real' work; and, inevitably, there was a good deal of corruption. These considerations dictated a switch to direct food aid in late spring 1847. At a maximum over three million soup rations were being doled out daily, even in the remotest regions. The soup failed to sustain many of those already weakened by malnutrition. Still, deaths took a downward turn in the summer of 1847. In August 1847 Whitehall declared the crisis over, and the burden of future relief shifted to the Irish Poor Law. While the tide had turned in most areas, mortality continued to be very high in the west in 1848 and 1849.

Death and Migration

The death toll cannot be measured with precision, but dispassionate estimates suggest that about one million died as a direct result of the crisis. The poor were the main casualties, though others who came into contact with the poor in the course of their work, such as medical practitioners and the clergy, also perished in numbers. Children and old people were most likely to succumb, but that was so in normal times too. Indeed famine mortality seems to have mirrored normal mortality by age and sex. An important feature of mortality was its long-drawn-out character; excess mortality was still significant four or five years after the first attack of blight.

Mass emigration was also a central feature of the Famine years. Between the mid-1840s and mid-1850s nearly two million people left Ireland for good. Most headed for the United States, but Great Britain and Canada were also important destinations. However, the entire outflow of the late 1840s must not be attributed to the Famine, because long-distance migration from Ireland had already been established by 1845. Assisted emigration was a much more important feature during the Famine than before, though most migrants still travelled without state or landlord assistance. This probably meant that poverty prevented many of the very poor from leaving, and that the emigrants were disproportionately from small farm rather than labouring backgrounds. Thus among famine casualties the poor tended to die and the not so poor to emigrate. Nevertheless, emigration from Ireland during the Famine differed markedly from earlier outflows in that the poorest counties now supplied more than their proportionate share of emigrants. At the outset, an unregulated market in passenger traffic across the Atlantic exploited desperate and ignorant emigrants, and mortality on the Atlantic passage was very high in 1847. However, after several scandals and disasters, legislation to control the traffic in passengers led to improvements in subsequent years.

Losers and Gainers

The most obvious losers from the Great Famine were the million or so who perished.

Yet the Famine adversely affected people across the whole socio-economic scale. Landlords found their rent receipts down, and their poor rate bills up. Farmers may have benefited from the rent reductions, but the wage they were required to pay to maintain a labour force capable of working rose. Among farmers, only those specializing in grazing are likely to have benefited from the price shifts caused by the Famine. Lawyers, waxing fat on the massive number of property transfers occasioned by the tragedy, are another group who benefited in the short run; their numbers rose between 1841 and 1851. In the longer run, fewer people meant less pressure on the land and higher wages for those who survived.

Aftermath

The population of Ireland continued to decline, and by 1900 had nearly halved. The decline was largely restricted to rural areas, so Ireland was a good deal more urbanized in 1900 than in 1850. At first it may have seemed as if the vacuum created in some western areas severely thinned by the Famine would be filled again. In such areas people continued to marry young, farms continued to be subdivided, and the potato continued to play a leading role in the diet. Some isolated parishes even experienced population growth in the 1850s and 1860s. Overall, however, between the Famine and World War I decline was greatest in the west. Emigration was largely responsible; over four million people left for good between the early 1850s and 1914. A reduction in nuptiality also reduced the rate of natural increase. Living standards rose. Real wages jumped in the wake of the Famine, but the rise persisted, and real wages in 1900 were more than double their level half a century earlier. Rising labour costs and relative price shifts caused agricultural output to shift towards livestock. The quality of housing improved, and diet became more varied.

All these developments followed in the wake of the Famine. Would they have occurred regardless? Several historians have answered this counterfactual question in the affirmative. In support, the experience of other European countries quite unaffected by the blight suggests that emigration from Ireland after mid-century would have been high anyway. Moreover, the changes in agriculture were in large part induced by world market trends. Besides, we have seen that demographic adjustment of a kind was under way even before 1846. However, the famine 'mattered'. First, it prompted a long-distance migration by the very poor that might have been slower to take hold otherwise. Second, the changes in the agricultural labour force and output cannot be accounted for by relative price shifts alone. After all, the decline in potato yields was famine-induced, and that alone was bound to force a shift to pasture. Taking a longer perspective, the reduction in the labour force suggests a redistribution of income from land to labour. Landlords were saved from such a shift for some decades by the drift towards pasture and dairying. Though it led to higher living standards, the Famine also traumatized those who survived it.

Reading

Bourke, A., *The Visitation of God? The Potato and the Great Irish Famine* (Dublin: Lilliput Press, 1993).

Crawford, E.M. (ed.), *Famine: The Irish Experience* (Edinburgh: John Donald, 1989).

Edwards, R.D. and Williams, T.D. (eds), *The Great Famine: Studies in Irish History* (Browne and Nolan, 1956).

Mokyr, J., *Why Ireland Starved*, 2nd edn (London: Allen and Unwin, 1985).

Ó Gráda, C., *The Great Irish Famine* (Macmillan, 1989).

——— *Ireland: A New Economic History 1780–1939* (Oxford: Oxford University Press, 1994).

Woodham-Smith, C., *The Great Hunger* (Harmondsworth: Penguin, 1990).

CORMAC Ó GRÁDA

fantastic 'The literary fantastic' represents, for suitable literary texts, an alternative to traditional generic approaches, and is based upon Todorov's notion of readers' hesitation as to whether the explanation for literary plot events is ascribable to realistic or non-realistic (supernatural, paranormal or 'marvellous') causes. Legend and folk or fairy tale, in Irish literature as in any other, regularly adopt the marvellous. What may be in many other ways realist literature, from the gothic period onward, frequently contains ambiguous elements, which may be resolved sooner or later into either realism or the supernatural, or may remain unresolved, and thus stay within the realm of the 'pure fantastic'.

A number of Anglo-Irish writers are leading candidates for consideration here, alongside such European or American authors as E.T.A. Hoffmann and Edgar Allen Poe. Charles Robert Maturin, a Gothic writer of wide European reputation, is one of the first. His masterpiece, *Melmoth the Wanderer* (1820), is a remarkable remix of a number of well-worn gothic themes, presented through multiple viewpoint in a multi-layered form of stories within stories, so extreme both in content and structure as ultimately to call into question its own purportedly and overtly Satanic credibility. Sheridan Le Fanu followed this tradition with his own variation of the demon lover in Schalken the Painter (1839), and the ghostly stories of his cycle *In a Glass Darkly* (1872), as well as in his better novels, most notably the remarkable Swedenborgian narrative *Uncle Silas* (1864), in which a fantastic dualism may be seen to lurk behind the surface plot of the almost conventional Victorian novel of sensation. Oscar Wilde employed the mode in 'The Canterville Ghost' (1887) and especially in *The Picture of Dorian Gray* (1890–1), a colourful reworking of Faustian bargain and double motifs in a secular context. The century is rounded off by Bram Stoker's *Dracula* (1897), descended in part from Melmoth and Le Fanu's 'Carmilla', in which the device of multiple narration once again calls into question the plausibility of events.

In the twentieth century, the breakdown of traditional genres under Modernism and, more recently, postmodernism has led to hybrid forms, in which the fantastic and 'fantasy' achieve considerable prominence. In the wake of James Joyce, the fiction of Flann O'Brien may at times yield to a fantastic reading. Traditional forms continued in the short (or ghost) story, as in Elizabeth Bowen's 'The Demon Lover'. More recently John Banville revisits such gothic clichés as the fallen house, the double and Faustian temptation in his associated pair of novels (published 13 years apart), *Birchwood* (1973) and the remarkably enigmatic *Mephisto* (1986).

Reading

Todorov, Tzvetan, *The Fantastic: A Structural Approach to a Literary Genre*, trans. Richard Howard (Cleveland and London: Case Western Reserve, 1973).
Cornwell, Neil, *The Literary Fantastic: from Gothic to Postmodernism (New York and London: Harvester Wheatsheaf, 1990).*

NEIL CORNWELL

Farquhar, George (1678–1707) Dramatist. Born Derry; died London. Farquhar's father was a clergyman of the established church. He had his early education in Derry, followed by a year or so in Trinity College, Dublin. A career on the stage in Dublin was brought to an abrupt end when he accidentally stabbed a fellow actor. He then went to London, where he began writing for the stage. In 1698 his first play, *Love and a Bottle*, was produced at Drury Lane. This was followed in 1699 by *The Constant Couple*, which was a great success. *Sir Harry Wildair*, in which he later made a return to the Dublin stage, was first produced in 1701, *The Inconstant* and *The Twin Rivals* in 1702, *The Stage Coach* (from the French) in 1704, *The Recruiting Officer* in 1706 and *The Beaux Strategem*, arguably his best, in 1707. In between Farquhar succeeded in getting a commission in the army at the behest of Lord Orrery. *The Recruiting Officer* is based on his army experiences. Although he had powerful patrons in the Duke of Ormond and Lord Orrery, he appears to

have been a prey to financial worries when he died, pathetically consigning his two little daughters to the care of the actor Wilks. Leigh Hunt had this to say of him: 'He was becoming gayer and gayer, when death... called him away as from a pleasant party, and left the house ringing with his jest.' The house is ringing still.

Reading

Connelly, Willard, *Young George Farquhar* (London: Cassell, 1949).
Farquhar, George, *Complete Works*, ed. C.A. Stonehill (London: Nonesuch Press, 1930).

PATRICK FAGAN

Farrell, Eibhlis (1953–) Born Rostrevor, County Down, 27 July. Farrell Studied at the Queen's University of Belfast, then gained an MMus in composition from Bristol University under Raymond Warren. She lectured at St Mary's College of Education, Belfast, before being appointed deputy principal and head of theory at the Dublin College of Music in 1983. From 1988 to 1990 she studied with Charles Wuorrinen on a composition fellowship at Rutgers University, New Jersey and was awarded her PhD in May 1991.

Her music is strong and atonal, using flexible rhythms, polyrhythms and melodic cells. She prefers extended, one-movement works, often in arc form. The aggressive writing of earlier years has given way to a more lyrical, romantic style with lighter, sparser textures.

SARAH BURN

Farrell, J.G. (1936–79) Born Liverpool. Farrell's family had close Irish connections. He was educated at Brasenose College, Oxford, and after graduating in 1960, taught in France for a number of years, and travelled. At the time of his death he was living in West Cork.

Of Farrell's seven novels, three command particular attention: *Troubles* (1970), set in a County Wexford hotel during the Anglo-Irish war; *The Siege of Krishnapur* (1973), dealing with the Indian Mutiny; and *The Singapore Grip* (1978), which depicts the fall of Singapore. These works are not merely narratives of the decline and fall of the British empire. Beneath their wealth of meticulous period detail and historical knowledge is a sophisticated meditation on catastrophe's peculiar norms, and on the marginality of such human resources as spirit and reason when confronted by the impersonal powers of change and enmity. These novels' sceptical anatomy of change is sustained by an increasingly deft management of ever more crowded canvases and by a tone which is a mordant combination of irony and entropy.

GEORGE O'BRIEN

Farrell, Micheal (1940–2000) Painter. Born in Kells, County Meath. Farrell studied at St Martin's Schools of Art, London (1957–61). He spent much of his career in France. He works in series; in the 1960s his work was abstract, exploring formal relationships and using traditional Celtic forms, such as the circle and spiral (Cairn series, 1966–7). Pop art has been a major influence, as can be seen in the Presse series (1970) of initially abstract work, which began to include representational elements in response to the worsening political troubles in the North (1975). Farrell abandoned abstraction, feeling that his work should have political and social content, a decision exemplified in *Miss O'Murphy or the Very First Real Irish Political Picture* (1977), based on Boucher's painting. His work has continued to explore political and personal subjects in a figurative mode.

FELICITY WOOLF

Farrington, Benjamin (1891–1974) Scholar. Born Cork, 10 July; died Hampshire, 17 November. Educated at University College, Cork, and Trinity College, Dublin, Farrington taught at Queen's University, Belfast, from 1916 to 1920, and from 1920 to 1935 at Cape Town University, where he was appointed professor of Latin in 1930. In 1936 he became professor of classics at University College, Swansea, retiring in 1956. His Marxist, humanist and rationalist faith informed his studies in the history of ideas and the relationship between science and practical life. This is the central theme of his best-known book, *Greek Science*. His 11 books include works on Aristotle, Epicurus, Francis Bacon and Darwin as well as studies in classical literature. In 1935 he married Ruth Schechter and in 1943 Cecily Sells; they had one daughter.

DAVID SMITH

Faulkner, George (1703–75) Bookseller and printer. Born Dublin, 3 April; died there, 29 or 30 August. Faulkner's father is said to have been a butcher. After his apprenticeship to Thomas Hume, printer, he set up shop in Dublin, but from 1726 to 1729 he left his kinsman and partner, James Hoey, in charge and spent much time in London working for the printers William Bowyer (father and son). His friendship with Bowyer junior was life-long and to their mutual advantage in the exchange of copyrights. Faulkner made other valuable contacts in London, and married there in 1730.

He became the most considerable bookseller–printer in eighteenth-century Ireland. His press was needed primarily for his newspaper; as a printer he was competent but not innovative. The *Dublin Journal* (1725–1825) survived through its apolitical policy of dull reliability and is remarkable for its stability and long life. Faulkner's own importance depends on his enterprise, energy and flair in his publishing activities. He joined with others in reprinting London titles, negotiated Dublin reprint rights in popular authors such as Samuel Richardson, and published first editions of many Irish writers including Patrick Delany, George Berkeley and William Dunkin. His fortune was probably made by his association with Swift, which began in 1730. He served as Swift's amanuensis and goad during the collection and editing of the *Works*, first issued in 1735, and was instrumental in conserving pieces that would otherwise have been lost.

Faulkner became an alderman in 1770. He was well known in literary circles in both Dublin and London, and renowned for his hospitality, numbering lords Chesterfield and Townshend amongst his dinner guests. He seems to have been a curious mixture of wit, pomposity and great ability.

Reading

Anon., 'Authentic memoirs of the late George Faulkner', *Hibernian Magazine* (Sept. 1775).

Ward, R.E. (ed.), *Prince of Dublin Printers: The Letters of George Faulkner* [*Not Already in Print*], (Lexington KY: University Press of Kentucky, 1972).

M. POLLARD

Fay brothers Frank (1871–1931), actor; William (George) (1872–1947), actor and director. Born in Dublin, they joined the Irish Literary Theatre in 1902, having run their own fit-up company the Ormonde Players. Both believed in the future of a serious Irish drama. William was largely responsible for the economic style of production and playing for which the Abbey Theatre became famous from 1904. He was also a character actor of immense versatility, creating Peter Gillan and Johnny Bacach (Yeats), Bartley, Martin Doul and Christy Mahon (Synge), Bartley Fallon, Michael Cooney and the Ballad Singer (Gregory), and Sganarelle (Gregory after Molière). Frank was noted for his verse speaking and created Forgael, Naoise and Cuchullain (Yeats). He also possessed a rich gift for comedy, as seen in Hyacinth Halvey (Gregory) and Shawn Keogh (Synge). By 1907 William, as producer, was dissatisfied with the haphazard administration and the predominance of peasant drama. Hoping to rectify these matters he requested managerial powers, which the directors refused to grant. In 1908 both Fays resigned from the Abbey Theatre, performing on stage and screen in Britain and America for the rest of their lives.

Reading

Fay, William, *The Fays of the Abbey Theatre* (London: Rich and Conran, 1935).

Robinson, Lennox, *Ireland's Abbey Theatre* (London: Sidgwick and Jackson, 1951).

CHRISTOPHER FITZSIMON

feminist writing Maria Edgeworth's satire on Rousseau's ideas for women's education in *Belinda* (1801) indicates that Enlightenment feminism had left its trace on the Irish novel. Lack of research on women's writing in the nineteenth century makes it difficult to ascertain how feminism fared until it resurfaced in the campaign for women's suffrage. The rediscovery of the work of such writers as Katherine Cecil Thurston, George Egerton (Mary Chavelita Dunne) and Emily Lawless, attention to the papers and documents of the suffrage movement itself, and the evidence of the persistence of feminist ideas in Irish women's writing in the 1930s and 1940s indicate that the suffrage movement had a very significant impact on Irish culture and literature. Many women writing in the nineteenth and early twentieth centuries did, however, give priority to the national question, though the women most involved in nationalist politics were often influenced by the ideas and ideals of the women's suffrage movement.

Feminism survived a long period of intense social conservatism in Ireland, North and South. Jenny Wyse Power and Kathleen Clarke used the Senate as a forum for feminist opposition to restrictions on women's employment and to a variety of conservative measures proposed by both Cumann na nGaedheal and Fianna Fáil during the period 1922–37. Women's discontent with the sexual conservatism of the new southern state surfaced into public protest on a number of occasions, notably in opposition to de Valera's constitution, with its emphasis on Catholic 'family' values and its intensely confining definitions of women's role in the new Ireland. In the literary sphere, writers such as Kate O'Brien and Elizabeth Bowen and critics such as

Brigid J. MacCarthy kept feminist ideas alive. MacCarthy's remarkable, scholarly, two-volume history, *The Female Pen* (1944, 1947), dealt with women's contribution to the novel form from 1621 to 1818, took Woolf's *A Room of One's Own* as its starting point, and sought to justify women's 'claims to free activity'.

The Irish women's movement which emerged in the next wave of feminist agitation in the sixties and seventies has developed within the social paradox of conservatism of aspiration and legislation in the context of enormous changes in Irish society, in sexual roles and in family structures. Feminist literature has developed and flourished since the 1970s despite the resistance of both the conservative and radical critical and literary establishments. Two feminist publishing houses can take a great deal of credit for this flourishing, the pioneering Arlen House (now defunct) and Attic Press, initally specializing in handbooks, information and polemical feminist work, but developing a strong fiction list (Attic is now an imprint of Cork University Press). A number of established women poets, Eavan Boland, Eiléan Ní Chuilleanáin and Medbh McGuckian in English, Máire Mhac An tSaoi and Nuala Ní Dhomhnaill in Gaelic, have put women's writing on the literary agenda in Ireland, though most of the publishing and reviewing outlets remain unamenable to the work of women writers and women writers were seriously neglected in the three-volume *Field Day Anthology of Irish Writing* published in 1991. The issue of gender is acknowledged in the fourth and fifth volumes of the *Anthology, Irish Women's Writing and Traditions* (2001). Fiction written by women is routinely dismissed as dreary 'confessional realism'. The diverse and innovative work of writers such as Eilis Ní Dhuibhne, Moy McCrory and Anne Enright effectively undermines such stereotypes, and these writers, with poets like Paula Meehan, Julie O'Callaghan, Rita Anne Higgins and Biddie Jenkinson, pose an invigorating challenge to the way in which Irish literature is defined and read.

Reading

Boland, Eavan, 'A Kind of Scar: The Woman Poet in a National Tradition', LIP Pamphlet (Dublin: Attic Press, 1989).

Colby Quarterly, Special Issue: 'Irish Women's Writing', XXVII, no. 1 (Mar. 1991).

Luddy, Maria and Murphy, Cliona (eds), *Women Surviving: Studies in Irish Women's History in the Nineteenth and Twentieth Centuries* (Dublin: Poolbeg, 1990).

O'Brien Johnson, Toni and Cairns, David (eds), *Gender in Irish Writing* (Open University Press, 1991).

Smyth, Ailbhe (ed.), *Wildish Things: An Anthology of New Irish Women's Writing* (Dublin: Attic Press, 1989).

GERALDINE MEANEY

Fenianism The *Fianna* (warriors) of Irish legend inspired the naming of the Fenian Brotherhood, founded in New York in 1859, from which was derived the informal designation 'Fenian' applied by friend and foe to a series of conspiratorial societies on both sides of the Atlantic devoted to the winning of Irish independence by military means. The societies on the American side expended most of their energy on Irish-American concerns, but what few resources (mainly financial) they directed to Ireland were the lifeblood of their Irish counterparts.

Beginning with the organization established by James Stephens in Dublin in 1858, Fenianism was founded on the premise that a successful Irish revolution was conceivable only when British power would be hamstrung by an international war. The point was reinforced when through failure of leadership a section of the Irish Fenians stumbled into a doomed rebellion in March 1867. At various times Fenians sought or envisaged alliances with the USA, France, Spain, Russia and imperial Germany. A new leadership emerging after 1867 effectively created a new Irish organization and formally adopted the designation Irish Republican Brotherhood (IRB), creating a supreme council and a three-man executive with a presidency which survived until 1924, when (it is generally believed) the IRB dissolved. There were always breakaway, dissident or alternative Fenian groupings.

In the middle and late 1860s Fenianism had scores of thousands of adherents in Ireland and among the Irish in Britain; but the more usual figure was a few thousand. Majority Irish nationalist opinion supported parliamentary politicians, but dead or imprisoned Fenians quickly assumed popular heroic status. Parnell converted most of the post-1867 IRB leaders to parliamentary politics. When the Irish Parliamentary Party lost its authority during World War I, the new contenders for nationalist leadership used the IRB as one of their main vehicles: through its offices the 1916 Rising was plotted, the Sinn Féin electoral triumph of December 1918 was masterminded, and a Dáil Éireann majority was secured for the Anglo-Irish Treaty of 1921.

Reading

Ó Broin, Leon, *Revolutionary Underground: the story of the Irish Republican Brotherhood, 1858–1924* (Dublin: Gill and Macmillan, 1976).

Comerford, R.V., *The Fenians in Context: Irish Politics and Society, 1848–82* (Dublin: Wolfhound Press, 1985).

Moody, T.W. (ed.), *The Fenian Movement* (Cork: Mercier Press, 1968).

D'Arcy, William, *The Fenian Movement in the United States, 1858–86* (Washington DC: Catholic University of America Press, 1947).

O'Brien, William and Ryan, Desmond (eds), *Devoy's Post Bag*, 2 vols (Dublin: Fallon, 1948, 1953).

R.V. COMERFORD

Ferguson, Howard (1908–) Pianist and composer. Ferguson studied at the Royal College of Music, London, with R.O. Morris. He was professor of composition at the Royal Academy of Music from 1948 to 1963. After producing a small number of works, he abandoned composition in 1959 and turned to editing the keyboard works of Purcell, Croft, Schubert, Picchi and others, and publishing *Keyboard Interpretation* in 1975. His finely crafted compositions are written in a basically diatonic style. They include two sonatas for violin and piano (op. 2 and 10), an octet (op. 4), *Five Irish Folksongs* (op. 17) for voice and piano, *Four Diversions on Ulster Airs* (op. 7) and *Overture for an Occasion* (op. 16) for orchestra, the piano concerto (op. 12), and *Amore langueo* (op. 18) and *The Dream of the Rood* (op. 19), both for solo voice, chorus and orchestra. Most are published by Boosey and Hawkes and the manuscripts are deposited in the Bodleian Library.

PETER DOWNEY

Ferguson, Samuel (1810–86) Poet, antiquarian and critic. Born Belfast, Samuel Ferguson's earliest published work consists of a handful of poems in the nationalist *Ulster Magazine* (1830–1), but his literary career began in earnest with his first contribution to *Blackwood's Edinburgh Magazine*, 'The Forging of the Anchor' (1832). He spent a brief but influential period in Edinburgh in 1832, becoming acquainted with the Blackwood circle before returning to Ireland and enrolling as a student at Trinity College, Dublin. In Dublin he balanced his professional training for the bar with extensive literary and journalistic activities, and while maintaining his contact with Blackwood's he also wrote for the *Dublin University Magazine* (*DUM*), established in 1833 as an organ of Irish Tory Unionism.

Ferguson expressed a commitment to Irish culture and history, and in pursuit of his avowed ambition to 'raise the matter of Ireland to a dignified level' he published between 1833 and 1836 the *Hibernian Nights' Entertainments*, a series of prose romances exploring various stages of Irish history and closely modelled on Scott. While privately condemning the Orange tendencies of the *DUM*, he frequently indulged in anti-papist jibes, and in 1834 he published four articles in the magazine attacking James Hardiman's collection *Irish Minstrelsy* (1831), which he rebuked as a pernicious combination of weak translation and strong nationalist piety. This extensive review is cited as having set an agenda for Protestant participation in a Gaelic national heritage, but its impact is complicated by Ferguson's attempts to ground his argument in a fashionable but crude historicist analysis of Ireland's retarded social development.

In the 1840s Ferguson's political affiliations became confused as he came into contact with the Young Irelanders, particularly Thomas Davis, whom he held in high esteem as an ideal of Irish Protestant manliness. His disillusionment with the Union was exacerbated by his belief that Westminster had mishandled Famine relief, and by his fears that the creeping policy of centralization was about to put into effect the transfer of the Irish law courts to London. He became a founder member of the Protestant Repeal Association but his political apostasy was short-lived, and by the end of 1848 he had withdrawn from public debate. In the same year he married Mary Catherine Guinness, author of *The Irish Before the Conquest* (1868).

Much of Ferguson's later life was devoted to antiquarianism, and to the production of his epic poems, including *Congal* (1872) and *Deirdre* (1880) – highly stylized Victorian versions of Gaelic legend. *Lays of the Western Gael* was published in 1864 and his *Poems* in 1880. He was knighted in 1878 and elected president of the Royal Irish Academy in 1881.

EVE PATTEN

fiction to 1830 The Irish novel in English has a long history, with prose fiction written, variously, in Ireland, by Irish-born writers, for Irish readers, on Irish subject matter, or revealing what later came to be thought characteristic Irish preoccupations dating from at least the early 1700s.

Sarah Butler's *Irish Tales* (1716) is set in Ireland's pre-Norman Gaelic past but concerned very much with the country's post-Williamite present. Reaching its climax with Brian Boru's victory over the Norse alliance at the Battle of Clontarf in 1014, the work argues on behalf of Ireland's Gaelic and Catholic people, suffering under unjust laws imposed by foreign invaders, and foretells the restoration of lands, rights, and power to the country's original inhabitants. If the Jacobite implications of *Irish Tales* are unexpected, and unusual in eighteenth-century fiction generally, then Butler's spirited defence of Irish culture against English prejudice is prophetic of much subsequent Irish fiction in English.

Also sympathetically concerned with Gaelic culture are *Memoirs of Several Ladies of Great Britain* (1755) and *The Life of John Buncle, Esq.* (1756–66), by the eccentric Thomas Amory (?1691–1788). Formally, the latter's anecdotal structure owes much to Irish oral narrative, specifically *seanchas*, in relating the experiences of the six-times-married Unitarian polymath hero as he travels through Ireland and the English Peak district. Amory offers vivid glimpses both of the Gaelic aristocracy in the west and of the middle-class culture of English-speaking Dublin. If the anecdotal structure is prophetic of later Irish writing, the defence of contemporary Ireland is characteristic of much eighteenth-century writing.

William Chaigneau's *The Life of Jack Connor* (1752) was recognized even by British reviewers as making 'smart reprizals upon the *English*, for their national and vulgar prejudices against their brethren of *Ireland*'. While Chaigneau's values are strongly Protestant, the Huguenot writer shows considerable sympathy for the poor Catholic Irish in a novel set partly in counties Limerick, Tipperary and Kildare, and in Dublin. *Jack Connor* confronts problems of contemporary cultural identity in the person of its hero – born of a Protestant father and Catholic mother – who, on leaving Ireland for England, is persuaded to change his name to avoid prejudice, a change uniquely indicated by a change of name on the title page of the novel's second volume: *The Life of Jack Connor; now Conyers*.

Though the picaresque mode Chaigneau took from Le Sage became increasingly unfashionable in later eighteenth-century fiction, *The History of Jack Juniper* (1774) and

The Adventures of Anthony Varnish (1786), both attributed to the Limerick-born Charles Johnstone, are worth noting, for they contain Irish scenes remarkable for their day. These novels confront English prejudice against Ireland, as does Johnstone's earlier and most successful fiction, *Chrysal; or the Adventures of a Guinea* (1760–5), a *roman à clef* whose wide-ranging satirical depiction of a vicious world does not preclude a concern with Ireland, especially in a Swiftian denunciation of English economic exploitation.

Johnstone's cosmopolitan values nevertheless militated against a narrowing of his concerns to Ireland, and mid-century cosmopolitanism combined with literary self-confidence to ensure that Irish writers did not place themselves outside of the mainstream of European fiction by restricting themselves to matters of merely Irish concern. If Oliver Goldsmith wrote on occasion out of his Irish experience, no attempt to see *The Vicar of Wakefield* (1766) in narrowly national terms can be adequate, and Goldsmith's own cosmopolitanism is well indicated by the title he chose for his essays on a Chinese in London: *The Citizen of the World.*

The cosmopolitanism of contemporary fiction is indicated in part by the rapidity with which works were translated from one language into another. Frances Sheridan learnt much from French novelists like Marie-Jean Riccoboni and the Abbé Prévost, the latter translating into French the first part of Sheridan's *Memoirs of Miss Sidney Bidulph* (1761–7) within a year of its appearance. Nominally set in Queen Anne's England, Sheridan's masterpiece easily invites a specifically Irish reading as its heroine struggles between the dull and faithless English husband she has married from a misplaced sense of duty and the wild, romantic Irishman, Orlando, she loves. Duty prevails but the price of following her conscience is high, and Sidney Bidulph looks for no compensation or consolation for her sacrifice in this life. That Sheridan was one of the most talented novelists of her day is evident also

from the much-admired *The History of Nourjahad* (1767), an Oriental tale – a popular mid-century form also practised successfully by Charles Johnstone, whose *The History of Arsaces* (1774) is a thinly disguised allegory of the conflict between Britain and her American colonies.

Unlike Johnstone, Sheridan used the Oriental tale to further her exploration of moral problems in a sentimental manner, and sentimentalism came increasingly to dominate later eighteenth-century fiction. Among successful Irish works of the kind were Hugh Kelly's *Memoirs of a Magdalen* (1767) and *Letters of Henry and Frances* (1757) by Richard Griffith and his wife Elizabeth. Richard Griffith was also the author of *The Triumvirate* (1765) and *The Posthumous Works of a Late Celebrated Genius Deceased* (1770), one of many contemporary imitations of Laurence Sterne, whom Griffith knew. Henry Brooke, another fine novelist of the period, began writing under the influence of *Tristram Shandy* and ended by paying homage to Sterne's most sentimental manner. His *The Fool of Quality* (1765–70) is a thesis-novel on education, written after the example of Rousseau's *Emile* (1761) yet with a decidedly Sternean playfulness. The playfulness, however, fades out of the novel's later volumes and Brooke's increasing sentimentalism is clearly apparent in his final novel, *Juliet Grenville; or the History of the Human Heart* (1774).

Sentimentalism continued to dominate Irish fiction until almost the end of the century, its ready appeal indicated to readers by the titles of such works as the thoughtful *The Triumph of Benevolence* (1772), once ascribed to Goldsmith, or the more characteristically inept *Harcourt: A Sentimental Tale* (1780). Occasionally titles could deceive, and the unpromisingly named *The Triumph of Prudence over Passion* (1781) provides a welcome corrective to commonplace sentimentality with a challenging feminist and political awareness, the heroine thwarting conventional expectations by refusing to marry the hero, while arguing for women's right to speak up for Protestant nationalist values in the era of the Free Trade debate and the Volunteer Movement.

An increasing national awareness is one of the main features of Irish fiction in the last three decades of the eighteenth century. This manifested itself in part in developing historical fiction touching on issues of identity (though in ways mostly far removed from Butler's *Irish Tales*); among the more interesting examples may be noted *Longsword* (1762) by Thomas Leland, the historian, and Anne Fuller's *Alan Fitz-Osborne* (1786) and *The Son of Ethelwolf* (1789). Both of Fuller's novels were subtitled 'An Historical Tale'. Increasingly, however, writers drew attention to the national concerns of their works. Such titles as *The Irish Guardian* (1776) or *The Irish Heiress* (1797) became more popular, while *The Triumph of Prudence over Passion* was described as 'An Hibernian Novel' on its first English publication in 1783.

The most famous work of this kind was Maria Edgeworth's own 'Hibernian Tale', *Castle Rackrent* (1800), which, while ostensibly bidding farewell to the Ireland of the years before the 1782 constitution, marked the beginning of a revived interest in Irish nationalist fiction in a period immediately following the Act of Union, when Romantic notions of national identity were replacing Enlightenment ones. Though Edgeworth's narrator, the steward Thady Quirk, tells of the fall of the Rackrent family in a voice very different to that his creator employed elsewhere, Edgeworth returned to explore Ireland's political, economic and cultural problems in such works as *Ennui* (1809), *The Absentee* (1812) and *Ormond* (1817), the last an ambitious novel whose hero, like Chaigneau's Jack Connor, embodies two different and frequently conflicting cultures: a potentially vibrant Protestant landed ascendancy and a dying Gaelic Catholic aristocracy. The optimism still evident in *Ormond* did not long survive and Edgeworth eventually disclaimed any ability to express in fiction her concern for an Ireland changing beyond her comprehension.

Nor did Edgeworth show any great interest in the nationalist fiction of such Irish writers as Sydney Owenson, Lady Morgan, whose third novel, *The Wild Irish Girl* (1806), boasted a heroine, Glorvina, who, with her beauty, resolution, and taste for poetry and music, came to personify the untamed west of Ireland for an audience in England as well as at home. Despite an implausible narrative and a setting as much influenced by Salvator Rosa as Connaught, Owenson nevertheless made large claims for the essential truthfulness of *The Wild Irish Girl*, helping to shape England's image of Ireland for some decades. Lady Morgan never repeated the success of *The Wild Irish Girl*, though she continued to write novels on Irish themes, including *The O'Briens and the O'Flahertys* (1827), with its more comprehensive rendering of Irish cultural complexity: Gaelic aristocracy and peasantry, renegade Catholics, Gaelicized Protestants, plantation families, and English landowners, in Dublin and Connaught.

Among writers influenced by Lady Morgan's work, Charles Robert Maturin is pre-eminent. His first novel, *Fatal Revenge* (1807), had been an example of rationalized gothic, a form made famous in England by Ann Radcliffe and practised in Ireland by Regina Maria Roche, author of the long-celebrated *The Children of the Abbey* (1796) and other works including *The Munster Cottage Boy* (1820) and *The Tradition of the Castle; or, Scenes in the Emerald Isle* (1824). However, in *The Wild Irish Boy* (1807) and *The Milesian Chief* (1812), Maturin paid obvious homage to Sydney Owenson's example, before writing of Calvinist circles in contemporary Dublin in *Women; or Pour et Contre* (1818). Maturin's greatest work, *Melmoth the Wanderer* (1820), is arguably the finest Irish novel between *Castle Rackrent* and *Portrait of the Artist as a Young Man*. Melding the gothic with myth – the Wandering Jew, Faust and the Ancient Mariner – *Melmoth* concerns itself in no ordinary way with the questions that preoccupied other Irish novelists of the day, with Maturin offering a troubled investigation of his own place, as a Protestant Irish clergyman with strongly anti-Catholic views, in a country he knew to be his own yet whose nature he only dimly understood. Yet if Maturin's was the most powerful articulation in fiction of the differences within contemporary Ireland, his work may be seen as exemplary of attempts by Irish novelists for over a century to explore specifically Irish problems in writings which both acknowledged the inescapable influence of contemporary English fiction and asserted Ireland's legitimate involvement with wider issues of European culture.

IAN CAMPBELL ROSS

Field Day Theatre Company Has been described as 'like the Irish Literary Theatre, a concept, not a building'. It was founded in Derry in 1980 by playwright Brian Friel and actor Stephen Rea with the intention of an annual touring venture of a production which, starting off in Derry, might bring something like political theatre to a wide, general audience in the South as well as the North. It is proper to say 'something like' political theatre because the aim was not propagandistic. Thus Friel's *Translations* (1980) was the first production, and his version of Chekhov's *Three Sisters* (1981) the second: the latter had art and not politics as its brief. Succeeding productions have been similarly diverse, down to Seamus Heaney's *The Cure at Troy* (1990) and Thomas Kilroy's *The Madame MacAdam Travelling Show* (1991). At the same time, Field Day bears within it a deliberate resemblance to the initial Abbey Theatre, 'in that it has within it the idea of a culture which has not yet come to be in political terms' (Seamus Deane, one of the directors). Accordingly, the plays usually address questions of identity, history and language in a non-sectarian fashion.

In 1983 Field Day began to publish pamphlets on the issues surrounding cultural nationalism, and to some extent these pamphlets (published three each year for five years) liberated the Theatre Company from the dilemma of art and politics within the same

programme; but the pamphlets also raised a cloud of dust obscuring what the Theatre Company stood for. Because the first three pamphlets were by three Field Day directors – Tom Paulin's 'A New Look at the Language Question', Seamus Heaney's 'An Open Letter' and Seamus Deane's 'Civilians and Barbarians' – they carried the stamp of authority. Whereas the polemical issues raised and debated here bear upon such plays as *Translations*, Kilroy's *Double Cross* (1986) and Friel's *Making History* (1988), it seems clear that they also initiated an intellectual if not an ideological structure which tended to be viewed by critics of Field Day as applicable also and without qualification to the dramatic productions. This development has been injurious to the enterprise of the company. It can be no accident that within a decade Friel was staging his new plays elsewhere. In 1991 the *Field Day Anthology of Irish Writing* (3 vols) was published under the general editorship of Seamus Deane. This massive project is perhaps the culmination of the directors' literary and cultural ambitions.

Reading

Deane, Seamus 'What is Field Day?', programme note for *Three Sisters* in a new translation by Brian Friel, Field Day Theatre Company, September 1981.

—— 'Introduction', in *Nationalism, Colonialism, and Literature: Terry Eagleton, Fredric Jameson, Edward W. Said. A Field Day Company Book* (Minneapolis: University of Minnesota Press, 1990).

Etherton, Michael, 'The Field Day Theatre Company and the New Irish Drama', *New Theatre Quarterly*, 3, no. 9 (1987), pp. 64–70.

Pine, Richard, *Brian Friel and Ireland's Drama* (London: Routledge, 1990).

Richards, Shaun, 'To Bind the Northern to the Southern Stars: Field Day in Derry and Dublin', *Irish Review*, 4 (Spring 1988), pp. 52–65.

—— 'Field Day's Fifth Province: Avenue or Impasse?' in Eamonn Hughes (ed.), *Culture and Politics in Northern Ireland 1960–1990* (Milton Keynes and Philadelphia: Open University Press, 1991).

CHRISTOPHER MURRAY

Field, John (1782–1837). Composer and pianist. Born Dublin, July; died Moscow, 23 January. Son of a theatre violinist, Field made his debut as a pianist aged 9. In 1793 the family moved to London, where he was apprenticed to the pianist and piano-maker Clementi. He performed his First Piano Concerto to great acclaim in 1799 and was subsequently much in demand in London. Accompanying Clementi on a European tour in 1802, he remained in St Petersburg after Clementi's departure in 1803. Apart from a European concert tour between 1831 and 1835, by which time he was already in declining health through alcoholism and cancer, he lived for the remainder of his life in St Petersburg and Moscow. The decade 1812–22 marks the peak of his career as both composer and pianist.

Field was one of the leading and most influential pianists of his time. He developed an intimate and expressive style of playing most evident in his nocturnes, a form invented by him and subsequently developed by Chopin. His compositions also include seven piano concertos and numerous rondos, variations, and other shorter pieces for solo piano.

Reading

Piggott, P., *The Life and Music of John Field 1782–1837* (London: Faber, 1973).

BARRA BOYDELL

film The first screening of a film in Ireland took place in 1896 at Dan Lowrey's Star of Erin Music Hall, Dublin; the first filmed images of Ireland were shown the following year; and Louis de Clerq produced the first Irish documentary, *Life on the Great Southern and Western Railway*, in 1904. *Irish Wives and English Husbands* (1907) was the first fiction film made in Ireland; its subject matter was Irish and its star, Kate O'Connor, came from Killarney, but its producer, Arthur Melbourne-Cooper, owner of the Alpha Picture Company, London, was English –

was it then an *Irish* film? Cast, crew, subject matter, location, financing: the question of what particular combination of elements constitutes an Irish film is still debatable in the multinational world of contemporary movie-making.

Irish-Canadian Sidney Olcott's adaptations in 1911 of Dion Boucicault's nineteenth-century plays *The Colleen Bawn* (itself an adaptation of Gerald Griffin's 1829 novel *The Collegians*) and *Arrah na Pogue* anticipated numerous subsequent interweavings of literature and film in Ireland. The Volta, Ireland's first permanent cinema, was opened in Dublin in 1909 by James Joyce, the Abbey Players frequently featured in Irish films, and playwrights like Lennox Robinson and Denis Johnston also felt the lure of the screen. The work of Irish writers such as Eibhlín Dhubh Ní Chonaill, William Carleton, Charles Kickham, J.M. Synge, Sean O'Casey, James Joyce and many others has been adapted for the screen by native and non-native directors.

The indigenous film industry has had a chequered history: pre-independence native films formed a silver if not golden age, but financial problems, political pressures and work practices disadvantageous to native talent prevented Ardmore Studios from becoming the centre of a national film industry in the 1960s. Recent critical work (such as *Cinema and Ireland*) has analysed the economic political and cultural reasons for the varying fortunes of the Irish film as well as the construction of cultural identity and perpetuation of national stereotypes in both Irish and Irish-related films.

The opening in 1992 of the archive at the Irish Film Institute facilitates the preservation of the past, while the maintenance of tax incentives has encouraged directors to film their screen plays in Ireland. The re-establishment of the Irish Film Board in 1993 has led to a considerable increase in the number of film projects receiving initial funding, thereby ensuring a future for new native talent to follow award-winning writer-directors like Neil Jordan, Jim Sheridan,

Thaddeus O'Sullivan, Bob Quinn, Pat Murphy, Pat O'Connor and Joe Comerford. Beginning with the critical success of Sheridan's *My Left Foot* in 1989, Irish films throughout the 1990s – from *The Field* (1990) to *The Butcher Boy* (1997) – have attested to a vigorous and challenging new Irish cinema.

Reading

Curran, Joseph M., *Hibernian Green on the Silver Screen: The Irish and American Movies* (London: Greenwood Press, 1989).

Gibbons, Luke, 'Romanticism in Ruins: Developments in Recent Irish Cinema', *Irish Review*, 2 (1987).

Kearney, Richard, 'Nationalism and Irish Cinema', in *Transitions: Narratives in Modern Irish Culture* (Manchester: Manchester University Press, 1988).

McIlroy, Brian, *World Cinema 4: Ireland* (Trowbridge: Flicks Books, 1989).

O'Connor, Barbara, 'Aspects of Representation of Women in Irish Film', *Crane Bag*, 8, no. 2 (1984).

Rockett, Kevin, Gibbons, Luke and Hill, John, *Cinema and Ireland*, 2nd edn (London: Croom Helm, 1988; first pub. 1987).

Slide, Anthony, *The Cinema and Ireland* (London: McFarland, 1988).

RICHARD HASLAM

fisheries Archaeological evidence shows that Ireland's earliest inhabitants were fish-eaters. Successive waves of settlers brought more fish catchers and better techniques, till late medieval Ireland became a prolific exporter of fish to most of Western Europe. Indeed greed to acquire the Irish fishing grounds and expel Continental fishermen sharing them with the natives was one motive behind the long, piecemeal English conquest of Ireland in the sixteenth century. After the definitive English occupation things were made difficult for the native fisheries: English fishermen came to fish Irish waters and the right to export fish was let to foreign governments. Nevertheless, Irish fishing communities obstinately survived, and there were periods,

as in the late seventeenth and late eighteenth centuries, when exports flourished.

During most of the nineteenth century, though there was a large fishing population, conditions were primitive, distribution difficult, and fishing communities despised and impoverished. The foundation at Baltimore in 1887 of Europe's first fishery school and intensive fishery research by the Royal Dublin Society heralded a remarkable revival. This ended with the establishment of the separate Irish state. In 1937 the fish catch fell to 10,000 tons, less than half what was exported a quarter of a century earlier.

Only in the 1960s, thanks to the persistence of the fishermen themselves and the pressure of public opinion, did a modern industry develop that quadrupled the annual catch in 30 years to 240,000 tons, contributing more to the national income yearly than the fishing industry of any EC country save Denmark.

Reading

Figueras, O.L. (ed.), *Local Boats*, Fourth International Symposium on Boat and Ship Archaeology, BAR International Series 438, i.

Ireland, J. de Courcy, *Ireland's Sea Fisheries: A History* (Dun Laoghaire: Glendale Press, 1981).

——*An Analysis of the History of Fish Exportation from Ireland* (Madrid: Comision Espanola de Historia Maritima, 1990).

McCaughlan, M., *Ethnology and Irish Boatbuilding Tradition* (Oxford).

JOHN DE COURCY IRELAND

FitzGerald family Dukes of Leinster. James FitzGerald, twentieth earl of Kildare, became the first duke of Leinster in 1766. He was the father of Lord Edward FitzGerald (see below). It was the nineteenth earl who bought back in 1739 the lands and house of Carton, Maynooth, County Kildare, to make it his principal residence, employing Richard Castle to enlarge the house. Various improvements were carried out to the house and demesne up to the end of the nineteenth century. However, further misfortunes fell on the family, with the sixth duke dying young and unmarried and the seventh duke, his younger brother (having, as a young man, signed away his expected inheritance for an annuity), could not afford to live in the family home. It was sold out of the family in 1949. The house has been in the care of a charitable trust for some years and is undergoing renovation as a national amenity.

Lord Edward Fitz Gerald (1763–98), fifth son of the duke of Leinster, inherited a legacy of active family rebellion against England in Tudor times. A military education led to distinguished conduct with the 19th Regiment during the American War of Independence. After his election as MP for Athy he went to Paris to witness the birth pangs of the Republic in 1792, lodging with Thomas Paine. During a meeting in Whites Hotel, Lord Edward publicly denounced hereditary titles and feudal distinctions, an outburst which led to his dismissal from the army. While residing in France he met and married Pamela de Genlis (1776?–1831), adopted but allegedly natural daughter of Madame de Genlis by the Duke of Orleans. Pamela, however, on a visit to England in 1791 had already agreed to marry the playwright and notorious philanderer Sheridan, whose recently deceased wife Elizabeth it is said she resembled. Perhaps it was this resemblance which also attracted Edward, for he had been Elizabeth's lover, and was rumoured to have fathered her last child. However, it was as director of military affairs of the United Irishmen that Lord Edward took his place as the quintessential Irish romantic hero and martyr, full of ardent candour and impulsiveness. After escaping arrest during 1798, he remained underground in Dublin for over a month, choosing to lead the insurrection rather than escape to France. After twice visiting his wife incognito, he was caught and fatally wounded, thus contributing another 'great might have been' to Irish history.

MÁIRE MACCONGHAIL AND
TREVOR BUTTERWORTH

FitzGerald, Lady Eleanor (c.1548–1638) Countess of Desmond. Born Kiltinan Castle, County Tipperary; died Sligo. Eleanor was the second daughter of Edmund Butler, Lord Baron of Dunboyne. Her life was overshadowed by the Desmond–Ormond feud and the Desmond Rebellions.

In 1564, she became the second wife of the 15th Earl of Desmond, Garnet FitzGerald. Following the first Desmond Rebellion, Eleanor struggled to help Garnet accept the Tudor monarch's plans of modernization and reformation. She counselled caution and diplomacy. She even pleaded with the queen. However, she failed to prevent the second Desmond Rebellion (1579–82), which led to the confiscation of the Desmond estates by the crown, and left Eleanor a widow and virtual pauper until she secured a pension from the crown in 1587. She later married Sir Donagh O'Conner of Sligo.

RACHEL FURMSTON

Fitzgerald, George Francis (1851–1901) Physicist. Born Monkstown. Educated by private tutors, Fitzgerald entered Trinity College, Dublin, at the age of 16 and went on to become one its leading characters towards the end of the century. He was the guiding spirit of the Maxwellians, an 'invisible college' of leading physicists (Lodge, Larmor, Heaviside, Hertz, etc.) who developed and applied Maxwell's electromagnetic theory. The 1887 experiment of Hertz, demonstrating the generation of electromagnetic waves, was foreseen by Fitzgerald some years earlier and brilliantly interpreted by him in a speech to the British Association meeting of 1888 ('We have snatched the thunderbolt from Jove himself, and enslaved the all-pervading ether'). Of his many fertile speculations on fundamental physics, that which is most remembered is the suggestion that a body must contract in the direction of its motion, in order to explain the result of the Michelson–Morley experiment. This 'Fitzgerald Contraction' is now enshrined in Einstein's theory of relativity.

He was passionately devoted to the application of science, and was the first in the British Isles to fly the Lilienthal glider. Frustrated with public policy in education at all levels, he devoted himself increasingly to its reform in his later years. In doing so, he may have driven himself too hard: like James Clerk Maxwell, in whose footsteps he followed, he just failed to survive a half century. He was remembered as 'a good man if ever there was one', 'the idol of the undergraduates and hope of the older men', and one of the greatest scientists that Ireland has ever produced.

Reading

Bell, John, 'George Francis Fitzgerald', *Physics World* (September 1992), pp. 31–5

Hunt, Bruce J., '*The Maxwellians*' (Ithaca NY: Cornell University Press, 1991).

Larmor, James (ed.), *The Scientific Writings of the late George Francis Fitzgerald* (Dublin: Hodges and Figgis, 1902).

DENIS L. WEAIRE

FitzGerald, Mary (1956–) Painter. Born Dublin. Fitzgerald trained in sculpture at the National College of Art and Design (1973–7). On graduation, she studied for two years in Japan; the minimalism implicit in Japanese design, and Japanese spatial organization, especially in architecture, have remained important to her. Her work is concerned with using the language of abstraction to respond to specific personal events. In formal terms she uses colour, abstract shapes and varying gestural marks to explore ambiguities of space. From 1989–91 her work became more sculptural, with materials such as wire, perspex or glass, plaster, bolts and pins applied to the canvas.

FELICITY WOOLF

Fitzgibbon, John (1749–1802) Lord chancellor. Born near Donnybrook. Fitzgibbon was educated at Trinity College, Dublin, and Oxford. In 1772 he was called to the Irish bar and also commenced his political career. Initially his rise in power and appointment as attorney general were welcomed by would-be reformers, but soon his violent opposition to Catholic emancipation and his staunch support for the government caused Grattan to campaign, unsuccessfully, for his removal. In 1789 Fitzgibbon was made lord chancellor and remained so until his death. In 1793 he was made viscount Fitzgibbon and in 1795 the earl of Clare.

Fitzgibbon was among the first to promote the idea of a Union and from 1793 he was secretly urging the plan on Pitt. Lecky gave him the title of 'the great father of the Union'. His disgust for the ignorance and barbarity, as he saw it, of the Irish was reciprocated, and his funeral procession was jeered and insulted by the mob. Peversely, he also held a reputation for kindness and would criticize other, less humane, landlords.

LUCINDA THOMSON

Fitzmaurice, George (1877–1963) Playwright. Born Bedford House, near Listowel, 28 January, to a Protestant clergyman, George, and his wife, Winifred O'Connor, a Catholic; died Dublin, 12 May. His parents' mixed marriage alienated the clergyman from his landlord family and George junior, one of 12 children, grew up poorly educated and quite eccentric. Yet he obviously absorbed the richness of language and wildness of imagination of the locality, because his plays, written for the Abbey Theatre, while reminiscent of J.M. Synge anticipated John B. Keane in their style, characterization and use of fantasy. *The Country Dressmaker* (1907), his first success, was followed by *The Pie Dish* (1908) and *The Magic Glasses* (1913), but the Abbey rejected *The Dandy Dolls*, now regarded as among Fitzmaurice's strangest and most original folk plays. His work was rediscovered by Austin Clarke in the 1940s, and since then his reputation has slowly grown.

Reading

Gelderman, Carol W., *George Fitzmaurice* (Boston: Twayne, 1979).

McGuinness, Arthur E., *George Fitzmaurice* (Lewisburg: Bucknell University Press, 1975).
Slaughter, Howard K., *George Fitzmaurice and his Enchanted Land* (Dublin: Dolmen, 1972).

C. MURRAY

Fitzwilliam estate The massive Fitzwilliam (earlier Rockingham, Wentworth and Strafford) estate in south Wicklow was a model showpiece of Irish landlordism. The estate was organized in the seventeenth century on exclusively Protestant lines, with its yeoman farmers, estate villages, demesne, and a functioning paternalism all mimetic of English examples. With their Yorkshire home at Wentworth, the Fitzwilliams were essentially absentee landlords, but their carefully managed and flourishing Irish estate was a conscious rebuke to easy denunciations of absenteeism. Politically Whigs, the family provided the doomed lord lieutenant of 1795. The Fitzwilliam estate records are one of the most informative series for studying Irish landlordism over a period of three centuries.

KEVIN WHELAN

Flanagan, T.P. (Terence) (1929–) Painter. Born Enniskillen, County Fermanagh. Flanagan studied at Belfast College of Art and has been active as a teacher and lecturer as well as a prolific painter. His work was included in the international exhibition 'ROSC: The Irish Imagination' (Dublin, 1971) and he has had many one-man shows, North and South. He became a Royal Ulster Academician 1964 and won the academy's gold medal in 1976. Flanagan is essentially a landscapist, equally adept at oils and watercolour; his early style was spare and allusive, but then his work became more traditional and also more colourful. He has also painted abroad, principally in Italy.

BRIAN FALLON

Fleischmann, Aloys (1910–92) Composer, teacher and conductor, of German origin. Brought up in Cork (BMus 1931, MA 1932), Fleischmann then studied in Munich.

Returning to Cork in 1934 he founded the Cork Symphony Orchestra, remaining its conductor for over 40 years. He was professor of music at University College, Cork (1934–80), and in 1954 was mainly responsible for establishing the Cork International Choral Festival, of which he became director, instituting notably successful public seminars on contemporary choral music. He obtained the DMus of the National University of Ireland in 1963, was awarded an honorary MusD of Dublin University in 1964, and in 1966 was elected a member of the Royal Irish Academy. He also received the Order of Merit of the German Federal Republic. His tireless work for the betterment of music and education in Ireland, and his research work in traditional music, left him little time for composition. Nevertheless, his boundless energy resulted in a significant and individual contribution to contemporary Irish music, which was recognized by his membership of Aosdána, and which continued undiminished in his eighties.

BRIAN BOYDELL

Fleming, Thomas (1593–1666) Franciscan and archbishop of Dublin (1623–66). He was a younger son of William Fleming, sixteenth baron Slane, and spent many years as a professor of theology at Louvain. Fleming played a central role in many of the political developments in the 1640s. He attended the October 1642 convention of the Catholic Confederacy at Kilkenny, and was appointed a delegate by the confederacy to the truce negotiations of 1644, though excluded at Ormond's insistence. In 1633 he was subjected to a series of literary attacks by Paul Harris, an English secular priest of Dublin diocese, who objected to the appointment of regulars to the hierarchy.

Reading

Franciscan Fathers (eds), *Father Luke Wadding: Commemorative Volume* (Dublin: Clonmore and Reynolds, 1957).

BRIAN DONOVAN

Flood, Henry (1732–91) Statesman and orator. Flood was educated in Trinity College, Dublin, and Oxford and initially practised law in England. He returned to Ireland in 1759 and was elected MP for Kilkenny. He quickly achieved a reputation for brilliant oratory and became the main figure around which the newly conceived patriot party came to be formed. Chiefly credited with forcing the introduction of the Octennial Bill limiting the duration of Parliament, he also campaigned for the reduction of pensions, the creation of a constitutional militia and, ultimately, the independence of the Irish legislature. The only liberal reform to which he was opposed was Catholic emancipation.

By 1775 Flood had become so powerful in opposition that the government saw the need to conciliate him. He accepted the position of vice-treasurer and a seat on the Privy Council. He hoped to be an effective and independent voice within government while still holding his position in the opposition. Neither aspiration proved possible. By 1781 the government would tolerate his lack of support and constant criticism no longer and forced his resignation. In the meantime Henry Grattan had assumed the position carved out by Flood as leader of the opposition and was not prepared to relinquish it. In 1783 Flood and Grattan fought irredeemably. Disillusioned and bitter, Flood turned to English politics and was duly elected, but failed to make an impression on Westminister. In 1790 he lost his seats in both Parliaments and 'at the age when most statesman are in the zenith of their influence he sank into political impotence', according to Lecky.

A compelling speaker and tireless reformer, Flood's greatest achievement was in proving for the first time that an opposition actually could influence legislation.

Reading

Lecky, W.E.H., *Leaders of Public Opinion in Ireland*, vol. 1 (London: 1903).

LUCINDA THOMSON

Flood, W.H. Grattan (1859–1928) Music historian, organist and teacher. Born Lismore, November; died Enniscorthy, 6 August. A school music teacher and organist at Enniscorthy Cathedral from 1895 until his death, Flood's activities in the field of church music earned him an honorary doctorate from the National University (1907) and the Order of Gregory from the Vatican (1922). He is chiefly remembered for his pioneering research into the history of music in Ireland. His major work, '*A History of Irish Music*', was first published in 1905. Unfortunately his tendency to make exaggerated claims, to overlook conflicting evidence, and seldom to acknowledge his sources, many of which have since been destroyed, renders his many publications suspect.

BARRA BOYDELL

Foley, John Henry (1818–74) Sculptor. Born Dublin, 24 May; died Hampstead, 27 August. The son of an English grocer and a Irish mother, Foley studied at the Royal Dublin Society's Schools (1831–4) and then at the Royal Academy in London. While the statue of Prince Albert and that of the group 'Asia' for the Albert Memorial in Hyde Park (1860) is his most famous work, he produced many statues of Irish significance: the O'Connell Monument in Dublin (1866–74), Burke and Goldsmith (Trinity College, Dublin, 1861–8).

Reading

Strickland, Walter, *A Dictionary of Irish Artists* (Shannon: Irish University Press, 1968).
Potterton, Homan, *The O' Connell Monument* (Ballycotton: 1973).
Turpin, John, *Dublin Historical Record*, 32 (March and June 1979).

FINTAN CULLEN

folklore The manuscript and other archive holdings of the Department of Irish Folklore at University College, Dublin, constitute the major resource for Irish folklore in the

English language. The holdings include two manuscript series: the Main Manuscripts, now amounting to 2,238 bound volumes containing in excess of one million pages (about one-quarter of which is in English), and the Schools' Manuscripts Collection, only slightly less extensive (about two-thirds of which is in English). There are also collections of sound recordings (on gramophone discs and audio tape, comprising many thousands of hours), photographs (about 40,000 in all), a substantial number of films and video tapes, and a variety of plans, sketches, diagrams and other pictorial representations of the visual aspects of tradition. The Department of Irish Folklore also boasts a specialist library of some 40,000 printed books, pamphlets and periodicals pertaining to Irish and comparative folklore and related fields, in which the vast bulk of publications on Irish folklore in English may be found.

The National Museum of Ireland houses large collections of artifacts and objects representative of multifarious aspects of folk life in Ireland in the past, together with numerous drawings, sketches, etc. and extensive photographic and film collections. In similar fashion, but with the addition of outdoor displays featuring relocated buildings, the Ulster Folk and Transport Museum at Cultra near Hollywood, County Down, concentrates on material folk culture, in this instance with particular reference to the northern third or so of the island of Ireland. The latter institution has library facilities for the study of Irish folk tradition, and is also a repository for manuscript and sound collections covering much the same ground as the collections held by the Department of Irish Folklore, though not as extensive.

Folklore materials and the study of them form the subject matter of two journals, the bilingual *Béaloideas* (Journal of the Folklore of Ireland Society) and *Ulster Folklife* (published by the Ulster Folk and Transport Museum), while the Folklore of Ireland Council (University College, Dublin) publishes Folklore Studies, a bilingual series which includes pamphlets as well as cassettes of folk music and folk narrative recordings. Included in this series are translations from classic collections in the Irish language, such as *Seán Ó Conaill's Book (Leabhar Sheáin Í Chonaill)*, which has been translated by Máire MacNeill. Excellent examples of folk narrative material translated from the Irish and drawn from the archives of the Department of Irish Folklore are also contained in *Folktales of Ireland*, *The Folklore of Ireland* and *Legends from Ireland*, all by Seán O'Sullivan (i.e. Ó Súilleabháin).

Reading

Danaher, Kevin and Lysaght, Patricia, 'A supplementary bibliography', *Béaloideas* 48–9 (1980–1), pp. 206–27.

Ó Danachair, Caoimhín, *A Bibliography of Irish Ethnology and Folk Tradition* (Cork: Mercier, 1978).

Ó Súilleabháin, S., *A Handbook of Irish Folklore* (Dublin: Educational Company of Ireland for the Folklore of Ireland Society, 1942).

—— *Folktales of Ireland* (London: Routledge and Paul, 1966).

—— *Legends from Ireland* (London: Batsford, 1977).

SÉAMUS Ó CATHÁIN

folk song in English A 'song' is a separate thing in Irish parlance: not 'music' though sung to an 'air', for 'music' is not what people sing but what they play – and singing and playing are separate things. For many centuries songs in English have been sung in Ireland, but the new language hardly took wing before the eighteenth century. It was then that native Irish songs in English – also called 'ballads' or 'come-all-ye's' without much discrimination – were beginning to outnumber borrowed songs from Britain, soon themselves to pass freely into British and also American tradition.

Early 'Anglo-Irish' songs are known today either from contemporary texts which some lucky intervention has preserved, like James Boswell's Belfast-printed song chapbooks of the 1760s, or occasionally, if they have found singers enough, from versions still sung in modern oral tradition. One of the oldest belongs to both categories: 'Skewball', a ballad about a horserace at the Curragh in 1752 and a prototype for later ballads of competitive sport. Quite a broad range of subjects and styles is represented by the small number of early texts preserved. It was a formative period in the use of a new language and in its special use for singing. Some songs took their inspiration, rather abstemiously, from cross-Channel lyrical and often narrative models. It is remarkable with what idiomatic propriety and how little apparent Gaelic flavour the Gaelic poet Eoghan Rua Ó Súilleabháin managed to celebrate in English an English naval victory of 1782 ('Rodney's Glory'). But there was plenty of room for other songs to mingle notions of culture, idiom and nationality. One Scots ballad (the 'Lass of Roch Royal') printed on London sheets in the 1790s had already been 'Hibernicized' from a sojourn in Ireland: the 'Lass of Aughrim'. Naturally the poetic skills and styles of Irish could leave a deep impression on Anglo–Irish songs, which thus turned out ornate or intricate in form, lyrically profuse or linguistically extravagant, ambiguous in meaning, or all these things at once. Though the old British narrative ballads were taken up eagerly, sequential narrative was not specially favoured in native song, and many Irish songs 'about' stories need explaining: a quality for which they are found admirable rather than deficient. People still 'make' songs, subject in varying degrees to inherited conventions.

Nationality is particularly difficult to recognize in song airs, many of which are shared with Britain. Airs in AABA or similar musical form, however, tend to sound Irish (as many no doubt are), such as 'Youghal Harbour'. The major is more common than the other heptatonic melodic modes, while pentatonality is strong in Ulster, perhaps as a result of Scots settlement. Songs are traditionally sung from memory – solo without 'music' (instruments) – and are generally 'recreative', that is, made or sung to 'pass the time', which does not mean that they need not be taken seriously. Singing style is little influenced by traditions of literacy, follows verbal rhythm, and is often *molto rubato* in slow songs. In the old-style performance and environment, personal approbation is preferred to the clapping of hands.

Reading

Carolan, Nicholas, *A Short Discography of Irish Folk Music* (Dublin: Folk Music Society of Ireland, 1987).

Carson, Ciaran, *Irish Traditional Music* (Belfast: Appletree Press, 1986).

Henry, Sam (ed.), ——*'s Songs of the People*, eds Gale Huntington and Lani Herrmann, with John Moulden (Athens GA and London: University of Georgia Press, 1991).

Munnelly, Tom, 'The singing traditions of Irish travellers', *Folk Music Journal*, 3, no. 1 (1975), pp. 3–30.

Shields, Hugh (ed.), *Shamrock Rose and Thistle: Folk Singing in North Derry* (Belfast: Blackstaff, 1981).

——*A Short Bibliography of Irish Folk Song* (Dublin: Folk Music Society of Ireland, 1985).

——*Narrative Singing in Ireland: Lays, Ballads, Come-All-Ye's and Other Songs* (Dublin: Irish Academic Press, 1992).

Zimmermann, G.D., *Songs of Irish Rebellion* (Dublin: Hodges Figgis, 1967).

HUGH SHIELDS

Ford, Michael (d. 1765) Mezzotint engraver. Died Dublin, 6 March. The son of an archdeacon of Derry, Ford studied with the artist Michael Mitchell in Dublin and is thought to have travelled and studied in London, France and Italy. From 1742 he worked and lived in Dublin where he taught drawing, produced reproduction prints and was also involved in publishing. He is thought to have learnt the art of mezzotint from Arthur Miller. His prints consist of reproductions of both contemporary portraits and historical figures such as Cromwell and William III.

Reading

Alexander, David, *Quarterly Bulletin of the Irish Georgian Society*, XVI (July–Sep. 1973).
Strickland, Walter, *A Dictionary of Irish Artists* (Shannon: Irish University Press, 1968).

FINTAN CULLEN

Forde, Samuel (1805–28) Painter. Born Cork; died there, 29 June. From a poor background, Forde did not receive any formal training until 1818 with the setting up of the Cork School of Art. Much admired for his decorative talents, he produced designs for both historical and religious subjects. David Wilkie, on visiting Cork some years after Forde's death, was full of praise for the young man's skill. He was patronized by the Cork architects Pain and Deane.

Reading

Irish Art in the 19th Century (Cork: ROSC, 1971).
Strickland, Walter, *A Dictionary of Irish Artists* (Shannon: Irish University Press, 1968).

FINTAN CULLEN

Foster, John (1740–1828) Last speaker of the Irish House of Commons. Foster was educated in Trinity College, Dublin, and called to the Irish bar in 1766. In 1761 he was elected to Parliament and embarked upon his varied and sometimes turbulent political career, which spanned 50 years. Part of a new breed of politicians who held power on merit rather than inherited position, he was relied upon by successive administrations for his grasp of economics and his support for domestic trade. He was briefly chancellor of the Exchequer from April 1784 until August 1785, when he was appointed speaker of the House of Commons. He held the position until its abolition with the Union in 1800.

On only two occasions did he adopt a non-pragmatic, highly principled stand in opposition to the government, but it is for these that he is remembered rather than the years spent in administration and economic study. In 1793 he opposed the Catholic Relief Bill, unsuccessfully and ingloriously, and in 1799 he led the opposition to the Union despite strenuous government attempts to conciliate him. His opposition to Catholic reform prevented him from approving an alliance between the anti-Unionists and the Catholic emancipationists, the one move which could conceivably have defeated the Union.

Almost uniquely among influential pre-Union politicians, he took his seat in the United Parliament and twice held the position of chancellor of the Irish Exchequer (1804–6, 1807–11). Despite his bitterness and disillusionment over the Union he was still a valuable politician, and Pitt went to considerable lengths to seduce him back into the government fold. He was created Baron Oriel of Ferrard in 1821.

Reading

Malcolmson, A.P.W., 'John Foster and the Speakership of the Irish House of Commons', *Proceedings of the Royal Irish Academy*, 72, sec. C, no. 11 (1972).
——*John Foster: The Politics of the Anglo-Irish Ascendency* (Oxford: Oxford University Press for the Institute of Irish Studies, Queen's University of Belfast).

LUCINDA THOMSON

Free Presbyterian church The first Free Presbyterian congregation was formed in 1951 when Crossgar Presbyterian church, County Down, seceded from the main Presbyterian body, accusing it of 'modernism' and hostility to old-style gospel preaching. Ian Paisley, then minister of Ravenhill Evangelical church, became the first (and so far only) moderator. In 1969 he opened his large and expensive Martyrs Memorial church in East Belfast. By 1990 there were over 50 congregations (one in the Republic). Services are a mixture of repetitive gospel preaching, extemporary prayer and jaunty hymn singing. Vehement opposition is as much to ecumenism and manifestations of modern secularism as to Catholicism.

W. HARVEY COX

The Freeman's Journal (1763–1904) A newspaper which bridged the gap between the old and the new Ireland without itself succeeding in making the transition. After 1853, when it was bought by Sir John Gray, its constitutional nationalism caught the temper of the times. It supported Parnell in the divorce controversy, but later changed sides, possibly for commercial reasons. James Joyce admired its – increasingly hesitant – anti-clericalism, and used it in *Ulysses* as a paradigm of the church–state relationship in Ireland. It was closed in 1924 by its last owner, a Dublin publican, and the title bought by William Lombard Murphy (son of the founder of the *Irish Independent*) for £24,000 to prevent it being acquired by sympathizers of Sinn Féin.

JOHN HORGAN

Freemasonry One of the oldest surviving fraternities in Ireland, with evidence for its existence dating back at least 300 years. Lodges elect officers annually and are organized on a regional basis, coming under the jurisdiction of Provincial Grand Lodges, which in turn are governed by the Grand Lodge of Ancient, Free and Accepted Masons of Ireland, based in Dublin.

The Grand Lodge was established during the 1720s and following the Grand Lodge of England is the second oldest in the world. Freemasonry flourished throughout Ireland in the eighteenth century, and several lodges were involved in the Volunteer Movement towards the end of the century. There is some evidence of Masonic involvement in the failed Rebellion of the United Irishmen in 1798.

Membership declined dramatically in Ireland during the 1820s when the papal bull of Pope Leo XII, prohibiting membership of secret societies, was published and widely enforced. One of the most famous members to have resigned from the Order at this time was Daniel O'Connell, who had represented the Grand Lodge in a court case in 1813.

Irish Freemasons, by way of emigration and colonization, have had a major influence on the fraternity world-wide, particularly in North America and Australia, and to this day there are Irish Lodges from Jamaica to New Zealand.

Reading

Crossle, P. and Lepper, J.H., *The History of the Grand Lodge of Ireland, Vol. 1* (Dublin: Lodge of Research, 1925).

Parkinson, R.E., *The History of the Grand Lodge of Ireland, Vol. 2* (Dublin: Lodge of Research, 1957).

ALEXANDRA WARD

French, Nicholas (1604–78) Catholic bishop of Ferns (1645–78). French played a prominent role on the Supreme Council of the Catholic Confederacy, and was a principal supporter of the papal nuncio Rinuccini. His support for the nuncio ended in 1648 when he supported the peace treaty concluded with the marquis of Ormond. Two years later he returned to Rinuccini's camp and signed the declaration of Jamestown condemning Ormond. In 1651, he left Ireland to solicit support from the duke of Lorraine. Not only did his mission fail, but he never returned to Ireland. While in Ireland, and later on the continent, he wrote numerous tracts on Irish affairs. His famous *Narrative of the Sale and Settlement of Ireland* (1668) was an indictment of the Acts of Settlement, written from the viewpoint of a Protestant gentleman. His hatred of Ormond never waned, and his last published work was a vicious attack on Ormond entitled *The Unkinde Desertor of Loyall Men and True Frinds* (1676).

Reading

Bindon, S.H. (ed.), *The Historical Works of Nicholas French*, 2 vols (Dublin: 1846).

Corish, P.J. 'Bishop Nicholas French and the second Ormond peace, 1648–9, *Irish Historical Studies*, vi (1948), pp. 83–100.

——'Two centuries of Catholicism in Co. Wexford', in K. Whelan (ed.), *Wexford: History and Society* (Dublin: 1987).

BRIAN DONOVAN

French Revolution Wolfe Tone described the French Revolution as 'the morning star of liberty' in Ireland. That star dawned in a peculiarly Irish constellation of political interests, against a background sky darkened for reformers by sharpening awareness that the vaunted 1782 settlement had produced merely the illusion of independence, while effectively copper-fastening the corrupt English connection. The stumbling block was the admission of Catholics to the political nation; the reform movement had bifurcated at this rock and the divided streams of reform increasingly diverged as the heady tide of early enthusiasm receded, exposing a barren political landscape as the decade subsided to a sullen end.

The instantaneous impact of the French Revolution was to break the sectarian gridlock of Irish politics, immobilized by the intransigent Protestant conviction that Catholics were inherently *incapaces libertatis* (incapable of liberty). The revolution provided the thrilling spectacle to reform-minded Protestants of French Catholics dismantling the *ancien régime* equation between popery, despotism and political slavery. The Irish implication was obvious; if French Catholics could display such political maturity, so too could Irish Catholics. Almost overnight, the political moulds of a century shattered; the French Revolution cleared a space amidst the debris of discarded certainties which could be occupied by a new, non-sectarian political movement. Tone's enormously successful pamphlet '*An argument on behalf of the Catholics of Ireland*' (1791) was written explicitly to persuade moderate Presbyterian opinion that the French lesson showed that the popish leopard could indeed shed its spots. The perceived decline of popery and its protective *ancien régime* shell was a necessary precursor to Presbyterian radicals making common cause with Catholics. It was at the flamboyant Belfast demonstration in July 1791, celebrating the fall of the Bastille, that plans were laid for the creation of the United Irishmen, who were to be the protagonists in Ireland of the French principles of liberty, equality and fraternity. Henceforth, attitudes to the French Revolution became the test of one's politics, with pros ('democrats') and antis ('aristocrats') polarizing on increasingly adversarial lines.

While for radicals, the French Revolution represented the triumph of Enlightenment principles, the victory of the future over the past, for conservatives it was a nightmarish assault on the principles of civilization itself. Burke's *Reflections* was an emotional assault on the concept that society could escape the gravities of their traditions, the conservative force-field of custom and precedent. His polemic was answered by Paine's *Rights of Man*, a defence of 'the swinish multitude', and the single most popular book in eighteenth-century Irish history. Paine's all too accessible arguments horrified previously unlikely bedfellows – the Dublin Castle establishment and the Catholic episcopacy, haunted by a vision of their congregations moving beyond their control, and being infected through Paine's poison with the French disease. This novel conjuncture led to the establishment in 1795 of Maynooth College as a deliberate counter-revolutionary ploy.

Outside the realm of high politics, the impact of the French Revolution stiffened the political stance of the hitherto ideologically invertebrate Defender organization. It also reignited the dormant fuse of millenarianism, sparking an eschotological effervescence in which the *Book of Revelations* was scoured for proleptic correspondences with the French Revolution. By the mid-1790s, as the revolution hurtled towards the *dérapage* of the Terror, as France itself began to explore the idea of exporting the revolution, and as the British and French states locked horns in the first modern (i.e. ideological) war, Ireland's situation *vis-à-vis* the revolution became critical. As British perceptions of Ireland's receptivity to French ideas (or even armies) increased, the Irish state moved to a war footing which involved massive doses of repression. The assault on the radicals drained the heady optimism of the early days of the revolution, and the United Irishmen metamorphosed into a revolutionary mass movement which looked to France for ideological and practical sustenance. The stage was now set for the gothic horrors of the late 1790s. The Irish window of opportunity opened by the French Revolution was forcibly closed. In the aftermath of 1798 and its rancorous polemics which peddled sectarian glosses, and given the changing international fortunes of 'popery' after Napoleon's concordat with the pope, the United Irish moment passed and croppies were forced to lie down. Despite its initial optimistic auspices, the French Revolution ushered in a phase of closure, not of opening, in Irish political life.

KEVIN WHELAN

Friel, Brian (1929–) Best-known Irish playwright of his generation. Friel was born in Omagh, County Tyrone, and reared from the age of 10 in Derry city. He was educated at Maynooth College and St Joseph's Teacher Training College, Belfast. Before becoming a professional writer in 1960, Friel taught at secondary level in Derry for 10 years. His early success came from short stories, many of which first appeared in the *New Yorker*. A period spent with the dramaturge Tyrone Guthrie in Minneapolis in 1963 proved a turning point, the most immediate product of which was one of his best-known international successes, *Philadelphia, Here I Come!* (1964).

The evolution of Friel's career from the early short stories to the plays of the 1970s and 1980s is an exemplary instance of the relationship between continuity and change in Irish writing since World War II. Friel's stories, set in his native north-west of Ireland, are written in the understated pastoral mode typical of Irish short fiction at mid-century. The plays draw on the same cultural landscape, but the imaginative ethos has been radicalized so that the material is a basis for critique, diagnosis and mythification. In the stories, community mores overpower individuality. For the plays' protagonists, empowerment is the problematical issue. Conflicts of empowerment are most comprehensively enacted in *The Freedom of the City* (1973), *Volunteers* (1975) and *Translations* (1980). These plays also present culture as a dialogue between individuals, communities and history, a thematic nexus also addressed in the popular successes *Aristocrats* (1979) and *Dancing at Lughnasa* (1990 which was made into a film in the late nineties).

As well as consistently seeking to enlarge its thematic scope, Friel's theatre – which has continued with *Wonderful Tennessee* (1993) and *Molly Sweeney* (1995) – is notable for its dramaturgical inventiveness. This commitment to formal innovation is expressive of Friel's sympathetic though persistent interrogation of the linguistic, historical and communal codes by which communities are sustained.

GEORGE O'BRIEN

Frömel, Gerda (1931–75) Sculptor. Born Schonberg, Czechoslovakia. Frömel studied in Stuttgart, Darmstadt and Munich before settling in Ireland in 1956. She died tragically, rescuing one of her children while swimming off a west-of-Ireland beach. She was influenced by Giacometti, Lehmbruck and Brancusi, but evolved her own delicate, ultra-sensitive style in which low modelling is a distinctive feature. She worked in bronze, stone and alabaster, as well as carrying out some large-scale commissions in steel (Carrolls Building, Dundalk) which are less personal and characterful. The most gifted sculptor of her generation in Ireland, and a woman of striking beauty and intelligence, she died just when her talents had come to full strength.

BRIAN FALLON

Froude–Lecky debate James Anthony Froude's *The English in Ireland in the Eighteenth Century* (3 vols, 1872–74) sparked off one of the most intensive controversies about the interpretation of Irish history and its significance for Irish politics. Froude's work was inspired by the conviction that the Irish were incapable of governing themselves. The flaws in the Irish character, according to Froude, were exacerbated by Catholicism, demagogues, unruliness and political failure. He believed that the English, whose duty it was to rule Ireland, had failed in that duty because of the policy of treating the Irish as equals. Froude drew down upon his head severe strictures from several Irish writers, of whom the most rational and scholarly was W.E.H. Lecky. Lecky's review (*Macmillan's Magazine*, January 1873, June 1874) criticized Froude's book as mischievous and misleading. He rejected its imperialist, anti-liberal, anti-democratic tone as well as its one-sidedness in dealing with historical evidence. Lecky's own volumes were directed largely towards providing a corrective to Froude. The refutation of Froude and the defence of the Irish character and of the eighteenth-century Irish parliament won Lecky the applause of nationalists and the extensive employment of his work in the campaign for home rule.

Reading

Dunn, W.H., *James Anthony Froude: A Biography 1818–1856* (Oxford: Clarendon Pess, 1961).

McCartney, Donal, 'James Anthony Froude and Ireland: a historiographical controversy of the nineteeth century', in T.D. Williams (ed.), *Historical Studies VIII* (Dublin: Gill and Macmillan, 1971).

Wyatt, Anne, 'Froude, Lecky and the humblest Irishman', *Irish Historical Studies*, xix, no. 75 (March 1975).

DONAL MCCARTNEY

G

Gaelic Athletic Association Founded by Michael Cusack and Dr. Croke, archbishop of Cashel, in 1884 to promote Irish national field sports, especially Gaelic football and hurling. These two games and also camogie, a version of hurling for girls, and handball were promoted nationwide from the last decade of the nineteenth century in preference to association and Rugby football, which were considered to be British in origin and consequently not acceptable to cultural nationalism.

Gaelic football and hurling as Irish pastimes have their origins in the countryside as popular parish games; of the two hurling is by far the older, figuring in the hero literature of the Gaelic language. Both games are played on rectangular, zoned, regulation-sized fields, with each team of 15 having a goalkeeper, six defenders, six in attack and two at midfield. Each player has a hurley, a bossed curved stick; the ball is three inches in diameter and has a ridged covering. The scoring system in both hurling and football involves a goal when the ball is placed in the net and a point when it is sent over the crossbar; one goal equals three points.

The all-Ireland championships are based upon county teams competing in provincial deciders and the finals held in September. The association's headquarters are at Croke Park in Dublin, where the annual finals attract over 70,000 spectators.

Gaelic football is played in all parts of the island, while hurling is located mainly in the south and south-east; handball is played in a walled court, in either singles of doubles format.

SEAMUS O'BUACHALLA

Gaelic, decline of as a spoken language – From the Middle Ages onwards English was the main spoken language of Dublin and most of the principal towns in Ireland, although these towns continued to contain many Gaelic speakers. It was also the language of some areas of settlement outside the towns in south-east Wexford, in the Pale area around Dublin, and, from the early seventeenth century onwards, in parts of Ulster settled from Scotland and England. Gaelic remained, however, the language of the vast majority of the population up to and during the seventeenth century.

During the eighteenth century, however, English spread outwards from the limited areas where it had previously been the principal language. By the 1770s Gaelic appears to have been spoken by only a minority of the younger generation in most of the eastern half of the island, subject to several exceptions. These exceptions were a Gaelic-speaking area stretching eastward from Granard in County Longford to the Irish Sea, and from Armagh to Navan, as well as, further south, most of Kilkenny and of the neighbouring counties of Waterford and Tipperary.

In the area west of the Shannon, and in Donegal except for some lowland areas in the hinterland of Derry, Gaelic was still spoken by the vast majority of the population at that time, and this was also true of almost the entire province of Munster. There were, however, some areas in Cork and around Limerick, as well as in the northern part of Tipperary, where English had by then made some inroads even in rural areas.

However, by the time of the Famine three-quarters of a century later Gaelic had ceased to be the principal language in any part of Ulster or Leinster save for west and north Donegal and isolated areas in Tyrone, the Cooley Peninsula, south Monaghan and south Kilkenny, and was spoken only by a minority of the younger generation in most of Tipperary and in north-east Limerick. It was, moreover, losing ground along the west bank of the Shannon in much of east Clare, south-east Galway, east Roscommon and south Leitrim. However, throughout south and west Munster, the greater part of Connacht and west Donegal, it was still spoken by the majority of the rising generation, although English was already making visible inroads in areas around ports such as Tralee, Galway, Westport and Sligo.

It was during the quarter of a century after the Famine that a further rapid spread of English isolated the four areas within which Gaelic survived, that is, south Kilkenny/west Waterford, west Cork/south Kerry, an area running from north Clare to north Mayo, and west Donegal. By 1870 the language continued to be spoken by a majority of the younger generation outside these regions only in a couple of isolated areas of mid-Tyrone, south Armagh/north-east Louth, and perhaps the Glens of Antrim – but during the

first half of the twentieth century it disappeared completely in these latter areas.

With the effective isolation of Gaelic-speaking in diminishing areas within the four regions mentioned above (which were later denominated as 'Gaeltacht' areas), a process of decline ensued as a result of which towards the close of the twentieth century Gaelic was the native language only of some tens of thousands of people in the four areas mentioned above.

Over the last century the decline of Gaelic as a native language was, however, accompanied by a move to revive the language throughout the educational system and the public service. As a result of this process some 30 per cent of the population of the Irish state reply positively to Census questions on Gaelic-speaking.

GARRET FITZGERALD

Gaelic society in the early modern period

The so-called 'Gaelic revival' of the fourteenth century had created in Ireland a society and culture which included both the Gaedhel and the Gall, the ruling elites of Anglo-Norman origin. Although it retained many archaic institutions – such as the role of the *fileadha* or poets, hereditary writers of praise-poems to lords – this society had absorbed many outside influences, not only from the former Anglo-Norman colony. The native practices of easy divorce and 'serial marriage', while they continued virtually unchanged, had come to be accommodated within a canon law framework of annulments, while – again under canon law influence – the native system of bride-price had given way to a typically Mediterranean system of dowry. The native Irish costume of the late sixteenth century – the object of hostile legislation by the English conquerors – seems to have been largely derived from the Western European costume of a century earlier.

The economic structure of late Gaelic Ireland was predominantly pastoral, based upon cattle rather than tillage, and cow-hides formed the most important element in Irish exports. With this pastoral economy went a great deal of mobility, the herds being moved not only on a seasonal basis from lowlands to uplands, where this was possible, but also from one district to another to escape local wars and disorders, or to make use of temporarily unoccupied grazings. Mobility was also encouraged by the practice of shifting the shares held by members of landholding lineages, in some areas even on a yearly basis. In keeping with this mobility, Irish dwellings – even those of persons of importance – tended to be flimsy and insubstantial, though a more permanent element was increasingly being provided by the spread of stone tower-houses or 'castles', a development which, however, had hardly reached Ulster by the close of the sixteenth century. Politically, the country was divided into a multitude of local lordships, the larger struggling for hegemony but always constrained by coalitions of hostile neighbours, the smaller seeking to assert the maximum degree of autonomy. All suffered from the same basic weaknesses, the defective mechanisms of succession, which, coupled with the proliferation of the ruling lineages and the principle of 'segmental opposition' by which the members out of power will unite against the actual ruler, led to constant unrest and revolts against the ruling lords. By the early sixteenth century, increasing lineage proliferation had led to a state of crisis in most Irish lordships, many of which had been divided between rival factions. In consequence of the growing secularization of the church, as its offices and revenues were taken over by the members of the dominant lineages, its traditional immunities were being increasingly violated, and a general economic decline and increase in disorder seem to be evident everywhere even before the start of the English reconquest.

Upon this, from 1534 onwards, there was imposed an English reconquest which, although always containing an element of conciliation, was committed not only to the imposition of the centralized English system of administration, which had no place (except as a temporary expedient) for indirect rule through local lords, but also (in contrast to contemporary English policy in Wales) to the elimination of native culture. It was enforced by a ruthless military policy, locally directed by unscrupulous adventurers, and the effect of English intervention was thus to bring not peace but further violence to a society already suffering from an excess of it. Some elements of traditional Gaelic society, such as the brehons or lawyers, found it easy to accommodate to English rule; others, like the poets, were targets of its particular hostility, though the execution of this policy was less thorough or efficient than has been sometimes supposed.

A further and in the event far more lasting condition of conflict was created by the fact that, owing to the virtual absence of native Reformers, and the consequent association of the Reformed doctrines with the intruding English, the people of Ireland had by the 1580s been drawn irreversibly into the Counter-Reformation camp. By the early years of the seventeenth century, while a new literary movement, typified by such as Geoffrey Keating (Seathrún Céitinn) was seeking both to reconcile traditional Gaelic learning with the New Learning of the Renaissance, and to provide a historiography which would explicitly unite Gaedhel and Gall in a single Irish nation whose bonding factor would be devotion to Counter-Reformation Catholicism, that same religious identity was merging them with the equally fervent Catholic 'Old English' of the Pale and the towns.

The early seventeenth century saw a rapid anglicization of the Gaelic elites, an approximation, however, not to the model provided by contemporary England but to that provided by the Old English. At the same time the period of peace which ensued after 1603 saw a rapid growth of population and so a movement of the rural economy to a more typically European model; of tillage and permanent settlement. It was the confiscations and plantations embarked on by the Stuart government, as well as its religious repression, which ensured that this transformation of Gaelic society was not in the end to provide a basis for a peaceful future.

KENNETH NICHOLLS

Gallaher's Blues Thomas Gallaher moved his tobacco-spinning factory from Derry to Belfast in 1891, and in 1902 started manufacturing cigarettes at his York Street factory in Belfast. The range included the series Blues, Greens (both untipped) and Reds (tipped). In their distinctive large packet, Blues looked like a set of piano keys and were generally regarded as a symbol of working-class prosperity before becoming a sign of cultural authenticity. Like other Gallaher's brand names, Blues disappeared into the international combines and lost market prominence in the tar-rated 1970s.

Reading

Carson, Ciaran, *The Irish for No* (Bloodaxe, 1988).

GERALD DAWE

galleries There are some 200 art galleries in Ireland. The majority of these show Irish art, though major state institutions such as the National Gallery of Ireland, the Hugh Lane Municipal Gallery of Modern Art and the Ulster Museum have permanent collections of work which include international art. While the greatest concentration of art galleries is in Dublin, followed by Cork, Limerick and Belfast, both the Arts Council of Ireland and the Arts Council of Northern Ireland have recently developed regional policies for the arts which include galleries and art exhibitions outside the main urban centres. The Orchard Gallery in Derry has achieved an international reputation since it opened in 1978. Over the last decade the Arts Council of Ireland has had a policy of creating regional Arts Centres and, within these, the art gallery is only one of several forums for the various arts. Despite the severe financial constraint, the Belltable in Limerick, the Garter Lane in Waterford and the Triskell

in Cork, among others, have conducted active visual arts programmes.

While the two Arts Councils in Ireland are now of crucial importance in the promotion and subsidization of contemporary art, it was initially the private art galleries which provided a forum for contemporary artists and a venue for new and sometimes progressive art. The first private galleries which operated in a truly professional sense were the Waddington Gallery, Leo Smith's Dawson Street Gallery and the Hendriks Gallery, all in Dublin. During the 1950s and 1960s these galleries played a significant role in supporting a new generation of Irish artists at a time when public funding for art and artists was not well established. None of these galleries has survived, but Leo Smith's gallery became the Taylor Galleries, which remains one of the most important private galleries in Ireland. Run by John Taylor and his brothers, the Taylor now has a large stable of artists from older and mid-generation to young.

The Taylor Galleries typifies Irish private galleries in being eclectic in its choice of artists and 'type' or style of art. It is assumed that with a small market, the galleries cannot afford to build a specific identity around a particular philosophy, attitude or style. Many private galleries in Ireland are closely associated with a broadly based local market, which indicates limited opportunity for the selling of luxury, consumer items such as art. It could be argued that this exceptionally small and conservative market has inhibited the development of an avant-garde in Irish art. Outside Dublin very few private galleries have achieved national reputations, one exception being the Riverrun Gallery, which, for a short time in the late 1980s, had venues in Limerick, Dublin and Galway. Belfast has had a very small number of private galleries. Only the Tom Caldwell Gallery has survived since the IRA campaign of the 1970s, and the main Caldwell art venue is now in Dublin.

In recent years several new private galleries have opened in Dublin. The most prevalent is the Kerlin Gallery. Its origins are in Belfast, where, over a short period in the mid-1980s, the two managers of what was then the *On the Wall Gallery*, Ken Kennedy and Dave Fitzgerald, built a close working relationship with a number of young artists. Since their move to Dublin in 1988 they have consolidated their position by attracting several established artists, as well as young southern Irish artists, to their stable. The Kerlin has managed to combine established repectability with a chic, fashionable image that has attracted a 'jet-set' following.

This type of marketing is new to the Irish art world and is in stark contrast to the older, more discreet relationship between artist and dealer eptitomized by the Hendriks and Taylor Galleries. It is also in stark contrast to the only private gallery in Ireland to take a single-minded approach to the kind of art to be promoted through its gallery space. The Oliver Dowling Gallery, which opened in 1976, advanced abstract and minimal art until its demise in 1993. The line it took might be considered principled but financially naive; however, it earned respect in many quarters for its consistency and insistence on a philosophy.

The influence of private galleries on the directions of Irish art is less strong today than in the 1960s, which is due in part to developments in tertiary education, assistance through subsidized studio spaces, and the increase in public galleries. Irish artists now have greater choice in regard to their career, even while public provision is regarded as woefully inadequate compared with many other European countries. The arts centre concept began with the Project Arts Centre in Dublin in 1967, and these centres have provided the main channel of opportunity throughout the Republic for young artists to exhibit their work. In Northern Ireland, the Arts Council of Northern Ireland Gallery in Belfast has provided similar opportunities.

At the upper end of the public galleries are those which show international exhibitions, retrospectives and theme exhibitions. The Royal Hibernian Academy Gallery in Dublin is a large space associated with traditionalist art, but lacks sufficient public or private funding to maintain a coherent policy. The Douglas Hyde Gallery in Dublin has acquired a reputation for establishing younger Irish artists and for introducing to Ireland new-tendency, international work. However, the Irish Museum of Modern Art (IMMA), which opened in the buildings of the Royal Hospital Kilmainham in 1991, under its director Declan McGonagle may prove to be a considerable influence on Irish art if it is given the level of funding necessary to run an ambitious programme.

IMMA is directly financed by government. This is indicative of another shift in the infrastructure of the visual arts away from the Arts Council as the arbiter for the funding of public venues for the exhibition of art. The Arts Council of Northern Ireland is meanwhile undergoing a much more dramatic reorganization away from being a centralized body which acts as the sole arbiter for public funding and towards decentralization. Greater plurality in the type of art venue within or linked to the public sector is a pattern in recent developments. One tendency is for universities to fund their own gallery. The Douglas Hyde Gallery is a precursor in its use of a space within Trinity College, Dublin, and a notable addition is the Fenderesky Gallery, now funded through Queen's University, Belfast. However, with its small population, Ireland will continue to have a relatively centralized support system for public galleries, and it has been true since the 1960s that few private art galleries have managed to survive for long.

Crawford Municipal Art Gallery, Cork

The red-brick and limestone building which now houses the Crawford Municipal Art Gallery was erected in 1724, as the Custom House for the city of Cork. Just over a century later, the Royal Cork Institution took over the building, installing their fledgeling school of art and a large collection of classical sculpture casts. The School of Art flourished, becoming a government school of design in 1850, and a part of the South Kensington schools system some years later. The building was remodelled in 1884, through the generosity of William Horatio Crawford, and galleries were added for the display of paintings and sculptures. The municipal art collection was built up steadily, so that when the School of Art relocated to new premises in 1979, the former studios were incorporated into what was now the Crawford Municipal Art Gallery, one the finest art museums in Ireland.

The art collections at the Crawford focus on British and Irish art from the eighteenth century to the present day. There are important works by James Barry, who trained as an artist in Cork, and Daniel Maclise, one of the first students at the School of Art in 1819. A famous fellow student of Maclise's, the neo-classical sculptor John Hogan, is also well represented, augmenting the classical cast collection. There is, logically, an emphasis on Cork art and artists, although the Crawford is distinguished by its fine collection of paintings from the Newlyn School. The Harry Clarke Room features paintings and stained glass work by this notable early twentieth-century Irish artist.

Other Irish artists represented are Walter Osborne, Sean Keating, Jack B. Yeats and Mainie Jellett. Contemporary Irish artists represented include Louis le Brocquy, Robert Ballagh and Maud Cotter. Recent acquisitions include works by Michael Mulcahy, Vivienne Roche, Mary Fitzgerald and Tony O'Malley. The temporary exhibition programme at the Crawford is diverse and broadly based, bringing both international and local exhibitions to the public.

The Douglas Hyde Gallery

The Douglas Hyde Gallery, housed in the new Arts Building in Trinity College, Dublin, opened in 1978. Jointly funded by the Arts Council and (TCD), the Douglas Hyde replaced the earlier College Gallery, with which it should not be confused. Its initial exhibition policy, however, reflected the eclecticism of its forerunner, ranging from historical shows such as 'The Peasant in French 19th Century Art' and 'Harry Clarke' to exhibitions of contemporary art by Agnes Martin and Edward Kienholz.

In 1984 the gallery was re-established on a more independent basis, with a director, instead of an exhibitions officer, at its head. During the following years, the Douglas Hyde initiated an impressive series of exhibitions by younger Irish artists, including Felim Egan, Michael Mulcahy and Dorothy Cross. These were accompanied by substantial publications – an important development in the field of contemporary Irish art. The gallery also held exhibitions by international artists, some of them well established, like Roy Lichtenstein and Philip Guston, and others, such as Judith Barry and Bill Viola, on the avant-garde end of the spectrum. The decade ended with a set of retrospective group shows of recent Irish art and a major exhibition by Anselm Kiefer.

Since its inception, therefore, the Douglas Hyde Gallery has increasingly devoted its attention to contemporary art. And following the foundation of the Irish Museum of Modern Art (IMMA), this has become its deliberate policy. With other institutions – IMMA, the Hugh Lane Gallery, and the Royal Hibernian Academy Gallagher Gallery – covering a broader span of twentieth- century art, the Douglas Hyde is now focusing on the more innovative side of current art practice.

JOAN FOWLER, PETER MURRAY AND
JOHN HUTCHINSON

Galway Founded as an Anglo–Norman medieval colony-town on the remote Atlantic seaboard, to provide a law-and-order garrison and a maritime trading post for native Irish exports, much as early Roman colonies were established at the extremities of empire. The inland Irish brought their goods into the walled city; English merchants despatched them abroad; the Irish were not permitted within the walls after each day's market. It was originally an apartheid city, an oligarchy of a few families known as the 'Tribes', very nearly a city-state, committed to doing sharp business for itself and by itself; and these characteristics have continued despite huge historical changes.

There is now a growing population of upwards of 45,000; a university; and an economy dependent on multinational high-tech industry and high-class 'cultural tourism' – the latter more reliable than the former. The old walled city is still an identifiable nucleus, surrounded by nondescript spreading suburbs, but filled with antique, restored-antique and postmodern 'streetscape-friendly' architecture, bookshops, galleries, pubs, restaurants. There is (as yet) no theatre or concert hall; but there are arts festivals, film festivals, street festivals, traditional music sessions, and much spoken Gaelic from Connemara and the Aran Islands; thousands come every year to enjoy them in an upmarket atmosphere of conviviality and apparent openness. To *initiate* them is not so easy, unless you are well dug in to a local twentieth-century cultural 'tribe' and the business community will not feel slighted by your notions of artistic expression. The medieval walls have all but disappeared; psychologically they are still in place; Galway looks after its own.

Reading

Hardiman, J., *History of the Town and County of Galway* (Dublin: 1820; repr. Galway: Kenny's, 1975).
O Cearbhail, Diarmuid (ed.), *Galway, Town and Gown, 1484–1884* (Dublin: Gill and Macmillan, 1984).

JOHN ARDEN

gardens While there is little evidence for gardens on a grand scale prior to the seventeenth century, the development of pleasure gardens during the second half of that century is well attested. During the reign of Charles II the gardens at Kilkenny Castle were elaborated and embellished with waterworks by a French gardener, and there are numerous references to English gardeners being employed by improvers all over the country. Most of this work in the French and Dutch styles has disappeared and can only be glimpsed in contemporary paintings or maps. Vestiges of baroque gardens remain at Antrim Castle, County Antrim, and at Thomastown, County Tipperary. A fortunate and remarkable surviror is the garden at Kilruddery, County Wicklow, with its long twin canals set in a lawn framed with trees leading to a half-mile-long avenue of limes. To one side is a formal area of lime beech and hornbeam hedges, long known as the 'Angles'. Elsewhere there is a large round pool surrounded by 20-ft-high beech hedges and nearby a sylvan theatre – an enclosed mini-amphitheatre.

The collecting and naturalizing of exotic plants seems to have been well under way at this time. About 1600 a Waterford cleric wrote 'the Irish climate is favourable to many plants which though neglected do better in Ireland than in the Countries from which they are imported'. Sir Arthur Rawdon (1662–95) of Moira, County Down, commissioned collectors in North America and the Caribbean to send seeds and exotics. A hothouse, probably the first in the country, was built to shelter many of the imports – one shipload of trees and shrubs from Jamaica arrived at Carrickfergus in 1692. Plants from Moira were distributed to Chelsea Physic Garden and the Bishop of London at Fulham, as well as to botanic gardens at Amsterdam, Leyden, Leipzig and Uppsala.

The eighteenth-century movement away from the formal Continental styles in England was initially influenced by Alexander Pope and William Kent, who sought to contrive more natural parks. The fashion reached Ireland through Pope's friends Jonathan Swift and Patrick Delany from the 1720s onwards. The Delany garden Delville on the outskirts of Dublin started in a rather formal style, but by the 1740s, when Delany had married the highly versatile and talented

Mary Granville, the newly fashionable natural style had been fully embraced and the place was replete with temple, grotto, groves, hills, river and islands. Their relatively modest garden has disappeared, as has the great landscaped park at Dangan, County Meath, seat of the Wesley family. Mary Delany was a frequent visitor there and she chronicled the transformation of the demesne during the second quarter of the century. Temples, lakes, fortifications, obelisks and pillars were interspersed among the gentle hillocks and extensive tree plantings, making it the most remarkable undertaking of its time.

Fortunately the great demesne at Carton, County Kildare, transformed from the mid-century, is still intact. Here the duke of Leinster and his able wife made a mildly Brownian landscape with gently sloping lawns and groves centred on the River Liffey, which was widened to form a grand basin of water. About the same time the earl of Charlemont created a sublime landscape at Marino on the edge of Dublin, and while this has been swallowed up by later development, his *chef d'oeuvre*, a casino of Portland stone designed by Sir William Chambers and erected in 1762, survives (now a national monument). It is undoubtedly the most accomplished and elaborate garden belvedere in the islands of Britain and Ireland.

In 1795 the Dublin Society, which since its foundation in 1731 had done much to encourage arboriculture, established a botanic garden at Glasnevin. The place flourished and has had a major influence on horticulture, gardening and plant collecting. Throughout the nineteenth century collectors sent plants, seeds and herbarium specimens to Glasnevin, to Trinity College, Dublin, and to the Royal Botanic Gardens at Kew. The most notable of the Irish collectors was Augustine Henry (1857–1930), who explored extensively in China while employed in the Imperial Chinese customs service between 1881 and 1900.

Among Irish nurseries and plant breeders, the daffodil specialists became renowned from the 1880s. William Hortland in Cork was the most prominent of the early breeders and the tradition continued until well into the mid-twentieth century, with Richardsons of Waterford and Guy Wilson of County Antrim being the most prolific. Rose breeding, through the firms of Dickson's and McGredy (both of County Down), became synonymous with Ireland during the early and mid-twentieth century.

William Robinson (1838–1935) might justly be regarded as Ireland's most famous gardener. He moved to London in 1861 and soon gravitated to journalism. In 1871 he started the *Garden* magazine, and there and in his books he campaigned extensively against the excesses of the nineteenth-century formal style, urging that plants and gardens be treated more naturally. A number of gardens in the Robinsonian style were made from the 1880s onwards, mainly in milder parts of Ireland, where many of the newer plants arriving from Asia and the Antipodes could thrive. These gardens contrast with the elaborate nineteenth-century creations based on formal architectural lines, the most famous of which – Powerscourt, County Wicklow – still survives.

During the twentieth century the very best gardens made have sought a balance between plant collecting and a wide botonical interest combined with strong elements of design.

The principal gardens to note, all of which open on a fairly regular basis, are as follows:

1 The National Botanic Garden, Dublin, is Ireland's premier botanical and horticultural establishment. There is a fine plant collection and a range of glasshouses built by Richard Turner between 1843 and 1969. However, the hand of bureaucracy lies heavily on the place and it is in need of considerable revitilization. Open all the year.
2 Killruddery, County Wicklow, the most elaborate baroque garden to survive in Britain and Ireland has a number of nineteenth-century features.

3 Powerscourt, County Wicklow, has an elaborate series of Italianate terraces in a majestic landscape and a good arboretum.

4 Mount Osher, County Wicklow, with a mild climate and acid soil, is planted in a Robinsonian style with an important botanical collection.

5 Annesgrove, County Cork, laid out in the early years of this century, has a renowned tree and shrub collection as well as a more formal walled garden. However, the place is somewhat in decline and is in urgent need of conservation.

6 Derreen, County Kerry, is a luxuriant woodland with many fine sub-tropical plants which have naturalized there.

7 Ilnacullin, County Cork, commonly called Garimish Island, has superb formal features designed by Harold Peto in the years before World War I, clothed with a world-class collection of plants.

8 Rowallane, County Down, famous for the rhododendron collection, contains extensive rock gardens as well as a walled garden.

9 Birr, County Offaly, unlike many of the larger gardens, is on an alkaline soil in the colder midlands. Here a superb arboretum around the lake is enhanced with extensive twentieth-century planting and formal gardens.

10 Castelwellan, National Arboretum, County Down, contains an outstanding collection of woody plants.

11 Mount Stewart, County Down, regarded as the most superb garden in Ireland, is largely the creation of the late Lady Londonderry between the 1920s and the 1950s. A series of formal gardens near the house extends into the woodlands, where many tender and sub-tropical plants thrive.

12 'Mount Congreue, County Waterford' is an eighteenth-century demesne transformed over the past 60 years into an extravagant woodland garden with major collections of camellias, magnolias and rhododendrons. There are borders and walled gardens on a grand scale such as is rarely encountered today (open by appointment only).

13 Glenveagh, County Donegal, is a late nineteenth-century woodland in a wild and remote valley, enhanced and embellished with formal features and exotic planting by its late American owner, Henry McIlhenny, with the help of Lanning Roper between the 1950s and the 1970s.

14 Heywood, County Laois, is a Lutyens-designed garden worthy of note, as is his Irish National War Memorial Garden at Islandbridge, Dublin.

15 The Talbot Botanic Garden at Malahide Castle, County Dublin, is primarily of interest for the collection of plants from the southern hemisphere amassed there in the mid-twentieth century by the late Lord Talbot.

16 The John F. Kennedy Arboretum, County Wexford, is a modern scientific collection with a particularly good range of shrubs.

17 Beech Park, County Dublin, a regency walled garden, is noted for a unique range of alpines and herbaceous plants.

18 The Dillon Garden, Dublin, and Butterstream, County Meath, are two late twentieth-century gardens on a human scale acclaimed for their plant collections as well as for their contribution to garden design and style.

JIM REYNOLDS

Gardiner, Luke (1745–98) Viscount Mountjoy. Politician and urban developer. Born Dublin, 7 February. The son and heir of Charles Gardiner, a wealthy landowner and property developer in Dublin he first came to political prominence in the 1770s, following his election to represent County Dublin in 1772. Of liberal inclinations, Gardiner established himself as one of the foremost parliamentarians of the day by guiding the Catholic relief measures of 1778 and 1782 through the Irish House of Commons. He cut his liberal links in the 1780s, when the desire for a peerage became the guiding principle in his political life. He was finally elevated to the peerage as Baron Mountjoy in 1789 (he was made a viscount in 1795), and he was killed leading his regiment of militia into Battle at New Ross on 5 June 1798.

Reading

Coyle, E.A., 'County Dublin elections (1790)', *Dublin Historical Record*, 44, (1991).

Craig, Maurice, *Dublin 1660–1860: A Social and Architectural History* (Dublin: Figgis, 1969).

JAMES KELLY

Garrett, James (1817–55) Ornithologist. Born 10 December; died 2 April. Garrett's father was an eminent Belfast solicitor, his mother a niece of Samuel Neilson, well-known editor of the *Northern Star*. Although he entered his father's firm, he became interested in science, especially ornithology, and William Thompson drew on his observations of northern Irish birds for the first three volumes of his *Natural History of Ireland* (1849–51). In his will, Thompson directed that in the event of his death his manuscript relating to the remainder of his *Natural History* be handed over to Robert Patterson and James Garrett. This happened upon Thompson's death in 1852, Garrett becoming responsible for Thompson's notes on mammalia, reptiles and fishes. Garrett himself died before the fourth and final volume of the *Natural History* could be published, and Patterson, with the help of George Dickie (professor of natural history in Queen's University, Belfast), brought the work to completion in 1856.

Reading

Deane, Arthur (ed.), *Belfast Natural History and Philosophical Society 1821–1921* (Belfast: BNHPS, 1924).

Dublin Natural History Review (July 1855).

Thompson, William, *The Natural History of Ireland*, vol. IV (1856).

JOHN WILSON FOSTER

Gate Theatre The Dublin theatrical company founded in 1928 by Micheál Mac Liammóir and his partner Hilton Edwards to play a wider repertoire of modern, Continental and classic plays than was then played by the Abbey. For the first two seasons the company used the tiny Peacock Theatre at the Abbey, but in 1930 they leased the Upper Music Room in the Rotunda, Parnell Square. Though critically successful, the original company met with financial difficulties in 1931. Lord Longford agreed to become a major shareholder and subsidized the theatre from his own private means. But a falling out in 1936 led to an arrangement whereby the original partners and Longford Productions shared the theatre for six months each.

The Gate Company toured in Egypt, the Balkans, England and America over the years, and during World War II and after played some seasons at the Gaiety, a larger Dublin venue. The range of the material was widened to include reviews and panto-style entertainments. Longford productions also played a wide range of plays, but the style was less polished.

The theatre began to have difficulties after the death of Lord Longford in 1961, and was even closed for a time. The government eventually agreed to subsidize the theatre, and after refurbishing the Gate was reopened in 1971. It celebrated its golden jubilee in 1978, the year in which Mac Liammóir died. Hilton Edwards survived until 1982. Though the founders' contribution was immense, the role of Lord and Lady Longford in the theatre should not be forgotten.

The Gate still thrives: in 1991 it staged a Beckett Festival and the building itself was extended in 1993. New plays and adaptations by such Irish writers as Hugh Leonard, Frank McGuinness and Brian Friel are now played, but classic and Continental plays are not neglected. Outside of the Abbey, the Gate is perhaps the most significant theatre in Ireland.

Reading

Cowell, John, *No Profit but the Name: The Long-fords and the Gate Theatre* (Dublin: 1988).

Luke, Peter (ed.), *Enter Certain Player: Edwards – MacLiammoir and the Gate 1928–1978* (Dublin: Dolmen Press, 1978).

PETER COSTELLO

Geldof, Bob (1954–) Founder member of the Boomtown Rats, a formative band of the post-punk seventies. Shocked in 1984 by the suffering of famine victims in Ethiopia, Geldof mobilized most of Britain's pop stars as Band Aid to record *Do They Know It's Christmas*, a song co-written with Midge Ure, and for many years the best-selling UK single. This success inspired Geldof to devise a global televised charity concert. With a cast of thousands working for nothing, and incredible technical and logistical problems, Live Aid (1986) became the biggest televisual event of all time. With 2,000 million viewers, campaigns in 22 countries and Geldof's plain speaking, charity revenue was in excess of $70 million. Geldof was wary of the accusations of self-publicity, and the most important event of 1986 for him was not the Nobel prize nomination or the honorary KBE, but his marriage to longstanding partner Paula Yates. In 1992 their company won the contract to provide a breakfast television show for Channel 4 in the UK. The couple divorced in 1996.

Reading

Geldof, Bob with Vallely, Paul, *Is That it?* (London: Sidgwick and Jackson, 1986).

TREVOR BUTTERWORTH

Geminiani, Francesco (1686/7–1762) Composer and violinist. Born Lucca; died Dublin. Geminiani arrived in England in 1714. He was nominated as successor to J.S. Cousser as Master of the King's Musick in Ireland in 1728, but M. Dubourg was appointed instead. Geminiani paid visits to Dublin between 1728 and 1733, when he settled there in his 'Great Musick Room' in Spring Gardens, off Dame Street. He was back in London in 1740, paid sporadic visits to Paris 1749–55, then lived in London until he was appointed music master to Mr Coote of Cootehill, County Cavan, in 1759. He was the author of several early and important treatises on performing practice, and composer of violin sonatas and many *concerti grossi* which were frequently played in Dublin throughout the eighteenth century.

BRIAN BOYDELL

genealogy An account of a person's lineage or the investigation of pedigrees or lineages as a form of research or study.

The oral genealogical or family history tradition has always had an important place in Irish society. Early Irish society was aristocratic and was structured into many petty kingdoms. A kingdom or *tuath* consisted of a population group with a distinct political entity, and many of the important families within these petty kingdoms had their own hereditary historian and genealogist. For example, the Mac Firbhisigh (MacFirbis/Forbes) family were the hereditary genealogists and historians to the Ó Dubhda family of Connacht.

These official historians and genealogists, who, unlike their respective leaders, had an accepted legal status outside their population group, were, it can be said, responsible for the cultural, linguistic and legal unity of early Irish society. When the assimilation of the Normans with the old Irish order came about during the thirteenth and fourteenth centuries, the Irish system of succession – based on an elected leadership through membership of the *deirbhfhine*, a family group consisting of four generations – was gradually superseded by the Norman and feudal system of the right of primogeniture, and gradually a unique corpus of medieval genealogical material accrued.

Rebellions, wars and British-government-sponsored land forfeitures and plantations during the sixteenth and seventeenth centuries saw the displacement, defeat or exile of the great Irish families. This dispossession and defeat strengthened the attachment to place and thus to origin and lineage that the Irish always had. By the middle of the eighteenth century many thousands of Irish had settled on the European Continent, and their desire for written, certified arms and pedigrees as evidence of their social and family standing created and stimulated work for a small group of scholars, among whom was Roger O Feral (O Farrell). He compiled in 1708 *Linea Antiqua*, the most important surviving record of pedigrees and arms of Old Irish families, which is preserved in the Genealogical Office. However, the majority of the present-day Irish population, together with those of Irish lineage around the world, are descended from non-propertied or small tenant-farming ancestors, for whom a minimum of relevant genealogical sources prior to 1800 exists.

Much valuable primary source material was destroyed when the Four Courts, together with the Public Record Office, were blown up in June 1922 during the Civil War, but significant efforts are being made to build up repositories, both national and local, and to have the sources available to the ever-increasing number of people within and without Ireland who have an interest in Irish genealogy.

Archival and Institutional Repositories
1   *National Archives* (most frequently used genealogical sources): Census returns and Census substitutes; testamentary records.
2   *General Register Office of Ireland*: state-registered births, marriages and deaths from 1864; Church of Ireland marriages from 1845–63.
3   *National Library*: microfilm copies of most of the Catholic parish registers; index to manuscript sources for the history of Irish civilization; manuscript, printed and family paper collections.

4   *Genealogical Office*: manuscript and printed sources relating to the granting and confirming of arms and pedigrees.
5   *The Registry of Deeds*: deeds, leases, wills and marriage settlements from 1708.
6   *The Library of the Church Representative Body*: manuscript and printed sources relating to members of the Church of Ireland.

Reading

Begley, Donal F. (ed.), *Irish Genealogy – A Record Finder* (Dublin: Heraldic Artists, 1981).
Irish Manuscripts Commission publications, including its periodical *Analecta Hibernica*, no. 1 (1930); no. 34 (1987).
MacLysaght, Edward, *The Surnames of Ireland* (Dublin: Irish Academic Press, 1978).
Ryan, James G., *Irish Records – Sources for Family Local History* (Ancestry Inc./Flyleaf Press, 1988).

MÁIRE MACCONGHAIL

Geology and geomorphology The oldest rocks in Ireland are located in two principal areas, the Kilmore Quay area of Wexford and the Mullet peninsula, Mayo. The rocks are gneisses and formed at great depths within the crust, their exposure at the surface today being due to uplift and erosion. They are c.1700–1900 million years old (Ma). Although now only 350 km apart, these two regions once lay on different sides of an ocean, Mayo being connected to the American plate and Wexford to the European plate. During the Cambrian (590–530 Ma), Ordovician (530–440 Ma) and Silurian (440–400 Ma), the ocean between the two plates received vast amount of sediments due to deposition from rivers.

The ocean (Iapetus Ocean) began to close when subduction zones formed along the northern and southern margins, producing a volcanic arc from Waterford to Arklow. As the ocean diminished in size, the vast amounts of thick sediment it contained became compressed and folded during a deformational episode termed the Caledonian Orogeny.

Major thrusts and slides developed to accommodate the stress, and rocks were transported many kilometres. The intense pressure and high temperatures associated with this closure caused the sedimentary rocks originally deposited in the ocean to be converted into metamorphic rocks (Dalradian Series). Sandstones were converted into quartzite (Errigal, Sugarloaf, Croagh Patrick) and limestone into marble (Connemara marble), and schists and slates formed from fine-grained sediments. These rocks can be found in Antrim, Tyrone, Donegal and Mayo. Granites were emplaced *c*.400 Ma (e.g. Leinster, Donegal, Galway, Mournes).

The Caledonian Orogeny was a long-lived event, though by the end of the Silurian closure of the Iapetus Ocean was essentially completed. The Iapetus suture runs across Ireland in a general north-east/south-west direction from the Shannon Estuary to Navan. By the end of this orogeny, a mountain belt crossed Ireland similar to the Himalayas, which stretched north-eastwards into Scandinavia and south-westwards along the east coast of America. The complex structural relationships observed in Ireland are not easily explained by a simple two-plate collision model. As the two plates approached, it is probable that a number of island-arcs and micro-continents were caught up in the collision process, resulting in Ireland being formed of a collage of terranes.

The Devonian (400–345 Ma) sediments are markedly different from the rocks laid down during the Cambrian, Ordovician and Silurian, indicating a major change in the palaeo-environment. Erosion of the uplifted mountains resulted in deposition in lakes, rivers and coastal plain. In Kerry and Cork several thousand metres of sandstones, mudstones and conglomerates were deposited. Old Red Sandstone outcrops are generally hard, resistant rocks; thus they often form mountainous areas (Knockmealdowns/Galtee Mountains).

The Carboniferous Period (345–280 Ma) is the most important in Ireland. Many of the important ore bodies (Navan) are hosted in Carboniferous rocks, which underlie about half of Ireland. During this period Ireland was gradually submerged as the ocean, which teemed with marine organisms, transgressed northwards, until most of Ireland south of about Sligo was submerged except for some upland areas. Initially calcareous sediments were deposited, forming limestones and reefs. Later on the type of sediment began to change: muds, sand and massive amounts of vegetation were deposited in swamps and lagoons. This vegetable matter was compressed and altered to produce coal.

Following the Carboniferous, closure of an ocean to the south of Ireland resulted in the older rocks being folded. This Variscan (Hercynian) Orogeny resulted in the formation of anticlines and synclines from Kerry to Waterford. Apart from northern Ireland, sedimentary rocks younger than Lower Carboniferous are not widespread. This is due to the uplift and erosion of these rocks. However, the Tertiary basalts in north-east Ireland protected rocks from Permian-Cretaceous from erosion.

The Permian (280–225 Ma) and Triassic (225–190 Ma) periods represent an arid environment in Ireland. Sandstone and mudstones are found in County Antrim and County Down, the outcrops over the rest of Ireland being eroded away except for a few isolated outliers (Cavan/Monaghan). In the arid climate, land-locked oceans dried up, leaving evaporite deposits. Today thick deposits of salt are mined at Carrickfergus. During the Jurassic (190–136 Ma), shallow seas spread over Ireland, which had been eroded down during the Permian and Triassic, within which mudstones and shale were formed. During this period ammonites, corals, bivalves and belemnites were abundant. The remains of microscopic coccoliths were compressed to form chalk layers.

At the end of the Cretaceous (65 Ma) a world-wide extinction of dinosaurs occurred. The Tertiary Period (65–2 Ma) in north-east Ireland was characterized by major igneous activity related to the Alpine Orogeny, which is continuing today. Vast amounts of basaltic lava poured onto the land as a constructive plate margin developed in relation to the opening of the North Atlantic. The lavas were fed from central vents (Slemish) or from vertical fissures which are now filled with igneous material (dykes). Igneous activity in the rest of Ireland was minimal, though crustal movements uplifted and downwarped different regions. Extensive erosion removed many kilometres of sediments.

About 2 Ma ago the temperature began to decrease and ice sheets in high northern latitudes moved southwards. Ireland was not permanently covered by ice during this time. There were glacial and interglacial periods, the temperature during the latter often being warmer than today. Even during glacial periods major ice sheets were absent, though very cold periglacial conditions existed. Ireland was completely covered by ice during the Munsterian glaciation, though a later glacial phase (Midlandian) did not reach the south coast, its greatest extent being marked by the Tipperary–Ballylanders end moraine. Local mountain glaciers also existed at this time. Major erosional features caused by the glaciers are generally confined to the mountains (corries and U-shaped valleys), whereas on the lowlands the glaciers and the rivers associated with them produced drumlins and eskers and deposited large quantities of till and fluvio-glacial deposits.

A number of widely used geological terms have specific Irish associations. The most important of these are as follows:

1 *Caledonian Orogeny*: Mountain-building process that occurred approximately 500 million years ago due to the collision of the European and the American plates.

2 *corrie/cirque*: An amphitheatre-shaped hollow on the flank of a mountain characterized by a steep backwall, which in Ireland was the site of a former glacier.

3 *Dalradian Series*: A suite of rocks, found mainly in Ulster, which were initially sediments deposited in the Iapetus Ocean but which have been converted into metamorphic rocks during the Caledonian Orogeny.

4 *drumlin*: A streamlined hill formed from till (boulder day) and produced by glacial action.

5 *dyke*: Igneous rock, often basaltic in composition, which was initially emplaced along a narrow fracture as magma.

6 *esker*: Long, narrow ridge of fluvio-glacial deposits which formed in a sub-glacial river.

7 *evaporite deposits*: sediments formed mainly by the evaporation of seawater. Progressive evaporation yields a sequence of precipitated minerals, salt only being deposited towards the end of the sequence.

8 *gneiss*: High-grade banded metamorphic rock composed mainly of coarse crystals of feldspar and quartz.

9 *Iapetus suture*: zone marking the collision site of the American and European plates.

10 *moraine*: An unsorted, heterogeneous accumulation of till deposited by a glacier.

11 *schist*: Metamorphic rock consisting of garnet, mica and feldspar and quartz. Formed during regional metamorphism.

12 *subduction zone*: Location where an oceanic plate is forced down into the underlying mantle.

13 *terrane*: An area of continental crust with distinct geological characteristics that are different from the surrounding areas of continental crust.

14 *Variscan Orogeny*: Mountain-building episode that occurred about 300 million years ago. Caused by the closure of an ocean to the south of Ireland, thus its compressional effects were not intense. Also referred to as the Hercynian or Armorican.

Reading

Davies, G.L. Herries and Stephens, Nicholas, *Ireland* (Methuen, 1978).

Holland, Charles (ed.), *A Geology of Ireland* (Scottish Academic Press, 1981).

Jurgen, Ehlers, Gibbard, Philip and Rose, Jim (eds), *Glacial Deposits in Great Britain and Ireland* (A.A. Balkema, 1991).

Murphy, F.C., et al., 'An appraisal of suspect terranes in Ireland', *Irish Journal of Earth Sciences*, 11, no. 1 (1991), pp. 11–41.

Nevill, W.E., *Geology and Ireland* (Allen Figgis, 1963).

Whittow, J.B., *Geology and Scenery in Ireland* (Penguin, 1974).

PAUL JUDE GIBSON

Georgian architecture Irish Georgian architecture can be studied as an architectural succession, with successive generations of practitioners starting as pupils or assistants and then succeeding to each other's practices or public posts. The distinctions between the practice of architecture, building and engineering were not as clear cut as they are today.

Unlike in Britain, where a fully baroque style developed under such architects as Hawksmoor and Vanbrugh in the 1720s, Palladianism was the unchallenged style of Irish Georgian architecture for the first two-thirds of the eighteenth century. The greatest of the Irish Palladians was Vanbrugh's cousin and pupil Sir Edward Lovett Pearce, who had travelled in France and Italy. His best-known public work was the Parliament House, obtained over the head of the surveyor general Thomas Burgh (whom he was to succeed in office) and begun in 1729. Pearce was also concerned in the completion of Castletown, County Kildare, Ireland's greatest classical house, begun for Speaker Conolly in 1722, probably after designs by Allesandro Galilei. Pearce's other domestic work included Summerhill, County Meath, the Archbishop's Palace at Cashel, and Bellamont Forest, County Cavan. He died in 1733, in his early thirties.

Pearce had recommended as his assistant for the Parliament House the architect Richard Castle, who had come from Germany via England. Castle was also Pearce's assistant on the Newry Canal, and designed the first of many country houses, Castle Hume (c.1729), for one of the canal commissioners. During almost 20 years of independent practice (he died in 1751), Castle dominated the architectural profession. While he held no government post, apart from superintending the canal works in 1734–6, he served as architect to Trinity College, designing the Printing House (1734), the Campanile (c.1740, demolished) and the Dining Hall (1741, rebuilt after 1758). He also designed a number of Dublin houses of varying size, including the first granite-faced mansion in the city, Tyrone House (1740) and Leinster House (1745), which has a country house plan. For the same patron, the earl of Kildare, he remodelled Carton, County Kildare (1739 onwards). Other rebuildings by Castle in the 1730s included Powerscourt, County Wicklow, and probably also the King House, Boyle, County Roscommon.

After Castle's death Kildare employed at both Carton and Leinster House the architect Isaac Ware, secretary of the English Board of Works. Ware, whose first Irish commission may have been the additions to Dublin Castle ordered in 1746 by his London patron, the viceroy Lord Chesterfield, was probably also responsible for the remodelling of some of the interiors at Castletown in the 1760s. At both Carton and Castletown there is plasterwork in the baroque style by the Lafranchini brothers, natives of Tichino on the Swiss–Italian border. From the 1750s a lighter, rococo style of stucco work was introduced, probably by Bartholomew Cramillion, best known for the chapel at Castle's Rotunda Hospital.

Among the last architects of the Palladian school was Davis Ducart, or Daviso De Arcourt, whose first documented building is the Limerick Custom House of 1765, and who went on to design the Mayoralty House in Cork (1766) and several country houses, such as Kilshanning, County Cork (1765) and Castletown Cox, County Kilkenny (1767).

Ducart was born in the alpine area of northern Italy where he trained as an engineer. His name may be derived from the town of Arcore, which is not far from the Lafranchinis' native Ticino. Like Pearce and Castle before him he was employed on the Ulster canals, carrying the system to the Tyrone coalfields in 1767–7. His assistant on this project, the Waterford quaker Thomas Penrose, was to serve as architect and inspector of civil buildings between 1784 and 1792.

Ducart is also credited with the grid plan of the Georgian new town of Limerick, drawn up by his associate Christopher Colles for Edmond Sexton Pery around 1769, and almost the exact contemporary of the similarly planned new town of Edinburgh (1766–7). From the 1760s much of Dublin was restructured by the Wide Streets Commissioners, whose architects designed long terraces of uniformly fronted houses. Cork too had its Wide Streets Commissioners, active in the 1820s. Formally designed streets were laid out in many of the larger towns – Armagh being a notable example, not just for the quality of its buildings but for it being one of the few places in Ireland where there is a consistent conservation policy.

Palladianism gave way in the 1770s to neo-classicism, as did rococo decoration. The Gothic revival had made a tentative appearance in two houses in the 1760s – Castleward, County Down, and Moore Abbey, County Kildare – but did not really become fashionable until the end of the century. Neo-classicism was popularized by British architects like Robert Adam, Sir William Chambers, James Wyatt and Athenian Stuart, all of whom worked in Ireland. For Lord Charlemont, Chambers designed two Dublin buildings, the Casino at Marino (1758 onwards) and Charlemont House (1763 onwards). Wyatt's Irish work included what is now the Senate Chamber at Leinster House (1775), Abbey Leix, County Laois (1773), Mount Kennedy, County Wicklow (1772, built 1782), the Gothic Slane Castle (1785) and Castle Coole, County Fermanagh (1790).

The executant architect at Mount Kennedy was Thomas Cooley, another Englishman, who won the Dublin Royal Exchange competition in 1769. He went on to serve as architect to the Irish Board of Works (1774–84), succeeding Joseph Jarratt. Jarratt designed the Palladian St Catherine's Church, Dublin (1759), which later formed the pattern for a rare Irish architectural export, the Town Hall at Lancaster (1781), designed by his colleague and kinsman Thomas Jarratt. In a period when English architects were much in vogue, the Irish name that stands out is Thomas Ivory, master of the Dublin Society drawing schools, whose chief works were the competition-winning Blue Coat School (1773) and the Newcomen Bank (1781).

After Cooley's death his architectural mantle fell to three individuals; Thomas Penrose, who succeeded him as government architect; his pupil Francis Johnston, who succeeded him as architect to Primate Robinson of Armagh; and the Englishman and Roman neo-classicist James Gandon, who took over his work at the Four Courts. Gandon and Johnston's official work is described under public buildings to 1922, but they also had private practices, though Gandon designed only one major country house, Emo Court, begun about 1790 but not completed until 1860. Johnston was the more eclectic architect, his styles ranging from the severe neo-classicism of Townley Hall, County Louth (1794), and the Gibbsian St George's Church, Dublin (1800), to the Gothick of Charleville Forest, County Offaly (1800), and Markree, County Sligo (1802). After he joined the public service in 1805, Johnston was succeeded as the leading country house architect by Sir Richard Morrison, who was later joined in practice by his son William Vitruvius. Joint works by the Morrison's include Ballyfin, County Laois (1822), and Fota, County Cork (c.1825). Like Johnston's, their work was eclectic, though the younger Morrison produced a more convincing domestic Gothic, examples including Hollybrooke, County Wicklow (c.1831) and Clontarf

Castle, Dublin (1836), as well as some fine neo-classical courthouses – Carlow and Tralee (both 1828).

In Ireland Georgian churches outside the cities tended to be relatively modest in size. Prior to 1800 the buildings of the Catholics and Protestant non-conformists were largely of the vernacular type. The cathedrals of the established church were mostly medieval foundations, though two notable new buildings were commissioned; Waterford (1774–9) and Cashel (opened 1783). The architect of the former, John Roberts, also designed the Catholic cathedral in the city (1792). Between c.1810 and 1833 a major parish church building programme (in the ubiquitous Perpendicular Gothic style) was undertaken by the Board of First Fruits, continued by their successors, the Ecclesiastical Commissioners.

Much of Ireland's building stock, particularly the centres of towns and many buildings in the countryside, dates from the Georgian era. For reasons related to the economy and falling population, most Georgian towns remained relatively unaltered until well into the twentieth century; macadamized roads, proliferating overhead wires, and brightly painted facades constituting the main changes. Unfortunately, since the 1980s, the traditional pattern of repair and maintenance has increasingly given way to intervention, where 'renovation' has become synonymous with the loss of wood sash windows, doors, natural slates and internal features. It is clear that if these trends continue unchecked, a significant and, by European standards, underappreciated part of Ireland's cultural heritage will have entirely lost its character and integrity within the span of a generation.

Reading

Bence-Jones, Mark, *Burke's Guide to Country Houses, Volume 1: Ireland* (London: Burke's Peerage, 1978; rev. edn, published as *A Guide to Irish Country Houses*, London: Constable, 1988).

——*Dublin 1660–1860* (London: Cresset Press, 1952; rev. edn, London: Penguin, 1992).

Craig, Maurice, *Classic Irish Houses of the Middle Size* (London: Architectural Press, 1976; New York: Architectural Book Publishing, 1977).

—— *The Architecture of Ireland, from the Earliest Times to 1880* (London: B.T. Batsford; Dublin: Eason and Son, 1982).

The Georgian Society Records of Eighteenth-Century Domestic Architecture and Decoration in Dublin, 5 volumes (Dublin: 1909–13; repr. intro. Desmond Guinness, Shannon; Irish University Press, 1969).

O'Brien, Jacqueline and Guinness, Desmond, *Great Irish Houses and Castles* (London: Weidenfeld and Nicolson, 1992).

O'Dwyer, Frederick, *Lost Dublin* (Dublin: Gill and Macmillan, 1981).

Rowan, Ann Martha (ed.), *The Architecture of Richard Morrison and William Vitruvius Morrison* (Dublin: Irish Architecture Archive, 1989).

FREDERICK O'DWYER

Gill, Michael Henry,

Gill, Michael Henry, (1794–1879) Printer, publisher and bookseller. Born Dublin; died there, 20 March. In 1813 Gill was apprenticed to the printers Graisberry and Campbell, and by 1842 had worked his way up to become printer at the Dublin University Press. He bought out James McGlashan, publisher and bookseller, in 1856, renaming the firm McGlashan and Gill. In 1874 he resigned as university printer and moved his printing plant to McGlashan and Gill's premises at 50 Upper Sackville Street. He died five years later. Members of the family have continued the business since.

Reading

Kinane, Vincent, *A History of the Dublin University Press* (Dublin: Gill and Macmillan, 1994).

VINCENT KINANE

Giordani, Tomasso (1730–1806) Composer. Born Naples; died Dublin. Giordani first visited Dublin with an Italian opera company at Smock Alley Theatre in 1764. Settling in Dublin in 1779, he remained associated with this theatre until its closure in 1787. In the following year he was appointed musical director of Crow Street theatre. He was active in Dublin also as a teacher and his pupils included Thomas Cook. A list of the operas and cantatas written by Giordani in Dublin is available in the *Musical Antiquary* (no. 6, January 1911). He wrote an oratorio, *Isaac*, and a *Te Deum* which was performed in Francis Street Chapel at a thanksgiving service for the recovery of the King in 1789.

HARRY WHITE

Glover, John William (1815–99) Music teacher, conductor, and occasional composer. A native Dubliner who lived his whole life in the city, Glover enjoyed a varied career, first finding employment as a violinist in a theatre orchestra. He was director of music at St Mary's pro-cathedral before being appointed the first professor of vocal music at the Normal Training School of the Irish National Board of Education in 1848. In 1851 he founded the Royal Choral Institute, a populist performing body which was largely middle class in constitution and decidedly Catholic in ethos. His original compositions include the oratorio *St Patrick at Tara* (1870); *One Hundred Years Ago* (1879), an ode to commemorate the centenary of the birth of the poet Thomas Moore, a figure much admired by Glover; and the opera, *The Deserted Village* (1880), after Goldsmith.

JOSEPH RYAN

Goldsmith, Oliver (1728–74) Writer. Born probably 10 November; died 4 April. Unfortunately the year was torn away from the family Bible in which Goldsmith's birth is entered. We can therefore only conjecture that his birthplace was Pallas, County Westmeath, although his father, Rev. Charles Goldsmith, shortly afterward became curate in charge of the parish of Kilkenny West, and as a result moved his family to the house in Lissoy where Oliver Goldsmith spent his childhood. Rev. Goldsmith seems to have been a clever but improvident man who

married young and was, for most of his adult life, short of funds with which to support his wife, three daughters and five sons. The eldest son, Henry, born 1723, inherited his parents' gifts. He did well at university, and in 1743 obtained a scholarship which would have served as a stepping-stone to any of the learned professions as well as making possible rapid advancement within the university itself. However, Henry, like his father before him, married for love, threw over his collegiate prospects, set up school in his father's neighbourhood, and 'buried his talents and acquirements for the remainder of his life in a curacy of forty pounds a year'. Rev. Charles Goldsmith died in 1747.

In that year, Oliver Goldsmith, who had followed his brother to Trinity College, Dublin, was admonished for his part in a student riot. This began as an attempt to free a fellow student from the clutches of the bailiffs. A rescue party was formed, the student was released, and the liberators, led by 'Gallows Walsh', then proposed marching on Newgate prison and breaking it open. Accompanied by a sizeable number of citizens they got as far as the outer walls of the prison, but were easily beaten back by rifle fire (two of the townsmen were killed and several wounded). The incident deserves to be noted because for all the efforts made to enlist Goldsmith as 'the most beloved of English writers' – the words are Thackeray's – there is good reason to think that he wanted to resist incorporation into the kind of tame Anglo-Irishness with which he is so often identified.

He eventually settled in London, but he might well not have done so. After gaining his degree from Trinity in 1750, but failing to gain ordination, he took himself off to Edinburgh to study medicine, from Edinburgh went on to Leyden, from Leyden travelled to Paris, and then undertook a reach-me-down version of the Grand Tour: Germany, Switzerland, north Italy, and back to Paris, which he reached in late 1755 and where he apparently began writing the poem that was eventually to be published as *The Traveller*. The following year he arrived in London, undertook some hack writing (an obvious enough way of making money), worked as an apothecary's assistant and a physician, and looked about for some more permanent post. In 1758 it seemed he had found what he was looking for. He was promised the post of civilian physician with the East India Company on the coast of Coromandel, on condition he paid his passage out. But he failed to obtain the post as hospital-mate on a ship bound for India and that, together with a growing amount of hack work, most importantly for the *Monthly Review*, appears to have been enough to make him decide that his future lay in the profession of letters. By the time of his death he was the author of at least one masterpiece in each of literature's major genres: the novel, the drama, and poetry.

Not that this guaranteed financial security. At various times in his life Goldsmith made good money from his writing, but at others he was penniless. And although by the end of the 1750s he was known as 'Dr Goldsmith' and could count on the friendship of, among others, Smollett, Burke (who had been a fellow student at Trinity) and Johnson, there is reason to believe that he never felt himself entirely at home with literary London. Garrick's epigram is of course famous: 'Here lies NOLLY Goldsmith, for shortness call'd Noll, / Who wrote like an angel, but talk'd like poor Poll.' That epigram was said to have been extemporized at a meeting of the Literary Club in January or February 1774, and inspired 'The Retaliation', Goldsmith's last major poem, which he left unfinished at his death on 4 April that year. Together with Johnson, Reynolds and Burke, Goldsmith was a founder member of the club, which had been formed in 1764 and whose members might well seem to compose a kind of literary and cultural establishment: monarchical, Tory, Anglican. Goldsmith might have talked like poor Poll, but in every other sense he was part of that establishment.

So at least the familiar account of him runs, whether it is offered in praise, as it is by Thackeray, Henry James and Donald Davie, or by way of criticism. Yeats, for example, damned Goldsmith with the faintest possible praise. He was, Yeats said, the type of Irishman who 'knows no wrong, and goes through life happy and untroubled, without any evil or sadness'. These words were probably at the back of Seamus Deane's mind when he criticized *The Deserted Village* (1770) for evading its own subject. The poem makes a 'most unconvincing attack upon "Luxury"', Deane argues; and the reason for this is that at a very deep level Goldsmith could not bring himself to see Ireland as a colony of England. 'It had to be, in some fashion, incorporated into English civilisation, an integral part of it.' And so, for all that Deane is prepared to allow that *The Vicar of Wakefield* (1766) has an ironic, subversive element which is 'consistently undermining the theme of the Vicar's inexhaustible benevolence', overall Goldsmith is too much the would-be literary Englishman. Even his dramatic comedies, *The Good-Natured Man* (1768) and *She Stoops to Conquer* (1773), are married by the very 'amenity' of the author's cast of mind, of which Henry James so approved. Goldsmith was the golden bird of literary London.

There is no doubt that he was prepared to play this part; hence Reynolds's remark that Goldsmith often put on an 'affected silliness' which Reynolds thought sprang from a desire to 'lessen himself'. Hence, too, that self-destructive streak which Johnson recognized and to which Boswell condescended. (He recounts an incident in which Goldsmith, having been out-argued by Johnson, made as if to leave but then chose to remain, hat in hand, 'like a gamester, who, at the close of a long night, lingers for a little while, to see if he can have a favourable opening to finish with success'. Eventually he interrupts Johnson out of 'envy and spleen' and earns from Johnson the rebuke, 'Sir, you are impertinent.') Golden birds should not sing out of turn.

They may, however, sing ever so subtly out of tune. None of Goldsmith's major works is quite what it seems. The Fielding-like Anglican benevolence of *The Vicar of Wakefield*'s eponymous hero is questioned, even undermined, by a narrative manner teasingly at odds with the novel's apparently enthusiastic endorsement of warmheartedness. And *The Deserted Village* is not merely a satire of 'Luxury'. Like *The Traveller*, its caustic account of the depradations of 'Pomp' connects with a view of the state as propped up by the injustices of law, whose tyrannical power is ultimately sanctioned by monarchy. Intermittently at least, Goldsmith is a far more radical writer than he is usually credited with being.

Reading

Balderstone, Katharine C. (ed.), *The Collected Letters of Oliver Goldsmith* (Cambridge: Cambridge University Press, 1928).

Batey, Mavis, 'Oliver Goldsmith: an indictment of landscape gardening', in P. Willis (ed.), *Furor Hortensis* (Edinburgh: Elysium Press, 1974).

Deane, Seamus, *A Short History of Irish Literature* (London: Hutchinson, 1986).

Friedman, Arthur (ed.), *The Collected Works of Oliver Goldsmith*, 5 vols (Oxford: Oxford University Press, 1966).

Ginger, John, *The Notable Man: The Life and Times of Oliver Goldsmith* (London: Hamish Hamilton, 1977).

Lonsdale, Roger (ed.), *The Poems of Gray, Collins and Goldsmith* (London: Longman, 1969).

Lucas, John, *England and Englishness* (London: Hogarth Press, Chatto & Windus, 1990).

Sells, A. Lytton, *Oliver Goldsmith: His Life and Works* (London: Allen and Unwin, 1974).

Swarbrick, A. (ed.), *Oliver Goldsmith: Critical Essays* (London: Vision Press, 1984).

JOHN LUCAS

Gonne, Maud (later MacBride) (1866–1953) Born in England, daughter of an Irish officer in the British Army and an Englishwoman. Maud was raised in Britain and France. She became an acknowledged beauty throughout Europe. While she was living in Auvergne, she had an affair with a married man, the French writer and politician Lucien Millevoye, with whom she had a daughter, Iseult (1895). The affair ended in 1899.

Return to Dublin, Maud met W.B. Yeats, who fell in love with her but whose proposal of marriage she declined. Her flat became a meeting place for Irish writers and nationalists and Maud was soon working for the nationalist cause.

In 1900, she joined Sinn Féin and resigned from the Irish Republican Brotherhood. She established a revolutionary women's society, Inghinidhe na Héireann.

Maud married John MacBride in Paris in 1903. Their son Seán was born in 1904, but the marriage failed and MacBride returned to Ireland. Maud did not return to Ireland until 1917 and was arrested a year later.

She worked for the White Cross during the War of Independence and took the anti-Treaty side in the Civil War. In her declining years she lived in the suburbs of Dublin. She published her autobiography, *A Service of the Queen*, in 1938.

Reading

Cardozo, Nancy, *Maud Gonne: Lucky Eyes and a High Heart* (Victor Gollancz, 1979).

RACHEL FURMSTON

Gookin, Vincent (1616?–59) Surveyor general of Ireland. Gookin was a staunch republican and supporter of Cromwell, and played a central role in the transplantation to Connaught and the Down survey. Though he supported the concept of transplantation, he differed significantly from certain members of the Committee of Transplantation over its projected extent. In his pamphlet *The Great Case of the Transplantation in Ireland Discussed* (1655), he argued that it was both impossible and pointless to transplant all the native Irish to Connaught. His arguments were savagely attacked as seditious by Colonel Richard Lawrence, who charged that he had been corrupted by the Irish. With the arrival of Henry Cromwell as chief governor of Ireland in 1655, the question was settled in Gookin's favour, and only Catholic landowners were transplanted.

Reading

Barnard, T.C., *Cromwellian Ireland* (Oxford: 1975).

Gardiner, S.R., 'The transplantation to Connaught', *English Historical Review* xiv (1899), pp. 700–34.

Prendergast, J.P., *The Cromwellian Settlement of Ireland*, 3rd ed. (Dublin: 1922).

BRIAN DONOVAN

Gothic revival The early Irish Gothic revival, in restored fortresses of the Pale, or in Palladian cubes remodelled with varying panache to suggest the family's tenure since time immemorial, or in rural Catholic churches awakening to emancipation, happily co-existed with the classical until the advent of Pugin. This bearer of knowledge into that garden of Eden was inspired by ruined Irish monasteries to produce his cathedrals of Killarney and Enniscorthy and his convents in Birr and Waterford. His son Edward and son-in-law George Ashlin formed a precarious partnership against disciples such as Goldie and Hardwick and the prolific J.J. Mc Carthy with four rival cathedrals: Armagh, Thurles, Derry and Monaghan. Pugin bridged the sectarian divide, influencing Atkins, Welland and Slater. His institutional ideals were realized not by himself at Maynooth but rather by the 'godless' Queen's Colleges, Belfast by Lanyon and Lynn and Cork by Deane and Woodward.

Woodward, influenced by Ruskin and the pre-Raphaelites, evolved into neo-Byzantine with the Trinity Museum and the nearby Kildare Street Club. These were to influence Dublin's commercial architecture but not Belfast, dominated by Lanyon, Lynn and the short-lived William Barre – endowed with every gift but taste. This was not an essential ingredient of High Victorian Gothic, which relied on archaelogical exploration charged by stylistic inventiveness,

as in St Finbarre's Cathedral, Cork, by Burges, Street's Ardamine and Christchurch Cathedral, Dublin, and the lost rural churches of Welland and Gillespie. Their secular counterparts, Dromore Castle by Godwin and Dunboy Castle by Christopher, achieve more authenticity as ruins. Humewood Castle improbably survives, although transformed by the next generation into an outpost of *la belle epoque*.

But good taste was to prevail at the expense of vitality. J.F. Fuller had to remodel Kylemore for a duke, having designed it 30 years before for an industrialist. At Ashford Castle Lord Ardilaun replaced him with the more fastidious Ashlin, whose secular work never matches a series of memorial chapels that enshrine bereavement by exorcizing all current trends. Only Lutyens was able to revive Gothic and predict the future, restoring the medieval castle of Lambay and adding a guest wing prophetic of Habitat.

Reading

Blau, Eve, *Ruskinian Gothic* (Princetown University Press, 1982).

Girouard, Mark, *The Victorian Country House* (Yale University Press, 1979).

Richardson, D.S., *Gothic Revival Architecture in Ireland* (1970).

Sheehy, Jeanne, *J.J. MacCarthy and the Gothic Revival in Ireland* (Ulster Architectural Heritage Society, 1977).

JEREMY WILLIAMS

Graham, Patrick (1943–) Painter. Born Mullingar, County Westmeath. Graham won a three-year scholarship to the National College of Art and Design, Dublin (1959–63). He was an extraordinarily gifted young draughtsman and painter, although he now presents these early successes as counterproductive. His work is highly expressionistic in terms of imagery and technique. Although he remains fundamentally a painter, he also uses collage, applying found objects to canvases which are ripped apart to expose the stretcher and further layers of canvas. Graham frequently deals with religious and sexual themes, and includes enigmatic captions or lines of poetry in his compositions. His work is highly acclaimed in both Ireland and the USA, and he is one of the most influential artists of his generation in Ireland.

Reading

Patrick Graham, (Dublin: Hendriks Gallery, n.d.).
John Hutchinson, 'An interview with Patrick Graham', in *Patrick Graham* (Los Angeles: Jack Rutberg Fine Arts, 1989).

FELICITY WOOLF

Grattan's Parliament (1782–1800) Title commonly given to the Irish legislature during the period between the attaining of legislative independence and the Act of Union. Henry Grattan (1746–1820) was one of the principal promoters of the 1782 settlement. Others played no less a role in its attainment, but through political circumstances and also by way of a certain personal showmanship on his part, Grattan was credited by many contemporaries with the achievement of legislative independence. A grateful parliament voted him £50,000 as a reward for his services, thus enabling him to continue for as long as he wished as an 'independent' popular politician. Until recently the part taken by Grattan in the creating of the new 'constitution' of 1782 was greatly overstated by historians. His legend was established largely by his son's five-volume biography, the hagiographical approach of which was echoed in most later historical and biographical treatments until 1986. Buoyed up by his 1782 political credibility, Grattan played a prominent but again often overstated role in opposition politics until the Union.

Ever since the dismissal of the Undertakers in 1770 and the repossession of their patronage powers by the lord lieutenant and chief secretary, the many divisions in the Irish Parliament had been subsumed for most politically important purposes into the two broad phalanxes of government and opposition. Whereas for much of the century the main conflict in the Irish Parliament had been between the government and the Undertakers, with secondary conflicts taking place amongst the Undertakers themselves or between the Undertakers and the objects of their patronage, the principal collision after 1770 (and one which was well established by 1782) was between the government and the opposition, of which the Undertakers still formed a prominent part.

The government side of the Irish Commons was led by the chief secretary, usually an English career politician. His leadership was followed by principal members of the Dublin Castle administration, who were regarded as political as well as civil servants of the regime. Necessarily the largest group in the Commons was the mass of members who were recipients of government patronage or of promises of such patronage; both groups were described in the parlance of the time as having 'entered into a confidential arrangement' with the minister. The opposition was a more heterogeneous body, the largest groups of which were led by the former Undertakers; during the 1782–1800 period these were the Shannons, the Leinsters and the Ponsonbys. Other groups, sometimes merely assortments of unconnected individuals, were likely to vary in terms of size and identity. On occasion the financially independent among them (the 'country gentlemen') could form themselves into a small but determined group and hold the balance of power. But the most obvious were the resigned or the resentful who had failed in their applications for Castle patronage and who bided their time in various states of impatience. The fact that these members were united by nothing other than rapaciousness made any group coherence difficult to maintain and vulnerable to government inducement.

Greater group awareness was to be found amongst the Patriots, with whom Grattan was closely associated. The Patriot group was handicapped by the relative impecuniousness

261

of some of its ablest members, and by the fact that some at least of its liberal policies were unattractive or irrelevant to the more powerful of the opposition or to its rank and file. These policies included the curbing of government patronage powers, particularly jobs and pensions, and a bill 'to secure the responsibility of the servants of the Crown', as well as measures supportive of Catholic relief and free trade. The persistent defeat of these measures made leadership of the Patriot group unattractive to Grattan, who courted a shallow personal popularity to the point where he distanced himself at times from opposition as clearly as from government. He exerted his showmanship skills to emerge as Patriot spokesman only at the rare moments during the 1780s when the government's humiliation appeared imminent.

One such moment was brought about by the government's attempt in 1785 to extend to Ireland 'an almost unlimited communication of commercial advantages' in return for an Irish commitment to contribute financially to the upkeep of the empire. Intense activity by fearful business interests in England led to disastrous emendations in the Commercial Propositions, as they became known. This, together with uncertainty amongst many Irish members as to the political implications of the deal for their cherished legislative independence, ultimately brought about the government's near-defeat on the reintroduction of the propositions in the Irish Commons on 12 August 1785. This was one of the few occasions in the history of Grattan's Parliament when the legislature actively repulsed what it saw as an attack on its legislative independence. It was also one of the first concrete indications to the British government of the constitutional dangers posed to the interregnal connection by the 1782 settlement.

The government's forbodings in this regard were copper-fastened during the regency crisis of 1789, an incident brought about by George III's apparently permanent illness. Largely due to the king's recovery, the administration of William Pitt the Younger survived at Westminster in the face of a threat from the Foxite Whigs, who supported the Prince of Wales and a regency. But the news of the king's recovery arrived too late in Dublin to prevent the mass defection of hitherto loyal government members to the opposition, and the defeat of the lord lieutenant in his bid to forestall the presentation of an address to the Prince of Wales. The king's recovery restored the status quo to Irish parliamentary politics, but much damage had been done. It had become clear that severe constitutional difficulties could ensue should the Irish Parliament, as in 1789, adopt a stance different from that decided on at Westminster.

Pitt nevertheless perserved with Irish legislative independence, using the old instruments of patronage and the Castle to ensure that British government policy rather than Irish Patriotism was the controlling factor in Irish political affairs. By these means Catholic relief measures were imposed by London on a reluctant Irish Parliament during the early 1790s. The end of the legislature had its true beginnings in French revolutionary fervour, whose effect on Ireland was not unrelated to the clear inability of the Irish Parliament to reform itself on more democratic lines. Grattan and the sadly depleted Patriot group withdrew from Parliament in 1797 in protest at the government's efforts to coerce the Irish countryside into total submission. Normal parliamentary politics then came to an end in Grattan's Parliament, to be revived briefly two years later as the Castle exerted every ounce of its legendary patronage and more to secure the Union, and the Patriots exerted all of their no-less legendary oratorical skills in a vain effort to frustrate that end. Grattan's Parliament expired on 1 January 1801 as the Act of Union came into effect.

Reading

O'Brien, Gerard, 'The Gratten mystique', *Eighteenth-Century Ireland* i (1986).

——*Anglo-Irish Politics in the Age of Grattan and Pitt* (Dublin: Irish Academic Press, 1987).

GERARD O'BRIEN

Graves, Robert James (1796–1853) Physician. Third surviving son of Richard Graves DD and his wife, Elizabeth Drought, Graves was born in Dublin on 28 March 1796 and studied at the School of Physic, graduating in 1818; he died at 4 (now 55) Merrion Square South on 20 March 1853, claiming as epitaph, 'he fed fevers'. The term 'Graves' disease' was popular, but his description of exophthalmic goitre was less valuable than his innovations (taken from continental schools) at the Meath Hospital, bedside teaching and the use of the stethoscope.

Reading

Taylor, Selwyn, *Robert Graves* (London: Royal Society of Medicine, 1989).

J.B. LYONS

Greatrakes, Valentine (1629–83) 'Stroker' or healer. The son of William and Mary Greatrakes, he was born on St Valentine's Day 1629 at Affane, County Waterford, and died there on 28 November 1683. Having served with Cromwell's Irish forces he lost his public offices after the restoration, but realized (or imagined) that he could cure the king's evil (scrofula) and other ailments by touching the afflicted. His aid was widely sought. Many successes were testified, but he failed to relieve Lady Anne Conway's headaches or John Flamsteed's rheumatism.

Reading

Fleetwood, John F., *History of Medicine in Ireland* (Dublin: Browne and Nolan, 1951).

J.B. LYONS

Grierson Constantia (*c.*1704–32) Classical scholar, press corrector and poet. Born between 1703 and 1705, County Kilkenny, of 'poor, illiterate country people'; died Dublin, 2 December. Her name was for long thought to be Phillips, but notes in Dix's copy of *The Dublin Scuffle* (1729) identify her as Crawley. After tuition by a country parson she came to Dublin to study obstetrics, but by 1724 was editing Virgil for pocket classics issued by George Grierson (king's printer, 1732–53). She married him in 1726; one child only survived infancy to succeed his father.

In 1730 the Griersons' petition to Parliament credited Constantia with advancing the art of printing in Ireland: 'the Editions corrected by her have been approved of, not only in this Kingdom, but in *Great Britain, Holland*, and elsewhere'. Numerous cancels present in, for instance, the Virgil (1724) and Terence (1729) show Constantia's editorial care.

She was a poet as well as a classicist. Swift described her as 'a very good Greek and Latin Scholar, and hath lately published a fine Edition of Tacitus, with a Latin Dedication to the Lord Lieutenant and she writes *carmina Anglicana non contemnenda*'. Six poems appeared in Mary Barber's *Poems on Several Occasions* (1734), and a manuscript containing new poems has recently been identified as hers by Dr A.C. Elias, Jr.

Reading

Elias, A.C., Jr, 'A manuscript book of Constantia Grierson's', *Swift Studies* 2 (1987).

M. POLLARD

Griffith, Arthur (1871–1922) Political leader. Born Dublin, 31 March 1871. The son of Arthur Griffith, a printer, and his wife Mary Phelan, Griffith was educated by the Christian Brothers and served his apprenticeship as a compositor. An ardent admirer of Parnell, he became active in nationalist politics while he was still a boy. Like many young people of the time he considered Parnell's fall to be a national humiliation for Ireland, and sought ways of concentrating the force of public opinion on self-determination. He joined the

Gaelic League and the secret, oath-bound Irish Republican Brotherhood, which perpetuated the ideals of the Fenians and the United Irishmen. This separatist tradition, rejected by the parliamentary nationalists, was rapidly gaining ground among the young.

In 1896 Griffith emigrated to South Africa, where he worked for a while in the diamond mines of the Transvaal before settling in Johannesburg and founding a newspaper there. Meanwhile in Ireland the anniversary of the 1798 insurrection had stimulated the formation of 'Ninety-eight' clubs, and when Griffith came home in 1899 he helped to found the *United Irishman*, a weekly newspaper which he edited until 1906. In its columns he forcefully expounded his own formula for the achievement of Irish independence. Always pragmatic, he argued that Ireland's economy would prosper once the country was politically free, but he did not believe that freedom could be won either by physical violence or by action in Parliament. Instead he preached a doctrine of self-reliance, advocating that Ireland's representatives should withdraw from Westminster and set up an assembly in Dublin. If it had the support of the Irish people, it would render government by the British no longer possible. Griffith's hero was Francis Deák, the Hungarian moderate politician whose efforts led to the restoration of his country's constitution when the principle of dual monarchy was conceded by the establishment of the Austro-Hungarian empire in 1867. Griffith hoped that a similar *Ausgleich* might be achieved for Britain and Ireland, and bring about economic prosperity for the latter. He published his ideas in a pamphlet, 'The Resurrection of Hungary', in 1906, and to promote them he founded the movement known as Sinn Féin ('We ourselves').

Sinn Féin was thus founded on conservative and monarchist principles rather different from the Republicanism it came to represent, and it enjoyed relatively little popular support until the Easter Rising of 1916. Though Griffith himself took no part in the Rising, the fact that the rebels were widely (and erroneously) referred to as 'Sinn Féiners' indicated the increasing popularity of Griffith's gospel of separatism and self-reliance. However, at the national convention of 1917, Griffith had to relinquish the leadership of the movement to Éamon de Valera, who was thus able to combine the military and political wings of Republicanism. In the general election of 1918, Sinn Féin candidates won 73 of the 105 seats, and the old parliamentary party was virtually eliminated. Pledged not to take their place at Westminster, the Sinn Féin members set up Dáil Éireann in Dublin in January 1919. The Republic of 1916 was reaffirmed, and Griffith was effectively its deputy president.

Though still doubting the efficacy of violence, Griffith was carried along by the force of events as the guerrilla war intensified. He was again arrested in 1920, but while in prison he was visited by an emissary from Lloyd George, and he was released when a truce was arranged in July 1921. Always more concerned with the substance than the form of independence, Griffith was disposed to reach a settlement with the British government, and he was the natural choice to lead the Irish delegation when negotiations resumed in the autumn. The Dáil had, somewhat inconsistently, appointed the delegates as plenipotentiaries, while instructing them not to sign any agreement without consulting Dublin. Though Collins and the others were not prepared to go as far as Griffith in meeting British demands, Griffith persuaded them to accept the final terms offered in the early hours of 6 December 1921, and the Articles of Agreement for a Treaty were signed, bringing the Irish Free State into existence. They were immediately rejected by de Valera and his followers, and in the bitter Dáil debates which ensued, they were ratified by seven votes.

Griffith, whose health was failing, now faced a Herculean task. The state whose rights he had won had still to be created, and meanwhile Ireland was drifting into civil war. Exhausted by the strain, he died suddenly while tying his shoelace on 12 August 1922. Posterity has judged him contrastingly as a man whose ideals were vindicated by the subsequent course of the Free State's history, or one who, in Stephen Mackenna's words, 'made such a chaos of Ireland as must cloud his eternity'.

Reading

Colum, Padraic, *Arthur Griffith* (London: Browne and Nolan, 1959).

Davis, Richard P., *Arthur Griffith and Non-Violent Sinn Féin* (Dublin, Anvil Books, 1974).

O'Luing, Sean, 'Arthur Griffith, 1871–1922: Thoughts on a centenary', *Irish Historical Studies*, lx, no. 238 (summer 1971).

Younger, Calton, *Arthur Griffith* (Dublin: Gill and Macmillan, 1981).

TONY STEWART

Grogan, Nathaniel (*c*.1740–1807) Painter. Born and died Cork. The son of a turner and block maker, Grogan was self taught. He spent most of his youth at sea, returning to Cork *c*.1778. Although primarily a genre painter, in the late 1780s Grogan painted murals in the home of Sir Henry Hayes at Vernon Mount, Douglas, County Cork. His most interesting work was as a recorder of folk customs of the Irish peasantry, where he mixed Dutch realism with grotesque satire, producing a sufficiently negative view of the Irish to satisfy a London audience. He exhibited at the Free Society of Artists in London in 1782. Grogan also painted attractive landscape views along the river Lee. These are of a conventional sylvan type, but his success in Cork is proof of the possibilities that existed in the late eighteenth century for artists to flourish outside of Dublin.

Reading

Crookshank, Anne, and the Knight of Glin, *The Painters of Ireland c. 1660–1920* (London: Barrie and Jenkins, 1978).

Pasquin, Anthony, *Memoirs of the Royal Academicians and an Authentic History of the Artists of Ireland* . . . (London: 1796).

Strickland, Walter, *A Dictionary of Irish Artists* (Shannon: Irish University Press, 1968).

FINTAN CULLEN

Groocock Joseph (1913–97). Musician and teacher. Born Croydon, 23 November; died 13 August. Educated in England, Groocock came to Ireland in 1935. For many years he taught music at St Columba's College and conducted the choral society at Trinity College, Dublin, where he was on the music staff from 1970; he also taught at the College of Music. In addition his work included adjudicating, accompanying and organ playing. In 1964 he was awarded an honorary doctorate by the University of Dublin. Groocock's reputation was above all as a teacher of counterpoint and of the music of Bach. This is reflected in his compositions, which include chamber and choral music often written to stimulate the interests of particular performers.

BARRA BOYDELL

Grubb, Thomas (1800–78) and **Howard** (1844–1931) Mechanical and optical engineers. Father and youngest son, both born, brought up and educated in Ireland, Thomas and Howard Grubb managed an engineering enterprise from 1825 to 1922. Their tradition continued into the 1980s in the form of Sir Howard Grubb, Parsons & Co. of Walkergate, Newcastle-upon-Tyne. In succession in Dublin, Grubbs made machine tools, telescopes, banknote printing machines, telescopes, optical accessories, telescopes, periscopes for submarines, and finally telescopes.

From the very start, 'stability' and 'freedom from excessive friction' were the watchwords of Grubb telescope design, with ingenious devices to assist the intended convenience of the user, not always achieved. Howard Grubb was disappointed, after two special journeys to distant California, not to secure the contract for the Lick telescope of 1888; he received a small payment for his ideas, which were utilized in that first major mountain-top telescope. The Grubbs' largest telescopes were the 48-inch reflector built for Melbourne in the 1860s, parts of which are still in use in Canberra, and the 27-inch refractor of 1885 erected in Vienna. Their most successful were the world-wide series of seven 13-inch Astrographic telescopes, c.1890, that incorporated good pendulum-controlled drives; the Radcliffe, Thomson and Victoria refractors at Oxford, Greenwich and Cape Town respectively; and a tiny coelostat used with a 4-inch lens at the famous solar eclipse of May 1919, which helped to verify Einstein's Theory of Relativity.

Even if the Bank of Ireland banknote printing machines did not make *them* money, the periscopes used in British submarines in World War I should have made Sir Howard's fortune. But the firm went into receivership in 1925; both Grubbs were honest and helpful in all their dealings, and jealous in preserving their reputation, in the tradition of the entrepreneurship of the Irish Quaker community, where their roots were.

Reading

Mollan, Charles, Davis, W., and Finucane, B. (eds), *Some People and Places in Irish Science and Technology* (Royal Irish Academy, 1985).
—— *More People and Places in Irish Science and Technology* (1990).
Mason, T.H., 'Dublin opticians and instrument makers', *Dublin Historical Record* 6, (1944), pp. 133–49.
Fitzgerald, W.G. 'Sir Howard Grubb, F.R.S., F.R.A.S., Etc., Etc.', *Strand Magazine* 12, (1896), p. 369.
Burnett, J.E., and Morrison-Low, A.D., *Vulgar and mechanick* (Dublin: Royal Dublin Society, 1989).
King, H.C., *The History of the Telescope* (Griffin, 1955).

PATRICK A. WAYMAN

Guilds of Dublin The merchants' guild was the first municipal organization to be recognized in Anglo-Norman Dublin (1192).

Craft guilds came later; none was formally incorporated before the 1400s, and the last (the apothecaries') received its charter in 1747, bringing the total to 25. The craft guilds gradually established their right to representation on the city corporation, but their members were less likely than the merchants to rise in the city hierarchy.

After the Restoration the Protestant gentry were determined to maintain the corporate towns as bastions of Protestantism. Guild officials, however, sought to maintain the principle of guild regulation of all who practised a trade. Hence the adoption of a quarterage system, by which Catholic tradesmen, disqualified from becoming freemen, could pay a quarterly fee allowing them to trade. When Catholic merchants successfully challenged this system in the mid-1700s, the guilds campaigned for statutory recognition for quarterage. The failure of this campaign undermined the guilds' economic role, but they retained much vitality: their triennial procession attracted visitors from abroad. A new merchants' guild hall was built as late as the 1820s.

Dublin's growth in the 1700s encouraged the freemen, led by Charles Lucas, to seek to overturn the aldermanic oligarchy in Dublin. The Dublin City Corporation Act (1760) allowed the guilds to choose their own municipal representatives, who also gained a role in the selection of magistrates. Many guild members supported the parliamentary Patriot opposition, calling for legislative independence. But their ethos remained staunchly Protestant, and when membership of guilds was opened to Catholics in 1793, few Catholics were admitted. Though the guilds were not formally dissolved by the Municipal Reform Act (1840), their link with the city corporation was terminated, and an attempt to revive their economic functions in the mid-1840s failed.

JACQUELINE HILL

Guinness family The numerous descendants of Richard Guinness of Celbridge, a small landowner whose son Arthur (1725–1803) founded the famous Dublin brewery in 1759. Contrary to popular belief, they constitute not a tightly knit dynasty of inherited wealth but an extensive matrimonial network whose members often marry within the clan. Arthur used a £100 legacy from the archbishop of Cashel to buy a small brewery in Leixlip in 1756. Subsequently he married an heiress, and bought the Dublin brewery where the original porter stout was made. His grandson, Sir Benjamin Guinness, laid the foundations of the 'brewery' line's enormous wealth by developing the export of the stout. An MP, philanthropist and lord mayor of Dublin, he also began the ascent of the family into the higher echelons of Irish and British society.

The senior (and non-moneyed) line descends from Arthur's eldest son, the Rev. Hosea Guinness, and has produced a succession of scholars, churchmen and missionaries. A third branch, which stems from Arthur's youngest brother Samuel, a gold-beater by trade, has built up a vast empire in banking. Edward Cecil Guinness, first earl of Iveagh, was Benjamin's son. His grandson, the statesman and traveller Walter Edward Guinness, first Baron Moyne, was assassinated by Stern Gang terrorists in 1944. Desmond Guinness, the present Baron Moyne was a founder member of the Irish Georgian Society, which campaigns to preserve the Irish architectural heritage of this period.

The Guinness name is rarely absent from the society gossip columns, and a succession of tragedies and business scandals has given rise to the legend of a 'Guinness curse'. Less publicity is devoted to the Guinness record of philanthropy and good works.

Reading

Mullally, Frederic, *The Silver Salvo: The Story of the Guinness Family* (London: Granada, 1981).
Guinness, Michele, *The Guinness Legend* (London: Hodder and Stoughton, 1989).

TONY STEWART

Guthrie, Sir (William) Tyrone (1900–71) Theatrical and operatic director. Born Tunbridge Wells, Kent, 2 July. Guthrie's father was a Scots doctor. His mother, Norah Power, came from Annaghmakerrig, County Monaghan, where Guthrie was largely brought up and where he died 15 May, having willed the house to the state as a workplace for artists. Educated at Wellington College, and St John's College, Oxford, after freelance theatre work he became a radio producer (1924) with the BBC in Belfast and London, and subsequently with CBC in Montreal. He was in charge of play production at the Old Vic (1933), becoming administrator (1937–45) and director (1951–2). With Tanya Moiseiwitsch, he developed the idea of the open stage, first at Stratford, Ontario (1953–7), emulated world-wide, then at the Guthrie Theatre, Minneapolis (1963–7). He directed in the West End and on Broadway, and in Ireland (at the Abbey, Gate and Gaiety in Dublin, and the Opera House, Belfast), Australia, Finland and Israel. Knighted 1961, he was made chancellor of Queen's University, Belfast, 1963–70.

Reading

Forsythe, James, *Tyrone Guthrie* (London: Hamish Hamilton, 1976).
Guthrie, Tyrone, *A Life in the Theatre* (London: Hamish Hamilton, 1960).
Rossi, Alfred, *Astonish Us in the Morning* (London: Hutchinson, 1977).

CHRISTOPHER FITZSIMON

Gwynn family Descended from a Welsh cleric who came to Ulster c.1660, almost every subsequent generation of this family included one or more Church of Ireland clergymen. Yet the Gwynne Institution in Derry, endowed c.1829 by a lay collateral for the education of needy boys, was designed to benefit Anglicans, Presbyterians and Catholics in equal numbers. In 1862 the Rev. John Gwynn, later regius professor of divinity at Trinity College, Dublin, and editor of the *Book of Armagh*, married Lucy, daughter of the 1848 rebel leader William Smith O'Brien. The union produced 10 children, in whom the academic Gwynn strain was leavened by the poetry, idealism and mild eccentricity of the O'Briens. Four, Edward, Robin, Lucy and Lucius, became respectively provost, regius professor of divinity, lady registrar and fellow of Trinity College, sometimes flippantly termed at this time 'Gwynnity College'. Edward, who was also lecturer in Celtic languages, edited the *Metrical Dindshenchus* and other texts, while the Rev. 'R.M.' or Robin Gwynn attracted some attention when in 1913 he made his rooms in Trinity available for the first meeting of James Connolly's Citizen Army. Best known was the eldest brother, Stephen Gwynn (1864–1950), poet, writer and Redmondite MP for Galway 1906–18, author of *Highways and Byways in Donegal and Antrim*, *Experiences of a Literary Man*, etc. Stephen's children, who with their mother were received into the Catholic church in 1902, included the Rev. Aubrey Gwynn SJ (1892–1983), professor of medieval history in University College, Dublin, and the Catholic journalist and author, Denis Gwynn (1893–1971).

KATHERINE SIMMS

H

Hall, Patrick (1935–) Painter. Born Tipperary. Hall studied at the Chelsea and the Central Schools of Art in London. Upon graduation in 1960 he exhibited at the Independent Artists exhibitions in Dublin. In the 1980s Hall's career gained impetus with a series of group exhibitions in Dublin, Boston and Cambridge. He has held individual exhibitions in the Lincoln and Temple Bar Galleries of Dublin, the Federensky Gallery of Belfast, and the Pentonville and Todd Galleries of London. A member of Aosdána, Hall has lived in Spain and New York. The powers of earth and fire inform his intense and darkly articulated paintings.

Reading

Sharpe, Henry J., 'Patrick Hall', in *Making Sense*, catalogue essay (Dublin: 1982).
Cooke, Harriet, Exhibition review, *Irish Arts Review* (1985).
Dunne, Aidan, *Life Lines: The Paintings of Patrick Hall*, catalogue essay (London: 1987).

DERVAL TUBRIDY

Hamilton (Abercorn) family Senior surviving branch of the Scottish house of Hamilton in the male line, the dukedom of Hamilton having passed through a female in the mid-seventeenth century. James Hamilton, first earl of Abercorn, was one of the major promoters of the Plantation of Ulster and received a grant of virtually the whole of the barony of Strabane, County Tyrone, in 1610. Subsequently, the family lost their Scottish estates at Paisley and in Linlithgowshire and concentrated their energies on Ireland. The fourth earl forfeited his Irish estates for his loyalty to James II, but his successors, the fifth and sixth earls, more than retrieved the situation. The seventh earl (1685–1744) was an FRS and wrote treatises on harmony and magnets; his younger brother, the Hon. Charles Hamilton of Painshill, Surrey, was a noted horticulturist. The eighth earl acquired the Duddingston estate, outside Edinburgh, in 1745, where Sir William Chambers built a mansion for him in the 1760s, and at Paisley he also built and town-planned extensively on the family's former property, which he reacquired in 1764. His successor, the ninth earl, employed John Soane to remodel the eighth earl's Tyrone seat, Barons Court, and the Middlesex seat which the ninth earl had himself acquired in the 1780s, Bentley Priory, Stanmore. Created first marquess in 1790, he was a leader of fashion, a friend of Pitt the Younger, and the first considerable political figure in the family. His grandson, the second marquess, was lord lieutenant of Ireland twice (1866–8, 1874–6), and in 1868 was created a duke (Ulster's only one, Ireland's second and the UK's second last). The second duke was a friend of Edward VII's and held various royal household appointments (1866–1901). The third duke was the first governor of Northern Ireland (1922–45).

Reading

Malcomson, A.P.W., 'Introduction to the Abercorn Papers, P.R.O.N.I., D. 623' (March 1990).

A.P.W. MALCOMSON

Hamilton, Hugh Douglas (1740–1808) Portrait painter. Born Dublin; died there 10 February. Of an artisan background, Hamilton trained at the Dublin Society Schools under the tutelage of Robert West. Hamilton is especially remembered for his pastel portraits, which on his move to London *c*.1760 brought him great success. From 1779 to 1792 the artist lived in Italy, where he enjoyed the company of other expatriate artists, such as John Flaxman, and befriended the sculptor Antonio Canova. On returning to Dublin Hamilton painted almost exclusively in oils and produced a wide range of portraits of peers and commoners. A surprisingly large number of these portraits were of sitters strongly opposed to the Union.

Reading

Cullen, Fintan, *Walpole Society* 50 (1984).
Strickland, Walter, *A Dictionary of Irish Artists* (Shannon: Irish University Press, 1968).

FINTAN CULLEN

Hamilton, Letitia Marion (1878–1964) Painter. Born Dunboyne, County Meath; died Dublin. With her artist sister, Eva Hamilton, she studied under William Orpen, first exhibiting at the Royal Hibernian Academy (RHA) in 1909. She was a founder member of the Dublin Painters in 1920, and

contributed to the Irish exhibition in Paris in 1922. She travelled widely on the Continent, painting in Italy and Yugoslavia, while continuing to exhibit Irish landscape and hunting scenes. Her mature style reflects School of Paris influence, with a Dufy freedom, though remarkable for its thick, Van Gogh-like impasto. She was elected RHA in 1944.

Reading

Irish Women Artists (Dublin: National Gallery of Ireland, 1987);
McConkey, K., *A Free Spirit: Irish Art 1860–1960* (London: Antique Collectors Club with Pyms, 1990).

HILARY PYLE

Hamilton, William Rowan (1805–65) Mathematician. Born in Dublin. As a young boy Hamilton moved to Trim where his uncle, Rev. James Hamilton, ran a school. Under his uncle's tutelage the young Hamilton displayed a precocious talent: initially this was in languages and the classics but later in mathematics. His undergraduate performance in Trinity College, Dublin, was so outstanding that in 1827, the year in which he graduated, the Board of the College took the courageous step of appointing him, against significant competition, to the chair of astronomy, which had just become vacant. As Andrews Professor of Astronomy, and with the associated title of Royal Astronomer of Ireland, Hamilton took up residence in the College Observatory at Dunsink, which was to be his home for the rest of his life.

Observational astronomy was not Hamilton's principal interest; nevertheless, with the help of his assistant and to some extent his own two sisters, who lived with him, he endeavoured to see that the required programme of observations was carried out. His main efforts and his great achievements were in mathematics. There are three distinct areas in which he made major contributions: in optics, which was of course not irrelevant to his astronomical responsibilities; in dynamics;

and in his discovery and development of quaternions.

In optics Hamilton predicted an entirely new and totally unexpected phenomenon called conical refraction, which was then observed, at his instigation, by his Trinity colleague Humphrey Lloyd. This brought him fame and, in 1835, a knighthood. His methods in dynamics have been of crucial importance to the subsequent development of both classical and quantum dynamics, and the Hamiltonian function which he introduced retains a central role in most areas of theoretical physics. The discovery of quaternions opened up new horizons in algebra. These highly imaginative and original contributions justify a place for Hamilton among the great mathematicians.

Wordsworth and Coleridge were among his friends. It was Wordsworth who persuaded Hamilton that his time was better spent at mathematics than writing verse, despite his strong inclination towards the latter. Coleridge introduced him to the philosophy of Kant, which was to become a major influence. In 1833 Hamilton married Helen Bayly; they had two sons and one daughter, but the memory of Catherine Disney, with whom he had fallen in love as a young man, retained a special place in his affection.

Reading

Hankins, Thomas L., *Sir William Rowan Hamilton* (Baltimore: Johns Hopkins University Press, 1980).

DAVID SPEARMAN

Hammond, Philip (1951–) Broadcaster, music critic, journalist and perfomer. Hammond studied composition at Queen's University, Belfast, with Raymond, Warren and Adrian Thomas, and piano at the Royal Irish Academy, Dublin, with Rhona Marshall. Formerly director of music at Cabin Hill Preparatory School, he is presently performing arts officer of the Arts Council of Northern Ireland. His compositions, much influenced by twentieth-century French music, have been commissioned, performed and broadcast in Britain and Ireland. They include *Thanatos* for tape and voices (1978), *Narcissus* (1981) and *Chanson d'Automne* (1987), both for voice and ensemble, *Fanfare of Orchestra* (1984), and works for young performers.

PETER DOWNEY

Handel in Dublin The visit of George Frideric Handel to Dublin between 18 November 1741 and 13 August 1742 was a significant event which profoundly affected the subsequent development of music in that city in terms of anglophone culture. On his arrival, Handel announced a series of six 'Musical Entertainments' at Neale's new Music Hall in Fishamble Street, which had opened just prior to Handel's visit. A second series followed, ending on 7 April 1742. These subscription concerts included performances of *Acis and Galatea*, the *Ode for St Cecilia's Day*, *Esther*, *Alexander's Feast* and a concert version of *Imeneo*, announced as a serenata. *Messiah*, composed in London between 22 August and 14 September 1741, was publicly rehearsed on 9 April and performed in the Music Hall on 13 April 1742. On 17 April, *Faulkner's Dublin Journal* reported the enthusiastic reception afforded to *Messiah* and added: 'It is but justice to Mr Handel, that the world should know, he generously gave the Money arising from this Grand Performance to be equally shared by the Society for relieving Prisoners, the Charitable Infirmary and Mercer's Hospital, for which they will ever gratefully remember his name.' Handel conducted a performance of *Saul* on 25 May and repeated *Messiah* on 3 June. He left Dublin with his finances and his reputation both markedly enhanced. The outstanding success of the Dublin visit, moreover, determined him upon the cultivation of oratorios in English (as against operas in Italian), notwithstanding the difficulties which he subsequently encountered, particularly with regard to the early London performances of *Messiah*.

Three factors account for Handel's success in Dublin as against his repeated failures in London prior to the Irish visit. The first is that his increasing preoccupation with settings of English texts found an ideal outlet in Dublin, where the tradition of Italian *opera seria* that depended on the sway of aristocratic support was largely unknown. Handel's oratorical performances were given in a purpose-built Dublin concert hall, and thus were exempt from the puritanical suspicions and associations which dogged the performance of his oratorios in London at the King's Theatre in the Haymarket and at Covent Garden.

The second factor which ensured Handel's success was that he stood like a colossus amidst his composer colleagues in Dublin. His virtual monopoly of non-theatrical music, not only during his stay but for long afterwards, is a striking feature of the city's musical life throughout the second half of the eighteenth century. In the 1749–50 season, for example, the only choral and/or sacred-dramatic works not by Handel to be given in Dublin were single performances of the *Stabat Mater* by Pergolesi and a funeral anthem by Bononcini. *Acis and Galatea*, among several works by Handel, was given seven times in that season.

The third and most important factor in Handel's favour was the habitual performance of music for charitable purposes by several Dublin musical societies, which constituted a vital feature of music making in the city. Annual hospital benefits were common in Dublin, and many Dublin hospitals effectively managed a major portion of the musical season there. The element of moral justification and social usefulness which characterized the performance of Handel's music during his visit to Dublin endured in performances of his music for long after his departure. Quite apart from the annual Mercer's Hospital benefit performances of *Messiah* (Handel had presented a score of the work to the hospital), which began in 1743, virtually every Irish performance of *Acis* and of the oratorios was in aid of a public or private charity. Between 1745 and 1753, for example, seven performances of the oratorio *Deborah* were given in Dublin, at least four of which were for the benefit of the Inns Quay Charitable Infirmary. *Deborah* does not appear to have been given once in London during the same period. In sum, the use of Handel's music for charitable purposes in Dublin amounted to a performance condition which was by no means the rule in London.

The strong association drawn between Handel's music and the public good, which was made by later eighteenth-century music historians, has been correctly undermined by a more balanced assessment of this 'prince of public entertainers' and his shrewd business sense. Nevertheless, this perception of Handel's music as an agent of public virtue and good works was greatly fortified during the Irish visit and endured for long afterwards. Handel's stay clarifies the differences in context, ideological climate and conditions of public musical performance between London and Dublin during much of the eighteenth century.

Reading

Boydell, Brian, *A Dublin Musical Calendar 1700–1760* (Dublin: Irish Academic Press, 1988).

HARRY WHITE

Harland and Wolff, Belfast shipbuilding

Shipbuilding in Belfast was already under way in 1800, and in 1820, the first steamboat built in Ireland, the *Belfast*, was launched. In 1853 an iron shipbuilding yard, Hickson's, opened on Queens Island, and in 1854 Edward Harland arrived as yard manager, acquiring full control in 1858. In 1861 he took on, as partner, his German-born assistant, Gustav Wilhelm Wolff. At this time Harland and Wolff's employed about 1,500. Progressive innovations in ship design led to the 'island', by the 1880s launching 100,000 tons a year, including the largest ships afloat. If Harlands could claim to be the greatest shipyard in the world, across the Lagan Workman Clark's ('the wee yard') was itself the sixth biggest in the UK. Lord Pirie, chairman from 1895, further developed Harland's link with the White Star Line, launching huge transatlantic liners, including the *Titanic*, which foundered in April 1912.

At its peak Belfast shipbuilding employed some 25,000. With linen and engineering, it provided a basis for commonality of interest of capital and labour in rejecting Irish nationalism and identifying with the Mersey and Clyde industrial areas.

Heavily Protestant and Orange, the workforce frequently exerted itself against Catholic or nationalist infiltration. As early as 1864 a shipwrights' strike demanded the exclusion of Catholic 'police spies' from the labour force. In 1920, a 'loyalists only' labour policy was pressed by 'vigilance committees' and some 500 alleged Sinn Féiners did lose their jobs. Yard men later played a prominent part in the Ulster Workers' Council strike of 1974.

From 1918 the yard's fortunes dipped. The slump killed off Workman Clark's in 1935. World War II brought a revival, with some 139 ships, including six aircraft carriers, being launched, but thereafter the yard declined, only being rescued in 1971 by government intervention. A bold modernization plan introduced new welding and assembly techniques, and a new building dock was opened in 1969, with its distinctive skyline-dominating cranes, Goliath and Samson. In 1989 the company was privatized by management–employee buyout in association with the Norwegian Fred Olsen companies. The future lay with series production of 'Capesize' bulk carriers and a new generation of oil tankers. In March 1994 the workforce was some 1,100 – a telling symptom of the decline of the loyalist working class.

A revival of interest in the yard's history was inspired by the huge international success of the film *Titanic* in 1998.

Reading

Harland and Wolff Marketing and Business Development, *A Short History of Harland and Wolff* (Belfast: Harland and Wolff, 1992).

Bardon, Jonathan, *A History of Ulster* (Belfast: Blackstaff, 1992).
Patterson, Henry, *Class Conflict and Sectarianism* (Belfast: Blackstaff, 1980).

W. HARVEY COX

harp The most common symbol of Ireland after the shamrock, the harp is perhaps the only musical instrument to serve as a national symbol. Henry VIII introduced it into his Irish armorial bearings, and the first separate Irish coinage (1534) bore on the reverse side a crowned harp. The harp in association with the crown was the norm; the United Irishmen in the 1790s signalled their Republicanism by dispensing with the crown. The harp's high profile today stems from Guinness brewery's decision (1862) to use it as a trade mark, and to its use by the Irish government on printed documents.

BARRA BOYDELL

Harris, Walter (1686–1761) Historian, antiquarian and editor. Known principally as the selfless midwife to other people's work, Harris in fact exercised a quiet but deliberate influence over the development of Irish history writing at a crucial juncture. His reputation is founded on his formidable editorial feats – his revision and translation from Latin of *The Whole Works of Sir James Ware concerning Ireland* (1739, 1746); his *Hibernica* (1747, 1750), an anthology of historical tracts and other documents derived from several sources; and the massive collection of transcriptions concerning the political and ecclesiastical history of Ireland, prepared for publication from a wide variety of primary sources but never printed (now preserved as the Harris MSS in the National Library of Ireland).

The editorial voice evident in these labours seems at first hearing muted and modern: in his essay 'On the defects in the Histories of Ireland' appended to the first volume of *Hibernica* Harris emphasized the dangers of depending upon ancient chronicles or more modern descriptions which were written with pronounced cultural and political bias, and argued for deeper research based on legal and administrative sources and greater restraint in interpretation. Like a modern academic entrepreneur, he petitioned the government for a grant to fund the research and publication of a massive documentary history of Ireland, and in 1755 the Irish Parliament voted the massive sum of £2,660 to subvent the work. The full amount seems never to have been paid, but as a result of his efforts Harris secured larger parliamentary grants for the Royal Dublin Society and a personal pension of £100 a year.

Such commitment to the promotion of pure scholarship contrasts markedly, however, with the polemical tone of Harris's work as author. In the preface to his own major study, the *History of William III* (1749), he declared that the book, begun during the Jacobite scare of 1745, was intended 'to fortify the well-affected in their zeal... against those who would divide the reformed and make them prey to the ambition and tyranny of a foreign religion'; and in the 1750s he consumed a good deal of his energies in the bitter controversy over the massacres of 1641, in which he unwaveringly supported the extreme Protestant view that the Ulster Catholics were entirely to blame for the rebellion and the atrocities.

The underlying unity of the two Harris styles rests, however, on his own distinctive understanding of his concept of documentary evidence. For him the continuous history of 'a nation', as distinct from mere myths and chronicles, could be traced only in the sequential records of its governance. And he was confident that his archival research would reveal that real continuity in Irish history could be established only after 'the English conquest' (1172), and that such dependable evidence as could be extracted concerning earlier periods – the bare records of political and ecclesiatical successions – was that which anticipated and prefigured the fully formed governing structures established in Ireland after the conquest. For Harris, history was by

definition a validation of English government in Ireland and of the Anglican Protestantism which had been so naturally grafted on to it. In this way Harris helped to redefine the study of Irish history not simply as a rigorous intellectual discipline, but as a demonstration of 'the Protestant nation's' right to rule.

Reading

Hill, Jacqueline R., 'Popery and Protestantism, civil and religious Liberty: the disputed lessons of Irish history', *Past and Present* 118 (Feb. 1988), pp. 96–121.

McNeill, Charles (ed.), 'Harris: Collectanea de rebus Hibernicis', *Analecta Hibernica* 6 (1934), pp. 248–450.

CIARAN BRADY

Harrison, Francis (Frank) Llewelyn (1905–87) Musicologist. Born Dublin, 29 September; died Canterbury, 29 December. Frank Harrison's career as a musician began in 1912, when he was admitted as a chorister of St Patrick's Cathedral, Dublin. He subsequently studied at the Royal Irish Academy of Music, where his teachers included John Larchet, George Hewson and Michele Esposito. In 1926 he received his MusB from Trinity College, Dublin, and in 1930 his MusD from the same university. Harrison emigrated to Canada in 1931, where he was to remain for some 15 years, initially as organist at Westminster Presbyterian Church, New Glasgow, Nova Scotia, and afterwards as organist of Knox Presbyterian Church in Ottawa (1934–5). He subsequently became organist of St George's Cathedral in Kingston, Ontario, where he was appointed assistant professor of music at Queen's University (1940). Harrison's brief at Queen's was to create a department of music, and his success in this regard was marked some 34 afterwards when Queen's conferred an honorary degree upon him and named its new music building partly in his honour (Harrison–Le Caine Hall). From Queen's University Harrison moved to the USA, first as professor of music at Colgate University, Hamilton, and finally, in 1947, to Washington University, St Louis. He also held visiting appointments in Yale and, in 1958, in Princeton, but in 1952 he took up a permanent position as lecturer in Oxford, where he remained until 1970, when he was elected to the chair of ethnomusicology at the University of Amsterdam. In 1976 he took up a part-time professorship at the University of Utrecht. Throughout his career, he was the recipient of many awards and visiting appointments in the United States and elsewhere. In 1965 he was elected a fellow of the British Academy.

Harrison's many publications in medieval music, ethnomusicology and (in collaboration with his wife, the distinguished scholar Joan Rimmer) organology combine to make him a seminal figure in post-war musicology. As a historian and editor of early music, his *Music in Medieval Britain* (1958) and his monumental edition of *The Eton Choirbook* (1956–61) secured his reputation as among the most important scholars in this field in the second half of the twentieth century. His interest in early music endured throughout his long lifetime, and was further evinced by his prodigious work for the series 'Polyphonic Music of the Fourteenth Century' and the Early English Church Music project funded by the British Academy. At the time of his death he was near to the completion of a book on tropes and liturgical plays in Catalunya, and in his eightieth year he accepted a vice-presidency and the chairmanship of the Plainsong and Medieval Society. In a span of some 35 years, Harrison also concerned himself intermittently with the music of his own country: *Music in Medieval Britain* characteristically includes archival material on the reformulation of statutes pertaining to the organization of music in Christ Church Cathedral, Dublin, and subsequent papers on music in Ireland exemplify Harrison's concern with the contextual circumstances and meaning of Irish music, which in turn reflect the polarization of his musical thought.

One of the most vital of Harrison's many scholarly achievements was his exploration of the history and function of musicological thought. In several papers and essays throughout his career, he sought to revise and renew the very purpose of musical research, and his persuasive advocation of 'man-centred' musicology remains one of the most fruitful contributions to the development of musical thought in the present century.

Reading

Chadd, David, 'Francis Llewelyn Harrison 1905–1987', *Proceedings of the British Academy* LXXV (1989), pp. 361–80.

White, Harry, 'Frank Llewelyn Harrison and the development of postwar musicological thought', *Hermathena* CXLVI (1989), pp. 39–47.

HARRY WHITE

Hartlib Circle Group of intellectuals surrounding Samuel Hartlib. Hartlib, a Protestant refugee from Continental Europe based in London from the late 1620s, was a polymathic figure in seventeenth-century thought. He was the correspondent of scores of leading thinkers – including Milton and Comenius – all over Europe, on subjects from astronomy to horticulture, linguistic thought and the philosophy of education. Bacon's grand project for the rational understanding of the whole empirical world, and his sense of knowledge as a form of benign power, were the governing inspiration of Hartlib's life. The Ireland of the 1640s and 1650s was one among other spheres in which he sought to bring his intellectual plans to fruition. His correspondents included William Petty and several other participants in the parliamentary and Cromwellian administrations in Ireland. Hartlib and they had a grand plan to set up in this territory, by 1650 newly subdued to English rule and apparently available for the setting up of a millennial Protestant dispensation, an intellectual clearing house (called the Office of Address) for ideas from many sources. More concretely, they meant to plant lands there, in the interest and for the advancement of Protestant intellectuals, including Hartlib himself. These plans foundered at the Restoration; but Hartlib's enthusiasm and practical encouragement did help to generate the 1652 volume *Ireland's Natural History* by the Dutch physician-scientists Arnold and Gerard Boate (the latter himself a Tipperary planter), and subsequent important, albeit abortive, projects to collect all kinds of empirical data about Ireland according to a proto-encyclopedic method called the 'Interrogatories', which anticipates Enlightenment thought.

The Hartlib Circle viewed Ireland as a promising locale both for scientific experiment and for 'improvements' of all kinds, but their undeniably genuine intellectual curiosity is inescapably allied with their colonizing ambitions, prompting the question whether such enlightened, rationalizing projects might not always also be forms of domination.

Reading

Barnard, T.C., *Cromwellian Ireland* (Oxford: Oxford University Press, 1975).

Boate, Arnold and Boate, Gerard, *Irelands Naturall History. Being a True and Ample Description of its Situation, Greatnes, Shape and Nature* (London: 1652).

Coughlan, Patricia, 'Natural history and historical nature: the Hartlib Circle and the Irish natural history project', in Mark Greengrass, Michael Leslie and Timothy Raylor (eds), *Samuel Hartlib and Universal Reformation* (Cambridge: Cambridge University Press, 1994).

Webster, Charles, *The Great Instauration: Science, Medicine, and Reform 1626–1660* (London: Duckworth, 1975).

PATRICIA COUGHLAN

Harty, Sir (Herbert) Hamilton (1879–1941) Composer, conductor and pianist. Born Hillsborough, County Down, 4 December; died Hove, Sussex, 19 February. Harty first made his name as an accompanist, in Dublin and then (from 1901) London. As a conductor he was principally associated with the Manchester-based Hallé Orchestra, whose chief conductor he was from 1920 to 1933. He gave the first performances of Walton's First Symphony (1934) and Bax's Sixth (1935), and the first British performances of such works as Mahler's Ninth Symphony and Shostakovich's First. As pianist he gave the first public performance of Constant Lambert's *The Rio Grande*. He was also a notable champion of the music of Berlioz. The quality of his interpretations can still be appreciated on record.

Some of his early works were written for the *Feis Ceoil*, including the *Irish Symphony* (1904). Other works include *A Comedy Overture* (1906), *Ode to a Nightingale* (written for his wife, the singer Agnes Nicholls, 1907), Violin Concerto (1908) and tone poem *With the Wild Geese* (1910). The work which did most to establish him as a composer was his choral setting of Whitman's *The Mystic Trumpeter* (1913). His style is mainly rooted in the European Romantic tradition, to which is added a pronounced Irish flavour. He composed much less after his appointment to the Hallé, concentrating instead on arrangements of Handel (notably the *Water Music* suite) and Field (*A John Field Suite*). Only when the onset of cancer interrupted his conducting career was he able to return to original composition and produce a masterpiece in the tone poem *The Children of Lir* (1938). He was knighted in 1925, and received the gold medal of the Royal Philharmonic Society in 1934.

Reading

Greer, David, *Hamilton Harty: His Life and Music* (Belfast: Blackstaff Press, 1978; repr. New York: 1980).

——*Hamilton Harty: Early Memories* (Belfast: Queen's University, 1979).

——'The composition of *The Children of Lir*', in G. Gillen and H. White (eds), *Irish Musical Studies I* (Dublin: 1990).

Kennedy, Michael, *The Hallé Tradition* (Manchester: 1960).

DAVID GREER

Harvey, Beauchamp Bagenal (1762–98) Political activist. Born Bargy Castle. One of a liberal family of south Wexford Protestant gentry, and educated as a barrister, Harvey was part of a generation of Irish activists inspired by the new energies released by the American and French revolutions. His career followed the familiar trajectory of 1790s radical chic – involvement in local, liberal, Reform and pro-Catholic issues, participation in the United Irishmen from 1791 onwards, accelerating alienation from the political establishment, and, ultimately, leadership of insurrection. Essentially a political not a military figure, Harvey's career as commander of the Wexford United Irish army had a doomed nobility about it. He was executed on 25 June 1798, and his Protestant gentry background ensured his immediate elevation and continuing status in the nationalist pantheon.

KEVIN WHELAN

Haughton, Samuel (1821–97) Scientist. Born Carlow, 21 December; died Dublin, 31 October. He graduated in mathematics from Trinity College, Dublin, and was professor of geology there (1851–81) and senior fellow (1881–97). His study of fossils aroused his interest in medicine, and he graduated from Trinity medical school in 1859, becoming medical registrar of the school. His many academic honours included fellowship of the Royal Society in 1859 and presidency of the Royal Irish Academy in 1887.

Reading

Haughton, Samuel, *The Pretensions of the Museum of Irish Industry* (Dublin: Hodges, 1854).
—— *Manual of Tides and Tidal Currents* (London: Longman, 1865).

HENRY BOYLAN

Haverty, Joseph Patrick (1794–1864) Painter. Born Galway; died Dublin, 27 July. Haverty seems to have lived in Galway until about 1814, thereafter living mainly in Dublin, where he frequently exhibited at the Royal Hibernian Academy. Coming to maturity during the heady days of Catholic emancipation, Haverty's work resounds with the new optimism of Catholic Ireland. He painted many portraits of O'Connell, including the impressive full-length with an Irish mastiff in the Reform Club, London (1823–30). His Catholic subjects included altarpieces, various paintings of the sacraments, and the highly sentimental *Father Mathew receiving a Pledge Breaker* (Dublin, National Gallery of Ireland). He also exploited the contemporary nostalgia for a vanished Ireland, as in the *Blind Piper* (Dublin, National Gallery of Ireland), which was engraved and became very widely known.

Reading

Crookshank, Anne and the Knight of Glin, *The Painters of Ireland c. 1660–1920* (London: Barrie and Jenkins, 1978).
Stewart, Ann M., *Royal Hibernian Academy of Arts, Index of Exhibitors and their works, 1826–1979* (Dublin: Manton Publishing, 1985–6).
Strickland, Walter, *A Dictionary of Irish Artists* (Shannon: Irish University Press, 1968).

FINTAN CULLEN

Hayes, Michael Angelo (1820–77) Subject painter. Born Waterford, 25 July; died Dublin, 31 December. The son and pupil of Edward Hayes RHA (Royal Hibenian Academician), and himself an academician at the early age of 34, Hayes was well known in his day as a painter of horses. He lectured and published on the subject of depicting animals in motion and seems to have anticipated Muybridge et al. in his discoveries. Although he painted in both oils and watercolours, his most successful works are large-scale drawings of cavalry charges that reflect the optimism of Victorian High Imperialism.

Reading

Strickland, Walter, *A Dictionary of Irish Artists* (Shannon: Irish University Press, 1968).

Barrett, Cyril (ed.), *Irish Art in the 19th Century* (Cork: ROSC, 1971).

FINTAN CULLEN

Healy, Robert (1743–71) Painter. Born Dublin; died Dangan, County Meath, July. Healy trained at the Dublin Society Schools. Principally remembered for his delicately drawn pastels in grey and white, he excelled in both portraiture and animal painting. Only some 25 works have been firmly attributed to him. In 1768–9 Healy received a commission from Tom Conolly MP for nine pastel drawings to be executed at Conolly's seat, Castletown, County Kildare. These drawings offer a fascinating glimpse into the private pursuits of the Anglo-Irish ruling class; the drawings include scenes of horse-racing, ice skating, etc.

Reading

Crookshank, Anne and the Knight of Glin, *Painters of Ireland, c.1660–1920* (London: Barrie and Jenkins, 1978).
Guinness, Desmond, *Apollo* CXV (1982).

FINTAN CULLEN

Heaney, Seamus (1939–) Poet. Born Mossbawn, County Londonderry. Heaney was educated at St Columb's College and Queen's University, Belfast. He taught at St Joseph's College of Education (Belfast) and Queen's University and Carysfort Training College (Dublin) before spending five years as Professor of Poetry at Oxford, followed by a Professorship at Harvard until 1997.

Heaney's poetic career to date has been notably and justly decorated with honours: he has occupied the Boylston Chair of Rhetoric at Harvard University (previously occupied by Robert Lowell, for whom the Irish poet has indicated great admiration and whose poetry has influenced Heaney's); he has been professor of poetry at Oxford, winner of numerous poetry prizes, and recipient of honorary degrees; in 1995 he was awarded the Nobel Prize for literature. His readings attract enormous audiences, and he stands in reputation among the pre-eminent living poets of the world, alongside Miloscz, Murray and Walcott. Before achieving such honours and stature, he was the unofficial laureate of Ulster, where in the 1960s he emerged to lead an impressive revival of poetry, in company with Michael Longley and Derek Mahon, who lit the way for Frank Ormsby, Paul Muldoon, Tom Paulin, Medbh McGuckian and others.

Unusually, Heaney's debut volume, *Death of a Naturalist* (1966), simultaneously announced a rich thematic potential, registered a distinctive and warmly memorable voice (however much it owed to Frost, Hughes and others), and established a new name in the British and Irish poetry scene. The corpus of work since then has been significant and continuous, despite some noteworthy redirections of tone and subject matter.

Like that of his admired predecessor, Hughes, Heaney's early poetry attracted popular attention through a physical immediacy of image in the re-creation of country life and custom, though a sporadic lilt of language distinguished him from his elder contemporary. From the start, the typical voice of Heaney's poems was that of a man set apart: sundered from a traditional way of life by education, standing painfully between the warring factions of Ulster, yet occupying a poetically fertile no man's land. And early, too, most notably in *Wintering Out* (1972) and *North* (1975), his verse excavations of the remote Irish past became extended metaphors, even allegories, of the troubled present. By dint of this (notwithstanding the amoral status of ritual – however lethal – and the poet's evident sympathies with his own Catholic community), Heaney became for a time, like Atwood in Canada or Larkin in England, a kind of cultural spokesman or exemplar.

Latterly, an ideal poetry and the obstacles in the path of its creation have reflexively become the subject of Heaney's work. In *The Haw Lantern* (1987), *Seeing Things* (1991) and *The Spirit Level* (1996), Heaney attempts with mixed but always interesting results a poetry that will be lyrically buoyed up by the very forces that substantiate and ground it, and achieving this buoyancy in the act of declaring its own intentions. Heaney's superb criticism, collected in *Preoccupations* (1980) and *The Government of the Tongue* (1988), has been in parallel development with his poetry in the sense of mirroring its concerns, as well, of course, as engaging with the work of fellow writers, particularly poets. Both kinds of writing are for Heaney commemorative in the deepest sense; but in his recent poetry, remembering is now a necessary clearing away, and in the resulting clearances, Heaney hopes to write a poetry 'dilating in new light'. Whether he succeeds in this or not, his achieved body of work is a major contribution to English-language poetry in the second half of the twentieth century; he has had enormous influence on younger poets writing in English, and only Derek Mahon challenges him for the inheritance of Yeats's mantle in Ireland.

Reading

Buttel, Robert, *Seamus Heaney* (Lewisburg PA: Bucknell University Press; London: Associated University Presses, 1975).
Corcoran, Neil, *Seamus Heaney* (London: Faber, 1986).
Curtis, Tony (ed.), *The Art of Seamus Heaney* (Bridgend: Poetry Wales Press, 1982, 1985).
Foster, John Wilson, 'The poetry of Seamus Heaney' and 'Heaney's redress', in *Colonial Consequences: Essays in Irish Literature and Culture* (Dublin: Lilliput Press, 1991).
Morrison, Blake, *Seamus Heaney* (London: Methuen, 1982).

JOHN WILSON FOSTER

hedge schools The term 'hedge school' originated in the common English usage of 'hedge' as an attribute expressing contempt as in 'hedge-doctor', 'hedge-alehouse', etc... Given the informal nature of popular, especially Catholic education and the lack of accredited training for schoolteachers, the term 'hedge school' was applied in this opprobious sense as the debate on popular education intensified in the early nineteenth century, when the word made its first appearance. The application of the term to mean schools literally held in the open air is adventitious, but the original derivation has been totally occluded, beginning with Carleton's *Traits and Stories of the Irish Peasantry*, where the later meaning is first categorically enunciated. Since Carleton, the hedge schoolmaster has become a stock picaresque figure, often treated as an entré to the world of Gaelic Ireland, his school a site for picturesque deprivation (cf. Flanagan's *The Year of the French*, Friel's *Translations*). This by now conventional overblown romanticization elides the prosaic English-speaking mundanity of Irish popular education. The standard trope of contrasting hedge schools with their successors, the national schools, is also misleading; four fifths of the hedge schoolmasters recorded at the peak of this phenomenon in the 1820s were painlessly absorbed into the national school system itself.

KEVIN WHELAN

Hellawell, Piers (1956–) Composer and broadcaster. Born Chinley, Derbyshire, 14 July. Hellawell studied at Oxford University with Hugh MacDonald, James Wood and Nicholas Maw, and was appointed composer in residence at Queen's University, Belfast, in 1981 and lecturer in music in 1986. He has broadcast and written about music, and his compositions have been commissioned, performed and broadcast in Europe and America. His work has been influenced by isorhythm and by the folk music of Ireland and of other lands, and includes *Seal Songs* for flute (1987), *Sound Carvings from Rano Raraku* for quartet (1988), *How Should I Your True Love Know* (1986) and *The Erratic Aviator's Dance* (1989) for chamber ensemble, and *Xenophon* for orchestra (1985).

PETER DOWNEY

Hely-Hutchinson family Came into being in the mid-eighteenth century when John

Hely (1724–94), the son of Francis Hely of Gortroe, County Cork, added 'Hutchinson' to his surname on inheriting the Hutchinson seat at Knocklofty, County Tipperary, through his wife Christina Nixon. John Hely-Hutchinson was a lawyer and politician of commanding talent and, following a number of years in opposition after his election to Parliament in 1759, he used his formidable legal and political skills to the full to promote his own and his family's advancement. Appointed prime serjeant in 1762 and secretary of state in 1777, his most controversial appointment was to the provostship of Trinity College, Dublin (1774), which led to a series of unedifying legal and political disputes and a number of duels, which did nothing for the college's reputation. Subsequently, however, Hely-Hutchinson proved an efficient and innovative provost. He was also possessed of a strong public spirit, which led him to produce the important tract *The Commercial Restraints of Ireland* (1779) in support of free trade. His eldest son, Richard, first Earl of Donoughmore (1756–1825), possessed this sentiment in an even stronger measure, for he devoted his political life to the cause of Catholic emancipation. He was succeeded by his brother John (1757–1832), the second earl, a career soldier who enjoyed mixed fortunes as an army commander (he was humiliated at Castlebar in 1798, for example), before a triumphant campaign in Egypt in 1801 won him fame as well as fortune.

Reading

McDowell, R.B. and Webb, D.A., *Trinity College 1592–1952: An Academic History* (Cambridge: Cambridge University Press, 1982).

JAMES KELLY

Hennessy, Patrick (1915–80) Painter. Born Cork. Hennessy was educated in Scotland and studied art in Paris and Rome, returning to Ireland shortly before World War II. Elected Royal Hibernian Academician in 1949, he had many exhibitions in Dublin, notably at the David Hendriks Gallery. In later years he spent much time in Morocco and on the Continent. A solitary figure in Irish art, Hennessy combined *trompe l'oeil* effects with subtle colour and a quality of almost surreal tension. Though the quality of his imagination coarsened in his last years, the poetically charged, almost sinister mood of his pictures makes them, at their best, individual and haunting. He is represented in public collections in Dublin, Limerick and Cork.

BRIAN FALLON

Hennessy, Richard (*c*.1727–1800) Founder of the brandy house. Born Ballymacmoy, County Cork, between 1724 and 1727; died Cognac. Ballymacmoy was part of the only region in County Cork in which a substantial Catholic landed presence survived in the eighteenth century. One consequence was that Hennessy was connected not only with the Nagles (his great-grandmother was a Nagle) but with many Cork business families and with Edmund Burke. Burke and Hennessy grew up together in the Blackwater valley, and Burke's name recurs in his correspondence up to 1792, when Hennessy on a business trip to London spent a night with Burke at Beaconsfield.

Hennessy joined Clare's regiment of the Irish Brigade in 1748, serving in the ranks while awaiting a commission (there is much inaccurate lore about his army service). However, even before receiving his second lieutenancy in 1753, like many other young men in peacetime armies he drifted out of military service into business in Ostend. He settled as a brandy merchant in Cognac in 1765, then moved in 1776 to Bordeaux to conduct a distilling business, and returned to Cognac in 1789.

Hennessy was an extraordinarily likeable man, loved by all who knew him. He was less successful as a businessman, though unluckily for him his arrival in Cognac in 1765 and in Bordeaux in 1776 was soon followed on each occasion by the onset of exceptional business crises. However, his 1789 business, in which he was partnered by his forceful and ambitious son James and another Irishman Samuel Turner, laid the foundations of the present celebrated brandy house. On going to Bordeaux Richard had ceded his business in Cognac to an Irishman and friend, John Saule. James learned his business as a clerk under Saule, and following Saule's death in 1788, the new partnership conducted its business in the old premises, originally acquired by Richard in 1765.

L.M. CULLEN

Henry, Paul (1876–1958) and **Grace** (1868–1953) Painters. Paul Henry, after studying under Whistler in Paris in the late 1890s, moved to Achill in 1910 with his artist wife Grace. Inspired to move by the writings of Synge, the island life dominated their painting for the next decade. In 1919 both moved to Dublin, where Paul formed the Society of Dublin Painters in 1920 as a venue for young artists to display their work. Credited with developing a distinct school of Irish landscape painting, Paul separated from Grace in 1930, at the height of his career. Grace, somewhat overshadowed by her husband in the history of Irish art, moved to Europe to work and exhibit.

Reading

Kennedy, S.B., *Irish Art and Modernism, 1880–1950* (Dublin: Institute of Irish Studies at the Queen's University of Belfast for the Hugh Lane Municipal Gallery of Modern Art, 1991).

TREVOR BUTTERWORTH

heraldry Art or science of depicting armorial bearings; of tracing and recording pedigrees; and of deciding questions of precedence. Heraldry has its origins in feudal warfare and in the feudal system of hereditary devolution by primogeniture, practised by the Normans and introduced to Ireland upon their arrival in 1169.

Irish succession and property rights were based not on the right of primogeniture but on an elected leadership/kingship through membership of the *deirbhfhine* (a family group of four generations) without the individual's right to transmit land, property or title after death. With the assimilation and intermarriage of many of the Normans with the Irish nobility, the Normans became Hibernicizised and the Irish slowly adopted heraldry, together with the customs and rights of primogeniture, so that by the late fifteenth or early sixteenth century the pre-heraldic tribal or totem emblems of the Irish began to make their appearances as heraldic charges or symbols. With the appointment in 1552, by royal patent, of the first herald of Ireland with the title of Ulster king of arms, the king of England (who had in 1541 been declared king of Ireland) brought English influence to bear on heraldry and genealogy. Thus, it can be posited that Ireland has three distinct but complementary heraldic traditions: Norman, Anglo-Irish and Old Irish.

Some of the characteristics that single out Irish heraldry from the other two traditions are as follows:

1 The lack of ordinaries – ordinaries being the basic geometrical patterns on the shield.

2 The frequent use of the tincture vert – the colour green – which, except for Ireland, is rarely used in heraldry.

3 The frequency and recurrence of certain motifs, such as:
   (a) *dexter hand appaumé*: the red hand – a motif central to Irish heraldry, but as a symbol of great antiquity, possibly representing the pre-Christian Celtic deity Nuadu;
   (b) *twin rampant lions*: the possible symbol of Mil/Milesius the warrior/father figure, who was often represented in the Irish epics as a lion (leomhan). Both the dexter hand and the rampant lion are closely associated with the Uí Néill families;

(c) the *Stag*: this motif, which is synonymous with the Eoghanacht families
of the south of Ireland – MacCarthy,
O Sullivan, O Connell, etc. – is again
of some antiquity, but as a heraldic
device does not predate the sixteenth
century;

(d) the *tree*: oak, yew and ash were probably associated with the mystical
source of strength. The family of
O Conor Don and many other Connacht families connected with them
display an oak tree vert on their
shields.

4 Unique to Irish heraldry are the number
of mottoes in the Irish language which are
inseparably attached to the arms of certain
families.

Most of the motifs used in Irish ('Gaelic')
heraldry are based on pre-Christian religion
and mythology, family legend and folklore.

MÁIRE MACCONGHAIL

Heron, Hilary (1923–77) Sculptor. Born
and died Dublin. Heron studied at the
NCAD, whose academic teaching she soon
rejected. She also studied in France and Italy,
on a travelling scholarship. She was one of the
central personalities for many years in the Irish
Exhibition of Living Art, as both an exhibitor
and an organizer. With Louis le Brocquy, she
represented Ireland at the Venice Biennale in
1956. Heron worked in a variety of materials,
but her strongest and most original works were
in metal, reflecting her interest in primitive
and totemistic levels of meaning.

BRIAN FALLON

Hervey, Frederick Augustus (1730–1803)
Fourth earl of Bristol and fifth Baron
Howard de Walden, bishop of Derry. Born
1 August; died 8 July. Hervey was educated
at Westminster School and Corpus Christi
College, Cambridge. On 2 February 1767,
he was created bishop of Cloyne, and on
18 February 1768 he was translated to the
bishopric of Derry, where his improvements

won him freedom of the city. His tolerant
policies led to the act relieving Catholics
from the Oath of Supremacy.

At the Volunteer convention in Dungannon
in February 1782, he joined the corps of
Londonderry Volunteers. More extreme
than Grattan, he advocated reform of the
Irish House of Commons and extension of
the franchise to Catholics. In November
1783, at the grand convention in Dublin, he
arrived flamboyantly dressed in purple, and
attended by dragoons. The convention
ignored his advice to dissolve before Flood
introduced his bill to the House of Commons.
When the Volunteer movement collapsed,
Hervey withdrew from Irish politics.

FRED LOWE

Hewitt, John Harold (1909–87) Poet.
Born Belfast, the son of Robert Telford
Hewitt and Elinor (Robinson) Hewitt, teachers, and educated at Methodist College
and Queen's University, Belfast (BA 1930).
Hewitt began to work as an art assistant at the
Belfast Museum and Art Gallery, rising to
deputy director; political bias led to him
being passed over for the position of director.
From 1957 he was director of the Herbert Art
Gallery in Coventry. He retired to Belfast in
1972. In 1934 he married Roberta Black,
socialist and educational activist. During his
first literary career in Belfast he helped form
the Ulster Unit, with Luke, McGann and
Middleton; he was active in the development
of Ulster regionalism and was associate editor
of *Lagan* in 1945–6. His interest in the recovery of a regional Ulster tradition fed into his
MA thesis on 'Ulster Poets, 1800–1870', later
published as *Rhyming Weavers*; contributions
to the *Bell* included his autobiographical
Planter's Gothic (1953).

Hewitt represented his time in Coventry
as a period of exile, and his influence in
Northern Irish culture and politics was really
revived at his return to Belfast, where he was
re-established as mentor to the younger
Ulster poets, in public perception if not in
fact. He found a sympathetic local publisher

in Blackstaff Press, which he warmly supported. He was first writer in residence at Queen's University and first president of the Northern Ireland Fabian Society.

Since Hewitt's death his championship of regionalism has been recruited to a cultural politics emphasizing a separate Protestant tradition, about which he expressed reservations as well as sympathies. The socialism and anti-sectarianism which he proposed as his most significant contributions to political action receive less attention. His reputation as poet and regional philosopher has never been higher, and is annually reformed at the John Hewitt International Summer School.

Reading

Brown, Terence, *Northern Voices: Poets from Ulster* (Dublin: Gill and Macmillan, 1975).

Dawe, Gerald and Wilson Foster, John, *The Poet's Place: Ulster literature and Society, Essays in Honour of John Hewitt 1907–1987* (Belfast: Institute of Irish Studies, Queen's University of Belfast, 1991).

Heaney, Seamus, 'The poetry of John Hewitt', *Threshold* 22 (Summer 1969), repr. in Seamus Heaney, *Preoccupations: Selected Prose 1968–1978* (London: Faber, 1980).

Hewitt, John, *Conacre* (Belfast: privately printed, 1943).

—— *Collected Poems 1932–1967* (London: MacGibbon and Kee, 1968).

—— *Out of My Time: Poems 1967–1974* (Belfast: Blackstaff Press, 1974).

—— (ed.), *Rhyming Weavers and Other Country Poets of Antrim and Down* (Belfast: Blackstaff Press, 1974).

—— *Kites in Spring: A Belfast Boyhood* (Belfast: Blackstaff Press, 1980).

—— *Ancestral Voices: The Selected Prose of John Hewitt*, ed. and intro. Tom Clyde (Belfast: Blackstaff Press, 1987).

—— *The Collected Poems of John Hewitt*, ed. Frank Ormsby (Belfast: Blackstaff Press, 1991).

Olinder, Brita, 'John Hewitt's Belfast', in Maurice Harnon (ed.), *The Irish Writer and the City* (Genard's Cross: Barnes and Noble, 1984).

Warner, Alan, 'John Hewitt: honest Ulsterman', *Threshold* 38 (Winter 1986–7).

SIOBHÁN KILFEATHER

Hewson, George Henry Phillips (1881–1972) Organist, scholar and composer. Born Dublin. Heusan was educated at St Patrick's Cathedral Choir School and Trinity College, Dublin, where he graduated as Bachelor in Music in 1903, adding the doctorate in 1914. He succeeded C.H. Kitson as professor of music in 1935, and retired in 1962. Organist successively at the Chapel Royal, Trinity College, and (for 40 years) at St Patrick's Cathedral, he was for many years at the centre of Dublin musical life. His reputation was mainly that of an organist, which was recognized by the award of honorary fellowship of the Royal College of Organists. His publications include some church music, and arrangements of Irish airs.

BRIAN BOYDELL

Hickey, Anthony (d. 1641) Franciscan and theologian. Originally from County Clare, he studied in Louvain, and became a professor of philosophy and theology there, and later at Cologne. In 1619 he moved to Rome to collaborate with his friend, Luke Wadding, in publishing the works of Duns Scotus. The fruits of these labours appeared in three volumes in 1639 entitled 'R.P.F. Joannis Duns Scoti...'. In the same year he attained the prominent office of diffinitor of the Franciscan order. His untimely death in 1641 cut short his voluminous plans for a history and hagiography of Ireland.

Reading

Bigger, F.J., 'The Irish in Rome in the 17th century', *Ulster Journal of Archaeology*, ser. 2, 5 (1899), pp. 115–38.

Franciscan Fathers (eds), *Father Luke Wadding: Commemorative Volume* (Dublin: Clanmore and Reynolds 1957).

BRIAN DONOVAN

Hickey, Patrick (1927–98) Graphic artist. Born India. A formative figure in the development of Irish graphics, Hickey came to Ireland in 1948 where he studied architecture. After a scholarship to study etching and lithography at Scuolo de Libro in Urbino, he founded the Graphic Studio in Dublin in 1961 and went on to represent Ireland in several International Graphic Biennales. The French National Archives bought his illustrations to Dante's Inferno, while his semi-abstract painting of County Wicklow proved to be most successful. From 1985 to 1990 Hickey was head of painting at the National College of Art and Design in Dublin.

Reading

O'Regan, J. (ed.), *Works 3: Patrick Hickey 1986–90 (Essays)* (Dublin: Gandon Editions, 1991).

TREVOR BUTTERWORTH

Higgins, Aidan (b. 1927) Writer. Born Celbridge, County Kildare. Higgins was educated at Clongowes Wood College, and emigrated to England. A succession of odd jobs there led to a two-year sojourn in South Africa, recounted in *Images of Africa* (1971). Other lengthy periods abroad in Spain, Germany and London have also influenced his work.

Higgins's fiction confronts explicitly the artistic legacies of James Joyce and Samuel Beckett. Beginning with the short story collection *Felo de Se* (1960, republished as *Asylum*, 1973), his work has dwelt on varieties of stasis and decay. His two most accomplished novels, *Langrishe, Go Down* (1966) and *Balcony of Europe* (1972), portray doomed love affairs in sterile times. Later novels, *Scenes From A Receding Past* (1977) and *Bornholm Night Ferry* (1983), repeat themes of estrangement and futility without extending them. Higgins's sharp-eyed journalism and travel writing are collected in *Ronda Gorge and Other Precipices* (1989) and *Helsingfors Station* (1990). Higgins's painterly style, innovative sense of form, and critique of personality comprise a tart antidote to the stereotypes of modern Irish fiction.

GEORGE O'BRIEN

Higgins, Frederick Robert (1896–1941) Poet. Higgins was a minor but acceptable poet in the 'Celtic' manner developed by Padraic Colum and the young Austin Clarke. Higgins has been doubly unlucky; he died at an early age, before his sometimes uncertain voice could consolidate itself, and, championed as he was by Yeats (whom he only just outlived), he has too often been instanced as an egregious example of the elder poet's erratic taste. His 'Song of the Clatter-Bones' is refreshingly scabrous, and he developed a pleasing topographical lyricism, in early poems about the west of Ireland and in the pieces about Meath in his final collection, *The Gap of Brightness* (1940); his other collections were *Island Blood* (1925), *The Dark Breed* (1927) and *Arable Holdings* (1933).

PETER DENMAN

hiring fair In the pre-mechanized era, when manual labour lay at the core of agricultural production, complex circulation systems evolved to distribute agricultural labour between areas of surplus and deficit. In Ireland, and especially in Ulster, that interchange often took the form of the hiring fair, where potential workers paraded themselves on specified fair days for inspection by employers. In May and November, when six-months' agreements were made, young boys and girls gathered at recognized spots, sometimes carrying the insignia of their skills – scythes, spades, flails, etc. Such fairs were often located at the junction between big and small farm areas, as in the Laggan in Donegal.

These theatrical displays of harsh social and economic realities became a motif for Ulster novelists (Patrick MacGill, Peader O'Donnell Seamus Ó Grianna), where the fairs were common (at least 80 sites are recorded). The hiring fairs eventually petered out by the time of World War II.

KEVIN WHELAN

historians' terms The nomenclature of the various communities, native and settler, that made up Irish society in the early modern period presented increasing difficulty to contemporaries as the mix became more diverse, and the problem continues to trouble historians. The term 'Irish' was ambiguous in some contexts, and specificity was achieved by the usages 'wild Irish' and 'mere Irish' (where 'mere' was not derogatory, but simply meant 'pure'), or the collective 'Irishry'; similarly, the term 'English' needed the qualifications 'by blood' and 'by birth' to convey the difference more neatly expressed in Gaelic as 'Gall' and 'Saxanaigh'. Within the English 'by blood', the most relevant principle on which to differentiate between communities which had developed along divergent lines remained their relationship with government, and the familiar division between 'English rebels' and 'loyal subjects' was still in common official use in the first half of the sixteenth century. When new settlers arrived later in the century, however, the term 'queen's loyal subjects' lost its historic meaning, and confusion resulted.

The cumbersome categories of 'the English of Irish birth' and 'the English of English birth', old terms revived with a fresh application, captured a distinction that served certain purposes, but had the disadvantage of failing to preserve the politically sensitive differences within the established colonial community. The same defect attached to the more convenient term which began to be employed late in the century, the 'English-Irish' or 'Anglo-Hiberni', which indiscriminately bonded those who were, in the words of Mountjoy, 'obstinate in Popish superstition'. The religious connotation is significant: the uncertain new terminology derived from the pragmatic need to describe a new element in the community, but the confusion was partly due to the way in which the quality of the loyalty of the original 'loyal subjects' had been compromised by their failure to follow England in adhering to the reformed religion. For 'English rebels', the alternative term 'degenerate English' was apt and increasingly used: for the subset of the 'queen's loyal subjects',

no alternative was found until about the turn of the century, when the self-ascribed term 'old English' was adopted as an integral part of the colonial response to conquest.

The new name denoted a new sociopolitical reality, for it subsumed both 'loyal subjects' and 'English rebels', and signified the reuniting of the colonial traditions. In essence, the mantle of the loyal tradition and the associated claim to considerate treatment was extended to those who had not historically (or even recently) shared it. The name itself was a propagandist statement which affirmed both the colonial status of the established Catholic colonists and their priority over the Protestant 'new English' who had come to Ireland in recent years. Within a very short time, the terms 'Sean-Ghaill' and 'Nua-Ghaill' were incorporated into the Gaelic vocabulary, and the shift in terminology was completed by widespread acceptance of the complementary term 'old Irish'.

But this new terminology left the small group of Protestant descendants of old settlers without a label. It also coped a little untidily with the Scots, brought by plantation and informal settlement in the early seventeenth century, who were called Scots when precision was required, but were otherwise loosely included amongst the 'new English'. Some 'old Irish' preserved the buried distinctions by distinguishing between the 'old English' and the more Gaelicized colonists who retained a certain cultural residue, whom they called the 'mixed Irish'. Others, at the time of the rising in 1641, sought to mark the alliance of settler and native by addressing the 'old English' as 'new Irish'. From the English side also, dissent from the terminology usually involved a challenge to the political identity of the 'old English'. The threat was foreshadowed in the language of Lord Deputy Wentworth (1633–41), who habitually blurred local distinctions by speaking interchangeably of 'papists' and 'natives'. It was realized in the 1650s, when innocence and guilt became the sole principle of differentiation and the single category of 'Irish papist' was used to describe not only the 'old Irish' and the 'old English', but also 'new English' converts to Catholicism (most famously the descendants of Edmund Spenser) and the occasional families of Catholic Elizabethan settlers. While one distinction was thus obliterated, a new one was imported as newcomers reinforced the Protestant community of Ireland in the 1640s and 1650s. Attempts by the established Protestant community to appropriate the name 'old English' fortunately failed, and the terms 'old Protestant' and 'new Protestant' became common currency, hinting at religious difference as well as precedence.

The simplified terminology endured: after the restoration Catholics were judged less on their origins than according to their recent loyalties, to king or papal nuncio, while it ceased to be to the advantage of Protestants to preserve their own divisions. Although the term 'old Protestant' survived briefly, and although the conflict of 'old Irish' and 'old English' interests remained, surfacing sharply in the Jacobite Parliament in 1689, the need for nuance had passed, and 'papist' and 'Protestant' already sufficed before the Williamite degredation of the 'old English' extinguished the old colony and set the 'Protestant ascendancy' firmly in place.

The practice of historians has not been consistent. Most accept that the term 'Anglo-Irish' is best reserved for the eighteenth-century Protestant colony, while 'new English' and 'old and new Protestants' adequately describe its antecedents. 'Gaelic Irish', 'native Irish' and 'old Irish' are freely used and unproblematic throughout the early modern period, as is the use of 'old English' with reference to the seventeenth-century Catholic colonists. Recent usage, with the authority of *A New History of Ireland*, has sought to resolve an enduring difficulty by extending 'old English' to describe the historic colonial communities of the sixteenth century: the effect is to obscure the way in which the coinage of the name was bound up with the emergence of the group which it signified. It may be doubted whether six-teenth-century nomenclature can be made tidier than the reality it describes.

AIDAN CLARKE

Historical Memoirs of the Irish Bards

The *Historical Memoirs* by Joseph Cooper Walker (1786), which comprises a history of music in Ireland and nine appendices, is a major document in terms of its exclusive concern with music in Ireland. Walker attempts to chronicle his subject in an admixture of learned reference, antiquarian speculation and rhetorical persuasion. His account charts the 'state of music amongst the Ancient Irish' and its subsequently depressed condition in Elizabethan Ireland, which in turn leads to its lethargic condition in the present day (i.e. the mid-1780s). Conjecture and partisan enthusiasm predominate in much of the historical chronicle, which also includes aesthetic discriminations between Irish music as 'the voice of nature' and Italian music, which 'only trifles with the ear'. The gloomy context which Walker provides for his life of Carolan (appendix VI of the *Memoirs*) is one in which the 'despotic sway' of Italian music in London and Dublin combines with outright political oppression to erode the aesthetic genius of the native Irish music. Walker laments that harpers in the seventeenth century 'degenerated into itinerant musicians', while he recognizes that the 'last of this Order of men . . . was Turlough O'Carolan, a fine natural Genius, who died in the year 1738.'

Carolan's achievement in the *Memoirs* is equated with Handel's impact on music in England. The crucial distinction between the two composers, however, lies in the dislocated status implied by Carolan's mastery of a generally defunct tradition by comparison with Handel's reanimation of a living one. Walker's attempt to claim for Carolan (and for Irish music in general) a degree of artistry comparable to that of Handel and English music was bluntly rejected by Charles Burney in his review of the *Historical Memoirs*, which appeared in the *Monthly Review* for December 1787: 'It is impossible for any one, not totally ignorant of the subject of Mr Walker's book, to read many pages of it without discovering his knowledge of music to be small and his credulity in Hibernian antiquities to be great.' Burney, moreover, condemns the stylistic features of the 'rude' collection of melodies attributed to Carolan and others which form the last appendix to the book. The conflict of opinion between Walker and Burney graphically demonstrates the apparently insurmountable difficulties which attended the development of an enduring mode of musical discourse in Ireland.

Reading

White, Harry, 'Carolan and the dislocation of music in Ireland', *Eighteenth-Century Ireland* IV (1989), pp. 55–64.

HARRY WHITE

Hitchcock, Reginald Ingram Montgomery (1893–1950) Film maker. Born 18 January, Dublin; died 22 July, Hollywood. R.I.M. Hitchcock, known as Rex Ingram, son of Rev. F.M.R. Hitchcock, was educated at St Columba's College, County Dublin. He emigrated to the USA at 18 and began to work in films. In 1921 he launched *The Four Horsemen of the Apocalypse*, featuring Rudolph Valentino and Alice Terry; she became Ingram's wife and starred in his films. *Four Horsemen* was enormously successful, and Ingram became one of the most important film makers in Hollywood. He retired in 1933 to devote himself to sculpture, writing and travel.

HENRY BOYLAN

Hogan, John (1800–58) Sculptor. Born Tallow, County Waterford, 14 October; d. Dublin, 27 March. Hogan's father was a builder while his mother came from an Ascendancy background. In 1819, working in Cork for the architect Thomas Deane, Hogan was encouraged to carve. Under the patronage of William Paulet Carey, Hogan travelled to Rome in 1824, where he was influenced by international neo-classicism. Hogan was based in Rome for the next 25 years. His work was mostly religious, his main patrons being the re-emerging Catholic church of mid-nineteenth century Ireland. He sculpted a toga-clad image of Daniel O'Connell in 1843 (Dublin, City Hall).

Reading

Turpin, John, *John Hogan: Irish Neoclassical Sculptor in Rome, 1800–1858* (Dublin: Irish Academic Press, 1982).

FINTAN CULLEN

Holinshed's Chronicles (1st edition 1577; 2nd edition 1586–7) This collection of histories of England, Scotland and Ireland was originally compiled by Raphael Holinshed (d. 1580), a Cambridge graduate from London. The section on Ireland was, however, written by Richard Stanihurst, a noted Dublin-born antiquarian, who relied heavily on the work of his former mentor, Edmund Campion. Nevertheless, Stanihurst's contribution was not merely in editing Campion's work, and he included many of his own details and observations on recent Irish history. For example, there is a detailed history of the Fitzgeralds, earls of Kildare, which attempts to exonerate them from the revolt of Silken Thomas in 1534, and prove their unswerving loyalty to the English crown. Furthermore, Stanihurst revels in the political and cultural superiority of the Pale community, and expresses his own energetic support for the government's attempts to reform Gaelic society, though this support is tempered by his advancement of education rather than coercion in accomplishing this aim. The section on Ireland is dedicated to the lord deputy, Sir Henry Sidney.

The first edition of the *Chronicles* was immediately successful, though certain sections of Stanihurst's contribution were considered offensive by the government, and were ordered to be removed. After Holinshed's death in 1580, his publishers decided to update the *Chronicles*, employing John Hooker, alias Vowell, as the new editor. Though originally from Exeter, Hooker had spent some time in Ireland with Sir Peter Carew in the 1560s and 1570s, and personally undertook updating the sections on Ireland. This second edition was published in 1586–7, and continued the history of Ireland to that year. Overall the *Chronicles*, the combined work of Campion, Stanihurst and Hooker, are an extremely important addition to our understanding of Irish history.

Reading

Hogan, Edmund 'The blessed Edmund Campion's History of Ireland, and its critics', *Irish Ecclesiastical Record*, 3rd series, xii (1891), pp. 629–41, 725–35.

Lennon, C., 'Richard Stanihurst and Old English identity', *Irish Historical Studies* xxi (1978), pp. 121–43.

——*Richard Stanihurst, the Dubliner, 1547–1618* (Dublin: Irish Academic Press 1981).

Miller, L. and Power, E. (eds), *Holinshed's Irish Chronicle* (Dublin: Dolmen Press, 1979).

BRIAN DONOVAN

Holland, John Philip (1841–1914) Inventor. Born Liscannor, County Clare, 24 February; died Newark, New Jersey, 12 August. The son of a coastguard, Holland was educated at Limerick Christian Brothers School. He became a Christian Brother in 1858, but was dispensed from his vows in 1872 and went to the USA, where he continued teaching. After many years of experimentation, helped financially by John Devoy, he built a submarine which operated successfully. The US and British navies ordered Holland vessels, and he is generally recognized as the father of the modern submarine.

HENRY BOYLAN

Holloway, Joseph (1861–1944) Architect and diarist. Born Dublin. The son of a baker, Holloway was educated at Castleknock College and Dublin Metropolitan School of Art. He worked in an architectural office, setting up his own practice in 1896, and redesigned the Mechanics' Theatre for the National Theatre Society (1903). He attended almost every theatrical performance in Dublin from 1895 until his death, keeping an extensive journal, now preserved in the National Library (222 volumes). This work is more useful as a record of plays produced than for its critical insights; his aesthetic appreciation was limited, and his moral outlook narrow. Political events, such as the 1916 Rising, are occasionally noted.

Reading

Hogan, Robert and O'Neill, Michael, *Joseph Holloway's Abbey Theatre* (Carbondale: University Press, 1967).
——*Joseph Holloway's Irish Theatre*, 3 vols (Dickson: Proscenium Press, 1968–70).

CHRISTOPHER FITZSIMON

Home Rule A term first used in the 1860s, which came to dominate Irish political life between 1870 and 1920. It meant the restoration of an Irish Parliament in Dublin with responsibility for most domestic issues, but still subordinate to the British government in many important areas. The term became common from the 1870s; Isaac Butt founded the Home Government Association in 1870, which subsequently became the Home Rule League in 1873. The 1874 general election resulted in 50 Home Rulers being elected, and out of this group emerged the Irish Parliamentary Party, or Home Rule Party.

The vagueness of the term meant that it was interpreted in different ways by different people. Butt hoped that both Catholics and Protestants would support Home Rule in a movement aimed at giving Ireland a federal government within the United Kingdom. Butt's mild-mannered leadership lost him support, and he was challenged by the more aggressive and militant tactics of Charles Stewart Parnell, who became leader in 1880.

Parnell recognized that hostility to British Rule was the driving force behind Irish nationalism, but was publicly willing to accept Home Rule, with limited legislative powers for an Irish Parliament, in order to allay British fears that Home Rule would lead to separation of Ireland from Britain; privately he saw Home Rule as indeed a step towards this very goal. In the 1880s he won the support of Republican movements such as the Fenians and the Irish Republican Brotherhood, who wanted complete independence and total separation, but who were willing to accept Home Rule as a halfway measure in the late nineteenth century.

The prospects of success were greatly increased by the conversion of Gladstone and the majority of the Liberal Party to the Home Rule cause in 1885. The Conservative Party exploited this by opposing Home Rule and appealing to the British electorate on the grounds of defence of the empire and the integrity of the United Kingdom. For Irish Unionists, Home Rule meant a Dublin Parliament dominated by Catholics and a threat to the economic development of the North. Ulster Unionists, in particular, opposed this, and the Orange Order was revived in 1886. Gladstone's first Home Rule Bill was defeated by 341 votes to 311 in the House of Commons on 8 June 1886. He introduced a second Home Rule Bill in 1893, similar to the first, with Westminster retaining direct control over matters such as the crown, defence and foreign relations, but with 80 Irish MPs to sit at Westminster. Although it passed the Commons, the Bill was overwhelmingly defeated in the House of Lords, and thus vanished the two crucial occasions in the late nineteenth century when the whole nature of the Anglo-Irish relationships might have been greatly improved. The Liberals quietly dropped the Home Rule albatross, and it is not revived until 1910 when the prime minister, Asquith, needed the votes of the Irish Parliamentary Party, led by John Redmond, to stay in power, and promised Home Rule in return. The third Home Rule Bill was introduced in April 1912, but, due to the use of the House of Lords veto, did not receive royal assent until 18 September 1914. The Bill was vehemently opposed by Sir Edward Carson and the Ulster Unionists, and the Conservative Party, and although the possibility of excluding Ulster was discussed, no agreement had been reached by the outbreak of war in August 1914. Liberal leadership was weak and indecisive, and Asquith was much relieved to get all sides to agree to suspend the Act for the duration of the war.

World War I and the 1916 Rising greatly changed the situation in Ireland. Home Rule came to be seen as irrelevant and second best, and the party was challenged and eventually overwhelmingly routed by Sinn Féin in the December 1918 election; nationalist opinion now favoured a separate Republic. Eventually, under the Government of Ireland Act 1920 and the 1921 Treaty, a separate Home Rule Parliament was established in Northern Ireland, and a 26-county Irish Free State was accorded dominion status – not total independence, but a great deal more than had been offered in 1914. Revolutionary nationalism had produced some of the results long sought after by the constitutionalists.

Reading

Bew, P., *Conflict and Conciliation in Ireland, 1890–1910: Parnellites and Radical Agrarians* (Oxford: Oxford University Press, 1987).

—— *Ideology and the Irish Question: Ulster Unionism and Irish Nationalism, 1912–1916* (Oxford: Oxford University Press, 1994).

Boyce, D.G., *Nationalism in Ireland* (London: Routledge, 1991).

Loughlin, J., *Gladstone, Home Rule and the Ulster Question, 1882–1893* (Dublin: Gill and Macmillan, 1986).

Lyons, F.S.L., *Charles Stewart Parnell* (London: Collins, 1974).

McCartney, D. (ed.), *Parnell: The Politics of Power* (Dublin: Wolfhound Press, 1991).

Morton, G., *Home Rule and the Irish Question* (London: Longman, 1980).

O'Day, A., *Parnell and the First Home Rule Episode, 1884–87* (Dublin: Gill and Macmillan, 1986).

JIM O'HARA

Hone family

1 Nathaniel Hone RA (1718–84) Painter. Born Dublin; died London, 14 August.
2 Horace Hone ARA (1756–1825) Painter. Born London; died London, 24 May.
3 John Camillus Hone (1759–1836) Painter. Born London: died Dublin, 23 May.
4 Nathaniel Hone RHA (1831–1917) Painter. Born and died Dublin.

The eighteenth-century Hone family of painters were all miniaturists and portraitists. The most important figure is Nathaniel Hone RA, who apart from portraits occasionally produced subject pictures; Horace Hone ARA and John Camillus Hone were his sons. Nathaniel Hone RHA and the twentieth-century painter Evie Hone were descended from the younger brothers of Nathaniel Hone RA.

Nathaniel Hone RA was the son of a merchant of Dutch descent and most probably trained in the Dublin Society Schools. He was resident in London by the mid-1740s, having married an English woman. Hone excelled in enamel miniatures, exhibited with the Society of Artists and was a founding member of the Royal Academy in 1769, where he exhibited until 1784. Opposed to the dominant classical Italianate style and favouring a more Dutch-inspired air of domesticity, his best works are the numerous portraits he did of his large family. *A Piping Boy* (1769, Dublin, National Gallery of Ireland) is a portrait of the artist's son John Camillus Hone. He is especially remembered for one large subject painting of 1775, *The Pictorial Conjuror, Displaying the Whole Art of Optical Deception* (Dublin, National Gallery of Ireland). This is a clever and detailed attack on Joshua Reynolds's penchant for 'borrowing' from the great masters, but when first submitted to the Royal Academy it also carried an indecorous suggestion of a relationship between Reynolds and Angelika Kauffmann.

Hone was forced to remove this section of the painting and the oil was rejected for exhibition. He later exhibited the picture in one of the earliest recorded one-man shows.

Horace Hone ARA was a highly accomplished miniaturist who practised in Dublin from 1782 to *c*.1801. One of his most celebrated sitters was the actress Sarah Siddons, whom he drew when she visited Dublin in 1784. This miniature achieved great popularity through Bartolozzi's engraving of 1785. Horace Hone became miniature painter to the Prince of Wales in 1795.

John Camillus Hone was also a miniaturist, who trained under his father. He worked in Calcutta throughout most of the 1780s but settled in Dublin about 1790.

Nathaniel Hone RHA came from a professional Dublin background, graduating in 1850 with a degree in engineering and science from Trinity College, Dublin. After studying with Thomas Couture in Paris (1854), he moved to Barbizon and later Fontainebleau, staying in France for a total of 17 years, with an additional 18 months in Italy. While in France he befriended many of the artists of the realist school, in particular Harpignies. He painted many of the sites frequented by the naturalists. He was in Etretat *c*.1867; Courbet was there in 1869. Returning to Ireland in 1872, Hone settled down to a comfortable rural life in Malahide where he painted and exhibited almost annually at the RHA, becoming professor of painting to the Academy in 1894. His private income meant he did not have to sell.

Hone's work varied little over the years, his subjects changing from the forests of Fontainebleau to the shore at Malahide and the pastures on his estate. His best works are those that incorporate sky and water, but the routine fashion in which he painted skies can make the viewing of his work a somewhat tiresome business. His occasional forays into figure work were weak and unconvincing.

In 1901 Hone shared an important retrospective exhibition with his contemporary John Butler Yeats. Organized by Sarah Purser, the exhibition was a deliberate alternative to the stagnant academicism of the annual Royal Hibernian Academy Exhibitions. Hone's French-realist-influenced landscapes and Yeats's Whistleresque portraits were a revelation to Dublin and to Hugh Lane in particular. Hone thus played a key role in the introduction of the ideas of French naturalism to Ireland even if the style and subject matter of his paintings were, by 1901, somewhat *passé*.

Reading

Campbell, Julian, *Nathaniel Hone the Younger 1831–1917* (Dublin: National Gallery of Ireland, 1991).

Crookshank, Anne and the Knight of Glin, *The Painters of Ireland, c.1660–1920* (London: Barrie and Jenkins, 1978).

Foskett, Daphne, *A Dictionary of British Miniature Painters*, 2 vols (London: Faber, 1972).

Mulvany, T.J. and Gandon, J., *The Life of James Gandon, Esq.* (Dublin: 1846; repr. London: Cornmarket Press, 1969).

Penny, Nicholas (ed.), *Reynolds* (London: Royal Academy of Arts and Weidenfeld and Nicholson, 1986).

Smith, J.T. *Nollekens and his Times* (London: 1829).

Strickland, Walter *A Dictionary of Irish Artists* (Shannon: Irish University Press, 1968).

FINTAN CULLEN

horse racing Ireland has produced an extraordinary succession of giants of the turf – Arkle, Golden Miller, Brown Jack, Ballymoss, Red Rum, L'Escargot and Dawn Run among the horses, trainers Vincent O'Brien, Tom Dreaper, Paddy Prendergast and jockeys Pat Taaffe, Martin Molony, Pat Eddery, Jonjo O'Neill, Adrian Maguire and Ulster-born Richard Dunwoody among the humans. Recent horses of note include Giant's Causeway, Imperial Call, Istabraq, Sinndar and Vintage Crop.

The country owes its influence on world horse racing to the limestone-rich soil, temperate climate and lush pasture – ideal conditions for breeding bloodstock – and to an historically rural economy which has given the Irish a particular affinity with horses. That racing runs deep in Irish culture is testified by the central role of the running of the Ascot Gold Cup in James Joyce's *Ulysses*, W.B. Yeats's poem 'At Galway Races' or Jack Yeats's brooding painting *Before the Start* in the National Gallery in Dublin.

The Turf Club, the Irish equivalent of the Jockey Club, was founded in the late eighteenth century, by which time Mr Edmund Blake and a Mr O'Callaghan had made their singular contribution to racing history in 1752 with a private race across open country, from Buttevant Church in County Cork to the spire of St Leger Church at Doneraile four and a half miles away, which gave the sport a new code – steeplechasing.

Throughout the nineteenth century the Irish influence on racing in England steadily increased, with Irish breds regularly enjoying prominence in the Grand National, run at Aintree from 1839. The first Irish-trained horse to land the Derby at Epsom was Orby in 1907, whose victory prompted an old lady to greet trainer Frederick MacCabe with the words: 'Thank God and you, sir, we have lived to see a Catholic horse win the Derby!'

The greatest Irish horse of all was Arkle, trained by Tom Dreaper and winner of the Cheltenham Gold Cup three times from 1964 (when he beat the Irish-bred but English-trained Mill House in a famous showdown celebrated in song by Dominic Behan) to 1966. Arkle won a string of other big races in a career which brought 22 victories from 26 steeplechases before injury ended his stately progress in December 1966.

Tipperary trainer Vincent O'Brien, who retired in 1994, did more than any other individual to put Ireland on the world racing map. In the 1940s and 1950s he won the Champion Hurdle three times, the Cheltenham Gold Cup four times, and the Grand National three years in succession with different horses, and became even more successful when he turned his attention to the Flat, handling such horses as Ballymoss (in 1958 the first Irish-trained horse to win the Prix de l'Arc de Triomphe) and the 1970 Triple Crown hero Nijinsky – one of O'Brien's six Derby winners. O'Brien was instrumental in importing some of the best American blood-lines to Europe and establishing the Coolmore Stud, which now houses many of the world's top stallions.

There are 27 race courses in Ireland (including two in Ulster: Irish racing recog-nizes no border), with facilities ranging from top class at the Curragh (home of all the Irish Classics) to the once-a-year curiosity of Laytown, the last surviving race meeting in Europe run along the beach, where the only permanent building is the gentlemen's toilet.

Reading

Magee, Sean, *Racing and the Irish* (London: Stanley Paul, 1992).

Smith, Brian, *The Horse in Ireland* (Dublin: Wolfhound Press, 1991).

Watson, S.J., *Between the Flags* (Dublin: Allen Figgis, 1969).

Welcome, John, *Irish Horse-racing* (London: Macmillan, 1982).

Willis, Grania, *The World of the Irish Horse* (London: Weidenfeld and Nicolson, 1992)

SEAN MAGEE

Huguenots Out of all proportion to the numbers who eventually settled in Ireland, and to the space offered to them there, the Huguenots hold a special place in the collect-ive memory of the nation. Implicit in the fact that numbers of them settled in Ireland, and counter to some contemporary, unflattering stereotypes of bigotry in Ireland, is the recog-nition that the community which welcomed these first *réfugiés* (who gave us the word 'refugee') was tolerant, and also sensitive to their qualities of industry and technical skill. This is all the more striking for occurring in a context of religious persecution: at a time when Irish Catholics were suffering the consequences of Cromwellian administration and subsequent Caroline legislation on resettlement, the Huguenots (whose faith was Calvinist and who were fleeing Catholic persecution in France) settled in a manner which has left absolutely no record of local recrimination or violence. The dispossessed of both countries appeared to recognize the plight of each other.

Immigration began in the late 1660s, in the wake of the Act of 1662 'for encouraging Protestant strangers to inhabit and plant in the Kingdom of Ireland' (14 & 15 Carol. II), gathered momentum after the revocation of the Edict of Nantes (1685), and continued until the early eighteenth century, after the Williamite military campaigns in Ireland. Although the number of immigrants proposed by the early work of Samuel Smiles should be revised down to something under 10,000, the quality and range of their contri-bution have been increasingly appreciated. The first settlers were textile workers brought to Dublin by the viceroy, the duke of Ormond, who had known exile in France; the later ones were pensioned officers of the Williamite armies, some of whom had fought at Aughrim and the Boyne. The arrival of the earlier ones coincided with the expansion of Dublin as a modern metropolis; the later ones founded their own graceful county town of Portarlington with a bequest from the Huguenot Henri de Ruvigny, earl of Galway and lord chief justice of Ireland.

The separate cultural identity of the Huguenot community in Ireland was eroded successively by the pressure to conform to Anglican doctrine, and by the subsequent unpopularity in official circles of all things French after the outbreak of the French Revolution. The last sermons in French at Portarlington were delivered in the 1820s.

Merging into the life of the local commun-ities, the legacy and memory of the Huguenots survive in a tradition of craftsmanship (the woodwork carvings of Jacques Tabary at the Royal Hospital, Kilmainham, and work of silversmiths such as de Wuillaume or de Lamerie), the perfection of technical skills (as in the linen manufacture of the Crommelin family at Lisburn, or the work of the cartographer John Rocque), the institution of an enduring banking system by the Digues La Touche family, the impact on early urban planning (as in their contribution to the Wide Streets Commission in Dublin), and the growth in Franco-Irish relations with trade between the related houses of major Irish cities and French *comptoirs*. The myth has thus flourished of a gentle people, industrious and persevering, whose presence was not only an adornment to the Irish cultural heritage, but early confirmation that in Ireland was a society which was cosmopolitan and non-provincial.

Reading

Caldicott, C.E.J., Gough, H. and Pittion, J.-P. (eds), *The Huguenots and Ireland: Anatomy of an Emigration* (Dublin: Glendale, 1987).

Gwynn, Robin, *Huguenot Heritage: The History and Contribution of the Huguenots in Britain* (London: Routledge and Kegan Paul, 1985).

Lee, Grace Lawless, *The Huguenot Settlements in Ireland* (London: Longmans, Green, 1936).

St Leger, Alicia, *Silver, Sails, and Silk: Huguenots in Cork, 1685–1850* (Cork: 1992).

C.E.J. CALDICOTT

Hume, John (1937–) Politician. Born Derry, 18 January. Hume was educated at St Columb's College, Derry, and St Patrick's College, Maynooth. A leader of the Northern Ireland civil rights movement in the 1960s, he was elected to the Stormont Parliament in 1969 and the following year founded, with five other MPs, the Social Democratic and Labour Party (SDLP). He became its leader in 1979, in which year he was elected to the British House of Commons and the European Parliament. He served as a member of the Northern Ireland power-sharing executive from January to May 1974, and supported subsequent efforts to revive power sharing, but grew disillusioned with prospects for an internal settlement. His friendship with Garret FitzGerald, Sean Donlon, secretary of the foreign affairs department, and leading European and American politicians was a factor in the process which issued in the signing of the Anglo-Irish Agreement in 1985.

During the 1980s and early 1990s Hume concentrated on economic rather than political affairs, and succeeded in obtaining substantial EU and other funding for the development of Derry, which he sees as the future north-western focus of a united Europe. His courage, dialectical skill, subtlety of mind and acute understanding of how to work the levers of power have made him the most considerable political figure in Northern Ireland and, in the opinion of many, the outstanding Irish statesman of his generation. His reputation in the 1990s was greatly enhanced by his insistence on the inclusion of Sinn Féin in the Northern Ireland Peace Process. He was elected to the Northern Ireland Assembly in June 1998, but announced his resignation, on health grounds, in 2000. With David Trimble he was awarded the Nobel Peace Prize in 1998.

Reading

White, Barry, *John Hume: Statesman of the Troubles* (Belfast: Blackstaff Press, 1984).

JAMES DOWNEY

hunger strikes The Irish have a long tradition of starvation and the British a scandalous tradition of ignoring it. The most famous of the Irish hunger strikes took place in 1981 in the Maze prison (formerly Long Kesh), where Bobby Sands and nine other Catholic inmates serving sentences for terrorism starved themselves to death in order to reclaim the status of prisoners of war, having been demoted by the Thatcher government to ODCs, or 'ordinary decent criminals'. These protestors were following the example of Terence McSwiney, lord mayor of Cork, who died in 1920 in Brixton prison after 74 days without food, and who bequeathed his lethal philosophy of self-denial to the Republican movement, in particular the often-quoted formula that 'It is not those who can inflict the most, but those who can suffer the most who will conquer.'

However, suffragettes had been conducting hunger strikes in Ireland since 1912; and it was probably to conceal this precedent that the nationalists resurrected a medieval antecedent for the hunger strike in the civil code of Ireland, the *Senchus Mor*. Medieval Ireland, like medieval India, had a legal procedure of 'fasting to distrain', known as *tros-cud*, whereby a creditor could fast against a debtor, or a victim of injustice could fast against the injuring person. This tradition found its way into Christianity, and there are legends in which the patron saint of Ireland, St Patrick, hunger strikes against God. God always relents, because capitulation in the face of such self-sacrifice was regarded by early Christians as a mark of holiness. These legends suggest that religious abstinence may have originated in the civil practice of fasting with a hostile purpose against an enemy, although these traditions later grew apart. As F.N. Robinson has argued, the notion of compulsion exercised on a divinity represents a fundamental element in fasting and in other phases of religious asceticism; and what appears to the modern Christian as a form of sacrifice and humiliation may once have been, in some of its aspects, a way of taking the kingdom of heaven by violence.

Reading

Bamford, Christopher, and Marsh, William Parker (eds), *Celtic Christianity: Ecology and Holiness* (Stockbridge MA: Inner Traditions/Lindisfarne Press, 1987).

Beresford, David, *Ten Men Dead: The Story of the 1981 Irish Hunger Strike* (London: Grafton, 1987).

Bynum, Caroline Walker, *Holy Feast and Holy Fast: The Religious Significance of Food to Medieval Women* (Berkeley: University of California Press, 1987).

Kelly, Fergus, *A Guide to Early Irish Law*, Early Irish Law Series III (Dublin: Dublin Institute for Advanced Studies, 1988).

O'Malley, Padraig, *Biting at the Greave: The Irish Hunger Strikes and the Politics of Despair* (Boston: Beacon Press, 1990).

Robinson, Fred Norris, 'Notes on the Irish practice of fasting as a means of distraint', in *Putnam Anniversary Volume* (Cedar Rapids, IA: Torch Press, 1909).

Senchus Mor, vol. I (Dublin: Alexander Thom; London: Longman, Roberts, and Green, 1865).

Sheehy-Skeffington, Andrée D., *Votes for Women: Irish Women's Struggle for the Vote* (Dublin: n.d.).

MAUD ELLMANN

hysteria and the Great Revival (1859) In the wake of the religious revival which swept America in 1857–8, the Synod of the Reformed Presbyterian church, meeting in Derry in 1858, recommended the holding of 'special meetings of a devotional character, with a view to promote the revival of religion in the Church'. Ulster had been prepared for such an awakening by the growth of prayer meetings and Sabbath schools, like the 'fellowship meeting' held in a schoolhouse near Kells by four young converts, McQuilken, Carlisle, Wallace and Meneely, who became the centre of the revival.

It is accepted that the service which sparked the revival was held in Ahoghill on 13 March by the Rev. David Adams. Over 3,000 gathered outside the church, and continued praying afterwards. The next day, the first prostrations occurred. Events then developed in a rapid and peculiar manner. Massive prayer meetings, with people being stricken down, occurred in Ballymena, Coleraine and Belfast, all leading to hundreds of converts. They would feel a desperate conviction of sin, cry out in distress, and frequently fall prostrate. Other physical phenomena occurred: people would go into trance-like states, and predict when they would 'go away' and 'come back', and others would be stricken deaf, dumb and blind. They would grab Bibles and point out texts of mysterious suitability. In September, in Lisburn, stigmata appeared in force, and tourists flocked in to see these sights. One woman displayed her breasts, miraculously tattooed with the words 'Jeasus Christ'.

Controversy raged about the cause of these phenomena. Archdeacon Stopford of Meath argued it was hysteria, with the sermons on sin producing intense fear and excitement. The symptoms were then 'propagated by sympathy'. The *Lancet* called it 'a moral epidemic' of fanaticism, and *The Times* blamed Irish fervour, 'stronger in all its manifestations than that bestowed on the cooler headed and less easily moved Saxons'. Modern scholars have argued that the introduction to stern Ulster Calvinism of evangelical techniques, like impassioned hymn singing and sermons on impending doom, led to the hysteria. Others attribute the awakening to recently literate farm labourers and factory workers, to whom the revival was restricted, learning to use biblical language in a stirring way.

Whatever the cause, the effects were long lasting. The arousing of Christian conscience in the community led to strict observance of the Sabbath. Sixty churches were built or extended, and the Presbyterian religious outlook became associated with the Ulster character.

Reading

Donat, James G. 'Medicine and religion: on the physical and mental disorders that accompanied the Ulster Revival of 1859', in W.F. Bynum, Roy Porter and Michael Shepherd (eds), *The Anatomy of Madness*, 3 vols (London: Tavistock, 1988).

Paisley, I.R.K., *The 'Fifty-Nine Revival'* (Belfast: Publications Board, Free Presbyterian Church of Ulster, 1958).

Scott, A.R. 'The Ulster Revival of 1859', Dublin University unpublished PhD thesis, 1962.

FRED LOWE

1

Icarus Founded in Trinity term, 1950, under the chairmanship of Alec Reid and the initial editorship of Cecil Jenkins, Rosalind Brett-Jones and Peter Devlin. Sponsored by the Dublin University Modern Languages Society, the magazine made its debut in May of the same year and has since appeared thrice yearly in October, January and May, the editor(s) changing with each issue. No. 1 contained poems by Douglas Sealy, Bernard Share, Richard Kell and Alec Reid, and prose by Alec Reid and Harry Keating among others. Subsequent issues carried verse and prose by Donald Davie, Richard Weber, R.J. Wathen, Brendan Kennelly, Bruce Arnold, Michael O'Siadhail, Michael Longley, Edna Broderick, Eavan Boland, Augh Maxton, Jeremy Lewis, Deirdre Madden, Sara Berkeley and Michael West. Illustrators have included Pauline Bewick, Julian Campbell and Michael Mulcahy. The sixties saw several attempts to widen the scope of an essentially collegiate publication, and the seventies a rash of pretentious graphics and violent fiction, including a necrophiliac short story which provoked the confiscation of an entire print run by college authorities – a *cause célèbre* in its day. The magazine, probably at its best in the sixties, continues to appear at irregular intervals.

DEREK MAHON

Impressionism Many of the leading Irish artists of the late nineteenth and early twentieth centuries studied in ateliers in Paris and Antwerp. They soon became aware of the radical French artistic movements such as realism, *plein-air*ism and Impressionism. They shared the then popular enjoyment of 'painting from nature', working in the artists' colonies in the area of Fontainebleau and in Brittany. Some of them practised a skilled but cautious naturalistic style, in the manner of Bastion-Lapage. Some stayed on in France, others made their careers in England, while the majority returned home and established themselves in Ireland. Once away from the bright sunshine of France and the Mediterranean coast, their palettes tended to revert to the more subdued tones and overcast light of Ireland. Some had to forfeit landscape painting, to earn their living as portraitists.

For these reasons, there was not a school of Irish Impressionists, at least in the sense of a district, cohesive group, working in the same location, or with a common style or purpose. The majority of Irish artists tended to work as individuals, independently of one another. Their 'Impressionism' was more likely to be filtered through the examples of Sargent or Whistler than directly influenced by the

French artists. Some of the finest examples of 'Irish Impressionism' were as likely to be at home in Ireland or in places as distant as Morocco or Egypt as in France itself. Others were painted well into the twentieth century, long after the original movement in France was over.

In a narrow sense, the purest examples of Impressionism by Irish artists are found in the French landscapes of Roderic O'Connor in the late 1880s, and in the charming garden scenes and interiors painted by Walter Osborne in turn-of-the-century Dublin. However, in a wider sense an Impressionistic influence appears in the work of a remarkable member of important artists: from Nathaniel Hone in the 1860s to Sarah Purser, Aloysius O'Kelly, Frank O'Meara and John Lavery, Osborne and O'Conor, up to the work of William John Leech and Mary Swanzy in the twentieth century. Continued research into the period often discovers surprising and vital examples of Impressionism, by forgotton as well as well-known Irish artists.

In *Vale*, the third part of his autobiography *Hail and Farewell*, George Moore writes: 'I am the only one in Dublin who knew Manet, Monet, Sisley, Renoir and Pissarro – I knew them well at the Nouvelle Athenes', while Lavery, in his autobiography *The Life of a Painter*, claims that if he had not remained with his English-speaking circle, and if he had been able to speak French better: 'No doubt, I should have learned more and been more influenced by the influential and impressed by the Impressionists.' In spite of the humourous or ingenuous tone of these writers' remarks, neither of their claims is strictly true. Nathaniel Hone (the Younger) had been a fellow student of Manet's in Courure's in the mid-1850s – 25 years before Moore's meeting with Manet. Hone met some of the young Impressionists, such as Sisley, Monet, Renoir and Sazille, in the Forest of Fontaine-bleau in the 1860s. Although a member of the Barbizon school, Hone was the first Irish artist to appreciate the discoveries of the French Impressionists. Some of his woodland

paintings of the late 1860s are close to the early work by Sisley and others, in the Corot mode. Some of his small studies have a freshness of colour, and show a spontaneous use of paint, while his Mediterranean paintings such as *Petite Afrique* (c.1872, private collection) are advanced for their time in their sunny atmosphere, free brushwork and use of bright colour, for example pinks and blues, golds, maroons and greens.

Hone visited Greece and Egypt c.1891–2. His watercolours charmingly capture the Mediterranean light and atmosphere, with touches of pink, blue and gold. His oil painting *Baules of the Nile* (Hugh Lane Gallery, Dublin) has an Impressionistic brightness and warmth. Back home in Ireland, Hone remained true to his Barbizon training. But his free brushwork, and use of touches of blues and reds even in sombre Irish landscapes and seascapes, display his continued awareness of Impressionism.

In publications such as *Confessions of a Young Man* (1888) and *Reminiscences of the Impressionist Painters* (1906), George Moore recalls student days in Paris in the 1870s and his visits to some of the Impressionist exhibitions. He became friends with Manet (1879–80) and is said to have been the first writer in English on Degas. But Limerick-born artist Norman Garstin had written about Manet as early as 1884, admiring his 'delicious brightness and happiness...He lets in air and light.'

Sarah Purser studied at the Academie Julian in Paris in 1878–9. Her small portraits of the 1880s, for instance *Le Petit Dejeuner* (1884, National Gallery of Ireland), show that she had studied the work of Monet and Degas closely.

Aloysius O'Kelly, born in Dublin c.1853, studied with Gerome in Paris, and visited Brittany in the 1870s and 1880s. Some of his Breton beach and harbour scenes have a light touch, and use vivid hues such as turquoise, pink, ultamarine and gold, while *Corpus Christie Procession, Brittany* (Allied Irish Banks Collection, Dublin) is surprisingly

'Impressionistic' in its sketchy, sunlit atmosphere. However, when O'Kelly visited Cairo in the late 1880s, he reverted to a more academic, literal style, in the manner of Gerome.

Henry Thaddeus Jones, and Walter Osborne with a group of Dublin friends, visited the artists' colonies in Brittany in the early 1880s, while Frank O'Meara, John Lavery and Roderic O'Connor painted in Grez-sur-Loing near Fontainebleau. O'Meara's *Towards Night and Winter* (1885, Hugh Lane Gallery, Dublin) and Lavery's *Under the Cherry Tree* (1884, Ulster Museum, Belfast) are both quintessential *plein-air* paintings of the mid-eighties. Yet both show an awareness of Impressionism. O'Meara's even, grey-green tonality is heightened by touches of green, blue and pink, and some of Lavery's river scenes have a vigorous, sketchy treatment, while his later *Bridge at Grez* (*c*.1900, Ulster Museum, Belfast), apparently painted in one sitting, shows his free, fluid treatment of water in a classic Impressionistic mode. He had a studio in Tangiers, and his small Moroccan paintings of the 1890s and 1900s charmingly capture carefree bazaar scenes, white-robed figures and the glare of sunlight on earth walls, with a few deft brushstrokes.

Roderic O'Connor adopted the free brushwork and pure blues of the French Impressionists more wholeheartedly than any other Irish artist. His early French landscapes, for example *Road and Farm Buildings* (*c*.1889, private collection), are characterized by impastoed brushstrokes and bright colours such as reds and oranges, blues and yellows, showing that he had closely studied paintings by Sisley, Monet and others at first hand. O'Conor is said to have met Van Gogh, and was an associate of Gauguin at Pont Aven. His Breton landscapes of the 1890s, such as *Yellow Landscape, Pont Aven* (Tate Gallery, London), use heavy impasto and dazzling colour, in the manner of Van Gogh, although with O'Conor's distinctive 'striped' technique. *La Ferme at Lezaven* (National Gallery of Ireland) has a more dappled, Impressionistic surface. O'Conor is more truly 'post-Impressionist than Impressionist. He remained independent of some of the Pont Aven Circle, and his fiery Breton seascapes of the late 1890s anticipate the Fauves in their vigour and 'hot' palette.

In the same period, in Ireland, Walter Osborne was quietly developing an individual Impressionist style. He admired English contemporaries and, on a visit to Paris in 1895, was critical of modern French painting. His work of the 1880s had had the sombre tonality and careful handling of the '*plein-air*' style, but his outdoor studies in the nineties, such as *In the Phoenix Park* (1895, National Gallery of Ireland), show increasing interest in sunlight and shadow. By the turn of the century, through the influence of J.S. Sargent and perhaps Berthe Morisot, Osborne's figure studies in interiors and landscapes had developed a much looser, more dappled atmosphere, culminating in masterly impressionistic paintings, such as *Tea in the Garden* (1902, Hugh Lane Gallery) and *In a Rathmines Garden*' (private collection), rendered in sunny tones and loose, curving ribbons of paint. The setting is suburban Dublin, but Osborne is practising a pure Impressionism, given special charm by his sympathy for women and children.

Osborne's student W.J. Leech painted small Impressionistic sketches in Brittany *c*.1910, and larger paintings contrasting bright sunlight and deep shadow. His best-known painting, *Convent Garden, Brittany* (1912?, National Gallery of Ireland), showing nuns in a lush, sunny garden, demonstrates a more studied, 'frozen' Impressionism than Osborne's. As a student in Paris before World War I Mary Swanzy became exposed to the even more radical influences of Fauvism and Cubism. Her later sketches of the Mediterranean and Czechoslovakia are Impressionistic in their bright palette and bold manner of painting. Her Samoan paintings of the early 1920s became more bright and Fauve.

Osborne may have claims to have been Ireland's only true Impressionist, who would have gained an international reputation had he lived longer. But sadly his career was cut short by his early death in 1903, thus closing a bright door of possibility in Irish Art.

JULIAN CAMPBELL

industrial building in the early twentieth century In the early years of the twentieth century there was a distinct change in the architecture of industrial buildings in Ireland. A major influence was from America, and in particular the work of the Chicago School with its bold new structures of multi-storey steel frames. The first building in Ireland to adopt the 'American' way of building was the huge Market Street Store House for Arthur Guinness in Dublin. Completed in 1904, the Guinness building is nine storeys high and the structure is composed of a steel frame with the outer part encased in brick. This major early modern industrial building was designed by A.H. Hignett and the engineering staff of Guinness Brewery, and the steelwork design was by Sir William Arrol. The invention of reinforced concrete and its large-scale development through the Hennebique system, in the first decade of the twentieth century, resulted in many large-scale mills and warehouses throughout the country in this new material. The first of these, in 1904, was the five-storey linen factory for Thomas Somerset in Belfast by architect W.J.W. Roome. Other notable early reinforced concrete buildings included R. and H. Hall's Granary in Waterford by engineer W. Friel, Bonded Whiskey Store in Dublin for John Jameson of 1906, and Hely's building in Dame Street, Dublin, of 1906 by architects Batchelor and Hicks.

When the new Irish Free State was established there was an early and far-seeing decision, in terms of the modern development of Ireland, with the planning of a national electricity supply based on the harnessing of the river Shannon. This work was carried out by the German firm of Siemens-Schuckert and this, the largest engineering and industrial project ever carried out in the country, lasted from 1924 until 1929. The power station at Ardnacrusha was constructed in steel framing with a high-pitched roof and tall windows, giving it a truly Germanic look. The huge dam and intake building, great reinforced concrete ship locks, and stark functional concrete bridges brought the quiet rural countryside abruptly into the twentieth century. In the late 1930s there was an expansion of the water-powered production of electricity by the construction of the large reservoir at Blessington in County Wicklow, and of a concrete dam with a powerful and dramatic form at the gorge of Poulaphuca. The ancillary buildings are white and functional and in a simple art deco style.

The earlier industry of gas production was modernized in the late 1920s by a series of new retort houses designed by West's Gas Improvement Company of Manchester. The function of the retort house was to burn coal and produce coal gas, with coke as a by-product. The Dublin Gas Company built two horizontal retort houses in 1922 but the new vertical house, erected in 1929, was a striking modern design owing much in appearance to the industrial architecture of Hans Poelzig in Germany. The Dublin vertical retort house was constructed of H-shaped steel framing with thin in-fill panels of Accrington engineering bricks and glass bricks, with open brickwork in some panels for ventilation. The retort houses had a lifespan of only 20 years and were replaced at intervals. The last Dublin retort house was demolished in 1985 with the advent of natural gas.

One of the earliest factory-building enterprises of the new Irish state was the construction of a number of industrial alcohol plants throughout the country. The government continued the policy of looking beyond Britain for advice and commissioned the Dutch architect J.D. Postma for the designs in 1934. Postma had wide experience of industrial building, and the new factories were constructed with steel framing, with bolted on steel panels. The design was in the international style, which was to dominate for most of the remaining century, particularly in the three decades after World War II, when there was an enormous expansion of industrial building.

SEAN ROTHERY

industrial revolutions The first industrial revolution can be characterized by the use of continuous mechanical power to turn machinery; typically millstones, a hammer for forging, or spinning and weaving machinery. These processes were subsequently rendered independent of a local water-power source by the invention of the steam engine. The rivers in Ireland, primarily in Ulster but also in the neighbourhood of Dublin, Cork and many Irish towns, were on a scale to enable them to be harnessed easily to give the few tens of horse power required for an industrial mill. Ruins of eighteenth-century water mills are a common sight in all parts of Ireland. Windmills are rare; Tacumshane in Wexford is preserved and Blennerville near Tralee has been restored.

There was another process at work which enhanced the industrial revolution in Britain. The use of charcoal to smelt iron had stripped the forests. When, in the 1750s, smelting with coal was developed, rapid expansion became possible; the need to pump the mines gave rise to the steam engine. This process, however, largely bypassed Ireland, though attempts were made in the 1840s to mate the coal and iron which surround Lough Allen, and some effort was put by Thomas Mulvany into the Shannon Navigation, with this and other industrial developments in mind. Mulvany went on to engineer the canals of the Ruhr, and he is commemorated in Essen with a statue. Steam, based on native coal from Coalisland as well as imported, became the main motive power for the Ulster mills, although water remained important, the water turbine being an Ulster invention.

A further enhancer of the industrial revolution in England was the accompanying agricultural revolution, associated with the name of 'Turnip' Townsend. Feeding cattle in the winter with harvested fodder provided a steady supply of meat and milk to feed the expanding cities. The Irish livestock industry has *to this day* managed to avoid taking this modest step into the nineteenth century, with the result that the industry remains bedevilled by quality and continuity problems. The 'mild winters' are invoked by some experts as an excuse, but less credibly as added value and continuity become increasingly important to the market.

The main impact on Ireland of steam was the railways. However, it could be argued that their role was to bleed the countryside and feed a parasitic metropolis. Consider their layout: the junctions outside Dublin are either in the middle of nowhere (Ballybrophy, Limerick Junction, Manulla, Farranfore) or else at the military garrison towns (Mallow, Athenry, Claremorris). The railway system never serviced direct interaction between the main urban centres outside Dublin. It serviced the emigration process and English-oriented commerce.

The electrical power revolution, when it came, had a very positive impact. The first wave was on the Edison direct current principle, and before 1914 most large and medium and some small towns were serviced, often with a small local hydro scheme on an eighteenth-century mill site. The 'second wave' (the 'Shannon Scheme') when it came in the 1920s for its time was quite visionary: it projected the production to several times the power then in use in all the urban generators, and laid down the basis for a national grid, taking advantage of the possibility of long-distance transmission at high voltage using alternating current. (This did not take place in Britain until after World War II.) The approach to Siemens-Schuckert in Germany was an assertion of independence from the hitherto well-trodden channels to England. The prime mover was Dr Thomas A. McLaughlan, a physicist turned engineer, who had served his time with Siemens in

Pomerania, where a regional grid existed on the Irish scale.

Developments were interrupted by the war, but in the 1950s the distribution system to rural areas was commenced, and by the end of the 1960s it was virtually complete. The use of single-phase 10kV lines was innovative, in response to the need to service isolated farmhouses. Elsewhere in Europe the rural community tends to live in villages, and isolated farmhouses are the exception. The case could be made that this was a technical fix for a peculiar Irish social situation, arising from the over dependence on a livestock-based economy. Had rural life been more village based, there would have been more of an opportunity for small local industry to develop. Rural electrification has allowed the isolated farmhouse to remain marginally viable longer perhaps than it deserved. This argument is a hypothesis put forward by the present writer; it needs to be researched.

The communications revolution brought about by the telegraph, telephone and radio where it touched Ireland has been episodic: the transatlantic cable and the early Marconi enterprises were implants servicing the needs of Britain. The use of radio in 1916 in broadcast (rather than point-to-point) mode for the first time in history is said to have ensured that the news of the Rising got to the USA via shipping; the fact that the effort was made with equipment commandeered from the naval radio school in O'Connell Street is well attested.

Less praiseworthy is the failure to make use of short-wave communications to keep the emigrants in touch. This became technically feasible in the 1930s, and was adopted effectively by the BBC for enabling the far-flung empire to be kept informed of British politics and culture. An attempt was made by de Valera to set this up during the war, with the aid of E.T.S. Walton in Trinity College, Dublin, and equipment was purchased in the 1950s for an RE World Service from Athlone, but later sold off at a loss.

The problem of supporting adequately the cultural needs of emigrants and expatriates remains, although the technology has been available since the 1930s.

The current wave of the industrial revolution is dominated by information technology. The first computer in the Republic, and perhaps in Ireland, was in use in the Irish Sugar Co. in Thurles in 1958. The Aer Lingus 'real-time' project of 1963–8, with which the present writer was associated, was a qualitative leap forward at the world state of the art. The universities followed suit. In 1992 there were some 400 firms in the *Kompass* directory listing 'software' among their products. Unlike earlier industrial revolutions, the information technology revolution is more than an implant; it seems to have put down roots in Ireland, and has the potential for becoming an accepted part of the culture.

ROY H.W. JOHNSTON

informers and spies Despite the fact that the later and more successful Irish nationalists of the 1919–22 period made effective use of informers and employed spies to infiltrate crown security networks, the tradition of informing carries a particular odium in Irish history. It was associated most commonly with the plight of the Catholic priests and bishops whose presence in eighteenth-century Ireland was largely prohibited by a set of penal laws, following the victory of the Protestant forces under King William III during the 1690s. The profession of priest-hunter was less common in Georgian times than has been believed, and its few more devoted followers appear to have led miserable and ill-rewarded lives. However, the faithless domestic servants or embittered clerical rivals on whom the priest-hunters depended for information may have been much more common, and the worst effects of informing were held in check only by official neglect or circumspection at the point of presecution.

Priest-hunters were protected to a point by officialdom; informers, however, were looked upon as akin to murderers and would, if identified and caught, be subjected to swift and usually fatal popular vengence. The mantle of the informer, far more than that of thief, rapist or murderer, would sit for generations on the family of offenders, to the disgrace of their descendants. The virulence of the popular attitude to informers sprang partly from the fact that they played a not-inconsiderable role in the downfall of substantial nationalist movements such as the United Irishmen. Leonard McNally (1752–1820), barrister and playwright, is remembered now not for his spirited songs and comic operas, but for his performance as defence attorney to the United Irishmen, from whom he accepted fees while simultaneously betraying them to the government for a substantial reward.

Despite the often elaborate precautions, none of the various Irish separatist movements was short of government infiltrators; the phenomenon existed alongside idealism as a curious mirror image of venality. Informers caused the collapse, respectively, of proposed and actual attempts at armed uprising by the Irish Republican Brotherhood in 1865 and 1867. Even in America, where the Fenian movement continued to flourish after the Irish failures of previous years, expeditions against Canada in 1866, 1870 and 1871 were reduced to a shambles largely by the work of Henri le Caron (1841–94), a spy of astonishing courage and endurance who lived to write his memoirs. Greater care in recruitment and swift, murderous revenge on detected offenders reduced the effectiveness of informers and spies during the Irish War of Independence of 1919–21, but they represented a danger which never quite faded. Informers within Dublin Castle in fact were then used with some success in the reduction of the British counter-terrorist efforts. The informer, however, in the guise of the 'supergrass', emerged yet again during the 1980s to threaten the effectiveness of both Republican and loyalist terror campaigns in Ulster. Patterns of behaviour and response were not markedly different to those which prevailed

two centuries ago; only the machinery of official protection and popular revenge had improved in response to modern technology.

GERARD O'BRIEN

Ingram, John Kells (1823–1907) Academic and economist. Born near Pettigo. In 1837 matriculated at the University of Dublin, while still in his fourteenth year. He graduated with a BA in 1843, in which year he also made himself famous by his poem, 'The Memory of the Dead'.

In Trinity College, Dublin, he held the chairs of oratory, English literature and Greek, and the Whately chair of political economy. At times he held these chairs simultaneously. In 1879, he was elected librarian to the college. His great service to the college came to an end in 1899, when he resigned the position of vice-provost.

Ingram's reputation as an economist began with his address to the British Association in 1878, in which he condemned the abstract method of economics by advocating a more historical and sociological approach to economic phenomena. He subsequently became, with Cliffe Leslie, the main spokesman of the English school of economic historians. Ingram achieved enormous success with his *History of Political Economy* (1888), which was translated into ten different languages. In his final years he expounded the principles of Comte's positivism as a religion and as a science of society.

Reading

Black, R.D.C., 'John Kells Ingram (1823–1907)', *Journal of the Statistical and Social Society of Ireland*, centenary vol. (1947).

Falkiner, C. Litton, 'A Memoir of the late John Kells Ingram', *Journal of the Statistical and Social Inquiry Society of Ireland* 12 (1908).

EAMONN SLATER

Institute of Public Administration Founded in 1957 by a group of public servants and academics to bring modern management thinking and practices into the public service. The institute offers management training and consultancy services to the Civil Service, local authorities, health boards and state-sponsored bodies. In 1993 it had 1,200 students taking its third-level degree and diploma courses. It publishes a wide range of descriptive and analytical material for students, practitioners and the interested public. Its *Administration Yearbook and Diary* is the most widely used reference book in Ireland. The institute undertakes administrative research projects. It also carries out work overseas.

Reading

Annual Report 1992 (Dublin: Institute of Public Administration, 1992).

JIM O'DONNELL

Insurrection Act (1796) The threat to the established order posed by the spread of the Defenders and the United Irishmen in the mid-1790s prompted a raft of counter-insurgency legislation from the Irish Parliament. The Insurrection Act, passed in February 1796, made it a capital offence to tender illegal oaths of association, and empowered the lord lieutenant to proclaim disturbed districts. This allowed magistrates to send suspects to the fleet and order searches for arms without observing due process.

Reading

McDowell, R.B., *Ireland in the Age of Imperialism and Revolution* (Oxford: Oxford University Press, 1979).

JAMES KELLY

internment Imprisoning Republican insurgents without trial has been a feature of all the main periods of conflict in Ireland in the twentieth century. In its objective of preventing insurrection it has had mixed results. Internment is central to the myth- and martyr-making process in Republicanism.

During World War I, 1,836 Republicans were interned at the Frongoch camp in north Wales, where, under the direction of Michael Collins, the core of the Republican Army which fought the War of Independence was formed. The hunger strike as a weapon of protest emerged, during this initial period, and attracted considerable public support for the protesters and internees. After Independence the largest-scale internment of the twentieth century took place, with up to 11,300 prisoners being held by the new Republic by the end of the Civil War in 1925. There were 82 executions during this period, and in spite of protests by prisoners this period of internment appeared to have the desired effect of quelling a major insurgent threat to the new state.

Internment was reintroduced on a much smaller scale during World War II and during the IRA's border campaign (1956–62). Again, internment was introduced virtually simultaneously on both sides of the border during these periods and was largely effective in its aims.

With the outbreak of serious communal violence in Northern Ireland, the then Stormont prime minister Brian Faulkner reintroduced internment on 9 August 1971. Some 260 Catholic men, including a small number of IRA members, were arrested in a major British army operation during the early hours of the morning. Most IRA members, well aware that internment was imminent, had left their homes before the raids. However, during the next three years a total of around 2,800 people were interned for periods ranging from weeks to years. Many of the initial internees were subjected to beatings and 'sensory deprivation' by soldiers, treatment later described as inhuman and degrading by the European Court of Human Rights. Of those interned, it is estimated that 2,060 were Republican and 109 Loyalist paramilitaries, the remainder being left-wingers or the politically uninvolved arrested as a result of mistaken identities.

The effect of Faulkner's decision was only to help establish a popular support base for the IRA among the Catholic working classes and to undermine the position of nationalist constitutional opposition within Northern Ireland. Violence rose dramatically, with deaths rising from 25 in 1970 to 174 in 1971 (mostly occurring after August) to 467 in 1972. The following year the Stormont government was replaced by direct rule from Westminster. Internment was eventually phased out in December 1985 and has not been used since.

JIM CUSACK

inter-party governments From the foundation of the state in 1922 to the end of 1998, Ireland had nine inter-party governments. One-party government was provided by Cumann na nGaedheal from 1922 to 1932 and by Fianna Fáil from 1932 to 1993, apart from 19 and a half years of inter-party government, as follows:

1 *February 1948 to June 1951*, a heterogeneous coalition of Fine Gael, Labour, National Labour, Clann na Poblachta, Clann na Talmhan and Independents. Fine Gael's John A. Costello became taoiseach and Labour's William Norton became tánaiste.

2 *May 1954 to March 1957*, again a coalition of all the other parties against Fianna Fáil, except that Clann na Poblachta did not join the government but pledged its support for it in the Dáil. Fine Gael's John A. Costello once more became taoiseach and Labour's William Norton became tánaiste.

3 *February 1973 to May 1977*, a coalition of Fine Gael and Labour. Fine Gael's Liam Cosgrave became taoiseach and Labour's Brendan Corish tánaiste.

4 *June 1981 to January 1982*, again a coalition of Fine Gael and Labour. Fine Gael's Garret Fitzgerald became taoiseach and Labour's Michael O'Leary became tánaiste.

5 *December 1982 to January 1987*, another coalition of Fine Gael and Labour. Fine

Gael's Garret FitzGerald became taoiseach and Labour's Dick Spring became tánaiste.

6 *June 1989 to November 1992*, a coalition of Fianna Fáil and the Progressive Democrats. Fianna Fáil's Charles J. Haughey became taoiseach and Fianna Fáil's Brian Lenihan became tánaiste.

7 *January 1993*, a coalition of Fianna Fáil and Labour. Fianna Fáil's Albert Reynolds became taoiseach and Labour's Dick Spring became tánaiste.

8 *January 1995* a centre-left, 'rainbow coalition' as it was called, of Fine Gael, the Labour and Democratic Left parties. Fianna Gael's John Bruton became taoiseach.

9 *June 1997* a coalition of Fianna Fáil and Progressive Democrats and independents. Fianna Fáil leader Bertie Ahern replaced John Bruton as taoiseach.

Reading

Chubb, Basil, *The Government and Politics of Ireland* (London: Longman, 1992).

Farrell, Brian, 'Coalitions and political institutions: the Irish experience', in V. Bogdanor (ed.), *Coalition Government in Western Europe* (London: Heinemann Educational, 1983).

JIM O'DONNELL

The *Irish Independent* (1904–) Effectively a relaunch of the undistinguished *Irish Daily Independent* (1891–1904) by William Martin Murphy, which capitalized brilliantly on technological and journalistic innovations pioneered by Northcliffe, and correctly identified a niche for a popular conservative newspaper. It is now the flagship of a three-paper organization (*Evening Herald*, 1891– and *Sunday Independent*, 1905–) published by a multi-media company, Independent Newspapers plc, which has diversified within Irish media and abroad, controlling or benefiting from substantial interests in Irish and Australian provincial papers, television distribution systems and outdoor advertising.

In the years after 1922, it broadly favoured the Cumann na nGael (now Fine Gael) party; more recently, it has extended critical support to governments which adopt conservative economic policies.

JOHN HORGAN

Irish Ireland This term originated in the decades around the end of the nineteenth century and represented a multi-dimensional concept which figured largely in the ethos of various political, cultural, literary, artistic and economic movements, ranging from the Society for the Preservation of the Irish Language (1876) and the Gaelic Union (1880) to the Gaelic Athletic Association (1884) and the Gaelic League (1893). One should also include such socio-political groups as Horace Plunkett's co-operative farming movement, the Land League and the Home Rule movement. These various associations did not constitute a formal coherent movement, all dedicated to the ideal of an Irish Ireland: rather they resemble in their total effect the work of F.H.S. Grundtvig and Kristian Kold in Denmark and that of Ugo Cygnaeus in the Fennoman movement in Finland in the same period.

Philosophically, the concept of 'Irish Ireland' owed much to the writings of Thomas Davis and the Young Irelanders of the 1840s and to the influence of their paper, the *Nation*. The immediate historical source may best be traced to the address of Douglas Hyde in 1892 on 'The necessity of de-anglicising Ireland'; this was the clarion call which convinced many of that generation of the need to promote a sense of separateness from England.

SEAMUS O'BUACHALLA

Irish Manuscripts Commission Founded by the Irish Government in 1928 to report on manuscripts relating to Irish history and literature and to publish editions and calendars of important manuscripts of Irish interest. Publications have ranged from facsimile reproductions of medieval manuscripts in Irish and Latin, such as the *Book of Lecan* and the *Book of Lismore*, to multi-volume printed editions of manuscripts such as the mid-seventeenth century *Civil Survey*. A periodical, *Analecta Hibernica*, is also published. The commission currently operates under the Department of Arts and Culture and its publishing projects are funded by the National Lottery.

Reading

Hogan, James, *The Irish Manuscripts Commission* (Cork: Cork University Press, 1954).

BERNADETTE CUNNINGHAM

Irish Republican Army The IRA (in Gaelic, Óglaigh na hÉireann) emerged in 1919 out of the Irish Volunteers and were the foremost Irish protagonists during the War of Independence, 1919–21. Following the establishment of the first Dáil Éireann in January 1919, the Irish Volunteers came to be recognized as the Army of the Republic. In conjunction with the political movement, Sinn Féin, the IRA fought an effective guerrilla campaign against British forces, which eventually led to the truce and Treaty of 1921. The Treaty, however, split the IRA; those who followed Michael Collins became members of the new National Army of the Free State, while those opposed to the Treaty (the Irregulars) took up arms against the new state in the Civil War of 1922–3. The bitterness of this war was to affect Irish life for generations.

The IRA continued to oppose the state and was outlawed by de Valera in 1936. Left-wing members such as Peadar O'Donnell failed to move it in a socialist direction in the 1930s, and in 1939 it declared war on Britain and Northern Ireland. A bombing campaign began in Britain during World War II, which led to the internment of hundreds of suspects in both states in Ireland, hunger strikes in prison, and the execution of some IRA members. During 1956–62 it began another military campaign against the

Northern Irish state, mainly aimed at police and military bases on the border. It had little success, failing to win the support of most Northern Irish Catholics, and in the 1960s gradually began to move away from its traditional physical force tradition to a more Marxist approach.

The outbreak of the Troubles in August 1969, with the consequent breakdown of law and order, left many Catholic areas in Belfast and Derry unprotected. In the aftermath of its helplessness, a group of mainly Northern IRA men in January 1970 purged itself of those supporting socialism and gradualism, and set up a separate Provisional command with a renewed emphasis on militarism. The Provisionals quickly acquired money and arms from Southern sympathizers, and as many Northern Catholics believed that the RUC and British Army were not acting in an impartial manner, the Provisionals took on themselves the role of defenders of Catholic areas and declared war on the security forces. From 1970 to 1994 a bitter and bloody war took place between the IRA and loyalist para-militaries and the British army, resulting in over 3,000 deaths, mostly civilian, and attacks in Britain and Europe, as well as Ireland. In August 1994 the IRA declared a ceasefire in order to enable its political wing Sinn Féin to enter political talks with the British and Irish governments. This terminated abruptly in February 1996, with a massive explosion in London's docklands, which killed two people and caused over £100 million worth of damage. Violence was resumed with several bomb attacks and sectarian killings, as the peace process in Northern Ireland faltered once more. Continuing deadlock over the decommissioning of IRA weapons led to Sinn Féin's being excluded from the peace talks. In April 1997 an IRA bomb warning succeeded in wrecking the British Grand National Meeting. A new round of peace talks in June pre-empted further violence and another ceasefire was announced by the IRA in August. In December 1997 British prime minister Tony Blair put the seal of approval on IRA co-operation in the peace process by inviting Sinn Féin leaders to Downing Street.

JIM O'HARA

Isdell, Sarah (*c*.1780–?) Playwright and novelist. A close relative of Oliver Goldsmith, Isdell was employed as a governess by the Denny family from Tralee, County Kerry. She wrote a very successful comedy, *The Poor Gentleman*, which was staged in Dublin in 1811 and later revived. She was also the author of a couple of novels, *The Irish Recluse* (1809) and *The Vale of Louisiana*.

RACHEL FURMSTON

J

Jacobitism In its broadest and best-understood sense Jacobitism was a Scottish phenomenon. It was a political and later largely a cultural movement which aimed at the restoration of the Stuart dynasty to the British thrones.

For the first half of the eighteenth century it was a politically active tendency of great potential, finding its supporters amongst the disaffected, idealistic or traditionally loyal Scottish noble families. Invasion scares were orchestrated over a prolonged period in consultation with the Stuart court in its places of European exile, and on two occasions, in 1715 and 1745, full-scale rebellions were put in hand. The second uprising saw a Scottish invasion of England and came too close to success for the Hanoverian regime to afford the Jacobite movement any further tolerance. Jacobitism in all its forms became the target of a determined government purge in post-1745 Scotland, and thereafter it ceased to have political teeth and became merely a cultural focus for anti-establishment sentiments.

Once the ousted James II had lost the Jacobite war in 1690–1, Ireland effectively ceased to be a Jacobite stronghold. Irish followers of the Stuarts followed James into exile and took with them such political commitment as Ireland had ever invested in Jacobitism. In Ireland, unlike Scotland, the Stuarts' significance had always been more religious than political, and they were associated primarily with Catholicism and the championing of the Irish and the remaining Old English against the Protestant establishment. Strong official belief in a possible Jacobite counter-blow through Ireland played a part in the enactment of virulent anti-Catholic legislation between 1695 and 1728. The Stuart Pretender (James III) from exile lent disastrous credibility to Irish Protestant fears by his insistence on an historic right to nominate Irish Catholic bishops, a practice which continued until his death in 1766. The Irish played no active part in the Jacobite uprisings of 1715 and 1745.

GERARD O'BRIEN

Jameson Anna, (neé Brownell) (1794–1860) Writer. Born 17 May; died March, Middlessex. Anna was the daughter of an Irish miniature painter. The family moved to England in 1798, and from 1800 she worked as a governess for several wealthy families, travelling with one of her pupils to Italy and France, where she wrote *The Diary of an Ennoyée* (1806). She married Robert Jameson, a young lawyer, in 1825. The marriage was a stormy one and they spent only a few years together. During her literary career she made many influential friends, including Lady Byron. A respected Regency writer, her works reflect her interest in art and religion (e.g. *Sacred and Legendary Arts*).

RACHEL FURMSTON

Jansenism A movement originating in seventeenth-century France, inspired by the theological ideas of C. Jansen, some aspects of which were condemned as heretical by Pope Innocent X in 1653, following lengthy debate. The theological pessimism of Jansenist doctrines concerning the necessity of divine grace and the irresistibility of that grace prompted extreme rigour in matters of morals and ecclesiastical discipline. Frequent use of the sacraments and regular communion were hallmarks of the adherents of Jansenism.

Early seventeenth-century Irish supporters of Jansen's teachings included Florence Conry, founder of the Franciscan college of St Anthony at Louvain, and John Sinnich, rector of the University of Louvain. In the early 1650s some Irish seminarians at Paris also joined the debate, which caused prolonged dissension within the Catholic church in France.

Reading

Oeyssens, Lucian, 'Florence Conry, Hugh de Burgo, Luke Wadding and Jansenism', in Franciscan Fathers (eds), *Father Luke Wadding Commemorative Volume* (Dublin: Franciscan Fathers, 1957).

O'Leary, Joseph S., 'The Irish and Jansenism in the seventeenth century', in Liam Swords (ed.), *The Irish–French Connection, 1578–1978* (Paris: Irish College, 1978).

Wall, Thomas, 'Irish enterprises in the University of Paris, 1651–53', *Irish Ecclesiastical Record*, ser. V, LXIV (1944).

BERNADETTE CUNNINGHAM

Japan, Irish studies in Studies in modern Irish literature have a long tradition in Japan. In the 1920s, representative figures of the Irish literary revival such as W.B. Yeats, J.M. Synge, Lady Gregory and Sean O'Casey began to enjoy a high fame particularly in the dramatic world of Japan. At present there are academic societies for certain individual Irish writers – Swift, Shaw, Yeats, Wilde and Joyce, for example – besides those for modern Irish literature in general. Studies in modern Irish history and church history began to flourish rather recently in Japan. A great many research papers and books of Irish studies, especially Irish literature, have been produced.

Reading

All the following are in Japanese.

Ken'ichi Matsumura (ed.) *A Companion to Irish Literature* (Tokyo: Kenkyusha, 1994).

Setsuko Mori, *The Religion and Culture of Ireland: A History of Adaptation of Christianity* (Tokyo: Japan Christian Publishers, 1991).

Shotaro Oshima, *Studies in Irish Literature* (Tokyo: Hokuseido Press, 1976).

KEN'ICHI MATSUMURA

Jehovah's Witnesses The first Jehovah's Witnesses congregations in Ireland were established in 1891. The response to their persistent door-to-door witnessing has been punctuated with bursts of violent opposition, although this is rare in recent decades. By 1992 more than 7,000 people worshipped in 101 congregations spread through every county in Ireland.

Reading

'Ireland', in *1988 Yearbook of Jehovah's Witnesses* (New York: Watchtower Bible and Tract Society, 1987).

JOSEPH LIECHTY

Jellett, Mainie (1897–1944) Painter. Born Mary Harriet Jellett Dublin; died Dublin. The child of a strongly Unionist family, Jellett studied in Dublin, in London under Sickert, and in Paris under André Lhote and Albert Gleizes. With her close friend and colleague Evie Hone, she is credited with introducing Cubism and abstract art into Ireland. Apart from her paintings, she was active and influential as a lecturer, organizer and propagandist for Modernism. Her Cubist phase has tended to overshadow the merits of her early, Orpen-influenced pictures and also her later development, in which religious art played a strong role. She died of cancer. A large exhibition mounted at the Irish Museum of Modern Art in 1992 did much to set the various phases of her career in clear perspective.

BRIAN FALLON

Jephson, Robert (1736–1803) Dramatist and poet. It is not clear where in Ireland Jephson was born, but he was educated in Dublin and died at Blackrock, County Dublin, 31 May. He was master of horse to several viceroys and was a member of the Irish Parliament from 1778. His plays include, *Braganza, The Law of Lombardy, The Count of Narbonne* and *The Hotel*.

PATRICK FAGAN

Jesuits The first Jesuits arrived in Ireland in 1542. They were succeeded by others at intervals over the next 250 years, always working under more or less hostile conditions to implement the Council of Trent's reforming decrees. Although under constant threat and usually short-lived, schools were developed in various urban centres outside Dublin and, from the middle of the eighteenth century, in the capital as well.

The first two Jesuits were foreigners. Their successors were Irish, drawn from both Gaelic and Anglo-Irish stock. After the almost world-wide suppression of the order (1773–1814), schools were opened once more, including Clongowes Wood College, County Kildare (1814), Belvedere College, Dublin (1832), Sacred Heart College, Limerick (now Crescent College Comprehensive, 1859). St Ignatius' College, Galway (1860), and Gonzaga College, Dublin (1950). These influenced the emergence of an educated

Catholic middle class in the nineteenth century and the development of the newly independent state in the twentieth.

Jesuit past pupils include Thomas Francis Meagher, John Redmond, James Joyce, Joseph Mary Plunkett and Austin Clarke. Jesuits were heavily involved in the genesis of the National University, through the work of men like Frs William Delaney and Thomas Finlay. Jesuits continued to exercise influence in University College, Dublin, through the work of some outstanding scholars, such as Frs Aubrey Gwynn and John Ryan. Other initiatives by the order, increasingly active in pastoral and social fields in the modern period, include the work of the Milltown Institute of Theology and Philosophy (1860), the review *Studies* (1912), the National College of Industrial Relations (1948), the Irish School of Ecumenics (1970), and the Centre for Faith and Justice. Fr Donal O'Sullivan was first director of the Arts Council.

Reading

McRedmond, Louis, *To the Greater Glory: A History of the Irish Jesuits* (Dublin: Gill and Macmillan, 1991).

BRUCE BRADLEY SJ

Jewish communities The history of the Jews in Ireland is one of the vicissitudes of immigration and emigration effected not only by medieval English anti-semitism in 1290, but also by more virulent European persecution in subsequent centuries. Despite a proposal in 1656 by James Harrington that Charles I should lease Ireland to the Jews to promote prosperity, the actual number of Jews resident in Ireland has always been small. That they exerted a profound influence disproportionate to their numbers is testified to by the extent and efficacy of Jewish aid from abroad during the Famine; yet census figures for 1881 record only 472 Jews in the 26 counties. By 1901 persecution in eastern Europe swelled the community to 3,769 – by far the majority concentrated in Dublin. The year 1904, however, bore witness to the only major act of blatant Irish anti-semitism when a campaign by a priest in Limerick led to most of the 100-member community fleeing.

While Joyce put a Jew and an Irishman at the centre of European literature, the exigencies of neutrality led Ireland to refuse entry to Jewish refugees from Nazism at the Evian conference of 1938. Despite the claims that there was not enough land for indigenous Irish or jobs for professionals, 25 refugees were admitted. In more recent years, Chaim Herzog, Belfast-born son of Ireland's first chief rabbi, Isaac Herzog, was elected president of Israel in 1983. In 1985 he returned to Ireland to open the Irish Jewish Museum, which records and celebrates the history of Ireland's Jews. Ireland's Jewish community gained its first minister in 1993 with Mervyn Taylor taking the portfolio for equality and law reform.

Reading

Hyman Louis, *The Jews of Ireland* (Irish University Press, 1972).
Shillman, Bernard, *A Short History of the Jews in Ireland* (Dublin: 1945).

TREVOR BUTTERWORTH

Johnston, Jennifer (1930–) Novelist and dramatist. Born Dublin, 12 January. The daughter of a playwright and an actress, Johnston attended Trinity College, Dublin, and is the recipient of three honorary degrees. Her nine award-winning bestsellers throughout the Troubles have influenced popular audiences through film, stage and television adaptations, and the school syllabus. Her ultra-feminine, maternal art considers time and consciousness as subtly as Woolf, with Austen's irony and Edgeworth's comic realism. Generally, she filters the disturbing now via the ghostly prism of history, focusing on illness as a metaphor for the betrayal of innocence. While her reiterated theme is the pity of war, her characters transcend the narrowness of Northern politics by crossing and recrossing tragically entrenched sociocultural divides. Her reassuring voice is both allusively witty and poetically fascinated by the meaning of words as actually spoken in conversation or monologue, wherein her genius lies.

Reading

Cahalan, J.M., *The Irish Novel* (Dublin: Gill and Macmillan, 1988).
Donnelly, B., 'The big house in the recent novel', *Studies* 64 (1975).
O'Toole, B., in *Across a Roaring Hill* (Belfast: Blackstaff Press, 1985).

MEDBH MCGUCKIAN

Johnston, (William) Denis (1901–84) Author and theatrical director. Born Dublin, 18 June; died Dublin, 8 August. The son of a Supreme Court judge, Johnston was educated at St Andrew's College, Dublin, Merchiston College, Edinburgh, Christ's College, Cambridge (MA, LLM, 1926) and Harvard Law School. He was called to the bar (1925) but worked with the Dublin Drama League and more importantly the Dublin Gate Theatre, to which he contributed *The Old Lady Says 'No!'* (1929), which made his name and brought to prominence the stage partnership of Hilton Edwards and Micheál MacLíammóir. Richly influenced by German Expressionism and the London productions of Peter Godfrey, it 'reads like the telephone directory and plays like Tristan and Isolde' (Edwards). This 'poetic satire' follows the meanderings of a concussed actor in the role of Robert Emmet through the pages of Romantic history and the foyers of post-revolutionary Dublin.

Johnston's most frequently performed play, *The Moon in the Yellow River* (Abbey, 1931), is an allegory on contemporary politics in which a new Free State power station is destroyed by the IRA; the style is heightened naturalism. *A Bride for the Unicorn* (Gate, 1933) concerns 'the triumph of banality in the modern world through its capacity to rob life of any value' (Cave). *Storm Song* (Gate, 1934), 'a sad little attempt at the popular market' (Johnston), is a satire on art appreciation. In *The Golden Cuckoo* (Gate, 1939) the Christ-like figure of Dotheright pits 'an inspired innocence against the forces of darkness' (Cusack). *The Dreaming Dust* (Gate/Gaiety, 1940), based on a radio play *Weep for Polyphemus*, explores the enigma of the life of Swift. *Strange Occurrence on Ireland's Eye* (Abbey, 1956) is an entertaining cross-examination of legal morality, and *The Scythe and the Sunset* (Abbey, 1858) a wryly detached counterblast to O'Casey.

Johnston joined the BBC (1936) as producer and reporter and during World War II broadcast from the Middle East and the Balkans. His 'speculative narrative' *Nine Rivers from Jordan* (1953) is a resonant response to these experiences. Other major prose works include *In Search of Swift* (1959) and *The Golden Horn* (1968). In 1928 he married the actress and director Shelah Richards; following their divorce he married the actress Betty Chancellor (1945). After the war he taught for many years in American universities, and was a founder of the Poets' Theatre, Boston. He was awarded the OBE (1946) and DLitt, New University of Ulster (1979).

Reading

MacLiammóir, Micheál, *All for Hecuba* (London: Methuen, 1946).

Ronsley, Joseph (ed.), *Denis Johnston* (Gerrards Cross: Colin Smythe, 1981).

CHRISTOPHER FITZSIMON

Joly, John (1857–1933) Geologist, physicist and Fellow of the Royal Society (1892). Joly studied modern literature and engineering at Trinity College, Dublin, and after working as a demonstrator in civil engineering and experimental physics he became professor of geology and mineralogy there in 1897. His varied academic pursuits led to significant research in several scientific areas, most importantly in the study of the earth and its crust. He sought to project the age of the earth by measuring the sodium content of the oceans, reviving theories first propounded by Edmund Halley in the eighteenth century. Joly believed that all the salts present in the oceans had precolated through from the land and had remained at a constant level throughout time. He published his theories in 1899, estimating the earth's age as being between 80 and 90 million years, a figure he revised upwards to 100 million years a few years later.

Joly also studied the radioactive content of the earth's crust in order to formulate a theory of thermal cycles, and examined the radioactive constituents of certain rocks as a means of deducing their age. His interest in radioactivity led to research in other areas – in particular his pioneering work with Walter Stevenson on the 'Dublin' method of radiotherapy. In 1914 he developed a method of extracting radium and applied its use to the treatment of cancer.

Joly is noted too for inventing a photometer for measuring light frequencies (1888), a constant volume gas thermometer, and a steam calorimeter to guage heat energy. He also experimented in colour photography techniques.

HELEN MCCURDY

Jones, Sir Thomas Alfred (1823–93) Painter. Died Dublin, 10 May. Of unknown parentage, Jones was brought up by the Archdales, a charitable Dublin family. He studied at the Royal Dublin Society Schools and later at Trinity College, Dublin. Primarily a portrait painter, he began exhibiting at the Royal Hibernian Academy in 1841 and submitted a painting nearly every year until his death. His life was in fact closely connected with the RHA, as he became an academician in 1860 and president in 1869. He was knighted in 1880. In 1871 he donated £1,000 towards the construction of a room for the life school of the academy.

Jones's solid and dull portraits include those of lord lieutenants, lord chancellors, prominent physicians, etc. His drawings and watercolours show more originality, exhibiting a nodding acquaintance with the high finish of the Pre-Raphaelite School, although the subjects are usually cloyingly sentimental.

Reading

Le Harivel, Adrian (ed.), *Irish Watercolours and Drawings* (Dublin: National Gallery of Ireland, 1991).
Strickland, Walter, *A Dictionary of Irish Artists* (Shannon: Irish University Press, 1968).

FINTAN CULLEN

Jones, Thomas (?1550–1619) Archbishop of Dublin (1605–19). Originally from Lancashire, after graduating from Cambridge and having been ordained Jones moved to Ireland. He married the sister-in-law of Archbishop Loftus, a move which enabled his rapid advancement in the established church in Ireland. He was made dean of St Patrick's Cathedral in 1581, and bishop of Meath in 1585. Furthermore he was made a privy councillor in the same year, and was to succeed Loftus as archbishop of Dublin and lord chancellor in 1605. Like many churchmen of his day, he was chiefly remembered for furthering his own family's and acquaintances' fortunes at the expense of the church. Jones was rabidly anti-Catholic, and identified with the reforming wing of the established church. He probably wrote the tract 'An Answer to Tyrone's Seditious Declaration sent to the Catholics of the Pale in 1596'.

Reading

Ford, A., *The Protestant Reformation in Ireland, 1590–1641* (Frankfurt: 1985).
Phillips, W.A., (ed.), *History of the Church of Ireland*, 3 vols (Oxford: 1933–4).

BRIAN DONOVAN

Jones, William Bence (1812–82) Agriculturalist. Born Beccles, Suffolk; died at 34 Elvaston Place, London, 22 June. Jones was educated at Harrow and Balliol College,

Oxford. In 1843 he undertook the management of his grandfather's estate of 4,000 acres at Lisselan, County Cork, farming one thousand acres himself. His farming methods were progressive, but he was attacked by Land League supporters as an unjust and rack-renting landlord. His refusal to accept Griffith's valuation for rent fixing led to his boycotting, and he left for London in 1881. He strongly opposed Gladstone's Land Act of 1881.

Reading

Jones, William Bence, *The Future of the Irish Church* (Dublin: Hodges, 1869).
—— *The Life's Work in Ireland of a Landlord* (London: Macmillan, 1880).

HENRY BOYLAN

journalism Irish journalism has traditionally been situated at the point where questions of national identity, political legitimacy and ethnic rivalry meet in a frothy maelstrom. Because of this, questions of press freedom have assumed a larger significance than in more settled cultures, and successive administrations, whether British or Irish, have been more sensitive to journalistic *lèse-majesté*, and for a longer period of time, than many of their counterparts elsewhere.

Initially, the development of journalism in Ireland mirrored that in the UK, in that it purveyed information that was primarily of commercial significance. The newsheet *An Account of the Chief Occurrences of Ireland together with some Particulars from England* appeared in 1659, the *Irish Intelligencer* in 1662. As organs of the commercial class, they and their immediate successors were politically monochrome, but from the middle of the eighteenth century the growth of factionalism in Irish politics, and the related attempts of the Irish authorities to curb disloyal and seditious publications, gave a new prominence to the newspaper over the pamphlet, and a new currency to the phrase 'freedom of the press'. The *Freeman's Journal*

(1763) was the harbinger of an era in which the spread of political intelligence and controversy, within the capital and across the country, became one of the press's primary functions.

A century later, the foundation of the *Nation* (1842), and the conversion of the *Freeman's Journal* to the cause of the Irish Parliamentary Party, marked a significant shift in emphasis away from complaints about English misgovernment and towards an assertion of Irish nationality. The growth of the Irish provincial media during the same period expressed the symbiotic relationship between nascent nationalism and the emerging Catholic middle class: the patterns laid down then are still evident a century and a half later. In the North, the *Belfast Newsletter* (1737) and the *Irish News* (1891) became the main standard bearers for their respective communities: the *Irish News* owed its origins (and its episcopal support) primarily to the Parnell split, in which the *Freeman's Journal* took Parnell's side.

Although not a party press in the Continental European sense, the Irish media in the late nineteenth and early twentieth centuries had their clearly defined loyalties. The *Irish Times* (1859) and the *Irish Independent* (1891, later incorporating the *Freeman's Journal*) mirrored the aspirations of the Protestant and Catholic middle classes respectively – not that this saved either of them, during the Civil War (1922–3) from the zealous attentions of a newly fledged government ever ready to discern threats to national security in the turn of a phrase of a careless caption. Nor was the government the only source of threats: Tim Harrington, editor of the *Irish Independent*, had to live in his own office for much of this period after warnings from the Irregulars.

Irish nationalists worsted in the Civil War lacked any mainstream media voice until 1931, when the foundation of the *Irish Press* closely followed the entry of Fianna Fáil into the Dáil. It would be too much to say that the Irish media spectrum was now complete; but it was certainly more rounded, and the new paper, under its energetic founding editor Frank Gallagher, quickly set new standards for journalistic brio and enterprise.

The climate within which Irish journalism operated after 1921 was characterized by a whole series of official and unofficial measures designed to marginalize those media outside a central consensus. The Cosgrave government's prosecution of Gallagher in 1931 for seditious libel was political in a party sense; but the actions taken by de Valera's subsequent governments, especially against the Communist and Labour press in the 1930s and 1940s, were no less severe, and considerbly more successful. The operation of a stifling censorship during the war years was a useful adjunct to this general policy, which extended at times beyond working-class publications to others – including Republican publications and some in the Gaelic language – whose cardinal sin was to imply that de Valera had been in some sense unfaithful to his principles, and that the legitimacy of the state he controlled could therefore be called in question.

During this period the *Irish Times* was adapting, chameleon-like, to its new habitat, under its charismatic editor R.M. Smyllie. The process was to be continued and enhanced by one of his successors, Douglas Gageby, an independently minded Belfast-born Protestant who had originally worked for the *Irish Press* Group. His appointment coincided with a number of changes, not only in the pattern but in the nature of Irish journalism. The creation of RTE introduced television journalism from the national broadcasting station to an eager public. Some of its early practitioners – Ted Nealon, David Thornley, Justin Keating – subsequently carved out careers in politics. Others, like Brian Farrell and Gay Byrne, became national institutions.

In the newspapers, there was a new irreverence in political reporting, symbolized by John Healy of the *Irish Times*. Tim Pat Coogan extended the journalistic boundaries of the by now somewhat staid *Irish Press*, and Louis MacRedmond was doing the same for the *Irish Independent*. Mary Kenny in the *Irish Press*, and Maeve Binchy and Mary Maher in the *Irish Times*, were among a group of young women journalists who, in their own way, were signalling to a younger and more vibrant readership the existence of a new agenda. It was, too, an age of increasing specialization. Up to the mid-1960s, politics and industrial affairs were the only acknowledged journalistic areas of special competence, but the development of new specialisms in education, women's affairs, property, religious affairs and media was a potent sign of the growing segmentation and targeting of media audiences that was taking place. Some titles, including the *Irish Press*, vanished; others – the *Sunday Tribune* among them – emerged. Periodical publications, and publications in Gaelic, waxed and waned, but mostly waned; a hardy survivor, the *Phoenix*, emerged to embody a tradition of scandal and gossip, despite considerable financial and legal odds.

Irish journalism is operating, as never before, in a multi-media environment, with strong internal competition sharpened by deregulation in the electronic media, and external competition from UK newspapers (traditionally a major element of the Irish media mix) and satellite media. To flourish in these circumstances, and to remain distinctively Irish, is a continuing challenge.

Reading

Brown, Stephen J.M., *The Press in Ireland* (New York: Lemma, 1971).
Glandon, V., *Arthur Griffith and the Advanced Nationalist Press: Ireland 1920–1922* (Peter Lang, 1985).
Inglis, Brian, *The Freedom of the Press in Ireland, 1784–1841* (Faber, 1954).
Munter, Robert, *The History of the Irish Newspaper 1685–1760* (Cambridge: Cambridge University Press, 1967).
Oram, Hugh, *The Newspaper Book* (Dublin: MO Books, 1983).
Stapleton, John, *Communication Policies in Ireland* (Paris: Unesco, 1974).

JOHN HORGAN

The Joyce Country A mountainous area largely devoted to sheep farming, west of the isthmus between Loughs Comb and Mask and having the Maamturks as its border with Connemara. It was settled by the Joyces, a Welsh family, under the aegis of the O'Flahertys in the thirteenth century. Trinity College, Dublin, had estates here from the time of the Cromwellian confiscations until the early twentieth century. Most of the Joyce Country lies within the Galway Gaeltacht, and there is a flourishing co-operative involved in afforestation. Tomás Ó Maille (1883–1938), professor of Irish at Queen's College (now University College, Galway), and his brother Pádraic, deputy speaker of the first Dáil, were born in the Maam Valley, and were active in the War of Independence there.

Reading

Ó Maille, Tómas, *Ant-iomaire Rua* (Dublin: 1939).
Robinson, Tim, *Connemara. Part I: Introduction and Gazetteer*, Part II: a one-inch map (Roundstone, 1990).

TIM ROBINSON

Joyce, James, works of More than those of any other twentieth-century writer, the works of James Joyce occupy a peculiarly totemic position in modern culture. Various scholarly, institutional and ideological factors have created and maintained this position. Biographical scholarship has increased awareness of the travail which accompanied the works' gestation and publication, thereby enlarging appreciation for them as human documents. Joyce's disregard for certain verbal and thematic taboos has given his works a spuriously sensational reputation on the one hand, while on the other it has placed them in the vanguard of opposition to censorship and support for artistic freedom. No other modern fiction has had more influence than

Joyce's on other authors within and beyond the anglophone world, and on fiction's aesthetic challenges and formal possibilities. And by virtue of being a by-word for stylistic complexity and recondite allusiveness, Joyce's works have become notorious for the number of exegetes which they have attracted and for the variety of hermeneutical approaches they have entertained. The comprehensiveness and persistence of these attentions constitute a set of intriguing asides on the sociology of culture, on the role of intellectuals and the power of the institution of criticism, and on the cultivation of taste in the second half of the twentieth century.

From an artistic standpoint, the uniqueness of Joyce's *oeuvre* may be perceived in the variety of dynamic interrelationships which exist within it. This is exemplified between works by the manner in which *A Portrait of the Artist as a Young Man* (1916) is a streamlined redaction of *Stephen Hero* (1904–5, 1944), and in the ways *Finnegans Wake* (1939) acts as the nocturnal complement of the diurnal *Ulysses* (1922). Among instances of the interrelationship's activity within works are the thematic patternings of the stories in *Dubliners* (1914), the characterization of Stephen Dedalus's development in *A Portrait of the Artist as a Young Man* in terms of phase and nexus, the masquerade of synonymity performed by the local and the universal in *Ulysses*, and the structure of Viconian cycles in *Finnegans Wake*.

Taking the Joyce corpus as a whole, the minor works establish some of the fundamental aesthetic interests and thematic preoccupations of all his writings. The verse of *Chamber Music* (1908) initiates the formal fastidiousness, verbal musicality and tonal subtlety characteristic of Joyce the stylist. The themes of attachment, usurpation, fidelity and betrayal, which Joyce's fiction treats with greater formal sophistication, receive their most explicit characterization in *Exiles* (1918), his solitary, seldom-performed play. Here too, and in *Giacomo Joyce* (1914, 1968), Joyce commits himself to those questions of

sexual identity which are central to both *Ulysses* and *Finnegans Wake*, and which are not the least of his contributions to Irish literature, despite Irish culture's reluctance to assimilate them.

Despite the conspicuous differences between each of Joyce's major works, and notwithstanding the fact that the articulation and recuperation of difference is one of Joyce's most significant cultural and imaginative achievements, his works constitute an intricate, carefully structured totality. As such, they are a formidable expression of artistic integrity, not only denoting the prismatic character of Joyce's creative intelligence but symbolizing the singular moral courage required to commission and sustain that intelligence. The very nature of the Joyce *oeuvre* conveys an exemplary power which, in addition to its radical contribution to European, Spanish-American and anglophone literature, gains additional significance when considered in the context of the formative years of Ireland's cultural renewal.

Joyce began his writing career as a poet and critic, and the influence of these two orientations recurs throughout his works. A synthesis of the aesthetic and the analytical is what Stephen Dedalus, hero of the autobiographical *A Portrait of the Artist as a Young Man*, tries to assert in the interests of his own self-realization. Language is the site selected for synthesis. The hero's desire to find a verbal code which might name his experience in its own terms is articulated in two opposing contexts. One is his acute subjective sensitivity to the plasticity of language. The other is his keen objective awareness of the clichés of institutional and other forms of public discourse, and of the moral stereotypes which such language evinces. Stephen's rejection of the commonplace in language is Joyce's means of emphasizing the nature, development and quality of Stephen's consciousness. The novel's implicit faith in growth aligns it with the European tradition of the *Bildungsroman*, while its self-consciously theoretical component underlines its Modernism. Regarded from a strictly Irish standpoint, Stephen is a singularly provocative representative of that generation in Ireland whose restless critical disposition came to historical term in the rebellion of Easter 1916.

The reconciliation of aesthetic theory with cultural critique which Stephen projects but fails to embody in *A Portrait of the Artist* forms the basis of Joyce's achievement in *Dubliners*. The cameos of *petit bourgeois* Dublin life which make up this collection of stories are also autobiographical, despite the impersonal veneer of their style. They constitute an autobiography of citizenship, rather than (as in *A Portrait of the Artist*) of temperament, and provide, by means of Joyce's skilful mimicry of local solecims of thought, speech, gesture and affect, an anatomy of political, religious, economic and moral conditions in a community so alienated from its own potential as to seem, in the author's own notorious formulation, paralysed.

In *Dubliners*, Joyce's sensitivity to the sound, texture and nuance of language articulates a poetics of the prosaic, and infuses his colourless material with revelatory power. This power, codified by Joyce in his theoretical writings as that of epiphany, attributes significance to the workaday world of a subject people by entitling it to speak on its own behalf and in its own terms. The influence of European literary models on the stories is also perceptible, as they reflect both Joyce's awareness of developments in the naturalistic *conte* and his admiration for the unflinching social diagnostics which he discovered in the plays of Ibsen. The stories are not only a landmark in the history of the form in English but a significant gesture of cultural solidarity with the virtually anonymous orphans, servants and petty functionaries who typify Dublin citizenhood in the years immediately preceding Irish independence.

Originally conceived as a *Dubliners* short story, *Ulysses* synthesizes the aesthetic strategies and cultural criticism of Joyce's early works. This work completes the dismantling of such narrative conventions as uniformity of perspective, pre-eminence of plot and linearity of development which Joyce's earlier fiction inaugurated. In their place are such innovations as the stream of consciousness, interactive and disjunctive levels of perception, and an eccentric patterning of event and stasis. In *Ulysses*, a fragmentary and socially entropic set of surfaces co-exists formally with epic form and thematically with a valorization of the labyrinthine resources of consciousness. Leopold and Molly Bloom, whose consciousnesses are the basis of the reader's epic journey, are Irish literature's most distinctive contribution to the family of European fictional characters, which includes not only Odysseus and Penelope but Don Quixote and Madame Bovary.

The parodic use of Homeric and other culturally sanctified materials draws attention to the fundamentally comic character of *Ulysses*. But if Joyce mocks epic, he also renews it by underwriting secular, contemporary versions of persistence, adaptability, dispassionateness and related qualities which epics traditionally uphold. Other aspects of epic tradition are reworked in *Ulysses* through the sophistication of its intertextuality and the ambition of its encyclopedism. Its recapitulation of history and consolidation of geography imaginatively endow Dublin with the lineaments of a capital city, so that in addition to its artistic attainments, *Ulysses* is also a complex cultural and political inscription of how Joyce, the exile, thinks of home as a place fit for the tribute of epic. Such an expression of both return and transformation makes *Ulysses* not only an analogue of the activity of memory but a powerful reformulation of the work of the poet-critic.

The principle of recycling to which the very title of *Ulysses* draws attention is brought to the fore in *Finnegans Wake*. The plethoric detail of *Ulysses* shows how the principle is sublimated, thereby assuming forms of social and cultural discourse. In *Finnegans Wake*, dream activity, the normative mode of sublimation, is deconstructed, unsettling the prescriptive and teleological implications of form and destabilizing not merely discourse but the origins of its cultural and linguistic integrity. The subversion of the idea of a native tongue in *Finnegans Wake* not only conveys Joyce's own polyglot experience of exile but acts as a poetically rendered critique of the putative synonymity of language and race, an ideological construct discredited both by the macaronic character of language in general and by the history of language in Ireland.

The resulting polyphony of sound and sense gives the principle of recycling lexical and textural pre-eminence through its dialectic of the dislocutionary and the combinative. But the text's neologistical energy is of more than structural and conceptual significance. It is also inescapable circumstantial evidence of the history of transgression which forms the narrative core of *Finnegans Wake*. Not only is language universalized, the themes which such a language might underwrite are inevitably universal, so that the localized story of the fall of H.C. Earwicker is both unique in itself and a pretext for a proliferation of analogues. Replications of different levels and modes of signification fuse form and content so indissolubly that, despite its extraordinary artifice, *Finnegans Wake* is literature's closest approximation to a work of nature. As such it is the ultimate expression of an imagination which initially presented itself to the world in the name of Dedalus.

GEORGE O'BRIEN

12th July The practice of celebrating King William's victory at the Boyne is as old as the Orange Institution itself. On 12 July 1796 processions, modelled partly on those used by the Masonic Order, took place at Portadown, Lurgan and Waringstown. The newly formed Grand Lodge of Ireland resolved in 1798 that 'we will annually celebrate the victory over James at the Boyne on 1st day of July, O.S., in every year, which day shall be our grand aera for ever'. Processions frequently led to sectarian disturbance in the nineteenth century. Acts against them, frequently defied, were passed in 1832 and again in 1850. One of the most violent affrays occurred on 12 July 1849 at Dolly's Brae, County Down. Over 1,200 Orangemen from Rathfriland, returning from a demonstration at Lord Roden's estate, Tollymore, encountered a crowd of Ribbonmen. 'Battle' ensued and over 30 Catholics were killed.

While generally the 18 or so processions each 'twelfth' pass off without incident, marchers traversing Catholic districts have sometimes sparked tensions on, for example, the Longstone Road (Mournes) in the 1950s, and in Obins Street ('the tunnel'), Portadown, in July 1986. An RUC rerouting of a march away from this pleased neither side and led to several nights' rioting. Potential trouble at the long-established Belfast 'twelfth' venue, on Finaghy Road North, by virtue of the encroachment of Catholic housing, was averted early in the 'Troubles' of 1968–98, when the Order moved its venue to an unprovocative site at Edenderry. However, since 1995, the Drumcree march has been the occasion of violent confrontations between loyalists and the security forces, as well as militant nationalist protests.

Reading

Dewar, M.W. et al., *Orangeism* (Belfast: Grand Orange Lodge of Ireland, 1969).

Bardon, Jonathan, *A History of Ulster* (Belfast: Blackstaff, 1992).

W. HARVEY COX

K

Kane, Michael (1935–) Born and lives in Dublin. Kane studied for two years at the National College of Art in Dublin. Subsequently he travelled and studied in Spain, Italy and Britain. Since the 1960s he has worked primarily in oil, gouache and woodcuts, and has exhibited, both individually and in group, throughout Ireland, Europe and even Cuba. He co-founded the Project Arts Centre in 1966, and currently is a member of Aosdána. Kane's images are primarily figurative. They reveal a strong influence of second-generation German Expressionism and are directly related to his perceptions of human sexuality, power and violence.

Reading

Knowles, Roderic, *Contemporary Irish Art* (Dublin: Wolfhound Press, 1982).
Sharpe, Henry, *Michael Kane, His Life and Art* (Dublin: Bluett, 1983).
The Arts Council of Ireland, RHA Gallery and the Dpt of An Taoiseach, *Irish Art, the European Dimension* (Dublin: Arts Council, 1990).

DERVAL TUBRIDY

Kane, Sir Robert John (1809–90) Scientist. Born Dublin, September; died there, 16 February. Kane was educated at Trinity College, Dublin, and became professor of chemistry at Apothecaries Hall, Dublin, in 1831. In 1832 he founded the *Dublin Journal of Medical Science*. In 1843 he delivered a course of lectures on the development of industries in Ireland; at his suggestion the government established a Museum of Irish Industry at St Stephen's Green, Dublin, in 1846 and he became director. In 1845 he was appointed president of Queen's College, Cork (opened 1849), and a member of the commission to enquire into the potato blight and the relief of distress. He was knighted in 1846 and elected fellow of the Royal Society in 1849. In 1873 he was appointed a commissioner of national education and in 1880 became vice-chancellor of the newly created Royal University of Ireland.

Reading

Kane, Robert John, *Elements of Chemistry* (Dublin: Hodges, 1841).
——*Industrial Resources of Ireland* (Dublin: Hodges Smith, 1844).

HENRY BOYLAN

Kavanagh, Patrick (1904–67) Poet, novelist and journalist. Kavanagh is best known for his poem *The Great Hunger* (1942), which definitively deromanticized Irish rural life. His novel *Tarry Flynn* (1948) treats similar material more comically. Kavanagh repudiated the literary revival because of its preoccupation with ethnicity. He cultivated a direct, vernacular casualness in prose and verse, but his poems are deceptively simple; whatever their apparent subject, they are usually meta-literary. *The Great Hunger* apart, he is most esteemed for the sonnets in which he celebrates 'the common and banal' aspects of country and town (e.g. 'Shancoduff', 'Advent', 'Epic', 'The Hospital', the Canal sonnets, 'October'); and the confessional lyrics in which he wryly and ruefully unmasks himself (e.g. 'I Had a Future', 'Prelude', 'Question to Life'). *Collected Poems* (1964) and *Complete Poems* (1972) have been reprinted several times. *Collected Prose* (1967) contains a selection of his prose.

ANTOINETTE QUINN

Kavanagh's Weekly (12 April–5 July 1952) A 'journal of literature and politics', written almost exclusively by Patrick Kavanagh and his brother Peter. In it they lambasted the Republic for its ineffectual materialism and mindless mediocrity, satirizing almost every institution of Irish life, in particular the Fianna Fáil government and the middle classes. Patrick was also scornful about recent and contemporary Irish writing. He countered its ethnicity by espousing the apparently contrary poetics of 'parochialism' (realist portrayal of the writer's parish) and 'personality' (self-portrayal and confessionalism). Due to lack of popular support or advertising revenue, the *Weekly* folded after 13 weeks.

ANTOINETTE QUINN

Keane, John Brendan (1928–) Playwright and fiction writer. Born Listowel, County Kerry, 21 July. Keane was educated locally. In 1951 he emigrated to England, where he worked as a labourer. Returning to Listowel in 1953 he married, and in 1955 bought a small public house, now very popular. His first play, *Sive*, won the All-Ireland Amateur Drama Festival in 1959. It was immediately successful countrywide and made his reputation. He has written a dozen plays, mostly on traditional themes, as well as poetry, essays and novellas cast in letter form. *The Field*, a powerful play about land hunger, was made into a successful film in 1990. He has also published novels, including *The Contractors* (1993) and *Christmas Takes* (1993).

HENRY BOYLAN

Keating family Sean Keating (1889–1977) was one of the leading Irish artists of the twentieth century. He studied at the Dublin Metropolitan School of Art, then worked under Orpen in London in 1915, becoming the most important of Orpen's pupils. He became professor at the National College of Art in Dublin in 1934. Elected to the RHA in 1919, he was its president from 1948 to 1962. A retrospective exhibition of his work was held in Dublin in 1963. A lifelong opponent of avant-garde 'anarchy'. Keating developed the academic tradition of Orpen in a 'social realist' and nationalistic direction – as in the problematically entitled *The Race of the Gael* (1939). His nationalism sometimes took a restrained form (*On the Run – War of Independence*, c.1924) and sometimes led in odd directions – *Men of the West* (1916) seems to evoke the American West as much as the west of Ireland. *Night's Candles are Burnt Out* (1928–9) is an interesting allegory of social 'development' consequent on electrification. While his portraits and landscapes are technically accomplished, he is at his best in paintings with a narrative dimension.

Keating, whose perceived aesthetic and pedagogical conservatism, in contrast with his political outlook, have contributed to a relative – and undeserved – scholarly neglect, was husband of socialist-feminist activist May Keating (née Walsh), and father of prominent writer, environmentalist and politician Justin Keating.

Reading

Sean Keating and the ESB (Dublin: Touring Exhibitions Service, n.d.).

Sean Keating, P.R.H.A. 1889–1977 (Dublin: Royal Hibernian Academy Gallagher Gallery, 1989).

PAUL O'BRIEN

Keating, Geoffrey (*c.*1580–*c.*1644) Historian, theologian and priest. Born Burges, County Tipperary; died near Clonmel. Keating was educated locally and at Bordeaux; he was a priest in Munster from about 1610 until his death. His early writings, *Eochair-Sgiath an Aifrinn* and *Trí Bhior Ghaoithe an Bháis*, were theological, adapted and translated from European Counter-Reformation texts, and intended for Irish preachers. Best known for his *Foras Feasa ar Éirinn*, a narrative compilation in Gaelic of sources for a history of Ireland to the coming of the Normans. Consciously, though sometimes uncritically, using primary source material, the history was written from the perspective of an Old English Counter-Reformation priest. It defended Ireland's reputation by reference to the legends and lives of past heroes. It promoted the image of an uncorrupted Irish Catholic church within a long-established diocesan structure. The history had considerable appeal for Irish Catholics and the Gaelic text circulated widely in manuscript form. The first printed edition was a (controversially) modified English-language edition by Dermod O'Connor, 1723.

Reading

Cunningham, Bernadette, 'Seventeenth century interpretations of the past: the case of Geoffrey Keating', *Irish Historical Studies* XXV, 1986.

Keating, Geoffrey, *Eochair-Sgiath an Aifrinn... An Explanatory Defence of the Mass*, ed. Patrick O'Brien (Dublin: 1898).

—— *Foras Feasa ar Éirinn: The History of Ireland*, eds D. Comyn and P.S. Dineen, 4 vols (London: Irish Texts Society, 1902–14).

—— *Trí Bhior Ghaoithe an Bháis: The Three Shafts of Death*, ed. Osborn Bergin (Dublin: Royal Irish Academy, 1931).

Ó Corráin, Donnchadh, 'Seathrún Céitinn, c. 1580–c. 1644: an cúlra stairiúil', in *Dúchas, 1983, 1984, 1985* (Dublin: Dúchas, 1986).

BERNADETTE CUNNINGHAM

Kelly, Hugh (1739–77) Journalist, novelist, essayist, dramatist. Born Killarney or Dublin; died London, 3 February. By trade a staymaker, Kelly went to London in 1760 to try his hand at writing. He had published several pamphlets, a novel about a prostitute and two volumes of essays under the title *The Babbler* before having his first play, *False Delicacy*, produced at Drury Lane in 1768. This was a highly successful play, although Johnson said of it that it 'was totally void of character'. A second comedy, *A Word to the Wise*, was produced at Drury Lane in 1770 and was followed by a blank verse tragedy, *Clementina*, at Covent Garden the following year. Three further comedies followed in quick succession – *The School for Wives* (1773), *The Romance of an Hour* (1770) and finally *The Man of Reason* (1776). Kelly had been called to the bar in 1774, and when *The Man of Reason* was damned by the critics, he decided to give up writing plays and to turn full-time to the law instead. But he failed dismally in this new career. He resorted to drink, got into debt, and died at Gough Square, Fleet Street, London.

Reading

Kelly, Hugh, *The Works of Hugh Kelly*, with 'life' prefixed (London: 1778).

PATRICK FAGAN

Kelly, Michael (1762–1826) Composer and singer. Born Dublin, 25 December; died Margate. Kelly studied music with a number of English and Italian composers (including Michael Arne) in Dublin, and in 1779 went to Naples to further his studies. He established himself as a singer in Vienna, where he remained about four years. There he became acquainted with Mozart, and sang in the first performance of *The Marriage of Figaro*, in which he doubled the roles of Don Basilio and Don Curzio.

On his return to England in 1787 he became principal tenor at Drury Lane Theatre, and in 1793 stage manager at the

King's Theatre. From 1801 to 1811 he ran a music shop in Pall Mall and was involved in the wine trade. During the later part of his career Kelly made a number of trips to Dublin, where his works were given at Crow Street Theatre.

Kelly wrote the music for some 60 dramatic pieces, although the extent to which he simply arranged the work of Italian composers must modify our understanding of his compositional achievement. He provided music for the following operas (which included material by other composers); *Bluebeard* (1798), *Cinderella* (1804), *Youth, Love, and Folly* (1805), *The Lady and the Devil* (1820), and other works.

Reading

Hogan, Ita M., *Anglo-Irish Music, 1780–1830* (Cork: 1966).

Walsh, T.J., *Opera in Dublin 1705–1797* (Dublin: A. Figgis, 1973).

HARRY WHITE

Kelly, Oisín (1916–84) Sculptor. Born Austin Kelly in Dublin; died Dublin. Kelly took an arts degree at Trinity College, Dublin, before studying at the NCAD. He exhibited regularly with the Irish Exhibition of Living Art from the late 1940s, and also with the Royal Hibernian Academy (RHA); he was elected RHA in 1966. Kelly was a deeply cultured man, whose interests ranged from medieval carvings to the work of Ernest Barlach. Extremely versatile and a fine craftsman, he carved, modelled and carried out public commissions such as his large statue of James Larkin (O'Connell Street, Dublin). A humorous, imaginative, very 'Celtic' quality runs through his work, which often features birds and animals among its subject matter. He also carried out church commissions (*Last Supper*, Knockanure, County Kerry).

BRIAN FALLON

Kelp The calcined ash of seaweed. Kelp manufacture started on the west coast in about 1700 in response to a demand for soda (for glass making and linen bleaching) and potash (for dyeing and gunpowder manufacture), and soon spread to Scotland's coasts and islands. For two centuries the laborious collecting, drying and burning of seaweed in simple kilns on the shore was an important source of income in such impoverished regions as Connemara. When other sources of alkali became more competitive, kelp was given a further lease of life by the discovery of iodine and its antiseptic properties, but the coming of penicillin led to its decline, and in Aran, for instance, the last kelp was burned in about 1948.

Reading

Clow, A. and Clow, N.L., *The Chemical Revolution* (London: Batchworth Press, 1952).

Ó Gaora, Colm, *Obair is Luadhain* (Dublin: Oifig Díolta Foillseacáin Rialtais, 1937).

Robinson, Tim, *Stones of Aran. Part I: Pilgrimage* (Dublin: Penguin, 1986).

TIM ROBINSON

Kennedy, Patrick (1801–73) Bookseller and folklore writer. Kennedy published a trio of books comprehensively recording Irish oral prose traditions: *Legendary Fictions of the Irish Celts* (1866), *The Bardic Stones of Ireland* (1871), and *Irish Fireside Stories* (1870), with 51 tales, such as 'Hairy Rouchy' and 'The Pooka of Baltracy', 'obtained from *bona fide* oral sources'. He was the first to recognize the impact on western folklore of the *Kalevala*, the Finnish national epic. He also contributed dozens of articles to the *Dublin University Magazine*, on subjects ranging from book lore to superstitions. He is credited with influencing Sheridan Le Fanu's return to more traditional Irish material in later stories; Le Fanu called Kennedy 'my quaint, kind and clever little bookseller'. Kennedy ran a bookshop in Anglesea Street, Dublin. His papers are in University College, Dublin.

AMY L. FRIEDMAN

Kennelly, Timothy Brendan (1936–) Poet. Born Ballylongford, County Kerry, 17 April. Kennelly was educated at Trinity College, Dublin, and Leeds University. In 1967 he won the AE Memorial Prize for Poetry. He was appointed professor of modern literature at Trinity in 1973. Early in his career he wrote two novels, one of university life and one on life in rural Kerry. One of the most prolific of contemporary poets, he has published more than a dozen collections of his work – including *Selected Poems* (1985) – as well as editing *The Penguin Book of Irish Verse* (1988), writing reviews and contributing to various international magazines.

HENRY BOYLAN

Keogh, John (1740–1817) Catholic agitator. Born Dublin; died there, 13 November. A successful Catholic businessman, John Keogh's first significant political act was the publication in 1784 of a pamphlet advocating the reform of the Irish House of Commons. A key figure in the Catholic Committee, he was one of leaders of the agitation that won Catholic freeholders the vote in 1793. Subsequently, Keogh all but withdrew from public life when he was accused of involvement with the United Irishmen.

Reading

Gwynn, Denis, *John Keogh* (Dublin: Talbot Press, 1930).

JAMES KELLY

Kickham, Charles J. (1828–82) Writer and Fenian. Born Mullinahone, County Tipperary, early May; died Blackrock, County Dublin, 22 August. The eldest child of John Kickham (shopkeeper) and Anne O'Mahony, Kickham was educated in the local 'classical' school. He was influenced as a youth by the romantic nationalism of the early *Nation*, which inspired him to write ballads, a few of which – 'Patrick Sheehan', 'Slievenamon', 'She lived beside the Anner' – have enjoyed enduring popular appeal. In the

1850s he dabbled in local journalism. A member of the Irish Republican Brotherhood (IRB) from 1861, he moved to Dublin in late 1863 to write for the new Fenian weekly, the *Irish People*. He now began to write creatively about his native place, producing *Sally Cavanagh* (probably his best book) in 1864. Arrested in late 1865 along with other leading Fenians, he remained in jail until March 1869. He returned to Mullinahone and began writing *Knocknagow* (1873), an unwieldly and many-sided evocation of rural life, and the book for which he is best known. In spite of serious deterioration of his sight and hearing he completed two further (and better crafted) novels in the next decade, *For the Old Land* and *The Eagle of Garryroe*. Meanwhile he was prominent in the reorganized IRB, becoming president of the supreme council. He was benevolently neutral towards Isaac Butt's Home Rule movement, disliked the obstructionists, bitterly opposed the 'new departure', and loathed the Land League.

Reading

Comerford, R.V., *Charles J. Kickham: A Study in Irish Nationalism and Literature* (Dublin: Wolfhound Press, 1979).

Maher, James (ed.), *The Valley near Slievenamon: A Kickham Anthology* (Mullinahone: the editor, 1942).

R.V. COMERFORD

Kiely, Benedict (1919–) Writer. Born near Dromore, County Tyrone. Kiely was educated by the Christian Brothers in Omagh. In 1937 he entered the Jesuit novitiate in County Laois, but during a lengthy convalescence from a tubercular spinal ailment the following year, he decided not to answer the call to clerical life. He enrolled at the National University in Dublin, from which he graduated with a BA in 1943. From 1945 until 1964, Kiely was a Dublin journalist. Between 1964 and 1968 he was a visiting professor of creative writing in American universities, returning to Dublin to lecture at University College, and thereafter becoming a full-time writer of novels, stories, newspaper features and reviews, as well as a frequent radio and television guest and broadcaster.

This biographical matter is worth rehearsing because it finds its way into the ten novels and four volumes of stories by a writer whose work bridges the post-World War II (post- Emergency) years in the Irish Republic (in the middle of what Maurice Harmon has called the 'era of inhibitions', 1920–60, during which Kiely had trouble with the censors) with the optimism and exuberance of the Sean Lemass years (the 1960s), and the despair and political breakdown in Northern Ireland of the following decade. The quiet integrity of an early novel such as *In a Harbour Green* (1949), followed by the unbuttoned energy of *Dogs Enjoy the Morning* (1968), succeeding to the angry anti-terrorist novella *Proxopera* (1977) chart the development of a novelist responsive to the history, geography, mores and creativity of an island that has exasperated and nourished him. He is by turns courageous realist and magician, chronicler and balladeer in prose. The best of his short stories, often as generous in form and content as his novels, were brought together in *Selected Stories* (1993). They put him at their best in the company of O'Connor and O'Faolain, and are impelled by a quite intense humanity. In 1997 Kiely published *As I Rode by Granard Moat: A Personal Anthology*.

Reading

Casey, Daniel J., *Benedict Kiely* (Lewisburg PA: Bucknell University Press, 1974).

Clarke, Jennifer, 'An interview with Benedict Kiely', *Irish Literary Supplement* (Spring 1987), pp. 10–12.

Eckley, Grace, *Benedict Kiely* (New York: Twayne, 1975).

Foster, John Wilson, in *Forces and Themes in Ulster Fiction* (Dublin: Gill and Macmillan, 1974; Totowa NJ: Rowman and Littlefield, 1974).

JOHN WILSON FOSTER

Kilkenny Despite the fact that Kilkenny is not the most 'central' or the largest or the oldest of the county's towns, it has always, apparently, been the principal urban focus within County Kilkenny. Pre-Norman Kilkenny, in common with many of the older Irish urban centres, seems to have begun life as a monastery. A happy coincident shift in the secular power base near the end of the ninth century led to the development of the town as a craft centre as well as a place of local administration.

Under the Normans Kilkenny became a show-piece of colonial development, the thirteenth century in particular witnessing the establishment of a number of monasteries, churches and hospitals. In common with the rest of Anglo-Norman Ireland, the colonial population of Kilkenny suffered from the process of assimilation which was to compromise the settlers' cultural independence. Alongside the English and French spoken in Kilkenny there prevailed Gaelic Brehon law and inheritance practices. The vulnerability of the Anglo-Normans (soon to become the Old English) to such incursions was increased by their growing isolation from their cultural heartlands in Europe. Much of the tone and character of the Kilkenny region was set by the Ormonde-Butler family, one of the most prominent and politically powerful dynasties in early modern Ireland.

Following the outbreak of the 1641 rebellion Kilkenny became the meeting place of the Confederation, a quasi-parliamentary body composed of Old English and Gaelic lords who had become effectively the Irish branch of Charles I's royalist cause. Cromwell's ultimate victory in 1650 led unavoidably to significant though limited changes in the property and power network. The Protestant yeomanry, envisioned by Cromwell as supplanters of the Catholics, did not materialize. Instead the new regime was represented by a small group of (mainly absentee) Protestant landowners. The tenantry continued to be Gaelic and Catholic, though its ranks were now swelled by a number of Old English ex-landowners whose political fortunes had changed for the worse.

Even more significant changes, however, were brought about by the Williamite confiscation which followed the Jacobite war of the early 1690s, at which point the remaining Old English power base was practically destroyed. The social and economic development of Kilkenny in the seventeenth and eighteenth centuries was characterized by an unusual degree of continuity, bearing in mind the amount of political and military tension that had centred on Kilkenny for much of the seventeenth century. Political and religious unrest in fact was of much less significance than the parallel tensions between the county's prosperous farmers and their less prosperous small tenantry. The new Protestant political order of the eighteenth century saw the emergence of the Ponsonbys, whose wealth and far-reaching connections made them a considerable and influential force in the Irish Parliament. Their gradual decline after 1770 assisted the re-emergence of a Butler-Ormonde interest, and both groups consolidated their positions after the Act of Union of 1800; this legislation cost Kilkenny six of its boroughs.

Kilkenny was one of the earliest participating counties in the Tithe War of the 1830s. By the early nineteenth century (30 years in fact before the advent of the National Board of Education) all Kilkenny schools were said to use the English language, producing probably the first generation of schoolchildren to do so. Older people, particularly in the more remote parts of the county, were monoglot Gaelic-speakers, and Irish remained the language of casual discourse and leisure for some considerable time. Catholic priests preached in both languages, but more generally in Gaelic.

GERARD O'BRIEN

Kilkenny, Confederation of The term 'Confederation of Kilkenny', dating from the 1840s, describes the organization established on 24 October 1642 as an umbrella body for those at war in Ireland. It termed itself the 'Confederated Catholics of Ireland', highlighting its role as a loose body of individuals bound together by the oath of confederation and not in opposition to the legitimate Dublin Parliament. Its motto, 'Pro Deo, pro Rege et pro Patria unanimis', indicates that it was not in opposition to the king but a negotiating body to secure concessions for the government of Ireland and Catholicism. Such a body was needed by the Old English after their expulsion from the Dublin Parliament on joining the Ulster insurgents at the end of 1641. The Catholic clergy also needed a body to manage the war in favour of the Catholic religion, and the initiative came from the Synods of Kells in March 1642 and Kilkenny in May 1642.

The confederation was made up of two bodies, the Supreme Council and the General Assembly. The assembly, about 300 members, was composed of the Catholic bishops, the Catholic nobility and a body elected on a parliamentary franchise. The assembly was summoned by writ on nine occasions to deal with specific matters such as peace negotiation strategy. While many of the members were former MPs, the style of the assembly was not that of a Parliament. It had only one chamber and no speaker, only a chairman who was not addressed in debate. The council had 24 members, of whom at least 12 had to be in Kilkenny at any one time, six elected from each province. The council held executive, legislative and judicial power when the assembly was not in session. Provincial commanders were appointed for the army, with no overall command except for special expeditions. A system of provincial and county councils was established in late 1642 and a judiciary in August 1644.

From its earliest meeting the confederation was split by internal factions. The main division was between the Old English, who wished to conclude peace with the king as soon as possible, and the Old Irish, who saw the prosecution of war as their main hope of salvation. The Old English dominated the confederation, and a cessation was agreed in 1643 with a peace in 1646. The Old Irish interests coincided with those of the papal nuncio Giovanni Battista Rinuccini, who felt the peace did not provide sufficient guarantees for Catholicism. Backed by the Ulster general Owen Roe O'Neill, he purged the confederation in 1646 and excommunicated those who accepted the treaty. In 1646 and 1647 the Old English regrouped sufficiently to stage a counter *coup d'état*, and in a worsening political situation they threw in their lot with the general royalist war effort in Ireland by concluding a peace with the lord lieutenant, the Duke of Ormond, in 1648. This was again condemned by Rinuccini, who was outflanked and fled the country. The 1648 peace formally dissolved the confederation.

Reading

Beckett, J.C., 'The Confederation of Kilkenny reviewed', in *Confrontations* (London: Faber, 1972).

Corish, P.J., 'The crisis in Ireland in 1648: the nuncio and the Supreme Council', *Irish Theological Quarterly* xxi (1955).

Cregan, Donal, 'Some members of the Confederation of Kilkenny', in Sylvester O'Brien (ed.), *Measgra i gouimhne Mhichil Ui Chleirigh* (Dublin: Assisi Press, 1944).

——'The Confederation of Kilkenny', in Brian Farrell (ed.), *The Irish Parliamentary Tradition* (Dublin: Gill, 1973).

Lowe, John, 'Charles I and the Confederation of Kilkenny, 1643–9', *Irish Historical Studies* xiv (1964–5).

RAYMOND GILLESPIE

Kilkenny, Statutes of A set of laws passed in 1366 to define the difference between 'the King's English subjects' and 'the King's Irish enemies'. The aim was partly to deter English colonists in Ireland from adopting Gaelic cultural practices (as was increasingly the case – the statutes proved ineffective in stemming this trend), and partly to demarcate the constitutional extent of the king's lordship in Ireland. The statutes invoke ethnocentric criteria of civility as the defining properties of political identity: to be Irish is to be a savage – uncivilized, non-citizen. Henry VIII's becoming king (instead of lord) of Ireland in 1543 abolished this status of Irish non- subjects and so rendered the statutes obsolete; but his cultural legislation shows their abiding influence.

JOEP LEERSSEN

Kilroy, Thomas (1934–) Playwright and novelist. From Kilkenny, Kilroy was a former college lecturer at University College, Dublin, and has held various visiting professorships in the US. He was professor of English at University College, Galway, before returning to write full-time in 1989. Since *The Door* was a BBC prize-winning play in 1967, Kilroy's plays have included *Tea & Sex & Shakespeare* (1976), the highly acclaimed *Talbot's Box* (1977), dealing with the life of a self-martyred working-class religious, *Double Cross* (1986) and *Madame MacAdam's Travelling Show* (1991). He has also written versions of Chekhov's *The Seagull* (1981) and *Ghosts* (1989). The long-awaited sequel to his award-winning novel, *The Big Chapel* (1971), promises both the imaginative inventiveness and intellectual confidence which are the hallmark of Kilroy's writing as a whole. He is a board member of Field Day and is a regular contributor to radio, journals and magazines. In 1997 his play *The Secret Fall of Constance Wilde* was premièred at the Abbey Theatre.

Reading

Kilroy, Thomas, *The Big Chapel* (London: Faber, 1971).

——*Double Cross* (London: Faber, 1986).

——*Madame MacAdam's Travelling Show* (London: Methuen, 1991).

GERALD DAWE

King, Cecil (1921–86) Abstract artist and collector. After leaving school King worked for a printing firm in Dundalk and began painting in his spare time. In 1963 he gave up his job to become a full-time painter, and held successful exhibitions of his work in Ireland, England, Europe and America. His prosperous family background also provided him with the means to build up his own private art collection, and as well as being a founder member of the Contemporary Irish Art Society, he also gave support to up-and-coming young artists.

HELEN MCCURDY

King, William (1650–1729) Archbishop of Dublin, philosopher, statesman and author. The son of Scots Presbyterian immigrants from Aberdeenshire, King was educated at Trinity College, Dublin (BA 1670, MA 1673), where he was converted to the Anglican church. Ordained in 1674, King became rector of St Werburgh's, Dublin, in 1679. Here he displayed theological and other intellectual interests, joining the Dublin Philosophical Society (Ireland's earliest scientific body) in 1684. Under James II, King emerged as a leader of the threatened Protestant community in Dublin. On James's arrival in 1689, King was twice imprisoned as a spy, and only released by William III's victory at the Boyne in July 1690. In 1691 King published *The State of the Protestants in Ireland under the Late King James's Government*, justifying resistance to the Stuart sovereign. An anonymous answer by Charles Leshe led to three expanded editions in 1692, with more than a dozen reprints to 1770.

King was created bishop of Derry in January 1691. His efforts to re-establish the church after the Jacobite war antagonized local Presbyterians, while his polemical *Discourse Concerning the Inventions of Man in the Worship of God* (1694) stirred wider controversy. He also became involved in the long-running dispute between the bishops of Derry and the Irish Society of London over church lands and fisheries. King's legal victory in the Irish House of Lords in 1697 was overturned by the English Lords in 1698, resulting in the loss of the appeal jurisdiction of the Irish peers. As archbishop of Dublin from March 1703 King proved an active administrator, creating new parishes in the growing city. After 1714, despite serving on four occasions as one of the lord justices (who deputized for the viceroy), King vigorously championed Protestant settler interests. The British Declaratory Act of 1720 asserting legislative and jurisdictional supremacy over Ireland was directly provoked by his actions in the *Sherlock* v. *Annesley* case the previous year. But in the instances of the national bank proposal in 1721 and the Woods's Halfpence Patent in 1724–5, King headed a 'nationalist' opposition that forced withdrawal of both measures. From the 1690s he had concerned himself with Ireland's economic difficulties, particularly the plight of the poor. On his death in 1729 King left the bulk of his fortune for religious and philanthropic purposes; his wide range of intellectual and practical interests was reflected in a library of over 7,000 volumes.

King's major philosophical work, *De Origine Mali*, appeared in 1702; criticisms were published by Bayle in 1705 and Leibniz in 1710, and an English translation with explanatory notes by Edmund Law appeared in 1731. Physical evil was accounted for by the necessary imperfection of created matter, while moral evil was the consequence of deficient choice by beings possessing free will. The perfection of the creator ensured, however, that the universe as a whole manifested the highest possible degree of good, specific evils existing only to promote greater good elsewhere.

Reading

Ehrenpreis, Irvin, *Swift: The Man, his Works, and the Age*, 3 vols Harvard University Press, 1967–83).

Theodore Hoppen, K., *The Common Scientist in the Seventeenth Century* (Routledge and Kegan Paul, 1970).

Kelly, Patrick, 'Archbishop William King and colonial nationalism', in Ciaran Brady (ed.), *Worsted in the Game: Losers in Irish History* (Dublin: 1989).

King, C.S. (ed.), *A Great Archbishop of Dublin: William King D.D., 1650–1729* (Dublin: Longmans, Green, 1906).

Lovejoy, Arthur O., *The Great Chain of Being* (Cambridge MA: Harvard University Press, 1936).

Matteson, Robert, 'Archbishop William King and the conception of his library', *Library*, 6th ser., 13 (1991), pp. 238–54.

PATRICK KELLY

Kinsella, John (1932–) Composer. Born Dublin. One of the most progressive members of the modern school of Irish composition, Kinsella studied violin and viola with John McKenzie, but is unusual in being largely self-taught as a composer. He abandoned a career as a computer programmer and systems analyst to join the music department of Radic Telefis Eireann in 1968, rising to assistant director in 1972 and head of music in 1983. He resigned his position in 1988 in order to devote his time entirely to creative work. An exponent of modernist compositional techniques, his extensive catalogue of works includes two symphonies, two violin concertos, and numerous works for other media, including much chamber music, which reflects his especial interest in this area.

JOSEPH RYAN

Kinsella, Thomas (1928–) Poet and translator. Born Dublin. If there is a 'fugitive' aspect to post-yeatsian poetry in Ireland, then Thomas Kinsella is its most thorough advocate and practitioner. Starting with some very brief facts issued by the Dolma Press in its early days, Kinsella has pursued a vocation of unrelenting self-scrutiny and effacement. Though the first two collections, *Another September* (1958) are *Downstream*, (1962) display a fastidious concern with 'the well made poem', from *Nightwalker and Other Poems* (1968) onwards order and disorder are interrogated simultaneously, at the personal, national and even cosmic level. *Butcher's Dozen* (1971) sounds a transition to a less accessible poetry, for which the old

guidelines of identity and form are no longer adequate. The Peppercanister series of poems and sequences published by Kinsella's own imprint and beginning in the 1970s is now has continued into the 1990s (now issued from the Dedalus Press). *A Technical Supplement* (1976) in the most striking of its many instalments. Major collections of Kinsella's poetry appeared in *Blood and Family* (1988) and *Collected Poems 1956–1994* (1996).

As a translator, Kinsella is particularly remembered for his version of *The Táin* (1969), the poem of ancient Ireland; but his commitment is also enclosed in *An Duanaire*.

W.J. MCCORMACK

Kirk, Thomas (1781–1845) Sculptor. Born Cork; died Dublin, 19 April. The son of a Scottish father and Irish mother, Kirk studied at the Dublin Society Schools and was apprenticed to Henry Darley, a Dublin stonecutter. Kirk's most famous statue was his 13-feet-high Portland stone representation of Nelson that once stood on top of the Pillar in Sackville (later O'Connell) Street, Dublin (1808). He was a founding member of the Royal Hibernian Academy in 1823 and soon became one of the most important sculptors working in Ireland in the first half of the nineteenth century. Funerary reliefs became a speciality and can be found in chuches throughout Ireland, his most frequent motif being the Good Samaritan. He also did many portrait busts, including one of Thomas Moore in the Royal Irish Academy, Dublin.

Reading

Potterton, Homan, *Irish Church Monuments 1570–1880* (Belfast: Ulster Architectural Heritage Society, 1975).

Strickland, Walter, *A Dictionary of Irish Artists* (Shannon: Irish University Press, 1968).

FINTAN CULLEN

Kirwan, Richard (1783–1812) Chemist. Born Cloughballymore, County Galway; died Dublin. Kirwan abandoned his studies

327

in a Jesuit novitiate on inheriting a large estate, moved to London and studied chemistry. He was elected fellow of the Royal Society in 1780 and received its highest honour, the Copley Medal, after 18 years of experimental work. He returned to Ireland, where he became inspector general of his majesty's mines. He was president of the Royal Irish Academy from 1790 to 1812 and was elected to many foreign academies, including those of Berlin, Stockholm and Philadelphia.

Reading

Kirwan, Richard, *Elements of Mineralogy* (London: Printed for P. Elmsley, 1784).
——*Essay on Human Happiness* (Dublin: Printed by Graisberry and Campbell, 1810).

HENRY BOYLAN

L

labour and trade union movement
Small, local craft societies emerged from the
class tensions within the guilds in the eighteenth century. Surviving records for Limerick stonecutters (1740s) and Belfast
cabinetmakers (1780s) indicate traditional
concerns for controlling entry to trades,
maintaining standards, bidding up 'prices'
and providing welfare. Further evidence is
found in that of repression. The Irish Parliament proscribed numerous organizations,
and many people were hung, imprisoned or
transported for their 'criminal activities'.
Driven underground, trade unions survived,
dealing with their enemies in often brutal
ways as in late eighteenth-century Dublin.
The Combination Acts, passed by the
Union Parliament, outlawed all trade unionism and its increasing connections with radical agitation. Irish unions still flourished,
however, and were identified with the campaign for the Repeal of the Combinations
Acts, achieved in 1824.

Trade societies after 1824 were localized,
craft exclusive and male. Particularly in the
south, they operated in a pre-industrial or
deindustrialized society. They recognized
the need for tariffs to protect native industry
and some measure of self-government to
achieve that end. Labour thus supported
O'Connell. Subsequent national movements
attracted labour sympathy in attempts to
reverse economic stagnation or decline.

After 1850, British-based 'new model'
unions such as the Amalgamated Society of
Engineers, expanded into Ireland, often
through the absorption of the existing local
unions. For the remainder of the century,
trade unions were increasingly incorporated
into British structures, although their political outlook continued to reflect Irish concerns, nationalist or Unionist. In 1880 the
Trades Union Congress (TUC), founded in
1868, met in Dublin with few Irish delegates
and little reference to Irish issues. The emerging trades councils in Belfast (1881) and
Dublin (1886) reflected the growing stability
of organization and the desire by labour to
influence local politics transformed by franchise extensions.

The 'new unionism' of the late 1880s
brought organization down to the unskilled,
a previously neglected force in the largely
casual Irish labour market. Again, British
unions such as the National Union of Gas
and General Labourers, National Amalgamated Union of Labour, Workers' Union
and National Union of Dock Labourers
(NUDL) were to the fore. Paradoxically, a
number of attempts to organize an Irish

Trade Union Congress (ITUC) finally succeeded in 1894. After the TUC met in Belfast in 1893, trades councils were excluded from the executive, moving Belfast and Dublin councils together to establish the ITUC. It was seen as neither challenge nor alternative to the TUC but a forum to discuss otherwise neglected Irish matters. Socialist politics was eschewed but was beginning to develop outside the unions. James Connolly became organizer for the Marxian Irish Socialist Republican Party in 1896 and rural radicalism, stirred by Michael Davitt and the Land War, demanded land reform, cottages for labourers and self-determination. The ITUC represented a small organized section of the urban working class, and did so in a cautious, conservative manner.

James Larkin's arrival in Ireland as NUDL organizer in 1907 quickly taught him the constraints of a colonizing trade union structure. A desire for modernization, a perception of nationalism as an opportunity to combine and promote a socialist agenda, and a responsive, impatient working class ready to be led saw Larkin found the Irish Transport and Workers' Union (ITGWU) in 1909. Employers tried to smash the new union. They attacked Larkin as papist, Orangeman or anti-Christ as occasion demanded. In 1913 they combined to lock out 25,000 workers and attempted to break the ITGWU with the weapons of starvation and repression. Nothing worked. The ITGWU emerged from the lock-out bloodied but intact. Significant liaisons were forged between labour and Republicans during the conflict and, after Larkin's departure for America in 1914, the ITGWU under James Connolly increased its involvement in the national struggle. Events in 1916 divided the trade union movement and Thomas Johnson, at the ITUC in Sligo, called for remembrance of Irish workers killed in Dublin and the trenches. The ITUC had added 'Labour Party' to its title in 1912, but it was an ungainly and unsure alliance.

Larkinism, that unpredictable, passionate maelstrom of action and rhetoric, gave way to syndicalism. The ITGWU grew to over 100,000 members by 1919, organizing in every county and seeking to combine industrial unionism with socialist politics. In Northern Ireland, shipyard expulsions and sectarian violence heralded partition and created a permanent handicap for a divided labour movement. After the collapse of the post-war expansion, the ITUC retreated from industrial unionism and was forced into a defensive mode by economic circumstance and aggressive tactics by the new state. The remaining inter-war years saw continuing division and dissension.

A clash between Larkin and William O'Brien divided the ITGWU and reverberative schisms throughout the movement. Larkin was involved in the foundation of the Worker's Union of Ireland (WUI) in 1924. National concerns and an increasingly internalized perspective, compounded by a global depression, created a movement that reflected a society hostile to socialism. Irish-based unions questioned the legitimacy of British-based unions and thus generated intensive conflict, a weakness readily exploited by employers, favoured by economic decline at the bargaining table. There were heroic episodes: the brief cross-community unity in the Outdoor Relief Strike, Belfast, 1935; the agitation in defence of the Spanish Republic; the valour of the Connolly Column International Brigaders; and an unquenchable capacity to fight as in the Dublin building strike, 1937. The Labour Party separated from the ITUC in 1930 and allowed its constitution to be vetted by the Catholic hierarchy as evidence of labour's passive subjection.

Tensions came to a head as World War II ended. Mass Communist activity in Northern Ireland industry radicalized the unions, and the new welfare state was an attractive reward for the privations of war. In the South, militant socialist activity in Dublin witnessed huge demonstrations against the Trade Union Act, 1941, and the Wages Standstill Order, 1942. Larkin and his son James Junior were at the heart of these battles in the unions and Dublin corporation. O'Brien and the ITGWU were compromised by their antagonism to Larkin, distrust of socialism and closeness to a government that offered 'one big union' by legislation. When the ITGWU loaned the state £50,000 to help cope with the Emergency, it all smacked of corporatist collusion between O'Brien and Fianna Fáil. Inevitably, on the pretext of avoiding contamination by Communism at the World Trade Union Congress, the ITGWU broke from the ITUC to form Comhar Ceard Éireann (Congress of Irish Unions, CIU). A parallel split occurred in the Labour Party with the formation of the ITGWU-dominated National Labour Party.

O'Brien's retirement in 1946 and Larkin's death in 1947 removed the major protagonists. Throughout the depressed and depressing 1950s, as tens of thousands took the boat, John Conroy (ITGWU), James Larkin Junior (WUI) and Norman Kennedy (Amalgamated TGWU) steered the ITUC and CIU towards reunification. The Irish Congress of Trade Unions (ICTU) was formed in 1959, with much autonomy for its Northern Ireland Committee (ICTU-NIC). James Larkin Junior's influence was apparent in the pressure for economic planning, social partnership and ordered bargaining. The 'great switch' in economic policy, away from tariff-protected home industry to attracting foreign multinational capital, was supported by ICTU. The EI dispute in Shannon established trade union organization in the arriving, largely American companies.

The 1960s tested the ICTU's authority with major disputes of bank officials, bus workers, and construction, electricity and maintenance workers. The government's patience was tried as they attempted to woo foreign capital and prepare for European entry. ICTU rationalized its picketing policy, imposed new disciplines and refined centralized wage bargaining. Developments politically were slower, although the decade ended optimistically with a mistaken belief that the 'seventies would be socialist'. Economic advance in the South was balanced by the decline of engineering, textiles and shipbuilding in Northern Ireland. Civil rights movements in America and liberation struggles in Vietnam and Africa inspired the emergence of the Civil Rights Association, strongly supported by the unions, releasing tensions that convulsed Northern society.

Irish trade unionism today maintains high levels of organization, with 100 per cent density in areas of the civil and public sector, power and transport. Many members, however, are captive products of closed shop agreements and deduction-at-source collection of subscriptions. A plethora of individual rights legislation and reference of most claims to the Labour Relations Commission and Labour Court increasingly tribunalizes large areas of industrial relations, an elimination of worker involvement compounded by sophisticated centralized bargaining, such as the Programme for National Recovery, Programme of Economic and Social Progress, and Programme for Competitiveness and Work. The 'industrialization' of the 1970s and 1980s did not generate class consciousness, and Labour continued to struggle politically. Modernization, urbanization, and the confidence and expectations of a new, highly educated generation led to increasing intolerance of corrupt and unresponsive political systems and church authority. As women entered the workforce they joined unions in large numbers and, in pursuing equality, challenged patriarchy, radicalized union agendas and sustained pressure for reform of social policy. The 500,000 marching for tax reform in the late 1970s and early 1980s exposed narrow vested interests. The Labour Party, under Dick Spring, gave voice to the new demands in Dáil Éireann and made an inspired choice in nominating Mary Robinson for president in 1990. In 1992, Labour captured 33 seats, its best ever performance. Its coalition with Fianna Fáil (1992–94) cost the party 16 seats in the 1997 general election, repeating the experience of previous coalitions with Fine Gael. In Northern Ireland, the NIC has successfully contained sectarianism in the workplace and, especially since direct rule, become an effective opposition in the absence of real politics.

ICTU celebrated its centenary in 1994 and can be proud of its past and confident of its future. Trade union amalgamations such as the coming together of the ITGWU and the WUI as SIPTU (Services, Industrial, Professional and Technical Union) are rapidly producing a more effective structure, and long years of campaigning on economic and social issues have legitimized many of these issues and set the agenda across wide areas of policy. Liaison with groups representing the aged and disabled has been complemented by a nationwide network of centres for the unemployed. ICTU is represented at all levels within the new structures created to dispense and utilize the incoming European funding. At the workplace, world class manufacture presents a challenge as it exploits a weakness of local organization, but new policies on pensions, worker participation and health and safety maintain a relevance and vibrancy for trade unionism, recognized by government and employers alike as a key component in the development of contemporary Ireland.

Reading

Boyle, John W., *The Irish Labour Movement in the Nineteenth Century* (Washington DC: Catholic University of America Press, 1988).

Cody, Seamus, O'Dowd, John and Rigney, Peter, *The Parliament of Labour: One Hundred Years of the Dublin Council of Trade Unions* (Dublin: DCTU, 1986).

Connolly, James, *Collected Works, Volume One* and *Volume Two*, (Dublin: New Books, 1988).

Cradden, Terry, *Trade Unionism, Socialism and Partition: The Labour Movement in Northern Ireland* (Belfast: December Publications, 1993).

D'Arcy, Fergus and Hannigan, Ken, *Workers in Union: Documents and Commentaries on the History of Irish Labour* (Dublin: National Archives, 1988).

Greaves, C. Desmond, *The Life and Times of James Connolly* (London: Lawrence and Wishart, 1961).

McCarthy, Charles, *The Decade of Upheaval: Irish Trade Unions in the 1960s* (Dublin: Institute of Public Administration, 1973).

—— *Trade Unions in Ireland, 1894–1960* (Dublin: Institute of Public Administration, 1977).

Milotte, Mike, *Communism in Modern Ireland: The Pursuit of the Workers' Republic Since 1920* (Dublin: Gill and Macmillan, 1984).

Mitchell, Arthur, *Labour in Irish Politics, 1890–1930* (Dublin: Irish University Press, 1974).

Morgan, Austen, *James Connolly: A Political Biography* (Manchester: Manchester University Press, 1988).

O'Connor, Emmet, *Syndicalism in Modern Ireland, 1917–1923* (Cork: Cork University Press, 1988).

——*A Labour History of Ireland, 1824–1960* (Dublin: Gill and Macmillan, 1992).

Patterson, Henry, *Class Conflict and Sectarianism: The Protestant Working Class and the Belfast Labour Movement, 1868–1920* (Belfast: Blackstaff, 1980).

Saothar, Journal of the Irish Labour History Society, annual.

FRANCIS DEVINE

Ladies Land League Formed 31 January 1881, Michael Davitt being the instigator. The league was designed as a response to the British government's Coercion Act, which made it only a matter of time before the Land League leaders were arrested (female organizations fell outside the terms of the Act).

The Land Leaguers thought the women would only be capable of providing a semblance of an organization. However, the Ladies Land League provided a militant campaign, organizing resistance from the ground. The next 18 months saw the emergence of a remarkable group of women, including Anna Parnell, who was appointed organizing secretary. On 16 September 1881, the Government suppressed the Ladies Land League. Its leaders were quickly arrested and convicted. Unlike their male counterparts they were treated as common criminals, not as political prisoners. However, repression backfired and scores of women volunteered their services.

In the end it was the male land leaguers, embarrassed by the women's militancy, who brought about the disbanding of the Ladies Land League in August 1881.

Reading

Ward, Margaret, *Unmanageable Revolutionaries: Women and Irish Nationalism* (Pluto Press, 1983).

RACHEL FURMSTON

Lalor, James Fintan (1807–49) Politician. Born Tinnakilly, County Laois; died Dublin. The son of a gentleman-farmer and MP, Lalor was educated at Carlow College and because of ill-health led a secluded life for many years. He became interested in agrarian reform and contributed articles to the *Nation* advocating 'the land of Ireland for the people of Ireland'. He formed a tenant-right league in Tipperary, took charge of the *Irish Felon* after the arrest of Mitchel, and tried unsuccessfully to organize a rising after the failure of the 1848 attempt.

HENRY BOYLAN

landscape *c*.1750–1990s In contrast to the situation in France or England, landscape painting in Ireland in the mid-eighteenth century should be seen in relation to the historical forces of colonialism. The great period of the confiscation of Irish lands by the New English settlers (sixteenth and seventeenth centuries) was not so far distant, and the Protestant Ascendancy had been assured by the Williamite campaigns of the end of the seventeenth century and secured in turn by the anti-Catholic Penal Laws. Their aims included not only the disenfranchisement of the Catholic majority but the transfer of the remaining Catholic lands into Protestant ownership through either dispossession or conversion. It is within this context of territorial acquisition that the mid-eighteenth century topographical views of the new Anglo-Irish estates should be considered. They range from the relatively schematic mapping of features of terrain and their proximity or distance from the great house to the more sophisticated and quite durable genre of the 'house portrait', of which Thomas Roberts's *Lucan House and Demesne* (1770, National Gallery of Ireland – NGI) is a good example. During the 1798 rebellion the building of military roads and forts in areas such as the Wicklow Mountains opened up territory for military surveillance and artistic contemplation alike – even if the repressive mechanisms of colonialism are largely absent from the images of landscape themselves. These mechanisms do persist, however, in the social relations of art and artists, in the artists' dealings with their landowning patrons, for example, or in the necessity to travel to London in search of both a more sustained art market and a degree of prestige.

Other factors in late eighteenth-century landscape painting are not so immediately reducible to the needs of colonialism, although they could do its ideological work if required. Increased naturalism in Irish art during the latter part of the century may be regarded as due at least in part to an emphasis on observation and enquiry like that which characterized the intellectual phenomenon of the Enlightenment in the rest of Europe: it is at this point also that artists such as Roberts undertook projects to observe and record different types of landscape throughout Ireland. Meanwhile an interest in classicism was not solely confined to the Claudian pictorial format of idealized landscape favoured by the aristocracy of Britain and Ireland. The European Enlightenment's study of the ruins of imperial Rome may be seen as echoed in Ireland by moves to investigate and record indigenous archaeological remains: landscapists such as Roberts, Jonathan Fisher or William Ashford all contributed watercolours, for example, to Francis Grose's *Antiquities of Ireland*.

Other key concerns of late eighteenth-century Irish landscape painting, however, emerge within the work of George Barret. Under the early patronage of Viscount Powerscourt he painted numerous views within the Powerscourt demesne and along the nearby valley of the Dargle. Around 1763 Barret moved to London, where not only was he a founder member of the Royal Academy but his work proved to be highly popular, resulting in a close rivalry with his British contemporary Richard Wilson. A painting such as *Powerscourt Waterfall* (1760, NGI) demonstrated the successful format developed by Barret quite early in his career. The scale of the waterfall in relation to the small foreground figures and the golden-coloured cascade against its darker background of rocks exemplify a familiarity with distinctions between notions of the 'beautiful' and the 'sublime' developed by Edmund Burke during the 1750s, but not published until 1767 as *A Philosophical Enquiry into the Origins of Our Ideas about the Sublime and the Beautiful*. Burke had been an early supporter of Barret; his own thesis provided a major contribution to an aesthetic debate which, throughout the eighteenth-century, had come to provide clear guidelines for the painters of landscape and their aristocratic patrons alike. To the 'Sublime' and the 'Beautiful' was soon added the category of the 'Picturesque', within which imaginative composition and lighting, conjoined with an evocation of the viewer's emotion, often superseded the value of topographic accuracy. The sublime's evocation of grandeur and terror reached a particular culmination during the early nineteenth century in the work of the emigré Francis Danby, whose *Liensfiord Lake* (1841, Victoria and Albert Museum – V&A) suggested a wild remoteness whose dangers could be vicariously experienced within the safe urban confines of the British Royal Academy.

Yet it was Danby's friend James Arthur O'Connor whose later works employed the characteristics of the picturesque in the service of a highly romanticized view of Ireland. Any evidence of contemporary agrarian unrest is excluded from O'Connor's work; instead paintings such as *The Poachers* (1835, NGI) address the emotions of their predominantly English audience through strategies of composition and lighting. His version of the often-painted tourist site *The Eagle's Rock, Killarney* (1831, private collection) clearly evokes a sense of solitude and Romantic melancholy in considerable contrast to an earlier view of a similar setting – Joseph Peacock's *The Patron of St Kevin at the Seven Churches of Glendalough* (1813, Ulster Museum), which combines the picturesque exaggeration of the scale of both the round tower and its surrounding mountains with a close observation of the festivities beneath.

In the mid-nineteenth century the practice of landscape painting became bound up with pervasive social forces affecting art on a more international scale. Previously it had been common for artists to move between Ireland and Britain in search of an expanded market. As the former relationships of aristocratic patronage were gradually eroded in the late eighteenth and early nineteenth centuries with the economic and political growth of the middle classes, the accompanying cultural changes meant that landscape painting was no longer required to represent the domination and possession of territory. Within the Romanticism of O'Connor and others, landscape became a sounding board for the viewer's emotion – a level of response which subsequently became devalued within the concerns of mid-nineteenth century realism. The possibility of an objective record of the surrounding environment was an artistic project formed in the context of the increasing materialism accompanying the growth of industrial capitalism. Landscape painting from the mid-nineteenth century onwards acquired a certain significance for the increasingly urban, middle-class audience for whom it embodied a changing relationship to the land itself – now a site of relaxation, enjoyment or even exoticism. In the artistic groupings focused on Paris, these new themes were concurrent with a concerted attack on both the institutional practices and the obsession with technical perfection dominating the academy.

This cluster of interests coalesced into an emergent avant-gardism characterized also by its internationalism, and including a large number of Irish landscape painters. The precedent was established in the 1850s by Nathaniel Hone, who for approximately 13 years lived in the artistic colony of Barbizon south of Paris. His approach to landscape was similar in its freshness and occasional spontaneity to some early Impressionist paintings, but only at times did his work approach the social critique of either Millet or Pissarro (e.g. *Old Woman Gathering Sticks*, dated probably after his return to Dublin *c*.1872, NGI). The degree of technical radicalism characterizing Hone's painting was typical of the developing avant-garde and was also a feature of Roderic O'Conor's views of Britanny, where he painted with Gauguin during the 1890s. By comparison the pictorial method and subject matter of both the early Lavery and Walter Osborne were closer to the naturalism of Bastien-Lepage, which combined fidelity of appearances with a rural setting. By the 1880s this method had lost any connotations of innovation, and Osborne's combinations of landscape with genre themes, as in *Apple Gathering, Quimperle* (1883, NGI), represent a highly conservative and sentimentalized view of rural Breton life.

The focus of Irish landscape painting during the nineteenth century therefore seems to have been mainly located outside Ireland itself. This degree of displacement into the European avant-garde has a particular consequence, however; it reasserts the severing of the making of art from the political conflicts over land which took place within Ireland throughout the century. The views of prosperous country estates around Dublin painted by James Richard Marquis during the 1850s had already excluded any reference to the devastation of the land during the Famine of the previous decade. Struggles over landownership throughout Ireland crystallized in the form of the Irish National Land League in 1879: nothing of this, for example, is acknowledged in the later works of Hone, whose return to Malahide to take up a career as a gentleman-farmer must certainly have precluded him from even considering allusions to agrarian conflict.

Similar to late nineteenth-century perceptions of Britanny, the notion of a region's being geographically marginal yet central to cultural developments acquired a major significance in Ireland. Douglas Hyde's foundation of the Gaelic League in 1893 marked an upsurge of interest primarily in Irish literary culture; in 1907, however, Jack Yeats illustrated Synge's *The Aran Islands*, while the prolonged visit of Grace and Paul Henry to Achill in 1910 also signalled an increasing interest in the west among artists. This was a process far from unique to Ireland, in that a hundred years after their recognition as the sites of the sublime the peripheral regions of Europe were once more becoming a source for artistic renovation. Initially both the landscape of the west of Ireland and the peasantry who worked it tended to be seen in primitivist terms. The harmonious and rhythmic integration of figures with the land they inhabit can be read in Paul Henry's *The Potato Diggers* (1910–11, private collection) as signifying not only a closeness to nature and instinctual rather than intellectual qualities, but also a source of spiritual renewal for largely metropolitan audiences. The representation of the peasant as hero, closely derived from Millet, had further resonances within the mythology of the west, which was meanwhile taking shape in the literature of the period.

During the 1920s the cultural requirements of the new, politically conservative Free State involved the construction of a 'true' Irishness, believed to reside in the isolated Gaeltacht areas along the Atlantic seaboard. This quality of authenticity could be read in Henry's paintings through the insistence on certain motifs – cottage, bog, mountain and (in earlier works) rustic peasant. The vocabulary of Irishness thereby established is both formally simplistic and culturally pervasive. Not only was it taken up by other painters such as George Humbert Craig, but a work by Henry appeared in 1932 on the cover of the Irish Free State Handbook. The peaceful and timeless appearance of works such as *Lakeside Cottages* (*c*.1923–30, Hugh Lane Municipal Gallery, Dublin), however, masks certain contradictions, not the least being that the pre-industrial economy and the isolation of many rural areas were inexorably if slowly changing during the 1920s and 1930s.

The preoccupation with landscape themes which emerged in Yeats's paintings of the late 1930s also works to convey a sense of 'Irishness', but by different means. The emphasis in many of these works is on a combination of mythology with nostalgia for an unspecified past – as in *The Path of Diarmuid and Grainne* (1945, private collection), which is itself located in a wild and rugged west similar to that of *The Plank Road* (1955–6, private collection). The isolated figure making its way across the bog is indicative of the frequent appearances of the alienated individual in these later landscapes, inviting readings of melancholy and loneliness. The looseness of paint handling is not only far removed from the clearly defined planes of Henry's views of the west or the formal simplifications of John Luke's Northern landscapes; this reliance on visual codes of Expressionism encourages the viewer's projection of emotion onto the landscape, reinforced by a romantic identification with the figure in the picture plane. Both the mythology of the west and the stereotype of the Irish national character as determined by melancholia are particularly powerful ideological mechanisms. That Yeats could acquire the accolade of 'Ireland's national painter' is doubtless due at least in part to the efficacy of such underpinnings. It is significant meanwhile that the increasingly Expressionist landscapes of Evie Hone or Nano Reid from the 1930s and 1940s tend to lack these particular emotional resonances, a factor which in addition to their gender has doubtless contributed to the marginalization of their work within historical accounts of Irish landscape painting. The common interest in the alienated individual on the part of European and American figurative painters after World

War II is also of some significance here, notably in the light of the depoliticization of many artists and writers in the cultural climate of the Cold War.

In post-Emergency Ireland the myth of the west could be seen to have exhausted its ideological impetus, at least in so far as the needs of the state had themselves shifted towards a greater focus on modernization. No longer laden with the overt connotations of history or mythology in the service of a cultural nationalism, the artist's response to the landscape could be construed solely at the level of individual perception and intuition. This is the case with Camille Souter's paintings of Achill from 1959–60, and a continuing fascination with the 'authenticity' of experience at Ireland's peripheries must also account for the successful reception of the Tory Island painters during the 1960s. The visual language of Yeats, which mingled abstraction and Expressionism, could be re-employed by a younger generation for whom Modernism implied an increased concern for the properties of paint itself, as in Camille Souter's *Fields in Calary* (1964, Ulster Museum), while the Northern painter T.P. Flanagan also applied a Modernist interest in space and form to his readings of the landscape around Lough Erne in the 1960s. The need to identify a successor to Yeats meanwhile had become focused on Patrick Collins, whose candidature was strengthened in that, like Yeats, he was from Sligo and hence could be easily incorporated into the revised myth of the west, divorced from its previous connotations. In Collins's work of the 1960s, a Yeatsian melancholia became redefined through a Modernist simplification of forms and a restriction of the palette to a range of blues, greys and greens. Although closely allied to assumptions of an essential Irish character through works such as *Tinker's Moon* (1967, private collection) or indeed Collins's *Homage to Paul Henry* (1867, private collection), in the Breton paintings of the 1960s there is an overspill into generic Celticness.

Throughout the 1970s, characterized by what appeared to be polarizations between

Expressionist concerns of intuition and empathy and formalist priorities of surface, materials and structure, the painting of landscape tended to rely more on the former tendency. Clear precedents had already been established by Yeats and Collins, whose contemporary Tony O'Malley, an Irish painter in exile in Cornwall, gained gradual recognition in Ireland throughout the decade. Within Ireland other artists as diverse as Barrie Cooke, and Basil Blackshaw and Sean MacSweeney continued to mine this celebratory vein of landscape painting; the 1980s, however, saw the advent of radical challenges to previous assumptions of the validity of all forms of visual representation, the status of landscape painting, and ultimately that of 'nature' itself. For many among a younger generation of artists, the formerly empathetic views of landscape appeared bankrupt within an Ireland increasingly challenged by environmental concerns and reassessments of its concepts of national identity. Particularly within the North, the political significance of landscape has become inescapable; albeit in a different form, the surveillance implicit in the military activities of the British army has resurrected the eighteenth-century concerns of the regulatory gaze within the topographical vista. The politics of the gaze within landscape have been taken up to great effect in the photoworks of Willie Doherty, mainly in the context of his native Derry; the Northern landscape as contested territory, often overlaid with environmental concerns, meanwhile informs the paintings of Dermot Seymour.

Ideological associations between landscape and the female body have also been critically reassessed by Kathy Prendergast in a series of watercolour and ink drawings, *Enclosed Worlds in Open Spaces* (1983, private collection); much of Prendergast's work, such as the installation *Land* (1990) shown at the Tate Gallery Liverpool's *Strongholds* exhibition of 1991, involves a radical engagement with preconceptions of landscape. Yet the Expressionist tendency still flourishes within the practice of painters such as Gwen

O'Dowd or Cecily Brennan: the work of both not only restates the validity of painting itself in the face of considerable postmodernist challenges, but reconstitutes Romanticist ideas of landscape as embodying values and emotions beyond the human scale. Notably in Cecily Brennan's paintings from Iceland, such as *Where Lava Meets the Sea* (1990, private collection), a concern with the sublime reasserts itself; what designates this work as belonging to the 1990s is that the sublime is no longer of 'neutral' gender, but is resolutely allied to female experience.

Reading

Fowler, Joan, 'Art and independence', *CIRCA* 14 (January/February 1984), pp. 6–10.

Gibbons, Luke, 'Displacing landscape', in *Cecily Brennan* (Dublin: Douglas Hyde Gallery, 1991).

Hutchinson, John, *James Arthur O'Connor* (Dublin: National Gallery of Ireland, 1985).

Schapis, Meyer, 'The nature of abstract art' (1937; repr. in *Modern Art, 19th and 20th Centuries*, London: 1978).

FIONA BARBER

Lane pictures controversy Sir Hugh Percy Lane (1875–1915), art dealer and gallery director nephew of Lady Gregory, had made a fine collection of representative modern works, mainly French Impressionists. In 1913 he had offered these to the City of Dublin, if the corporation would build a gallery for them. Disputes over the nature of the gallery and disdain for the collection by some led Sir Hugh to withdraw the offer. In a properly witnessed will of 1913 he left the collection to the English National Gallery in London. But in an unwitnessed codicil of February 1915 he bequeathed them to Dublin as he had originally planned.

Sir Hugh died in the sinking of the *Lusitania* on 5 May 1915, and the pictures were kept by London. This was disputed by the Dublin Municipal Gallery and by many in Ireland, encouraged by Lady Gregory and her supporters. Eventually, it was agreed in 1959 that the collection (the highlight of which was Renoir's

Les Parapluies) would be shared between the two galleries, each having half the pictures for display for a period of five years in turn.

PETER COSTELLO

language: varieties of spoken English today When Irish people speak English they use a dialect which is distinctive in its sounds as well as in idioms and structures. The dialect is called 'Hiberno-English', a term which suggests more than simply 'English spoken in Ireland': it implies a close influence from one language (Gaelic) onto another (English).

Irish people use the sounds of the Gaelic language to pronounce English words; the closer to places in Ireland where the Gaelic language was recently spoken as the normal medium, the more likely is the speaker to use undiluted Irish sounds – hence, 'tree' for 'three', 'wondher' for 'wonder', 'shtar' for 'star', 'sthrip' for 'strip', 'filum' for 'film', and so on. Similarly, expressions such as 'I'm after having my tea', 'I have the letter written', and 'He asked her was she a stranger' also reflect Gaelic influence. The Gaelic verbal system is evident in forms such as 'I do be here every day' and 'Is it yourself that's in it?' Gaelic words also regularly crop up in conversation; for example, 'Stop foostering' (Gaelic *fústar*, 'fuss') or 'You're talking rawmaish' (Gaelic *ráiméis*, 'nonsense'). Another distinctive feature of Hiberno-English is the wide use of words which are no longer found in general use in Standard English; for example, 'cog', to cheat in an examination, 'bowsey', disreputable drunkard, 'delph', crockery. Irish people also tend to put the stress in longer words nearer the end of such words than speakers of Standard English, as in 'committēe', 'disc̄ipline', 'advertīsement'.

Some or all of these distinctive features are to be found in Irish speakers of English, but it seems that the more educated the speaker, especially if he or she lives close to Dublin, the smaller number of these traits occur. An educated Dubliner would be unlikely to say 'He fell out of his standing' (meaning 'He fell over') which is obviously non-standard, but he or she might say 'Don't be talking', which is equally non-standard, but less obviously so. There is a considerable difference between speakers of Hiberno-English in Northern Ireland and those to the South, mainly for historical reasons, in particular the very strong influence from the idiom of Scottish Gaelic and Ulster Scots.

In general, by contrast with the levelling effect of Standard English in England, which is based on the educated dialect of London, there is no equivalent 'Standard Hiberno-English', because each dialectal area retains some local characteristics; although these are tending to be lost, not out of a desire to imitate an educated Dublin-based norm, but because of the universalizing effect of radio and television. The English language will remain the dominant language in Ireland, even though it is technically, according to the Constitution of Ireland, only 'recognized as a second official language'. However, thanks to the continuous interference from Gaelic, 'the first official language', the influence of which many Irish users of English are unaware of, the Hiberno-English dialect displays the linguistic energy of both languages.

T.P. DOLAN

languages in the early modern period Gaelic, English and Latin were the three principal languages of early modern Ireland. Before the mid-sixteenth century, Latin was the standard language used in most legal agreements, and it continued to be used up to the mid-seventeenth century for inquisitions as well as for works of scholarly theology and in the liturgy. Latin was the main medium of instruction in grammar schools and at university until the eighteenth century. It was frequently used as the language of communication between Gaelic-speaking Irish lords and the English administration, though by the end of the sixteenth century there were few Irish lords who did not also understand some English.

Gaelic was the dominant language of everyday conversation in sixteenth-century

Ireland. In the course of the seventeenth century the classical Gaelic preserved by bardic poets ceased to be used in literary compositions, and was replaced by the ordinary Gaelic dialects in everyday use. Although some religious works in Gaelic were published on the Continent, no Gaelic books were published in Ireland in the seventeenth century.

Among the Anglo-Irish of the Pale and the towns, English was common, but the extent of interaction with Gaelic areas meant that a knowledge of Gaelic was useful to the gentry of the Pale also, and Gaelic was regularly heard on the streets of Dublin and other towns in the sixteenth century. During the seventeenth century English gradually became established as the language of law and of commerce. While written English conformed to the standard in use in England, in conversation several dialects were used; lowland Scots was spoken extensively in Ulster as a result of the early seventeenth-century plantation there. In south Wexford, the dialect of English used was peculiar to the baronies of Forth and Bargy.

Anglo-Norman French or 'law french' was also used in legal proceedings.

Reading

Adams, G.B. (ed.), *Ulster Dialects* (Cultra: Ulster Folk Museum, 1964).

Bliss, Alan, 'The English language in early modern Ireland', in T.W. Moody, F.X. Martin and F.J. Byrne (eds), *A New History of Ireland. Vol. III: Early Modern Ireland, 1534–1691* (Oxford: 1976).

——*Spoken English in Ireland, 1600–1740* (Dublin: 1979).

Ó Cuív, Brian, 'The Irish language in the early modern period', in T.W. Moody, F.X. Martin and F.J. Byrne (eds), *A New History of Ireland. Vol. III: Early Modern Ireland, 1534–1691* (Oxford: 1976).

O'Rahilly, T.F., *Irish Dialects Past and Present* (Dublin: 1972).

Stanford, W.B., *Ireland and the Classical Tradition* (Dublin: Allen Figgis, 1976).

BERNADETTE CUNNINGHAM

Lansdowne Road The Irish Champion Athletic Club was founded in 1872 by H.W.D. Dunlop, a prominent Trinity College, Dublin, sportsman, to organize the premier championship in Irish athletics. Its first meeting was held in that year in the College Park. Dunlop then obtained a lease from the Pembroke estate on a field near Landowne Road Station. There he developed a sports complex catering initially for archery, tennis, cricket and croquet, with a cinder track for athletics. The ground became the home of the Lansdowne Football Club (1872) and, in 1907, the headquarters of the Irish Rugby Football Union. Besides being the venue for international rugby, and until 1960 for occasional athletic meetings, Landsdowne Road has, in recent years, been the setting for the Republic of Ireland's home international soccer matches.

TREVOR WEST

Larchet, John F. (1884–1967) Teacher, arranger, composer, and mentor to a whole school of Irish composition. Born Dublin. Larchet studied at the Royal Irish Academy of Music (RIAM) with Esposito and later at Trinity College, Dublin, with C.H. Kitson and Dr Joze, taking his MusB (1915) and MusD (1917). He was director of music at the Abbey Theatre (1908–34), where with his small orchestra he provided incidental music for plays and ballets and arrangements of Irish airs for the interval. Larchet believed passionately in the need for a comprehensive system of music education in the newly independent state, a goal he was well placed to pursue as senior professor of composition, harmony, and counterpoint at the RIAM (1920–55). He was concurrently appointed to the chair of music at University College, Dublin (1921–58). In his music he sought to forge a distinctive national idiom through a synthesis of the indigenous folk song heritage with the broader European tradition. His was not a conspicuous, individual creative voice; he was more the craftsman, and a miniaturist. But his finest achievements – the songs 'Padraic the Fiddler' (1919), 'An Ardglass Boat Song' (1920) and

'The Cormorant' (1947), along with the orchestral *Lament for Youth* (*c*.1920), and characteristic pairings 'Dirge of Ossian' and 'Macananty's Reel' (1940), and 'Carlow Tune' and 'Tinkers' Wedding' (1952) – attest to the quality of his writing. Some of his most profound original writing is to be found in his final work, the set of *Three Motets* (1961).

JOSEPH RYAN

Lardner, Dionysius (1793–1859) Physicist and encyclopedist. Born 3 April; died 29 April, Naples. Son of a County Clare solicitor, Lardner entered Trinity College, Dublin, in 1812. A brilliant student, he won almost all the available prizes in mathematics and philosophy as an undergraduate; he took the BA, MA, LLB and LLD degrees and worked as a 'grinder' of students. Lardner had a reputation as a mathematician. His textbook on analytic geometry (1823) was recommended to the 18-year-old William Rowan Hamilton by John Brinkley, astronomer royal of Ireland. Lardner took holy orders, probably because he had his eye on a lucrative fellowship. As well as being an energetic author, he fathered an illegitimate son, who became the successful playwright, Dion Boucicault. In 1828 Lardner moved to London to become the first professor of natural philosophy and astronomy in the newly founded, and radical, University (College) of London. A showman-like public lecturer, he early identified the clamour for knowledge of things scientific and gave himself over completely to the publishing enterprise by which he is best remembered, the production of the 133-volume Cabinet encyclopedia. A heavy pressure on Lardner to make this publishing enterprise a success arose because he needed a sum of £8,000 to pay compensation to a cavalry officer whose wife he seduced and subsequently married. He died a wealthy man.

Reading

Bellot, Hugh, H.L., *University College London, 1826–1926* (London: UCL Press, 1929).

Lardner, Dionysius, *The Cabinet Cyclopaedia* (London: Longman, Orme, Rees, Brown et al., 1830–49).

Davis, William, J., in Charles Mollan, William Davis and Brendan Finucane (eds), *More People and Places in Irish Science and Technology* (Dublin: Royal Irish Academy, 1990).

WILLIAM J. DAVIS

Larkin, James (1876–1947) Trade union leader. Born Liverpool, 21 January; died Dublin, 30 January. The son of poor Irish parents, Larkin began work as a labourer at the age of 9. After a period as a seaman, he became a foreman on Liverpool docks in 1894, but lost the job when he joined the men under him on strike. Working for the National Union of Dock Labourers (NUDL), he organized a wave of strikes in Belfast, 1907, including one by the police. His militant methods alarmed the NUDL, and he was transferred to Dublin in 1908, where, suspended by the union, he founded the Irish Transport and General Workers' Union (ITGWU) in 1909. His success worried employers, who, led by William Martin Murphy, attempted to prevent workers joining the ITGWU, resulting in the lock-out of 1913. In 1914, Larkin went to the USA to raise funds, but became involved in the American labour movement, and stayed for nine years. In 1920, he was sentenced to 10 years' imprisonment for 'criminal syndicalism', but was released in 1923 and returned home to a tumultuous reception. He attempted to regain control of the union, but was expelled, after which he founded the Workers' Union of Ireland. In 1924, he visited Russia as representative of the Irish section of the Comintern. He was a deputy in Dáil Éireann 1927–32, 1937–8, and, for the Labour Party, 1943–4. His last main achievement was securing a fortnight's holidays for manual workers after a 14-week strike. His statue stands in O'Connell Street, Dublin.

JAMES KEMMY

Latham, James (1696–1747) Portrait painter. Born County Tipperary; died Dublin,

26 January. Latham studied in Antwerp with the Guild of St Luke (1724–5). An early and unusual commission, given the Penal Laws, is a portrait of Christopher Butler, Catholic archbishop of Cashel (*c*.1720, Kilkenny Castle). Well established by 1731, Latham painted the portrait of Charles Tottenham (Dublin, National Gallery of Ireland), recording the famous patriotic incident of 'Tottenham in his Boots'. He particularly excelled in double portraits, such as that of Bishop Clayton and his wife (*c*.1730, Dublin, National Gallery of Ireland), or in dynastic portraits, as in the various paintings of the Cosby family of Stradbally.

Reading

Crookshank, Anne, *The GPA Irish Arts Review Yearbook* (Eton Enterprises, 1988).
Pasquin, Anthony, *Memoirs of the Royal Academicians and an Authentic History of the Artists of Ireland...* (London: 1796).

FINTAN CULLEN

Lavery, Sir John (1856–1941) Painter. Born 26 March, Belfast; died Kilkenny. The son of a publican, and left an orphan at 3, Lavery was cared for by his uncle, a farmer in County Down, and another relative who was a pawnbroker at Saltcoats in Scotland. After an unhappy childhood he was apprenticed to a photographer in Glasgow, from whom he learned the art of tinting photographs. Later, when his own studio was destroyed by fire, he used the £300 insurance money to pay for art studies in London, and in Paris at the Academie Julien, where he encountered the techniques of the rising young French painters of the time. He painted for a spell with the artists' colony at Grez-sur-Loing before returning to Scotland, where he soon found recognition as the most cosmopolitan of the 'Glasgow Boys'. A commission to paint Queen Victoria's visit to the Glasgow Exhibition in 1882 changed his life, launching him on a career as an international society painter. Many honours were bestowed on

him, and in 1918 he was knighted for his work as a war artist. His fluent and accomplished style is seen at its best in his portraits of women. After his second marriage, to a beautiful American widow, Hazel Martyn, the couple played an active role in the Irish cultural renaissance, and Lady Lavery's portrait as an Irish colleen appeared on the banknotes of the Irish Free State. She died in 1935. Lavery died at his step-daughter's home in 1941.

Reading

Crookshank, Anne and the Knight of Glin, *The Painters of Ireland, c. 1660–1920* (London: Barrie and Jenkins, 1978).
McConkey, Kenneth, *Sir John Lavery, R.A., 1856–1941* (Belfast: Ulster Museum and Fine Art Society, 1993).
——*Sir John Lavery* (Edinburgh: Canongate Press, 1993).

TONY STEWART

Lavin, Mary (1912–96) Short story writer. Lavin first took as her territory the almost invisible, frustrated lives of the Midlands, where custom and social pressure reinforce an innate tendency to avoid taking risks. Stories like 'The Will' and 'Frail Vessel' contrast the openness of a single vital character with the stultification of conformists who only dimly perceive what they are missing. Lavin often uses a female protagonist, although her central characters can be of either sex and from any social circumstance or role in life.

Her range later extended to stories set in Dublin, some, including 'In a Café', drawing on her own experience of widowhood. Her mature stories, reflecting the increased complexity of Irish society, show characters trapped less by social pressures than by their own internal limitations. Nevertheless her depictions of marriage are often terrifying presentations of the inability of couples to retain a fruitful intimacy.

Lavin writes in the tradition of Chekhov, where plot and incident are important only in so far as they serve to reveal character. Most of her works, remarkably consistent in quality, are collected in three volumes in *The Stories of Mary Lavin* (1964–85), although there are also some impressive later pieces.

RUTH SHERRY

Lawless, Emily (1845–1913) Novelist and poet. Born Kildare. The daughter of the third Lord Cloncurry, Lawless's first fiction, *Hurrish* (1882), analysed the legal position of the Irish tenant farmer and was admired by Gladstone, who became an occasional correspondent. Nine subsequent novels included *Grania* (1892), a mawkish romantic saga which vividly depicts landscape and life on the Aran Islands, and *Maelcho* (1894), a competent historical novel which recounts in sanguinary detail the warfare between Elizabethan and native forces during the Desmond rebellion in 1583. Her poems, published as *With the Wild Geese* (1902), sustain a historical interest in ballad and lyric form but fail to achieve the quality of her fiction. Other works include the pseudo-historical document *With Essex in Ireland* (1890) and a biography of Maria Edgeworth published in 1904. Lawless spent her final years in England, where she lived as a recluse. Frequently described as an Ascendancy writer, she in fact defies such classification and has resultantly suffered critical neglect.

EVE PATTEN

Lawless, Matthew James (1837–64) Painter and illustrator. Born Dublin; died London, 6 August. The son of a solicitor, Lawless was educated in Bath. He studied art under J.M. Leigh, founder of the Newman Street drawing school in London, and later with Henry O'Neill RA at the Langham School. Lawless never returned to Ireland and was primarily an illustrator to London magazines such as *Once a Week*, *London Society* and *Punch*. He died at the age of 27.

Lawless seems to have been particularly fond of period subjects, evidenced most especially in one of his few known paintings,

The Sick Call (1863, Dublin, National Gallery of Ireland), where a solemn priest and a group of acolytes travel by rowing boat to a possible death bed. Going by the architecture, the scene is set in northern Europe. In terms of style and content, Lawless exhibits an affinity with the Pre-Raphaelites. In the foreground of *The Sick Call* he plays close attention to the symbolical significance of vegetation.

Reading

Butler, Patricia, *Three Hundred Years of Irish Watercolours and Drawings* (London: Weidenfeld and Nicolson, 1990).
Strickland, Walter, *A Dictionary of Irish Artists* (Shannon: Irish University Press, 1968).

FINTAN CULLEN

Leahy, Edward Daniel (1797–1875) Painter. Born London; died Brighton, 9 February. The son of Irish parents, Leahy studied at the Dublin Society Schools. Although he lived his adult life in England, he frequently exhibited at the Royal Hibernian Academy, specializing in historical themes, such as Mary Queen of Scots and subject pictures like *Catching the Expression* (the expression belonged to Thomas Moore). He painted a few portraits, such as the representation of Father Matthew now in the National Portrait Gallery, London.

Reading

Stewart, Ann M., *Royal Hibernian Academy of Arts, Index of Exhibitors and their Works, 1826–1979* (Dublin: Manton, 1985–6).
Strickland, Walter, *A Dictionary of Irish Artists* (Shannon: Irish University Press, 1968).

FINTAN CULLEN

Learned societies Seventeenth-century scientists felt that the universities, dominated by old-fashioned theocentric attitudes, failed to provide a congenial forum for the exchange of scholarly ideas. As a result, non-university learned academies were set up, precursors being the Collège de France and the

Académie Française. The Royal Society was founded in 1662, most scientific academies in Europe following suit around the opening of the eighteenth century, in the early Enlightenment. The type of scholarship cultivated there was usually practical, oriented towards experiment and the 'natural' sciences. Swift (a staunch conservative) lampooned the institution as the Academy of Lagado.

In Ireland, the example of Newton's Royal Society was emulated in the Dublin Philosophical Society (established 1684), among whose original members were the celebrated chemist Robert Boyle and William Molyneux. In Ireland, such societies tended to take on a 'patriotic' profile: thus the Dublin Society, founded in 1732 as a patriotic improving society, was in part of its activities also a learned society. In 1744, its members pursued their more learned interests in the Physico-Historical Society. Later again, in 1772, the Dublin Society set up a select committee, which was the precursor of a Hibernian Antiquarian Society (1779), which in turn merged into the newly founded Royal Irish Academy (RIA, 1782), Ireland's definitive 'official' academy of sciences. Throughout the eighteenth century, men of 'patriotic' sympathies like Molyneux and Sir Lucius O'Brien were involved in these developments.

Besides an ongoing interest in experimental 'natural philosophy', learned societies in Ireland cultivated a growing interest in Irish antiquity. All the above-mentioned forerunners of the RIA were strongly antiquarian in orientation. As a result, it became possible for the Anglo-Irish elite to develop, in a climate of political friction, a scholarly interest in Ireland's Gaelic past; and these learned societies became the most important medium though which native lore was passed to the elite culture. That pattern continued after the Union, not only in the work of the RIA itself, but also in a number of antiquarian or philological societies, which sponsored invaluable Gaelic scholarship in the decades before Celtic philology became a university discipline: the Dublin Gaelic Society (1808); the

Iberno-Celtic Society (1818), the Ulster Gaelic Society (1830), the Irish Archaeological Society (1840), the Celtic Society (1845), the Ossianic Society (1853), and a number of local antiquarian associations. The RIA is still active; its function as a learned state institution is now complemented by the Dublin Institute of Advanced Studies.

Reading

Hoppen, K.T., 'The Dublin Philosophical Society and the new learning in Ireland', *Irish Historical Studies* 14 (1964–5), pp. 99–118.
Leerssen, Joep, *Mere Irish and Fíor-Ghael* (Amsterdam and Philadelphia: John Benjamins, 1986).

JOEP LEERSSEN

Lecky, William Edward Hartpole (1838–1903) Historian. Born Newtownpark, County Dublin, 26 March; died London, 22 October. The Leckys, of Scottish origins, had settled in the north of Ireland in the seventeenth century, and became prominent in the public life of Derry. One member of the family moved to Carlow and established the branch of the family from which W.E.H. Lecky sprang. The historian's paternal grandmother belonged to the Hartpole family once prominent in the affairs of Queen's County. The inherited Hartpole and Lecky property, although modest, allowed Lecky's father, John Hartpole Lecky, to live as a gentleman of independent means. The historian's mother, Mary Anne Tallents, the daughter of a Newark solicitor, died when Lecky was only a year old, and his father married Isabella Eliza Wilmot of Queen's County.

Cheltenham College was among the schools Lecky attended before entering Trinity College, Dublin. The most remarkable thing about Lecky's days in Trinity College (1856–60) was that they culminated in a pass degree, a second-class divinity testimonium and the anonymous publication of three small books – *Friendship and other Poems* (1859), *The Religious Tendencies of the*

Age (1860) and *The Leaders of Public Opinion in Ireland* (1861).

Lecky spent the greater part of the 1860s on the Continent wandering from one library to another. The outcome of what he called 'an immense amount of literary vagabondage' was two books, *The History of the Rise and Influence of the Spirit of Rationalism in Europe* (1865) and *The History of European Morals from Augustus to Charlemagne* (1869). Settled in London, he turned to the political history of England and Ireland. A second enlarged edition of his *Leaders of Public Opinion in Ireland*, containing essays on Swift, Flood, Grattan and O'Connell, was published in 1871. That same year he married Elisabeth, Baroness Van Dedem, a maid of honour to Queen Sophia of the Netherlands. They had no children. His *History of England in the Eighteenth Century* was published in eight volumes between 1878 and 1890 and set the seal on Lecky's reputation as a historian. The Irish and English chapters were published separately in 1892, with seven volumes devoted to England and five volumes to Ireland. *Democracy and Liberty* was published in 1896.

Lecky was elected to Parliament for Dublin University in a by-election in December 1895. He served in the Liberal Unionist interest until his resignation for health reasons in 1902. His *Map of Life* (1899) was based on thoughts and observations he had written down in his commonplace books over the years. *Historical and Political Essays* (1908), published posthumously, was a collection of occasional pieces written during the early 1890s. The third revised and enlarged edition of his *Leaders of Public Opinion* (1903) was published in the year of his death, which occurred in his library.

Lecky's works on the history of rationalism and morals, written while he was very much under the influence of Henry Thomas Buckle, were pioneering adventures into the new sociological history of ideas, and won for him wide acclaim. Although enjoying great popular success in their own time, these books have exhibited none of the staying qualities of his more political history of England and Ireland in the eighteenth century. The accolades that greeted the volumes on the eighteenth century compared him with Gibbon, Macaulay, Carlyle and Froude. The qualities that won him loudest praise were impartiality, judiciousness, moral tone and liberal sympathies. His *England in the Eighteenth Century*, though important in any survey of the course of British historiography, has long been replaced as the leading textbook on England in the eighteenth century. Although devoting some sections to social and religious issues, his work is now considered weakest on economic and cultural history. Only at their peril, however, may historians even today ignore Lecky's *Ireland in the Eighteenth Century*. Those chapters dealing especially with the 1790s were based largely upon original records. He remained, however, one of the last survivors of the great tradition of amateur historians, convinced that his work ultimately had more to do with literature than with the new science of history coming out of Germany.

Lecky's historical writings were among the most influential contributions ever made to Irish nationalism. Liberal leaders, including Gladstone, and Irish Home Rulers all quoted Lecky in support of their cause. With the Home Rule and land agitations in Ireland very much in his mind, Lecky's *Democracy and Liberty*, while being a defence of individual freedom, was also a diatribe against the dangers of democracy. The combination of democracy, nationalism and socialism which, in Lecky's view, had produced Parnellism found in him a horrified and determined opponent. To counter the nationalism which he had helped to foster in his books, he turned to Unionist propaganda, but Lecky the Unionist pamphleteer was no match for Lecky the historian.

Reading

Auchmuty, J.J., *Lecky: A Biographical and Critical Essay* (Dublin: Hodges Figgis, 1945).

Hyde, H.M. (ed.), *A Victorian Historian: Private Letters of W.E.H. Lecky, 1859–1878* (London: Home and Van Thal, 1947).

Lecky, Elisabeth, *A Memoir of the Right Hon. William Edward Hartpole Lecky, By his Wife* (London: Longmans, Green, 1909).

McCartney, Donal, 'Lecky's *Leaders of Public Opinion in Ireland*', *Irish Historical Studies* xiv, no. 54 (Sept. 1964).

—— *W.E.H. Lecky: Historian and Politician 1838–1903* (Dublin: Lilliput Press, 1994).

Phillips, W.A., *Lecky: A Lecture in Celebration of the Centenary of Lecky's Birth* (Dublin: University Press, 1939).

DONAL MCCARTNEY

Leech, W.J. (William John) (1881–1966) Painter. Born Dublin; died Guildford. The son of a professor of law, Leech studied under Walter Osborne and later attended the Académie Julien in Paris. Leech belonged to a generation which looked to France, where he lived and worked from 1903 to 1916, before settling in England. He never returned to Ireland, though he had been elected Royal Hibernian Academician in 1910 and continued to exhibit in Dublin; he also showed in London at the Royal Academy and with the New English Art Club. Essentially a late *plein-airiste*, he painted landscapes, interiors, nudes and occasional portraits, showing a special sensitivity to light. His oil sketches show him at his purest and most spontaneous. His early *Goose Girl* (National Gallery of Ireland) has become one of the most reproduced and popular pictures by an Irish painter.

BRIAN FALLON

Le Fanu, Joseph Thomas Sheridan (1814–73) Novelist. Born Dublin. Le Fanu's parents brought together the contrasting legacies of Huguenot rectitude and Sheridan flamboyance. Educated privately, he passed his childhood in the Phoenix Park (where his father had a clerical appointment) and later at Abingdon, County Limerick (Le Fanu senior was now Dean of Emly). He studied at Trinity College and the Kings Inns, Dublin,

but practised little as a barrister. By 1840, he had an interest in two Dublin newspapers; press ownership provided an income for many years. In 1861, he acquired the *Dublin University Magazine*. Editing it till 1869, he published serial novels by numerous women, most notably his niece, Rhoda Broughton. Le Fanu married Susanna Bennett in 1843; they had four children, and she died in 1858.

Le Fanu began to write fiction during the Tithe War of the 1830s, and his writing can be divided into two phases. The first – including *The Purcell Papers* (1838–40, collected 1880, *The Cock and Anchor* (1845) and *The Fortunes of Colonel Torlogh O'Brien* (1847) – utilized an eighteenth-century Irish setting. The second – notable for *Wylder's Hand* (1864), *Uncle Silas* (1865) and *In a Glass Darkly* (1872) – favoured contemporary British settings. *The House by the Churchyard* (1863) is a complex transitional work, which Joyce drew on for *Finnegans Wake*.

Le Fanu's best work is remarkable for its nervous brilliance in conveying sensation, its preoccupation with ambiguities of religious belief, and its occasional investigations of sexual identity. (There is a good deal of less than best work, however.) His influence is traceable in Somerville and Ross, in Yeats, in Joyce and in Bowen.

W.J. MCCORMACK

legislative independence A term commonly used to describe the Irish constitutional position between 1782 and the Union. The product of a bitterly fought campaign by the Patriot opposition, the 'independence' consisted of the repeal of the 1720 Declaratory Act, largely a symbolic gesture, and the amendment of a Poynings' Law procedure – after 1782 the Irish privy council could not alter or suppress an Irish parliamentary measure. The nature of the 1782 settlement was such that the balance of power which had existed throughout the century between the Irish Parliament and the Dublin and London administrations shifted dramatically in favour of the Irish Parliament. The English privy council, whilst it retained its right to alter and suppress Irish measures, was reluctant to court political unrest in Ireland thereafter by using this power. The overall effect, therefore, was to standardize the existing power of legislative veto possessed by both parliaments so that each could defend itself on equal terms from incursions by the other. The policies, wishes and actions of the non-government members of the Irish Parliament, which hitherto had been merely of academic consequence, were now invested with a very real significance. The Irish opposition, whether Patriot or venal, had acquired a share in the exercise of legislative power in Ireland. Since the London and Dublin administrations were now obliged to share their mandate for the making of Irish policy with the elected Irish MPs, legislative power rested not only between Dublin and London but between both administrations and the Irish parliament. An experiment in power sharing had come into being.

GERARD O'BRIEN

Lever, Charles James, (1806–72) Novelist. Born Dublin; died Trieste. Educated at Trinity College, Dublin, Lever practised medicine in County Derry and Brussels before becoming a professional novelist. He edited the *Dublin University Magazine* from 1842 to 1845, when he left Ireland and settled in Italy. Between 1852 and 1867 he served as British vice-consul at La Spezia, and at the time of his death was consul at Trieste.

Lever's career as a novelist falls into two parts. In the first, he produced a series of best-selling military novels featuring tearaway subalterns. From these, Lever's reputation for superficiality and stage-Irishness derives. This reputation obscures later works which thoughtfully diagnose the falling from power, through its own misjudgement, complacency and failure of nerve, of the Anglo-Irish landed aristocracy. Such novels as *The Martins of Cro' Martin* (1856), *Luttrell of Arran* (1865) and *Lord Kilgobbin* (1872), though not free of

their predecessors' formal inadequacies, show how developments in English politics and society exposed incurable flaws in Irish conditions. Central to an assessment of Victorian Ireland, and to the cultural preconditions of the Irish Literary Revival, these works also provide a firm basis for a reappraisal of Lever's undervalued and misunderstood career.

GEORGE O'BRIEN

libraries The development of libraries in Ireland has followed a similar pattern to that of events in England, though at a slower pace and at a lower quality of provision. Although private collections have formed the basis for many libraries in the public domain, their development is not considered here. The pattern has been the early development of a university library, the later establishment of libraries for special interest groups of the educated classes, clergy, doctors, etc., in the eighteenth century, and the rise of reading societies for gentlemen at the end of that century. The early nineteenth-century spread of literacy and earnest desire for 'improvement' among the lower middle and artisan classes is seen in the foundation of Mechanics' Institutes and Repeal Reading Rooms. At a higher social and educational level was the foundation of the Queen's Colleges in mid-century to provide further opportunities for university education. Finally, there was the slow establishment in the 1880s of rate-supported public libraries.

This entry deals principally with those libraries which are, or have been, in some measure open to the public. The history of modern Irish libraries begins with the foundation of Trinity College, Dublin, in 1592. Once book purchasing began in earnest in 1601 the library grew rapidly to impressive size, having 4,000 volumes by 1610. Archbishop James Ussher's collection of 10,000 volumes was the major seventeenth-century accession. Three important bequests came in the eighteenth century, from Theophilus Butler in 1723 (1,000 volumes), Archbishop

William Palliser in 1726 (4,000 volumes) and Claudius Gilbert in 1743 (13,000 volumes). Two events at the start of the nineteenth century boosted the collections greatly. The library of Greffier Hendrik Fagel of Holland was purchased in 1802, and the Copyright Act of 1801 allowed the library the privilege of claiming a copy of every book published in Great Britain and Ireland, a privilege which continues to this day. Although the take from this source was small at first, improved coverage from the 1840s set the pattern for remorseless expansion, which has brought the College Library to its present size of three million volumes.

For a century, Trinity College Library was the sole institutional library in the country. In 1673 the first of a series of diocesan libraries was founded for the benefit of clergymen of the established Church of Ireland. Over the following 180 years such libraries were set up in over half the dioceses. The first, at St Canice's Cathedral in Kilkenny for Ossory diocese in 1693, was followed by Derry in 1709, Cathedral Library in Cork in 1720, Cashel in 1730, Raphoe in 1737 (amalgamated with Derry in 1881), Waterford in 1745, Down and Connor in 1854, and Tuam in 1881. The seventeenth-and eighteenth-century foundations were based on gifts of private libraries, and their content ranged more widely than the professional interest in theology. The nineteenth-century ones were more narrowly focused. Each, from the start, suffered from a lack of sufficient recurrent funding to enable it to keep up with publication even in the professional subjects. As a result what had, at their establishment, been reasonable professional and leisure libraries became fairly quickly fossilized, of antiquarian interest only. In most cases neglect followed, with, in many cases, piecemeal sale of the better books, or, in the case of the Clogher Diocesan Library, complete dispersal in the 1950s. In recent years, with a rise in appreciation of the cultural value of historical collections, their futures have improved. The Cathedral Library in Cork has been taken over by University College, Cork, while that at Tuam has established a connection with University College, Galway. The principal ones which are open to the public, albeit for restricted hours, are Derry, Cashel (now called the Bolton Library), and St Canice's Library, Kilkenny.

The restrictions on access to Trinity College Library to the provost, fellows and resident bachelors prompted Archbishop Narcissus Marsh to found a public library in 1701. This was incorporated as a public library by Act of Parliament in 1707. The bookstock was composed of three major collections: Marsh's own library, that of Bishop Edward Stillingfleet, and that of Dr Elias Bouhéreau, an emigré Huguenot physician who became the first librarian in 1701. The most substantial subsequent accession was of 3,000 volumes from the library of Bishop John Stearne in 1745. Marsh had only one imitator, Richard Robinson, who, when archbishop of Armagh, founded the public library there in 1771 (subsequently incorporated by Act of Parliament in 1773) with the gift of his own collection of 8,000 volumes.

A cluster of societies founded libraries in the eighteenth century as an adjunct to their main activities. The Dublin Society, later the Royal Dublin Society, was founded in 1731 with the aim of improving husbandry, manufactures and arts and sciences, and almost at once began a collection. By the mid-nineteenth century it had built up major collections in science and history, which were further strengthened by the gift of the Joly Collection in 1863. Parliamentary recommendation that, as a body in receipt of public funding, it should open to the public led to the library operating as a public library between 1836 and 1877, when the bulk of the collection in the humanities was transferred to the newly established National Library. The Royal College of Physicians in Ireland, though founded in 1667, seems not to have had a library before the bequest by Sir Patrick Dun (d. 1713) of his books. Poor, sometimes dishonest, administration meant that the library was not established on any reasonably firm basis until 1785. The Royal College of Surgeons in Ireland, founded in 1784, set up a library within a few years. Both collections developed through the nineteenth century on fairly strict professional limits. The barristers, too, set up their library in the 1780s, with the purchase of the professional portion of Judge Christopher Robinson's library in 1787. Their society, the Honourable Society of King's Inns, had in fact been in existence since 1541. Their library enjoyed legal deposit status from 1801 until 1836, when the society compounded the privilege for an annual payment of £400. One other major society library was founded in the 1780s, that of the Royal Irish Academy (RIA), established in 1785 for the study of history, antiquities, literature and pure science. Collecting began at once, though the collection which makes the RIA uniquely important among Irish historical libraries, the Haliday collection of tracts, was not received until 1867.

The 1780s also saw the beginning of private subscription libraries for the middle classes with the foundation of the Belfast Reading Society, renamed the Belfast Society for Promoting Knowledge in 1792 and now universally known as the Linenhall Library. Similar societies, now all deceased, were founded in Dublin in 1791, Cork in 1792, Limerick in 1809 and Kilkenny in 1811. These supplemented the provision of reading matter supplied by commercial lending libraries, which, in Dublin, existed in considerable numbers from the mid-eighteenth century and which also occurred in Cork, Limerick and Belfast.

Until the nineteenth century there was little provision of books for the poorer members of society. Occasionally, small collections of 'improving' books were held at schools, given by societies dedicated to the moral improvement of the working class. A rising interest in education, particularly in technical education, led to the founding of Mechanics' Institutes in the 1820s, first in Dublin in 1824, Belfast in 1825, and Galway in 1826. By 1852 at least 20 of these institutes had libraries. Enthusiasm faded gradually and by the 1870s most had disappeared, drowned in debts. An attempt to encourage a patriotic consciousness in the early 1840s was made with the concept of Repeal Reading Rooms. Between 1842 and 1845, 71 of these were established, providing newspapers and books, but virtually all of these were extinct by 1850.

The foundation for rate-supported public libraries in Ireland was laid with the passing of the Public Libraries Act (Ireland) in 1855, enabling authorities in towns of over 5,000 inhabitants to levy a rate of one penny in the pound to set up a library. Although Dundalk successfully opened a library in 1858, taking over 1,600 volumes of the former Mechanics' Institute, and latterly called the Dundalk Literary and Scientific Institution, in most towns the produce of the rate was insufficient to accomplish the purposes of the act, and no further libraries were established. The next town to follow was Sligo in 1880. The modern network was essentially established in the following 30 years, encouraged by legislation in 1894, the Public Libraries (Ireland) Act, and a similarly titled act in 1902, which eased the restrictions on fund raising and allowed for co-operation between adjoining authorities. Great, if at times overgreat, advances in library buildings were made after the extension of the Carnegie grants to Ireland between 1897 and 1927. Following the partition of the island, public libraries developed separately in each jurisdiction, those in Northern Ireland faring better financially. There, in 1973, the existing county structure was abandoned and five area boards were established to run the service. In the Republic the organization by county has remained.

With the establishment of the Queen's Colleges in Belfast, Cork and Galway in 1845 and the founding of the Catholic University of Ireland in 1854, the era of modern university education began. Library provision in each was limited until the beginning of the century. Queen's College, Belfast, which developed into the Queen's University of Belfast in 1910, enjoyed better financial support than the other colleges, particularly after the establishment of Northern Ireland. The two other colleges became, with the ultimate successor of the Catholic University in Dublin, University College, constituent colleges of the National University of Ireland. These became Irish copyright libraries under the copyright Act of 1927.

Two foundations originally established to prepare candidates for the religious ministry – St Patrick's College, Maynooth, founded in 1795 for Catholics, and Magee College, Derry, founded in 1865 for Presbyterians – have acquired large historical collections. Both have been taken into the university system, as St Patrick's College became part of the National University of Ireland and then a legal deposit library for Ireland (1963). Magee College was part of the Royal University of Ireland from 1880 to 1909 and thereafter prepared students for degrees from the University of Dublin. It then formed part of the New University of Ulster in 1968, and was later subsumed into the University of Ulster.

A quite remarkable collection was presented to the Republic of Ireland in 1968. This was the private library of Western European printed books and Oriental manuscripts and artifacts assembled by Sir Alfred Chester Beatty. At a stroke the country became a leading holder of Arabic manuscripts. The strength of the printed books is particularly great in illustrated works.

In the 1970s and 1980s library provision in Ireland at last reached levels appropriate to the needs of a modern industrial nation. The provision of public library services in Northern Ireland is more generous than in the Republic, where successive crises in state and local government funding led on occasion to cuts in book funds in the 1980s. The level of acquisition of current material in the universities is, at the least, adequate, and in some cases liberal. In the Republic every university library has legal deposit status. It is dismaying that only two institutions in the island, the National Library

and Trinity College Library, are acquiring any significant number of older printed books. There are, however, welcome signs of a greater appreciation of historical libraries, and many of the smaller collections, though woefully underfunded, are being made more accessible to readers. Inclusion of their holdings in international databases such as the Eighteenth Century Short Title Catalogue will ensure wider recognition and greater security for them. In the 1990s government cutbacks on library funding sadly led to a halt in growth, and the threat of closure faced many smaller public libraries.

CHARLES BENSON

Liddiard, Anna (*c*.1785–*c*.1830) Poet. Born Anna Wilkinson in County Meath. She married William Liddiard, an Anglican clergyman of Knockmark, County Meath. She was one of a number of Anglo-Irish Protestant ladies (e.g. Charlotte Brooke, Lady Wilde, Fanny Parnell and Lady Dufferin) who, despite their Ascendancy backgrounds, interested themselves in the Gaelic language and/or the lives of the ordinary people. Anna Liddiard published several volumes of mainly patriotic verse, including *Poems* (1810) and Mount Leinster (1819). Other works included *The Sgéalaighe or a Tale of Old* (1811), *Kenilworth, a Mask* (1815) and *Theodore and Laura, or Evening after the Battle, a Tale in Verse* (1816).

PATRICK FAGAN

Limerick Soviet In April 1919, the funeral of Bobby Byrne, a Republican prisoner and union activist who was killed in a rescue attempt, was attended by 15,000 people. Alarmed, the military authorities invoked martial law under the Defence of the Realm Act, requiring a pass to enter or leave the area. In protest, on 14 April the Trades and Labour Council called a general strike, named a Soviet by international journalists in the city covering the proposed transatlantic flight by Major Woods. The workers took control of the city, organized the distribution of essentials, and issued their own currency and *Daily Bulletin*. Lacking outside financial support, the strike ended on 24 April when the Catholic bishop and the mayor reached an agreement with the British commander.

JAMES KEMMY

Limerick, Treaty of (3 October 1691) Brought the Williamite war in Ireland to an end. William III's desire for peace to deploy his forces elsewhere and the worsening Jacobite military position in 1691 made a peace necessary, and at the second seige of Limerick two sets of articles were concluded. The military ones permitted the Jacobite forces to serve James II overseas, and the civil ones offered Catholics the religious privileges held under Charles II, with guarantees on security of property. The articles were to be confirmed by Parliament. In drawing up a fair copy for signature a clause was omitted by the clerk, thus leaving the lands of civilians in Limerick, Clare, Kerry, Cork and Mayo open to confiscation.

The treaty was not well received by either side, Jacobites thought too many concessions had been made and Williamites thought not enough had been extracted. It was unlikely therefore that Parliament would ratify the articles, and no attempt was made to obtain ratification without modification. It was 1697 before William, in the face of pressure from Ireland, agreed to a modified form of the treaty, which was ratified. This did not provide for the religious freedoms promised and the 'missing clause' was not restored. Despite this the bill passed only narrowly.

Reading

Simms, J.G., 'Williamite peace tactics', *Irish Historical Studies* viii (1963).
Troost, Wouter, *William III and the Treaty of Limerick* (privately published, n.d.).

RAYMOND GILLESPIE

linen Became Ireland's most profitable export to Britain in the eighteenth century. After industrialization in the early nineteenth century, Ulster became the most important region for the manufacture of linens in the world.

Although flax had been spun and woven into linen cloth in Ireland since ancient times, the origins of a commercial linen industry in Ulster date from the immigration of English and Scottish settlers in the seventeenth century. The bulk of the flax used in the industry was grown by local farmers. They 'retted' or steeped the flax and then 'scutched' it to remove the woody stems from the fibres. Women 'heckled' or combed these fibres and spun them into yarn. Men wove because early handlooms were heavy and cumbersome. They carried their webs of cloth to public markets in the towns, where the Board of Trustees of the Linen and Hempen Manufacturers (created in 1711 by the government to promote and regulate the industry) organized the inspection of yarn and cloth in its brown or unbleached state before it was purchased by linen drapers. The bleaching of linen was a long and expensive process, but in time Ulster bleachers gained a high reputation for harnessing water power to drive wash mills and beetling engines, as well as for their readiness to employ chemicals to reduce the bleaching period. In time they became the capitalists of the industry and the entrepreneurs of industrialization.

The white or bleached linens were carried south to the White Linen Hall in Dublin, where factors financed its sale in London. Rapidly increasing exports required more weavers, and cash earnings attracted rural smallholders. Landlords on many mid-Ulster estates were prepared to grant long leases for farms of 5–10 acres to the best-paid weavers, and these districts in time became the most densely populated in Ireland. Elsewhere weavers continued to pay farmers in labour for their holdings and so remained members of the cottier class. Confidence was reflected also in the development of the urban network. Landlords competed to attract drapers to their linen markets by providing better facilities, while weavers purchased oatmeal, their staple food, and candles to light their work.

After 1780 the domestic linen industry began to suffer from competition with cotton, which was much cheaper to finish and print. Then the invention of dry-spinning linen yarn by machinery destroyed the handspinning trade. Although some contemporaries foresaw the death of the linen industry in Ulster, its capitalists responded by erecting mills to produce fine yarns by the wet-spinning process. Weaving by power loom was not mechanized until the 1850s. By 1900, however, Ulster had gained many gold medals in international exhibitions for the quality of its linens.

After World War I, linen suffered from a severe world-wide contraction, but Ulster held its share of world markets. After World War II it had to face growing international competition, as well as the introduction of synthetic fibres and paper napkins and handkerchiefs. Nevertheless, today Ulster exports linen yarn and cloth to the value of £120 million each year.

Reading

Crawford, W.H., 'The origins of the linen industry in north Armagh and the Lagan Valley', *Ulster Folklife* 17 (1971).
—— *The Irish Linen Industry* (Belfast: 1987).
—— 'The evolution of the linen trade in Ireland before industrialization', *Irish Economic and Social History* XV (1988).
—— *Handloom Weavers in the Ulster Linen Industry* (Belfast: 1993).
Gill, Conrad, *The Rise of the Irish Linen Industry* (Oxford: 1925).
McCutcheon, W. Alan, *The Industrial Archaeology of Northern Ireland* (Belfast: 1980).

W.H. CRAWFORD

literary criticism since 1960 The publication in 1959 of both Richard Ellmann's *James Joyce* and *The Third Voice* by Denis Donoghue initiates the narrative of Irish literary criticism since 1960 and articulates some representative themes in it. Such a context identifies Ellmann's biography as a significant cultural document for reasons other than its undoubted forensic mastery, while Donoghue's status as the most eminent Irish literary critic of the contemporary period becomes more than a matter of personal attainment. Broadly speaking, these two critics' theory and practice typify the most visible trajectory of Irish literary criticism since 1960, and highlight important methodological and ideological considerations which subsequent critical developments implicitly, though unsystematically, have sought to revise.

As the most notable achievement of the leading American scholar of his generation to concentrate on Irish literature, *James Joyce* crystallizes the complex interaction of American institutional and cultural practices with the largely undeveloped condition of documentary and other sources of Irish literary culture. Commonly regarded as a monument to its subject, the work paradoxically revokes Joyce's exile by making him a citizen of the world, including Dublin. This process of domestication contrasts intriguingly with Ellmann's earlier work on Yeats. Surpassing in scope and resourcefulness more obviously exegetical interventions in the Joyce canon by such Ellmann contemporaries as Harry Levin, Hugh Kenner and William York Tindall, *James Joyce* is a landmark in the internationalization of modern Irish literature. The critical method which accommodated such a development essentially derived from the New Criticism, a major cultural discourse of the Cold War. Ellmann's historicized adaptation of the method was directed towards a characterization of his subject, rather than towards a reassessment of the texts' significance in Irish literary culture.

As though to reciprocate international critical interest in Irish literature, *The Third Voice* represents the first systematic reading of a range of modern texts by an Irish critic. In tone, subject matter and overall conception of the critic's task, it supersedes other works of criticism by Irish authors with international outlooks, such as Frank O'Connor's *The Mirror in the Roadway* (1956), Sean

O Faolain's *The Vanishing Hero* (1956) and Conor Cruise O'Brien's *Maria Cross* (1954), revealing as these works are regarding problems of critical method and ideological orientation. Yet, despite its originality and acumen, *The Third Voice* has greater cultural than critical importance, since it inaugurates the commitment to the spectrum of Modernism which gives Donoghue's career its exemplary significance.

Notwithstanding his readings of modern Irish writers, Donoghue's critical interests have continued to dwell on the aesthetic practices of international Modernism, rather than on its specifically Irish manifestations, as well as on the function of criticism at the present time. In addressing such concerns, Donoghue reveals not only his mastery of certain intellectual idioms of a predominantly American intellectual community, many of which derive from New Criticism, but an implicit repudiation of cultural insularity. Though Donoghue retains a keen awareness of the historical and ideological preconditions of modern Irish literature, it is the rhetorical resources and ideational underpinnings of international Modernism which provide him with the context for the most effective authentication of matters of Irish literary value. The hieratic Yeats which Donoghue's work privileges is a complement to, rather than in conflict with, Ellmann's demotic Joyce, both critical constructs being the outcome of a shared, if differently nuanced, sense of critical purpose.

The influence of the professional standards established by Ellmann's and Donoghue's works may be seen at both the scholarly and interpretative levels of subsequent projects. Both these levels have shown a general conservationist, institutionalizing tendency. Despite facilitating important archival work by mainly American scholars, this tendency has not shown itself to be a particularly flexible intellectual instrument. Not only has its consolidation coincided with a diminution of the traditional role of the artist as critic in Irish letters, it has not proved particularly committed to diversifying its lines of inquiry.

The possibilities of synthesis explored in Vivian Mercier's *The Irish Comic Tradition* (1962) have largely not been pursued. The subject of his *A Reader's Guide to The New Novel* (1971) is a reminder that, among other issues, internationalism has remained a synonym for anglo-centricity. Mercier's *Beckett/Beckett* (1977) remained the most substantial study by an Irish critic of a modern Irish author until Anthony Cronin's *Samuel Beckett: The Last Modernist* appeared in 1996.

In addition, the establishment of criticism as an essentially academic enterprise, based on a conception of literature as a discipline and carried out in the name of strictly methodological presuppositions, raised important questions about more traditional views of literature as an agent of Irish culture. These views represented a highly socialized view of writing, and perceived imaginative literature itself to be a critical activity. Accordingly, literature is seen as a fundamentally public act with direct public consequences, representation is considered to be synonymous with interpretation, and a writer's authority derives not from biographical particularity or aesthetic cerebration but from the manner in which his or her work, by entailing an audience, is a manifestation of self-conscious cultural activism.

Attempts since the mid-1970s to reinstall a more culturally oriented and ideologically combative sense of literature constitute, in part, a critique of the disjunction between text and context in New Criticism and of that methodology's pre-eminence in an anglophone world in which the Irish polity has a largely client status. This tacit invocation of more flexible and wide-ranging models of discourse also coincides with an increased scepticism generally regarding Anglo-American ideology. In part, also, the shift in emphasis – encapsulated by the titles of two works of criticism by Anthony Cronin, *A Question of Modernity* (1966) and *Heritage Now* (1982) – is a reflection of the revisionism which has pervaded recent Irish cultural debate and of the subsidiary but no less intense debate regarding the quality, character and legitimacy of revisionism. Relevant texts include Seamus Deane's *Celtic Revivals* (1985), W.J. McCormack's *The Battle of the Books* (1986) and Edna Longley's *Poetry in the Wars* (1986).

Identity, community and tradition are the terms in which attempts to reinscribe both literature and criticism as public resources are typically conveyed. The perception of these terms' utility is based on their history in previous moments of cultural self-consciousness. But the frequency with which they recur in contemporary debate exposes the variety of ideological emphases which they encode. They reveal at once a more complex, less hegemonic sense of Irish culture and anxieties regarding the aims and structure of Irish critical discourse. The clearest manifestation of, and response to, these new conditions of diversity and uncertainty is *The Field Day Anthology of Irish Writing* (1991). The contents of this epic undertaking not only provide a much more elaborate and broad-ranging conspectus of the cultural and historical materiality of Irish writing than had hitherto been acknowledged but, by doing so, highlight the degree to which issues fundamental to literary criticism, such as canonicity, periodization and genre, have been inadequately characterized.

Of equal importance is the perspective which the anthology's various editorial apparatuses provide on at least a nascent diversification of Irish literary critical practices. Though necessarily limited, this perspective also identifies the possibility of much more detailed engagement with such areas as Irish literary history, the sociology of Irish literature, comparative literature and critical theory *The Field Day Anthology* also signals, in part, the emergence of an intelligentsia with an orientation which is not entirely defined by institutionalized and professionalist contexts. Despite the resistance which this complicated and even somewhat ill-defined generational shift has met, it extends the possibility that the development of a conceptually sophisti-cated, socially responsive and ideologically self-critical criticism of literature has become both a viable intellectual task and a desirable cultural objective.

In 1997 the critical debate over James Joyce was revived with the publication of a new edition of *Ulysses*, edited by Danis Rose. Whilst some greeted this as an important addition to Joycean scholarship, many other critics vilified it for its intensive editing.

GEORGE O'BRIEN

literary periodicals Twentieth-century Ireland has rarely been without at least one literary or cultural periodical; while none achieved international stature, they provided a forum for discussions urbane and committed. The more noteworthy titles are listed here chronologically.

Dana (May 1904–April 1905, monthly) was edited by Frederick Ryan and John Eglinton (W.K. Magee). Combining agnostic rationalism and *belles-lettres*, it published work by Joyce, AE, Colum, Dowden, Gogarty and Moore. *The Irish Review* (1911–14, monthly) carried commentary on social issues and a distinguished literary content. A number of those associated with it were later prominent in the Easter Rising of 1916. The *Dublin Magazine* (1923–5, monthly; 1926–58, quarterly) was a literary periodical edited by Seamus O'Sullivan (James Starkey) until his death; Stephens, O'Flaherty and the poets of the post-Yeatsian generation were among its contributors. *Ireland Today* (1936–8, monthly) was remarkable in that, during an isolationist period in Ireland's history, it took an enlightened international line. It carried some thoughtful film criticism, and published early work by poets such as Coffey and Devlin. It prepared the way for the *Bell*, which is the subject of a separate entry.

Irish Writing (1947–56, quarterly) and its sister publication *Poetry Ireland* were published in Cork, and *Rann* (1948–53, quarterly) and *Threshold* (1957–61, quarterly, thereafter occasional) were published in Belfast; the two Ulster titles were avowedly regionalist in impulse. One of the most distinguished magazines of the post-war years was *Envoy* (1949–51, monthly); edited by John Ryan, it included work by Kavanagh, Beckett, Stuart and Mary Lavin. The *Kilkenny Magazine* (1960–70, quarterly) and the *Dubliner* – later the *Dublin Magazine* – (1961–72, quarterly) provided useful literary outlets but without ever entering into urgent contact with Irish society. *Atlantis* (1970–3, quarterly), the *Crane Bag* (1977–85, semi-annually) and the *Irish Review* (1986–, semi-annually) in turn offered a platform for cultural debate, but opted for substance at the expense of frequency, while the purely literary periodicals tended to concentrate more and more on poetry: the *Lace Curtain* (1969–78, irregular), *Poetry Ireland* new series (1962–8, irregular), *Cyphers* (1975–, irregular), the *Honest Ulsterman* (1968–, monthly), *Poetry Ireland Review* (1981–, quarterly) and *Metre* (1996–, quarterly).

PETER DENMAN

Lloyd, Humphrey (1800–81) Scientist. Born Dublin, 16 April; died in the provost's house, Trinity College, Dublin, 17 January. Lloyd was educated at Trinity College, Dublin, and became professor of natural and experimental philosophy there, and provost in 1867. He contributed papers on his researches into physical optics and magnetism to many learned journals, was president of the Royal Irish Academy (1846–51), president of the British Association (1857), a fellow of the Royal Societies of London and Edinburgh, and an honorary member of many other learned societies in Europe and America.

Reading

Lloyd, Humphrey, *Lectures on the Wave-Theory of Light* (Dublin: Andrew Milliken, 1841).
——*Elements of Optics* (Dublin: Hodges and Smith, 1849).
——*A Treatise on Magnetism, General and Terrestrial* (London: Longmans, 1874).

HENRY BOYLAN

lock-out, Dublin 1913 The Irish Transport and General Workers' Union (ITGWU), founded by James Larkin in 1909, threatened employers with militant tactics of sympathetic action and picketing infused with an assertive socialist perspective. After Larkin stopped William Martin Murphy's trams during Horse Show week, August 1913, and extended unionization to his *Irish Independent* newspaper, the employers responded with the decision to lock out workers until they denied the ITGWU, and to force home their advantage through hunger and repression. Murphy persuaded 404 employees to join him and by early September 25,000 were locked out. Larkin, who attacked Murphy at mass public meetings and through the pages of the wonderfully scurrilous *Irish Worker*, galvanized the workers, inspired them through his oratory and passion, and provided sustenance through the food ships *Hare* and *Fraternity*.

Bloody Sunday, 31 August, witnessed Larkin's arrest, after he had been hidden and disguised by Countess Markiewicz, and terrible scenes of police brutality that outraged public opinion. The employers' obduracy and refusal to respond to the various mediation attempts by George Askwith's Board of Trade Inquiry or the Trades Union Congress (TUC) leadership generated much sympathy among Dublin's intelligentsia. The TUC held a special congress in London in December but, annoyed by Larkin's 'divine mission of discontent', his attempts to extend industrial action to Britain, and his personalized attacks on the TUC leaders, they offered charity rather than industrial support. Dublin was isolated. James Connolly's shrewd management of the dispute ensured stalemate but, as early as December 1913, the ITGWU was urging members to return to work, avoiding signing the employers' 'document' if they could. The torment continued until February, when the battle was over and the employers claimed a victory they had not the strength to enforce. Connolly argued for a draw.

The ITGWU not only survived but had created an image of 'heroic Dublin', sung of today in the song '*Dublin City*', written by Donagh MacDonagh, son of executed 1916 leader Thomas MacDonagh. The lock-out inspired Oisín Kelly's sculpture of Larkin that stands proudly today in O'Connell Street, Dublin, and James Plunkett's celebrated novel *Strumpet City*. Some have argued that the Irish Citizen Army, formed as a workers' defence force, and the *rapprochement* between labour and Republicans cemented the cornerstone for events in 1916. The deaths of James Nolan, James Byrne and Alice Brady, together with the brave sacrifice of Eugene Salmon, killed rescuing victims of a tenement collapse, more importantly are part of labour's heritage, its sense of its own strength and the price paid for its position as a founding partner in the creation of the new state. Over time, 1913 has proved an inspiring victory.

Reading

Brown, Kenneth D., 'Larkin and the strikes of 1913: their place in British history', *Saothar 9*, (1983), pp. 89–99.

Curriculum Development Unit, *Divided City, Portrait of Dublin 1913* (Dublin: O'Brien Educational, 1978; repub. as *Dublin 1913*).

Greaves, C. Desmond, *The Irish Transport and General Workers' Union: The Formative Years, 1907–1923* (Dublin: ITGWU/Gill and Macmillan, 1982).

Keogh, Dermot, *The Rise of the Irish Working Class: The Dublin Trade Union Movement and Labour Leadership, 1890–1919* (Belfast: Appletree Press, 1982).

Larkin, Emmet, *James Larkin, 1876–1947, Irish Labour Leader* (London: Routledge and Kegan Paul, 1965).

Nevin, Donal, (ed.), *1913: Jim Larkin and the Dublin Lock-Out* (Dublin: Workers' Union of Ireland, 1964).

Saothar 4 (1978), Journal of the Irish Labour History Society special commemorative issue.

FRANCIS DEVINE

Locke, John (1632–1704) The writings of the English philosopher were of crucial importance in the intellectual formation of eighteenth-century Ireland. This influence can be traced to the success of his friend William Molyneux in persuading Provost Ashe to include *An Essay concerning Human Understanding* (1690) on the Trinity College, Dublin, curriculum in 1692. Locke's *Essay* shaped the field of philosophical inquiry in Ireland from Berkeley's *New Theory of Vision* (1711) to Burke's *Inquiry into the Origins of the Sublime and Beautiful* (1759). A similar Lockian influence can be traced in Irish theological writings from John Toland's *Christianity not Mysterious* (1696) to Robert Clayton's *New Theory of Spirit* (1757). The publication of Locke and Molyneux's correspondence in *Some Familiar Letters between Mr John Locke and Several of his Friends* (1708), reprinted in the 14 editions of Locke's *Works* to 1826, helped sustain Irish interest in Locke's writings.

Molyneux's *The Case of Ireland's being Bound by Acts of Parliament in England, Stated* (1698) was one of the earliest works to make explicit reference to Locke's *Two Treatises of Government*. It drew on Locke's natural rights theory to demonstrate the legislative independence of the Irish Parliament. By the late 1770s Locke's *Second Treatise of Government* (known as *Locke of Government*) had become the standard Trinity textbook on politics, and its influence on Irish political pamphleteering can be traced from 1779. Locke's authority was appealed to by Irish writers on both sides of the debate on the French Revolution, and Locke was the most widely cited political writer in the controversy over union with Great Britain in 1798–1800. In 1798 Thomas Elrington produced the first annotated edition of *Locke on Government* to sanitize Trinity students against revolutionary readings of the book, such as that of Thomas Paine. Locke's educational theories, which had been applied by William Molyneux in the upbringing of his son Samuel, enjoyed a considerable vogue in eighteenth-century Ireland; his writings on money were also well known and influenced, amongst others, Swift, Berkeley and Thomas Prior.

Reading

Berman, David 'Enlightenment and counter-Enlightenment in Irish philosophy', *Archiv für Gesichte de Philosophie* 64 (1982).

Kelly, Patrick 'Perceptions of Locke in eighteenth-century Ireland', *Proceedings of the Royal Irish Academy* 89 (1989).

McDowell, R.B. and Webb, D.A., *Trinity College, Dublin* (Cambridge: Cambridge University Press, 1981).

PATRICK KELLY

Loftus family Adam (?1533–1605), archbishop of Dublin (1567–1605), was the founder of the Loftus family in Ireland. Originally from Yorkshire, he came to Ireland in 1560 as chaplain to Lord Lieutenant Sussex. Loftus was elevated to the archbishopric of Armagh in 1561, and thereafter became the head of the commission for ecclesiastical causes, which attempted to enforce the Elizabethan Act of Supremacy across Ireland. His zeal in executing these offices was rewarded in 1567 with the archbishopric of Dublin, and in 1581 with the important office of lord chancellor, both posts he held until his death in 1605. He played a central role in the government of the country, being appointed lord justice on three occasions (1582, 1597, 1599). Furthermore he was principally involved in founding Trinity College, Dublin, in 1592, and acted as its first provost. Though his religious convictions bordered on the Puritan, he was known for his astute acquisition of estates and ready display of wealth. Moreover he fathered 20 children, who constituted the basis of the powerful Loftus network for the ensuing two centuries.

Adam (?1568–1643), first viscount Loftus of Ely, was a nephew of Archbishop Loftus, a connection which enabled him to rise rapidly within both the church and the administration. In 1597 he was made archdeacon of Glendalough, and the following year a master in Chancery. After his uncle's death in 1605, he was made a member of the Privy Council and was politically close to the lord deputy,

Sir Arthur Chichester. In 1619, he attained the lucrative office of lord chancellor. Thereafter his career was beset with disputes with the incumbent lord deputies, first with Falkland and in the 1630s with Wentworth.

Dudley (1619–95), third son of Sir Adam Loftus of Rathfarnham Castle, and great-grandson of the archbishop, was educated in Trinity College (BA) and Oxford (MA), and became a talented Orientalist and Latin scholar. His earliest published works included an introduction to Aristotilian philosophy and *Logica Armeniaca in Latinam traducta* (both published in 1657), but much of his later work centred on the translation of texts by Dionysius Syrus. He was an avid collector of manuscripts, in Arabic, Hebrew, Irish, Persian, Syriac and many other languages. Furthermore he was a prominent jurist in the Dublin administration, chiefly occupying the post of master in Chancery from 1655.

Reading

Ford, G.A., *The Protestant Reformation in Ireland, 1590–1641* (Frankfurt: Lang, 1985).

Kearney, H., *Strafford in Ireland, 1633–41* (Cambridge: Cambridge University Press, 1989).

Phillips, W.A. (ed.), *History of the Church of Ireland* (Oxford: Oxford University Press/H. Milford, 1933–4).

BRIAN DONOVAN

Logue, Michael (1840–1924) Cardinal. Born Carrigart, County Donegal, 1 October; died Armagh, 19 November. Logue was educated at Maynooth, became professor of dogmatic theology at the Irish College in Paris in 1866, and returned to Maynooth in 1876 as dean and professor of Irish and theology. He became bishop of Raphoe in 1879, archbishop of Armagh in 1888, and a cardinal in 1893. He denounced Parnell after the O'Shea divorce case and remained afterwards suspicious of the Irish Party. Although protesting strongly against partition, he accepted the Anglo-Irish Treaty of 1921.

HENRY BOYLAN

Lombard, Peter (*c.*1554–1625) Theologian and archbishop of Armagh. Born Waterford; died Rome. Born into a Waterford merchant family, Lombard attended Peter White's classical school in Waterford and, from 1572, Le Faucon College, Louvain. A professor of philosophy and of theology at Louvain, by 1598 he was the university's representative at Rome. He was consecrated archbishop of Armagh in 1601, but never returned to Ireland; David Rothe, bishop of Ossory, acted as his vicar. In 1600 he wrote a propagandist account of Irish history, *De Regno Hibernise Sanctorum insula commentarius*, defending the war of Hugh O'Neill, earl of Tyrone, against Elizabeth I as a religious war for Catholicism. After 1607, however, the pragmatist Lombard promoted the view, voiced by Pope Clement VIII, that James I was the legitimate king, worthy of the loyalty of Irish Catholics. A leading theologian in Rome, he was arbitrator in a controversy over supernatural grace (1602–7), and later promoted papal toleration of secular states. In 1616 he presided over the theologians who condemned Galileo.

Reading

Lombard, Peter, *De Regno Hiberniae Sanctorum insula Commentarius*, ed. Patrick, F. Moran (Dublin: James Duffy, 1868; first pub. 1632).
Silke, John J., 'The Irish Peter Lombard', *Studies* XLIV (1975).

BERNADETTE CUNNINGHAM

Longford, Christine (née Trew) (1900–80) Playright. Born Cheddar. Educated in Wells High School and Somerville College, Oxford, Christine married Edward Pakenham, sixth earl of Longford, in 1925. Two years later they moved to Ireland and she adopted it as her native land. She became a distinguished figure in Irish theatrical life. She wrote over 20 plays for the Gate Theatre and for her husband's company, and helped him to manage his theatre. She continued to run the Gate Theatre for some years after her husband's death in 1961.

Her plays include *Queen and Emperors* (1932), *Stop the Clock* (1955) and *Stephen Stoney* (1960). She also wrote some well-received novels, including *Printed Cotton* (1935) and *Sea Change* (1940).

RACHEL FURMSTON

lord lieutenancy 1690–1800 As the king's representative in Ireland, the lord lieutenant was the head of the Dublin Castle-based Irish executive and commander in chief of the Irish army. He was responsible for ensuring that British government in Ireland was kept on an even keel and, for this reason, he was a member of the British cabinet for most of the eighteenth century, even though he was effectively prohibited from attending cabinet meetings after Lord Townshend (1767–72) determined that lord lieutenants should reside in Ireland for the duration of their term in office. Townshend's decision had enormous implications for Irish politics as well as for the lord lieutenancy, and was a key moment in the history of Irish administration in the eighteenth century.

The lord lieutenant in Ireland wielded extensive powers. He could pardon all but the most serious crimes, and remit fines; in association with the Privy Council, he could issue proclamations; he could appoint to all but the highest lay and clerical offices in the land, grant warrants authorizing expenditure, bring all revenue officers to account, give orders to the military and appoint lord justices. Despite these powers, the lord lieutenancy was not a popular posting. Lord Northington described it in 1783 as 'honourable banishment'; and while there were generally sufficient candidates ready to accept the position, there were many more for whom the prospect of a term in Ireland was so intolerable that they were not prepared to accept the position under any circumstances.

The main cause of the opposition of English politicians to serving as Irish lord lieutenant was not the prospect (unpleasant though it was for many) of having to reside, either permanently or temporarily, in Ireland.

The financial rewards of office (£16,000 a year from the early 1760s and £20,000 per annum after 1783) more than compensated for this; what they did not compensate for was the tension and travail associated with mediating between Britain and Ireland on sensitive constitutional and commercial issues, and with securing a parliamentary majority that would approve the legislation on which the smooth administration of the kingdom of Ireland depended.

The centrality of efficient management to the maintenance of the Anglo-Irish nexus and to the preservation of political harmony in Ireland was highlighted by the first Parliament convened after the victory of the Williamite armies in 1690–1. The lord lieutenant, Lord Sydney, faced the Irish Parliament with an inadequate support base, and quickly found himself forced to prorogue the Parliament when MPs controversially affirmed that they had the 'sole right' to originate money bills. Sydney's inability to deal with this challenge more effectively boded ill for the future of British government in Ireland, but his successor, Lord Capel, identified a way forward. Capel established a *modus vivendi* with key interests in the Irish Parliament whereby, in return for their support on vital financial matters, he met their wishes on other issues. Capel's pragmatism ensured the 1695 session was a success, and though a series of commercial and constitutional disputes in the late 1690s threatened the future of such a strategy, the decision of the earl of Rochester, who was appointed lord lieutenant in 1700, to reside in Ireland only when Parliament was meeting, and the obvious merit of Capel's recourse to parliamentary 'managers', ensured that managers of one form or another became an integrated part of the Irish Parliament in the early eighteenth century. Indeed, in a curious way, the rise of party in the reign of Queen Anne (1703–14) served to affirm rather than to weaken the lord lieutenants' dependence on parliamentary managers. With the exception of the duke of Ormonde (1703–7, 1710–13), who was knowledgeable about Irish affairs,

none of the other Whig or Tory lord lieutenants appointed between 1703 and 1717 (earl of Pembroke, 1707–8; earl of Wharton, 1708–10; duke of Shrewsbury, 1713–14; earl of Sunderland, 1714–17) were sufficiently *au fait* with or interested in Irish politics to get by without help. All depended to a greater or lesser degree on the caucuses that led the Whig and Tory party interests, though all endeavoured to steer a course between party diehards.

The decline of party following the accession of the Hanoverians in 1714 did not prompt a redefinition of the role and nature of the office of lord lieutenant. On the contrary; the Irish viceroyalty was seen and used on several occasions by political leaders in England in the reign of George I as a means of 'banishing' their rivals (earl of Sunderland, 1714–17; Viscount Townshend, 1717; Lord Cartaret, 1724–30), and this, combined with the growing restlessness of Irish Protestants due to the poor performance of the economy and differences with England over the appellate jurisdiction of the Irish House of Lords and Woods' Halfpence, ensured that successive lord lieutenants remained dependent on managerial support. The dukes of Bolton (1717–20), Grafton (1720–4) and Lord Cartaret had to choose between William Conolly, the most skilful political operator of his day, and the more erratic St John Broderick. Conolly was preferred, which allowed him to emerge in the late 1720s as the politician who actually undertook to secure parliamentary approval for legislation on behalf of the lord lieutenant. This development was not afforded an unequivocal welcome in the highest political circles, but though Cartaret and his successor, the duke of Dorset (1730–7), endeavoured to avoid becoming dependent on one 'Undertaker', this did not prove possible. Dorset was obliged in 1733 to have recourse to Henry Boyle, who assumed command of the Brodrick interest in the late 1720s, and who was to provide him and his successors (duke of Devonshire, 1737–45; earl of Chesterfield,

1745; earl of Harrington, 1746–50) with secure parliamentary majorities. By this means, domestic Irish politics were kept on an even keel for most of the 1730s and 1740s. Indeed, except for Chesterfield, whose openness, common sense and tolerance won much praise, none of the lord lieutenants appointed to serve in Ireland in the 1730s and 1740s possessed either the imagination or the strength of will to reshape the political administration of Ireland in a manner that would enable the lord lieutenant to play a more central and decisive political part.

The most threatening development in these years for domestic political stability was the encouragement given the ambitious Ponsonby family by the duke of Devonshire. This did not excite especial concern until the late 1740s, when the Ponsonbys, now allied with the primate, George Stone, endeavoured to take Henry Boyle's place as the leading Undertaker interest in the Irish House of Commons. They received the opportunity they craved with the reappointment of the duke of Dorset to the lord lieutenancy in 1750, but his decision to place his confidence in the Ponsonby–Stone interest inaugurated a period of instability in Irish politics, which served only to make British politicians acutely aware of the power exercised by leading Irish politicians and the weaknesses of current arrangements as far as the security of the Anglo-Irish nexus was concerned. The upshot was that they began to reassess the role of the lord lieutenant in the Irish administration. One strategy pursued by successive lord lieutenants in the late 1750s (earl of Hartington, 1755–7; duke of Bedford, 1757–60) was not to rely exclusively on any one individual or alliance of interests in the Irish House of Commons. This proved only partly successful, however, and English opinion gradually came round to the view that something more radical had to be done to prevent Ireland succumbing to what one observer termed 'the frenzy of independency'. Many suggestions were advanced, but the most feasible and the one that found favour was that future lord

lieutenants should reside in Ireland for the duration of their appointment. The advantage of this was it would deprive the Undertaker of the status and influence he derived from the fact that traditionally he was appointed to fill one of the places in the commission of lord justices created each time the lord lieutenant left the kingdom. By extension, it would, of course, also strengthen the power of the lord lieutenant, by obliging him to reside in Ireland and to exercise the power of his office for the duration of his appointment. A resolution to this effect was approved by the British cabinet in February 1765, but the decision was not implemented for several years because of the refusal of several appointees (Viscount Weymouth, – 1765; earl of Hertford, 1765; earl of Bristol, 1766–7) to reside in Ireland. Finally, however, Lord Townshend – an experienced soldier with firm views on imperial management – chose to give effect to this policy. Townshend was not directed to reside, but he perceived the refusal of the leading parliamentary interests in the Irish Parliament to support his legislative programme, unless he first responded to their demands, as so intolerable that he chose to become resident and undertook to break the influence of the Undertakers by assuming the responsibility for creating a pro-Castle majority in the House of Commons. Townshend experienced his share of setbacks before he finally departed Ireland in 1772, but by then he had effectively destroyed the Undertaker system, and inaugurated a new era in Irish politics in which the lord lieutenant and the Dublin Castle executive took a more active political role.

After 1772, Dublin Castle was the key player in the management of the Irish House of Commons. Under the direction of the lord lieutenant, the chief secretary and his allies used a combination of lures and promises to create a sufficiently weighty phalanx to enable them to carry vital legislation. Townshend's successor, Earl Harcourt (1772–6), proved quite skilled at this, and his administration passed off without any serious crises.

However, the combination of political ineptitude and the emergence of Protestant nationalism as a strong political force in the late 1770s ensured that his successor, the inept earl of Buckinghamshire, had a torrid time. His successors, the earl of Carlisle (1781–2), the duke of Portland (1782) and Earl Temple (1782–3), were more capable, but they were kept on the defensive politically by the level of popular support for Protestant nationalism, and obliged to preside over the most fundamental dilution of English constitutional authority in Ireland in centuries. But the lord lieutenancy under the direction of Lord Northington (1783–4) and the duke of Rutland (1784–7), re-established itself as the main source of political power in the kingdom.

The last five lord lieutenants of the eighteenth century were the marquess of Buckingham (1787–9), the earl of Westmorland (1789–94), Earl Fitzwilliam (1794–5), Earl Camden (1795–8) and the marquess of Cornwallis (1798–1801). Each faced dramatic political changes. Buckingham and Fitzwilliam essentially misjudged the temper of the kingdom, with the result that they both left office under a cloud. Westmorland and Camden relied on conservative advisers who put political control and the security of the Anglo-Irish connection above domestic harmony in Ireland. Cornwallis, by contrast, was much more independent-minded, and he displayed admirable fairness and not a little deftness in dealing with the problems thrown up by the 1798 Rebellion and the decision to attempt a legislative union. The Act of Union had enormous implications for the lord lieutenancy, moreover. The office survived the constitutional changes effected in 1800, but the combination of residence and the continuing rise in the status of the chief secretaryship had the effect of downgrading the role and influence of the lord lieutenancy.

Reading

Hayton, David, 'Ireland and the English ministers 1707–16', Oxford University, DPhil thesis, 1975.

Johnston, E.M., *Great Britain and Ireland 1760–1800* (Edinburgh: University Court of the University of St Andrews/Oliver and Boyd, 1963).

Kelly, James, 'The search for a commercial arrangement: Anglo-Irish politics in the 1780s', University College, Dublin, PhD thesis, 1985.

McCracken, J.L., 'Central and local administration in the reign of George II', Queen's University, Belfast, PhD thesis, 1949.

JAMES KELLY

Lough Derg (1971) A long narrative poem by Patrick Kavanagh. Written in June 1942, it participates in a literary discourse on the Lough Derg pilgrimage to which William Carleton, Denis Devlin, Sean O'Faolain and Seamus Heaney have also contributed. Kavanagh's narrator is a pilgrim-poet who records his shifting responses to Irish Catholicism, but also questions the poetic enterprise of documenting a people's spiritual life. The poem eschews the narrative and philosophical certitudes of *The Great Hunger*, and admits a tension between subjective interpretation and accurate representation. Ultimately, Kavanagh abdicated the authority of authorship by declining to publish it.

ANTOINETTE QUINN

Lucas, Charles (1713–73) Patriot, physician and political agitator. Elected to the lower house of Dublin Corporation in 1741, he began his life-long campaign against the abuse of political power in general and the usurpation of power by the aldermen in particular. In 1749 he stood for Parliament, but his writings and outspoken criticisms of the government brought him charges of sedition and the threat of Newgate. He fled to England, where he qualified as a doctor. He returned to Ireland in 1761, and held a seat in Parliament until his death.

A prolific, passionate and highly critical writer and campaigner, dubbed the 'Wilkes of Ireland', his enthusiasm was not matched by literary talent. He was greatly loved by the masses of Dublin, despite a reputation for anti-Catholic bigotry.

Reading

Murphy, Sean, 'The Lucas affair: a study of municipal and electoral politics in Dublin 1742–49', MA thesis, University College, Dublin, 1981.

LUCINDA THOMSON

Luce, Arthur Aston (1882–1977) Philosopher and churchman. Born Gloucester, 21 August; died Dublin, 28 June. The third son of the Rev. John James Luce, Luce was educated at Eastbourne College. He matriculated at Trinity College, Dublin, in January 1901, and proceeded as an extern student to a pass BA in 1905, taking a supplemental moderatorship in 1906. His election to a life fellowship in classics and philosophy (the longest tenure in the history of the college) came in 1912. Ordained to the ministry of the Church of Ireland in 1907, he began a life-long association with St Patrick's Cathedral as treasurer's vicar in 1909, later becoming canon (1930–6), chancellor (1936–52) and precentor (1952–73). In World War I he served in France with the 12th Royal Irish Rifles, being promoted captain (1916) and winning the MC (1917). He gained his DD in 1920, and his appointment as Donnellan Lecturer in 1921 led to a book on Bergson's doctrine of intuition. The Berkeleian research that was later to absorb all his intellectual energies began in 1930. He held the chair of moral philosophy from 1934 to 1949, and a personal chair from 1953 to 1977. He was vice-provost under E.H. Alton from 1946 to 1952, and was honoured with a LittD by Queen's University, Belfast, in 1953. In December 1918 he married a Trinity graduate (Lilian Mary Thomson), and they had two sons and a daughter.

J.V. LUCE

Lundy, Robert (fl. 1689) Governor of Londonderry. A Scots Protestant, Lundy became governor 21 December 1688. His ineffective attempts to defend the city allowed the Jacobites to force the Williamites into a disorderly retreat behind the walls. The citizens blamed him for their plight and in April 1689 Lundy's successor, Walker, had to help him escape the city in disguise. Protestants subsequently made 'Lundy the traitor' a symbol, burning his firework-filled effigy, hanging from the Walker pillar, every 18 December. More a defeatist than a traitor, Lundy's true significance was that, as a non-Ulsterman, his commitment was limited.

Reading

Lacy, Brian, *Seige City* (Belfast: Blackstaff, 1991).

W. HARVEY COX

Lynn, Samuel (1834–76) Sculptor. Born Fethard, County Tipperary; died Belfast, 5 April. Lynn studied at the Belfast School of Art and later at the Royal Academy School in London and in the studio of the Irish sculptor, Patrick McDowell. In the mid-1860s he assisted Foley on the statue of Prince Albert for the Kensington Gardens Memorial. London had by then become his home, but he accepted commissions for public statues in Dublin, Belfast, Cavan Town, Hillsborough, County Down and Manchester. He has the distinction of having produced the first monument to a Presbyterian minister in Belfast, *Dr Henry Cooke*, a bronze in College Square East, erected in March 1876. He was made an associate of the Royal Hibernian Academy in 1872.

Reading

Strickland, Walter, *A Dictionary of Irish Artists* (Shannon: Irish University Press, 1968).

FINTAN CULLEN

M

MacBride, Seán (1904–88) Revolutionary, lawyer and politician. Born Paris, 26 January; died Dublin, 15 January. MacBride joined the Irish Volunteers, opposed the Treaty of 1921, and became chief of staff of the IRA in 1936. On the enactment of the Constitution of 1937 he resigned from the IRA and began a successful career at the bar. In 1946 he founded Clann na Poblachta, became minister for external affairs, and influenced the declaration of a Republic in 1949. He became prominent in international bodies working for peace and received the Nobel Prize for Peace in 1974.

HENRY BOYLAN

McCormack, John (1884–1945) Operatic and concert tenor. Born Athlone, County Westmeath, 14 June; died Booterstown, County Dublin, 16 September. McCormack won a gold medal at the Dublin Feis Ceoil in 1902, then studied in Italy under Sabatini, and made his operatic debut at Covent Garden in 1907. After successful operatic seasons he turned to the concert stage and achieved extraordinary popularity, being acclaimed as the greatest living lyric tenor. His hundreds of records sold in great numbers. He was made a hereditary papal count in 1928 for his services to Catholic charities.

HENRY BOYLAN

McCormick, F.J. (1889–1947) Actor. Born Peter Judge at Skerries, County Dublin. A civil servant with an ineradicable interest in the theatre, McCormick joined the Abbey Players in 1918. He played over 500 parts on the Abbey stage, excelling in deeply observed comic characterizations. Among his most remarkable creations were Seumas Shields, Joxer Daly and Jack Clitheroe (O'Casey), Professor Tim (Shiels), Faustus Kelly (Flann O'Brien), Oedipus (Yeats), Dobelle (Johnston) and Stephen Moore (Mayne). In established parts he excelled as General Burgoyne and Caesar (Shaw), Haroun al Rashid (Flecker) and Lear. His most famous film role was in *Odd Man Out* (1946).

Reading

Robinson, Lennox, *Ireland's Abbey Theatre* (London: Sidgwick and Jackson, 1951).
Hunt, Hugh, *The Abbey* (Dublin: Gill and Macmillan, 1979).

CHRISTOPER FITZSIMON

McCracken, Henry Joy (1767–98) United Irishman. Born High Street, Belfast, 31 August; hanged Belfast market house, 17 July. With Wolfe Tone and Thomas Russell, McCracken founded the first Society of

United Irishmen in Belfast in 1791. He commanded the insurgents in County Antrim during the Rising of 1798, but his attack on Antrim town was defeated by the British troops. He hid for some months in the Slemish mountains but when about to escape to America he was seized, tried by court martial and condemned to death.

HENRY BOYLAN

MacDonagh, Thomas (1878–1916) Writer, teacher, Republican. Born Cloughjordan, County Tipperary, 1 February; executed Kilmainham Gaol, 3 May. MacDonagh's first book of poems, *Through the Ivory Gate* (1902), was dedicated to W.B. Yeats. There followed five books of poems, ending with the selected *Lyrical Poems* (1913). His play *When the Dawn is Come* was staged at the Abbey in 1908. He joined Patrick Pearse as teacher of English and French at his new school, St Enda's, in September 1908. In January 1912 he married Muriel Gifford (sister of Grace, who was to marry his friend Joseph Plunkett). A founder member of the Irish Volunteers (November 1913), he became its director of training. He was the last of the Signatories to the 1916 Proclamation to join the Military Council planning the Rising in early April 1916. During the Rising he commanded the 2nd Battalion from Jacob's Factory.

MacDonagh's most significant literary work is the critical study *Literature in Ireland*, published after his death in July 1916. Here he formulates an inclusive theory of the Irish literary tradition. In what he called the 'Irish Mode' he tried to show that the distinctive speech patterns and rhythms of the Gaelic language, and the native mentality expressed in Gaelic literature, were in the course of passing from the Gaelic language to Hiberno-English as spoken and written by native Irish and Anglo-Irish alike. This culturally ecumenical idea was not popular with Gaelic-language revivalists such as Daniel Corkery in the twenties and thirties, who downplayed MacDonagh's ideas in favour of Patrick Pearse's.

Reading

Norstedt, Johann A., *Thomas MacDonagh: A Critical Biography* (University Press of Virginia).

Parks, E.W. and Parks, A.W, *Thomas MacDonagh: The Man, The Patriot, The Writer* (Georgia: 1967)

PAT COOKE

McDonald, Walter (1854–1920) Theologian. Born Mooncoin, County Kilkenny, June; died Maynooth, 2 May. McDonald was educated at St Kieran's College, Kilkenny, and Maynooth seminary, and was appointed professor of moral theology in Maynooth in 1881. Between 1898 and 1903 be wrote six volumes of theology, but all were refused an imprimatur and so could not be published. Two later works on ethical questions received an imprimatur from the Westminister censor and were published in London. At no time did the bishops attempt to dismiss him.

Reading

McDonald, Walter, *Some Ethical Questions of Peace and War* (London: Burns and Oats, 1919).

——*Reminiscences of a Maynooth Professor*, ed. Denis Gwynn (London: Cape, 1925).

HENRY BOYLAN

MacDonogh, Patrick (1902–61) Poet. Born Dublin. MacDonogh is remembered as the poet of a few near-perfect lyrics such as 'Be Still As You Are Beautiful' and 'The Widow of Drynam'. He was educated at Avoca School and at Trinity College, Dublin, and worked for most of his life in Guinness's. His first volume, *Flirtations: Some Occasional Verses* (1927), was not an auspicious debut and the second, *A Leaf in the Wind* (1927), used some but not all of the ample room for improvement. His pamphlets *The Vestal Fire* (1941) and *Over the Water and Other Poems* (1943) were published by Seamus O'Sullivan's Orwell Press in Dublin; the former is a 750-line meditation on love. In the 1940s and 1950s MacDonogh's poems appeared in periodicals on both sides of the Atlantic, and most of them were gathered in his final and most achieved collection, *One Landscape Still and Other Poems* (1958).

PETER DENMAN

McGahern, John (1934–) Novelist and short story writer. McGahern was brought up in Roscommon and Leitrim, the rural terrain of his fictions, where he himself has returned to live and farm. His novels and short stories, beginning with *The Barracks* (1963), break with post-revival realism, because their vision is ruthlessly existential, refusing the consolations of Catholicism. He has sometimes been underestimated as a worthy, traditional novelist because of his understated, plain style and his characters' rural roots. However, though he contextualizes his unhappy, migrant or settled Irish characters with remorseless accuracy, their situations serve as metaphors of the bleakness of the human condition.

McGahern is an obsessive writer who returns with changed focus to the same small family of characters: tyrannical father, alienated son, compliant stepmother, terminally ill older woman, rejected or disenchanted lover. Happiness renders him mawkish, and he is at his best when chronicling lives of quiet desperation with black or unobtrusive humour, especially in the short story collections *Nightlines* (1970), *Getting Through* (1978) and *High Ground* (1985). A collected edition of his stories was published in 1992. The award-winning *Amongst Women* (1990) is his masterpiece: a compassionate analysis of familial power relations, the culmination of a life-long fascination with the centrality of the image, and with syntactical and structural repetition and rhythm in narrative.

The outcry over the banning of McGahern's *The Dark* (1965) was almost upstaged by the furore over his first Abbey play, *The Power of Darkness* (1991), where his discomfiting vision of Irish life is revealed without any of his customary resonance and reticence.

ANTOINETTE QUINN

MacGowran, Jack (1918–73) Actor. MacGowran began his stage career in 1944, making his first London appearance in 1953. A distinguished artist, his work with Samuel Beckett set him apart. From 1955 his intense interpretations of Beckett's spare texts were the most authoritative: his lean features and large protuberant eyes gave his distinctive appearance a most effective focus. In 1961 he was British Television Actor of the Year, and in 1971 gained the Actor of the Year award of the York Critics for his performance as Vladimir in *Beginning to End*.

PETER COSTELLO

McGrath, Miler (1523?–1622) Archbishop. Born into a notable native Irish family, McGrath was educated at Rome, became a Franciscan friar, and was appointed by the pope to the bishopric of Down and Connor in 1565. Accommodating himself to the established church, he was appointed bishop of Clogher in 1570, and then in 1571 was translated to the archbishopric of Cashel, which he held with Emly until his death in 1622. Initially a shrewd and influential political figure, in 1582 he acquired the dioceses of Waterford and Lismore. By the early seventeenth century, however, he was seen by the English leaders of the Church of Ireland as an unreliable native Irish time-server more interested in enriching himself and his family than serving the church, and he was squeezed out from positions of influence, retreating to the remote dioceses of Killala and Achonry, which he also held from 1611 till his death. His vigorous personality, flexible principles and chequered career have made him into a colourful historiographical figure.

Reading

Jackson, R.W. *Archbishop Magrath the Scoundrel of Cashel* (Dublin: 1974).

Marron, Lawrence (ed.), 'Documents from the state papers concerning Miler McGrath', *Archivium Hibernicum* xxi (1958).

ALAN FORD

MacGreevy, Thomas (1893–1967) Poet and critic. Born Tarbert, County Kerry. MacGreevy was educated at Trinity College, Dublin (1919–21). His artistic career began in 1921, only after an early career in the British Civil Service, and after having served in the Royal Field Artillery in the closing years of the Great War. In 1928 he went to Paris, becoming part of the Modernist *avant-garde*, where he tapped into a greater European Catholic heritage rich in music and the visual arts. His poetry, self-consciously Modernist, at times deliberately obscure, and at its best a marriage of the political and the spiritual, had more in common with contemporary French or American poetry than Irish. He was an early advocate of Irish Modernist art, and particularly of many of the artists who later formed the nucleus of the Irish Exhibition of Living Art. In 1950 MacGreevy became director of the National Gallery of Ireland. His far-ranging plans, many of them realized only after his resignation in 1963 due to failing health, brought the gallery at long last into the twentieth century.

Reading

MacGreevy, Thomas, *T.S. Eliot: A Study* (London: Chatto and Windus, 1931).
—— *Poems* (London: Heinemann, 1934).
—— *Jack B. Yeats: An Appreciation and an Interpretation* (Dublin: Waddington, 1945).
Schreibman, Susan, *Collected Poems of Thomas MacGreevy: An Annotated Edition* (Dublin: Anna Livia Press; Washington DC: Catholic University of America Press, 1991).

SUSAN SCHREIBMAN

McGuckian, Medbh (1950–) Poet. Born Belfast. McGuckian's stylistically provocative *Portrait of Joanna* (1980) and *The Flower Master* (1982) combined psychological intensity with mesmeric paraphasia. The follow-up collections *Venus and the Rain* (1984) and *On Ballycastle Beach* (1988) confirmed McGuckian's breakthrough into a new and distinctive poetic mode, but were met with accusations of emotional hermeticism and abstraction. Her recurrent motifs, particularly of flowers, houses and colours, have been dismissed by some as redundant architectural ornament, but others have welcomed the rich verbal texture and conceptual free-fall of her writing, while debate about her work has called attention to the question of difference in masculine and feminine responses to language and form. Her most recent collections, are *Marconi's Cottage*, (1991), *The Flower Master and Other Poems* (1993) and *Captain Lavendar* (1994).

EVE PATTEN

McGuinness, Frank (1956–) Playwright and former lecturer in English at St Patrick's College, Maynooth. Born Buncrana, County Donegal. McGuinness studied at University College, Dublin (1971–4). One of the finest younger Irish playwrights, he has won several major literary awards. His work demonstrates a linguistic lyricism and a willingness to experiment with dramatic form. He is particularly adept at using humour as a foil for emotionally searing subjects. His best work, *Observe the Sons of Ulster Marching Towards the Somme* (1985), *Innocence* (1986), *Carthaginians* (1988) and *Someone Who'll Watch Over Me* (1992), sensitively questions clichéd notions of identity (national and sexual), explores the complexity of human relationships, and celebrates human endurance in the face of the unspeakable and unbearable. McGuinness has also successfully adapted Lorca, Ibsen Chekhov, and most recently, Brecht. In 1994, McGuinness published *Booterstown*, his first collection of poems. The first volume of his selected plays appeared in 1996.

Reading

Etherton, Michael, *Contemporary Irish Dramatists* (London: Macmillan, 1986).
Maxwell, D.E.S., 'Northern Ireland's political drama', *Modern Drama* 33, no.1 (March 1990), pp. 7–9.

KARLIN J. LILLINGTON

McGuinness, Norah (1903–82) Painter. Born Derry. McGuinness studied in Dublin, in London and under André Lhote in Paris. She was associated for many years with the Irish Exhibition of Living Art, of which she was president from 1947 to 1971. She represented Ireland at the Venice Biennale, 1950. A retrospective exhibition was held in Trinity College, Dublin, 1968. Her style, strongly influenced by the clear bright colours of Dufy and other French painters, applied a Modernist format to an essentially traditional, lyrical sensibility. There are works by her in Dublin, Belfast, Washington and Coventry.

BRIAN FALLON

MacHale, John (1791–1881) Churchman. Born Tirawley, County Mayo, 6 March; died Tuam, 7 November. Of farming and trading stock, MacHale was educated locally, in Castlebar, and at Maynooth. Ordained there in 1814, he at once joined the teaching staff. In 1820, under the pen-name 'Hierophilos', he launched a series of open letters in which Catholic grievances, especially concerning schooling, were vigorously set forth. In 1825 he became co-adjutor bishop of Killala, and the first wholly Irish-educated Catholic bishop since the sixteenth century. In the campaign for Catholic emancipation he gained a nationwide reputation and was promoted in 1834 to the archbishopric of Tuam, which he was to occupy for 47 years. In the 1840s he figured prominently in the repeal agitation. But the Great Famine wrecked his world, and after 1850 Archbishop Cullen outmanoeuvred him in ecclesiastical politics. Henceforth they differed on most questions, including the opportuneness (which MacHale questioned) of defining papal infallibility at the Vatican Council. MacHale preached in Gaelic regularly, published extensive translations into Gaelic, and promoted the study of the language at St Jarlath's College, Tuam.

Reading

O'Reilly, Bernard, *John MacHale: His Life, Times and Correspondence*, 2 vols (New York: 1890)
Corish, Patrick J., 'Cardinal Cullen and Archbishop MacHale', *Irish Ecclesiastical Records* xci (1959).

R.V. COMERFORD

McKenna, Siobhán (1923–86) Actress. Born Belfast. McKenna was raised in Galway, and studied at University College, Galway (1940–4). She was an internationally known and, in Ireland, much-beloved stage and screen actress. The Gaelic-speaking McKenna's 1940 debut was with An Taibhdhearc in Galway. Her close association with the Abbey Theatre began in 1944 with *The Countess Kathleen*, launching a career of vivid portrayals of the stage's great women characters. One of her finest roles was Joan in Shaw's *Joan of Arc*, which ran on Broadway in 1956. Other major roles were Pegeen Mike in film and stage versions of *The Playboy of the Western World* and her acclaimed portrayal of Irish literary heroines in her one-woman show *Here Are Ladies*. Her final role as Mommo in *Bailegangaire* was considered a *tour de force*. McKenna was married to actor Dennis O'Dea (d. 1978).

Reading

Mikhail, E.H. (ed.), *The Abbey Theatre: Interviews and Recollections* (London: Macmillan, 1988).

KARLIN J. LILLINGTON

MacKenna, Stephen (1872–1934) Journalist and translator. Whatever his reputation during his lifetime as an essayist and conversationalist, Stephen MacKenna is remembered today for just one thing, his great translation of the works of the Greek neo-Platonist philosopher Plotinus, as *The Enneads of Plotinus*. MacKenna was born in Liverpool, son of a flamboyant and improvident Irish former officer in the Indian Army (and then unsuccessful novelist), who died when Stephen was just 11. He was supported by two maiden aunts, who saw to his education. He excelled at school in classics and English, but failed the entrance examination in English to London University, and was put to work in a bank, now back with his aunts in Dublin.

He was not fated, however, to be a bank official. He kept up his literary interests, and in 1896 produced an English translation of the *Imitation of Christ*, and had it accepted by a Dublin publisher. He now decided to break loose from respectability, and become a writer. His brother, who was in journalism, got him a job in London with a daily paper, from which position he quickly moved to Paris, as the Paris correspondent for an English Catholic journal.

This began a particularly formative period of his life. He became a close friend of the playwright J.M. Synge, and of a number of other Irish exiles, political or aesthetic. He also became friendly with Armenian and Greek exiles. In the spring of 1897, he went off to join an international brigade, led by the son of Garibaldi, to help the Greeks against the Turks, though he was never involved in fighting, and arrived back in Paris penniless in the autumn.

In the midst of all these adventures, MacKenna was developing a philosophy, or view of life, which comes close to that of the man to whom he was to devote his life, Plotinus. Entries in diaries and journals he kept in these years show belief in a pure spirit which is the only true reality. He also had strong views on aesthetics and literary style. Such a man was plainly not going to be long satisfied as a journalist either.

In 1902 he met and married a young American girl, Mary Bray, and for a while (between 1903 and 1907), attained a prosperity and success to which he never again rose, first as a correspondent for the *New York Herald*, and then as European representative of the *New York World*. In the course of his duties, he was covering the 1905 Revolution in St Petersburg when in a bookstore he came upon a copy of Creuzer's edition of Plotinus'

Enneads, which he began to struggle through. By March 1907 he had resolved that his life's work must be to translate Plotinus.

He now quarrelled with his boss, Joseph Pulitzer, resigned his position, and moved to London, and then, in the autumn of 1908, back to Dublin, where he joined the *Freeman's Journal* as a leader writer, being supported also by his wife, who had a small income. In 1908 he produced a first attempt at a Plotinus translation, in the form of the essay *On Beauty* (*Enn.* I 8), and this was published in an edition of 300 copies by A.H. Bullen (which sold out, though without much profit to the author).

MacKenna now plunged into nationalist politics and the learning of Gaelic, making the acquaintance of such figures as AE, Thomas Bodkin, the Celtic scholar Osborne Bergin, and the young poets Padraic Colum, James Stephens and Thomas MacDonagh (later to be one the leaders of the Easter Rising). From 1908 to 1913, the MacKennas' house was a meeting place, on Saturday evenings, for all these and others, and the conversation was sparkling.

Nothing further, however, was done with Plotinus, until an unexpected letter arrived in January 1912 from a certain Ernest Debenham, a wealthy British industrialist with literary and philosophical interests. Debenham had read and liked the *Essay on Beauty*, and wondered when more might be expected. This put MacKenna on the spot, and he wrote a rather waffling reply, whereupon Debenham offered to subsidize him, to give him leisure to complete the work. This MacKenna initially refused, but Debenham disguised his help by getting Philip Lee Warner, publisher to the Medici Society, to offer MacKenna an advance against publication, and he was thus effectively hooked.

The next dozen years, to 1924, were a period of ever-increasing stress for MacKenna. He was an extreme, though peaceful, nationalist (he had offered his services to the 1916 rebels, but was politely turned down), and he was disgusted by the compromise represented by the Treaty of

1921. He was tormented by (possibly psycho-somatic) illnesses, and in 1923 his wife died of a real, though rather mysterious, one. He was about to abandon the whole project of translation, when Debenham stepped in again, invited him over to England, and set him up in Bournemouth, thus saving his health and the project.

MacKenna never returned to Ireland, though he kept in touch with many Irish writers and scholars, such as AE, James Stephens and W.K. Magee ('John Eglinton'). For the next six years, in various locations, and living on a shoestring, he toiled at his task (though complaining much to his friend E.R. Dodds, the Northern Irish Greek scholar, and others), and in May 1930 the last proofs were sent off to the printers.

His life's work was now done, but he lived on till 1934, working to master the Gaelic language, and his other great love, the playing of the accordion, though without great success at either. He died on 8 March of that year, at the age of 62.

Reading

Dodds, E.R. (ed.), *The Journal and Letters of Stephen MacKenna* (London: Constable, 1936).

JOHN DILLON

McLaverty, Michael Francis (1907–92)

Novelist and short story writer. Born Carrickmacross, County Monaghan. Early formative influences on McLaverty included several childhood years on Rathlin Island. He was educated at St Malachy's College, Belfast, and at Queen's University. A teacher of mathematics and headmaster for all of his professional life, McLaverty produced a veritable stream of novels and stories. He is best remembered, perhaps, for his earliest effort, *Call My Brother Back* (1939), which was set in early 1920s Ulster. McLaverty's last, most popular book was *Billy Boogles and the Brown Cow* (1982). His *Collected Short Stories* were published in 1978.

GERARD O'BRIEN

Mac Liammóir, Micheál (1899–1978)

Actor who transformed the Irish theatre. Born Alfred Lee Willmore in Willesden, north London, 25 October; died 6 March. Micheál Mac Liammóir made his first stage appearance in 1911 in London. After a period in Europe, he returned to Ireland in 1928 with Anew MacMaster's company, in which he met Hilton Edwards.

They founded the Gate Theatre in 1928 specifically to widen the repertoire of plays for Dublin audiences. For the first two years they played in the Peacock before moving to the company to the Rotunda in 1930.

Though he was involved in over 300 productions and toured England, America, Egypt and the Balkans, Mac Liammóir was also a distinguished writer in Gaelic and English; *All for Hecuba* (1946) and *Enter A Goldfish* (1977) are autobiographies. His one-man shows, beginning with *The Importance of Being Oscar* (1963), brought him international fame.

Reading

O hAodha, Micheál, *The Importance of Being Micheál* (Dingle: 1990).

PETER COSTELLO

Macklin, Charles (*c*.1697–1797)

Actor and dramatist. Born McLaughlin in the North of Ireland; died Covent Garden, London, 11 July. Macklin was educated in Dublin and was a strolling player in England for some years before he played his first part in Drury Lane Theatre in October 1733. He turned to writing plays *c*.1745, and over the next 20 years had the following produced: *King Henry VII*, *A Will and No Will*, *The Suspicious Husband Criticised*, *The Fortune Hunters*, *Love à la Mode*, *Married Libertine*, *The True-Born Irishman* and *The Man of the World*. The last named was one of the most successful comedies of the century.

Reading

Parry, Edward A., *Charles Macklin* (London: 1891).

PATRICK FAGAN

Maclise, Daniel (1806–70) Painter. Born Cork, 2 February; died London, 25 April. The son of an immigrant Scot, Maclise trained at the Cork Institute, copying the recently acquired Greco-Roman casts from the Vatican. Through the sale of studio pencil portraits he earned enough to go to London, exhibiting at the Royal Academy (RA) in 1828 and becoming RA in 1840. His historical and literary pictures were strongly influenced by German painting and he was noted for his own exactitude in matters of historical detail, and for the scale of his more important canvases. He was also an illustrator, and published caricatures in *Fraser's Magazine*.

Reading

Crookshank, A. and the Knight of Glin, *The Painters of Ireland, c. 1660–1920* (London: Barrie and Jenkins, 1978).

Ormond, R., and Turpin, J., *Daniel Maclise 1806–1870* (London: Arts Council of Great Britain, 1972).

Turpin, J., 'Maclise as a book illustrator', *Irish Arts Review* 2, no. 2 (1985).

HILARY PYLE

McNamara, Brinsley (John Weldon) (1890–1963) Actor, playwright and novelist. In 1910 McNamara joined the Abbey Theatre, Dublin, as an actor and toured the USA with the company in 1911. Disappointed at the failure of his acting career, he turned to writing and went back to his home in Delvin, living in obscurity for several years until he published the first of his seven novels, *The Valley of the Squinting Windows*, in 1918. This realistic portrayal of Irish rural life brought him unwelcome notoriety and estangement from his home and in 1922 he settled in Dublin, where he went on to publish novels, short stories and plays.

The Abbey Theatre staged nine of MacNamara's plays, including the powerful drama *Margaret Gillan* (1933) and the two more commercial comedies *The Glorious Uncertainty* (1923) and *Look at the Heffernans* (1926). MacNamara later became drama critic for the *Irish Times* and was a founding member of the Irish Academy of Letters in 1932. He is best remembered for his novel *The Various Lives of Marcus Igoe* (1929), which is generally considered one of the best twentieth-century Irish novels.

HELEN MCCURDY

MacNeice, Louis (1907–63) Poet. Born Belfast. MacNeice was born into a clerical family. He spent his childhood in the town of Carrickfergus on the northern shore of Belfast Lough, where his father was rector of the local Church of Ireland parish. He was educated in England at Sherbourne, Marlborough and Oxford, where he read classics. In the 1930s his name was associated with the Auden group and with the popular left-wing enthusiasms of that decade. MacNeice caught the mood of pre-war London in a series of highly charged, doom-laden lyrics and in his long poem of 1939, *Autumn Journal*, the most accomplished production of the first phase of his career. He worked as a classics don both in Birmingham and in London, but in 1941 he joined the British Broadcasting Corporation, in whose employ he remained for 20 years.

During World War II (in which he served as a fire warden during the blitz on London) he wrote and made many broadcasts and in the post-war years he was a significant presence in the highly creative Features Department of the BBC. MacNeice developed considerable skill as a radio producer and dramatist; his play of 1946, *The Dark Tower*, is reckoned a classic of the genre. During this second phase of his career MacNeice also produced much literary journalism, did translations, and travelled widely. His career as a poet, however, seemed to have run somewhat into the sands, although he continued to publish regularly, to mixed notices. In the final six years of his life MacNeice experienced a poetic renaiassance, and his last three volumes, *Visitations* (1957), *Solstices* (1961) and the posthumous *The Burning Perch* (1963), display all the old lyrical skill, with an added note of almost Beckettian desperation and black-comic élan.

MacNeice was in many respects a displaced person. His early poetry expressed a profound ambiguity of feeling about his native Ulster and about independent Ireland. England, however, never became truly home for him, and from his characteristically Anglo-Irish ambivalencies of feeling he made an art of settled scepticism and pervasive alienation, redeemed only by moments of love, friendship and sensory delight. A master of melancholy, his poems are saved from subjective self-indulgence by a classical temper, a Yeatsian devotion to the craft of poetry (he published a still-useful book-length study of Yeats in 1941), and a marked metrical skill – all of which made him one of the most distinctive and distinguished of twentieth-century poets writing in English. He is buried in Carrowdore churchyard in County Down, in a province in which his work has proved inspirational for a subsequent generation of poets, for whom the publication of his *Collected Poems* (1966), edited by his friend and fellow-Ulsterman E.R. Dodds, regius professor of Greek in the University of Oxford, was a cultural landmark.

TERENCE BROWN

MacNeill, Eoin (1867–1945) Academic and statesman. Born Glenarm, County Antrim, May; died Dublin, October. MacNeill married Agnes Moore (1896) and had seven children. Educated in Belfast and Dublin, he was appointed professor of early (including medieval) Irish history in University College, Dublin (1909). A prominent figure in the Irish cultural and political movements which led to the foundation of the modern Irish state in 1922, his major achievements were founding, with Douglas Hyde, the Gaelic League (1893) and the Irish Volunteers (1913), and the establishment of an academic basis for Irish studies.

MacNeill was first minister for finance (1919), ceann comhairle (speaker) in the second Dáil during the Treaty debate, and minister for education (1922). He was the Free State member on the Boundary Commission, and head of the Free State delegation to the League of Nations and to the Imperial Conference in London. He was elected TD for Clare and the National University (1923).

His contributions to Irish life were obscured by his controversial opposition to the Easter Rising (1916) and membership of the Boundary Commission (1923). Retiring from political life (1927), he embarked on further scholarship and served as president of several learned societies (Irish History Society, 1935–45; Royal Society of Antiquaries of Ireland, 1937–40; Royal Irish Academy, 1940–3). He received many honours, including election to the Academie des inscriptions et des Belles Lettres of France.

C.P. Curran said that 'MacNeill's study was not a cell, but the sally-port from which our state was established.' MacNeill was a quintessential scholar revolutionary, initiating a cultural revolution in Irish studies, founding the Irish Volunteers from which derives the modern Irish Army, and thereafter playing a seminal role in the nascent state. He was without any personal political ambition. With a suspicion of doctrinaire politics typical of an Antrim glensman, his self-effacement and lack of political ambition led to his virtual exclusion from a national pantheon whose very existence sprang from his unique initiatives.

Reading

Curran, C.P., 'Obituary', *Sunday Independent* (21 October 1945).

MacNeill, Eoin, 'A plea and a plan for the extension of the movement to preserve and spread the Gaelic language in Ireland', *Gaelic Journal* 6 (March 1893).

——'The North began', *Claideamh Soluis* 15, no. [34] 814 (5 November 1913).

Martin, F.X. and Byrne, F.J. (eds), *The Scholar Revolutionary* (Shannon: Irish University Press, 1973).

Tierney, Michael, *Eoin MacNeill: Scholar and Man of Action, 1867–1945* (Oxford: Clarendon Press, 1981).

BRIDÍN TIERNEY

McNeill, Janet (*b*.1907–) Novelist. Born Dublin, 14 September. The daughter of a minister, McNeill was educated in England and Scotland (MA, St Andrew's University). Before marriage, she was a journalist with the *Belfast Telegraph*. She was chair of the Belfast Centre of PEN (Ireland) and between 1959 and 1964 served on the Advisory Council of the BBC. After many years in Belfast, she moved to Bristol.

Well known as a writer of novels for children, McNeill has also written a number of stylish novels for adults, most of them charting the complex, mundane territory of middle age with perception and intelligence. The confidence and polish of these novels belie the sexual and psychological insecurities of her chief characters; so too do the middle-class, middle-brow exteriors of their lives. McNeill's settings are chiefly middle-class Belfast to begin with, seamlessly and effortlessly switching in later novels to middle-class England. *The Maiden Dinosaur* (1964) is one of the best Irish novels of its generation, successfully blending regional colour with broader, at times existential concerns. *Talk to Me* (1965) and *The Small Widow* (1967) are also notable amidst a quiet stream of highly readable, at times disturbing novels. Her most recent works are *Tea at Four O'clock* (1988) and *We Three Kings* (1992).

Reading

Cronin, John, 'Prose', in Michael Longley (ed.), *Causeway: The Arts in Ulster* (Belfast: Arts Council of Northern Ireland, 1971).

Foster, John Wilson, in *Forces and Themes in Ulster Fiction* (Dublin: Gill and Macmillan, 1974; Totowa NJ: Rowman and Littlefield, 1974).

JOHN WILSON FOSTER

Maconchy, Elizabeth (1901–94).Composer. Of Irish lineage, Maconchy is a graduate of the Royal College of Music in London, where she studied with Charles Wood and Ralph Vaughan Williams; she pursued further studies in Prague with Octavia Scholarship.

The suite for orchestra *The Land* was performed at the Promenade Concerts in 1930, and she was awarded the *Daily Telegraph* chamber music prize for her oboe quintet in 1933. Her work demonstrates a forward-looking style which is yet founded on tonality. The large output covers many genres and includes operas – for some of which she either adapted or provided her own libretto – orchestral works, vocal and choral pieces – including settings of six pieces by Yeats for soprano, female choir and small ensemble – and chamber music. The 13 string quartets (1933–79) are among her most personal statements and provide a good introduction to her work. Of her craft, she records: 'Being a composer is a life-sentence from which there is no escape.'

JOSEPH RYAN

McQuaid, John Charles (1895–1973) Churchman. Born Cootehill, County Cavan, 28 July. McQuaid was educated at St Patrick's College, Cavan; at Blackrock College, Dublin; at Clongowes Wood College; at University College, Dublin; and in Rome. His outstanding intellectual and administrative ability was early recognized. He became president of Blackrock College in 1931, and archbishop of Dublin in 1940. His episcopate of over 30 years was characterized by formidable energy in administration, intense compassion for the poor and weak, and rigid transmontane authoritarianism. His achievements included the construction of scores of churches and secondary schools, the foundation in 1950 of the Dublin Institute of Catholic Sociology (now the Dublin Institute of Adult Education), and the establishment of the Catholic Social Service Conference (1941) and the Catholic Social Welfare Bureau to help emigrants (1942). He imposed an iron discipline on his priests; favoured total segregation of the sexes in education; decreed the dissolution of organizations set up to promote Catholic dialogue with Protestants and Jews; forbade Catholics, 'on pain of mortal sin', to attend Trinity College, Dublin, without

371

episcopal permission; and played a leading role in the mother–and–child scheme controversy. In private life he was kind and humorous. The key to his character and actions may lie in his conviction that he was personally responsible for the salvation of every soul in his archdioces.

Reading

Whyte, John H., *Church and State in Modern Ireland* (Gill and Macmillan/Barnes and Noble, 1980).

JAMES DOWNEY

McWilliam, F. E. (1909–92) Sculptor. Born Banbridge, County Down; died London. The son of a doctor and christened Frederick Edward, McWilliam studied at Belfast School of Art and at the Slade School in London, before making a lengthy stay in Paris. Returning to London, he showed with the English surrealists and was a respected avant-garde figure when war broke out. He served with the RAF, and after the war taught at the Slade until 1968, while acquiring an international reputation as an artist (Sao Paolo Biennale, 1957). A versatile craftsman, working in bronze, wood, stone and even cement, he ranged from abstract works to large-scale figure pieces such as *Princess Macha* (Altnagelvin Hospital, Derry). The leading Irish sculptor of his generation, he is represented in many collections, both Irish and overseas, including the Tate Gallery, MOMA in New York, and in Antwerp, Ottawa, Chicago, Perth and Adelaide. Retrospectives were mounted in Belfast and Dublin in 1981, and at the Tate in 1989.

BRIAN FALLON

Madden, Anne (1932–) Painter. Born London. Of Irish and Anglo-Chilean origin, Madden grew up in Ireland and now lives and works in the south of France. She studied at the Chelsea School of Art, London, and has exhibited in Dublin, London, Paris, Barcelona and New York since the 1950s. In 1965 she represented Ireland at the *Quatrième Biennale de Paris*. Retrospective exhibitions of her work have been held at the Ulster Museum in 1974 and at the Royal Hibernian Academy Gallagher Gallery in 1991. Primarily abstract, Madden's paintings derive their power from a sense of place – the Burren, County Clare – and more recently the sea.

Reading

Kearney, Richard, 'Interview with Anne Madden', *Crane Bag* 4, no. 1 (1980).
Towle, Tony, 'Anne Madden at Armstrong', *Art in America* (February 1987).
Dunne, Aidan, 'Introductory essay', in *Anne Madden* (Dublin: RHA Gallagher Gallery, 1991).

DERVAL TUBRIDY

Madden, Richard Robert (1798–1886) Writer. Born 9 Wormwood Gate, Dublin, 20 August; died 3 Vernon Terrace, Booterstown, County Dublin, 5 February. Madden studied medicine in Paris, London and Naples and practised in the Near East between 1824 and 1827. He served as a magistrate in Jamaica, Havana and Africa, showing reforming zeal there and later as colonial secretary for West Australia. He was secretary of the Local Loan Fund Board in Dublin from 1850 to 1880, and wrote books about his travels and experiences and a notable history of the United Irishmen.

Reading

Madden, Richard, *The United Irishmen, Their Lives and Times*, 7 vols (London: James Madden, 1842–6).
—— *The Slave Trade and Slavery* (London: James Madden, 1843).
—— *The Connexion between the Kingdom of Ireland and the Crown of England* (Dublin: Duffy, 1845).

HENRY BOYLAN

Madden, Samuel (1686–1765) Writer and philanthropist. Born Dublin, 23 December; died Manor Waterhouse, County Fermanagh, 31 December. Madden was educated at

Trinity College, Dublin, took holy orders, and obtained a living at Newtownbutler, County Fermanagh, near family estates be inherited in 1703. He helped to found the Dublin Society in 1731 and presented premiums of £300 a year to encourage manufacturers and the arts. He also contributed to premiums for students at Trinity College. His tragedy *Themistocles* was successful in London. His *Reflections and Resolutions* advocated measures to improve the distressed state of the country.

Reading

Madden, Samuel *Themistocles, a Play* (Dublin: Rock, Ewing and Smith, 1729).
——*Reflections and Resolutions* (Dublin: Ewing, 1738).

HENRY BOYLAN

Maginnis, Kenneth (Ken) (1938–) Politician. Maginnis has been Ulster Unionist Party (UUP) MP for Fermanagh-South Tyrone since 1983 and was assembly member for the same constituency 1982–6. A teacher by profession, he served in both the Ulster Special Constabulary and the Ulster Defence Regiment. He has been UUP security spokesperson since 1982 and sought stronger security measures against the IRA in border areas (there were 220 murders in his constituency during the Troubles). There were several attempts on his life. He is a politician of independent outlook and is a long-time supporter of 'responsibility sharing', pioneering the concept on Dungannon District Council. In 1987 he served a brief prison sentence for refusal to pay car tax in protest against the Anglo-Irish Agreement. In November 1990 he drew praise (from nationalists) and criticism (from the Democratic Unionist Party) for attending the inauguration of President Mary Robinson and the installation of Archbishop Cahal Daly. He was a key participant in the 1991–2 Brooke–Mayhew talks. He has argued the Unionist case throughout the Republic and was the first senior Unionist to participate in television debates with Sinn Féin members. A staunch supporter of the Good Friday Agreement, he allied himself with First Minister David Trimble to defend the new poltical order in Northern Ireland. In January 2000 he announced that he would not be a candidate in the next Westminster election.

PATRICK GILLAN

Maguire, Brian (1951–) Painter. Born Dublin. Maguire studied at Dun Laoghaire School of Art (1968–9) and the National College of Art, Dublin (1969–74). He is one of the most successful of the new Irish Expressionists, and is particularly indebted to the work of Patrick Graham. His paintings are about individual isolation, often representing the failure or ambiguity of personal and sexual relations. He also deals with themes of poverty, powerlessness and alienation in the city. Stylistically, his paintings are dark in tone and deliberately coarse in execution. In 2000 he was appointed Head of Fine Art at the NCAD.

Reading

Kuspit, Donald, 'Brian Maguire', in *Brian Maguire: Paintings 1982–1987* (Dublin: Douglas Hyde Gallery, 1988).
Sharpe, Henry J., Lynch, Jim and Dunne, Aidan, *Patrick Graham Brian Maguire: Paintings 1984* (Belfast: Octagon Gallery, 1984).

FELICITY WOOLF

Mahon, Derek (1941–) Poet and verse translator. Born Belfast. Mahon writes sophisticated, amusing and tautly controlled lyrics, whose vision is bleakly metaphysical. His Northern Irish background is usually only an oblique presence in poems that meditate on the complex relationship between art and violence, civility and barbarism, such as 'The Snow Party'. Mahon's secular verses deglamorize the world, reducing it with prophetic irony to a technological scrapyard. Urbanely apocalyptic, he likes to regard humanity as a 'foreclosed species' and takes pleasure in contemplating the aftermath of our civilization. He also transcends a contemporary *Zeitgeist* with witty sympathy by projecting the viewpoint of 'mute phenomena', abandoned habitations, derelict sites ('A Disused Shed in Co. Wexford'), and minor or maverick writers. His is a terminally ironic art where dread is darkened by humour. His published work includes *The Hunt by Night* (1982), *Antartica* (1985) and *Collected Poems* (1999).

ANTOINETTE QUINN

Malone, Edmund (1741–1812) Shakespearean scholar. Born Dublin. Malone entered Trinity College, Dublin, in 1756. In 1763 he went to the Inner Temple in London as a law student, beginning work on the Munster circuit in 1767, a year after his father had been made judge of common pleas. In 1776 he started an edition of Oliver Goldsmith's works, moving (with the aid of an inheritance from his father) to London in 1777, publishing the edition in 1780. He had met Dr Johnson's circle in the 1760s, and now rejoined it. Boswell's *Tour to the Hebrides* was dedicated to Malone in 1785. Later he helped Boswell with the *Life of Johnson*.

Shakespeare had taken up Malone's time before the edition of Goldsmith was completed. In 1778, as a supplement to the second Steevens edition of Shakespeare, he published the first part of his life's main work, an enquiry into the much-disputed chronology of the plays, giving them a sequence and dates that are still close to the received wisdom. His use of the early quartos with their dates, entries in the Stationers' Register and the records of performances at court, together with internal allusions and similar references, set a pattern which has never been replaced. His metrical analysis of the development of Shakespeare's verse style also broke new ground. His place near Johnson also gave him access to Johnson's 1780 edition, in which he published an extensive supplement. This was the first of his studies into the still-unpublished records of Shakespeare's life and stage. Working with the discoveries made by

previous generations of antiquarians, he transcribed most of the records regarded as important today, including Henslowe's papers and Henry Herbert's working diary (now extant only in Malone's notes), with a meticulous care for accuracy. In his edition and in the related essays he established the principle of authenticity in antiquarian studies, and inaugurated the concern to identify the original theatre conditions that has been the dominant principle in Shakespeare studies ever since.

Reading

de Grazia, Margreta, *Shakespeare Verbatim. The Reproduction of Authenticity and the 1790 Apparatus* (Oxford: Clarendon Press, 1991).

Schoenbawn, S., *Shakespeare's lives*, new edn (Oxford: Clarendon Press, 1991).

A.J. GURR

Mangan, James Clarence (1803–49) Translator. A gifted if precocious student, Mangan resented becoming the family breadwinner at the age of 15. However, he cultivated a shaky income from freelance journalism while ostensibly in the successive employment of a solicitor, the Ordnance Survey Department and Trinity College Library. Initial humorous verses gave way to more lucrative translations of fashionable foreign poetry, mostly German, for the *Dublin University Review*, which first appeared in 1833. Mangan was often at best a loose translator and frequently fraudulent when it came to works of more exotic an origin than Germany. However, there are moments when his musical ear for language erupts in works of brilliance, Rueckert's 'Dying Flower' for example. He reached his zenith with his translations of Irish poetry, begun in 1841. Writing for the *Irish Penny Journal* and the *Nation*, his nationalist sympathies produced translations emblematic of Ireland's mournful oppression. 'Dark Rosalleen', translated from the sixteenth-century 'Roisin Dubh', is in Lionel Johnson's words 'the chivalry of a nation's faith struck on a sudden into the immortality of music'. Sacked from Trinity in 1848. Mangan slipped into destitution, aided by a long, studious apprenticeship to alcohol. Renowned for his wit, this errant, eccentric genius died during a cholera epidemic in 1849.

Reading

Mangan, James Clarence, *Poems by James Clarence Mangan* (New York: 1870).
—— *Essays in Prose and Verse* (Dublin: 1884).
—— *The Autobiography of James Clarence Mangan* (Dublin: Dolmen Press, 1968).

TREVOR BUTTERWORTH

Marcus family Emigrated from Lithuania to Ireland in the 1880s. The children of Solomon Marcus and Frances Rebecca (née Goldberg) were born and educated in Cork and now reside on both sides of the Irish Sea. Three members of the family are based in London: **Abraham** (1919–), MB BCh, medical correspondent of the *Observer* (1958–72) and subsequently medical publisher; **Elkan** (1923–), MB BCh, general practitioner; and **Nella** (1929–), LTCL (Music), executive with Decca Record Company (1959–72), music consultant and author of *Careers in Classical Music* (1983) and *Fifty Plus* (1991). Two brothers live in Dublin. **David** (1924–), BL, translator, poet and novelist, is the founder of *Irish Writing* (1946–54) and *Poetry Ireland* (1948–54) and literary editor of the *Irish Press* (1968–86). He is the editor of numerous anthologies, the translator of *The Midnight Court* (1953), and the author of *Six Poems* (1953), *To Next Year in Jerusalem* (1954), *A Land Not Theirs* (1986), *A Land in Flames* (1987), and *Who Ever Heard of an Irish Jew?* (1988). He is married to the Irish novelist, Ita Daley. **Louis** (1936–), BA (Hons), professional film maker, is a member of the Academy of Motion Picture Arts and Sciences (1972) and fellow of Aosdána (1989), with over 50 documentaries and nearly 20 festival awards (including two Academy Award nominations) to his credit. His cinema documentaries in Gaelic for Gael-Linn in the 1960s include *Fleadh Cheoil, Capallology* and *Poc ar Buille*; and his subsequent work for television comprises *The Heritage of Ireland, The Entertainers* and *Hidden Lives*.

FIONA MACINTOSH

Marsh, Narcissus (1638–1713) Archbishop of Armagh. Born 20 December, Hannington; died 2 November. Educated at Oxford, Marsh was ordained deacon and priest in 1662, but resigned when a simoniacal marriage was expected. His success as principal of St Alban Hall led the duke of Ormonde to make him provost of Trinity College, Dublin, in 1678. During extensive rebuilding, the library became inoperative, so he proposed building one 'for public use, where all might have free access'. This became Marsh's library, which was incorporated in 1707, and remained the only public library in Dublin for about 150 years.

It contains three episcopal libraries: that of Edward Stillingfleet of Worcester, the basis of the collection; that of John Stearne of Clogher; and Marsh's collection, largely Oriental texts. It also contains the books of Elias Bouhéreau, a Huguenot refugee, physician, theologian and Greek scholar, and Marsh's first librarian. The fifth library is that of Dr Dudley Loftus, canonist, historian and Orientalist.

Marsh was the first to employ a teacher of Gaelic at Trinity, so that the 30 scholars required by statute to be of Irish extraction should also be able to read and write Gaelic. He helped prepare for publication Bishop Bedell's translation of the Old Testament into Gaelic. An ardent musician and mathematician, he founded the Royal Dublin Society with Petty and Molyneux. He was bishop of Leighlin and Ferns, and archbishop of Cashel, of Dublin and finally of Armagh in 1703. He is buried in St Patrick's Cathedral.

FRED LOWE

Martin, John (Cornelius the Irishman) (1549?–75) Cabin boy and heretic. John's father, a sacristan at Cork cathedral, died when John was a youth. His mother then married a tailor called Cornelius, who renamed the lad 'William Cornelius'. The family left Ireland 'due to great privations', and settled in Padstow, England, where the tailor died. John's mother became blind, and he led her from door to door, begging. Next, John joined the flagship of John Hawkins's expedition of 1567–8 as a cabin boy: his incompetence meant he was soon demoted to the even lower rank of 'sweeper'. With the defeat of Hawkins by the colonial Spanish authorities off the coast of Mexico in 1568, John was amongst the 80 men taken prisoner. After an initial period of surveillance the prisoners were allowed to settle in Mexico: John eventually established himself as a barber-surgeon with a wife and child in the remote village of La Trinidad in Guatemala.

We know so much about this unpromising Irish migrant because, in 1572, most probably in response to the raids of Francis Drake, the Inquisition was established in Mexico, and the records of its interrogations have survived. The English prisoners were rounded up, questioned, tortured, and assigned various punishments. One, George Reaveley, was executed. 'Juan Martinez', in distant Guatemala, was missed in that first round-up. He was located and brought to Mexico City in 1574. If Reaveley has been hailed as the first Protestant martyr in America, poor John Martin can be seen as a martyr of another kind, the powerless, solitary migrant, making his way, as best he can, in a world he cannot influence. Ground between the mill-stones of the Reformation and the Counter-Reformation, the offences of which he was accused were too intellectual, too theological for his understanding. Had he betrayed his Irish Catholic faith when he settled in 'Lutherite' England? What the Inquisitors wanted from John Martin was abject submission expressed in a consistent narrative, and this he was unable to supply. He was garrotted and his body burnt at the *auto-da-fé* in Mexico City on 6 March 1575.

Reading

Hair, P.E.H., 'An Irishman before the Mexican Inquisition, 1574–5', *Irish Historical Studies* XVII, no. 67 (March 1971).

Quinn, David B., *Ireland and America: Their Early Associations, 1500–1640* (Liverpool: Liverpool University Press, 1991).

Unwin, Rayner, *The Defeat of John Hawkins: A Biography of his Third Slaving Voyage* (London: Allen and Unwin, 1960).

PATRICK O'SULLIVAN

Martin, Philip (1947–) Pianist and composer. Born Dublin. Martin was educated at Read Pianoforte School, at the Royal Academy of Music in London, and privately with Louis Kentner. Martin has an established reputation as a performer, regularly appearing as soloist with major orchestras. Later occasional creative influences included Franz Reizenstein, Lennox Berkeley, Elizabeth Maconchy and Richard Rodney Bennett. Compositions include over 100 songs written for his wife, the soprano Penelope Price Jones. Alongside the many chamber works and compositions in smaller forms are two piano concertos. The first was completed in 1986 and premièred by the composer with the RTE symphony orchestra in Dublin in 1987. The second, with the Joycean subtitle *A Day in the City*, was commissioned to commemorate Dublin's position as the European City of Culture in 1991. Cast in one continuous movement, it was first given in June of that year by the composer with the National Symphony Orchestra, conducted by Howard Williams.

JOSEPH RYAN

Martyn, Edward (1859–1923) Playwright. Born 31 January; died 5 December. Martyn was the elder of two sons of John Martyn JP of Tulira Castle, Araranan, County Galway, and his wife Anne Mary Josephine Smith, daughter of James Smith JP or Masonbrook, County Galway. He was educated by the Jesuits in Ireland, at Beaumont College, and then at Christ Church, Oxford. He died unmarried. Tulira Castle passed to his father's first cousin Mary, wife of the 3rd Lord Hemphill.

MÁIRE MacCONGHAIL

Martyn, Francis Victor (Ferenc) (1899–1986). Painter. Born 16 June, Hungary. Martyn was the son of Arthur Martyn and Grizella Piatsck. His grandfather Robert Martyn of Doebeg, County Sligo, who was a major in the Austrian Service, married in 1802 a Hungarian and settled there. Arthur Martyn (Ferenc's father) was a fifth cousin of Edward Martyn, playwright. Their common ancestor was Oliver Martyn of Tullira, County Galway, MP for Galway (1689).

MÁIRE MacCONGHAIL

Marx, Karl (1818–83) wrote a considerable amount about Ireland, mainly in the form of newspaper articles, speeches, in correspondence to his friends, and fleetingly in *Capital*. Interest in his opinions on Ireland has revolved around an attempt to come to grips with Marx's understanding of colonialism.

Marx argued that Ireland's poverty and misery were caused by British oppression and exploitation: 'Every time Ireland was about to develop industrially, she was crushed and reconverted into a purely agricultural land...''Land is Life''. Land became the great object of pursuit. The people had now before them the choice between the occupation of land, *at any rent*, or *starvation*.' Consequently Marx argued that the main cause of industrial decline in Ireland was the absence of tariffs needed to protect this industry from British competition. Therefore he advocated Irish independence and an agrarian revolution. By 1869, while mobilizing the General Council of the First International to support the Irish amnesty movement (to free a number of the Fenians condemned for terrorist activities), Marx went so far as to say that: 'The English working class will *never accomplish anything* before it has got rid of Ireland. The lever must be applied in Ireland. That is

why the Irish Question is so important for the social movement in general.'

Marx's assertion that national liberation in Ireland had to precede the proletarian revolution should not be seen as a general rule to be applied to the colonies. Most of his discussions of Ireland were of an empirical nature, and therefore they lack the necessary rigour of his theoretical pronouncements in *Capital*. However, although Marx lacked an adequate theory of capitalism's international relations between countries, he did begin with Ireland and India in the colonial context. If one is to develop a theory of colonialism within the Marxist framework, Ireland is probably the case study to begin from.

Reading

Hazelkorn, Ellen, '*Capital* and the Irish Question', *Science and Society* 44 (1980).

Marx, K. and Engels, F., *Ireland and the Irish Question* (Moscow: Progress Publishers, 1971).

Vujacic, Ivan, 'Marx and Engels on development and underdevelopment: the restoration of a certain coherence', *History of Political Economy* 20, no. 3 (1988).

EAMONN SLATER

mathematics, contributions to The interest during the seventeenth century in surveying and cartography, and in particular the Down Survey carried out by Sir William Petty in 1655–6, provided an important stimulus to mathematical studies in Ireland. The first professorship of mathematics in Dublin University was established by the parliamentary commissioners in 1652, with the intention of producing trained surveyors. Another important development was the founding in 1684, at the instigation of William Molyneux, of the Dublin Philosophical Society, which promoted the scientific renaissance, the new learning, in Ireland. Yet although there was some serious interest in mathematics through the eighteenth century, and this was encouraged and given a new focus with the establishment of the Royal Irish Academy in 1785, one has to wait until the 1820s and 1830s to find major Irish contributions to mathematics and theoretical physics (or natural philosophy as it was then called).

The key development, which laid the foundation for the Dublin mathematical school, was the radical reform of the Trinity College, Dublin, mathematical curriculum by Bartholomew Lloyd, who was professor of mathematics from 1813 to 1822 and later became provost. Lloyd brought the syllabus up to date, introducing, in particular, the new ideas which had recently been and continued to be developed in France. The result was that able students were brought into contact with the subject as it was actually developing and could share in the excitement of current research.

The most brilliant of those students was William Rowan Hamilton, whose profoundly original contributions in several quite different areas of mathematics – optics, dynamics and algebra – have earned him a place among the great mathematicians.

James Mac Cullagh, who graduated in 1828 just four years after Hamilton, was a superb geometer who in turn trained and inspired a new generation of students. His own most important research contribution was the construction of a model of the aether which was both self-consistent and in accord with the observed phenomena of light propagation. A proud and patriotic man, he was appalled at the lack of interest in his country's heritage and history, and used his savings to buy the Cross of Cong for the academy as the start of a national collection. Mac Cullagh was unfortunately prone to depression and took his own life at the age of 38.

George Salmon, born in Cork in 1819, was the most distinguished of Mac Cullagh's students. He made significant original contributions in geometry and in the theory of invariants, but is best known for his four textbooks in geometry and in algebra. Translated into several languages and published in many editions, these books exercised a major influence. Salmon was also a theologian of distinction and was provost of Trinity College from 1888 to 1904.

In 1849, George Boole was appointed to the chair of mathematics in the Queen's College in Cork. Although not an Irishman by birth, Boole settled in Cork and his major work was carried out there. *The Laws of Thought*, published in 1854, laid the foundations of mathematical and symbolic logic. The symbolic calculus which he developed, now known as Boolean algebra, has proved to be central to the analysis of logical processes in computer design.

George Gabriel Stokes (1819–1903) was one of the leading mathematical physicists of his time, but although born and brought up in Ireland his entire working career was in Cambridge, where he was Lucasian professor of mathematics. His successor in the Lucasian chair, Joseph Larmor, was also an Irishman, who held the chair of mathematics in Queen's College, Galway, before his Cambridge appointment.

The most prominent Irish mathematician of the present century was J.L. Synge (born 1897). Synge was a versatile and original applied mathematician who worked on a wide variety of problems. His most important contribution was in relativity theory; the powerful geometrical intuition which he brought to bear on this significantly influenced its subsequent development.

Reading

McConnell, A.J., 'The Dublin mathematical school in the first half of the nineteenth century', *Proceedings of the Royal Irish Academy L* 75–88 (1945).

Spearman, T.D., 'Mathematics and theoretical physics', in T. O'Raifeartaigh (ed.), *The Royal Irish Academy: A Bicentennial History, 1785–1985* (Dublin: 1985).

——'Four hundred years of mathematics', in C.H. Holland (ed.), *Trinity College Dublin and the Idea of a University* (Dublin: Trinity College Dublin Press, 1991).

DAVID SPEARMAN

Maturin family Of Huguenot descent, Maturins served the Church of Ireland through several generations. The Rev. Peter Maturin (d. 1741) was dean of Killala and his son, the Rev. Gabriel James Maturin (1700–46), succeeded Swift as dean of St Patrick's Cathedral, Dublin, in 1745. Gabriel's son, William (b. 1745), employed in the Irish postal service, was father of the novelist, dramatist and religious controversialist, the Rev. Charles Robert Maturin (1780–1824). Maturin's first novel, *Fatal Revenge* (1807) – rationalized gothic after the manner of Ann Radcliffe – was succeeded by *The Wild Irish Boy* (1808) and *The Milesian Chief* (1812), influenced by Sydney Owenson, Lady Morgan. A much-admired tragedy, *Bertram* (1816), acted in London by Edmund Kean, was followed by two less successful plays, *Manuel* and *Fredolfo*, and a novel, *Women; or Pour et Contre* (1818), a study of religious divisions in contemporary Dublin. Though the high church sympathies of his son, the Rev. William Maturin (1803–87), were later to arouse extreme Protestant anger, Maturin's own religious convictions are evident in his *Sermons* (1819), *Five Sermons on the Errors of the Roman Catholic Church* (1824) and his final novel, *The Albigenses* (1824). Maturin's masterpiece, *Melmoth the Wanderer* (1820), is a study of obsession which fuses the gothic with a reworking of myth – Faust, the Ancient Mariner, and the Wandering Jew – in a narrative of extraordinary complexity beginning and ending in contemporary Ireland. *Melmoth* was extravagantly admired in the nineteenth century, by none more so than by Baudelaire, who compared Maturin, in his treatment of melancholy and incurable despair, with Beethoven, Byron and Poe. Following his imprisonment, Oscar Wilde chose as a *nom d'éxil* 'Sebastien Melmoth'.

IAN CAMPBELL ROSS

Maxton, Hugh (b. 1947) Poet, translator and art reviewer. Born outside Aughrim, County Wicklow. Maxton was educated at Trinity College, Dublin. His early work (*Stones*, 1970, and *The Noise of the Fields*, 1974, a Poetry Book Society Choice) was deeply marked by archaeological and historical images. *Jubilee for Renegades* (1982) signalled a turning towards contemporary political themes, and *At the Protestant Museum* (1985) brought together a personal history and a Continental European frame of reference. This latter is also exemplified in his translation of several Hungarian poets into English (see in particular *Between: Selected Poems of Agnes Nemes Nagy*, 1988). *The Engraved Passion: New and Selected Poems 1970–1991* (1992) contains his best work to date, though *Swiftmail*, a poem in regular rhyming stanzas dedicated to Derek Mahon, indicates a deepening satirical commitment. Maxton's work is noted for its experimentalism, cultural and political radicalism, and hermetic tendencies. He has also published several important critical studies, including *Dissolute Characters: Irish Literary History through Balzac, Le Fanu, Yeats, and Bowen* (1993).

GERALD DAWE

May, Frederick (1911–85) Composer. Born Dublin. The Irish composer with the most original creative voice of his generation, May commenced musical education in his native Dublin with Larchet at the Royal Irish Academy of Music and then at Trinity College, Dublin (MusB 1931). He moved to the Royal College of Music, London, where he continued studies for three years with Gordon Jacob and with R. Vaughan Williams, whom he greatly admired. May's first major work was completed there, the short *Scherzo for Orchestra* (1933). It helped win him a travelling studentship to Vienna to study with Alban Berg. But Berg's untimely death in December 1935 meant May worked under Egon Wellesz instead. The String Quartet in C minor on which he was engaged at this time remains one of his finest achievements, and one of the first great musical statements of the era by an Irish composer. It is an intense work in one continuous movement with three subsections, which lasts in total some 30 minutes. A number of independent orchestral pieces separate the quartet from his other towering expression, *Songs from Prison*, written for baritone and enlarged orchestra. It is a work of conscience, completed in 1941, which reflects his strongly held political views. Increasing deafness, caused by otosclerosis, was but one of many troubles that diverted May from composition in his later years. Thus the orchestral work *Sunlight and Shadow* (1955) stands alone as his last major work.

JOSEPH RYAN

medicine, contributions to An impression of the rather narrow scale of Ireland's early contributions to medicine may be obtained from an authorative source, *Bibliotheca Osleriana*. This catalogue of Sir William Osler's collection illustrating the history of medicine and science acknowledged just three Irish contributors to its 'Bibliotheca Prima' – 'the essential literature grouped about the men of the first rank'. These were the cherists, Boyle and Black, and the philosopher George Berkeley. Nine from Ireland (some of whom are referred to below) figure as authors in the 'Bibliotheca Secunda'.

The propriety of including Joseph Black, discoverer of 'fixed air' (carbon dioxide), on an Irish roll of honour is arguable (born in Bordeaux, where his father, a native of Belfast, followed the wine trade, his early education was imparted in Ireland and completed in Scotland, where his life's work was accomplished), and illustrates a possible distortion of medical history when the bias of patriotism is introduced. But ideas know no boundaries and it is proposed that in this outline the significant advances of Irish contributors, whether made at home or abroad, shall be credited to Ireland's medical schools. These did not exist in the medieval period. Medicine was then practised as a hereditary right by certain families whose members had access to texts based on Greco-Arabic sources.

The first medical book printed in Dublin was *Pathologia hereditaria generalis* (1619) by Dermot O'Meara, whose son, Edmund, ventured in 1665 to criticize Thomas Willis's teachings on fever. The latter's polemic defence by Richard Lower evoked support for Edmund O'Meara's reactionary viewpoint two years later from Conlan Cashin. The interest in scientific matters evinced by Edmund O'Meara's contemporaries in Ireland led to the foundation of the Dublin Philosophical Society, and Allen Mullen (author of *An Account of the Elephant*, 1682) demonstrated the vascularity of the lens of the eye. Bernard Connor (elected a fellow of the Royal Society in 1695) sent a description to the *Philosophical Transactions* of a skeleton displaying what is now called ankylosing spondylitis.

Ireland was in the van of an eighteenth-century movement to provide hospitals for the poor. The Charitable Infirmary founded by six Dublin surgeons was the first 'voluntary hospital' in the British Isles. The first lying-in hospital, the forerunner of the Rotunda Hospital, was established by Dr Bartholomew Mosse in George's Lane in 1745. The urge to explain patients' ailments in the new hospitals and to expedite their cures was a potent stimulus to research. Abraham Colles, Robert W. Smith and Edward Hallaran Bennett described certain common fractures, and 'a Colles' or 'a Bennett' are terms that remain in clinical parlance. William Wallace demonstrated the infectivity of the secondary stage of syphilis and introduced potassium iodide as an ameliorative remedy for that distressing disease. The terms 'Cheyne-Stokes breathing' and 'Stokes Adams syndrome' designate important disorders first described in Dublin. Robert Graves recognized a glandular disorder commonly called 'Graves disease', and with his colleague, William Stokes (author of the first book in English on the stethoscope), introduced bedside teaching at the Meath Hospital. The Dublin Pathological Society founded in 1838 set a pattern copied elsewhere. James Bovell, one of Sir William Osler's mentors, was a founder member.

Samuel Haughton, who was both a divine and a medical doctor, won Osler's approval with papers on diabetes and the composition of urine. His more important contribution was to devise a formula to calculate the length of the drop, which transformed judicial hanging from slow strangulation to immediate death. Sir Dominic Corrigan and Robert Bentley Todd, surprisingly, did not gain entry to 'Bibliotheca Secunda'. Corrigan, the first Catholic to play a leading role in the College of Physicians, described aortic incompetence and popularized 'Corrigan's button' to apply counter-irritation. Todd settled in London and was a founder of King's College Hospital; he described 'Todd's paralysis' (temporary weakness following an epileptic seizure) and introduced the useful terms 'afferent' and 'efferent' into neurophysiology.

Anatomy remained a life-long interest for nineteenth-century surgeons, and eponyms claimed for Ireland include Alcock's canal, Ball's valve, Crampton's muscle, Houston's fold, Jacob's membrane, etc. Arthur Jacob, a pioneer eye-surgeon, also described 'Jacob's ulcer', now called basal cell carcinoma. Sir William Wilde, one of the founders of otology in the British Isles, introduced 'Wilde's incision' in mastoid surgery and published an influential textbook, *Practical Observations on Aural Surgery* (1853).

Hypodermic medication was first administered by Francis Rynd in 1844 at the Meath Hospital; Sir Francis Cruise devised a distally lit cystoscope; the 'Freyer' and 'Millin' methods of prostatectomy were introduced by Irish surgeons working in London. Irish graduates who excelled in neurology include Sir Gordon Holmes and Robert Foster Kennedy, working in London and New York respectively. Minor advances, however useful, may fail to gain kudos for their discoverers, in which category is a curative technique for treating ingrowing toe-nails with phenol, devised by Royal Army Medical Corps surgeon, Charles J. Holmes (a graduate of Queen's College, Cork), during the Boer War, and rediscovered recently by chiropodists.

Adrian Stokes (a grandson of William Stokes) took a motor-cycle and sidecar with him to France in 1914 and provided the British Army's first mobile laboratory. His experience with gassed soldiers enabled him to improve methods of giving oxygen. He used the rhesus monkey as an experimental animal to study yellow fever in West Africa, where he died in 1928.

Osler was impressed by the presence of Irish medical graduates wherever he went, but the Rockefeller Foundation, appealed to for funds in the early 1920s, noted that Belfast, Cork and Galway each had its medical school, with three in Dublin for good measure, and reported adversely on this multiplicity. Unsympathetic to sectarian divisions and local political pressures, the Rockefeller Foundation did little to assist the Irish schools, but gave considerable support to the Irish Free State's emerging public health system and helped selected individuals in the university departments. The financial plight of the clinical departments was ameliorated in the 1930s by the Irish Hospitals Sweepstakes, which contributed to a newly established Medical Research Council.

Edward Conway, first professor of biochemistry at University College, Dublin, invented a microburette and diffusion unit ('the Conway unit') to facilitate microanalysis. His basic research was concerned with the movement of ions across cell membranes. Vincent Barry worked on the chemotherapy of tuberculosis and leprosy. He introduced drugs effective in the treatment of the latter which have been used in the Third World.

The eponyms 'Kerley's lines', 'Burkitt's lymphoma' and 'Swan-Ganz catheter' relate to Irish contributions fashioned abroad, but the 'Romano-Ward syndrome' commemorates a contemporary Dublin paediatrician. For a country of its size and resources, Ireland's medical profession manages to maintain high standards in treatment, teaching and research. Its lecturers are invited to distant forums, and its researchers are represented in prestigious foreign journals. The 'Fegan' treatment of varicose veins, the invention of an artificial knee, the manifestations of coeliac disease, the benefits of the cardiac ambulance, the surgery of epilepsy, the molecular biology of vulnerability to malignant hyperthermia, the elucidation of the biochemical fault underlying subacute combined degeneration of the spinal cord, and the discovery of the gene associated with retinitis pigmentosa are among the diverse subjects fruitfully studied in Ireland in recent decades.

J.B. LYONS

Mercier, Vivian Herbert Samuel (1919–89) Literary scholar and critic. Born Dublin. Mercier was educated at Portora Royal School and Trinity College, Dublin. He went to the United States in 1947, where he taught English literature successively at Bennington College, the City College of New York, the University of Colorado at Boulder, and the University of California, Santa Barbara. Author of *The Irish Comic Tradition* (1952), and editor, with David H. Greene, of *1000 Years of Irish Prose* (1952), Mercier, whose research had focused on Anglo-Irish writing, addressed himself to contemporary French literature with *The New Novel: From Queneau to Pinget* (1971). This book, which emphasizes the contributions of Joyce and Beckett to the theory and practice of the New Novel, was followed by *Beckett/Beckett* (1977). Of *Waiting for Godot*, Mercier memorably remarked that it was 'a play in which nothing happens, *twice*'.

MARY LYDON

Merriman, Brian (*c.*1749–1805) Poet. Born, reputedly illegitimately, in Ennistymon, County Clare. Merriman spent most of his life teaching and farming in Feakle before moving to Limerick city around 1802, where he lived until his death. He is remembered for a single poem, *Cúirt an Mheán Oíche* (*The Midnight Court*), composed around 1780. The poem, rightly regarded as the greatest comic work in Gaelic literature, focuses on aspects of sexual life in late eighteenth-century Ireland as debated by a young girl and an old man before an imaginary assembly of women. The vigorous advocacy, ribald

humour and radical rhetoric of their polemic account for much of the poem's lasting popular appeal.

Reading

Ó Crualaoich, Gearóid, 'The vision of liberation in *Cúirt an Mheán Oíche*', in *Folia Gadelica* (Cork: Cork University Press, 1983).
Ó Tuama, Seán, 'Brian Merriman and his court', *Irish University Review* 11 (Autumn 1981), pp. 149–64.

LIAM HARTE

Methodist church After Ireland's first Methodist society was formed in Dublin in 1747, Methodist leader John Wesley soon came calling. It was the first of 21 visits spread over 42 years.

These were years of impressive growth. The undogmatic, experiential piety, disciplined personal life and intense community experience characteristic of Methodism proved attractive to many. By 1791, the year of Wesley's death, Irish Methodists numbered 14,158 members (*c*.42,000 adherents), and it was an increasingly Irish movement. In 1752 the first Irish Methodist Conference was dominated by English preachers; by 1789 nearly all the 50 preachers were Irish.

These were also years of controversy. Already in 1752 Irish Methodism suffered its first division. Many Church of Ireland leaders were incensed by Methodism's disdain for ecclesiastical protocol. Methodist preachers drew the suspicion of Catholic clergy by preaching whenever and wherever possible (sometimes in Gaelic), which also attracted sometimes volatile crowds. Calvinist fellow evangelicals despised Methodism's Arminian theology.

After Wesley's death, growth continued (to a high of 44,314 members in 1844), and so did controversy. Although the old external conflicts remained, perhaps the dominant one was internal. Wesley wanted Methodism to remain an Anglican reform movement, but in 1816 Irish Methodism split into Wesleyans, who organized as a separate church, and Primitive Wesleyans, who retained the Church of Ireland connection. Methodist unity was restored in 1878, after disestablishment of the Church of Ireland (1870) had weakened Primitive loyalty.

Today Methodism is much reduced in numbers; there were 19,217 members and a total community of 58,741 at the end of 1991. The reasons are complex, but the most important is probably emigration – which has also made the Irish hugely influential in world Methodism. Relations with other churches are long since transformed, and Methodists are integrally involved in ecumenism and in a range of pan-evangelical organizations.

Reading

Cole, R. Lee, *History of Methodism in Ireland, 1860–1960* (Belfast: Irish Methodist Publishing, 1960).

Crookshank, Charles H., *History of Methodism in Ireland*, 3 vols (Belfast and London: T. Woolmer, 1885–8).

Hempton, David, 'Methodism in Irish society, 1770–1830', *Transactions of the Royal Historical Society* 36 (1986).

Hempton, David and Hill, Myrtle, *Evangelical Protestantism in Ulster Society, 1740–1890* (London and New York: Routledge, 1992).

Taggart, Norman, W., *The Irish in World Methodism, 1760–1900* (London: Epworth Press, 1986).

JOSEPH LIECHTY

Miami Showband Dublin-based five-member band. Returning from a Banbridge dance on 31 July 1975, the popular band's minibus was stopped at a bogus Ulster Defence Regiment roadblock near Newry. When two men were blown up attempting to plant a bomb in the minibus, the patrol opened fire, killing three Miami Showband members. Apparently the Ulster Volunteer Force intended to make it appear the band were smuggling arms over an underpatrolled border. Two men were convicted. The incident was considered one of the most horrific sectarian attacks of 1975.

Reading

Bruce, Steve, *The Red Hand: Protestant Paramilitaries in Northern Ireland* (Oxford: Oxford University Press, 1992).

KARLIN J. LILLINGTON

Middleton, Colin (1910–83) Painter. Born Belfast. Middleton worked from 1927 to 1947 as a damask designer, but won a scholarship to Belfast College of Art in 1932. He belonged to the strikingly gifted Northern generation of Dillon, Campbell, O'Neill, etc., and like them he exhibited regularly at the Irish Exhibition of Living Art in Dublin; he also had many one-man exhibitions, including a number at Tooth's gallery in London. He was created an MBE in 1969. A retrospective exhibition was mounted in Belfast and Dublin in 1976. There are works by him in public collections in Dublin, Belfast and Melbourne. Middleton's frequent changes of style sometimes baffled his admirers, since he used Expressionist, surreal and abstract elements when he chose, but there is a rugged, painterly integrity which is constant through all these.

BRIAN FALLON

missionary activity overseas The earliest overseas missionary work of the post-Reformation Church of Ireland took place under the auspices of the Society for the Propagation of the Gospel and the Church Missionary Society (the latter a product of the evangelical movement), whose Irish auxiliaries were founded in 1701 and 1814, respectively. Three indigenous societies were the Leprosy Mission (1874), which was interdenominational, and two, part of a wider university movement, that had their origins in a meeting in Trinity College, Dublin, in 1885: the Dublin University Mission to Fukien (now the Dublin University Mission to the Far East) and the Dublin University Mission to Chota Nagpur (1892), whose primary and secondary schools for girls and boys, teaching hospital, and St Columba's third-level co-educational college continue to serve the Church of North India. By 1992 the association of missionary societies active within the Church of Ireland listed 14 member bodies, who fielded a total of 65 missionary workers (expatriates), mainly in East Africa, Nepal and South America, in such varied work as Bible college lecturing, clean-water supply, famine relief, rural development, community-based care, and education.

KENNETH MILNE

Mitchel, John (1815–75). Nationalist and political journalist. Born Camnish, County Derry, 3 November; died 20 March. The son of John Mitchel, a radical presbyterian minister with strong Unitarian sympathies, and his wife, Mary Haslett, Mitchel was educated at Newry and between 1830 and 1834 at Trinity College, Dublin, apparently under the country list system (a scheme which enabled poorer students to receive tuition at home while coming to Dublin only to take examinations). At any rate, he played no part in the political or cultural debates then current among undergraduates, and appears to have had no contact at that time with Thomas Davis or any of the other Trinity-educated Young Irelanders with whom he would later be associated. After a brief spell as a bank clerk in Derry, Mitchel began practice as a solicitor in Banbridge in 1840. His private correspondence at this time shows a growing interest in politics, and in 1845 he abandoned the law to join the staff of the *Nation*, the organ of the forward Young Ireland pressure group who were growing impatient with the moderate tactics of O'Connell.

As the Irish Famine worsened, Mitchel rapidly moved beyond his colleagues, and a series of incendiary articles which he published resulted in the paper's editor, Charles Gavan Duffy, being prosecuted for seditious libel. Early in 1848 Mitchel founded his own paper, the *United Irishman*, where his own uncompromising calls for a general rebellion led to a charge of sedition and his conviction

under the emergency powers of a new Treason Felony Act. Sentenced to 14 years' imprisonment in the penal colony of Van Diemen's Land, Mitchel recorded his disillusion with conventional Irish politics, his hatred of British imperialism and his personal education as an extreme insurrectionary in his *Jail Journal*, a powerful piece of prison literature, which became a central text in the canon of Irish revolutionary nationalism.

In the summer of 1853 Mitchel escaped from the colony, with the help of Irish-American sympathizers, and established in New York the *Citizen*, a paper designed to give voice to radical Irish-American anti-British opinion. But the editor soon confused and disappointed his readership by displacing emigrant concerns with an increasingly virulent defence of southern slavery. Mitchel himself soon made clear that he regarded the defence of slavery as a priority by resigning his post, settling in Tennessee, going on tour as a public spokesman for the south and eventually, in 1857, founding the *Southern Citizen* as a mouthpiece for the slave cause. Thereafter, through war and defeat, Mitchel remained a stalwart defender of the south, quarrelling even with Jefferson Davis, whom he regarded as too moderate, and earning by his characteristically unrepentant writings a second (brief) term of imprisonment, this time at the hands of the federal administration in 1865.

After the war Mitchel resumed his interest in Irish politics by founding another paper, the *Irish Citizen*, in New York, but he refused to identify himself either with the Fenian Brotherhood (then commanding much support in the US) or with the cause of Home Rule, while devoting much of the paper's space to the so-called continuation of his *Jail Journal*, a series which was in fact a vehicle for the rehearsal and vindication of his pro-slavery views. The paper failed to gain readers and ceased publication in 1872. In 1875 Mitchel made a final dramatic return to Irish politics, winning election to Parliament for the Tipperary constituency. The election was invalidated on the grounds that Mitchel was a convicted felon. Again elected with an increased majority, he was on the point of provoking something of a crisis when he died suddenly, and his opponent was returned unopposed.

By the time of this last foray, Mitchel was, in any case, little more than a political symbol. But the defence of slavery which alienated much potential political sympathy and helped marginalize him from mainstream Irish-American politics was more than a piece of reckless self-indulgence. It had its roots in Mitchel's tramautic experience of the Irish Famine and of the events which led up to it. More than any of the Young Irelanders, Mitchel was appalled by what he saw as the predetermined nature of the Irish crisis, of the way in which in its stages it bowed inexorably to the diktats of political economy. Outraged by the doctrine of classical political economy, with its resigned acceptance of inevitable contraction and collapse, but overwhelmed, like so many of his generation, by what appeared to be its powerful and inescapable logic, Mitchel vowed to oppose the operations of this system politically, by radical action and polemical intellectual warfare. This was the object of all of his public utterances in the years after 1847, in his composition of the revolutionary *Jail Journal*, in his contemporary popular histories – notably his *The Last Conquest of Ireland (Perhaps)* – in his editorial work and most ambitiously in his unyielding defence of slavery.

For Mitchel, southern slavery represented the last vestiges of an economic system that was wholly antagonistic to the brutal international capitalism legitimated, if not celebrated, by the doctrines of political economy. It created a culture which for all its abuses generated stability and order and did not subordinate itself to the dictates of a nihilistic determinism. Thus whether slavery could survive or not, its defence as a means of economic production and social organization alternative to commercial capitalism provided a fine polemical means of demonstrating the

viciousness and cruelty of the modern world system, which had brought misery and ruin to Ireland. And so Mitchel, who had already consciously refashioned himself in the pages of *Jail Journal* as the apotheosis of the Irish patriot, now projected a further image as the unwavering apologist for slavery without any sense of contradiction. It was to prove a foolhardy and costly commitment; but it is full measure of the degree to which Mitchel was prepared to sacrifice himself in waging war against the dominant culture that he believed was destroying his own native land.

Reading

Dillon, William, *The Life of John Mitchel*, 2 vols (London: 1888).

Donnelly, James F., Jr, 'The great famine: its interpreters old and new', *History Ireland* 1, no. 3 (Autumn 1993).

Genovese, Engene, in *The World the Slaveholders Made* (New York: 1969).

Mitchel, John, *The Last Conquest of Ireland (Perhaps)*, author's edn (Glasgow: 1876).

——*Jail Journal* (Dublin: M.H. Gill, 1913).

CIARAN BRADY

Mitchel, John, *Jail Journal* **of** First published serially by the New York *Citizen* in 1854. The *Jail Journal* is one of the most important textual links in the chain which binds the individual to history in Irish nationalist ideology. The first part, the 'Introductory Narrative', is a concise and eloquent Romantic nationalist reading of the Irish past, linking a history of national conquests and persecutions to Mitchel's arrest, imprisonment and exile in 1848. 'The general history of a nation', he writes, 'may fitly preface the personal memoranda of a solitary captive.' The *Jail Journal* proper then develops Mitchel's radical, often sardonic, critique of coercive concepts such as 'civilisation', 'progress' and 'amelioration' as he records his imprisonment in Bermuda, South Africa and Tasmania. At the centre of the text is a dialogue between 'The Ego' and the 'Doppelganger', which builds to the apocalyptic conclusion that 'the world needs to be cleared by a wholesome tornado'. The *Jail Journal* has been almost continuously in print since the mid-nineteenth century, and its influence on generations of militant nationalists has been immense.

CHRIS MORASH

Mitchell, George Francis (1912–) Environmental scientist and historian. Born Dublin. Mitchell was educated at the High School and Trinity College, Dublin. While still in college he was selected to join Professor Knud Jessen of Copenhagen as field assistant during his pioneer studies of Irish bogs. This was the start of a career which was to embrace studies of botany, geology, geography, archaeology, zoology and art. His whole professional life was linked to Trinity College, where he was elected fellow in 1944 and later became professor of quaternary studies. He is the father of the study of quaternary ecology in Ireland, tracing environmental changes since the most recent glaciations. He is a fellow of the Royal Society and an honorary graduate of Queens University, Belfast, the National University and Uppsala University. Mitchell has published numerous accounts of his work, as well as writing on the Irish landscape, in *Where has Ireland Come From?* (1994) and *Reading the Irish Landscape* (1997, joint author).

Reading

Mitchell, Frank, *Shell Guide to Reading the Irish Landscape* (Dublin: Country House, 1986).
—— *The Way that I Followed* (Dublin: Country House, 1990).

MICHAEL JONES

Mitchell, Susan Langstaff (1866–1926) Poet and satirist. Born Carrick-on-Shannon, 5 December; died Dublin, 4 March. Sub-editor of Plunkett's *Irish Homestead*, Mitchell rapidly developed her satirical powers as both journalist and versifier, commenting spicily and sometimes wickedly on the personalities prominent in politics, literature and art during the Irish cultural renaissance. She was a member of the Dublin Hermetic Society. A close friend of AE (George Russell) and the Yeatses, the two opposing sides of her personality are best illustrated in her books *Aids to the Immortality of Certain Persons in Ireland* and *The Living Chalice* (both 1908).

Reading

Kain, R.M., *S. L. Mitchell* (Lewisburg: Bucknell University Press, 1972).
Pyle, H., 'External things and images', in *Irish Arts Review Yearbook* (1991–2).
—— *Susan L. Mitchell* (London: Colin Smythe, 1992).

HILARY PYLE

Modernism may be defined in terms of formal experimentation, including a tendency to abstraction; the subversion of received modes of representation and indeed of the traditional notion of the art work itself; an intensive dialogue with technology; the importance of the 'sublime' and the unconscious; the emancipation of form and colour; and the tendency for a rigid distinction to exist between 'high' (Modernist) art and the generally despised 'mass culture'. Modernism was the dominant artistic practice of the first half of the twentieth century, and is now generally agreed to have been superseded by post modernism, though what the latter term actually means, and whether it involves a continuation of or a radical break with Modernism, is a matter of widespread debate.

In contrast to the leading role played by Modernist writers such as James Joyce, Modernism in the visual arts in Ireland has always lagged behind developments in Europe. This is due in part to the lack of a strong visual tradition in Ireland, which in turn may be traced to the historical defeat of its natural patrons, the Gaelic aristocracy and the Catholic church, as well as to such factors as the Act of Union and general economic impoverishment. Other elements hindering the development of a genuinely innovative Modernism along Continental lines were the post-revolutionary ideal of a 'national school', which laid emphasis on life in the west of Ireland, the pervasive influence of Romanticism, and the widespread absence of a theoretical perspective among Irish Modernists.

Thus, Irish Modernist painters tended to retain a nineteenth-century approach to subject matter, while using techniques based on contemporary Continental styles. Irish artists of the twenties and thirties paid little heed to such European phenomena as Dada or surrealism, the aesthetic and social radicalism of the Bauhaus, or the social and political concerns that motivated some of their Continental counterparts such as Dix, Grosz and Heartfield. Irish Modernists functioned, by and large, to bring about an awareness in Ireland of some recent European artistic developments, rather than to act as innovators. In the key text *Irish Art and Modernism*, S.B. Kennedy traces the origins of Modernism in Ireland to the annual exhibition of the Dublin Sketching Club in December 1884, which included paintings by Whistler. This was the first of a number of exhibitions to be held in Dublin which stimulated some consciousness of modern developments, through exposing the community to artistic influences from abroad. The exhibition '*Modern Paintings*' was held in Dublin in April 1899, including a number of pictures by the French Impressionists. In 1901 Nathaniel Hone and John Butler Yeats held an exhibition arranged by the portrait painter Sarah Purser, an important event in that it stimulated an interest on the part of the art dealer Hugh Lane in both Irish and modern art.

Lane devoted himself to the ideal of a gallery of modern art in Dublin, in order to help bring about an Irish school of painting by exhibiting modern Irish works together with contemporary works by non-Irish artists. The exhibition of modern painting he organized in Dublin in 1904 was the most comprehensive yet seen in the British Isles. Dublin Corporation voted to establish a gallery of modern art, which eventually opened in a temporary premises in 1908 with Lane as its honorary director. But disputes between Lane and the corporation regarding the design and siting of the permanent gallery led to a complicated and long-lasting legal struggle between the Irish and British over the ownership of 39 of the pictures.

In 1920 Paul Henry founded the Society of Dublin Painters, which was important in fostering Modernist painting in Ireland, though characterized by a certain element of dilettantism and a somewhat passive adoption of Continental models. Jack B. Yeats, the son of John Butler Yeats, and generally regarded as the most important Irish painter of the century, was a member of the society from 1920 to 1923. His work is influenced by Van Gogh and Rouault among others.

A striking feature of Irish Modernism is the leading part played by women artists, who unlike their counterparts in other countries have never been 'marginalized'. These included Letitia Hamilton, May Guinness (who was influenced by Matisse), Mary Swanzy (in whose work may be discerned some elements of Expressionism and Futurism), Evie Hone and Mainie Jellett. Jellett and Evie Hone became the only true Irish Cubist painters, though other Irish artists influenced by Cubism included Norah McGuinness, Louis le Brocquy and Colin Middleton. Swanzy, Jellett and Cecil Salkeld probably represent the high point of achievement of the Dublin Painters' Society in terms of Modernism.

English pacifist expatriates Basil Rákóczi (whose work ranged in style from Expressionist to surrealist) and Kenneth Hall (who anticipated in some ways abstract Expressionism) formed the core of the White Stag Group, which held its first exhibition in 1940, including works by Mainie Jellett. In Kennedy's view the most significant event to be arranged by the group was the exhibition of subjective art held in 1944, and he sees the work of the White Stag Group as having influenced the founding of the Irish Exhibition of Living Art – the first exhibition being held at the National College of Art in Dublin in 1943. Notable names to emerge from the IELA were Louis le Brocquy, a largely self-taught artist whose work embodies a quintessentially Modernist ('existentialist') sense of individual isolation; and Colin Middleton, the most prominent Irish surrealist. Modernist sculptors of note include Jocelyn Chewett, F.E. McWilliam (whose 'fragmented' approach was influenced by Picasso) and Laurence Campbell.

Other artists who continued the Irish Modernist tradition included Nano Reid, Anne Madden, Camille Souter, Patrick Collins, Patrick Scott, Cecil King and Tony O'Malley. Abstract art generally, and possibly the new Expressionism, continue elements of the Modernist tradition, while it is a matter of debate how the hyper-realism of prominent artists like Robert Ballagh or Martin Gale should be classified.

The prominent role played by women in Irish Modernism, the lingering influence of 'naturism' and Romanticism, the links and disjunctions between Irish painting and Irish literature, the tensions between cultural nationalism and Modernism, all combine to make of Irish Modernism a peculiar entity, whose analysis in terms of such factors as class, gender and nationality is as important as it is embryonic.

Reading

Arnold, Bruce, *Irish Art: A Concise History* (London: Thames and Hudson, 1977).

Kennedy, S.B., *Irish Art and Modernism: 1880–1950* (Belfast: Institute of Irish Studies/Queens University Press, 1991).

McConkey, Kenneth, *A Free Spirit: Irish Art 1860–1960* (London: Antique Collectors Club/Pyms Gallery, 1991).

National Gallery of Ireland/Douglas Hyde Gallery, *Irish Women Artists: From the Eighteenth Century to the Present Day* (Dublin: NGI/DHG, 1989).

PAUL O'BRIEN

modernization The emergence of economic relations, political formations and social institutions which are identifiable as 'modern' constitute the process of modernization which has shaped Irish society since the late sixteenth century. In the economic sphere, property relations were transformed by the undermining of the old Gaelic and feudal systems as conquest was completed in the seventeenth century. The rise of the Anglo-Irish Ascendancy through the eighteenth century was founded on political hegemony and a landlord system which asserted the absolute rights of private property. The growing integration of the Irish economy with the British market, in turn being shaped by the industrial revolution, generated patterns of economic organization and class structure which were becoming identifiably modern by the second half of the eighteenth century. The commercialization of agriculture, the growth in trade, and the rise of an educated and influential Catholic middle class based in commerce and the professions represented key structural changes in Irish society in this period.

It is in the nineteenth century, however, and more particularly in the post-Famine period, that political and social forces emerged which accelerated the modernization process. The Famine itself decisively altered the balance in Irish society by decimating and undermining traditional forms of agriculture and the populous communities on which they were based. The decline in the Gaelic language, for example, reflected both the disproportionate impact which the Famine had on regions and classes where Gaelic had been most widely spoken and also the fact that it came to be associated with a traditional and poverty-stricken way of life. Traditional forms of religion, which typically expressed themselves in a creative mixture of Christianity and pagan practices, were also undermined by the Famine. Indeed, the onward march of a resurgent, centralizing, modernizing Catholic church was one of the most powerful forces shaping Irish society in the second half of the nineteenth century.

Throughout the nineteenth century, many of the changes in Irish society were driven by the increasing role of the state and its institutions in the ordinary lives of citizens. In the areas of health, education and local government Ireland was regarded as a 'social laboratory', and many policies enacted were in advance of anything known in England. It has been claimed that Ireland had one of the most advanced health services in Europe in the early nineteenth century, with a network of 600 district dispensaries and 10 district mental asylums under state administration by 1840. While the level of care available in these institutions may have been rudimentary by modern standards, the system nevertheless represented an essential framework for adequate medical care for the poor, which would remain in place for almost a century.

Underpinning the modernization of Irish society through the nineteenth century were the dramatic improvements in education and literacy achieved from the 1830s onwards. The National Board of Education, established in 1831, sought to put in place a country-wide system of national education. Inevitably beset by religious controversies, the system nevertheless saw the number of schools in operation rise from 4,500 in 1850 to nearly 9,000 by the end of the century. In terms of children attending, numbers rose from about 800,000 in 1860 to 3,000,000 by 1890. Improvements in literacy in the post-Famine decades are reflected in rising levels of newspaper circulation, which in turn contributed to the growing sense of regional and national identities.

It is in the spheres of politics and state institutions that developments through the mid-nineteenth century had most impact in furthering the modernization process. Daniel O'Connell's Repeal Movement and the campaign for Catholic emancipation represented the first genuine mobilization of popular politics. Prefiguring modern political parties, the Catholic Association, founded by O'Connell in 1823, was a mass movement funded by penny-a-month contributions from hundreds of thousands of cottiers and small farmers.

A series of spectacular election victories through the 1820s established the legitimacy and efficacy of this form of politics. Formally opposed to the traditional world of secret societies and agrarian violence, O'Connell's mass movements and monster rallies represented a decisive expression of modern forms in the political sphere. With the eventual emergence of the Home Rule party led by Parnell in the late 1870s, organized parliamentary nationalism came to play a sophisticated and influential role at Westminster.

In terms of the modernization process, subsequent political developments that centred on the independence movement, culminating in the setting up of the revolutionary Dáil in 1919, illustrate the extent to which Irish politics was committed to modern political forms. The 1919 Dáil, legitimized by election, continued in being as a parliamentary assembly through revolution and war. In 1922, despite its rejection by de Valera, the duly elected government enjoyed widespread recognition. Later, the formation of Fianna Fáil, and the smooth transfer of power to that party in 1932, underline the extent to which democratic values and acceptance of modern democratic institutions had become core values in Irish political culture.

PETER CONNELL

Moeran, Ernest John (1894–1950) Composer. Of mixed Irish and English parentage, Moeran was born and educated in England but was emotionally attached to Ireland, a country he had first visited in 1917 for a period of convalescence after sustaining a severe head injury while serving with the British army in France. Composition did not come easily to Moeran and his works betray the many influences to which he was susceptible. Early works such as *Lonely Waters* (1924) and *Whythorne's Shadow* (1931) demonstrate his empathy with Elizabethan music, while the *Serenade* (1948) is redolent of Delius. He was also appreciative of folk song, and his output contains arrangements of traditional airs from both Norfolk and Kerry. The latter became his spiritual home and some of his finest works were conceived there, including the *Symphony in G minor* (1937) and the *Violin Concerto* (1941). Despite these successes, Moeran was essentially a lyrical writer more comfortable with smaller forms, and his original songs, such as the *Seven Poems of James Joyce* (1929) and the *Sinfonietta*, are among his most compelling achievements. A troubled and lonely life was brought to a close when he drowned off the pier at Kenmare on 1 December 1950.

Reading

Self, G., *The Music of E. J. Moeran* (Toccata Press, 1986).

JOSEPH RYAN

Molesworth, Robert (1656–1725) Political writer. Born Dublin. Molesworth attended Trinity College, Dublin. A prominent supporter of William of Orange, he was appointed in 1692 envoy to Denmark, where his Republican and anti-clerical sympathies made him unpopular. His *An Account of Denmark as it was in 1692* (1694) is probably his most influential work. Its preface, in particular, became a rallying cry for enlightened opinion.

Molesworth became a member of both the British and Irish parliaments. He was created Viscount Molesworth of Swords in 1719. His colonial nationalism, evident in *Considerations for Promoting Agriculture* (1723), was admired by Swift, who dedicated the fifth of his *Drapier's Letters* to him. Molesworth is also important as a patron and mentor of Irish Enlightenment thinkers, most notably John Toland and Francis Hutcheson.

Reading

Robbins, Caroline, *The Eighteenth-Century Commonwealthman* (Cambridge MA: Harvard University Press, 1959).

DAVID BERMAN

Molyneux family Influential in Dublin from the later sixteenth century to the early nineteenth. Its founder, Thomas Molyneux (1531–97), who came from Calais *c*.1570 as a protégé of Archbishop Loftus, became chancellor of the Irish Exchequer in 1590. (The claim that he was knighted is apparently without foundation.) His grandson Samuel Molyneux (1616–93), master gunner of Ireland, who was the first of the family to display mathematical and scientific interests, established himself as a landowner at Castle Dillon in Armagh in 1664. By then the family had established marriage links with the Usshers and other prominent Dublin dynasties.

Distinguished later members included William Molyneux FRS (1656–98), scientist and political writer, who founded Ireland's first scientific body, the Dublin Philosophical Society, in 1683. William's most important scientific work, *Dioptrica Nova* (1692), brought him the friendship of the philosopher Locke, for whom he propounded the perceptual problem known as the Molyneux problem, subsequently published in the second edition of Locke's *Essay* (1694). His friendship with Locke became widely celebrated through the publication of their correspondence in Locke's *Familiar Letters* (1708). William Molyneux is best known, however, for his political pamphlet, *The Case of Ireland's being Bound by Acts of Parliament in England, Stated* (1698), which argued the case for Ireland's legislative independence on the basis of legal and historical precedent. The work also developed natural right arguments from Locke's *Two Treatises of Government* (1690) in order to demonstrate that no one society has a right to dominate another. Described in 1779 as 'the manual of Irish liberty', Molyneux's *Case* was reprinted nine times up to the recovery of legislative independence in Grattan's Parliament in 1782, and has continued to be held in high regard.

William's brother, Thomas Molyneux FRS (1661–1733), was a distinguished physician, member of the Dublin Philosophical Society, and a prolific contributor to the *Philosophical Transactions* of the Royal Society. Educated at Dublin and Leiden, he was made state physician in 1715 and regius professor of medicine at Trinity College, Dublin, in 1717. Created a baronet in 1730, he established the family seat at Castle Dillon. In 1731 he was associated in the establishment of the (Royal) Dublin Society. William's son, Samuel Molyneux FRS (1689–1728), was an astronomer and secretary to George II, as prince of Wales. Notable for his improvements to the reflecting telescope, he collaborated with James Bradley in observations of stellar parallax, which led to the latter's discovery of the aberration of light. Sir Capel Molyneux, fourth baronet (1750–1832), Irish MP and writer of political pamphlets, published a privately printed history of the family, entitled *An Account of the Family and Descendants of Sir Thomas Molyneux Kt....* in 1820.

Reading

Hoppen, T.K., *The Common Scientist in the Seventeenth Century* (London: Routledge and Kegan Paul, 1970).

Kelly, Patrick, 'William Molyneux and the spirit of liberty in eighteenth-century Ireland', *Eighteenth-Century Ireland* 3 (1988).

Morgan, M.J., *Molyneux's Question* (Cambridge: Cambridge University Press, 1977).

Simms, J.G., *William Molyneux of Dublin* (Dublin: Irish Academic Press, 1982).

PATRICK KELLY

Molyneux problem Celebrated philosophical-scientific thought experiment devised by William Molyneux. He asked whether a man blind from birth would upon gaining his sight be able to distinguish (visually) a sphere from a cube. The problem was first published in Locke's *Essay concerning Human Understanding* (2nd edn, 1694), Molyneux having previously sent it to Locke on 2 March 1692/3. Locke agreed with Molyneux's negative answer. The first (extant) positive answer was also given by an Irishman, Edward Synge, in a letter of 1695.

However, it is Berkeley's answer, in his *Essay of Vision* (1709), that is philosophically most important. Berkeley used the problem to justify and illustrate the *Essay*'s central thesis: that touch and sight are entirely heterogeneous. Another Irish philosopher who grappled with the problem was Francis Hutcheson. In a letter of 1727 he rejects the negative answers of Molyneux, Locke and Berkeley, arguing that there is something in common between visual and tangible extension. Hutcheson's solution is remarkably similar to that offered by Leibniz in his posthumous *New Essays* (1765).

A Molyneux-like problem was also used crucially in theology by Synge and Berkeley, as well as by Peter Browne and William King. Jonathan Swift, too, seems to advert to it in, for example, *Gulliver's Travels*, and Edmund Burke uses it innovatively in his 1757 *Philosophical Enquiry* to explain the role of synaesthesia in aesthetic appreciation.

Reading

Berman, D., 'Francis Hutcheson on Berkeley and the Molyneux problem', *Proceedings of the Royal Irish Academy* 74 (1974).

Morgan, M.J., *Molyneux's Question* (Cambridge: Cambridge University Press, 1977).

DAVID BERMAN

Monck, Mary (d. 1715) Poet. The second daughter of Robert Molesworth, first Viscount Molesworth, and Lititia, the third daughter of Richard, Lord Coloony. Mary married George Monck of St Stephens Green, Dublin. She taught herself Spanish, Italian and Latin and studied English literature. On her deathbed she wrote a number of poems to her husband, which were printed in Barber's Collection of *Poems by Eminent Ladies* (1755). Some of her other poems appeared shortly after her death under the title *Marinda, Poems and Translations Upon Several Occasions*. She died at Bath.

RACHEL FURMSTON

Montague, John (1929–) Poet. Born Brooklyn. Montague is a consummate craftsman, a poet in constant quest of the perfect visual or sculpted image to contain and control chaos. Since *Tides* (1970) he has tended to arrange and rearrange his attenuated lyrics into sequences. His poetry is essentially autobiographical. His love lyrics are tender and sensual, but not erotic; memorializing a past or passing passion gracefully. Virtually orphaned and 'transplanted' to Tyrone at age 4, he has personalized the nightmare of Northern Irish history. In his most acclaimed sequence, *The Rough Field* (1972), colonial dispossession and technological despoliation are an extension of his own trauma of deracination. In *The Dead Kingdom* (1984) he bids a simultaneous farewell to mother and motherland. Later work includes a novella, *The Lost Notebook* (1987), *Mount Eagle* (1988), *New Selected Poems* (1989) and *The Figure in the Cave and Other Essays* (1990). Montague held the Ireland Chair of Poetry (1998–2001).

ANTOINETTE QUINN

Montgomery, Henry (1788–1865) Founder of the remonstrant synod of Ulster. Born Boltnaconnell House, Killead, County Antrim, 16 January; died 18 December. Montgomery attended Glasgow College, graduating MA in 1807, and was licensed by Templepatrick presbytery the next year, when he was ordained by Bangor presbytery, his parish until his death.

From 1813 he advocated Catholic emancipation, and in 1817 he was made headmaster of the English school in the Belfast Academy. In 1818, he was elected moderator of the general synod. He proclaimed himself an Arian, and began a life-long struggle against the campaign against Arianism led by Henry Cooke. Montgomery's speech at Strabane (1827) in favour of religious liberty and tolerance won him the acclaim of various denominations, including Catholics, though Cooke won the battle to make members of the synod accept the doctrine of the Trinity.

Montgomery and his followers were forced to withdraw. In 1828, these non-subscribers to the Westminster confession proposed a 'remonstrance', and the first remonstrant synod was held in May 1832.

Though in favour of Irish disestablishment, and the national system of education, attacked by Cooke, Montgomery opposed O'Connell's campaign to repeal the Union, and lost the support of many liberals as a result. He won a notable victory against Cooke when he defeated his attempt to exclude Arians from the chair of theology in the Belfast Academy in 1841. Though he became more conservative in later years, he continued to advocate non-subscribing until his death.

FRED LOWE

Moore, Brian (1921–99) Novelist. Born Belfast. Moore's work and life enact the conflicts of belief, tradition and modernization in Irish society. He emigrated to Montreal in 1948, where he published two acclaimed novels set in Belfast: *The Lonely Passion of Judith Hearne* (1955) and *The Feast of Lupercal* (1957). In 1959 Moore moved to the United States, publishing *The Luck of Ginger Coffey* (1960) and *An Answer from Limbo* (1962), both dealing with the dislocation of values attendant upon the experience of emigration. These early novels explore the consequences of rejecting religious certainties, a theme developed in a sequence of novels which expand Moore's grimly realistic style, beginning in 1972 with *Catholics*, and moving through *The Great Victorian Collection* (1975), *The Mangan Inheritance* (1979) and *The Cold Heaven* (1983). Moore's later works, *Black Robe* (1985), set amongst Jesuits in seventeenth-century Canada, *The Colour of Blood* (1987) *Lies of Silence* (1990), *No Other Life* (1993), and *The Statement* (1995) indicate a move beyond the rejection of Catholicism to an exploration of the conditional nature of all belief. Moore was a novelist with an international reputation, twice recipient of the Canadian Governor General's Award and twice short listed for the Booker Prize. Five of his novels have been filmed.

Reading

O'Donoghere, Jo, *Brian Moore: A Critical Study* (Gill and Macmillan).

CHRIS MORASH

Moore, George (1852–1933) Novelist. Born into a well-known family of landlords and public servants at Moore Hall, Ballyglass, County Mayo. Moore was educated at Oscott College, Birmingham, and originally intended to become a painter. He lived in London and Paris, where Zola, Manet and Whistler became influences. His failure as a painter was initially reciprocated by his attempts to write fiction. It was not until the naturalistic *A Mummer's Wife* (1885) gained notoriety that his reputation as a novelist was firmly established, to be consolidated by *A Drama in Muslin* (1887; ineffectually reworked as *Muslin*, 1915) and, particularly, *Esther Waters* (1894).

In the same year as *A Drama in Muslin*, Moore also published a book of incisive sketches entitled *Parnell and his Island*. These two works combine to give a jaundiced but worldly dissection of Ireland at the height of Parnell's fame, and reveal powers of satirical observation which are only intermittently exercised in his later fiction. Moore returned to Ireland in 1901, immersed himself in Dublin cultural life, and was instrumental in developing the theatrical initiative which culminated in the Abbey Theatre. These experiences were distinguished by bouts of intense ill-will on the part of all concerned, but had the welcome outcome of prompting a vivid expiation in Moore's autobiographical trilogy, *Hail and Farewell* (*Ave*, 1911; *Salve*, 1912; *Vale*, 1914). Other works of this period are *The Untilled Field* (1903) and *The Lake* (1905), the former a landmark development in Irish short fiction. Returning to London permanently in 1911, Moore spent the remainder of his career polishing his silvery prose style by writing historical romances, the best known of which are *The Brook Kerith* (1916) and *Heloise and Abelard* (1921).

Nothing that pre-dated Moore's career and output could have anticipated them. His career, and the tissue of new departures which constitute it, resemble those of his illustrious contemporaries, John B. Yeats and J.M. Synge. The exemplary impact of these careers' non-conformity on an emerging Irish cultural consciousness has yet to be thoroughly assessed.

Moore's interest in, and adaptation of, the European conception of the artist's task contributed to the introduction of a whole new repertoire of effects and concerns to the novel in English. The banning in England of *A Mummer's Wife* is an indication of this contribution's significance. Moore's time in Paris, together with his reading of Balzac and Turgenev, enabled him to develop his own techniques to represent the new subject matter of art discovered by Impressionism and naturalism. The self-consciousness of his identification with contemporary aesthetic developments in the novel had a liberating effect on the form. With Moore, Irish fiction comes of age and finally outgrows the generic and ideological constraints of the eighteenth-century forms on which it had hitherto been largely modelled. Of equal significance is his adventurous adaptation of autobiography. A form of cultural apologetics in nineteenth-century Ireland, in Moore's hands its expressive rather than its exculpatory potential are released.

Moore's career is both defined and undermined by its transitional character. Definition is provided by the type of commitment which enabled Moore to find the new forms necessary to establish his literary identity. Undermining results from his apparent need to revise that identity without finding sufficiently persuasive alternative forms in which to do so. This weakness is revealed by his misguided but compulsive rewriting of his work, and by the revision's privileging of style as an end in itself. Nevertheless, Moore's

393

major works represent crucial developments in imaginative prose in Ireland, and are also of value as repositories of themes and perspectives which are not addressed by other participants in the Irish literary revival.

GEORGE O'BRIEN

Moore, Thomas (1779–1852) Poet and miscellaneous writer. Born at 12 Aungier Street, Dublin, 28 May, died Sloperton, near Devizes in Wiltshire, 26 February. Moore's parents were well-to-do grocers who saw to it that their only son had a good education at Samuel Whyte's academy in Grafton Street, Dublin, at Trinity College, Dublin, and at the Middle Temple, London. A dabbler in verse since he was a boy, Moore appears to have devoted much of his time as a student in Trinity College to a metrical translation of the Greek poet Anacreon. When published in 1800 the translation earned him some plaudits from the critics, and the *Morning Post* dubbed him Anacreon Moore. His *Poems of the Late Thomas Little* (1801) were regarded as licentious by the more strait-laced of the time.

Meanwhile Moore had established himself in high-life circles in England, mainly through his talents as a singer and musician and through a highly attractive personality. A post in Bermuda turned out to be a sore disappointment, but he turned it to advantage with a tour of the United States and Canada, which was to provide him with some satirical material for his *Odes and Epistles* (1806). In the following year there appeared the first instalment of his *Irish Melodies*, with music by Sir John Stevenson. Over the next 27 years, further instalments appeared at irregular intervals, and provided him with a steady income, averaging £500 a year.

In 1817 Moore's magnum opus, *Lalla Rookh*, appeared. It had been commissioned by Longmans for the then enormous sum of £3,000. *Lalla Rookh* relates and celebrates the journey of the princess Lalla Rookh from Delhi to Kashmir to wed the king of Burcharia. Moore put into this work a prodigious amount of research, but too much striving after effect eventually becomes oppressive. Nevertheless the section 'Paradise and the Peri' deserves to be remembered, as well as some intermittent songs, including the well-known 'Bendemeer's Stream'.

The Fudge family in Paris (1818) is a satirical look in verse at the antics of the English abroad, and *The Loves of the Angels* (1823) is another poem on an Eastern theme. Moore had meantime become a close friend of Byron, and the latter some years before his death entrusted to Moore his memoirs. While these were destroyed because of their explicitness in circumstances in which Moore played a part, he made amends to some extent with his highly acclaimed biography of Byron (1830). His lives of Sheridan (1825) and of Lord Edward Fitzgerald (1831), and a four-volume history of Ireland, were, however, less successful.

Moore's reputation today rests solidly and almost exclusively on his *Irish Melodies*, which over nearly two centuries have enjoyed a world-wide popularity which shows no sign of waning.

Reading

Moore, Thomas, *Poetical Works*, 10 vols (London: 1840–1).
White, Terence de Vere, *Tom Moore the Irish poet* (London: Hamish Hamilton, 1977).

PATRICK FAGAN

Moore, Thomas and music Moore's *A Selection of Irish Melodies* began to appear in 1807; the last of them was published in 1834. These had accompaniments and 'symphonies' (pianoforte introductions) by Sir John Stevenson. Part of Stevenson's work was revised by Henry Bishop. The *Melodies* went through several reprints and editions, with the accompaniments newly set or revised by Michael Balfe (1859), George McFarren (1859–61), John Glover (1860), etc. Moore also published *Sacred Songs* (arrangements of traditional Irish airs) in 1816, again with arrangements by Stevenson.

His *A Selection of Popular National Airs* (1818–28) includes the 'Melologue upon National Music', originally published in 1811. Moore's own texts and poems were widely set by English and European composers (Bantock, Kelly, A. Rubinstein, J. Jongen, Berlioz, Hindemith, etc.). He enjoyed a huge reputation as a reciter and singer of his own texts.

Moore's *Irish Melodies* dominate the whole question of music in Ireland during the nineteenth century. Their sources, textual history, immense popularity and political ramifications stimulated a wide-ranging debate which touched upon many of the central problems associated with music in Ireland. Moore's use of Edward Bunting's collection of melodies (*Ancient Music of Ireland*, 1796) led to a controversy between the two men, which was illustrative of the conflict between the antiquarian (and scholarly) pursuit of traditional music as a vital component of past culture and the reanimation and popular dissemination of these melodies, adapted to suit the needs of Moore's verse. This conflict was never resolved (although Moore came to understand Bunting's resentment and even inclined to blame Stevenson in his journal for the modification of the original airs). Instead, the quarrel was aggravated by successive editors of, and commentators on, the melodies (including Charles Stanford), whose objections and counter-objections underlined the enduring difficulty of reconciling an ethnic tradition of music in Ireland with clear political connotations and a European mode of musical articulation which equally connoted oppression or callous disregard.

From the vantage point of the present day, it is possible to regard Moore's *Melodies* themselves as part of the fundamental musical experience of Irish life, cultural and otherwise.

Reading

Jordan, Hoover H., *Bolt Upright: The Life of Thomas Moore* (Salzburg, 1975).

HARRY WHITE

Moravian church Descended from the pre-Reformation Unitas Fratrum, Moravians founded their first Irish congregation in 1749. Moravians everywhere typically devoted as much energy to renewing other churches as to building their own, which is consequently small. In Ireland 450 regular participants worship in five congregations, all in Northern Ireland. Gracehill, County Antrim, still retains something of the character of a typical eighteenth-century Moravian settlement.

JOSEPH LIECHTY

Mornington, first earl of (Garrett Colley Mornington Wesley), (1735–81) Composer and amateur violinist. The family name was later changed to Wellesley. Mornington succeeded as second Baron Mornington in 1758, and was created Viscount Wellesley and earl of Mornington in 1760. He became first professor of music (1764) at the University of Dublin, in which year he received his MusD. He resigned from the chair in 1774. A godson of Mrs Delany, and father of the first duke of Wellington, he was very active in Dublin musical life, especially in connection with hospital charities, and in the foundation of the 1757 Musical Academy. He published 11 collections of glees, catches, etc., and composed a well-known Anglican chant.

BRIAN BOYDELL

Morrison, Van (1945–) Singer-songwriter. Born George Ivan Morrison in Belfast. Morrison was educated at Orangefield Boys School. From early jazz and rythm-and-blues influences, the Morrison-led band *Them* recorded popular hits in the mid-1960s with 'Baby Please Don't Go', 'Gloria' and 'Here Comes the Night'. Dissatisfied with the British music scene and business, Morrison moved to New York to work with Bert Berns. From 1968 he released a string of innovative albums such as *Astral Weeks* (1969), *Moondance* (1970) and the classic 'live' album, *It's Too Late To Stop Now* (1974). *Veedon Fleece* (1974) marked the return, after an eight-year absence, of Morrison to Belfast and a deepening encounter with Irish musical and literary traditions. His blend of mysticism, poetic utterance and biblical imagery makes for a thoroughly distinctive lyrical ambition in contemporary popular music, as albums from *No Guru, No Method, No Teacher* (1986), *Avalon Sunset* (1989), *Enlightenment* (1990), *Hymns to the Silence* (1991), *The Healing Game* (1997) amply portray. In 1998, *The Philosopher's Stone* a major two-CD retrospective collection of Morrison's early career from 1971 to 1988 was released.

GERALD DAWE

mother-and-child scheme This major controversy began with the proposal by Dr Noel Browne, health minister in the 1945–51 coalition, to introduce free medical care for mothers and their children. The scheme was opposed by the medical profession and the Catholic hierarchy, and the opposition of the latter carried the day. Browne's resignation precipitated the downfall of the government, and the publication by the *Irish Times* of the correspondence between the minister and the hierarchy caused a sensation. In the magisterial *Church and State in Modern Ireland*, Professor John Whyts identifies no villains in the piece, but the image of an earnest reforming minister driven from office by over-mighty bishops has never been eradicated.

JAMES DOWNEY

Mulcahy, Michael (1952–) Painter. Born Cork City. Mulcahy studied at the Crawford School of Art (1969) and at the National College of Art and Design, Dublin (1970–3). Mulcahy's work is semi-abstract, consisting of heads or strong calligraphic marks or symbols floating on richly coloured grounds. The subjects and images in his work are drawn from the mythologies of various non-industrialized societies, such as the Australian Aboriginals and the Dogon people of Mali, with whom Mulcahy spent several months. He conceives of the artist as a shaman or healer, whose paintings can mediate between the earthly and the spiritual.

Reading

Dunne, Aidan, 'The limits of Desire', in *Michael Mulcahy* (Dublin: Douglas Hyde Gallery, 1989).
Scott, David, 'Figuring matter', in *Michael Mulcahy*, (Dublin: Taylor Galleries, 1991).
Walker, Dorothy, 'From Alice Springs to Kanganaman', *Irish Arts Review* 2, no. 4 (Winter 1985), pp. 45–8.

FELICITY WOOLF

Muldoon, Paul (1951–) Poet. Born Armagh. Muldoon's first collection, *New Weather* (1973), revealed a precocious and innovative talent, which matured gradually in subsequent collections *Mules* (1977) and *Why Brownlee Left* (1980). His multi-layered imaginative reach and his subversive use of form – particularly his manipulation of the sonnet – were given full vent in *Quoof* (1983), in which Muldoon exploited his interest in the American Indian trickster cycle and simultaneously displayed his sophisticated lyrical abilities. After *Meeting the British* (1987) he produced *Madoc: A Mystery* (1990), a mock epic account of a Coleridgean pantisocratic community envisaged through a phantasmagoric collage of historical, philosophical and fictional detail, with the poet revelling in obscure terminology and enigmatic cross-reference. Muldoon's ludic tendencies have not prevented the growth of his reputation as the most original voice of the Heaney slipstream. He is now resident in the USA, and while his Northern roots have been irretrievably blended into his international canvas, his work has proved to be an enduring influence on a younger generation of Irish poets.

EVE PATTEN

Mulready, William (1786–1863) Painter. Born Ennis, 1 April; died London 7 July. Mulready's family moved to London, where he received his first instruction from John Graham, Thomas Banks the sculptor, and

Fuseli at the Royal Academy (RA) Schools. As a young man he 'tried his hand at anything from a miniature to a panorama'. He first exhibited at the RA 1804, being elected RA in 1816. Influenced by David Wilkie, he developed an original style of genre painting, particularly featuring boys. His style is notable for its clean line, sculptural forms, and agreeable though sometimes turgid colouring, admired by the Pre-Raphaelites.

Reading

Crookshank, A. and the Knight of Glin, *The Painters of Ireland, c. 1660–1920* (London: Barrie and Jenkins, 1978).
Pointon, M., *Mulready* (London: Victoria and Albert Museum, 1986).
Strickland, W.G., *A Dictionary of Irish Artists* (Shannon: Irish University Press, 1968).

HILARY PYLE

Mulvany, George Francis (1809–69) Painter and administrator. Born and died Dublin. Mulvany was the son of Thomas James Mulvany, keeper of the Royal Hibernian Academy (RHA). After initial training in the RHA School he studied in Italy and was a member of the RHA at the age of 26. He succeeded his father as keeper in 1845. In 1862 he was made the first director of the National Gallery of Ireland. An able administrator, Mulvany established a collection of some 200 paintings as well as drawings and casts after the antique. He also published the first catalogue of the collection (1864). Apart from some historical pieces Mulvany's output as a painter was mainly in portraits, many of which were first exhibited at the RHA. These included likenesses of John Banim, Frederick William Burton, Charles Kean as Hamlet and a Daniel O'Connell now in the National Gallery of Ireland.

Reading

National Gallery of Ireland. Illustrated Summary Catalogue of Paintings, intro. Homan Potterton (Dublin: National Gallery of Ireland, 1981).

Strickland, Walter, *A Dictionary of Irish Artists* (Shannon: Irish University Press, 1968).

FINTAN CULLEN

Mulvany, Thomas (1779–1845) Painter. Born and died Dublin. Mulvany studied under Francis Robert West at the Dublin Society Schools. One of a dynasty of artists deeply involved in Dublin artistic life throughout the first half of the nineteenth century, and a founding member of the Royal Hibernian Academy (RHA) in 1823, he became its first keeper. Primarily a landscape painter, he frequently exhibited Mayo scenes, most of which were views within the Brabazon estate. He also exhibited paintings of horses and was one of the first artists to paint scenes of Killarney and similar beauty spots repeatedly. His view of *Kilmallock* in the National Gallery of Ireland is a mixture of antiquarian interest and sentimental anecdote. Mulvany was also an historian; he edited the *Life of James Gandon* (1846) and wrote an important series of biographical articles on Irish artists for the *Citizen* and *Dublin Monthly Magazine*.

Reading

Crookshank, Anne and the Knight of Glin, *The Painters of Ireland c. 1660–1920* (London: Barrie and Jenkins, 1978).
Strickland, Walter, *A Dictionary of Irish Artists* (Shannon: Irish University Press, 1968).

FINTAN CULLEN

Murdoch, Jean Iris (1920–99) Novelist and philosopher. Born Dublin. Of Anglo-Irish parents, Murdoch was educated at Oxford, where she took up a post in philosophy after a short period as a Treasury civil servant. Her first novel, *Under the Net* (1954), a satirical account of an angry young man in post-war London, revealed her skill with comedy and even farce, but intellectualism soon emerged as Murdoch's dominant characteristic, and subsequent novels marked out her definitive territory in rigorous philosophical explorations of moral, social and sexual relationships. Among the best known are *The Bell* (1957), set in a closed religious community, *The Black Prince* (1973), loosely worked around *Hamlet*, and *The Sea, The Sea* (1978), which was awarded the Booker Prize. *The Message to the Planet* (1989) and *The Green Knight* (1993) confirmed both her scope and contemporary relevance. A disciple of Sartre, on whom she published *Romantic Rationalist* in 1953, her influences also included Wittgenstein and Elias Canetti. Her 1961 essay 'Against dryness', published in *Encounter* Magazine, made a significant contribution to modern fictional theory. In 1992 she published *Metaphysics as a Guide to Morals*.

EVE PATTEN

Murphy, Arthur (1727–1805) Actor, dramatist and translator. Born Clooneyquin, County Roscommon; died Knightsbridge, London, 18 June. Following the death of Murphy's father the family moved to London in 1735, and Murphy was sent to the English College of St Omer in France. After spells as a clerk in Cork and London, he turned to acting, whence he progressed to play-writing. He had four farces produced before turning to more serious themes with *The Orphan of China*, a tragedy, and *The Desert Island*, a dramatic poem. There followed a string of adaptations from French authors, and then *The Grecian Daughter*, his best-known tragedy. And all this was the work of a man who scarcely had an original idea in his life, but borrowed freely from other authors and sources. He also edited the works of Fielding, wrote a biography of Garrick, and translated the works of the Roman historians Tacitus and Sallust.

Reading

Murphy, Arthur, *The Works of Arthur Murphy*, 7 vols (London: 1786).

PATRICK FAGAN

Murphy, Richard (1927–) Poet. Murphy embodies the tension not only of the Irish Protestant tradition at home but of the British colonial service abroad. Out of each he has formed his carefully crafted poems. History and contemporary events violently collide in the balanced stanzas and rhymes of *The Battle of Aughrim* (1968), a dual tale of stupidity and treachery where 'the past is happening today'. In *The Price of Stone* (1985) the strict sonnet form unfolds a personal history spoken by the buildings that have shaped an outsider's 'privileged' life. More recently, a return to his childhood home in Sri Lanka has freed Murphy's verse to echo the love plaints of the ancient Sinhalese graffiti on *The Mirror Wall* (1989).

JOHN B. BRESLIN

Murphy, Thomas (1935–) Playwright. Born Tuam, County Galway. Murphy originally trained as a metalwork teacher before the 1961 London success of his first full-length play, *A Whistle in the Dark*, which had been rejected by the Abbey, enabled him to give up teaching. After a period in England writing for British television (1962–70), Murphy returned to Ireland and, since 1969 with *A Crucial Week in the Life of a Grocer's Assistant*, most of his plays have been first produced at the Abbey. These include the fairy-tale-style *Morning After Optimism* (1971), the Expressionist *Sanctuary Lamp* (1976), which caused controversy over its supposed anti-clericalism, the outstandingly successful Faust-based *Gigli Concert* (1983) and *Too Late for Logic* (1989). A very fruitful period as writer in association with the Galway Druid Theatre (1983–5) resulted in productions in 1985 of *Conversations on a Homecoming*, a revised version of the earlier *The White House*, concerned with the disenchantments of 1970s' Ireland after the idealism of the 1960s, and *Bailegangaire*, with its latter day Cathleen Ni Houlihan, the senile, story-telling Mommo.

Long established as one of Ireland's leading contemporary playwrights, on the Abbey Theatre board of directors 1972–83, Murphy's reputation abroad grew more slowly, but with new London productions of *A Whistle in the Dark* (1989) and *The Gigli Concert* (1992) and the publication of collections of his plays, this changed. His imagination is restless, even wayward, but in his best work – *The Gigli Concert* and *Bailegangaire* – he has achieved a romantic and obsessional drama of extraordinary force and resonance. In 1994 Murphy published his first novel *The Seduction of Morality*.

Reading

Murphy, Tom, *After Tragedy: The Gigli Concert, Bailegangaire, Conversations on a Homecoming* (London: Methuen, 1988).
——*A Whistle in the Dark and Other Plays* (London: Methuen, 1989).
O'Toole, Fintan, *The Politics of Magic: The Work and Times of Tom Murphy* (Dublin: Raven Arts, 1987).

NICHOLAS GRENE

Murphy, William Martin (1844–1919) Capitalist. Born Bandon, County Cork, 21 November; died Dublin, 25 June. Murphy was educated at Belvedere College, and took over the family building business at 19 when his father died. His enterprise and business acumen brought rapid and successful expansion; he built churches, schools and bridges throughout Ireland, founded the *Irish Independent* in 1905, and acquired the Dublin Tramway Company. He was Nationalist MP for St Patrick's, Dublin (1885–92), and led the employers against the unions in the lockout of 1913.

HENRY BOYLAN

Murray, T.C. (1873–1959) Playwright. Born Macroom, 17 January; died in Dublin, 7 March. Murray was headmaster of the Model School in Inchicore (1915–32). His importance as a playwright lies in his development after the death of J.M. Synge of a new, understated tragic realism. *Birthright*, staged at the Abbey in 1910, explores the Irish passion for land, which can lead, as here, to the killing of brother by brother. *Maurice Harte* (1912) describes another version of Irish tragedy, a young man's loss of religious vocation, while *Autumn Fire* (1925) quietly reveals the self-destructiveness of a widower's marriage to a young beauty who falls in love with his son. Murray also wrote several one-act plays of lasting merit, such as *Sovereign Love* (1913), *The Briery Gap* (1917) and *Spring* (1918), written in that combination of fidelity to the details of rural life and delicate insight into tragic situations which gives Murray's work its distinction. It is noteworthy that when the Abbey Players toured the USA in 1911, Murray's early work made a strong impact on the young Eugene O'Neill. Although Murray's plays are now out of fashion he is in his own way as good an example of the Irish imagination true to its sources as O'Neill's first, one-act plays are an expression of the emergent, self-defining American consciousness.

Reading

Ó hAodha, Micheál, *Plays and Places* (Dublin: Progress House, 1961).
Sahal, N., *Sixty Years of Realistic Irish Drama (1900–1960)* (Bombay: Macmillan, 1971).

CHRISTOPHER MURRAY

music associations and institutions A number of institutions support music in Northern Ireland. Queen's University, Belfast, and the University of Ulster offer degree and postgraduate courses, and the latter is also responsible for the training of music teachers for secondary-level education (age 11–18). In Belfast, Stranmillis College and St Mary's College train teachers with specialist music training to service the primary sector (age 4–11). The five education and library boards maintain music services providing specialist instrumental tuition in schools, and they, together with the independent Ulster College of Music in Belfast, also offer advanced evening tuition and group activities to talented children in a number of music centres.

Weekly recitals, an annual November Festival and the alternating Early Music and Sonorities Twentieth-Century Music festivals are all promoted by Queen's University. Belfast also supports annual civic and folk festivals, a community arts festival and promenade concerts, and a recital series is organized by the Belfast Music Society. Campuses of the University of Ulster in Jordanstown, Coleraine and Derry, together with a network of Arts Committees across Northern Ireland, ensure that concerts and recitals are presented in all the major towns. Northern Ireland Opera presents two seasons of opera per year in Belfast, and opera is also presented at Castle Ward, near Strangford. Concerts given by young performers are promoted by the music services of the five Education and Library Boards.

The Sonorities Festival includes a composition competition, and regional heats of the BBC Young Musician of the Year and Choir of the Year contests also take place. Competitive music festivals and *feiseanna*, which include western and traditional music sections, feature strongly; the Northern Ireland Bands' Association organizes contests for brass, military, accordion and flute bands; and the many amateur operatic societies participate in the annual Waterford Festival of the Association of Irish Musical Societies.

PETER DOWNEY

music education Recent welcome advances cannot conceal the fact that Ireland's low level of musical activity is in large measure attributable to the historical paucity of opportunity for music education. The indigenous practice is an oral tradition and has been passed from generation to generation in this manner. The experience of art music was confined to the eastern littoral and to major urban centres; consequently music had little place in general education prior to the establishment of E.G. Stanley's national school system of 1831. Even then music was optional and equated with sight-singing, employing the methods of John Hullah or John Curwen. In 1851, of 204 schools examined only six were teaching music. Some early concern regarding the musical proficiency of aspiring teachers was indicated by the appointment in 1848 of John William Glover as professor of vocal music at the Normal Training School of the Irish National Board of Education. Further improvement was managed by the dedication of inspectors of schools such as Patrick Keenan – who from 1858 advocated the provision of harmoniums to schools – and Peter Goodman, whose appointment in 1899 coincided with one of the most fruitful periods for music education at the primary level. Music in secondary schools presents a more dismal account not only as a consequence of denominational wrangling, but particularly because the universities were for long ill equipped to provide the specialized training necessary for teachers at this level.

The obvious requirement for a school of music concentrating on performance was addressed in the middle of the nineteenth century by a group of dedicated individuals, which included: John Stanford, father to the composer; Dr John Smith, professor of music at Trinity College, Dublin; his eventual successor in this appointment, Robert Prescott Stewart; and the leading violinist, R.M. Levey. Their first venture, established in 1848, met with only partial success, but was sufficient to encourage a second endeavour, which resulted in 1856 in the creation of the Academy of Music. Generous legacies from Miss Elizabeth Coulson and Mr Ormsby Vandeleur, along with an annual grant voted by Parliament in 1870, ensured the survival of the fledgeling institution. The title 'Royal', bestowed in 1872, attests the standing achieved by the academy, which quickly earned a high reputation for excellence, notably in its schools of keyboard and string teaching.

Among the early members of the teaching staff were Joseph Robinson and his wife, formerly Miss Fanny Arthur, a gifted English pianist. Of necessity, many of the tutors came from abroad and notable were the string teachers Herr Lauer, Guido Papini, Adolf Wilhelmj and Achille Simonetti; the singing teacher Adelio Viani; and especially the Neapolitan pianist and composer Michele Esposito, who, from 1882 until his return to Italy in 1928, was the central dynamic force in all the academy's activities. The surpassing piano school which he developed was continued by, among others, his pupil Dina Copeman, and continues to this day under the guidance of John O'Conor.

A sister institution, the Dublin Municipal School of Music, was one element in a chain of technical schools established following the Artisans Exhibition of 1885 held in the city. Initially it was under the auspices of the Royal Irish Academy of Music (RIAM), and indeed it was intended that it complement the older institution through a concentration on wind and percussion. However, it soon departed from this original design and under a later designation, the College of Music, largely replicated the work of the academy. Under the direction of Frank Heneghan, it enjoyed an excellent reputation, particularly for its school of vocal studies headed by Veronica Dunne. In the 1990s, the College of Music was re-structured as the Dublin Institute of Technology (DIT) Conservatory of Music and Drama.

It was precisely the requirement for wind and percussion players which prompted the Free State's first minister for defence and chief of staff, General Richard Mulcahy, to propose the army as the ideal host for a school of music concentrating on these areas. With the advice of Professor John Larchet of University College, Dublin, the Army School of Music was founded in 1923 under the direction of an eminent German bandmaster and conductor, Wilhelm Fritz Brase (1875–1940). With singular dedication and the assistance of his compatriot, Friedrich Christian Sauerzweig (1881–1953), he created four fine military bands and furnished a succession of able executants capable of contributing to the development of orchestral

music, and a number of proficient conductors who were to guide the development of the symphony orchestra of the broadcasting service in its formative decades.

The concentration of such institutions in Dublin, which occasioned an imbalance in the opportunity for an education in music, was further emphasized by the the creation of the Leinster School of Music (1904) and the Read School of Pianoforte Playing (1915). Encouraged by a novel scheme of grants designed to promote the teaching of music, a Municipal School of Music was founded in Cork in 1878. However, its impact was at first limited by the fact that it had places for only 180 pupils. Not until 1902, when it moved from the Grand Parade to more spacious accommodation on Union Quay, could it expand its influence. Attempts to establish a similar institution in Belfast met with less success. The Belfast City School of Music, founded in 1891, survived just over a decade, while the Belfast Conservatoire (1894) and the Ulster Academy of Music (1899) met with a similar fate. Not until 1965 was a permanent municipal school of music established in the city.

Trinity College, the sole constituent college of the University of Dublin, awarded its first music degree in 1615, the recipient being the madrigalist Thomas Bateson. The first professor to be appointed was Garret Colley Wesley, the Earl of Mornington (1735–81), father to the Duke of Wellington, who held the chair for a decade from 1764. It lay vacant for some 70 years before John Smith, the recipient of an honorary doctorate from the university in 1827, was appointed in 1845. Thereafter there was a regular succession, although Trinity's influence was for long circumscribed by being an examining body rather than a teaching centre. Hormoz Farhat succeeded Brian Boydell as professor in 1982.

A total concentration on religious music meant that St Patrick's College, Maynooth, historically exercised a limited impact on general musical developments. Its first professor of music was the energetic German scholar, Revd Heinrich Bewerunge (1862–1923). The growth in the secular role of the college in recent decades has been reflected in the broader scope of its musical programmes, currently under the direction of Professor Gerard Gillen. A chair of music was established in University College, Dublin, in 1913, but remained a part-time appointment until 1944. Professor John Larchet was the incumbent from 1921 until he was succeeded by his erstwhile pupil, Dr Anthony Hughes, in 1958. Hughes was succeeded in 1993 by Harry White. The first third-level provision for music in Cork had been the creation of a part-time lecturership in the Queen's College in 1906, which was retained under the National University. This was converted to a part-time professorship and was not made a full-time position until 1948. Dr Aloys Fleischmann was head of the department from 1934 to 1980. Nicholas Sandon was appointed in 1986. In 1994, David Harold Cox was appointed professor. Queen's University, Belfast, is home to the endowed Hamilton Harty chair of music, which was established in 1947 and later held by Adrian Thomas, and Jan Smaczny. The founding of the Irish World Music Centre at the University of Limerick in 1994, under the direction of Professor Mícheál Ó Súilleabháin, has resulted in a new focus for graduate studies in music and musicology in Ireland.

JOSEPH RYAN

music ensembles 1660–1990, Dublin The Restoration proved a period propitious to artistic pursuits, and the fashionable penchant for visiting musicians did not wholly impede the formation of musical ensembles in the capital. The most venerable was the Hibernian Catch Club, founded *c*.1680 by the vicars choral of the two metropolitan cathedrals, who were to the fore in many of the enterprises over the succeeding centuries. Instrumental music was provided by the small theatre orchestras, the first of which, the Theatre Royal in Smock Alley, opened in 1661. Music associated with theatrical productions became a feature in the life of the city and ensembles were formed in Aungier Street (1734) and Crow Street (1758). Occasional ensembles were gathered for the presentation of oratorio, which was exceedingly popular, or for the many charity concerts, which were important occasions of musical activity. Amateur endeavour was catered for by the Anacreontic Society, established in the second quarter of the eighteenth century, an ambitious if unbalanced orchestral combination which survived over a century. Burgeoning interest in the indigenous tradition, as demonstrated in the Granard and Belfast harp festivals in the late eighteenth century, led to the foundation in 1809 of the Harp Society of Ireland.

Choral music was particularly favoured during the nineteenth century when Francis Robinson, the immigrant patriarch of an eminent musical family and organist at both Christ Church and St Patrick's, founded the large choral group the Sons of Handel (1810) exclusively for the performance of oratorio. He was also one of the initiators of the Philharmonic Society (1826), which survived some 40 years as one of the mainstays of musical life in the city, giving many first performances in Ireland including that of Beethoven's Choral Symphony in 1856. This society was regularly conducted by Robinson's youngest son, Joseph, who was also the first conductor of the University of Dublin Choral Society, founded in 1837 with an intention 'to cultivate choral music in general'. This energetic figure also established the Antient Concerts, which flourished from 1834 until 1863, affording Dubliners the opportunity to hear not only established works but even the most modern creations of such as Mendelssohn. The preponderance of Protestant endeavour found a Catholic counterpart in the Royal Choral Institute, inaugurated by John William Glover in 1851. Chamber music, both choral and instrumental, was sponsored by the unheralded violinist R.M. Levey, who demonstrated his versatility in 1863, by presenting both the Dublin Madrigal Society and the

Dublin Quartette Union. However, the choral ascendancy continued to the close of the century: Joseph Robinson established the Dublin Musical Society, dedicated to the presentation of the major works of the repertory, in 1876, while St Patrick's Oratorio Society (1880) was initiated and conducted by Charles George Marchant, organist of the Dublin cathedral. It is a telling reflection that the first professional orchestra in the city independent of a theatre was the Dublin Orchestral Society, founded in 1899 by Michele Esposito. In the same year a contemporary immigrant musician, James C. Culwick, established and conducted the Orpheus Choral Society; his daughter, Florence, continued this tradition with the Culwick Choral Society. Vincent O'Brien's Dublin Oratorio Society was active from 1906.

Opera was provided for from 1928 by the Dublin Operatic Society and from 1941 by the Dublin Grand Opera Society, while the Rathmines and Rathgar Musical Society is the most venerable of the many groups enjoying the pleasures of light opera. The much-vaunted Irish Musical League was initiated in 1926 by Hester Travers Smith and others, but never attracted sufficient support to realize its ambitions. One of its principal advocates, Colonel Wilhelm Fritz Brase, director of the Army School of Music, then set about forming the Dublin Symphony Orchestra. In July 1927 it formally amalgamated with Turner Huggard's Philharmonic Choral Society to form the reincarnated Dublin Philharmonic Society, which for a decade was the most active ensemble in the city. Brase was also active at this period developing the four military bands of the Irish Army, the first of which, the Army No. 1 Band, was created in 1923 and achieved a standard that offered a lead to the city's many amateur bands, the oldest of which, St James's, had been founded in 1800.

Permanent ensembles were provided by the national broadcasting organization, which commenced service under the call-sign 2RN in 1926. The station orchestra was gradually increased in size until it reached a complement of 60 players in the 1940s; performing since 1990 as the National Symphony Orchestra, it remains the one permanent professional orchestra in the capital, with a strength of some 80 instrumentalists. In 1943 it was joined by Cor Radio Eireann, expanded in the 1980s by Colin Mawby to include a children's choir, Cor na nog, chamber choir, now termed the National Chamber Choir, occasional chorus, and larger RTE Philharmonic Choir, and in 1948 by the smaller Radio Eireann Light Orchestra, now called the RTE Concert Orchestra. The threat to these groups and the decision to disband the station's Vanbrugh String Quartet (appointed 1986), resulting from revised broadcasting legislation in 1990, represented a major reversal, now subsequently overcome (1998).

The welcome expansion in activity since the end of World War II has led to the emergence of many amateur bodies. Terry O'Connor's Dublin String Orchestra achieved an high standard and gave many first performances of works by young Irish composers during the 1930s and 1940s. Constance Hardinge and Havelock Nelson created the Dublin Orchestral Players in 1939, while the younger Dublin Symphony Orchestra, which emerged from the Orchestra of the Keating Branch of the Gaelic League, gives an annual series of concerts currently under the direction of John Hughes. The concise resources of the professional Irish Chamber Orchestra, formed in 1970, allow it to explore a repertoire which complements that of the National Symphony Orchestra, while the National Youth Orchestra, conducted by Hugh Maguire, offers invaluable experience to emerging instrumentalists. Jane O'Leary's Concorde concentrates on the presentation of contemporary music. The Dublin Baroque Players (1965) is a chamber orchestra with a penchant for touring. Numerous smaller choral groups have appeared, of which St Stephen's Singers, based at University College, Dublin, achieved a particularly laudable standard during the 1970s. Many such choirs were motivated by an interest in earlier music, which found an instrumental counterpart in the Consort of St Sepulchre. Our Lady's Choral Society, formed in 1945 from members of Catholic church choirs, is representative of a number of large choral unions at work in the city.

JOSEPH RYAN

music ensembles, Northern Ireland As a result of the disbandment of the BBC Northern Ireland Orchestra, the Ulster Orchestra, previously of chamber proportions, was enlarged in 1981. Expansion has continued over the years to the current playing strength of 64. In addition to giving regular concerts both in Belfast and at various regional centres, the orchestra accompanies the performances of the Belfast Philharmonic Society and Northern Ireland Opera. Its imaginative educational programme is assuming increasing importance. The orchestra's standing has been enhanced by frequent radio and television broadcasts, a series of commercial recordings of a wide repertoire (including the orchestral music of Harty and Stanford), and tours of Britain and Europe.

The work of the Ulster Orchestra is complemented by the Belfast Baroque Consort, the Harty Ensemble, the Northern Sinfonia and the Western Sinfonia, which consist largely of professional and semi-professional players. In Londonderry the Guildhall Chamber Orchestra provides an opportunity for those studying at conservatoires in Britain and elsewhere to make music together during vacations. The principal amateur orchestras are the Studio Symphony Orchestra and the Northern Ireland Symphony. The availability of instrumental tuition at many primary and secondary schools, as well as through the music centres serviced by the five education and library boards, has been of paramount importance, with the various regional youth orchestras and wind ensembles in particular achieving impressively high standards of performance.

Members of the Ulster Orchestra constitute 15 independent chamber and other ensembles. Prominent among these are the Adelphi and Orion String Quartets, the Belfast Wind Quintet, Ulster Brass, the Amalgamation Jazz Band, and Carousel. Another professional chamber group, Sequenza, specializes in the performance of contemporary music.

While many of Ulster's numerous flute, pipe, brass and accordion bands are closely associated with either Loyalist or Republican parades, others confine themselves to concert giving. Unique among these is the Killycoogan Accordion Orchestra. Using high-quality accordions supported by a synthesizer and a full percussion section, this ensemble presents a very varied selection of music.

Ulster's choral tradition continues to flourish. In Belfast, performances of major choral works are given by the Belfast Philharmonic Society and the St George's Singers. Civic choirs are found in Bangor, Enniskillen, Larne, Londonderry, Newry, Newtownards, Omagh and Armagh, where the Armagh City Choir represents a conspicuously successful attempt to bridge sectarian divisions. The Armagh City Junior Choir also draws its members from both the Protestant and Catholic communities.

The Renaissance Singers and the Priory Singers are two of the province's best-known chamber choirs. There are male-voice choirs in Ballyclare, Ballymena, Donaghadee and Portadown, in addition to those in Belfast. The Mossgrove Singers is perhaps the most notable of the comparatively few ladies' choirs. Of the many school choirs, that of Grosvenor High School (Belfast) has an outstanding record of achievement. Amateur operatic productions range from Gilbert and Sullivan to modern musicals, with some of the leading companies frequently receiving awards in such competitions as those at the annual Waterford Festival of Light Opera. At the Queen's University, Belfast, and the University of Ulster there is considerable choral and orchestral activity, with the performance of contemporary music being particularly encouraged.

HARRY GRINDLE

music festivals and *feiseanna* In an Irish context, the music festival may generally be interpreted as an annual event or series of events at a specific venue and consisting of concerts, recitals, workshops and lectures, as well as competitive and non-competitive elements. In some cases these events are worked around a deliberate theme, such as opera. In others musical performances are accommodated under a broad cultural umbrella, which also covers speech and drama, art and dance; such activities often form the kernel of an arts festival or arts week. Whatever its make-up, the festival aims to foster and inspire a standard of excellence in musical performance primarily among the local population and sometimes with a national and even international sphere of influence.

The first celebrated Irish festival was the isolated Belfast Harp Festival of 1792, now famous as much for the discovery of the young Edward Bunting as for the impressive and unique gathering of all of the country's exponents on the instrument. In its more familiar form, the festival took root at the end of the nineteenth century and modelled itself on similar events in Britain. Very soon it articulated a separate identity which referred to historical, religious and cultural issues. The Irish words *feis* and *féile* were frequently adopted, and traditional music often participated on an equal footing with classical. Now, over 100 years later, distinctions between the festival and *feis* are reduced to the likelier involvement of established foreign artists in the former and the more probable content of competition in the latter.

The inauguration of the Dublin Feis Ceoil in 1897 created a format which was eventually imitated throughout the country, notably in Belfast (the Belfast Musical Festival), Cork and Dublin (the Fr Mathew Feis), Derry (the Londonderry Feis and Feis Dhoire Cholmcille), Sligo (the Sligo Feis Ceoil and Feis Shligigh) and Limerick (Féile Luimnighe), and also in such towns as Arklow, Ballina, Dundalk, Enniskillen, Kilcoole, Newry and Omagh. Here vocal, choral and instrumental classes in classical music may be supplemented by competitions in traditional music, jazz and composition.

Some of the most successful festivals have taken a central theme and subsequently developed into truly international events. Among these must be mentioned the Wexford Opera Festival, which retains its original objective in staging unfamiliar works, Belfast's Sonorities, a festival which concentrates exclusively on performances of twentieth-century music, the Cork International Choral and Folk Dance Festival, which among other achievements has promoted the work of many Irish composers, the Dublin International Organ Festival, in which an organ-playing competition attracts contestants from all over the world, and the Waterford International Festival of Light Opera. An unusual and imaginative idea gave rise to the GPA Music Festival in great Irish houses, while the Dublin Festival of Early Music combines the best of native and foreign specialists in the field. Other more general festivals which merit inclusion here are the Belfast Festival, Kilkenny Arts Week and Adare Festival. Finally the AXA Dublin International Piano Competition, established in 1988, now features firmly on the festival calendar.

JOSEPH RYAN

music: history and performance 1700–1990s The condition of music in Ireland within the anglophone tradition has been characterized by two principal factors since the beginning of the eighteenth century. One concerns the relationship of Anglo-Irish music with the indigenous repertory; the other is its relationship with English music and the wider European tradition. A third factor which bears upon both ethnic and art music traditions is the increasingly polarized perception of these traditions, which stems directly from the political and social circumstances in which music in Ireland has been written and performed.

In the assessment of that music which follows here, these factors prevail over the detailed recapitulation of biographical and other information, which is available in the entries on individual composers, on genres and on performance included in this *Companion*.

Conditions for the development of music in anglophone culture were enhanced by the comparatively stable political climate in Ireland at the beginning of the eighteenth century. Nevertheless, a notable indifference to the claims of high culture and serious patronage determined much of Ascendancy musical life, and despite the popularity of ballad opera in Dublin, the cultivation of most European forms of serious musical entertainment, especially *opera seria*, held no interest for Anglo-Irish society. Jonathan Swift's well-known disdain for European norms of musical expression sharply apostrophized a general antipathy towards the complex and demanding aesthetic of Italian music in particular. As against this general indifference, the periodic appointment of gifted musicians from the continent, such as Johann Sigismond Cousser, Matthew Dubourg and Francesco Geminiani, to court or theatre positions in Dublin resulted in a significantly active musical life. Music as recreation and even as a means of social comment was much in evidence and on occasion was specially composed for Dublin. Music as the expression of political or ecclesiastical well-being, music as an analogue of great architecture or painting, was on a less secure footing. Even the distinctive and regular feature of Dublin's non-theatrical music – the performance of major choral works for charitable purposes – failed to stimulate an urban musical culture independent of London norms. The considerable range of musical entertainment in evidence in Dublin throughout the eighteenth century rarely excited intellectual commentary. For the most part, music lay remote from the Anglo-Irish intellect.

Sporadic attempts, moreover, to reconcile (or at least identify) the distinct traditions of Gaelic and Ascendancy musical culture failed to narrow the gulf that lay between them. While Joseph Walker in his *Historical Memoirs of the Irish Bards* (1786) sought to identify Turlough Carolan (1670–1738) as the proper focus of Irish musical endeavour, Charles Burney contemptuously dismissed the role of the Irish bard as 'little better than that of piper to the *White Boys*, and other savage and lawless ruffians'.

This kind of disparity is best understood within the context of music in Dublin during the eighteenth century. Three kinds of public music making, in church, in the theatre and in purpose-built concert rooms and halls, illustrate how closely music in Ireland depended upon English tastes and how generally unconnected it was with the ethnic, Gaelic tradition. Church music was the least cultivated of these three. Swift's vehement denial that he had permitted members of St Patrick's Cathedral choir to participate in the first performance of the *Messiah* (1742) is an extreme formulation of the perception of concerted music of sacred character as a harbinger of popery and Italian decadence. The generally enthusiastic reception of the *Messiah* and several other of Handel's choral works, however, allows us to establish that the performance in Dublin in aid of a deserving charity or allied cause was much welcomed in Ireland.

Brian Boydell's exhaustive researches of music in Dublin throughout the period 1700–60 firmly demonstrate the pre-eminence of Handel's sacred-dramatic works, which were regularly given both before and after the composer's visit to the city in 1741–2. 'Giant Handel' (Pope) stood like a colossus among his composer colleagues in Dublin.

Music in the theatre was largely given over to the hybrid form, ballad opera. The production of *The Beggar's Opera* in London on 29 January 1728 was followed by an Irish production at Smock Alley theatre on 16 March of the same year. Its immediate popularity in Dublin led to a host of imitations, which were either imported from London or newly composed. The immense appeal of these productions, which burlesqued or drastically simplified the musical style of *opera seria*, demonstrates the complete absorption by the Irish Ascendancy and bourgeoise of English taste in this regard.

Although collections of ethnic Irish music had been published on occasion throughout the 1700s, it was not until the appearance of Edward Bunting's *Ancient Music of Ireland* (3 vols, 1796, 1809, 1840) that the Anglophone tradition took any real cognizance of the native repertory. Thomas Moore's selections of *Irish Melodies*, which appeared in serial publication between 1808 and 1834, represent the first sustained attempt to integrate ethnic and ascendancy traditions. Then as now, Moore's alterations and juxtapositions of newly composed texts and sometimes patently distorted airs induced considerable criticism. The antagonism between Moore and Bunting in this regard recalls the earlier dispute between Walker and Burney, and despite the fact the publication of the *Melodies* disseminated Irish music on a scale previously unknown, the practice and composition of music in Ireland remained distinctly polarized.

Although the Act of Union in 1801 and the abolition of an Irish Parliament have long been regarded as inhibiting factors in the development of music in Ireland, this polarization of the two traditions was well established by the last decades of the eighteenth century. In terms of anglophone culture, the period 1760–1830 produced a number of composers, among them Charles Thomas Carter, the earl of Mornington (Garrett Colley Wellesley), Phillip Cogan, Michael Kelly, Sir John Andrew Stevenson and Thomas Cooke, all of whom made a serious contribution to the cultivation of music in Ireland. They ought to be distinguished from those post-union figures (John Field, Michael William Balfe, Vincent Wallace, etc.), whose reputations were made outside Ireland. Of these composers it was Stevenson who most nearly encountered the native tradition in the

'symphonies and accompaniments' which he provided for Moore's *Irish Melodies*. Philip Cogan's assimilation of European structural norms, especially evident in his extant keyboard sonatas, and Kelly's prolific output as a composer of popular operas staged in London and Dublin (which achievement largely post-dated his years as a singer), both testify to a creditable degree of professional competence. Little in the way of original development, particularly with regard to the potential of the ethnic repertory, is manifest in the work of this group.

When practitioners from within the anglophone tradition did encounter the native tradition, as in Stevenson's case, the problems (aesthetic as well as purely musical) were quickly realized: J. Gamble's observation in 1819 that 'I respect Sir John's talents as a general composer, but he appears to me to be totally unfitted to do justice to Irish music. In almost every instance he seems to have substituted in place of the wonderful charm of melody the ostentation of science and mere trick execution' is a formulation of one commonly perceived difficulty. The ethnic repertory, once published and restored, could not afford to lose its integrity within contemporary European musical discourse.

Throughout the nineteenth century, both traditions, native and anglophone, continued to develop along parallel lines. Notwithstanding the antiquarian pursuit of the ethnic repertory by important collectors (among them Forde, Hudson, Pigot and Goodman), the linguistic, social and cultural differences between town and country, as between Protestant Ascendancy and Catholic peasant, endured and hardened.

The publication of George Petrie's *The Ancient Music of Ireland* in 1855 exemplifies the general tendency to set the old melodies to new texts in English, a practice which was also maintained by the Young Irelanders in their quest for a musical diction appropriate to their political aspirations. It was not until the appearance of Patrick Weston Joyce's *Irish*

Music and Song in 1888 that both words and music were derived from original sources.

Within the anglophone tradition, the performance of music by choral societies and associations, instrumental groups (including military and civic bands) and opera companies, was well established by mid-century. The Theatre Royal in Dublin, which opened in 1821, was perhaps the most important of a number of similar venues in Dublin, Cork and Belfast where the international operatic works of the period – including operas by Irish-born composers such as Wallace and Balfe – were regularly given within a few years of their première performances in Europe.

One of the by-products of this surge of musical activity was the articulation of a distinctly conservative movement in Catholic church music, which fostered ties with the European Continent and above all with Germany. Irish priests, including L.J. Renehan and Nicholas Donnelly, sought to establish the principles of the Cecilian movement in Dublin and elsewhere, by which the music of the Counter-Reformation (that of Palestrina above all) and later music in direct emulation of this repertory would be performed in church virtually to the exclusion of everything else. The journal of the Irish Society of St Cecilia, *Lyra Ecclesiastica* (1878–), and the appointment of the young priest Heinrich Bewerunge as professor of church chant and organ at Maynooth University in 1888, were two among several elements which signify the pervasive importance of a musical issue that was beyond the domain of mere entertainment and which was wholly unrelated to the polarized condition of secular music in Ireland in the nineteenth century. Bewerunge's prodigious energy, his critical acumen and his forceful personality registered a musico-religious habit of mind that owed much to his Irish colleagues and their effort to secure for Irish church music a severely Roman countenance. The foundation of the Palestrina Choir at St Mary's Pro-cathedral in Dublin (1902) confirmed these ambitions. Given the long-standing traditions of Anglican music maintained at St Patrick's and Christ Church cathedrals, these developments at the pro-cathedral may be read as an attempt to establish a correspondingly distinctive practice within the Catholic position.

The foundation of the Feis Ceoil (Festival of Music) and the Oireachtas in 1897 can be regarded as the musical outgrowth of the cultural and political nationalism which characterized Ireland's movement towards independence in this period. The fact that the festivals quickly separated to pursue different goals once more illustrates the apparently irreconcilable differences in the two traditions of music in Ireland. Other attempts to overcome these differences were directly inspired by the literary revival and the foundation of a national theatre. The incidental music written by John F. Larchet for plays performed at the Abbey (including J.M. Synge's *Deirdre of the Sorrows* (1910) and the Irish opera *Eithne* by Robert O'Dwyer (1910) reflect an effort to merge the resources of European musical structures and Irish subject matter, which only partly succeeded. A more abstract and therefore more successful assimilation of these elements was apparent in the tone poems of Hamilton Harty, whose *With the Wild Geese* was based on an Irish legend.

The wider provision for music education which became evident in the last decades of the nineteenth century in Dublin and Cork (and to a lesser extent in Belfast) meant that for the first time advanced vocal and instrumental training was available to Irish people at home. The achievements of Michele Esposito in this respect, together with the consolidation of the Royal Irish Academy of Music and the founding of municipal schools (later colleges) of music in Dublin and Cork, reflect a heightening of musical awareness in Ireland which was necessarily frustrated by the political turbulence of the 1916–22 period. Many of the already difficult questions of authenticity and expressive resource which attended the effort to create a durable mode of Irish art music were further complicated by the advent of Modernism in Europe and more immediately by the crisis of nationalism at home. In the decades after independence, composer-teachers such as O'Dwyer and Larchet appeared to retire from these questions, which were vigorously if sporadically debated on the periphery of the larger and more central arguments about Irish identity, politics and literature in the new state. Although a sense of musical awareness benefited the scholarly pursuit of the ethnic tradition, the impasse between European techniques and the native repertory widened. While critics recognized that a cosmetic arrangement of Irish melodies was a poor substitute for a wholly developed and manifestly Irish idiom in contemporary art music, few appeared willing to challenge the viability of the latter. There was indeed an abrupt discontinuity between Ireland as a provincial centre of European and English music, and Ireland as the projected locale of a new mode of musical expression which would answer the demands of nationalist aspirations. Alienated perhaps by the raw politicization of music in such terms, composers such as Frederick May, Arthur Duff, Ina Boyle and Hamilton Harty quietly sidestepped the issue in favour of a more muted or allusive Irish presence in their works.

Since the end of World War II, many of the problems which hindered the development of music in the anglophone tradition have been resolved, even if the fragmentary and often hermetic nature of contemporary musical discourse has worked against the emergence of a compositional style which would harness the ethnic repertory (other than figuratively) to the technical resources of the art tradition. Seán Ó Riada (1931–71) clearly mastered both traditions but signally failed to reconcile them, and his increasing preoccupation with the native repertory towards the end of his life silently suggests that he doubted the possibility of doing so, given the vastly complicated aesthetic of contemporary music and the distinctly different ideology underlying traditional music.

Five aspects of music in Ireland in the postwar period clarify the current state of the art music tradition in relation to the native repertory. First, opportunities to hear and perform music have increased at an unprecedented rate since 1945. Seasons and festivals of opera in Belfast, Dublin, Wexford and Waterford have become annual fixtures. Touring opera companies from Belfast, Cork and Dublin have brought productions of the standard repertory to smaller towns and cities. Three professional orchestras in Belfast and Dublin have made access to live performance of the orchestral repertoire a matter of course. The relocation of the Irish Chamber Orchestra to Limerick (1995) has also helped to widen access to the chamber repertory in the south-west. Dublin at last has a concert hall adequate to its needs. Festivals of twentieth-century music, of early music, as well as international competitions such as the Dublin International Organ Festival and the GPA (subsequently AXA) Dublin International Piano Competition attest to the creative insight, organizational flair and sheer musical ability of such musicians as Geoffrey Spratt, T.J. Walsh, Aloys Fleischmann, John O'Conor, Gerard Gillen and many others. A host of concert and recital series in the main urban centres has enriched musical life in Ireland far beyond the precedents established before the war. Many Irish performers now enjoy an international reputation.

Second, as a vital adjunct to performance, the range and depth of music education in Ireland within the past 25 years has regenerated the study and practice of music, to the extent that the older pattern of dependence on musical personnel from abroad has lessened significantly in favour of persons trained in Ireland, or more frequently Irish persons who train in Ireland and subsequently study further in Britain, Europe or North America.

Third, radio and television have also advanced art music in Ireland, and the national broadcasting service, Radio Telefis

Éireann (RTE), has been seminal not only in its effective management of orchestras but also in its commitment to smaller professional vocal and instrumental ensembles. If this commitment has waned occasionally as a result of funding reductions, it is nevertheless fair to credit RTE with a major role in the fostering of art music generally and in the provision of a forum for contemporary Irish music in particular. The development of a radio channel exclusively devoted to art music is another instance of RTE's vital commitment in this regard.

A fourth development in post-war music is, strictly speaking, beyond the scope of an assessment of the anglophone tradition. But the emancipation of ethnic Irish music and its revival by professional and amateur musicians throughout the country since the early 1950s have had important implications for the perception and practice of music in Ireland. The artistry and expressive virtuosity of the Chieftains, for example, have greatly heightened awareness of traditional music and its communicative potential. It remains to be seen whether some form of cross-fertilization between this music and the techniques of art music will yield fresh resources for the contemporary Irish composer.

The fifth and final aspect is at once the most plainly evident and the most difficult to summarize. The access to music education in Ireland and an unprecedented exposure to European art music have resulted in a large number of Irish composers who work within the European tradition. The older generation of these composers include A.J. Potter, Brian Boydell, Gerard Victory, Aloys Fleischmann, James Wilson, John Kinsella and Séoirse Bodley. Michael Alcorn, Gerald Barry, David Byers, John Buckley, Rhona Clarke, Frank Corcoran, Jerome de Bromhead, Eibhlis Farrell, Roger Doyle, Phillip Edmondson, Raymond Deane, Phillip Hammond, Piers Hellawell, Michael Holohan, Fergus Johnston, Philip Martin, David Morris, Kevin O'Connell, Jane O'Leary, Eric Sweeney, Adrian Thomas and Kevin Volans belong to the younger generation.

This list – by no means exhaustive – gives some indication of the rate at which composition in Ireland has accelerated within the past 20 years. The association of Irish composers and the Contemporary Music Centre also reflect the high level of creative work in contemporary Irish music. If senior figures such as Bodley and Victory have tended to merge established genres and exploratory techniques (e.g. symphonic and operatic structures imbued with ethnically derived material), younger Irish composers have shown comparatively little interest in the native repertory except as an element which contributes to the admixture of electronic, aleatoric and textural experiment in contemporary composition. A keenly felt aesthetic problem has evolved from the historically based tension between art and ethnic elements in Irish music. The surge of composition in Ireland occurs during a period when the atomization of musical expression and style undermines the possibility of a fertile exchange between the two traditions. Nevertheless, the current difficulties of much contemporary compositional technique, together with the sometimes bewildering range of musical expression which this technique brings in its wake, cannot impair the integrity of the ethnic repertory itself. Given the very recent but unmistakable questioning of such techniques by American composers in particular, it is by no means inevitable that the resources of Ireland's musical past will permanently remain irrelevant to the objectives of contemporary composition.

Reading

Boydell, Brian, *A Dublin Musical Calendar 1700–1760* (Dublin: 1988).

Gillen, Gerard and White, Harry (eds), *Irish Musical Studies*, 5 vols (Dublin: 1990–).

Hogan, Ita, *Anglo-Irish Music, 1780–1830* (Cork: 1966).

Walsh, T.J., *Opera in Dublin, 1705–1797* (Dublin: 1973).

White, Harry, *The Keeper's Recital: Music and Cultural History in Ireland, 1770–1970* (Cork and Indiana: 1998).

HARRY WHITE

music: performers

Conductors

The dearth of native ensembles and the reliance on visiting groups meant that for long there was little call, or opportunity, for home-based conductors. The earliest practitioners were immigrant musicians, while the few indigenous conductors tended to combine direction with another activity, such as performance or teaching. Johann Cousser (b. 1660, Bratislava) settled in Dublin in 1707, where his facility as arranger and conductor saw him appointed master of the state music. His influential successor was Matthew Dubourg, a pupil of Geminiani, who arrived in Ireland in 1724 and was appointed to lead the Viceroy's Band in 1728. Dubourg was largely responsible for the successful premiere of Handel's *Messiah* in 1742. Thomas Arne was the most distinguished of directors: he conducted various performances during his three extended visits to Ireland in the mid-century. Theatre orchestras offered another source of employment; Thomas Pinto was leader of the band at Smock Alley from 1773 to 1779 – where Tommaso Giordani was one of his predecessors – and one of a succession of directors at Dr Mosse's Round Room or Rotunda at the same period. The English organist, conductor and occasional composer Jonathan Blewitt arrived in Ireland in 1811, and succeeded Thomas Cooke as director of the theatre in Crow Street in 1813.

But the decline in patronage and in social activity consequent on the Act of Union (1800) encouraged, and even necessitated, the gradual emergence of native conductors. Henry Bussell, one of the founders of the Philharmonic Society (1826), was eventually succeeded as conductor of this organization by the energetic Joseph Robinson. Robert Prescott Stewart, who followed Robinson as conductor of the University of Dublin Choral Society, was also to the fore until his death in 1894. The appointment by Edward Martyn of Vincent O'Brien as the first director of the Palestrina Choir, established in 1903 in St Mary's Pro-cathedral, first introduced the name of this Dublin musician to his fellow citizens.

The industry of foreign musicians was still keenly felt. Achievements in the choral domain by the English-born J.C. Culwick complemented the work in the orchestral sphere of the Neapolitan Michele Esposito. None had a greater impact on the field of conducting than the German musician Wilhelm Fritz Brase, who had come to Ireland in 1923 to establish the Army School of Music. Not only was he a leading exponent of the art, whose work with the Dublin Philharmonic Society in the decade from 1927 provided the major focus of musical enterprise, but he also encouraged a group of native conductors including Arthur Duff, James Doyle, Dermot O'Hara and Michael Bowles, who played a significant part in the development of the broadcasting service, the Dublin Grand Opera Society, and smaller ensembles. Dependence on the immigrant musician was even more notable in provincial centres: music in Cork was beholden to the Milanese Ferruccio Grossi, to Heinrich Tils, and to the Fleischmanns, father and son, a legacy of commitment that brings us to the present day. German musicians were also to the fore in Belfast: Francis Koller succeeded Adolf Beyschlag as conductor of the Belfast Philharmonic Society in 1887, an organization founded by yet another foreigner, Henry Stiehl. From 1912 the society came under the discerning guidance of E. Godfrey Brown. The North provided the most exceptional talent in the person of Hamilton Harty, who was to achieve international fame with his tenure at the Hallé Orchestra (1920–33).

The expansion of the Radio Éireann Symphony Orchestra in the 1940s necessitated the engagement of experienced foreign conductors. The popular Jean Martinon, Hans Smidth-Isserstedt, Norman del Mar and Jean Fournet were at the start of a succession which included Milan Horvat and Tibor Paul, and that has latterly led to contracts for Bryden Thompson, Janos Furst, George Hurst Kasper de Roo and Alexander Anissimov. The skills of Hans Waldemar Rosen, Eric Sweeney and currently Colin Mawby have all been put to the service of RTE's commitment to choral music. However, the lack of any systematic training for aspiring conductors reflects the dearth of opportunity for employment here; Eimear O'Broin, Colman Pearce and Proinnsias O'Duinn are the leading contemporary native conductors, while the younger Robert Houlihan has had to move abroad to find a permanent post.

Wind Players: Woodwind and Brass
A persistent obstacle to the development of ensembles and full orchestras in Ireland was the absence of any tradition of wind playing, a situation which has been tackled only within the last century. Visiting soloists had appeared here but were never as attractive a proposition as were pianists and string players, although Egon Petri (1881–1962), the celebrated pianist, did appear in the RDS playing horn. The establishment of the Municipal School of Music in Dublin in 1890, with an initial concentration on woodwind, brass and percussion, suggested that some thought had been given to rectifying the previous imbalance in instrumental instruction. However, it was not until the creation of the Army School of Music in 1923 that a systematic scheme of education and a regular opportunity to perform were offered to aspiring wind players. Many of the leading executants, including those who peopled the early 2RN (the call-sign of the national broadcasting organization) and Radio Éireann (RE) orchestra, had emerged from the Army No. 1 Band and its sister bands. The clarinettist Frederick Ashton was one such, later exponents of this instrument being the foreign musicians Wolf Adler and Michele Incenzo, who were followed by Brian O'Rourke and John Finucane. Andre Prieur

was an outstanding flute player, as was Herbert Leeming in an earlier generation. The latter's influence as a teacher has been carried on by Doris Keogh in the Royal Irish Academy of Music (RIAM), while Evelyn Grant has had impressive success in Cork. Principal contemporary exponents are William Dowdall, Madeleine Staunton and Deirdre Brady. Edward Beckett has pursued his career abroad, as has the hugely successful James Galway. Other woodwind players of note are Helmut Seeber, Albert Soliveres and the younger Matthew Manning, who perform on the upper double-reeds, and Gilbert Berg and John Lyons on bassoon. Kenneth Edge has recently emerged as a distinctive solo saxophonist.

Standards of brass playing have not in general kept pace with the improvements in the woodwind sector. The horn player Leopold Laurent was one of the many immigrants attracted to Ireland by positions in the orchestras and in the technical schools. He played alongside Harry Woods and the current manager of the National Concert Hall, Frank Murphy. Victor Malirsh was not only a fine exponent of French horn but also a seminal influence on younger players, among whom Fergus O'Carroll ranks as a leading performer. Many of the principal trumpet players emerged from the Army No. 1 Band, including Tommy McCurtan and Con Fury. Novema Salvadori played orchestral trombone and taught in the RIAM, where Sean Cahill is his successor. His pupil Donal Bannister is pursuing his career in Britain. Hartmut Pritzel and Niall Doyle are among the principal exponents of the tuba.

String Players
As with other instrumental disciplines, Ireland was fortunate in attracting to its shores string players of quality to serve its needs. R.M. Levey was the leading resident performer and teacher during the middle years of the nineteenth century. He was an early member of the staff of the RIAM, which later attracted the impressive succession of

Guido Papini (1891–9), Adolf Wilhemj (1900–12) and Achille Simonetti (1912–20) as senior violin professors. They did much to raise the general standard of string playing, but the lack of opportunity for advancement meant that student numbers were modest. A colleague on the staff was Arthur Darley, who also performed within the traditional idiom; he was the first musical director of the Abbey Theatre following its foundation in 1904. The Milanese Ferruccio Grossi was also a member of staff, although he is best remembered for his work in Cork. These teachers and their successors were responsible for the emergence of a talented school of native performers.

In the early years of the Free State, ensembles such as the Dublin Philharmonic Society depended on the talents of a small but energetic pool of players including violinists Joshua Watson, Nancy Lord and Petite O'Hara, who also played viola, as did George Brett; and cellists Ida Starkey-O'Reilly and Clyde Twelvetrees, the latter of whom was to lead that section of the Hallé Orchestra. Terry O'Connor was the first leader of the 2RN orchestra, a post she retained for two decades. She also founded and conducted the Dublin String Orchestra and she heralds the noticeable ascendancy of women in the area of string performance. Geraldine O'Grady has an established reputation as a soloist, orchestral player and teacher, as has Therese Timoney, leader of the New Irish Chamber Orchestra. Many of this generation, including Margaret Hayes and Mary Gallagher, were influenced by the excellent teaching of the Czech Jaroslav Vanecek at the RIAM. His industry found a counterpart in the College of Music through the work of Michael McNamara and his son Brian, while Hugh Maguire has proved particularly inspirational to younger players through his work with the Irish Youth Orchestra. Cork too can boast an impressive teaching record with guidance from such as John Vallery, Constantin Zanidache, Adrian Petcu, Josef Calef and, again, Michael McNamara.

The orchestras of the broadcasting service have traditionally been the principal source of employment for executants. John Ronayne was a distinguished leader and a contemporary of another leading violinist, Clodagh McSwiney. Audrey Collins is his successor in what has been since 1990 the National Symphony Orchestra, where she worked alongside her husband, the late Archie Collins, leader of the viola section, a position also occupied by Maire Larchet. At the first desk of the cello section of this ensemble was Vincenzo Caminiti, a position later occupied with grace by Aisling Drury Byrne who, together with Fionnuala Hunt (violin) and Una Hunt (piano), formed the Dublin Piano Trio. The female hegemony was broken by Alan Smale, leader of the RTE Concert Orchestra and active with a number of smaller ensembles. Maighread McCrann (violin) and Daire Fitzgerald (cello) are representative of the emerging generation, while Brendan O'Brien (violin) and David Daly (double bass) are amongst the leading Irish players pursuing careers in Britain. Individual members of the RTE Vanbrugh Quartet, particularly Gregory Ellis, have also begun to contribute as important teachers.

Keyboard Players

The development of music education in Ireland from the last decades of the nineteenth century onwards is especially borne out by the work of Michele Esposito, whose tenure at the RIAM from 1882 until his death resulted in a tradition of piano teaching which is sustained to the present day. In more recent years, the achievement of outstanding teachers (who include J.J. O'Reilly, Elizabeth Costello, Elizabeth Heuben, Frank Heneghan and Mabel Swainson) in Dublin, Cork, Limerick and Belfast has ensured the widespread popularity of the piano throughout Ireland, not only as a form of entertainment but as an object of intensive study.

Since the early 1920s, Irish pianists have studied abroad (often in London), but it is only since World War II that they have found what limited employment there is for the professional pianist in Ireland (as a performer). The career of Charles Lynch (1907–84) illustrates the difficulty facing Irish performers in their quest for a livelihood at home. Lynch's pre-war livelihood as a pianist was largely made outside Ireland.

The 1960s and 1970s produced leading exponents of the instrument, including Veronica McSwiney, John O'Conor, Micheal O'Rourke and Phillip Martin. In the 1980s, the emergence of Hugh Tinney and Barry Douglas gave further evidence of the success of Irish teaching North and South. Douglas's victory in the 1986 Moscow International Piano Competition, and O'Conor's founding artistic directorship of the GPA Dublin International Piano Competition in 1988, are two outstanding events in the recent history of the instrument in Ireland. Other prominent young players include Anthony Byrne, Jan Cap and Roy Holmes, each of whom may be taken here to represent individual trends which lend depth and interest to pianists working in Ireland. Holmes, for example, is representative of a significant number of gifted accompanists (including Jeannie Reddin and Gillian Smith) who play a vital role in Irish musical life. Byrne likewise has been noted for his performance of piano music by contemporary Irish composers (in particular John Buckley): such a rapport between performers and musicians deserves more widespread emulation than it has received; meanwhile, the Arts Council of Ireland and other funding bodies remain sympathetic to the idea of Irish pianists commissioning work from Irish composers.

Other keyboard instruments have also been widely cultivated in recent years. Organists such as Gerard Gillen, Desmond Hunter and Peter Sweeney have achieved an international reputation and have done much to maintain a high standard of teaching and playing in Ireland. The Dublin International Organ Festival and regular series of recitals in churches throughout the country have greatly increased the audience for the instrument since the 1970s.

The harpsichord has also come into prominence among Irish players in the recent past. Emer Buckley, Malcolm Proud, Ann Heneghan and Christopher Stembridge each pursue busy careers at home or abroad as soloists and continuo players, which reflect the somewhat earlier achievements of John Beckett as a harpsichordist of the first rank.

Singers
The phenomenal success of Irish singers who made their careers in opera abroad early in the twentieth century is not perhaps directly related to the evolution of music as a cultural force in Irish life. Nevertheless, it is impossible to ignore the achievement of John McCormack (1884–1945) and Margaret Burke Sheridan (1889–1958) simply because they did not (as a rule) perform frequently in Ireland. Even earlier, Michael Kelly (1762–1826) may be said to have inaugurated a tradition of Irish-born singers who have won fame as operatic or concert artists on the Continent and elsewhere. Kelly's success as a tenor in Vienna, where he created the roles of Don Basilio and Don Curzio in Mozart's *The Marriage of Figaro*, has been emulated by Irish singers to the present day. Such artists as Particia Bardon, Heather Harper, Mary Hegarty, Ann Murray and Suzanne Murphy are among those of the present generation who have attained distinction as members of English or European opera companies. Margaret Sheridan de Bruin, Veronica Dunne and Bernadette Greevy also enjoyed significant success on the concert platform abroad, and there are many others, including Frank Patterson, Collette McGahon, Regina Nathan and Finbar Wright, who have sustained this distinguished tradition. And even these names are merely representative of a larger cadre of successful artists.

That many of these singers have won acclaim at international level is due in significant measure to the contribution of such distinguished teachers as Veronica

Dunne, Mary Brennan, Paul Deegan, Deirdre Grier Delaney and others. In domestic terms, the opportunities afforded to Irish singers by companies such as Opera Northern Ireland, DGOS Opera Ireland, Opera Theatre Company, Cork City Opera and the Wexford Festival Opera have greatly increased within the past 25 years.

JOSEPH RYAN AND HARRY WHITE

music printing and publishing Music publishing in Ireland has seldom catered significantly for the needs of composers. On the other hand, at various periods there has been considerable activity in the printing and publication of Irish and of other music in response to public demand.

Nathaniel Thompson of London and Dublin printed music on occasion between 1666 and 1688, but the earliest record of music printing specifically in Ireland was by Robert Thornton of Dublin, who in 1686 advertised 'choicest New Songs, with Musical Notes...engraven on Copper Plates'. Isolated examples of music were printed in Dublin around the turn of the eighteenth century, and Samuel Terry from Liverpool is recorded as a music printer and publisher in Cork (1721–2) and Limerick (1722–5), but significant activity did not begin until the 1720s.

In Dublin, John and William Neale published collections of instrumental and vocal music from 1723, including the earliest collection of Irish music in 1724. This was followed by a dramatic increase in activity throughout the eighteenth century, reaching a peak during the 1820s when over two dozen music sellers, including printers and publishers, were active in Dublin. Amongst the more prominent were the Rhames family (1750–1810), the Lee family (1752–1821), Maurice Hime (1790–1820), Smollet Holden (1800–18), J.B. Logier (1809–46), and Edward (and later James) McCullagh (1821–51). Certain prominent London publishers, most notably Goulding and Co. (1803–16), maintained branches in Dublin. The music published

consisted almost exclusively of popular works aimed at the amateur market: songs and arrangements from ballad or comic operas, glees, dances and, increasingly from the late eighteenth century, drawing room arrangements of Irish melodies.

From the 1840s music publishing declined, with only a handful of companies operating. Amongst these was Samuel Pigott, who started c.1825 and, later as Pigott and Co., continued as a publisher mainly of Irish songs, part songs, and instrumental arrangements until 1968. In the twentieth century the growing sense of national identity following independence was reflected in many publications of Irish music, often as arrangements, by Waltons (founded 1924), by An Gúm (founded by the government 1926), and by numerous other publishers, especially in recent years.

The opportunities for publication within Ireland of music by living composers remain extremely limited. As well as housing a large collection of scores, the Contemporary Music Centre, set up in 1986, publishes a limited number of works by composers from North and South. Numbers of smaller, often private publishers are active, but without access to effective distribution it remains difficult for Irish composers to achieve international notice unless represented by major publishing houses abroad.

BARRA BOYDELL

music sources The earliest extant musical sources of Irish origin consist of manuscripts which contain extracts of either plainsong or three-part sacred polyphony. A gradual from the second half of the twelfth century was associated with the Benedictine monastery at Downpatrick, County Down. More famous is the three-part colophon *Cormacus scripsit hoc psalterium*, which dates from the early thirteenth century. In these manuscripts the music is written in square notation on staves of four lines in different colours. Of a slightly later origin are the *Dublin Troper* (dated c.1360), an Augustinian missal and Sarum processional, the latter two intended for churches in Dublin in the fourteenth century. All of these sources are located in British libraries.

The fifteenth century enjoys a much greater representation of surviving musical material, mostly in the form of antiphonals and processionals. Certainly the most unusual items are four fragments of slate which are inscribed with mensural notation. The slates were rescued from the ruins of a church at Smarmore, County Louth, and are now preserved in the National Museum of Ireland.

Sources of instrumental music originate in the sixteenth century. These include the so-called *Dublin Virginal Manuscript* (*c*.1570), Ireland's oldest keyboard anthology, and a number of volumes of lute music, the best known being *Thomas Tallis Pupil's Lute Book* (dated 1583) and the *Ballett Lute Book*. These contain not only original compositions but transcriptions of Italian madrigals, French chansons and Latin motets, as well as English and Dutch songs. Dances also feature widely here. The music is usually presented in six-line French tablature form.

Vocal music from this period is served by a small collection of surviving partbooks, chief amongst which are the *Thomas Wode Partbooks*, a series of manuscripts of Scottish provenance which at some point made their way to Dublin. These volumes, like their contemporary sources of instrumental pieces, refer for the first time to the works of specific composers such as Janequin, Tallis, Byrd, Philips, Dowland and a host of minor figures.

By the end of the sixteenth century the rapid development and increased circulation of printed music had inevitably replaced the laborious copying of manuscripts, and the attention of both performer and librarian now switched to publication as the more accessible and reliable musical format.

Libraries
Most musical collections in Ireland today are found in general libraries which provide at least some degree of access and certain limited

borrowing facilities for the public. The collections may comprise any combination of the following material: reference tools, manuscripts and/or printed copies of music, literature on music, and specific gifts or bequests, which are often preserved intact.

1   The National Library of Ireland incorporates in its music holdings five important gift collections. Areas covered by these relate to Irish music as well as some early examples of printed music. The library of the Royal Irish Academy specializes in manuscripts and printed works of Irish interest and contains some musical items.

2   The largest music collection in Northern Ireland is to be found in the library of Queen's University, Belfast. It includes a large stock of specialist music literature, music periodicals, *opera omnia* editions, and copies of theses on musicological and ethnomusicological subjects. A number of early nineteenth-century prints of part songs and chamber music, which originally belonged to the Belfast Anacreontic Society, and of sacred vocal music have also been deposited there. Of particular interest are the personal library of Sir Hamilton Harty, which includes his own annotated conducting scores and the autographs of most of his works, and the Edward Bunting manuscript collection of Irish folk melodies. The music library of the Belfast Central Library includes music texts, some *opera omnia* editions, music periodicals, recorded music and a large stock of performance materials. A special Irish music section includes the Henry, Bunting, Hardebeck and O'Neill collections, and also a collection of broadside ballads. The Linenhall Library, Belfast, which dates from the 1780s, is concerned mainly with modern collections of Irish folk music. However, copies of the Bunting manuscripts are kept there, while some early Anglican service books with music are to be found in the largely uncatalogued collection of early printed

books. The University of Ulster library includes printed music, music texts and music periodicals.

The Republic possesses four university music libraries, foremost of which is the fine one in Trinity College, Dublin. Its considerable holdings include manuscripts and early prints as well as the library of Ebenezer Prout. The collection of University College, Dublin, contains the Count John McCormack bequest and some manuscripts of Sir Arnold Bax. Eighteenth-century English operas are featured in the Sperrin-Johnson collection at University College, Cork, while works devoted to church music represent an important category in the library of St Patrick's College, Maynooth, County Kildare.

3 The Royal Irish Academy of Music (RIAM) was fortunate enough to acquire the works of Sir Charles Villiers Stanford as a gift for its library. Lord Monteagle's bequest occupies a central place here. The library of the College of Music is of a more recent origin.

4 The music holdings of Christ Church Cathedral and St Patrick's Cathedral are typical of Irish cathedral libraries in their emphasis on sacred works formerly performed in their liturgies.

5 Archbishop Marsh's Library in Dublin ranges in its musical material from fifteenth-century sources and early printed editions of Italian madrigals to twentieth-century additions. Its principal contents date from the seventeenth century. The Diocesan Library at Cashel, County Tipperary, contains both manuscript and printed music. The oldest item, which dates from 1168, resembles a general compendium which includes a tract on music. The most modern library is the Music Library, a division of the Central Library at the ILAC Centre in Dublin since 1986. As well as scores, books and periodicals on music, the library contains collections of records, cassettes (audio and video) and compact discs. Users also enjoy on-site listening and viewing facilities. Finally, many county libraries include small sections on music.

Collections

1 *Books*. In 1863 the National Library of Ireland was presented with the library of Jasper Robert Joly (1819–92). The 6,000 items include Irish and Scottish songs and dances, early ballad operas and eighteenth-century songsheets.

The library acquired the music collection of George Noble Count Plunkett in 1942. Consisting of *c*.400 volumes, the collection includes works by Philip Cogan, and transcriptions of songs and instrumental pieces. Smaller gifts to the library are those of Banks, Omeath and Hamilton.

After the death of Ebenezer Prout (1835–1909), Trinity College, Dublin, purchased his library of *c*.1200 volumes. This is a comprehensive collection which ranges from scores and biographies to volumes on acoustics and criticism.

2 *Instruments*. The largest collection of musical instruments in Ireland is located in the National Museum. It comprises 350 individual items, half of which are European in origin. The Ulster Folk Museum at Cultra maintains an archive of Ulster folk music. Among the Irish musical instruments preserved at the Ulster Museum are Bronze Age horns and trumpets, a medieval wooden trumpet, some late eighteenth-century military bugles and drums, harps and uillean pipes of the nineteenth and early twentieth centuries, and fragments of a tambourine and of a fretted string instrument from the Armada wreck, the *Girona*.

Finally, several collections of keyboard and stringed instruments in private houses in Ireland do exist, but for reasons of security these remain unadvertised to the general public.

PETER DOWNEY AND PETER DEVINE

music venues This entry is confined to public venues for formal music, and does not include small or ephemeral accommodation unless of special significance.

BARRA BOYDELL

Dublin

From medieval times the cathedrals of St Patrick and Christ Church, with their professional choirs, played a central part in musical life, the significance of which diminished as public concerts developed during the eighteenth-century. St Andrew's Round Church was notable for some decades after 1736 as the venue for the annual benefit for Mercer's Hospital. The relative importance of Dublin Castle, where royal odes were performed, diminished for a similar reason.

The Musick Hall in Crow Street, opened in 1731, was the first major concert hall, supplanting society rooms in taverns. Mr Neal's Great Musick Room in Fishamble Street, built by Richard Cassels for the Charitable Musical Society, was opened in October 1741, in time for Handel's visit. With a capacity of 700 (without hoops and swords) it was the venue for the first performance of the *Messiah*. After the opening of the Rotunda in 1767 its importance declined, and it was converted into a theatre in 1777 in time for the first season devoted to full-scale productions of Italian opera. It was finally converted into an ironworks in 1867.

In the 1740s, the Crow Street hall was being used more for assemblies and balls, and the Philharmonick Society's oratorios and orchestral concerts were being performed in their room a short distance up Fishamble Street from Neal's hall. The Philharmonick Room ceased to figure in the 1750s, and Crow Street was converted into a theatre in 1757, continuing as such until 1820.

In the mid-eighteenth century 'concerts of Vocal and Instrumental Musick' performed in ornamental gardens during the summer months contributed significantly to Dublin musical life. The chief locations were Spring Gardens in St Stephen's Green, Marlborough Street Bowling Green, Great Britain Street Gardens (where the Lying-in Hospital and Rotunda were built, largely on the proceeds) and the City Bason (*sic*) in St James's Street.

Apart from some concerts in the Exhibition Rooms in William Street between 1790 and 1820, the Rotunda and its adjacent Assembly Rooms in Rutland Square became the chief concert venue until the opening of the Antient Concert Rooms in Brunswick (now Pearse) Street in 1843. Accommodating just over 1,000, it remained the chief Dublin concert hall until 1916. From then until the opening of the National Concert Hall in Earlsfort Terrace in 1981, the capital city had no suitable concert hall. In the meantime, public orchestral concerts were given in the acoustically unsuitable Gaiety Theatre (seating 1,075) and other unsatisfactory venues, such as the Metropolitan Hall in Abbey Street, the St Francis Xavier Hall, the Round Room of the Mansion House, and the Capitol Theatre. Chamber music and recitals usually took place in hotel ballrooms; though increasing use was more recently made of the fine eighteenth-century Examination Hall in Trinity College, the Baroque Room of the National Gallery, and Georgian churches such as St Anne's and St Stephen's. The Royal Dublin Society posesses a hall where it has promoted an annual series of recitals since the last century. More recently, the hall and chapel of the restored seventeenth-century Royal Hospital at Kilmainham has provided an attractive venue for chamber music and smaller concerts. Very large audiences for such attractions as Paverotti and popular music have been catered for in the Royal Dublin Society exhibition hall; and since 1989 the Point Theatre, with a capacity in excess of 6,000, has been available.

At least until the nineteenth-century, when spoken drama became distinctly separated from opera and musical plays, the function of the theatre as a venue for musical performances was of great importance. In addition to ballad and comic operas performed by 'singing actors', there was elaborate incidental and interval music. Little is known of the productions at the first Dublin theatre, which opened in Werburgh Street in 1637, and had to close four years later with the outbreak of rebellion. With the advent of the Restoration, the Smock Alley Theatre was opened in 1662. The Williamite war caused its closure between 1688 and 1692, but thereafter it remained active until 1787. The first ballad opera, *The Beggar's Opera*, met with great success there in 1728; and the first Italian operas heard in Dublin, in the form of one-act burlettas, were performed there in 1761. With its resident band of instrumentalists, it made an important contribution to Dublin's experience of dramatic music. There was rivalry for a short time when the Aungier Street theatre was opened in 1734, though poor acoustics and other disadvantages led to its closure after 1753. The conversion of the Crow Street hall into a theatre in 1758 provided rivalry again, added to by two theatres in Capel Street, which were ephemerally active in promoting opera.

The Crow Street theatre finally closed in 1820, to be followed after a year by the opening of the Theatre Royal in Hawkins Street. This was burned down in 1880. Meanwhile, the Gaiety Theatre had been opened in 1871, and has ever since been the home for operatic performances in Dublin.

Belfast

Belfast did not become a major centre for the performing arts until the nineteenth-century. Some concerts took place in the Old Market House in High Street before the building of the Exchange Rooms in Waring Street, which became the main concert venue from the 1770s until well into the nineteenth-century. The meeting of the harpers in 1792 took place there. The first purpose-built concert hall was the Music Hall in May Street, opened by the Anacreontic Society in 1840. The Ulster Hall, with its excellent acoustics, was opened in 1862, and has remained the principal venue for orchestral and large-scale concerts.

Queen's University has two venues for recitals: the Harty Room and the Elmwood Hall. Larger concerts are sometimes held in the Whitla Hall of the university.

Belfast had a theatre in the 1730s, known as 'the Vaults' from its situation in wine vaults. There was a succession of theatres until, in 1793, the theatre in Arthur Square was opened. Performances of Arne's *Comus* took place in 1788 and 1793. The Theatre Royal succeeded it on the same site in 1871. It was burned down and swiftly rebuilt. The proprietor also built a second theatre, the Grand Opera House in Great Victoria Street in 1895. After extensive renovation in 1980, this still survives.

Cork

The Charitable Musical Society in Cork held concerts in the 1730s, a meeting at the Joiners' Hall being noted in 1732, and weekly concerts took place in 1749 in the Assembly House on Hammond's Marsh. Reports of concerts at the Assembly House in George's Street are noted from 1759 well into the nineteenth-century. In 1770, a larger room with a music gallery was opened in Turkey Street. These venues supplied the needs of the city until more spacious accommodation was offered by the Assembly Rooms in the 1870s, and then by the City Hall. The latter was burned down in 1920, and replaced in 1926 by the present City Hall, which is ideally suited to orchestral and other performances involving large numbers. Some concerts were held at the Clarence Hall in the first decade of the century, and in 1902 the Exhibition Hall supplied accommodation for an audience of 2,000.

Since the early nineteenth-century, sacred music and oratorios were often performed in churches, especially Christ Church. Catalani thrilled the Cork audience with a recital in North Chapel in 1814.

The Old Playhouse (1736–59) was replaced in 1760 by the Theatre Royal opened by Spranger Barry, manager of the Crow Street theatre in Dublin. This was where visiting companies presented opera thereafter, until

1840, when it was burned down after a performance of Bellini's *La Sonnambula*, leaving Seymour's establishment (opened in 1838 at 26 Cooke Street) as the only considerable theatre in Cork until the rebuilding of the Theatre Royal in 1854. The Opera House, opened in 1888 and recently rebuilt, then became the venue for opera, ballet and musical drama.

Chamber music recitals are now given in the halls of the university and of the School of Music.

Smaller Provincial Towns

Much research has yet to be done concerning the history of the limited amount of musical activity in smaller provincial towns. Although certain performances are noted as having taken place in towns such as Derry and Drogheda, precise information concerning the venues for these is not available. At present, music is usually performed in the halls of local convent or technical schools, and occasionally in a town hall or courthouse.

BRIAN BOYDELL

musical instruments The decline in Gaelic music and instruments from the seventeenth century coincides with the beginnings of what was to develop into a local but significant tradition of musical instrument making in Ireland along anglo-Continental models. The Irish harp had reached a peak of development in examples such as the (now fragmentary) Dalway harp of 1621. Irish harps were highly esteemed abroad in the seventeenth century, even being made in England and possibly on the Continent. Although several harps from the eighteenth century survive, the form and size had altered and they are rougher in finish, reflecting the decline of the culture and society to which they belonged. The emergence of the Union (or uilleann) pipes during the early eighteenth century is perhaps the most significant development in native Irish musical instruments during the ensuing period.

Interest in the Irish harp was revived in the early nineteenth century amongst the educated classes. John Egan (fl. *c*.1804–after 1841) of Dublin met this fashionable demand with instruments influenced by contemporary concert harp design, with hand-operated levers to alter the pitch of the strings, with gut rather than metal strings, and often elaborately decorated with shamrocks. Only in recent years have some Irish harp makers begun to return again to earlier historic models.

Although the Dublin city musicians from the later fifteenth century are known to have played wind instruments, a payment in 1696 specifically refers to these being bought in England. However, a drum and trumpet bought in 1616 make no mention of their being imported. The first clear evidence for instrument making in Dublin is mention in 1651 of 'Adrian Strange the virginall maker'. In 1662 George Harris (of Dublin?) built an organ for Christ Church Cathedral, and in 1667 the Cambridge organ builder Lancelot Peace came to Ireland. His instruments included an organ for Trinity College, Dublin, in 1684. The leading English organ builder Renatus Harris built organs at St Patrick's and Christ Church Cathedrals in 1696/7, as well as St Mary's Abbey, and his pupil Jean-Baptiste Culville was active throughout the country in the early eighteenth century. The Hollister family of Dublin (Thomas (fl. 1695–1730), Philip (d. 1760) and William Castels (d. 1802)) were prominent organ builders in the eighteenth century, but the leading maker was Ferdinand Weber (d. 1784), who arrived from Saxony in 1739 and built organs for St Werburgh's and other Dublin churches, as well as in Tuam, Cork and elsewhere. Weber was also an important maker of harpsichords.

Significant numbers of organ and harpsichord (later piano) makers were active especially in Dublin in the later eighteenth and early nineteenth centuries. These include Henry Rother (fl. 1762–82), by whom a clavicytherium survives in the National

Museum, and William Southwell (1756–1842), a pupil of Weber who contributed important innovations in the action of square and cabinet pianos. However, as with other instruments, where named instruments are not extant it is not always possible to distinguish between those who made and those who merely sold or repaired harpsichords and pianos.

While the manufacture of pianos ceased in Ireland with the introduction of the metal-framed piano during the mid-nineteenth century, organ building continued. The most important maker was William Telford, who set up in Dublin in 1830 and built organs throughout Ireland and abroad, as far afield as New Zealand. His organ in Killala Cathedral (1839) is still in playing condition. In modern times Kenneth Jones (since 1973) has established an international reputation, his organs including that in the National Concert Hall, Dublin (1991).

The mid-eighteenth century also saw the development of non-keyboard instrument making in Ireland. Violin makers are first documented from the 1730s, including Thomas Molyneux (d. 1757) of Dublin. Irish violin making reached its apogee in the work of Thomas Perry (b. ?Dublin 1744 or c.1757; d. 1818). The finest of Perry's instruments are highly regarded, but after his death his partner William Wilkinson continued to use his name on instruments of poorer quality. Numbers of violin makers were active thoughout Ireland during the nineteenth and twentieth centuries. In the 1880s J. Bennett of Cork produced instruments of idiosyncratic design without side-ribs, and from 1900 to 1926 G. William Hofmann worked in Dublin, succeeded by his son William, now the doyen of Irish violin makers and repairers. However, few Irish violin makers attracted attention overseas. The founding of a violin-making school in Limerick in 1975, and a short-lived school in Cork in the 1970s–80s, have produced numbers of younger violin makers trained to a high standard.

Wind instrument making developed significantly during the eighteenth century, reaching a peak during the 1820s. Flutes were made in Dublin certainly from the 1740s, and early nineteenth-century wood-wind makers, including Andrew Ellard and John Dollard, also made flageolets. The stationing of many military regiments in Ireland, especially after the 1798 Rebellion and the Act of Union, resulted in an increase in the demand for band and military instruments. Traditional players subsequently adopted the flutes of the military bands, ensuring a continuation up to our own time of wooden flute playing in Ireland. Numbers of brass instrument makers were also active in Ireland at a time when makers throughout Europe were seeking means of providing brass instruments with a full chromatic range. Although by then no longer resident in Ireland, Waterford-born Charles Clagget patented a 'Cromatic [sic] Trumpet and French Horn' in England in 1788. In 1810 Joseph Haliday, bandmaster of the Cavan Militia, added keys to the military bugle, producing the Royal Kent or keyed bugle, which proved to be an important and influential development. A curiosity was the 'Hibernicon', a contrabass horn with keys and fingerholes patented by the Rev. Cotter from County Cork in 1823, an example of which was made by Thomas Key of London. After the middle of the century the number of military bands declined, and with them brass-wind making died out in Ireland.

While only a handful of instrument makers could be counted around the middle of the twentieth century, in recent decades there has been a noticeable increase, largely in response to the growing numbers of people playing traditional and folk music. The instruments most widely represented today are: the violin family, uilleann pipes, harp, wooden flute, guitar and bodhrán.

Reading

Boydell, Brian, *A Dublin Musical Calendar, 1700–1760* (Dublin: Irish Academic Press, 1988).

Pye, Joyce, *Ireland's Musical Instrument Makers* (Galway: Salmon, 1990).

Rimmer, Joan, *The Irish Harp* (Cork: Mercier for the Cultural Relations Committee, 1969).

Teahan, John, 'A list of Irish instrument makers', *Galpin Society Journal* XVI (1963).

BARRA BOYDELL

musicology The publication of Aloys Fleischmann's *Music in Ireland* (1952) can be advanced as an event which heralded the advent of musicology in Ireland, although important work in the collection and preservation of folk music had been for many years previously an important exception to the dearth of scholarly research in music throughout Ireland. Prior to the development of research on a regular basis, a wide range of musical discourse – some of which could reasonably be classified under the broad heading of musicology – can be found in Irish periodical literature from the middle of the nineteenth century onwards. Journals including the *Dublin University Magazine*, the *New Ireland Review*, the *Irish Theological Quarterly* and the *Irish Ecclesiastical Record* carried extensive contributions from musicians and musical antiquaries which debated the (then) current condition of music in Ireland, particularly at the turn of the nineteenth century. Heinrich Bewerunge, Robert Dwyer and Edward Martyn are among those who featured in this debate. Bewerunge, in his detailed assessment of various theories and editions of plain chant, produced work of scholarly significance that went beyond the question of music in Ireland. His contributions to *Lyra Ecclesiastica* and the *Irish Ecclesiastical Record*, as well as to *Kirchenmusikalisches Jahrbuch* (Bonn), are especially noteworthy in these respects. From about 1940, other journals, including the *Bell*, the *Journal of the Royal Society of Antiquaries in Ireland* and the *Proceedings of the Royal Irish Academy* have occasionally carried general or specialized material of musical significance.

Within the field of traditional music, the long-established cultivation of research which began with Edward Bunting's *Ancient Music of Ireland* (three volumes, 1797, 1809, 1840)

was advanced by the work of later collectors including Petrie, Forde, Pigott and Joyce. The volumes of the Irish Folk Song Society (1909ff) and in particular the research of Donal O'Sullivan and Charlotte Milligan Fox kept scholarly musical inquiry alive in Ireland in the early decades of the twentieth century. More recently, two journals in particular, *Ceol* (1963–86) and *Irish Folk Music Studies* (1971–), have provided fora for work in native music. Many scholars, including Breandán Breathnach, Nicholas Carolan, Hugh Shields, Tom Munnelly and Breandán Ó Madagáin have contributed significantly to this area of research. Fleischmann's *The Sources of Irish Traditional Music* (1996) is an outstanding example of the application of modern musicological techniques to the ethnic repertory.

Since about 1970, a significant development in other areas of musical research has taken place as Irish university departments of music have expanded and developed programmes which reflect the unprecedented growth of musicology in Europe and North America in the post-war era. Masters' and doctoral programmes in musicology are now widely available in Ireland and Irish musicologists participate regularly in international meetings and congresses of musicology. The first such event to be held in Ireland, however, was as recently as 1995, when the Maynooth International Musicological Conference took place. The series of volumes *Irish Musical Studies* (1990–) is another marker in the development of Irish musicology, and has addressed such issues as 'Musicology in Ireland', 'Music and the Church' and 'Music and Irish Cultural History'. The following is a brief list of individuals and research interests which affords some idea of the scope of musicology as it is practised in Ireland

Martin Adams (Purcell)

Ita Beausang (music in Dublin, 1780–1800)

Barra Boydell (Renaissance organology; music in seventeenth- and eighteenth-century Dublin; music iconography)

Brian Boydell (music in eighteenth-century Dublin)

Hilary Bracefield (contemporary music in Northern Ireland)

Anthony Carver (late Renaissance choral music)

Denis Collins (history of canon; computer applications in music)

David Harold Cox (contemporary British and American music)

Gareth Cox (Webern; contemporary music in Ireland)

Kieran A. Daly (church music in Ireland)

Patrick F. Devine (Bruckner; Czech music)

Peter Downey (Renaissance and baroque organology)

Máire Egan-Buffet (Goudimel; modal theory; Irish liturgical MSS)

Robin Elliott (music in Canada; nineteenth and twentieth-century European music)

Paul J. Everett (Vivaldi)

Hormoz Farhat (music in Persia; ethnomusicology)

Gerard Gillen (early organ music; history of the organ)

Desmond Hunter (early keyboard music)

Andrew Johnstone (Renaissance polyphony)

Paul McGettrick (ethnomusicology; Irish music)

Anne Murphy (requiem in European music)

Michael Murphy (music in Poland; nationalism and music)

John Morgan O'Connell (music in Turkey)

Mícheál Ó Súilleabháin (ethnomusicology; music in Ireland)

John Reidy (Brahms; analysis)

Michael Russ (Bartók and Mussorgsky)

Joseph Ryan (nationalism and music in Ireland)

Jan Smaczny (Czech music)

Thérèse Smith (ethnomusicology; African-American music; Irish music)

Harry White (Johann Joseph Fux; music and cultural history in Ireland)

Ian Woodfield (organology; British music in India)

Reading

White, Harry, 'Musicology in Ireland', *Acta Musicologica* 60 (1988), pp. 290–305.

HARRY WHITE

N

Nagle, Honora (1728–84) Founder of the Presentation Order. Born Ballygriffin, near Mallow, County Cork; died Cork City, 20 April. After some private tutoring at home, Nagle went to Paris for further education. In the 1750s she came back to Ireland with the intention of devoting her life to the education of the poor, and she used her own fortune to start a school in Cork for poor Catholic girls. She was unable to make a success of this school without charging fees, and so she later handed it over to the Ursuline Order, who catered for the more well-to-do classes. Nagle continued to pursue her aim of education for the children of the poor, and in 1775 she founded the Presentation Order for that purpose. This order has been remarkably successful and, in addition to its many schools in Ireland, it has schools in Britain, the US, Canada and Australia.

Reading

Walsh, T.J., *Nano Nagle and the Presentation Order* (Dublin: Browne and Nolan, 1959).

PATRICK FAGAN

Nary, Cornelius (1658–1738) Catholic controversialist and activist. Born Tipper, Naas, County Kildare; died Bull Lane, Dublin, 3 March. Nary received his early education in Naas and was ordained a priest before going to the Irish College in Paris. He took a doctorate in both canon and civil law at the University of Paris. He went to London *c.*1695 as tutor to the son of the earl of Antrim and in 1696 published his first work of controversy, a defence of Catholic doctrine in reply to the sermons of Archbishop Tillotson of Canterbury. He returned to Ireland *c.*1698 and shortly afterwards was appointed priest of St Michan's parish in Dublin. He spent some 10 years on a translation of the New Testament, a project which was to get him into bad odour with Rome. In 1724 he published 'The case of the Roman Catholics of Ireland', a pamphlet in answer to the 1723 Popery Bill which proposed more repressive measures against the Catholic clergy. He supported the Protestant Archbishop Synge's proposal for a special oath of loyalty to the king for Catholics to the extent that he himself drafted a form of oath. His declining years were occupied with a long-drawn-out, but quite gentlemanly, controversy on doctrinal matters with Archbishop Synge. The historian Lecky described Nary as 'probably the ablest priest then living in Ireland', but, strangely, he has been quite neglected by modern historians.

Reading

Fagan, Patrick, *Dublin's Turbulent Priest: Cornelius Nary (1658–1738)* (Dublin: Royal Irish Academy, 1991).

Nary, Cornelius, *The New Treatment of Our Lord and Saviour Jesus Christ* (place of publication unknown: 1718).

——*A New History of the World* (Dublin: 1720).

PATRICK FAGAN

The *Nation* Weekly newspaper associated with the Young Ireland faction of the Repeal Movement in the 1840s. Founded by Thomas Davis, John Blake Dillon and Charles Gavan Duffy in 1842, and later edited by John Mitchel, the *Nation* provided a forum for many of the most popular Irish poets of the nineteenth century, including James Clarence Mangan and Speranza, setting their work in the context of the cultural nationalist essays of its editors. After giving rise to a number of similar periodicals, including John Mitchel's *United Irishman*, the *Nation* was suppressed in 1848. Relaunched in 1849 (and published until 1892), it never matched the readership or importance achieved in the period 1842–8. The poems and essays of its leading writers, however, became the staples of Irish anthologies, including the best-selling *Spirit of the Nation* (1843). The most frequently anthologized *Nation* poems support the charge by later critics – notably W.B. Yeats – that the *Nation* promoted only agitprop ballads. This neglects, however, the wide range of material published in its pages, including translations from many literatures (principally French and German), parodic pieces, and active cultural debate. Because the contents of the original *Nation* were so widely available in the later nineteenth century, those involved in its publication (such as Gavan Duffy and A.M. Sullivan) were able to use their experience as a touchstone of authenticity which increased their standing in the movement, while others, notably John O'Leary, turned to the *Nation* as a model for their own cultural nationalist agendas.

CHRIS MORASH

National Land League of Ireland Founded 21 October 1879 with the object of obtaining 'such reforms in the laws relating to the land as will enable every tenant to become the owner of his holding by paying a fair rent for a limited number of years'. Its foundation followed the failure of Gladstone's Land Act of 1870 to protect tenants from eviction. The goal of full peasant ownership seemed utopian in 1879 – particularly against a background of an agricultural depression and the widespread evictions that were commonplace at the time. Final victory was achieved only after a land war lasting more than 20 years, which was led in the first crucial phase by Charles Stewart Parnell and Michael Davitt.

The Land League quickly became a powerful national organization, a symbol of the New Departure, and was organized mainly by ex-Fenians. Mass demonstrations in support of reduced rents were staged and many evictions were successfully resisted. Victims of eviction were given shelter and support. The Land League operated on the margins of the law, combining legal protest with physical force (thus providing a model of political organization that survives to the present day), although the leadership disavowed violence. Its formal policy of non-violence enabled the Land League to enlist the support of the Catholic clergy, who proved powerful allies. Landlords were forced to reduce rents and were in many instances prevented from carrying out evictions.

The success of the Land League prompted both a tough Coercion Act and the second Land Act of 1881. The latter granted the three Fs long sought by land reformers: *fixity of tenure*, provided the rent was paid; *free sale* by the tenant of the tenant's interest and improvements in a holding on his vacating it; and *fair rents* to be determined by a government Land Court. Although revolutionary in its day, the measure fell short of radical demands for a total transfer of the land to the people. And for adherents of the New Departure, land reform was secondary to national independence. On the other hand,

425

conservatives strongly supported the measure. In order to keep both sides happy Parnell devised the formula of 'testing the act', whereby the Land League initiated a number of test cases to establish what actual reductions in rent the government was really prepared to give, thus placing the onus of co-operation on the government.

The continued enforcement of the Coercion Act resulted in demands for militant action, particularly in America. Parnell sought to reassure Irish America with tough anti-British speeches. These led to his arrest, and he was soon joined by other prominent Land Leaguers in Kilmainham gaol. From there they issued the 'No Rent Manifesto', whereupon the government suppressed the Land League. In reality, it was already breaking up, a victim of its own success. The Land Act satisfied most tenants. Outstanding issues – most notably the question of tenants with heavy arrears – were dealt with by the Kilmainham Treaty negotiated by intermediaries on behalf of Gladstone and Parnell. The terms included repeal of the Coercion Act and the release of Parnell and his fellow detainees in return for an end to land agitation and co-operation in working the Land Act.

The Phoenix Park murders, involving prominent members of the Land League, were a major setback for the new accord. However, the Land League's objective was ultimately realized: by the time of the Anglo-Irish Treaty of 1921, out of 470,000 holdings, 400,000 were owned by their occupiers.

PATRICK GILLAN

National Literary Society Founded in Dublin in 1892 by W.B. Yeats, with John O'Leary as president, this was a branch of the Irish Literary Society founded in London by T.W. Rolleston and others in 1892, with Sir Charles Gavan Duffy as president. The general idea was to fill the cultural vacuum left by the death of Parnell. Yeats wanted the publication and dissemination of popular imaginative literature but had to settle for lectures and the raising of membership,

aided by Maud Gonne. Committees and sub-committees proliferated, one of these becoming the Gaelic League in 1893. The Irish literary renaissance was thereby initiated, with a raising of consciousness of Irish history, Irish mythology and Irish culture. The National Literary Society was a sower of seeds among the people: of hope, of education and of national identity.

CHRISTOPHER MURRAY

Neal(e) family The most important members of this family were as follows:

1 John (died Dublin, after 1740). Music printer and publisher; instrument-maker and importer, at Christ Church Yard from 1721. After 1734 he was in partnership with his son William.
2 William (c.1700–69) continued to run his father's music shop until 1740, when he became treasurer of the Charitable Musical Society, in which capacity he was responsible for building the Music Hall in Fishamble Street.
3 John (c.1733) The son of William, and an Amateur violinist who first appeared in 1743 'aged 10' playing a violin concerto at a benefit for the hautboy player John Neal (no relation). Described as 'one of the finest private violin performers in Europe', he played to George II at St James's and was a violinist in the 1757 Musical Academy. He was surgeon to the Charitable Infirmary (1756–89).

BRIAN BOYDELL

Neilson, William (1760–1821) Grammarian. Born County Down; died Belfast. Neilson received a classical education under John Young, afterwards professor of Greek at Glasgow, and was ordained a Presbyterian minister. He served at Dundalk, where he kept a school. His *Greek Exercises* became popular for schools and went into eight editions. His *Introduction to the Irish Language* is a faithful representation of the Gaelic then spoken in County Down. In 1817 he became professor of Greek and Hebrew in Belfast College, a training college for Presbyterian ministers, associated with Belfast Academical Institution.

Reading

Neilson, William, *Greek Exercises in Syntax, Ellipsis, Dialects, Prosody and Metaphrasis*, (Dundalk: printed by J. Parks, 1804).
——*An Introduction to the Irish Language* (Dublin: Wogan, 1808).

HENRY BOYLAN

Nelson, Havelock (1917–96) Born Cork, 25 May; died August. Piano accompanist, organist, adjudicator, conductor and composer. Nelson achieved doctorates in both science and music at Trinity College, Dublin, and also studied at the Royal Irish Academy of Music. After war service in the RAF, he was appointed conductor of the BBC Northern Ireland Orchestra in 1947. Founder and director of the Studio Symphony Orchestra, the Ulster Singers and the Studio Opera Group, he has received many awards and honours in recognition of his services to music. In addition to radio, television and film scores, and arrangements of Irish airs, his compositions include a sonatina for clarinet and piano (1949), the song cycle *Love's Joy and Pain* (1952), a concertino for piano and orchestra (1955), and a *Sinfonietta* (1951). Much of his vocal music has been published.

PETER DOWNEY

ne temere **decree** (1907, effective 1908) Governed the marriage of Catholics, including mixed marriages. Thus, any marriage between a Catholic and a non-Catholic was declared invalid and punishable by excommunication, unless it took place before a duly authorized Catholic priest. To obtain dispensation for such a marriage to take place the following conditions were to be signed by both partners:

1 There shall be no interference with the religion of the Catholic party or his (or her) practice of it.

2 The Catholic party shall endeavour in every reasonable way to bring the non-Catholic party to the faith.
3 All the children of the marriage shall be baptized and brought up in the Catholic faith.
4 The parties shall not present themselves, either before or after the Catholic marriage, before a non-Catholic minister of religion for any religious ceremony.

The subsequent Vatican regulations have revoked the penalty of excommunication (*Matrimonia mixta*, 1966) and abolished (1970) the promise of the non-Catholic partner, while still requiring of Catholic partners a promise 'to do all in their power' within the unity of the marriage to ensure that all the children will be baptized and brought up in the Catholic church.

KENNETH MILNE

New Departure In the 1870s Clan na Gael, guided by John Devoy, became the leading Irish republican organization in America and established close formal links with the Irish Republican Brotherhood (IRB) in Ireland. In October 1878 Devoy moved to carry both organizations into an alliance with the obstructionist wing of the Home Rule party, by sending a telegram to the IRB in Dublin for transmission to Parnell setting out conditions of co-operation. The IRB supreme council refused to go along with this 'New Departure', and in little over a year Parnell effectively secured the support of the IRB rank and file on his own terms.

Reading

Moody, T.W., *Davitt and Irish Revolution, 1846–92* (Oxford: Clarendon Press, 1981).

R.V. COMERFORD

new learning Programme associated with the English philosopher Francis Bacon and the central European refugees Comenius and Hartlib. It sought to substitute observation and experiment for received tradition and

427

speculation as the basis for enquiries into the natural world. Its first supporters in Ireland were clergymen and officials brought from England by Wentworth in the 1630s.

Under the Cromwellians in the 1650s, the tasks of surveying and redistributing confiscated lands, coupled with the challenge of developing Ireland's agricultural and commercial potential, lured over adepts of the new learning, notably William Petty, Benjamin Worsley, Robert Wood and Miles Symner. Their endeavours, topical and utilitarian, carried moral and religious messages: to recover mastery over nature, to penetrate the mysteries of creation and so to further spiritual regeneration.

By 1683 more settled conditions, a larger Protestant population and the example of the Royal Society in London encouraged the systematization of hitherto loosely organized activities with the foundation of the Dublin Philosophical Society. Presided over by the ageing virtuoso Petty, its leading light was William Molyneux. Meetings were held regularly in Dublin, information about experiments, curiosities and inventions was collected and then publicized in the hope that it might have practical applications. A natural history, planned on a county basis, though partly written, was not published.

The society, suspended during warfare, revived between 1693 and 1708. Dependent on the official and ecclesiastical elites of Protestant Ireland, it only occasionally drew on or drew in Irish Catholics. Yet the society, if short-lived, promoted practical and utopian schemes which catered simultaneously to the self-interest and altruism of Irish Protestants, and inaugurated collective schemes of improvement which would be continued by the Royal Dublin and the Physico-Historical societies.

T.C. BARNARD

Ní Chuilleanáin, Eiléan (1942–) Poet. Born Cork City. Ní Chuilleanáin was educated at University College, Cork, and Oxford. Since her first collection of poems,

Acts and Monuments (1975), she has published *Site of Ambush* (1975), *Cork* (with illustrations by Brian Lalor, 1977) and *The Rose-Geranium* (1981). A founder editor of the literary magazine *Cyphers*, Ní Chuilleanáin edited the important volume of essays *Irish Women: Image and Achievement* (1985). Her most recent collections, *The Magdalene Sermon* (1989) and *The Brazen Serpent* (1994) bring together in poems of formidable lucidity and confidence the enduring concerns of her art with the physical and spiritual condition of women at various times and in different places, ranging from the Irish present to the mythologized past.

Reading

Ní Chuilleanáin, Eiléan, *Irish Women: Image and Achievement* (Dublin: Arlen House, 1985).
—— *The Second Voyage* (Dublin: Gallery, 1986).
—— *The Magdalene Sermon* (Oldcastle: Gallery, 1989).

GERALD DAWE

Nine Years War The English conquest of Ireland was completed at the turn of the sixteenth century. British historians call this final phase 'Tyrone's rebellion' after the feudal title of the crown's main antagonist, Hugh O'Neill. Most Irish historians use the less perjorative 'Nine Years War' to refer to the tumultuous decade between the revolt of Maguire in April 1593 and the treaty of Mellifont in March 1603. The history of this conflict has been distorted in recent times. Nineteenth-century historians made much uncritical use of Ó Cléirigh's *Beatha Aodha Ruaidh Ó Domhnaill*, a eulogistic biography of Hugh O'Donnell, the junior partner in the Gaelic leadership. The problem was compounded in 1940 by Sean O'Faolain's ever-popular book *The Great O'Neill*, which combined crass romanticism with faulty revisionism. Consequently the politically engaged accounts of contemporary writers such as Camden, Moryson and Lombard remain the best available in default of a full-scale modern history.

The conflict was caused by the crown's attempt to replace the autonomous Gaelic lordships in Ulster with an English pattern of inheritance and government. The Gaelic lords were shocked by the execution of Hugh MacMahon for minor offences in 1590 and the subsequent division of his lordship and its transmutation into the county of Monaghan. A major beneficiary was Sir Henry Bagenal. His ambition to become lord president of Ulster excited the growing hostility of his erstwhile brother-in-law, Hugh O'Neill, whose family were by tradition provincial overlords. It is not surprising that this reform policy went wrong, because it was undertaken by Lord Deputy Fitzwilliam in a high-handed manner wholly contemptuous of power relations in the north. Lord Burghley, who had direction of English policy after the death of Secretary Walsingham in 1590, must also be held responsible in that he gave his client Fitzwilliam a free hand despite mounting evidence that the lord deputy was corrupt.

O'Neill had strengthened himself for a possible conflict by opening channels with Spain and by springing Hugh O'Donnell, his son-in-law, from prison in Dublin Castle. An oath-bound confederacy of Ulster lords linked to O'Neill by blood, marriage and fosterage was established. O'Neill's tactics, intended to confuse government officials, have also confused many historians. At the outset he fought proxy wars through dependents whom he claimed to be unable to control. He even campaigned against Maguire himself in order to win time. By these subterfuges he avoided being proclaimed a traitor until June 1595. The crown was forced soon afterwards to respond to O'Neill's offer of submission. The arrival of Spanish agents in the spring of 1596 with a promise of military intervention aborted a negotiated compromise. Nevertheless O'Neill tried to keep the new departure secret by turning over 'the king of Spain's letter' to the Dublin authorities. The unexpected death of the vigorous Lord Deputy Burgh saw a further round of negotiations in the winter of 1597/8 and the final exasperation of government commissioners with the wily O'Neill, who raised his demands each time he offered to submit.

Confederate successes at the negotiating table were backed up by successes in the field. O'Neill welded together an effective army aided by veterans from English and Spanish service. Traditional guerrilla tactics were modernized with the increased use of firearms. The Elizabethan regime, racked by factional disputes and committed financially and militarily on the Continent, was slow to respond to the challenge. Its Irish army was badly supplied and worse led. The command was divided between Russell and Norris in 1596 and 1597; between governorships, the self-interested strategy of Ormond prevailed; the generalship of Bagenal, who had succeeded his father as marshal of the army, was inept. O'Neill's greatest victories – large-scale ambushes at Clontibret in 1595 and the Yellow Ford in 1598 – were over Sir Henry. These victories, coupled with the fall of strategic forts, facilitated the spread of the Irish revolt to the west, where the Gaelic lords were dissatisfied by the Composition of Connacht, and to the south, where the original lords had been dispossessed by the plantations of Laois/Offaly and Munster. Finally the disastrous governorship of the earl of Essex left the confederates in charge of most of the country, but unable to conquer the towns because they lacked the necessary artillery, siege equipment and training.

Outright victory required either the defection of the townsmen or a successful Spanish invasion. O'Neill tried to win over the English-speaking inhabitants of the towns and their hinterlands by appealing to them on the grounds of common nationality and religion. This was a revival of a confessional nationalism originally proclaimed by James Fitzmaurice Fitgerald after his return from the Continent, where Irish exiles had combined Renaissance patriotism with militant Catholicism. The townsmen, fearful that religious zeal masked Gaelic despotism, remained aloof. The concept of faith and fatherland which had successfully united the Netherlanders in their struggle against Spain proved a failure in Ireland. Main force was no more successful than persuasion. A Spanish expedition eventually landed at Kinsale in 1601, but the confederate forces, which marched the length of the island to its relief, committed themselves to a pitched battle and were decisively beaten.

Lord Deputy Mountjoy, the victor of Kinsale, thereafter destroyed Ulster in a war of attrition. An amphibious landing at Derry wrought havoc behind Gaelic lines, a scorched earth policy reduced the country to famine, and a constellation of small garrisons drove O'Neill into hiding. Final victory in the war, which cost £2,000,000 sterling, was only achieved after the debasement of the Irish currency. The crown of England enjoyed functional sovereignty throughout Ireland for the first time; Gaelic lordship was terminated symbolically by the destruction of the inaugural seat of the O'Neills at Tullaghoge. After his surrender at Mellifont, O'Neill was dependent on Mountjoy's good offices at court. His room for manoeuvre lessened with the sudden death of his conqueror turned patron in 1606. Fearing arrest and the discovery of further conspiracy with Spain, O'Neill and the other northern lords departed for the Continent in the summer of 1607 in an episode immortalized as 'the flight of the earls'. This fateful abdication of leadership opened the road for 'the plantation of Ulster'.

HIRAM MORGAN

Nobel prize winners Nobel prizes have been awarded eight times to Irish recipients. The best known of these is W.B. Yeats, who won the Literature prize in 1923. The least-known winner is Richard L. Synge, an English-born member of the playwright's family, who shared the Chemistry prize in 1953 for, in particular, his work on partition chromatography. The eminent international jurist, Sean MacBride, won the Peace prize in 1974, partly in recognition for his role in the difficult birth of Namibia as a sovereign state. In 1976, the same prize was awarded jointly to Betty Williams and Mairead Corrigan, organizers of the mid-1970s Peace People series of marches in Northern Ireland. George Bernard Shaw, in 1926, Samuel Beckett, in 1969, and Seamus Heaney, in 1995, also received the Literature prize. The 1998 Peace prize was shared by John Hume and David Trimble. Yeats recorded the liturgical and ideological content of the prize-giving ceremony in *The Bounty of Sweden*. Shaw used some of the prize's proceeds to fund the propagation of Swedish literature in England. Beckett marked the occasion by holding his peace in a hotel in Tunisia. Heaney's success was the occasion of great popular celebration.

Superficially, these welcome gestures of international recognition have a largely emblematic significance. Yet, by rewarding attainments which have not derived from conventional national pieties or local institutional support, the prizes possess a more than exhibitionistic claim to attention. They emphasize the varieties of exile within the Irish experience. This emphasis, together with some of the prizes' contexts and orientations, provides a basis for assessing the relationship in Irish society between individual and community. By drawing attention to these two areas, Ireland's Nobel laureates unwittingly but tellingly evoke two centrally problematic stress points in Irish life. Ireland's Nobel prize winners are undoubtedly a source of national pride. Some doubts persist, however, regarding the strength, utility and best application of their contribution to the national being.

GEORGE O'BRIEN

O

O'Brien, Conor Cruise (1917–) Writer, journalist and controversialist. Conor Cruise O'Brien was born into an Irish Catholic political family. His maternal grandfather, David Sheehy, was a Nationalist MP at Westminister, and his grand-uncle Eugene Sheehy was a Land League priest. David Sheehy was one of the majority declaring against Parnell in the famous Committee Room 15 of the House of Commons. This act has often worried O'Brien and as a young man he thought that 'the great primal and puzzling event was the fall of Parnell'. O'Brien's father Francis was a leader writer with the *Freeman's Journal* and his mother Catherine Sheehy was a vocational teacher. He was educated at Sandford Park School and Trinity College, Dublin (BA, PhD).

O'Brien was a diplomat in the Department of Foreign Affairs (1944–61) and the representative of the secretary-general of the UN in Katanga (1961). He resigned from both services amid controversy (1961). He became a Labour Party TD in 1969, government minister for post and telegraphs (1973–7), and a member of the Seanad (1977–9). He has held a number of important academic posts in Ghana, the US and the UK, as well as being pro-chancellor of the University of Dublin.

Following O'Brien's entry into Irish politics and public life (1969), his commentaries on the unification of Ireland, the IRA and violence, and questions of faith and morals aroused and continue to arouse much passionate dissent and anger. His persistent and merciless pursuit of those, and politicians in particular, whose rhetoric on unification sustained violence and the IRA, as he saw it, has brought about a more careful and considered approach in the language of public discourse about the future of Northern Ireland. O'Brien has functioned very much as a critic of the Irish mind, political, lay and clerical, and in that role 'his penchant for arguing his cases from logic, and the awkward conclusions that logic sometimes reached, created culture shock in conventional political circles.'

His close attention to the actions and words of Charles Haughey since the Arms Trial (1970) enabled him to add a new word to Irish political vocabulary. In August 1982, a double-murder suspect was arrested at the home of Haughey's attorney, General Patrick Connolly, SC. Haughey described the event as 'grotesque, unprecedented, bizarre and unbelievable'. O'Brien coined the acronym 'GUBU', which he used to describe other happenings in the Haughey administration. 'GUBU' has entered into common usage.

As an essayist and biographer O'Brien is one of the master stylists of prose in English of this century, and his books on Parnell and Burke are outstanding of their kind. He has written regularly for the *Irish Times* and the London *Times/Sunday Times*, and was editor in chief of the *Observer* (1979–81). Currently contributing editor of the *Atlantic* (Boston), he now writes a weekly column for the *Irish Independent* and contributes to the London *Daily Telegraph* and *Sunday Telegraph* as well as the London *Times*.

His publications include *Maria Cross* (1952), *Parnell and his Party* (1957), *To Katanga and Back* (1962), *Writers and Politics* (1965), *The United Nations: Sacred Drama* (1967), *Camus* (1969), *The Suspecting Glance* (1972), *States of Ireland* (1972), *Herod* (1978), *Neighbours* (1980), *The Siege* (1986), *Passion and Cunning* (1988), *God Land* (1988), *The Great Melody: A Thematic Biography and Commented Anthology of Edmund Burke* (1992) and *Memoir: My Life and Themes* (2000). He co-authored with Máire Mhac an tSaoi (poet, married to O'Brien 1962) *A Concise History of Ireland* (1972). He has edited Burke's *Reflections on the Revolution in France* (1969) and a Thomas Davis Lecture series *The Shaping of Modern Ireland* (1959). He has also written four plays: *Murderous Angels* (1968), Herodes Ludens: (1) *King Herod Explains*, (2) *Salome and the Wild Man* and (3) *King Herod Advises* (1978).

In 1996, O'Brien was selected to sit in the Northern Ireland Forum as a Unionist.

MUIRIS MacCONGHAIL

O'Brien, Edna (1930–) Novelist. Born Tuamgraney, County Clare, 15 December. O'Brien was educated at the Convent of Mercy, Loughrea and attended Pharmaceutical College. She began writing for the Irish press in 1948, and moved to England in 1959. O'Brien's heroines, from the early *Country Girls* trilogy of the 1960s to the 1990 collection of short stories *Lantern Slides*, are victims of their own belief in the ideology of love, as well as of the men on to whom they project their desire for emotional rescue, and of the society which prohibits such rescue. Lovers are frequently inadequate substitutes for mothers. The loss of mothering, whether through the actual loss of a mother in death or exile or through the powerlessness and victimization which she suffers and bequeaths to her daughter, is the most powerful strand in O'Brien's work. This loss of the mother for which no compensation is possible is linked to O'Brien's myth of 'Mother Ireland' as a bitter, destructive, yet idealized and desired place. O'Brien's declared concern is with 'insubstantial Ireland', a changeless, gothic landscape for doomed heroines. The unwillingness to deal with substantial and changing Ireland is part of a much wider problem in O'Brien's work, which tends to naturalize and even eroticize feminine victimization. Her most recent novel is *Wild December* (1999).

Reading

Eckley, Grace, *Edna O'Brien* (Associated University Presses, 1974).

GERALDINE MEANEY

O'Brien, Kate (1895–1974) Novelist. Born 3 December, Limerick, died 13 August, Faversham, Kent. She was educated in Laurel Hill Convent and at University College, Dublin. She lived for many years in Britain, where she worked as a journalist and critic before becoming known first as a playwright and then as a novelist. She also worked briefly as a governess in Spain, about which she wrote throughout her career, but from which she was expelled for over 20 years because of the anti-Fascist views expressed in her travel book, *Farewell Spain* (1937). O'Brien's work was also suppressed in Ireland: *Mary Lavelle* (1936), *The Land of Spices* (1941) and *That Lady* (1946) were banned. Novels like *The Ante-Room* (1934) and *The Last of Summer* (1943) deal with the repressive claustrophobia of conventional Irish middle-class living. O'Brien consistently identifies sexual, political and artistic freedom. *That Lady*, an historical novel set in Philip II's Spain, is a complex parable of resistance to Fascism which develops one woman's claim to sexual freedom into an act of political defiance. Through symbols as diverse as the bullfight, a schoolgirl's face and operatic training, O'Brien formulated an aesthetic which could accommodate her concerns as a woman and a writer and her political convictions. *As Music and Splendour* (1958), O'Brien's last and most interesting novel, is the apotheosis of this strand in her work, exploring two young Irish women's progress from singers to operatic artists. Interestingly this novel is also the one where O'Brien finally deals directly with an ongoing and openly lesbian relationship. The conventionality of O'Brien's prose is deceptive: her innovations in form and material are subtle, but her novels question our fundamental assumptions about sexual, political and artistic identity.

Reading

Dalsimer, Adele, *Kate O'Brien* (Dublin: Gill and Macmillan, 1990).
Reynolds, Lorna, *Kate O'Brien: A Literary Portrait* (Gerrards Gross: Colin Smythe, 1987).

GERALDINE MEANEY

O'Brien, Terence Albert (1600–51) Dominican and martyr. Originally from Limerick, he entered the Dominican order in 1620 and spent eight years at Toledo, where he was ordained a priest. He played a prominent role in the Catholic Confederacy as the provincial of the Irish Dominicans. He signed the declaration of 1646 against the peace with Ormond, and thereafter was a principal supporter of the papal nuncio Rinuccini. It was with the help of the nuncio that he was appointed to the bishopric of Emly in 1647. In 1650 he signed the declaration of Jamestown, excommunicating Ormond's followers, and the following year he was at Limerick whilst it was besieged by parliamentarian

forces. Once the city was taken he was hanged, and his head displayed over St John's gate.

Reading

Coleman, A., *The Dominican Order in Ireland* (Dublin: 1926).
O'Heyne, J., *Irish Dominicans in the Seventeenth Century* (Dundalk: 1902).
Mould, D.C.P., *The Irish Dominicans* (Dublin: Dominican Publications, 1957).

BRIAN DONOVAN

O'Brien, William Smith (1803–64) Nationalist. Born Dromoland, County Clare, 17 October; died Bangor, Wales, 16 June. The son of Sir Lucius O'Brien, he was educated at Harrow and Cambridge University. He was Conservative MP for Ennis in 1825 and for County Limerick in 1835, but then became a convinced repealer and Young Irelander. For his part in the abortive rising of 1848 he was sentenced to death, commuted to penal servitude for life, but was released from Tasmania after five years. He returned to Ireland but took little part in politics.

HENRY BOYLAN

Ó Cadhain, Máirtín (1906–70) Novelist, short story writer, pamphleteer. Born An Cnocán Glas in the Galway Gaeltacht. Ó Cadhain trained as a national school teacher but was dismissed in 1936 for IRA activities. His internment followed, briefly in 1939, and then from 1940 to 1944, an experience which greatly accelerated his intellectual development. A collection of his prison letters, *As An nGéibheann* (1973), reveals his pro-German sympathies. He worked as a Dáil translator from 1947 until his appointment as a lecturer in the Department of Irish, Trinity College, Dublin, in 1956. He became professor in 1969.

Ó Cadhain is the finest creative prose writer in Gaelic since the seventeenth century. The lexical and syntactic possibilities of the Gaelic language on the one hand, and the limitations of communication through language on the other, are dominant obsessions in his work. The characters in his only published novel, *Cré na Cille* (1949), are corpses in a Gaeltacht graveyard who have brought with them all their spite and factiousness, ceaselessly speaking at rather than to each other, while simultaneously bringing all the copiousness of the Gaelic language to their locquacious contention. His early stories accommodated themselves to the vision of the Gaeltacht dominant in the Gaelic Revival, but his work quickly developed in both depth of characterization and breadth of concern. For copyright reasons, only work from the first two of his six short story collections has been translated (*The Road to Brightcity*, 1981, translated by Eoghan Ó Tuairisc) and the absence of translations has greatly restricted his influence. A translation of *Cré na Cille* by Joan Keefe (PhD thesis, University of Berkley, 1984) remains unpublished.

PROINSIAS Ó DRISCEOIL

O'Casey, Sean (1880–1964) Dramatist. Born Dublin, 30 March, died Torquay 18 September. O'Casey's parents were lower middle-class Protestants. His eyesight was early affected by disease, but he read widely. Reduced to poverty by his father's early death, he worked as a labourer, an experience which marked both his plays and the public positions he adopted.

Though involved with the Gaelic League, the Gaelic Athletic Association and the Irish Citizen Army, the misconceived Easter Rebellion of 1916 dismayed him.

The early trilogy on the Troubles for the Abbey, *Shadow of a Gunman* (1923), *Juno and the Paycock* (1924) and *The Plough and the Stars* (1926), despite an initial hostile reception, were quickly accepted as classics. Breaking with the Abbey when Yeats refused *The Silver Tassie* in 1928, O'Casey went to live in England. His later, more experimental plays were less well received. His best later work is in his remarkable autobiographies, *The Mirror in the House* (1939–54), which evoke in a painful and dramatic way his early impressions and later opinions.

Though his compassion is often marred by sentimentality, and his sense of character unsure when he moves beyond the working classes, he gave a voice to all the inarticulate thousands whose lives were ruined by Irish patriotism.

Reading

Krause, David, *Sean O'Casey: The Man and his Work* (London: Collier Books, 1960).
O'Casey, Eileen, *Sean* (London: Papermac, 1971).
O'Connor, Garry, *Sean O'Casey* (London: Paladin, 1988).

PETER COSTELLO

O'Connell, Daniel (1775–1847) Lawyer and politican. Born 6 August, Carhen, near Cahirciveen, County Kerry; died 15 May, Genoa. O'Connell was the eldest of 10 children born to Morgan and Catherine (née O'Mullane) O'Connell. He was fostered out to a tenant of his father and later adopted as heir by his uncle, Maurice O'Connell, nicknamed Hunting Cap, who lived at Derrynane House, near Caherdaniel, County Kerry. Daniel was educated successively by a hedge-school master, then at Father Harrington's school at Cove, near Cork, and from 1791 at St Omer, Douai, London and Dublin, where he was called to the bar in 1798.

O'Connell's career spans the first half of the nineteenth century, aptly called 'the Age of O'Connell'. He had the most formative influence of any single personality of Irish political culture: his efforts gave birth to modern Irish democracy. He has remained the touchstone of Irish political attitudes and movements. During his era Ireland experienced the transition from the *ancien régime* to the modern world.

O'Connell first entered politics with a public speech in 1800 to protest against the Act of Union. His early career was marked by outstanding success as a lawyer: he became one of the best-known advocates in Ireland. His oratory was essential to his success. He was extremely effective not only in the court room but at public meetings and later in Parliament. He was one of Ireland's greatest orators. His legal set-pieces reinforced his political profile, as with his defence of John Magee in 1813: this ranks as one of the great court-room orations of modern times.

O'Connell became known as 'the Counsellor', the legendary champion of the oppressed Catholic people. A murder case in which he was defence counsel became the theme of Gerald Griffin's novel *The Collegians* and later of Dion Boucicault's play *The Colleen Bawn*, eventually becoming the subject of Julius Benedict's opera *The Lily of Killarney*. The most dramatic of all his cases was the Doneraile Conspiracy trials of 1829, later featured in Canon Sheehan's novel *Glenanaar: A Story of Irish Life*.

O'Connell was quickly involved in the Catholic Committee, which sought Catholic emancipation. He advocated constant agitation and opposed vigorously giving 'securities' to the government to facilitate concessions to Catholics in the 'Veto' controversies. He opposed the vetoist policy even to the extent of rejecting papal interference in Irish affairs.

He established a number of political organizations such as the Catholic Board, but years of failure to achieve Catholic emancipation led eventually to his most creative political action, when he founded the Catholic Association in 1823. He called for the collection of a Catholic rent from the whole population and through its collection developed the first great popular democratic organization of the modern world. O'Connell was the outstanding pioneer in the new era of mass democratic politics, and the basis of Irish democracy was laid through his efforts for Catholic emancipation. His novel political organization at local level soon contested Protestant landlord control and won seats for pro-emancipationist candidates, notably in Waterford in the 1826 general election.

O'Connell was elected MP for County Clare in 1826, being the first Catholic to stand for Parliament since the seventeenth century. His election led to the crisis from which he won Catholic emancipation in 1829. This confirmed his popular title 'the Liberator' amongst the Catholic people of Ireland, and his international reputation as one of the great men of his age.

He created the first Irish parliamentary party in Westminster during the 1830s, where he became the leading radical, supporting a wide range of reforms. These included ensuring the passage of the Great Reform Act 1832; the extension of the suffrage; support for the Tolpuddle martyrs, Poles persecuted by Czarist Russia, Jewish Emancipation, and free trade; the repeal of the Corn Laws; and the abolition of slavery. O'Connell devised and explored the repertoire of options and techniques of popular parliamentary politics which were deployed and refined by later Irish leaders. His belief that reform was a necessary prologue to repeal of the Act of Union led to co-operation with the Whigs, notably in the 'Lichfield House Compact' in 1835. He had important, if partial, success in obtaining a more equal administration of justice as a result.

O'Connell founded the Repeal Association in 1840 upon the prospect of Robert Peel's return to office. He became the lord mayor of Dublin of the reformed corporation in 1841, and thereby the first Catholic lord mayor since the 'Glorious Revolution' of 1689. He developed a major public campaign for repeal in 1842 and 1843, but called off the Clontarf 'monster meeting' in October 1843 when the Peel government proscribed it. O'Connell was prosecuted and tried in January 1844 for seditious conspiracy and sentenced to a year's imprisonment in May 1844. The sentence was subsequently quashed by the House of Lords in September 1844.

His career ended as he clashed with the Young Irelanders, an important element within the repeal movement, in 1845 and 1846. The conflict with Young Ireland may be seen as the Irish expression of the struggle between liberalism and cultural nationalism, which arose in Europe as a result of the Romantic movement. The clash led to a split in the Repeal Association in July 1846 on the question of violence: O'Connell insisted on the principle of moral force to the total exclusion of the use of violence to achieve self-government and constitutional change. He made efforts to come to terms with the onset of the Great Famine, making a last appeal to the House of Commons to save famine-stricken Ireland before he set off on a pilgrimage to Rome, dying en route at Genoa.

O'Connell was the last and most important political embodiment of the still co-existing and interacting English and Gaelic traditions. He bestrode two cultural worlds: Gaelic Ireland and Anglo-Irish law and politics. His Gaelic background in County Kerry gave him a remarkable and unique rapport with the pragmatic survival political impulses of Gaelic Ireland: he was the last great Gaelic hero for Gaelic-speaking writers and versifiers of his day. Balzac hardly exaggerated when he said O'Connell 'incarnated a whole people'. Yet O'Connellite politics were equally shaped by the radical political thought he absorbed as a student in the 1790s. He transmitted to Irish politics the historic liberal tradition of the Enlightenment, with his profound commitment to the march of rational progress and individual liberty. He believed that violent revolution in the Irish context would not only halt progress but would defeat the ends of liberty: the means were fundamental to the ends.

For O'Connell, the key to every beneficial change lay in the mobilization of the people and the enlistment of public opinion. O'Connellism represents commitment to democratic change, to political equality for all citizens, to humanitarian reform, and to anti-imperialist and anti-racialist politics. Uniquely among Catholic statesmen of his time O'Connell espoused complete separation of church and state. His significance has been at the centre of many attempts to reinterpret Irish history since his death. The classics include John Mitchel's *Jail Journal*, Lecky's

Leaders of Public Opinion in Ireland, Charles Gavan Duffy's *Young Ireland* and Sean O'Faolain's *King of the Beggars*. Recent historical scholarship has served to reappropriate for contemporary discourse the liberal democratic legacy of O'Connell's protean heritage.

The pervasive and prolonged disparagement of O'Connell's democratic achievement by later Irish nationalists has been addressed by historians. W.B. Yeats's harsh political poem 'Parnell's Funeral' commences 'Under the Great Comedian's tomb the crowd'. The poet's perception is of an Irish people culturally and spiritually degenerate when O'Connellite democracy gave full scope to 'the contagion of the throng' to bring Parnell down. The poem contributes little to our understanding of O'Connell's liberal and democratic heritage.

Reading

Grogan, G.F., *The Noblest Agitator: Daniel O'Connell and the German Catholic Movement 1830–50* (Dublin: Veritas, 1991).

Houston, A., *Daniel O'Connell: His Early Life and Journal, 1795–1802* (London: Sir Isaac Pitman and Sons, 1906).

McCartney, D. (ed.), *The World of Daniel O'Connell* (Dublin and Cork: Mercier, 1980).

MacDonagh, O., *The Hereditary Bondsman: Daniel O'Connell 1775–1829* (London: Weidenfeld and Nicolson, 1988).

—— *The Emancipist: Daniel O'Connell 1830–47* (London: Weidenfeld and Nicolson, 1989).

Macintyre, A., *The Liberator Daniel O'Connell and the Irish Party 1830–1847* (London: Hamish Hamilton, 1965).

Nowlan, K.B. and O'Connell, M.R. (eds), *Daniel O'Connell: Portrait of a Radical* (Belfast: Appletree Press, 1984).

O'Connell, John (ed.), *The Select Speeches of Daniel O'Connell M.P.* (Dublin: James Duffy, 1862).

O'Connell, M.R. (ed.), *The Correspondence of Daniel O'Connell* 8 vols (Shannon and Dublin: for Irish Manuscripts Commission, 1972–1980).

—— *Daniel O'Connell: The Man and His Politics* (Dublin: Irish Academic Press, 1990).

—— *Daniel O'Connell, Political Pioneer* (Dublin: Institute of Public Administration, 1991).

O'Ferrall, F., *Daniel O'Connell* (Dublin: Gill and Macmillan, 1981).

——*Catholic Emancipation: Daniel O'Connell and the Birth of Irish Democracy 1820–30* (Dublin: Gill and Macmillan, 1985).

FERGUS O'FERRALL

O'Connell in folklore If one is to believe the folk tradition, Daniel O'Connell, as befits all heroes, was predestined for greatness, and his poetess grandmother, Máire Ní Duibh, foretold it. He was elevated to the status of folk hero while he was still alive, a phenomenon that did not go unnoticed in his time. This process of being transmuted from a human into a superhuman must have been understood by a man of O'Connell's perception, familiar as he was with Gaelic lore; and the process of being given the characteristics of the great *Laochra* of long ago, must have amused him as much as it must have pleased him in strengthening his *locus standi* among his own.

It was expected that the new hero's birth and early life should be invested with fantastical qualities. A Kerry story has it that the local priest foretold at the first Mass said in a chapel which had been built by O'Connell's childless parents that they would soon have the child they so much wanted: 'and nine months after that Daniel O'Connell was born. And when he was born there was a cross on his back like you'd see on an ass, and that was a sign that he'd be a famous man and that he's emancipate the Catholics.'

A folk hero should have a distinguished pedigree, and O'Connell was, according to a West Cork tradition, descended from Dian Cecht, the physician of the Tuatha Dé Danann. His baby-clothes were passed around from house to house, and when he grew to manhood bits of his cloak were in great demand, as they too were thought to have great curative properties.

As a schoolboy he was able to win law cases; and the myriads of stories told of the great Counsellor are full of malicious inventiveness in the face of overwhelming odds. His forensic and political oratory was so powerful 'that when he practised his speeches in his garden the birds used to stop singing to listen in admiration.'

He was invincible, except in the heel. He was a devil for the women; but were not all the heroes of old? His mistresses included Queen Victoria; and the town of Rathkeale stands shamed for failing to provide a woman for his bed.

All the stories about him are the product of the people's imagination, but, as has been said, imagination is not the faculty of making something out of nothing, but of using, in more or less different form, something already present in the mind. Almost single-handed Daniel O'Connell had lifted a nation from its knees; and the people, in return, paid him their supreme compliment by including him in their pantheon.

DIARMAID Ó MUIRITHE

O'Connor, Frank (1903–66) Writer and translator. Born Michael O'Donovan. O'Connor was one of the towering figures of the mid-century. His international reputation is based on short stories and translations of poetry from Gaelic, but he was also a literary critic and historian, novelist, dramatist, autobiographer, and newspaper controversialist. *An Only Child* (1961), O'Connor's autobiography, gives an unsurpassed account of life in the slums of Cork early in the century and the changes wrought by the struggle for independence.

O'Connor is often thought of as a humorist by those who know him mostly from autobiographical stories of childhood such as 'My Oedipus Complex' and 'First Confession', but many of his best stories, including 'Guests of the Nation', present a bleak and anti-fanatical view of political commitment. Elegiac accounts of the Gaelic way of life are found in stories like 'The Majesty of the Law' and 'Uprooted'. Less familiar, but historically important, are his later probings of provincial middle-class life. The cream of O'Connor's short fiction is found in the American

Collected Stories (1981); a good sampling is in *My Oedipus Complex and Other Stories* (1963).

O'Connor's translations of poetry from Irish are still the most extensive and best known of the century, and most are collected in *Kings, Lords and Commons* (1959).

RUTH SHERRY

O'Connor, James Arthur (1792–1841) Landscape painter. Born Dublin; died London, 7 January. The son of a printseller and engraver, O'Connor may have studied at the Dublin Society Drawing Schools. His first major commissions were for estate portraits of Westport House and Ballinrobe House, both in County Mayo (1818–19). These sedate views of well-controlled Irish estates are valuable representations of how the west of Ireland underwent 'improvement'. From 1822 onwards O'Connor was based in London. He travelled widely, visiting Brussels and Paris as well as journeying for some six months along the Saar and Moselle in Germany. Always short of cash, O'Connor's output was largely composed of easy-to-sell pot-boiler landscapes, which over the years ranged from picturesque views of Ireland or England to more dramatic and usually highly imaginative mountain scenes (Dublin's National Gallery of Ireland holds a representative collection).

Reading

Bodkin, Thomas, *Four Irish Landscape Painters* (Dublin and London: 1920, repr. intro. Julian Campbell, Dublin: Irish Academic Press, 1987).

Crookshank, Anne and the Knight of Glin, *The Painters of Ireland c. 1660–1920* (London: Barrie and Jenkins, 1978).

Hutchinson, John, *James Arthur O Connor* (Dublin: National Gallery of Ireland, 1985).

Mulvany (?), George, *Dublin Monthly Magazine* (April 1842).

Strickland, Walter, *A Dictionary of Irish Artists* (Shannon: Irish University Press, 1968).

FINTAN CULLEN

O'Conor, Roderic (1860–1940) Painter. Born 17 October, Milton, County Roscommon; died 18 March, Neuil-sur-Layon. Of a legal and landed background, O'Conor attended Ampleforth from 1873 to 1878. Between 1879 and 1881 he studied at the Metropolitan School of Art in Dublin and at the Royal Hibernian Academy. A student at the Antwerp Academy from 1881 to *c*.1884, he later moved to Paris, where he worked under Carolus-Duran until 1888.

O'Conor's professional career was spent exclusively in France. His relationship with Ireland was slight, although in 1904 he exhibited at the Irish exhibition in Guildhall Art Gallery organized by Hugh Lane. His work has to be seen in the context of turn-of-the-century French avant-garde developments, where he worked closely with Gauguin and Serusier. The empirical nature of his approach to Modernist language influenced such English painters as Roger Fry, Matthew Smith and Duncan Grant but had little effect on painting in Ireland.

Reading

Bell, Clive, *Old Friends: Personal Recollections* (London: Chatto and Windus, 1956).

Campbell, Julian, *The Irish Impressionists: Irish Artists in France and Belgium, 1850–1914* (Dublin: National Gallery of Ireland, 1984).

Johnson, Roy, *Roderic O'Conor 1860–1940* (London: Barbican Art Gallery, 1985).

FINTAN CULLEN

O'Dea, James Augustine (1899–1965) Comedian. Born Dublin; died there, 7 January. O'Dea qualified as an optician in Edinburgh. Returning to Dublin, he took part in his spare time in amateur productions of Ibsen and Chekhov. In 1927 he took to the stage full-time and formed a partnership with Harry O'Donovan, who created for him his most famous part, Biddy Mulligan, 'the Pride of the Coombe'. In a successful career in pantomine and 'on the halls', he toured Ireland and England for many years.

HENRY BOYLAN

O'Doherty, William James (1835–69) Sculptor. Born Dublin; died Berlin. O'Doherty studied at the Royal Dublin Society Schools (1848–53). He moved to London in 1854, exhibiting at the Royal Academy and receiving patronage from the marquis of Downshire and others. He travelled to Italy in 1864 but died young, at the age of 34.

Reading

Art Journal (1868).

Strickland, Walter, *A Dictionary of Irish Artists* (Shannon: Irish University Press, 1968).

FINTAN CULLEN

O'Donnell, Manus (d. 1564) Lord of Tyrconnell. O'Donnell was inaugurated as chief of the O'Donnells in 1537 following the death of his father, Aodh Dubh O'Donnell. He was deposed by his own sons Calvach and Hugh in 1555 and died at Lifford in February 1564. Under the surrender and regrant initiative of Lord Deputy St Leger, Manus submitted to the king on 6 August 1541, agreeing to hold his lands from him, to renounce papal authority, to attend Parliament, to attend hostings and to serve the king at his own expense, in return for the promised protection and support of the lord deputy and council. He was generally loyal to the Dublin administration thereafter. He is remembered as a patron of learning and also composed poetry himself. An O'Donnell poem book was compiled for him in 1534, and a Gaelic life of St Columcille was written under his direction at Lifford castle.

Reading

Bradshaw, Brendan, 'Manus "the magnificent": O'Donnell as Renaissance prince', in Art Cosgrave and D. McCartney (eds), *Studies in Irish History presented to R. Dudley Edwards* (Dublin: University College Dublin, 1979).

BERNADETTE CUNNINGHAM

O'Donnell, Peadar (1893–1986) Novelist. Born Meenmore, County Donegal. O'Donnell trained as a teacher at St Patrick's College, Dublin, and became an organizer for the Irish Transport and General Workers' Union and a socialist republican activist. He served in the War of Independence and the Civil War, and was interned. The latter experience is detailed in *The Gates Flew Open* (1932). As *There Will Be Another Day* (1963) records, O'Donnell's activism continued throughout the 1930s with the Republican Congress. He visited Spain immediately prior to the Civil War and his support for the Republicans is documented in *Salud! An Irishman in Spain*. O'Donnell edited the *Bell* from 1946 to 1954. Thereafter he was an influential supporter of numerous political causes, including Irish opposition to the Vietnam war.

O'Donnell is best known as a novelist, and is both the major regional, and most explicitly political, novelist of his generation. His artistic commitment is to the authentication of the Republican conception of the people. Novels such as *Islanders* (1928), *Adrigoole* (1929) and *The Knife* (1930) are a cogent critique of nativism, and of the social and psychological consequences of the economic conditions which maintain it. These works, rather than O'Donnell's more popular though more muted post-war fiction, raise questions concerning the social destiny of rural Ireland, and the novel's capacity to do them justice, with which Irish culture is still coming to terms.

GEORGE O'BRIEN

O'Donnell, Red Hugh (Aodh Ruadh) (1572–1602) Gaelic lord. The son of Sir Hugh O'Donnell and Fionnuala (Inion Dubh) Mac Donnell, he was favoured as the heir to the O'Donnell title in preference to his older half-brother Domnall, due to his mother's insistence. Having been captured by Lord Deputy Sir John Perrot, he was imprisoned in Dublin Castle from 1587 to 1590, when he escaped but was recaptured, escaping again at Christmas 1591. He was inagurated as O'Donnell in May 1592, although his father was still alive. Red Hugh was one of the Gaelic leaders in the Nine Years War against the

English administration, and an active seeker of Spanish support. Following defeat at the battle of Kinsale in 1601, he immediately departed for Spain to seek further help, but died there in September 1602, and was succeeded by his younger brother Rory.

Reading

Silke, J.J., 'Red Hugh O'Donnell: a biographical survey', *Donegal Annual* no. 5, (1961).

Walsh, Paul, (ed. and transl.), *Beatha Aodha Ruadh Uí Dhomhnaill*, 2 vols (London: Irish Texts Society, 1948, 1957).

BERNADETTE CUNNINGHAM

O'Donnell, Rory (?1575–1608) First earl of Tyrconnell. Younger son of Sir Hugh (Aodh) O'Donnell, chieftain of Tir Conaill, and the influential Fionnuala (Inion Dubh) Mac Donnell, Rory O'Donnell came to prominence during the Nine Years War in support of Red Hugh O'Donnell, his elder brother. When Red Hugh departed for Spain in the immediate aftermath of the battle of Kinsale, Rory assumed interim leadership of his kinsmen, an arrangement which became permanent on Red Hugh's death in 1602.

Rory surrendered to Lord Deputy Mountjoy along with Hugh O'Neill in 1603 and was received at court by the new king, James I. He was knighted in Christ Church Cathedral, Dublin, in September 1603 and created first earl of Tyrconnell. Although title to most of the O'Donnell territories was confirmed to him after the Nine Years War, he was dissatisfied with the concessions made to him after his surrender. Rory O'Donnell was one of the instigators of the 'flight of the earls' in 1607, and though he survived the arduous journey to Rome, arriving in April 1608, he died there in July of the same year.

Reading

Walsh, Paul, (ed.), *Beatha Aodha Ruaidh Uí Dhomhnaill*, 2 vols (London: Irish Texts Society, 1948, 1957).

BERNADETTE CUNNINGHAM

O'Donovan, Gerald(1871–1942) Novelist. Born Jeremiah O'Donovan in Rostrevor, County Down. O'Donovan was ordained a priest in 1895 at Maynooth. Enthusiasm for contemporary progressive social, cultural and clerical tendencies led to trouble with his diocesan superiors. In 1904, he left Ireland and the priesthood. The remainder of his life was spent in England where, between 1913 and 1922, he published six novels. In his later years he was closely associated with the English novelist Rose Macauley.

O'Donovan is best known for *Father Ralph* (1913). Like many Irish novels of the period, this autobiographical work deals with a young man's trial by consciousness, and reveals the moral tensions and intellectual strains of Catholic middle-class ambition at the turn of the century. O'Donovan's other novels are essentially *romans-à-these* on such matters as intermarriage (*Waiting*, 1914), the condition of contemporary Ireland (*Conquest*, 1920), and the Home Front (*How They Did It*, 1920). The title of *Vocation* (1921) speaks for itself, though O'Donovan's last novel, *The Holy Tree* (1922), suggests a change of artistic direction and is of some psychological interest.

GEORGE O'BRIEN

O'Duffy, Emar Ultan (1893–1935) Writer. Born Dublin. Educated at Stonyhurst and University College, Dublin, O'Duffy became a captain in the Irish Volunteers, and in that capacity spent Easter 1916 in Belfast. Subsequent political events disillusioned him. In 1925, O'Duffy left Ireland for England, where he spent the remainder of his life.

A versatile and prolific writer, O'Duffy's most noteworthy works are *The Wasted Island* (1919; rev. edn 1929) and the Cuandine trilogy. The former, a novel, is a bitter though unco-ordinated critique of his generation's idealism. The trilogy consists of *King Goshawk and the Birds* (1926), *The Spacious Adventures of the Man in the Street* (1928) and *Asses in Clover* (1934), of which the first two works are far superior to the third. These extravagant satirical fantasies take aim at targets unveiled in *The Wasted Island*. In the history of Irish satire, they also mark the transition from the whimsy of James Stephens to the austerity of Flann O'Brien. O'Duffy also wrote a popular treatise on the econometrics of Major Douglas, *Life and Money* (1932; third edn 1935).

GEORGE O'BRIEN

O'Dwyer, Robert (1862–1949) Teacher and occasional composer. Born Dwyer in Bristol. Of Irish parentage, O'Dwyer commenced his career in Bristol, conducting the Rousby Opera Company (1891–6). In the following year he settled in Dublin, where he was at different periods a conductor, composer, teacher and critic. As the last, he contributed to D.P. Moran's *Leader*, which doubtless honed his strongly nationalist views. These found further expression in 1902 in the creation and subsequent direction of the Oireachtas Choir, and in the addition of the fashionable patronymic prefix. He was sympathetic with the aims of the Gaelic Revival and his principal work, the opera *Eithne*, was written for the Oireachtas of 1909, with a libretto by Rev. Thomas O'Kelly of Sligo, which was later translated into Gaelic. While the influence of the broader operatic tradition lies uncomfortably with the conscious attempt to portray an Irish idiom, it is yet an ambitious work which gives especial prominence to choral and ensemble writing. On the strength of the opera's success, O'Dwyer was appointed professor of Irish music in University College, Dublin, a part-time post sponsored for a period by Dublin Corporation, which he held until his retirement in 1939.

JOSEPH RYAN

O'Faolain, Sean (1900–91) Writer, and founder of the *Bell*. O'Faolain is usually labelled a writer of short stories although, like his friend, rival and Cork contemporary Frank O'Connor, he was a central figure operating on many cultural and political fronts. In addition to fiction he produced book-length studies of Daniel O'Connell, Constance Markievicz, Hugh O'Neill, Éamon de Valera and Cardinal Newman. He also wrote literary criticism, autobiography and travel books.

Educated partly at Harvard, O'Faolain had a cosmopolitan outlook and some credentials as a scholar. The relatively frank treatment of sexuality in some of his early fiction subjected him to opprobrium and censorship, but he attempted to combine enlightened Catholicism with high intellectual and literary standards.

O'Faolain's achievements in fiction are in fact uneven, a few subtle stories like 'The Lovers of the Lake' standing beside sensational and over-coloured ones like 'The Small Lady'. His collected short fiction is available in three volumes under the titles *Midsummer Night Madness, The Heat of the Day* and *Foreign Affairs*.

O'Faolain is more likely to be remembered in future generations for the variety of his commitments, and for his cultural commentary, than for his fiction. His highest achievement is indisputably his founding in 1940 of the *Bell*, a monthly review which provided the sole forum for intelligent political and cultural debate in a period of stagnation, isolation and conformity. It also published the work of many established writers and gave openings to new ones like James Plunkett and John Montague.

His daughter Julia is also a leading writer.

RUTH SHERRY

O'Flaherty, Liam (1896–1984) Novelist and short story writer. Born Inishmore, Aran Islands. O'Flaherty travelled widely in Europe and the Americas, but lived mostly in Dublin from 1946 until his death. He wrote 15 novels, the most powerful of which – *The Informer* (1925), *Skerrett* (1932), *Famine* (1937), *Land* (1946) – are starkly naturalistic dramatizations of the conflict between the forces of instinct and intellect in rural and urban Ireland. In O'Flaherty's primitivist universe courage and endurance ennoble, whereas materialism and urbanization corrupt. His short stories contain his best writing, especially those inspired by his awed admiration for human and natural beings driven by a pure, primal energy, which he renders in sensuously pictorial prose.

Reading

Averill, Deborah M., *The Irish Short Story from George Moore to Frank O'Connor* (New York and London: University of America Press, 1982).
Sheeran, Patrick, *The Novels of Liam O'Flaherty* (Dublin: Wolfhound Press, 1976).

LIAM HARTE

O'Halloran, Sylvester (1728–1897) Surgeon and historian. Born 31 December, Caherdavin, County Clare, died 11 August, Limerick. The youngest son of Michael O'Halloran, a Catholic farmer, and his wife, Mary McDonnell, O'Halloran studied surgery abroad and died a leading surgeon and an honoured citizen. He published inventive and critical surgical monographs, an overcredulous history of Ireland, and *Proposals for the Advancement of Surgery*, the blueprint for a College of Surgeons in Ireland.

Reading

Lyons, J.B. 'Sylvester O'Halloran', *Irish Journal of Medical Science* (1963), pp. 217–32, 279–88.

J.B. LYONS

O'hEodhusa, Giolla Bride/Bonaventura (d. 1614) Franciscan, theologian and poet. Though originally an Ulster poet patronized by the Maguire family, he opted in mid-life to become a Franciscan. Giolla Bride left Ireland for the Continent with the collapse of the Nine Years War. He was educated at Louvain, where he became a lecturer in philosophy and theology, and ultimately guardian of the college. Furthermore he was a talented poet, and wrote many catechisms, such as his well-known *Teagasc criosdaidhe*. Though most of his poetry was either devotional or in praise of various Irish chiefs, he wrote one religious polemic, entitled *Truagh liom, a chompain, do chor*. This was

directed at Miler Magrath, an apostrate bishop who turned Protestant and became archbishop of Cashel. O'hEodhusa's work is typical of the emerging Irish religious literature founded on Counter-Reformation ideology.

Reading

Carney, J., *The Irish Bardic Poet* (Dublin: Dolmen Press, 1967).
Cunningham, B., 'Native culture and political change in Ireland, 1580–1640', in *Natives and Newcomers* (Dublin: Irish Academic Press, 1986).
O'Cuir, B., 'The Irish language in the early modern period', in *A New History of Ireland. Vol. 3: Early Modern Times* (Clarendon Press, 1976).
O'Riordan, M., *The Gaelic Mind and the Collapse of the Gaelic World* (Cork: Cork University Press, 1990).

BRIAN DONOVAN

An Óige Irish Youth Hostels Association. Formed in Dublin in 1931 by a group of walkers enthused by the success of the hostel movement in Germany. Amongst its founders, most of whom were associated with Trinity College, Dublin, was Thekla Beere, later to be the first woman to head a government department. An Óige opened its first hostels in County Wicklow and, aided by grants from the Carnegie Trust and other benefactions, gradually developed a network of hostels throughout the 26 counties. Unlike many such organizations, An Óige eschewed politics and militaristic trappings completely, concentrating on providing accommodation rather than on regimenting its members. In 1992 it had some 15,000 members, and ran 42 hostels.

EUNAN O'HALPIN

O'Keefe, John (1747–1833) Playwright. Born Dublin; died Southampton. Known, unfortunately, as 'the English Molière' – his plays are nothing like Molière's, and he was not English – O'Keefe was a much more prolific playwright than his contemporaries Oliver Goldsmith and Richard Sheridan, though a less enduring one. He studied painting at Mr West's Academy in Dublin, but turned to acting at Smock Alley and on tour in Ireland, and, from c.1770, to writing plays, chiefly in London. His whimsical comedy *Wild Oats* (1791) remained in the repertoire for over a century and was brilliantly revived by the Royal Shakespeare Company in 1976. His plagiaristic sequel to *She Stoops to Conquer*, *Tony Lumpkin in Town* (1773), was immensely popular, as were his comic operas to music arranged from Carolan, *The Shamrock* (1777) and *The Banditti* (1781). He wrote comedies, pantomimes, farces and afterpieces, many with Irish settings, such as *Harlequin Teague* (1782) and *The Wicklow God Mines* (1796). His *Recollections* (1826) reveal a modest and good-natured man.

CHRISTOPHER FITZSIMON

O'Leary, Arthur (1729–1802) Catholic priest and opinion maker. Born county Cork; died London. O'Leary trained as a Capuchin priest at St Malo in Brittany. Following his return to Ireland in 1771, he produced a series of pamphlets in which he advocated that Irish Catholics should ally themselves with the Protestant state, and challenged the view of many Protestants (notably John Wesley) who averred that 'the Popish religion is inconsistent with the safety of a free people and a Protestant government'. This won him a national reputation with the Catholic public, and prompted Dublin Castle to try to buy his services, but he appears to have continued to pursue an independent course. He acquitted himself well in an acrimonious controversy with Bishop Woodward in the mid-1780s, in which he was accused of supporting the Rightboys' anti-tithe agitation, but he chose, subsequently, to leave Ireland for London, where he spent the remainder of his life.

Reading

Buckley, M.B., *The Life and Writings of the Rev. Arthur O'Leary* (Dublin: 1868).

England, T.R., *The Life of Arthur O'Leary* (London: 1822).

Kelly, James, 'Interdenominational relations and religious toleration in late eighteenth century Ireland', *Eighteenth-Century Ireland* iii (1988).

JAMES KELLY

O'Leary, Jane (1946–) Composer. Born 13 October, Hartford, Connecticut. O'Leary studied music at Vassar College and completed her PhD in composition under Milton Babbit at Princeton University. She moved to Ireland in 1972 and lives in Galway. Her first international recognition as a composer came in 1978 when she was awarded the W.K. Rose Fellowship in Creative Arts from Vassar College. Membership of Aosdána has enabled her to be a full-time composer. She became chairperson of the Contemporary Music Centre in Dublin, a member of the executive board of the International League of Women Composers, and a director of the National Concert Hall. In 1981 she was a founder of Music for Galway (a concert promotion organization) and was appointed chairperson in 1984. She founded and is pianist/director of Concorde, the twentieth-century music ensemble.

Her early works explore structural elements that arise from predetermined pitch patterns. Since 1983 she has adopted a freer approach to composition which expresses itself in a concern with longer melodic lines, beauty of sound and fluid textures. A particular influence has been the poetry of Brendan Kennelly, several of whose poems she has set.

SARAH BURN

O'Leary, John (1830–1907) member of the Fenian movement. O'Leary was notable for his influence on the cultural debates of the 1890s. In 1863, with Charles Kickham, he founded the *Irish People*, an anti-clerical nationalist newspaper, for which he was imprisoned and later exiled. Returning to Dublin in 1885, O'Leary promoted Irish culture and nationalism, giving lectures and writing *Recollections of Fenians and Fenianism* (1896). W.B. Yeats uses O'Leary as a symbol of a chivalric, heroic nationalism in several poems. 'From O'Leary's conversation, and from the Irish books he lent or gave me, has come all I have set my hand to since.'

CHRIS MORASH

O'Malley, Tony (1913–) Self-taught painter. Born Callan. County Kilkenny. O'Malley has a growing international reputation. He developed his interest in painting in the 1940s during a prolonged illness. Employed as a bank official, he eventually left to take up art on a full-time basis. He settled among the artistic community in St Ives, Cornwall, in 1959, which undoubtedly had the effect of raising his profile on the international art scene. He has also maintained a home in County Kilkenny, and is a regular visitor to the West Indies. In 1981 he was awarded the Douglas Hyde Gold Medal in the Oireachteas Art Exhibition in Dublin. In the same year he was elected a member of Aosdána. A retrospective exhibition of his work, organized by the Arts Council, took place in the Douglas Hyde Gallery in Dublin in 1984. He received the Irish American Cultural Award for painting in 1989. He exhibits in Cornwall and with the Taylor Galleries in Dublin. His paintings, whether responding to his native Ireland or to the West Indies, tend towards abstraction and are inspired both by nature and history. While eschewing perspective, his work explores the texture of surfaces. O'Malley's work is in the tradition of Irish Romantic, poetic 'naturism', though it perhaps raises some philosophical questions concerning the ascribed depiction of natural 'essences'.

Reading

Fallon, Brian, *Tony O'Malley: Painter in Exile* (Dublin/Belfast: Arts Council/An Chomhairle Ealaion/Arts Council of Northern Ireland, 1984).

PAUL O'BRIEN

ombudsman The Ombudsman Act 1980 provided for the appointment of an ombudsman with power to investigate complaints of maladministration against government departments and offices and to report annually to the Oireachtas. No appointment was made until January 1984, when Garret FitzGerald's coalition government chose a distinguished journalist, Michael Mills, as Ireland's first ombudsman. In 1985 the jurisdiction of the ombudsman's office was extended to local authorities, health boards, Telecom Éireann and An Post.

JAMES DOWNEY

O'Meara, Frank (1853–88) Painter. Born Carlow, 30 March; died there of malaria, 15 October. The son of a medical doctor, O'Meara trained at the atelier of Carolus-Duran in Paris (1873–4). Part of an international group of artists who lived at Grez-sur-Loing, near Fontainebleau, O'Meara was virtually unknown in Ireland until after his death. Heavily influenced by the French *plein-air* movement of the 1870s–80s and a lingering Pre-Raphaelitism (a similarity he shared with John Butler Yeats), O'Meara produced a small *oeuvre* dominated by a wistful melancholia often represented by means of an isolated woman and encroaching winter.

Reading

Campbell, Julian, *Frank O'Meara 1853–1888* (Dublin: Hugh Lane Municipal Gallery of Modern Art, 1989).

FINTAN CULLEN

O'Meara, Kathleen (1839–88) Writer. Born Dublin; died Paris, 10 November. O'Meara moved to Paris as an infant and spent most of her life in France, seldom, if ever, returning to Ireland. She began writing under the pseudonym of Grace Ramsey, and gained a reputation as a writer of quality novels and biographies. For many years she was the Paris correspondent of the *Tablet* newspaper. Her novels include *A Woman's Trials* (1867), *Iza's Story* (1869) and *Are you my Wife?* (1878). Her biographies include *The Life of Thomas Grant, First Bishop of South-*

wark (1874) and *The Life of Frederic Ozanman* (1876).

RACHEL FURMSTON

O'Neill, Francis (1849–1936) Collector of traditional music and general superintendent of police, Chicago. Born Tralibane, County Cork. Reportedly 'intended for the Irish Christian Brothers', O'Neill ran away to sea in 1865 and after an extraordinary career, which included shipwreck in the Pacific, made his way to Chicago, where in 1873 he joined the police force, eventually becoming general superintendent.

His passion for collecting traditional Irish music and song led his critics to complain that during his tenure of office the Chicago Police Force contained an unusually high proportion of Irish musicians. Be that as it may, Chicago proved an ideal base for a collector of Irish music, for emigration brought to Chicago musicians from all over the island of Ireland, and from Scotland. Between 1903 and 1922 O'Neill published five compilations of Irish traditional music and two books about the subject.

More than any other one person, O'Neill is responsible for the survival of a living Irish music tradition within the Irish diaspora: yet, of course, at the same time his work helped bring about the homogenization of Irish music. In 1931 O'Neill donated his collection of books and music to the University of Notre Dame, Indiana. He died unaware of the respect which would accrue to his life work: Irish musicians still refer to O'Neill's 1907 collection, *1001 Gems*, as 'The Book'.

Reading

Fuderer, Laura Sue, *Music Mad: Captain Francis O'Neill and Traditional Irish Music – An Exhibition from the Captain Francis O'Neill Collection of Irish Music* (Notre Dame IN: Department of Special Collections, University Libraries, University of Notre Dame, Indiana, 1990).
O'Connor, Nuala, *Bringing It All Back Home: The Influence of Irish Music* (London: BBC Books, 1991).

O'Neill, Francis, *The Dance Music of Ireland: 1001 Gems* (Dublin: Walton's 1907).
——*Irish Folk Music: A Fascinating Hobby, with Some Account of Allied Subjects including O'Farrell's Treatise on the Irish or Union Pipes and Touhey's Hints to Amateur Pipers* (Chicago: Regan Printing House, 1910).
Smith, Graeme, 'My love is in America: emigration and Irish music', in *The Creative Migrant*, vol. 3 of Patrick O'Sullivan (ed.), *The Irish World Wide: History, Heritage, Identity* (London: Leicester University Press, 1994).

PATRICK O'SULLIVAN

O'Neill, Hugh (*c*.1550–1616) Gaelic lord. Born Dungannon; died Rome, 20 July. O'Neill, third baron of Dungannon and second earl of Tyrone, was the second son of Feardorcha (Matthew) O'Neill, baron of Dungannon, and Joan Maguire. After the death of his father at the hands of Shane O'Neill in 1558, Hugh was made a ward of the crown and was reared in the household of Giles Hovenden, a New English settler in the Pale, and his Anglo-Irish wife Elizabeth Cheevers. His elder brother, Brian, was murdered in 1562, and from the late 1560s Hugh was frequently supported by the Dublin government as a check on the power of Turlough Luineach O'Neill within the O'Neill lordship. The longer-term consequence of the English administration's policy of using Hugh to advance their schemes to reform Ulster was that he became the most powerful man in the province. Hugh pursued power in Ulster using both Gaelic and English methods as expedient. He sat in the Dublin Parliament of 1585 as earl of Tyrone, but sought the traditional Gaelic title also and was eventually inaugurated as O'Neill in May 1593, two years before the death of the ageing Turlough Luineach.

His close allies in the 1590s, when the Gaelic Ulster chiefs became embroiled in military hostilities with the Dublin government, were Hugh Roe O'Donnell and Hugh Maguire. Despite some successes in guerilla-style warfare, most notably at the Yellow Ford in 1598 against the English forces led by his father-in-law Sir Nicholas Bagenal, the Nine Years War showed O'Neill's lack of skill as a military leader in regular warfare. The combined Irish and Spanish forces under the command of Hugh O'Neill, Hugh Roe O'Donnell and Don Juan d'Aquila were defeated at Kinsale in December 1601 by the army of Lord Deputy Mountjoy. O'Neill submitted to Lord Mountjoy in 1603, renouncing his Irish title and his links with foreign princes, and undertaking not to interfere with the lesser lords in his territories. O'Neill was received at court by James I in June 1603 and had his English title and his lands confirmed to him, but four years later, on 14 September 1607, he left Ulster permanently, sailing from Rathmullen with Hugh O'Donnell and many of their kinsmen and friends, travelling via the Low Countries to arrive in Rome in April 1608. Attempts to secure further Spanish military assistance in support of his ambitions in Ireland were unsuccessful, and O'Neill died isolated and desolate.

Reading

Canny, Nicholas P., 'Hugh O'Neill, earl of Tyrone, and the changing face of Gaelic Ulster', *Studia Hibernica* X (1970).

Morgan, Hiram, *Tyrone's Rebellion* (Dublin: Gill and Macmillan, 1993).

Walsh, Micheline Kerney *'Destruction by Peace': Hugh O'Neill after Kinsale* (Armagh: Cumann Seanchais Ard Mhacha, 1986).

BERNADETTE CUNNINGHAM

O'Neill, Owen Roe (?1582–1649) Soldier. Born north Armagh; died Cloughoughter Castle, County Cavan, 6 November. O'Neill was the youngest son of Art Mc Baron O'Neill, who was half-brother to the earl of Tyrone. In 1604 or early 1605 he left Ireland and joined the Irish regiments in Spanish Flanders, where he remained until 1642. His European experience was not a happy one. Although a talented soldier, he was overshadowed by the political necessity of accommodating the descendants of the earls of Tyrone and Tyrconnell in the Irish army of Flanders, and did not receive the promotion to which he felt entitled.

O'Neill's European experience was important since, while based at Louvain, he made contacts among the Irish Franciscan exile community which shaped his political views and his loyalty to Counter-Reformation Catholicism. On the outbreak of war in Ireland in late 1641, disillusioned with his promotion in Europe, O'Neill deserted and returned to Ireland. He landed at Doe castle in Donegal on 6 July 1642. He was acknowledged by the Ulster army as their commander at Clones in August. He attended the first session of the Confederation of Kilkenny in October and was appointed commander in Ulster. The Old English did not trust him and throughout the 1640s were not prepared to appoint him to a more senior post. O'Neill's main problem was the organization of the ad hoc Ulster army into a European-style force, and by 1646 he had achieved some measure of success, as evidenced by his victory at the battle of Benburb. Politically, after 1645, he supported the papal nuncio, Rinuccini, which alienated him from the Confederation. He refused to support the Ormond peaces of 1646 or 1648, was proclaimed a traitor by the confederation, and his command was rescinded.

Reading

Casway, Jerrold, *Owen Roe O'Neill and the Struggle for Catholic Ireland* (Philadelphia: University of Pennsylvania Press, 1984).

Gillespie, Raymond 'Owen Roe O'Neill', in Gerard O'Brien and Peter Roebuck (eds), *Nine Ulster Lives* (Belfast: Ulster Historical Foundation, 1992).

RAYMOND GILLESPIE

Opera

1660–1800

During the seventeenth and eighteenth centuries, the term 'opera' in Ireland, as in

England, could refer to any theatrical performance including music, usually in the form of
plays with substantial numbers of songs. It is
in this sense that the earliest reference to
opera in Ireland should be understood, when
John Ogilvy was granted a licence in 1661 'to
represent Comedyes, Tragedyes and Operas'
in Dublin.

From the late seventeenth century, increasing numbers of English and Continental singers and musicians visited Dublin. Although
opera hardly featured in the early eighteenth
century, *The Island Passion*, with music by
Daniel Purcell, Jeremiah Clarke and others,
staged at the Smock Alley Theatre in 1705/6,
is considered to be the first true opera performed in Ireland. The fashion for Italian
opera which reached London in the early
1700s failed to reach Dublin. This was despite
the visits of Italian singers, including the castrato Niccolini, who gave a concert in 1711,
and the presence from 1707 until his death in
1727 of Cousser, who had an international
reputation as an opera composer but produced none while in Dublin.

The success of *The Beggar's Opera*, first
performed in Dublin in March 1728, led to
ballad operas and their successors, English
comic operas, becoming amongst the most
popular theatrical entertainments throughout
the rest of the eighteenth century. Thomas
Arne, Charles Dibdin, William Shield and
Stephen Storace were amongst the leading
composers in this field. Dublin had to wait
until 1761 for its first full Italian operas, when
a visiting company presented burlettas and
opera buffa, including Pergolesi's *La Serva
Padrona*. The first Italian *opera seria* performed was Giordani's *L'Eroe Cinese* in
1766, although Arne's *Artaxerxes*, an English
opera seria, had been staged the previous year.
In the latter part of the century English translations of Continental operas, including
Gluck's *Orfeo ed Euridice*, were sometimes
performed.

Although Dublin companies occasionally
visited other provincial towns, Cork and
Belfast were the only other musical centres
of significance. As in Dublin, ballad and
comic operas were popular during the later
part of the eighteenth century. The castrato
Tenducci, who lived in Dublin and sang in
operas mainly at Smock Alley between 1765
and 1786, visited Cork in 1766. In Belfast,
visiting companies periodically performed
ballad operas from 1750, with a local company
being set up in 1773.

BARRA BOYDELL

1800–1900

At the beginning of the nineteenth century a
taste for opera was well established in Dublin,
where of all forms of music making it had the
largest following. The Crow Street theatre,
which was closed in 1820, was supplanted by
the Theatre Royal in Hawkins Street, with a
seating capacity of 3,800. It was burned down
in 1880, but the Gaiety Theatre which had
been opened in 1871 was available to take its
place. Seating 1,075, this acoustically unsatisfactory theatre, with restricted stage space,
has been the venue for operatic performances
ever since.

In the nineteenth century it was chiefly
Italian opera that really established itself in
Dublin. In the second decade, Mozart's *Cosi
fan tutte*, *Don Giovanni* and *Figaro* were introduced without notable success; but with the
advent of easier travel, touring opera companies paid regular visits and succeeded in
implanting an enthusiasm for opera that left
a permanent mark on Irish musical life. By
1840, having been introduced to Rossini,
Italian opera began to reach full flower with
great singers in the operas of Bellini and
Donizzetti, followed in the 1850s by Verdi.
A remarkable feature was the short time-lag
between the production of new operas in
London and on the Continent and their performance in Dublin. Verdi's *La Traviata* and
Il Trovatore, for instance, were produced in
Dublin in 1855, two years after their first
performance.

Of German opera sung in German there
was none; though Weber's *Der Freischütz* and
Oberon met with considerable success when

produced in English translation remarkably soon after their original productions. Wagner's *Lohengrin* was given in Italian in 1875, and *Der Fliegende Holländer* in English by the Carl Rosa company in 1878. Visits were made by French companies in 1824, 1850, 1870 and 1875, bringing operas by Boildieu, Auber, Offenbach, Hérold and Halévy, among others of lesser note. The Irish composers Balfe and Wallace were not unexpectedly very popular in Dublin, both receiving the ultimate compliment of having an opera performed in Italian.

The popularity of opera had already spread to Belfast, where a suitable theatre had been opened in 1793. In the early part of the century, it was eighteenth-century English opera, usually built around engagements of eminent singers such as Braham and Horn, that provided the main operatic fare. By the mid-century, seasons of Italian opera were given by companies visiting Dublin and by the English opera company, which included Sims Reeves.

The growth of the industrial city, and the replacement of its eighteenth-century theatre by the larger Theatre Royal in 1871, put Belfast on the major British Isles touring circuit. The Carl Rosa company included Belfast in its touring schedules throughout its existence. In the early 1890s there was a golden age for opera, when in the space of three years there were nearly 50 performances by one company or another of 33 different operas, 18 of them being heard in the city for the first time. There was sufficient inducement to build a second theatre, and the Grand Opera House was opened in 1895.

The companies engaged in Dublin and Belfast made occasional visits to Cork, though the high fees demanded by soloists of international standing precluded fully staged performances in provincial towns with a small audience potential. Even in Cork, it was often considered necessary to present operas in shortened form, adding a popular farce to the evening's entertainment in order to induce a less sophisticated audience to fill the house.

Cork was visited regularly in the 1870s and 1880s by such companies as the Grand English Opera Company, the D'Oyly Carte Company, and the Italian Opera Company of Covent Garden. Local amateur opera developed later than in Dublin but prior to that in Belfast, for in 1883 the Cork Amateur Operatic and Dramatic Society presented *The Pirates of Penzance* at the Opera House during the Industrial Exhibition. The popularity of opera in Cork can be judged from the fact that in 1896 five different opera companies gave seasons at the Opera House, bringing the usual repertoire, but also lesser-known comic operas by Dibdin, Cellier and Audran.

In the earlier part of the century, smaller provincial centres could enjoy occasional performances of the popular English comic operas and musical plays of the eighteenth century, which did not demand the participation of 'star' singers. This genre of light opera sowed the seeds which were later fertilized by tours by the D'Oyly Carte Company to give rise to the great popularity of Gilbert and Sullivan and similar operettas, which sustained amateur societies throughout the country from the end of the nineteenth century to the present day.

The nearest approach to Grand Opera which could be enjoyed outside Dublin, Belfast and Cork was occasional visits of famous singers giving concert performances after appearing in the capital.

BRIAN BOYDELL

1900–90s

The experience of opera in the early years of the twentieth century was largely restricted to the cities and dependent on visiting companies such as the Carl Rosa, Moody-Manners and O'Mara companies. In 1928 Signor Adelio Viani, professor of singing in the Royal Irish Academy of Music, established the Dublin Operatic Society as a first resident enterprise designed to serve the opera-loving public of the metropolis. This body lasted but a short time; however, its successor, the Dublin Grand Opera Society, founded in

1941, quickly established a reputation and continues to make its contribution to the cultural life of the city. The ambitious annual Wexford Festival which concentrates on producing lesser-known works in intimate surroundings, was founded in 1951 by T.J. Walsh, and the high standard of production has earned international approbation. Many an aspiring vocalist has had a first experience of operatic performance in the less formal setting of Irish National Opera (1965), which tours the country and employs piano accompaniment for its productions. This company has more recently been succeeded by the Opera Theatre Company. Opera Northern Ireland is active north of the border.

Success in presentation has not been matched by commensurate creative endeavour. It is indicative of the general low level of musical activity that opera, that primary vehicle of the music of commitment, should have made such a tardy response to the cultural and political nationalism evident in this period. It is true that the first operas produced at the start of the century were imbued with the character of the Celtic Revival and were equally a rejection of the anglocentric 'jolly Irish' image promulgated by Stanford in his *Singspiel*, *Shamus O'Brien* (1895); but these are the exception. *Muirgheis* by the Kerry-born O'Brien Butler (?1862–1915) and Robert O'Dwyer's *Eithne* were both inspired by the ideals of the Gaelic League; both, while originally written in English, were translated into Gaelic. *Muirgheis*, a love story based on an Irish saga realized in the libretto by Nora Chesson, was first given in the Theatre Royal, Dublin, in December 1903. While it is an uneven work, it has much to recommend it. *Eithne* was written for the Oireachtas of 1909 to a libretto by Rev Thomas O'Kelly of Sligo. It was first given in Dublin in August that year, and again in the third week of May the following year. Like O'Brien Butler's work, it is a grand opera inasmuch as it has no spoken dialogue, but it is less folksy and is altogether more challenging. O'Kelly also collaborated

on yet another opera in this vein, *Sruth na Maoile* (*The Waters of Moyle*), by the organist and composer Geoffrey Molyneux Palmer, who was born in Middlesex in 1882 but had settled in Ireland in 1910 and whose work evinces his espousal of the dominant nationalist sentiment. The opera was first given in the Gaiety Theatre in July 1923 under the direction of Vincent O'Brien. Another such opera, *Sean the Post* by Dermot Macmurrough (the *nom de plume* employed by the critic and teacher Harold White), was premièred in the capital the following year as one of the musical contributions to the revived Tailteann Games.

A number of composers in subsequent generations have attended to the form. Eamonn O'Gallchobhair (1906–82) has produced a number of short works for the stage, while Gerard Victory has proved the most prolific writer of his generation. A.J. Potter's *The Wedding* was given in 1981, while the most notable of recent productions was Gerald Barry's ambitious creation *The Intelligence Park*, a three-act opera to a libretto by Vincent Deane premièred in London in 1990.

BARRA BOYDELL, BRIAN BOYDELL AND

JOSEPH RYAN

Orangeism and the Orange Order
Orangeism traces its birth to the meeting in Exeter Cathedral in 1688 which offered the crown of Britain to William III, Prince of Orange. Other antecedents included the Aldermen of Skinner's Alley, who continued to meet in Dublin when James II sought to remove Protestants from public office, and officers of the 4th of Foot who formed the Loyal and Friendly Society of the Blew and Orange.

Local land wars and employment opportunities lay behind the battle of the Diamond in Armagh on 21 September 1795. The inappropriately named Defenders attacked from Faughart Hill, wrecked Dan Winter's cottage and sought to seize the Diamond Hill. Protestants, thus attacked, won and formed themselves into the Orange Society. Their mission statement was 'to defend themselves, to support the Protestant Religion and to uphold the King and Constitution'. The Grand Lodge was formed in Dublin in 1798. The Order has often been maligned and misunderstood, occasionally through foolish and misguided actions by some members.

During the mid-1800s several Acts of Parliament were passed, mainly aimed against ribbon societies – a source of agitation. The year 1825 saw the Act against unlawful association, which, at the request of pro-Catholic elements at Westminster, was extended to Orange Lodges. Accordingly, the Grand Lodge dissolved itself on 18 March. Two House of Lords Select Committees were set up to investigate the Order. The chairman of the English Committee, a radical, Joseph Hume, had no pretence of impartiality. The Irish Committee included one O'Connellite MP who described Orangemen as 'a race of reptiles raised in blood and cherished in crime'.

Ambiguous in their decisions, the committees presented an unfinished report to the Lords. Orangemen did not consider themselves guilty of disloyalty and continued to meet in subordinate lodges. With the expiration of the Party Processions Act, they came out openly in 1845 and the Grand Lodge was reconstructed in 1847.

The Famine of 1847, the rise of the Ribbonmen in 1849, and their attack on an Orange Walk via Dolly's Brae on 12 July 1849 led to the Party Processions Act of 1850. The subsequent Party Emblems Act of 1860 was not fairly enforced. Orangemen were jailed, while no notice was taken of a mammoth demonstration in Dublin in memory of O'Connell. As a result, William Johnston led a march from Newtownards to Bangor. Imprisoned, and subsequently elected as Independent Orange Candidate in South Belfast, he saw the Acts repealed in 1870.

The Order has grown and spread worldwide. As a Benevolent Society, it cares for its members, widows and orphans. Its halls, often the only public hall in the community, are used for social and cultural activities, prayer meetings and evangelistic missions. Although so used, and for non-profit-making activities, they only earned a right of rebate on rates after the demise of Stormont. Participating in diverse church services, members learnt to respect other forms of worship and particular doctrines. Despite being anti-papist, members are encouraged not to be antagonistic to Catholic people. Thus, bands have shared instruments with Catholic bands and Hibernians have exchanged banner poles with Orange Lodges. During the Famine, lodges aided famine relief; and Derriaghy and Belfast Orangemen, because of their concept of civil and religious liberty, contributed to build chapels. Politically, the Order seeks to represent the best interests of people and has argued their case with both Westminster and Stormont administrations. On occasions, to the detriment of all in Northern Ireland, its voice was not heeded.

Members remain committed to their faith and loyal to their country, though never subservient to any prevailing political opinion.

Reading

Dewar, Michael W., Brown, John and Long, Samuel Ernest, *Orangeism: A New Historical Appreciation* (Belfast: Grand Orange Lodge of Ireland, 1967).

Senior, Hereward, *Orangeism in Ireland and Britain 1795–1836* (London: Routledge and Kegan Paul, 1966).

—— 'The early Orange Order, 1795–1870', and McClelland, Aitken, 'The later Orange Order', in *Secret Societies in Ireland* (Dublin: Gill and Macmillan, 1973).

Sibbett, R.M., *Orangeism in Ireland and Throughout the Empire* (London: Thynne, 1939).

REV. MARTIN SMYTH

Ó Rathaille, Aogán (*c.*1670–*c.*1726) Poet. Born Scrahanaveal, County Kerry. Ó Rathaille appears to have had a privileged upbringing and education, but was deprived of his holdings following the Jacibite defeats of 1690–1 and lived out the later part of his life in poverty. He is buried in Muckross Abbey, Killarney. He is widely regarded as the greatest poet in Gaelic literature. He is primarily a poet of displacement and dispossession, the première elegist of Gaelic civilization in decline. His poetry reflects the ever-changing socio-political realities of the early Penal era as they are borne in upon his tortured imagination. His aislings – 'Gile na Gile' ('Brighness Most Bright'), 'An Aisling' ('The Vision'), 'Mac an Chennaí' ('The Redeemer's Son') – are among the most celebrated in the language, yet more impressive are such poems as 'Is Fada Liom Oíche Fhírfhliuch' ('The Drenching Night Drags On') and 'Cabhair Ní Ghairfead' ('No Help I'll Call'), in which expressions of personal suffering open out into plangent evocations of national desolation.

Reading

Jordan, John, 'Aogán Ó Rathaille', in Seán Mac Réamoinn (ed.), *The Pleasures of Gaelic Poetry* (London: Allen Lane, 1982).

Ó Tuama, Seán, *Filí Faoi Sceimhle* (Dublin: Stationery Office, 1978).

LIAM HARTE

Ordnance Survey Official department established under military direction in the 1790s to produce a trigonometrical survey and topographical map of Great Britain. In 1824 the Survey's field of operations was extended to cover Ireland. There was already a habit of strong central government participation in Irish local affairs, and the first Irish Ordnance maps were intended less for military purposes than to facilitate the taxation of land and buildings on a county basis. Published at six inches to one mile between 1833 and 1846, they were more accurate and detailed than anything the department had yet produced in Britain. Their construction entailed a careful study of Irish place-names, an episode later to be described vividly but erroneously in Brian Friel's play *Translations*, and during the 1830s this programme was developed under the inspiration of Captain Thomas Larcom into a scheme for publishing an account of Ireland's physical and human geography. Larcom's 'memoir' project captured the imagination of many Irish patriots, but it was discontinued in 1840, partly on grounds of expense and partly because the military authorities came to regard it as foreign to the character of a cartographic survey.

The Survey's Dublin office remained in being with its terms of reference more narrowly defined, and from the mid-century onwards its output was governed by a policy designed for Britain. But since British cartographic needs were now expanding rapidly, Ireland acquired a richer legacy of official maps than an autonomous national government would have been likely to countenance, notably town plans at 60 or more inches to the mile and maps of virtually all enclosed rural landscapes at about 25 inches to a mile.

In 1922 two new survey departments, both called Ordnance Surveys, were established in Dublin and Belfast. Both have striven to carry nineteenth-century cartographic standards into a new age of technological revolution and accelerating landscape change. The results have inevitably differed from North to South according to the resources available, but both Surveys continue to map their territories on a wide range of scales, and since the 1970s they have each been publishing at the new scale of 1:50,000 within an all-Ireland framework of sheet-lines.

Reading

Andrews, J.H., *A Paper Landscape: The Ordnance Survey in Nineteenth-Century Ireland* (Oxford: Oxford University Press, 1975).

An Illustrated Record of Ordnance Survey in Ireland (Dublin and Belfast: Ordnance Survey of Ireland and Ordnance Survey of Northern Ireland, 1991).

J.H. ANDREWS

Ó Riada, Seán (1931–71) Composer and arranger. Born John Reidy in Cork, 1 August;

died London, 3 October. Ó Riada received his early musical education in Cork, where he graduated with a BMus from University College in 1952. Thereafter he became assistant musical director at Radio Éireann (until 1956). Later appointments included a period as music director at the Abbey Theatre (1956–62) and as lecturer in music at University College, Cork (1962–71).

Ó Riada's career as a composer of music unrelated to the traditional music of Ireland overlapped with his involvement with traditional music as an arranger and performer. Although most of his original compositions make no attempt to incorporate traditional Irish airs, the latter occupied much of his time in Radio Éireann, and throughout the late fifties and early sixties, when he established the group Ceoltóirí Chualann as an 'experiment' in the pursuit of traditional Irish music arranged for 'folk orchestra' (Paddy Moloney's description). Ó Riada also wrote a considerable body of film music for conventional orchestral resources, much of which demonstrates his craftsmanship in the arrangement of traditional melodies for large resources. The film scores for *Mise Eire* (1959), *Saoirse?* (1960) and *The Playboy of the Western World* (1962) are all important in this regard. His music for Thomas Kinsella's radio version of the Irish epic *The Tain* (1970) is an admixture of traditional and original elements.

Ó Riada also made several vocal arrangements of Irish music, and he composed two settings of the Mass in Irish which can be classified as original compositions written in the manner and style of the traditional repertory. His long-held interest in the music and person of Turlough Carolan culminated in the mid-sixties, when he sought to reanimate Carolan's cross-fertilization of ethnic and European musical elements in his arrangements, performances and recordings with Ceoltóirí Chualann (Ó Riada played the harpsichord on many of these recordings).

In his assessment of the original compositions, Séoirse Bodley nominates the first, second and fourth of Ó Riada's *Nomos* works (1957–8) as among the most significant he produced. *Nomos* no. 1, *Hercules Dux Ferrariae*, is scored for string orchestra, and its eight sections manifest a control of structural and formal technique which reflect the composer's interest in a modified application of serialism and other (then) Modernist techniques. Ó Riada characteristically combined such techniques with modal structures (as in the modal theme derived from the vowels of the work's title) and traditional means of textural elaboration, including fugue and ground-bass.

Nomos no. 2, regarded by Aloys Fleischmann among others as the most important of Ó Riada's original compositions, is a large-scale work for choir and orchestra of some 50 minutes' duration. Its text is drawn from the Theban cycle of Sophocles (Ó Riada's abiding interest in Greek drama is a significant factor in his work) and reflects on fate, life and death. The musical approach throughout *Nomos* no. 2 is deliberately eclectic, in that the work attempts to trace the history of musical styles by means of references to plain chant, modal scales, organum, and a direct quotation of the *L'homme armé* melody. Quotations from Beethoven, Brahms and Mozart are sharply contrasted with harsh discords. The work also embraces serial techniques. In spite of its uneven quality and occasionally naive theatricality, it succeeds as a large-scale musical unity.

Ó Riada's other orchestral works, his original song settings (of texts by Pound, Kinsella, Arp, Hölderlin, Montague and Heaney, among others), and his musical output as a whole strongly suggest that within the comparatively short span of his lifetime, the composer failed to find a style answerable to the demands of his musical imagination. His intensified interest in traditional music, which followed the production of his most important original works, only served to reinforce this stylistic crisis. Notwithstanding his own volatile temperament, Ó Riada's development as a composer of outstanding promise was also inhibited by his acute awareness of the dislocated and subsequently marginalized position of the creative musician in Ireland during his lifetime and for centuries beforehand.

Reading

Fleischmann, Aloys, 'Ó Riada, Sean', in Stanley Sadie (ed.), *The New Grove Dictionary of Music and Musicians* (London: Macmillan, 1980), vol. 13.

Freyer, Grattan and Harris, Bernard (eds), *The Achievement of Séan Ó Riada* (Ballina and Pennsylvania: Irish Humanities Centre/Dufour Editions, 1981).

HARRY WHITE

Orientalism Defined by Edward Said as 'a Western style for dominating, restructuring, and having authority over the Orient'. Said's *Orientalism* cross-fertilizes literary criticism, history, politics, sociology and anthropology. Drawing upon Michel Foucault's concepts of 'discourse' (an internally regulated assemblage of events, utterances and texts) and 'the archive' (the code of rules which controls what may be said), as well as Antonio Gramsci's idea of 'hegemony' (the manner in which rulers successfully persuade the ruled of the validity of their rule), Said examines the parts, parties and partialities of representation: those who represent (the Orientalists); those who are represented (the peoples of the Orient); and those to whom the representation is addressed (the peoples of the West). One of *Orientalism*'s wry epigraphs is Karl Marx's disparaging comment in *The Eighteenth Brumaire of Louis Bonaparte* (1852) about the French smallholding peasants: 'They cannot represent themselves, they must be represented.' Said's methodology involves 'strategic location', which describes a writer's placing in a text with respect to the material written about, and 'strategic formation', which involves analysing how texts affiliate to form the discourse that bolsters an intellectual hegemony. In tracing the development of Orientalism from Aeschylus to the present, Said raises questions about the role of the intellectual, what it means to represent another culture, and whether racial, religious and cultural distinctions are more important in human relations than socio-economic, political and historical factors.

Said's work has attracted the attention of critics of Irish writing, since Ireland like the Orient has long suffered under and struggled against imposed representations (one area of convergence is in the work of prominent Orientalist Ernest Renan, who sought in 'The Poetry of the Celtic Races' (1859) to define the essence of the Celt). David Cairns and Shaun Richards's *Writing Ireland* (1988) acknowledges debts to *Orientalism*; Seamus Deane's 'Civilians and Barbarians' (1983) and Declan Kiberd's 'Anglo-Irish Attitudes' (1984), both Field Day pamphlets, employ methods akin to Said's with greater success than Said's own Field Day pamphlet 'Yeats and Decolonization' (1988), which treats Yeats as a decolonizing poet. Irish writers like Thomas Moore, in *Lallah Rookh* (1817), and James Clarence Mangan, in his late 1830s and 1840s series of real and sham translations *Litterae Orientales*, sometimes indulged in the Orientalist mode, but George Bernard Shaw, in his 1906 'Preface for Politicians' to *John Bull's Other Island* (1904), linked the Denshawi atrocity in Egypt with misrule in Ireland, exposed the stratagems of British Orientalism, and espoused Home Rule for Ireland and the other countries of the empire, while James Joyce's short story 'Araby' (1905) can be read as – amongst other things – a subtle critique of the vanity and blindness of Orientalism.

Reading

Said, Edward W., *Orientalism* (London: Routledge and Kegan Paul, 1978).

—— *The World, the Text, and the Critic* (Cambridge MA: Harvard University Press, 1983).

—— 'Orientalism Reconsidered', in Francis Barker (ed.), *Europe and its Others*, vol. 1 (Colchester: University of Essex, 1985).

——'Yeats and Decolonization', (Derry: Field Day, 1988).

——*Culture and Imperialism* (London: Chatto and Windus, 1993).

Sprinkler, Michael (ed.), *Edward Said: A Critical Reader* (Oxford: Blackwell, 1992).

RICHARD HASLAM

Orpen, Sir William (1878–1931) Painter and graphic artist. Born Stillorgan, County Dublin. Orpen was one of the few Irish artists to win international fame in his lifetime. The son of a lawyer, he was a teenage prodigy, winning many prizes at the Metropolitan School of Art in Dublin and later at the Slade School in London. For a time, he ran an art school in London with Augustus John. Elected to the Royal Academy and to the New English Art Club, he built up a major reputation as a portrait painter, though he retained his links with Ireland and returned regularly to Dublin for teaching stints. The 1916 Rebellion antagonized him and he became estranged from his homeland.

Orpen served as an official war artist at the Western Front and painted the delegates to the Versailles Conference. At one stage, his portrait practice was so large that he maintained studios in London and Paris. His reputation sank rapidly after his death, but since his centenary year it has risen steadily again.

Like Sorolla in Spain, Zorn in Sweden, and Liebermann in Germany, Orpen was an international eclectic who grafted the brilliant brushwork of Manet onto a late realist style. In spite of the fame of his portraits, much of his best work is in his interiors and genre pieces. *Homage to Manet* (Manchester Art Gallery) contains portraits of George Moore, Steer, Tonks and other contemporaries. As a teacher, Orpen left a lasting mark on the Irish generation of Sleator, Whelan, Keating and Tuohy.

BRIAN FALLON

Orr, James (1770–1816) Poet. Born Broadisland, County Antrim; died Ballycarry, County Antrim, 24 April. A United Irishman, Orr escaped to America after the rebellion of 1798, but returned to Ireland after a short time. Many of his poems are in the Antrim dialect.

Reading

Orr, James, *Poems* (Belfast: 1817).

PATRICK FAGAN

Osborne, Walter (1859–1903) Painter. Born Rathmines, 17 June; died Dublin, 24 April. Osborne was from a middle-class Protestant family; his father, William Osborne RHA, was English and a well-known painter of animals. Osborne was educated at Rathmines School and then at the Royal Hibernian Academy (RHA) School (1876), where he won a Taylor Scholarship in 1881. Later that year he moved to Antwerp and stayed 18 months, studying at the Academic Royale under Charles Verlat.

Antwerp was the making of Osborne, as he learnt to draw with speed and panache and in colour. A Rubens influence has been cited as lying behind this change from the more drab teaching of the Dublin Academy, but the advocacy of a freer use of colour together with a looser administrative structure allowed for greater personal development. In Antwerp he met Blandford Fletcher, who introduced him to *plein-air* painting, and he started going on painting expeditions to Brittany in 1883. There Osborne met other English artists such as Clausen and Stanhope-Forbes. His subject matter at this time was realist depictions of peasant girls gathering apples or quiet corners of an English country garden.

In many ways Osborne's favourite habitat was the south of England, but family duties called him back to Dublin, where he turned to genre scenes of Dublin street life and domestic, middle-class homes. These Dublin paintings of the 1890s are his most memorable achievement and were executed in both oils and watercolour. There is a solitary melancholy about much of his work, perhaps complemented in his own somewhat lonely

life. For economic reasons he took up portraiture in the 1890s and produced solid and
respectable portraits of Dublin society and
of professional gentlemen. He was friendly
with George Moore, Stephen Gwynne,
Nathaniel Hone and Walter Armstrong, a
one-time director of the National Gallery
of Ireland, with whom he travelled in Europe
in 1895–6. He declined a knighthood in
1900.

Reading

Bodkin, Thomas, *Four Irish Landscape Painters*
(Dublin: Talbot Press, 1920; repr. intro. Julian
Campbell, Irish Academic Press, 1987).

Campbell, Julian, *The Irish Impressionists: Irish
Artists in France and Belgium, 1850–1914*
(Dublin: National Gallery of Ireland, 1984).

McConkey, Kenneth, *A Free Spirit: Irish Art
1860–1960* (Woodbridge: Antique Collectors'
Club, 1990).

Sheehy, Jeanne, *Walter Osborne* (Dublin: National
Gallery of Ireland, 1983).

Strickland, Walter, *A Dictionary of Irish Artists*
(Shannon: Irish University Press, 1968).

FINTAN CULLEN

Otway, Caesar (1780–1842) Author. Born
County Tipperary; died Dublin, 16 March.
Otway was educated at Trinity College,
Dublin, and took holy orders, serving in a
country parish for 17 years and then as assistant chaplain in Leeson Street Magdalen
Chapel in Dublin. In 1826 he founded a
religious magazine, the *Christian Examiner*,
with J. H. Singer, and was the first to publish
stories by William Carleton. He founded the
Dublin Penny Journal with George Petrie in
1832. His books give interesting contemporary accounts of Irish life. Ill health curtailed
his literary activities.

Reading

Otway, Caesar, *Sketches in Ireland* (Dublin:
William Curry, 1827).
——*A Tour of Conaught* (Dublin: William Curry,
1839).

HENRY BOYLAN

Owenson family Born Robert MacOwen in
Mayo, Robert Owenson (1744–1812), as he
called himself, enjoyed a successful acting
career in England, specializing in Irish roles.
Leaving London for Dublin in 1776, he
became co-proprietor of the Crow Street
Theatre; subsequent attempts to manage
Irish provincial theatres were not successful.
His daughter, Sydney Owenson (1776?–
1859), later Lady Morgan, published two
mildly successful novels, *St Clair* (1804) and
The Novice of St Dominick (1805), before
finding fame with the immensely popular
The Wild Irish Girl (1806). This novel, of
considerable descriptive power and narrative
improbability, embodied national sentiments
perfectly attuned to an age still engrossed
with debating the authenticity of *Ossian*.
The Wild Irish Girl was an important influence on early nineteenth-century Irish
Romantic fiction, especially Maturin's, and
allowed its author to impersonate her heroine,
Glorvina, to great applause in the salons of
Dublin and London. Further novels on Irish
themes included *O'Donel: A National Tale*
(1814), *Florence M'Carthy* (1816) and her most
ambitious work, *The O'Briens and the O'Flaher-
ties* (1827), which attempted a comprehensive
treatment in fiction of Irish cultural complexity.
Sydney Owenson's prolific output included
successful books on France (1817) and Italy
(1821) – the latter praised by Byron and proscribed by the pope – and a life of Salvator Rosa
(1824), the painter whose influence informs
the portrayal of landscape in her fiction.

IAN CAMPBELL ROSS

P

Pacata Hibernia, *Ireland appeased and reduced; Or an historie of the warres of Ireland especially within the province of Mounster under the government of Sir George Carew* (edited by Thomas Stafford) Published in London in 1633 by Robert Milbourne in a large folio volume comprising almost 200,000 words and illustrated with 17 original maps, *Pacata Hibernia* is the largest and most detailed single account written by a contemporary about the Elizabethan wars in Ireland. Concentrating only on Munster in the years 1600 to 1603, it offers a full account of the conduct of Sir George Carew as president of the province. Internal evidence suggests that it was composed at a time close to the events it relates (there is little retrospection and no commentary on figures who later became more significant), but its authorship remains uncertain. It has been assumed that the editor Thomas (later Sir Thomas) Stafford was in fact the author. Stafford, who was rumoured to be an illegitimate son of Carew, served with him in Munster, and inherited all of Carew's books as well as the manuscripts upon which *Pacata* is based. But he makes no claim to authorship, and he is not known to have published anything further. It has also been speculated that Carew himself composed the text. A man of deep historical and antiquarian and historical interests, who counted Camden, Sir Robert Cotton and Sir Thomas Bodley among his friends, he carefully preserved the documents gathered during his Irish service and added greatly to them over time: they formed the basis of the very large collection of Irish materials now housed in Lambeth Palace Library. Carew is also credited with a history of the reign of Henry V and the translation of two French accounts of Irish history in the Middle Ages, all of which appeared anonymously. So it is possible that his diffidence extended to claiming credit for *Pacata*.

Pacata differs significantly from the typical expressions of English views on Ireland at the time in which it was written. Unlike Spenser, Moryson and Rich, its author makes no attempt at pseudo-anthropology, justifying the coercive methods adopted in Ireland in relation to the barbarous or unregenerate nature of its people. Equally, there is little reference to history as a means of asserting the English crown's right to govern Ireland unopposed; and no other determinist framework is imposed to explain the inevitable conflict between English and Irish. The underlying tropes of the narrative, rather are psychological, medical and ideological in that order. The conduct of rebel lords is explained by their pride, avarice or fear; rebellion is a contagion which infects a mildly disaffected people and can be cured by vigorous ministration. Religious convictions inflame those who would otherwise be loyal and obedient. The model which determined the structure, argument and style of the work is the classical military memoir derived from Caesar and affected by several public men (Blaise de Monluc in France, Sir Henry Sidney in Ireland) in the later sixteenth century. Its assessment of character and motivation and its underlying assumptions as to how history works are influenced by the cynical or realist political commentaries of the later Renaissance, in particular Guiccidiardini's *History of Italy*, which enjoyed great popularity among figures of Carew's generation.

The intellectual and literary influences behind the text are more obvious than the circumstances which prompted its publication. Commercial and charitable motives are evident: the title page announces that part of the profits were to be devoted to the maintenance of the children of the late lexicographer and antiquarian John Minsheu. But in the year which saw Sir Thomas Wentworth take up his appointment as lord deputy, political considerations may also have been at work. The editor declares that edificatory lessons were to be found in the work for both English and Irish readers: for the English, showing how deadly rebellion and invasion might be defeated by courage and ingenuity; for the Irish how loyalty to their lawful prince yielded a greater reward than the false promises of rebels and their foreign inciters. This appeal to unity under the authority of a common sovereign was most certainly suited to the policy of Wentworth, who was determined to become a tool of neither the native nor planter interest in Ireland, and proposed instead to rely on the unquestioning support of the king to impose his will on both sides. The same affirmation of the unity of all inhabitants of Ireland under the crown was made, it should be noted, by Ware in his introduction to his set of Irish Chronicles, which was

more overtly aligned to Wentworth's government.

The concern to marginalize rebels, to subordinate cultural and ethnic difference, and to assert the natural obedience of the majority of the Irish to English government which is the underlying imperative of the *Pacata* seems, at any rate, to have been its most attractive characteristic to later generations of readers. It was reprinted in Dublin by Hibernia Press in 1810 within a decade of the Union and the troubles which surrounded it. And in 1896, in a lengthy introduction to his edition (a modernized and annotated version of the 1810 text), Standish O'Grady, at the expense of discounting religious conflict (one of the central themes of the work) underlined its value to anti-Home Rule, anti-Land League Tories as a demonstration of how political unrest and social upheaval could be suppressed among the Irish by strong, fair and consistent government.

CIARAN BRADY

Paisley, Rev. Ian Richard Kyle (1926–) Leader of the Democratic Unionist Party and Moderator of the Free Presbyterian Church. Born Killylea, County Amagh, 6 April. The most prominent Unionist of the second half of the twentieth century, Paisley was the son of Kyle Paisley, a Baptist minister, and his wife Isabella, née Turnbull. Brought up in the Unionist and Protestant heartland of Ballymena, County Antrim, where his father was posted as a preacher when Paisley was in his infancy, Paisley became imbued with the staunch traditions of evangelistic preaching and political militancy. He began preaching at the age of 16 and had set up his own church, the Free Presbyterians, in 1951. He is regarded as a powerful preacher of the 'fire and brimstone' variety, although he is also capable of entertaining or moving oratory. His abrasive preaching and politicking prevented his acceptance into the conservative worlds of the Unionist Party and the Orange Order, where firebrand preachers were viewed with suspicion.

In the early 1960s Paisley embarked upon the first of his confrontational protests against what he and his supporters saw as threats to the Protestant-Unionist ethos. Such threats included any sign of weakening in Unionism, particularly when it involved improving relations with Dublin; popery; liberalization of sexuality laws (he led a campaign under the banner 'Save Ulster from Sodomy'); and any form of ecumenical behaviour between any other Protestant church and the Catholic church. The worst of his confrontations led to serious riots in the Catholic Divis area in the summer of 1964, when he threatened to march there and remove a tricolour from the local Republican Party offices unless the Royal Ulster Constabulary (RUC) did so. The RUC obliged and several days of violence ensued.

Paisley became the leader of extreme Unionism and attracted followers who were also involved in the paramilitary Ulster Volunteer Force. This group carried out two sectarian murders of Catholic men in the mid-1960s, and nationalists tend to regard these killings as the first important acts of violence in the decades of conflict which followed. In the ensuing years of turmoil Paisley's demagoguery guaranteed his political rise and he set up his own party, the Ulster Democratic Unionist Party. However, in spite of huge personal votes he never succeeded in overturning the Unionist Party. He topped the poll in the 1984 European elections with 230,251 votes and held both European and Westminster parliamentary seats.

Ironically, after a lifetime of railing against the Republic's government, in July 1992 he found himself sitting at the negotiating table with ministers from Dublin during discussions on political settlement proposals for Northern Ireland. Throughout the 1990s Paisley reluctantly took part in negotiations towards a peace settlement, but he and the Democratic Unionists refused to accept the outcome of the 1998 referendum and promised to do all in their power to obstruct the workings of the new Northern Ireland Assembly. In the changing political climate in Ireland the hardline stance of Ian Paisley is becoming increasingly marginalized.

Reading

Bruce, Steve, *God Save Ulster: The Religion and Politics of Paisleyism* (Oxford: Oxford Press, 1986).

Marrinan, Patrick, *Paisley: Man of Wrath* (Dublin: Anvil Books, 1973).

Moloney, Ed and Pollack, Andy, *Paisley* (Dublin: Poolbeg, 1986).

'Protestant ideology and politics in Ulster', *European Journal of Sociology* XIV (1973), pp. 213–80.

Walltis, Roy, and Bruce, Steve, *No Surrender! Paisleyism and the Politics of Ethnic Identity in Northern Ireland* (Belfast: Queens University, 1986).

JIM CUSACK

Pakenham, Edward Arthur Henry seventh earl of Longford (1902–61) Playwright and producer. Born 29 December; died 4 February. Pakenham was educated at Eton and Christ Church, Oxford, where he met his future wife Christine Trew. In 1931 Lord and Lady Longford became major shareholders in the Gate Theatre, for which they wrote plays and translations. From 1936 their own company used the theatre for half of the year. Lord Longford was also a distinguished poet and translator of Gaelic poetry, including Brian Merriman's notorious classic *The Midnight Court* (1949).

Reading

Cowell, John, *No Profit But the Name: The Longfords and the Gate Theatre* (Dublin: 1988).

PETER COSTELLO

Palatines In 1709 over 800 Protestant families, refugees from Louis XIV's occupation of the Palatinate of the Rhine, came to Ireland under a government scheme. Some of them, after a short stay in Dublin, returned to their homeland. Most of them settled in

Limerick and Kerry, and Arthur Young attributed their relatively high standard of husbandry to the long leases they obtained from their landlords. According to Young, 'a few beneficial practices were introduced, but never travelled beyond their own farms'. Their memory survives in family and place-names, such as Palatine in County Carlow and Palatine's Rock in County Limerick.

KENNETH MILNE

Pale Although the term belongs strictly to the last phase of the medieval lordship of Ireland, it is often casually applied to earlier periods. This is unfortunate since it creates an unduly constricted image of the English lordship.

In the late twelfth and thirteenth centuries the English crown and baronage had extended their power over most of Leinster and Munster and parts of Ulster and Connacht, consolidating it through a network of counties, liberties and major boroughs. This network, which was administered through a substantial, though unevenly distributed, settler gentry and urban elite, was given solidity in the south and east by peasant immigration from England and Wales. Around 1300 the Dublin exchequer raised revenues from a widespread colonial society, while the court of the king's justiciar held frequent sessions from the borders of Ulster to Cork and Limerick. By 1300, however, the impetus of expansion had ceased; a defensive outlook is apparent in the use of the term 'land of peace' to describe the core areas of the lordship, whose defence against the native Irish and unruly English of the 'land of war' was becoming a priority of the Irish Parliament.

It was only gradually that the 'land of peace' came to be identified soley with the hinterland of Dublin. This development was connected with the difficulty of protecting the Barrow valley, the key overland route between Dublin and the south. As control of the Barrow was lost, administrative separation grew between the Dublin region and the English communities of south Leinster and east Munster. From the late fifteenth century

the term 'Pale', meaning a defended area with defined boundaries, was applied to the English parts of the four countries around Dublin which were subject to direct royal government. In 1488 a statute saw it as covering the coast from Dundalk to beyond Dalkey and extending inland to embrace the towns of Kells, Trim and Naas. Even at this period the Pale and its outskirts did not represent the full limits of English influence. English institutions survived also in the cities of Cork, Waterford and Limerick, in towns such as Carrickfergus, Galway and Kilkenny, and in the rural communities of the river valleys that lay within the remnants of the county and liberty jurisdictions of the south. The Pale has been aptly described as 'a fulcrum for action', a base from which the chief governor could command a measure of obedience further afield and conduct diplomacy with Gaelic and Gaelicized lords. Yet though the king's authority mattered elsewhere in Ireland, it was only in the Pale that it could be exercised routinely and intensively.

Reading

Cosgrove, A., *Late Medieval Ireland 1370–1541* (Dublin: Helicon, 1981).

—— (ed.), *A New History of Ireland, II. Medieval Ireland 1169–1534* (Oxford: Oxford University Press, 1987).

Frame, R., *Colonial Ireland 1169–1369* (Dublin: Helicon, 1981).

—— *English Lordship in Ireland 1318–1361* (Oxford: Oxford University Press, 1982).

Lydon, J.F. (ed.), *The English in Medieval Ireland* (Dublin: Royal Irish Academy, 1984).

Otway-Ruthven, A.J., *A History of Medieval Ireland* (London: Benn, 2nd edn, 1980).

R.F. FRAME

Parke, Dorothy (?–1990) Composer. Born Derry died Belfast. Parke studied piano and composition at the Royal Academy of Music, London. She composed and published music for voice(s) and piano, written in an unashamedly diatonic manner and often with young performers in mind. Anglo-Irish poetry was her main inspiration. Her songs, many of which were printed, include 'A snowy field' and 'As it was windy weather' for SATB choir to texts by James Stephens, and the cycle *By Winding Roads* for voice and piano on poems by St John Irvine. She also published a number of arrangements of Irish airs.

PETER DOWNEY

Parker, Stewart (1941–88) Playwright. Born in east Belfast, Parker was educated at Queens University. His *Irish Times* 'High Pop' column was an important guide in the 1970s to the world of popular music and culture. This unique blend was the creative source of his own plays, such as *Spokesong, Catchpenny Twist* and *Nightshade*. His television plays – *I'm a Dreamer, Montreal; Blue Money* and *Irish in the Traffic, Ruby in the Rain*, and *Lost Belongings* (1987), a six-part series dealing with interpretations of the Deirdre myth – draw upon the comedy of everyday life in a refreshingly light-hearted yet poignant fashion. In the 'Three Plays for Ireland' – *Northern Star* (1984), *Heavenly Bodies* (1986) and *Pentecost* (1987) – published shortly after his untimely death from cancer, Parker unravelled what he called 'the whole Irish–British cat's cradle...of multiplying dualities: two islands, two Irelands, two Ulsters, two men fighting over a field'.

Reading

Parker, Stewart *Catchpenny Twist* (Dublin: Gallery, 1980).
——*Spokesong* (London: French, 1980).
——*Nightshade* (Dublin: Co-op Books, 1980).
——*Three Plays for Ireland* (Birmingham: Oberon Books, 1989).

GERALD DAWE

Parliamentary Register There is no surviving record of what was said in the Irish Parliament for most of the eighteenth century. (The *Journals* and *Votes* record only was done.) Sir James Caldwell did produce a two-volume account of the deliberations of the House of Commons in the 1763–4 session anonymously in 1766, but it was not until 1782, with the publication of the first volume of *The Parliamentary Register, or History of the Proceedings and Debates of the House of Commons of Ireland* during the momentous 1781–2 session, that a regular series was commenced. Seventeen volumes were produced in all, and they contain the fullest surviving record of debate in the House of Commons and, occasionally, in the House of Lords between 1781 and 1797. It is not entirely clear why publication ceased with the 1797 session, but it is probably connected with the arrest of Patrick Byrne, its main publisher, for seditious activities, and his subsequent emigration to the United States. As a result, there is no equally full record on the short 1798 session or of the Union debates that dominated parliamentary proceedings in 1799 and 1800.

The *Parliamentary Register* does not offer a verbatim record of what was said in the House of Commons on any issue. Speeches and debates are presented in reported form, which allowed the compliers to compress what was said and to exclude procedural and other ancillary matter. One negative consequence of this is that the *Register*'s reports on debates are not always complete or totally accurate. Individual contributions were frequently foreshortened and sometimes omitted. Where particularly detailed contextual points are being explored, the *Register* should be used in tandem with sources like Sir Henry Cavendish's manuscript notes of proceedings in the Irish House of Commons and newspaper reports in order to secure as reliable as possible a guide to what was said.

Reading

The Parliamentary Register, or History of the Proceedings and Debates of the House of Commons of Ireland, 17 vols (Dublin: 1782–99).
Malcomson, A.P.W., 'Sir Henry Cavendish and the proceedings of the Irish parliament' (unpublished paper, 1981).

JAMES KELLY

parliaments In Ireland, as in England, the origins of Parliament are to be found in the growing power of the Crown and its constant need for money. By the end of the thirteenth century Parliament had become an identifiable institution, with a lower house consisting of representatives of the shires and boroughs, and an upper house of spiritual and temporal peers. Throughout its history, however, the Irish institution mirrored the development of its English counterpart. With the shrinking of the Anglo-Norman colony in the later Middle Ages, Irish parliaments represented only the four 'obedient shires' around Dublin. In the sixteenth century Parliament became more important because of the Reformation and the attempts to exert royal authority over the whole of Ireland, but Tudor and Stuart monarchs summoned their Irish parliaments only for specific purposes. Elizabeth convened three, and only six met during the entire course of the seventeenth century.

From 1494 the Irish Parliament was shackled by the famous 'Poynings' Law', named after one of Henry VII's English deputies. In effect it subjected all proposed Irish legislation to the veto of the council, and it remained in force, with some modifications, until 1782. Originally intended as a safeguard against the abuse of power by an over mighty Irish chief governor, it was welcomed as such by the inhabitants of the Pale, but in time it became a clog on the legislative initiative of Parliament, and a burning grievance.

Attempts by the Irish Parliament to extend its power by control of revenue generally failed. The Parliament summoned by James II in 1689, and subsequently known as the 'patriot Parliament', was of constitutional significance because, by then, William III had ascended the English throne. James was still king of Ireland, and in theory the apparatus of government was entirely separate. The Irish Catholic nobility hoped that James would use Parliament to overturn the land settlement and establish the primacy of the Catholic church, but in the event he acted as an English king, preoccupied with English affairs. The

dilemma was resolved by his defeat and exile, which also had the effect of securing the ascendancy of the Protestant landowners for a century to come. An extensive code of penal laws, passed by both parliaments, excluded Catholics from all political influence.

Yet it was in the eighteenth century that the Irish Parliament achieved the summit of its power and dignity, and became the focus for the assertion of Ireland's rights as an independent nation. From Anne's reign onward, the Irish Parliament met regularly, for six months in every two years, exerted some control over taxation and jealously guarded its rights and privileges, mostly assumed in imitation of the mother Parliament. In the early years of the century the Irish House of Commons was managed in the government interest by 'Undertakers', powerful borough owners, in return for a share of official patronage. They exerted great influence, and were often able to advance Irish interests as well as their own. When the government intervened more directly, the question of the independence of the Irish Parliament surfaced once again. In reality, the situation of the Irish Parliament was very different from that of its model. In Ireland government rested not in Parliament but in the lord lieutenant, who was the king's representative, and had no responsibility to the House. To complicate matters, the English House of Commons exerted the right to legislate for Ireland. The relationship between the two parliaments was therefore complex, and a source of friction. After the overthrow of the Undertakers, a 'Patriot' opposition began to draw up a programme of reforms to restore the independence of the Irish Parliament, and in 1782 a Whig administration in Britain, chastened by the loss of the American colonies, and the rise of a citizen volunteer army in Ireland, suddenly conceded most of the Irish demands. Poynings' Law and other restrictive Acts were repealed, and Henry Grattan, the leading Patriot orator, was hailed as Ireland's champion. But the 'Constitution of 1782' proved to be an illusion while the Irish Parliament still lacked the capacity to control the executive. Radical demands for a reform of Parliament and the extension of the franchise to Catholics mixed potently with resurgent Irish nationalism to produce the insurrection of 1798, and two years later the Irish Parliament was abolished by the Act of Union, passed through both legislatures.

The legislative Union of Great Britain and Ireland lasted until 1920, when, at the height of the Anglo-Irish War, Lloyd George passed the Government of Ireland Act, establishing separate parliaments at Dublin and Belfast. The southern parliament never functioned, because nationalist members had already set up Dáil Éireann in 1919. After the signing of the Treaty in 1921, the Dáil became the official Assembly of the Irish Free State, and King George V opened the first Parliament in Belfast, which continued to operate and provide the devolved government of Northern Ireland, until it was extinguished by Edward Heath in 1972. In June 1998, after the signing of the Good Friday Peace Accord, a referendum held in Northern Ireland resulted in a vote of 71 per cent in support of the establishment of a new Northern Ireland Assembly. This referendum was endorsed by a vote in the Irish Republic to drop Ireland's constitutional claim over Northern Ireland, in existence since 1937.

Reading

Beckett, James Camlin, *The Anglo-Irish Tradition* (London: Faber 1976).

Curtis, Edmund and McDowell, Robert Brendan, *Irish Historical Documents, 1172–1922* (London: Methuen, 1943).

Falkiner, Caesar Litton, *Essays Relating to Ireland* (London: Longmans, Green, 1908).

Farrell, Brian (ed.), *The Founding of Dáil Éireann: Parliament and Nation-Building* (Dublin: Gill and Macmillan, 1971).

—— *The Irish Parliamentary Tradition* (Dublin: Gill and Macmillan, 1973).

Johnston, Edith Mary, *Great Britain and Ireland, 1760–1800* (Edinburgh: Oliver and Boyd, 1963).

Lawrence, R.J., *The Government of Northern Ireland* (Oxford: Oxford University Press, 1965).

Mansergh, Nicholas, *The Government of Northern Ireland: A Study in Devolution* (London: Allen and Unwin, 1936).

A.T.Q. STEWART

Parnell family Thomas Parnell (1625–85) of Congleton in Cheshire came to Ireland at the time of the Restoration. He purchased an estate in Queen's County. He had two sons: the eldest, Thomas, won some fame as a poet. The second, John, became an MP, as did his son, Sir John. The second Sir John Parnell (1744–1801) became chancellor of the Irish Exchequer and was dismissed from office for refusing to support the Union. He had inherited or acquired a considerable amount of property including Avondale, County Wicklow. His children included Henry Brooke (1776–1842) first Baron Congleton, and William (1777–1821). Henry Brooke Parnell sat in the last Irish Parliament and after the Union sat in Westminster. He served in various administrations – a lord of the Treasury in 1806, secretary of war, treasurer of the navy, and paymaster general. His brother, William, wrote *An Enquiry into the Causes of Popular Discontents in Ireland* (1805) and *An Historical Apology for the Irish Catholics* (1807). He served as an MP in the UK parliament. William's grandchildren included Charles Stewart Parnell (1846–91), Fanny (1849–82) and Anna (1852–1911).

DONAL MCCARTNEY

Charles Stewart Parnell

Charles Stewart Parnell (1846–91) political leader, was born 27 June at Avondale, County Wicklow, and died 6 October at Brighton. He was the son of John Henry Parnell and his American wife, Delia Tudor Stewart. Of the 11 children of this family who survived birth, Charles was the seventh. Parnell's paternal great-grandfather, granduncle and grandfather were all members of parliament. His maternal great-grandfather was a member of the House and Senate of Massachusetts and served briefly as secretary of state. His maternal grandfather, Admiral Charles Stewart,

'Old Ironsides', had won fame as a naval commander in the 1812 war against the British.

Because of his mother's frequent moves with her family, Parnell's formal education in a number of schools in England left much to be desired. On the death of his father in 1859 he inherited Avondale. He attended a private school at Chipping Norton, Oxfordshire, in preparation for his admission to Magdalene College, Cambridge, in 1865. Before taking his degree, however, Parnell was fined in the courts and sent down for a term in 1869 because of his involvement in a scuffle between students and townspeople. He never returned to Cambridge to take his degree. In 1871 he spent some months visiting his brother in America. Back in Ireland he became involved in Isaac Butt's Home Rule movement. He was defeated for County Dublin in the by-election of 1874, but the following year he contested and won the parliamentary seat for County Meath. In the House of Commons he joined the obstructionist wing of the Home Rule Party. His interjection in the House in defence of the Manchester Martyrs, in which he stated that 'I do not believe, and never shall believe, that any murder was committed at Manchester', attracted the attention of the Irish Republican Brotherhood.

Within two years of his entry into Parliament, Parnell had asserted his leadership over the extreme wing of the party, and was elected president of the Home Rule Confederation of Great Britain. Impressed by Parnell's politics, John Devoy, as spokesman for Clan na Gael, the American Fenian organization, proposed a 'new departure' in October 1878. The thrust of this proposal was that there should be cooperation between the advocates of physical force and those who believed in constitutional agitation. What Devoy advocated was a general declaration in favour of self-government and a vigorous agitation of the land question on the basis of a peasant proprietary. Deteriorating economic conditions in the west of Ireland gave rise to agrarian agitation, during which Parnell advised the tenants at Westport, County Mayo, on 8 June 1879 'to hold a firm grip of your homesteads and lands'. The agricultural crisis led to the foundation of the National Land League in October 1879 with Parnell as president. The League aimed at the reduction of rack-rents and the transfer of the ownership of the land to a peasant proprietary. When Parnell was also elected chairman of the Irish parliamentary party in May 1880 he found himself at the head of three powerful, interlinking forces which previously had often been opposed to each other in Irish politics: constitutionalism, physical force nationalism, and agrarianism. In a speech at Ennis (September 1880) he initiated as one of his weapons in the Land War: the system of boycotting landlords, their agents and all who associated with them or broke the tenants' 'unwritten code of laws'. Parnell and some of his followers were arrested for incendiary speeches and confined in Kilmainham jail (October 1881–May 1882).

From prison the leaders issued the 'No Rent Manifesto', and the government countered by declaring the Land League an illegal organization. Following negotiations between Parnell and Gladstone, the so-called Kilmainham Treaty was concluded, whereby it was informally agreed that the no-rent policy would be abandoned and Parnell would use his influence to discourage violence and end the agrarian agitation. In return for this the government would amend the Land Act in order to deal satisfactorily with the problem of tenants' arrears. On his release Parnell suppressed the Ladies' Land League, which had taken the place of the proscribed Land League; condemned the murder of the new chief secretary, Lord Frederick Charles Cavendish, and the permanent undersecretary, Thomas H. Burke (May 1882); and founded the Irish National League (October 1882) to concentrate on the political objective of Home Rule. The widespread support in the country which by the early 1880s he enjoyed as 'the uncrowned king of Ireland' was reflected in the contribution of over £37,000 for the Parnell Tribute to relieve the financial difficulties of his Avondale estate. He had also got the strong support of the bishops when in 1884 they made the party the guardian of Catholic educational interests. After Gladstone's government fell in 1885, Parnell found himself able to enter into a bargaining position with both the Conservatives and the Liberals on the question of Home Rule. When it appeared that the Conservatives were prepared to offer more than the liberals on the issue of self-government for Ireland, Parnell issued a manifesto calling on the Irish in Britain to vote Conservative. The result of the election was Liberals 335 seats, Conservatives 249; the Irish party with 86 held the balance, and supported the Conservatives for government. Shortly afterwards it was announced that Gladstone favoured Home Rule.

A new land crisis in 1886 led to renewed agitation and the Plan of Campaign to withhold rents. When the Conservative government introduced a coercion bill to deal with the situation, Parnell switched his party's support to the Liberals; Gladstone introduced the first Home Rule Bill and as a consequence lost some of his supporters, who became Liberal-Unionists and voted against the bill. The Bill was defeated 341 to 311 and Parliament was dissolved. In the ensuing election the anti-Home Rule Conservatives won a majority of 118 over the combined Liberal and Irish parties. That same year of 1886 Parnell took up residence at Eltham with Mrs Katharine O'Shea, and his appearances in the House of Commons became less frequent between 1886 and 1890, partly due to health reasons. A series of articles entitled 'Parnellism and Crime' which appeared in *The Times* in 1887 accused him and his colleagues of conniving at crime and outrage during his Land League days.

A special parliamentary commission was established to examine the charges and Parnell's denials. During the hearings it was established that Parnell's alleged letters were forgeries, the fabrications of a disreputable Dublin journalist, Richard Pigott. In 1889

Captain O'Shea filed for divorce from his wife, naming Parnell as co-respondent. O'Shea's case was not opposed and he was given custody of Parnell's two children. Parnell gradually lost the support of the liberal non-conformists, Gladstone, the leaders of the Irish party and the Catholic hierarchy. At a meeting in Committee Room 15 of the House of Commons in December 1891 the party split on the question of the termination of Parnell's leadership. A majority (45) walked out of the room, leaving Parnell behind with 27 supporters. Parnell married Katharine O'Shea on 25 June 1891. In three by-elections following the split his candidates were defeated by the anti-Parnellites. He gave his last defiant speech in Ireland at Cleggs on the Roscommon–Galway border, where he spoke bareheaded in a downpour. A sick man, he travelled home to Brighton, where he died in his wife's arms.

In the course of a relatively short career Parnell succeeded in skilfully uniting under his leadership all shades of nationalist opinion in the 'new departure'. Parnellism enlisted the suppressed or submerged rebellion that had sometimes come to the surface in the secret agrarian societies and in Fenian outrage, and placed them in the service of the constitutional or parliamentary party. In his leadership of this national front, Parnell performed one of the greatest tight-rope acts in Irish history. He created and led what has been considered by many to be the first modern political party machine in the United Kingdom. He and his well-disciplined party had converted Gladstone and the Liberals to the principle of self-government for Ireland, and the Conservatives to a policy of conciliation and concession as a substitute for Home Rule. The Land League, under his leadership, had succeeded in smashing the old landlord system and had begun the process of transferring the ownership of the land to the tenant farmers. He had bequeathed to Irish politics and to Dáil Éireann a legacy of constitutional and democratic nationalism, as well as a spirit of defiance to the 1916 generation of political activists. Parnell failed to achieve Home Rule or to conciliate Ulster unionism, however, and his uncompromising stand on the leadership crisis split the party into two factions. He has been seen by some biographers and commentators as a titanic figure hewn from Wicklow granite but carrying in his make-up a structural flaw – the political leader who was brought down by the weaknesses in his own personality. Although he himself showed no interest in literature, he has been immortalized in the work of the two most famous writers of his time in Anglo-Irish literature, W.B. Yeats and James Joyce, as the proud and tragic hero brought down by lesser men.

Thomas Parnell

Thomas Parnell, (1679–1718) poet is remembered today largely because he was one of the Scriblerians, and because Charles Stewart Parnell was descended from his younger brother. Born in Dublin, and educated at Trinity College, Dublin, he was ordained after he received his MA in 1700, and was made archdeacon of Clogher in 1705, the year he married Anne Minchin. They had two sons, who died young, and a daughter. From 1709 to 1711, Parnell was chairman of the committee appointed to make recommendations on printing the Bible and liturgy in Irish, and providing Irish priests, to help convert Catholics.

Parnell never recovered from his wife's death in 1711, and he took to heavy drinking. Swift befriended him, and got Archbishop King to transfer his prebend of Dunlavin to him. In 1713, Parnell was a popular member of the Scriblerus Club, and had ambitions in London until Queen Anne's death. In 1716 he was made vicar of Finglas, but he died suddenly in Chester while he was returning to Ireland.

A selection of his precise and cultivated poems, with a moralizing stance, were published in 1722 by Pope, who also added polish to them. Goldsmith claimed Parnell's 'A Nightpiece on Death' created the vogue for graveyard poems, of which Gray's 'Elegy' is the best known. Other poems of note are '*Rise of Woman*', '*The Hermit*', '*Pervigilium Veneris*', and '*Allegory on Man*'. Johnson found he was too derivative, but praised his 'easy sweetness of diction', and added that 'he always delights but never ravishes'. Few could disagree.

Reading

Bew, Paul, *C.S. Parnell* (Dublin: Gill and Macmillan, 1980).

Boyce, George D. and O'Day, Alan (eds), *Parnell in Perspective* (London and New York: Routledge, 1991).

Callanan, Frank, *The Parnell Split 1890–91* (Cork: Cork University Press, 1992).

Côté, Jane McL., *Fanny and Anna Parnell, Ireland's Patriotic Sisters* (Dublin: Gill and Macmillan, 1991).

Forster, R.F., *Charles Stewart Parnell: The Man and his Family* (Brighton: Harvester Press, 1976).

Kee, Robert, *The Laurel and the Ivy: The Story of Charles Stewart Parnell and Irish Nationalism* (London: Hamish Hamilton, 1993).

Lyons, F.S.L., *The Fall of Parnell 1890–91* (London: Routledge and Kegan Paul, 1960).

——*Charles Stewart Parnell* (London: Collins, 1977).

McCartney, Donal (ed.), *Parnell: The Politics of Power* (Dublin: Wolfhound Press, 1991).

O'Brien, Conor Cruise, *Parnell and his Party 1880–1890* (Oxford: Clarendon Press, 1957, 1964).

O'Brien, R.B., *Life of Charles Stewart Parnell*, 2 vols (London: Smith, Elder, 1898).

DONAL MCCARTNEY AND FRED LOWE

patriotism Originally, the term denotes the 'politics of virtue', in particular the virtue of loving one's country and exerting oneself for the common good. It was a civic ideal based on Roman models as extolled by authors like Livy and Tacitus. Thus, Bishop Berkeley defined a patriot as 'one who heartily wisheth the public prosperity, and doth not only wish, but also study and endeavour to promote it'. The ideology of public-minded civic spirit began to thrive in Ireland in the course of the eighteenth century and led to works of public utility such as the Lying-in Hospital and the Grand and Royal canals. The (subsequently Royal) Dublin Society, founded in 1731, had such patriotic aims as promoting husbandry, agriculture, science and the useful arts. Also, the cultivation of letters and polite learning was considered a 'patriotic' activity (hence the patriot affiliation of many learned societies), since it was held to redound to the honour of one's country. As such, patriotism is a typical Enlightenment ideology, with a belief in human perfectibility and social progress, and in the contractual basis of society as an association of free-born equals.

In most European countries, patriotism became most pronounced among the bourgeois classes and opposed itself to arbitrary government and to the aristocracy, which was considered corrupt, decadent, and irresponsible. Hence, in Germany, the United Provinces and France, patriotism became a democratic, proto-liberal ideology. In Ireland, where 'aristocracy' and 'arbitrary government' were coterminous with the 'English interest', England came to be seen as the source of all political corruption. Thus, Irish patriotism (like its counterpart in the American colonies) tended to exhibit a mixture of anti-English separatism and anti-aristocratic bourgeois democracy. Both these aspects converged in the call for greater, autonomous powers for the Irish Parliament. In the 1780s, the Patriot movement in Ireland, led by Henry Grattan and supported by its armed wing, the Volunteers (a civic militia which had formed, in true Patriot spirit, in order to resist a threatened French invasion), culminated in the constitutional emancipation of the Irish House of Commons. The bourgeois character of Irish patriotism is shown by the fact that on the whole it evinced little active solidarity with the proletarian (Catholic) mass of the people, and that it evaporated with the disappearance of its proper forum, an Irish House of Commons, under the Union.

The most inspiring representatives of Irish patriotism in the course of the eighteenth century were James Molyneux, Jonathan Swift, Bishop Berkeley, Charles Lucas, Henry Flood and Henry Grattan. The anti-English element in their political thought has often been read in a 'nationalist' Irish light; however, eighteenth-century patriotism should not be interpreted as an early type of nationalism. Post-1800 Irish nationalism had different antecedents and drew on a different class of the population. In most European countries, the ideology of patriotism after the French Revolution led into liberalism; but in the nineteenth-century Irish context, liberalism was not a viable political programme.

Reading

Beckett, J.C., *The Anglo-Irish Tradition* (London: Faber, 1976).

Deane, Seamus, 'Edmund Burke and the ideology of Irish Liberalism', in R. Kearney (ed.), *The Irish Mind. Exploring Intellectual Traditions* (Dublin: Wolfhound, 1985).

Leerssen, Joep 'Anglo-Irish patriotism and its European context', *Eighteenth-Century Ireland* 3 (1988), pp. 7–24.

McDowell, R.B., *Ireland in the Age of Imperialism and Revolution, 1760–1801*

JOEP LEERSSEN

Payne, Robert (*c*.1550–*c*.1620) Agriculturalist. Born Nottinghamshire. Payne was known for his writings on agricultural techniques. However, with the advent of the Munster plantation in the late 1580s, he was appointed by his neighbours to scout out the merits of moving there. His notes and comments were completed in 1589 and published the following year as *A Briefe Description of Ireland*. He emphasized the good quality of the land, the effectiveness of the Munster presidency in administering justice, and the availability of cheap labour and produce. Payne was sufficiently satisfied to move to County Cork himself.

Reading

MacCarthy-Morrogh, M., *The Munster Plantation* (Oxford: Clarendon Press/Oxford University Press, 1986).

Payne, R., 'A briefe description of Ireland...', *Tracts relating to Ireland, vol. 1* (Dublin: Irish Archaeological Society, 1841).

BRIAN DONOVAN

Peacock Theatre The pocket theatre of the Abbey Theatre. Opened in November 1925 with a policy of presenting new and experimental dramas, it was also used by other companies such as the Gate and by amateur groups. Its smaller-scale productions were a training ground for students at the Abbey School of Acting through the Abbey Experimental Theatre (from 1937). Jack Yeats, de Nerval and Lorca were among the authors played. After the Abbey was destroyed by fire in 1951, the Peacock went into limbo, but was reopened in the rebuilt Abbey Theatre in 1972.

Reading

Robinson, Lennox, *Ireland's Abbey Theatre* (London: Sidgwick and Jackson, 1951).

PETER COSTELLO

Pearse, Patrick Henry (1879–1916) Nationalist, poet and founder of St Enda's school. Born Dublin, November; executed Dublin, May. The son of James Pearse, an English-born monumental sculptor and Margaret Brady, from Dublin's northside, Pearse was born at 27 Great Brunswick Street (now named Pearse Street), the second eldest of four children. His short life was characterized by deep involvement in the cultural nationalism of the Gaelic League, by a deep and active interest in education reform, by a literary output in Gaelic and English which, if not extensive, is significant, and finally by a growing realization that self-determination for Ireland could be achieved only by armed insurrection. This realization and conviction found dramatic expression in the 1916 Easter Rising, in which Pearse, as president of the Provisional Government, read the Proclamation at the General Post Office; on surrender of the insurgents, Pearse and his six fellow signatories were executed.

While at school and university, Pearse developed an interest in and knowledge of the Gaelic language, which led him inevitably to membership of the Gaelic League. He served on its central committees, spoke at public meetings and cultural festivals, and represented the League abroad, where he acquired an interest in bilingualism. His major contribution in the League was his six years as editor of its weekly bilingual newspaper, *An Claidheamh Soluis*, in which he sought to promote 'the intellectual independence of Ireland'. In Pearse's view, that independence required education reform as well as political self-determination.

His progressive bilingual school, St Enda's, founded in 1908, was characterized by 'freedom and inspiration', the two essentials; its curriculum provided a balance of practical and academic subjects, reflecting in its spirit the philosophy of the New Education Movement in the Europe of the period. His school ceased to function in 1935.

Of the political figures of twentieth-century Ireland, Pearse has exercised a sustained and widespread influence on national self-identity, on language policy and in later years on education policy.

SEAMUS O'BUACHALLA

penal laws A relatively modern term. The common term in the eighteenth century was the 'Popery Acts', to denote a body of legislation which began in 1695 and was not completed until well into the following century. There was of course preceding legislation from the sixteenth and from the seventeenth centuries. However, there had been a near-hiatus in new legislation after mid-century, and under Charles II a large measure of *de facto* toleration existed. Thus, when the Treaty of Limerick was signed, one of the inducements to the defeated Catholic Jacobites was the assurance of the rights they had enjoyed under Charles II. Ambiguous in itself, and a measure less of toleration than of the fact that no Irish Parliament had sat from 1667 to 1692, the assurance was broken in letter and in spirit from 1695 onwards by the introduction of new legislation in the Irish Parliament. The key measures banished regulars and ecclesiastical dignitaries (1697), provided for the registration of the remaining clergy in terms which allowed for no successors (1704), required Catholics in certain circumstances to take an oath of abjuration (1704 and 1709 – this explicitly violated an assurance in the Treaty), and in 1704 and 1709 addressed property matters, prohibiting Catholic purchase of property in fee, limiting rights in leasehold, and confining rights of succession and enjoyment of property in various ways. Other provisions affected firearms, schooling, tutoring and both education and military service abroad. The right to vote was explicitly removed from Catholics in 1727.

The last 'penal' legislation affecting Catholics was that passed in the 1745–6 Parliament and the measure against military service abroad in 1755–6, though as late as the 1770s new measures were unsuccessfully proposed in the Parliament. However, they were really intended as a counter to the various mortgage bills which in securing loans by Catholics would have effectively undermined the property code. The repeal of the penal laws had been first broached by the registration bills of 1755 and 1757, which were not the persecuting measures that Catholic writers have taken them to be but the first effort, however abortive, at providing for legal recognition of the Catholic church.

Much modern writing has stressed that the penal code was primarily intended to deprive Catholics of property. However, as political rights depended on the ownership or occupation of property, the property clauses should more accurately be seen as an effort to exclude Catholics from political power. Moreover, there was a belief, especially among the Protestant bishops, that converts could be made: the draconian property code would compel propertied Catholics to conform, and in the wake of their conformity the conversion of the lower orders would take place. In the second half of the nineteenth century, when

the Church of Ireland before or after its disestablishment was under fire from its opponents, the property aspects of the code were emphasized as the less ugly face of past discrimination, and one which would shift responsibility from the bench of bishops to the lay members of the old Parliament.

This seemed plausible, because Catholics themselves had emphasized the property code from the 1750s. However, this was primarily a result of their belief that the religious clauses were already in abeyance and that the real sufferers were the propertied laity rather than the clergy. These arguments were taken up by Edmund Burke, and through his writings powerfully influenced William Lecky. Burke's views on the code are not an objective, detached account but a powerful polemic by a man with a Catholic background and an intimate connection with the Catholic leaders in Ireland.

The penal code never represented a unanimous view of Irish Protestants. Its introduction had involved debate, and hence when, in the 1750s, more liberal sentiments began to emerge, the idea of change attracted support from such elements in the Irish Parliament. These views are well represented in the thought of Lord Charlemont, who was well disposed to all relief provided that it did not reach to voting rights and the right to carry firearms. Indeed, without liberal support to introduce measures of repeal, they would have been self-defeating: attempts to impose them on the Parliament would have resulted in their rejection. Burke, his views coloured by his experience of Irish parliamentarians, believed from as early as the late 1760s (very wrongly as events later showed) that anti-Catholic animus had shrunk and was limited to a minority who manipulated relgious issues for their own political advantage. He failed to see that it commanded a wide constituency of support, and he was not alive to the issues in the new debate which began after property rights had been conceded in 1778 and 1782. Burke had always argued, in private, that property rights could only be guaranteed by political rights, and in introducing the legislation in 1782, Luke Gardiner (who was close to Burke's thinking) conceded that the question of firearms would be adressed in the fullness of time. He thus unwittingly contributed to the debate on Catholics in the volunteers and on firearms, which was at the heart of the troubles in, significantly, Charlemont's county of Armagh in the 1780s and indirectly behind the emergence of the Orange Order in the sane county in 1795.

The main residue of the penal code was removed in 1792 and 1793. When major political rights, including the right to serve as a magistrate, sit on grand juries and vote in parliamentary elections, were conceded in 1793, the concessions prompted the issue of Protestant Ascendancy; that is, of taking steps to ensure that, when Catholics got political rights, they would not get power. This object was feasible only through alliance between hardline Protestants and the Dublin government headed by the lord lieutenant, with his ministers and officers who sat in the Irish Parliament. Hence, contrary to the simplistic interpretation of a Catholic–Protestant divide, the real divide in Ireland revolved around a Catholic–liberal–Protestant alignment versus a Protestant and ministerialist one, which was emerging in thc 1780s but firmed up in the early 1790s. The shortlived Fitwilliam viceroyalty in 1795 and the debacle it led to was not about Catholic rights but about power in Irish political life. The ministerial alliance with the ultras was itself a radical departure from the traditional situation, in which the lord lieutenant had sought to moderate anti-Catholic animus or, from the 1750s, to encourage relief measures, and its novelty added to the swelling depth of bitterness in Irish life in the 1790s. The failed Catholic relief bill of 1795 was the first one lacking ministerial backing: it attracted a surprising amount of parliamentary support, and Charlemont too in the twilight years of his life changed his views on political rights for Catholics The issue of power also explains why, in the aftermath of the rebellion, there was much liberal support,

undeterred by the excesses of the rebels, both for a benign treatment of rebels and for the Union, which was seen as the dispatch into the night of the discredited administration of the 1790s and of its minions.

The penal laws were a failure not only in their religious dimensions but in the property clauses, which neither reduced Catholic land-ownership nor prevented access to leasehold property. However, there is a modern tendency to underestimate their importance. The failure of the property code depended both on collusive or friendly 'discoveries' and on conformity, which by real or nominal 'conversion' helped to keep property in the same family. Apart from the religious and legal delicacies of these steps, the injustice to Catholic landowning lay less in the code itself than in the confiscations of the seventeenth century in the wake of every war, which deprived the defeated party of further land. On non-property issues, resentment of the code was fuelled by selective enforcement, itself invariably prompted by the exigencies or tensions of county politics. On obscure issues at local level in several counties, the future was built, and Catholic landowners became a much more obvert and national force in the 1790s. In such circumstances the failure to deliver the promised relief (access to high office and to seats in Parliament) in the wake of the Union, and the fact that it was conceded only under threat of civil war in 1829, determined the future direction of Catholic Ireland. The Fitzwilliam lord lieutenancy in 1795 and the magisterial administration of Cornwallis in 1798–1801 had breached the political alliance of conservatives and ministerialists in Ireland. Under the Union, the implicit promise of evenhanded dealing was delivered only under the Liberal alliance of O'Connell and the Melbourne ministry in the second half of the 1830s (an achievement whose significance has still not had its full recognition), a failure which sealed the ultimate fate of the Union.

Both before and after the disestablishment of the Church of Ireland, a hardline and increasingly politicized clergy, wearing the often unattractive face of a progressively more impotent intolerance, was confronted by a new Catholic triumphalism and assertiveness. This was compounded variously of old memories and, in the wake of the collapse of the Gallican church in France, a growing alliance of the Irish bishops with the ultramontane forces of the Vatican. The Vatican feared civil governments, and ironically the now-ultramontane Irish church did better in securing its hold on education than it would have under a Catholic power.

The penal laws need study. The law courts were impartial in the interpretation of the law, which caused much political consternation, and legal compendia, such as Howards's *Several Special Cases on the Laws against...Popery* (1775), are a prime source for understanding the realities of Ireland. Legal aspects apart, they were not studied in the eighteenth century. Burke's writings on the penal laws, not published at the time, have later been taken as an authoritative summary of the situation, whereas they are magisterial and essentially Catholic polemic. Arthur Young's account likewise relied on access to Burke's opinions and probably his writing. In the 1790s the United Irishmen took up the penal laws, with Simon Butler publishing a useful and informative survey in 1792. Ironically, in debate within the United Irishmen on the Catholic question, those least sympathetic to the Catholics, such as Butler and Drennan, wanted to make an issue of the distinction between the Catholics and the rest of the population, as a useful political gambit to widen the quarrel with the ministry, whereas the Catholic United Irishmen and the ultra-radicals wanted to stress the common cause of Catholics and Protestants in a radical crusade in which political victory would lead to all redress.

In the interval before Catholic 'emancipation' in 1829, several Catholics, notably Scully, O'Connor and Wyse, wrote accounts. Later studies tended to be exclusively Catholic, and were often triumphalist, and at times superficial, versions, magnifying the undoubted resilience of Catholic survival. As writings they are disfigured by the ugly face of Irish sectarianism, both in themselves and equally in the intolerance they were responding to. Moreover, deeply influenced by the ultramontane concerns of a church fearful of anti-clericalism (represented in Ireland by the appeal of Fenianism), they were also motivated by an urge to identify as far as possible Catholics and the Irish nation as one, and to assert the central role of the church in the achievement of survival and recovery. In contrast to the past, the great bulk of Catholic accounts were now by churchmen. In the Catholic literature the converts were branded as perverts, an attitude which would have been unthinkable in the past.

Lecky's account of the penal laws, while very generous in its attitudes, is unduly influenced by Burke. A series of studies is badly needed of what is, despite the universal agreement on its significance, a singularly unstudied subject. First and and foremost in these needs is study of the legal aspects of the penal laws. Second, the parliamentary history of their passing, maintenance and repeal, which is an intriguing one of parliamentary politics often at both its most noble and ignoble, is a rich field for investigation. Third, the historiography of the penal laws merits attention, because it was from the time of Burke a subject which acquired a life of its own harnessed variously, depending on the period, to political, national or church purposes.

Reading

Cullen, L.M. 'Catholics under the penal laws', *Eighteenth-Century Ireland* 1 (1986), pp. 23–36.

—— 'Burke, Ireland and revolution', *Studies in the Eighteenth Century 8: Papers Presented at the Eighth David Nichol Smith Memorial Seminar, Eighteenth-century Life* 16, n.s. (1992), pp. 21–42.

Osborough, W. N. 'Catholics, land and the poperty acts of Anne', in T.P. Power and K. Whelan (eds), *Endurance and Emergence: Catholics in the Eighteenth Century* (Dublin: Irish Academic Press, 1990).

Wall, M., *The Penal Laws 1691–1760: Church and State from the Treaty of Limerick to the Accession of George* (Dublin: Dundalgan Press for the Irish Historical Association T.P. Power and K. Whelan (eds), 1961).

L.M. CULLEN

Petrie, George (1789–1866) Collector of Irish folk-songs, painter and violinist. Born Dublin: died Dublin, 17 January. Employed as an official of the Government Ordnance Survey Office, Petrie had ample opportunity to travel and transcribe melodies from traditional musicians all over the country. In 1851 he was largely responsible for the foundation of the Society for the Preservation and Publication of the Melodies of Ireland, which published his *Ancient Music of Ireland* (a collection of 147 airs with commentary) in 1855. His entire collection of 1,582 tunes was edited by Stanford and published (1902–5) as *The Complete Collection of Irish Music as noted by George Petrie, L.L.D., R.H.A.*

Reading

Breathnach, Breandan, *Folk Music and Dances of Ireland* (Cork: Talbot Press, 1971, rev. edn Mercier, 1977).

O'Neill, Francis, *Irish Folk Music* (Chicago: 1910, Wakefield: 1973).

GERARD GILLEN

Petty, Sir William (1623–87) Scientist and economist. Born the third of six children of a clothier at Romsey in Hampshire, Petty went to sea aged 13. According to his contemporary biographer, John Aubrey, sailors on his ship were jealous of his ability and abandoned him in France. He certainly entered the Jesuit college at Caen. At the outbreak of the English Civil War in 1642 he was serving in the Royal Navy, but left to study in Europe at Utrecht and Amsterdam. In 1644 he entered Leyden to study medicine, and the following year was in Paris studying anatomy with Thomas Hobbes. He returned to England in 1646, and after a brief period as a clotheir went to

Oxford, where he took the degree of doctor of medicine in 1649. Under the Commonwealth he had influential friends, and was appointed professor of anatomy at Oxford in 1650 and physician general to the army in Ireland in 1652. When in Ireland he was also employed to direct a survey of Ireland, the Downe Survey, and this created friction with Benjamin Worsley, then surveyor general, whose survey schemes were rejected. Allegations of land fraud were later made against Petty, but his connections with Henry Cromwell, to whom he was secretary, protected him. After the army coup of 1659 accusations were renewed and he fled to London. There he joined a scientific group meeting at Gresham College, which in 1662 became the Royal Society, with Petty as a founder member.

Under the Restoration land settlement Petty, as a supporter of the new order, retained most of his Irish estate, although litigation continued until his death about his lands. Having lost his posts in Oxford he made Dublin his main residence until 1685, when he moved to London. He became a judge in the Irish admiralty court and president of the Dublin Philosophical Society. On his estates he undertook a number of important improvements in the areas of mining and fishing. His major contribution to intellectual life, both in Ireland and England, was in the area of 'political arithmetic'. His main writings on the Irish economy were the *Political Anatomy of Ireland*, written in 1672 but not published until 1691, and his 1687 *Treatise on Ireland*, not published until the nineteenth century.

Reading

Fitzmaurice, Lord Edmund, *The Life of Sir William Petty* (London: Murray, 1895).

Hull, C.H. (ed.), *The Economic Writings of Sir William Petty*, 2 vols (Cambridge: Cambridge University Press, 1899).

Strauss, E., *Sir William Petty: Portrait of a Genius* (London: Bodley Head, 1954).

RAYMOND GILLESPIE

471

Petty-Fitzmaurice family Derives from the marriage in 1693 of Anne, daughter and ultimate heiress of the self-made Sir William Petty, and Thomas Fitzmaurice, twentieth lord and first earl of Kerry, the head of an Anglo-Norman family established in County Kerry since the twelfth century. Lady Anne's younger grandson, John Petty-Fitzmaurice, first earl of Shelburne, succeeded to Petty's *c.*270,000 acres in south Kerry in 1751. Meanwhile, the north Kerry lands owned by her elder, Fitzmaurice grandson, the third earl of Kerry, dwindled to nothing, and at his death in 1818 his titles merged with those of his Petty-Fitzmaurice cousin, Henry, fourth earl of Shelburne and third marquess of Lansdowne. By this time, the Petty-Fitzmaurices had established themselves in English landed society, at Bowood, Calne, Wiltshire, and Lansdowne House, Berkeley Square. Successive marquesses of Lansdowne have held high political office as prime minister (1783–4), chancellor of the Exchequer (1806–7) and viceroy of India (1888–93).

Reading

Lansdowne, Sixth Marquess of, *Glanerought and the Petty-Fitzmaurices* (London: 1937).

A.P.W. MALCOLMSON

photography The work of Irish photographers Willie Doherty, Karl Grimes, Paul Seawright, Billy Stickland and others has achieved international acclaim, but has not been widely recognized in Ireland. Photography has not been accorded the high status it enjoys in other countries, most notably France, Germany and the United States. Its low profile does not reflect a lack of talent or enthusiasm. In the Republic alone, there are over 50 camera clubs, and the large number of submissions to publications such as *One Day for Life in Ireland* (1990) attests to widespread amateur photographic activity. Rather, it is historical factors that have inhibited the development of a more dynamic, professional photographic culture.

In the debates over Irish cultural identity during the first half of the twentieth century, photography was of marginal interest in a climate where appeal was made to literature, drama and music for cultural definition and the development of a national self-image. Given these concerns, the validation of photography by the international art institutional complex, a process that drew on and supported various forms of Modernist experimentation, did not, by and large, impinge on Ireland. Indeed, it was not until 1978 that a photographer (Tony Murray) was awarded a bursary from the Arts Council, and photographic work remains under-represented in the council's collections.

Emerging from this historical context, Irish photographic discourse has been dominated by two opposing strands. The first consists of commercial work for the tourism industry on both sides of the border. Constructing an 'Ireland of impossibly blue skies', this tradition is characterized by the rural romanticism of the John Hinde studios. The genre has been supplemented with work by Liam Blake, Tom Kelly, Walter Pfeiffer and Peter Zoller, which embodies more voguish, but equally romanticized, visual styles.

The second main strand in photographic representations of Ireland comprises photojournalistic reportage, particularly of sectarian violence in the North. Both photojournalist and tourist imagery cater largely to international audiences and can thus afford to gloss over the complex issue of how Irish people perceive and represent their lived experiences.

Since the late 1970s, the inadequacies of these representational genres have been addressed by a number of photographers and artists working in the medium. A more critical, independent photography sector has emerged in tandem. Crucial to its development was the establishment of the Irish Gallery of Photography (IGP) in Dublin in 1978. Administered by Christine Redmond, the gallery's programme of exhibitions, lectures and workshops has played a fundamental role in raising the critical profile of Irish photography. With the consolidation of photography in secondary and tertiary educational institutions, and various community initiatives (e.g. Belfast Exposed, the Rivermount Workshop), Irish photography has opened out and now includes a diverse range of styles and subject matter.

Major group exhibitions such as 'Out of the Shadows' (1982) and the shows by the Contemporary Irish Photography group (1987, 1989) give some idea of this new diversity. They feature Expressionist work (Patricia Langlois, Amelia Stein, Eilish McCarrick), portrait series (Christine Bond, Fergus Bourke, Gene Lambert) and more formalist studies (Geoff White, Peter Morgan, Brian Cross).

One-person shows operate within similarly diverse agendas. Karl Grimes's recent work juxtaposes the cultural traditions of Ireland, North Africa and Continental Europe. Through an innovative use of collage, the unifying aesthetic principles of the classical Greek heritage are subtly subverted. Pointing up the refraction and local inflections of the classical tradition, Grimes's work opens up a more heterogeneous notion of European identity.

The conventions of the European fine art tradition are humorously reworked by emerging photographer Michael Boran. In his 1992 show, Boran posed kitschy, sentimentalized toy animals in a series of hand-tinted tableaux. His quizzical approach contrasts with the main body of recent photographic work in Ireland, which is oriented towards social documentary (David Farrell, Tom Grace, Kate Horgan, Tony Murray, Kevin O'Farrell, Tom Shortt, Rod Tuach). In this field, there is a new trend towards documenting urban themes and issues, with leading work by Tony O'Shea, Daniel de Chenu and Anthony Haughey and phototexts by Mick O'Kelly. Though each has developed an individual approach, working-class areas of Dublin form their common focus. Their work breaks from the nostalgic emphasis on fair days and religious events in rural Ireland that characterized earlier documentary output. However, in general, the new independent photography has not turned the lens to the urban middle class, and work from specific feminist perspectives has not been developed. Moreover, in the absence of a magazine of Irish photography (and with only a nascent archive in the IGP), the work itself is not well documented, which limits its currency to the period of public exhibition.

In the field of press photography, consistently strong work is produced by Billy Stickland, James Meehan, Peter Thursfield, Dara MacDonaill, Bob Hobby, Bryan O'Brien and Brenda Fitzsimons. However, newspapers in Ireland are unadventurous in their handling of pictures. There is little commitment to collaboration between photographer and journalist, and extended photoessays are rarely published. With the exception of the *Irish Times* and the *Sunday Business Post*, photojournalism remains poorly served by most titles. This situation has prompted the Press Photographers Association of Ireland and the IGP to mount a continuous exhibition of press work. Independent photojournalist Derek Speirs has also exhibited in a gallery context. His highly disciplined body of work sets events of the last decade in their broader social context. Eschewing the construction of violence as universal drama, Speirs's images from Northern Ireland cast a critical eye on the complicity between the news media and political systems.

Concern with the politics of representation also characterizes the work of Northern artist Willie Doherty. In large-scale phototexts, his native city of Derry appears very normal, even banal. Drawing on devices developed by conceptual artists, Doherty overlays the images with short, spare text in anonymous, commercial lettering. Through the juxtaposition of word and image, and through the absence of people, of dramatic focus and of authorial presence, the initial impression of normalcy is subtly unsettled and the scene becomes charged with a sense of hidden tension. In work from the late 1980s, Doherty uses colour to reframe the dominant romanticism of nationalist aspirations, conveying a sense of stasis, loss and suspended temporality.

Victor Sloan's exploration of the Loyalist marching season displays a similar concern with temporal structures. In series such as *Drumming* (1986) and *Demonstration at the Castle* (1987), a tension is set up between a certain admiration for the stubborn determination of Orangemen, and a sense of the anachronism of their siege mentality. A painter by training, Sloan subverts the instantaneity of the photographic process by intervening at the printing stage. His negatives are scratched and violently scored, and the prints are tinted and defaced with gouache and crayon. Sloan's work was featured in the 1987 touring show 'Magnetic North' along with photoworks by Peter Neill, Maurice Hobson and Barbara Freeman. This exhibition was selected by critic Brian McAvera, whose work has contributed greatly to raising the profile of Northern Ireland photography. Newer voices include Paul Seawright (whose controversial series on sectarian murders was purchased by the Arts Council in Britain), Errol Forbes, Hazel McNeill, Tony Corey and Martin Nangle.

TANYA KIANG

Pilkington, Matthew (*c.*1700–74) and **Pilkington, Laetitia** (1712–50) Poets. Matthew was born at Ballyboy, Offaly, and died probably at Donabate, Dublin. He was educated at Mr Neile's school in Dublin and at Trinity College, Dublin. He was ordained in the established church and shortly afterwards married Laetitia Vanlewin. Matthew published a collection of verse in 1730 and around this time the Pilkingtons were introduced to Swift, who was impressed by the pair. But he was to change his tune later when, due to Laetitia's adultery, the marriage ended. He then called Matthew 'the falsest rogue' and Laetitia 'the most profligate whore in either kingdom'. Matthew complied (*pace* what the *Dictionary of National Biography* says to the contrary) *The Gentleman's and Connoisseur's Dictionary of Painters*, first published in 1770. Laetitia's fame rests principally on her *Memoirs*.

Reading

Pilkington, Laetitia, *Memoirs of Mrs Laetitia Pilkington wherein are ... All her Poems* (Dublin: 1748).
Pilkington, Matthew, *Poems on Several Occasions* (Dublin: 1730).

PATRICK FAGAN

Pinto, Thomas (Tomasso) (1714–83) Violinist. Born London; died Dublin(?). Pinto came to Ireland in 1773 and was leader of the Smock Alley Theatre orchestra until 1779. In 1776 he led the orchestra at Crow Street Theatre for Michael Arne's season of English opera. He conducted the orchestra and performed violin concertos at concert seasons given in the Rotunda (1780–2). He also gave concerts in Cork and Limerick.

Reading

Hogan, Ita, *Anglo-Irish Music 1780–1830* (Cork: 1966).

HARRY WHITE

plantation Term and concept applied to certain developments in Ireland from approximately the middle of the sixteenth to the middle of the seventeenth century. Earlier incursions, whether of Vikings, Normans, English or others, have not been thus described, although some had features in common with the later 'plantations'.

What principally distinguished the incursions of the mid-sixteenth to mid-seventeenth century was that they occurred within a context of British 'expansion' and, perhaps more important, within a classically derived language and mental architecture regarding that process. Thus, there was no 'plantation' before the self-conscious political consolidation of the Tudor monarchy gave rise to adventures in Ireland and America which could be likened to the colonial enterprises of ancient Rome. The underlying notion was that soldiers/settlers/citizens would go forth to establish 'colonies' abroad, for their own benefit and that of their nation.

The use of the word 'plant' to mean 'to settle (a person) in a place ... [or] establish [a person] as a settler or colonist' dates from at least the beginning of the fourteenth century, but the use of the word 'plantation' to mean 'a settlement in a new or conquered country' was apparently not established until the late sixteenth century. It occurs in the celebrated tract of 1584 by Richard Hakluyt, *A Discourse of the Western Planting*, which enthusiastically advocated New World British settlements as a panacea for the domestic and international ills of the day. By the early seventeenth century, British settlements in Ireland were commonly called 'plantations', and there was a growing literature advocating their growth and proliferation, both in Ireland and abroad.

By that time, not only were the terminology and concepts in place, but so were palpable and visible British settlements in Ireland to which they could be applied. These settlements differed from those of the medieval lordship in that they were less adventitous. Instead, they were coherent, planned and systematic efforts to inject new populations into specified areas for specified governmental purposes. As a possible English policy for dealing with Ireland, the idea of plantation is first found in 1521, but not until the late 1540s and 1550s did it begin to be put into practice. Then it was an outgrowth of the two great forts, Governor and Protector (later Philipstown and Maryborough), which were established in the reign of Edward VI (1547–53) to defend the western border of the Pale from the depredations of Gaelic Irish living in Leix and Offaly.

Sir Edward Bellingham, lord deputy (1547–8) and secretary of state (1548–9), urged that women be brought to join soldiers in the forts, and that the adjacent areas be cultivated. In the subsequent reign of Queen Mary (1553–8) these efforts culminated in the official 'plantation' of Leix and Offaly, a con-

certed plan to settle the area with a more civil and obedient population. Although slow to take actual shape, it was, arguably, the first English plantation anywhere, and was to be succeeded by variations on the theme in both Ireland and America.

In Ireland, enterprises large or small, successful or disastrous, were for a century called 'plantations' without distinction. In the 1570s, several were attempted in Ulster, most memorably those of Sir Thomas Smith and Walter Devereux, first earl of Essex. These efforts, though small, introduced the important apparatus of joint stock capitalization and vigorous promotion. But the only momentous plantation before the death of Queen Elizabeth (1603) was that of Munster, developed between 1585 and 1594.

The distinctive features of the Munster plantation were, first, that it was concentrated on some 600,000 acres of what were presumed to be the former lands of the rebellious earl of Desmond; second, that the new settlers were almost exclusively English-born Protestants; and third, that the former occupants, whether 'Old English' or Gaelic, were extruded from the area. The inchoate plantation was destroyed by rebellion (1598–1603), but slowly re-established itself thereafter and left a permanent imprint of English culture and influence in the settled area, especially the coasts and river valleys of Cork and Waterford. The numbers of planters (or 'Undertakers' as they were called) attracted was relatively small, and most came from the south-western countries of England. Some areas of Munster must have resembled Somerset, Devon and Cornwall.

The English defeat of the northern earls in the opening years of the seventeenth century completed the Elizabethan conquest of Ireland, and eventually opened Gaelic Ulster to the plantation phenomenon, which had first been initiated on a large scale in Munster. In Ulster, six of nine counties were found to have escheated to the crown as a consequence of the rebellious activity of their Gaelic masters. Plans for an ambitious plantation were drawn up (1609–10), and although the necessary immigration from England and Scotland was slow to begin (and the capital investments which were to accompany it reluctant and halting), the Ulster plantation, in a century of development, was to prove far the most consequential of all the Irish plantations.

Not only did it embrace the largest area, but it attracted an unprecedentedly large number of immigrants. Antrim and Down, although not part of the official plantation, were simultaneously attracting numerous Scottish (mainly Protestant) settlers, and in the course of the seventeenth century Ulster, as a whole, became a major site of lowland Scottish immigration, thus transforming the character of the province down to the modern day. The City of London temporarily acquired an interest in County Coleraine, which, together with its principal town, was renamed Londonderry. Although English immigration to the Ulster plantation has been less extensively studied than Scottish, evidence points to substantial numbers coming from the north-west counties, and it is sometimes argued that, together with their lowland Scottish counterparts, they constituted a less skilled and wealthy immigrant population than the new – predominantly West Country English – planters of Munster.

Because the term 'plantation' was, in this period, applied to almost every effort to introduce British immigrants, there were, in addition to the major plantations of Munster and Ulster, numerous miscellaneous early seventeenth-century 'plantations', including those in Longford, Leitrim, Wexford and Wicklow, and one – associated particularly with the career of Thomas Wentworth (later earl of Strafford) – in Connacht. None of these had an impact to compare with the larger plantations, especially that of Ulster.

After the Irish rebellion which began in October 1641 and the decade of warfare which followed, the kind of British immigration and settlement which had characterized 'plantation' did not cease – indeed the second half of the seventeenth century seems to have been critical – but it was given different names. The scheme initiated in March, 1642, for instance, which resulted in the distribution in the 1650s of some million acres of Irish land to those who either fought for the reconquest of Ireland or contributed money to finance it, was called an 'adventure' rather than a plantation. The crucial English acts of the 1650s and 1660s which determined who would hold, lose or recover land in Ireland were called acts of 'settlement', not plantation, and the process which followed the Jacobite rising of 1688–91 was very much of a piece.

In retrospect it can be seen that the hundred-year period of 'plantation' was an anomaly in the Anglo-Irish relationship of the period 1167–1922. For reasons having to do with the novel ambitions, powers and institutions of the Tudor monarchy; with the perplexing (to the men and women of the time) religious cleavage which opened in the Islands in the second half of the sixteenth century; and with the dramatic threat posed by that colossus, the Spanish empire, English statesmen, monarchs and political writers briefly regarded large portions of Ireland as if they were new lands either lacking inhabitants, or containing inhabitants who could be legitimately and effectively dispossessed. The concept of plantation died as an older truth – that of Ireland as a connected kingdom rather than an exotic colony – reasserted itself. Ireland was not a new land but an old one. Its inhabitants could not be enduringly dispossessed, for they retained both the constitutional means and the instinct to press their former rights, and energetically did so until some, if not all, of the marks of plantation were effaced.

Late twentieth-century historians, reacting against the frequent condemnation of plantation by nineteenth-and early twentieth-century Irish nationalists, have often emphasized the economic, technical, and cultural benefits which the plantations – particularly that of Munster – introduced, along with

their more obvious iniquities and depradations. Whether the era of plantation is to be
celebrated or lamented, it constitutes a crucial
phase of the history of modern Ireland.

Reading

Bottigheimer, K.S., *English Money and Irish Land*
(Clarendon Press, 1971).

Brady, Ciaran, and Gillespie, Raymond (eds),
*Natives and Newcomers: The Making of Irish
Colonial Society, 1534–1641* (Irish Academic
Press, 1986).

Butler, W.F.T., *Confiscation in Irish History* (1918,
and later reprints).

Canny, Nicholas, P., *The Elizabethan Conquest of
Ireland* (Harvester Press: 1976).

Gillespie, Raymond, *Colonial Ulster: The
Settlement of East Ulster, 1600–1641* (Cork
University Press for the Irish Committee of
Historical Science, 1985).

MacCarthy-Morrogh, Michael, *The Munster
Plantation: English Migration to Southern
Ireland, 1583–1641* (Clarendon Press/Oxford
University Press, 1986).

Moody, T.W., *The Londonderry Plantation, 1608–
41* (W. Mullan and Son, 1939).

Perceval-Maxwell, M., *The Scottish Migration to
Ulster in the Reign of James I* (Routledge and
Kegan Paul, 1973).

Quinn, D.B., *The Elizabethans and the Irish*
(Cornell University Press for the Folger
University Library, 1966).

Robinson, Philip, *The Plantation of Ulster* (Gill and
Macmillan, 1984).

K.S. BOTTIGHEIMER

police Since the mid-nineteenth century,
policing in Ireland has been a national rather
than a local matter, a pattern which differ-
entiates Ireland from most European countries. With the exception of Dublin, which
had its own Dublin Metropolitan Police until
1925, under British rule all of Ireland was
policed by the Royal Irish Constabulary
(RIC) under the direct control of Dublin
Castle. The RIC, an armed police force, was
regarded as the eyes and ears of the government. Despite its inability to control
insurgency after 1919, and its adulteration

in 1920 and 1921 by uncontrollable and
untrained temporary recruits – the Black
and Tans and the Auxiliary Cadets – the
force was admired for its discipline and resilience, not least by the key separatist strate-
gist Michael Collins. When, after a disastrous
start, the new state successfully established a
national police force, the Garda Siochana,
this bore a close resemblance to the old RIC
with the important exception that it was a
mainly unarmed force. In Northern Ireland,
the full-time Royal Ulster Constabulary
(RUC) was simply the Ulster RIC renamed.
There, however, the government also established part-time and temporary police units,
most notoriously the B Specials, eventually
disbanded in 1969. These gained a reputation
as partisan, sectarian groups concerned simply to cow the nationalist minority.

Over the years the Garda Siochana, like the
RIC they replaced, were given a miscellany of
functions by central government, many of
them with no direct bearing on police work.
This, while it may have hampered such work,
kept them in very close touch with the communities they served. That in turn may
explain what survey data suggest: that the
force, in contrast to its European analogues,
continues to command remarkably widespread public respect and trust. This is
despite its political policing role, the responsibility of its Special Branch. In Northern
Ireland, however, the RUC has always been
regarded with mistrust by the nationalist
community, although the force has changed
enormously since the early 1970s and has
made considerable efforts to demonstrate
an evenhanded approach to public order
problems.

EUNAN O'HALPIN

political economy, study of Richard
Whately, archbishop of Dublin (1831–63)
and former Drummond professor of political
economy at Oxford, was by far the most
influential figure in the propagation of political economy in nineteenth-century Ireland.
Its formal teaching was inaugurated in 1832

when he founded the first Irish chair in the discipline at Trinity College, Dublin. Professors were selected by competitive examination and held office for five years as at Oxford. Also in 1832 Whately became a Commissioner of National Education and the *de facto* head of the board, using his influence to have political economy taught to children and even writing the textbook himself – *Easy Lessons on Money Matters*. In 1834 John Barrington, a Dublin businessman, set up the Barrington Trust to teach political economy to the working classes throughout the towns and villages of Ireland. In 1847 the Dublin Statistical Society (later to become the Statistical and Social Inquiry Society of Ireland) was established mainly by the Whately professors (especially William Neilson Hancock), perhaps at Whately's instigation but certainly with his strong support. One of its chief aims was to promote the study of political economy and to apply its principles to social questions. In 1849 it took over the administration of the Barrington lectures, which had been in abeyance until then. In the same year the Queen's Colleges (Belfast, Cork and Galway) opened their doors to students and each had a combined chair of jurisprudence and political economy. The Whately professors and ex-professors, as well as their colleagues in the Queen's Colleges, were particularly active in mid-century in disseminating political economy, not only to their students and through their publications, but also in the proceedings of the Statistical Society, in their involvement in the Barrington scheme, and in lectures delivered to the flourishing literary, philosophical and scientific bodies, and to Mechanics' Institutes throughout Ireland.

Following a suggestion by Marian Bowley, R.D. Collison Black, in 1945, contended that Mountifort Longfield (1802–84), the first Whately professor (1832–6), founded a 'Dublin School' which included such of his successors as Isaac Butt, J.A. Lawson, Hancock, Arthur Houston and, to a lesser extent, R. Hussey Walsh. These 'Irish dissidents', who were clearly indebted to Whately and his friend Nassau Senior, broke with the dominant classical Ricardian paradigm with its emphasis on production and with a labour or cost-of-production theory of value. They were precursors of the 'marginalist revolution' of the 1870s in their advocacy of a 'subjective' or 'utility' theory of value. More radically, W.E. Hearn placed wants and the means of satisfying them at the centre of his analysis. Ideologically the focus of attention on consumption rather than on production involved a substitution of a harmonious model of social progress for the class conflict implicit in classical theory. A corollary was that the theory of distribution was subsumed under and became a special case of the theory of value, in sharp contrast with the classical approach. But John Elliot Cairnes (1823–75), the sixth occupant of the Whately chair (1856–61), vigorously defended the Ricardo–Mill tradition.

Longfield, Butt, Cairnes and especially Bastable made significant contributions to the theory of international trade, and Bastable was a leading figure in the new field of public finance. The other main area to which Irish political economists contributed was methodology. The early Whately professors were inductivists but Cairnes defended deductivism, through, in effect, he practised historical materialism in his applied economics and especially in his influential study of the political economy of slavery, *The Slave Power* (1862). Cliffe Leslie and John Kells Ingram were pioneers in historical economics in the English-speaking world, and Hearn is regarded as the first author to apply the Darwinian theory of organic evolution systematically to political economy, in his *Plutology* (1863). In economic policy Butt was the only academic economist in Great Britain or Ireland of his day to defend protectionism, while, in the words of Keynes, Cairnes was perhaps the 'first orthodox economist to deliver a frontal attack upon *laissez-faire* in general'.

There was a widespread view in the nineteenth century that political economy was little known and not highly regarded in Ireland and that the Irish and Catholic 'characters' were allergic to its principles and possessed virtues inimical to economic progress. So political economy was identified as the chief means of establishing hegemony over the Irish, by promoting the economically progressive virtues (seen as English and rational) of self-interest and individualism, the socially desirable objective of neutralizing class antagonisms, and the political objective of 'tranquillizing' Ireland and assimilating it to English norms. In a deeply divided society consensus was sought in that allegedly value-free and incontrovertible form of knowledge, political economy.

The Great Famine of 1846–7 provoked a popular Irish outcry against political economy and especially *laissez faire*. The ideological establishment strenuously defended the discipline, but within 10 years a moral critique from within seriously questioned its scientific status. A historical and comparative approach impugned the deductivism of political economy, its abstractionism, its homogenizing cosmopolitanism, its anglocentrism. Nationalist critics condemned the policies of free trade and *laissez faire* and, in the fashion of Carlyle and Ruskin, subjected the utilitarian philosophy which underpinned political economy to unrelenting moral and aesthetic attack. In general, a political economy based on English ideas and experiences was rejected for Ireland and the notion was embraced that Ireland should be governed by 'Irish ideas'. Various Irish Land Acts undermined the 'English' ideas of the sacredness of contract and of absolute property in land. Such basic tenets of political economy as individualism and self-interest were challenged in the name of social and co-operative values, and some authors argued that the family rather than the individual was the basic unit of society. In the end, despite spectacular early success, political economy failed in its ideological missions and was itself, in part, changed in its engagement with Irish history.

Reading

Black, R.D. Collison, 'Trinity College, Dublin, and the theory of value, 1832–1863', *Economica* 12 (1945), pp. 140–8.

—— 'Economic studies at Trinity College, Dublin – I', *Hermathena* LXX (1947), pp. 65–80.

—— *The Statistical and Social Inquiry Society of Ireland Centenary Volume 1847–1947: With a History of the Society* (Dublin: 1947).

—— 'Economic studies at Trinity College, Dublin – II', *Hermathena* LXXI (1948), pp. 52–63.

—— *Economic Thought and the Irish Question 1817–1870* (Cambridge, 1960).

Boylan, Thomas A. and Foley, Timothy P., 'John Elliot Cairnes, John Stuart Mill and Ireland: some problems for political economy', in Antoin E. Murphy (ed.), *Economists and the Irish Economy from the Eighteenth Century to the Present Day* (Dublin: Irish Academic Press, 1984).

—— '"Tempering the rawness": W.E. Hearn, Irish political economist, and intellectual life in Australia', in Seamus Grimes and Gearóid Ó Tuathaigh (eds), *The Irish-Australian Connection: An Caidreamh Gael–Astrálach* (Galway: 1988).

—— *Political Economy and Colonial Ireland: The Propagation and Ideological Function of Economic Discourse in the Nineteenth Century* (London: Routledge, 1992).

Koot, Gerard M., 'T.E. Cliffe Leslie, Irish social reform, and the origins of the English historical school of economics', *History of Political Economy* 7 (1975), pp. 312–36.

Moss, Laurence S., *Mountifort Longfield: Ireland's First Professor of Political Economy* (Ottawa IL: Green Hill, 1976).

TIMOTHY P. FOLEY

Ponsonby family An Anglo-Irish family of wealth and distinction, the Ponsonbys came to Ireland with Cromwell and settled at Bessborough towards the middle of the seventeenth century. The family pursued political interests both in Ireland and in England, but it was in Ireland that they fared best. Its most significant member perhaps was John Ponsonby (1713–89), who was speaker of the Irish Commons from 1756 until the conflict between the Undertakers and Lord Townshend drove him from office.

The family remained a loosely knit but numerically strong and powerful body in Irish politics which no lord lieutenant could afford to ignore. They opposed the Union but afterwards continued to represent Irish constituencies at Westminster. Eighteenth-century connections by marriage with the Duke of Devonshire gave solidity and a degree of continuity to the family's power base. Nineteenth-century Ponsonbys included prominent soldiers, cricketers and novelists.

GERARD O'BRIEN

popular music As defined by the emerging commercial music industry of the 1920s, this faced strong resistance in seeking to establish itself in Ireland. The new Irish state adopted a defensive Gaelicism hostile to 'alien' influences and a puritan Catholic morality as its official culture. The state radio service founded in 1926, 2RN, was dedicated by Douglas Hyde at its inauguration to 'emphasis[ing] what we have derived from our Gaelic ancestors, from one of the oldest civilisations in Europe, the heritage of the Os and the Macs'. 'Irish ballads', 'Gaelic songs', 'Irish pipe music' and the singing of the station's director, Seamus Clandillon – 'inventor' of the ceili band – and of his wife, Mairead Ní Hannagain, featured prominently in the station's programming. At the same time, radio receivers were sold with the promise of 'nights of pleasure', notably dance music, which could be heard on foreign channels.

Éamon de Valera, as leader of Fianna Fáil in opposition in the late 1920s, had linked the evils of drink to those of jazz. The Catholic bishops denounced jazz and jitterbugging in a 1932 Lenten pastoral. As controversy raged about the licensing of dance halls in 1933, a County Louth parish priest wrote to the *Irish Independent* of the 'human wreckage from the devil's workshops'.

But political and ecclesiastical strictures merely slowed the adoption of popular music. The same *Irish Independent* which gave such prominence to the church's attacks on dance halls also hosted performances from the roof of its Dublin headquarters by English singer Gracie Fields and by Jack Hilton and his band, the most successful of the English dance bands. In the years after World War II, dance bands flourished throughout Ireland. Some, like Mick Delahunty's band, based in Clonmel, County Tipperary, toured the country extensively. The tempo was strict, the band suits were formal, and the venues were unlicensed. In the 'ballrooms of romance', women and men stayed apart except for the time spent dancing.

Bill Haley's mid-1950s film *Rock Around the Clock* and Radio Luxembourg brought a taste of something much less inhibited. Some time in the late 1950s a northern dance band, The Clipper Carlton got out from behind their music stands and stood up to play. The bass guitar and the electric guitar eventually replaced the double bass and piano, giving the musicians greater freedom to move. The showband was born. In a few years, ballroom owners, dance promoters, band managers and some musicians had made millionaire-equivalent fortunes or, at least, were living an ostentatious lifestyle suggesting they had. Showbands mixed current pop 'hits', material in more or less rock-and-roll style, novelty and comedy numbers, and sentimental country and western songs. The flashy suits and on-stage routine all stressed the 'show' element. In the typical line-up of eight or nine musicians, several played more than one instrument. The showbands could handle anything from dixieland jazz *à la* Acker Bilk to Beatles hits – whatever was in demand. As traditional music found new popularity, the showbands added reels and jigs to their repertoire. When the Clancy Brothers and the Dubliners began to sing Irish ballads lustily to guitar accompaniment, the showbands belted out 'The Holy Ground' as well.

In 1965, Brendan Bowyer and the Royal Showband, from Waterford, started a new dance craze with their hit 'The Hucklebuck'. In that same year, Trinity College, Dublin, history student Ian Whitcomb went to number 8 in the American pop charts with 'You Turn Me On', Belfast band Them, with singer Van Morrison, had a hit in Britain with 'Baby Please Don't Go' and Ireland first took part in the Eurovision Song Contest. Since then, Irish songs have won the contest seven times. The showbands continued to dominate the main venues but they no longer had the popular music scene to themselves. It was the 'beat groups' which first reversed the flow of popular music into the country.

Popularity in this context equates with commercial success, and the Irish pop and rock market was – and is – too small to provide a solid commercial base. The international recording contract was to become the mark of having 'arrived'. Indeed, international acceptance remains a condition for major success in Ireland. From the emerging rock movement of the late 1960s came Rory Gallagher, Phil Lynott and Gary Moore, who were all to break the international barrier. Twenty years later, Van Morrison, Gallagher and Moore continue to play to international audiences, Morrison in particular being universally respected. He started his musical career in the Monarchs showband in the early 1960s; he has returned to different Irish roots in recent years by recording with traditional musicians and singing Irish ballads.

By the late 1970s, the showbands were in terminal decline, though many of their stalwarts continue to perform in the 1990s, some (like Big Tom, formerly with Big Tom and the Mainliners) playing a strictly bound country and western-based music also referred to as 'country and Irish', and others (like Dickie Rock, formerly with the Miami Showband) performing on a cabaret circuit of hotels, theatres and larger public houses. Joe Dolan, formerly Joe Dolan and the Drifters, remains a major attraction. The locales have changed, however. Most of the 'dry' ballrooms which were built in the 1960s have ceased to function. Pubs and hotels added lounges and function rooms which could accommodate the dancers – and serve them alcoholic drink. In some cases, these have been adapted later as discos, live music being displaced altogether.

In the post-showband years, the formerly quite separate musical worlds of traditional, folk, pop and rock have increasingly overlapped. From folk group Sweeney's Men in the late 1960s, through Planxty and Clannad, formed in 1970, the Bothy Band (mid-1970s) Moving Hearts (early 1980s), and Davy Spillane in the 1990s, the quest has continued for a contemporary approach to traditional music, marrying, for instance, electric keyboards and uileann pipes. Donal Lunny, the moving musical spirit of several of those groups, is one of the single most influential figures in contemporary Irish popular music as producer, arranger and accompanist on recordings in a wide range of modes. Christy Moore, an associate of Lunny in Planxty and Moving Hearts, has become one of the most broadly popular performers in Ireland, also touring abroad regularly. He sings narrative, bantering songs and social-issues in a deceptively simple manner.

As their music has acquired a more 'pop' and cosmopolitan flavour, Mary Black, former singer with traditional group De Danann, and Enya, a former Clannad member, have won international audiences. Paul Brady moved from 'beat' to folk, with the Johnstons and Planxty, to a highly individual approach to rock, with a strong Irish inflection and deep personal engagement. His commercial success has not matched his critical acclaim, though his songs have been taken up by American singers Tina Turner and Bonnie Raitt among others. From a rock background, Thin Lizzy and Horslips had sought in the early 1970s to infuse a 'Celtic' element into their music. Thin Lizzy's 'Whiskey in the Jar', a rock rendering of an Irish ballad, went into the British pop charts in 1973. The band became best known for a harder style of rock, though lead singer Phil Lynott (deceased 1986) also showed a softer, vaguely mystical side.

The anger and aggression of the 'new wave' of the mid-1970s was reflected in the deliberate provocations of the Boomtown Rats, led by Bob Geldof. After a series of international hits with the band, Geldof has had a solo career of mixed fortune but maintained a high profile with his leading role in Band Aid, the international music industry's contribution to relief of the mid-1980s famine in Ethiopia. The Rats' arrival, self-propelled to prominence, came as Dublin pirate radio stations were emerging, playing rock and pop music through the night. By 1979, RTE, the state broadcaster, had to respond with its own popular music channel, Radio 2. Later commercial radio stations boast how little they interrupt the stream of music. Popular music has become a means to deliver an audience to advertisers.

In the year in which Radio 2 was launched, a Dublin band emerged from the chaos of sessions by young punk bands in a disused bottling plant in central Dublin to record their first single, 'Out of Control'. U2 were, in fact, highly controlled. In the punk movement proper, Belfast band Stiff Little Fingers and Derry band the Undertones had made more of an impact than any of the Dublin contenders. But as U2's music took shape, it moved far from the fury of punk, acquiring an other-worldly feel. Marking the extent to which acceptance of popular music has been seen as a necessary part of modernization, U2's success has been celebrated by the political, if not the ecclesiastical, powers. Following U2's tour of north America in 1987 the then taoiseach, Charles Haughey, accorded the band a government reception. There could be no question about their status: *Time* magazine had put them on its cover. The band's achievements won Dublin the status of 'epicentre of world rock'. Talent scouts from major record labels have hunted Dublin and Ireland for the successors to U2. Contracts have been signed but no band has lived up to the hopes.

The biggest impact by an Irish popular music performer since U2 has been made by Sinead O'Connor, with her haunting voice and naive stage presence. In her musical associations, she has contrived to span the distance between Christy Moore and American funk musician Prince. The best-known acts to subsequently achieve international success are the Corrs and the expertly-marketed boybands, Boyzone and Westlife.

London-Irish band the Pogues, with their uninhibited approach to ballad-singing, had a line-up in the 1990s which reflected further how diverse musical strands have crossed. It included Joe Strummer, a leading light of the 1970s punk scene with London band the Clash, Terry Woods, a veteran of Sweeney's Men, and Philip Chevron, formerly with Radiators from Space, contemporaries of the Boomtown Rats.

The Pogues' style has influenced that of bands like the Sawdoctors. They proudly proclaim their origins in Tuam, in east County Galway, heartlands of the 'country and Irish' scene. The Sawdoctors sing vigorously of their love of the N17, the road into Tuam. Big Tom sings in melancholy manner of 'Four Roads to Glenamaddy' (also in east Galway). In 1933, it was the archbishop of Tuam, Dr Gilmartin, who warned that 'a terrible judgement must await those who organise immodest dances'. The Sawdoctors make immodesty a virtue.

BRIAN TRENCH

Portraiture, pre twentieth-century Dublin of the eighteenth and nineteenth centuries boasted good training schools for artists, exhibitions were held, reviews were written and above all, portraits were produced. It is important to stress this last point. The production of portraiture was the only economically viable solution open to the native artist. History and landscape painting by Irish artists did not enjoy extensive local patronage, leaving face painting as the only outlet for those who wished to stay. Even then many left for the more lucrative attractions of London, while others sent work for exhibition there. Letters of the leading portraitist of the late eighteenth century, Hugh Douglas Hamilton, written from Dublin to his friend, the sculptor Antonio Canova in Rome, tell of the feeling of isolation and cultural despair felt by a Dublin-based artist *c*.1800. Hamilton complains of his physical exhaustion at having to produce an infinite number of portraits and of how he would much rather be painting history paintings. A study of the exhibitions held in Dublin in the very early years of the nineteenth century, to which Hamilton was an active contributor, show that portraiture accounted for some 85 per cent of all paintings and drawings submitted. 'Portraiture is at present so much the rage', an anonymous Dublin diarist of 1801 informs us, that 'had the artists practising in Ireland, inclination, ability and sale for composition... they have not leisure for any other branch of study.'

The setting up of the Dublin Society School of Figure Drawing in the 1740s created, under the tutelage of the French-trained Robert West, a generation of excellent portraitists. Pastel drawing was particularly encouraged, and artists such as Hamilton and Matthew William Peters earned international reputations for the speed and elegance of their crayon heads. James McArdell, the mezzotint engraver who gained early fame by reproducing the portraits of Sir Joshua Reynolds, as well as James Barry, who occasionally indulged in portraits, were also to benefit from the teaching of West and his family. Three generations of Wests were to run the Dublin Society Drawing School and each in his day was a competent portraitist. In terms of establishment success their most illustrious pupil was the portraitist Martin Archer Shee, who in 1830 was elected President of the Royal Academy (RA) in London. In Ireland four of the nine nineteenth-century presidents of the Royal Hibernian Academy (RHA) were portraitists.

It is ironic that in the eighteenth century, when Ireland had its own Parliament, the majority of lords and commoners who wished to have their portrait painted ventured to London; see, for example, the amazing pomposity of Reynold's portrait of Charles Coote, third earl of Bellamont (1774, Dublin, National Gallery of Ireland). After the Act of Union and into the nineteenth century the financial rewards for Irish-based portraitists improved. Stephen Catterson Smith (1806–72), a Yorkshire-born portraitist, gave up a respectable business in London, where clients had included the royal family, to become portrait painter to the lord lieutenant of Ireland, a post he held for almost 30 years. His private commissions were extensive and he also found time to be elected president of the RHA twice.

Later nineteenth-century artists, such as Walter Osborne and John Butler Yeats, exhibit in their portraits an interest in the then new stylistic developments emanating from France. Osborne was a most reluctant portraitist, only doing it for the money. Yeats by contrast was a born pursuer of character. In his drawings he strove to express an intensity and a presence in his sitter that reflects his own supremely cerebral approach to human relations. He never made any money out of portraits, but he conveyed a conviction in his creations that places artists such as Catterson Smith in the shade.

Reading

Crookshank, Anne and the Knight of Glin, *Irish Portraits 1660–1860* (London: Paul Mellon Foundation for British Art, 1969).

——, and the Knight of Glin, *Painters of Ireland c.1660–1920* (London: Barrie and Jenkins, 1978).

Cullen, Fintan, *Walpole Society* 50 (1984).

—— *The Drawings of John Butler Yeats* (Albany NY: Albany Institute of History and Art, 1987).

ROSC, *Irish Art in the 19th Century* (Cork: ROSC, 1971).

Sheehy, Jeanne, *Walter Osborne* (Dublin: National Gallery of Ireland, 1983).

Strickland, Walter, *A Dictionary of Irish Artists* (Shannon: Irish University Press, 1968).

FINTAN CULLEN

Postmodernism Defined by Jean-François Lyotard as 'incredulity towards metanarratives'. Responding to Lyotard's call for the replacement of such metanarratives as capitalism, communism and Enlightenment values by a proliferation of micro-narratives, Richard Kearney argues that Ireland is currently experiencing an ideological crisis, and suggests that postmodern 'radical pluralism' offers a means of reimagining the socio-cultural and political relationships between region, nation and European federation.

Postmodern literature's ludic mode employs parody, pastiche, hybridism and self-reflexivity, in texts mixing 'high art' with 'popular culture': Irish examples include Flann O'Brien's *At Swim-Two-Birds* (1939) – anticipating postmodernism's strategies three decades before the term achieved widespread recognition – Stewart Parker's play *Northern Star* (1985), and Paul Muldoon's *Madoc* (1990). Postmodern literature's melancholic mode is exemplified in Samuel Beckett's trilogy of novels *Molloy, Malone Dies* and *The Unnamable* (first published in French, 1950–2), whose ontologically attenuating narrators bear incessant witness to the dent in identity, the hole in wholeness.

Reading

Kearney, Richard (ed.), *Across the Frontiers* (Dublin: Wolfhound Press, 1988).
—— 'Postmodern Ireland', in Miriam Hederman (ed.), *The Clash of Ideas* (Dublin: Gill and Macmillan, 1988).
Lyotard, Jean-François, *The Postmodern Condition*, trans. Geoff Bennington and Brian Massumi (Minneapolis: University of Minnesota Press, 1988; first pub. in French 1979).

RICHARD HASLAM

potato The humble potato became 'the great multiplier of mankind' (*Times*, 1864) in Ireland; by 1841, three million (the potato people) relied exclusively on it as a diet, when it still enjoyed a healthy freedom of the fields. The potato had multiple advantages – it tolerated the prevalent poor soils and wet climate; it was a nutritious food source requiring no technology or processing; it was palatable even as a mono-diet. The potato loosened the leash on population

growth, permitting the massive surge in the century before the Famine, and indelibly stamping itself as a definitive symbol of Irish poverty and exceptionalism. But total reliance sharpened the ecological knife edge on which the potato people were ever more precariously perched. The malignant blight of the 1840s pushed them over the potato precipice – into death (for one million) and subsequent emigration (for two million).

KEVIN WHELAN

Potter, A.J. (Archibald James) (1918–80) Composer and broadcaster. Born 22 September, Belfast; died 5 July, Greystones, County Wicklow. Poor home circumstances as a child led to Potter's living with relatives in Kent from 9 years of age. He was educated through scholarships at All Saints Choir School (London), Clifton College, and the Royal College of Music, where he studied with H.C. Colles, George Thalben Ball (organ) and Vaughan Williams (composition). After army service in World War II (including the Russo-Finnish 'Winter War' and fighting in the Indian Army against the Japanese in Burma), he worked for the United Africa Company in Nigeria before settling in Dublin in 1950. He became vicar Choral (bass) in St Patrick's Cathedral, and taught singing and composition at the Royal Irish Academy of Music (RIAM). Appointed professor of composition at RIAM in 1955, he gained a DMus from Dublin University in 1953. His *Missa Brevis* won the Festival of Britain (NI) Prize in 1950, and he won the first two Radio Éireann Carolan Competitions with the orchestral diptych *Overture to a Kitchen Comedy* and *Rhapsody under a High Sky* (1950) and *Concerto da Chiesa* (1952). He received the Jacobs Award in 1968 for an outstanding contribution to Irish Radio. Potter regularly broadcast his own radio series *Listening to Music* and *The Young Student's Guide to Music*, and was a frequent contributor to radio and periodicals. He became a full-time composer after the 1972 Finance Act.

Potter was an extremely prolific and versatile composer in a wide range of musical styles, characterized by the use of instrumental colour and striking melodic ideas, ranging from modal motifs to 12-note themes. The rumbustiousness, puns and humour of his music, as well as the most deeply felt personal works, all reflected aspects of his complex personality. He was a distinguished arranger and orchestrator, and made hundreds of orchestral and choral arrangements of traditional tunes for RTE.

SARAH BURN

poverty Ireland has long been viewed as one of the poorest countries in Western Europe. The Royal Commission of Inquiry into the Conditions of the Poorer Classes in Ireland published three reports in 1835 and 1836. These contained harrowing descriptions of widespread destitution. The Great Famine of 1845–7 led to starvation, diseases and a dramatic growth in emigration. While there was a slow but real decline in destitution during the rest of the century, it still remained very high in some areas, notably in Dublin.

In the twentieth century the incidence of absolute poverty slowly declined with gradual improvements in income support, housing and public services. Thus in recent years few people have lacked the barest minimum of food, housing and clothing necessary for survival. However, many people have continued to live in conditions of considerable poverty, and emigration has remained one of the few escape routes. In 1971 Seamus O'Cinneide estimated that 25 per cent of Irish people were living in poverty. In 1986 the government responded to the growing evidence of poverty by establishing a semi-state agency, the Combat Poverty Agency, to advise government, to initiate projects to undertake research, and to create a greater public awareness of poverty. Over the period 1987–92 public concern about poverty continued to grow. Opinion polls showed that poverty was, along with unemployment, emigration and health, one of the four issues of greatest concern to the general public.

By 1992 research showed that, depending where you draw the line, somewhere between 20 and 30 per cent of the population were living in some degree of poverty and that over a 20-year period the proportion of those living in poverty had risen. Over the same period the proportion of the poor who were elderly had declined, while there had been an increase in the significance of unemployment. About a third of households who were living in poverty were headed by someone who was unemployed, while almost one-quarter were farm households. Particularly at risk of poverty are larger families and single-parent households. There are also small but significant groups, such as Travellers and the homeless, who experience particularly acute poverty. Comparisons within the European Community show that only Portugal has a higher proportion of people living in poverty.

Living in poverty means being excluded from a minimally acceptable standard of living based on what is the norm for other people. People experiencing poverty have severely restricted access not only to income but also to other essentials like employment, housing, education and cultural, health and legal services. Being poor involves feelings of exclusion, isolation and a sense of powerlessness. It involves real pain, anxiety and psychological distress. Poverty has also been closely connected to the extraordinary lack of social mobility in Ireland. Children growing up in poverty are less likely to do well educationally or ultimately to get jobs.

While the degree and intensity of poverty have varied over time, the underlying causes have not. In Ireland poverty has always been a structural problem. It results primarily from the fact that resources and opportunities are distributed very unequally within Irish society. This was true at the time of the Great Famine and is still true today. It also means that in spite of economic growth the benefits have not been distributed fairly between countries and regions. Previously as

485

a colony of the United Kingdom and now, with the greater mobility of international capital, as a peripheral region of the European Community, Ireland has transferred much of its gross domestic product out of the country. Poverty has thus been a product of a wider economic dependence. It has also been a cause. The extent to which poverty has persisted both north and south of the border since independence has continued to undermine self-confidence and self-esteem and has diminished the degree to which it has been possible to develop a confident, outward-looking and vibrant society.

Poverty is the manifestation of an increasingly divided society, with growing concentrations of multiple disadvantage in selective urban areas and peripheral rural communities. It has forced many people to emigrate. Thus, much of the potential energy and leadership that would have pressed for greater modernization of Irish society has been lost, and there has been much apathy amongst those that have remained. This has enabled outdated political and social structures and attitudes to survive. There has been a close connection between the acceptance of poverty and the conservative nature of Irish churches. For much of the twentieth century the emphasis in relation to poverty has been far more on a charitable response rather than on arguing for a political response to the underlying causes.

Reading

Burke, H., *The People and the Poor Law* (Women's Education Bureau, 1987).
Callan T., *Poverty, Income and Welfare in Ireland* (Economic and Social Research Institute, 1989).
Commission of the European Communities, *Final Report on the Second European Poverty Programme 1985–1989*, COM(91) Final (Brussels, 1991).
O'Cinneide, S., 'The extent of poverty in Ireland', *Social Studies* 1 (1972).

HUGH FRAZER

Prendergast, Kathy (1958–) Sculptor. Born Dublin. Prendergast trained at the National College of Art and Design, Dublin (1976–80,

1982–3), and at the Royal College of Art, London (1983–6). One of several successful woman sculptors of her generation, she also makes works on paper. Her sculptures are in many media, including bronze, stone, cloth and chalk. She is primarily interested in landscape and its relationship, both physical and psychological, to human experience. She uses conventions from cartography to make 'maps' in two and three dimensions of the human body and other forms. Ambiguities of scale are often a crucial element in her work.

Reading

Dunne, Aidan, 'Kathy Prendergast', in *Edge to Edge: Three Sculptors from Ireland: Eilis O'Connell, Kathy Prendergast, Vivienne Roche* (Dublin: Gandon Editions, 1991).
Joyce, Conor, 'Kathy Prendergast: a geography,' in *Kathy Prendergast* (Douglas Hyde Gallery, Dublin/The Arts Council of Northern Ireland, Belfast, 1990).
ROSC 1988 (Dublin: 1988).

FELICITY WOOLF

Presbyterian churches Presbyterianism was the faith of seventeenth-century Scottish planters in Ulster. They formed their first presbytery amidst the chaos of 1642, and when Charles II and Anglicanism were restored in 1660, Presbyterians, circumscribed by penal laws, became the largest and most powerful group of Protestant dissenters. Through the centuries the Scottish connection remained vital. Even today, many ministers study in Scotland, while Presbyterians are most numerous in areas of north-east Ulster where Scottish settlers predominated.

Divisions created a Presbyterian network, each group making a different appeal to the same constituency. Despite often vehement disagreements, the varieties of Presbyterianism functioned as a safety valve for individual bodies; disgruntled liberals or conservatives were far more likely to join a different Presbyterian group than to join another church.

By 1800 Irish Presbyterianism comprised five groups. The most rigorously orthodox and strictly disciplined was the Reformed Presbyterian Church (or Covenanters). Characterized by relentless adherence to national Covenants of 1638 and 1643, which advocated a firmly Presbyterian establishment in church and state, Reformed Presbyterians were never numerous, but their costly commitment to a radical expression of Presbyterian principles made them an important reminder of Presbyterian origins. The Burgher and Anti-Burgher Secession Synods originated in Scottish divisions over church government issues irrelevant in Ireland. However, the Seceders' tremendous energy and slightly less radical adherence to essentially the same principles as Covenanters attracted many Irish Presbyterians. The Synod of Ulster was the broad church of Irish Presbyterianism, numerically dominant and relatively diverse in practice and doctrine. In 1726 the synod's capacity for accommodation was finally exceeded over the issue of clerical subscription to the strongly Calvinist Westminster Confession of Faith of 1643, the touchstone of Presbyterian orthodoxy. The synod's solution was to place the non-subscribing liberals in a small and partially separate Presbytery of Antrim. Conservatives saw the Presbytery as dangerously heterodox; the Presbytery understood itself as the champion of religious liberty from 'human tests of divine truths'.

After 1800 a series of unions and divisions gave Irish Presbyterianism the configuration it essentially retains today. Only the Covenanters, marginalized by uncompromising adherence to the Covenants, were not involved. By the early 1990s the Reformed Presbyterian Church remained vital but small, numbering about 3,700 members. The first union occurred in 1818, when Burghers and Anti-Burghers joined to form a Secession Synod. The Synod of Ulster followed with a new division over a perennial issue, subscription to the Westminster Confession. In 1829, 17 liberal congregations, alienated by increasingly stringent doctrinal standards, withdrew to form a Remonstrant Synod. However, two enduring unions emerged from this split. The

departure of the liberals brought rapprochement between the Synod of Ulster and the Seceders, who formed the Presbyterian Church in Ireland in 1840. It remained by the early 1990s by far the largest Presbyterian church, containing about 28 per cent of the population of Northern Ireland and about 10 per cent of that of the whole island. For their part, the Remonstrants joined with the Presbytery of Antrim and the Synod of Munster to form the Non-Subscribing Presbyterian Church in Ireland, in the early 1990s numbered about 4,500 members.

The twentieth century added one group to the Presbyterian network, the Free Presbyterian Church, led since its foundation in 1951 by Ian Paisley. Although Paisley's background was independent Baptist, using the Presbyterian title is not only a shrewd appropriation of its cachet in Northern Ireland, it also partially indicates the new church's position in Protestantism. Like eighteenth-century Covenanters and Seceders, Free Presbyterians offer a conservative option to liberal churches, and former Presbyterians are the largest group among approximately 11,500 Free Presbyterian members.

Reading

Brooke, Peter, *Ulster Presbyterianism: The Historical Perspective, 1610–1970* (Dublin and New York: Gill and Macmillan/St Martin's Press, 1987).

Bruce, Steve, *God Save Ulster! The Religion and Politics of Paisleyism* (Oxford and New York: Oxford University Press, 1986).

Hempton, David and Hill, Myrtle, *Evangelical Protestantism in Ulster Society, 1740–1890* (London and New York: Routledge, 1992).

Holmes, Finlay, *Henry Cooke* (Belfast, Dublin and Ottawa: Christian Journals, 1981).

—— *Our Irish Presbyterian Heritage* (Belfast: Publications Committee of the Presbyterian Church in Ireland, 1985).

Loughridge, Adam, *The Covenanters in Ireland* (Belfast: Cameron Press, 1984).

Stewart, A.T.Q. *The Narrow Ground: The Roots of Conflict in Ulster*, 2nd edn (London and Boston: Faber, 1989).

Stewart David, *The Seceders in Ireland* (Belfast: Presbyterian Historical Society, 1950).

JOSEPH LIECHTY

Preston, Thomas (1860–1900) Physicist. Thomas Preston was one of many who bene-fited from the inspiring example of George Francis Fitzgerald of Trinity College, Dublin. A quiet and industrious Ulsterman, Preston surpassed that example at least in the production of books, writing two major texts (*Theory of Light, Theory of Heat*) before he was 35. Up to that point he was regarded as a worthy but unoriginal scientist. In a startling change of direction, he embarked upon experiments at the Royal University which were to bring him honours as the discoverer of the Anomalous Zeeman Effect. The Zeeman Effect (for which Zeeman and Lorentz later received the Nobel prize) is the change in the light emitted by atoms when a magnetic field is applied. In fact it was Preston who first found the true form of this effect, and the appellation 'Anomalous' is a misnomer, except in the context of the classical theory of the atom which prevailed at that time. His early death, apparently from overwork, robbed him of much of the lasting recognition which this discovery deserved.

Reading

Weaire, D. and O'Connor, S., 'Unfulfilled renown', *Annals of Science* 44 (1887), pp. 617–44.

DENIS L. WEAIRE

provinces The Gaelic word for province is *cúigeadh* (Old Ir. *cóiced*), a 'fifth'. The sim-plest explanation for this expression is that it was coined when the country was considered as divided into five over-kingdoms, Munster, Leinster, Connacht, Meath and Ulster. Using the evidence of an early Irish poem attributed to Mael Mura of Fahan (d. 887). T.F. O'Rahilly has argued that this five-fold pat-tern arose when the midland over-kingdom of Mide or Meath developed, displacing an earlier division of Ireland into four provinces only, namely Ulaid (Ulster). Galióin (Leinster), Muma (Munster) and Fir Ól nÉcmacht (Connacht). As an explanation for the notor-ious inconsistency among early Irish *literati* over the identity of the fifth province (variously accounted for by a second Munster, a second Leinster, or a small area around Uisnech in Westmeath). O'Rahilly's theory retains its attraction, though modern scholarship would question his chronology. Alwyn and Brinley Rees posit an earlier and indeed mystical origin for the concept of Ireland as a unit divided into five fifths, but their argument draws on literary sources of significantly later date than the poem used by O'Rahilly. F.J. Byrne has pointed out that the learned classes of eleventh and twelfth-century Ireland were quite capable of seeing the country as divided into seven sevenths or six sixths in response to changing political situations.

Moreover, the boundaries between the pro-vinces were by no means immutable. The modern County Clare at one time formed part of Connacht, and later became annexed to Munster, while the kingdom of Osraige (nowadays represented by the diocese of Ossory) belonged at different times to Munster or Leinster. Indeed the debatable border between these two provinces was the subject of a humorous twelfth-century tale. 'The Quarrel about the Loaf'.

In the course of the twelfth century the political collapse of the provincial kingdom of Meath was to be reflected in the disposi-tions made at the reforming synod of Kells-Mellifont in 1152, when Ireland was divided into a mere four ecclesiastical provinces, of Armagh. Tuam, Cashel and Dublin, corre-sponding to the former secular provinces of Ulster (with Meath), Connacht, Munster and Leinster respectively. In the wake of the Norman invasion (1169) the provincial over-kingdoms themselves were initially succeeded by the great Norman lordships of Leinster. Meath, Connacht, the earldom of Ulster and an early county of Munster covering Limerick and Tipperary only. These territorial jurisdictions became obsolete with the partition of Leinster and Meath between hieresses and the redrawing of county boundaries, but the Anglo-Irish colony remained conscious of the historic division of Ireland into provinces, perhaps reminded by differences in Irish dialects and political groupings. In 1332 a Limerick jury accused Maurice FitzThomas, the rebellious first earl of Desmond, of plotting to make himself king over Ireland, allotting Munster and Meath to himself, Connacht to Walter de Burgh, Leinster to William de Bermingham and Ulster to Henry de Mandeville, an interesting fourfold division which none the less retained the pre-Norman pattern of five provincial kingdoms.

In 1562, when the earl of Sussex planned the decentralization of the English government in Ireland into regional presidencies, he used the names of the well-remembered provincial kingdoms rather than the ecclesiastical provinces. Through the subsequently established Munster and Connacht presidencies, the old divisions once more assumed a jurisdictional reality in the early modern period.

KATHERINE SIMMS

psychiatry Long before psychiatry became a separate discipline, Ireland had developed a system of lunatic asylums largely controlled by the medical profession. In the eighteenth century, only two institutions for the mentally ill existed in Ireland. St Patrick's, founded by the will of Jonathan Swift, opened in 1757, and one opened in Cork, owing to the work of Dr William Saunders Hallaran, who wrote a treatise on the causes and cure of insanity. In 1815, the governors of the Dublin House of Industry opened a separate lunatic asylum, named after the Earl of Richmond, which was soon unable to cope with the numbers sent to it from all Ireland. A bill in 1817, therefore, set up a system of district lunatic asylums, and by 1835, nine were constructed, years before England planned such a system. The asylums had visiting physicians, who increasingly took control, and in 1845 their role was formalized by the foundation of a lunacy inspectorate. Francis White, surgeon to the Richmond, was the first inspector. He was instrumental in transferring the asylums from lay to medical management. Revised rules in 1862 established the authority of the 'resident medical superintendent' and made him responsible for the moral and medical treatment of all patients. When psychiatry emerged as a new branch of medicine, it took over existing structures of control. In 1947, St Patrick's became a teaching hospital, and Professor J.N.P Moore the medical director. A chair of academic psychiatry was established at Trinity College, Dublin, in 1968, and the new professor, Peter Beckett, organized training, with the help of the Royal College of Psychiatrists, throughout the Republic.

FRED LOWE

public buildings to 1922 From 1613 until 1763 the construction and maintenance of military and state buildings in Ireland was largely entrusted to the office of the director general, later surveyor general, of the fortifications and buildings. The office holders were initially military engineers, but between 1670 and 1733 the post was held by architects of high repute. The first of these, Sir William Robinson, designed the Royal Hospital Kilmainham (1680–7), the earliest major public building in Ireland in the classical style. He also drew up a master plan for the reconstruction of Dublin Castle after the state apartments were destroyed by fire in 1684. This involved the partial demilitarization of the castle and the progressive demolition of its defensive walls. The new state apartments and civil offices were continued by Robinson's successor Thomas Burgh between 1700 and 1730, though not finally completed for another three decades. Burgh's successor, Sir Edward Lovett Pearce, died young in 1733, but his erudite Parliament House on College Green, designed in 1728, ranks among the great European buildings of the eighteenth century.

In 1763 the functions of the surveyor general were taken over by the Barrack Board and Board of Works, which established a civil department. Its architect from 1774 was Thomas Cooley, an Englishman who had won the competition for the Dublin Royal Exchange (now City Hall) in 1769. In 1776 Cooley began the new law offices on Inns Quay, continued after his death in 1784 by James Gandon, who introduced a domed centre block to house the Four Courts. Gandon had been brought over from London in 1781 by John Beresford, chief commissioner of the revenue, to design the Custom House. The sophistication of his architecture was perhaps matched by that of only one other eighteenth-century practitioner in Ireland – Pearce, whose Parliament House he extended (1784–90).

In 1802 the civil side of the Board of Works was reorganized, operating until 1831 when the present Board or Office of Public Works came into being. Pre-eminent in the early nineteenth century was Francis Johnson, who converted the Parliament House into the Bank of Ireland (opened 1808) and, in his capacity as architect and inspector of civil buildings from 1805, designed the Chapel Royal at Dublin Castle (1807) and the Dublin General Post Office (1814). Johnston also added porticos to the Vice-Regal Lodge, which had been acquired in 1781 as a summer residence for the lord lieutenants. He oversaw a major gaol-building programme undertaken by the local authorities and, with his cousin William Murray, designed the first nine district lunatic asylums (1820–34). During this period the grand juries erected a series of fine neo-classical court houses, including some elaborate porticoed examples in the county towns (Cork, Tralee, Dundalk, Carlow, Tullamore, Ennis, etc.).

From 1832 to 1891 the architectural department of the new Office of Public Works was run by the Owen family, originally from north Wales. Jacob Owen altered and extended several of the Dublin public buildings, as well as overseeing the construction of the Queen's Colleges and a further batch of district lunatic asylums (mostly in the Gothic style) in the 1840s. His sons J.H. and E.T. Owen presided over the expansion of the board's architectural activities outside Dublin in the 1860s and 1870s, when large numbers of coast guard stations, police barracks, post offices and standard-plan national schools were built.

The principal public buildings erected in Dublin in the late Victorian and Edwardian eras were the National Library and Museum (1885–90) and the College of Science and Government Buildings (1904–22). The replacement of the grand jury system with new county councils in 1898 was not followed by any great rush of civic building, though the period saw the construction of two important municipal buildings in Ulster, the sumptuous baroque City Hall in Belfast (1896–1906, by Alfred Brumwell Thomas) and the Town Hall, Enniskillen (1898–1901, by Anthony Scott and Son).

Reading

Locber, Rolf, *A Biographical Dictionary of Architects in Ireland, 1600–1720* (London: John Murray, 1981).

McParland, Edward, *James Gandon. Virtuvius Hibernicus* (London: Zwemmer, 1985).

O'Dwyer, Frederick, 'The architecture of the Board of Public Works 1831–1922', in Ciaran O'Connor and John O'Regan (eds), *Public Works* (Dublin: Architectural Association of Ireland, 1987).

FREDERICK O'DWYER

Purser family The descendants of a prosperous flour miller in Dungarvan, County Waterford, who have distinguished themselves academically and culturally. John Mallet (1839–1929), a physician, and Louis Claude (1854–1932), a classicist, both had chairs in Trinity College, Dublin; their niece, Olive Purser, one of the first women to gain a degree, was Women's Dean. In the present generation, John W. Purser (1942–) is poet, playwright and composer.

Sarah Henrietta Purser (1848–1943) is perhaps the most widely known as painter, patron, collector, wit, and promoter of the Irish cultural renaissance, as well as founder of An Túr Gloine, the stained glass studios. After her father's bankruptcy in 1873 and a move to Dublin, she studied at the Metropolitan School of Art and the Academie Julien in Paris, producing some of her best work – intimate, relaxed portraits – shortly afterwards. Her career as a portrait painter in Dublin was highly successful, though her style was uneven and she was generally better at painting men. Her salons at Mespil House gathered together Dublin's foremost artists and intellectuals.

Reading

Coxhead, E., *Daughters of Erin* (London: Secker and Warburg, 1965).

Irish Art, 1900–1950 (Cork: Crawford Municipal Art Gallery, 1975).

Irish Women Artists (Dublin: National Gallery of Ireland, 1987).

HILARY PYLE

Q

Quakers When the Friends (or Quakers) came to Ireland in the 1650s, they brought radical testimonies against tithes, oaths, and war. Not only was each testimony an affront to the establishment in church and state, Friends propagated them boldly and relentlessly, with the predictable result that they spent a lot of time before magistrates.

From 1663 persecution eased and Friends flourished. A combination of Quaker immigrants and the success of travelling preachers among Puritan settlers raised membership as high as 6,000 by 1688. The next century, however, was a period of consolidation. While eighteenth-century Friends stubbornly maintained the same testimonies as their forebears, they did so quietly now, withdrawing into a subculture. Cut off from many professions and bolstered by frugality and a reputation for painstaking truthfulness, some Friends became successful entrepeneurs. The resulting wealth brought anxiety about excess, and the Friends' rigorous discipline included a scrupulous, even stylized, simplicity.

Friends also became indefatigable campaigners for humanitarian causes, as epitomized in Ireland by their work against the Great Famine. Their whole-hearted efforts, untainted by the slightest hint of proselytism, earned them a place of honour in Irish mythology.

Although in this century membership has fallen steadily (to 1,630 in 1991), the Friends remain an important part of Irish society. Social changes have reduced the direct significance of testimonies against tithes and oaths, but violence is a greater scourge than ever, and any Irish movement for world peace or local reconciliation is likely to enjoy the influence of Friends.

Reading

Wigham, Maurice J., *The Irish Quakers: A Short History of the Religious Society of Friends in Ireland* (Dublin: Historical Committee of the Religious Society of Friends, 1992).

JOSEPH LIECHTY

R

Raftery, Anthony (1779–1835) Poet and musician. Born Kiltamagh, County Mayo; died Croughwell, at Christmas. 'Raiftearaí' spent most of his adult life in County Galway as a travelling poet and musician. Although blind from early childhood, and unable to read or write, his hedge-school education gave him a deep knowledge of Irish history and the classics. He became very well known in his lifetime and he seems to have been an opinion former on political and religious matters among the local population. Many of his poems are sermon-like, didactic works. Raftery's best-known poem is *Eanach Dhúin*, commemorating a boating accident on Lough Corrib on 4 September 1828 when many people from Annaghdown were drowned.

Reading

Ó Coigligh, Ciarán (ed.), *Raiftearaí: amhráin agus dánta* (Baile Átha Cliath: An Clóchomhar, 1987).

BERNADETTE CUNNINGHAM

Ralahine The Ralahine Agricultural and Manufacturing Co-operative Association was a pioneering co-operative society founded on his 618-acre County Clare estate by John Scott Vandaleur in 1831, as an alternative for his tenantry to agrarian secret societies. Consisting of 52 men, women and children and governed by a committee of nine, elected twice yearly, its aim was to acquire common capital and thereby improve the quality of life of its members. It was to pay Vandaleur £700 rent yearly until capital to purchase the estate was acquired. The experiment lasted only two years, foundering on Vandaleur's reckless gambling. He fled the country, and his creditors refused to recognize the commune and seized the estate. *History of Ralahine* by Thomas Craig, who advised on its establishment, was translated into several Continental languages.

JAMES KEMMY

recusancy Recusants were those who refused to attend their parish church for Church of Ireland worship on Sundays and holy days as required by the Irish Acts of Uniformity of 1560 and 1660. The fine for not attending was 12 d, levied by the parish churchwardens. Both dissenters and Catholics were fined. In practice fines were collected only sporadically and were seen more as a potential source of income for the state than a mechanism for changing religious allegiance. They were abolished for dissenters by the 1710 Toleration Act and for Catholics by the 1793 Catholic Relief Act.

BERNADETTE CUNNINGHAM

Red Hand of Ulster Originally, a red right hand cut off at the wrist was the emblem of the O'Neills of Ulster. In the province's arms it appears on a small shield at the centre of a red cross upon a gold field. The legend associating it with a chieftain who served his hand and threw it ashore to claim possession lacks substance, as it also appears elsewhere. Some authorities suggest a connection with the red branch knights. Confusingly, a red *left* hand became the badge of the English order of baronets, created by James I to raise funds for the defence of the Ulster plantation. It has become a Unionist symbol, widely employed in loyalist iconography, perhaps connoting a hand raised in loyalty or in bloodily signifying 'no'. The Red Hand Commandos, a small paramilitary grouping, emerged in 1972.

Reading

Belfast Museum and Art Gallery Bulletin 1, no. 4 (1951).

W. HARVEY COX

Redmond, John (1856–1918) Politician. Born County Wexford. Redmond was the son of an MP and educated in Dublin at Clongowes Wood College and Trinity College. He was elected MP from 1881 to 1918, and became a principal lieutenant of Charles Stewart Parnell. He supported Parnell during the split over the divorce case in 1890, and led the minority Parnellite section of the Irish Parliamentary Party until it reunited in 1900, when he was accepted as leader. His support kept Asquith's Liberal government in power after the 1910 elections, and, in return, he secured the introduction of the Third Home Rule Bill in 1912. A believer in the British empire and Ireland's role in it, he urged the Irish Volunteers in 1914 to join the British army. Militant nationalists opposed this, and Redmond increasingly misjudged the changing mood of Irish public opinion, especially after the 1916 Rising. Opposed to partition, he was never able to secure Home Rule and died a disappointed man. Within months his party was overwhelmed by Sinn Féin in the December 1918 general election.

Reading

Bew, Paul, *Conflict and Conciliation in Ireland, 1890–1910: Parnellites and Radical Agrarians* (Oxford: Oxford University Press, 1987).
—— *Ideology and the Irish Question: Ulster Unionism and Irish Nationalism, 1912–1916* (Oxford: Oxford University Press, 1994).
Laffan, M., 'John Redmond and Home Rule', in C. Brady (ed.), *Worsted in the Game: Losers in Irish History* (Dublin: Lilliput Press, 1989).
Lyons, F.S.L., *The Irish Parliamentary Party 1890–1910* (London: Greenwood Press, 1975).
—— 'Dillon, Redmond and the Irish Home Rulers', in F.A. Martin (ed.), *Leaders and Men of the Easter Rising: Dublin 1916* (London: Methuen, 1967).

JIM O'HARA

referendums Amendments to the constitution, itself approved by plebiscite in 1937, must be sanctioned by popular referendum. The first attempted amendment, in 1959, failed when the electorate narrowly rejected a Fianna Fáil proposal to abolish proportional representation. A second attempt to achieve the same aim failed, by a much larger majority, in 1968. Subsequent referendums, with one exception, have had greater success. In 1972 the electorate approved Irish entry into the European Community, and in the same year amendments were carried which reduced the voting age from 21 to 18 and which delated the Article according a 'special position' to the Catholic church. In 1979 two more referendums permitted a reform of adoption law and a change in Seanad university repesentation. The controversial 1983 referendum inserted in Article 40 this subsection: 'The state recognises the right to life of the unborn and with due regard to the equal right to life of the mother, guarantees in its laws to respect and as far as practicable by its laws to defend and vindicate that right.' In 1984 a referendum approved voting rights in Ireland for citizens of other EC countries, and in 1987 another referendum permitted the government to ratify the Single European Act, which had been judged unconstitutional by the Supreme Court. Meanwhile, in 1986 a proposal to remove the ban on divorce from the consitution was heavily defeated.

In 1992 the government revived the abortion issue with another referendum on the subject, as a result of which, the electorate voted for the provision of information on abortion and the right to travel abroad. In 1995 a referendum on divorce was passed by a small majority in favour of allowing divorce in cases where the couple had lived apart for four years or more.

More importantly, on the political front, a referendum held in June 1998, gave the taoiseach, Bertie Ahern, an overwhelming mandate in favour of dropping Ireland's Constitutional claim over Northern Ireland, a move which considerably aided the achievement of a peace settlement after 30 years of 'the Troubles'.

JAMES DOWNEY

Reformation The European Reformation of the sixteenth century was an immensely complex phenomenon. It started in 1517 as a rather recondite theological challenge to the orthodoxy of the later medieval Catholic church by a German Augustinian, Martin Luther; it rapidly developed into a widespread reform movement, as Protestant preaching gained a popular hold; it was soon sucked into the vortex of diplomacy and politics, as kings and princes sought to impose religious uniformity upon their subjects and exploit the Reformation for their own ends; and finally the Reformation was inextricably linked to the changing social and economic circumstances of the transition from medieval to early modern Europe.

Each country was unique in the way these forces combined. In England, secular issues predominated: it was Henry VIII's desire for a divorce which led him to break with the papacy. Though there was a group of committed Protestants in Henry's England, the English Reformation under Henry was essentially concerned not with doctrine but with authority – substituting the king for the pope as head of the church following Henry's quarrel with the papacy over his divorce. It was not till the reigns of Edward VI (1547–53) and Elizabeth (1558–1603) that it is possible to describe the English Reformation as Protestant. Even quite late in the sixteenth century, the degree of progress which Protestantism had made at a parochial level varied considerably in different areas of England.

In Ireland as in England the Reformation was imposed as a result of dynastic politics: in 1536 the Irish Parliament followed the example of its English counterpart by declaring Henry supreme head of the church. But though the English Reformation provided a powerful model for the progress of the Reformation in Ireland, the Irish context was substantially different, and, of course, the end result totally contrary. In England state, church and people became Protestant: in Ireland church and state adopted the Reformation, but the people remained resolutely Catholic.

The importance of the Reformation for Irish history is therefore very different from that of England or Continental countries, where it marked a decisive shift in religious loyalties, from Catholic to Protestant uniformity. The historical significance of the Reformation in Ireland is that, in its vital popular dimension, it failed, and in failing, created a basic and continuing divide in Irish history – that between Protestant and Catholic, between a Protestant state and established church on the one hand, and a largely Catholic people on the other. Into this basic framework of religious division, the further complexities of political, social ideological and economic divisions have to be woven, giving rise to the subtle complexities of Irish early modern and modern history.

Though the end result of these historical processes is self-evident – an Ireland divided between Protestant minority and Catholic majority – the processes through which this emerged, and the way in which the various forces combined to produce such a result, are much more difficult to trace, and, as a consequence, the disentangling of cause and effect in the first hundred years of the Irish Reformation constitutes a considerable challenge to historians. Traditionally, there has been a tendency, not unnatural given the depth of the religious divide in later centuries, to read these later antitheses and confessional attitudes back into the early Reformation. The authoritative account of relations between church and state in the Reformation period attributed the country's loyalty to the pope to its 'Fundamentally Catholic disposition', and repeatedly pointed to the intense popular distaste for and resentment at the imposition of religious changes during Henry's reign. The standard (Protestant) history of the Church of Ireland attributed the failure of the Reformation to the backwardness of the Irish people, their lack of education, subjection to ignorant chieftains, dependence upon superstitious priests, and 'slipshod . . . moral conduct'.

In recent decades, however, historians have been looking anew at the development of the division between Catholicism and Protestantism in early modern Ireland, re-evaluating casual assumptions about the inevitability of the success of the former and the failure of the latter, assessing when precisely the division arose, and trying to understand the nexus of forces that gave rise to it. In order to do this, the different stages of the Reformation have to be examined separately, first the Henrician enforcement of royal supremacy, then the beginnings of the Protestant Reformation under Edward VI and Elizabeth, and finally the consolidation of the two religious traditions under James I and Charles I.

Henry VIII

The main impact of the Reformation upon Ireland in its first two decades was threefold. First it made the king head of the church. At parochial level this probably made little difference, but for bishops it meant that they had to take the oath of supremacy, and accept their see from Henry rather than the pope. The extent to which Irish bishops did so has been the subject of vitriolic debate amongst Irish historians in the nineteenth century. Modern scholars have concluded that the Dublin government was relatively successful in gaining support for royal supremacy, even from bishops outside the Pale and those areas subject to the direct influence of royal writ. Second, it led to the dissolution of the monasteries. Traditionally this has been seen as a religious, social and cultural calamity, as the traditions and endowments of centuries were swept away, leading to 'the disorganisation of religion and the retarding of all religious development throughout Ireland, for nearly three centuries'. A more recent study has substantially revised this view, arguing that many of the monastic houses which were dissolved were in any case 'sick to death', that the local communities, far from being deeply resentful at the destruction of their religious heritage, hardly reacted at all to the dissolution, and finally that 25 years after Henry VIII's death 'it is difficult to find evidence of the ill effects of the suppression'.

The third way in which the Reformation affected religious life was in the changes that were made to liturgical and popular religious practice. Some of these were minor, such as the removal of references to the papacy in prayers, but others have been painted as major assaults upon indigenous piety. Again, however, traditional assumptions have recently been revised: the official campaign to destroy shrines and images in the Pale (1538–9), seen by one historian as deeply alienating the religious public, is portrayed by another as a moderate attempt to counter the fraudulent use of images which aroused little popular opposition.

The sum of these revisions is a much less pessimistic picture of the progress of the Reformation. It is true that it still laboured under immense handicaps: the Dublin government had only limited power to enforce royal supremacy, even in the areas it did control; in the remoter areas of Ireland the church continued in its familiar medieval style; the ideal of a vernacular Bible was unattainable because of the government's distaste for proselytizing in Gaelic; little preaching or evangelizing took place for want of committed and trained clergy. It is true that there is very little evidence for the emergence of indigenous Protestantism. But the very lack of doctrinal thrust, and the very caution of the government in its approach to enforcing the Reformation, both ensured that alienation and hostility to its message were limited. So long as the Reformation was limited to the enforcement of royal supremacy, it stood a chance of success.

Edward VI and Elizabeth

The problem was that this cautious *modus vivendi* could not be sustained. The Reformation was not a vague Erasmian reformist movement. It became apparent in the reign of Edward VI and Elizabeth that it was a Protestant Reformation, which involved doctrinal choice on the part of clergy and laity. At roughly the same time, political, economic and cultural elements combined further to polarize Irish society. As a result in the second stage of the Reformation, in the second half of the sixteenth century, the familiar division between Protestant and Catholic begins to appear.

Various components contributed to this polarization. In the established church, bishops who had conformed under Henry VIII found the liturgical changes of Edward's reign, with their markedly Protestant emphasis, unacceptable. Increasingly, the Dublin authorities turned to England to find committed (though not always competent) protestant replacements. The foundation of Trinity College, Dublin, in 1592 represented a belated attempt to train doctrinally committed clergy in Ireland. The growth in the power of the state, which by 1603 extended to the whole of the island, was paralleled by a similar extension of the ambit of the established church. The extent of its ministry at a parochial level was severely limited, however, by impoverishment – benefices were poor, and several had to be combined in order to support one preaching minister; by a consequent shortage of clergy; and by the inability of those ministers the church did secure to preach in the language of the people, and in some cases by their outright hostility to the Gaelic language. The result was that the Protestant church tended to cater only for those who were already Protestant – recent immigrants, settlers, Dublin officials.

On the Catholic side, the 1570s and 1580s saw the development of a new sense of self-consciousness, as, following the excommunication of Elizabeth, the arrival of seminary-trained priests and missionaries in Ireland, and the increasing resort of Irish students to Counter-Reformation educational centres on the Continent, Catholics in Ireland began to absent themselves from the services of the Church of Ireland, resist the attempts of the state to force them to conform through legal action and fines, and develop a separate, often underground Catholic church. In the political, the policy of plantation, the entrusting of official positions increasingly to recent new English administrators, the gradual exclusion of the Catholic Anglo-Irish from positions of responsibility, and the imposition of cess and other taxes and duties upon the populace by the Dublin government all combined to place under strain the relations between government and governed. Culturally the determination of the English-born leaders of the Church of Ireland to link Protestantism to anglicization, and their persistent denigration of Gaelic culture, widened the gulf between the native Irish population and the established church.

There was, in short, a fortuitous combination of four elements – Protestantization of the Church of Ireland, increasing Catholic religious consciousness and assertiveness, political tensions, and cultural alienation – which conspired to produce by the early seventeenth century two distinctive communities divided by religion.

Whether the Catholic assertiveness predated Protestant failure and elitism is far from clear. On the one hand, the inability of the Church of Ireland to win over the Irish people can be accounted for in terms of its own internal problems, inadequacies and inherent contradictions. On the other hand it can also be attributed to the strength of the Catholic opposition and resurgence in the second half of the century. It is possible as well to downplay the significance of purely religious motivation, and argue that political and cultural alienation played an equally important part in the increasing conflict and division in late sixteenth century Irish society.

Whatever the precise causation, it is apparent that at some stage in the 1570s and 1580s, or maybe even earlier, the familiar division between Catholic and Protestant begins to emerge distinctly in Irish history, as, for the first time, religious labels are applied to individuals, and religious motivation comes to the fore in public fora such as Parliament, and in the endemic rebellions and revolts of early modern Ireland.

James I and Charles I

The early seventeenth century as a result marked the third stage of the Irish Reformation, the consolidation of the Protestant position in church and state. As the failure to convert the Irish population began to be absorbed as a more than temporary possibility, the patterns of Protestant thought and policy were explored and established, and a distinctive Protestant outlook and intellectual tradition constructed. The Irish Articles of Faith of 1615 spelt out at length the distinctive Calvinist theology of the Church of Ireland. The development of anti-Catholic polemical theology further re-examined and reinterpreted on both sides of the religious divide to bolster each side's claim to be the true church. James Ussher, archbishop of Armagh, the outstanding intellect amongst the Protestant hierarchy, in his book published in 1631, *A Discourse of the Religion Anciently Professed by the Irish and British*, sought to demonstrate that the early Irish church had been, to all intents and purposes, Protestant in its doctrine, and that the Irish Reformation had, consequently merely rescued this pure church from the 'Roman superstition' into which it had sunk in the later Middle Ages.

The Reformation in Ireland, then, combined in a unique way with the dramatic political, social, economic and military events of the sixteenth century to produce by the early seventeenth century a remarkable religious settlement. In an era that saw uniformity in religion as essential for the safety of both state and souls, Ireland stood the standard Reformation dictum, *cuius regio, eius religio* (the head of a state determines its religion), on its head. Rather, the Counter-Reformation had in Ireland managed to succeed directly against the wishes of the head of state. The resulting anomaly was laden with tensions and ambiguities, which became apparent in subsequent centuries as the established Protestant church tried to come to terms with its role and position in a largely Catholic land.

Reading

Bottigheimer, K.S., 'The failure of the reformation in Ireland: *une question bien posée*', *Journal of Ecclesiastical History* xxxvi (1986).

Bradshaw, B.I., 'George Brown, first reformation Archbishop of Dublin', *Journal of Ecclesiastical History* xxi (1970).

—— *The Dissolution of the Religious Orders in Ireland under Henry VIII* (Cambridge: Cambridge University Press, 1974).

——'The Edwardian reformation in Ireland, 1547–53', *Archivium Hibernicum* xxxiv (1976–7).

—— 'Sword, word and strategy in the reformation in Ireland', *Historical Journal* xxi (1978).

Canny, N., 'Why the reformation failed in Ireland: *une question mal posée*', *Journal of Ecclesiastical History* xxx (1979).

Clarke, A., 'Varieties of uniformity: the first century of the Church of Ireland', in W.J. Sheils and D. Wood (eds), *The Churches, Ireland and the Irish* Studies in Church History, xxv (Oxford: Blackwell, 1989).

Edwards, R.D., *Church and State in Tudor Ireland* (Dublin: Longmans, Green, 1935).

Ford, A., 'The protestant reformation in Ireland', in C. Brady and R. Gillespie (eds), *Natives and Newcomers* (Dublin: Irish Academic Press, 1986).

—— *The Protestant Reformation in Ireland, 1590–1641* (Frankfurt: Peter Lang, 1987).

Knox, R.B., *James Ussher, Archbishop of Armagh* (Cardiff: University of Wales Press, 1967).

Phillips, W.A. (ed.), *History of the Church of Ireland*, 3 vols (London: Oxford University Press, 1933–4).

ALAN FORD

Reid, J. Graham (1945–) Playwright. Born Belfast. Reid gave up schoolteaching following the success of *The Death of Humpty-Dumpty* (1979) and *The Closed Door* (1980). Other plays include *Dorothy* (1980), *The Hidden Curriculum* (1982) and *Remembrance* (1984). Violent interactions of terrorism, sexuality and guilt feature strongly in Reid's writing, which, since *The Billy Trilogy* (BBC, 1982–4), is mainly for television.

GER FITZGIBBON

Reid, Nano (1905–81) Painter and graphic artist. Born and died in Drogheda, County Louth. Reid studied at the Metropolitan School of Art in Dublin, in London under Bernard Meninsky, and later in Paris. She was one of the strongest personalities identified with the Irish Exhibition of Living Art in its early, creative years, and a close friend and associate of Dillon, Campbell, etc. From relatively conventional beginnings, she evolved via a lyrical, personal Expressionism into a style close to that of the Action Painters in America, though on a modest scale. Often working in rather low, ochrous tones, she created a web of brushstrokes through which a buried radiance seems to struggle. A retrospective exhibition was seen in Belfast and Dublin in 1974–5, and a large memorial exhibition was mounted in the Drogheda Arts centre in 1991.

BRIAN FALLON

religious orders Whatever the ambiguities and uncertainties of the immediate post-Reformation years, it became clear at an early date that there would be no place for religious community life, either for men or for women in the new order. The dissolution of the monasteries (of which the great majority were Cistercian) was a fairly rapid process, and painless only for a minority of abbots and other office holders who accepted compensatory pensions or preferment within the reformed establishment. Some monks and nuns survived dispersal by living in as close conformity to their rule as was possible in the circumstances, and by 1600 the Cistercian remnant was joined by a small contingent of their brethren from Spain. The other monastic foundations – Knights Hospitallers, Trinitarians, Benedictines and one small Carthusian community – died out, and of these only the Benedictines were re-established in Ireland (in the twentieth century).

The case of the friars is different. Franciscans, Dominicans, Augustinians and Carmelites were well established in priories and convents from the twelfth and thirteenth centuries, in Dublin and the other towns, and in the countryside where they enjoyed both Gaelic and 'Old English' patronage. But even the most 'conventualized' among them retained something of their original pastoral vocation as mendicants and, to some extent, itinerants (not sharing the *stabilitas* of monasticism). And 'observant' revivals and devotional movements had made considerable ground during the century preceding the Reformation.

These developments were strongest amongst the Gaelic communities, whose growing influence in this period led to greater independence for their orders. Generally speaking it can be said that, despite some defections, the friars maintained a sturdy opposition to the new ordinances, and that their religious convictions were not untinged by a nascent 'national' consciousness.

On the eve of the Reformation they formed some 250 communities, most of them scattered by the reign of Elizabeth I, though conditions in some areas made a discreetly continued observance still possible. Some friars retired completely into secular life, while others went into exile, joining communities of their respective orders on the Continent. This exodus was to form the basis for what may be seen as the great Irish contribution to the Counter-Reformation. Certainly their strong Continental links, especially with Rome, were to stand the friars in good stood, and would be a significant resource for the Irish church in difficult times.

The Stuart succession to the English throne was generally welcomed by Irish Catholics as signalling a new era of tolerance, if not restoration. In fact, the first half of the sixteenth century was a period of intensive colonialism (although unevenly administered), during which internal church reform and redevelopment were pursued with varying success. This revival was supported by the first wave of 'new priests' from the Irish colleges and seminaries which had been set up in Catholic Europe, and these included friars, chiefly Franciscan and Dominican from Louvain and Rome. A newly constituted branch of the Franciscan family also appeared in Ireland in 1615, in the person of the Capuchin, Francis Nugent: ten years later the first Carmelites arrived. The story of their first mission is brief and tragic: their communities were erected into a province in 1638, but dissolved 15 years later, the result of Cromwellian persecution.

Indeed, following the brief exhilaration of the Confederation years (1641–9), Cromwell's military campaign, conducted with all the ruthless fanaticism of a crusade, came as a savage blow to Catholic hopes not only of renewal but even of survival. Friars of all orders are to be counted among the Cromwellian martyrs, and after 'pacification' many of the surviving brethren suffered imprisonment or deportation. For those who remained it was the era of the Mass-rock and the priest-hunter, while for the people as a whole it was a time of large-scale dispossession and confiscation.

The Restoration of 1660 heralded another false dawn for Catholic hopes. The reign of Charles II did provide considerable relief from some of the worst aspects of life under the Commonwealth, but toleration, while widespread, was liable to sudden relapses into severe discrimination, and, after the 'popish plot' episode (1678), outright persecution. Institutionally the church had to reorganize once again, and this time the role of the friars can be seen as somewhat ambivalent, at least in the case of the Franciscans, a considerable number of whom, especially in the northern province, were at odds with the Primate, archbishop Oliver Plunkett (now canonized), and among whom a few individuals were involved in his downfall and heroic death. And the fact that one of the Franciscans' number, Peter Walsh, was a leader of the highly controversial 'Remonstrance' movement (denounced as disloyal to the pope) did not help matters. To Walsh, incidentally, we are indebted for an estimate of the numbers of the friars in the country in 1665, including some 400 of his own order, with 200 Dominicans and 100 Augustinians, as well as some smaller groups including 20 Capuchins and 25 Discalced Carmelites (newly reconstituted). These figures are probably inflated but, undoubtedly, numbers had been swollen since the Restoration, mainly by new recruits, many of whom were accommodated in makeshift novitiates throughout the country (these were to be a long-term matter for dispute and disciplinary disapproval), but also by a new wave from the Continent.

Certainly those who looked forward to complete freedom for Catholics under a Catholic monarch, whose accession seemed certain, saw that the needs of the faithful could only be met by an enlarged priesthood, and that the friars would play a valuable part in this new pastoral situation. When James II did come to the throne (1685), there were indeed a few short years of exuberent activity. The Dominican and Franciscan habits were worn with pride in town and country, and in new schools of philosophy and the humanities. But once again hopes were dashed, and the Williamite wars, culminating for the Irish in the Treaty of Limerick (1691), were soon succeeded by the dark decades of the penal laws.

These 'laws against popery' were mainly directed against Catholic property and political rights, in order to prevent any possible recrudescence of Catholic power. In this they were very largely sucessful – by 1778 only 5 per cent of Irish land was in Catholic hands. But a steady increase in the Catholic population (1.67 million in 1766 as against 0.68 million Protestants) provided the sinews for what by the end of the century was a new, emerging 'Catholic nation', the great majority of whom were desperately poor, but with a modestly prospering minority in both the tenant farmer and commercial classes.

Against this background, it is possible to see the 'penal days' as a highly unpleasant phase in Irish social history with little direct effect on Catholic life as such. But in fact, the first half of the century was marked by severe interference with religious practice, amounting in the first decades to active persecution. Bishops and members of religious orders had been ordered to leave the country by 1 May 1688, and for the few who defied the order it was a repeat of the Cromwellian experience.

In 1704 a system of registration for parish clergy was set up: their activities were sharply restricted, and any breach of the regulations under which they laboured was punishable – in some cases by death. Some 1,089 priests were registered, but of these only 33 remained legally in office after 1708, when the vast majority refused an anti-Stuart oath which pledged support to 'the Protestant succession'. Soon the priest-catcher was back in business, and what has been described as 'active if sporadic persecution of the clergy' continued until about 1730. Nevertheless, by that year nearly all dioceses had bishops, and that other forbidden species, the friars, were openly ministering in 'mass-houses' in a number of centres – and not only friars, but Jesuits and even at least one Cistercian monk.

The fragmented remains of the religious orders, friars in particular, did in fact show a remarkable tenacity, and indeed grew in numbers over the first half of the century. Conditions of course varied from place to place, and in some, local officers of the law were disposed to turn a blind eye. In Galway, for example, an account book of the Augustinian priory records a sum of 1 shilling and 1 penny 'for a bottle of wine for the sheriffs', while the Dominicans noted spending twice that sum 'for claret to treat the sheriffs in their search'.

Needless to say, the search proved negative, although we know that, as well as the two communities mentioned, there were at least one other friary (Franciscan) and three 'nunneries which the papists commonly call boarding-schools'. These three were a relatively new feature of the Catholic landscape (there were few such convents in the country before the Reformation), but convents were by now established in Dublin, Drogheda, Loughrea (Discalced Carmelites) and possibly Cork. Devoted to the education of young women, these sisters (mainly Franciscan, Dominican and Augustinian) attracted little unfavourable attention. Most of them had returned from Continental convents, to which a steady *émigré* stream, beginning in the early seventeenth century, would continue through the eighteenth, even surviving the upheavals of the French Revolution – as in the case of the Irish Benedictine nuns at Ypres, now at Kylemore, County

Galway. We must also note the Irish Dominican convent of Born Successo in Lisbon. Founded in 1639, it continued to flourish throughout the following centuries (the sisters escaped injury in the great earthquake of 1755) and down to our own time: in 1991 the community received the first woman president of Ireland, Dr Mary Robinson.

But Ypres, Lisbon and a very few others were exceptional cases: most Irish nuns in exile lived their lives in Continental communities, and our record is partial – even of their names. Only a small proportion returned to Ireland, compared with their brethren from colleges in Rome, Louvain, Prague, Lisbon and elsewhere, who continued to swell the ranks of their orders at home in the first half of the eighteenth century and gave bishops to several dioceses, including one archbishop of Dublin, the Dominican John Troy. In the north, however, many – especially among the Franciscans – were the product of hasty recruitment and inadequate formation. So, by 1750, higher authority decided to call a halt. A decree of Pope Benedict XIV, subjecting all religious orders to strict episcopal discipline and limiting their work in parishes, led to a rapid decine in their numbers and their influence. Over 150 years were to pass before the friars recovered anything like their old vitality. But their pastoral ministry, if restricted, continued to provide a much valued service, especially in Dublin and certain other towns. Nineteenth-century Ireland owed much to the Capuchin Father Theobald Mathew, the 'apostle of temperance', to the Dominican patriot preacher Father Tom Burke; to the Augustinian bishop Doyle, reformer and pamphleteer, commonly known as 'JKL'; and to the Carmelite John Spratt, a pioneer of practical social concern in Dublin's inner city.

Concern for the poor, in town and country, had in fact become an ever more urgent aspect of religious commitment from the last decades of the eighteenth century, in view of a population explosion in the 'lower strata' of Irish society, until the Great Famine of 1847–8 with its toll of millions in death and emigration. The pioneers among the new 'social' religious were three women: Nano Nagle, Mary Aikenhead and Catherine McAuley, foundresses respectively of the Presentation Sisters (1775), the Irish Sisters of Charity (1815) and the Sisters of Mercy (1831). Their work in teaching and care of the sick was quite outstanding. Two societies of men teachers, the Irish Christian Brothers and the Presentation Brothers, were set up in 1802 (by Edmund Ignatius Rice, a Waterford merchant), to be followed in 1808 by the Patrician Brothers, and later (1881) by the De La Salle and Marist Brothers.

These Irish foundations were joined by Irish branches of Continental sisterhoods: Ursulines (1771), Loreto (1821) and Sacred Heart (1841), Little Sisters of the Poor (1868) and others. And the nineteenth century saw a considerable incursion of 'modern' congregations of men religious, begining with the Vincentians in 1835 and including Passionists, Redemptorists, Oblates, Holy Ghost and Marist Fathers and Rosminians. As preachers and educators, these played a very significant part in 'modernizing' the post-emancipation church, and in the formation of an Irish version of the prevailing Franco-Italian religious culture.

The national revival – political, social, cultural – which marked the first decades of the twentieth century was matched by a resurgence in the life of the Catholic Church, not least among the religious orders, new and old. As well as world-wide missionary activity (including that of new Irish organizations such as the Columban and Kiltegan Fathers and the Medical Missionaries of Mary), there was a notable, growing involvement by the friars and other religious in Irish life, especially following the establishment of the Irish state in 1922. (The first papal nuncio was an Irish-born Franciscan, Archbishop Paschal Robinson.) And they continued to play a significant part in the spiritual life of the faithful. Numbers steadily rose until the aftermath of the Second Vatican Council (1962–5), since when there has been a decline – part of a common phenomenon, in Western Europe especially. But Irish friars, Jesuits and other religious have been among the leaders of Catholic renewal in recent years.

One remarkable aspect of religious life in the twentieth century has been a flourishing monastic revival. The Cistercians, who were re-established in the Abbey of Mount Mellary, have several new foundations in or near old sites. The Premonstratensians are in County Cavan, and the Benedictines in their first Irish abbey in Glenstal, County Limerick, have become a national focus for ecumenical and liturgical activity.

Indeed, monks, friars and the religious orders generally have also a considerable influence on the wider culture. Individuals have been leaders in a much-needed renewal of church art and architecture, and in this and in the literary and musical fields have done much to bridge the gap between sacred and secular. They follow an honourable tradition. The *émigré* friars of the seventeenth century, who became part of the Counter-Reformation movement in theology and pastoral care, did not escape the influence of the baroque, which has been called the artistic idiom of that movement. The Franciscans especially, in their literary output printed and published in Louvain and Rome and Prague, did more than provide spiritual reading for Irish Catholics: they made a very significant contribution to the evolution of modern literature in the Gaelic language. They were not alone: in Ireland, the Dominican Padraigín Haicéad was one of the most imortant seventeenth-century poets, and, in the following century the Augustinian Liam was a considerable figure in the literary life of the 'Hidden Ireland'. His verse shows a preoccupation with European affairs, of which he was clearly a keen observer. And here we have a pointer to what has been perhaps the principal element in the cultural influence of the religious orders over the centuries. In fair weather and foul, the Continental link was maintained, and an often close involvement in developments at home – secular as well as ecclesiastical – has never been allowed to obscure the larger vision. This has had a valuable effect on Irish thought and practice, notably in education both formal and informal, and in the cultivation of the arts, and may be seen as serving the development of an idea of nationality placed within a European framework.

SEÁN MAC RÉAMOINN

Repeal The Repeal of the Act of Union of 1801 was the political *idée fixe* of Daniel O'Connell. In its pure essence, the Repeal demand was a demand for the re-establishment of an independent Irish Parliament, equal in status to the Westminster Parliament, but under a common crown. Throughout the campaign, the constitutional purity of Repeal was frequently diluted by O'Connell, though he never wavered in his expressions of political and personal loyalty to the crown.

O'Connell launched his Repeal campaign almost immediately after his campaign for Catholic emancipation had achieved its goal in 1829. Despite some encouraging evidence of continuing popular support in nationalist Ireland (though with Ulster Unionism already unshakeably hostile), the early phase of the Repeal campaign, lacking support from any significant section of British parliamentary opinion, had run into the ground by 1834. For the remainder of the decade O'Connell suspended the Repeal campaign, and contented himself with seeking 'justice for Ireland' by instalments, in partnership with the Whig-Liberal government. Warning signs of the impending return to office of his arch-enemy, Peel, prompted O'Connell to relaunch his campaign, styled the Loyal National Repeal Association, in July 1840, and he soon began to deploy again the impressively full repertoire of his skills of political agitation.

'Monster' meetings were held at historic sites; Repeal reading rooms were established as centres of evangelism for the cause; local leaders (styled 'Repeal wardens') were to be

503

sober in every sense of the word, giving moral as well as political example. The Catholic clergy rowed in with strong support. The *Nation* newspaper (from 1842) led a formidable wave of propogandist writings. A rich store of nationalist symbols was deployed in creating and mobilizing a large popular following for Repeal, Resorting to his familiar brinkmanship, O'Connell declared 1843 'the Repeal year'. It was not to be. Peel determined to face down the challenge. A 'monster' meeting planned for October 1843 at Clontarf was banned by the government, with a strong show of military force. O'Connell cancelled the meeting to avoid bloodshed, and, while the momentum of his campaign did not immediately slacken, his hand had been called. He would not risk serious violence, and his followers were prepared to obey him. The threat that rebellion and anarchy would follow, if the people's demands were ignored, was exposed as an empty one.

A prison sentence helped keep O'Connell's stock high. But, gradually, divisions opened up within the Repeal ranks on matters of policy and of personality. In particular, the disagreements between O'Connell and the Young Irelanders became increasingly bitter. The deepening crisis of the famine and the waning of O'Connell's powers provided a grim backdrop to the lingering death of the Repeal movement. Despite the energetic, if politically inept, efforts of O'Connell's son John to keep the campaign alive, the Repeal movement, already deeply riven and losing coherence, was finally overwhelmed by the catastrophe of the great Irish famine.

Reading

Boyce, D. George, *Nationalism in Ireland* (Dublin: Gill and Macmillan, 1982).

Kerr, D., *Peel, Priests and Politics: Sir Robert Peel's Administration and the Roman Catholic Church in Ireland, 1841–46* (Oxford: 1982).

MacDonagh, Oliver, *O'Connell: The Life of Daniel O'Connell 1775–1847* (London: Weidenfeld and Nicolson, 1991).

Macintyre, A., *The Liberator: Daniel O'Connell and the Irish Party 1830–1847* (London: 1965).

Nowlan, K.B., *The Politics of Repeal: A Study of the Relations between Great Britain and Ireland 1841–50* (London: 1965).

M.A.G. Ó TUATHAIGH

Republicanism before 1860 Until the rise of the Fenian movement in the late 1850s, the Republican 'tradition' in Ireland had been a short-lived one. Attempts to separate the two kingdoms were not new even by the 1790s, but Republicanism as an expression of Irish separatist aspirations is now seen as having originated with the United Irishmen's failed rebellion against British rule in 1798. The republican sentiment which would later inform the ideology of the Irish Republican Brotherhood and later still that of the Irish Free State and Republic began with the French Revolution. The doctrine of classless, creedless rebellion, however, was ill suited to the Georgian and Victorian Irish environment and was slow to spread with any conviction to the lower classes. The Young Ireland movement of the 1840s attempted, unsucessfully in the short term, to 'Gaelicize' the Republican sentiment, removing it from its French antecedents and infusing it with strong home-grown cultural overtones, some of which were rooted in historical fiction.

GERARD O'BRIEN

Roberts, Michael (1817–82) Mathematician. Born Cork, 18 April; died Dublin, 4 October. Roberts graduated from Trinity College, Dublin, in 1838, and became a Fellow in 1843. He was professor of mathematics 1862–79. He published important papers on the properties of geodesic lines and lines of curvature on the ellipsoid, and on the trigonometry of hyperelliptic functions.

DAVID SMITH

Roberts, Thomas (1748–78) Painter. Born Waterford; died Lisbon. The son of an architect, Roberts is sometimes confused with his brother Thomas Sautelle Roberts (*c.*1760–1826). He attended the Dublin Society's School from 1763 and was the pupil of Mannin, Mullins and Butts. By 1766 he was exhibiting at the Society of Artists. He was patronized by the duke of Leinster, Lord Powerscourt and others. His early topographical views soon gave way to Romantic landscapes of the highest quality, evoking poetically the changing moods of the Irish landscape. Some were engraved by Milton in his *Collection of Select Views* (1783–1793).

Reading

Crookshank, A. and the Knight of Glin, *The Painters of Ireland, c. 1660–1920* (London: Barrie and Jenkins, 1978).

Strickland, W.G., *A Dictionary of Irish Artists* (Shannon: Irish University Press, 1968).

Wynne, M., *Thomas Roberts 1748–1778* (Dublin: National Gallery of Ireland, 1978).

HILARY PYLE

Robinson, Esmé Stuart Lennox (1886–1958) Playwright and theatre director, and a major figure in Irish drama. Born Cork; died Dublin. Robinson wrote over 20 plays, mostly gently satiric comedies of provincial life. The term 'the well-made play' is particularly applicable to his work; the influence of both Ibsen and Chekhov may readily be seen. His enduring comedy *Drama at Inish* (1933) concerns actors and audiences who take message-plays too seriously. Several of his plays were produced in the West End and on Broadway, but now they are generally revived only in Ireland; the best are *The White-Headed Boy* (1916), *The Big House* (1926) and *The Far-Off Hills* (1928). *Church Street* (1934) is deliberately Pirandellan. He held managerial and production posts at the Abbey Theatre, where he directed over 100 plays. He wrote *Ireland's Abbey Theatre: A History 1899–1951* (1951) and edited John B. Yeats's *Letters* (1920) and Lady Gregory's *Journals* (1946).

CHRISTOPHER FITZSIMON

Robinson, Mary (1944–) First female president of the Republic of Ireland. Born Ballina, County Mayo. Both Robinson's parents were doctors, and she was educated at convent boarding school in Dublin, Trinity College, Dublin, and Harvard University. At 25 years of age, she became Trinity's youngest professor of law and subsequently barrister and senator. She became both well known and controversial for her support for radical reforms in human and civil rights, and her campaigning for feminist causes in areas such as birth control and divorce. She joined the Labour Party but was twice defeated (1977, 1981) in elections to the Dáil. She resigned from the party in 1985 as the result of Labour's support for the Anglo-Irish Agreement, claiming that Ulster Unionists had not been properly consulted, yet in 1993 publicly shook hands with Gerry Adams. In 1990 she stood as an independent candidate for the presidency, with the support of Labour and other smaller parties and, against all expectations, won the election in November. Her election was viewed by many as a turning point, representing a new, younger, liberal, pluralist Irish society with a prominent role for women. Her energy, eloquence and intelligence made this first female president the most popular in history. In 1997 Robinson stood down to take on the role of United Nations High Commissioner for Human Rights, and immediately took up the causes of Rwandan refugees and Somalian fanine victims.

Reading

Finlay, Fergus, *Mary Robinson: A President with a Purpose* (Dublin: O'Brien Press, 1990).

O'Sullivan, Eoin, 'The 1990 presidential elections in the Republic of Ireland', *Irish Political Studies* (1991).

O'Sullivan, Michael, *Mary Robinson: The Life and Times of an Irish Liberal* (Dublin: Blackwater Press, 1993).

JIM O'HARA

Roche, Sir Boyle (1743–1807) Soldier and politician. Best known for his inimitable 'bulls' (self-contradictory propositions) in the Irish House of Commons, Roche served in the British army in the American War of Independence before entering politics. First elected to represent the constituency of Tralee in 1777, he was not sufficiently affluent to maintain an independent political stance. A supporter of Dublin Castle, he cultivated an acquaintance with the Catholic earl of Kenmare in the early 1780s hoping that this might prove advantageous. This came to nothing, but Roche ensured the long-term good will of Dublin Castle, and his faltering political career, by providing George Ogle with a forged letter (reputedly by Lord Kenmare) which disrupted the Grand National Convention of Volunteer Delegates convened in Dublin in November 1783 to advance the cause of parliamentary reform.

Reading

Kelly, James, 'The parliamentary reform movement and the Catholic question 1782–85', *Archivium Hibernicum* 43 (1988).

McLysaght, E. (ed.), *Kenmare Manuscripts* (Dublin: Irish Manuscripts Commission, 1942).

JAMES KELLY

Rodgers, W.R. William Robert (1909–69) Presbyterian minister and poet. Born County Antrim. Rodgers's first collection of poetry, *Awake! And Other Poems* (1941), led Louis MacNeice to invite him to join the BBC. Over a 20-year period, Rodgers recorded accounts of W.B. Yeats, James Joyce and others by those who had known them, including Austin Clarke and Oliver St John Gogarty. The transcripts of these interviews were published as *Irish Literary Portraits* (1972). Rodger's second, highly accomplished collection of poetry, *Europa and the Bull*, appeared in 1952, winning praise for its controlled, inventive use of language. His *Collected Poems* appeared posthumously in 1971.

CHRIS MORASH

Romanticism The development of an interest in regional culture is an important ingredient of Romanticism, which in the case of Ireland ironically coincides with the demise of an independent Parliament and the passing of the Act of Union in 1800. James Barry's inclusion of Ossian with an Irish harp in his mammoth painting *Elysium and Tartarus or the State of Final Retribution* (1777–84, London, Royal Society of Arts), a heavenly based portrait gallery of human achievement, is one of the earliest representations of the periphery, Ireland, forcing itself on the centre, London. In the post-Union period paintings produced in Ireland or paintings of Irish subjects produced elsewhere were in the main dictated by the tastes of the Royal Academy (RA) in London. A case in point is the colourful canvas painted by the Scottish-born artist David Wilkie (1745–1841) entitled *The Peep-O-Day Boy's Cabin, in the West of Ireland* (London, Tate Gallery), which was exhibited in 1836. The result of a trip to Ireland in the early 1830s, the painting is set within an Irish cabin: a watchful wife protects her husband from possible capture, a tale seemingly relating to Ireland's recent violent agrarian wars. In this and in another painting, *The Irish Whiskey Still* (RA, 1840; Edinburgh, National Gallery of Scotland), Wilkie reduced Ireland to a series of generalizations: a rustic interior, quaint customs and modes of dress, striking beauty in the women and colourful mischievousness in the children.

And yet it is ironic to note that in *The Peep-O-Day Boy's Cabin* Wilkie is in some confusion over what exactly it is he is representing. The Peep-O-Day Boys were a Protestant group active in Ulster in the 1780s, who in early morning raids attempted to rob Catholics of their weaponry. A close viewing of the painting reveals a major problem with regard to Wilkie's title. The woman in the centre of the canvas holds in her left hand, directly above the head of her sleeping husband, a rosary. There is obviously something wrong here. Wilkie has confused his Irish secret societies. In fact, one can go so far as to say that Wilkie does not know what he is painting. His is a confused view of Irish political agitation. Exhibited in the wake of the granting of Catholic emancipation, the painting displays a novel interest in Irish subject matter but at the expense of accuracy. Perhaps encouraged by the popularity of the Captain Rock story, which had spawned a lengthy tome in 1824 from Tom Moore, Wilkie decided to satisfy a London appetite for generalized and Romantic representations of the Irish character. To Wilkie, Ireland for the painter was an undiscovered country, and he recommended that English artists come and paint the 'primeval simplicity' of the people. Obviously not concerned with truth, Wilkie was interested in the picturesque potential of the west of Ireland: the red petticoats of the women reminded him of Titian, while the naked children had the beauty of a Correggio cherub. The centre, London's RA, is here imposing its imaginative perceptions on the periphery, depriving it of an authentic existence yet framing it within the acceptable language of an old master painting.

With his representation of a subject that would be expected to attract popular interest in London, Wilkie in the 1830s is granting Ireland a historical past separate from that of England. In this he is going a step further than the repetitive idealized views of the Irish landscape produced by the previous generation of artists, both native and foreign (for example, Thomas Roberts and William Ashford), who depicted Irish demesnes as little Englands or indeed as little Italian campagnas, after the fashion of the seventeenth-century artist Claude Lorraine. In the Wilkie, difference is recognized but is proved ineffectual because it has no teeth. His cabin dwellers are not fiece rural guerillas but rearranged figures from a sixteenth-century Italian Holy Family or Lamentation.

The representation of the native Irish became a not uncommon but not widespread subject in the early decades of the nineteenth century. The English-born Maria Spilsbury

(1773–1823) produced lively scenes full of folk customs and amusing anecdote; so too did Joseph Peacock (c.1783–1837), whose large *The Patron, in Glendalough* (1813, Belfast, Ulster Museum) is an important reference for the study of folk history. George Petrie (1790–1866), eminent both as an archeologist and as a watercolourist, favoured the native landscape and antique remains over the inhabitants. Yet in such a large exhibition piece as *Clonmacnoise, The Last Circuit of Pilgrims* (c.1838, Dublin, National Gallery of Ireland), he isolates a heavily cloaked old woman on a ridge above the Shannon next to the ruined Round Tower. Is this figure the visual personification of Ireland so beloved of eighteenth-century aisling poems, or is she the beginnings of a Romanticization of Ireland as the lonely mother deprived of her children through poverty and emigration?

London played a vital role in Irish visual production throughout the nineteenth century. Most artists were forced to emigrate; those that stayed, such pillars of the Royal Hibernian Academy (RHA) as George Francis Mulvany, Sir Thomas Alfred Jones, etc., produced dull portraits of lord lieutenants and physicans. In Ireland patronage did not really exist for anything beyond portraits. Daniel MacLise (1806–70) left Ireland at the age of 21 and never returned. One of his most famous Irish paintings, *The Marriage of Strongbow and Eva* (1854, Dublin, National Gallery of Ireland), was originally painted for the newly built Palace of Westminster. Here we find a splendidly large-scale summation of the historicizing trend in the representation of Irish subject matter. Maclise included all he knew or could discover about early Ireland: gold torcs on the arms of his Irish warriors, an early Irish harp (the broken strings symbolizing a defeated Ireland), a romanesque doorway in the background, and so on. But just as in the Wilkie example, we soon begin to notice compositional borrowings from the great Italians of previous centuries. Ireland can only be represented in the language of Leonardo (the acolytes in the right foreground), Guido Reni (the distraught mother in the left foreground), and perhaps Velazquez (the Norman knights in the right background). Universalism has conquered over regionality.

An antidote to the heady antiquarianism and art historical erudition of Maclise is the Irish work of yet another Scottish-born painter, Erskine Nicol (1825–1904). Nicol lived in Ireland for a few years in the late 1840s and was later to return on an annual basis. In many ways he took up Wilkie's challenge to paint the Irish, but he sought a more humorous expression. His cabinet-sized peasant paintings were immensely popular in London and were produced in great number. They created an identifiable type of Irish buffoon which pre-date by at least a decade the more famous images of Sir John Tenniel. Nicol's Paddy is a colourful example of exotica: tall and fit with a scrubby beard and slight simian features (e.g. *Paddy at Versailles*, 1856, Belfast, Ulster Museum). Gentle ridicule is forever present in Nicol's work, as is an underlying anti-Catholicism. In *Notice to Quit* (1862), the wretched inhabitants of a bare cabin, a man, a woman and a sick child, are faced with immediate eviction, their only defence being the pathetic wielding of a crucifix by an aged grandmother in the face of the baliff. The painting is a convincingly realistic capturing of the interior of an Irish hovel of the mid-nineteenth century. The strong lighting and the lengthy gap that divides the baliff from the family increase the drama of the scene, yet the tone is immediately softened by the ridiculous crucifix, which would have perpetuated the London audience's view of the backwardness of Irish Catholicism.

The literary historian Thomas Flanagan has written of how the audience for Irish books in the first half of the nineteenth century was in part at least a British one. Substituting 'painter' for 'writer' one could state, as he does, that artists were concerned to 'interpret' Ireland, to exploit as local colour or as provincial genre painting whatever

seemed unique, particular or 'Romantic' in Irish life. In true Romantic terms the Ireland of the nineteenth century had entered, like the Middle East, Spain and Northern Africa for French and English artists, that select group of what Wilkie called the 'untouched and new' areas waiting to be discovered.

Reading

Chiego, William J., *Sir David Wilkie of Scotland* (Raleigh NC: North Carolina Museum of Art, 1987).

Crookshank Anne, and the Knight of Glin, *The Painters of Ireland c. 1660–1920* (London: Barrie and Jenkins, 1978).

Daniel Maclise 1806–1870 (London: Arts Council of Great Britain, 1972).

Flanagan, Thomas, 'Literature in English, 1801–91', in W.E. Vaughan (ed.), *A New History of Ireland, V, Ireland Under the Union, I* (Oxford: 1989).

Gibbons, Luke, ' "The shadowy narrator": history, art and Romantic nationalism in Ireland 1750–1850', in Ciaran Brady (ed.), *Ideology and the Historians* (Dublin: Lilliput Press, 1991).

Hutchinson, John, *James Arthur O'Connor* (Dublin: National Gallery of Ireland, 1985).

Irish Art in the 19th Century (Cork: ROSC, 1971).

McConkey, Kenneth, *A Free Spirit: Irish Art 1860–1960* (Woodbridge: Antique Collectors' Club, 1990).

Portraits and Prospects: British and Irish Drawings and Watercolours from the Collection of the Ulster Museum, Belfast (Belfast: Ulster Museum, 1989).

Strickland, Walter, *A Dictionary of Irish Artists* (Shannon: Irish University Press, 1968).

White, James, *Apollo* 84 (October 1966).

FINTAN CULLEN

Ros, Amanda M'Kittrick (1860–1939) Writer and (perhaps unconscious) humorist. Born 8, December near Ballynahinch, County Down. The daughter of headteacher Edward Amlane M'Kittrick, Ros was educated at Marlborough Training College, Dublin. She became a teacher at Larne, County Antrim. She married Andrew Ross, Larne station master, in 1887 (d. 1917) and

Thomas Rodgers, farmer, in 1922 (d. 1934). She published her own novels and poems, in which she attacked critics (notably Barry Pain) and other enemies. Her extraordinary linguistic inventiveness, which veers between regional brusqueness and an almost parodic sentimentality, has made her a cult figure. In contemplation of dead literary predecessors she wrote 'Some rare bits of brain lie here / Mortal loads of beef and beer'.

Reading

London, J., *O Rare Amanda!* (London: 1954)

Ormsby, F., *Thine in Storm and Calm: An Amanda McKittrick Ros Reader* (Belfast: 1988).

Ros, Amanda M'Kittrick, *Irene Iddlesleigh* (Belfast: 1897).

—— *Delia Delaney* (1898).

—— *Poems of Puncture* (London: 1913)

—— *Fumes of Formation* (Belfast: 1933)

—— *Helen Huddleson* (London: 1969).

SIOBHÁN KILFEATHER

Roseingrave family

1 Daniel (died Dublin 1727). Organist and composer. After serving as organist of Gloucester (1679–81), Winchester (1682–92) and Salisbury (1692–8), he was appointed to both Dublin cathedrals in 1698. He retired (unofficially) in 1719 in favour of his son Ralph.

2 Daniel Jr (born Winchester, 1685; died Dublin before 1724). Organist and composer, the eldest son of Daniel. He entered Trinity College, Dublin, in 1702, became a scholar in 1705, and was organist of the College Chapel.

3 Thomas (born Winchester, 1688; died Dunleary, near Dublin, 1766). Composer and organist, the second son of Daniel. He was given a grant of £10 by St Patrick's Cathedral to travel to Italy in 1710, where he became friendly with the Scarlattis. He later did much to introduce Domenico Scarlatti's harpsichord music in England.

He was probably back in Dublin 1713–17, after which he went to London, becoming organist at St George's, Hanover Square, in 1725. A mental breakdown led him to vacate his post in 1737. He returned to Dublin in 1749, where a concert performance of his opera *Phaedra* was given in 1753. He composed much fine organ music and a number of anthems. His major verse-anthem 'Arise, Shine', written in Venice in 1712, shows him to have been a composer of outstanding individuality and merit.

4 Ralph (born Salisbury, *c*.1695; died Dublin, 1747). Organist and composer, third son of Daniel. He was acting organist of both Dublin cathedrals 1719–27, when he was officially appointed to his father's post.

BARRA BOYDELL

It is difficult to ascribe the cathedral music of the four Roseingraves to any one member of the family, as part-books usually give the surname only.

BARRA BOYDELL

Rosse, earls of (Parsons family) In the early 1840s an extraordinary construction was undertaken on the estate of William, third earl of Rosse, in County Offaly. Using local labour he designed and built what was to remain the world's largest telescope until partially dismantled in 1914. During much of the nineteenth century a visit to Parsonstown to view the Leviathan was *de rigeur* for scientists, intellectuals and the merely curious. They were often disappointed on account of the Irish weather or the condition of the great mirror which lay at the heart of the instrument and required regular polishing. But this was no mere architectural folly or heroic feat of amateur engineering. Using it, the earl discerned for the first time the structure of spiral nebulae: his achievements were recognized by his election as president of the Royal Society. He was not alone in his enthusiasm for things scientific and technical. His wife Mary was a notable early photographer, and his successor Laurence continued his astronomical researches. His youngest son, Charles Parsons, produced the first successful steam turbine, with which he startled the British fleet at Spithead in 1897, in a publicity stunt which ensured subsequent government funding.

Sir Laurence Parsons was granted the castle in 1620. Apart from occasional displacement by force of arms the family has lived there ever since: it inherited the earldom of Rosse in the eighteenth century.

The present (seventh) earl and his wife, Brendan and Alison, have clung tenaciously to the traditions of the family, conserving Birr Castle and its estate through difficult times. There are active plans to restore the telescope and develop the estate for exhibitions, education and tourism. In addition to its role in astronomy, it was a favourite home for precious specimens brought back by the exploring botanists of the Victorian era. The gardens contain a thousand catalogued species and the earl takes part in expeditions which regularly augment the collection.

There is in Ireland today a warmer appreciation of the historic role of the Anglo–Irish aristocracy than in the recent past. Great estates may be regarded as the 'multinational companies' of their day, providing employment and, in the case of Birr, inspiring examples of the use of wealth for the advancement of knowledge and technology.

Reading

Mills, John FitzMaurice, *The Noble Dwellings of Ireland* (London: Thames and Hudson, 1987).

Parsons, W., *The Scientific Papers of William Parsons, Third Earl of Rosse*, ed. C. Parsons (Bradord and London: Lund, Humphries, 1926).

DENIS L. WEAIRE

Rowan, Archibald Hamilton (1751–1834)

United Irishman. Born Rathbone Place, London, 12 May; died Dublin, 1 November. Rowan's grandfather beqeathed him considerable wealth, and he was educated at Westminister School and Queen's College, Cambridge. He settled in County Kildare and, influenced by Wolfe Tone, joined the United Irishmen in 1791. Sentenced to two years' imprisonment for sedition in 1794, he escaped from Newgate, Dublin, to France. He went to America in 1795, and when pardoned in 1803 settled on his estate at Killyleagh Castle, County Down. He was a strong supporter of Catholic emancipation.

HENRY BOYLAN

Royal Black Preceptory

Often regarded as the senior and elite section of the Orange Order, it is in fact a separate institution, though equally dedicated to the defence of Protestantism and the Union with Great Britain. Like the Order it is quasi-Masonic in ritual and organization. Its proper title is the Imperial Grand Black Chapter of the British Commonwealth, and it has a considerable membership outside Ireland, in Britain, the United States, Canada, Australia and New Zealand, as well as in some African countries. It holds annual parades in the North of Ireland on the last Sunday in August, when about 30,000 'Black' men walk with banners and bands.

A.T.Q. STEWART

Royal College of Physicians and Surgeons

The Fraternity of Physicians established by John Stearne at Trinity Hall (1654) was incorporated as the College of Physicians of Dublin in 1667. It was styled the King and Queen's College of Physicians in Ireland under a charter of William and Mary in 1692, when Patrick Dun was president, changing its title to the Royal College of Physicians of Ireland in 1890. The college building in Kildare Street was opened in 1864.

A charter was granted by George III to the Royal College of Surgeons in Ireland in 1784. Situated temporarily to the rear of Mercer's Hospital, more suitable premises for its flourishing medical school were provided on

St Stephen's Green in 1810 and enlarged in 1825. A building programme in the 1970s provided modern lecture halls and laboratories, and a new library was opened in 1991 in the Mercer building, which the college acquired when Mercer's Hospital closed in 1983.

Reading

Lyons, J.B., *The Quality of Mercer's* (Dublin: Glendale Press, 1991).
Widdess, J.D.H., *A History of the Royal College of Physicians of Ireland, 1654–1963* (Edinburgh: Livingstone, 1963).
—— *The Royal College of Surgeons in Ireland and its Medical School 1784–1984*, 3rd edn (Dublin: RCSI, 1984).

J.B. LYONS

Royal Dublin Society Founded 25 June 1731, by 14 members of the philosophical society of Trinity College, Dublin, the Dublin Society's aim was 'improving Husbandry, Manufactures, and other Arts and Sciences'. Originally, every member was expected to carry out research to advance agricultural knowledge. In 1795, the society developed the Botanic Gardens, and subsequently helped found the National Museum, the National Art Gallery, the Veterinary College, the College of Science, the National College of Art and the National Library. In 1880, the RDS moved to a permanent site in Ballsbridge, where its Spring and Dublin Horse Shows continue to promote agriculture and country pursuits in Ireland. By 1992 it had over 14,000 members.

FRED LOWE

Royal Hospital Kilmainham 'The Hospital of King Charles the Second for Ancient and maimed officers and soldiers of the Army of Ireland' was, at the time of its construction, the largest secular edifice in Dublin and the first major building in the classical style. It was designed by the Irish surveyor general Sir William Robinson. The foundation stone was laid in April 1680 by the viceroy, the duke of Ormonde, the first inmates being admitted just four years later. While the concept of the hospital may be related to Louis XIV's Hotel des Invalides in Paris, begun in 1670, the planning is firmly rooted in the precedents of English medieval collegiate and hospital architecture. The RHK was built on the site of the old priory of the Knight's Hospitallers, the (rubble) stones of its chapel being used in the new chapel, which contains some fine timber carving the work of James Tabary. The ceiling is a *papier mâché* replica of the original, dating from 1902. The spire was not completed (by Thomas Burgh) until the early 1700s. The hospital was originally surrounded by four flankers, on the site of one of which is the deputy master's house (1762, extended 1797). In the master's garden is a dining pavilion attributed to Sir Edward Lovett Pearce (*c*.1730, restored 1990). Other buildings include two by Francis Johnston; the adjutant general's Office (pre-1820) and the West Gatehouse (1808, moved to this location in 1847). Johnston was also responsible for major renovations to the hospital proper in 1805.

Since 1837 the RHK has been in the care of the Office of Public Works. In the decades after 1927, when the last of the old soldiers were moved to Chelsea, the fabric of the building deteriorated. In the late 1960s the tower and the roof of the Great Hall were restored, but the major reconstruction programme, under the architectural supervision of Costello Muray and Beaumont, did not get under way until 1980. This was completed in 1985. Following the government decision, in 1987, to house the Irish Museum of Modern Art at the RHK, further works of adaptation were undertaken in 1988 and in 1990–1, the architects for the final phase being Shay Cleary, in consultation with Noel de Chenu of the Office of Public Works.

Reading

Costello, Murray and Beaumont, *An Introduction to The Royal Hospital Kilmainham – Its Architec-*

ture, *History and Restoration* (Dublin: CMB, 1987).

O'Dwyer, Frederick and Igoe, Vivien, 'Early views of the Royal Hospital Kilmainham', in *The GPA Irish Arts Review Yearbook 1988* (Belfast: Eton Enterprises, 1988).

Olley, John, 'Sustaining the narrative at Kilmainham', in *Irish Arts Review Yearbook 1991–1992* (Dun Laoghaire: Eton Enterprises, 1991).

FREDERICK O'DWYER

rundale system Up until recently the rundale system was part of the 'hidden Ireland'. It is the historical geographers who have rediscovered this aspect of the lives of the lower peasantry in the eighteenth and nineteenth centuries. The system occupied a large area in the north, west and south-west of pre-Famine Ireland, but its origin remains obscure. Whether it was a product of the switch to tillage in the eighteenth century or a survival of Gaelic Ireland cannot be said with certainty. This unanswered question leaves the nature of the system problematic.

The 'plachan' (the exclusive form of the rundale village) and the land attached to it were usually coterminous with a townland. Arable land in the infield was held jointly, although individual shares were intermingled. These shares manifested themselves as 'lazy beds', which were widely scattered in the infield to include land of different qualities. Lord George Hill cited the extreme example in Gweedore of a small field of half an acre in which 26 people held possession rights. In some districts these individual plots were periodically redistributed in a lottery, the 'changedale'. Cropping tended to follow a continuous rotation of grain (barley or oats) and potatoes, mostly without fallow. The only visible division of land was a temporary fence of mud bank and loose wattle between the infield and the outfield. The outfield was the main source of the community's pasture land. It was supplemented by 'booleying', the summer transhumance of livestock to the mountain uplands, and by allowing the stock to graze on the stubble of the infield in winter time.

There was an essential dualism of communality and individualism in this system of agriculture, and these opposing forces shaped its nature. Individuals gained access to the land not through the rental structures of landlordism but through their relationship to the community as a whole, usually by kinship, and produced their own products under the overall direction of the commune. It was the community as a whole that made decisions about the organization of production, such as the time of booleying. We need to look at this system of land tenure in greater detail in order to explicate the nature of the lower peasantry who lived outside the control of the landlord in the pre-Famine period.

Reading

Buchanan, R.H., 'Field systems of Ireland', in A.R. Baker and R.A. Butlin (eds), *Studies of Field Systems in the British Isles* (London: Cambridge University Press, 1973).

Hill, Lord George, *Facts from Gweedore* (London: 1887).

McCourt, D., 'The decline of rundale, 1750–1850', in Peter Roebuck (ed.), *Plantation to Partition* (Belfast: Blackstaff Press, 1981).

EAMONN SLATER

rural organizations The most significant of these are as follows:

1 *Irish Farmers' Association*: founded as the NFA in 1955 to represent farmers' interests.
2 *Irish Creamery Milk Suppliers' Association*: founded in Limerick in 1950 to organize Irish farmers nationally and internationally.
3 *Macra na Féirme*: founded in Athy in 1944 to promote personal development, social and cultural training and leadership among young farmers and rural youth.
4 *Irish Countrywomen's Association*: founded in Bree, County Wexford, in 1910 to improve rural life: runs an Adult Education

and a Horticultural College at An Grianán, Termonfeckin, County Louth.

5 *Foróige – National Youth Development Organization*: founded as Macra na Tuaithe in 1955: became Foróige in 1981. Its purpose is the involvement of young people in their own development and in the development of society.

ALAN DUKES

Russell, George William (AE) (1867–1935) Painter, mystic, poet and co-operator. Born 10 April, Lurgan, County Armagh; died 17 July, Bournemouth. After his birth Russell's family moved to Dublin, where he completed his education at the Rathmines School. From the age of 12 he studied at the Metropolitan School of Art, where he met W.B. Yeats.

After working as a clerk in a brewery, and in Pim's, the Dublin drapery store, he joined the Irish Agricultural Organization. Russell devoted the rest of his life to espousing the practical and ethical aspects of rural co-operation. Writing under the anonym 'AE', he edited the *Irish Homestead* (1906–23) and the *Irish Statesman* (1923–30). The influence of the co-operative movement was wonderfully beneficial for Irish life.

His early ambition to be a professional painter faded after he joined the Dublin Theosophists. His paintings have been admired, but the technique is often poor and the themes repetitive. His poetry (two collected editions, 1913 and 1926) is often lacking in power and precision, but such poems as 'Germinal' and 'On Behalf of Some Irishmen not Followers of Tradition' show him at his best.

Reading

Johnson, Raynor C., *The Light and the Gate* (London: 1964).

Summerfield, Henry, *That Myriad Minded Man: A Biography of George William Russell* (Gerrards Cross: 1975).

PETER COSTELLO

S

Sacramental Test (Test Act) The requirement that holders of crown office should take communion according to the Anglican rite was introduced in England, but not Ireland, in 1673. A sacramental test was introduced in Ireland as part of the 1704 Act 'to prevent the further growth of popery'. The motivation for its inclusion in this Act is unclear, but it was inserted by the English Privy Council, probably by the secretary of state, the earl of Nottingham. Despite pressure from Ulster Presbyterians, especially in the 1730s, it was in force until 1780, although the 24 indemnity acts that were passed suggest the requirement was flouted.

Reading

Beckett, J.C., *Protestant Dissent in Ireland, 1687–1780* (London: Faber, 1948).
Simms, J.G., 'The making of a penal law (2 Anne c. 6), 1703–4', *Irish Historical Studies* xii (1960).

RAYMOND GILLESPIE

Sarsfield, Patrick (?1655–93) Soldier. Born probably at Lucan. Sarsfield was the second son of Patrick Sarsfield, an Old English gentleman, and Anne, daughter of Rory O'More, one of the planners of the 1641 rising. He left Ireland in 1675, probably to serve in one of Charles II's regiments in France, before going to England in 1678 to take up a commission in the English army. He was dismissed later that year as part of the reaction to the popish plot. He returned to Ireland but in 1685 was appointed by James II as a lieutenant colonel in the English army.

In 1686 Sarsfield fought against Monmouth at Sedgemoor and was promoted to a full colonel. After the landing of William III he fought for James at the battle of Wincanton and fled to France with the exiled king. In March 1689 he arrived in Ireland with James. He became a privy councillor and member of the Jacobite Parliament for County Dublin, but his main role was as a military commander, being appointed a brigadier at the instigation of the earl of Tyrconnel and the comte d'Avaux, the French ambassador. For most of 1689 he served in the north-west of Ireland containing the Enniskillen force. After the relief of Derry he retreated south, but took Sligo in October. He remained in Dublin for the winter but was present at the battle of the Boyne in July 1690.

After the defeat of the Jacobite forces Sarsfield retreated west and successfully repulsed the first siege of Limerick in August 1690. Throughout the winter of 1690/1 he was marginalized by the promotion over his head of Charles St Ruth and Thomas Maxwell. He and St Ruth disagreed on strategy, St Ruth arguing for the need for a dramatic victory and electing for a battle at Aughrim, at which the Jacobite force was defeated. Sarsfield retreated to Limerick, where, after a siege, he was forced to surrender on 24 September 1691.

Under the terms of the treaty of Limerick he, and a substantial portion of the army, sailed to France to serve Louis XVI. Sarsfield left Cork on 22 December 1691. He was fatally wounded at the battle of Lander on 19 August 1693 and died soon after.

Reading

Simms, J.G., *Jacobite Ireland, 1685–91* (London: Routledge and Kegan Paul, 1969).

Wauchop, Piers, *Patrick Sarsfield and the Williamite War* (Dublin: Irish Academic Press, 1992).

RAYMOND GILLESPIE

St Enda's School Founded by Patrick Pearse in September 1908 at Cullenswood House, Ranelagh, as Ireland's first bilingual secondary school for boys. Its founder's aim was to instil in his pupils a love for Gaelic language, games and traditions. He also brought to the school others of his own distinctive passions, including a love for nature, and admiration for the ancient heroic tales and the more recent tradition of militant nationalism. In 1910 he moved his school to the Hermitage, Rathfarnham. After Pearse's execution the school reverted for a while to Ranelagh. It returned to Rathfarnham in 1919, where it endured under constant financial difficulties until its closure in 1935. By the early 1990s it housed the Pearse Museum.

Reading

Edwards, Ruth Dudley, *Patrick Pearse: The Triumph of Failure* (London: Faber, 1977; reissued Dublin: Poolbeg, 1990).

O Buachalla, Seamus, '*Patrick Pearse: A Significant Irish Educationalist*, (Cork: Mercier, 1979).

PAT COOKE

St Leger family The surname St Leger is of Norman origin. William de Saint Leger, Constable of Carmarthen, came to Ireland in 1192 with the earl of Pembroke. He was invested with much land in counties Kilkenny, Laois and Westmeath. The sixteenth century saw the descendants of William as substantive landowners with Edmund St Leger of Tullaghanbrogue, Kilkenny, in conflict with the Friars Preachers and Minors because he disputed gifts made to convents by his ancestors. He was excommunicated in 1509 by the bishop of Ossory. His son, Oliver St Leger, styled 'lord of Tullaghanbrogue and baron of Rosconnel', was elected sovereign of Kilkenny in 1533, but in 1537 he was found guilty by verdict of the Corporation of the town of Kilkenny for charging their tenants 'with Coyn and Livery'.

Patrick, his son and heir, was styled the baron St Leger. In April 1550 the lord of Upper Ossory 'accompagnied by divers evil disposed persons' invaded the manor of Rosconnel, expelling the St Legers' tenants. That the law suit that followed favoured Patrick was due in no small way to the assistance of Sir Anthony St Leger of Ulcombe, near Maidstone, a distant relative, ancestor of the viscounts of Doneraile, who had been appointed in 1540 lord deputy of Ireland.

Reading

St Leger, Moya Frenz, *St Leger – The Family and the Race* (Chichester: Phillimore, 1986).

MÁIRE MacCONGHAIL

St Patrick By the 1700s St Patrick's feast day on 17 March was being observed by the Irish abroad as well as at home. The saint was acceptable to both Catholics and Protestants; Archbishop Ussher had portrayed him as a forerunner of Protestantism. As Williamite anniversaries became contentious, liberal

Protestants in the early 1800s offered St Patrick's day as the national festival for all creeds. Though Orangemen objected, the state lent some support to this. The Irish Parliamentary Party supported the campaign which made St Patrick's day a bank holiday (1903); its importance today owes much to the Irish diaspora.

Reading

Alter, Peter, 'Symbols of Irish nationalism', *Studia Hibernica* xiv (1974).

Crimmins, John D., *St Patrick's day: Its Celebration in New York and Other American Places, 1737–1845* (New York: published by the author, 1902).

Hill, Jacqueline, 'National festivals, the state and "Protestant Ascendancy" in Ireland, 1790–1829', *Irish Historical Studies* xxiv (1984).

JACQUELINE HILL

satirical novel in the twentieth century
Satire had something of a renaissance in the twentieth century. Disillusioned and angered by the censorship and repression manifested after 1922, Eimar O'Duffy, Austin Clarke and Mervyn Wall were remarkable for their rejection of formal realism and their re-fashioning of the popular mythologies of the revival period in satires which attack the orthodoxies of the new state.

Eimar O'Duffy (1893–1935) was heavily involved with the Irish Volunteers, and despaired about the Easter Rising. His trilogy of novels, *King Goshawk and the Birds* (1926), *The Spacious Adventures of the Man in the Street* (1928) and *Asses in Clover* (1933), written after his permanent departure from Ireland, uses a fantastic premise (the return to modern Ireland of Cuchulain's half-human, half-divine son, Cuanduine) as the basis for an episodic wander through contemporary Ireland and England. As Cuandine experiences modern life, O'Duffy exposes the evils of modern warfare, contemporary politics, popular music, mass circulation newsprint, censorship and millionaire commodity brokers. O'Duffy is remarkable for

his incorporation of many styles, for the comic juxtaposition of the heroic and the modern, and for his prophetic awareness of commercial realities.

Austin Clarke (1896–1974) returned to the world of eighteenth-century Ireland in his three 'Romances', *The Bright Temptation* (1932), *The Singing Men at Cashel* (1936) and *The Sun Dances at Easter* (1952). Using a palimpsest of myth, history and contemporary reference, Clarke satirized the overdominance of the Catholic church, particularly in matters of sexuality and church/state relations. Clarke's celebration of the artistic achievements of the period, and, especially, his lambent descriptions of the natural world are more effective than his more pointed comments in exposing, by contrast, the body-denying Jansenism of the church.

Mervyn Wall (Eugene Welpy, 1908–97) has demonstrated a keen sense of the absurd, surreal world of the Civil Service, in which he spent much of his working life. His best-known novel, *The Unfortunate Fursey* (1946), set in tenth-century Ireland, again satirizes the pride, power-hunger and obsession with sex of the clergy and asserts that innocence and goodness can find no place in Ireland. More influenced by European tales of witchcraft than by Irish sources, less interested in rhetorical effects or lapidary prose than O'Duffy or Clarke, Wall achieves his broadly comic effects by means of a narrative which relies on the creation of unexpected and absurd situations.

If the choice of fantastic, quasi-mythological or historical settings was prompted by a desire to evade censorship, it was unavailing. All three writers were banned.

ANNE CLUNE

Scott, Patrick (1921–) Painter, designer and graphic artist. Born Kilbrittan, County Cork. Scott studied architecture in Dublin, working for many years as a graphic designer before turning to painting full-time. He represented Ireland at the Venice Biennale in 1960, won a Guggenheim Award the same year, and was included in the 'Irish

Imagination' exhibition (Dublin, 1971). Scott was a pioneer of abstract art in Ireland, sometimes applying gold leaf to an unprimed canvas, and stressing an almost Oriental elegance and spareness. He is also a noted designer of tapestries. Apart from Irish collections, he is represented in museums in New York and Washington.

BRIAN FALLON

Scott, William (1913–90) Painter and graphic artist. Born Greenock. Scott grew up in Enniskillen, his father's native town, and studied at the Belfast College of Art. In the 1930s he spent much time in France, and served as a sapper in World War II. During the 1950s he began to acquire an international reputation, and he was one of the first British artists to make personal contact with the New York School of Pollock, Rothko and others. From a style akin to the Euston Road School, he moved through a Picasso-inspired phase into total abstraction, though he continued to draw and paint figuratively when he chose. A large retrospective exhibition was mounted at the Tate Gallery in 1972.

BRIAN FALLON

Scully, Denys (1773–1830) Barrister and Catholic activist. Born Kilfeacle, County Tipperary, 4 May; died there, 25 October. A behind-the-scenes operator rather than an orator, Scully was nevertheless seen by many as the most influential figure in Catholic politics between 1804 and his retirement from public life after 1817. His anonymous *A Statement of the Penal Laws* (1811–12) led to the prosecution of the printer, Hugh Fitzpatrick. Scully's papers are a central source for post-Union Catholic politics.

Reading

MacDermot, Brian (ed.), *The Catholic Question in Ireland and England 1798–1822* (Dublin: Irish Academic Press, 1988).

SEAN CONNOLLY

Scully, Sean (1945–) Abstract artist. Born Dublin. Scully studied at the Croydon College of Art in London. He later taught at Newcastle University, the Chelsea School of Art and Goldsmith's College, London. Since 1975 he has worked and exhibited in New York. An exhibition of his work was shown in the Douglas Hyde Gallery in 1982, and a major exhibition covering 1982–8 took place at the Whitechapel Art Gallery, London, in 1989. His taut, Mondrian-influenced work is characterized by grids and stripes. There is little doubt about his importance on the international art scene, though doubts may be raised about Ireland's claim to Scully (he left the country as a child).

Reading

Poirier, Maurice, *Sean Scully* (New York: Hudson Wills Press, 1990).

PAUL O'BRIEN

sculpture In Ireland as in other northern European countries, sculpture has not as high a profile within the arts as has painting. Sculpture was slower to establish itself in the first Irish art schools, the Dublin Society Schools and the Royal Hibernian Academy, a legacy which continued into the twentieth century in art education, where sculpture has attracted fewer students. This has not enhanced sculpture's status or identity, which in turn has perpetuated a common perception that 'art' and 'painting' are virtually synonomous. Economic factors are at least part of the explanation: traditionally, sculpture is relatively expensive to produce and to purchase, and larger-scale sculpture requires space for display. Despite these limitations, sculpture is a strong influence in the visual arts, especially since the 1970s, when, in common with those in Western Europe and North America, the more radical artists extended the definitions of Irish sculpture to include aspects of performance, video, installation and photographic art.

Irish sculpture developed as a craft as much as a fine art, with many sculptors from the eighteenth century to the present earning their living through modest commissions in, for example, tombstone carving and architectural decoration. Fine art commissions as such were, and are, few and far between, and production costs restricted the extent of non-commissioned work. While sculpture is privately produced and circulated in much the same way as painting, sculpture also assumes a significant role as public art, where the sculptor's role is more akin to that of the architect in the negotiation of public works rather than in the expression of private desires. The scope of sculpture is therefore remarkably broad, from its relationship with the crafts to its public and private roles. The vast majority of sculpture of the eighteenth, nineteenth and early twentieth centuries was to serve as religious, commemorative, colonial or national monuments. Since the mid-twentieth century gallery sculpture, as work in and for itself, has assumed much greater importance as Modernism – and latterly post-modernism – have encouraged individuated concepts of art and artists.

While Ireland cannot claim the flambuoyant and idealized art styles of nineteenth-century Europe, there was considerable expansion of statuary in towns and cities throughout the century. Today these monuments are not highly regarded as artworks; rather they have become very much part of the town or cityscape and as such have not survived unscathed by the effects of weathering, car fumes and graffiti. Yet, until the mid-twentieth century, these public sculptures often embodied potent cultural and political symbols. For example, the early eighteenth-century equestrian statue of William III in College Green, Dublin, was the focal point for an annual Orange parade until its prohibition in 1882 on the grounds that it was a threat to law and order. The William statue, along with many other monuments to British authority, disappeared from public view after the Irish Free State was

established. In more recent times the most famous surviving monument to British rule was Thomas Kirk's statue of Admiral Lord Nelson on top of what was commonly known as Nelson's Pillar in Dublin, until the IRA managed to blow up most of the pillar in 1966. The importance of such monuments is largely social and sometimes political. In the latter part of the twentieth century this perception has subsumed their value as art.

The history of Irish sculptors (as distinct from earlier artists invited to Ireland to work on commissions) begins in the late eighteenth century and coincides with the neo-classical style. Christopher Hewetson (c.1739–94) spent most of his career in Rome, but his neo-classical work is seen at its best in his monument to Provost Baldwin (1784) in Trinity College, Dublin. John Hogan (1800–58) also spent most of his career in Rome, which is an indication not only of the continued importance of neo-classicism and the ideal of the antique, but of the difficulty of finding sufficient work in Ireland. Hogan returned home in 1848 and during the remainder of his career he completed several religious sculptures as well as a number of portraits. The neo-classical style was perpetuated by Thomas Kirk (1781–1845) and John Edward Carew (c.1782–1868). Carew is almost unique in Irish sculpture as the long-term recipient of single patronage. He worked under Lord Egremont in England, which allowed him to pursue a pure neo-classicism unhindered by more pragmatic concerns. This was in stark contrast to Hogan, whose work is regarded as having suffered due to too few commissions. Neo-classicism was very much the style of the educated gentry. The Catholic church was not a committed patron of neo-classicism, which is a significant factor given the church's expansive buildings programme after Catholic emancipation in 1829.

Two of the most acclaimed sculptors between the late eighteenth and late nineteenth centuries are Edward Smyth (1749–1812) and John Henry Foley (1818–74). Between them they represent extremes in regard to their work context as sculptors of the period. Edward Smyth is remembered because he worked on designs for James Gandon's buildings, including the Custom House and the Four Courts in Dublin. Where Smyth was essentially a craftsman, John Henry Foley belonged to the fine art tradition. In Foley, we witness the successful transition in style from idealized neo-classical casts to the naturalistic bronze statues that seem so much a part of the materialist ethos of Victorian Britain. Foley build his career in England, where he owned a studio large enough to allow him to work exclusively on modelling while several assistants produced the finished sculpture. Several of Foley's bronze sculptures are located in public places in Ireland and the best of these are the intimate, single-figure statues, such as Goldsmith (1861) and Burke (1868), which stand at the entrance to Trinity College, Dublin, or Lord Rosse (1876), which is in the town of Birr. For all its technical virtuousity, his group of figures around the drum of the monument to Daniel O'Connell (completed 1883) in O'Connell Street, Dublin, is both imposing and strained due to the overwhelming complexity of the figure arrangement.

While Foley's reputation is not as great as it once was, this is even more marked in the example of Thomas Farrell (1827–1900), a popular Dublin sculptor of the late nineteenth century. There was an emphatic twentieth-century reaction against Victorian tastes and values, and in the Irish Republic there was also a reaction against commemorations of the British monarch and empire. This is evidenced by, for example, the removal from the grounds at Leinster House of the national monument to Queen Victoria (1908), the only substantial public work by John Hughes (1865–1941). More in keeping with trends in the early twentieth century in both its national sympathies and its awareness of a shift from naturalism and late Victorian over elaboration is the Parnell Monument (1911) in O'Connell Street, Dublin, by Augustus St Gaudens (1848–1907). The reductive

lines of the bronze figure of Parnell, set in a two-dimensional manner against a wall, is exceptionally 'modern', and the inscription on the wall behind the figure is suggestively nationalist. Two other Irish Americans worked in Ireland after the Irish Free State was established. Andrew O'Connor (1874–1941) completed a large crucifixion scene entitled *Christ the King*, now standing in Dun Laoghaire. Jerome Connor (1876–1943) spent many years working on the Lusitania Memorial in Cobh, a memorial which suffered from cash-flow problems and a sculptor who changed his mind on the design on several occasions.

The first half of the twentieth century was an impoverished period for Irish sculpture. Successive Free State governments were constrained by a weak economy and were not particularly sympathetic to the arts anyway. Church patronage was equally limited and church sculpture rarely rose above the most stereotyped of religious representations. Two sculptors who are known for their Rodinesque and naturalistic modelling are Oliver Sheppard (1864–1941) and his pupil, Albert Power (1883–1945). Sheppard's naturalism ranges from the powerfully stated bust of James Mangan (1908) in St Stephen's Green, Dublin, to the absurdly idealized bust of Patrick Pearse (1936) in the Dáil Éireann Collection. He is closely associated with nationalism, largely because of his 1798 memorials at Wexford and Enniscorthy and his *Death of Cuchulain* (1911), which was later placed in the General Post Office in Dublin as a commemoration of the 1916 Rising. Such work is in stark contrast to contemporary European sculpture, where modelling had been rejected in favour of carving, an extension of the 'truth to materials' philosophy of early Modernism. This eventually took root in Ireland through a younger generation which included Laurence Campbell (1911–68), though Irish identity continued to be expressed in the self-conscious use of local stone. The shift towards Modernism did not begin until the 1950s. F.E. McWilliam

(1909–92) emigrated to London at an early stage of his career and there are few Irish references in his work, an exception being his *Women of Belfast* series of the 1970s. The first sculpture dealing with abstraction is attributed to the Czech-born immigrant Gerda Fromel (1931–75).

By the 1960s and 1970s Irish society was in a process of change from a rural to a more urban economy, and modern art and architecture quickly adapted to the new urban identity, which was encouraged by government sponsorship. This is well represented by Gerda Fromel's sculpture at Carroll's factory in Dundalk, and Michael Bulfin's (1939–) sculpture at the Bank of Ireland headquarters in Dublin. Abstract and minimalist tendencies have continued in the sculpture of Michael Warren (1950–). The more radical tendencies since then have emerged through gallery-oriented work. In the 1970s Brian King (1942–) completed projects which were process based and relied on photographic documentation. The most challenging of recent work is conceptually oriented and works in multimedia rather than traditional sculptural materials. Kathy Prendergast (1958–) and Dorothy Cross (1956–) are notable examples of younger-generation sculptors. Temporary installation, as opposed to the permanent art object, is now an acceptable option for both artists and curators. However, sculpture continues to suffer from severe financial constraints despite the political lobbying of the Sculptors Society (formed 1980), and it continues to attract only a small audience despite its enhanced reputation within the arts.

Reading

Harbison, P., Potterton, H. and Sheehy, J. *Irish Art and Architecture from Prehistory to the Present* (London: Thames and Hudson, 1978, 1993).

Kennedy, S.B., *Irish Art and Modernism 1880–1950* (Belfast: Institute of Irish Studies, Queen's University Belfast).

Read, B., *Victorian Sculpture* (New Haven CT and London: Yale University Press, 1982).

JOAN FOWLER

seafaring All the ancestors of the Irish arrived by sea, and no people has a better claim than the Irish to have 'the sea in its blood'. Archaeologist Gordon Childe wrote that the Irish Sea swarmed with 'neolithic argonauts'. Irish raiders helped overthrow the Roman empire, and the pre-Christian 'Immrama' tell of seafarers launching into the unknown to seek the unattainable. During five centuries missionaries sailed all Europe's seas, and reached Iceland: the Brendan story, told throughout medieval Europe, epitomizes their adventures. Late medieval Irish seafarers visited all Western Europe's chief ports.

The definitive seventeenth-century English occupation did not prevent Irish ownership of ships, which by the eighteenth century frequented the Mediterranean and Caribbean. Other Irish seafarers became pirates (like Cork's Ann Bonny), privateers for Algiers, shipbuilders for Spain, admirals for France, captains for the Netherlands and Portugal, or explorers of the Amazon. In 1820 Bransfield of Ballinacurra was the first to sight Antarctica. In 1915 Shackleton from Kildare made polar exploration's greatest open-boat voyage. Famous sea shanties recall numberless Irish crews of nineteenth-century windjammers. Halpin of Wicklow laid the first ocean cables, admirals Mackau (McCoy) and Casy (O'Casey) were ministers of marine in France in the 1840s, Brown of Foxford founded Argentina's navy, Holland from Clare designed the first successful submarine, the *Fenian Ram*, and for years in this century Harland and Wolffe's Belfast shipyard was the world's biggest. Today, uniquely for a town so small, Arklow runs a fleet of 27 modern cargo ships.

Reading

Bowen, E.G., *Britain and the Western Seaways* (London: Thames and Hudson, 1972).

Forde, Frank, *Maritime Arklow* (Dun Laoghaire: Glendale Press, 1987).

Ireland, J. de Courcy, *Ireland and the Irish in Maritime History* (Dun Laoghaire: Glendale Press, 1986).

——*Ireland's Maritime Heritage* (Dublin: An Post, 1992).

JOHN DE COURCY IRELAND

Second Reformation Flourishing from about 1820 to 1860, the Second (or New) Reformation sought successfully to revitalize the Protestant churches and unsuccessfully to convert Catholics. Its dual legacy has been strongly evangelical Protestantism and heightened sectarian tension, the first resulting from patient labour in the churches and the second from the bitter, public religious controversy that accompanied conversion efforts.

Reading

Bowen, Desmond, *The Protestant Crusade in Ireland, 1800–70* (Dublin: Gill and Macmillan, 1978).

JOSEPH LIECHTY

secret societies These have played an important and often understated role in Irish politics for over two centuries. Rural society was infested by such organizations at local level from the middle of the eighteenth century, and increasingly politicized secret societies penetrated the towns and cities from the time of the French Revolution. As time went on, the local groups tended increasingly to link up with each other in regional and occasionally provincial or even island-wide networks. The Irish diasporas in England and America also were penetrated by the secret societies. The modern Irish party systems in both Northern Ireland and the Republic are descended, in great part, from secret organizations of a revolutionary, pseudo-revolutionary or counter-revolutionary nature. Freemasonries of various kinds, such as the Freemasons themselves and the Knights of Columbanus, have furthered the interests of Catholics and Protestants in the twentieth century. In the late eighteenth and early nineteenth century, the Combination Acts caused trade unions to organize themselves as secret societies.

Clandestine organizations can be classified very roughly as falling into four main types: those of agrarian and/or labour defence; sectarian; political; military/revolutionary. The boundaries between these groups is difficult to draw, and many organizations partook, at the same time or at different times, of the character of more than one of these categories. Furthermore, it is not always clear from the historical record and from the often prejudiced opinions of outside observers and internal apologists what the exact nature of a particular society was at a particular time. Also, organizations sometimes absorbed each other or split over issues that may be obscure; thus, in the 1830s, there were, apparently, two Ribbon-Hibernian organizations, one with American and the other with British connections. Since 1970, there have been several Irish Republican Armies. The Treaty Split of 1921–2, although enacted in public, is nearly as obscure in its original causes as that between the Three-Year-Olds and the Four-Year-Olds of the early nineteenth century.

What is clear is that Irish rural people showed an impressive capacity for collective organization for purposes of agitation from the middle of the eighteenth century on. In the west of the island agrarian groups existed even earlier, but it was in Tipperary that the first great Whiteboy outbreak occurred in 1760, during the middle of the Seven Years War. The war and the British industrial revolution had increased the demand for Irish cattle, and subsistence tenants were being pushed off their farms by big graziers. Whiteboyism was in part a defence against this, and also a resistance against ecclesiastical charges, whether Protestant or Catholic. Later societies enforced a crude land law and resisted tithes. The generic name referred to the custom of using white shirts and ribbons as disguises and marks of identification.

Classic Whiteboyism of the late eighteenth century was notably effective at communication. The local elected captain proclaimed the 'Rules of the Parish', and these rules were communicated by messengers to the neighbouring parishes, with the instruction that the rules be similarly proclaimed and passed on. By means of this chain-letter technique, entire provinces could be mobilized in a few weeks. On one occasion in 1786, the Rightboy movement threatened to take over peasant society on the entire island from its focus in central Munster, and was prevented only by determined patrolling of the rivers Nore and Shannon by the militia.

Early rural secret societies appear to have had little sectarian or nationalist feeling, although a certain residual Jacobitism seems to have been present. Later societies, however, quickly became associated only with one or other of the great religious blocs. The exception that, in a sense, proves this general rule was, of course, the United Irishmen. Agrarian secret societies appeared in Ulster in the 1870s in the form of the Protestant Hearts of Oak and Hearts of Steel organizations of agrarian defence, their names suggesting an assertion of both political loyalty and insistence on a sturdy defence of their rights as tenantry.

The emergence of Defenderism and of what evolved into the Orange Order was a crucial event. Stimulated by the Volunteer movement, by the American war and by Catholic and Protestant competition for land in the borderlands of Ulster, federations of secret societies confined to Catholic and Protestants, respectively Defenders and Peep-o'-Day Boys, sprung up in south Ulster and north Leinster in 1784. By 1790 the Defenders were a network of local societies stretching from Donegal to Louth and had begun to penetrate the towns as well. During this decade the United Irishmen, founded in Dublin and Belfast by middle-class men in 1791, tried to take over the Defenders. They had some local success, but it appears that the bulk of the Defender organization remained aloof from the revolutionaries. In 1795, the British government suppressed the United Irishmen and tolerated the emergence of the Orange Order as a militant Protestant defence association. Both the United Irishmen and the Defenders had penetrated the militia, thus encouraging the government to raise a new and more reliable force, the yeomanry, from the Orange Order.

The defeat of the rebellion of 1798 meant the end of the United Irishmen, but both the Defender and Orange traditions persisted, the Defenders evolving into the Ribbon organizations of the northern half of Ireland after the Napoleonic wars. The Orange Order was suppressed in 1836 because of its involvement in a treasonous attempt to alter the succession to the crown. Ribbonism divided into two networks, one associated more with Belfast and the other with Dublin. It crossed the Irish Sea and the Atlantic in the 1820s and, in the gentler political climate of Britain and the United States, came into the open as the Ancient Order of Hibernians. Hibernianism was later re-exported from the United States into Ireland. Similarly, Scottish Hibernianism linked up with the Ulster societies.

Pre-Famine secret societies were characterized by an intense localism which tended to stultify any attempt to build large-scale networks, by a distrust of the written word and by a fondness for passwords, secret grips and 'quarrelling words', which were, in principle at least, changed every three months. The passwords were carried around the country by people whose occupations justified continual travelling: pedlars, itinerant schoolmasters, canal workers, coachmen and artisans. Local publicans commonly were the local officers or captains of the Ribbon organizations. Local agrarian societies seem often to have been led by the most athletic and popular of the farmers' sons. Whereas Ribbon organizations appear to have been prone to a form of Tammanyism, and whereas local societies sometimes became the enforcers of a folk land code through terror, it appears also that at times the societies were an attempt to achieve democratic political action in a society which prevented such action.

Certainly, both constitutional and unconstitutional political leaders realized the potential of these local organizations. O'Connell attempted to substitute his Catholic Association for the Ribbonism and Whiteboyism of the parishes, and local poets such as Anthony Raftery urged the people to give up nightwalking and to trust to O'Connell's leadership. Parnell quite explicitly assimilated 'Ribbon-Fenianism' to the Land League organization of the 1880s. The Fenian organization, founded in Dublin in 1858, also tried to take over local Whiteboy and Ribbon clubs, with considerable success.

Fenianism, or the Irish Republican Brotherhood (IRB), was the best known of the military-revolutionary societies that nineteenth-century Ireland evolved. From it, through a penetration of the Volunteer and Gaelic League organizations of the pre-1914 decade, are descended all of the political parties of the present-day Irish Republic with the exception of the Labour Party. Similarly, it was the originator of the tradition of the Irish Republican Army (IRA). Its first attempt at an Irish revolution failed in 1867, but it went on to play a significant part in the Land War. It penetrated the Gaelic Athletic Association in 1884. A generational change occurred in the IRB at the beginning of the twentieth century, and the young revolutionaries succeeded in taking over the Gaelic League in 1911. The Irish Volunteers of 1913 were controlled by the secret society, and its was a faction within the IRB – a secret society inside a secret society – that engineered the 1916 Rising. With the formation of the Second Sinn Féin Party, the IRA and the founding of the Dáil, the IRB became less important. However, it was one of the networks used by Michael Collins to run the War of Independence and to gain the revolutionaries' consent to the Anglo-Irish Treaty of 1921. Distrust of the IRB on the part of Éamon de Valera and many other political and military leaders was a primary cause of the mutual distrust that split the movement in 1922 and caused the Irish Civil War. The society died in the early 1920s.

The establishment of the independent Irish state and of Northern Ireland had the effect of partitioning the underground world of the secret societies as well. The IRA, for example, was faced with very different circumstances in the two parts of Ireland. In the 26 counties, it gradually was worn away by the twin processes of political co-option and military and police suppression. The formation of the army and the Civic Guard in 1922 attracted many IRA Volunteers into these new legal organizations. The Civic Guard, in particular, was an ingenious device by which young Volunteers were disarmed and converted, by ex-Royal Irish Constabulary instructors, from guerrillas into policemen. Parenthetically, the new Free State Army was ex-IRA only at officer level; its NCOs were recruited from disbanded Irish regiments of the British army, and its private soldiers were recruited mainly from young men who had had no connection with the old IRA.

When Fianna Fáil came into the Dáil in 1927, it brought with it the bulk of the rest of the 26-county IRA. Subsequent visitations to the political Canossa of Leinster House (the Irish Parliament) were made by the MacBride Republicans in the 1940s and the Official Republicans in the 1980s. The Provisionals dropped their policy of abstention from Dáil Éireann in 1986, but have achieved no political reward from the electorate for this belated bow to democracy. The swan-song of the southern IRA was the border campaign of 1956–61, which, significantly, generated little support north of the border. In 1957, abstentionist Sinn Féin, the IRA's political arm, actually won four Dáil seats, but its refusal to take the seats damaged it politically in the Republic. The 'secret army' persists in the South, but in attenuated form, and is mainly a reflection of events north of the border. Its relevance to the politics of the Republic is slight, however, cannot be discounted.

In Northern Ireland, the situation was, of course, very different, and the IRA has persisted to the present day. After 1922, it remained quite strong in Catholic areas, but gradually it lost initiative and enthusiasm, as the Northern state asserted itself and showed itself to be implacable in its efforts to defeat revolutionary Republicanism. However, by comparison with the South, the Northern IRA remained strong. This was partly due to the failure of the Stormont regime to offer genuine political life to the Catholics, and party to the discriminatory and repressive policies it pursued.

The organization virtually came back from the dead in 1969–71, and waged a guerrilla war against the British government and the government of Northern Ireland upto 1994. In 1970, it split into Provisional and Official wings; the latter has become virtually extinct as such and has mainly 'gone legal'. Elements have engaged in criminal activity. The Provisionals reorganized themselves into a cell structure in 1977, thereby reverting, perhaps unconsciously, to the structure used by the original Fenians. The movement has also shed various splinter groups since 1970, in particular the Marxist Irish People's Liberation Army.

Other essentially secret organizations have specific religious connections. The Orange Order, although technically no longer a secret organization, has many of the features of such a body. Its penetration of British Conservatism in late Victorian times in both Ireland and Britain was not inconsiderable, and it virtually controlled the Ulster Unionist Party in power after 1922. Its power has weakened considerably since the fall of Stormont in 1972, but it still an important feature of the North's political landscape.

Freemasonry, important in the last years of British Ireland because of its apparent penetration of much of Irish business, has declined since independence. A Catholic organization, the Knights of Columbanus, founded in imitation of the Freemasons at the beginning of the twentieth century, became a considerable political force after independence because of the support it received from the Catholic bishops, some Catholic businessmen and civil servants. It was particularly powerful in the Northern Catholic middle class, and in the towns of Dundalk, Drogheda and Limerick in the Republic. At least one president of the Republic, Sean T. O'Kelly, was a knight, to the apparent displeasure of de Valera. At one stage many officials of the Revenue were in the organization. It seems to be less important now than it used to be, and also appears to be less an organization of mutual career enhancement and more purely charitable than it once was.

The secret society tradition in Ireland is of great historical importance. Ireland is not unique in having such a tradition of secret politics, but the peculiar character of Irish political development has prevented the usual western process by which open competitive electoral politics replaces conspiratorial styles of political action from completing itself. The Republic has succeeded in shaking off more of the tradition of secrecy than has the North, but even in the Republic, political culture remains clandestine and a truly open and public style of government has yet to be achieved fully.

TOM GARVIN

sectarianism Viewed from a narrowly North Atlantic perspective during the 1970s and 1980s, Irish sectarianism, as manifested in the Troubles, could seem a baffling aberration. This required ignoring contemporary hotspots, notably the Middle East and Sri Lanka, and the widespread presence of similar dynamics in European and North American societies from the Reformation through to World War II, but it could be done. In recent years, however, the explosion of ethnic conflicts, some involving religion, in the former USSR and Yugoslavia has made Northern Ireland seem depressingly normal, perhaps even a mild case.

The Irish usage of 'sectarianism' is a local one not elucidated by church/sect typology, which could falsely suggest that responsibility lies with small, sect-like groups, or by dictionaries, which tend to define sectarianism in church/sect terms or in too-simple terms of religious bigotry. 'Sectarianism', as commonly used in Ireland, might be defined as 'a complex of attitudes, beliefs, behaviours, and structures in which religion is a significant component and which (1) infringes civil or religious rights or (2) influences or causes conflict'. This definition suggests three key characteristics of sectarianism.

1   Sectarianism is a religious problem. In recent times, the specifically doctrinal content of sectarianism has lowered – always allowing for the extreme importance for many conservative Protestants of centuries-old objections to Catholic teaching on the Mass, purgatory, Mary's role, etc. However, doctrinally derived issues can still generate searing sectarian heat in society. The outstanding recent examples are constitutional referendums which supported the absolute prohibition of divorce and abortion in the Republic of Ireland, positions justified by the Catholic bishops in terms of the greatest good for the greatest number, but interpreted by many Protestants, and others disaffected from Catholicism, as the sectarian imposition of Catholic standards.
2   Sectarianism is not, however, a 'purely' religious problem. Sectarianism typically involves a union of religion with political, economic, or cultural considerations – as the divorce and abortion examples illustrate. Northern Catholics use the language of sectarianism, not simply injustice or aggravation, when objecting to Orange Order marches, discriminatory employment practices, and the like, because religious, political and economic factors are entwined. Similarly, Northern Protestants brand the Irish state as sectarian, not merely discriminatory, because they perceive a pernicious blend of religion and politics.
3   Sectarianism causes injustice and conflict. An emphasis on negative consequences helps to distinguish sectarianism from simple religious difference or from benign intersections of religion and politics, which are only sectarian when they lead,

directly or indirectly, to injustice or conflict. The abuse of power to impose standards or deny opportunities is likely to loom large when the language of sectarianism is employed.

The sources of Irish sectarianism can be named in terms descriptive of ethnic conflicts everywhere: assuming the superiority of one's own community, demonizing enemies, curbing the rights of dissenters. But the specific form of Irish sectarianism reflects its Reformation origins. Churches became the key defining element of community identity, and conflict between the three largest communities – Church of Ireland, Presbyterian and Catholic – was partly couched in religious terms: our church is the one true church outside of which is no salvation, and error has no right. Although the Church of Ireland won the privileges of state establishment, the other two were frustrated establishments in waiting, differing only as to which was the true church, who was outside salvation, and who had no rights.

During this century the three main churches have acknowledged each other's salvific integrity and rejected the idea that error has no right. Although sectarianism will not be swept away quickly by the change, it may be a watershed. Previously the use of power to impose one church's teaching on society could claim a theological rationale. Now such behaviour violates explicit church teaching.

JOSEPH LIECHTY

self-portraiture in the twentieth century The broadest statement on Irish self-portraiture is made by the works in the National Self-Portrait Collection owned by (and housed in) the University of Limerick. This is somewhat of a forced statement in that very few of the 150 portraits which comprise this collection were made spontaneously: many of the artists, in responding to a formal invitation, found themselves faced with an art practice quite alien to their own.

The resulting works, which span a wide range of styles and media, include photo-realist images by abstract painters and detailed pencil drawings by minimalist sculptors. Thus the existence of an 'Irish self-portraiture' genre remains questionable.

As to whether Irish self-portraiture is distinctive in its Irishness, this is an equally doubtful reality. One could argue that, being a race with a reputation for 'beating around the bush', it is no surprise that many of these portraits possess a distant, indirect quality: so often the sitters' eyes are averted from the viewer. The works by women, although in the minority, are a notable exception to this general lack of commitment. Perhaps it is no coincidence that most of these women were born before the middle of the century, and therefore were making art at a time when a more resilient self-questioning and self-motivating streak was demanded of them than of their male counterparts who dominated the world of Irish fine art.

The majority of works in this collection do not rate very highly. As studies in how a selection of twentieth-century Irish artists have chosen to portray themselves to the Irish public, they create quite a curiosity.

Reading

Brett, David, 'The possibility of portraiture', *Circa* 57 (May/June 1991).

Finlay, Sarah, *The National Self Portrait Collection of Ireland* (University of Limerick Press, 1989).

Maxton, Hugh, 'Portrait of the nation as a young gallery', *Circa* 49 (January/February 1990).

SARAH FINLAY

sexuality In pre-modern societies, sex, reproduction and kinship were intertwined with the economic functioning of society. Eighteenth-century pre-Famine Ireland was characterized by very early marriage for males and females among the poorer classes. This probably explained the huge population increase from 2 million in 1754 to over 8 million in 1841. Economic decline from 1820 and the potato famine of the 1840s led to mass emigration and starvation, drastically reducing the labourer and cottier classes. Survival at subsistence level in an agricultural economy required population control and the consolidation and reorganization of farms. Sexual control and restraint played a major role in this social transformation, as postponed marriage and high rates of permanent celibacy controlled population growth. The abandonment of land subdivision and its replacement by a single farm inheritor consolidated holdings. Emigration continued as both employment and marriage prospects were low. This pattern persisted, so that by the 1950s Ireland had the lowest marriage rate in Europe and very high celibacy rates, with 30 per cent of men and 25 per cent of women aged 55 unmarried. The average marriage age was 33 for men and 28 for women. High levels of celibacy co-existed with high fertility rates within marriage. This era survived in Ireland almost until the 1960s.

The adoption of Catholic values and ideals facilitated the sexual restraint required by celibacy and postponed marriage. Through its teaching and in particular by its role in education, the church helped to civilize the peasant population. The church contribution in turn served to advance their power, leading to a theocratic state when Ireland gained its independence.

The civilizing process was initiated by building churches as separate places of devotion. Attendance at Mass, respectful dress and behaviour in church were promoted. Schools under the control of religious orders and priests were established. Religious voluntary effort provided Ireland with an educational system which greatly exceeded its economic capacity. The social practices which emerged were Catholic ones, inspired and directed by Catholic church teaching.

Catholic social teaching on women was based not on equality with men but on either complementarity or subsidiarity. Men had a natural right to rule the family, women were best suited for work in the home. Within Catholicism the Cartesian/Augustinian legacy saw the body or 'flesh' as a source of evil. Sexual passion had to be controlled. In the confessional the penitent's sexual practices and thoughts were investigated. This practice inculcated a sense of private guilt about sexual matters. Sex (as sinful) became such a preoccupation that immorality became virtually synonymous with sexual immorality. This was exacerbated by a failure to provide any form of sex education and by a general view that these matters should be repressed and not discussed publicly.

Catholic teaching did not permit men greater sexual freedom, but stressed women's responsibility for controlling men's sexual passions. Women, because of original sin, had a weakness; they could be the temptress or seductive Eve. Their sexual passions must be controlled, and when controlled the refined, delicate nature of women could be revealed. A Catholic education emphasized modesty in conduct and dress, and devotion to Our Lady was encouraged. She embodied the mutually exclusive roles of virgin and mother. Her virginity role model generated an esteem for celibacy, inspiring women to become nuns or 'brides of Christ'. Christ himself was celibate and provided a male role model. The church's message encouraging sexual restraint and control, albeit supported by persistent economic recession in Ireland, was successful if judged by the number of men and women who remained celibate, or joined religious orders. Pregnancy outside marriage was lower among Catholics, and such fallen women often ended up in asylums.

Irish mothers were empowered within the home by the church, which valued their dissemination of Catholic values and beliefs, and their encouragement of vocations. Given the devotion within Catholicism to Jesus and Mary and their ascetic lifestyles, it is not surprising that sex within marriage had to have a procreative purpose. While Irish married women had high fertility rates, little is known about their sexual practices, except that due to general ignorance, sex was often deemed an obligation.

The 1937 constitution legally enshrined key aspects of Catholic social teaching. Defensive censorship legislation was enacted which banned any work considered indecent or obscene, as well as literature advocating birth control. The narrow emphasis on sex meant the banning of the work of major Irish writers. This theocratic state remained virtually unchallenged until the seventies. Catholic church teaching on birth control was strictly adhered to. The essential core of this teaching was that every 'act of marriage' must, in itself, stay open to human procreation. For Catholics, contraception was morally prohibited; in Ireland it was legally prohibited also. The church vehemently, if eventually unsuccessfully, resisted its legalization.

In the 1990s, unwanted pregnancies and attendant abortions in England co-exist with strong opposition to legalized abortion and even to sex education in schools. The legalization of homosexuality, mandatory as a result of a European Court verdict, is not yet on the political agenda. While gay and lesbian rights groups are gaining support, diverse sexual proclivities and attendant lifestyles are simply not recognized. Irish attitudes to sexuality remain conservative.

This retention of the link between sex and reproduction is a crucial one in interpreting the role of sexuality in society. The family gives sex a legitimacy. Sexuality as a distinct personal entitlement or experience cannot easily exist if sexual behaviour is bound up with reproduction. In modern society, contraception, limitation of family size and the possibility of technological reproduction remove reproduction from 'nature' to social control. The separation of sexuality from reproduction brings a series of attendant life practices: homosexuality, lesbianism and the transformation of intimacy in new, equal, consensual relationships. Once sexuality becomes an integral component of social relations, heterosexuality is no longer the standard by which everything is judged. Such an approach to sexuality is consistent with modernity, a process as yet only begun in Ireland.

Reading

Clear, C., *Nuns in Nineteenth Century Ireland* (Dublin: Gill and Macmillan, 1987).

Curtin, C., 'Marriage and family', in P. Clancy, S. Drudy, K. Lynch and L. O'Dowd, *Ireland: A Sociological Profile* (Dublin: Institute of Public Administration, 1986).

Foucault M., *The History of Sexuality. Vol. 1* (Harmondsworth: Penguin, 1978).

Giddens, A., *The Transformation of Intimacy* (Cambridge: Polity Press, 1992).

Humphreys, A., *New Dubliners: Urbanization and the Irish Family* (London: Routledge and Kegan Paul, 1966).

Inglis, T., *Moral Monopoly* (Dublin: Gill and Macmillan, 1987).

Lee, J., *Ireland 1912–1985* (Cambridge: Cambridge University Press, 1989).

Luddy, M., 'Prostitution and rescue work in nineteenth-century Ireland', in M. Luddy and C. Murphy (eds), *Women Surviving: Studies in Irish Women's History in the 19th and 20th Centuries* (Dublin: Poolbeg, 1990).

Maddox, B., *The Pope and Contraception* (London: Chatto and Windus, 1991).

Mahon, E., 'Women's rights and Catholicism in Ireland', *New Left Review* 166 (November/ December 1987).

O'Dowd, L., 'Church, state and women: the aftermath of partition', in C. Curtin, (ed), *Gender in Irish Society* (Galway: Galway University Press, 1987).

Tussing, A.D., *Irish Educational Expenditures – Past, Present and Future* (Dublin: Economic and Social Research Institute, 1978).

Whyte, J., *Church and State in Modern Ireland 1923–1979*, 2nd edn (Dublin: Gill and Macmillan, 1980).

EVELYN MAHON

Shackleton family One of Ireland's best-known Quaker families. Of yeoman stock in the West Riding of Yorkshire, Abraham (1696–1771) came to Carlow in 1720 as tutor to the Ducketts of Duckett's Grove, County Carlow, and the Coopers of Cooper's Hill, King's County, returning in 1726 to settle and found Ballitore boarding-school in County Kildare (which closed in 1836, some thousand pupils later). His son, Richard (1728–92), friend to Edmund Burke, succeeded him as master at Ballitore in 1756 and had a mill there in 1776. Richard's daughter, Mary Leadbeater (1758–1826), wrote the *Annals of Ballitore* (printed by R.D. Webb in 1862), an exemplary record of daily village life from 1766 to 1824. Richard's grandson, George (1785–1871), took over the milling business at Ballitore in 1823, expanding to Lyons Mill at Straffan in 1853 (burnt 1903), Anna Liffey Mill at Lucan in 1859 (sold to Roma Foods 1980), and Grange Mill at the twelfth lock, Lucan, in 1865 (sold 1978). George's daughter Lydia (1828–1914), one of 13 children by Hannah, was a noted botanical artist under Sir Frederick Moore at Dublin's National Botanic Gardens. George's brother, Ebenezer (1784–1856), was father of Richard, who built the first steel roller mill in Ireland at Carlow, and Henry, whose son Ernest (1874–1922), born in Kilkea, County Kildare, was an outstanding Antarctic explorer, coming within 97 miles of the South Pole and receiving a knighthood in 1909. Ernest's brother Frank (1876–1941) was a Dublin Herald implicated in the theft of the Insignia of the Order of St Patrick in 1907. Ernest's son Edward (1911–) was created a life peer in 1958 and became Labour leader of the House of Lords from 1968 to 1970. David Shackleton (1923–88), plant collector, established a garden of international repute at Beech Park, Clonsilla, County Dublin.

ANTONY FARRELL

Shakespearean scholars Edmond Malone (1741–1812), Ireland's pre-eminent scholar of Shakespeare, was preceded in his studies by the earlier antiquarian John Monck Mason (1726–1809), and followed by others such as Nicholas Halpin (1790–1850). The pre-eminent Irish Shakespearean was Edward

Dowden (1843–1913). Born in Cork, he was educated at Trinity College, Dublin, where he was given the newly founded chair of English literature in 1867. The book he published eight years later, *Shakspere, His Mind and Art*, presented a psychological and moralistic view of Shakespeare that helped to set the predominant tone of Shakespeare appreciation for the next half-century. In more recent years, James K. Walton, educated in Dublin, the UK and the USA, was a scholar whose concept of Shakespearean textual studies and in particular the text of *Richard III* was some decades ahead of its time. (The minority view he voiced in the 1960s was substantiated in the New Oxford edition of 1988.)

Probably the most notorious of all the early Shakespeareans, William-Henry Ireland (1775–1835), owes Ireland nothing but his name. His forgeries of Shakespeare plays, stimulated by Edmond Malone's work on the manuscripts, and which Malone played a signal part in exposing, brought him fame and then notoriety in 1795.

Reading

Schoenbaum, S., *Shakespeare's Lives*, new edn (Oxford: 1991).

A.J. GURR

Shaw, George Bernard (1856–1950) Dramatist and critic. Born Dublin, 26 July; died Ayot St Lawrence, 2 November. When Bernard Shaw died at the age of 94, he was one of the most famous writers in the world: author of over 50 plays, five novels, volumes of theatre and music criticism, political essays, journalism on every subject imaginable, an *oeuvre* to be listed in a thousand-page bibliography. Where did it all come from, what did it amount to?

George Bernard Shaw was the son of George Carr Shaw, ne' er-do-well businessman and closet drunk, and Lucinda Elizabeth Gurly, amateur singer later turned music teacher. Of a class described by Shaw himself as

the 'downstarts', younger sons of younger sons, Protestantism and landed connections kept the family just within the bounds of middle-class gentility, though association with the charlatan musician George Vandaleur Lee, with whom the Shaw parents shared a *ménage à trois*, must have put that status at risk. Leaving school at 15, Shaw spent nearly five years as a clerk in a Dublin land agency office, before leaving to join his mother and sister in London in 1876. Unemployed for most of the nine years that followed, he wrote novel after unpublished novel and educated himself as, among other things, a radical socialist. From 1885 he began to make a living as a journalist, reviewing books, art and (most notably) music, while also building a reputation as a public speaker in advanced socialist circles. An apostle for a European avant-garde in art, his advocacy of Wagner in music was matched by his crusade for Ibsen in the drama which informed his theatre criticism for the *Saturday Review* (1895–8) and his own early plays in the same period.

Shaw's first play, *Widower's Houses*, produced in 1892, was a challenging Ibsenian problem play about slum landlordism. His characteristic technique in these plays of the 1890s was to transform a popular theatrical form by subverting audience expectations, whether the 'woman with a past' play (*Mrs Warren's Profession*), military romance (*Arms and the Man*) or farce (*You Never Can Tell*). Unable to find commercial productions for his plays, he took the then unusual step of publishing them in two volumes of *Plays Pleasant and Unpleasant* in 1898, with his *Three Plays for Puritans* following in 1901. In 1898, also, he married Charlotte Payne-Townshend, a well-to-do Irish woman from Cork and Fabian Society associate, and gave up regular journalism. His breakthrough as a playwright came in 1904–7, when the repertory seasons of Granville Barker and Vedrenne at the London Royal Court Theatre brought him outstanding successes with *John Bull's Other Island*, his one full-length play about Ireland, *Major Barbara*, and *Man and*

Superman, the gigantic 'comedy and philosophy' written some years earlier without a view to being staged. From that point on, Shaw's international fame as a playwright was assured, though it was not until 1911, with *Fanny's First Play*, that he had a long run in the West End, and not until 1914, with *Pygmalion*, that he had his first major popular success.

Always deliberately provocative in his public attitudes, Shaw outraged the English with his long pamphlet *Common Sense About the War*, which he rushed out in November 1914, though he was to support the Allied cause and later even assist in army recruiting. Politically opposed to Irish national separatism, he nevertheless defended the leaders of the Easter Rising in 1916 and attempted to draft a defence for Roger Casement. His one major play written during the war, *Heartbreak House*, was not well received when it was published in 1919, and *Back to Methuselah* (1921), his cycle of five plays dramatizing the doctrine of creative evolution, appeared unstageable. His reputation more than recovered, however, with the international success of *Saint Joan* (1923) and the award of the Nobel prize for literature in 1926. His other most important work of the 1920s was *The Intelligent Woman's Guide to Socialism and Capitalism* (1928).

Though his political satire *The Apple Cart* (1929) was reasonably successful, and he found a vehicle for his new plays in the Malvern Festival, in extravaganzas such as *Too True to be Good* (1932) and *The Simpleton of the Unexpected Isles* (1935) Shaw's dramatic inventiveness seemed to slacken. Admirers were shaken by his positive enthusiasm for Stalin (whom he met briefly on a visit to Russia in 1931), and his lack of condemnation for Mussolini and Hitler, quite genially caricatured in *Geneva* (1938). He went on writing through his eighties and into his nineties, and his earlier plays continued to be much revived in the theatre and successfully filmed, but it was as public figure, sage, and grand old man that he was most valued in his last years.

One final measure of his popularity was the swift sales of the 'Shaw Million', 100,000 copies each of ten of his works, published by Penguin Books for his ninetieth birthday in 1946.

'I am not enamoured of failure, of poverty, of obscurity, and of the ostracism and contempt which these imply; and these were all that Dublin offered to the enormity of my unconscious ambition.' Fleeing the Ireland where he was nobody, Shaw was determined to reconstitute himself as somebody in the cosmopolitanism of London. In the created persona of G.B.S., his Irishness was always to be retained as a feature of defining difference, along with his vegetarianism, his teetotalism, and his belief in all-wool clothing. Shaw wanted to remake not only his initally unsatisfactory self, but also the unsatisfactory world in which he found that self. His conversion to socialism gave him a cause and a system with which to identify his desire for fundamental social reform. Though a heterodox socialist, whose reading of Marx was subsequently overlaid by a conversion to Jevonian economics, his tireless work with Beatrice and Sydney Webb in the Fabian Society (which he helped to found), and his part in the immensely influential collection of *Fabian Essays in Socialism* (1889), contributed substantially to the development of social democracy in Britain. Never content to be a man of letters merely, Shaw often felt a sense of frustration at his failure to achieve the degree of public influence he would have liked. This frustration, along with a longstanding impatience with the inefficiencies and hypocrisies of the democratic system, gave him his preference for totalizing political solutions such as equality of incomes in *The Intelligent Woman's Guide*, and his admiration for the 1930s dictators.

Shaw's distinction involved a peculiar combination of clarity and singularity in thought and style. Through the period of his intellectual evolution in the 1880s and 1890s, he absorbed ideas from Hegel, Marx, Nietzsche (Shaw was the writer who gave the word 'superman' to the English language), William Morris, Ibsen and Wagner, but he transformed them into an amalgam which was all his own. His central creed of creative evolution, the idea that a life force was working through the human species towards ever greater powers of self-realization, was a means of marrying his individualism to a comprehensible and determining world view. The brilliant discursiveness of so much of his writing, and its didacticism in both plays and prefaces, helped to make Shaw disciples, but have also resulted in his anomalous standing as a figure in world literature. The standard charge against Shaw, in his own time and since, has been that he is not a playwright but a preacher, a preacher whose views have become increasingly irrelevant and outmoded.

On the face of it, the charge is ridiculous. The most popular of Shaw's plays continue to hold the stage across the world; in St Joan he wrote one of the great female leading roles in the theatrical repertoire; no playwright in English since Shakespeare has created anything like his range of stage characters. By its crackle and thrust, turn and counter-turn, Shaw's dramatic rhetoric continues to live, though the ideas may be dated as the dodo. Yet the hostility towards Shaw's plays persists, partly as a reaction against the relentlessness of his ideological control and the unyielding certainty of his style. In the second half of the twentieth century, when literary critics have valued texts above all for multivalence, ambiguity and discordance, Shaw's assured and assertive writings have been increasingly ignored. So the paradox remains of a writer displaced and dismissed within the academy who yet continues to have an exceptionally wide readership, the status of a classic playwright, and the unquantifiable influence of ideas diffused by quotation through the language.

Reading

Bentley, Eric, *Bernard Shaw: A Reconsideration* (New York: New Directions, 1947).

Gordon, David J., *Bernard Shaw and the Comic Sublime* (Basingstoke and London: Macmillan 1990).

Grene, Nicholas, *Bernard Shaw: A Critical View* (Basingstoke and London: Macmillan 1984).

Holroyd, Michael, *Bernard Shaw*, 3 vols (London: Chatto and Windus, 1988–91).

Laurence, Dan H., *Bernard Shaw: A Bibliography*, 2 vols (Oxford: Clarendon Press, 1983).

Meisel, Martin, *Shaw and the Nineteenth-Century Theater* (Princeton NJ: Princeton University Press, 1963).

Shaw, G.B., *The Works of Bernard Shaw: Standard Edition*, 37 vols (London: Constable, 1931–51).

NICHOLAS GRENE

Shawcross, Neil (1940–) Painter. Born Kearsely. Shawcross attended art colleges in Bolton and Lancaster but has lived in Northern Ireland since 1968. He has had many exhibitions in Dublin and Belfast, and was included in 'The Delighted Eye' at London in 1980. Shawcross's style, influenced by Bonnard and Matisse, is colourful and distinctive, with softly brushed contours and a strong element of wit. More recently, he has experimented with collage-like effects. His portrait of the novelist Francis Stuart (Ulster Museum) shows him at his best and most characteristic. Shawcross has also been active in Belfast as a teacher and art lecturer.

BRIAN FALLON

Shee, Sir Martin Archer (1769–1850) Painter. Born Dublin, 20 December; died Brighton, 19 August. The son of a merchant, Shee grew up in County Wicklow. A student at the Dublin Society Schools aged 12–14, he set up as a professional while still a teenager. On moving to London in 1788 he sought further instruction and was a student at the Royal Academy (RA) School for about a year. Assisted and influenced by Gilbert Stuart, Joshua Reynolds and others, Shee specialized in portraits becoming RA in 1800. In 1830 in competition with David Wilkie he succeeded Sir Thomas Lawrence as president of the RA a surprising achievement for a Catholic-born Irishman. He was knighted in the same year.

Reading

Crookshank, Anne, and the Knight of Glin, *The Painters of Ireland c. 1660–1920* (London: Barrie and Jenkins, 1978).

Shee, Martin Archer, *The Life of Sir Martin Archer Shee* (London: 1860).

Strickland, Walter, *A Dictionary of Irish Artists* (Shannon: Irish University Press, 1968).

FINTAN CULLEN

Sheehy, Nicholas (1728–66) Catholic priest. Born Fethard, County Tipperary educated in France, Sheehy was parish priest of the County Tipperary parish of Clogheen and Newcastle in the early 1760s, when the Whiteboy disturbances were at their height. A champion of the poor, and prosecuted on several occasions for involvement with the Whiteboys, he was charged in February 1766 with the murder of an informer. Sheehy denied the charge, but sectarian animosities had become so enflamed in County Tipperary that Protestant jurymen had no difficulty in acceding to the directions of their social superiors, who wanted a guilty veredict. Sheehy was hanged in 1766 and, as a result, became a folk hero with the local Catholic population.

Reading

Bric, Maurice, 'The Whiteboy movement 1760–1800', in W. Nolan (ed.), *Tipperary: History and Society* (Dublin: Geography Publications, 1985).

Griffith, Amyas, *Miscellaneous Tracts* (Dublin: 1788).

JAMES KELLY

Sheehy Skeffington, Owen (1909–70) University lecturer and senator. Sheehy Skeffington was the only son of Hanna Sheehy and Francis Skeffington. Hanna (born County Cork, 1877) was the eldest daughter of David Sheehy, MP (1844–1932), niece of Father Eugene Sheehy, the 'Land League Priest' (1841–1917), and of the same family as Fr. Nicholas Sheehy (1728–66), who was executed at the height of the Whiteboy alarms. She was a leader in the Irish women's suffrage movement and active in Sinn Féin. Francis (Frank, born County Cavan, 1878), was an early feminist, pacifist and socialist. He was shot without trial in April 1916, by a British officer later declared guilty but insane.

In 1934, after two years teaching in the École Normale Supérieure, Paris, Sheehy Skeffington became lecturer in French at his *alma mater*, Trinity College, Dublin, where he remained until his death. Elected to represent the college in Seanad Éireann in 1954, he remained active here also. In 1935 he married Andrée, née Denis, of Amiens, by whom he had two sons, Francis and Alan, and a daughter, Micheline.

Socialist, liberal, pacifist, he started or got involved in many controversies, for freedom of conscience and expression against state, church or party authoritarianism, in favour of humane social legislation and a more egalitarian society. Many of his battles were fought in articles or correspondence to the newspapers, one of the more notable and extended subsequently being published by the *Irish Times* with the title *The Liberal Ethic*. He is remembered as a champion of minority causes, who spoke out fearlessly and persistently at a time when this took courage.

Reading

Sheehy Skeffington, Andrée, *Skeff – The Life of Owen Sheehy Skeffington* (Dublin: Lilliput Press, 1991).

ANDRÉE SHEEHY SKEFFINGTON

Sheridan family Rev. Denis Sheridan (born County Cavan), an Irish speaker, was brought up a Protestant in the house of John Hill, dean of Kilmore, ordained 10 June 1634 by William Bedell, bishop of Kilmore, and is said to have assisted Bedell in translating the Old Testament into Gaelic. He married an Englishwoman and had the following children:

1 William (1636–1711). Born Togher, Kilmore, County Cavan. He became Bishop of Kilmore (he was Bishop Bedell's godson). He entered Trinity College, Dublin, 15 May 1652 aged 17 years. He was imprisoned and deprived of the bishopric for refusing to take an oath of loyalty to King William III. He married Mary O'Reilly, and had a son, Donald.
2 Patrick (c.1638–82). Born near Enniskillen, County Fermanagh. He was appointed Bishop of Cloyne (1679). He entered Trinity College, Dublin, 15 May 1652, aged 14 years.
3 Thomas (c.1646–88/1712). Born St John's, near Trim, County Meath. He was a Jacobite and author. He entered Trinity College, Dublin, 17 January 1660/1, aged 14 years. He became collector of customs in Cork. He was imprisoned during the 'popish plot' scare in 1680; in 1688 he became private secretary to James II in exile. He married (?natural daughter of James II), and had a daughter who married Col. Guillaume, aide-de-camp to William III and a son, Thomas the younger (1684–1746), who became tutor in exile to Prince Charles 'the Pretender', and fought at Culloden.
4 James (c.1649–?). Born near Trim, County Meath. The entered Trinity College, Dublin, 11 May 1665, aged 16 years.

Rev. Dr Thomas Sheridan (1687–1738) was the nephew of William, bishop of Kilmore, and of Thomas, the Jacobite and author; he was probably the son of James. Born in Cavan, he entered Trinity College, Dublin, 18 October 1707, aged 20 years. A noted scholar and close friend of Dean Jonathan Swift, he had a distinguished school for boys in Capel Street, Dublin. He married Elizabeth, only daughter and heiress of

Charles MacFadden of Quilca, County Cavan, and had the following children:

1 James (d. 22 August 1724). He is buried in St Mary's, Dublin.
2 Richard, of North Earls Street, Dublin. He entered Trinity College, Dublin, 14 March 1731/2, aged 16 years. His will is dated 15 May 1782, proved 10 March 1787. He married Elinor and had at least five children.
3 Thomas (1719–88).
4 Elizabeth, of Camden Row, Dublin. She died November 1784, aged 70 years.
5 Anne, who married (1735) John Sheen of Custom House, Dublin.
6 Esther, who married John Knowles of Dublin.
7 Meliora.

Thomas Sheridan (1719–88) was an author, actor, theatre manager and elocution teacher. He was born at 12 Dorset Street, Dublin, and entered Trinity College, Dublin, 26 May 1735, aged 16 years. In 1743 he made his debut as an actor at the Theatre Royal, Smock Alley, Dublin; in 1745 he became manager of Smock Alley. He left with his family for London in 1754. Swift was his godfather. In 1747 Sheridan married Frances, daughter of Rev. Philip Chamberlayne, archdeacon of Glendalough. Frances Chamberlayne Sheridan (born Dublin, 1724) was a successful writer and dramatist; the family settled in Blois, France, in 1764, where she died (20 September 1766). Thomas, her husband, then went back to England and settled in Bath, where he taught elocution. There were five children:

1 Thomas (1748–50).
2 Charles Francis (1750–1806), author and politician. He was born in Dorset Street. Dublin. Elected MP for the Borough of Belturbet in 1776, he became MP for Rathcormack in 1780. He was secretary of war in Dublin (1782–9). In 1783 he married Letitia Christiana, daughter of

Robert Bolton of Dublin. He died in Tunbridge Wells.

3   Right Hon. Richard Brinsley Sheridan (1751–1816).

4   Alicia, author of a memoire of her mother. Born in 1753, she married Joseph Le Fanu (11 October 1871).

5   Anne Elizabeth Hume Crawford. Her letters to Alicia were published in 1960. Born in 1758, she married Henry Le Fanu, Captain of 56th Foot, in 1789.

Right Hon. Richard Brinsley Sheridan, dramatist, orator and politician, was born 30 October 1751 at Dorset Street. He left Ireland with his parents and never revisited. Manager and subsequently owner of Drury Lane Theatre (1776–1809), he became MP for Stafford (1780–1812). In 1782 he was made under-secretary of state for foreign affairs, and in 1783 secretary of the Treasury. He is buried in Westminster Abbey. In 1773 he married Elizabeth, daughter of Thomas Linley; she was a vocalist, and they had one son, Thomas. In 1795 Richard married Esther Jane, daughter of Dr Ogle, Dean of Winchester; they had a son, Charles Brinsley, who died 1848.

Thomas, son of Richard, 'Tom' Sheridan married Caroline Henrietta, daughter of Col. James Callander (afterwards Sir James Campbell) and of his wife Lady Elizabeth Helena, youngest daughter of Alexander Macdonnell, fifth earl of Antrim. 'Tom' died (1817) in the Cape of Good Hope, where he was posted with his family as colonial treasurer. Caroline Henrietta Sheridan returned to London with her seven children (four sons and three daughters). She was a novelist and died 1851. Their eldest son was Richard Brinsley Sheridan, MP for Shaftersbury (1845–52). In 1835 he married Marcia Maria, only surviving child of Lieut.-Gen. Sir Colquhoen of Frampton Court; they had nine children. He died 1888.

'Tom' and Caroline Henrietta Sheridan's eldest daughter was Helena Selina Sheridan (1807–67), a songwriter, wife of Commander Price Blackwood, baron of Dufferin and Clandeboye.

MÁIRE MACCONGHAIL

silver Silver and gold were worked in Ireland in three identifiable periods. From approximately 2000 BC to AD 500 the principal manufacture was in gold ornaments for personal adornment. The second period from AD 500 to 1500 began shortly after the introduction of Christianity, when silver took the place of gold and was used with a combination of other metals such as gold, copper and bronze, the church being the main patron. The final period from 1500 onwards continues with church plate, mostly chalices, and this is extended until 1637 and the complete organization of the Company of Goldsmiths, with a charter stipulating recognized standards for precious metals that apply to the present day. No domestic silver plate survives which is known to have been made in Ireland before the institution of the Company of Goldsmiths in 1637, due mainly to the outbreak of rebellion on 23 October 1641, when the government was forced to raise funds for the relief of the army: a warrant of 5 January 1642 ordered all persons to deliver half or more of their plate for sale.

It is only with the restoration of the monarchy in 1660 that it becomes possible to start a serious study of domestic plate. The styles in silver conformed to English and European influences. After the Edict of Nantes in 1685, several Hugenot silversmiths arrived and brought with them new ideas, including the baluster shape. From about 1700 to 1740 domestic silver was made of heavy-gauge metal. It was a time of plain surfaces and elegant proportions.

By 1740 this plain period had drawn to a close and the elaborate rococo style became fashionable. The asymmetrical designs in ornamentation were born in France in the 1720s and took about 20 years to arrive in Ireland. The chaser's art flourished, and farmyard animals were becoming popular in decoration from about 1760.

By 1770 society had begun to tire of the disorderly designs of this period, and a new generation with modern town-houses demanded something different. The spirit of antiquity and the neo-classical or Adam period had arrived in Ireland. The classical shapes of metal were covered with a variety of engraved designs and motifs, including borders and festoons of husks, palm and acanthus leaves. After 1800 this influence began to lose popularity. The nineteenth century saw the expansion of retail shops, and silver articles became heavy in weight as both the silver metal and labour were cheap compared with the eighteenth-century rates. For the first half of the nineteenth century there was no particular theme in decoration. Heavy chasing with a stippled background was fashionable. In the 1840s there was a reawakening of interest in ancient artifacts, and copies of brooches in the Royal Irish Academy were being manufactured. In 1894 the Arts and Crafts Society was formed and several silversmiths exhibited at their shows in 1896 and 1899.

The silver trade moved into the twentieth century still copying old designs. The Catholic church, after the Catholic Emancipation Act of 1829, encouraged the manufacture of ecclesiastical vessels, and was one of the main patrons of the silver trade until Vatican II ordered a cutback in elaborate altar furnishings.

The golden period for design in silver was the eighteenth century. The silver trade continues today with not a single apprentice in the whole of Ireland and is faced with increased competition from England, Germany and Italy, together with various Asian countries.

DOUGLAS BENNETT

Sinn Féin The name, meaning 'ourselves', was current for years before Arthur Griffith adopted it as the title of one of his many newspapers. Soon afterwards the first Sinn Féin party was founded (1907), and for the next few years it propagated Griffith's policies of economic independence, the abstention of Irish representatives from Westminster, and the revision of Anglo-Irish relations along the lines of an idealized Grattan's Parliament or an idealized Austro-Hungarian dual monarchy. The party was a failure; at its peak it claimed only 128 branches, it lost the one by-election it contested, and it soon faded away. After 1913 the Irish Volunteers took over the role which had been played briefly by Sinn Féin, that of radical nationalist challenger to the Parliamentary Party.

However, the name 'Sinn Féin' was soon applied to the Volunteers, and subsequently to the Easter Rising as well. The result was that when political separatism revived in 1917, Griffith and his ideas played a more prominent role than might otherwise have been expected. A second Sinn Féin party was formed, which won mass support, and by the end of the year it had over 1,200 branches throughout the country. Like its predecessor, it was a coalition of different elements; it was dominated by Volunteers and former rebels, many of whom regarded political activity as an unworthy, distasteful and temporary substitute for their proper role: fighting the British. None the less they proved skilful and successful politicians, and some of them were weaned away from their narrow military ideas. Sinn Féin defeated the Parliamentary Party in a series of by-elections and replaced it as the principal voice of nationalist Ireland.

Griffith was replaced as president by Éamon de Valera, the senior surviving leader of Easter Week, and, despite the opposition of moderates who knew that such a policy must lead to war, the party committed itself to the aim of securing an Irish Republic. Socially it was conservative, and it was determined to avoid all involvement in conflicts which would distract the Irish people from 'national' objectives; one of its more remarkable innovations was the establishment of a series of arbitration courts aimed at defusing class tensions. In 1918 the party's position was strengthened by its prominent role in the fight against conscription, and its triumph was completed in the general elections of December 1918, when it routed the Parliamentary Party and won 73 of the 105 Irish seats. The following month Sinn Féin MPs met and proclaimed themselves Dáil Éireann, or the Irish Parliament. Implementing Griffith's policies, they established a cabinet and a bureaucracy and tried to act as a normal government in opposition to Dublin Castle and the British forces.

The resumption of widespread hostilities between 1919 and 1921 restored the Volunteers' pre-eminent role; while they took the lead in the war with Britain, Sinn Féin was forced underground for nearly two years and its activities were severely restricted. Many of the powers which it had exercised were now taken over by the Dáil and its bureaucracy; although the circumstances were abnormal, the party's experience was astonishingly 'normal', and followed the pattern whereby parties tend to lose influence to the state machinery as their leaders move from opposition to government.

Sinn Féin, like the cabinet, the Dáil and the army, was divided over the terms of the Anglo-Irish Treaty. Although the overwhelming majority of its members were less radical than some of their leaders (or than the bulk of the army), and supported the agreement as an acceptable compromise, the party avoided any formal decision on the question. In the meantime rival pro- and anti-Treaty organizations were formed and campaigned against each other in anticipation of a general election. Sinn Féin was left as little more than a fragile aspiration to unity, and was governed by an officer board carefully balanced between the opposing factions. The party had fallen apart precisely and predictably on the question of 'the Republic', the issue which had proved so divisive when the coalition between the different elements had been formalized in October 1917.

In May 1922 its fortunes seemed to have been revived by the Collins – de Valera pact, according to which pro- and anti-Treaty elements should run candidates in a joint 'Sinn Féin panel' in proportion to their strength in the existing Dáil; only the right of 'other' parties to run candidates could prevent the unopposed return of every sitting TD. In the event enough other candidates ran to ensure meaningful elections, and this enabled the electorate to vote decisively in favour of the Treaty. Pro-Treaty Sinn Féin won 58 seats, Republicans 36 and 'others' (all pro-Treaty) 34. The large anti-Sinn Féin vote could be seen as a repudiation of the party's recent record. Soon afterwards the long-simmering civil war finally exploded, and politics once more took second place to military action.

Supporters of the Treaty decided to discard Sinn Féin and start afresh with a new organization, Cumann na nGaedheal. De Valera moved to fill the vacuum. Even though the Republicans were strongest in the army, and were in many cases contemptuous of politics and politicians, it was they who tried to retain the name, structures and assets of the old Sinn Féin party, which their enemies had unwisely discarded.

Despite a break in institutional and legal continuity, a new (third) Sinn Féin party emerged in 1923 as the political wing of the Republican or anti-Treaty movement. It was committed to abstention from the Free State Dáil, just as its predecessor had been to abstention from Westminster. The party contested the 1923 elections and performed surprisingly well, winning 27.6 per cent of the first-preference votes, but its abstention policy doomed it to irrelevance. De Valera became increasingly frustrated at being excluded from the country's political life, but was unable to convince a majority of his colleagues of the need for even minimal flexibility. In 1926 he and many of his followers left the Sinn Féin party and founded Fianna Fáil, which, a year later, became the dominant voice of Irish republicans. Ever since then Sinn Féin has been little more than an auxiliary to successive forms of the IRA. In 1998 the organization was poised to finally achieve political credibility, with the election to the Executive of the Northern Ireland Assembly of its candidates Báirbre de Brún and Martin McGuinness.

Reading

Boyce, D.G. (ed.), *The Revolution in Ireland, 1879–1923* (Dublin: Gill and Macmillan, 1988).

Curran, Joseph, *The Birth of the Irish Free State, 1921–1923* (Alabama: University of Alabama Press, 1980).

Davis, Richard, *Arthur Griffith and Non-Violent Sinn Fein* (Dublin: Anvil Books, 1974).

Farrell, Brian, *The Founding of Dail Eireann* (Dublin: Gill and Macmillan, 1971).

Fitzpatrick, David, *The Geography of Irish Nationalism, Past and Present*.

Garvin, Tom, *Revolutionary Nationalists in Ireland, 1858–1924* (Oxford: Oxford University Press).

Glandon, Virginia, *Arthur Griffith and the Advanced Nationalist Press in Ireland, 1900–1922* (New York: Peter Lang, 1985).

Laffan, Michael, 'The Unification of Sinn Fein in 1917', *IHS* xvii (1971).

Lee, J.J., *Ireland, 1912–1985: Politics and Society* (Cambridge: Cambridge University Press, 1989).

Ó Luing, Sean, *Art Ó Griofa* (Dublin: Sáirséal agus Dill, 1953).

Rumpf, Erhard and Hepburn, A.C., *Nationalism and Socialism in Twentieth Century Ireland* (Liverpool: Liverpool University Press, 1977).

Walker, B.M. (ed.), *Parliamentary Election Results in Ireland, 1801–1922* (Dublin: Royal Irish Academy, 1978).

MICHAEL LAFFAN

Sirr, Henry Charles (1764–1841) Deputy town major and town major – effectively, head of police – in Dublin (1795–1828). In 1798 Sirr was in charge of the party which arrested Lord Edward Fitzgerald after a desperate struggle, in which one of the group received a wound 'so large that his bowels fell out on the floor'. Sirr fired at Fitzgerald and wounded him. Sirr was also involved in the subsequent investigations of the United Irishmen's conspiracy. In 1803 he organized the capture of Robert Emmet and other revolutionaries after Emmet's abortive rebellion.

EUNAN O'HALPIN

Sixteenth (Irish) Division (1914–22) It was one of three divisions through which Irish Catholics and Protestants responded to Lord Kitchener's appeal and John Redmond's persuasion. The division was prominent in some of the best-remembered engagements of the war, including Messines, the Somme, and the Third Ypres. By November 1918 over 4,000 of its troops had perished. With Irish independence came the disbandment of most of the division's regiments and also (until very recently) the historical demise of the division, as its achievements were ignored and supplanted by panegyrics on the nationalist insurrection of 1916.

GERARD O'BRIEN

Sloane, Sir Hans (1660–1753) Physician. Born Killileagh, County Down, 16 April. Sloane studied medicine in Paris and Montpelier, graduating MD from the University of Orange in 1683. He went as ship's doctor on an expedition to Jamaica in 1687 and returned with a collection of 800 plants. He settled in Bloomsbury Square. He was secretary of the Royal Society from 1693 to 1712, reviving the *Philosophical Transactions*, and in 1696 he published his catalogue of the plants of Jamaica, a book still valued by botanists. He received his MD from Oxford in 1701, and medicine made him a fortune, but it was his love of botany that made him a name. In 1707, he published his great natural history book, *A Voyage to the Islands of Madera, Barbadoes, Nieves, St. Christopher and Jamaica*, and was elected as foreign member of the French Academy of Sciences the next year. On the death of Newton, he became president of the Royal Society, a post he held from 1727–1741. In 1721, he founded the Botanic Garden at Chelsea, but his lasting fame came from his gift to the nation of his specimens and books, for his trustees purchased Montague House to hold them, thus founding the British Museum.

FRED LOWE

Smerwick 1580 In 1579 the first volley of the Desmond revolt (1579–83) was fired, when James Fitzmaurice arrived at Smerwick bay with 60 Italian troops and built a small fort. The troops had been originally raised by Thomas Stuckley, under the patronage of the pope, though it was not until 1580 that the majority of them arrived. This later arrival of 600 Italians and Spaniards refortified Smerwick, under the command of Bastiano di San Giuseppi, and helped bolster the failing position of the earl of Desmond. The Dublin government, deeply concerned at these developments, transported thousands of troops to besiege the fort, and blockaded the bay with five frigates. The Italians and Spaniards, aware that the siege could not be lifted by Desmond, surrendered on 10 November 1580. They lay down their weapons in expectation of mercy, but were promptly butchered by Lord Deputy Grey de Wilton's troops. Furthermore, the massacre was supported by the government and Queen Elizabeth. The enormity of the event had widespread repercussions amongst the populace of Munster, and continued as a rallying cry for the Irish for many years thereafter.

Reading

Ellis, S., *Tudor Ireland* (London: 1985).
Falls, C., *Elizabeth's Irish Wars* (London: 1950).
Jones, F., 'The plan of the Golden Fort at Smerwick, 1580', *Irish Sword* i (1954), pp. 41–2.
O'Rahilly, A. *The Massacre at Smerwick, 1580* (Cork: 1938).

BRIAN DONOVAN

Smock Alley Theatre The chief public theatre in Ireland (1662–1787) was founded by John Ogilby, a Scottish dancing teacher, publisher and former member of the lord deputy's household at Dublin Castle, who had run Dublin's earliest theatre at Werburgh Street (1637–40). 'Smock Alley' was the first purpose-built Restoration-style theatre in the British Isles, and its company became noted for its 'clear and bold elocution', especially under Joseph Ashbury (1638–1720). Many Irish actors of repute started their careers at Smock Alley, and many English actors, including Garrick and Siddons, performed there. Smock Alley mounted very few first productions of plays by Irish writers, though most of the plays of Southerne, Congreve, Farquhar, Murphy, Goldsmith, Sheridan, O'Keefe and others were produced by the Smock Alley management soon after their initial London presentations.

CHRISTOPHER FITZSIMON

Smyth, Edward (1745–1812) Sculptor. Born County Meath; died Dublin, 2 August. The son of a stone-cutter, after basic training at the Dublin Society Schools Smyth was apprenticed to Simon Vierpyl. Smyth's most famous work is his architectural sculptures for James Gandon's Custom House in Dublin (1781–91), especially the vigorous riverine heard and the superb armorial arrangements at the ends of the north and south fronts, where for patriotic reasons it was decided to include the arms of Ireland as opposed to those of the king. One of Smyth's most successful free-standing sculptures is the monument to the Marquis of Buckingham in St Patrick's Cathedral, Dublin, *c*.1788.

Reading

Lenehan, Patrick, *The GPA Irish Arts Review Yearbook* (1989–90).
Potterton, Homan, *Irish Church Monuments 1570–1880* (Ulster Architectural Heritage Society, 1975).
Strickland, Walter, *A Dictionary of Irish Artists* (Shannon: Irish University Press, 1968).

FINTAN CULLEN

Solemn League and Covenant After the introduction of the Third Home Bill in April 1912 by Asquith's Liberal government, Ulster Unionists led by Edward Carson and James Craig were determined to resist Home Rule by all means at their disposal. The Solemn League and Covenant was part of a strategy aimed at pressuring the government by organizing mass protests in Northern Ireland. As a propaganda exercise it was highly successful. Saturday 28 September 1912 was proclaimed 'Ulster Day', and hundreds of thousands of Protestants signed the covenant, inspired by a sixteenth-century Scottish covenant, pledging themselves before God to resist and refuse to recognize the authority of any Irish Parliament forced upon them. It was eventually signed by some 220,000 adult males, and an even greater number of women signed their own separate declaration. In the covenant, Ulster Protestants proclaimed their loyalty to the king, George V, while refusing to accept the right and authority of the Westminster Parliament to pass Home Rule for Ireland, and declared their intention to use 'all means which may be found necessary to defeat the present conspiracy to set up a Home Rule Parliament'. One of these means was to be the formation of the Ulster Volunteer Force in January 1913. The conditional loyalty to Britain, both explicit and implicit in the covenant, was one of the paradoxes of Ulster Unionism.

Reading

Boyce, D.G., 'Edward Carson and Irish Unionism', in C. Brady (ed.), *Worsted in the Game: Lessons in Irish History* (Dublin: Lilliput Press, 1989).

Miller, D., *Queens Rebels: Ulster Loyalism in Historical Perspective*, (Dublin: Gill and Macmillan, 1978).

Stewart, A.T.Q., *The Ulster Crisis* (London: Faber, 1969).

——*Sir Edward Carson* (Dublin: Gill and Macmillan, 1981).

JIM O'HARA

Solomons, Estella Francis (1882–1968) and **O'Sullivan, Seumas (James Sullivan Starkey)** (1879–1958). Painter; writer. Both born and died in Dublin. Solomons and O'Sullivain epitomize the plurality of the Irish cultural renaissance. Of Jewish and Methodist stock, they were married in Dublin in 1926. Estella Solomons trained in Dublin under Osborne and in London under Orpen, and a visit to Rembrandt's tercentenary exhibition in Amsterdam led to a chiaroscuro manner in her portraiture. Later, her style became more colourful and Expressionist. She painted landscape all over Ireland, particularly in the Dublin locality, and was also an accomplished etcher. She was a member of Cumann na mBan. Seumas O'Sullivan's first poems were published in the *United Irishman* and the *All Ireland Review*. In 1905 he published his first collection, *The Twilight People*, which established his dreamy romantic manner. With the able assistance of his wife, he founded the *Dublin Magazine* (1923–58), the renowned monthly, later quarterly, literary and art magazine.

Reading

Irish Women Artists (Dublin: National Gallery of Ireland, 1987).

Miller, L. (ed.), *Retrospect: The Work of Seumas O'Sullivan and Estella F. Solomons* (Dublin: Dolmen Press, 1973).

O'Sullivan, S., *Collected Poems* (Dublin: Orwell Press, 1940).

HILARY PYLE

Somerville, E. Œ and Ross Martin Edith Œnone Somerville (1858–1949) and Violet Martin (1862–1915). Writers. 'The Irish Cousins' are internationally famous for their humorous sketches and stories, especially *Some Experiences of an Irish R.M.* (1899) and its successors, the source for a popular television series in which their characters were retained but their plots soon abandoned. These hilarious tales provide a cross-section of rural society and view the intricate interrelations of all its classes and conditions (not least the animal) with an unparalleled combination of cynicism and affection. No group is spared their sardonic thrust, but the mainspring of the joke is the helplessness of well-meaning English incomers in a culture which superficially appears familiar but proves as alien as any tropical jungle.

Somerville and Ross brought to perfection the use of dialect for literary purposes, somewhat in advance of Lady Gregory and J.M. Synge, who are more often given credit for the accomplishment. The darker side of their work is less well known, with its powerful studies of the decline of the Ascendancy and its pessimistic view of the relations between the sexes in novels like *The Real Charlotte* (1894) and *The Big House of Inver* (1925).

Feminists, they chose to be professional writers in defiance of conventional expectation, and their unique partnership was achieved against many odds. Somerville, a Paris-trained artist, provided illustrations for their work which sometimes take priority over the text. She believed that she was still in communication with her cousin after Martin's death, and gave Martin credit for joint authorship to the end of her long and productive life.

RUTH SHERRY

Souter, Camille (1929–) Painter. Born Evelyn Holmes in Northampton. Souter moved to Ireland as a baby. Later, she worked for a time in England as a nurse, but has been active as a painter since the 1950s. She rarely has solo exhibitions, but has exhibited at many group exhibitions both at home and abroad, and was included in 'The Delighted Eye' in London (1980). A retrospective exhibition was mounted in Trinity College, Dublin (1981). Her early work was mostly abstract and gestural, but she has since developed as a kind of intimist, painting still life, landscape, old buildings and generally humble subject matter. Her style is painterly and subtly colourful; her more recent work

reflects her love of flying a small plane. For many years she lived and worked in Wicklow, and then she moved to Achill, in the west.

BRIAN FALLON

Special Air Services The 22nd Special Air Service (SAS) Regiment was formed during World War II and carried out disruptive attacks behind enemy lines, particularly in the desert. The regiment subsequently became the principal anti-insurgent British military force. Its questionable activities, described as 'counter-terrorist' or 'covert', only really emerged in the West when it was sent to Northern Ireland. In 1978 the SAS shot dead a County Antrim teenager, John Boyle, whose family had told the Royal Ulster Constabulary of an arms cache left by the IRA near their home.

The SAS shooting of three IRA members in Gibraltar (March 1988) caused international controversy. About 30 people, mostly IRA members, have been shot dead in SAS ambushes. The largest loss of life in a single incident occurred at Loughgall, County Armagh (May 1987), when eight IRA members on a bombing mission and an innocent passerby were shot dead by the SAS.

JIM CUSACK

Spenser, Edmund (1552?–99) Poet and planter. Spenser arrived in Ireland in 1580 during the Desmond Rebellion as secretary to the newly appointed deputy, Lord Arthur Grey, whose policy of 'thorough' repression he fully supported. There ensued such notorious incidents as the massacre of some 600 disarmed mercenaries at Smerwick and the deliberate precipitation of famine in Munster, both of which Spenser later defended. After his patron's dishonourable recall, he acted successively as clerk to the Faculties and secretary to the lord president of Munster. In recognition of these services he received a grant of some 3,200 acres in the plantation of Munster, centring upon Kilcolman and bordering upon the estate of Sir Walter Raleigh.

The indigenous Celtic population he regarded as a 'salvage nacion' in need of political, social and religious reform, although he acknowledged the skill of the Celtic bards, samples of whose work he had translated into English. The cultural 'degeneration' of the Old Norman families, many of whom had grown 'as Irishe as O'Hanlans breeche', he particularly lamented, advocating a policy of strict racial segregation designed to insulate the New English settlers from similar 'contagion'. In *A Vewe of the Present State of Irelande*, largely a pre-emptive tract designed to forestall imminent rebellion, he advocated the suppression and plantation of Ulster as a prelude to the obliteration of Celtic culture through the destruction of the clans. The Gaelic language was to be supplanted by English, for 'the speache beinge Irishe the harte muste nedes be Irishe'. The vehemence of such racial and political attitudes – cogently debunked in Geoffrey Keating's *Foras Feasa ar Eirinn* – reflects an increasing insecurity on the part of the New English settlers, occasioning a failure of confidence in former policies of gradual civic reform.

Celtic influence upon Spenser's poetry is both pervasive and profound. Like Camoens's *Os Lusiads*, *The Faerie Queene* is very much a colonial epic, just as concerned with 'reducinge [Ireland's] salvage nacion to better gouerment and cyvilitye' as with 'fashioning' the manners of courtly English gentlemen. The landscape of the first instalment (1590) is everywhere redolent of the 'wild' ethos beyond the Pale, and the implacable hostility to Catholicism attests to prevalent fears of imminent Spanish invasion. However, although the dedicatory sonnets convey a desperate sense of cultural isolation in 'a savage soil far from Parnasso mount', the natural beauty of the Irish countryside evokes some of Spenser's most memorable verse, such as the celebrated pageant of Irish rivers in 'The Legend of Friendship'. Further evidence of ambivalent attitudes is afforded by *Colin Clouts Come Home Again* (1595), where Ireland provides an apparently preferable, if politically imperfect, alternative to the corruptions of Gloriana's court. The second instalment of *The Faerie Queene* (1596) presents a highly contentious defence of Lord Grey's Irish campaign through the transparent medium of explicit historical allegory. The failure of Grey's policies is primarily attributed to the malice of enemies at court and, by implication, to the irresolution of the Queen.

In attempting to refute the 'sinister suggestions of cruelty' attaching to his patron's reputation, Spenser endorses the doctrine of political 'necessity' or *raison d'état*, thereby severely compromising the moral basis of his poetic vision. By consigning Grey's violence to the iron man Talus, he seeks to insulate his hero from the taint of blood-guilt while at the same time implying the necessity for renewed hostilities. Such passages were doubtless designed to lend support to the recommendations of the *Vewe*, entered in the Stationers' Register that same year but fated to remain unpublished, probably through government disapproval, until 1633, when Sir James Ware tactfully deleted all material offensive to the Old Norman families. Set in Munster's Galtee Mountains, the fragmentary 'Mutabilitie Cantos' (posthumously published in 1609) eloquently voice the despair of the remaining planters or 'in-dwellers' in the face of inevitable rout. Their rising panic receives dramatic expression in Spenser's final Irish tract, *A Brief Note of Ireland*, written in the crisis of rebellion to petition for immediate military action – or immediate recall. In the event, Spenser did not live to witness the disastrous intervention of the earl of Essex, his own preferred candidate for the office of lord lieutenant. Upon the sacking of Kilcolman by Celtic forces in 1598 he fled first to Cork and thence to London, where he died, possibly in straitened circumstances, in 1599. Of his political vision for Ireland Yeats wrote perhaps the perfect epitaph: 'he was the first of many Englishmen to see nothing but what he was desired to see'.

Reading

Coughlan, Patricia (ed.), *Spenser and Ireland: An Interdisciplinary Perspective* (Cork: 1989).

Greenblatt, Stephen, *Renaissance Self-Fashioning: From More to Shakespeare* (Chicago: 1980).

Henley, Pauline, *Spenser in Ireland* (Cork: 1928).

Judson, Alexander, *The Life of Edmund Spenser* (Baltimore: 1945).

McCabe, Richard A., *The Pillars of Eternity: Time and Providence in 'The Faerie Queene'* (Dublin: 1989).

—— 'Edmund Spenser: Poet of Exile', *Proceedings of the British Academy* (1991).

O'Connell, Michael, *Mirror and Veil: The Historical Dimension of Spenser's 'Faerie Queene'* (Chapel Hill NC: 1977).

Yeats, W.B. (ed.), *Poems of Spenser* (Edinburgh: 1906).

RICHARD A. MCCABE

Spring, Richard (Dick) (1950–) Politician. Born Tralee, County Kerry. Spring was leader of the Labour Party (1982–97). A barrister by profession, he was first elected to Dáil Éireann in 1981, succeeding his father, who had held the seat since 1943. He was tánaiste during the Fine Gael/Labour government (1982–7) and was a leading participant in the New Ireland Forum (1984–5). He also took part in the negotiations that led to the Anglo-Irish Agreement of 1985. Spring was responsible for arresting the decline in support for the Labour Party, which was at a low ebb in the mid-1980s. His most adroit political move was to nominate Mary Robinson for the presidency in 1990. Labour reaped the reward in the 1992 general election, when the party doubled its vote and won 33 seats. Many Labour voters were angered when Spring decided to join Fianna Fáil in government. (This anger was forcefully expressed in the general election five years later.) He was appointed tánaiste and minister for foreign affairs and retained both positions in the Rainbow Government formed in December 1994. His presence in cabinet ensured continuity in the peace process, although he increasingly attracted Unionist criticism, and was described by John Taylor MP as 'the most detested politician in Northern Ireland'. In tandem with his close involvement in the peace process, he oversaw the Irish presidency of the European Union in the latter half of 1996. He suffered a major setback in the 1997 general election, when the number of Labour's seats was halved and the Rainbow Government lost office after which he resigned as party leader.

PATRICK GILLAN

stained glass There is as yet no evidence of any natively produced stained glass before the eighteenth century in Ireland, when three of the leading glass painters in England were Irish born or Dublin trained. In the nineteenth century, among the artists and many studios, Michael O'Connor and Thomas Earley provide Irish links with Pugin and the Gothic Revival. By 1900 eminent Irish firms were easily undercut by the large English and German commercial firms. With romantic nationalist fervour, Edward Martyn and Sarah Purser encouraged the Dublin Metropolitan School of Art to train native craftsmen and women and set up the co-operative studio of An Túr Gloine in 1903. Thus, through Michael Healy, Wilhelmina Geddes, Harry Clarke and Evie Hone, Irish stained glass achieved international renown. Maud Cotter and James Scanlon are revitalizing the craft today.

Reading

Bowe, Nicola Gordon, Caron David, and Wynne, Michael, *A Gazetteer of Irish Stained Glass* (Dublin: Irish Academic Press, 1988).

NICOLA GORDON BOWE

Stanford, Sir Charles Villiers (1852–1924) Composer, teacher and conductor. Born Dublin. Stanford spent the greater part of his life in England. The only son of a lawyer, who was a keen amateur cellist and singer, his early musical education was at the Royal Irish Academy of Music, where he exhibited remarkable early gifts as a composer and pianist. In 1870 he entered Queen's College, Cambridge, as a choral scholar, and within three years was fulfilling important musical duties normally reserved for his seniors, including those of organist of Trinity College, Cambridge. He was allowed periods of absence for study in Leipzig and Berlin. In 1883 he was appointed professor of composition at the newly opened Royal College of Music, and in 1887 became professor of music at Cambridge. He pursued both these duties with untiring energy until his death.

The most influential teacher of composition of his time, he was largely responsible for the renaissance of a school of English composition. His influence on twentieth-century Irish composition was strong for a time, but has more recently been criticized as advocating an unsuitable marriage between nineteenth-century Teutonic harmony and traditional Irish melodies. He was a prolific composer in every medium. The reputation of much of his excellently crafted music has suffered from changes in fashion, particularly in the case of works consciously imbued with an Irish flavour. His solo songs, church music and smaller choral pieces deservedly escaped the prejudices of contemporary taste, and a fresh evaluation of his extensive output is overdue.

JOSEPH RYAN

Stanihurst, Richard (1547–1618) Writer. Born Dublin; died Brussels. Stanihurst, son of James Stanyhurst, speaker of the Irish House of Commons, was educated at Peter White's classical school and subsequently at Oxford University and the Inns of Court. His later years were spent in self-imposed exile in the Low Countries, where he converted to Catholicism and apparently took Holy Orders. Stanyhurst's *Description of Ireland* was published in Holinshed's *Chronicles of Ireland* (1577). He collaborated with Edmund Campion in writing a *History of Ireland* for the same publication. His Latin writings included *De Rebus in Hiberniae Gestis*, on the early history of Ireland, published at Antwerp in 1584, and a life of St Patrick. His writings on Ireland were criticized by seventeenth-century historians including Geoffrey Keating.

Reading

Lennon, Colm, *Richard Stanihurst, the Dubliner* (Dublin: Irish Academic Press, 1981).

BERNADETTE CUNNINGHAM

statistical surveys of counties One of the main obstacles the Dublin Society perceived in the way of its endeavours to foster the development of Irish agriculture in the late eighteenth century was the shortage of accurate information on existing practices. In an attempt to remedy this deficiency, a questionnaire-style survey was undertaken in the 1770s, but this did not answer all needs. Following the publication of Sir John Sinclair's impressive 27-volume statistical account of Scotland in the 1790s, the Dublin Society was emboldened to undertake to emulate his example with a comprehensive county survey of Ireland. The sum of £15,000 was secured from the Irish Parliament in 1800 to answer the cost of such an ambitious undertaking, and individuals were commissioned to prepare surveys which would 'contain an accurate statement of the extent and mode of agriculture; of planting, size of farm houses; manufactures; roads; draining; breed of cattle; nature of soil; the state or probabilities of mines; with observations on all defects in practice, and the possible remedies and improvements in every particular'. The scheme began promisingly; the first survey was published in 1801, and before the end of 1802, 15 were in print. However, only eight of the remaining 17 counties were completed, though all were commissioned and manuscripts prepared. Like most collaborative enterprises, the Dublin Society's statistical surveys are uneven; at their best they are insightful and informative; at their worst they are prejudiced and banal. Together they offer an unparalleled vista on the Irish economy and society in the early nineteenth century.

Reading

Berry, H.F., *A History of the Royal Dublin Society* (London: 1915).

Meenan, James and Clarke, Desmond (eds), *The Royal Dublin Society* (Dublin: 1981).

JAMES KELLY

Steele, Sir Richard (1672–1729) Essayist and dramatist. Born Dublin. Steele was educated at Charterhouse, with Joseph Addison, and at Merton College, Oxford. He relinquished his studies, and a legacy in Ireland, to become a cadet in the Horse Guards. He became Secretary to Lord Cutts, who gave him a commission. His reckless nature led him into at least two duels, fathering a child by Jacob Tonson's daughter, and constant debt. His love of the high life was balanced by a zeal to reform others through his writing. An early tract, *The Christian Hero*, was followed by three comedies, which established him as a successful dramatist.

He found his metier when debt led him to produce the *Tatler* in April 1709, which appeared thrice weekly and for which he effectively invented the periodical essay. This mock newspaper, inspired largely by Jonathan Swift, contained essays which were supposed to emanate from coffee houses noted for their special interests, such as Will's for poetry, and the Grecian for learning. This format allowed Steele to cover a wide range of fashionable topics catering for all tastes. It was a considerable advance on Defoe's *Review*, in both variety of content and flexibility of style. The idea was Steele's, and Addison did not contribute until no. 18. The *Tatler* ceased publication in January 1711 and was followed in turn by the *Spectator* (1711–12), the *Guardian* and the *Englishman*. The emphasis by later critics on form rather than content has caused Steele's reputation to suffer. Though Addison's masterly prose overshadowed Steele's cruder style, too little credit is given to Steele for being the creative intellect behind both the concept and the central group of characters in the enormously successful *Spectator*.

When Steele left Ireland at the age of 12, he adopted England. He became an ardent Whig, and was elected MP to Stockbridge in 1713. Though high political office eluded him, he was made gazetteer in 1711, became a justice of the peace, commissioner of the Stamp Office, surveyor of the Royal Stables at Hampton Court, governor of the Royal Company of Comedians, commissioner of 'Forfeited Estates in Scotland', and deputy lieutenant of Middlesex, and was knighted in 1715. Despite this service to England, his Irishness was constantly used against him. John Dennis, when attacking Steele, wrote:

> His ancestors flourished in Tipperary long before the English ever set foot in Ireland... [God] stamped his native country on his face, his understanding, his writings, his actions, his passions, and, above all, his vanity. The Hibernian brogue is still upon all these, though long habit and length of days have worn it off his tongue.

None the less, as Steele himself said, whatever the quintessentially English Addison had given him, it was he who gave Addison to the world.

FRED LOWE

Steevens' Hospital Built *c.*1721, Dublin but did not formally open its doors until 1733. It was designed by the architect Thomas Burgh, who is chiefly remembered for his design of the Library in Trinity College, Dublin. Dr Richard Steevens bequeathed his estate to his twin sister, Madam Grizel Steevens, for her lifetime, and on her death to be used for the building of a hospital. She, however, decided that the hospital should be built immediately. Jonathan Swift was one of the early governors, and several famous doctors and surgeons have been associated with this hospital, including Abraham Colles, who first described a fracture of the wrist,

'Colles fracture'. The hospital closed in 1987 and the building was purchased by the Eastern Health Board. It was superbly restored and became the headquarters of the board.

MURIEL MCCARTHY

Stephens, James (1825–1901) Fenian. Born Kilkenny; died Blackrock, County Dublin, 29 April. With T.C. Luby, Stephens founded the Irish Republican Brotherhood or Fenian movement, and made successful fund-raising visits to America in 1858 and 1864. In 1863 he founded a successful newspaper, the *Irish People*, to forward the cause. When he failed to lead a rising in 1865 as promised, the American Fenians denounced him and he fled to Paris. A public subscription raised by friends in Ireland enabled him to return in 1886 and end his days in comparative comfort.

HENRY BOYLAN

Stephens, James (1880–1950) Poet and storyteller. Born Dublin, probably 9 February; died London, 26 December. Stephens was reared in an orphanage and worked as a solicitor's clerk in Dublin. By 1912 he had won recognition as a prose writer of originality, close to genius. He was registrar of the National Gallery, Dublin, from 1915 to 1924, when he removed to London, and in his later years enthralled listeners with his verse and stories on the BBC. He was a founder member of the Irish Academy of Letters and received a civil list pension in 1942.

HENRY BOYLAN

Sterne family Of English origin, one branch of the Sterne family settled in Ireland during the seventeenth century, a John Stearne marrying a niece of James Ussher, archbishop of Armagh. His son, John (1624–69), who studied at Trinity College, Dublin, and Cambridge, and was successively lecturer in Hebrew and professor of law and medicine in the university, founded the Irish College of Physicians in 1667. His son, also John (1660–1745), who immediately preceded Jonathan

Swift as Dean of St Partick's Cathedral, Dublin, was later bishop of Dromore (1713) and Clogher (1717) and became vice-chancellor of the University of Dublin in 1721. The English branch of the family, meanwhile, established itself in Yorkshire, Richard Sterne (1596?–1683) becoming archbishop of York in 1664. His great-grandson was the novelist, Laurence Sterne (1713–68), born in Clonmel, where his ensign father was temporarily stationed, though he left the country in 1723 or 1724 and never returned, spending most of his life as an Anglican priest in rural Yorkshire. In 1759, Sterne published, in York, the first two volumes of *The Life and Opinions of Tristram Shandy, Gentleman* (1759–67), which brought him celebrity throughout Europe. He consolidated his initial success with *Sermons of Mr Yorick* (1760–6) and in the year of his death published the first volume of *A Sentimental Journey through France and Italy*. Though the importance to his art of his Irish birth may be disputed, Sterne influenced later Irish novelists, most notably James Joyce (who instanced *Tristram Shandy* as a model for *Finnegans Wake*), Flann O'Brien and Samuel Beckett.

IAN CAMPBELL ROSS

Sterne/Stearne, John (1624–69) and **John** (1660–1745) Scholar; churchman. The elder John Sterne was born at Ardbraccan, County Meath, and died in Dublin, 18 November. He was enducated at Trinity College, Dublin, and fled to England to escape the Rebellion of 1641. After studying medicine at Cambridge, be returned to Trinity in 1656, lectured in Hebrew, became MD, and founded the College of Physicians in 1660. He was first president, and in 1662 became president for life, and life professor of medicine in Trinity. A man of the world, be contrived to stand well with both Cromwellian and Royalist parties.

His son, John, was born in Dublin and died at Clogher, 6 June. He was educated at Cathedral School and Trinity College, Dublin, and took holy orders. He became

Dean of St Patrick's Cathedral and joined the social circle of Jonathan Swift, Stella and their friends. He became bishop of Dromore in 1713, supported by Swift, whose friends wanted the deanery for him, and was translated to Clogher in 1717. He had ample means, was very hospitable, and gave £1,000 for a printing house in Trinity and legacies to Swift's and Steevens' hospitals.

Reading

Stearne, John, MD, *Clarissimi viri* (Dublin: Printed by Wm Blanden, 1660).

Stearne, John, bishop, *Tractatus de Visitatione Infirmorum, typis Joseph Ray, impensis Jacobi Milner* (Dublin: 1697, trans. 1840 as *The Curate's Manual*, London).

HENRY BOYLAN

Stevenson, Sir John Andrew (1761–1833) Composer. The son of a violinist in the State Band of Dublin, Stevenson became a chorister at Christ Church Cathedral in 1771. Thereafter he was associated with the choirs of both Dublin cathedrals, becoming a vicar-choral of St Patrick's in 1783, and of Christ Church in 1800. He was awarded an honorary MusD by Dublin University in 1791, and was one of the earliest musicians to be knighted (1803). The composer of theatrical music, some church music, and innumerable songs, glees and catches, he is best known for his 'symphonies' and accompaniments for Thomas Moore's *Irish Melodies*.

BARRA BOYDELL

Stewart, Robert (Viscount Castlereagh and second marquess of Londonderry) (1769–1822) Statesman. Born 18 June, Dublin. Castlereagh, known best by his courtesy title, was born at the house of his grandfather, Alexander Stewart, a Presbyterian merchant of Whiggish principles. His mother, Lady Frances Seymour Conway, a daughter of the earl of Hertford, died when he was an infant. Originally of Scottish planter stock, settled in Donegal, the Stewarts acquired great wealth and influence by a succession of judicious marriages, and Castlereagh's father purchased an estate in County Down and built Mountstewart.

Castlereagh entered the Irish Parliament in 1790 as a Whig member for Down, but soon aafter his marriage to Lady Amelia (Emily) Hobart, he turned Tory and became an admirer of Pitt. Influenced by his stepmother's brother, Earl Camden, who was lord lieutenant of Ireland 1795–8, he sought a career at the centre of British politics. He was appointed chief secretary to his uncle in 1797. In this capacity he helped to suppress the United Irish insurrenction in 1798, ordering the arrest of many of his father's tenants. The radical Presbyterians never forgave this apostasy, which was compouned when Castlereagh masterminded the passing of the Act of Union in 1801. That measure was not accompanied by Catholic emancipation, as he had hoped, and he resigned with Pitt. He was defeated in the Down election of 1805, but continued as an MP for an English constituency.

His talents were recognized by high office in succeeding administistations. As war minister, and as foreign secretary from 1812, he worked tirelessly to construct the alliances which eroded Napoleon's hegemony in Europe, and the success of the Congress of Vienna in 1815 marked the zenith of his career. As a politician he was just, honourable and diligent, and his mastery of foreign policy won the admiration of Metternich, but his icy self-control alienated public opinion.

In the summer of 1822 he suffered a mental breakdown, brought on by overwork, and possibly by an exaggerated dread of blackmail. At an audience on 9 August 1822 the king was so alarmed by his manner that he urged Castlereagh to seek medical advice, but three days later Castlereagh committed suicide by cutting his throat with a penknife. In the main, posterity has overlooked his achievements and remembered only his unpopularity.

Reading

Hinde, Wendy, *Castlereagh* (London: Collins, 1981).

Hyde, H.M., *The Rise of Castlereagh* (London: Macmillan, 1933).

A.T.Q. STEWART

Stewart, Sir Robert Prescott (1825–94) Organist, composer, conductor and professor. Born Dublin, 16 December; died there, 24 March. Stewart showed an early talent for music, becoming organist of Christ Church Cathedral at the age of 19 and later also of St Patrick's Cathedral. From 1846 he conducted the Choral Society at Trinity College, Dublin, where he attained his MusD in 1851 and became professor of music in 1862. He also taught at the Royal Irish Academy of Music and conducted the Dublin Philharmonic Orchestra. Stewart was a dominant and respected figure in Irish musical life. His compositions include cantatas, glees, church music and organ music.

BARRA BOYDELL

Stoker, Abraham (1847–1912) Writer. Born Dublin. The sickly 'Bram' was educated at home until he entered Trinity College, Dublin, in 1664. Though a civil servant for years, his interest lay in drama, and in 1871 he began as critic for the *Dublin Mail*. In 1876 he started working with his idol, Henry Irving. He joined him at the Lyceum, London, in 1876, staying until Irving's death in 1897. That year he published *Dracula*, the most famous of his 12 novels. Inspired by *Carmilla*, the vampire story by Sheridan Le Fanu, he made the notorious Romanian Count Dracula a vampire, and so created one of the great evil characters in literature.

FRED LOWE

Stokes family The best-known members of the family are as follows:

1 Whitley (1763–1845), physician and polymath. The son of Gabriel Stokes, a clergyman, he was born in Waterford, studied at Trinity College, Dublin, and was elected Fellow in 1787. He took the MD with a thesis 'On Respiration', was Donegall professor of mathematics and lecturer on natural history, but fell under suspicion of favouring the United Irishmen. He was professor of medicine at the College of Surgeons (1819–28), physician to the Meath Hospital, and in a different sphere of interest published *Observations on the Necessity of Publishing the Scriptures in the Irish Language*. He died at 16 Harcourt Street, Dublin, on 13 April.

2. William (1804–78), physician. He was born in Dublin to Mary Ann Picknell, wife of Whitley Stokes, in July. A private education preceded professional studies in Dublin and Edinburgh. He published the first work on the stethoscope in English while still a student, then joined the staff at the Meath Hospital, attaining a leading position in Irish medicine. International recognition was accorded to his textbooks on the heart and chest. His name still features in the eponyms 'Cheyne-Stokes breathing' and 'Stokes-Adams syndrome'. In retirement he lived at Howth, and died there on 6 January.

3. Sir William (1839–1900), surgeon. The son of Dr William Stokes and his wife Mary Black, formerly of Glasgow, he was born at 50 York Street, Dublin, 10 March, and while serving in the Boer War died of typhoid fever at Pietermaritzburg on 19 August. Appointed surgeon to the Meath Hospital in 1864, he moved to the Richmond Hospital four years later and was an early advocate of 'Listerism'. He was president of the Royal College of Surgeons in Ireland (1886–7).

4. Adrian (1887–1927), pathologist. The son of Henry Stokes of the Indian Civil Service (and grandson of the celebrated physician), he was born in Lausanne, 9 February, fated to die from yellow fever in Lagos, Nigeria, 19 September. A graduate in medicine of Trinity College,

Dublin, he specialized in pathology and served with the Royal Army Medical Corps in the Great War. The granting of Irish independence caused him to leave Ireland. He accepted a chair at Guy's Hospital. Invited to join the Rockefeller Foundation's West African Yellow Fever Commission in 1927, he was infected accidentally in the laboratory.

Reading

Lyons, J.B., 'A great Dublin medical family', *Proceedings of the XXIII Congress of the History of Medicine* (London: Wellcome Institute, 1973).
Stokes, Sir William, *William Stokes* (London: Fisher Unwin, 1898).

J.B. LYONS

Stopford family Edward Adderley Stopford was appointed rector of Kells and archdeacon of Meath in 1844 by his father, the bishop of the diocese. He was a moderate evangelical (like his father), assiduous in his pastoral duties, particularly during the Famine years. A practical man, who enjoyed book-binding and the construction of steam engines, he also had scholarly tastes. He wrote a textbook on ecclesiastical law, and many pamphlets, engaging in the theological controversies of the time, yet he was ready to question what he considered to be the sensationalist aspects of the Ulster Revival of 1859. Of unquestioned loyalty to the establishment, Stopford strove to reduce to the minimum the dangers to church – state relations inherent in divided opinions over the national schools, which he supported. Similarly, and of even greater significance, he was one of the few dignitaries of the Church of Ireland to adopt a realistic, conciliatory attitude to Gladstone's disestablishment proposals. The prime minister responded to Stopford's offer of assistance by inviting him to Hawarden for discussions, 'co-operation under protest', which were continued by correspondence. With Gladstone's approval, the archdeacon exercised his good offices in both political and ecclesiastical

circles, putting at the disposal of government his unrivalled knowledge of the Irish church and its law, while strenuously arguing its case. Following the passing of the Irish Church Act, he took an active part in the convention that drafted the constitution of the disestablished church.

Archdeacon Stopford had a worthy daughter, his seventh child and third daughter, Alice (1847–1929), 'a passionate historian'. She married the historian J.R. Green, and collaborated in his work, but was a historian in her own right, and as Alice Stopford Green published such influential works as *The Making of Ireland and its Undoing* (1908). Like her father, she was practical in those causes in which she believed. She espoused home rule, raised funds for the Irish Volunteers, and was nominated by W.T. Cosgrave to the first Senate of the Irish Free State.

KENNETH MILNE

sublime The concept of 'the sublime' was a most important formative influence on the rise of Romanticism in the late eighteenth century. Introduced into critical discourse by translations of the first century AD treatise *On the Sublime* by Longinus, it owed its widespread popularity to Edmund Burke's remarkable early work, *A Philosophical Enquiry into the Origin of our Ideas of the Sublime and Beautiful* (1757). On account of its success in establishing vastness, wildness and terror as legitimate sources of aesthetic experience, Burke's *Enquiry* is generally credited with helping to shift artistic and cultural sensibility from the artifice of both 'beauty' (order, symmetry, decorum) and the 'rhetorical sublime' associated with Longinus, which considered sublimity as an effect of language (figurative expressions, heightened diction, etc.).

In emphasizing the self-centred character of the sublime, Burke's treatise certainly contributed to the taste for primitivism, wild scenery and Romantic solitude which constituted 'Nature' as an aesthetic norm in the eighteenth century. In the eyes of some

English critics, such as Richard Payne Knight, Burke's Irish background gave him a head start on such matters, and it is not surprising to find Ireland itself portrayed as an outpost of the 'natural sublime' in much subsequent travel writing and Romantic literature. This was not how it appeared to those critics *within* Ireland who came under the influence of Burke. They sought to retain and elaborate the connection with the 'rhetorical sublime', dissociating the concept from its grounding in nature and reworking it in linguistic and social terms.

In James Usher's *Clio, or, a Discourse on Taste* (1767), Burke's contoversial equation of the sublime with obscurity is enlisted in support of an anti-Lockean theory of meaning, which proposed that the most powerful uses of language serve to *conceal* rather than to reveal reality. In Richard Stack's 'An Essay on Sublimity of Writing' (1787), the remit of the sublime is extended beyond individualism, and the possibilities of harnessing its energies for more sociable or political ends, such as national identity, is explored. These ideas are further developed in George Miller's 'An Essay on the Origin of our Idea of the Sublime' (1795), where a more concerted effort is made to link the sublime with patriotism and what Miller calls 'moral sublimity' or 'active benevolence'. These early forays by Irish critics into aesthetic theory can be seen as part of an attempt to fuse the terror of sublimity with the social and communal sentiments of beauty – a fusion of aesthetics and politics that was to prove combustible in subsequent Irish culture.

LUKE GIBBONS

suburbs Dublin has become a suburban city, with less than one in twelve of its population still left inhabiting its historic core – the oval-shaped area between the two canals. And Dublin, in this context, may be seen as a paradigm for Ireland as a whole, where the suburbs are now strung out along nearly every country road.

According to architect Arthur Gibney, Dublin is losing its urban sensibilities as a result of being over-run by 'the inhabitants of its hinterland' (a polite way of saying 'culchies'), with their provincial values. 'After two generations of suburban living, the myth and memory of city life has nearly disappeared', he complains. Indeed, the city has become a colony, ruled by people who drive in from the suburbs. The suburbs might even be seen as a purgatorial half-way house between the hell of city life, immortalized by such as Sean O'Casey, and the heavenly ideal of so many of Ireland's *nouveau riche* – the bungalow bliss of living in the countryside, perhaps even in an ostentatious example of the phenomenon known as the *palazzi gombeeni*, those grandiose Southfork-style houses built just for show.

It could even be argued that the middle classes have been deserting the city since there was a middle class in Ireland, from the mid-nineteenth century onwards. No doubt this flight was prompted by a desire to escape from the poor and the constant daily sight of poverty, which helps to explain why Dublin is now one of the most socially segregated cities in Europe, with ghettoes for the rich as well as the poor.

The drift from the core to the periphery was, of course, encouraged by the 'garden city' ideal and its notion that fresh air and a garden in which to grow vegetables would provide a *rus in urbi* antidote to the squalor and congestion of inner-city living. It was an ideal adopted with great zeal in Britain and the United States and, inevitably, Ireland's planners followed suit, with enthusiasm. The suburbs they created, starting in Marino in the 1920s, gave way to bastardized versions as time went on, to produce the repetitive low-density housing estates which characterized suburban sprawl from the 1960s onwards. Though classified as 'neighbourhoods', they were largely designed for cars rather than people, with wide, straight roads which encourage speeding, to the detriment of anyone on foot. They are also largely featureless, because little or no attempt was ever made to preserve links with the past; indeed, the first casualty of any housing scheme was usually the manor house which stood on the land being developed. This was reinforced by the obsessive provision of 'open space', no matter how uncontained, with shopping centres surrounded by vast car parks as the single social focus.

Because the suburbs were based on the mad notion of the 'motorized city', many people are marginalized because they do not have cars. In the meantime, of course, the cities and towns experienced a spiral of decline, with the centre of Dublin reduced to little more than a largely unemployed working-class ghetto, littered with derelict sites and prey to the road-widening schemes to cater for those who do.

But despite the huge suburban expansion of the past 25 years, it remains a staggering fact that 'one-off' houses – largely in the countryside – now account for over half of the total national output of private housing. In other words, for every house built in an urban or suburban setting, at least one other house is built in the middle of nowhere – usually on land sold off by farmers in half-acre plots. And as the suburbs of Ireland colonize the countryside with reckless abandon, not only is the rural landscape being eroded at an alarming rate, but the cities and towns have become increasingly dead after dark. There are few people left to inhabit the upper floors of shop premises, so the buildings – some of significant architectural quality, but all important to the streetscape – fall into decay. That is why the Temple Bar area project in Dublin is so crucial. It is the first time in living memory that a three-dimensional plan has been prepared for any part of a city or town in Ireland. By the 1990s the official goal was to have at least 3,000 people living there within the next five years, helping to redefine the city as a truly European capital with a vibrant culture of its own.

FRANK MCDONALD

Supremacy, Act of Two Acts of Supremacy were passed in sixteenth-century Ireland. The 1536 Act, which declared that King Henry VIII was 'the only supreme head in earth of the whole Church of Ireland', was criticized by contemporaries who maintained that 'the supremacy ... is maintained only by power and not reasoned by learning'. The 1560 Act of Supremacy declared Queen Elizabeth to be supreme governor of the church but allowed her less personal ecclesiastical control than Henry enjoyed under the 1536 Act. The 1560 Act imposed an oath of supremacy on office holders of the state and the church, on those suing livery of their estates and on those taking university degrees. The Court of High Commission used to enforce the 1560 legislation was ineffective, and strict enforcement would have left a shortage of office holders.

Reading

Ellis, Steven G., *Tudor Ireland* (London: Longman, 1985).

BERNADETTE CUNNINGHAM

Surrender and regrant A term given by historians to a policy of the Tudor administration in Ireland initiated under Lord Deputy St Leger in the early 1540s, whereby principal Gaelic and Gaelicized lords surrendered their lands to the crown and received new grants of those lands to be held directly from the crown. In some instances the lords were also given English-style titles of nobility. Thus, for example, Conn Bacach O'Neill became first earl of Tyrone in 1542, and Ulick Burke became first earl of Clanricard in 1543, having first surrendered their lands to the crown and received new grants. It was intended that lords who surrendered and were regranted their lands would hold those lands by royal patent and, in contrast to the Gaelic custom, succession would be by primogeniture, though there were some compromise arrangements on succession in the initial stages. It was hoped that the strategy would extend royal authority throughout Ireland in line with the 1541 Act for the kingly title; early surrenders usually also included a renunciation of papal authority. The idea of principal Gaelic lords holding land directly from the crown continued as a key Tudor policy down to the end of the sixteenth century, and the surrender and regrant strategy was used as occasion warranted.

The principal problems with the scheme lay with inheritance, since most of the extended kin group from among whom the successor to a Gaelic lord was traditionally elected were excluded from access to power under the English-style system, where a lord was succeeded by his eldest son. The scheme appealed to Gaelic chiefs who could use it to gain rights over land more extensive than their entitlements under Gaelic law. Over time, it allowed a Gaelic lord the opportunity to transform his lordship into an English-style landed estate, the freeholders who were his followers being reduced to the status of tenants.

Reading

Bagwell, Richard, *Ireland under the Tudors. Vol. I* (London: Longmans Green, 1885).
Bradshaw, Brendan, *The Irish Constitutional Revolution* (Cambridge: 1979).
Brady, Ciaran, 'The O'Reillys of East Breifne and the problem of "Surrender and Regrant"', *Breifne* VI, no. 23 (1985).

BERNADETTE CUNNINGHAM

Swanzy Mary (1881–1978) Painter. Born Dublin; died London. Swanzy was educated in Dublin before moving to Paris to study under the artists Delacluse and La Grandara, and at the Grande Chaumiére and Colarossi schools. In Dublin (1913) she held her first one-woman show, and in 1914 she exhibited at the Salon des Independants in Paris. She continued to exhibit in Dublin, Paris, London, Brussels and California while travelling to Eastern and Southern Europe, Samoa and the USA. In 1968 a retrospective was held in Dublin. Her style encompasses Cubist

and Fauvist influences, and is distinctive in its rich and textured colouring.

Reading

Arnold, Bruce, *A Concise History of Irish Art* (London: Thames and Hudson, 1977).
Hobart, Alan and Hobart, Mary, *Mary Swanzy HRHA* (London: Pyms Gallery, 1986).
Pyle, Hilary, *Irish Art 1900–1950* (Cork: Crawford Municipal Art Gallery, 1976).

DERVAL TUBRIDY

Sweeney, Eric (1948–) Composer, conductor, teacher Born Dublin Sweeney studied at Trinity College, Dublin, and abroad before becoming a lecturer at the College of Music, Dublin, and at Trinity College, and choral director at RTE (1978–81). Since 1981 he has been head of music at Waterford Regional Technical College. A member of Aosdána, he was appointed to the Arts Council in 1989. He is also active as a choral conductor, accompanist and organist. Sweeney's compositions have attracted international commissions. His Symphony No. 2, performed in Paris in 1989, marked a change from an earlier atonal style to a more direct idiom in which Irish traditional elements provide a basis for a minimalist approach.

BARRA BOYDELL

Sweetman family From Wexford. They offer an emblematic example of the background from which the leaders of the Catholic community emerged in the eighteenth and nineteenth centuries. After 1641, they were dispossessed of their ancestral estate and became middlemen at Newbawn near New Ross. Their 1690s house is still standing – an instructive blend of vernacular and formal styles, exactly embodying their newly ambiguous social position. From here, the Sweetmans elaborated a powerful kinship network, moving into church and trade at home, on the Continent and in the New World, as well as farming successfully. The money gained from trade was reinvested in leaseholds and prestigious houses, creating clusters of related families fanning out from the Newbawn base. Reflecting their prominence in the local community, the Sweetmans supplied clergy, maintained a schoolmaster, and patronized the local church, which acted as a nucleus for the chapel village of Newbawn. They also played a powerful political role, including in the Catholic Committee and the United Irishmen; Wolfe Tone's friend, Edward Sweetman, was active in both, and Edward's brother Nicholas was prominent in the 1798 Rebellion in Wexford.

The Sweetmans saw themselves and were seen as natural leaders of the Catholic community: highly conscious of their origins and prior status, they belonged to an underground Catholic gentry which had its own cohesive structure and momentum, lubricated by the kinship mechanism. They bridged multiple worlds and were brokers on a number of levels – social, cultural and political. They were the hubs and hinges on which Catholic society revolved, the solid and stiffening backbone of the Catholic nation in the modern period.

KEVIN WHELAN

Swift, Jonathan (1667–1745) Writer. Born 30 November, 7 Hoey's Court, near St Patrick's Cathedral, Dublin; died in the deanery there. Swift lived most of his life in Ireland, and his greatness is indissolubly linked with his Irish association, although he would always contest the claim. His perpetual interest was the human condition in all its aspects, comic or tragic, ridiculous or inscrutable, and his judgements were intended to be of universal application.

His upbringing took place in a world in which the English Civil War, the march of Cromwell's armies, was the most sensational memory of most of his contemporaries; his own grandfather had been the victim of the Puritan rage in his Herefordshire church, and Swift would not forget. And yet he lived to see with his own eyes the establishment of a system in which English money and arrogance marked Irish subjection and Irish poverty. He shaped and reshaped his version of the English language to lash the perpetrators of this infamy, and for this offence, among others, he was never forgiven.

However, his emergence as the Hibernian patriot, the exponent of Irish independence, was a gradual development against all his predilections, against his will. He was educated at Kilkenny Grammar School and Trinity College, Dublin, but he showed no love for his native land. Whenever the chance was offered, he accepted a post in England. He worked for years in the homes of the leading English statesman, Sir William Temple. He acquired there a taste for English politics, but discovered also after several painful disappointments that his most convenient way to earn a livelihood was to become ordained as a priest in the Irish church. He was appointed prebend of Kilroot in Ulster in 1695, and later vicar of Laracor and prebend of St Patrick's Cathedral in Dublin in 1700.

All his life he was a prodigious reader, and the addiction was fostered in Sir William's library. His own beloved authors were so dear to him that they were always part of his real world. He naturally tried his own hand at the art, first with some adulatory odes addressed to prominent political figures and next with a mild political polemic against the newly developing party politics of the age. Neither mode seemed to test his capacities properly, but he could turn easily to other pursuits. He would charm the men and, more especially the women in his immediate circle. His wit, his humour, his raillery were irrepressible, and he could weld them all into an ironic view of the world around him.

Years later this combination of gifts was to find expression in his poetry, but some time in his early thirties, when he was brooding but not too irredeemably in Kilroot on one of his early love affairs, he started to conceive and execute the wonder which was to be published to the world under the title of *A Tale of a Tub*, the tub being the one which the seamen have when they meet a whale to fling out by way of amusement, to divert violence from laying hold of the ship. This diversion was designed in particular to protect the interests of the Anglican church, which gave Swift his livelihood, but the exercise was done with such a blasphemous exuberance that most of his fellow churchmen, with Queen Anne at their head, raised their hands in horror.

Looking back years later, Swift himself is supposed to have cried: 'Good God! What a genius I had when I wrote that book', and no present-day reader is likely to dissent. The twists in the satire seem endlessly renewed; the morals to be drawn may be obscured but the language is all the more pungent; the author seems always to derive much more delight from the way his weapon is wielded than from the cause which he serves.

When *A Tale of a Tub*, 'written for the Universal Improvement of Mankind', was published in 1704, along with the even less consequential *Battle of the Books*, the mystification was excusable and Swift could stay his enemies; but who were his friends?

> As for Us, the Antients, We are content with the Bee, to pretend to Nothing of our own, beyond our Wings and our Voice: that is to say, our Flights and our Language; For the rest, whatever we have got, has been by infinite Labor, and search, and ranging thro' every Corner of Nature: The Difference is, that instead of Dirt and Poison, we have rather chose to fill our Hives with Honey and Wax, thus furnishing Mankind with the two Noblest of Things, which are Sweetness and Light.

The force and beauty of that sentence were invoked to defend some heroes in a mock battle. Swift always enjoyed devoting his gifts to the lighter side of mankind's or womankind's affairs. He exposed the astrologers who paraded as major prophets or the god of love, 'whose usual trade is / To pick up sublimary ladies'. He became the honoured friend of some of the leading literary figures in London, Joseph Addison, Richard Steele

and William Congreve. Everyone who ever met him could be captivated by his talk, and soon they were reacting with fear or delight to the products of his pen.

The England, the London, to which Swift had been sent by his friends in Dublin was at war with Louis XIV's France, but this at first was no part of Swift's business. Dynastic contests could be fought to a finish, without exhausting the combatants. But Swift became friends with some of the political leaders who, for whatever reason, wanted to make a peace. Swift started to put their case in the Tory newspaper the *Examiner*, and then, at the critical moment in the argument, produced *The Conduct of the Allies*, which described what the profits of the war were like for those who profited most, notably the captain general and commander in chief, the duke of Marlborough, and what the killing was like for those who were killed.

The Swift who had taken the trouble to see what the war truly meant was never quite the same man again. He could laugh and mock and make love. He never stopped writing riddles and invectives, and compounded them all best in the *Verses on his Death*, just about the most joyous poem in the English language, and one which, like his own epitaph graven on the wall of St Patrick's Cathedral, contains not a scintilla of religious veneration.

When in 1713 he was appointed dean of St Patrick's, it was no more than a poor consolation prize for one who had cut such a figure in the political world of London. He hated especially the severance from his new circle of friends, headed by his fellow poet, Alexander Pope. And how his enemies – and he had plenty – mocked in their appeal to St Patrick: 'Convert the Dean on this great day / or else God save the People.'

He came back to Esther Johnson, the Stella whom he had loved since he had first met her as a child in Sir William Temple's household: his *Journal to Stella*, directed in particular to a description of these years, showed how true was that love. However, he also loved Esther Vanhomrigh, the heroine of his own poem,

Cadenus and Vanessa, the longest and most sensitive he ever wrote. It was convenient no doubt to keep them separated by the Irish Sea. But when Swift seemed to be banished, Vanessa pursued him, establishing herself first in Dublin and then at her family's house at Celbridge, 12 miles outside. There he renewed her tuition, with the notable aid of Michel de Montaigne.

But Swift could not be defeated by any combination of circumstances, and more than ever he could feel the power which he wielded through his mastery of the English language. Soon his difficulty seemed to be to choose the best form: his poetry achieved a new rhythm and resonance, and could be compared with Pope's; his satire was enriched with new complexities and challenges, but first and foremost he demonstrated his own down-to-earth doctrine that government was no mystery to be left to interested, self-appointed experts; all the necessary arguments could be stated in plain words which were also somehow a summons to action. Swift's *Drapier's Letters* of the 1720s set the standard for all great English pamphleteers – Thomas Paine, William Hazlitt, Robert Blatchford and many more.

Of course, the cause was pre-eminently a good one: it was the spectacle of Irish poverty and the manner in which English power sought to deal with it which stirred Swift so deeply. The *Drapier's Letters*, which dealt with the immediate insult of Wood's half-pence, prepared the way for the full exposure of imperialism and war in *Gulliver's Travels*, or *The Modest Proposal* denouncing Irish landlords and moneylenders, the most damning indictment of that breed of malefactors since Jesus of Nazareth drove them from the temple.

Gulliver's Travels carried the argument still further until it covered the whole realm of man's inhumanity, or woman's inhumanity, for that matter, although he was more forgiving there than he was often given credit for – witness the sorrel nag who came to Gulliver's rescue in the land of the Houyhnhnms. 'I see myself accused', wrote Swift himself when he was preparing notes for the authoritative 1735 Faulkner edition, 'of reflecting upon our great States-Folk; of degrading human Nature (for so they have still the confidence to stile it) and of abusing the Female Sex.' He might be thought to be placing all those accusations on the same level, but of course he was not. He would often thus incriminate himself. It is safer to accept the verdict which he himself inscribed for St Patrick's Cathedral. He served human liberty. He did, and still does.

MICHAEL FOOT

Synge Street School The Christian Brothers School (Synge Street, Dublin), established in 1864, is one of the large Dublin schools for boys run by the religious Congregation of the Christian Brothers of Ireland, which was founded in 1803 by Edmund Ignatius Rice of Waterford to serve and educate the poor. Sited first at Mill Street (1818), and later moving to Francis Street (1846), the Synge Street school gained a reputation for thorough and rigorous academic education. From the outset it drew pupils from a wide social background, and the initial fee was only 1d per week. From 1878 the school entered pupils for the Intermediate Board public examinations with marked success, and many past pupils have distinguished themselves in the public, commercial and artistic life of Ireland. Among these are Cearbhall O'Dalaigh, president of Ireland (1974–6), Liam Cosgrave, taoiseach (1973–7), and Eamon Andrews and Gay Byrne (TV personalities).

Reading

CBS Synge Street – 125 Year Book (Dublin; Enro PR Marketing, 1989).

Coldrey, B., *For Faith and Fatherland – the Christian Brothers and the development of Irish Nationalism, 1838–1921* (Dublin: Gill and Macmillan, 1988).

Normoyle, M.C., *A Tree is Planted – The Life and Times of Edmund Rice* (Dublin: 1976).

SUSAN PARKES

T

The Tailor and Ansty (1942) A book by Eric Cross gathering the fireside recollections and observations of the pensioner 'Tailor' Buckley, who lived in west Cork with his wife Ansty (Anastasia). Some early sections were serialized in the *Bell*, where O'Faolain hailed it as being in the line of *The Islandman* and *Twenty Years A-Growing* – rather too large a claim for this mix of anecdotal whimsy and homespun wisdom. The book became a *cause célèbre* when it was banned, one of the more ludicrous consequences of the 1929 Censorship Act. The decision was debated in the Senate and, although the banning was overwhelmingly supported there, the affair did initiate a re-examination of the workings and effects of the Censorship Board.

PETER DENMAN

An Taisce Founded 1946 to act as the National Trust for Ireland. An Taisce is a voluntary body which receives no state support. Dedicated to conserving Ireland's heritage and environment, it became a prescribed body under the 1963 Planning Act. This gives it the right to monitor and the responsibility to comment on all planning proposals.

TREVOR BUTTERWORTH

Talbot, Matt (1856–1925) Lay ascetic. Born Dublin, 2 May; died there, 7 June. The second of 12 children, Talbot left school at 12, to work as a labourer. A heavy drinker, he took the pledge in 1884, beginning a new life of penitential austerity and spiritual cultivation. This was only publicized when he died in Granby Lane on his way to Mass: it was found that his arms, waist and one knee were bound with chains and cords. He was unmarried. Recognized as a 'Servant of God', he was declared venerable by the Catholic Church on 3 October 1975 (a step towards canonization). His remains are enshrined (since 1972) in Sean McDermot Street church.

Reading

Glynn, Sir Joseph, *The Life of Matt Talbot 1856–1925* (Catholic Truth Society of Ireland, 1928; rev. edn 1977).

Purcell, Mary, *Matt Talbot and his Times* (M.H. Gill, 1954; new edn 1975).

—— *Remembering Matt Talbot* (Veritas, 1990).

PETER COSTELLO

Talbot, Peter (1620–80) Catholic archbishop of Dublin. Talbot was the son of Sir Richard Talbot of Malahide and elder brother of Richard Talbot. Educated in Portugal, he entered the Jesuit order in 1655. Links with the Spanish court made him influential in Charles II's court in exile. On the death of Oliver Cromwell he went to England to support the cause of the king's restoration. The Jesuits ordered him back to Europe and he left the order. He returned to England after the restoration but was impeached for treason and fled to France. In 1668 he was appointed archbishop of Dublin; he was in Dublin by August 1670, when he held a diocesan synod. After the failure by his brother to reverse the restoration land settlement, he was banished from Ireland in 1673. He returned to Ireland in poor health in 1678, but was implicated in a plot and imprisoned in Dublin Castle, where he died in 1680.

Reading

D'Alton, John, *Memoirs of the Archbishops of Dublin* (Dublin: 1838).

Moran, P.F., *History of the Catholic Archbishops of Dublin since the Reformation* (Dublin: James Duffy 1864).

Renehan, L.F., *Collections on Irish Church History*, ed. Daniel McCarthy (Dublin: C.M. Warren, 1861).

RAYMOND GILLESPIE

Talbot, Richard (1630–91) Politician and lord deputy. Talbot was the youngest son of Sir Richard Talbot of Malahide. He served in the Confederate army in the late 1640s and was at Drogheda during the Cromwellian seige. He went to Europe and served during the 1650s in the household of the Duke of York, later James II, apart from a brief period in England as part of an abortive assassination attempt on Oliver Cromwell. At the restoration he became part of the royal court in London, acting as agent for the restoration of Old English Catholics to their estates. He was the main agent for their petition in 1670 to reverse the restoration land settlement, and with its failure in 1673 he was banished from court, fleeing to France. He returned to

Ireland in 1678 but was implicated in the popish plot and after a period in prison returned to France.

On the accession of James II in 1685, Talbot returned to court, was appointed earl of Tyrconnell, and exercised a growing influence on Irish policy, culminating in his appointment as lord deputy in 1686. He began increasing the numbers of Catholics in the judiciary and the army, and also granted new charters to towns enabling Catholics to be members of corporations. His principal aim was the reversal of the restoration land settlement, and after a meeting with the king at Chester in 1687 he began preparing legislation. On James II's arrival in Ireland after the Glorious Revolution of 1688 a Parliament enacted this legistation. It could not be carried out because of the Williamite victory. Talbot died suddenly in August 1691 at the seige of Limerick, at the end of the Williamite war.

Reading

McGuire, J.I., 'Richard Talbot, earl of Tyrconnell, and the Catholic counter revolution', in Ciaran Brady (ed.), *Worsted in the Game: Losers in Irish History* (Dublin: Lilliput, 1989).

Miller, John, 'The earl of Tyrconnell and James II's Irish Policy', *Historical Journal* xx (1977).

Simms, J.G., *Jacobite Ireland* (London: Routledge, 1969).

RAYMOND GILLESPIE

tánaiste The member of government who acts 'for all purposes in place of the taoiseach' if the latter dies, is incapacitated or is absent. The tánaiste, who is nominated by the taoiseach, is required to be a Dáil deputy. The title, derived from early Irish law, suggests 'next-in-line or heir apparent', but there is no established right of succession in modern usage. Typically in Fianna Fáil governments a senior minister is appointed; an exception was Ray McSharry, promoted over former tánaiste Brian Lenihan in 1982. The Labour Party leader has been tánaiste in all Fine Gael–Labour coalition governments.

BRIAN FARRELL

Tandy, James Napper (1740–1803) Political radical. Born Dublin, 1737 or 1740; died Bordeaux, 24 August. Born into a Church of Ireland family near the Liberties, Tandy embraced the cause of radical politics in the 1760s as a confidant of Charles Lucas. Following Lucas's death in 1771, Tandy established himself as one of the city's leading radicals, and he played a prominent part in the popular campaigns against the American War of Independence and in support of free trade and legislative independence. In 1784, he was the prime mover in the radical agitation for parliamentary reform, and though this failed, Tandy remained the most prominent radical of the day. He was a leading light in the Dublin Society of United Irishmen, until a series of indiscretions forced him to flee the country in 1793. He finally settled in Paris, but his lack of discretion and heavy drinking alienated him from Wolfe Tone. He participated in a failed French military expedition to Ireland in 1798, but was captured and sentenced to death at Lifford assizes in 1800. The sentence was commuted, and he lived his last years virtually penniless and alone in Bordeaux.

JAMES KELLY

taoiseach Early Gaelic term meaning 'chief' or 'leader'. It was introduced into Éamon de Valera's 1937 constitution, replacing the title 'president of the Executive Council' used in the Irish Free State constitution. The taoiseach is the prime minister in an Irish parliamentary cabinet system closely following the British Westminster model. Constitutionally required to be a Dáil deputy, the taoiseach is invariably the leader of either Fianna Fáil or Fine Gael; John A. Costello a Fine Gael deputy (taoiseach 1948–51, 1954–7) is the only exception. To date all taoisigh have been male.

Nominated by vote of the Dáil, formally appointed by the president, the taoiseach is head of government. He selects ministers (not fewer than seven, not more than 15) usually from senior party members in the Dáil, allocates them to departments and may change their portfolios. However, government reshuffles and ministerial resignations, forced or otherwise, are rare in the Irish legal system. On the resignation of the taoiseach, the other ministers are deemed to have resigned but carry on their duties until successors are appointed; the same rule is applied during general election periods. The constitution requires the taoiseach to resign upon 'ceasing to retain the support of a majority in Dáil Éireann'; the exact implications of this provision are unresolved and became controversial after the inconclusive outcome of the 1989 election.

The taoiseach generally chooses the dates of parliamentary elections and is responsible for official communication with the president. The decisive strategic role of the taoiseach in managing public affairs has been described by the longest-serving Irish cabinet secretary, Dr Maurice Moynihan:

> he is the central co-ordinating figure, who takes an interest in the work of all Departments, the figure to whom Ministers naturally turn for advice and guidance when faced with problems involving large questions of policy or otherwise of special difficulty and whose leadership is essential to the successful working of the Government as a collective authority.

These functions include determining the agenda, chairing and steering cabinet meetings towards decisions. But, as in other democracies, the taoiseach's role is multi-functional: chief executive, commonly party leader, in effect principal legislator, national spokesman, target of media attention and available scapegoat when things go wrong.

A suggested typology has distinguished two broad types of incumbent, chairman or chief. In recent decades the prominence of the taoiseach in international affairs has been enhanced through European Community and Anglo-Irish summits. Somewhat unexpectedly, to date most incumbents have been Dublin deputies.

BRIAN FARRELL

Tate, Nahum (1652–1715) Poet and dramatist. Born Dublin; died London, 12 August. Soon after graduating from Trinity College (1672), Tate went to London, where he launched his writing career. As a dramatist he is best known for his adaptations of Shakespeare; his revised *King Lear*, with a happy ending, was performed until about 1840. He wrote the libretto for Purcell's *Dido and Aeneas* (1689), and was appointed poet laureate in 1692; some critics think him the worst poet to have held this office.

Reading

Spencer, C., *Nahum Tate* (New York: Twayne, 1972).
Tate, Nahum, *The History of King Lear*, ed. J. Black (London: Edward Arnold, 1976).

DAVID SMITH

Taylor, Jeremy (1613–67) Writer and churchman. Born Cambridge; died Lisnagarvey (Lisburn), County Down, 13 September. Taylor graduated from Caius College, Cambridge, in 1634, having already taken holy orders. He attracted attention by his preaching, and became a Fellow of All Souls' College, Oxford, and a chaplain to Archbishop Laud and to the king. As a loyal anti-Catholic Anglican and royalist, he accompanied the king's army in the Civil War, and was captured in 1645. Set free, he lived at Golden Grove, Carmarthenshire, where he wrote his best known works, *Holy Living* (1649) and *Holy Dying* (1650). He was twice imprisoned in the 1650s, but in 1658, through royalist patronage, became assistant lecturer at Lisnagarvey. In 1660, after the Restoration, he was appointed bishop of Down and Connor, and vice chancellor of the University of Dublin. Presbyterians locally – 'such intolerable persons' – and Catholics nationally gave him trouble until his death. He married Phoebe Landisdale in 1637, and Joanna Bridges in 1655; none of their children seems to have survived. His prose style has been much admired.

Reading

Stranks, C.J., *The Life and Writings of Jeremy Taylor* (London: SPCK, 1952).
Taylor, Jeremy, *Holy Living* and *Holy Dying*, ed. P.G. Stanwood (Oxford: Clarendon Press, 1989).

DAVID SMITH

technology Political, economic and historical writers in the Irish context have tended to ignore technology, despite its fundamental nature as an activity of *Homo sapiens*. Tool-using inhabitants of Ireland have been working in stone and metal for millennia, and Irish metal-working craftsmen in the golden age were celebrated throughout Europe. Technology was integral to the culture. As the technological processes became more industrial, and with greater dependence on scientific knowledge, the gap between them and what was perceived as Irish culture widened. This process can be followed by studying the interactions between the native Irish culture and the successive waves of foreign influences.

It can be argued that the fertility of Ireland, and the ease with which a livestock-owning culture could maintain itself in prosperity, removed the stimulus for taking an interest in those areas of technology associated with capital accumulation. A pure livestock culture, given mild winters, can get by with relatively simple technology. Once crops become important, the development of technology to the proto-industrial level becomes inevitable: milling, iron ploughs, roads, bridges, brewing, distilling. Norman Ireland was moving in this direction, and would perhaps have evolved on the European model had it not been for the wars of Elizabeth and then Cromwell. The process resumed again after Cromwell, but with a wider culture gap between the planted Ascendancy and the natives, comparable to what we have seen more recently in Kenya or Rhodesia (now Zimbabwe). In this situation, the control of technology was in the hands of the Ascendancy; the native culture saw it as pure destruction. The forests were stripped to smelt iron and to build the English navy.

This culture gap again began to narrow, as the eighteenth century progressed and manufacturing became established, primarily in the north-east but also elsewhere where there were good maritime communications (e.g. Cork). There emerged by the 1790s a technically competent bourgeoisie, which looked politically and philosophically to France, and sought to develop, on a secular democratic basis, a modern nation which was inclusive of the old native culture. This, as a colonial nationalist model, was innovative, and in contrast to the American practice, which tended towards genocide.

The Royal Dublin Society at this time constituted a focus of applied research support for industry, of European stature, and was verging on the role of a college of technology; there was noticeable French influence. This process of integration of technology into the culture was, however, again aborted by the unsuccessful attempt to establish a republic on the French model in 1798, and by the subsequent Act of Union.

An important aspect of technology underpinning the emergence of modern European nation states was the mastery of travel by sea to all parts of the world. In the post-Union disapora, many talented people were exported who contributed to the development of the maritime interests of the USA, Latin America, and various European maritime powers, as well as Britain. Had the political climate been congenial, these people would have serviced Irish needs.

In the nineteenth century, the emerging technological elite continued to be creamed off by the increasing pull of opportunity within the British empire, in the USA, and on the continent. Typical perhaps was the evolution of Charles Parsons, of steam turbine fame. A younger son of the earl of Rosse, he served his time in the workshops associated with the great telescope at Birr Castle, while studying for engineering in Trinity College, Dublin, but went into business in England. The Grubb optical works in Rathmines, also a spin-off from the Birr telescope, supplied the British navy with gunsights, as well as most of the world with asronomical telescopes. This was 'cutting-edge' high technology, right up to the time it moved to St Albans 'for strategic reasons' in 1921.

The emerging Irish leadership in the 1916–22 period had few, if any, people of influence who were in a position to appreciate the importance of industrial technology, increasingly based on science, as the key to national economic development. Those who were technologically aware would have emerged primarily via Trinity College, Dublin, and tended to look to the British empire. We can attribute this cultural gap to the ban on the 'godless colleges' imposed by Cardinal Cullen in the 1840s. This put barriers in the way of access to leading-edge scientific technology for the emerging Catholic component of the bourgeoisie. The Mechanics Institutes, the Dublin Technical Colleges, the Royal University, the College of Science and then finally the National University of Ireland emerged to fill the gap, but the 'intellectual partition' of the country remained a palpable barrier, right up to the 1950s.

The full integration of scientific technology into the perceived Irish cultural canon remains on the agenda. Sources useful in the quest for support for this process include the Royal Irish Academy and the Institution of Engineers of Ireland.

ROY H.W. JOHNSTON

television Contemporary television culture in Ireland is extremely cosmopolitan. It could even be argued that the Irish viewer occupies a privileged position with respect to exposure to the best of the world's television. In addition to four Irish indigenous channels (RTÉ 1, Network 2, TV3 and the Irish-language station TG4), most of the population receives via cable all British terrestrial channels (BBC 1, BBC 2, ITN/UTV and Channel 4), as well as a number of satellite channels (Sky 1, Sky News, Super, Lifestyle, etc.). The number of satellite channels varies according to local cable arrangements, as well as on a subscription basis, movie channels being the most attractive in this area.

All of the terrestrial channels, Irish and British, carry a high level of indigenous programming, both in-house and commissioned out, as well as much imported programming. The latter comes primarily from the USA, but its sources have expanded considerably over the past decade. The tolerance of English-speaking audiences for subtitled or dubbed material is still comparatively low, but the persistence of a public service ethos in European broadcasting assures such material an airing for the specialized audience who want it, despite low ratings. By far, however, the largest amount of imported material consists of US prime-time series, mini-series and TV movies. Australian productions have come to occupy more and more of the schedule across the channels in the past decade.

Radio Telefis Éireann is financed both by licence fee and by advertising revenue and has thus always been influenced by both public service and commercial considerations. The emergence of the privately-owned commercial channel TV3 has ended RTÉ's monopoly within the Republic of Ireland, and RTÉ has lost some high-profile soaps and sports programmes to its commercial rival. RTÉ has never, however, had a monopoly on its audience. Ulster Television, part of the British Independent Network, has long competed with it, along with the British Broadcasting Corporation, which preceded it.

Indigenous Irish programming has always developed in the context of its exposure to international television, on the part of both its audience and its producers. Its production

standards have tended to be relatively high because of this exposure. Its programme formats have reproduced those originated elsewhere: news, current affairs, drama serials, quiz shows, arts shows, talk shows, sports coverage, etc. It nevertheless has its distinctiveness, sometimes in pioneering formats, more importantly in its positioning in relation to the community, whose collective consciousness it creates and reflects.

This is most true of its talk shows, most particularly its longest running programme, *The Late, Late Show*, which began broadcasting in 1962. So intertwined with all of the trials and traumas of Irish society over the years has it been that it would be impossible to write a credible social history of Ireland without dealing with it. Its former presenter, Gay Byrne, is often credited with playing a crucial role in the liberalization of Irish society, but he did so more as a sensitive barometer of what the society could bear, of what currents could no longer be contained, than as a conscious and committed initiator of social change.

The Riordans, long off the air but still strong in the folk memory, was a long-running (1965–79) rural drama serial, which broke new ground in its production methods in its time by combining the immediacy of video technology with the authenticity of location shooting. It also played out many of the social tensions of the era in its storylines.

Nighthawks, a mixed-format live programme set in a fictional diner, involving satirical sketches, music and ironic interactions of real personalities with fictional ones, was being seen as a vanguard experiment in postmodernist programming. It also pushed forward the parameters of the permissible in social and political satire.

RTÉ has long been an arena of confrontation and combat between the forces of conservatism and modernization in Irish society. Traditionalists have veered between railing against television as the source of heretical ideas and alien values and fighting to use television in the service of their own ideas and values. In its early years, television was full of liturgical ceremony and pious commentary, presented in a mode of address which assumed its audience was 100 per cent Catholic. This has eroded over the years, but it persists, most notably in *The Angelus*, which still comes over the airwaves twice every day.

Television, however, by its very nature, could not but be an agent of modernization. Itself the product of industrial and technological development, its presence brought even the most remote rural dwelling into a complex web of implication in the forms of perception and rhythms of response embodied in the culture which brought it forth. On one level, the overt opening of Ireland to other cultures, providing constant points of comparison and contrast to its own culture, was bound to have a powerfully relativizing effect. On another level, a sort of subliminal seduction into the whole pace and texture of its dense and discontinuous flood of stimuli has most probably had even more far-reaching consequences.

However, the old order has not gone down without kicking and screaming. The history of RTÉ has been littered with repeated skirmishes and full-scale battles: floods of letters and telephone calls of complaint, resolutions of condemnation from county councils, dismissal of the RTÉ authority by the government, denunciations, apologies, programmes taken off air in mid-run.

Although conservative opinion has always mobilized itself more effectively than liberal opinion in putting pressure on RTÉ and has won many battles, it was never possible for it to win the war. The conflict continues, but the balance has relentlessly shifted in favour of liberalism. The dominance of a liberal consensus, although it gives some scope for expression to other views, can be as frustrating to those to the left of it as to those to the right of it.

Despite the fragmentation of television audiences elsewhere and despite heavy viewing of imported programmes and foreign channels, home-produced programmes still have privileged access to their audience and play a central role in a society still talking to itself. This is because Irish society, despite its diversity and debate, is still a society in a way that other television audiences have ceased to be.

News and current affairs programmes are at the cutting edge of this process. RTÉ coverage of Irish political, economic and cultural life is an influential force within the flow of it all. *Today-Tonight*, and later *Prime Time*, have probed various strands of political and economic scandal in the best traditions of investigative journalism. RTÉ coverage of international affairs tends to align itself to the wire service orthodoxy prevailing worldwide. Its coverage of events in Eastern Europe in 1989–90, for example, was quite conformist. However, its treatment of the Gulf War in 1991 embodied a critical and independent dimension that was in sharp contrast to the coverage the same audience saw on American and British channels.

Drama has declined noticeably in recent years. The single play has virtually disappeared, as have dramatic series and miniseries. After a rich history of studio-based single plays in the 1960s, more on-location series and mini-series in the 1970s, and more expensive co-production in the 1980s, all that was left in the early 1990s were two serials, *Glenroe* (axed in 2000) and *Fair City*, neither of which distinguished itself in its sensitivity to the texture of the times. Arts, books, sports, quiz, music, variety, youth and talk shows continue, but with an ever-accelerating turnover of formats.

However, Roddy Doyle's controversial series *Family* (1994), and the excellent adaptation of John McGahern's *Amongst Women* (1998) proved that RTÉ remains capable of producing television drama of the highest standard. Likewise, the documentary series, *States of Fear* (1999), along with the *Irish Empire* (1999) and *Seven Ages* (2000) were in the best tradition of public service broadcasting.

HELENA SHEEHAN

Temperance Movement (1838–1849) Took place against a background of similar anti-drink crusades in England and Wales. However, as the industrial revolution had never materialized in Ireland, the Irish campaign lacked the broader economic motives which elsewhere in the British Isles reflected a growing anxiety about regular hours, output and industrial competitiveness. The absence of worried entrepreneurs was more than compensated for by the enthusiasm of Fr Theobald Mathew (1790–1856), with whom the Irish crusade is most closely associated. Mathew enjoyed considerable success, some 50 per cent of the Irish adult population 'taking the pledge', and government revenue from duty on spirits was slashed. Race memory of his impact on Irish urban drinking habits (it was in towns that the worst problems prevailed) has obscured the fact that he was not a unique messianic figure but rather part of a tradition. There had been previous Irish temperence societies, always conservative in outlook, and they had modelled their approach on similar organizations in America – 'It was not the drunkard but the moderate drinker who was to be persuaded to change his ways.' The earliest such reformers were Presbyterian clergymen. The Lancashire-type teetotalism which was typical of British anti-drink crusades was first brought to Ireland by John Finch, who began his operations in Strabane.

Reading

Kerrigan, Colm, *Father Mathew and the Irish Temperence Movement 1838–1849* (Cork: Cork University Press, 1992).

GERARD O'BRIEN

terrorism The term is both pejorative and dangerous, its definition as slippery as the political circumstances which give rise to it.

To the Israelis, terrorism is any form of armed resistance to Israeli occupation: to the Palestinians, it represents any Israeli military operation. To the Soviet army in Afghanistan in 1980, it meant Afghan resistance: to the Afghans, it meant Soviet repression. To the British army in Northern Ireland, it means any form of violent IRA activity; to the IRA it means the very presence of crown forces in the six counties. The BBC often referred to Palestinian 'terrorism', never referred to bomb explosions by the ANC in South Africa as 'terrorism', but always called the IRA 'terrorists'. American news agencies do not hesitate to use 'terrorism' in relation to Arab attacks on westerners or Israelis, rarely use the word about the IRA – there are, of course, many Irish Americans among the agencies subscribers – and never refer to Israeli 'terrorism' (even when this involves Jewish bomb attacks on Palestinians).

The US State Department tried to define 'international terrorism' in 1976, claiming that it involved politically motivated assassination, murder or kidnapping which transcended national boundaries. This definition would certainly indict the bombers of the Lockerbie airliner, IRA hit squads in Northern Ireland and Britain, 'Islamic Jihad' kidnappers in Lebanon, the Columbian drugs cartel and sundry others. The State Department did not suggest – as was the case – that this definition would also condemn Israel (which kidnapped a Moslem cleric from Lebanon in 1989 and assassinated another in 1991, while murdering numerous Palestinian leaders in Lebanon and Tunisia). For Irish nationalists, it would include any shoot-to-kill policy carried out by British army or Royal Ulster Constabulary squads in the North of Ireland. It would certainly be impossible to exclude the numerous CIA operations intended to liquidate America's enemies in south east Asia and Latin America.

'Terrorism', as a definition, thus tends to be a political contrivance, an attempt – however justified – to deprive one's opponents of legitimacy. 'Terrorists' are those who use violence against the side that is using the word. To understand this, one has only to ask how the world chose to respond to the worst act of 'terrorism' committed in the Middle East in the 1980s – the massacre of hundreds of Palestinian civilians by Lebanese Christian militiamen in September 1982. Shock and horror were expressed, but not a single western newspaper or agency or television report referred to the slaughter as an act of 'terrorism'. For, as the world knew, the Christian murderers were militiamen armed and trained by the Israelis, who had been sent into the Palestinian camps by the Israelis to search – and here is the rub – for Palestinian 'terrorists'.

In Ireland, we may ask how anyone can question the use of the word 'terrorism' in relation to bombs and assassinations. What alternative semantics is available to encompass a bomb at a war memorial, the sectarian murder of Protestant and Catholic civilians, a car bombing in Belfast or Dublin? Few Britons would find fault with describing those who kill British soldiers as 'terrorists' – but few Britons would have used the word about Afghan guerrillas who killed Soviet troops in Kabul.

To reject the word 'terrorism' does not imply approval of any act of violence, merely a refusal to accept a term which has become as immoral in its use as it has become meaningless in its definition. Unless the word is employed about all acts of 'terrorism' – which it is not – then every reference turns us into participants in a war. For not only is it pejorative: it is persuasive because it prevents us examining the reasons why men and women move so far beyond the bounds of civilized behaviour in their desire to achieve their aims. It thus also precludes us from making our own judgement on the degree of moral condemnation which the perpetrators of violence deserve. Governments prefer it that way. So do those who kill the innocent. Wars against 'terrorism' are easy to justify when we can forget history.

ROBERT FISK

theatre The Gaelic culture, while producing several remarkable literary works in dialogue form, did not embrace the theatre genre in the sense of organized performances where participants enact a fable, portraying characters other than themselves. After the Anglo-Norman invasion the European tradition of religious drama was instituted in some of the chief towns, particularly Dublin and Kilkenny, where processional plays at Easter or Corpus Christi were performed by the trade guilds and greatly encouraged by the corporations.

Lord Deputy Wentworth engaged a Scots dancing master, John Ogilby, to provide secular entertainments in Dublin Castle (*c*.1633). Ogilby subsequently opened the earliest purpose-built theatre in the British Isles outside London, in Werburgh Street, Dublin (1637). It closed under the Cromwellian interdict four years later. In 1661 Ogilby was granted a patent to erect theatres anywhere in Ireland; he confined himself to a site at Smock Alley, Dublin, where the Theatre Royal – the first in the 'French' or 'Restoration' style in the British Isles – flourished until 1787. Many of the greatest Irish and English players performed there. A theatre in Aungier Street designed by (Sir) William Lovett Pearce, opened in 1733, only survived 13 years. During the eighteenth century there were other short-lived theatres in Rainsford Street and Capel Street.

Smock Alley declined due to competition from the Crow Street Theatre (opened 1758), but it in turn failed in 1821. Its patent was transferred to the new Theatre Royal in Hawkins Street, which became the number one Dublin venue for cross-channel companies. Burned in 1880, immediately rebuilt and rebuilt again in 1897, the site was cleared for the huge 4,000-seat Theatre Royal in 1937, the largest in the British Isles, creating a vogue for 'cine-variety'. It was also Dublin's major venue for celebrity concerts till demolished in 1963.

Two handsome Victorian theatres were replaced by office blocks in the same decade, the Capitol (formerly La Scala) in Prince's Street, and the Queen's (formerly Adelphi) in Pearse Street. The Queen's was notable for its neo-Celtic plasterwork (*c*.1908); it was the chief house for melodrama until as late as the 1920s. The only surviving nineteenth-century theatres are the Gaiety in South King Street and the Olympia (formerly Empire Palace, and prior to that Dan Lowery's Music Hall) in Dame Street. These splendid old theatres continue to house opera, musicals, pantomime and, to a surprising degree since the 1970s, a greatly expanded programme of plays.

The present Abbey and Peacock Theatres, home of the National Theatre Society Ltd and designed by Michael Scott (1966), occupy the site of the original Abbey Theatre (opened 1904) which was formerly the theatre of the Mechanics' Institute, and had first been known as the Theatre Royal in Abbey Street (1837–9). The only other permanent theatre on the north side of the Liffey is the Gate in what were the Assembly Rooms of the Rotunda Hospital (1784), leased by Dublin Gate Theatre Productions in 1933.

Theatres known (according to changing fashions) as 'art' or 'experimental' or 'fringe' come and go quite rapidly – except for the Abbey and Gate, which started in this vein but, founded upon solid administrative structures, kept developing artistically. Edward Martyn's Hardwick Street Theatre at the turn of the twentieth century, and Madam Bannard Cogley's Studio Theatre, Barry Cassin and Nora Lever's 37 Theatre Club and Alan Simpson and Carolyn Swift's Pike Theatre Club at mid-century, were among those which helped to expose the latest theatre modes. Similarly Deirdre O'Connell's Focus Theatre and the Project Arts Centre continued to supply this essential ingredient, the premises of the latter providing a secure base for several impressive companies, such as Rough Magic. A popular urban drama has also evolved in Dublin through the work of the Passion Machine. The most useful new Dublin venues since the close of the 1980s have been the Andrew's Lane and Tivoli theatres.

Outside Dublin there was very little organized theatre until well into the eighteenth century, though sporadic productions are known to have been given in Cork from 1713, and in Belfast from 1730. Cork's first Theatre Royal (1736) was superseded by another of the same name in 1760; the Athenaeum (1866), subsequently renamed the Opera House, was burned in 1955 and replaced on the same site 10 years later. The nineteenth-century Palace became a cinema, but reverted to theatre production in 1990. The Group Theatre (fl. 1958–74) and the Southern Theatre Group (fl. 1959–71) kept local drama alive, as did the Everyman and Cork Theatre companies in more recent times.

Plays were occasionally presented in Belfast at the Vaults (1730) and subsequently at successive theatres in Castle Street (1768), Mill Gate (1770), Ann Street (1778), Rosemary Street (1784) and Arthur Square (1793) – the last survived for 140 years. The late nineteenth-century Alhambra and Empire have been demolished and the Hippodrome converted to a cinema. Belfast's most opulent theatre, the Grand Opera House (designed by Matcham, 1895), was restored in 1980, and restored again after a street explosion in 1991. The Ulster Literary Theatre, a copy of the National Theatre Society, presented new plays in the early years of the twentieth century. The Ulster Group Theatre (fl. 1940–72) was another localized version of the Abbey. The Arts Theatre (1946) and the Lyric Players Theatre (1951) continue; the latter is Belfast's leading production company.

The earliest purpose-built theatre (1770–1818) in Limerick was managed by Tottenham Heaphy. The only other of significance was the Theatre Royal (1841–1922). In 1981 the Belltable Arts Centre, a reconstruction of the awkwardly shaped Coliseum, filled an unfortunate void. In Wexford the Theatre Royal (1830) became a cinema, but was purchased by Wexford Festival Opera and has been running as a theatre since 1951. A fine theatre was placed in the Waterford City Hall (1784), was remodelled in the mid-nineteenth century, and is now the oldest in continuous operation in Ireland. The Garter Lane Arts

Centre, home of the enterprising Red Kettle Theatre Company, has added greatly to Waterford's theatrical life since the 1980s.

There have been theatrical performances in Galway since 1739 in a number of venues. Taibhdhearch na Gaillimhe was instituted in 1928 but has failed to produce the anticipated surge of new Gaelic-language drama. Its excellent auditorium is situated near the premises of the Druid Theatre Company (1975), where an English-language repertory has been highly successful.

There are modern theatre buildings in Coleraine, Enniskillen, Sligo, Tallaght and Tralee; the last is the home of the National Folk Theatre (Siamsa Tíre).

The theatres of Ireland are less notable than the work of the playwrights which is produced within them. There is no adequate theatre building in Londonderry, but the Field Day Theatre Company has its headquarters in the city, and presents its work on tour in Ireland and abroad. It is probably true that more new plays are professionally presented annually in Ireland than in any other western country; it is certainly true in proportion to the country's size and population.

Reading

Clark, W.S., *The Irish Stage in the Provincial Towns* (Oxford: Clarendon Press, 1955).
FitzSimon, Christopher, *The Irish Theatre* (London: Thames and Hudson, 1983).
Kavanagh, Peter, *The Irish Theatre* (Tralee: Kerryman, 1946).

CHRISTOPHER FITZSIMON

Thomas, Adrian (1947–) Composer, lecturer and Head of Music, BBC Radio 3. Born Cornwall. Thomas was educated at the University of Nottingham and Krakow Conservatory. In 1972 he joined the music department of Queen's University, Belfast, as lecturer and subsequently Hamilton Harty professor of music. Major compositions include *Busonku* (1978) and *in wild quiet* (1980) for instrumental septet; *Intrada* (1981)

for orchestra; *Elegy* (1983) for violin and piano; *Rau* (1985) for string octet; *Kuoan Variations* (1987) for viola and *Black Rainbow* (1989) for mixed choir. In 1985 his book *Grazyna Bacewicz: Chamber and Orchestral Music* was published in Los Angeles, and in 1989 he was awarded the medal of the Polish Composers' Union for distinguished services to contemporary Polish music.

E. O'KELLY

Thompson, William (1785–1833) Political economist and social reformer. Born into a position of wealth and privilege, Thompson had a strong sense of social injustice that led him to study the economic problems of rural deprivation, as exemplified in the pitiful lives of his tenants. He saw landed wealth as lying at the root of many of society's problems and considered that the key to political and economic change lay in its fair and equal redistribution. In this respect he echoed the views of his contemporaries Robert Owen and Jeremy Bentham, and his 1824 treatise *An Enquiry into the Principles of the Distribution of Wealth Most Conducive to Human Happiness* later influenced the theories of Karl Marx. Thompson also campaigned for the rights of women in *Appeal of One Half of the Human Race, Women, against the Pretensions of the Other Half, Men to Retain them in Political, and thence in Civil and Domestic Slavery* (1825). True to his beliefs, Thompson bequeathed most of his wealth to the poor, but 25 years' tortutous litigation eventually overthrew his last request.

HELEN McCURDY

Titanic The loss of the 66,000-ton White Star liner *Titanic* with 1,503 lives, when it struck an iceberg off Newfoundland during the night of 14–15 April 1912, gave rise then and later to folklore and legend. There have been several feature films, a number of poems and a radio play about it; and novels of the period sometimes refer to the disaster, so great was the suggestiveness of the (Promethean) myth. There is Hardy's poem

'The Convergence of the Twain', Conrad's *Reflections on the loss of the 'Titanic'*, and, for its Spenglerian resonance, a mention in Thomas Mann's *The Magic Mountain* (1927). Stella Rodney, visiting an Irish country house in Elizabeth Bowen's wartime psychological thriller *The Heat of the Day* (1949), notices, 'stuck to an alien frame', a magazine photograph of 'a liner going down in a blaze with all lights on, decks and port-holes shining', over the caption, 'Nearer, my God, to Thee: the *Titanic*, 1912'. The ship was built by Harland and Wolff, and glimpsed by the 5-year-old Louis MacNeice as it sailed down Belfast Lough to its sea trials. 'Death of an Old Lady' remembers a dream of 'shipyard voices at five in the morning' and 'a boat so big it was named Titanic'. The poem, about the death of his grandmother, was collected in *Visitations* (1957). In *The Iceberg*, by Stewart Parker, first broadcast on BBC Radio 3 in January 1974 and published in *The Honest Ulsterman* (Winter 1975), two ghosts, Danny and Hugh, are overheard discussing the doomed liner under construction in the Belfast shipyard. Anthony Cronin's longish poem *R.M.S. Titanic* (1980), a cinematic montage of scene and incident, dramatizes ethical and philosophical questions and tries to answer them with word-pictures of the ship in hubristic relation to the universe – 'huge against the stars'.

In the late 1990s the story of the *Titanic* was revived on an unprecedented scale in fictionalized form. The publication of Beryl Bainbridge's highly praised novel *Every Man For Himself*, which won the 1996 Whitbread Prize, was soon eclipsed by the box office phenomenon of James Cameron's Hollywood blockbuster *Titanic*, which scooped 11 Academy Awards. The success of the film rekindled considerable interest in the Belfast ship-building tradition and the Harland & Wolff shipyards where *Titanic* was built.

DEREK MAHON

Toland, John (1607–1722) Writer and philosopher. Toland's Christian names ('Joannes Eugenius' or 'Janus Junius'), his date and place of birth (30 November in Londonderry or on Inishowen in the parish of Clonmany?), and his parentage (the bastard son of a Catholic priest?), are all matters of controversy. He was educated at the universities of Glasgow, Edinburgh and (apparently) Leiden and Utrecht. He died at Putney on 11 March.

Toland's career was controversial also, and his contemporary reputation mixed at best. Acquainted with people of power and influence – Locke, Shaftesbury, Bayle, Liebniz, Robert Harley, the earl of Oxford – Toland squandered opportunity after opportunity as if courting unpopularity by 'talking against the Scriptures, commending Commonwealths, justifying the murder of K[ing] C[harles] 1st, railing against Priests in general, with a Thousand other Extravagancys'.

Toland's notoriety – and his troubles – stemmed in large part from his deist pamphlet, *Christianity Not Mysterious* (1696). He was accused of being a Socinian, a member of 'a secret Club, who set themselves with a great deal of Industry to destroy all Reveal'd Religion'. Locke promptly severed his connections with the disgraced writer, although Shaftesbury (with whom Toland was said to correspond 'as tenderly as if they used to lye with one another') kept in touch for several years more until finally convinced that Toland's 'prophane & loose Ways overballance all the Good (I think) that either he has done or can do'.

Toland found new friends such as Robert Harley, and gained a reputation as a 'Commonwealthman' by writing propaganda and editing the works of Milton, Ludlow and Harrington as part of the Country opposition's campaign against the government of William III. After the publication of *The Art of Governing by Partys* and *Anglia Libera* in 1701, Toland accompanied the 'atheist' earl of Macclesfield to Hanover to present the dowager duchess Sophia with a copy of the Act of Settlement.

Toland found favour with Sophia for a time but, his credit with her ministers (and with Liebniz) soon wearing out, he was forced to approach Harley once more, publishing *The Memorial of the State of England* (1705) at the secretary of state's 'direction'. Still the financial independence Toland craved failed to materialize. Harley used him as an agent in Germany but refused to grant him a regular government pension. Toland hoped in vain for better things on the change of ministry in 1710. However, his association with Harley having compromised his relations with the Whigs, Toland spent the remainder of his life trying unsuccessfully to regain their favour. By 1718 he was reduced to lodging in the friend's house in Putney in which he died.

More polemicist than philosopher, Toland was a tireless propagandist for a host of strange ideas – pantheism, Rosicrucianism, and the hermetic writings of Giordano Bruno, to name but a few. He is best remembered for his demystification of superstition and religion in *Christianity Not Mysterious* and the *Letters to Serena* (1704), for which he was reviled by many writers, including Jonathan Swift, who went out of his way to declaim against 'the Trumpery lately written by *Asgill, Tindall, Toland, Coward,* and Forty more'.

Reading

Carabelli, Giancarlo, *Tolandiana: materiali bibliografici per lo studio dell'opera e della fortuna di John Toland (1670–1722)* (Florence: La Nuova Italia, 1975).

Daniel, Stephen H., *John Toland: His Methods, Manners, and Mind* (Kingston and Montreal: McGill-Queen's University Press, 1984).

Desmaizeaux, Pierre, (ed.), *A Collection of Several Pieces of Mr. John Toland*, 2 vols (London: J. Peele, 1726).

Downie, J.A., *Robert Harley and the Press: Propaganda and Public Opinion in the Age of Swift and Defoe* (Cambridge: Cambridge University Press, 1979).

Jacob, Margaret C., *The Newtonians and the English Revolution, 1689–1720* (Ithaca NY: Cornell University Press, 1976).

Simms, J.G., 'John Toland (1670–1722), a Donegal heretic', *Irish Historical Studies* 16 (1969).

Sullivan, Robert E., *John Toland and the Deist Controversy: A Study in Adaptations* (Cambridge and London: Harvard University Press, 1982).

Worden, A.B., (ed.), *Edmund Ludlow, A Voyce from the Watch Tower: Part Five, 1660–1662* (London: Royal Historical Society, 1978).

A.J. DOWNIE

Toler, John (1745–1831) Lawyer. Born Tipperary. Educated in Trinity College, Dublin, Toler was called to the Irish bar in 1770 and elected MP for Tralee in 1776. As leader of the government opposition to Catholic emancipation, he was largely responsible for the rejection of Grattan's Catholic Relief Bill in 1795. He rose rapidly in power, unencumbered by scruples or principles, and was successively solicitor general (1789–98), attorney general (1798–1800), and finally justice of the Court of Common Pleas (1800–27). He prosecuted the leaders of the 1798 rebellion and presided at the trial of Robert Emmet.

Toler was described by Lecky as 'a violent, selfish and unprincipled advocate', and his position as chief justice was felt to be an insult to Catholics and a mockery of justice. He was only bought off the bench in 1827, aged 82, by his advancement in the peerage as Viscount Glandine and the earl of Norbury.

Reading

Lecky, W.E.H., *History of Ireland in the Eighteenth Century* (Chicago: 1972).

LUCINDA THOMSON

Tone, Theobald Wolfe (1763–98) Political radical and United Irishman. Born Dublin, 20 June; died, by suicide, Kilmainham Jail, 19 November. Tone's middle-class background pointed to a commercial rather than a professional career, but his intelligence led him to Trinity College, Dublin, where he manifested his incipient radicalism. He was elected to the committee of seven nominated by students in July 1784 to consider the feasibility of convening a meeting of students to elect delegates for Napper Tandy's reform congress. Nothing came of this, and Tone devoted his time in subsequent years to wooing Martha Witherington, who became his wife, and to fulfilling the requirements necessary to enable him to practice law. In truth, Tone had little interest in the law, but when a number of alternative schemes failed to come to pass, he practised for a short time in the late 1780s.

Tone was attracted by politics, but though a pamphlet he published in 1790 on 'the conduct of administration' brought him to the notice of the Irish Whigs, it did not win him political patronage. Instead, he found himself drawn once more towards radicalism, and he became friendly with a number of Dublin-based radicals, of whom Thomas Russell and William Drennan are the best known. The influence of events in France, now in the throes of revolution, created an atmosphere particularly conducive to the dissemination of radical ideas, and conviced a number of radical spirits in Belfast as well as Dublin of the need for a society transcending the sectarian divide, which would advance the cause of parliamentary reform. Jone's contribution to the foundation and his involvement with the United Irishmen in the early 1790s was more modest than is usually assumed. He was recruited early in 1792 by the Catholic Committee, which was impressed by his 1791 tract *Argument on behalf of the Catholics* to act as their agent. Tone proved a very effective agent. He travelled the country enjoining Catholics to return delegates for the Catholic Convention, which met in December in Tailor's Hall, and accompanied the delegates who presented the petition of the convention to George III. The enfranchisement of Catholic freeholders in 1793 left Tone without employment, but the polarization of Irish politics between radical and conservative in the mid-1790s directed him towards Republican separatism. He was implicated in a seditious communication with France by William Jackson, and following the disastrous

Fitzwilliam viceroyalty and the embrace by the United Irishmen of revolution, he determined to go to Paris to convince the French authorities of the merits of sending a military force to Ireland to enable the United Irishmen to achieve their ends. Tone had effectively been transformed into a revolutionary by events; only an independent Irish republic, he believed, would provide the population with a political system that was non-denominational and representative.

Tone arrived in Paris, via Philadelphia, in 1796, and undertook the forbidding challenge of convincing the Directory to send a military expedition to Ireland. He proved an especially adroit diplomat, but when Lazare Hoche led an expedition to Ireland in December 1796, it was wrecked by poor weather. Despite this reverse, Tone did not give up, though a combination of factors reduced the prospects of the French dispatching another expedition in 1797 and in early 1798. It was not until rebellion broke out in Ireland, in May 1798, that the French were finally galvanized into activity, but by then it was too late. Three small expeditions hurriedly set sail, but none made any impression. Tone was captured following a naval engagement off the coast of Donegal, but following a court martial which refused to allow him the soldier's right of death by firing squad, he chose to end his own remarkable life.

Reading

Elliott, Marianne, *Wolfe Tone: Prophet of Irish Independence* (London: Yale University Press, 1989).

Tone, William T.W., *The Life of Theobald Wolfe Tone*, 2 vols (Washington DC: 1826).

JAMES KELLY

Tories Deriving from *tóraidhe* (literally a pursuer) the term, meaning bandits or outlaws, came into general use in Ireland during the 1660s, although isolated references occur earlier. The term 'raparee' is used synonymously with Tory in the seventeenth and eighteenth centuries. Tory replaced the older 'woodkern' and indicated a greater organization of bandit groups, usually under a captain, such as Redmond O'Hanlon in south Armagh. This use of the term declined in the early eighteenth century. After the defeat in England of the second exclusion bill in 1679 it was used as a term of abuse, associating the duke of Ormond and his followers with Irish outlaws. The word did not enter parliamentary language until after 1690.

Reading

Duffy, R. Quinn, 'Redmond O'Hanlon and the outlaws of Ulster', *History Today* xxxii (1982).

Connolly, S.J., 'Violence and order in the eighteenth century', in Patrick O'Flanagan, Paul, Ferguson, Paul and Whelan, Kevin (eds), *Rural Ireland 1600–1900* (Cork: Cork University Press 1987).

William, Robert, 'The origin of "Whig" and "Tory" in English political language', *Historical Journal* xvii (1974).

RAYMOND GILLESPIE

An Tostal In the 1950s many towns and villages eagerly participated in the Tostal festival, initiated by what is now Bord Fáilte in the hope of extending back to early June the all-too-short Irish tourist season, but gradually abandoned the term *tostal* (gathering). The event has survived under that name, largely thanks to the work of Councillor Joseph Mooney, only in Drumshanbo, County Leitrim, where the emphasis is on traditional music. However, the festival idea caught fire, and countless thematic celebrations are held annually throughout Ireland.

JAMES DOWNEY

tourism Large-scale tourism was initiated by the train, which was the first mode of transport comfortable and cheap enough to make travelling for pleasure attractive. Also, because a railway line needs to carry large numbers of people to meet its fixed costs, railway companies built luxury hotels and set out to fill them, the Great Southern and Western Railway alone building five in Kerry, at Killarney, Kenmare, Parknasilla, Caragh Lake and Waterville. Other railway hotels were built in Galway, Mulrany, Sligo, Bundoran, Rostrevor, Warrenpoint and Greenore, while in Dublin private hotels sprang up around every terminus.

The introduction of steam-powered ferries between Britain and Ireland also encouraged pleasure travel, because visitors no longer ran the risk of being delayed for days by unfavourable winds. Much later, aircraft cut journey times and made Ireland a more convenient destination for people from North America and the Continent. So, when boat and air fares fell steadily in relation to incomes in the post-war years, tourist numbers began to grow. In 1960, only 25,000 Continentals visited Ireland, but by 1989, the figure had risen to 744,000. The increase from the US was less marked, rising from 69,000 to 443,000 over the same period, while the number of British visitors, who had long had easy access, only doubled.

Overall, the number of overseas visitors to Ireland almost tripled in the 30 years between 1961 and 1991, rising from 1,012,000 to 3,015,000. However, as the lower fares and shorter journey times enabled progressively less wealthy visitors to come, the average tourist spent less money and stayed fewer days. In 1961, a typical visitor spent £367 in Ireland in 1990 terms. By 1991 that figure had dropped to £275.

The new, poorer, visitor demanded cheaper accommodation and, while the number of families offering bed and breakfast soared, the number of hotels fell from 707 offering 12.7m bed-nights in 1978 to 643 with 12.4m bed-nights in 1985. By 1990, the number of hotels (at 658) had started to recover, but the growth rate of the sector was greatly exceeded by that of the cheapest type of accommodation of all – the independent hostel, offering beds at £4 a night. There was also a rise in the number of visitors in camper vans and German coaches with sleeping trailers. These tourists spent very little in Ireland and some imported most of their food.

Even wealthy visitors to Ireland spent less than they had done previously, no longer regarding it as the journey of a lifetime from which they must return with lavish presents for all their friends. However, although attracting more visitors was spoiling the nature of the holidays Ireland offered and inescapably meant attracting a less wealthy clientele, the government responded to a suggestion from the Irish Hotel Federation in 1987 and set itself the target of doubling the number of arrivals over the following five years, bringing it to 4.2 million by 1992. By the late 1990s the Irish tourist trade was worth over $2\frac{1}{2}$ billion dollars a year.

Despite the rapid expansion, the overall impact of post-war tourism has been good so far. Early 1950s Ireland was drab and grim, with little local pride, but this began to change when the Irish Tourist Association (ITA) encouraged communities to hold events as part of the 1953 Tostal Festival. Many current festivals date back to these efforts. The ITA's successor, Bord Fáilte, has also made rural Ireland pleasanter for both visitors and local people by its sponsorship of the annual Tidy Towns contest.

In addition, the visitors' interest in natural history and archeology has rubbed off on Irish people, and many pleas for conservation have been made in the name of tourism when, in reality, the protestors wanted the features preserved for themselves. The growth of bed and breakfast has spread income from tourism widely throughout the community.

There are signs, however, that the limits to visitor growth have been reached, even breached, in the most popular tourist areas. It is now necessary to queue for admission to Newgrange at the busiest times of year, and the sheer number of day-trippers overwhelms the people of Inis Mór in the Aran Islands, damaging both the community and the archaeological and landscape features the visitors come to see. With the inception of the peace process in Northern Ireland in the mid-

1990s and the cessation of hostilities between sectarian groups, tourists are flooding into Ireland. This boom in tourism, particularly by people seeking to redisover their Irish roots, has also been fostered by huge international interest in traditional Irish music and dance.

RICHARD DOUTHWAITE

Townsend, Richard (1821–84) Mathematician. Born Baltimore, County Cork, 3 April; died Dublin, 16 October. Townsend graduated from Trinity College, Dublin, in 1842, and was elected Fellow in mathematics in 1845. In 1870 he became professor of natural philosophy. He was well regarded as a teacher. He published numerous mathematical articles, being best known for his work in pure geometry. He published *Chapters on the Modern Geometry of the Point, Line and Circle* (1862–5).

DAVID SMITH

trade unions Although little trace of the relevant legislation can be found in the statutes, it is probable that the sixteenth-century English prohibition of workers' combinations extended also in practice to Ireland. The prevalence of labour unrest, however, is suggested by measures enacted in 1729 and 1743 to outlaw combinations. Both laws were ignored by the workers, who continued to form trade unions. Further legislation in 1757 and 1763 prescribed harsh penalties for those who persisted in organizing such unions. In 1764 the first clearly identifiable trade union, the Regular Carpenters of Dublin, was formed. Middle-class nationalists such as Daniel O'Connell and the Fenians feared and opposed Chartism and trade unionism, and the movement did not become associated with nationalism until the latter end of the nineteenth century.

After the establishment of the 'new model' trade unions in Britain in the 1850s, the Irish unions were affected increasingly by competition from these new bodies for their members. Mergers between the older Irish and newer

British unions occurred but generally these were not to the advantage of the Irish groups, and the question emerged as to whether Irish unions should remain independent or become branches of British organizations. Irish unions, however, were subject to British law, and Ireland was included in trade union legislation passed in 1871, 1906 and 1913. The political settlement of 1921 allowed the new Irish Free State to enact its own trade union legislation, but in the event the old British measures were continued and eventually written into the Irish constitution in 1937.

Home-grown labour laws in southern Ireland have been few; perhaps the most significant measure was the 1946 Act, which established a labour court for the settlement of industrial disputes. While a strong socialist ideology was and is often lacking, most trades and professions in present-day Ireland are unionized.

GERARD O'BRIEN

transport Inland transport in Ireland is dominated by road transport. In 1994 there were 9,230,000 kilometres of public roads in the Republic (RI) and 2,417,000 in Northern Ireland (NI). The network is extensive and lightly used. In 1994 there were 38 inhabitants per km of road in RI and 66 in NI, compared to 156 in Great Britain (GB). RI had 12 vehicles registered per km of road, compared to 22 in NI and 69 in GB. There were 1.3 million road vehicles registered in RI and 0.6 million in NI. Road expenditure in NI in 1994 was planned at £118m and the network was generally considered adequate. In RI the proposed capital expenditures in 1994 were £192m on the national primary and secondary roads and £75m on regional and local roads. Backlogs of investment on the primary roads are being eliminated, but a severe problem of potholed rural roads has resulted from spending only about a third of road tax revenues on roads, and from the abolition of local authority revenues from rates on residential dwellings.

Buses are the dominant form of public transport, with 80 million journeys a year in NI and 240 million in RI by the state company CIE (in 1994). There is a private bus fleet in RI, which is large than CIE, but its passenger numbers are not published. There is also a large shared taxi service in Belfast and Derry, with fares which are similar to competing bus fares.

Railways accounted for about 4 per cent of passenger km and 10 per cent of freight in RI in 1994. NI Railways (NIR) do not run freight trains, but CIE uses NIR track for some rail freight. NIR carried 5.2m passengers per year, compared to 25.8 million on CIE in 1994. The CIE mainline rail system carried 7.6m passengers, with the remaining 18.2m using the Dublin suburban services in 1994. Railway subsidies are greater than customer receipts in RI. In NI capital grants of 80 per cent were paid in respect of investments between 1985/6 and 1991/2, in addition to revenue grants of 40 per cent of turnover.

Air and sea transport play a key role in an island economy with one of the highest ratios of foreign trade to GNP in the world. RI airports handled 9m passengers and NI airports almost 3m in 1994. Traffic has grown rapidly since deregulation of Ireland/UK routes in 1986, and there have been substantial reductions in fares. The London–Dublin route is the second busiest international air route in Europe. Dublin airport accounts for about half the traffic, while Belfast provides an interesting example of competition between its International and City airports. New airports in recent years at Derry, Donegal, Sligo, Knock, Galway, Waterford and Kerry have found it difficult to attract airline service. Air freight accounted for 18 per cent of RI foreign trade by value in 1994, and volumes have increased rapidly in recent years.

Seaports handled 42.4m tonnes in 1990. The leading ports by tonnage were Belfast (18 per cent market share), Dublin (15 per cent), Limerick and Cork (14 per cent each) and Larne (9 per cent). The major passenger ports are Larne, Dun Laoghaire, Dublin and

Rosslare. These also cater for roll-on roll-off freight. Belfast, Warrenpoint, Waterford and Dublin are major lift-on lift-off freight ports.

Reading

Barrett, Sean D., *Transport Policy in Ireland in the 1990s* (1991).
Northern Ireland Economic Council, *Transport Infrastructure and Policy in Northern Ireland* (1993).
Report of the Review Group on Commercial Harbours and Pilotage Policy and Legislation (Dublin: 1992).

SEAN D. BARRETT

Travellers Irish Travellers are an indigenous nomadic ethnic group. In the early 1990s the Traveller population in Ireland was estimated at 20,000, making up nearly 0.5 per cent of the total population. Over 50 per cent were located in the countries of Cork, Dublin, Limerick and Galway. There were also a further 15,000 Irish Travellers estimated to be in Britain. The Travellers bring an important element of cultural diversity to a society that effectively defines itself as monocultural. It was only in 1995, in the report of the Task Force for Travelling People, that Traveller culture was officially recognised.

In the past the Travellers were largely a rural people with an economy based on tinsmithing and horse dealing. The mass production of tinware and plastics, the mechanization of farming and the exodus from the rural areas created an economic crisis for the Travellers from the 1940s onwards. The Travellers responded to this crisis by moving to the towns and developing new economic activities, particularly in the area of waste recycling and scrap dealing.

Nomadism plays an important role within the Traveller economy, giving Travellers access to a market large enough to make marginal activities profitable. The wealthier Travellers tend to be the more mobile, in particular those engaged in trading. Nomadism also has important social and even psychological functions that ensure the smooth functioning of Traveller society. Changing technology and new economic opportunities have meant that Traveller nomadism itself has taken new forms.

According to the first survey of Traveller's attitudes published in February 2001, almost seven out of ten Travellers said they had been discriminated against by publicans, 40 per cent by owners of clubs and discos, 38 per cent by gardaí, 37 per cent by shop owners, 33 per cent by county councils and housing authorities, and 26 per cent by the Department of Social, Community and Family Affairs. Nevertheless, 71 per cent of Travellers declared themselves 'satisfied' or 'very satisfied' with their lives, though this figure dropped to 59 per cent amongst Travellers living in temporary or roadside accommodation. Most Travellers regard better education for their children as a priority.

Travellers still face serious accommodation problems. Many local authorities are failing to respond to the housing needs of the travelling community and to adopt specific accommodation programmes as required by the Traveller Accommodation Act of 1998.

Reading

DTEDG File – Irish Travellers, New Analysis and New Initiatives (Dublin: Pavee Point Publications, 1992).
Joyce, Nan with Farmer, Anna, *Traveller* (Dublin: Gill and Macmillan, 1985).
Liegeois, J.P., *Gypsies and Travellers* (Strasbourg: Council of Europe, 1987).
Pavee Pictures (Dublin: Dublin Travellers Education and Development Group, 1991).
Rottman, Dale-Tussing and Wiley, *The Population Structure and Living Circumstances of Irish Travellers* (Dublin: Economic and Social Research Institute Paper No. 131, 1986).

NIALL CROWLEY

Trench, Richard Chenevix (1807–86) Writer. Trench succeeded Richard Whately in the see of Dublin, and resembled his predecessor in his academic accomplishments, though in little else. A writer of distinction in the fields of literature and philology, he was also a recognized poet, and altogether left a considerable corpus of publications. He is credited with the original plan for the *Oxford English Dictionary*.

Irish by birth, his childhood was passed in England. At Cambridge he was influenced by F.D. Maurice (of the Christian Socialist movement) and moved in literary circles with Tennyson and Hallam. He held the chair of divinity at King's College, London, was later dean of Westminster, and then archbishop of Dublin.

His episcopate coincided with the turbulent period prior to and following disestablishment, to which he was implacably opposed, seeing no place for compromise. 'If the battle is lost, then, totally rejecting the process of gradual starvation to which Disraeli would submit us, to go in for instant death at the hands of Gladstone.' It was left to men like Archdeacon Stopford to protect Church of Ireland interests by a more conciliatory tone. Trench is seen to better advantage in the years of reconstruction that followed the passing of the Irish Church Act. A sympathizer (unlike Whately) with the Oxford Movement and a friend of Pusey, he sought with success to preserve the prerogatives of the bishops under the new constitution, and in the newly established general synod he worked to secure the retention of the integrity of the Book of Common Prayer (while wishing to see the Irish missionary saints introduced to the Calendar: 'the dogmatic can never be rightly understood except in the light of the historic'). He was conscious of the pressures that might be brought to bear on tractarian clergy in Ireland in the aftermath of disestablishment, and was dubbed 'Puseyite Trench' for his stand on their behalf.

KENNETH MILNE

Trevor, William (William Trevor Cox) (1928–) Novelist and short story writer. Born Mitchelstown, County Cork, 24 May.

Trevor had an unsettled education, because his father James William Cox was by profession a bank manager and was frequently transferred. Trevor's secondary education was completed in Dublin, at Sandford Park and St Columba's College, after which he took his BA at Trinity College (significantly in history) in 1950. Having married in 1952 he moved to England in 1953, at first teaching and then taking up sculpture for a time. He settled in Devon, where he still lives.

Including the early *A Standard of Behaviour* (1958), Trevor has written 15 novels up to *Death in Summer* (1998) and nine volumes of short stories up to *The Hill Bachelors* (2000). Apart from the first-mentioned, these have been well received, and *Reading Turgenev* (1991) was nominated for the Booker Prize. Several stories have been televised with great success, notably 'The Ballroom of Romance' and 'Events at Drimaghleen'. An indifferent play, yet infused with Trevor's historical interests, *Scenes from an Album*, was staged at the Abbey in 1981. His first book for children, *Juliet's Story* (1991), reminds one how important children are in Trevor's fiction generally. Trevor has also edited the *Oxford Book of Irish Short Stories* (1989) and published his collected essays, *Excursions in the Real World* (1993).

Trevor straddles two literary traditions, the English (exemplified especially by Dickens and Hardy) and the Irish (exemplified particularly by Joyce but also by O'Connor and Bowen), and his work oscillates expertly between both traditions. This duality is his great strength, allowing a detachment which penetrates to the heart of human affairs, whether English or Irish. Since the mid-1970s, however, his fiction has persistently undertaken the tragic matter of Irish history, especially in *Fools of Fortune* (1983) and *The Silence in the Garden* (1988).

Reading

Mortimer, Mark, 'William Trevor', *Ireland Today* 1031 (September 1986), pp. 7–10.

Schirmer, Gregory A., *William Trevor: A Study of his Fiction* (London and New York: Routledge, 1990).

Stinson, John J., 'Replicas, foils, and revelation, in some "Irish" short stories of William Trevor', *Canadian Journal of Irish Studies* 11, no.2 (1985), pp. 17–26.

CHRISTOPHER MURRAY

Trimble, (William) David (1944–) Leader of the Ulster Unionist Party since 1995 and MP for Upper Bann since 1990. Born 15 October. A barrister and law lecturer at Queen's University, Belfast, he was VUPP Convention member for South Belfast (1975–6). He supported voluntary coalition, including the Social Democratic and Labour Party (SDLP), after which the Vanguard Party split; he joined the Ulster Unionist Party (UUP) in 1978. He was associated with the Ulster Club's campaign of civil disobedience against the Anglo–Irish Agreement in the mid-1980s before being elected to the UUP executive, of which he became honorary secretary. In December 1993 he accused Taoiseach Albert Reynolds of offering Unionists 'surrender by stages'. With Ian Paisley he was honoured by the Orange Order for his role in a confrontation between Orange marchers and Catholic residents at Portadown in July 1995. He was again at the centre of the Drumcree stand-off in 1996, which caused widespread nationalist anger. Trimble's leadership of the UUP was strengthened when the party gained an extra seat in the 1997 Westminster election. Despite bitter criticism from both the Democratic Unionist Party and the United Kingdom Unionist Party, he subsequently led the UUP into talks at Stormont which included Sinn Féin and which resulted in the carrying of a referendum to establish a new Northern Ireland Assembly in 1998. Outfacing his UUP opponents, Trimble was elected Northern Ireland's First Minister in July 1998. Later that year, he and John Hume were jointly awarded the Nobel prize.

PATRICK GILLAN

Trollope, Anthony (1815–82) Civil servant and novelist. Trollope's successful Civil Service career took him to Ireland for most of 1841–51 and 1853–7. Newly married to Rose Heseltine, he was first stationed in Banagher, as the postal surveyor's (or district superintendent's) clerk. Finding living expenses low, he bought a horse and began a lifetime infatuation with both hunting and hacking. Ireland was the launching pad for Trollope's triumphant Post Office career, particularly from his assignment to the Southern Postal District from 1848. Here he initiated a significant extension of rural postal deliveries, often ascertaining route feasibility on foot or on horseback. 'It was the ambition of my life to cover the country with rural letter-carriers', he recorded in his *Autobiography*. His affection for the country on the whole was restrained: he found Dublin 'a nice city enough' and wrote in 1854 that 'tho' the North of Ireland is not the choicest permanent residence, it has some charms for the tourist'. None the less, his duties touring many areas certainly fired his literary imagination. Ireland features as the setting for his first two novels, both completed in Ireland, *The Macdermots of Ballycloran* (1847), and *The Kellys and the O'Kellys* (1848), largely set in County Galway. (*The Times* liked the 'humour' and 'bold reality' of the characters.) Two later novels have Irish settings, *Castle Richmond* (1860), set chiefly in County Cork, and *An Eye for an Eye* (1879), set in County Clare. The short stories 'Father Giles of Ballymoy' and 'The O'Conors of Castle Conor' are also set in Ireland. For *The Landleaguers*, set mostly in County Galway and unfinished at his death, the ageing author undertook a tour of Ireland in the summer of 1882 to research his theme of agrarian insurgency, immersing himself in 'Irish difficulties and Irish rebels'. Trollope also wrote an unpublished *Handbook to Ireland*.

AMY L. FRIEDMAN

Troy, John Thomas (1739–1823) Archbishop of Dublin. Born Porterstown, County Dublin; died Dublin, 11 May. Troy was educated in Rome at the Irish Dominican College of San Clemente, where he was later rector. He was appointed bishop of Ossory in 1776 and was translated to Dublin in 1784. In both dioceses he vigorously opposed all movements which sought to attain their ends by unconstitutional means – the Whiteboys in Ossory and the Defenders and the United Irishmen in Dublin. In 1792 he disavowed long-held papal pretensions in the matter of absolving subjects from their allegiance to the king and so influenced the passing of the Catholic Relief Act of 1793. He supported the Act of Union because he believed there was a much better chance of Catholic emancipation from a London Parliament than from a Dublin one. However, he opposed, with one brief lapse, the proposal that the king could exercise a veto on the appointment of Catholic bishops.

PATRICK FAGAN

tuberculosis and its eradication Eradication was part of a global phenomenon. Hereditary physicians in Gaelic Ireland certainly had a book knowledge of tuberculosis (phthisis, consumption), but we have no indication of its prevalence (in records or in bones) before 1673/4, when it accounted for 15 per cent of Protestant burials in Dublin. W.A. Wilde's *Report on the Census of 1851* shows that the disease spread from the garrison towns and planter communities after the seventeenth-century plantations. In the hinterland the infection ran riot in virgin families sustained by Outdoor Relief after the Famine.

The permissive rather than mandatory nature of the Tuberculosis Prevention (Ireland) Act of 1908, which stemmed from Lady Aberdeen's crusade, frustrated its provisions with regard to notification and the construction of sanatoria and dispensaries. The lethargy still affected native governments, and by the time sufficient funds were made available to make the Health Act (1947) effective, a new departure had been made in specific chemotherapy.

Plotting the tuberculosis death rate per 100,000 population in England and Wales logarithmically reveals the abrupt substantial fall following the introduction of effective chemotherapy in 1947. The sharp 1947 inflection is even more pronounced in the Irish curve, coming after an uneven plateau over the previous 25 years. The Irish experience was not unique; it was not the work of a thaumaturge, despite strident claims to the contrary. A major contribution to the rapid decline in morbidity from tuberculosis in childhood and adolescence was made by metropolitan and national BCG vaccination services, although a countrywide tuberculosis dispensary service as sophisticated as the sanatorium network (1947–55), which hastened the decline in new cases, was never established.

Reading

Aberdeen, Ishbel, *Ireland's Crusade Against Tuberculosis* (Dublin: Maunsell, 1908).

Barrington, Ruth, *Health, Medicine and Politics, 1900–1970* (Dublin: Institute of Public Administration, 1987).

Lowell, A.M., 'A review of tuberculosis . . . 1947–1962', *Adv. Tuberc. Research* 15 (1966), pp. 55–124.

Newsholme, A., 'Poverty and disease, . . . typhus fever and phthisis in Ireland', *Proceedings of the Royal Society of Medicine 1: Epidemiological Section* (1908), pp. 1–44.

Wilde, W.A., *Report on the Census of Ireland 1851. Part V* (Dublin: Thom, 1856).

C.S. BREATHNACH

Tyndall, John (1820–93) Scientist. Born Leighlinbridge, County Carlow, 2 August; died 4 December. The son of John Tyndall and Sarah McAssey, Tyndall was educated locally. He worked in the Ordnance Survey, then with a firm of railway engineers, and later taught mathematics and surveying. He was awarded his PhD at Marburg University. He was elected Fellow of the Royal Society, and appointed professor of natural philosophy at the Royal Institution in 1853 and its superintendent in 1867. He married Louisa Hamilton in 1876. He died as a result of chloral being accidently administered by his wife.

Tyndall's chief contributions were on radiant heat, which had meteorological significance; on bacteria, which influenced the development of antiseptic surgical methods; and on the movement of glaciers. Although not as eminent as some of his contemporaries, Tyndall was nevertheless a central figure in the history of Victorian science and regarded as one of its most popular and successful expositors.

Reading

Brock, W.H., McMillan, N.D. and Mollan, R.C. (eds), *John Tyndall: Essays on a Natural Philosopher* (Dublin: Royal Dublin Society, 1981).

Eve, A.S. and Creasey, C.H. *Life and Work of John Tyndall* (London: Macmillan, 1945).

DONAL MCCARTNEY

Tyrell, Charles (1950–) Painter. Born Trim, County Meath. Tyrrell trained as a painter at the National College of Art and Design (1969–74). Since 1984 he has lived and worked in the Beara Peninsula, West Cork. Tyrrell's initial interests were strictly formal; in the 1980s his paintings had a clearly drawn geometrical skeleton relating to the square support, which remained visible through layers of splashed, stained and heavily worked paint. Although still primarily abstract, his most recent *Borderland* series (1991) in colouring, surface and structure suggest some elements of the rugged landscape of West Cork.

Reading

Crozier, William, *Charles Tyrrell: New Work at Taylor Galleries* (Dublin: 1991).

Kelly, Liam, *Theo McNab, Charles Tyrrell: Surface and Structure* (Dublin: Douglas Hyde Gallery, 1987).

FELICITY WOOLF

U

U2 Dublin rock band; by the late 1980s, a true pop 'supergroup'. Members Paul 'Bono' Hewson (1960–), Dave 'The Edge' Evans (1961–), Adam Clayton (1960–) and Larry Mullen (1962–) formed the band in 1976 while in school. Bono's voice and The Edge's distinctive guitar style are U2 trademarks. Their third LP, *War*, brought them a world-wide audience; successive albums like *The Unforgettable Fire* and *The Joshua Tree* were massively popular. Ringing rock anthems and an embracing of social 'causes' defined the band in the 1980s. U2's continuing uncanny (and daring) ability to remake themselves creatively was demonstrated with the critically acclaimed, harder-edged *Achtung Baby* in 1991. The band continues to enjoy critical and commercial success with albums such as *Zooropa* (1993), *Pop* (1997) and *All That You Can't Leave Behind* (2000).

Reading

Dunphy, Eamon, *The Unforgettable Fire* (Harmondsworth: Penguin, 1988).

Stokes, Niall, *The U2 File: The Hot Press U2 History* (London: Omnibus, 1985).

KARLIN J. LILLINGTON

Ulster Defence Association Various Protestant vigilante groups and other small paramilitary groups came together to form what was the largest private army in Europe in the late summer of 1971. It was claimed that the UDA had 40,000 members in the early 1970s.

The organization was involved in the mass intimidation of Catholics living in religiously integrated working-class suburbs of Belfast, and it is estimated that 85 per cent of the 60,000 people forcibly moved from their homes in Belfast between 1969 and 1975 were Catholics, mostly intimated by the UDA. It also carried out regular assassinations of Catholic civilians, and a number of its victims were kidnapped and tortured before being shot. The high point of the UDA's power occurred in 1974, when it provided the muscle behind the Unionist campaign to destory the power-sharing executive government at Stormont.

In spite of its activities the UDA remained an entirely legal organization, while its paramilitary counterparts, the IRA and Ulster Volunteer Force, were proscribed. However, after a resurgence of UDA violence it was eventually banned by the British government in August 1992.

Reading

Bruce, Steve, *The Red Hand* (Oxford: Oxford University Press, 1992).

JIM CUSACK

Ulster Defence Regiment The indigenous Northern Ireland regiment of the British army, which was raised from April 1970 as a replacement to the Royal Ulster Constabulary's (RUC) Special Constabulary, or B Specials, disbanded because of its partisan behaviour towards Catholics in the early part of the conflict.

Catholics were encouraged to join the newly formed UDR to ensure that it would not reassume the sectarian character of the B Specials. For the first years it did achieve a membership which was up to 18 per cent Catholic, but this quickly dropped off because of attacks by the IRA on Catholic UDR members and because of disenchantment among Catholics about sectarianism among their Protestant fellow members. Catholic membership settled at around 3 per cent.

The role of the UDR was to support the RUC and British army. Its membership was largely part-time and those living in rural areas where the IRA was active suffered a high attrition rate. A total of 197 UDR members were killed by the IRA. The regiment's public image suffered from the frequency with which members were arrested and charged with involvement in loyalist crimes, including several murders. It was also found that members regularly leaked information to loyalist paramilitaries. The UDR was disbanded in July 1992 and its nine battalions incorporated along with the Royal Irish Rangers into the Royal Irish Regiment.

Reading

Ryder, Chris, *The Ulster Defence Regiment – An Instrument of Peace?* (London: Methuen, 1991).

JIM CUSACK

Ulster Folk and Transport Museum The museum's aim is to illustrate the social history of the people of Northern Ireland. It consists of two main components. First, there is the Witham Street Gallery (formerly the Belfast Transport Museum); exhibits include a collection of railway rolling stock, motorcycles and motor cars, trams, bicycles and carriages. Second, there is the Open Air Museum, which exhibits buildings removed from Ulster's countryside and carefully reconstructed at Cultra. At present this part of the museum contains 24 exhibits, including three urban terraces, a Catholic chapel and a Church of Ireland church, various buildings involved in the linen industry, four farm houses, cottier dwellings, two national school buildings and a court house. In addition to these authentic buildings there is a replica of the Northern Banking Company's premises in Portglenone, County Antrim.

The museum holds craft courses for the public throughout the year. These include courses on spinning, weaving, quilting and lace making. Additionally the Ulster Folk museum hosts one-off lectures and exhibitions.

RACHEL FURMSTON

Ulster Group Theatre Recognizing the need for a locally based professional company in Belfast, Harold Goldblatt, James Mageean, R.H. McCandless, Joseph Tomelty and others formed the Group Theatre in 1941. The players augmented small salaries by regular engagements with the prolific drama department of BBC Northern Ireland. Among the 50 original plays produced were *The Old Broom* by George Shiels, *My Brother Tom* by St John Irvine, *Danger, Men Working* by John D. Stewart, *Traitors in our Way* by Louis MacNeice, *The Bonefire* by Gerald McLarnon, *The Randy Dandy* by Stewart Love, and Tomelty's celebrated *All Souls' Night* and *Is the Priest at Home?* The Group broke up in 1958 when the actor James Ellis formed a company to produce Sam

Thompson's *Over the Bridge*, which was thought too controversial to stage. Other leading Group actors were Colin Blakeley, Stephen Boyd, J.G. Devlin, Denys Hawthorne, Maurice O'Callaghan, Elizabeth Begley, Margaret D'Arcy and Doreen Hepburn.

CHRISTOPHER FITZSIMON

Ulster Literary Theatre Inspired by the formation in Dublin of the Irish Literary Theatre in 1898 (transformed into the National Theatre Society in 1903), the Ulster Literary Theatre was founded in Belfast by Bulmer Hobson, David Parkhill and others in 1904. Rutherford Mayne's early plays *Turn of the Road* (1906), *The Drone* (1908) and *Red Turf* (1911) helped to establish the company, but his later and superior work was produced in Dublin. Several satirical comedies by Gerald Macnamara, including *The Mist that Does Be on the Bog* (1909) and *Thompson in Tir na nOg* (1912), helped to popularize the movement. Fifty original plays were produced over 19 years. St John Ervine, George Shiels and Lynn Doyle, among others, contributed substantial material, but the company ultimately failed through lack of energy and direction, generally ascribed to 'the Troubles', though its Dublin counterpart flourished through revolution and civil war.

CHRISTOPHER FITZSIMON

Ulster Museum The national museum for Northern Ireland. It is an interdisciplinary institution, with curatorial departments of antiquities, art, botany and zoology, geology and local history. The art collections comprise European paintings 1500–1800, British paintings and sculptures 1700– present, Irish paintings and sculptures from the seventeenth century to the present, and a distinguished collection of applied arts, costumes and fabrics dating from *c.*1600 to the present. Although the pre-twentieth-century fine art collections include a number of important works – Turner's *Dawn of Christianity*, Jordaens's *St Christopher Carrying the Christ Child*, and Van Oost's, *The Holy Family with St John and St Elizabeth*, for example – it is for more recent works that the museum is best known. These include a small, but prestigious group of American abstract expressionist and colour field paintings, European paintings and sculptures by the COBRA group of artists, the German Group Zero, the Düsseldorf School and the more recent Expressionists, a number of 'Hard Edge' paintings from the 1970s, and 'op', kinetic and pop art works by British and European artists. The collections of contemporary British, Irish and European ceramics and glass are amongst the most important in the British Isles.

S.B. KENNEDY

Ulster Volunteer Force Established in January 1913 by the Ulster Unionist Council, the UVF aimed at resisting the implementation of Home Rule. It attracted 100,000 recruits, and in April 1914 successfully landed guns and ammunition from Germany. This initiative served as an example to Irish nationalists, who formed a similar organization, the Irish Volunteers, to defend the Home Rule proposal. During the Great War the UVF was incorporated into the 36th (Ulster) Division of the British army, and suffered very heavy casualties at the Somme in 1916. During the 1920 sectarian riots most UVF members joined the new Ulster Special Constabulary, the B Specials, an overtly sectarian force. The UVF was revived in 1966 by loyalist militants and carried out many notorious attacks on Catholics, as well as political assassinations, during the Troubles. It participated in the loyalist paramilitary cease-fire of 1994; many of its members, tired of 30 years of violence, voted 'yes' in the 1998 referendum, in the hopes of at long last bringing an end to sectarian conflict in Northern Ireland.

Reading

Bardon, Jonathan, *A History of Ulster* (Belfast: Blackstaff Press, 1992).

Boulton, David, *The U.V.F, 1966–1973* (Dublin: Torc Press, 1973).

Bruce, Steve, *The Red Hand: Protestant Paramilitaries in Northern Ireland* (Oxford: Oxford University Press, 1992).

Howie, J., 'Militarism in society. The Ulster Volunteer Force, 1912–14', in A. O'Day and Y. Alexander (eds), *Ireland's Terrorist Dilemma* (Kluwer-Hijkoff, 1986).

JIM O'HARA

Undertakers Parliamentary managers who 'undertook' to pilot legislation through the Irish House of Commons on behalf of non-residential lord lieutenants in return for power and preferment. They evolved out of the managers who, in one form or another, were a feature of the Irish House of Commons from 1695. William Conolly was the first politician to serve in this capacity, in the years immediately prior to his death in 1729. After a brief period of instability in which Dublin Castle experimented with a number of different options, Henry Boyle undertook to secure a majority for government legislation. He did this remarkably efficiently for nearly two decades, until the Money Bill dispute of 1753 exposed the limits of this political arrangement and prompted British politicians to contemplate alternatives. Nothing was done until the late 1760s, when Lord Townshend was so enfuriated by the unco-operativeness of the leading figures in the House of Commons that he put an end to the undertaker system, and restored the initiative in parliamentary management to Dublin Castle.

Reading

Bartlett, Thomas and Hayton, D.W. (eds), *Penal Era and Golden Age* (Belfast: Ulster Historical Foundation, 1979).

JAMES KELLY

Uniformity, Acts of The two Irish Acts of Uniformity were designed, like their English counterparts of 1549, 1552, 1559 and 1662, to ensure that the nation followed a single Protestant liturgy. The first Irish Act of 1560 committed the Church of Ireland to the Elizabethan Book of Common Prayer, and prescribed punishments for both ministers who failed to use it and laity who refused to come to service. The latter incurred a fine of 12 d, which, together with ecclesiastical censures, became the main weapon open to government and established church in their efforts to impose Protestantism. The difficulty, of course, was that the Irish people remained loyal to their Catholic faith, despite sporadic attempts to enforce the Act of Uniformity in the late sixteenth and early seventeenth centuries. By the 1630s an uneasy compromise had been reached, with the government reluctant to try to enforce what was an unworkable Act, but unwilling to make any concession on the established status of the Church of Ireland.

The continued formal commitment to uniformity was reiterated in the second Irish Act of 1666. In addition to tightening up provisions to ensure the conformity of schoolmasters, it was also directed at Presbyterians. Again, it was more effective in stating the ideal of uniformity than enforcing the reality.

ALAN FORD

Unionism 1690–1972 As an organized political movement Unionism in Ireland dates from 1885–6; as a popular political war-cry it developed in the first half of the nineteenth century. But the intellectual roots of Irish Unionism extend into the seventeenth and eighteenth centuries, and to the polemical writings of William Molyneux, Jonathan Swift, and other colonial champions of Irish representative rights. Molyneux pronounced in his *The Case of Ireland* (1698) that the Irish political nation 'should be willing enough to embrace' Irish representation at London, while Swift's *Story of an Injured Lady* (1707) compared Ireland's constitutional position unfavourably to that of Scotland at the time of the Anglo–Scots union. Unionism was born, therefore, as a political ideal for those colonial patriots of the late seventeenth century who were angered by an unrepresentative English Parliament's determination to impose legislation on Ireland.

From these beginnings as a debating proposition for Irish students of Locke, Unionism developed at the end of the eighteenth century in close association with public discussion on Catholic civil rights. With the emergence of a politically articulate and assertive Catholic middle class by the 1780s and 1790s, influential English and Irish Ascendancy politicians re-examined the merits of a constitutional Union. Imaginative English conservatives like William Pitt (probably a convert to Union from 1784–5) viewed the usefulness of this measure from a very different vantage to that of Ascendancy intellectuals such as John Fitzgibbon, Lord Clare (c.1748–1802) – but each tacitly defined the Union in relation to the Catholic question. For Pitt the Union offered an opportunity to balance Irish Catholic and Protestant political interests, permitting a grant of political equality to Catholics – but within a constitutional Union where British Protestant interests would dominate Irish rivalries. For Pitt, the Union bill of 1799–1800 was to have been the preliminary to a measure of Catholic relief, and Catholic bishops, informally briefed, accepted the Union as part of a broader package of reform. But Fitzgibbon, and other Ascendancy Unionists, saw the survival of the Protestant gentry class as inextricably linked to the British connection, and saw the strengthening of that connection as a long-term security against Catholic political challenge. Different interest groups had thus different and incompatible expectations of the Union. On the whole it was Fitzgibbon's definition – the Protestant one – which proved to be the most realistic and enduring. Catholic relief did not automatically follow the Union, as Pitt had hoped and promised. The Protestant gentry, on the other hand, emerged from the Act of Union not merely unscathed, but (however temporarily) politically enhanced.

The Union passed into law in January 1801, because Pitt, as with his anti-French coalitions, had been able to construct an improbable and precarious supporting alliance. The Union had the convinced allegiance of his own governing circle, and the approval of the ablest Irish defenders of the Ascendancy interest; it had the muted and qualified blessing of the Irish Catholic hierarchy. But the measure had little coherent popular support, and certainly not in Ulster. Ulster Protestants were as divided over the Act of Union as they had been over the 1798 Rising. The northern Presbyterian community had broken in 1798, and remained fractured in its attitudes to the Union: for Dr William Drennan, a Presbyterian founder of the United Irishmen, the Unionists of 1799–1800 were plain 'rogues'. The predominantly Anglican Protestants of Armagh, Tyrone, and Fermanagh – the heartland of the newly formed Orange Order and of sectarian division – were no less anti-Unionist, and yet far removed from the United Irish ideals of a Drennan. For them the Union meant the demise of a Protestant Parliament which had carefully nurtured Protestant interests.

In 1800 there was no popular base to Unionism in Ulster – and so the emergence of a mass movement in the later nineteenth century was in no sense predetermined. Popular Unionism depended upon a more unified sense of Protestantism and a more coherent sense of Britishness than existed in 1800; Protestant unity and a reinforced Britishness depended in turn upon the economic development of Ulster, the cultural anglicization of much of Ireland in the nineteenth century, and (indirectly) upon the political and institutional consolidation of Irish Catholicism.

Ulster Protestants appeared to be the main economic beneficiaries of the Union. After 1800 the north-east of Ireland became the most industrialized region of the island, with the mechanization of the linen industry promoting other related trades (such as engineering). The shipbuilding industry developed with the benefit of English capital and expertise, and grew rapidly in the second half of the nineteenth century. Economic diversity in Ulster made for a strong regional economy – an economy more diversified than that of the rest of Ireland, and more akin to that of the north of England and the Clyde estuary. Eastern Ulster shared in the economic growth of Victorian Britain, and experienced only in a diminished form the disastrous experiences of agrarian Ireland. The regional economy was controlled by Protestants, who unhesitatingly attributed their prosperity to the Union.

Unionism was promoted by economic diversity and by religious unity – by the relative political and doctrinal unity of the main Protestant denominations. In the nineteenth century 'Protestant' ceased to be a synonym for 'Anglican', and became a collective noun for the reformed faiths of the settler communities. Presbyterianism, influenced by the Rev. Henry Cooke (1788–1868) in the second quarter of the nineteenth century, became politically and theologically more conservative, and increasingly more tolerant of Anglicanism. The Church of Ireland and the Presbyterians were further united by a shared evangelicalism: evangelical faith and expression became the shared language of most Irish Protestants in the nineteenth century. Legislative challenges to the Church of Ireland – especially the legal disestablishment of the Church in 1869–70 – provoked considerable Presbyterian sympathy. In 1885–6, at the time of the first Home Rule Bill, Unionist organization built upon the talents of politicians Presbyterian *and* Anglican. In 1885–6 Unionist organization built upon a heightened feeling of unity among Irish Protestant, and upon a more coherent sense of Protestant identity.

This identity emerged partly as a reaction to the consolidation of Irish Catholicism in the nineteenth century. Daniel O'Connell's mass mobilization of Catholics in the 1820s tended to intimidate and to unite Protestants, even though there was widespread support for Catholic relief. In 1834–5, under Henry Cooke's direction and in the context of O'Connell's parliamentary influence, there was a regrouping of some Presbyterian and Anglican voters behind Robert Peel's new Conservatism; by 1841 Cooke could lead a unified Protestant opposition in Ulster to O'Connell's campaign for a repeal of the Act of Union. Protestant unity, then, was partly a reaction to the mobilization and politicization of the Catholic interest. This more coherent and more acerbic Protestantism was an essential precondition for the organization of Irish Unionism in 1885–6.

Irish Unionist organization emerged in 1885–6 in the wake of a revitalization of Orangeism and Conservatism, which, in turn, had its origins in a reaction to the Land War of 1879–81. By 1883 the intermittent successes of the Home Rule movement and the Land and National Leagues in the outer counties of Ulster had alarmed northern loyalists and had provoked Orange and Conservative counter-attacks. Electoral reform in 1884–5 created a more representative, and therefore more Catholic, electorate in Ireland, and threatened to annihilate a still directionless and divided loyalism. It was in response to this combined Home Rule and electoral challenge that a group of Orange Conservatives, including Edward Saunderson (1837–1906), a Cavan landowner, sought to create a coalition which stretched beyond the traditional bounds of loyalism – the Orange Order and the Irish Conservative party. In February 1885 the first Irish loyalist parliamentary group had been created, while in the summer of 1885 a popular base was being added in both Belfast and Dublin. By March 1886, when Gladstone introduced the Home Rule Bill, a coherent Unionist organization was in place both inside and outside the House of Commons. The strength of this organization lay in the fact that it was *not* an immediate response to Gladstone's challenge; it drew instead on long-term developments within the Protestant communities, as well as on the revamped loyalist institutions which had begun to emerge in 1880–1.

The Unionist movement which opposed the first Home Rule Bill in 1886 and the second Bill (in 1893) was characterized by good relations with English Conservatives, by landlord domination, and by a unity of feeling binding its bases in Belfast and Dublin. Between 1885–6 and 1920, when Ireland was partitioned, these characteristics changed, and with them the nature of Unionism in Ireland. By 1920 Irish Unionism had more equivocal relations with its English support, it was more middle-class and urban in leadership, and it had splintered into northern and southern fragments.

Southern Irish Unionists (numbering at most 250,000) were primarily landed and Anglican, and provided considerable financial and organizational direction to Unionists in all of Ireland. In common with other economic elites, southern Unionists were over-represented in both houses of the British Parliament. Unionists claimed in the 1880s and 1890s to be part of a movement which embraced the entire island, and southern Unionists, though numerically slight, were important in lending credibility to this claim.

Southern Unionist decline, in the Edwardian period and after, occurred partly because of the rapid economic and political decline of Irish landlords at the end of the nineteenth century, and partly because of the gradual development of popular Unionist organization in Ulster. In 1904–5, moved by English Conservative neglect and local internal challenge, a group of young, middle-class Unionists (including James Craig, 1871–1940) created the first centralized and representative organization for all Unionist activity in the north of Ireland: the Ulster Unionist Council. The UUC spearheaded a more militant and localized Unionism, based in Belfast and reflecting narrowly northern concerns. It was this council which directed the Unionist campaign during the passage of the third Home Rule Bill (1912–14), and which lent this campaign its popular and threatening tone.

Ulster Unionist domination of the movement led to a modification of its rhetoric and strategy. Under the charismatic Edward Carson (1854–1935), a unique mass mobilization of northern Unionists was achieved. Potentially explosive popular emotions were cultivated by Carson and his lieutenant Craig, and guided into the paramilitary Ulster Volunteer Force (UVF, 1913) and into regimented protest demonstrations. Unionist claims to repudiate Home Rule for all of Ireland were qualified, while emphasis was given to the rights of the popular and by now more coherent Protestant community in Ulster. By July 1914 Ulster Unionists had abandoned the all-Ireland Unionism of 1886 and 1893, and were prepared to negotiate for a partition settlement, based upon the exclusion from Home Rule of the six most Unionist counties of Ireland. Equally, by July 1914 Ulster Unionists had abandoned the essentially constitutional strategies of 1886 and 1893, and were importing large quantities of weapons (most spectacularly at Larne in April 1914), and otherwise preparing for civil war.

Superficially the outbreak of World War I in August 1914 defused the constitutional crisis, for the operation of Home Rule was suspended for the duration of the war. Yet the war helped to further the geographical polarization of Irish politics, indirectly promoting the division of Irish Unionism, and broadening the distance between Unionism and Nationalism. The UVF was transformed into the 36th (Ulster) Division of the British army, and was to be decimated on the Somme in July 1916: this sacrifice served to reinforce the loyalty of loyalism, while simultaneously heightening its expectations of political reward. It was the immolation of an *Ulster* division, and the commemoration of this fact tended to reinforce a peculiarly northern sense of identity. While Ulster Unionists grew more particularist, southern Unionists, weakened by immense wartime losses, and horrified by the development of Sinn Féin, grew more pragmatic: southern Unionist representatives at the Irish Convention of

1917 were prepared to endorse Home Rule. This apostasy helped to confirm the partitionism of Ulster Unionists. When the constitutional debate was revived in 1919–20, Ulster Unionists voted for a six-county partition scheme, abandoning with some regret the small Ulster Unionist minority in Cavan, Donegal and Monaghan, and abandoning with fewer qualms the now alien Unionists of Leinster, Munster and Connacht. A divided Unionism had been an essential precondition for a divided Ireland.

In 1920 the UUC accepted the British Parliament's Government of Ireland Act, a measure which created a six-county territory, Northern Ireland, governed by a Home Rule assembly and executive in Belfast. Unionism, which had emerged as a coalition opposed to Home Rule, and demanding the maintenance of a united Parliament in London, had become the majority party in a devolved Parliament, and the guarantor of a Home Rule and partition settlement. This rapid change of function helped to promote ideological shifts inside Unionism. Partitionist polemic had predated the Government of Ireland Act, but a devolved Parliament had never been an Ulster Unionist ideal. Yet, during the lifetime of the Northern Ireland Parliament (1921–72), Unionism became progressively devolutionist in tone. By 1972 the transformation of Victorian Unionism was complete: from an all-Ireland movement opposing Home Rule in 1886, to an Ulster movement demanding exclusion from Home Rule in 1914, Ulster Unionism had become, by 1972, a movement committed to maintain Home Rule within a partition settlement.

As a governing party Unionism faced two fundamental challenges – Catholic alienation and economic retraction – and to each it proved incapable of any effective response. Of the one and a half million residents of Northern Ireland, over one-third were Roman Catholic; and most of these rejected the partition settlement and its political institutions. Nationalist animosity, combined with poor popular sectarian relations, drew out the anti-Catholicism of many early Unionist ministers (Dawson Bates at Home Affairs was a notable offender), and made concessions to any form of Catholic opinion rare. The judiciary and police forces were directed in particular against Nationalist subversion, with the result that Catholics suffered disproportionately from official invasion of civil liberties. The Civil Authorities (Special Powers Act) of 1922 and the Ulster Special Constabulary emerged as particular sources of grievance for northern Catholics. This law and order issue, in combination with the restrictive local government franchise and the maladministration of local government, helped to inflame civil rights protests against Unionist government after 1967.

If the Unionist government never adequately addressed Catholic alienation, then the economic condition of Northern Ireland prove equally beyond its capacity. The relentless contraction of those industries which had promoted the Victorian boom in Belfast combined with greater efficiency in agriculture to maintain uniformly high levels of unemployment. Large-scale unemployment tended to encourage civil unrest, and to weaken the already vulnerable finances of the Northern Ireland government; large-scale unemployment tended to sustain Catholic alienation, and to force Unionist governments into greater financial and political dependence on Westminster. In 1972, when the Northern Ireland Parliament was summarily prorogued, the extent of this political dependence was sharply exposed.

The economic difficulties of Unionist government also occasionally threatened the solidarity of its own support. Yet, before the 1960s, Unionism was characterized more obviously by stability than by internal dissent: only in 1943, in the exceptional circumstances of World War II, was a Unionist prime minister deposed after a party coup. Unionism faced no serious electoral challenge after 1920, and, after 1922, Unionist government easily overcame the sporadic offensives of the IRA.

Electoral stability did not, however, help to encourage normal democratic political skills; nor did this stability permit Unionism to develop beyond its original limitations as a primarily Protestant protest movement. Under the pressure of a unique combination of challenges which emerged after 1966, the Unionist party of Terence O'Neill (prime minister 1963–9) fractured irreparably. O'Neill, a well-meaning but insensitive politician, sought to force through a policy of modernization, but rapidly lost touch with the fundamentalist Protestantism of, in particular, his rural support. Confounded by popular political passions – the street protests of the civil rights movement, a renascent republicanism, and Ian Paisley's militant Protestant Unionism – O'Neill resigned in April 1969. By September 1971, with the creation of the Democratic Unionist Party, the divisions inside Unionism had become thoroughly institutionalized.

O'Neill demonstrated that the traditional Unionist party could not be a vehicle for even a moderate reform of community relations. Unionism was not a finely regulated political machine under the firm discipline of its leaders. Historically Unionism had developed as a decentralized coalition, capable of occasional demonstrations of unity, but incapable of sustained unity and coherence. O'Neill was a victim of his party, and a victim of political opportunism; he was a victim of his own limitations. But he did not divide Unionism. By 1972 Unionism, which had developed so remarkably in terms of its central tenets, had simply broken down into its original components. Unionist ideology had changed, but Unionism remained the fissile loyalist coalition of the 1880s.

Reading

Buckland, Patrick, *Irish Unionism. I: The Anglo-Irish and the New Ireland, 1885–1922* (Dublin: Gill and Macmillan, 1972).

—— *Irish Unionism. II: Ulster Unionism and the Origins of Northern Ireland* (Dublin: Gill and Macmillan, 1973).

—— *The Factory of Grievances: Devolved Government in Northern Ireland, 1921–1939* (Dublin: Gill and Macmillan, 1979).

Gibbon, Peter, *The Origins of Ulster Unionism: The Foundations of Popular Protestant Politics and Ideology in Nineteenth Century Ireland* (Manchester: Manchester University Press, 1975).

Harbinson, John, *The Ulster Unionist Party, 1882–1973: Its Development and Organisation* (Belfast: Blackstaff Press, 1973).

Harkness, David, *Northern Ireland since 1920* (Dublin: Helicon, 1983).

Holmes, R. Finlay, *Henry Cooke* (Belfast: Christian Journals, 1981).

Hyde, H. Montgomery, *Carson: The Life of Sir Edward Carson, Lord Carson of Duncairn* (London: Heinemann, 1953).

Jackson, Alvin, *The Ulster Party: Irish Unionists in the House of Commons, 1884–1911* (Oxford: Clarendon Press, 1989).

Kennedy, Liam and Ollerenshaw, Phillip, *An Economic History of Ulster, 1820–1939* (Manchester: Manchester University Press, 1985).

Patterson, Henry, *Class Conflict and Sectarianism: The Protestant Working Class and the Belfast Labour Movement, 1868–1920* (Belfast: Blackstaff Press, 1980).

Stewart, A.T.Q., *The Ulster Crisis* (London: Faber, 1967).

ALVIN JACKSON

United Irishmen Founded in 1791 in Belfast by a secret committee of radical, Presbyterian Volunteers. The aims of the movement were comprehensive parliamentary reform, Catholic emancipation, and a union of Protestant and Catholic Irishmen to achieve them. Yet the methods employed to implement this revolutionary programme were reformist, drawing heavily on the Volunteer campaign of the previous decade. A loose association of affiliated clubs, the most prominent one in Dublin, focused on mobilizing middle-class public opinion to pressure an intransigent Irish government into reforming itself out of existence. Frustrated in these efforts by prohibitive legislation and isolated as treacherous malcontents once war commenced with revolutionary France in 1793, the United Irishmen adopted an insurrectionary strategy based on forging an alliance with France, mass recruitment of the lower classes of town and countryside, and reorganization on a paramilitary basis. According to their own records, the United Irishmen claimed membership of over 300,000 by the end of 1797, with strong representation among the petty bourgeoisie, especially in Dublin and the counties of Antrim and Down.

The vulnerability of Ireland to the twin assault of internal rebellion and foreign invasion was fully appreciated by the government and its supporters, who pursued a policy of ruthless repression. United Irish leaders resolved to rise without French support, but their plans were thrown into confusion when the leadership was arrested on the eve of the insurrection. Local rebellions occurred in May and June of 1798, the most formidable in County Wexford. A small French forced arrived in August, too little and too late, to find the United Irish movement shattered and the government engaged in a brutal mopping-up operation. Nevertheless, remnants of the organization lingered on in Wicklow and the north-east, contributing to Robert Emmet's insurrection in Dublin in 1803.

Regarded as the progenitors of modern revolutionary Republicanism in Ireland, the United Irishmen aroused bitter sectarian hostility and facilitated William Pitt's efforts to foist the Act of Union on a wary Anglo-Irish Ascendancy. Despite populist appeals to woo the lower classes, United Irish aims and ideology more accurately reflected the classically liberal agenda of the movement's middle-class leadership – representative government, equal opportunity, and economic individualism. The liberalism of the United Irishmen, however, left only faint footprints in the sand, while the calls for Ireland's separation from Britain provided a more enduring legacy.

Reading

Curtin, Nancy J., *The United Irishmen: Popular Politics in Ulster and Dublin, 1791–1798* (Oxford: Clarendon Press, 1994).

Dickson, David, Whelan, Kevin and Keogh, Daire (eds), *The United Irishmen: Republicanism, Radicalism and Rebellion* (Dublin: Lilliput Press, 1993).

Elliott, Marianne, *Partners in Revolution: The United Irishmen and France* (New Haven CI and London: Yale University Press, 1982).

Gough, Hugh and Dickson, David (eds), *Ireland and the French Revolution* (Dublin: Irish Academic Press, 1990).

Smyth, Jim, *The Men of No Property: Irish Radicals and Popular Politics in the Late Eighteenth Century* (New York: St Martin's Press, 1992).

NANCY J. CURTIN

universal language Changing social and cultural conditions in the seventeenth century confronted European scholars with two linguistic problems which had, to some extent, existed for centuries, but for which solutions had now become urgent. First, the expansion of mercantile horizons to the New World and the Far East created special difficulties for those who had to communicate with speakers of hitherto unknown languages, and second, the development of experimental science, where record and communication needed absolute accuracy, called for vocabularies less ambiguous and imprecise than those of the vernaculars.

It was Francis Bacon who first commented publicly on these two different types of problem and their solutions. For international communication he suggested the creation of a written symbolism, or 'character', which would be universally comprehensible because it would represent 'things and notions' directly, not via the words of individual vernaculars. As a solution to lexical ambiguity he proposed the explicit definition of terminology before men entered into debates and discussions; and he also looked for a 'new remedy', the search for which inspired the seventeenth-century quest for a universal 'philosophical' (i.e. 'scientific') language, which was to find its most successful realization in John Wilkins's *Essay towards a Real Character, and a Philosophical Language* (1668).

In Ireland, there were serious problems of communication between native speakers and the English clergy. William Bedell, Provost of Trinity College, Dublin (1627–9), found that the only solution was to learn Gaelic himself; but he was also interested in problems of ambiguity, and persuaded a Trinity colleague, John Johnson, to complete a plan which he himself had drawn up for some kind of universal character or philosophical language. Johnson succeeded in doing so in his *Wit-spell*, but the plates were destroyed in the rebellion of 1641, and Johnson himself was killed. A draft (now lost) of *Wit-spell* was taken to Oxford in the early 1650s, and was probably known to Wilkins.

Several other scholars with Irish connections, such as Robert Boyle and William Petty, were interested in solutions to the problem of ambiguity, but the only relevant project actually to be published in Ireland was the invention of an English physician, Nathaniel Chamberlain. It survives in a unique copy in Marsh's library.

In his *Tractatus*, Chamberlain recounts how he set to work on his project at Oxford in the 1630s, later discussing it with Sir Thomas Urquhart (an enthusiast for 'philosophical' language) and the Dublin schoolmaster William Hill. Chamberlain claims that anyone who understands his linguistic system will be a scientist, because the names of objects will reveal their characteristics. The language, when complete, would contain a limited number of 'radical' words, denoting basic conceptual classes, to which affixes could be appended to show both semantic and grammatical modifications. Chamberlain devised not only a written language, but also a 'universal' sound system for its spoken realization.

In 1685 John Keogh presented a paper on 'universal character' to the Dublin Philosophical Society; although it was never published, it may have been known to Jonathan Swift as one of the targets for his satire on universal language in *Gulliver's Travels* (1726). Scepticism like Swift's about the possibility of creating such a language persuaded later scholars to devote their attention either to the creation of quasi-vernaculars like Esperanto, for ordinary conversation, or to specialized forms either of terminology, like that of botany, or of symbolization, like that of chemistry.

Reading

Chamberlain, Nathaniel, *Tractatus de literis et lingua philosophica* (Dublin: 1679).

Robins, R.H., *A Short History of Linguistics* (London and New York: Longman, 3rd edn 1990).

Salmon, Vivian, 'The development of universal language schemes', in V. Salmon, *The Works of Francis Lodwick: A Study of his Writings in the Intellectual Context of the Seventeenth Century* (London: Longman, 1972).

—— 'William Bedell and the universal language movement in seventeenth-century Ireland', *Essays and Studies* NS 36 (1983), pp. 27–39.

—— 'Nathaniel Chamberlain and his *Tractatus de literis et lingua philosophica (1679)*', in E.G. Stanley and D. Gray (eds), *Five Hundred Years of Words and Sounds for E.J. Dobson* (Woodbridge: Boydell and Brewer, 1983).

—— 'Missionary linguistics in seventeenth-century Ireland and a North American analogy', *Historiographia Linguistica* 12 (1985), pp. 321–49.

—— 'Caracteristiques et langues universelles', in S. Awoux (ed.), *Histoire des Idées Linguistiques* (Liège: Mardaga, 1992).

Slaughter, M.M., *Universal Languages and Scientific Taxonomy in the Seventeenth Century* (Cambridge: Cambridge University Press, 1982).

VIVIAN SALMON

universities/higher education Unlike many other European countries, Ireland did not benefit from the foundation of a university in medieval times. It was not until 1591 that its first university, the University of Dublin, Trinity College, was founded as

587

part of the Elizabethan policy of colonization, linked to the spread of the religious policy of the Reformation. For most of its history, even after the 1793 Relief Act had opened Trinity College to non-Anglicans, the college was associated predominantly with the Protestant church and pro-English political interest. This was exacerbated by a Catholic ban on attendance there, imposed in 1875, and not formally lifted until 1970. Many of the impressive buildings of the contemporary, fine city-centre campus date from the eighteenth century, and coincided with the Georgian elegance of the 'second city of the empire'.

The late eighteenth century saw two significant initiatives in the area of higher education. One was the establishment of the Royal Irish Academy in 1785, to promote scholarly work in science, polite literature and antiquities. The other was the founding of St Patrick's College, Maynooth, by Act of Parliament, as a seminary for the Catholic priesthood. This represented a significant shift from the penal policy of the previous century. In 1899 Maynooth got approval to award degrees of the Pontifical University in Rome in philosophy, theology and canon law. It became a recognized college of the new National University of Ireland, in 1910.

The issue of providing university education for lay Catholics was one of the great political questions in the second half of the nineteenth century. In May 1845 Prime Minister Sir Robert Peel took the initiative and introduced an Irish Colleges Bill. It provided for the setting up of three Queen's Colleges, to be sited in Belfast, Cork and Galway. The colleges would be non-denominational and state-funded. Any theological teaching would have to be privately funded. The colleges were to be non-residential, with low fees, and the curriculum was to be along modern utilitarian lines with three faculties – arts, law and medicine. The Bill caused bitter controversy. The Catholic hierarchy and Daniel O'Connell, the celebrated lay

Catholic leader, opposed the measure. The Irish Colleges Bill received royal assent on 31 July 1845. Impressive building plans for the new institutions were put into effect and the colleges opened for the academic year 1849–50. In 1850 the Queen's University was established to act as the examining and degree-awarding body for the colleges, with its headquarters in Dublin Castle. The same year saw a clear affirmation of Catholic opposition to the Queen's Colleges at the Synod of Thurles. Despite the potential of the Queen's Colleges for promoting higher education in post-famine Ireland, the sustained opposition of the Catholic church proved to be a daunting obstacle to the colleges realizing that potential, particularly in the case of Cork and Galway.

As a counter-measure to the Queen's Colleges, the Synod of Thurles initiated a fund-raising campaign for the establishment of a Catholic university in Ireland. John Henry Newman, the distinguished scholar of Oriel College, Oxford, and a recent convert to Catholicism, was appointed rector of the new university in 1851. His views on university education are set forth strikingly in his *Discourses on University Education* and in his *University Sketches*. The Catholic University was formally established in 1854 at St Stephen's Green, Dublin. A blow to the infant university was the resignation of Newman as rector in 1858. Fundamental problems continued to inhibit the university in the refusal of the government to grant it a charter for the award of degrees and the lack of state financial support. By the mid-1860s it was clear that neither the Catholic University nor the Queen's Colleges were fulfilling the expectations held for them.

An effort by Gladstone in 1873 to resolve the university question by establishing one federal university for Ireland failed in Parliament, and led to the fall of the Liberal government. A more successful initiative was taken by Disraeli's government in 1879 with the establishment of the Royal University in 1879, to replace the Queen's University. The

Royal University was a purely examining body open to male and female students from any college, or by way of private study. The Catholic University got a lease of life from the distribution of fellowships from the Royal University. The Catholic University came under the control of the Jesuits in 1883 and became known as University College. At the time James Joyce attended there, about 180 students were enrolled.

The Royal University was not regarded as a permanent solution to the university problem, and its critics maintained that its existence undermined genuine university education by encouraging grinding for examinations. Many proposals were made to devise a satisfactory solution to what everybody agreed was a difficult problem. Most notable were the recommendations of the Robertson (1901) and the Fry (1907) Commissions. However, it was the solution of Chief Secretary Augustine Birrel which proved to be the successful way forward, as reflected in his Irish Universities Act of 1908. This Act allowed the University of Dublin, with its single college, Trinity College, to continue its existence, unaffected by other institutions. The Royal University was abolished. In its place Queen's University Belfast and a new National University of Ireland (NUI) were established. This latter was to be a federal university, with the old Queen's Colleges at Cork and Galway (now called University College, Cork, and University College, Galway, respectively) joined with University College, Dublin, as constituent colleges of the NUI. Provision was made for the association of 'recognized' colleges, which Maynooth became in 1910. Both Queen's Belfast and the NUI were to be non-denominational and non-residential, with student attendance at courses necessary to enter for the university examinations. Ireland now had three universities, which reflected the politico-religious complexion of Ireland of that time. The 1908 Act proved to be a very durable solution, which only came under serious re-examination in the 1960s.

Following the great debates and initiatives which Irish university education had experienced over the 60 years prior to 1908, the subsequent 50 years were ones of considerable calm. Concerns shifted from structural and administrative reform to the quieter work of academic affairs and the general organization of university life.

The political partition settlement of 1922 caused no significant change. Any hopes which were entertained for greater financial support by an independent Irish government did not materialize, but the new governments in both parts of Ireland did not interfere with the academic autonomy of the universities. In an undeveloped economy, with much social deprivation, university education was regarded as a minority concern, whereby well-positioned families sought a secure future for their children through access to careers facilitated by graduation from universities. The universities adopted a low public profile, coped with inadequate resourcing, and did little to inform public opinion on the potential role the university could play in the intellectual, social and economic life of post-partition Ireland.

The increase in student numbers in the university colleges reflected a slow, if steady growth. In 1920–1 the number of students in Trinity College and the colleges of the NUI was 3,600. On the eve of World War II, in 1939, it was almost 5,000. Twenty years later, 8,600 students were in attendance. The greatest expansion had taken place in University College, Dublin, where numbers grew from 1,500 in 1931 to almost 4,000 by 1960, although it was the institution which was least equipped with suitable buildings. The Report of the Commission on Accommodation Needs of the NUI colleges in 1959, in effect, was a searing indictment of the general neglect of the provision of suitable accommodation within all the NUI colleges. The report recommended the transfer of University College, Dublin, to a suburban, green-field site at Belfield. The government decided to take this course of action in 1959.

While the existing university facilities were overcrowded, it was also the case that less than 4 per cent of the age cohort proceeded to university in the early 1960s, and among these, grave imbalances occurred in the socio-economic and geographic background of the students.

In 1960 the government appointed the first comprehensive Commission of Inquiry into higher education since independence, with very wide terms of reference. It approached its work in a thorough and painstaking manner, but by the time the Commission's Report was published in 1967 the government had moved towards a binary policy for higher education, with the decision to establish regional technical colleges as a non-university sector. The government rejected the commission's recommendations on giving independence to the NUI colleges and, instead, opted for a merger between Trinity College and University College, Dublin, a proposal which aroused great controversy. This was never put into effect, and the NUI colleges were not made independent universities. The report of the commission highlighted the parlous state of many aspects of university education, and various reforms were put into effect. The first state grants for students were instituted in 1968, linked to merit and means test criteria. Also in 1968, the Higher Education Authority (HEA) was set up to act as a planning and budgetary agency between the government and the individual colleges.

The sixties saw higher education come centre stage in Irish political and educational debate for the first time since independence. The decades which followed witnessed a remarkable era of expansion in the university sector and in the new and rapidly expanding non-university sector. The number in higher education increased from 9,000 in 1960 to 85,000 in 1993, and it is envisaged that it will reach 115,000 by the year 2000, or about 50 per cent of the age cohort. Expenditure in higher education increased from about 12 per cent of the expenditure on education in 1966 to 22 per cent in 1992. In 1972 a National Council for Educational Awards was established to approve courses and grant certification to the non-university institutions. In 1989 the government brought in legislation which established two of these institutions as independent universities – the University of Limerick and the City of Dublin University, the first universities set up since independence. In 1992 legislation gave the ten regional technical colleges greater autonomy and modernized their governing arrangements.

Access to universities, particularly the professional faculties, is highly competitive and is based on a points system linked to performance in the final post-primary school examinations. Applications are processed through a Central Applications Office.

In line with developments in many other countries, the government has been taking a more directive role with regard to university affairs. It is pressing the institutions to take more of the aspiring students. Both the government and the HEA are encouraging greater course modularization, with credit transfer arrangements between the institutions. Unit cost funding schemes are being introduced, with greater accountability procedures. There is concern for greater quality assurance, and the use of performance indicators is being promoted. Universities have been establishing closer links with industry and cultivating more international links. A Distance Education Unit for Higher Education has been established in recent years.

Many of these developments have been proceeding without much controversy, but concern is being voiced about the more intrusive role of the state, about its economical and utilitarian emphases, and about inadequate resourcing of research in the universities. Despite the great expansion of participation in the universities, there is concern too at the persistent socio-economic imbalance in the representation within the universities, with some direct measures being adopted to seek to alleviate this problem. Overall, by the 1990s higher education in Ireland had experienced three decades of great expansion and diversification, a new dynamism and innovative spirit was in evidence, and a confidence existed about the role of higher education in society and in the standards being achieved.

Reading

Coolahan, John, *Irish Education: History and Structure* (Dublin: Institute of Public Administration, 1981).

Hyland, A. and Milne, K. (eds), *Irish Educational Documents*, vols 1 and 2 (Dublin: Church of Ireland College of Education, 1987, 1992).

McDowell, R.G. and Webb, D.A., *Trinity College Dublin* (Cambridge: Cambridge University Press, 1982).

McGrath, Fergal, *Newman's University – Idea and Reality* (Dublin: Browne and Nolan, 1951).

Moody, T.W. and Beckett, J.C., *Queen's Belfast, 1849–1949*, 2 vols (London: Faber 1959).

Tierney, Michael (ed.), *Struggle with Fortune* (Dublin: Browne and Nolan, 1954).

JOHN COOLAHAN

Ussher family before 1600 According to family legend, the Usshers originated in Yorkshire and first came to Ireland with Prince John in 1185 in the wake of the Norman invasion. Whereas a Yorkshire origin is likely, documentary evidence suggests a much later arrival, and the alleged association with Prince John doubtless represents a retrospective attempt to justify and reinforce the Usshers' increasing prominence amongst the Anglo-Norman Ascendancy of the sixteenth and seventeenth centuries.

The first member of the family to achieve civic distinction was Arland or Arlantor Uscher, a wealthy Dublin merchant who served as city bailiff in 1461 and as lord mayor eight years later. He may have been descended from a certain John le Ussher, appointed constable of Dublin Castle in 1302 by Edward I and reappointed to the same office under Edward II. Arland fortified his social position by marrying into the old established families of Taylor and Berford,

and by pursuing a similar marital strategy, his sons John and Christopher effectively assured the continuing fortunes of the Irish Usshers. From this time onwards their name is seldom absent from the civic, legal or ecclesiastical records of the Pale.

Amongst Christopher's descendants was Sir William Ussher, secretary to the Council of Ireland from 1593 to the Interregnum and patron of the first Celtic version of the New Testament. Sir William was a distant ancestor of Arthur Wellesley, first duke of Wellington. Amongst the descendants of Arland's elder son John were the great Ussher families of Dublin, Santry and Birr, notable in all generations for their combination of wealth, prestige and intellectual attainment. Religious divisions emerged at the time of the Reformation, however, and led ultimately to the decline of certain branches of the family though forfeiture of ancestral estates.

One of the most influential of the Protestant Dublin branch was Henry Ussher, brother-in-law of Primate John Garvey and archbishop of Armagh from 1595 to 1613. Educated at Magdalene College, Cambridge, and University College, Oxford, Henry was instrumental, along with Archbishop Loftus and Luke Chaloner, in the foundation of Trinity College, Dublin (1592), and was appointed to be its first fellow, having personally petitioned the court for the granting of its charter. This marked the beginning of an involvement in the affairs of the college which continues to the present century. Henry's nephews Ambrose and James (the future archbishop) were amongst its first alumni (both being the sons of Arland Ussher, one of the six clerks of Chancery and registrar of Chancery Appeals), while his son Robert was elected master in 1629 but proved to be 'of too soft and gentle a disposition to rule so heady a company'.

The enormous intellectual and political influence of the Usshers in every department of the civic and intellectual life of the Pale prior to 1600 must be accounted an important formative factor in the development of an emergent Anglo-Irish culture.

Reading

Wright, William Ball, *The Ussher Memoirs; or Genealogical Memoirs of the Ussher Families in Ireland* (Dublin and London: 1889).

RICHARD A. McCABE

V

Valois, Ninette de (1898–2001) Dancer, choreographer and dance director. Born Edris Stannus, of Huguenot stock, second daughter of Lt Col. Stannus and Lilith Graydon-Smith at Baltyboys House, Blessington, County Wicklow, 6 June. Moving with her family to Walmer, Kent, in 1905, de Valois joined Lila Field's Academy in 1912 and made her West End debut as leading dancer in *Jack and the Beanstalk* at the Lyceum in 1914. Training with Espinosa and Cecchetti, she danced with Diaghilev's Ballets Russes (1923–5), guesting until 1928. In 1926, she founded the London Academy of Choreographic Art and, in 1927, the Abbey Ballet School in Dublin, choreographing and performing in Yeats's *Plays for Dancers* until 1934. In 1931, she became founder-director with Lilian Baylis of the Vic-Wells Ballet. This became the Sadler's Wells Ballet and, 10 years after the company moved to the Royal Opera House, Covent Garden, in 1946, the Royal Ballet. She also directed the Royal Ballet School and was patron of Irish National Ballet. The first woman to receive the Dutch Erasmus Prize (in 1964), she was awarded the DBE in 1951 and the Legion d'Honneur in 1959. Choreography includes *Job* (1931), *The Rake's Progress* (1935) and *Checkmate* (1937). Publications include *Invitation to the Ballet* (1937), *Come Dance With Me* (1957), *Step By Step* (1977) and *The Cycle* (1987). In June 1998 Dame Ninette's 100th birthday was celebrated with several gala performances throughout Britain, including a revival of her little-seen wartime ballet *The Prospect Before Us* (1940). These and other TV programmes and press articles provided a fitting tribute to a woman who for 70 years devoted herself to British ballet.

Reading

Bland, Alexander, *The Royal Ballet, the First Fifty Years* (New York: Doubleday, 1981).

Walker, Kathrine Sorley, *Ninette de Valois, Idealist Without Illusions* (London: Hamish Hamilton, 1987).

CAROLYN SWIFT

Van Nost, John (d. 1787) Sculptor. Most probably born London; died Dublin. Van Nost was the son of a sculptor of the same name, with whom he trained. In Dublin *c*.1750 he soon became the leading sculptor of the period. He attracted commissions from major figures and institutions there: the founders of the Dublin Society (busts of Samuel Madden and Thomas Prior, Royal Dublin Society, 1751–6), Dublin Castle (the figures

593

of Justice and Mars over the gateways to the Upper Castle Yard, 1752), Bartolomew Mosse (busts in Rotunda Hospital, mid-1750s), the corporation (an equestrian statue of George II for St Stephen's Green, 1756–8, now destroyed), etc. He is of great importance for the development of sculpture in Ireland in the eighteenth century, as he was employed as a teacher by the Dublin Society and had such pupils as Patrick Cunningham and Christopher Hewetson.

Reading

Crookshank, Anne and the Knight of Glin, *Irish Portraits 1660–1860* (London: Paul Mellon Foundation for British Art, 1969).

McParland, Edward, *Eighteenth Century Ireland* 2 (1987).

Strickland, Walter, *A Dictionary of Irish Artists* (Shannon: Irish University Press, 1968).

FINTAN CULLEN

Vatican Councils Forty years after emancipation, the First Vatican Council (1869–70) gave an international role to the Irish Catholic church. Paul Cullen, archbishop of Dublin, was a leader of the 'opportunist' party which favoured a declaration of papal infallibility, and it was he who presented to the council the formula containing the substance of the final definition of the doctrine. His formidable rival, Archbishop John McHale of Tuam, took the opposite view, and he and Bishop Moriarty of Kerry maintained the 'inopportunist' position to the end (while actually abstaining in the final vote).

Infallibility, once defined, caused little difficulty for Irish Catholics, who had a long tradition of loyalty to the Holy See, and most of whose leaders were strongly ultramontanist. But the definition had an unexpected effect in another direction. W.E. Gladstone, on whom so many of Irish nationalist hopes were then placed, found infallibility too much to swallow, both as a Liberal and as a devout Anglican, and popular Protestant opinion in England was

vociferously critical. And while the fall of Rome to Italian revolutionaries was seen there as a victory for liberty and enlightenment, Irish sympathy and support for a beleaguered pope knew no bounds. The Liberal–nationalist honeymoon was over.

Vatican 2 (1962–5) was a very different matter. This time there was little or no Irish input, either in debate or in the formulation of the several conciliar constitutions and decrees which signalled a radical renewal – a revolution, some called it – of Catholicism. But this renewal has, over the past 30 years or so, certainly transformed the Irish church in its worship (now in the vernacular – Gaelic as well as English – and involving much lay participation), in its relations with other Christian bodies, and in its thinking and discipline. The two latter aspects of change have also been of no small import in the church's role in what may certainly be called a cultural revolution, which began in the 1960s. The economic developments of that decade, a move from rural to urban hegemony, events in the North since 1969, and membership of the European Community as well as the Women's Movement, a growing youth culture and the influence of both Irish and British television have combined to provide a new context and a new agenda for a Catholicism which has itself been both an agent and an object of change.

SEÁN MAC RÉAMOINN

Veto Controversy Began in 1808, when Grattan and other parliamentary supporters of emancipation suggested, as a safeguard to reassure Protestant opinion, that Catholic episcopal appointments should in future be subject to approval by the crown. The proposal was supported by most English Catholic leaders, and by a minority, including the small but hitherto influential Catholic landed class, in Ireland. Thomas Moore, in *A Letter to the Roman Catholics of Dublin* (1810), argued forcibly that such arrangements were compatible with Catholic doctrine and practice. However, O'Connell and others on the

Irish Catholic board aggressively rejected what they presented as the subordination of their church to state control, and popular feeling was strong enough to force the Irish bishops to retreat from earlier declarations of support for some such arrangement. The dispute continued into the early 1820s.

Reading

Vaughan (ed.), W.E., *A New History of Ireland, V* (Oxford: Clarendon Press, 1989).

SEAN CONNOLLY

Victory Gerard (1921–95) Composer, Born 24 December; died 14 March. Victory was a graduate of University College, Dublin, and the University of Dublin (Trinity College), where he was awarded a DMUS in 1972. He worked as a producer in Radio Éireann from 1953, and became director of music there in 1961. The recipient of many awards and commissions, he was especially well known for his film and television scores, chamber music and large-scale orchestral and choral works. Victory's contributions to many major European music festivals and to the Dublin festival of twentieth-century music resulted in a body of important work which considerably advanced the scope and reach of contemporary Irish music. Victory's symphonic portrait of Jonathan Swift (1972), his four symphonies and his five operas are especially significant works, which have been heard in Europe as well as in Ireland. Other major works include *Ultima Rerum*, *Kriegeslieder* and *Homage to Petrarch*.

HARRY WHITE

Volunteers Founded in the mid-1770s to combat internal disaffection and to compensate for the reduction in the Irish army establishment caused by the redeployment of troops to fight in the American War of Independence, the Volunteers represent the apogee of the civil defence tradition of eighteenth-century Irish protestantism. Unlike their predecessors and successors,

the corps that constituted the Volunteers were independent foundations and were not under the control of the Irish administration. The earliest corps were established in Leinster to combat Whiteboyism, but it was the apprehension of a French invasion of the kingdom in 1778 and 1779 that prompted the rapid acceleration in recruitment that made the Volunteers a truly impressive and formidable force. Reliable statistical information is elusive, but numbers rose from an estimated 12,000 to 40,000 in 1779 alone, and they continued to grow till they reached a peak of nearly 100,000 in 1782.

These are contemporary figures, and there is probably more than a tincture of hyperbole attached to them. What cannot easily be exaggerated is the political impact of this vast armed movement. Once they had aligned themselves behind the campaign run by the Patriot leadership for the removal of the commercial and constitutional restrictions binding Irish trade and the Irish Parliament, they provided it with a countrywide network and an intimidating paramilitary arm which the English-appointed administration simply could not ignore. Their most famous and decisive interventions occurred on 4 November 1779, when they hijacked the annual Williamite commemoration to make a most telling statement in support of free trade, and on 15 February 1782, when delegates representing hundreds of Ulster corps gave the flagging campaign for legislative independence a much-needed boost.

With free trade and legislative independence secured, the middle-class and radicalized elements in the Volunteers that had contributed to the success of the campaigns for free trade (1780) and legislative independence (1782) endeavoured to commit the movement to the advocacy of the cause of parliamentary reform in order to secure full access to the representative system. They elected delegates for a further convention, which was held in Dublin in November 1783, but this and further initiatives in 1784–5 to reform Parliament came to grief.

595

Already weakened by the defection of its more conservative elements, as a result of the conclusion of hostilities in America and differences over the meaning of legislative independence (the renunciation crisis of 1782–3), the Volunteers' advocacy of the cause of parliamentary reform campaign hastened its decline. Numbers fell rapidly till there were few more than 18,000 members in the autumn of 1784, and the Castle administration felt emboldened to contemplate their abolition and replacement with a militia that was under its control. Legislation to this effect was ratified in 1785, but it was not put into effect, because the Volunteers chose to eschew political involvement for the remainder of the 1780s. However, when the United Irishmen endeavoured to revitalize the movement in the winter of 1792–3, Dublin Castle wasted little time prohibiting the organization and replacing it with a militia that was more compliant.

Reading

Kelly, James, 'A secret return of the Volunteers of Ireland in 1784', *Irish Historical Studies* 26 (1989), pp. 268–92.

MacNevin, Thomas, *The History of the Volunteers of 1782* (Dublin: 1846).

Smyth, P.D.H., 'The Volunteer movement in Ulster 1745–84', PhD thesis, Queen's University Belfast, 1974.

—— 'The Volunteers and parliament 1779–84' in D.W. Hayton, and T. Bartlett (eds), *Penal Era and Golden Age* (Belfast: 1979).

JAMES KELLY

W

Wadding, Luke (1588–1657) Franciscan historian. Born County Wateford, 16 October; died Rome, 18 November. Classically educated in Waterford, Wadding then studied at the Irish College, Lisbon, from 1603, and Coimbra (1609–13). He was ordained at Vizeu, Portugal, (1613), and studied and taught at Salamanca. He founded the Irish Franciscan College of St Isidore, Rome (1625), and was its rector for 14 years. He established the Ludovician College for Irish secular priests at Rome (1627). He was appointed to the Holy Office by Paul V, but despite duties in Rome, he maintained contact with Irish bishops, clergy and scholars. After 1641 he acted as confederate ambassador at Rome and promoted Cardinal Rinuccini's appointment as papal nuncio to Ireland. A prolific scholar, his publications include *Annales Ordinis minorum*, a history of the Franciscan order to 1540 (8 volumes, 1625–4) and the first critical edition of Duns Scotus's *Opera Omnia* (16 vols, 1639).

Reading

Franciscan Fathers, *Father Luke Wadding: Commemorative Volume* (Dublin: Clonmore and Reynolds, 1957).

Jennings, Brendan (ed.), *Wadding Papers* (Dublin, Irish Manuscripts Commission, 1953).

BERNADETTE CUNNINGHAM

Wakefield's *Ireland* (1812) Edward Wakefield (1774–1854) is remembered principally for writing *An Account of Ireland, Statistical and Political*. The two volumes formed a more compact and coherent accompaniment to the (ultimately incomplete) Royal Dublin Society enquiries, which were then in progress. The first volume described the physical and industrial characteristics of Ireland. The second volume gave an account of Irish national finances, the governing system, schools and churches, and included a chapter on popular customs and habits, as well as a short piece on the 1798 rebellion. The work, begun at the instigation of the former speaker of the Irish Commons, John Foster, took four years to complete.

GERARD O'BRIEN

Walker, George (1618–90) Soldier and churchman. Rector of both Lissan and Donaghmore, Walker raised a regiment at Dungannon following the breakdown of order in Ulster in 1688. In 1689 the regiment took refuge in Derry. Walker assumed the joint governorship of Derry after the expulsion of Governor James Lundy in April, resigning his office to the Williamite Major General Kirk in July 1689 after the siege. In August he left for London to present a loyal address to William III. He was promised the bishopric of Derry by William, but died at the battle of the Boyne. While in London he published *A True Account of the Siege of Londonderry*, which ran to five editions, including ones in Dutch and German. His account was challenged by the Presbyterian John Mackenzie, Walker producing *A Vindication* in reply.

Reading

Dwyer, Philip (ed.), *The Siege of Londonderry in 1689* (London: Elliot Stock, 1893).

Macrory, Patrick, *The Siege of Derry* (Oxford: Oxford University Press, 1980).

Milligan, C.O., *A History of the Siege of Londonderry* (Belfast: 1951).

RAYMOND GILLESPIE

Walker's *Historical Memoirs* (1786) Joseph Cooper Walker's *Historical Memoirs of the Irish Bards*, which comprises a history of music in Ireland and nine appendices, is a major document in terms of its exclusive concern with music in Ireland. Walker attempts to chronicle his subject in an admixture of learned reference, antiquarian speculation and rhetorical persuasion. His account charts the 'state of music amongst the Ancient Irish' and its subsequently depressed condition in Elizabethan Ireland, which in turn leads to its lethargic condition in the present day (i.e. the mid-1780s). Conjecture and partisan enthusiasm predominate in much of the historical chronicle, which also includes aesthetic discriminations between Irish music as 'the voice of nature' and Italian music, which 'only trifles with the ear'. The gloomy context which Walker provides for his life of Carolan (appendix VI of the memoirs) is one in which the 'despotic sway' of Italian music in London and Dublin combines with outright political oppression to erode the aesthetic genius of the native Irish music. Walker laments that harpers in the seventeenth century 'degenerated into itinerant musicians', while he recognizes that the 'last of this Order of men ... was Turlough O'Carolan, a fine natural Genius, who died in the year 1738'.

Carolan's achievement in the *Memoirs* is equated with Handel's impact on music in England. The crucial distinction between the two composers, however, lies in the dislocated status implied by Carolan's mastery of a generally defunct tradition by comparison with Handel's reanimation of a living one. Walker's attempt to claim for Carolan (and for Irish music in general) a degree of artistry comparable to that of Handel and English music was bluntly rejected by Charles Burney in his 1787 review of the *Historical Memoirs*: 'It is impossible for any one, not totally ignorant of the subject of Mr Walker's book, to read many pages of it without discovering his knowledge of music to be small and his credulity in Hibernian antiquities to be great.' Burney, moreover, condemns the stylistic features of the 'rude' collection of melodies attributed to Carolan and others which form the last appendix to the book. The conflict of opinion between Walker and Burney graphically demonstrates the apparently insurmountable difficulties which attended the development of an enduring mode of musical discourse in Ireland.

Reading

White, Harry, 'Carolan and the dislocation of music in Ireland', *Eighteenth-Century Ireland* IV (1989), pp. 55–64.

HARRY WHITE

Wallace, (William) Vincent (1812–65) Pianist, violinist and composer. Born Waterford, 11 March; died Vieuzos, France, 12 October. During the first part of his restless (and according to some accounts adventurous) life, Wallace became celebrated the world over – from Australia to South America to the Caribbean to North America – as barn-storming pianist and violinist, sometimes playing concertos for each instrument in the same concert. A popular favourite was his *Cracovienne* variations, which he would play on either instrument. In London in 1845 he scored a huge success with his first opera *Maritana*, which was subsequently performed in many of the opera houses of Europe and North America. This work owed its success to Wallace's ability to write a big tune in the manner of Meyerbeer, to adopt a convincing Spanish flavour that anticipates Bizet, and to compose an extended finale. Other operas followed, the most successful of which was *Lurline* (first performed 1860). Together with Michael Balfe, Sir Julius Benedict and others, Wallace played a part in the attempt to create an English grand opera tradition. He also composed a great quantity of piano music, some of it of great difficulty.

Reading

Temperley, Nicholas (ed.), *Music in Britain: The Romantic Age 1800–1914* (London: 1981).
White, Eric Walter, *A History of English Opera* (London: 1983).

DAVID GREER

Walsh, Peter (*c*.1616–88) Franciscan priest and controversialist. Born County Kildare; died London, 15 March. The 'son unto a poore and beggarly channtler' and a Protestant mother, Walsh studied at the Irish college of St Anthony at Louvain before returning to Ireland in 1639. He taught theology at Kilkenny, but was removed following his opposition to Cardinal Rinuccini in 1648. His conviction that the spiritual allegiance of Catholics to Rome in no way compromised their political loyalties was central to his 1661 'Irish Remonstrance', which declared the loy-alty of Anglo-Irish Catholics to Charles II, outlined their grievances, and sought their protection from persecution. Despite lay sup-port, it incurred clerical opposition. Walsh was excommunicated in 1670 and thereafter lived mostly in London, continuing to write defending the remonstrance. Despite his insubordination he believed the Catholic church was 'safer to die in', and repented his controversialism on his deathbed.

Reading

Walsh, Peter, *The History and Vindication of the Loyal Formulary or Irish Remonstrance* (London: 1674).

BERNADETTE CUNNINGHAM

Walsh, Samuel (1950–) Painter. Born London. Of Irish parents, Walsh attended Limerick School of Art (1969–74). He lives and works in Limerick. Walsh's paintings are austere abstractions, made up of symmetrical geometric formations. Predominantly light on dark, with limited use of colour, the paint-ings could suggest ordered planes superim-posed on landscape, although any such visual references are not made overt. Subsequently Walsh has used more colour in the series *14 Points of Entry*, which is based on the Stations of the Cross.

Reading

Dunne, Aidan, *Samuel Walsh: The Arena Paintings 1987–89* (Limerick: 1989).

FELICITY WOOLF

Walton, Ernest Thomas Sinton (1903–95) Physicist. In 1951 the Nobel prize for physics was shared between E.T.S. Walton and J.D. Cockcroft, in recognition of their 1934 experiment, often described as 'splitting the atom'. More precisely, it was the first transmutation of an element by artificially excited particles (protons). As such it was the 'alchemists' dream come true, as a con-temporary headline declared. It also provided the first test of Einstein's $E = mc^2$ for a nuclear reaction, and might be regarded as the prototype of subsequent generations of experiments in fundamental physics. Indeed one might wonder why these two students of

Ernest Rutherford had to wait so long for the prize. Walton's own ascetic and self-effacing personality may have had much to do with this. He always emphasized the dominant role of Rutherford in the Cavendish Laboratory of that time, but his own technical skills in developing the Cockcroft–Walton accelerator have been regarded as crucial in realizing the experiment. He even attributed his acceptance as a research student in the Cavendish to Rutherford's respect for the work of John Joly, who recommended him.

He returned to the land of his birth and education not long afterwards, to devote the rest of his career to the physics department of Trinity College, Dublin. The eventual award of the Nobel Prize changed the lifestyle of this modest man hardly at all. Despite retiring in 1974, he continued to give inspiring occasional lectures until he was in his eighties.

Reading

Weber, R.L. *Pioneers of Science* (London: Institute of Physics, 1980).

DENIS L. WEAIRE

Ware, Sir James (1594–1666) Antiquarian and historian. Born 26 November; died 1 December. Ware is remembered primarily as an antiquarian, a compiler of annals lists and other records, and a collector and conserver of ancient manuscripts. His scholarship, however, cannot be separated from the larger political and ideological concerns of his time. Educated at Trinity College, Dublin, between 1610 and 1616, when he graduated MA, he came to the attention of one of its most renowned scholars, James Ussher (later archbishop of Armagh), who cultivated his antiquarian and historical interests. Under Ussher's influence he published his first antiquarian collections, *Archiepiscoporum Casseliensium et Tuamensium Vitae* (1626) and *De preaesulibus Lageniae* (1628), which were designed as part of Ussher's larger project to write a general history of the Church of Ireland proving that the Irish church in both origin and tradition was quite independent of Rome.

In the 1630s Ware entered public life. In 1632 he succeeded his father as auditor general of the Irish treasury. Two years later he sat for the University of Dublin (Trinity College) as MP. Nominated to the seat by Lord Deputy Wentworth, who applied some persuasions to have him elected, he identified himself closely with the administration, acting as government teller on a number of divisions. Under Wentworth's favour he was appointed to the powerful Commission for Defective Titles in 1636, was nominated by the deputy to the commission to hear appeals from the ecclesiastical courts, and in 1639 was appointed a privy councillor. During these years Ware's scholarly work was strongly influenced by his political concerns. In 1633 he published his edition of *Ancient Irish Histories*, reprinting Edmund Campion's *Histories* (1571) and publishing for the first time the chronicles of Meredith Hanmer and Henry Marleburgh, and Edmund Spenser's controversial *View of the Present State of Ireland* (1596). In dedicating these editions to Lord Deputy Wentworth, Ware overtly regretted the harshness and violence of several of Spenser's observations and silently censored the text, excising its adverse reflections on the Anglo-Irish lords and moderating its most critical descriptions of the customs of the native Irish. In doing so Ware was partially motivated by concern for the house of Ormond, whose current head, the twelfth earl, was a patron and a principal Irish ally of Wentworth. But there were also larger matters at stake. For Ware was determined to show that underneath the upheavals and conflicts of the past there lay no fundamental or irreconcilable differences, as Spenser had argued, but merely the accidents of history, which had been resolved by history itself in the most recent past, so that 'now we may truly say, *Iam cuncti gens una sumus*' [now we are all one people]. This desire to emphasize the unity of the people of the realm of Ireland is evident also in Ware's publication of

Hanmer's chronicle of ancient Ireland, which provided a detailed discussion of the common origins and features of Irish and British mythical history, and in his second publication in these years (also dedicated to Wentworth), *De scriptoribus Hiberniae* (1639) he again underlined the common intellectual interests of native-born and English writers in writing about Ireland and in relating Ireland to the broader cultural currents of Christendom.

The crisis years of the 1640s and 1650s seriously disrupted Ware's political and scholarly career. Though forced to testify against Wentworth at his trial, he remained a staunch royalist. He represented Ormond in negotiations with the Irish confederates in 1643. Despatched to Oxford to report to Charles I on the state of the royalist cause in Ireland, he was captured by a parliamentary ship on his return voyage and imprisoned in the Tower (1645–6). On his release he returned to Dublin. Under constant suspicion (he was once used as a hostage for the city by parliamentary forces), he was at length forced into exile in 1649, and after a short stay in France took up residence in London. At the Resoration he sat in the Irish Convention in 1660, resumed his office as auditor general, and served on the commissions of settlement and appeals (1661–2). But he appears to have played no further part in high politics.

During his years of exile Ware extended his antiquarian researches in Oxford, Paris and London, publishing two editions of his *De Hibernia et antiquitatibus eius Disquisitiones* (1654, 1658). And after the Restoration, in addition to a short set of early Tudor annals (*Rerum Hibernicarum Annales, 1485–1558*, 1664) he published the completion of the ecclesiastical history he had begun in his youth, *De praesulibus Hiberniae Commentarius* (1665). In these later works Ware was particularly indebted to the Gaelic scholar Duald Mac Firbis, with whom he appears to have become acquainted some time in the later 1640s, and who supplied him with transcriptions and translations from the corpus of Gaelic annals, genealogies, law tracts and poetry. In his patronage of Gaelic scholarship and his respect for Gaelic materials in general, Ware was remarkable among antiquarians of his time, and to him belongs credit for the preservation of many manuscripts (especially in the Clarendon collection in the British Library) that would otherwise have been lost. But Ware's collection and organization of material continued to be dominated by his own master interpretation of Irish history, which, in recategorizing difference and discord as curiosity and antiquity, suppressed much that was central to the history of Gaelic Ireland, and sought to enforce a spurious continuty through church history and lists of episcopal succession.

CIARAN BRADY

Warren, Michael (1950–) Artist and sculptor. Born Dublin. Warren studied at Bath Academy of Art (1969–70), Trinity College, Dublin (1970–1), and the Accademia di Belle Arti di Brera, Milan (1971–5). He now lives and works in County Wexford. He makes large-scale sculptures in wood, many of which are displayed in prominent public sites in Ireland and abroad (RTÉ, Donnybrook, and Hakone Open Air Museum, Japan). The sculptures, usually combinations of elongated rectangles, appear to relate to minimalist theory, but in fact Warren's work belongs to the tradition of Modernism, which represents the spiritual through abstraction. In his sculptures he explores notions of struggle and equilibrium.

Reading

Hutchinson, John *Silence and Necessity: The Sculpture of Michael Warren*, (Dublin: Douglas Hyde Gallery, 1989).
Mulcahy, Rosemary, *ROSC 1984* (Dublin: 1984).
Ruane, Frances, 'Michael Warren', *Irish Arts Review* 2, no. 3 (1985).

FELICITY WOOLF

Warren, Raymond (1928–9) Composer. Born Weston-super-Mare, 7 December. Warren studied with Robin Orr (at Cambridge), Michael Tippett and Lennox Berkeley. From 1955 he was successively lecturer, professor of composition and professor of music at the Queen's University of Belfast. He held the chair of music at Bristol University (1972). Such major works as the oratorio *The Passion*, the opera *Graduation Ode* (libretto by the Ulster novelist Janet McNeill), the two symphonies and the violin concerto were all first performed in Belfast by largely local forces. His output has also included pieces for Belfast schools, incidental music for productions of 11 of W.B. Yeats's plays at the Lyric Theatre, and settings of poems by Yeats and Seamus Heaney.

Reading

Acton, Charles, 'The music of Raymond Warren', *Musical Times* cx (October 1969).
Ramsey, Basil, 'Raymond Warren', *Musical Times* cv (August 1964).

HARRY GRINDLE

water colouring to the 1990s Topographical views dominated the early uses of watercolour as a medium in Ireland. A public curiosity about the landscape of one's nation led artists, both native and foreign, to visit grassy demesnes, inaccessible stretches of the River Dargle in Wicklow, Killarney, choice spots along Dublin Bay, and such natural marvels as the Giant's Causeway. Subsequently engraved, these views proved lucrative for painter, engraver and printer. Innumerable English artists came to Ireland between *c.* 1770 and 1860 to exploit the natural beauty of the countryside; William Ashford specialized in country seats, Francis Wheatley produced a series of large drawings of country fairs, and in 1771 William Pars accompanied Henry Temple, second Viscount Palmerston, on a tour of the latter's estates in Sligo and Kerry. The result was a comprehensive visual account of one man's landed wealth.

James Malton's famous views of Dublin (1790s) were first produced in watercolour and later published in aquatint, a form of engraving invented so as to approach as closely as possible the delicate wash of the original. These superbly crafted drawings celebrated the city's new buildings and still enjoy an honoured place in the visual culture of both Dubliners and tourists. George Petrie's antiquarian interests led him to produce large-scale drawings that awakened many a visitor to the annual Royal Hibernian Academy exhibitions to the delights of Ireland's early history. Petrie was the first full-time watercolourist to be a member of the academy. He eventually became president in 1857.

Watercolour had long been popular as both a professional and an amateur pursuit. Given the restrictions on the social life of women in the nineteenth century, the production of watercolour drawings became a common pastime. In 1871 a group of well-connected women organized an exhibition in Lismore, County Waterford. Further exhibitions were held in Clonmel, Carlow and Dublin. This informal group eventually formed itself in 1888 into the Watercolour Society of Ireland, and held an annual exhibition in Molesworth Hall, Dublin. Mildred Anne Butler, one of the most gifted watercolourists of her day, exhibited with the society in the 1890s.

In the twentieth century watercolour was important for the preparation of designs in stained glass, the manufacture of which was a vital cultural force in the early years of the century. Evie Hone, Michael Healy and others were all most proficient in the medium. More recently, Pauline Bewick has attracted great public interest in her sensuous use of watercolour for both illustrative and large-scale works.

Reading

Butler, Patricia, *Three Hundred Years of Irish Watercolours and Drawings* (London: Weidenfeld and Nicolson, 1990).

Le Harivel Adrian, (ed.), *Irish Watercolours and Drawings* (Dublin: National Gallery of Ireland, 1991).

Strickland, Walter, *A Dictionary of Irish Artists* (Shannon: Irish University Press, 1968).

FINTAN CULLEN

Waterford glass Drinking glasses, bottles and 'other' articles were made near Waterford from approximately 1720 to 1735. As far as is known no specimens of glass survive from this period. In 1783 George and William Penrose advertised that they were producing 'plain and cut flint glass, useful and ornamental'. This was at Penrose Lane, adjoining the Quays at Waterford. By the end of the century Jonathan Gatchell and others had taken over the business, where fine-quality domestic glass was made until 1851, after which no lead-crystal glass was made in Waterford until the establishment of the modern factory in 1951. One notable name associated with the Penrose period is John Hill, a glassmaker from England who was employed as overseer and brought over with him 'the best set of workmen'. Another is Samuel Miller, foreman cutter during the 1820s and 1830s. His patterns survive and are in the National Museum of Ireland.

The Waterford glassworks took particular care to produce a clear and colourless glass. The products were of a wide variety, including decanters, some impressed on the base 'PENROSE WATERFORD'; large fruit bowls, circular or boat-shaped; wine glasses of various sizes, some in the same form as the circular fruit bowls; and butter coolers, sugar bowls and celery vases. From the late eighteenth century large quantities of wine glasses were exported to Jersey, Jamaica, Newfoundland, New York, the West Indies and other destinations. The success of modern Waterford Crystal can be gauged by the increase in the number employed which rose from 50 in 1951 to a figure variously stated as between 2,000 and 4,000 in 1973, establishing Waterford as being one of the largest centres in the world producing

hand-blown glass that is cut and engraved on the premises.

Reading

Dunlevy, Mairead, *Penrose Glass* (National Museum of Ireland, 1989).

Warren, Phelps, *Irish Glass* (London: Faber, 1981).

Westropp, M.S.D., *Irish Glass* (London: Herbert Jenkins 1921; rev. edn ed. Mary Boydell, Dublin: Allen Figgis, 1978).

MARY BOYDELL

Wellesley, Arthur (1769–1852) Duke of Wellington. Born Dublin, 29 April; died 14 September. Wellesley was educated at Eton and Pignerol's military academy at Angers. He was commissioned in 1787 and appointed aide-de-camp to the lord lieutenant of Ireland, until 1793. From 1790 to 1797, he was MP for Trim in the Irish Parliament. After service in India, he returned to politics, and from 1807 to 1809 he was chief secretary of Ireland. He laid the foundations for the Irish constabulary by reorganizing the Dublin police.

In 1825, he campaigned for Catholic emancipation and the preservation of the Protestant Ascendancy as the only solution to the Irish problem. Fearing wider reforms, he resigned from Canning's government with Peel in 1827.

As prime minister in 1828, he reformed the Test and Corporation Acts that penalized non-conformists. When Daniel O'Connell was elected to Clare, Wellington split the Tories by making Catholic emancipation law in 1829. He also enacted a bill to suppress the Catholic Association.

His obdurate opposition to parliamentary reform, which he called 'revolution by due course of law', forced his resignation. He thwarted the 1832 Reform Bill until the constitutional crisis led him to persuade his followers to absent themselves to allow its passage. Nevertheless, radical mobs stoned his house. He received a heraldic funeral. He was glorified for his victories over

Napoleon, and the opprobrium heaped on his reactionary policies was forgotten.

FRED LOWE

Wentworth, Thomas (1593–1641) Earl of Strafford and lord deputy. The eldest son of Sir William Wentworth of Wentworth-Woodhouse in south Yorkshire, Thomas was educated in St John's College, Cambridge, and the Inner Temple. He was elected to the 1614 Parliament for Yorkshire and was also a member of the 1621, 1624 and 1628 parliaments. He emerged as an opponent of the court faction lead by the Duke of Buckingham and rapidly became one of the most influential figures in the Commons. He was arrested for his refusal to pay the forced loan. After Charles I's capitulation to Parliament with the acceptance of the Petition of Right in 1628, Wentworth was created a baron, later a viscount, and appointed as lord president of the Council of the North. After the assassination of Buckingham in 1629 the faction to which Wentworth adhered rose to influence. He was appointed a privy councillor in 1629 and lord deputy of Ireland in January 1632, arriving in Dublin in July 1633.

In Ireland, as in England, Wentworth was concerned about the balance of power between crown and subjects, which in Ireland he believed had swung too far in favour of the subject. Through the activities of the 1634–5 Parliament, the establishment of a commission on defective titles, and a revitalization of the Court of Castle Chamber and the Court of Wards, he attempted to reverse this trend. This brought him into conflict with the main settler lords, especially Richard Boyle, earl of Cork. His reactivation of the policy of plantation and the refusal to confirm measures which would have guaranteed Old English land titles also alienated him from this group. His attempts to move the Church of Ireland from its Calvinist position towards a more Laudian outlook and to recover church lands through the Court of High Commission upset many. Ulster Presbyterians resented the 'Black Oath' imposed by him, which held the king to be head of the church. The calling of the Irish Parliament in 1640, intended to provide money for the waging of the Bishops' Wars in Scotland, brought all Wentworth's enemies together, and in collaboration with the newly summoned Long Parliament in England Wentworth was recalled and impeached. He was executed 12 May 1641 on Tower Hill.

Reading

Kearney, Hugh, *Strafford in Ireland, 1633–41* (Manchester: Manchester University Press, 1959; repr. with new introduction, Cambridge: Cambridge University Press, 1989).

Ranger, Terence, 'Strafford in Ireland: a revaluation', *Past and Present* 19 (1965).

RAYMOND GILLESPIE

Wesleys Visiting in shifts from August 1747, Methodist leaders John and Charles Wesley spent much of the next two years nurturing Ireland's nascent Methodist movement. John persevered: by 1789 the time he spent in his 21 visits added up to over five years.

John's visits were feats of endurance, as his circuit-riding work of preaching, visiting, examining members and settling conflicts covered vast areas. His controversial and very public ministry drew crowds, sometimes violent and sometimes connived at by authorities. 'I am still a wonder to myself', he wrote in 1771 after passing his sixty-eighth birthday in the midst of another exhausting tour. He marvelled at the 'huge applause and huge opposition' he inspired. 'I think there is not such another nation in Europe so "Impetuous in their love and in their hate".' His persistence was rewarded with an increasingly self-reliant Irish Methodism, comprising 14,010 members by his final visit in 1789.

Reading

Haire, Robert, *Wesley's One-and-Twenty Visits to Ireland* (London: Epworth Press, 1947).

Wesley, John, 'Letters and Journals', in *The Works of John Wesley*, 34 vols (Oxford: Clarendon Press, and Nashville TN: Abingdon, 1975–).

JOSEPH LIECHTY

West, Francis Robert (*c.* 1749–1809) draughtsman and art teacher. Probably born Dublin; died there, 24 January. Son of the draughtsman Robert West, the founder of the Dublin Society Drawing School, West trained in Dublin under his father. In 1777 he succeeded his father as master of the Dublin Society Figure School. He tutored his pupils through engravings of the old masters and curated a cast collection. Privately he worked in pastel in the manner of Hugh Douglas Hamilton and exhibited in both Dublin and London.

Reading

Herbert, J.D., *Irish Varieties for the Past Fifty Years* (London: 1836).
Mulvany, T.J., *Citizen* 24 (October 1841).
Turpin, John, *Dublin Historical Record* 40 (December 1986, March 1987).

FINTAN CULLEN

West, Robert (d. 1770) Draughtsman and art teacher. Born Waterford; died Dublin. Described as 'one of the most important figures in the development of Irish art', West yet remains 'maddeningly elusive'. The son of an alderman, he may have trained in England and France, returning to Dublin *c.*1740. For some years West ran his own drawing school in Dublin, but in 1744 was employed to teach figure drawing for the newly founded Dublin Society. He thus became the first known teacher of drawing in an institution in Ireland, training any number of important artists of the second half of the century. The drawing academy that he founded ran for over a century. He excelled in chalk drawings and seemed to favour a somewhat old-fashioned rococo style.

Reading

Crookshank, Anne and the Knight of Glin, *The Painters of Ireland c.1660–1920* (London: Barrie and Jenkins, 1978).
Mulvany, T.J., *Citizen* 24 (October 1841).
Turpin, John, *Dublin Historical Record* 40 (December 1986, March 1987).

FINTAN CULLEN

West, Robert Lucius (*c.* 1774–1850) Painter. Died Dublin, 3 June. The grandson of Robert West, founder of the Dublin Society Drawing School, West was the son of Francis Robert West, also a draughtsman and teacher. In turn in 1809 he succeeded his father as master of the Dublin Society Figure School, a post he held until 1845. His retirement brought to an end 100 years of dynastic control by the West family of art training in Dublin. After training with his father he specialized in portraits, being greatly influenced by Hugh Douglas Hamilton, whose work he also copied. A founding member of the Royal Hibernian Academy, he exhibited regularly until 1849.

Reading

Crookshank, Anne and the Knight of Glin, *The Painters of Ireland c.1660–1920* (London: Barrie and Jenkins, 1978).
Strickland, Walter, *A Dictionary of Irish Artists* (Shannon: Irish University Press, 1968).
Turpin, John, *Dublin Historical Record* 39 (March 1986).

FINTAN CULLEN

Whaley/Whalley, Thomas 'Buck' (1766–1800) Politician. Born 86 St Stephen's Green, Dublin; died Knutsford, 2 November, on his way to London. At 13 Whaley inherited £7,000 a year and £60,000 in cash. He accepted a wager, said to be for £20,000, to travel to Jerusalem and back within two years. He left Dublin in September 1788 and was back in June 1789, a feat that made him famous. He was MP for Newcastle, County Down, and for Enniscorthy. Sir Jonah

Barrington said that he accepted bribes, first to vote for the Union and then against it.

Reading

Sullivan, Sir Edmund (ed.), *Buck Whaley's Memoirs* (London: De La More Press, 1906).

HENRY BOYLAN

Whately, Richard (1787–1863) Academic and cleric. Church of Ireland archbishop of Dublin (1831–63), Whately came to Ireland from being Drummond professor of political economics at Oxford, a scholar and a lively writer of note. He knew little about Ireland or the Church of Ireland, but, nothing daunted, assumed with (apparently) a high degree of confidence the position of leadership that his office conferred with the opportunities it provided for him to express his views. In Church of Ireland eyes, he was more accommodating to government than many would have wished in the working out of the implications of the Church Temporalities Act and of tithe legislation. Moreover, the didactic and often insensitive manner in which he criticized the academic level of the ordained ministry did not endear him to the clergy (or Trinity College, Dublin).

A believer in religious toleration, he had as an Oxford don supported Catholic emancipation. However, his critics would have said his excessively broad-churchmanship had little sympathy with the Anglo-Catholic movement within the Church, 'Puseyism', and though he and Newman were neighbours in Dublin (after the latter's conversion and as rector of the Catholic University), Whately hurtfully cut his former pupil.

Evangelicals and other conservative members of the church were affronted by Whately's espousal of the newly created national schools, accusing him of showing bias against those who found the schools unacceptable on theological grounds in his appointment to preferment. As one of the commissioners of national education (with Archbishop Murray, to whom he related well) and chairman in all but name, he showed a total commitment to the principles of mixed secular and separate religious education, even writing some of the textbooks. The archbishop was officially designated chairman of a royal commission of inquiry into the condition of the poor in Ireland, whose report of 1835–6 showed concern for those who had 'a miserable existence in a state of frightful destitution', and made far-reaching, though to the government unrealistic, recommendations, including the funding of emigration on a large scale.

KENNETH MILNE

Wheatley, Francis (1747–1801) Painter. Born London; died there 28 June. Wheatley trained at Shipley's Drawing School, was a pupil of Richard Wilson, and became director of the Society of Artists in 1772. However, he painted his best pictures during the four years he spent in Dublin eluding his creditors. He depicted the more exciting events of the Irish Volunteer Movement as they unfolded, in particular Henry Grattan's speech on the Repeal of Poynings Law; and this led to commissions for his vivacious landscape portraits and topographical views. He is especially noted for his lively Irish genre scenes, influenced by Wouwerman.

Reading

Crookshank, A. and the Knight of Glin, *The Painters of Ireland, c. 1660–1920* (London: Barrie and Jenkins, 1978).

W.G., Strickland, *A Dictionary of Irish Artists* (Shannon: Irish University Press, 1968).

Webster, M., 'Wheatley's Lord and Lady Antrim', *Irish Arts Review* 1, no. 1 (1984).

HILARY PYLE

Whitaker, Thomas Kenneth (Ken) (1916–) Economist. Born 8 December, Rostrevor, County Down. Whitaker entered the Irish Civil Service in 1934. He became secretary of the Department of Finance (1956–69), governor of the Central Bank of Ireland (1969–76), and a member of Seanad

Éireann (1977–82). He began an in-depth study of the Irish economy in January 1957. In December 1957, he received government approval to pursue and complete the work. In November 1958, the study, *Economic Development* (popularly known as the 'Grey Book'), was published by the government, with authorship credited to Whitaker, together with a government White Paper entitled 'Programme for Economic Expansion'. *Economic Development* was the first official work to describe the Irish economy, analyse its strengths and weaknesses, attempt to describe the influence on development of external forces, and recommend policy options in a five-year framework.

Whitaker not only initiated a new process of economic programming, but, more importantly, he introduced systematic analysis into Irish economic policy making. He has received numerous honours, including the French Légion d'Honneur in 1976. From 1976 to 1996 he served as Chancellor of the National University of Ireland.

Reading

Interests: T.K. Whitaker (Dublin: Institute of Public Administration, 1983).
McCarthy, John F. (ed.), *Planning Ireland's Future: The Legacy of T.K. Whitaker* (Dublin: Glendale Press, 1990).

ALAN DUKES

White Stag Group Founded in London in 1935 by Basil Rákóczi (1908–79) and Kenneth Hall (1913–46) for the advancement of subjectivity in psychological analysis and art. (The white stag is a Hungarian emblem for creativity.) From early 1940 the group was centred in Dublin in Lower Baggot Street, as Rákóczi, Hall and Dr Herbrand Ingouville-Williams (1896–1945), founder with Rákóczi in Bloomsbury of the Society for Creative Psychology, had moved to Ireland. They were joined as associates by other, primarily English, pacifist artists, including Nick Nicholls, Georgette Rondel, Stephen Gilbert, Jocelyn Chewett and Phyllis Hayward. Their philosophy attracted a number of radical Irish intellectuals and artists. Amongst these were Brian Boydell, Thurloe Conolly, Ralph Cusack, Mainie Jellett, Patrick Scott and Doreen Vanston.

Whilst artists were free to express their own individuality, the underlying philosophy was the release of subconscious imagery, expressed with an emphasis on line and form. Regular lectures and exhibitions were held, culminating in the controversial 1944 Exhibition of Subjective Art at the White Stag Gallery. The exhibition raised public awareness of contemporary trends in art and led to the publication of *Three Painters*, a study of the work of Rákóczi, Hall and Scott. The group dispersed when war ended, although Rákóczi and Hayward maintained links with Ireland until the 1950s.

Reading

Ingouville-Williams, H.A.C., *Three Painters* (Dublin: Three Candles, 1945).
Kennedy, S.B., *Irish Art and Modernism* (Belfast: Institute of Irish Studies, Queen's University, 1991).

ELISABETH GUINNESS

Whiteboyism Term derived from the appellative 'Whiteboy', applied by contemporaries to describe those responsible for agrarian unrest in eighteenth- and early nineteenth-century Ireland. The term 'Ribbonism' gained currency in the early nineteenth century also. As terms which purport to embrace all manifestations of agrarian radicalism between 1760 and 1850, both 'Whiteboyism' and 'Ribbonism' are deficient. Most scholars today follow James Donnolly in confining their usage of the term 'Whiteboy' to the particular outbreaks of agrarian unrest that occurred in Munster and south Leinster in the 1760s and 1770s, when bodies of marginalized tenants came together to oppose enclosure because it reduced the availability of common land, the levying of tithes and high conacre rents. 'Whiteboy' is quite apposite in these instances, because those responsible draped themselves in white sheets. It is probable that this reflected atavistic affection for the Jacobite cause in the same way as wearing a white rose on 10 June, but the main thrust of Whiteboy agitation was the preservation of traditional rural practices at a time of rapid commercialization and population growth.

The essentially conservative character of the Whiteboys was replicated by such near contemporary movements as the Oakboys and Steelboys, who rose to secure remedies to different grievances in Ulster, and the Rightboys of the 1780s, whose main objects were the tithe and the dues sought by Catholic priests. These eighteenth-century movements were secretive and oath-bound, and their *modus operandi* involved recourse to whatever violent and intimidatory tactics they believed necessary to enforce their 'rule'. This seldom resulted in the assassination of defaulters, but following the emergence of such avowedly sectarian agrarian organizations as the Peep O'Day Boys and Defenders in south Ulster in the 1780s, and 'the end of the moral economy' in the 1790s, murderous violence became an integral feature of early nineteenth-century agrarian protest. Bodies like the Threshers (1806–7), Shanavests and Caravats (1809–11), Carders (1813–17), Rockites (1819–23), Whitefeet (1830–34) and Terry Alts (1831–8, 1844–7) reflected the intensifying economic problems experienced by modest-sized farmers and labourers. They could do nothing to influence the international economic environment in their favour, but their recourse to intimidation, assault and murder served to warn landlords, their agents, large farmers and other tenants that their interests could not be ignored, and they effectively acted as a brake on economic change in land use and occupation. This came as a consequence of the population loss occasioned by the Great Famine. Thereafter, circumstances were no longer conducive to 'Whiteboyism' and the nature of agrarian unrest in rural Ireland changed fundamentally.

Reading

Bartlett, Thomas, 'An end to moral economy: the Irish militia disturbances of 1793', *Past and Present* 99 (1983), pp. 41–64.

Beames, M.R., *Peasants and Power: The Whiteboy Movements and their Control in Pre-Famine Ireland* (1983).

Donnolly, J.S., 'The Rightboy movement 1785–8', *Studia Hibernica* xix (1978), pp. 7–73.

—— 'The Whiteboy movement 1761–5', *Irish Historical Studies* xxi (1978–9), pp. 20–54.

—— 'Irish Agrarian Rebellion: the Whiteboys of 1769–76', *Royal Irish Academy Proceedings* 83C (1983), pp. 293–331.

JAMES KELLY

Wild Geese (*Na Geanna Fiaine*) Probably first used as a code word to signify those Irishmen who were recruited clandestinely in Ireland during the seventeenth and first half of the eighteenth centuries to serve as soldiers in the armies of Europe, particularly in those of France and Spain. It applied to the Irish exiles who went to Europe after the cessation of the Williamite war (1689–91) and the signing of the Treaty of Limerick (October 1691), and subsequently it was used to include their descendants. Revenue correspondence, dated 6 September 1726, refers to 'those persons commonly called wild geese'. The term was used in Irish poetry of the early part of the eighteenth century: the hoped-for success of the Jacobite cause and thus the return of 'na geanna' (the geese) to Ireland in triumph was a recurring theme.

Due to political and economical disabilities in the seventeenth century, many Catholics in Ireland sought refuge or exile in Europe. France, Spain, Rome and the Lowlands (under Spanish governors) gave Irish Catholic immigrants sustenance, both material and spiritual. France declared war on Spain in 1635, and with the tacit support of Charles I of England the French actively recruited in

Ireland. Among the estimated 3,000 troops who arrived at French ports were Michael, Garrett, Richard and Edmund, the four younger sons of William Wall of Coolnamuck, County Waterford, and his wife Catherine, daughter of Walter Walsh, lord of the mountain. They raised an Irish regiment of their own name in France, which was possibly the first such regiment in exile.

In 1689 King James II arrived in Ireland, and to assist him France undertook an exchange of French troops to Ireland for Irish troops to France. Thus, in March 1690, Justin MacCarthy, Viscount Mountcashell, arranged for 5,000–6,000 recruits to be sent to France, and on the return voyage a greater number of French landed in Cork. These Irish recruits were formed into three regiments: Mountcashell's own, later known as Lee's and Bulkeley's; Lord Clare's, commanded by the O'Brien family until 1775, when it was amalgamated with Berwick regiment; and Dillon's regiment, commanded by Dillon's and in 1775 amalgamated with Bulkeley's. These regiments were considered part of the foreign unit of the French army.

An essential condition of the surrender of Limerick and part of the subsequent treaty was that all those Irish officers and soldiers of James's army who wished to go to France would be transported there together with women and children. It is estimated that 12,000 men went with Patrick Sarsfield to France, where, under James's control until 1697 but paid for by the French king, they formed the kernel from which the Irish brigades expanded to distinguish themselves in the service of the French during the eighteenth century.

Irish immigration and exile to Europe had reached its pinnacle. With the Treaty of Ryswick in 1697, Louis XIV of France recognized William as king of England; thus James could no longer control an army. As a result many Irishmen, if not absorbed into French units of the army, found themselves unemployed. They looked to other European countries – Spain, the Austrian Empire, Russia.

Little is recorded of the rank-and-file 'wild geese'; on the other hand, the officers, in order to gain access to the royal courts and armies of Europe, found it necessary to establish their lineage. This stimulated their interest in genealogies and 'wild geese' family history, which in many families was kept alive and recorded.

Reading

Gallwey, Hubert, *The Wall Family in Ireland 1170–1970* (Leinster Leader, 1970).

Hayes, Richard, *A Biographical Dictionary of Irishmen in France*, M.H. Gill (Dublin, 1949).

Holohan, Renagh, *The Irish Chateaux* (Dublin: Lilliput Press, 1989).

O'Callaghan, J.C., *History of the Irish Brigades in the Service of France* (Glascow, 1870).

Simms, J.G., *The Irish on the Continent 1691–1800: A New History of Ireland*, vol iv (Oxford University Press, 1986).

MÁIRE MacCONGHAIL

Wilde family Jane (Elgee) Wilde (pseudonym 'Speranza') (1821–96), poet, folklorist, translator and journalist, claimed a distant Italian ancestry and a distinguished Irish clerical and legal background. Her mother's family had included a friend of Jonathan Swift and later the novelist Charles Maturin. Her paternal ancestors had been farmers in County Down, her grandfather was an archdeacon and her father a lawyer. She was born in Wexford and as a young woman she was a regular and enthusiastic contributor of poetry and essays to the *Nation*. Her article 'Jacta Alea Est' (July 1848) was attributed to Gavin Duffy and mentioned in sedition charges against him. When Duffy was interrogated about the article in his prosecution, Jane Elgee rose in the public gallery to claim its authorship. In 1851 she married William Wilde (1815–76), doctor, antiquarian and topographical writer, whose *Beauties of the Boyne* she had reviewed for the *Nation*, possibly the occasion of their meeting. They lived at 1 Merrion Square, Dublin.

William Wilde was born in County Roscommon and came from a family of merchants, physicians and farmers. Wilde was an eye and ear specialist, trained in London, Vienna and Berlin; he founded St Mark's Hospital, Dublin (1844), the first Irish hospital to offer aural treatment. He was census commissioner for the 1851 census, collecting medical statistics including the first statistical record on eye and ear diseases. William Wilde was knighted in 1864. He had three children by unknown mothers before his marriage to Jane Elgee: Henry Wilson went into his father's practice; Emily and Mary Wilde died together in an accidental fire in 1871. William Wilde's reputation was damaged shortly after his knighthood, when Mary Travers, a former patient, claimed that he had drugged and raped her. The case was made public when Mary Travers sued Jane Wilde for libel, after the latter had protested to Travers's father about the accusation. Travers won the case, but with only a farthing damage.

William and Jane Wilde had three children: William Robert Kingsbury Wills Wilde (1852–99), lawyer; Oscar Fingal O'Flahertie Wills Wilde (1854–1900), poet, novelist and dramatist; and Isola Wilde (1857–67). Oscar Wilde was educated at Portora Royal School, Enniskillen; at Trinity College, Dublin; and at Magdalen College, Oxford. At Oxford (1874–8) Wilde was influenced by John Ruskin's lectures on the aesthetic and by his own reading of Hegel. He was also a talented classical scholar, and he won a major poetry prize. There he began to be noted for the affectations of dress, speech and manner then characterized as the attributes of aestheticism, which have subsequently contributed to his status as an icon of camp culture. A lecture tour of the USA in 1882 contributed to his literary fame. In 1884 he married Constance Lloyd (1858–98). They had two sons: Cyril (Wilde) Holland (born 1885), died in World War I; and Vyvyan (Wilde) Holland (born 1886), writer and family biographer. Wilde was already known as the author of poems, stories, journalism

and a striking gothic novel, *The Portrait of Dorian Gray*, when he met Lord Alfred Douglas in 1891, and the two became lovers. In the following four years Wilde produced a number of very successful plays and the couple travelled extensively in Europe. In February 1895 Douglas's father, the marquess of Queensbury, insulted Wilde, and Wilde sued for libel and lost. He was then charged with indecent acts, convicted at his second trial, and spent his two-year sentence in Pentonville, Wandsworth and Reading prisons. While he was in prison, Jane Wilde died.

Wilde had been made bankrupt as well as imprisoned and after his release he lived in France and Italy, sometimes with Douglas, on an allowance from Constance Wilde and, after her death, from her estate. Wilde died at Paris in 1900 and is buried in the *Père Lachaise* cemetery. His first lover, Robert Ross, was his literary executor and befriended Wilde's orphaned sons.

The Wilde family exemplify some features of later nineteenth-century Protestant, middle-class Irish nationalism, from antiquarianism to enthusiasm, but they were all more than usually radical in the politics and aesthetics. Jane and Oscar Wilde are now best remembered for the ways in which they challenged normative sexual values and social decorum. Oscar Wilde's interest in women's rights owes something to his mother and wife as well as to his own interrogation of the boundaries between masculine and feminine. The family's love of elaborate names and pseudonyms is part of a shared fascination with masquerade, which in Oscar found its fruition in 'posing as a Sodomite' and as Irishman abroad. Wilde's best-known works, his comic drama *The Importance of Being Earnest* and his confessional protesting *Ballad of Reading Gaol*, are two sides of a commitment to style as the site of national and social reformations.

Reading

Bartlett, Neil, *Who Was that Man? A Present for Mr Oscar Wilde* (London: 1988).

Douglas, Alfred, *Oscar Wilde and Myself* (New York: 1914).

Ellman, Richard, *Oscar Wilde* (London: 1987).

Holland, Vyvyan, *Son of Oscar Wilde* (London: 1954).

Hyde, H. Montgomey (ed.), *The Trial of Oscar Wilde* (New York: 1962).

Showalter, Elaine, *Sexual Anarchy: Gender and Culture at the Fin de Siècle* (New York: 1991).

White, Terence de Vere, *The Parents of Oscar Wilde* (London: 1967).

Worth, Katherine, *Oscar Wilde* (London: 1983).

SIOBHÁN KILFEATHER

Wilson, James (1922–) Composer. Born 27 September, London. Wilson, a civil servant, served in the Royal Navy in World War II, and afterwards studied piano, harpsichord and composition (with Alec Rowley) at Trinity College of Music, London. He settled in County Dublin in 1948, taught composition at the Royal Irish Academy of Music (*c.*1969–80), and founded and organized the May in Monkstown music festival. He is a co-director of the Ennis Composition Summer School, which has a valuable role in composer development in Ireland. Secretary of the Association of Irish Composers in 1970s, he was a founder member of Aosdána and is a director of the Irish Music Rights Organization.

Wilson's first work to attract public attention was the children's opera *The Hunting of the Snark* (1965). *Twelfth Night* was staged at the 1969 Wexford Opera Festival. He now works principally in Ireland and Denmark, where a number of his main works have been produced, including *Grinning at the Devil*, an opera on the life of Karen Blixen (20 performances in Copenhagen, 1989); *King of the Golden River*, a children's opera (TBF Copenhagen, 1993); and *The Little Mermaid*, a puppet play. He has written music in most genres and his style is eclectic. He aims for transparency and his recent works, in particular, demonstrate fine melodic lines and a telling use of orchestral colour.

SARAH BURN

Witherow, Thomas (1824–90) Divine and historian. Born Ballycastle, County Antrim, 29 May; died Derry, 25 January. Witherow was educated at the Royal Belfast Academical Institution. In 1845 he was ordained a Presbyterian minister, and he became professor of church history and pastoral theology at Magee College, Derry, in 1865. In 1878 he was elected moderator of the General Assembly, and in 1883 made honorary doctor of divinity by the Presbyterian Theological Faculty, Ireland. He wrote a number of works on religious and historical subjects and was one of the editors of the *Presbyterian Review*.

Reading

Witherow, Thomas, *The Apostolic Church* (Belfast: Shepherd and Aitchison, 1856).

—— *Historical and Literary Memorials of Presbyterianism in Ireland (1623–1731)* (London and Belfast: Mullan, 1879).

—— *Three Prophets of Our Own* (Londonderry: James Davidson, 1880).

HENRY BOYLAN

women artists Relatively little is known about Irish women painters during the eighteenth century, a situation compounded by probable misattributions of their work to other artists. Yet despite the efforts of feminists and others, the problem is not one to be solved by the identification of authorship alone. The making of art is not gender-free: rather it is bound up with the social construction of femininity at particular historical moments, which certainly during this earlier period helped to ensure that art made by women was considered to be as marginal as it generally was elsewhere. This was a period when the practice of art was becoming increasingly professionalized, signalled by the formation of the British Royal Academy in 1768, which included two male Irish artists among its founder members. By comparison the wash drawings of Anglo-Irish women artists, such as Mary Delany or her friend

Letitia Bushe, tend to be regarded as of amateur status. Unlike oil, watercolour or pastel could safely form part of a lady's accomplishments, similar to embroidery; while Mary Delany's letters provide a valuable record of the arts in Ireland she was also renowned for her needlework skills, her shell decorations or her flower collages, which accurately detail the different species. Unless there were professional artists within the family, as in Susannah Drury's case, or they were members of the gentry, women also tended to lack any access to art education.

Susannah Drury's career remains highly obscure beyond her two pairs of views of the Giant's Causeway, painted probably in 1739. Her only other known work is an untraced view of London, which suggests that she may have trained there before coming to Ireland. Significantly, none of these paintings uses oils; they are small, painstaking works in gouache on vellum, again indicating the pervasive gender distinction in the use of materials. However, the engraving of her two views by Francois Vivares made these works available to an audience within Britain and Europe, where they contributed to major geological debates over the origins of crystalline rocks. Drury's views of the Causeway's east and west prospects (now in the Ulster Museum and the collection of the Knight of Glin) provided the most accurate records to date of both alignment and formation of the basalt columns. The central bulk of these in the Ulster Museum *East Prospect* is exaggerated in scale and distinguished in tone from its surroundings, yet its awesome qualities are mediated by the oblivious picnickers beneath and the fishermen at the far right.

Despite the containment of women's activities mainly to the domestic sphere, their work on occasions registered other historical processes. This need not have been on a conscious level, however, Lady Florence Cole's pencil drawing of *Crom Castle* (n.d. but probably early nineteenth century, National Trust) is not merely a picturesque view of a local scene; it represents the County Fermanagh

site of a major battle in 1689, which had helped to secure the Protestant Ascendancy of which Cole was herself a member. Meanwhile the pencil and wash drawings of Caroline Hamilton (e.g. *Society*, 1801, private collection) at times more explicitly acknowledge the effects of wider political developments within the feminine domain of the home. Unusually for a woman artist at this time, Hamilton's work also engages with current satirical trends which characterized political and social commentary of the late eighteenth and early nineteenth centuries; the non-conformism inherited from her mother may well have facilitated a degree of ironic distance from the mores of the gentry, of which she was still a part.

Extant work by women from the early nineteenth century mainly consists of portraits, landscapes or genre scenes, often featuring children or family members; again, the delicacy of handling required by the medium of watercolour or wash drawing was appropriate to the notion of femininity such women were expected to fulfil. Their exclusion from academic training ensured that they lacked the skill in painting the figure which was the basis for prestigious historical subjects, while the extremity of emotional response required within the Romantic category of the sublime was clearly incompatible with the perceived fragility of female sensibilities. However, challenges to this ideology of femininity began to develop in the mid-nineteenth century, with the emergence of Paris as a focus for artists within the early avant-garde.

Like their male counterparts, Irish women artists were clearly drawn to Paris as a site of artistic innovation, yet there was an additional attraction for women in the existence of a more liberal art education than was largely available elsewhere. During the 1860s the first atelier began to accept women students; the first Irish woman artist, Harriet Osborne O'Hagan, arrived in 1863. However, the city's Bohemian reputation prompted some families to provide chaperones for their daughters. Edith Somerville, for example, was accompanied by various relatives on her first visit to Paris in 1884. Irish women also participated in the artistic colonization of Britanny, and although Helen Mabel Trevor's depictions of Breton women are still located within the familiar domain of the home, figure studies such as *The Fisherman's Mother* (1892, National Gallery of Ireland) register the emergence of new forms of realism in art by Irish women. By this date it was also increasingly common for women to work in oil on canvas – one indicator that they were beginning to compete professionally with men.

Indeed Trevor's *Self Portrait* (1890s?, National Gallery of Ireland) depicts her in painter's clothes and holding a palette. The bulk of the figure within the picture frame and the steady gaze addressing the viewer signify a lack of idealization of her own image: that the portrait can uncompromisingly be read as that of an artist indicates that new identities were beginning to emerge for Irish women. The democratization of painting practices proposed by realism affected both male and female artists visiting France. The further significance for women lay in its enabling them to become professional painters, not only through a devaluation of the standards of the academy, but in allowing many of them to construct an identity outside their families for the first time. From this point onwards women were to play significant roles in the development of Modernism within Irish painting.

One of the key figures was certainly Sarah Purser, and the importance of her subsequent roles as an organizer and facilitator of the emergence of Irish Modernism should not be allowed to detract from her significance as a painter. At the age of 30 Purser travelled to Paris (1878) so that she could make her living as a portrait painter, and is thus a prime example of this emergent professionalism among Irish women artists. Paintings like *Le Petit Dejeuner* (1881/2, National Gallery of Ireland) indicate a receptiveness to the realist concerns with modern subject matter current within Paris and depicted with an increasingly non-naturalistic handling of paint. This method of working was also transferred to paintings executed after her return to Ireland, including *Lady With A Rattle* (1885, National Gallery of Ireland). This choice of subject matter normally depends on the perception of caring for children as a 'natural' female activity – yet the awkwardness of the pose and the impassivity of the facial expression introduce a disturbing tension within this scenario. Apart from having a highly successful career as a portrait painter, Purser became renowned as a collector and organizer of exhibitions of modern works, in addition to making funds available in 1934 to support the study of art history in Ireland. In 1903 she also founded the stained glass workshop An Tur Gloinne (the Tower of Glass).

While the experience of Paris enabled a number of women artists to establish their careers, other forms of professionalism were taking shape within Ireland. The emergence of the Arts and Crafts movement in Ireland during the late nineteenth century was mainly due to the efforts of women; its emphasis on such traditional skills as lace-making, weaving or embroidery involved an extension of acceptable female roles rather than the challenge to these posed by becoming an artist. Consequently such craft-based activities were admirably suited to the needs of a range of philanthropic institutions and individuals in training young working-class women. However, by the turn of the century other organizations, including the Gaelic League, were beginning to offer training in similar areas to more affluent women. The revival of traditional crafts in addition to a study of Gaelic language and music had an obvious application to the cultural nationalism of the period. They helped to give concrete form to usable versions of the Celtic past,- through the various activities promoted by the Dun Emer Guild (established in 1902 by Evelyn Gleeson), the stained glass production of An Tur Gloinne, or the Cuala Press (set up by Elizabeth Yeats in 1908). For some artists, however, Celtic revivalism became subsumed into more pressing political concerns, as in the case of Constance de Markiewicz; for others, such as Grace Henry, the associations implied between the west of Ireland and cultural renewal proved to be so valuable that she spent eight years working on Achill Island, off the west coast of Ireland.

Paris still continued as an important focus for Irish women artists during the early part of the twentieth century. For Eileen Gray avant-gardism supplied an escape from her family, in addition to providing her with both skills and clientele necessary for a career as an influential Modernist designer and architect. Unlike Gray, who remained in Paris from 1902 until she died in 1976, the majority of Irish women, such as Mary Swanzy or May Guinness, tended to stay only for relatively short periods before return-ing. These visits were important in that they contributed to an awareness of Modernist ideas within Ireland, although this was clearly insufficient to mediate the critical response to Mainie Jellett's abstract paintings, exhibited at the Society of Dublin Painters in 1923. Studying first with Lhote and then with Gleizes from 1921 onwards, Jellett and Evie Hone had collaborated in the development of a rigorous pictorial construction derived from Cubism. Within Jellett's concern for 'pure painting' any possible reading of Modernism as ideologically engaged with post-colonial Ireland was at least initially missing, which may be at least partly explained by her family's problematic position as formerly powerful Southern Unionists within the new Free State. When she did reintroduce such subject matter it was in the form mainly of religious imagery (e.g. *Homage to Fra Angelico*, 1928, private collection), a direction taken also by Evie Hone in her stained glass work of the 1930s. However, despite the close working relationship between the two women during the twenties, it was Jellett who was the public apologist for Modernism within Ireland, giving lectures and broadcasts

while continuing to paint until shortly before her death in 1944.

The deserved significance of Mainie Jellett's work should not be allowed to over-shadow other women painters for whom abstraction was not an issue. Landscape was a predominant theme in the work of women artists including Letitia Hamilton and Estella Solomons; Beatrice Glenavy's paintings of the 1930s, such as *The Intruder* (1933, private collection), have, however, strong elements of fantasy and shared characteristics with the dream state of surrealism. During the war years Cubist-derived work was represented by the involvement of Doreen Vanston with the White Stag Group, while in 1943 the foundation of the Irish Exhibition of Living Art demonstrated the full-scale participation of women in the visual arts. Founded by Sybil le Brocquy, Living Art had as initial chair-woman Mainie Jellett, succeeded by Norah MacGuinness, who carried out the difficult task of combining the necessary administrat-ive duties with her work as a painter. MacGuinness's work of the 1940s has on occasions been criticized as formulaic, relying on a fragmented pictorial space and restricted palette in the now familiar Cubist idiom. Yet, as with Sarah Purser before her, this belies her crucial role in championing the arts in Ireland over some 26 years, until 1970 when she resigned her presidency. Significantly, MacGuinness was also one of two artists – both women – selected to represent Ireland at the Venice Biennale in 1950. Nano Reid, the second painter, was of the post-war genera-tion notably the only woman whose work resembled the type of gestural painting epitomized by American Abstract Expression-ism – whose global dominance would actually be consolidated through the 1950 Biennale. Reid and MacGuinness were certainly not chosen on the basis of their gender; they did, however, represent two differing tendencies current within Irish art – the Cubist-aligned and the Expressionistic. Reid's work bore clear similarities to the position established by Jack Yeats's landscapes, over the previous decade: her own paintings, such as *A Wild Day* (1959, private collection), rely, however, upon increasingly agitated brushwork and application of colour to evoke an emotional response from the viewer.

Throughout the 1950s and 1960s, Living Art was notable for both the high degree of involvement by women and its promotion of international Modernist art; the emergence of concerns with a 'pure', self-referential art practice now began to demonstrate evidence of links with post-war American painting and sculpture rather than Cubism. Although she subsequently worked primarily in sculpture, Deborah Brown's first experiments with abstraction were in pictorial form; she often discussed her ideas with Alice Berger-Hammerschlag, whose concerns were similar. The fibreglass sculptural forms which Brown developed subsequently have frequently been perceived as cementing the position of Irish art within European Modernism, a relationship further reinforced by the work of two other European women sculptors working in Ireland. Both Gerda Fromel and Alexandra Wejchert evolved working practices involving the use of industrial materials, such as stainless steel or perspex, which proved to be highly suited to the needs of corporate patronage emerging in Ireland during the 1960s. Meanwhile the figurative sculptures of Hilary Heron, such as *Crazy Jane* (*c.*1960, Jury's Hotel, Dublin), combined formal concerns with an interest in primitivism, emphasizing the individual's response to nature, which had also characterized paintings by Camille Souter or Anne Madden. The work of Madden in particular has used the language of abstraction to address the representation of landscape as permeated by the prehistoric past.

As a means of constituting pictorial practices, Modernism has certainly been important for women artists within Ireland, yet this legacy has increasingly been perceived as problematic. The generation of students in art education during the 1970s, informed by both feminist developments in art practice in Britain and America and a growing women's movement within Ireland, increasingly began to question Modernism's perceived inability to address areas of women's experience. Many of these artists, such as Pauline Cummins, Alanna O'Kelly and Dorothy Cross, were to develop such concerns in their work of the eighties, a decade when the politics of gender finally became recognized as a crucial part of Irish art practice.

Reading

Angelsea, Martyn and Preston, John, 'A philosophical landscape: Susanna Drury and the Giant's Causeway', *Art History* 3, no. 3 (September 1980, pp. 252–73).

Arnold, Bruce, *Mairie Jellett and the Modern Movement in Ireland* (New Haven CT and London: 1991).

Campbell, Julian, *The Irish Impressionists: Irish Artists in France and Belgium, 1850–1914* (Dublin: 1984).

Day, Angelique (ed.), *Letters from Georgian Ireland: The Correspondence of May Delany 1731–68* (Belfast: 1991).

Irish Women Artists from the Eighteenth Century to the Present Day (Dublin: National Gallery of Ireland and Douglas Hyde Gallery, 1987).

Kennedy, S.B., *Irish Art and Modernism* (Belfast: 1991).

FIONA BARBER

women, position of The Irish constitution, adopted in 1937 and generally held to reflect closely the social ideas of Éamon de Valera, recognizes not the individual but *the family* as the fundamental unit of society. That the family so recognized is conceived as one on the 'traditional' model, consisting of one provider (male), one homemaker (female) and their children, is rendered explicit in article 41.2.1, where 'the State recognises that by her life in the home, woman gives ... a support without which the common good cannot be achieved'. In order to guarantee that support, the state in turn would 'endeavour to ensure that mothers shall not be obliged by economic necessity to engage in labour to the neglect of their duties in the home'.

The prescriptive and limiting nature of this definition of woman's role and possibilities was quite deliberate: de Valera explicitly rejected a suggested amendment diluting the phrase 'life within the home' to 'work for the home'. As in other key areas of the de Valera philosophy reflected in the constitution, there was a considerable gap between the ideal and the actual. For almost a full generation after the enactment of the 1937 constitution, the 'economic necessity' de Valera aspired to subjugate remained a particularly pressing reality for the majority of Irish people. Male unemployment and low wages conspired to provide conditions which saw many Irish women moving into paid employment. A low marriage rate and a tendency towards late marriage were also significant factors.

For many women, however, the economic and social opportunities they sought could be found only through emigration. Throughout the mid-century period, Ireland tended to have a much higher ratio of female to male emigration than comparable societies on the European mainland. This haemorrhage of chiefly young Irish women provoked a moral panic among some commentators, concerned at the alleged spiritual dangers to which the emigrants would be exposed in the more culturally and religiously diverse – and less policed – environments of Britain and America. Women were strongly urged to be content with their lot and warned that their aspirations for a more fulfilled and perhaps more exciting life abroad were illusory celluloid dreams. A legal ban being found to be impractical, however, female emigration continued at a high level, and while for many women the improvement in their economic condition abroad must have been relatively modest, for others, particularly those working in the fields of education or nursing, emigration not only brought financial rewards but significantly enhanced personal independence and status.

If Irish women were felt by many in authority to be particularly at risk abroad, they were not considered safe at home either. The report of the Committee on the Criminal Law Amendment Acts (1880–5) and on Juvenile Prostitution found that the number of births outside marriage had been increasing 'at an unprecedented rate' in the latter half of the 1920s. The Garda Commissioner also reported a very significant increase in sexual crimes against young girls, only a small minority of which were actually prosecuted. Police sources estimated the number of under-age (between 16 and 21) prostitutes operating in Dublin in the late 1920s to be about 100. All concerned agreed that this disquieting information, so much at odds with Catholic Ireland's vision of itself, would be best kept from the public.

Modernity – in the shape of motor cars, mass public entertainment and new fashions in music, particularly jazz – was seen as a severe threat to the morals of Irish people, and in particular Irish women, who were considered to be entirely passive sexually, somewhat weak-minded and more than a little innocent. Bishops and priests were much concerned at 'the misuse of... motor cars for luring girls' at country dances. One advisory committee of bishops went so far as to suggest to the authorities that young girls should be afforded admittance to such places of entertainment only if accompanied by their parents.

Young women who found themselves pregnant were often faced with a choice between emigration and entering the 'refuge' of a convent, where in some cases they would remain as virtual slaves (known as 'magdalens') for the rest of their lives, deprived of their babies, who were put up for adoption, and permanently disowned by their families. This unsavoury example of Ireland's methods of treating its social problems in the middle decades of the century received a public airing only in the 1990s.

The view of the fundamental importance of the family enshrined in the 1937 constitution necessarily involved also attributing a central place to the founding act of the family, marriage. The state, therefore, pledged itself 'to guard with special care the institution of marriage, on which the family is founded, and to protect it against attack'. Specifically, no law could be enacted providing for the grant of a dissolution of marriage. This ban on civil divorce, applying to Protestants and other minority faiths as to Catholics, was to persist in Ireland for 58 years.

The conservative social views of de Valera and Fianna Fáil – indeed of almost all sectors of official political opinion – were not entirely unopposed. Feminism had been a significant strand in the struggle for national independence in the first 20 years of the twentieth century. Distinguished figures such as Constance Markievicz (1868–1927), Helena Molony (1884–1967), Maud Gonne (1866–1953) and Hanna Sheehy-Skeffington (1877–1946) operated through a variety of organizations, such as Inghinidhe na hÉireann (Daughters of Ireland), Cumann na mBan (the Society of Women) and the Irish Women's Franchise League, usually in alliance with the more radical wing of the nationalist movement. Markievicz (née Gore-Booth) was the first woman to be elected to the House of Commons – though she did not take her seat – and was to become minister for labour in the first Dáil.

The ideological radicalism of many of the pre-1920 republicans did not, however, long survive the achievement of independence. Indeed the positions held by some self-declared feminists could be surprising. 'We all believe that woman's place is in the home provided she has a home', said Helena Molony, a former secretary of the Irish Women Workers' Union and president of the Irish Trades Union Congress. The provisions of article 41 of the constitution were strongly opposed by the National University Women Graduates' Association. For their pains they were sneered at in the Fianna Fáil newspaper, the *Irish Press*, as 'learned ladies' deficient in patriotism and national spirit. The constitutional ban on divorce was not seen as particularly a 'women's issue'. Such opposition to it

as was voiced came largely from those concerned that the 7 per cent of the population which was not Catholic and which did not necessarily share the Catholic church's views on divorce would be diminished in its civil rights.

Individual feminist voices persisted in Ireland throughout the middle years of the century, but they were on the whole isolated and found little popular echo in a state where the majority were concerned with economic subsistence and many of the more adventurous had emigrated. The 'second wave' of feminism, which emerged in the 1970s, shared areas of concern and action with its sister movements in America and Europe – the right to work and rights at work, violence against women, media representation of women's role and exploitation of women's bodies. Given the distance that remained to be travelled, Irish feminists were also even more concerned than their counterparts in more liberal societies with issues relating to the control of fertility.

Section 17 of the Criminal Law Amendment Act of 1935 had prohibited the importation and sale of contraceptive devices. For those who were determined enough – and had the means – such devices remained available in Northern Ireland and, to a limited extent, on the black market, but the ban was nevertheless effective, and the vast majority of Irish couples were effectively denied control of fertility by any means other than celibacy or the notoriously unreliable but church-sanctioned 'rhythm method'.

Reform of contraception legislation was eventually achieved in the 1970s by an increasingly bold campaign of public defiance of the law, and through a key constitutional case which forced the legislature to act. Mrs Mary McGee was a mother of four children who had suffered serious complications in each of her pregnancies, to the extent that her doctor warned that another could threaten her life. In alliance with the Irish Family Planning Association, McGee took an action against the Irish Customs, who had seized spermicidal jelly she imported from Britain. McGee's action was upheld on appeal to the Supreme Court in 1973.

In the following year, the Dáil sought to give legislative effect to the court decision but the Bill was defeated, the taoiseach, Liam Cosgrave, voting against his own government's proposals. Legalization of a kind eventually came in 1977 when Health Minister Charles Haughey successfully introduced a Bill making contraceptives available for '*bona fide* family planning purposes' – that is, for married couples. In effect, contraceptives had already become fairly widely available through a network of family planning clinics in urban centres, as groups of liberals and feminists gained the confidence to defy the law. Haughey's description of his compromise solution – 'an Irish solution to an Irish problem' – was widely interpreted as a sardonic acknowledgement of a prevailing hypocrisy in the country on questions of sexual morality.

A similar disjunction between the actual and the officially allowable was seen on the question of abortion. In 1983 an anti-abortion pressure group, the Pro-Life Amendment Campaign, succeeded in having a referendum held on the insertion of an amendment into the constitution specifically upholding 'the right to life of the unborn'. There had never been legal provision for abortion in Ireland and the campaign for such provision enjoyed only minority support. Nevertheless, anti-abortion groups, fearing the possibility of a repeat of the McGee action on the abortion front, decided on a pre-emptive strike. They were spectacularly successful, the amendment being carried after a bitter campaign by a margin of two to one. Meanwhile, throughout the 1980s, between 3,000 and 4,000 Irish women annually continued to travel to Britain for terminations. It was, as cynics remarked, an English solution to an Irish problem. A further referendum in 1992 was required after a successful Supreme Court challenge to an attempt to prevent a pregnant 14-year-old from travelling to England for an abortion. On this occasion the electorate affirmed the right to information on abortion services available outside the state and the right to travel to avail oneself of these services.

An attempt to remove the constitutional ban on divorce in 1986 was decisively rejected after a campaign which relied heavily on exploiting women's fears of desertion and poverty – this in spite of evidence from other countries indicating that most divorce petitions were filed by women. While the backbone of the divorce campaign was provided by personnel from the feminist movement, in alliance with other liberal and left-wing elements, many women saw matters in a different light. For Alice Glenn, a colourful conservative Dáil deputy, women voting for divorce were 'like turkeys voting for Christmas'.

The divorce battle was refought in 1995, with the government on this occasion more adequately prepared than previously to deal with queries on property rights and provision for the first family. The card of fear of desertion was again played by the anti-divorce lobby, but this time with less success. The electorate voted, by the narrowest of margins, to remove the constitutional ban, clearing the way for eventual divorce legislation. Analysis of voting patterns revealed a continuing move away from conservative social values among the young and the urbanized. The sector showing the greatest shift in attitudes between 1986 and 1995 appeared to be urban working-class women. Ireland finally appeared prepared to accommodate its laws and constitution to the visible reality of a small, but increasing, rate of marriage breakdown. Nevertheless, the people's decision was immediately challenged in the courts by the anti-divorce lobby on the grounds of alleged improper use of public funds by the government to urge a 'Yes' vote.

The gradual move away from the absolute dominance of conservative social values in Irish life from the 1970s onwards was fostered by new voices in the media, many of them women. Journalists such as Mary Kenny, Nell

McCafferty and Maeve Binchy spoke to the readers of the *Irish Press* and *Irish Times* with a confidence and irreverence which found a ready echo among a more educated and impatient generation. RTE's Gay Byrne, through both his television and radio talk shows, shone a light on hidden corners of Irish life and subjects which had previously been considered taboo, many involving patriarchal oppression and cruelty within the family. Daytime 'talk radio' with a predominantly female listenership, most notably Marion Finucane's *Liveline* programme, continued into the 1990s to be a powerful force in validating the opinion and experience of women. And women's voices in the media have not been entirely ghettoized into 'appropriate' areas: women such as Olivia O'Leary, Geraldine Kennedy and Emily O'Reilly in fact dominate in the area of mainstream political commentary.

Much of the progress recorded in certain aspects of the struggle for women's rights in the 1970s and 1980s was, however, attributable more to Ireland's membership of the European Economic Community than to any powerful organic movement for change. This was particularly the case in the areas of access to employment and social welfare equality. The Anti-Discrimination (Pay) Act of 1974 established the right to equal pay for work of equal value. The Employment Equality Act of 1977 prohibited discrimination on grounds of sex or marital status and attempted to ensure equality of access to training and opportunities for promotion. Progress has, however, been slow in overcoming discrimination at work, because of both resistance to change and a generally unfavourable employment situation. The conditions of working-class women are particularly difficult, with the decline of those industrial sectors which traditionally provided employment outlets and a sharp deterioration in the social fabric in areas of high unemployment.

On the positive side, there has been a significant increase in the number of women in higher education and the beginnings of a penetration into traditionally all-male areas of study, though what effect this will eventually have on the 'glass ceiling' effect, in the absence of significant improvement in the areas of child care and flexible working arrangements, remains to be seen. While there is still a wide disparity in wages and in labour force participation (32.7 per cent for women as against 66.3 per cent for men), the state appears more committed than ever before to positive action in favour of women. Measures have been implemented to foster the leadership role of women in deprived communities, and financial support for rape crisis centres and women's refuges is slowly increasing.

Women have played an important part in Irish cultural life in the twentieth century. As distinguished practitioners and champions of the Modernist movement in the visual arts, Evie Hone and in particular Mainie Jellet were involved in public battles with the artistic and political establishment. Notable contemporary women artists include painters Alice Maher, Kathy Prendergast, Eithne Jordan, Cecily Brennan and Gwen O'Dowd and sculptor Cathy Carman. Leading literary figures in the early and mid-century periods included the Anglo-Irish Elizabeth Bowen and short story writer Mary Lavin. Novelist Kate O'Brien fell foul of the draconian Irish censorship legislation in 1942 when her novel *Land of Spices* was banned over a single line hinting at a homosexual act.

More notorious still were the 1960s novels of Edna O'Brien, including *The Country Girls* and *Girls in their Married Bliss*, which though banned were nevertheless very widely read, circulating through clandestine copies brought in from Britain. O'Brien's novels were particularly obnoxious to the authorities, both patriarchal and clerical, promoting a view of female sexuality in which women were not potential victims to be protected from the wiles of male seducers but sexual beings in their own right – 'two Irish girls full of yearnings and desire. Wicked!', as their creator put it. Later prominent figures

Y

Yeats family Despite the mythologizing of the familial past by the poet W.B. Yeats, there was nothing so particularly distinguished about the Yeats name and the family's Irish history as to account easily for the quite extraordinary contribution made to Irish life and to world art and letters by the Yeatses in modern times. Like many a Protestant family in Ireland they must trace their origins to the seventeenth century, when a merchant, Jervis Yeats, plied a trade as a Dublin linen merchant. Commerce and ecclesiastical service in the Church of Ireland remained the family's primary focus until the birth of the poet's father John Butler Yeats in 1889, even if the family had its moments when higher destiny seemed to beckon and when more conventional forms of enoblement seemed possible. A Yeats, John (1774–1846), was a friend of Robert Emmet and in 1803 during a failed rebellion was very briefly imprisoned, only to finish his days as reactor of Drunmcliffe in County Sligo in the heart of what is now known as the Yeats country. And Jervis's grandson did marry a Butler in 1773, connecting the Yeats name to that of the great Norman family of the Ormondes, while the poet's grandfather, rector of Moira in County Down, married into a family of Armstrongs and Corbets who could claim military traditions and a relationship to the owner of the pretentiously named Sandymount Castle in Dublin.

John Butler Yeats was born in the north of Ireland in Tullyish in County Armagh, but educated on the Isle of Man, where he met the male scions of the Pollexfen family of County Sligo, whose sister he was to marry in 1863. He entered Trinity College, Dublin, in 1857 and was subsequently called to the bar. He claimed that his marital alliance with the famously taciturn, morose and Puritanical Pollexfens (a Devonshire family settled in Sligo) gave 'a tongue to the sea cliffs'. Be that as it may, the marriage was less than successful, because of both Susan Yeats's rather difficult temperament and subsequent serious illnesses (she died in 1900) and John Yeats's constitutional inability to provide for a burgeoning family. He refused to practise in the legal profession; his patrimony was less than ample and was fairly swiftly eroded. It had never really been sufficient to support the four surviving children of the marriage (two other children died in infancy) in that decent respectability which Victorian Ireland (and certainly the Pollexfen family) considered its minimum entitlement.

If, however, Yeats *père* never established for his family the economic security he might have done (necessity enforced frequent moves and several sojourns in London in hopes of better times), he did give to his children the inestimable gift of independence of mind. An outspoken sceptic and freethinker in the notably conventional world of Dublin's middle class, and a gifted conversationalist, he made no concessions to respectability and, despite many vicissitudes, allowed himself (given an undeniable dilatory quality in his nature) to become the quite remarkable portrait painter he did. As such he left to posterity the magnificent images of the writers and thinkers who, from the 1880s onwards, were to constitute a renaissance of artistic and literary life in the country.

John Yeats was elected to the Royal Hibernian Academy in 1892. In 1901 he was exhibited in Dublin along with Nathaniel Hone, coming to the attention of the New York lawyer and patron John Quinn. And it is from the years between this and his departure to settle in New York in 1909 that many of his most memorable portraits derive. In the last decade of his life he was a literary journalist, occasional portrait painter and dedicated correspondent (particularly with his son W.B. Yeats). A selection of his correspondence made by the poet Ezra Pound (*Passages from the Letters of J.B. Yeats*) was published 1917. John Yeats died in 1922 and was buried in the village of Chestertown in the Andirondacks. His *Early Memoirs* was published in 1923 by the Cuala press.

Reference to the Cuala Press is a reminder that it was not only the male progeny of John Yeats and Susan Pollexfen who possessed unusual gifts and who made signal contributions to contemporary arts. Both Susan Mary Yeats ('Lily', 1866–1949) and Elizabeth Corbet Yeats ('Lollie', 1868–1940) were involved in the late Victorian Arts and Crafts movement and in the establishment in Dundrum, near Dublin, with Evelyn Gleeson of the Dun Emer Industries, to engage in embroidery, weaving and the making of tapestry as well as the hand-press printing of books and other artifacts. Lolly Yeats was in charge of the Dun Emer Press (modelled on William Morris's Kelmscott Press and on the Doves Press), in which her brother W.B. Yeats served as editor. Eleven books and a series of *broadsides* were published under the Dun Emer imprint, until the name was changed to the Cuala Press in 1908. The Cuala Press issued 66 books before it closed in 1946, many of them being works by the family's poet himself. The company, although it produced work of very high quality, was less than a commercial success and, after the marriage of W.B. Yeats to Georgina Hyde-Lees in 1917, was often beholden to her good offices as literary diplomat and dependent on her sound financial sense. She took over the management of the industries and the press after Lolly's death in 1940. The Cuala Press was revived in 1969/70 by W.B. Yeats's son and daughter Michael and Anne Yeats, along with the poet Thomas Kinsella and the publisher/printer Liam Miller.

The Dun Emer and Cuala presses also issued various occasional publications, such as greeting cards, calendars, etc. Among the most popular of these were the hand-coloured prints that brought the work of Jack Yeats, brother of Lily, Lollie and William, to popular attention (though he himself deprecated the fact that the prints were often taken for originals). These were issued from 1904 onwards, in the period when Jack Yeats was committed as an artist to an illustrative record of the Irish world of pedlars, fishermen, tinkers, circus performers, sportsmen, jockeys and tramps that had been so much a part of his Sligo childhood experience.

Jack Yeats was born in London in 1871, but from 1879 to 1887 he lived with the Pollexfen grandparents in County Sligo. It was in Sligo that he acquired that love of Irish landscape and people that was to make him perhaps the first truly national painter, whose subject remained Ireland throughout a long and enormously productive life. Yeats studied art at a number of London art schools, and in the 1890s and the early years of the twentieth century he made a living as a book and magazine illustrator. He continued until 1941 to contribute to the humorous magazine *Punch* under the name of W. Bird. In 1894 he married an independently wealthy woman, Mary Cottenham White, and the couple initially settled in Devon. In 1910 they moved to Greystones, County Wicklow, and in 1917 they settled in Dublin, where they would remain for the rest of their lives. By the time of their move of Ireland, Jack Yeats was already deemed one of the most Irish of contemporary artists. His work indeed was reckoned in several respects the visual equivalent of the poetry and drama of the Irish literary revival, sharing its rural preoccupations, its romanticism and its relish for the wild and untamed in Irish reality. Jack Yeats illustrated John Synge's prose account of his Aran visits and designed the costumes and the set for Synge's *The Playboy of the Western World* (1907).

It was after he had settled in Ireland, where he was elected to the Royal Hibernian Academy in 1916, that Jack Yeats was to begin his exploration of oil paint as a medium, in which, in the next 45 or so years, he was to produce the numerous masterpieces on which his international reputation now depends. He developed a highly individual style of romantic Expressionism, which never lost touch with the artist's roots in and commitment to the landscape and people of his homeland. He was honoured in 1942 by a retrospective exhibition in the National Gallery in London in 1942, a loan exhibition at the Tate in the same city in 1948, and an American retrospective in several cities in 1951.

Jack Yeats was deeply affected by the Easter Rising of 1916 and remained a resolute Republican throughout his life. He was unquestionably a Yeats and a Pollexfen in the individualism and integrity of his art and in his markedly self-possessed social expression. Where his brother had begun adult life as a member of the Irish Republican Brotherhood, whose dialectical public development would encompass a senatorship in the Free State Parliament and flirtation in the 1930s

with the anti-democratic Blueshirt movement, Jack Yeats quietly remained true to a vision of life which, although intensely private in its imagery, seems grounded in a democratic humanism of feeling. He was indisputably his own man, whether before a canvas or publishing the whimsical novels and writing the three strange plays that the Abbey staged in the late thirties and forties, even as he must have seemed to his contemporaries to be overshadowed by his brother, the ostentatiously self-dramatizing Nobel laureate for literature (1923).

The poet in this family of painters and craftswomen was born in Sandymount, Dublin, in 1865, but spent much of his childhood in Sligo, though less happily than brother Jack. Intensely shy as a young man, while he was at art school in Dublin in the 1880s William Butler Yeats encountered the old Fenian John O'Leary and the young men with whom he shared his developing interest in magic and hermeticism. Both nationalism and the occult gave force to his protean, complex, constantly developing personality, empowering the young man, who as the elder son and first-born felt especially the inhibiting influence of a dominant father. These preoccupations became the basis of much of his writing for the stage as well as the page. Like his brother, W.B. Yeats took Ireland for his subject, but unlike his brother he contrived, though few of his contemporaries remarked on the fact, to spend protracted periods of his life abroad. In the eighties and nineties he was in London, where he was associated with the *fin de siècle* poets of the Cheshire Cheese. In his middle years he was often in Oxford and made tours of the United States to help raise funds for the Abbey Theatre, which grew out of the Irish Literary Theatre founded by W.B. Yeats, Lady Gregory, Edward Martyn and George Moore in 1899. And in old age he resided, in failing health, in the south of France, where he died in January 1939.

In 1891, W.B. Yeats met Maud Gonne in Dublin. She was a famous beauty and revolutionary nationalist. The poet's love was unrequited but was to be the basis of many of his most charged love poems. In 1903, to Yeats's chagrin she married Major John MacBride, the veteran of the Boer War who was to be executed by the British in 1916 for his part in the Rising in Dublin of that year. Yeats himself was to remain single until 1917, when he married an English woman, Georgina Hyde-Lees; but not until he had pressed his suit yet again with Maud and then with her daughter Iseult.

The power and originality of W.B. Yeats's early poetry depended on the exploitation of Celtic mythology and saga material, which the poet endowed with a profound sense of mystical implication and heroic national significance. Indeed, he made Cuchulain the hero of the *Tainan*, an image of Irish possibility. In mid-career W.B. Yeats as poet renewed his art by making it much more attentive to current Irish experience and history, and from the publication of his volume *Responsibilities* in 1914 to his death he published many resonant public poems which dramatize the poet's angry, bitter, fearful and exalted responses to an era which saw revolution, imperial defeat and civil war. More and more attracted to a version of radical conservative authoritarianism (like a number of the great Modernist writers with whom his name is associated) than to Republican politics, W.B. Yeats became in the second half of his career a defendant of a mythologized Anglo-Irish past and a celebrant of Big House courtesies, finding Lady Gregory's home, Coole Park in County Galway, an epitome of an imagined tradition. Yeats himself purchased Thoor, Ballylee, a Norman keep near Lady Gregory's house and estate, which he renovated as a private dwelling in which he and his wife lived for some brief periods. He considered the tower his symbol, associating it with his lonely, proud mind and the highly individual quality of his persistent broodings on occult learning, magic and spiritual potentialities (in 1928 his finest single volume of verse was published under the title *The Tower and*

Other Poems). In 1926 *A Vision* outlined an esoteric system culled from his idiosyncratic reading and ostensibly from spirit messages communicated by his wife's automatic writing.

W.B. Yeats, like his brother, remained artistically vital until his death (his *Last Poems* were published posthumously), but where his brother's work remained optimistic to the end in its fundamental sense of life, W.B. Yeats's late poetry is haunted by a tragic sense, an almost Swiftian horror at ageing and decrepitude, and a deep antipathy for the modern, materialistic, democratic world. There is indeed something awesome in the spectacle of the contrast between the two brothers at the last: the one hoping in his seventies for a destructive war out of which a new rule of kin might emerge, the other at the age of 84 painting in *My Beautiful, My Beautiful* (1953) an image of lyrical joy, in which a man with a horse expresses humankind's indestructible love of living.

The Yeats name is now universally renowned. Several living family members in Ireland also keep it before the public eye. W.B. Yeats's son Michael has served in the Irish senate and remains influential in public life. His daughter is a painter of distinction. Michael's wife Gráinne is a noted harpist and interpreter of Irish traditional music. A granddaughter of the poet, Síle Yeats, is an RTÉ radio producer. But in Sligo, that seedbed of genius, no Yeats or indeed Pollexfen remains, giving special poignancy to Samuel Beckett's famous words about the painter Jack Yeats, which might serve as a kind of motto and general epigraph for this astonishing family: 'The artist who stakes his being is from nowhere, has no kith.' They 'brought light, as only the great dare to bring light, to the issueless predicament of existence'.

TERENCE BROWN

Yelverton, Barry (1736–1805) Politician. Born near Cork. Educated at Trinity College, Dublin, Yelverton pursued high legal office both directly and by way of the Irish Parliament. He was a prominent figure in the Patriot ranks, his eloquence compensating for mediocre legal intellect. His role in the securing of legislative independence in 1782 has been greatly understated. A supporter of government from 1783, he became chief baron of the exchequer, and a viscount in 1800.

GERARD O'BRIEN

Young Ireland On 15 October 1842 the first issue of a new weekly newspaper called the *Nation* was published. Its guiding spirits were a group of young journalists and intellectuals, the principals being Thomas Davis, Charles Gavan Duffy and John Blake Dillon. Later called the Young Irelanders by Daniel O'Connell, their project was, in essence, the definition of an inclusivist version of Irish identity and the propagation of an ideology of cultural nationalism based on that definition. Initially fully supportive of O'Connell's Repeal movement, from 1843 onwards the Young Irelanders found themselves increasingly at odds with O'Connell on issues of political style and substance.

The inevitable break finally came in 1846 on the abstract issue of whether or not violence could be justified in pursuit of political objectives, O'Connell taking the pacifist position. New members and the Famine crisis combined to produce new strains of social radicalism in the Young Ireland movement (notably James Fintan Lalor and John Mitchel), and finally provoked the remnants of the movement into a military gesture of rebellion in 1848. The legacy of the writings and of the failed rebellion exerted significant influence on later generations of Irish nationalists – cultural as well as political.

Reading

Boyce, D. George, *Nationalism in Ireland* (Dublin: 1982).

Davis, R., *The Young Ireland Movement* (Dublin: 1987).

Hutchinson, John, *The Dynamics of Cultural Nationalism* (London: Allen and Unwin, 1987).

M.A.G. Ó TUATHAIGH

Young's *Tour* (1780) Arthur Young (1741–1820), English agricultural writer and traveller, visited Ireland on two occasions. The first was between June and October 1776 and the second from September to October 1777. After the 1777 tour he was appointed as resident agent on the Kingsborough estate at Mitchelstown, County Cork. He returned to England in 1778. The result of his experiences were published by subscription in London and entitled *A Tour in Ireland with General Observations on the Present State of that Kingdom*. The *Tour* is in two parts, the first being a record of Young's travels and the second a more analytical account of the Irish economy and society, underpinned by statistical data gathered by Young on his tour. It is these data which are the most important part of Young's work. His method was to visit the main landed families. He took pains to report average rather than advanced farming methods, but he did take a special interest in specific schemes for agricultural improvement. In addition to specific projects he also tried to describe the regional context of such schemes.

Reading

Young, Arthur, *A Tour in Ireland, 1776–9*, ed. A.W. Hutton (London: George Bell, 1892; repr. Shannon: Irish University Press, 1970).

RAYMOND GILLESPIE

Z

'Zozimus' Michael, Moran (1794–1846) Balladeer. Born Faddle Alley, in Dublin's Liberties; died 3 April. Moran was blinded by illness when two weeks old. He was more of a reciter than a singer, and became known as 'Zozimus' from his recitation of the history of St Mary of Egypt, who was found in the desert by the Blessed Zozimus. Many of his ballads, such as 'St Patrick was a Gentleman' and 'The Finding of Moses', have survived to this day. He was buried in Glasnevin cemetery, where a monument to him was unveiled on 6 April 1988.

HENRY BOYLAN

Appendix

(2001)

asylum seekers and refugees The family of the fictional Leopold Bloom would never have been allowed to enter Ireland if the Irish Department of Justice had any say in the matter. In the 1930s Ireland refused to accept Jewish refugees, and after World War II the Department of Justice refused entry to 100 child survivors of the concentration camps, describing Jews as a 'potential irritant in the body politic'. (A small number of children were later accepted on a strictly short-term basis on condition that they were financially supported by the Jewish community.) In 1956 over 500 Hungarians were accepted but, arising from their experiences, the majority left for Canada as soon as they could.

There are two categories of refugee: (1) *programme refugees* comprise a group of people deemed by the government as being in special need of protection and they enjoy the same rights as Irish nationals; and (2) *convention refugees* are judged case-by-case in line with the 1951 Geneva Convention Relating to the Status of Refugees and, when granted refugee status, enjoy the same rights as Irish nationals. In the 1970s, groups of programme refugees arrived from Chile and Vietnam. Few Chileans remain and a small Vietnamese community survives. In the 1980s, 26 Iranian Baha'is were admitted to the country and in the 1990s the break-up of Yugoslavia resulted in the arrival of larger groups of Bosnians and Kosovo Albanians.

In Europe as a whole the number of asylum seekers (people applying for refugee status) reached almost 700,000 in 1992 (although only 39 applied in Ireland). The response was to limit access as much as possible. The European Union adopted the 'first country application' policy (the Dublin Convention) which allows a person to apply for asylum only in the first EU member state they arrive in. By 1998 the number of asylum seekers in Europe had dropped by more than half the 1992 figure. Other measures were taken which in 1997 resulted in only 11 per cent of applicants in Europe being recognized as refugees under the 1951 Convention.

In contrast, during the years following 1992 there was a rapid rise in asylum applications in Ireland. There were 424 in 1995, 3,833 in 1997, 4,626 in 1998, 7,724 in 1999, and 10,938 in 2000. But the Department of Justice's processing system failed to keep pace with the growing numbers. Consequently in November 2000 the number of asylum seekers awaiting decisions on their applications stood at 11,437. Since 1991 members of more than 100 nationalities have sought refuge in Ireland and in recent years Nigeria and

Romania have been the main countries of origin. The Irish government has concluded agreements with both countries for the deportation of unsuccessful asylum seekers.

It was not until 1996 that the out-dated Aliens Act 1935 was superseded by the Refugee Act. The Act was welcomed as 'one of the most progressive models of refugee legislation' in Europe. Despite some flaws, it marked a watershed in Irish asylum policy. It incorporated key international provisions of refugee protection into Irish law and set out a detailed statutory framework and appeals process.

However, the spirit of the Act was undermined by an action of the Rainbow Government that had introduced it. This was the abolition of the Common Travel Area between Ireland and the United Kingdom by way of an Aliens Amendment Order. Under the Order immigration officers were granted powers to refuse entry to any persons arriving from Britain or Northern Ireland. The Fianna Fáil /Progressive Democrat coalition further undermined the Refugee Act by including it as an amendment to the Immigration Act 1999 which is mainly concerned with deportations. The main amendment to the Immigration Act accepted by the government gave asylum seekers waiting for more than twelve months on a determination of their case the right to work.

On the streets, asylum seekers are subjected to racism which often takes the form of violent physical attacks. Up to April 2000, asylum seekers could avail of social welfare payments and were given rent allowances. Since then the State pays their accommodation and living expenses and gives them an allowance of £15 per week (£7.50 for children). A policy of dispersal has been implemented and many asylum seekers have been moved from Dublin to country towns and villages where they have not always been made welcome. In one location a hotel which was selected to accommodate asylum seekers was burned down.

Racism has been fuelled by politicians seeking to exploit fear and ignorance for electoral gain. Newspapers have published misleading and sensational reports with such headlines as: 'Services face overload as refugee flood continues' (*Sunday Business Post*, 18 May 1997); 'Floodgates open as new army of poor swamp the country' (*Sunday World*, 25 May 1997); 'Gardaí move on dole fraud by daytrip refugees' (*Irish Independent*, 7 June 1997); 'Refugees rob names from children's graves' (*Sunday Times, Irish Edition*, 13 August 2000).

Ireland will in time come to wholeheartedly welcome asylum seekers and the contribution refugees can make to Irish society but this will require political leadership, media balance and the development of positive attitudes to multiculturalism. Political parties should not tolerate the slightest hint of racism from elected representatives and the media should take note of the 1989 Prohibition of Incitement to Hatred Act.

PATRICK GILLAN

Bacon (Francis) Studio 7 Reece Mews, Kensington, London, housed the home and studio of Irish-born painter Francis Bacon (1909–92) for the last 30 years of his life. On his death, the premises passed into the ownership of John Edwards, Bacon's companion of 16 years and heir to his English estate. At the time Edwards stated his intention of preserving the house and studio exactly as it was. 'I am going to live in it until I die and then donate it to the nation,' he said. 'When I pop off, then it's up to them what they to do with it.' It was not practical to preserve the studio *in situ* as a public space and it was offered to several major British galleries, but there were no takers. Edwards then decided to donate the studio to the Hugh Lane Municipal Gallery of Modern Art in Dublin. The gallery appointed a team of archaeologists and conservators to catalogue and remove the entire studio contents. The reconstructed studio features the original walls, floor, ceiling and shelves. The cluttered studio contents comprise a vast archive of material that highlights the eclectic nature of Bacon's influences and his unorthodox painting techniques. The chaotic state of the studio was a source of inspiration to Bacon. 'I feel at home here in the chaos,' he once said, 'because chaos suggests images to me.' The studio is augmented by an audio-visual room, an exhibition gallery featuring unfinished paintings, and a micro gallery that provides access to the most important items in the archive.

PATRICK GILLAN

Belfast (Good Friday) Agreement The parties to the agreement, concluded on 10 April 1998, were the British and Irish governments and the main political parties in Northern Ireland including Sinn Féin, but excluding the DUP and UKUP. It provided for a 108-member legislative Assembly with six members elected by PR from each of Northern Ireland's 18 constituencies. Headed by an Executive Committee, the Assembly was charged with establishing a North-South Ministerial Council to oversee co-operation in a number of areas. It was agreed that votes in the Assembly on matters of importance would require either a majority of both nationalists and unionists voting in favour or, alternatively, a weighted majority of 60 per cent, with at least 40 per cent of both nationalists and unionists present voting in favour. The Irish government undertook to recommend amendments to articles 2 and 3 of the Constitution of Ireland effectively to drop the territorial claim on Northern Ireland while retaining the aspiration to unity. The British government agreed to replace the Government of Ireland Act. The agreement provided for the establishment of a British–Irish Council consisting of representatives of the British and Irish governments, devolved institutions in Northern Ireland, Scotland and Wales, the Isle of Man and the Channel Islands. Provision was made for the early release of prisoners convicted of terrorist offences, the last prisoners to be released within two years. The participants agreed to use their influence to achieve the decommissioning of all paramilitary weapons within two years of the agreement being endorsed by referendums in Northern Ireland and the Republic. Provision was also made for the reform of policing in Northern Ireland, demilitarization and an end to emergency powers. The exact meaning of paragraph 25, which states that 'those who hold office should use only democratic, non-violent means, and those who do not should be excluded or removed from office...' was to become a bone of contention between republicans and unionists. The agreement was overwhelmingly endorsed in referendums held simultaneously in Northern Ireland and the Republic (where articles 2 and 3 were also amended) in May. However, an exit poll in Northern Ireland found that while 96 per cent of Catholics supported the agreement only 55 per cent of Protestants did so. The IRA expressed dissatisfaction with the agreement, while dissident republicans and unionists condemned it.

PATRICK GILLAN

Celtic Tiger The First Programme for Economic Expansion (1958) marked a sea change in Irish economic policy, effectively ending protectionism, encouraging significant inflows of foreign capital and boosting industrial growth among other things. Most importantly it laid the ground for the more enlightened economic-policy making that contributed to the Celtic Tiger. There were serious setbacks in the 1970s and also in the 1980s when remedial action was taken by the Fine Gael/Labour coalition government. Cuts in public expenditure were accompanied by increased taxation resulting in a substantial reduction in the exchequer borrowing requirement; inflation was reduced from 17 per cent to four per cent. But real personal income after tax fell by 12 per cent in the years 1980–6 and emigration returned, averaging 25,000 annually in the 1980s. Public expenditure cuts continued under Fianna Fáil which enjoyed the support of Fine Gael in line with the Tallaght Strategy espoused by party leader Alan Dukes. Later cuts consisted of reductions in the rate of increase of borrowing rather than cuts in spending. Positive results were achieved and current spending had broken even by 1994 with surpluses recorded in 1996 and 1997. The massive national debt, while still rising in nominal terms, fell from its 1987 peak to the mid-60 per cent of GDP in late 1997, close to one of the key Maastricht criteria.

Social partnership was another major factor in turning the economy around. The social partners through the National Economic and Social Council (NESC) agreed on a strategy to escape from the damaging combination of stagnation, rising taxes and growing debt. The NESC's 1986 *Strategy Report* formed the basis for the Programme for National Recovery (PNR) to run from 1987 to 1990. This was the first of a series of agreements that formed the economic and social consensus which was to underpin growth and prosperity. Initially there was some scepticism among trade unionists in relation to the PNR but, as social partnership began to bear fruit, support for it grew. Moderate pay increases went hand-in-hand with tax reductions which boosted take home pay. The agreements, each lasting three years, set wage increases and devised a common approach to a wide range of issues from tax reform and tackling social exclusion to exchange-rate policy and the Maastricht criteria. The PNR was followed by the Programme for Economic and Social Progress (1991–3) and the Programme for Competitiveness and Work (1994–7). The trade unions, business and farming organizations were joined by the community and voluntary sector together with unemployed and women's groups in negotiating agreements with the government. Partnership 2000 was agreed in 1997 and broke new ground in the culture of work by providing for partnership at enterprise level. It was followed by the Programme for Prosperity and Fairness which guaranteed wage increases of 15.7 per cent over three years. Rising inflation in the latter half of 2000 caused a revision of the programme which resulted in a 2 per cent additional pay increase from April 2001 and a one per cent lump sum payment in 2002. The main benefits of partnership have been steady, if modest, wage increases and greater industrial peace. The extension of partnership to enterprises has helped to achieve quality and competitive output.

The improved industrial relations climate increased competitiveness and made it easier to attract investment from abroad. Foreign direct investment (FDI) has played a major role in the Republic's economic success. The Industrial Development Authority (IDA) proved adept at attracting FDI by offering high grants, tax breaks, a skilled workforce and other incentives. The IDA targeted particular industries – chemicals, electronics, pharmaceuticals and software – that make up the expanding industrial sectors crucial to a modern developing economy.

EU membership made it attractive for multinational corporations, particularly US companies, to locate in Ireland. Investment in education in the 1960s was supplemented by education and training funds channelled through the EU structural and cohesion funds, making the Irish workforce one of the best educated in Europe. Cohesion funds were designed to enable poor and peripheral regions to keep pace with wealthy regions following the establishment of the Single Market. Substantial funds were invested in infrastructure as well as in human capital, especially in training. Public policy was adapted to make the maximum use of the funds which had an important effect in re-introducing developmental thinking and procedures in the public service.

Ireland's large-scale farmers have benefited greatly from the Common Agricultural Policy as has agribusiness. Employment in agriculture has dropped steadily and those who remain on the land enjoy highly subsidized incomes far in excess of what they could command in the free market. While this yields a net gain to the economy, it is at the expense of taxpayers and consumers. The Single

Market has had a much more positive effect. It helped to make the Republic an attractive location for multinational corporations; it provided new market opportunities for indigenous companies; it created the environment for a major expansion of the services sector; the free movement of capital has made it easier for Irish companies to access capital abroad; it created the incentive for Irish firms to become more competitive; greater EC monitoring and control of state aid has prompted improved performance by commercial state companies; and it requires public utilities to provide a better service.

The revolution in communications is another factor in economic success. Other contributory factors include fiscal reform, a restructured economy (a younger higher-skilled workforce, an expanded services sector and increased output from fewer farmers) and high industrial productivity. The fall in the dependency ratio has also played its part. While the population and labour force have increased, the birth rate has dropped and female participation in the labour force has risen substantially. The dependency ratio, having reached very high levels in the 1980s, is now close to the EU average and is set to become the most favourable in the EU.

Ireland's economic indicators show GDP per capita of £12,907, an annual growth rate of 8 per cent, and an unemployment rate of 3.7 per cent (down from 17 per cent in the mid-1980s). But inflation rose in 2000, reaching almost 7 per cent in October, and now stands at 5.5 per cent. Brussels has called for action to reduce it.

The signs of prosperity are evident throughout the country. New car sales have quadrupled and top-of-the-range cars clog the roads and city streets. Mobile phone ownership is higher than in Britain. House prices have risen by 70 per cent in seven years and modest terraced cottages in parts of Dublin are priced from £200,000 upwards. Gourmet food halls, top-class restaurants and well-stocked wine shops are now commonplace. Authentic Irish pubs are fast becoming a thing of the past and kitsch theme bars abound. Lap-dancing clubs are the latest addition to Dublin's nightlife. Jobs are plentiful and technology companies regularly advertise posts carrying salaries of £100,00. It is predicted that 350,000 new jobs will be created in the coming years with immigrants filling 200,000 of these. The government has established the Jobs Ireland Unit to recruit foreign workers.

Notwithstanding the Celtic Tiger, the gap between the poor and better off is widening. More than 20 per cent of the population live below the poverty line. Among EU member states average Irish wages are the third lowest and only Portugal has a higher proportion of its population (24 per cent) living on a low income. According to a report published by the National Economic and Social Forum published in 2000, Ireland 'is a deeply unequal country, marked by one of the most unequal distributions of income in Europe, massive class inequalities in educational participation and entrenched intolerance towards minorities such as Travellers'. Figures show that while Ireland's GNP and GDP per capita are among the highest in Europe, and indeed the world, the health service, schools and roads are among the worst. And the Economic and Social Research Institute (ESRI) in 2000 pointed out that social spending has fallen as a proportion of national income. While acknowledging that the economic boom has brought increased opportunities and improved living standards, the ESRI stated that 'meritocracy remains an aspiration'.

PATRICK GILLAN

de Paor, Liam (1926–98) Archaeologist and historian. Born Dublin. He was educated by the Christian Brothers at Choláiste Mhuire after which he enrolled at University College, Dublin, to study architecture. He found the experience 'absolutely terrible' and after two years left to join the Office of Public Works. His work in conservation led him to return to UCD to take a degree in archaeology. With his first wife, Máire McDermott, he collaborated on various projects and the couple spent a year in Nepal in 1964 when de Paor was appointed by UNESCO to advise the government on the conservation of national monuments. On his return to Ireland, he joined the teaching staff of UCD where he lectured in American history in addition to his more obvious specialisms. He was highly regarded by staff and students alike but was never completely at ease with UCD's 'Fine Gael atmosphere'. In the late 1960s he identified with the student radicals who launched the 'gentle revolution'. He joined the Labour Party in 1965 but resigned in the early 1970s over the issues of coalition and Northern Ireland though his allegiance to the left continued. He totally abhorred political violence and advocated Irish independence over Irish unity, a concept nationalists simply could not grasp. Consistent with this thinking, he disagreed with the Anglo-Irish Agreement of 1985. Deeply committed to Gaelic culture, he was a fluent Irish speaker and a regular and enthusiastic participant in the annual summer schools dedicated to the memory of the eighteenth-century Gaelic poet, Brian Merriman. He broadcast regularly on RTÉ and in the 1970s he wrote a highly-readable weekly column, 'Roots', for the *Irish Times* in which he examined the relationship between modern Ireland and the distant past. He retired from UCD in 1986 and spent much time in the United States. After the death of his first wife in 1994 he married Deirdre Glenn. His many publications include (with Máire de Paor) *Early Christian Ireland* (1958), *Divided Ulster* (1970), *The Peoples of Ireland: From Prehistory to Modern Times* (1993), *Saint Patrick's World* (1993), *Ireland and Early Europe* (1997) and *Landscapes with Figures* (1998). His last article, published in the journal *Times Change*, argued that the 1798 rebellion had left Ireland with a confused heritage and a legacy of division. The validity of his argument was tragically borne out when, on the day of his funeral service in Dublin, 29 people were killed in Omagh by a Real IRA bomb.

PATRICK GILLAN

Devlin, Patrick Joseph (Paddy) (1925–99) Politician and trade unionist. Born in Belfast into a working-class family, he began work at the age of 14 having completed an elementary education. A member of Na Fianna Éireann, he joined the IRA in 1940. In this capacity he gathered information about military installations which the IRA transmitted to the Nazis, something he later deeply regretted. He was interned from 1942 to 1945 and in 1948 moved to England. A trial with Coventry City FC led to the offer of a contract for the 1949–50 season but he had to return home for family reasons. Working as a milk roundsman he became involved in trade union activities. He had turned his back on the IRA and joined the Northern Ireland Labour Party. A fellow member introduced him to the works of Harold Laski, H. G. Wells and Emile Zola. Elected to Belfast City Council in 1956, he later became active in the civil rights movement and in 1969 won the Falls seat in the Stormont parliament in the teeth of conservative Catholic opposition. Following the outbreak of violence in Derry and Belfast, he addressed a street meeting in Dublin and declared that guns were needed to defend the Catholic community. This remark, made in the heat of the moment, came to haunt him. Unknown to him, forces were at work that spawned the Provisional IRA. In 1970 he joined Gerry Fitt and others to found the Social Democratic and Labour Party (SDLP). He worked hard to establish the party in Belfast, incurring the wrath of the Provisionals. Such was the level of hostility that he felt obliged to obtain a legally-held gun to protect himself and his family. Devlin was an early advocate of greater co-operation between the British and Irish governments in order to find a political solution to the escalating conflict. He served in the short-lived power-sharing executive that was brought down by the loyalist Ulster Workers' Council strike in 1974. He was elected to the Convention (1975–76) and was involved in several unsuccessful attempts to secure SDLP/Unionist co-operation. He then became Northern organizer of the Irish Transport and General Workers' Union. Disagreement with the SDLP's 'narrow nationalism' led to his explusion from the party. He lost his deposit in the 1979 European Parliament election and subsequent attempts to launch a non-sectarian party of the left proved futile. He withstood IRA pressure to support the H-Blocks hunger strikes in 1980–81 and was forced to move house after his home was besieged by republicans. As a Belfast councillor, he strongly supported the arts. He was active in saving Belfast's Linenhall Library and he championed the award of the freedom of the city to the poet John Hewitt. His degree thesis, on the joint efforts of Catholics and Protestants to fight poverty in the 1930s, formed the basis of a book, *Yes We Have No Bananas*. He wrote a newspaper column and had several plays produced. An autobiography *Straight Left* was published in 1993. He suffered from diabetes and failing eyesight forced him to abandon writing; he later became totally blind. In 1999 he was made a CBE which award he accepted as recognition of the Northern Ireland labour and trade union movement.

PATRICK GILLAN

Goulding, Cathal (1922–98) Republican. From a working-class republican family, he and his boyhood friend Brendan Behan joined Na Fianna Éireann in 1937. They both served their time as house-painters and in later life Goulding ran a small building business. He joined the IRA and in 1953 was arrested after an arms raid in England. He served an eight-year sentence in Pentonville Prison. (He spent a total of 16 years in prison.) He returned to Ireland in the dying days of the IRA's ill-fated border campaign and was quickly interned. He became chief-of-staff of a demoralized and almost defunct army, and took the first steps in reshaping the republican movement into a radical socialist organization. Arms were sold off to the Free Wales Army and he enlisted the help of Marxist intellectuals to

create a popular movement campaigning on such issues as housing, the defence of small farmers and, in Northern Ireland, civil rights. This did not please orthodox republicans (nor did the scrapping of the Rosary at republican commemorations) and tensions arose that culminated in the split of 1969–70 which resulted in the formation of the Provisional IRA. As leader of what became quaintly known as the Official IRA, and against the background of violence in Northern Ireland, he had to balance demands for military action with the need to develop a working-class political base. Military blunders such as the Aldershot bombing of 1972 (in retaliation for Bloody Sunday) led to a cease-fire that same year. The Officials, however, were drawn into intermittent violent feuds with the Provisionals and later with the Irish National Liberation Army. Politically the Officials made some electoral gains in Northern Ireland and their three members on Belfast City Council in the 1970s proved to be particularly effective. In 1981 the first Official Sinn Féin (later Workers' Party) TD was elected to Dáil Éireann, and in 1989 the party won seven Dáil seats and a seat in the European Parliament. By this time Goulding had vacated his leadership position although he remained on the WP's executive. Parliamentary aspirations did not sit easily with the republican tradition and growing differences within the WP could not be reconciled. Six of the party's TDs together with a majority of members in the Republic departed to form Democratic Left. Goulding remained committed to the revolutionary objectives that had renewed republicanism in the 1960s and stayed with the WP. However, the party's influence was greatly diminished while Democratic Left, having participated in the Rainbow Coalition government (1994–97), merged with the Labour Party in 1998. In conventional terms, Goulding's attempt to refashion republicanism could be judged to have failed. Yet one significant achievement cannot be denied. He steered a substantial number of republicans away from extreme nationalism that, had it remained unchecked, would surely have precipitated widespread sectarian slaughter in Northern Ireland.

PATRICK GILLAN

Guerin, Veronica (1958–96) Journalist. Born Dublin. On obtaining a Leaving Certificate she went to work for the Irish League of Credit Unions, and later took up employment in her father's accountancy practice. A one-time member of Ógra Fianna Fáil (the party's youth section) and a friend of taoiseach Charles Haughey's family, she was appointed to the governing body of the National Institute of Higher Education (now Dublin City University) in 1982. The following year she was appointed as an assistant to the Fianna Fáil delegation to the New Ireland Forum. Her first indirect involvement in journalism occured when she leaked a copy of the draft Forum report to the *Sunday Tribune*. She then worked in public relations, taking a year out to obtain a diploma in marketing management. In 1990 she turned to journalism, first with the *Sunday Business Post*, then with the *Sunday Tribune*, and finally, in 1994, with the *Sunday Independent*. From the outset she specialized in investigative journalism and was responsible for a number of exclusive reports concerning business and financial scandals. Some of her methods, however, were questionable and it appeared to colleagues that she would do anything for a story. At the *Sunday Independent* she concentrated on crime reporting and cultivated criminals and gardaí alike in pursuit of stories, often playing one criminal off against another. Her sometimes melodramatic reports won her celebrity status and she was featured prominently in the *Sunday Independent's* promotional campaigns. She became increasingly reckless in her dealings with criminals, calling to their homes and inviting them to hers. She was, according to a close acquaintance, 'besotted with crime'. Not all criminals welcomed her attentions. In October 1994 shots were fired into her house which she shared with her husband and young son. In January 1995 she was shot in the leg in the hallway of her home. She accepted garda protection for a time but it was removed at her request. Ignoring the advice of friends, she continued her investigation of Dublin's gangland. This led in September 1995 to an encounter with a career criminal, John Gilligan, who owned a £4 million equestrian centre on 300 acres in County Meath. Despite the elaborate security in place at the centre she managed to gain admission to the premises where it is alleged Gilligan assaulted her and threatened to rape her son. The *Sunday Independent* published a detailed report of the incident and Gilligan was later charged with assault. By mid-1996 rumours were circulating that she was to publicly name four criminals involved in the drugs trade. Her main criminal informant applied for a High Court injunction to prevent publication of an article concerning him. On 26 June 1996 Veronica Guerin was driving towards Dublin city centre when she was stopped at traffic lights at Clondalkin on the Naas Road. A motor cycle pulled up beside her car and the pillion passenger drew a gun and shot her dead. She was the first journalist to be murdered in the history of the Irish state. Two men were subsequently convicted of the murder but in March 2001 the self-styled 'chief suspect' John Gilligan was found not guilty by the Special Criminal Court although he was sentenced to 28 years' imprisonment for drugs-trafficking offences.

PATRICK GILLAN

Kemmy, James (Jim) (1936–97) Politician. Born in Garryowen, Limerick, he left school at 15 to serve his time as a stonemason, continuing a family tradition dating from the early nineteenth century. On the death of his father two years later, he became the family breadwinner on wages of 10d (about four pence) an hour. On completing his apprenticeship he went to London to ply his trade. There he was introduced to trade unionism and the classics of socialist literature. Returning to Limerick in 1960, he worked on the building of the Shannon industrial estate and became a branch secretary of the

635

Brick and Stone Layers' Trade Union. He was later elected president of the Limerick Trades Council. He joined the Labour Party and served on the party's administrative council. However, endless running battles with the conservative local Labour TD Stevie Coughlan prompted Kemmy and many supporters to leave the party and set up an independent socialist organization which published the *Limerick Socialist*. He was elected to Limerick City Council in 1974 and his stand against nationalism and the H-Blocks hunger strikes brought him to national attention. Active in Limerick's family planning clinic, he frequently clashed with Bishop Jeremiah Newman over this and other issues. In 1981 he was elected to Dáil Éireann and, while he supported the formation of the Fine Gael/Labour coalition, he opposed budgetary proposals in 1982 to impose VAT on children's shoes thereby contributing to the fall of the government. In the subsequent general election he was re-elected with an increased vote. He then founded the Democratic Socialist Party (DSP), a 'post nationalist' socialist party. His opposition to the proposed 'pro-life' amendment cost him his seat in November 1982 when the full force of Catholic Limerick was pitted against him. He regained his seat in 1987 and held it until his death. In 1990 the DSP merged with the Labour Party and he was elected party chairman in 1993. By this time Labour was in government with Fianna Fáil and he was at pains to preserve Labour's independent identity, and never shied away from criticism of Fianna Fáil when he felt it was warranted. Neither was he afraid to defend controversial measures such as the tax amnesty. In 1991, as Mayor of Limerick, he donated his £16,000 salary to offset cuts in the council's allocation to local organizations. He had a passionate interest in local history and edited the quarterly *Old Limerick Journal*. He was also editor of the well-received *Limerick Anthology* (1997). He sat on the Belltable Arts Centre advisory committee and was a member of Limerick Corporation's national monuments advisory committee.

PATRICK GILLAN

Lynch, John Mary (Jack) (1917–99) Politician. Educated at North Monastery CBS, Cork, and King's Inns, Dublin, he first worked in the civil service before pursuing a legal career. He was a GAA legend, winning six all-Ireland medals for Cork between 1941 and 1946 – five for hurling and one for Gaelic football. He won a seat for Fianna Fáil in the 1948 general election and became a parliamentary secretary in 1951. He later held, in turn, the education, industry and commerce, and finance portfolios before succeeding Seán Lemass as taoiseach and Fianna Fáil leader in 1966. Initially viewed as a 'caretaker', he consolidated his position by leading Fianna Fáil to a comfortable victory in the 1969 general election during which his campaign tour of convents underlined the party's adherence to traditional Catholic values. However, the outbreak of civil disturbances in Northern Ireland caused deep divisions in the government to surface and Neil Blaney in particular advocated a more aggressive Northern policy. Violence in Derry and Belfast in August 1969 increased the pressure on Lynch who responded with a television address to the nation, declaring that the Republic would 'not stand by'. Following a meeting with prime minister Harold Wilson later that month, Lynch agreed that the border could not be removed by force and that his government's policy was to seek Irish unity by peaceful means. Not all government members agreed with Lynch. Public monies were secretly used to purchase arms for the emerging Provisional IRA. As details of the conspiracy began to circulate in British and Irish security circles, Lynch was forced to act. He sacked Blaney and his finance minister Charles Haughey. Both were later acquitted by the courts on charges of the attempted illegal importation of arms (see Arms Trial, p. 30). There followed Lynch's most difficult period as Fianna Fáil leader, but he managed to hold the party together. Pragmatism became the norm in Anglo-Irish relations and Lynch contributed to the bipartisan policy on Northern Ireland that developed in the Dáil. In 1972 he travelled to Brussels to sign the treaty of accession to the EEC. He regarded this and the treaty's subsequent ratification in a referendum as high points in his career. After four years in opposition (1973–77) he led Fianna Fáil to its greatest ever election victory. But the victory was to rebound on Lynch as many of the incoming backbenchers supported Haughey who was now minister for health. Party discipline began to break down and Lynch's leadership was openly questioned. Poor results in European and local elections followed by the loss of two seats in by-elections in Cork set the scene for his resignation in 1979. He was succeeded by Haughey. Lynch resigned from the Dáil in 1981 and took no further part in public life. Under the Haughey regime he was effectively air-brushed out of Fianna Fáil history. A stroke in 1993 incapacitated him. The former Fine Gael leader, Liam Cosgrave, described him as 'the most popular Irish politician since Daniel O'Connell'.

PATRICK GILLAN

Northern Ireland, devolved government On 1 July 1998 the Northern Ireland Assembly elected David Trimble and Seamus Mallon as First Minister and Deputy First Minister respectively. However, differences over decommissioning delayed the appointment of an Executive Committee. An attempt to appoint the Executive in July 1999 was aborted when Trimble and his UUP colleagues boycotted the Assembly. Mallon resigned as Deputy First Minister in protest. The Assembly was adjourned and a review of the workings of the Belfast Agreement with George Mitchell as facilitator was scheduled for September. As the year drew to a close there were signs that Sinn Féin and the UUP better understood each other. Total commitment to the full implementation of the Belfast Agreement was expressed by the UUP, which

also reiterated its support for the principles of 'inclusivity, equality and mutual respect'. Gerry Adams, for Sinn Féin, declared that the conflict 'must be for all of us now a thing of the past, over, done with and gone.' Sinn Féin acknowledged that decommissioning was an essential part of the peace process. The IRA softened its line on the Belfast Agreement, and indicated that it would appoint a representative to liaise with the Decommissioning body once the political institutions were established. There was a tacit understanding that the deadline for a start to decommissioning was January 2000. By a narrow margin, Trimble won the support of the Ulster Unionist Council to enter a power-sharing executive. In December 1999 the 12-person Executive was appointed, with four ministers each from the SDLP and UUP and two each from the DUP and Sinn Féin. Martin McGuinness of Sinn Féin was allocated the education portfolio. The DUP announced that its ministers would not attend Executive meetings with Sinn Féin. Following the establishment of the Executive the IRA appointed an interlocutor to the Decommissioning body; the Irish government formally changed articles 2 and 3; and the North-South and East-West bodies met for the first time. The Executive worked well but by January 2000, in the absence of progress on decommissioning, it faced collapse. In order to avert a complete breakdown of the Belfast Agreement, Secretary of State Peter Mandelson suspended the institutions. There followed the publication of the Pattern Report on policing which put further pressure on Trimble who was then confronted by a damaging leadership challenge which he overcame. The British and Irish governments took a fresh look at decommissioning out of which a formula for the inspection of IRA arms dumps by independent third parties emerged. Sinn Féin responded positively and the IRA agreed to regular inspections of arms dumps as part of a process of putting arms beyond use. Trimble, for his part, proceeded with caution and secured concessions on a range of issues in order to strengthen his hand against his UUP opponents. The concessions enabled him to secure a narrow victory at the UUC for a return to power sharing. The Executive and Assembly were restored on 27 May 2000 and Mallon was re-elected Deputy First Minister. The normal work of government resumed and Northern Ireland's first budget for 30 years was introduced in October. However, the decommissioning and policing issues continued to fester and contributed to the UUP's loss of a seat to the DUP in the South Antrim by-election in September. Trimble's opponents called a UUC meeting for November. There he wrong-footed them by announcing that he would refuse to nominate Sinn Féin ministers to attend North-South Ministerial Council meetings until there was progress on decommissioning. Trimble carried the day and the Executive survived.

PATRICK GILLAN

political scandals In the Summer of 2000 there were 20 tribunals and inquiries investigating political corruption and other matters ranging from the supply of contaminated blood supplies to haemophiliacs to child abuse in state institutions. Following decades of concealment transparency, it seemed, was the order of the day. The **Beef Tribunal** (1991–94) had provided a glimpse of things to come. Serious malpractice in the beef industry, including massive tax evasion, were found to be commonplace. Some mid-ranking functionaries were charged and convicted by the courts on matters arising, but the 'persons unknown' with whom they had conspired remained at large. Suggestions of cronyism were ruled out and, curiously, political donations amounting to thousands of pounds were deemed by Mr Justice Hamilton to be 'normal'.

Around the same time, a series of political scandals drew attention to the existence of a 'Golden Circle' linking business and politics in shady multimillion pound deals. A complex network of accountants and lawyers concealed identities and kept transactions out of sight of the taxman. The then taoiseach, Charles J. Haughey, attempted to make light

of the matter. 'Look at London and New York,' he declared. 'There are scandals there which make anything that happens here seem in the halfpenny place.' Haughey had misjudged the public mood, however, and was forced to acknowledge 'the reprehensible behaviour of a small number of individuals in the business and financial sector'.

Six years later Haughey appeared before the **McCracken Tribunal**, established in February 1997 to examine payments by the head of the Dunnes' supermarket chain, Ben Dunne, to politicians including Fine Gael TD and former minister Michael Lowry. The tribunal uncovered the existence of the Ansbacher Deposits in the Cayman Islands. These deposits were part of a massive tax evasion fraud supervised by Des Traynor, manager of Haughey's finances, on behalf of 120 of Ireland's richest business people and involving several hundred million pounds. Payments to Haughey were channelled through the deposits. Haughey at first denied receiving payments (which amounted to £1.1 million) from Dunne and finally owned up only when evidence was produced to show that he had. Mr Justice McCracken found no political impropriety but stated that

> It is quite unacceptable that a member of Dáil Éireann, and in particular a Cabinet minister and Taoiseach, should be supported in his personal lifestyle by gifts made to him personally. It is particularly unacceptable that such gifts should emanate from prominent businessmen within the State. The possibility that political or financial favours could be sought in return for such gifts, or even be given without being sought, is very high, and if such gifts are permissible, they would lead in some cases to bribery and corruption.

Haughey's evidence to the Tribunal was referred to the DPP as a result of which he was charged with criminal obstruction.

Michael Lowry, a contractor to Dunnes Stores, was found to have been 'consistently benefiting from the black economy from shortly after the time he was first elected to Dáil Éireann'. Forced to resign as Minister for Transport, Energy and Communications because of his relationship with Ben Dunne, Lowry was also found to have opened offshore accounts for tax evasion purposes. The McCracken Tribunal Report described him as operating his business at two levels, 'on one level through the company which made a small profit and duly paid its taxes, and on a second level whereby large sums of money were paid to him personally in a clandestine manner'.

In August 1999 the Dáil Public Accounts Committee (PAC) undertook the **DIRT Inquiry** into bogus non-residential bank accounts. These accounts were opened in the 1980s and 1990s by people falsely claiming to be domiciled abroad and therefore not liable for Deposit Interest Retention Tax (DIRT). In most cases false names and British or American addresses were supplied by customers whose true names and addresses were known to the banks concerned. The Revenue Commissioners were aware of the practice. In 1988 documents issued by the Revenue in relation to the tax amnesty (1988) made specific reference to taxpayers who were holding money in Irish banks 'under non-resident names and addresses'. The number of bogus accounts is as yet unknown but the available evidence suggests that it is in the tens of thousands. The DIRT Inquiry was widely praised for its efficiency. Arising from the inquiry the Revenue Commissioners undertook an audit of 37 financial institutions to establish liability for unpaid DIRT. A total of £173 million in unpaid tax, interest and penalties was recovered. But the PAC's success was somewhat tarnished in January 2000 when it was revealed the committee's vice-chairman, Fianna Fáil TD Denis Foley, had £135,000 sterling in an Ansbacher account. He resigned from the PAC and was suspended from the Dáil for a week.

In a further development in March 2001, another Fianna Fáil TD Beverly Cooper-Flynn, resigned from membership of the PAC after she lost a libel case against RTÉ in which the jury found that as a National Irish Bank employee she had advised or encouraged people to evade tax. Ms Cooper-Flynn was ordered to pay the costs of the case, estimated at £2 million.

One of the most popular theatre shows in Dublin in the Summer of 2000 was *Will We Get A Receipt? Will We F..k!*, a revue based entirely on transcripts of the tribunals.

The **Moriarty Tribunal**, established in October 1997, took up where McCracken left off, inquiring into details of payments to Haughey and the source of money in bank accounts held by Haughey and Lowry. It was revealed at the tribunal that between 1979 and 1996 Haughey had received £8.5 million from businessmen, that he drew on the Fianna Fáil leader's account (expressly intended for political purposes only) to cover personal expenses and that he made deductions from donations given to him for Fianna Fáil. Contributions towards the medical expenses of his colleague Brian Lenihan given to Haughey ended up in the party leader's account. Haughey accepted all kinds of gifts. In 1990 the businessman and tax exile, Dr Michael Smurfit, presented Haughey with a painting for the state, *The Flag* by Sir John Lavery, 'to mark Mr Haughey's taking on the presidency of the EU'. (Ireland held the EU presidency for the first half of 1990). He took a 'spur-of-the-moment' decision to give Haughey a personal gift of a Jack B. Yeats painting, *The Forge*, valued at £55,000. Smurfit felt compelled to tell Haughey that he didn't want the painting sold:

> Yes I had it the back of my mind that it would look very bad if you gave a painting like that to somebody and they cashed it in the next day. It would look like a cash gift. I wasn't into that situation and I requested that he would hold it for a considerable period of time. I hoped it would become what is known as a family heirloom.

Another matter due to be dealt with by the Moriarity Tribunal concerns a cheque for $50,000 sent by a Norwegian telecom company, Telenor, to Fine Gael in May 1997.

639

Telenor claims it sent the cheque on behalf of Esat Digifone in which it had a stake, and which had been awarded a mobile phone licence by the Fine Gael-led Rainbow government in 1996. When the news broke in March 2001, Denis O'Brien, the former head of Esat Digifone, denied any involvement in the matter. The general secretary of Fine Gael described the news as 'political dynamite' (a remark he later sought to withdraw) and the party returned the cheque uncashed. The affair was deeply embarrassing for the newly-elected Fine Gael leader Michael Noonan who, in his first major public statement, promised that the party would campaign vigorously for a ban on corporate donations to political parties.

The **Flood Tribunal** was established in 1998 and is mainly concerned with investigating possible corruption related to planning and rezoning in North Dublin. It discovered that the former Dublin city and county assistant manager, George Redmond, had accumulated approximately £1 million in illicit payments from builders, developers and property owners. In April 2001 Redmond was brought before the courts on bribery and corruption charges.

A former Fianna Fáil government press secretary, Frank Dunlop, admitted to the tribunal that in the 1990s he paid £180,000 to Dublin county councillors on behalf of developers seeking to have lands rezoned.

Pádraig Flynn is due to give evidence to the tribunal in relation to allegations that he received £50,000 from a property developer in 1989 when he was minister for the environment. Flynn, a former EU commissioner, has never explicitly denied receiving the money but has denied that he 'took money from anyone to do a political favour as far as planning is concerned'. In 1999 the matter became the subject of a Dáil motion that called on Flynn to make a full statement on the allegations. His daughter, Fianna Fáil TD Beverley Cooper-Flynn, voted against the government, declaring 'A Flynn must support a Flynn.'

Ray Burke, a former cabinet colleague of Flynn's, was forced to resign from both the government and the Dáil in 1997 over conflicting accounts of payments he received in 1989. In 2001 Burke told the Flood Tribunal that he had received £275,000 in donations over a 20-year period which included £120,000 in 1989 when his gross salary was £40,000. Substantial monies were paid to him in cash, much of which was lodged in a Jersey-based company named Caviar. When questioned about breaches of currency regulations, he replied that as a politician it was his job to make laws but that it was for others to implement them.

Burke listed his political expenditure. During elections he had to look after his campaign workers, 'for drinks in the evening'. There was also ongoing 'expenditure in every pub or club you find yourself in, there would be drinks and entertainments on a daily basis, residents' associations and sports clubs, purchasing drinks and entertaining them generally, bringing groups into the Dáil, senior citizens, ladies' clubs, funerals, mass cards, that sort of thing...' And drinks had to be bought for the media in the Dáil. He needed money for 'sponsorships, putting up prizes at dinner dances, raffles, draws, golf outings, sponsored walks'. He was expected to host groups of up to twenty people at the Fianna Fáil president's dinner and the party's árd fheis (conference) was a 'very expensive weekend'. Members of the youth section had to be catered for at their gatherings. He was obliged to reimburse his wife for tea, coffee, and biscuits for constituents who turned up at his home – this came to £6,000. Then there were heating and electricity bills for that part of his home he used as a constituency office. There was no end to it: 'Often you would be touched for a few bob by people who had fallen on hard times.' For 'political expenditure' of this magnitude, Burke needed a ready supply of what he termed 'walking-around money'.

The Flood Tribunal found £2.6 million in unexplained lodgements to Fianna Fáil TD Liam Lawlor's accounts. He was happy to explain how, when it was inconvenient to get to the bank, a friendly publican would change a cheque for £38,000 for him. But he stubbornly refused to provide other details of his finances. He was imprisoned for a week in January 2001 for disobeying a court order to co-operate fully with the tribunal. On his release from Mountjoy Prison, Lawlor and a group of supporters repaired to the Dáil bar for celebratory drinks.

PATRICK GILLAN

Stuart, (Henry) Francis (Montgomery) (1902–2000) Writer. Born Townsville, Australia. In June 1999, Francis Stuart defeated the *Irish Times* in an out-of-court settlement. The ninety-seven-year-old novelist's libel action arose from an accusation of wartime anti-semitism. The proceedings echoed a long and farcical debate at the November 1997 meeting of Aosdana, the academy of Irish writers, musicians, and visual artists, founded by the perjuring tax-evader, C. J. Haughey. The Gaelic poet, Máire Mhac an tSaoi, had moved to have Stuart expelled from the organization but succeeded only in recruiting the support of her husband (Conor Cruise O'Brien) who was a non-member sitting noisily in the public arena. In defeat, Ms Mhac an tSaoi resigned from Aosdana, though not before she murmured the ultimate folly – alleging that perhaps Stuart had been a British agent all along!

Stuart was always surrounded by controversy. His father, Henry Irwin Stuart, an immigrant from Protestant Ulster, committed suicide in a mental asylum less than four months after the birth, believing himself to be 'a great criminal'. His mother Lily (née Montgomery) brought the boy home, and he grew up shifting between various Irish residences, including Benvarden, a gloomy house on the coast of Antrim. This was a society of collapsing landlordism and diminishing legacies for the coming generation, a seed bed of resentment. On the eleventh anniversary of Henry Stuart's commitment as a lunatic, Lily married her first cousin, Henry Clem-

ents, a retired alcoholic Texan cowboy fond of inviting his stepson to share a bath. Home life for the young Stuart was a hazard of maternal indifference and male irrationality. Apart from the traditional nanny, only an aunt who smoked a pipe and wore men's trousers showed the child any affection. He was sent off first to a prep school in Warwickshire, and then to Rugby which was brightened only by news of the Russian Revolution. The next logical step was Trinity College Dublin, but Stuart never took it. He was regarded as intellectually dim, a view occasionally endorsed by W. B. Yeats.

The great moment in his drifting life was an encounter with Iseult, daughter of Maud Gonne and John MacBride, but usually introduced as 'Madame's niece'. The wife-beating major had been executed after the 1916 Rising, and the beautiful widow (Yeats's inviolate rose) epitomized martyrdom, self-pity and a good deal of racialist bile. Iseult was very beautiful too, and lacked most of her mother's vices. The young pair eloped to London, but returned to Dublin where they were married a few weeks before the groom's eighteenth birthday. (Iseult at twenty-five had been already deflowered by Ezra Pound.) Given his new family's loyalties, Stuart had neither difficulty nor choice in embracing Catholicism and militant nationalism. He supported the Republicans during Ireland's civil war of 1922–3, and under his name appeared a pamphlet published by Sinn Fein, the text of a lecture on *Nationality and Culture* (1924). After his death, this obscure item in his bibliography was cited as evidence of his early anti-Semitism, though only one paragraph could be cited. Stuart had long ago disavowed any knowledge of giving the lecture and the larger argument of the pamphlet closely resembled the ideas of his mother-in-law Maud Gonne (borrowing here and there from Yeats).

The marriage was doomed, given Stuart's own confused immaturity, Iseult's disinclination towards sex, and the interference of both Gonne and Yeats. Incidents of domestic cruelty, in Stuart's hardly unique case, have never been forgiven by his detractors. The infant death of a daughter, Dolores, occurred in 1921 when Stuart had taken temporary leave of his wife. Yeats, in his astrologer's habit, had declared the girl should ideally marry into Yeats's own family, as if further to undermine Stuart as a father. In prison a year later he read and wrote, attracted to the visionary work of Dostoevsky. But when Stuart's first book of poems appeared in 1924, its title – *We Have Kept the Faith* – was taken from Rupert Brooke. While devoid of Yeats's genius, Stuart was something of a ghost-in-reverse for the Nobel Prize winner. The younger man could flirt with Catholicism and violence in a way Yeats, 'who ruffled in a manly pose', would not. Their apogee came in the short-lived magazine, *Tomorrow* (August 1924), for which Yeats wrote a purple editorial above the names of Stuart and a few others.

By the end of the 1920s, the Stuarts were living in County Wicklow at Laragh Castle, a British military blockhouse built after the rebellion of 1798. A son, Ion (sometime a sculptor) was born in 1926, a second daughter (Catherine, or Kay) in 1931 – the latter was suspected by one acute observer to be Yeats's child, not Stuart's. Lily Clements moved to Laragh also, and the entourage hoped to survive on the profits of poultry farming. Stuart had now turned to fiction. *Women and God* appeared in 1931. Better novels quickly followed – *Pigeon Irish, The Coloured Dome* (both 1932) and *Try the Sky* (1933). Yeats was now inclined to be approving, and Stuart became a founding member of the Irish Academy of Letters (1932). He philandered in London, drank everywhere with Liam O'Flaherty, and visited Samuel Beckett in pre-war Paris. As a writer, he was going downhill, too prolific, too undisciplined. He had other preoccupations, notably aeroplanes and horses. Both cost him money. *Racing for Pleasure and Profit* (1937) remains the rarest item for collectors of Stuart, and the passion for breeding and racing also ran strong in his only frankly autobiographical book, *Things to Live For* (1934). On the race course, he was always known as Harry, his father's son.

During the early 1930s, Yeats was flirting with Ireland's fascist movement, the Blueshirts, in which Stuart took no interest. 'Send war in our time, O Lord' was to be a death-bed cry of Yeats's, a theme investigated less noisily by Stuart in a forgotten novel, *The Angel of Pity* (1935). As the older man's extreme politics developed through an arcane symbolism, Stuart's complementary role became active and direct. He was implicated with the cartel of former IRB men who steered W. J. Maloney's *The Forged Casement Diaries* (1936) into print, and on 19 December 1938 published a letter in the *Irish Times* opposing the admission of refugees (e.g. Jewish refugees) into Ireland. These were journeyman tasks, compared to his destined master role. Stuart was to be conscripted as Yeats's posthumous anti-self. Shortly after the honoured poet died in January 1939, Stuart was invited to give readings in Germany. A month after the invasion of Czechoslovakia, he arrived in Berlin, returning to Ireland for the summer. In late September, he returned to Berlin on a university contract, and with some low-grade IRA contacts. This occurred weeks after the commencement of the War.

There was no causal relationship between Yeats's death and Stuart's departure, but it fell to the younger man's lot to work out much of what his mentor had preached – the hard, yet bogus, aristocratic credo in an age of mass-murder and ideological hatred. At thirty-seven, he was either culpably ignorant of what had already happened in Germany, or deliberately hostile to humane reasoning – or both. Irish neutrality had an undeniable basis in law, but its defence in moral terms required more energy than Stuart ever expended. Credited with the authorship of a book in German about Casement, he later conceded that it had eventuated only after Maloney had refused permission for his own work to be translated. Stuart was no democrat, and during four and a half years in the Reich he not only taught its undergraduates (in dwindling numbers) but also wrote and delivered broadcasts on its long-range radio service. (These have now been edited by Brendan Barrington, *The Wartime Broadcast of Francis Stuart, 1942–1944*. Dublin: Lilliput Press, 2000.)

Among the students was a Gertrud Meissner. IRA terrorism in Britain gave Stuart a certain éclat in the eyes of the Nazis, and in February 1940 he was asked to write scripts. In the words of Geoffrey Elborn, 'Stuart insisted he would not write anti-semitic material, and when told this was not required, he agreed.' One broadcast – on 16 December 1942 – certainly praised Hitler, though more were devoted to praising Irish neutrality. The Irish government protested to Berlin twice, on both occasions citing interference in domestic affairs. When Stuart's Irish passport expired, the Berlin Legation refused to renew it.

Characteristically, Stuart set about complicating his marital and sexual life. This he did by establishing a relationship with Meissner and by advising a German spy, bound for Ireland, to stay with Iseult at Laragh. Maud Gonne MacBride assisted in concealing Herr Goertz, but Iseult was arrested. In Germany, Stuart morally slept-walked through the Reich, until the saturation bombing disturbed his peace. As the Red Army advanced into Germany, Stuart and Meissner set out southwards in mid-September 1944, and spent months shunting about in the chaos of war's end. News of Hitler's death reached them at Dornbirn in Austria.

British and French troops were in the area, and in August 1945 Stuart was allowed to travel to Paris. In effect, he was free to go home. Madeleine – as she came to be renamed – had inspired in him a new kind of Christianity, anarchic and sentimental perhaps, but more attuned to their circumstances than the editorials of *Tomorrow*. Back in Dornbirn, the two lived contentedly until, on 21 November, they were arrested by the French authorities. Confusion over Meissner's Christian name added to their difficulties, but after six

months, both she and Stuart were released without charge.

They were transferred, however, to a villa in Germany where he was further interrogated; released into the French zone, they lived in relative freedom until October 1946 when Stuart alone was re-arrested and detained in Freiburg. Here things got tougher, but once again he was released without charge, though remaining under surveillance well into 1948. The novelist, Ethel Mannin, described the situation in *German Journey* (1948), though her account was coloured by her desire to re-establish herself in Stuart's eyes, he and Yeats having shared her affections before the War.

Stuart moved to Paris in July 1949, having completed three novels in Freiburg. Published by Victor Gollancz, *The Pillar of Cloud* (1948) and *Redemption* (1949) remain disturbing, unrivalled novels of physical privation and religious intensity, based more on the author's post-war experience than on the years in Berlin. Madeleine Meissner joined him in August. Though the new novels won some plaudits, an attitude of high caution pervaded the critical response. Basil Liddell-Hart, who had admired some of the pre-war work, corresponded with Stuart, but until closed Foreign Office and Irish External Affairs files are opened the real nature of their connection cannot be gauged.

The British authorities regarded the Goertz affair as damnable, but it was the Irish state which had been put at risk. The Irish made no moves to extradite Stuart, and the United Kingdom's Treachery Act (1940) could not be brought to bear on the issue of broadcasts. As for the French, they could not charge a neutral with collaboration. While this analysis of Stuart's escape from retribution is basically legalistic, it remains the case that no substantive evidence of anti-semitic behaviour or sentiments has been adduced to date. The same is true of Yeats.

While Iseult remained alive, it was impossible to bring Madeleine to Ireland, a situation made even worse when Stuart's brother-in-law (a former IRA chief) became Minister for External Affairs in 1948. Six years later, Iseult died. After her funeral at Glendalough, Stuart returned to London and married Madeleine on 28 April 1954, the day before his fifty-second birthday. In London, later in County Meath, and finally opposite Dublin's Central Hospital for the Criminally Insane, Francis and Madeleine Stuart lived the closest kind of married existence, until her death in August 1986. She was his salvation in several regards.

The post-war fiction – in which Madeleine is everywhere recognizable – passed through two repetitions of his 1930s pattern – good work, followed by a steady decline. Gollancz personally tried to persuade Stuart that his attitude towards Jews should be clarified; the result, *Victors and Vanquished* (1958), is perhaps the weakest of the post-war novels. Soon the author began a long silence, only broken in 1970 with *Blacklist Section H*.

Living in a cottage near Dunshaughlin, Stuart had worked on this auto-fiction for more than a decade. A younger writer, Tom MacIntyre, advised cuts which helped to make the book marketable while also eliminating valuable early material. Gollancz was dead. An extract appeared in the new journal, *Atlantis*, of which Derek Mahon was an editor. A Dublin publisher, keen to have an early viewing, turned *Blacklist* down flat. Southern Illinois University Press, advised by Harry T. Moore (a D.H. Lawrence expert), snapped it up. Issued in January 1972, it was greeted with amazement and respect, though not with warm enthusiasm. The most enduring of Stuart's novels, it provides an unvarnished account of H from childhood confusion to wartime disorientation. The cryptic H is Harry Stuart, son of Harry Irwin Stuart, step-son of Harry Clements, lost son and lost soul. The style is unadorned, at times awkward. But *Blacklist* established Stuart as

an Irish writer of rugged, even perverse, independence. Then a third decline in artistic control promptly began.

In the 1970s, the former republican flirted with Loyalist organizations in Belfast, but his search for a place among the condemned had little meaning in the new Ireland. There were too many such places. Protesting against Ronald Reagan in 1984, he was an elder statesman of dissent. Everywhere spoken against, yet honoured by Aosdana, Stuart's reputation was fuelled by accounts of an occasional barroom incident. He married for a third time, to Finola Graham, a painter, on the second last day of 1987.

No account of Francis Stuart should underestimate the influence of his profoundly dysfunctional family background. Nor was the triangle of Yeats, Iseult Gonne and Maud Gonne MacBride calculated to assist a confused teenager in the early years of marriage, especially as the older man had wished to marry both Maud and Iseult at different times, and to be husband and surrogate father to Stuart's wife at different times. To see Stuart as Yeats's bad karma is also to acknowledge the serpent-like cunning of the poet's commitment to fascism. Stuart admitted that he 'made mistakes' but never apologized for his German residence from 1940 to 1945: to have done so would have violated his amoralism. Intermittently villified in his last years, Francis Stuart served to distract attention from the iniquities of other, powerful Irish icons. As in Germany so in Ireland, the self-proclaimed outcast was manipulated more often than he could realize.

Stuart died on 2 February 2000 in County Clare. A press photograph of him in death gave rise rise to some disquiet, as did rumours that a favourite cat had been coffined with him.

W.J. McCORMACK

Select bibliography of recent publications

Andrews, J.H., *A Paper Landscape: The Ordnance Survey in Nineteenth-Century Ireland*. Oxford: Clarendon Press, 1975.

Beckett, J.C., *The Anglo-Irish Tradition*. Belfast: 1976.

Bew, Paul, and Gordon Gillespie, *Northern Ireland: A Chronology of the Troubles 1968–1999*. Dublin: Gill and Macmillan, 1999.

Black, R.D.C., *Economic Thought and the Irish Question, 1817–1870*. Cambridge: Cambridge University Press, 1960.

Bliss, Alan, *Spoken English in Ireland 1600–1740: Twenty-Seven Representative Texts*. Dublin: Dolmen Press, 1979.

Bolton, G.C., *The Passing of the Irish Act of Union*. Oxford: Oxford University Press, 1966.

Bourke, Austin, *The Visitation of God? The Potato and the Irish Famine*. Dublin: Lilliput, 1993.

Boyce, D. George, and Alan O'Day, *Modern Irish History: Revisionism and the Revisionist Controversy*. London, New York: Routledge, 1996.

Boyd, Andrew, *The Rise of the Irish Trade Unions*. Dublin: 1985.

Brady, Ciaran, *The Chief Governors: The Rise and Fall of Reform Government in Tudor Ireland*. Cambridge: Cambridge University Press, 1994.

Brady, Ciaran (ed.), *Interpreting Irish History: The Debate on Historical Revisionism, 1938–1994*. Dublin: Irish Academic Press, 1994.

Brown, Malcom, *The Politics of Irish Literature: From Thomas Davis to W.B. Yeats*. London: Allen and Unwin, 1972.

Brown, Stephen, *Ireland in Fiction*. Shannon: Irish University Press, 1969.

Brown, Terence, *Ireland: A Social and Cultural History*. London: Fontana, 1986. (2nd edn.)

Brown, Terence, *Ireland's Literature: Selected Essays*. Dublin: Lilliput Press, 1988.

Buckland, Patrick, *Ulster Unionism and the Origins of Northern Ireland 1886–1922*. Dublin: 1973.

Cahalan, James M., *Great Hatred, Little Room: The Irish Historical Novel*. Syracuse: Syracuse University Press, 1983.

Cairns, David, and Shaun Richards, *Writing Ireland*. Manchester: Manchester University Press, 1988.

Carter, R.W.G., and A.J. Parker (eds), *Ireland: A Contemporary Geographical Perspective*. London: Routledge, 1989.

Connell, Kenneth, *Irish Peasant Society*. Oxford: Oxford University Press, 1967.

Connolly, S.J., *Religion, Law and Power: The Making of Protestant Ireland 1660–1760*. Oxford: Oxford University Press, 1992.

Cosgrove, Art (ed.), *Marriage in Ireland*. Dublin: College Press, 1985.

Coughlan, Patrick, and Alex Davis, *Modernism and Ireland: Poetry in the 1930s*. Cork: Cork University Press, 1995.

Craig, Maurice, *The Architecture of Ireland from the Earliest Times to 1880*. London: Batsford; Dublin: Eason, 1982.

Craig, Maurice, *Dublin 1660–1860*. Penguin, 1992.

Cullen, L.M., *An Economic History of Ireland since 1660*. London: Batsford, 1972.

Cullen, L.M., *The Emergence of Modern Ireland 1600–1900*. London: Batsford, 1981.

Curtis, L.P., *Apes and Angels: The Irishman in Victorian Caricature*. Washington: Smithsonian Institution, 1971.

Deane, Seamus, *Celtic Revivals: Essays in Modern Irish Literature 1880–1980*. London: Faber, 1985.

Deane, Seamus, Carpenter, Andrew and Williams, Jonathan (eds), *The Field Day Anthology of Irish Writing*. Derry: Field Day Company, 1991. 3 vols.

Donnelly, J.S., *Landlord and Tenant in Nineteenth-Century Ireland*. Dublin: 1973.

Eagleton, Terry, *Heathcliff and the Great Hunger: Studies in Irish Culture*. London: Verso, 1995.

Edwards, R. Dudley, and T. Desmond Williams, *The Great Famine: Studies in Irish History, 1845–52*. Dublin: Lilliput Press, 1994. (New edn intro. Cormac O Grada.)

Elliott, Marianne, *Partners in Revolution: The United Irishmen and France*. London: Yale University Press, 1982.

Elmes, Rosalind, *Catalogue of Irish Topographical Prints and Original Drawings in the National Library of Ireland*. Dublin: Stationery Ofice, 1975. (2nd edn.)

Evans Estyn, *Irish Folk Ways*. Routledge, 1988.

Fabricant, Carole, *Swift's Landscape*. Notre Dame, London: University of Notre Dame, 1995. (2nd edn.)

Fallon, Brian, *Irish Art 1830–1990*. Belfast: Appletree Press, 1994.

Fanning, Charles, *The Irish Voice in America: Irish-American Fiction from the 1760s to the 1980s*. Lexington: University Press of Kentucky, 1990.

Foster, John Wilson, *Forces and Themes in Ulster Fiction*. Dublin: Gill and Macmillan, 1974.

Foster, John Wilson, *Fictions of the Irish Literary Revival: A Changeling Art*. Syracuse: Syracuse University Press, 1987.

Foster, R.F., *Modern Ireland 1600–1972*. London: Penguin, 1988.

Freeman, T.W., *Pre-Famine Ireland: A Study in Historical Geography*. Manchester: Manchester University Press, 1957.

Garvin, Tom, *The Evolution of Irish Nationalist Politics*. Dublin: Gill and Macmillan, 1981.

Garvin, Tom, *1922: The Birth of Irish Democracy*. Dublin: Gill and Macmillan, 1996.

Gibbons, Luke, *Transformations in Irish Culture*. Cork: Cork University Press, 1996.

Goldring, Maurice, *Pleasant the Scholar's Life: Irish Intellectuals and the Construction of the Nation State*. London: Serif, 1993.

Harbison, Peter, Potterton, Homan and Sheehy, Jeanne, *Irish Art and Architecture from Prehistory to the Present*. London: Thames and Hudson, 1978.

Hempton, David, *Religion and Political Culture in Britain and Ireland from the Glorious Revolution to the Decline of Empire*. Cambridge: Cambridge University Press, 1996.

Hempton, David, and Myrtle Hill, *Evangelical Protestantism in Ulster Society 1740–1890*. London: Routledge, 1992.

Innes, C.L., *Woman and Nation in Irish Literature and Society, 1880–1935*. London: Harvester Wheatsheaf, 1993.

Jeffares, A.N., *Anglo-Irish Literature*. London: Macmillan, 1982.

Kennedy, S.B., *Irish Art and Modernism 1880–1950*. Belfast: Institute of Irish Studies, 1991.

Kiberd, Declan, *Inventing Ireland*. London: Cape, 1995.

Kinsella, Thomas, *The Dual Tradition: An Essay on Poetry and Politics in Ireland*. Manchester: Carcanet, 1995.

Lee, Joseph, *Ireland 1912–1985: Politics and Society*. Cambridge: Cambridge University Press, 1990.

Leerssen, J.T., *Mere Irish and Fíor-Ghael: Studies in the Idea of Irish Nationality, its Development and Literary Expression Prior to the Nineteenth Century*. Amsterdam: Benjamins, 1986.

Leerssen, J.T., *Remembrance and Imagination: Patterns in the Historical and Literary Representation of Ireland in the Nineteenth Century*. Cork: Cork University Press, 1996.

Lloyd, David, *Nationalism and Minor Literature: James Clarence Mangan and the Emergence of Irish Cultural Nationalism*. Berkeley, London: University of California Press, 1987.

Lloyd, David, *Anomalous States: Irish Writing and the Post-Colonial Moment*. Dublin: Lilliput Press, 1993.

Long, Gerard (ed.), *Books Beyond the Pale: Aspects of the Provincial Book Trade in Ireland Before 1850*. Dublin: Library Association of Ireland, 1996.

Longley, Edna, *The Living Stream: Literature and Revisionism in Ireland*. Newcastle-on-Tyne: Bloodaxe, 1994.

Lyons, F.S.L., *Culture and Anarchy in Ireland 1890–1939*. Oxford: Clarendon Press, 1979.

Macafee, C.I., *A Concise Ulster Dictionary*. Oxford: Oxford University Press, 1996.

McCormack, W.J., *The Battle of the Books: Two Decades of Irish Cultural Debate*. Dublin: Lilliput Press, 1986.

McCormack, W.J., *From Burke to Beckett: Ascendancy, Tradition and Betrayal in Literary History*. Cork: Cork University Press, 1994.

McCutcheon, W.A., *The Industrial Archaeology of Northern Ireland*. Belfast: HMSO, 1981.

MacDonagh, Oliver, *States of Mind: A Study of Anglo-Irish Conflict 1780–1980*. London: Allen and Unwin, 1983.

McDowell, R.B., *Public Opinion and Government Policy in Ireland 1801–1846*. London: Faber, 1952.

McDowell, R.B., *Ireland in the Age of Imperialism and Revolution*. Clarendon Press/Oxford University Press, 1979.

Malcolm, Elizabeth, *Ireland Sober, Ireland Free: Drink and Temperance in Nineteenth-Century Ireland*. Dublin: 1986.

Malcomson, A.P.W., *John Foster: The Politics of the Anglo-Irish Ascendancy*. Oxford: Oxford University Press, 1978.

Mansergh, Nicholas, *The Irish Free State, its Government and Politics*. Allen and Unwin, 1934.

Maume, Patrick, *'Life that is Exile': Daniel Corkery and the Search for Irish Ireland*. Belfast: Institute of Irish Studies, 1993.

Mercier, Vivian, *The Irish Comic Tradition*. London: Souvenir Press, 1991. (2nd edn.)

Moody, T.W., and F.X. Martin (eds), *The Course of Irish History*. Cork: Mercier Press, 1984.

Moody, T.W., and Martin, F.X., *A New History of Ireland*. Oxford: Oxford University Press, 1980 onwards. (To be completed in 10 volumes.)

Morash, Christopher, *Writing the Irish Famine*. Oxford: Oxford University Press, 1995.

Nelson, E. Charles, and Wendy F. Walsh, *Trees of Ireland, Native and Naturalized*. Dublin: Lilliput Press, 1993.

O'Brien, Conor Cruise, *States of Ireland*. London: Hutchinson, 1972.

O'Day, Alan, and John Stevenson, *Irish Historical Documents since 1800*. Dublin: Gill and Macmillan, 1992.

O'Dowd, Liam (ed.), *On Intellectuals and Intellectual Life in Ireland*. Belfast: Institute of Irish Studies, 1996.

O'Ferrell, Fergus, *Catholic Emancipation: Daniel O'Connell and the Birth of Irish Democracy*. Dublin: Gill and Macmillan, 1985.

Ó Gráda, Cormac, *Ireland Before and After the Famine: Explorations in Economic History 1800–1930*. Manchester: Manchester University Press, 1993.

Ó Gráda, Cormac, *Ireland: A New Economic History, 1780–1939*. Oxford: Oxford University Press, 1994.

Pakenham, Thomas, *The Year of Liberty: The Story of the Great Irish Rebellion of 1798*. London: Hodder and Stoughton, 1969.

Pierce, David, *James Joyce's Ireland*. London: Yale University Press, 1992.

Pittock, G.H. Murray, *Poetry and Jacobite Politics in Eighteenth-Century Britain and Ireland*. Cambridge: Cambridge University Press, 1994.

Pollard, M., *Dublin's Trade in Books, 1550–1800*. Oxford: Clarendon Press, 1989.

Rafroidi, Patrick, *Irish Literature in English: The Romantic Period*. Gerrards Cross: Smythe, 1980. 2 vols.

Rauchbauer, Otto (ed.), *Ancestral Voices: The Big House in Anglo-Irish Literature*. Dublin: Lilliput Press, 1992.

Robinson, Tim, *Setting Foot on the Shores of Connemara and Other Writings*. Dublin: Lilliput Press, 1996.

Roche, Anthony, *Contemporary Irish Drama from Beckett to McGuinness*. Dublin: Gill and Macmillan, 1994.

Rockett, Kevin, and Luke Gibbons, *Cinema and Ireland*. London: 1988.

Rothery, Sean, *Ireland and the New Architecture*. Dublin: Lilliput Press, 1991.

Sheehy, Jeanne, *The Rediscovery of Ireland's Past: The Celtic Revival, 1830–1930*. London: Thames and Hudson, 1980.

Sloan, Barry, Tucker, Bernard, LSU College of Higher Education and Walsh, Oonagh, *Ireland's*

Ulster Crisis: Politics and Literature since 1969. Southampton: LSU Colege, 1994.

Stewart, A.T., *The Narrow Ground: Aspects of Ulster 1609–1969.* London: 1977.

Stewart, Bruce, *Literature in Twentieth-Century Ulster.* London: British Council, 1995.

Thuente, Mary Helen, *The Harp Re-Strung: The United Irishmen and the Rise of Irish Literary Nationalism.* Syracuse: Syracuse University Press, 1994.

Watson, George, *Irish Identity and the Literary Revival.* Washington: Catholic University of America, 1994. (2nd edn.)

Weekes, Ann Owen, *Irish Women Writers: An Uncharted Tradition.* Lexington: University of Kentucky, 1990.

White, Harry, *The Keeper's Recital/Music and Cultural History in Ireland, 1770–1970.* Cork and Indiana: 1998.

Index

Numbers in bold indicate main references.